The Wiley-Blackwell Handbook of Family Psychology

The Wiley-Blackwell Handbook of Family Psychology

Edited by

James H. Bray and Mark Stanton

WILEY-BLACKWELL

A John Wiley & Sons, Ltd., Publication

This edition first published 2009
© 2009 Blackwell Publishing Ltd

Blackwell Publishing was acquired by John Wiley and Sons in February 2007. Blackwell's publishing program has been merged with Wiley's global Scientific, Technical, and Medical business to form Wiley-Blackwell.

Registered Office
John Wiley and Sons Ltd, The Atrium, Southern Gate, Chichester, West Sussex, PO19 8SQ, United Kingdom

Editorial Offices
350 Main Street, Malden, MA 02148-5020, USA
9600 Garsington Road, Oxford, OX4 2DQ, UK
The Atrium, Southern Gate, Chichester, West Sussex, PO19 8SQ, UK

For details of our global editorial offices, for customer services, and for information about how to apply for permission to reuse the copyright material in this book please see our website at www.wiley.com/wiley-blackwell.

The right of James H. Bray and Mark Stanton to be identified as the authors of the editorial material in this work has been asserted in accordance with the Copyright, Designs and Patents Act 1988.

Library of Congress Cataloging-in-Publication Data

The Wiley-Blackwell handbook of family psychology / edited by James H. Bray and Mark Stanton.
    p. cm.
    Includes bibliographical references and index.
    ISBN 978-1-4051-6994-3 (hardcover : alk. paper)   1. Family—Psychological aspects.
2. Family psychotherapy. 3. Psychology—Study and teaching.   I. Bray, James H. II. Stanton, Mark.
    RC488.5.H328 2009
    616.89′156—dc22

                                                                                    2009006576

A catalogue record for this book is available from the British Library.

Set in 10.5/12.5pt Garamond by Graphicraft Limited, Hong Kong
Printed in Singapore by Markono Print Media Pte Ltd

1   2009

Contents

Contributors

Melissa A. Alderfer, PhD, Children's Hospital of Philadelphia, University of Pennsylvania School of Medicine

Harlene Anderson, PhD, Houston Galveston Institute, Taos Institute, Our Lady of the Lake University

Ryan Barker, BA, Smith College

Steven R. H. Beach, PhD, University of Georgia

Gary R. Birchler, PhD, University of California, San Diego School of Medicine, Department of Psychiatry

Danielle A. Black, PhD, The Family Institute at Northwestern University

Brent Bradley, PhD, AAMFT Approved Supervisor, University of Houston – Clear Lake

James H. Bray, PhD, Baylor College of Medicine, Department of Family and Community Medicine

Scott Browning, PhD, Chestnut Hill College

Cindy Carlson, PhD, University of Texas at Austin

Cheryl Cebula, MSW, ACSW, The Leadership Institute of Seattle/Saybrook Graduate School and Research Center, Bellevue, Washington

Marianne P. Celano, PhD, Emory University School of Medicine, Department of Psychiatry and Behavioral Sciences

Joseph M. Cervantes, PhD, ABPP, California State University, Fullerton, Department of Counseling

Anthony L. Chambers, PhD, The Family Institute at Northwestern University

Stephen Cheung, PsyD, Azusa Pacific University

Margaret Crosbie-Burnett, PhD, Fellow of the National Council on Family Relations, University of Miami

Thomas J. Dishion, PhD, University of Oregon, Child and Family Center

Lee J. Dixon, MA, University of Tennessee, Knoxville

Brian D. Doss, PhD, Texas A&M University

Lindsey A. Einhorn, MA, University of Denver

Ivan Eisler, PhD, AcSS, King's College London, Institute of Psychiatry

William Fals-Stewart, PhD, University of Rochester

Barbara H. Fiese, PhD, University of Illinois at Urbana-Champaign

Catherine L. Funk, MS, University of Texas at Austin

Jane F. Gilgun, PhD, University of Minnesota, Twin Cities School of Social Work

Abbie E. Goldberg, PhD, Clark University, Department of Psychology

Herbert Goldenberg, PhD, University of California, Los Angeles

Irene Goldenberg, EdD, ABPP, ABFCP, University of California, Los Angeles, Semel Institute

Kristina Coop Gordon, PhD, University of Tennessee, Knoxville

Marjorie Graham-Howard, PhD, Azusa Pacific University

Lyn Greenberg, PhD, Private Practice, Los Angeles

Ashly J. Hagen, MA, JD, Seattle Pacific University

Diane F. Halpern, PhD, Claremont McKenna College

David S. Hargrove, PhD, ABPP, Appalachian State University, Department of Psychology

Michele Harway, PhD, ABPP, Antioch University

Margaret Heldring, PhD, University of Washington, Department of Family Medicine

Scott W. Henggeler, PhD, Medical University of South Carolina

Richard E. Heyman, PhD, Stony Brook University, State University of New York

Gwynith Hoffman-Robinson, MA, Seattle Pacific University

George K. Hong, PhD, ABPP, California State University at Los Angeles

Viviana E. Horigian, MD, University of Miami Miller School of Medicine

Farrah M. Hughes, PhD, Francis Marion University

Sue Johnson, EdD, CPsych, University of Ottawa, Alliant International University, San Diego

Florence W. Kaslow, PhD, ABPP, Florida Couples and Family Institute

Nadine J. Kaslow, PhD, ABPP, Emory University, Department of Psychiatry and Behavioral Sciences

David M. Klein, PhD, Fellow of the National Council on Family Relations, University of Notre Dame

Lauren Knickerbocker, MA, Stony Brook University, State University of New York

Wendy (K. K.) Lam, PhD, University of Rochester

Erika Lawrence, PhD, University of Iowa

Jay Lebow, PhD, The Family Institute at Northwestern University

Terry Lee, MD, University of Washington

Harriet P. Lefley, PhD, University of Miami Miller School of Medicine

Ronald F. Levant, EdD, ABPP, University of Akron

Howard A. Liddle, EdD, ABPP, University of Miami Miller School of Medicine

Jeffrey J. Magnavita, PhD, ABPP, Glastonbury Psychological Associates, PC University of Hartford

Howard J. Markman, PhD, University of Denver

Diane T. Marsh, PhD, University of Pittsburgh at Greensburg

Olga L. Mejía, PhD, California State University, Fullerton, Department of Counseling

Victoria B. Mitrani, PhD, University of Miami School of Nursing and Health Studies

KimHoang T. Nguyen, MA, University of Texas at Austin

A. Rodney Nurse, PhD, FAPA, ABPP, Family Psychological Services/Collaborative Divorce Associates

Timothy J. O'Farrell, PhD, ABPP, Harvard Medical School

Spencer B. Olmstead, MEd, Florida State University

Daniela J. Owen, MA, Stony Brook University, State University of New York

Kay Pasley, EdD, Florida State University

Terence Patterson, EdD, ABPP, University of San Francisco

Willo Pequegnat, PhD, National Institute of Mental Health

William M. Pinsof, PhD, ABPP, The Family Institute at Northwestern University

Marsha Kline Pruett, PhD, MSL, Smith College and School for Social Work

Erica P. Ragan, MA, University of Denver, Department of Psychology

Kevin S. Reimer, PhD, Azusa Pacific University

Galena K. Rhoades, PhD, University of Denver

Michael S. Robbins, PhD, University of Miami Miller School of Medicine

Carleen Robinson, MSW, University of Miami Miller School of Medicine, Department of Psychiatry and Behavioral Sciences

Tziporah Rosenberg, PhD, University of Rochester School of Medicine and Dentistry, Departments of Psychiatry and Family Medicine, Institute for the Family

Mary T. Rourke, PhD, Children's Hospital of Philadelphia

Thomas L. Sexton, PhD, ABPP, Indiana University, Center for Adolescent and Family Studies

Ashli J. Sheidow, PhD, Medical University of South Carolina

Lauren J. Shelly, MA, Seattle Pacific University

Amy M. Smith Slep, PhD, Stony Brook University, State University of New York

Scott M. Stanley, PhD, University of Denver

Mark Stanton, PhD, ABPP, Azusa Pacific University

Elizabeth Stormshak, PhD, University of Oregon

José Szapocznik, PhD, AAMFT Approved Supervisor, University of Miami Miller School of Medicine, Department of Epidemiology and Public Health

Sherylle J. Tan, PhD, Claremont McKenna College

John Thoburn, PhD, ABPP, Seattle Pacific University

Peggy Thompson, PhD, Family Psychological Services/Collaborative Divorce Associates

Arlene Vetere, PhD, DipClinPsychol (BPS), University of Surrey

Froma Walsh, PhD, University of Chicago, Chicago Center for Family Health

William Watson, PhD, University of Rochester School of Medicine and Dentistry, Departments of Psychiatry and Neurology, Institute for the Family

Timothy Weber, PhD, MDiv, AAMFT Approved Supervisor, The Leadership Institute of Seattle/Saybrook Graduate School and Research Center, Bellevue, Washington

Robert Welsh, PhD, ABPP, Azusa Pacific University

Valerie E. Whiffen, PhD, Private Practice

Mark A. Whisman, PhD, University of Colorado at Boulder

Natalie Whiteford, MA, University of Colorado at Boulder

Christine M. Williams, MA, University of Akron

Jennifer M. Willett, BA, University of Tennessee, Knoxville

Marcia A. Winter, PhD, Syracuse University

Preface

Family psychology is a recognized specialty and has a growing number of doctoral and post-doctoral training programs. Family psychology has made great strides from its early beginnings as a part of the family therapy movement. The development of this Handbook comes from many years of study, teaching, and clinical practice in understanding and helping couples and families. The journeys of the editors took different paths, but led to a common goal: to provide the field with an overview of the field of family psychology.

James Bray first encountered family psychology in the late 1970s during his graduate training in clinical psychology at the University of Houston. The Houston-Galveston mental health community was one of the "hotbeds" of family therapy training and development. While this training was multi-disciplinary and included psychologists, psychiatrists, social workers, and nurses, some of the leading figures that later developed the specialty of family psychology were in the area. Harry Goolishian, Donald Williamson, and others were nationally recognized leaders and developing their unique brands of family therapy and psychology. In addition, the Houston-Galveston Family Therapy Consortium was an association of six institutions that sponsored workshops by the creators of the family therapy movement that included regular visits by Haley, Watzlawick, Weakland, Whitaker, Minuchin, McGoldrick, Boscolo, Cecchin, and many others.

As chance would have it, James Alexander, the creator of functional family therapy, interviewed for the director of clinical training at the University of Houston. James Bray was the graduate student on the search committee and had the opportunity to talk with Dr Alexander about his research and the burgeoning field of family psychology. James was unclear whether to focus on adults or children in his research and clinical work. Dr Alexander wisely told him that he should consider studying and working with families because one could work with both adults and children with this perspective. Because of this advice and the wonderful training offered by professionals in the Houston-Galveston

Family Therapy Consortium, such as Walter DeLange, Patrick and Carol Brady, Barbara Hoek, Donald Williamson, Harry Goolishian, and others, James decided to do both his pre-doctoral internship and post-doctoral fellowship in Houston. During these experiences he developed clinical and research collaborations with Donald Williamson and Harry Goolishian that strongly influenced his choice to focus on family psychology.

Mark Stanton was introduced to ecological systems theory and systemic thinking through the work of Urie Bronfenbrenner. Mark readily found a resonance with systemic concepts and quickly identified as a systemic thinker. While completing his doctoral degree in the School of Psychology at Fuller Seminary in the 1980s he was exposed to the work of the early leaders in the family systems movement under the tutelage of Dennis Guernsey, Jack Balswick, Cameron Lee, and Judy Balswick. Significant emphasis was placed on theory in his program, including sociological models as well as psychological theory, social work frameworks, and family systems conceptualization. He was influenced by a shift in the late 1980s away from the sole focus on families in the family therapy movement to create a more balanced model that included individual, interpersonal, and environmental factors (see Chapter 1). This is family psychology.

Mark's graduate clinical training included couples therapy and substance abuse treatment, creating in him an ongoing interest in each and in the intersection of the two. He was an early adopter of the Millon Clinical Multiaxial Inventory, an assessment of individual personality and psychopathology, but used it in the treatment of couples. He led family group therapy (groups of 3–5 families at a time) and an aftercare group in an outpatient substance abuse treatment center for several years and soon began to provide couples therapy for partners where one or both abused substances. A licensed psychologist, Mark was board certified in family psychology by the American Board of Professional Psychology in 2003.

Mark entered academia upon receipt of his doctorate. Recognizing the scarcity of graduate training in family psychology, he soon helped his university develop a doctoral degree in clinical psychology with an emphasis in family psychology and achieve American Psychological Association (APA) accreditation. He served as director of the program for over 10 years and developed an interest in graduate education in family psychology, interacting with other program leaders to identify programs with a track or strong emphasis in the specialty.

The editors have been involved in the development of family psychology through work in the APA's Society of Family Psychology (Division 43). James was an early leader within Division 43 and served as the 1995 president. Mark began as chair of the membership committee and then served as the editor of the division bulletin, *The Family Psychologist*, for five years, becoming acquainted with many of the leaders in family psychology as they contributed articles. He was president of Division 43 in 2005. It is in the Society of Family Psychology that James and Mark met and developed a professional relationship that led to co-editing this Handbook. Both of them share a passion for innovation and applying the systemic principles of family psychology in their research, teaching, and clinical work.

There are many people that we would like to thank who contributed to the development of the Handbook. Together, we thank the nearly 100 authors who contributed to the 54 chapters of the Handbook. We are privileged that these experts in the various aspects of the specialty have contributed the most recent research and detail for the Handbook.

James would like to thank his colleagues in Division 43 and at Baylor College of Medicine for their support over the years in developing family psychology theory and research and applying it in a variety of mental health and primary care settings. He is also appreciative of the support and encouragement of his wife, Elizabeth, and his children, Lindsey, Jessica, and Matthew, in teaching him about the personal side of family systems. We acknowledge the contributions of Jessica Bray and Robert J. Marker, Jr., in creating the indices for the book.

Mark would like to thank his executive assistant, Candi Adermatt, and doctoral research assistant, Teresa J. Hooker. Both read various chapters and provided valuable comments regarding APA style, references, grammar, syntax, and meaning. In addition, Candi facilitated communication with the chapter authors while Teresa helped with the details of chapter author information. Finally, of course, it is appropriate in a family psychology text to recognize the support and encouragement of his wife, Kathleen, and his children, April, Erin, Chelse, and Sean, over the course of completing the Handbook.

James H. Bray
Mark Stanton

Part I

Foundations of Family Psychology

Introduction

Any construction relies upon a solid foundation in order to build an enduring structure. This part of the Handbook describes the foundations of contemporary family psychology, including a focus on the epistemology and theory, history, demographics, diversity, research methods, competencies, and education that underlie the specialty. This part is placed first in the Handbook because we believe it is important to understand the foundations of the specialty before moving to treatment applications or particular areas of importance.

The specialty of family psychology is distinctive because it is founded on systems theory and a systemic epistemology is evident in the origins and evolution of the specialty. Chapter 1 describes the systemic epistemology of family psychology and the importance of systemic conceptualization for family psychology research design and clinical intervention.

The history of the evolution of systemic models of psychotherapeutic intervention is presented in Chapter 2. Many of these models originated with strong, charismatic individuals who championed particular ways of working with individuals, couples, and families, but the chapter describes a progression over time to more integrated and sophisticated models that rely on scientific evidence and outcomes more than individual personality.

Many theories may be understood to contribute to family psychology, and Chapter 3 provides an introduction to the meaning and purpose of theory and to several theories that are salient to a systemic perspective. Countering the rush to therapeutic intervention, the chapter stresses the importance of theory to provide adequate conceptualization to shape questions that result in beneficial applications and interventions.

The demographics of American family life have changed significantly in recent years, and Chapter 4 examines the sociodemographic trends that surround the practice of family psychology. For instance, the delay in marriage and the increase in cohabitation significantly impact society and psychotherapy, so the demographics provide a foundation for many chapters that follow in the Handbook. Chapter 5 continues this theme with a synopsis of diversity issues in family psychology, focusing especially on ethnic diversity to examine varying marriage and family patterns, as well as crucial sociocultural dimensions that may be considered for culturally appropriate psychotherapeutic intervention.

The relationship of research and research methods and the challenges to linking family psychology research and practice are addressed in Chapters 6 and 7. Family psychology emphasizes the science of psychology, and these chapters note the importance of solid research methodology and respect for research findings in the practice of family psychology. Both qualitative and quantitative methods are salient for understanding systemic dynamics.

The recent focus on the core competencies necessary for family psychology practice is underscored in Chapter 8 with delineation of the systemic elements of such competencies. Developmental markers are clarified and key aspects of competency are specified in the chapter.

Finally, Chapter 9 provides a review of contemporary graduate education in family psychology in the United States and the United Kingdom. Ultimately, education and training are the lifeblood of a specialty and this chapter details the contemporary trends and foci.

These topics constitute the foundation for the specialty and this Handbook. Students and clinicians may turn first to the clinical chapters or the chapters on specific dimensions of the specialty, but we hope that all will turn eventually to these chapters that address the foundations of the specialty.

1

The Systemic Epistemology of the Specialty of Family Psychology

Mark Stanton

Family psychology is a broad and general orientation to psychology that utilizes a systemic epistemology to provide an alternative to the individual focus of many psychological orientations (Nutt & Stanton, 2008). Although the specialty is sometimes confused with the practice of family therapy, family psychology is a broader term that recognizes that human behavior occurs within a contextual matrix of individual, interpersonal, and environmental or macrosystemic factors (Robbins, Mayorga, & Szapocznik, 2003; Stanton, 1999). A systemic epistemology includes systemic thinking (inculcation of systemic concepts and use of a systemic paradigm to organize thoughts) and application to clinical practice and research. A systemic epistemology provides a framework for the general conceptualization of human behavior and for psychological assessment, psychotherapeutic intervention, and family psychology research.

This chapter provides an introduction to the systemic epistemology of family psychology, including a definition of epistemology, the importance of an epistemological transformation to shift from an individualistic approach to a systemic approach to psychology, the delineation of a family psychology paradigm, and a description of important systemic factors. Finally, this systemic epistemology is applied to psychotherapeutic intervention and family psychology research.

Definition of Epistemology

We use the term epistemology here in a manner consistent with the work of Auerswald and Bateson (Auerswald, 1990; Bateson, 1972): a set of pervasive rules used in thought by large groups of people to define reality. Epistemology is a branch of philosophy that focuses on knowledge and the justification of knowledge by examining the origins, nature, and methods of knowledge. Understood more broadly, epistemology has "to do with the creation and dissemination of knowledge in particular areas of inquiry" (*Stanford Encyclopedia of Philosophy*, n.d.). More simply stated it is "how we know what we know." Epistemology often involves creation and use of a paradigm to organize information and knowledge.

The crucial issue for family psychologists is the role of one's epistemology in determining the sources and organization of knowledge, as these constitute what we know and believe to be true. In that sense, "reality" is a construct, based on what our rules say is real or not real. For instance, is the sound of a dog whistle "real"? Most humans cannot hear the sound, so if our rules limit reality to those things that can be directly experienced by human senses (i.e., sight, hearing, touch, feel) in an anthropocentric manner, the sound of the dog whistle is not real. This is problematic, because we can observe that when we blow the whistle all the dogs in the area respond, and we have learned that there are high-frequency sounds beyond our auditory range, so our rules may be challenged by other experiences or knowledge. If so, do we change our rules, or do we hold to them stubbornly because we "know" they are right? Rules may preclude consideration of novel ideas or exclude options without deliberation because they do not fit our "reality."

Many people have given little thought to the rules they follow in thinking. Most do not face an ambiguous situation, stop, determine the rules we intend to use to conceptualize that situation, and then address it. Instead, we automatically follow the rules into which we have been socialized. Family psychology challenges us to understand how we have been socialized and educated to think, and to consider new methods.

The Cartesian Method

Many people educated in the United States and Europe have inculcated the scientific method espoused by Rene Descartes in 1637 (Capra, 2002; Nutt & Stanton, 2008). The Cartesian method of critical thinking is so intrinsic to western thought that most of us use it automatically when we think, with little or no awareness that our methodology influences our thoughts and interpretations (see Nisbett, 2007, for a detailed depiction of the differences between eastern and western thought processes). There may be an implicit assumption in western psychology that this is the only way to think about issues and problems.

Elements of Descartes' model

Essential elements of the Cartesian model to be used in solving problems, drawn from Descartes' *Discourse on Method* (Descartes, 1999), include: (a) Cartesian doubt (i.e., seeking convincing evidence for every thought; never accepting anything as true without manifest knowledge that it is true); (b) dividing the whole into parts (i.e., breaking any problem down into as many parts as needed in order to solve it); (c) creating an orderly thought process by beginning with those aspects of the problem easiest to understand and ascending in steps to understand the most complex parts, without trying to follow any natural relationship between the parts; and (d) being thorough to ensure that nothing was left out.

In practice, these rules led to substantial scientific accomplishments (e.g., advances in medicine and other disciplines that enhance human experience) and the development of modern society. They also prove helpful in tackling problems. For instance, the challenge of writing a graduate term paper may be so daunting that students feel overwhelmed and unable to proceed. However, if they are encouraged to "break it down into sections," "create an outline," and "start with the section you know the most about," they are often able to accomplish the task.

Errors of Cartesian extremism

Extreme individualism. Alternatively, when taken to an extreme, these rules have fragmented the whole to the extent that the natural connection between parts of the whole is lost. In practice, Cartesian methods have resulted in extreme individualism (the tendency to frame reality through the lens of the individual rather than the collective whole). We see this in western psychology, where many theories and approaches to psychological intervention are focused on the individual as if she or he were entirely independent of any social system. These models of psychology minimize the attention provided to interpersonal and environmental factors in human behavior, focusing almost exclusively on the intrapsychic or individual psychological factors. These approaches tend "to study the individual by removing the person from the context of his or her life" (Cervone, Shoda, & Downey, 2007, p. 4).

Reductionism. Cartesian rules have also promoted reductionism (the idea that a complex system is only the sum of its parts, so it is possible to break any system down to its elementary levels for analysis, understanding, and problem solving) in a manner that limits our ability to understand the complexity of the whole. For instance, reductionistic thinking in psychology may result in a fragmented understanding of human behavior as particular psychologists focus only on the part of that behavior in which they specialize (e.g., some cognitive psychologists focus solely on mental representations, dismissing or discounting other factors, such as affect). The insight gained from such sole focus may be helpful, on the one hand, but ultimately misleading because it suggests that other factors are unrelated or unimportant. When reductionistic solutions are applied to complex phenomena, the solutions ultimately fail to address the complexity of the behavior. For example, there was a campaign some time ago to reduce the number and severity of automobile accidents. The thrust of the campaign was a slogan that encouraged drivers to leave one car length between them and the car ahead for every 10 mph of their driving speed. At initial glance, the simple logic of this suggestion makes sense; six car lengths at 60 mph allow plenty of room to stop or avoid an accident. In fact, this solution may make sense on a single-lane road. However, the solution is reductionistic when applied to the real world of multiple-lane highways traveled by most suburban and urban drivers. In that case, if one leaves significant space between cars it often results in other cars "cutting in front" of your car, increasing the potential for an accident. Reductionism may appear to solve a problem, but miss the complexity of an interactive system around the problem. This is similar to what occurs when a complex issue like substance abuse is understood as entirely an individual issue and the addict is treated on an inpatient unit until sobriety is achieved, then returned to the home and social environment in which the problem originated, only to relapse because the treatment did not address the complexity of the problem.

Linear thinking. In addition, Cartesian logic often leads to linear thinking (the idea that there is a simple cause-and-effect mechanism that may explain most acts as one explores them using logical, rational analysis). Such thinking typically excludes synergistic thinking (the understanding that combined effects are greater than the sum of individual effects) and integrative processes (the ability to join parts into a larger whole) that recognize the creative, complex, and unexpected pathways surrounding human acts. Linear thinking alone may be inadequate to understand and address life issues and circumstances.

Extreme objectivism. Similarly, Descartes' focus on objectivity is misleading, when taken to an extreme. When Descartes conceptually divided mind and matter he argued that a human scientist could observe the world objectively. Many contemporary scientists agree with him; they eschew any form of subjectivity in research. Only that which can be known through the scientific method, narrowly interpreted, is reliable knowledge. However, Capra (2002) argues that discoveries in quantum physics and theories of cognition overrule such an extreme focus on objectivity to recognize that science may be rigorous and disciplined without excluding the subjective dimension. A systems epistemology avoids the error of extreme objectivity, noting that all forms of knowledge may contribute to healthy functioning. This has important ramifications for psychotherapy and psychological research (e.g., the legitimacy of qualitative methods).

The legacy of Descartes is substantial and we would not easily discard his rules. When taken to an extreme, the Cartesian method lacks balance and requires reconsideration. There are systemic ways to conceptualize human behavior that are amenable to complexity and context; these may complement Cartesian methods.

Epistemological Transformation

Because many people have never considered the rules they observe automatically in their thought processes, it is difficult to change those rules. Mary Catherine Bateson (Gregory Bateson's anthropologist daughter and collaborator until his death) suggests that we need an "epistemological shock" to challenge our worldview and the fundamental framework we use to perceive the world (Bloom, n.d.). The Batesons used a variety of literary forms (e.g., metalogues: conversations that stretch our thinking), life examples, and arguments to help us break out of our assumptions to consider different ways of thinking.

Learning to learn

Gregory Bateson (an early leader in systemic conceptualization; 1972) provided a classic example of the struggle to comprehend new structures of thinking when he described a porpoise that was frustrated while learning to demonstrate new behaviors under the guidance of a trainer. The trainer put the porpoise through a series of presentations in which only one new noteworthy behavior was rewarded (by a whistle and food) in each session. This resulted in a pattern over 14 episodes: the porpoise would repeat the behavior rewarded in the prior session but go unrewarded until it evidenced some new behavior, not previously demonstrated, which would then be rewarded. But during the break between the fourteenth and fifteenth sessions, the porpoise was very excited and "when she came on stage for the fifteenth session she put on an elaborate performance including eight conspicuous pieces of behavior of which four were entirely new – never before observed in this species of animal" (p. 277). The porpoise finally understood that the trainer desired entirely new behaviors. She saw beyond each separate session to the pattern across all presentations. Bateson termed this "deutero-learning" or "learning to learn." It is at the core of an epistemological transformation.

According to conceptual change theory, there are several characteristics needed in the ecological surround to support change in one's worldview: (a) dissatisfaction with existing conception, (b) an intelligible new conception, (c) an initially plausible conception, and (d) the new conception holding the possibility of solving future problems (Gregoire, 2003; Sandoval, 1996).

The process of change involves identifying existing beliefs, making these tacit beliefs available for deliberate reflection, and systematic refutation of misconceptions. Conceptual change may be enhanced through the use of analogies, especially those generated by the changing individual (Duit, Roth, Komorek, & Wilbers, 2001). For example, when individuals are asked to work in groups to identify systemic metaphors or analogies, it often results in enhanced understanding of systems theory as an epistemology. They end up identifying natural or mechanistic systems all around them that evidence the qualities of a system (see below), such as the interactive parts and processes of the human body or the intricacies of a functioning automobile.

The disequilibrium created in the epistemological change process may result in negative affect for the person being challenged to change, so a supportive environment is needed (Demastes, Good, & Peebles, 1995; Gregoire, 2003). It is uncomfortable to find one's foundations of knowledge cracking or crumbling.

Paradigm shift: from individualistic approach to systemic

Family psychology requires a fundamental paradigm shift from western individualism to systemic complexity (Stanton, 2005). If we want to understand and treat individuals, couples, families, and larger social groups effectively, we need to conceptualize cases within the system in which they exist (the context and the meanings attributed to the context), assess the salient factors in the system, and intervene at identified points across the system.

This means that we need to "see" the system in which human life is embedded. One note-worthy metaphor comes from the work of Bronfenbrenner (1979), the author of the idea of development in ecological context. Bronfenbrenner suggested that the individual grows and develops within a nested structure of environments, comparing such context to the sets of Russian dolls that nest inside each other, with each one opening to reveal another level inside. Bronfenbrenner (1979) coined the terms microsystem (the immediate setting of development), mesosystem (the interrelationships between microsystems), macrosystem (higher-level systems), exosystem (settings beyond the immediate experience of the individual that influences development), and chronosystem (the evolving interconnected nature of the person, environment, and proximal processes over time) (Bronfenbrenner, 1986) to identify various levels and types of systemic context in which human life occurs.

Transformation in personal thought process for the psychologist usually requires facing the complexity of a clinical case or research question and finding reductionistic solutions inadequate. For instance, early conceptualization of child development and attachment focused on qualities of the mother in a somewhat unidirectional manner (i.e., how the mother influences child attachment). However, as research progressed, it became clear that there was a reciprocal interactive process between an individual child and the mother (i.e., the child evoked responses and responded to evocations from mother). In fact, mother–child relations may differ between the same mother and each of her children. Fathers eventually were included in the conceptualization of attachment etiology, at first primarily through their interaction with mother and later through the complexity of the mother–father–child system. Finally, other caregivers were understood to contribute to the development of internalized attachment, including members of the extended family and child-care providers (see Schermerhorn, Cummings, & Davies, 2008, for a review of the evolution of thinking about child development). The "old" idea of maternal influence on the child alone is no longer sufficient for understanding child development.

As one begins to see the system at work, the individualistic paradigm breaks down and there is room for the systemic paradigm. Apparently simple cause-and-effect explanations are demonstrated to be insufficient and more complex, systemic rationales evolve to take their place.

Once the transformation takes place, it is impossible to see things in the old way. Even if a clinician elects to work exclusively with individuals in clinical practice, the approach will be different because he or she will see the system in which the person lives and interacts. Of course, many such clinicians will now feel more comfortable working with couples, families, and larger social organizations because they have the framework to understand, assess, and intervene in the system. Additional training in systemic assessment devices, techniques, and evidence-based approaches enhances the assessment and intervention competencies, but they are founded on systemic thinking.

Delineation of a Systemic "Family Psychology" Paradigm

An epistemological transformation requires a new framework to organize knowledge. Typically, epistemological rules lead to structures that are used to arrange, categorize, and

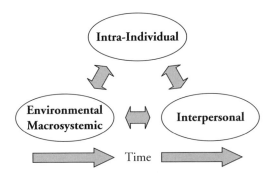

Figure 1.1   Systemic paradigm of family psychology

classify information. For example, when people in the western world consider human relations in the workplace, the Cartesian epistemology manifests itself in adoption of a hierarchical organizational chart. Such charts are familiar in the west because they evidence the hierarchical and linear individualism that results from excessive adoption of the Cartesian method. In these models, communication and decision-making flow from top to bottom, and individual components relate to others in a linear fashion, with power and status locked into roles within the hierarchy. The general focus of the organization is on individual building blocks (e.g., defining individual roles, responsibilities, and reporting relationships) rather than the whole.

By contrast, a systemic paradigm recognizes the dynamic reciprocity between individual, interpersonal, and environmental or macrosystemic factors over time in human behavior (Liddle, Santisteban, Levant, & Bray, 2002; Robbins et al., 2003; Stanton, 1999). Figure 1.1 presents this paradigm.

A systemic paradigm is helpful in psychology because it provides a framework for conceptualizing, assessing, treating, and researching human behavior. A family psychologist is one who internalizes this type of paradigm to the point that thinking is organized by it. The paradigm becomes a conceptual map that allows the family psychologist to navigate the system. For instance, a family psychologist automatically considers the variety of factors in these categories when commencing psychotherapy or consultation with an individual, couple, family, or larger social system. All factors apply regardless of the modality of treatment (e.g., interpersonal and macrosystemic factors are included in the treatment of an individual, even if other family members never come to treatment). The factors serve as a framework for conceptualization, assessment, and intervention.

Individual factors

Family psychology does not ignore the individual (Nichols, 1987). Intrapsychic and individual factors are an important part of understanding individual, couple, or family dynamics. A variety of individual factors may be considered salient to a particular situation (see Table 1.1).

Table 1.1   Individual, Interpersonal, and Macrosystemic Factors

Individual factors	*Interpersonal factors*	*Macrosystemic/Environmental*
• Individual development in context • Cognitive process and intelligence • Attachment and/or intrapsychic structures • Personality • Gender, age, sexual orientation, physical factors • Psychobiology • Neuropsychology • Personal strengths • Psychopathology • Personal beliefs or convictions	• Family development • Family life-cycle stage • Couple relations • Parent–child relations • Sibling relations • Family process • Family strengths • Family constructs • Social network relations (including social support)	• Socioeconomic status • Work • Cultural differences • Politics – political forces • Medicine, healthcare, health insurance • Physical environment • Safety: crime, terrorism • Community organizations • Religion – religious organizations • Media (internet, TV/cable, newspapers, magazines)

Any or all of these individual factors may be important to the etiology, progression, or treatment of issues presented in psychotherapy. There is substantial psychological research literature in each of these areas, often with clear treatment implications. Family psychologists consider these factors to determine which may be relevant to the presenting issue(s), assess them, and focus interventions on them. Family psychologists understand that change is initiated and maintained by individuals.

However, family psychologists consider individual factors as part of the interactive system with interpersonal and macrosystemic factors rather than as self-contained or stand-alone factors (see Chapter 11, this volume). Advances in the conception of individuals suggest that what had previously been considered a personality characteristic of the individual (e.g., conscientiousness) may not exist within the person but as "an emerging phenomenon that reflects the interplay among the components of the system that is a person" (Shoda, 2007, p. 331). Individual behavior reflects the manner in which the individual responds to a particular circumstance or context, not an isomorphic portrayal of an individual trait. This is so much so that personality varies across contexts or interpersonal circumstances; "an individual's 'personality signature' represents his or her variability across situations and reflects the patterning of the individual's responses while also being stable over time" (Andersen, Thorpe, & Kooij, 2007, p. 177). So, family psychologists consider personality, but not as a static, internal construct; family psychologists regard the interaction of personality (and other individual factors) with the interpersonal and environmental context.

Interpersonal factors

Interpersonal factors describe social dynamics, such as a couple, family, or larger social system and the relational aspects in those groups. Family psychologists may assess and treat a variety of interpersonal factors (see Table 1.1). Each of these interpersonal factors reflects a variety of underlying processes, such as the addition and departure of members (e.g., birth, death, divorce), role definition (i.e., who does what in the relationship), and communication patterns (e.g., egalitarian, hierarchical; unidirectional, omnidirectional). There is substantial family psychology literature around these factors in this Handbook.

Interpersonal factors interact reciprocally with individual factors (e.g., couple relations are a composite of the two individuals and the unique interactive process between them; a couple is more than a sum of the two individuals) and macrosystemic factors (e.g., family process interacts with the family's ethnic and cultural context).

Macrosystemic/environmental factors

A systemic epistemology recognizes that individual and interpersonal factors exist within the larger context of the environment and social macrosystem. These factors include a variety of global, regional, and local dynamics that interact with individual and inter-personal factors (see Table 1.1).

It used to be that local environmental or macrosystemic factors were more salient to the individual and interpersonal reality of most people, but that has changed. We now live in a global community and many of these factors regularly move from global to local in rapid fashion (Friedman, 2005). Individual and family perspectives intermingle with global perspectives, sometimes without our conscious awareness.

Some advocate for a global psychology in a manner that is consistent with systemic thinking. Marsella (1998) argues that international conditions are linked to our wellbeing; he suggests that western psychology must reconsider its fundamental premises in order to adequately incorporate the cultural, economic, political, and environmental forces that impose on our lives. There is evident need for family psychologists to recognize the import-ance of macrosystemic and environmental factors in the lives of those that present in our offices.

Time

Time cuts across the first three groups of factors. Time is often considered relevant to the individual (e.g., life-span development) as individual factors are assessed longitudin-ally in research. In addition, family psychologists recognize the important role of time in understanding all systemic factors. So, normative (i.e., events that happen to most people, such as aging) and non-normative changes (i.e., events that happen to some people, such as chronic illness or war) are life transitions that occur over time across the three systemic groups of factors. For instance, changes in the global economy may result in a job loss for an individual, resulting in individual developmental change at the particular stage in which the job loss occurs and possibly impacting family relations (e.g., divorce or family stress; impact on child development).

Family psychologists recognize the importance of time at the individual level (e.g., individual development in context), the interpersonal level (e.g., multigenerational transmission of family traits), and environmental or macrosystemic level (e.g., national or international events and circumstances that interact with individual and interpersonal factors, such as the way 9/11 impacted everyone old enough to understand it in a way that those who come after us will not share). In professional practice, family psychologists take an individual history, complete a multigeneration genogram (McGoldrick, Gerson, & Petry, 2008), and consider cohort effects that may impact the individual and couple or family dynamics in treatment.

Important Systemic Concepts

A final aspect of systemic thinking involves recognition of important concepts in order to ensure that they are part of the thinking process. Key concepts underlying the systemic paradigm include complexity, reciprocity, living open systems theory, self-organization, adaptation, and social constructivism and cognition.

Complexity

Complexity involves becoming comfortable with the ambiguity that often exists in real-life situations instead of seeking simplistic or reductionistic solutions. Complexity accords with the concept of non-summativity, which suggests that one cannot break complex systems down to component pieces for comprehension or treatment and then simply add them together again. Complexity posits that human behavior must not be reduced to simplistic levels for analysis or intervention. The suggestion that psychological concerns can be understood apart from the social and macrosystemic context is repudiated. There exist today complex analyses of systems that have conceptualized the interaction between levels of systems and developed means to measure systemic capabilities (e.g., see Ulanowicz, 1997, for his description of ascendency within systems, a form of power coordination and organization toward system goals). These analyses challenge family psychologists to grapple with the complexity of systemic interactions and transactions.

Complexity is related to chaos theory. Chaos theory suggests that complex systems are unpredictable, with abrupt and discontinuous change occurring at random points; such systems appear chaotic because it is difficult to explain the interaction of many variables in the system. Chaos means that we should not expect to predict and control our lives; rather we manage and adapt in the midst of the complex system (see McBride, 2005, for a brief overview of chaos theory). Concepts like the "butterfly effect" (Laszlo, 1996) suggest that relatively minor changes in one part of the global system impact other parts of that system (e.g., a slight increase in the ocean temperature in South America may impact weather patterns in North America). At first glance these ideas seem incredible or naïve, but upon consideration they point to the interconnectedness of all living organisms and systems. Chaos theory is relevant to family psychologists because it suggests the need to recognize unexpected and unpredictable results of interventions in the system.

For beginning family psychologists, the complexity of the epistemology and paradigm may be somewhat overwhelming. It is intimidating to think about the variety of systemic factors one must consider to provide family psychology treatment. On the other hand, screening for the salient factors in a particular case gets easier over time, and it is much better to struggle with the ambiguity of complexity than to settle for simplistic or reductionistic solutions to complex problems. It is typical for a particular clinical case to include some mix of individual, interpersonal, and macrosystemic factors, but not all of the factors noted above will be found in any one case.

For example, Kalisha was a 36-year-old African American woman who presented for psychotherapy because she was "feeling depressed," but it was evident in the intake session that there was a larger picture to be explored when her case was considered from a systemic perspective (i.e., personality factors, relationship problems, socioeconomic issues, and cultural prescriptions were all involved in her presenting symptoms). I began to conceptualize her case within the interactive matrix of these factors and to assess each area in more detail. It became clear that her dependent personality features, marital relationship, job loss, and need for social support were central factors involved in her depression. The presenting issues were prioritized for intervention.

Knowing the range of factors allows the family psychologist to monitor for them, but set aside those that do not seem important in this case in order to focus on the few that are significant.

Reciprocity

Reciprocity refers to mutual, interactive, non-sequential effects that occur between persons or circumstances. Capra defines reciprocity as human transactions that demonstrate a "simultaneous and mutually interdependent interaction between multiple components" (1983, p. 267). The central concept is a transition from linear causality (e.g., A leads to B) to recognition of a more complex process of interaction that is occurring continuously and simultaneously, with components influencing and being influenced. In this sense, it is impossible to isolate one distinct act as prior to another, because the first act is changing even as it occurs due to reciprocity with other acts that are taking place (e.g., it is impossible to say that a mother is influencing her child without concomitantly recognizing that the child is influencing the mother simultaneously; we cannot say mother did this, then the child did that, as if each act was distinct and followed the other in linear causality). So, in couple therapy, the family psychologist moves away from the typical idea held by each partner that his or her behavior was a reaction to the partner, and toward recognition that each partner is constantly acting and reacting to the partner in reciprocal fashion. This diminishes blame and promotes responsibility by both partners for the relationship dynamic.

For example, due to Kalisha's initial presentation of her concerns (above), I recommended that her husband be included in conjoint psychotherapy. She readily agreed to invite him because, she indicated, "I know my relationship with my husband is messed up and it makes me more depressed." Avoiding blame, we focused on how each person's actions perpetuated a cycle of negative interaction with the other.

Living open systems theory

The idea of living open systems draws upon the work of Bertalanffy (Bertalanffy, 1950) and Miller (Miller & Miller, 1993) to denote the way living systems interact continuously with their environment by exchanging energy, matter, and information in order to maintain life in the system. Closed systems do not interact with the environment in which they exist; they function based on whatever was built into the system until it is used up, so they tend toward entropy (increasing disorder and eventual exhaustion of the system over time) (Capra, 1996). For example, the automobile is a closed system, dependent upon its existing (unchanging) structure and the resources supplied to it by humans. Over time, it breaks down and fails to operate any longer (even recent advances that allow some cars to be "self-servicing" are only examples of redundancy built into a closed system). Human social systems evidence the qualities of open systems, including the ability to seek out and utilize resources to rejuvenate and maintain vitality in the face of serious challenges. For instance, a couple experiencing difficulty is not confined to that relationship; they may reach out in a variety of directions to seek input to revitalize the relationship. In Kalisha's case (continued from above), she decided to reach out more to her church for social support; "I always feel better after I go to those meetings."

Self-organization

An essential aspect for understanding living systems is recognition of the pattern of organization in the system, arranged in network manner. Each network is organized in a kind of enclosed loop that makes it a distinct system (or subsystem), yet allows it to interact with its environment. For instance, the brain may be understood as a complex web of subsystem networks that nest into a macrosystemic network (see Capra, 1996, for a thorough discussion of self-organization). Patterns are the basis of life in a system, and the primary reason systems cannot be reduced easily for reductionistic analysis. As Capra (1996) indicates, "What is destroyed when a living organism is dissected is its pattern. The components are still there, but the configuration of relationships among them – the pattern – is destroyed, and thus the organism dies" (p. 81).

Non-linear networks facilitate feedback mechanisms (i.e., a form of corrective communication) that enable the system to regulate itself, even while operating far from equilibrium (contemporary systems theory recognizes that living systems are in constant flux as they interact with lower and higher systems; social systems should not expect to maintain the status quo, but to continually adjust to reflect changes at the individual, interpersonal, and macrosystemic levels). This allows the system to dynamically reorganize itself when life circumstances require new behaviors or new structures within the complexity of reciprocal interactions in a living system.

Adaptation

This is the innovative elasticity of living systems and their ability to change in response to situational demands that is part of self-organization. All living systems adapt to the shifting demands of the environment in which they exist. Living systems evidence equifinality, the inner-directed creative ability to protect, restore, and advance wholeness in the system. Systems reorganize and restructure, creating new communication pathways and new interactive processes for survival. Life process (Capra, 1996) is "the activity involved in the continual embodiment of the system's pattern or organization" (p. 161). Ecological succession refers to the way a living system evolves over time.

One way to understand systemic treatment is to consider it a formal process for adaptation. The family psychologist joins the system to facilitate creative adaptation. In Kalisha's case, cutbacks in the state economy had eliminated her part-time job at the local elementary school, putting the family in financial crisis and contributing to her depression. Treatment helped her respond by changing some patterns in her life (strengthening her marital relationship, connecting with her church) to reorganize in the face of her current dilemma.

Social constructivism and cognition

Systemic models include communication and cognitive processes as important aspects of system functioning. Constructivism posits the idea that humans are active agents in their own development, continually constructing their reality in interaction with their social and physical environments; it views learning, knowing, and memory as the ongoing attempts of the body and brain to organize into patterns the engagements with the changing world (Mahoney, 1991). Mind (mental activity) and the process of knowing have been identified as a core element of the self-organization process in living systems; "The organizing activity of living systems, at all levels of life, is mental activity" (Capra, 2002, p. 34). This is a distinctly different understanding of cognition than that which locates it within the brain (Goldspink & Kay, 2004). Capra suggests that understanding mind as the process of cognition inherent in the process of life is a conceptual advance that prevails against the separation of mind and matter that originated with Descartes. Although they are not yet integrated ideas, the two strands of constructivism and cognition both are central to a systemic epistemology. Narrative approaches to psychotherapy capitalize on this dimension of systemic functioning (see Chapter 20, this volume).

Epistemology in Practice

The family psychology epistemology presented in this chapter (i.e., the systemic way of thinking, including recognition of key concepts and the adoption of a systemic paradigm) is directly applicable to professional practice. Family psychologists conceptualize cases through the systemic epistemology, assess for salient factors within the systemic paradigm, and use the paradigm to organize information and plan coherent interventions in the system. For example, a family psychologist treating an individual holds the paradigm (individual – interpersonal – environmental or macrosystemic factors) in mind as he or she listens to that individual. The individual describes the presenting concerns (in response to a general question, "What brings you here today?"), often touching on issues within each of the three systemic domains. The family psychologist sorts the information using the domains, asking further questions if little or insufficient information is presented to determine the salience of particular factors to the presenting concerns. This allows the family psychologist to conceptualize the case and to determine the need for additional assessment in particular areas. Assessment may include individual (e.g., history, personality, intelligence), interpersonal (e.g., 3–4 generation genogram, couple or family factors, social support), and environmental/macrosystemic factors (socioeconomic status, ethnicity/ culture, religion) (see Chapter 10, this volume).

Conceptualization and assessment facilitate determination of treatment focus and/or treatment modality (i.e., a family psychologist may begin treatment with an individual, but the conceptualization and assessment may result in a recommendation for a couple, family, or social network treatment modality). During treatment, the family psychologist expects complexity (and avoids reductionistic problem solving), clarifies reciprocal dynamics between people or factors to avoid blaming and encourage personal responsibility, facilitates reorganization or adaptation to current circumstances, and uses language (communication and/or social narrative construction) to enhance system process. Family psychologists recognize the systemic capacity for self-organization and creativity, so they understand that the system may reject "expert" input at times to go in the direction chosen by the system. Any of a variety of intervention models that incorporate systemic elements may be engaged for treatment (see Part II of this volume for examples of various forms of systemic treatment).

Epistemology in Research

Family psychologists also conduct research using systemic designs that consider the interaction of individual, interpersonal, and environmental or macrosystemic factors in the etiology, progression, and treatment of behavior. Family psychologists avoid reductionistic logic to consider the complexity of human behavior in real-life circumstances. Both qualitative (see Chapter 6, this volume) and quantitative (see Chapters 7, 11, and 29, this volume) designs may be appropriate in systemic research.

It is possible for family psychology research to bridge the gap between research and clinical practice, benefiting a common goal (see Chapter 7, this volume). Education and training in qualitative methods may enhance clinical abilities in interviewing and noting patterns or themes in verbal communication. Knowledge of quantitative methods promotes understanding and acceptance of evidence-based clinical practices (see Chapter 21, this volume). Clinical research may even inform the ongoing process in professional practice (see Chapter 29, this volume).

Conclusion

Family psychology is distinctive because it adopts a systemic epistemology and paradigm. For those educated in western countries, this usually requires a paradigm shift from the typical Cartesian worldview. Such an epistemological transformation may be difficult, but it provides a paradigm that is adequate for conceptualizing, assessing, treating, and researching human behavior in a complex world.

Resources

Capra, F. (2002). *The hidden connections: A science for sustainable living*. New York: Anchor Books.

Laszlo, E. (1996). *The systems view of the world: A holistic vision for our time*. Cresskill, NJ: Hampton Press.

References

Andersen, S. M., Thorpe, J. S., & Kooij, C. S. (2007). Character in context: The relational self and transference. In Y. Shoda, D. Cervone, & G. Downey (Eds.), *Persons in context: Building a science of the individual* (pp. 169–200). New York: Guilford Press.

Auerswald, E. H. (1990). Toward epistemological transformation in the education and training of family therapists. In M. P. Mirkin (Ed.), *The social and political contexts of family therapy* (pp. 19–50). Needham Heights, MA: Allyn & Bacon.

Bateson, G. (1972). *Steps to an ecology of mind*. New York: Ballantine.

Bertalanffy, L. V. (1950). An outline of general system theory. *British Journal for the Philosophy of Science, 1*, 134–165.

Bloom, J. (n.d.). Bateson @ 100: Multiple versions of the world [Electronic version]. Retrieved January 12, 2008, from http://www.ccaerasig.com/papers/05/BatesonConference.pdf

Bronfenbrenner, U. (1979). *The ecology of human development*. Cambridge, MA: Harvard University Press.

Bronfenbrenner, U. (1986). Ecology of the family as a context for human development: Research perspectives. *Developmental Psychology, 22*, 723–742.

Capra, F. (1983). *The turning point*. Toronto: Bantam.

Capra, F. (1996). *The web of life*. New York: Anchor Books.

Capra, F. (2002). *The hidden connections: A science for sustainable living*. New York: Anchor Books.

Cervone, D., Shoda, Y., & Downey, G. (2007). Construing persons in context: On building a science of the individual. In Y. Shoda, D. Cervone, & G. Downey (Eds.), *Persons in context: Building a science of the individual* (pp. 3–15). New York: Guilford Press.

Demastes, S. S., Good, R. G., & Peebles, P. (1995). Students' conceptual ecologies and the process of conceptual change in evolution. *Science Education, 79*, 637–666.

Descartes, R. (1999). *Discourse on method and meditations on first philosophy* (Donald A. Cress, Trans., 4th ed.). Indianapolis, IN: Hackett.

Duit, R., Roth, W.-M., Komorek, M., & Wilbers, J. (2001). Fostering conceptual change by analogies – between Scylla and Charybdis. *Learning and Instruction, 11*, 283–303.

Friedman, T. L. (2005). *The world is flat: A brief history of the twenty-first century.* New York: Farrar, Straus, and Giroux.

Goldspink, C., & Kay, R. (2004). Bridging the micro–macro divide: A new basis for social science. *Human Relations, 57*, 597–618.

Gregoire, M. (2003). *Effects of augmented activation, refutational text, efficacy beliefs, epistemological beliefs, and systematic processing on conceptual change.* Unpublished doctoral dissertation, University of Florida.

Laszlo, E. (1996). *The systems view of the world: A holistic vision for our time.* Cresskill, NJ: Hampton Press.

Liddle, H., Santisteban, D., Levant, R., & Bray, J. (Eds.). (2002). *Family psychology: Science-based interventions.* Washington, DC: American Psychological Association.

Mahoney, M. (1991). *Human change processes.* New York: Basic Books.

Marsella, A. J. (1998). Toward a "global-community psychology:" Meeting the needs of a changing world. *American Psychologist, 53*, 1282–1291.

McBride, N. (2005). Chaos theory as a model for interpreting information systems in organizations. *Information Systems Journal, 15*, 233–254.

McGoldrick, M., Gerson, R., & Petry, S. (2008). *Genograms: Assessment and intervention.* New York: Norton.

Miller, J. L., & Miller, J. G. (1993). Greater than the sum of its parts: II. Matter–energy processing subsystems. *Behavioral Science, 38*, 151–163.

Nichols, M. P. (1987). *The self in the system.* New York: Brunner/Mazel.

Nisbett, R. E. (2007). Eastern and western ways of perceiving the world. In Y. Shoda, D. Cervone, & G. Downey (Eds.), *Persons in context: Building a science of the individual* (pp. 62–83). New York: Guilford Press.

Nutt, R., & Stanton, M. (2008). Family psychology specialty practice. *Professional Psychology: Research and Practice, 39*, 519–528.

Robbins, M., Mayorga, C., & Szapocznik, J. (2003). The ecosystemic "lens" to understanding family functioning. In T. Sexton, G. Weeks, & M. Robbins (Eds.), *Handbook of family therapy: The science and practice of working with families and couples* (pp. 21–36). New York: Brunner-Routledge.

Sandoval, J. (1996). Constructivism, consultee-centered consultation, and conceptual change. *Journal of Educational and Psychological Consultation, 7*, 89–97.

Schermerhorn, A. C., Cummings, E. M., & Davies, P. T. (2008). Children's representations of multiple family relationships: Organizational structure and development in early childhood. *Journal of Family Psychology, 22*, 89–101.

Shoda, Y. (2007). From homunculus to a system: Toward a science of the person. In Y. Shoda, D. Cervone, & G. Downey (Eds.), *Persons in context: Building a science of the individual* (pp. 327–331). New York: Guilford Press.

Stanford encyclopedia of philosophy. (n.d.). Retrieved October 4, 2007, from http://plato.stanford.edu/entries/epistemology/#SEP

Stanton, M. (1999). Family psychology. In D. Benner & P. Hill (Eds.), *Baker encyclopedia of psychology and counseling* (2nd ed., pp. 438–439). Grand Rapids: Baker.

Stanton, M. (2005). Developing family psychologists: Epistemological transformation. *The Family Psychologist, 21*, 26.

Ulanowicz, R. E. (1997). *Ecology: The ascendant perspective.* New York: Columbia University Press.

2

The Revolution and Evolution of Family Therapy and Family Psychology

Herbert Goldenberg and Irene Goldenberg

The revolution is over! Long live the revolution!

The revolution we refer to, in this case, began a half century ago, when a number of leading scientists, engineers, mathematicians, and social scientists proposed a new paradigm – one that emphasized systems, a cybernetic epistemology, and in general an outlook that underscored the role that context and interaction play in understanding individual behavior. Within this new conceptual leap, each person's experiences, attitudes, and sets of problems could now be defined as occurring within a framework such as a family. Rather than seek out the person's intrapsychic problems, clinicians were now urged to direct the attention to the family context in which the behavior occurred and to the interpersonal sequences taking place between family members. Focusing on *what* was occurring in the present as families interacted, and *how* each participant influenced (and in turn is influenced by) other family members, began to replace the search for explanations of *why* problems developed as a result of past trauma. As the outlook of reciprocal causality (or circular causality) replaced linear explanations, clinicians learned to attend to the dysfunctional family unit and not merely the symptomatic person (Goldenberg & Goldenberg, 2008).

During its heyday in the 1970s and 1980s, as the family systems outlook gained prominence, a number of seasoned clinicians, formerly psychodynamic in viewpoint, converted to its tenets. They, as well as many fledgling clinicians, were attracted to its basic notion that behavior occurs in context, that problems exist between people rather than within each person, and that seeking to uncover and gain insight into unconscious conflicts was not nearly as therapeutic as helping families change ongoing dysfunctional interactions. Fraenkel (2005) recalls from his student days, after becoming convinced of the therapeutic worth of systems intervention, that "family therapy was an unstoppable revolutionary movement, which would radically change the mental health field, and even our larger society" (p. 33).

Today, much of that fervor has passed, inevitably replaced by new approaches, yet the systems viewpoint is far from dead. On the contrary, it has permeated all forms of psychotherapy, and while no longer so revolutionary, has entered middle age and become part of mainstream therapeutic endeavors.

In this chapter, we intend to tell family psychology's story – from the early clinical trailblazers offering innovative if often radical ideas and approaches without benefit of research support, to the present effort to establish an evidence-based set of procedures to more scientifically justify family therapy procedures. Credit must also be extended to the behavioral psychologists, gaining prominence at the same time that family theories emerged, who also directed attention to observable behavior rather than the more traditional (but less measurable) intrapsychic viewpoint. The behavioral outlook, applied to families, helped fuel the focus on family interactional patterns.

The Pioneers

Pioneers are often iconoclastic; they enjoy swimming against the prevailing tide, and they typically dismiss the value of current ways of doing things. The early systems theorists and practitioners were no exception; having discovered the "truth," many argued that earlier viewpoints, focused on the individual's internal world, were simplistic, reductionistic, and outmoded. For them, the wave of the future was in an interpersonal (not intrapsychic), here-and-now (not uncovering or reconstructing the past) contextual examination of how people within a family repetitiously (and sometimes ineffectively) deal with one another, and how the appearance of problems or symptoms in a family member was a function of a faulty or dysfunctional family system (and not the result of unresolved conflict within the identified patient).

Early efforts at systems thinking began more modestly, starting with the Macy Foundation Conferences in the 1940s, as interdisciplinary conferees grappled, among other things, with improving communication, regulation, and control of wartime weapons problems (e.g., guided missiles and rockets). Slowly, a new paradigm emerged – one based on a systems view that self-regulation could be achieved by reinserting the results of past performance into current functioning. Thus, a way was beginning to be developed regarding changing patterns of performance by altering feedback mechanisms. Anthropologist Gregory Bateson, an attendee, in particular, saw the relevance to human interactive behavior patterns of this cybernetic notion that systems are governed by self-regulating feedback loops that correct for deviations and thus restore stability. Later, he led a Schizophrenia Communication Research Project (Bateson, Jackson, Haley, & Weakland, 1956) that issued the famed, if flawed, *double-bind theory* that took the unorthodox position that the disorder was a consequence of failure in the family's communication system, not of the internal conflicts of the identified patient.

The family psychology pioneers in the 1950s focused on family systems research, not yet on treatment. At least four major research groups launched scientific investigations regarding the role of the family in the development of schizophrenia in one of its members. In addition to Bateson's project, Theodore Lidz at Yale (Lidz, Cornelison, Fleck, & Terry, 1957), Murray Bowen (1960) at the National Institute of Mental Health, and later, succeeding Bowen at NIMH, the group led by Lyman Wynne (Wynne, Ryckoff, Day, & Hirsch, 1958) were all beginning to study the impact of family dysfunction on the appearance of schizophrenia in a family member. By 1957, these researchers met at the national convention of the American Orthopsychiatric Association, and family psychology studies took on a more cohesive form as researchers exchanged views and visited each other's facilities (Broderick & Schrader, 1991).

By the 1960s, many therapists, trained to work therapeutically with individuals, were beginning to take notice of systems theory and to consider the value of intervention at the family level, first with schizophrenics and later with other troubled clients. Don Jackson (1965), from the Bateson group in Palo Alto, California, saw the therapeutic implications of family research, and formed the Mental Research Institute (MRI), recruiting social worker Virginia Satir and communication specialist Jay Haley. On the east coast, Nathan Ackerman (1958), a child psychiatrist, organized the Family Institute in New York devoted to treating families. In New England, psychologist John Bell (1961) began experimenting with group therapy for the entire family. Carl Whitaker (1958), having initially worked with individuals, began, with a co-therapist, to treat entire families, often several generations at a time. Salvador Minuchin (Minuchin, Montalvo, Guerney, Rosman, & Schumer, 1967), later in the decade, offered a pioneering study of working with urban slum families at the Wiltwyck School in upper New York State, where he developed many techniques which later became the basis for structural family therapy. In the 1960s, Ackerman and Jackson together helped launch the first and still the most influential journal in the field, *Family Process*, with Jay Haley as its first editor.

So who deserves recognition as the founder of family therapy? That honor is shared by several prominent names – Ackerman, Bell, Jackson, Bowen, and Whitaker. During its formative years, Haley, Satir, Wynne, and Minuchin played significant roles in developing theoretical and/or clinical models of family therapy. Less well known, but nevertheless important, is the contribution of Christian Midelfort (1957), who presented the first paper on treating psychiatric patients by including their families. Unfortunately, Midelfort's efforts are all but forgotten today, because his geographic location in La Crosse, Wisconsin, and his lack of an academic or training center isolated him from family therapy's mainstream activity.

The Golden Years

The 1970s and 1980s were the golden years for family therapy. Family therapy journals proliferated, some 300 freestanding family therapy training institutes came into being, and new professional organizations (such as the American Family Therapy Association and the Division of Family Psychology of the American Psychological Association) were established. Membership in the interdisciplinary American Association for Marriage and Family Therapy (AAMFT) swelled over seven-fold in one decade – from 1,000 members in 1970 to 7,500 by 1979.

A variety of ground-breaking interventions (most without benefit of having first been submitted to empirical testing regarding effectiveness) were introduced during this exploratory period. In Vermont, Laqueur (1976) treated several families with hospitalized schizophrenic members in group therapy procedures (called multiple family therapy), while in Texas a group led by Robert MacGregor (MacGregor, Ritchie, Serrano, & Schuster, 1964) brought families together for an intensive two-day period of continuing interaction with a team of mental health professionals (multiple impact therapy). A third group, in Philadelphia, led by Speck and Attneave (1973), carried out network therapy by working in the client's home with a large, extended group, including family, friends, neighbors, and employers.

Perhaps most significant during this expansive period was the emergence and elaboration of a half dozen major models of family therapy practice. These at times contentious "camps" were all systems-based, usually followed an inventive, charismatic leader, and, despite insistence as to their uniqueness, often showed considerable overlap in both theory and technique. However, each typically allowed students to learn a set of therapeutic procedures and to determine for themselves which style "fit" for them. (The danger, of course, was the risk of blindly following the leader.).

Major models

Psychodynamic therapies.   Nathan Ackerman, trained as a psychoanalyst, became an early family therapist who nevertheless retained his psychodynamic orientation and thus never lost sight of each family member's needs, wishes, and longings. Psychologist James Framo (1981), another first-generation family therapist, emphasized the relationship between the intrapsychic and interpersonal, offering an amalgam of psychodynamic and systems concepts. In England, object relations theorists, following the early lead of child psychoanalyst Melanie Klein (1946), focused attention on the infant's attachment (emotional bonding) experiences in relationship to the mother as the primary determinant of adult personality formation.

Transgenerational therapies.   Murray Bowen, earlier trained in psychoanalysis, turned to an examination of the family's emotional system for most of his career. He viewed families as *natural systems*, and thus saw the human family as one type of living system. Bowen's set of interlocking theoretical concepts (differentiation of self, triangles, family projection process, etc.) remain in the forefront of family psychology theory today. (See Chapter 19, this volume, for an overview of Bowen theory.)

Experiential therapies.   Virginia Satir (1964) was more renowned for her inspiring training demonstrations with families than for theory-building. Humanistic in value, and determined to stimulate an inherent growth-producing process in families, Satir emphasized open communication and emotional experiencing, usually by demonstrating these qualities in her own behavior with families, a position her followers attempted to emulate. Carl Whitaker (Whitaker & Bumberry, 1988) viewed theory as largely a therapeutic hindrance, and in its place offered families an encounter experience in which therapist and family together probed and gave voice to their impulses and fantasies. Each family member was encouraged to maximize his or her growth potential rather than seek solutions for specific problems.

Structural therapies. Salvador Minuchin (1974) offered a transaction-based theory regarding how families organize or structure their lives; these arrangements, usually unstated and often unrecognized by the participants, govern their interactions. Family subsystems, boundaries, alignments and coalitions within the family were investigated. Therapeutically, Minuchin developed a set of interventions for joining the family, assessing its transactional patterns, clarifying boundaries, and helping restructure what the family considers to be outmoded or no longer workable rules that hamper optimum functioning.

Strategic therapies. Originally associated with the efforts of the Mental Research Institute in Palo Alto, emphasizing what gets communicated between family members, and how it gets communicated, this approach later came to be linked with the work of Jay Haley (1963).

Here, family hierarchies, triangles, and transactional sequences are all studied in an effort to see how the presenting problem is maintained by the family, before the therapist customizes a strategy aimed at alleviating the specific problem the family wishes to resolve. In Italy, Mara Selvini-Palazzoli and her associates (Selvini-Palazzoli, Boscolo, Cecchin, & Prata, 1978) offered a related set of strategic intervention procedures, but urged families to examine their *belief systems* (attitudes, thoughts, meanings attributed to events) rather than helping change their interactive patterns.

Behavioral and cognitive-behavioral therapies. Behavioral couples therapy (Liberman, 1970; Stuart, 1969) and behavioral parent training (Patterson, 1971) represent efforts to bring the scientific method to bear in working therapeutically with families. In this practical approach, more likely to be researched than the others so far discussed, presenting symptoms are seen as learned maladaptive patterns rather than the manifestation of an underlying disorder or disease process. Careful assessments (tests, questionnaires, personality inventories) have been employed, and the contingencies of reinforcement for problematic behavior examined. Skills training is emphasized, and, among cognitively oriented behavioral therapists, distorted beliefs and expectations are guided to be restructured. *Functional family therapy*, a therapeutic approach based on systems theory, cognitive theory, and behavioral principles, in which clients are helped to understand the function or interpersonal payoff of certain of their behaviors, has been especially noteworthy in providing strong evidence-based findings for its therapeutic efforts with at-risk adolescents and their families (Sexton & Alexander, 2003).

The Feminist Challenge

The articulation of feminine concerns jolted family therapy's growing self-satisfaction in the second half of the 1970s. Having viewed themselves as rebellious and avant garde because they had moved beyond traditional linear views of behavior, most practicing family therapists considered themselves above the growing feminine critique of most forms of long-term psychotherapy. Thus, they were unprepared for critics such as Rachel Hare-Mustin (1978), who offered the eye-opening argument that the then current family therapy models were rife with gender bias – extolling values typically considered male (autonomy, independence, control), while devaluing those nurturing and relationship values more customarily considered female. Feminists contended that by being inattentive to such family issues as gender roles and wife battering, theoreticians (almost all male) were, often inadvertently, reinforcing patriarchal attitudes as well as masculine and feminine stereotypes.

Drawing attention to the social and political context in which families live, feminists insisted that such systems notions as reciprocity and circularity, in which all participants share responsibility for the ensuing transactions, were oblivious to the differences in power between the persons involved. In the case of family violence, for example, feminists disputed as oversimplified the notion of equal responsibility and equal blame, since such a formulation failed to acknowledge the typically crucial differences in power, economic earning power, and physical supremacy of males in the relationship.

Family therapists, having grown up in a sexist society, according to feminists, were urged to examine their own built-in values, attitudes, and beliefs that could be detrimental if they were to help all family members, male as well as female, feel empowered. One major consequence of the feminist critique was to force therapists to look beyond a simple systems view within the family to the broader view of the impact of historical, political, social, and community forces on family functioning. Another was to stimulate men's studies, especially how men too were subject to role restraints and disadvantaged as a result of sexist attitudes in society. Levant and Philpot (2002) later suggested that such restraint was traumatic for many men because it truncated their natural emotionality.

The Postmodern Critique

As family psychologists struggled with examining their own patriarchal ideas, and in making their therapeutic interventions more gender-sensitive, they were forced to deal with the further criticism that their assumptions of what constitutes a "normal" family, passed on by the pioneers, was too fixed and unbending. Postmodernists, beginning in the 1980s, challenged the assumption that there is an objective set of truths awaiting discovery as a result of objective observations and measurement. Part of the postmodern critique in literature, education, science, and religion then taking place, deconstruction efforts were underway to reexamine assumptions previously taken for granted. To the postmodern family therapists, multiple views of reality exist and the absolute truth can never be known. Numerous family lifestyles (single-parent-led families, stepfamilies, gay and lesbian couples, and so forth) exist side by side and may or may not thrive, but they should not be judged by the formal standard of the intact heterosexual marital unit.

Postmodernists such as Gergen (1985) argued that our beliefs about the world – what constitutes reality – are not an exact replica of what is out there, but are social inventions that arrive from interactions with others over time. Such a constructivist epistemology (how we subjectively perceive or construct the world rather than how the world objectively exists) flies in the face of simple cybernetic concepts. That is, attention is paid to the family's belief system and the assumptions they make about their problems, rather than viewing their difficulties in terms of interactional behavior and feedback loops. Collaboratively helping families seek new meanings through mutual inquiry replaces the therapist as objective expert who stands apart from the dysfunctional family and attempts to reprogram their interactions from the outside. Postmodern therapists do not claim to have the answers to the family's problems; on the contrary, their efforts are directed at working in partnership with the family to deconstruct old family assumptions and co-construct new narratives or realities that are less saturated with past problems or past failed solutions. Narrative therapists such as Michael White (White & Epston, 1990) and collaborative therapists such as Harlene Anderson and Harry Goolishian (1988) were especially influential clinicians in promoting the postmodern viewpoint.

Postmodernism and Diversity Awareness

By highlighting the pluralistic nature of society, postmodernists forced many family therapists to revisit their views of some families as "dysfunctional" because they did not conform to the prevalent picture of American middle-class family life. By the 1980s, family therapists were being urged to attend to a client family's cultural heritage or ethnicity and to appreciate the primacy of diversity in our society (race, social class, gender, sexual orientation, and so forth). Values, rituals, common transactional patterns, ways of communicating – all called for inclusion if an accurate, unbiased, and comprehensive family evaluation could be completed. The publication of a landmark text, *Ethnicity and Family Therapy* by McGoldrick, Pearce, and Giordano (1982), presented descriptions of common family patterns for a variety of ethnic groups (expanded to over 40 groups in the latest 2005 edition), emphasizing the different family issues important to them as well as the resources, values, and customs they commonly bring to problem solving. The interaction of ethnicity with economics, race, social class, religion, politics, geography, the length of time since their ancestors migrated to this country, the degree of discrimination they experienced, and so forth were especially relevant in any efforts at understanding and clinical intervention.

To become *culturally competent*, therapists were directed to take client family's cultural histories into account before undertaking assessments, forming judgments, and initiating intervention procedures. At the same time that they maintain cultural sensitivity, therapists must not blindly stereotype all members of a particular group as homogeneous, since a variety of factors – educational level, social class, religion, stage of acculturation into American society – also influence family behavior patterns (Falicov, 1995). Without an appreciation for diversity and the acceptance that we live in a pluralistic society, therapists run the risk of mislabeling attitudes, beliefs, and cultural patterns unfamiliar to them as abnormal when they may be appropriate to the family's cultural background. On the other hand, we must take care not to overlook, minimize, or dismiss certain deviant values or beliefs in unfamiliar families by simply attributing them to cultural differences. Family therapists themselves were directed to examine their own corresponding attitudes, values, and cultural patterns in order to reduce bias in their assessments and treatment.

By the last decade of the twentieth century, most family therapists were beginning to appreciate the central role that a family's cultural background is likely to play in their assumptions about the world. For some, this meant de-emphasizing the systems metaphor to concentrate on the family's belief system, and how those sets of beliefs help shape the family's collective perceptions as well as their actions.

The Emergence of Social Constructionism

If, indeed, our perceptions are not an exact duplicate of the world, but rather represent a point of view constructed through the limiting lens of assumptions about people, then some therapists, such as Anderson and Goolishian (1988), directed their therapeutic efforts at engaging in dialogues with families, helping families investigate their perceptions and beliefs, opening up the possibility of seeing their problems in a fresh way, and in the process freeing themselves from burdensome, entrenched beliefs. In this collaborative undertaking, the therapist does not direct the family toward his or her notion of what constitutes happiness or normality, but rather takes a "not knowing" attitude and engages in a mutual inquiry with them about new ways of understanding their problems and seeking new solutions.

Constructivism is rooted in the biology of cognition – each of our perceptions is filtered through our individual nervous systems, so that no one ever sees all that is out there. Instead we each bring our own assumptions to the same situation; we each construct reality differently. Social constructionism expands this viewpoint, asserting that what we do construct from what we observe comes from the language system, relationships, and social context we share with others. It is through learning and conversations with others that we learn the prepackaged thoughts of our society, and through the process of socialization that we learn to share the values and ideology of our language system and the culture in which we live (Becvar, 2000). The reality each of us constructs emerges from our relationship with other people.

Social Construction Therapeutic Models

How do postmodern therapists propose helping families deconstruct fixed ways of thinking so that they may explore new assumptions and develop new constructions about their beliefs? At least four related efforts can be differentiated.

Solution-focused therapies.   This brief, pragmatic, cognitive approach emphasizes the therapeutic conversation between therapist and family members directed at constructing new solutions to their presenting problems, rather than searching for explanations concerning why the problem initially emerged. Led by husband and wife Steve de Shazer (1988) and Insoo Berg (1994), families were helped to get "unstuck," that is, to change outmoded beliefs, and to actively create new, empowering stories about themselves, ones that reconstruct their sense of their ability to bring about change. Central to this approach is the search for exceptions (times in the past when the problem did not occur) in the service of building on past successes in problem solving. Miracle questions (asking family members to imagine what life would be like if they woke up next morning and their problem was solved) help them to identify goals and, together, reveal potential solutions. (See Chapter 14, this volume, for a more thorough description.)

Collaborative therapies.   This postmodern approach, especially attentive to language and communication, focuses on an egalitarian relationship between therapist and family members in which they jointly generate new meanings, new outlooks, and the ultimate dissolution of the family's presenting problem. Advocates of this linguistically oriented model, such as Anderson and Goolishian (1988), do not offer a specific set of intervention procedures, nor do they consider themselves objective experts regarding family problems, but rather take a "not knowing" position, respectfully listening to the clients' unfolding story. Without a set idea of how the family needs to change, they view their role as conversational partners with the family as they mutually search for new meanings, attitudes, narratives, and behavior. To collaborative therapists, problems are stories that people have agreed to tell themselves (Hoffman, 1990). Consequently, the therapist's task becomes reconstructive, to co-construct new stories intended to free the family from dysfunctional self-accounts in order to make way for alternative accounts, ascribe new meanings to their experiences, and discover possibilities for new options for action and change. Problems, having been created through language, are dissolved by the same process, as alternative meanings and new solutions emerge, enabling the client to no longer experience the previously distressing matter as a problem.

Narrative therapies.   Narrative therapists contend that our sense of reality is organized and maintained by the stories we tell about ourselves, and that certain dominant stories from the past form the basis for our current thoughts and actions. These therapists see their task as helping clients liberate themselves from destructive or self-limiting, problem-saturated stories (dead-ended self-narratives and cultural narratives) and, together with them, construct alternative stories that provide new options and future possibilities. Australian Michael White (1995), narrative therapy's leading exponent, engages clients in respectful, non-blaming narrative conversations in which clients are assumed to have the competence to deconstruct old interpretations of events and construct more positive stories about themselves. Narrative therapists help clients externalize a restraining problem – an unwelcomed outside narrative they have acquired and not an internal deficiency or pathological condition – and then help them look for unique outcomes when the hampering story did not dominate their lives. All of these efforts are intended to aid clients as they begin to feel trapped by problematic stories and to gain a sense of other feasible, more open-ended, preferred stories about their future.

Reflecting teams.   This boundary-breaking technique is aimed at opening up the therapist–consultation team dialogue. Instead of the traditional post-session case conference in which professionals behind a one-way mirror emerge to discuss in private what they have observed about the family, here they do so as the family watches. Employed by various postmodern therapists, this democratization of the therapeutic process calls for professionals to watch families during a therapy session, then to change places with them to discuss their impressions of what they have just observed as the family, now behind the one-way mirror, watches them. Later, the family and their therapist return to the consultation room to reflect on the observations they have just witnessed. Developed by Norwegian psychiatrist Tom Andersen (1991), and consistent with social constructionist thinking, reflecting teams offer a stimulating, non-hierarchical, collaborative procedure in which clients are free to select fresh perspectives from what they have heard, encouraging them to develop new dialogues among themselves.

The Impact of Managed Care: A Changing Medical Care Delivery System

No history of family therapy's evolution would be complete without noting the upheaval to ways of practicing caused by the introduction of managed care, a health insurance system by which third party payers regulate and control the cost, quality, and terms of providing clinical services. Unlike the earlier, unrestricted golden years, when health costs soared as independent practitioners billed insurance companies on a fee-for-service delivery system, employers, who pay the bulk of healthcare costs for their employees, turned in the mid-1980s to managed care insurance programs to control escalating expenses. Health maintenance organizations (HMOs), a form of managed care, have since emerged as the dominant healthcare delivery system in the United States, forcing most practitioners into unfamiliar, time-limited, cost-conscious ways of offering their services (Hersch, 1995).

If practitioners complain that HMO micromanagement and cost containment seem to take precedence over quality of care, HMOs argue that their restrictions have offered clinicians an incentive to account for their interventions by developing brief, effective interventions, such as solution-focused therapy. One positive, if not necessarily intended consequence, as we shall see later, has been the efforts by various clinicians to attempt to develop evidence-based clinical practices.

New Directions in Family Therapy and Family Psychology

Now in its adult years, and no longer the radical movement of a half century ago, family therapy today must compete in the marketplace with a variety of newly minted, newly glamorized therapeutic approaches. While much of the early evangelical fervor has abated, systems thinking has influenced all contemporary psychotherapy, and family therapy has taken its place among one of many therapeutic modalities available to clinicians. Ironically, many family therapists, attracted to the newer social construction models, have themselves de-emphasized systems theory.

Differences between "schools" of family therapy have faded, as clinicians understand that no one approach fits all and that it makes sense to borrow concepts and techniques from one another when appropriate to a specific family or situation. Eclecticism (select-ing concepts or intervention techniques from a variety of sources by a therapist on the basis of his or her experience that a specific approach works with a certain set of prob-lems) involves a pragmatic and case-based effort that has gained popularity. Integration, more complex, calls for a combining of parts of various theories and treatment processes into a higher-level theory crossing theoretical boundaries. Lebow (1997) suggests most family therapists today are eclectic or integrative, recognizing that no one school has a monopoly on effectiveness with all populations. Integrative couples therapy (Jacobson & Christensen, 1996) represents one such effort to combine behaviorally based thera-peutic strategies while promoting more collaborative attitudes (e.g., partner acceptance) between couples in distress. Postmodern thinking has made clear that there are many versions of the "truth" within families, and that the therapist is a collaborative partner and no longer the expert who reprograms a family from the outside.

In addition, in part a response to managed care's restrictions on practice, many family psychologists have moved beyond the consultation room into a number of exciting roles: business executive coaching, divorce mediation, child custody evaluators, forensic speci-alists as consultants to the courts, and workshop leaders conducting public forums. Others have had to modify the nature of their work as family life changes, new popu-lations are served, and cultural differences between themselves and clients (e.g., immi-grant populations) require greater sensitivity and understanding.

Community consultation.   Family psychologists, having expanded their view beyond the individual to examine the family system, have begun to enlarge that framework further, in effect examining the interlocking effect of systems within systems. If the beliefs, actions, and lives of family members are interconnected, then families themselves are embedded in complex extended family, neighborhood, institutional, class, ethnic, and cultural sys-tems (Goldenberg & Goldenberg, 2008). From such an ecosystemic, multidimensional outlook, these "external" factors are likely to influence family functioning (Robbins, Mayorga, & Szapocznik, 2003). No longer confined to the consultation room, some family therapists fan out into the community, delivering services in schools, medical facilities, community agencies, the courts, the welfare system, and on occasion the home. The focus here is on strengthening relationships between the family and the community's available resources rather than working directly at repairing family dysfunction (Henggeler & Borduin, 1990).

Schools offer a clear example of working with an enlarged system. The schoolchild is at the same time a member of a classroom, the school itself, and the school district, all with their own structures and interactive processes, as well as the home, with his or her family structures and processes. These two major systems (school and home) interface and form a new, larger system in which the child brings the struggles, accomplishments, triumphs, and failures being experienced in one system into the other (DeHay, 2006). The family psychologist, called in as consultant to the school to assess the schoolchild's behavioral problem (truancy, dropout, violence, drug use), needs to remain aware of the interaction of the two systems – the family functioning and the school culture – and whether the child is having problems in one or both, before determining how to proceed. A number of intervention programs have been proposed for chronic behavioral and emotional problems in adolescents. One especially promising example is *multisystemic therapy* (Henggeler & Cunningham, 2006), a family-based treatment program that evaluates the multisystemic set of causal and sustaining factors: the family psychologist assesses how much of the problem is associated with characteristics of the child, family, peers, school–family trust of one another, and the community subculture and its support, or lack of support, for academic success before offering a comprehensive set of interventions. (See Chapters 34 and 35, this volume, for additional information on school-based interventions.)

Interdisciplinary teamwork.   A clear example here can be found in the growing field of *medical family therapy* (McDaniel, Hepworth, & Doherty, 1992), in which family psychologists, together with medical personnel, attempt to deal with the complex interface between family relationships and family health. Beyond the simple and traditional physician–patient medical model, medical family therapy calls for a *biopsychosocial* approach, an integrated effort by a team that calls attention to the inevitable impact of chronic illness not only on the personal life of the patient but also on the interpersonal life of the family.

  This collaborative, holistic approach recognizes that no medical event occurs without psychosocial consequences that impact all family members. How well the family adapts is likely to be influenced by its belief system regarding illness, its communicative skills, its customary style of functioning and view of the world, its resources to cope with the possible trauma or crisis in the family's life, and frequently the influence of its ethnic background regarding illness. Just as physicians can enlighten therapists about the cause, likely progression, and prognosis of the illness, so psychologists can enlighten the medical team about helping the family cope better and comply with the prescribed medical regime. Family therapists are often called upon to tend to the family's emotional needs after patient surgery as the physician tends to the biomedical needs. Families can be helped to gain some power and influence over pending medical decisions and to utilize their inherent resiliency to deal more effectively with a possible life-changing situation.

Psychoeducational program facilitator.   Psychoeducational programs are intended to impart information to a variety of distraught families, educating them so that they might develop skills for understanding and coping with a disturbed family member or a troubled family relationship. Such programs include those aimed at supporting and empowering families with schizophrenic members (McFarlane, Dixon, & Lukens, 2002), those struggling with chronic illness (Rolland, 2003), those wishing to improve their marital relationship (Guerney, Brock, & Coufal, 1986), or those learning new skills before forming a stepfamily (Visher & Visher, 1996). What these diverse approaches have in common is the effort by the therapist to form a collaborative, supportive partnership with the family, harness their strengths and resiliencies, teach skills-building and stress-management techniques, and in general help the family gain a sense of mastery, as far as possible, over their situation.

  Family psychologists offering a psychoeducational approach typically follow an empirically derived eclectic approach that usually involves a combination of cognitive-behavioral, educational, and family systems interventions. Such efforts follow one of two formats: (a) working with individual couples or families (e.g., tailoring a program for the family with a schizophrenic member in order to reduce relapse and re-hospitalization), or (b) working with multiple families simultaneously (e.g., weekend workshops for couples stressing relationship enhancement). In all cases, strategies are taught to reduce conflict and learn to prevent problems before they occur in order to head off future distress.

Evidence-Based Family Therapy

Family psychology first gained a foothold among clinicians as a research undertaking. The idea of seeing families for therapeutic purposes came later and followed from research discoveries and subsequent theorizing. The family therapy pioneers, however, perhaps in a rush to develop intervention programs, for the most part did not stop to provide research-based documentation for their theories and techniques. This, in and of itself, is not unusual when ground-breaking ideas are offered, but by today's standards it falls short of what scientific endeavors demand. In recent years, pressure from managed care insurance third party payers, as well as increased funding by government agencies such as the National Institute of Mental Health, has led to greatly expanded family-focused research, particularly in the area of outcome research in psychotherapy. More specifically, some family psychologists have answered the call for providing greater accountability by attempting to establish an empirically validated basis for delivering their services, improving clinical effectiveness and reducing healthcare costs (Goodheart, Kazdin, & Sternberg, 2006).

Academically based clinicians have led the way in developing models of effective treatment programs under rigorous and controlled conditions (e.g., a homogeneous client population, matched groups of clients randomly assigned to treatment or no-treatment groups, therapists trained and monitored in carrying out specific interventions following treatment manuals, multiple outcome measures scored by independent judges, and follow-up evaluations extended over lengthy periods of time). To date, certain integrated approaches, such as multisystemic therapy for treating chronic behavioral problems in adolescents, have shown promise, as have specific parent management training programs (Webster-Stratton & Hammond, 1997). Some psychoeducational programs, such as the Prevention and Relationship Enhancement Program (PREP), have been shown to be effective in increasing marital relationship satisfaction (Markman, Renick, Floyd, Stanley, & Clements, 1993). To date, most evidence-based research has focused on behavioral procedures, which better lend themselves to such investigations.

Many family psychologists are now actively engaged in carrying out evidence-based studies directed at specific disorders or supporting specific therapeutic approaches. There are now numerous evidence-based studies, as reflected in this volume, that address depression, anxiety, children's behavior problems, schizophrenia, etc., in addition to marital therapies and some family therapies. The task is costly, and complicated by the number of variables involved within a large and complex unit such as the family that is in a constant state of change. For example, some members change more than others, they change in different ways, and some may improve while others find their situation has worsened. Then, there is the issue of attending to types of families, their stage in the family life cycle, their ethnic and social class background, level of family functioning, and so forth. In addition, despite mounting evidence, experienced clinicians are often resistant to limiting their therapeutic efforts to approved techniques, which in many cases do not match the family with whom they are working. Many, too, do not wish to be bound by following manualized guidelines, especially in complex cases.

Clinicians of the future face a new set of challenges brought about by the search for evidence-based interventions. The field has faced challenges before (the feminist critique, multiculturalism, postmodernism and social constructionism, managed care) and it has continued to evolve, as it will no doubt continue to do.

The revolution is over. Long live the revolution!

References

Ackerman, N. W. (1958). *The psychodynamics of family life.* New York: Basic Books.

Andersen, T. (1991). *The reflecting team: Dialogues and dialogues about dialogues.* New York: Norton.

Anderson, H. D., & Goolishian, H. A. (1988). Human systems as linguistic systems: Preliminary and evolving ideas about the implications for clinical theory. *Family Process, 27,* 371–393.

Bateson, G., Jackson, D. D., Haley, J., & Weakland, J. (1956). Towards a theory of schizophrenia. *Behavioral Science, 1,* 251–264.

Becvar, D. S. (2000). Human development as a process of meaning making and reality construction. In W. C. Nichols, M. A. Pace-Nichols, D. S. Becvar, & A. Y. Napier (Eds.), *Handbook of family development and intervention* (pp. 65–82). New York: Wiley.

Bell, J. E. (1961). *Family group therapy* (Public Health Monograph No. 64). Washington, DC: U.S. Government Printing Office.

Berg, I. K. (1994). *Family-based services: A solution-focused approach.* New York: Norton.

Bowen, M. (1960). A family concept of schizophrenia. In D. D. Jackson (Ed.), *The etiology of schizophrenia.* New York: Basic Books.

Broderick, C. B., & Schrader, S. S. (1991). The history of professional marriage and family counseling. In A. S. Gurman & D. P. Kniskern (Eds.), *Handbook of family therapy: Vol. 2* (pp. 3–40). New York: Brunner/Mazel.

DeHay, T. L. (2006). The rewards of training in school-based family practice. *The Family Psychologist, 22,* 15–16.

de Shazer, S. (1988). *Clues: Investigating solutions in brief therapy.* New York: Norton.

Falicov, C. J. (1995). Training to think culturally: A multidimensional comparative framework. *Family Process, 34,* 373–388.

Fraenkel, P. (2005). Whatever happened to family therapy? *Psychotherapy Networker, 29,* 23–27.

Framo, J. L. (1981). The integration of marital therapy with sessions with family of origin. In A. S. Gurman & D. P. Kniskern (Eds.), *Handbook of family therapy* (pp. 133–158). New York: Brunner/Mazel.

Gergen, K. J. (1985). The social construction movement in modern psychology. *American Psychologist, 40,* 266–275.

Goldenberg, H., & Goldenberg, I. (2008). *Family therapy: An overview* (7th ed.). Belmont, CA: Thomson.

Goodheart, C. D., Kazdin, A. E., & Sternberg, R. J. (Eds.). (2006). *Evidence-based psychotherapy: Where practice and research meet.* Washington, DC: American Psychological Association.

Guerney, Jr., B. G., Brock, G., & Coufal, J. (1986). Integrating marital therapy and enrichment: The relationship enhancement approach. In N. D. Jacobson & A. S. Gurman (Eds.), *Clinical handbook of marital therapy*. New York: Guilford Press.

Haley, J. (1963). *Strategies of psychotherapy*. New York: Grune & Stratton.

Hare-Mustin, R. T. (1978). A feminist approach to family therapy. *Family Process, 17*, 181–194.

Henggeler, S. W., & Borduin, C. M. (1990). *Family therapy and beyond: A multisystemic approach to treating the behavioral problems of children and adolescents*. Pacific Grove, CA: Brooks/Cole.

Henggeler, S. W., & Cunningham, P. B. (2006). School-related interventions and outcomes for multisystemic therapy (MST). *The Family Psychologist, 22(1)*, 4–5, 28–29.

Hersch, L. (1995). Adapting to health care reform and managed care: Three strategies for survival and growth. *Professional Psychology: Research and Practice, 26*, 16–26.

Hoffman, L. (1990). Constructing realities: An art of lenses. *Family Process, 29*, 1–12.

Jackson, D. D. (1965). The study of the family. *Family Process, 4(1)*, 1–20.

Jacobson, N. S., & Christensen, A. (1996). *Integrative couple therapy: Promoting acceptance*. New York: Norton.

Klein, M. (1946). Notes on some schizoid mechanisms. *International Journal of Psychoanalysis, 27*, 99–110.

Laqueur, H. P. (1976). Multiple family therapy. In P. J. Guerin, Jr. (Ed.), *Family therapy: Theory and practice*. New York: Gardner Press.

Lebow, J. (1997). The integrative revolution in couple and family therapy. *Family Process, 36*, 1–17.

Levant, R. F., & Philpot, C. L. (2002). Conceptualizing gender in marital and family therapy research: The gender role restraint paradigm. In H. A. Liddle, D. A. Santisban, R. F. Levant, & J. H. Bray (Eds.), *Family psychology: Science-based interventions*. Washington, DC: American Psychological Association.

Liberman, R. P. (1970). Behavioral approaches to family and couple therapy. *American Journal of Orthopsychiatry, 40*, 106–118.

Lidz, T., Cornelison, A., Fleck, S., & Terry, D. (1957). The intrafamilial environment of schizophrenic patients: I. The father. *Psychiatry, 20*, 329–342.

MacGregor, R., Ritchie, A. N., Serrano, A. C., & Schuster, F. P. (1964). *Multiple impact therapy with families*. New York: McGraw-Hill.

Markman, H. J., Renick, M. J., Floyd, F. J., Stanley, S. M., & Clements, M. (1993). Preventing marital distress through communication and conflict management training: A 4- and 5-year follow-up. *Journal of Consulting and Clinical Psychology, 61*, 70–77.

McDaniel, S. H., Hepworth, J., & Doherty, W. J. (1992). *Medical family therapy: A biopsychosocial approach to families with health problems*. New York: Basic Books.

McFarlane, W. R., Dixon, L., & Lukens, E. (2002). Severe mental illness. In D. H. Sprenkle (Ed.), *Effectiveness research in marriage and family therapy* (pp. 255–288). Alexandria, VA: American Association for Marriage and Family Therapy.

McGoldrick, M., Pearce, J. K., & Giordano, J. (1982). *Ethnicity and family therapy*. New York: Guilford Press.

Midelfort, C. F. (1957). *The family in psychotherapy*. New York: Viking Press.

Minuchin, S. (1974). *Families and family therapy*. Cambridge, MA: Harvard University Press.

Minuchin, S., Montalvo, B., Guerney, Jr., B. G., Rosman, B. L., & Schumer, F. (1967). *Families of the slums: An exploration of their structure and treatment*. New York: Basic Books.

Patterson, G. R. (1971). *Families: Application of social learning to family life*. Champaign, IL: Research Press.

Robbins, M. S., Mayorga, B. A., & Szapocznik, J. (2003). The ecosystemic "lens" for understanding family functioning. In T. L. Sexton, G. R. Weeks, & M. S. Robbins (Eds.), *Handbook of family therapy: The science and practice of working with families and couples* (pp. 21–36). New York: Brunner-Routledge.

Rolland, J. S. (2003). Mastering family challenges in illness and disability. In F. Walsh (Ed.), *Normal family processes: Growing diversity and complexity* (3rd ed., pp. 460–489). New York: Guilford Press.

Satir, V. M. (1964). *Conjoint family therapy.* Palo Alto, CA: Science and Behavior Books.

Selvini-Palazzoli, M., Boscolo, L., Cecchin, G. F., & Prata, G. (1978). *Paradox and counterparadox: A new model in the therapy of the family in schizophrenic transaction.* New York: Aronson.

Sexton, T. L., & Alexander, J. F. (2003). Functional family therapy: A mature clinical model for working with at-risk adolescents and their families. In T. L. Sexton, G. R. Weeks, & M. S. Robbins (Eds.), *Handbook of family therapy: The science and practice of working with families and couples* (pp. 323–348). New York: Brunner-Routledge.

Speck, R., & Attneave, C. (1973). *Family networks: Rehabilitation and healing.* New York: Pantheon.

Stuart, R. B. (1969). Operant-interpersonal treatment of marital discord. *Journal of Consulting and Clinical Psychology, 33,* 675–682.

Visher, E. B., & Visher, J. S. (1996). *Therapy with stepfamilies.* New York: Brunner/Mazel.

Webster-Stratton, C., & Hammond, M. (1997). Treating children with early-onset conduct problems: A comparison of child and parent training interventions. *Journal of Consulting and Clinical Psychology, 65(1),* 93–109.

Whitaker, C. A. (Ed.). (1958). *Psychotherapy of chronic schizophrenic patients.* Boston: Little, Brown.

Whitaker, C. A., & Bumberry, W. M. (1988). *Dancing with the family: A symbolic-experiential approach.* New York: Brunner/Mazel.

White, M. (1995). *Re-authoring lives: Interviews and essays.* Adelaide, Australia: Dulwich Centre.

White, M., & Epston, D. (1990). *Narrative means to therapeutic ends.* New York: Norton.

Wynne, L. C., Ryckoff, I. M., Day, J., & Hirsch, S. I. (1958). Pseudomutuality in the family relationships of schizophrenics. *Psychiatry, 21,* 205–220.

3

The Fascinating Story of Family Theories

Margaret Crosbie-Burnett and David M. Klein

This chapter creates a conceptual and historical context for the variety of family theories in this volume and for their explicit or implicit applications. The chapter includes issues in the development and use of family theories, a brief history of family theories, snapshots of prominent, current family theories, and our predictions about the future of family theories. The chapter covers neither international family theories nor research methods, which are intertwined with theory construction and development. Where appropriate, we refer the reader to related chapters in this volume and to fully developed accounts of family theories.

Why are Theories Important?

Theory! Who needs it? Actually, human beings, and other animals, need theory to survive, and so even before birth our brains attempt to organize and make sense of the cacophony of information that enters our bodies through the senses. For example, an infant uses elements of theory to meet survival needs. Consider the proposition, "If I cry, my caretaker might give me attention." This allows infants to predict caretaker behavior, and to control it to some extent. As children and adults, we all create theory about our own family life. Theories provide explanations of observable and non-observable data (information and events). Theory gives structure, a way to perceive and organize data. If we understand why things happen, we may be able to control or at least predict events.

As scholars increasingly assumed the role of theory construction in the early twentieth century, the focus of the search for the "truth" about life on earth shifted from the writings of "authorities" to scientific methods of research. In the social sciences, theories of reality, as perceived by scholars, formed the basis of social policy, educational policy, and later, therapeutic interventions. With rare exception, those scholars were formally educated, upper-class men of the dominant culture, a small percentage of the population. Therefore, theories were created from their worldviews and values regarding society, including families. They defined "the American family" as the traditional, nuclear family. Defining the construct we label "family" is a prerequisite to theorizing about families.

Definition of Family

Like beauty, family is in the eyes of the beholder. The construct "family" is within the purview of most social, behavioral, and biological sciences. To a *biologist*, family is a group of individuals related genetically. To an *attorney*, family is a legally defined group or lineage of individuals, who have legally defined rights and responsibilities to each other, based on birth and legal marriage or adoption. To a *communications* scholar, family is a group of intimates who encode and decode verbal and non-verbal symbols that have shared meanings; the transactions express both content and information about the relationships between the intimates. To a capitalist *macroeconomist*, family is a household that produces goods and services and consumes goods and services. To a *microeconomist* or *home economist*, family is a household with members who have a division of labor (some types of labor being valued more than other types) both inside and outside of the household.

To a *sociologist*, family is the smallest unit of society and is a network of persons who behave according to specific family roles, who share a past and a future, and are bound by marriage, biology, or commitment. Family is the site of reproduction and the most important force in socializing children. Families are categorized by demographic characteristics like social class, culture, immigration status, composition, religion, age cohort, urban versus rural, and stage of development (e.g., birth of first child). To a *psychologist*, family is a group of individuals who are connected to each other emotionally, cognitively, and usually behaviorally, regardless of legal ties and physical locations, potentially even including deceased persons. Psychologists explain *how* children become socialized and *how* families promote pro-social and antisocial behavior, mental health, and mental illness.

Defining family is not simple. For example, some stepchildren include their non-residential biological parent with whom they have not communicated in years as family, but exclude the stepparent who has financially supported them and with whom they have lived for many years. Consider sperm donors and surrogate mothers. Are they part of the families of their offspring? Clearly, some disciplines would include them and some would not. Consider other aspects of the definition of family: the clans of Southeast Asian Americans; chosen families of gay, lesbian, bisexual, and transgendered people; fictive kin of African Americans (e.g., non-biological "aunts"); godparents of Hispanic/Latino children; deceased ancestors of Native American Indians.

In recognition of the diverse definitions of family, the National Institute of Mental Health defined family as "a network of mutual commitment" (Pequegnat & Bray, 1997). Thus, persons who fulfill relationship roles heretofore traditionally specified by biological or legal relationships are now considered family members for the purpose of supporting each other and understanding their social network. For the purpose of this chapter, we use the NIMH definition. Historically, family scholars have used narrower, more traditional definitions of family. For a detailed analysis of what constitutes "family," see White and Klein (2007). Also, we focus on our diverse array of American families. For a perspective on international families, see Adams and Trost (2005).

While the *definition* of family varies widely, there is some agreement, at least among sociologists and psychologists, about the *function* of families. Functional families: (a) support the physical development of members, including food, clothing, shelter, (b) educate and socialize children, (c) create an environment supportive of the sexual needs of couples, (d) care for the dependency needs of young, old, ill, and disabled family members, and (e) care for the human emotional needs for affiliation, belonging, and feeling valued.

Issues in the Development and Use of Family Theories

Researchers and clinicians often rely on one or more theories to make sense of their data or case materials. They may draw upon theories ahead of time to help shape their inquiries, or they may take existing data and seek an explanation that makes sense of the data. While scholars and practitioners sometimes attempt to develop new theories, they most often draw upon existing theories in their professions and apply those ideas to the topic at hand. Below are crucial considerations that help to *guide the choice of a relevant theory*. There seldom is a single best answer across all situations, but thinking about the range of possibilities may improve the quality of the solution.

1   Is the purpose to describe or explain? For example, how current family members adjust to the arrival of a new member is a matter of describing the adjustment process. Why one adjustment process tends to be more successful than another is a matter of explanation. We must satisfactorily describe something before we can adequately explain it. The descriptive and explanatory aspects of theory are often used together. The key is to keep the differences between these two purposes in mind, and in particular to resist thinking that even a richly detailed description explains anything.
2   If the goal is to explain, should the explanation be derived from general principles, or is it better to search for cause-and-effect relationships? For example, to argue that leadership styles in small groups can be directly applied to leadership styles in families is to draw upon general principles for a particular application (deductive logic). The derivation is logical if families are viewed as small groups. In contrast, one could use an inductive process to create a theory of leadership styles in family by directly studying the factors that influence leadership styles in families, and creating a theory based on the findings.
3   Is it better to rely on one orienting theoretical framework or paradigm, or can aspects of more than one framework be combined? For example, suppose we are interested in comparing families having open boundaries with those having closed boundaries. It may be very useful in this case to draw upon family systems theory. However, if we have

observed that families change the openness of their boundaries over time, we may want to combine systems theory with a developmental theory to understand the process.

4   Which units or levels of analysis are most relevant to the issue at hand? Stated in different terms, who are the relevant social actors? Several levels are potentially important for theories about the family: individuals, dyads (the couple; parent–child), triads (triangulated families), whole families (which may be small or large, nuclear or extended), neighborhoods or communities in which multiple families co-reside, social networks embracing multiple families or perhaps the partially separate networks of each family member, and other geographic or cultural entities like societies, nations, and ethnic groups.

Sometimes theories will consistently address a given unit of analysis. For example, marital communication theories focus on the couple, and family stress theory focuses on the nuclear family. Often, however, we may be interested in cross-level effects. How do families affect their individual members? How do persons influence the families of which they are a part? What does "family psychology" really mean if not the intersection of two different units of analysis, one at the individual level and one at the group level?

5   What is the best way to address time? Do family theories acknowledge it at all? Is a theory static or dynamic? Which time unit is most relevant–centuries, lifetimes, episodes lasting a minute, or something else? Biographical time leads us to consider changes in individuals and families over the life span or life course of an individual. Historical time leads us to consider broader images of time, such as eras, epochs, generations, or cohorts. The notion of "family time" leads us to consider many connotations, (e.g., individuals "make time" for family).

6   How should external sources of influence be incorporated? Some theories include macrolevel external sources like social class or religion; others include microlevel external sources like a teen's friend or a therapist. To fully capitalize on the belief that your actions can influence your clients' lives, you need to be able to theorize about how change agents outside of families influence those families. Therapeutic theories are designed explicitly for this purpose – focusing on interventions that influence family interactions.

7   Would a macrolevel or microlevel theory be more relevant? Most sociological theories are created to guide social policy for the benefit of families in general. Psychological theories are created to guide prevention and remediation of problems, and can be adapted to particular families. Family studies integrates sociological and psychological, using a wide range of theories to educate audiences as diverse as families and government leaders, regarding life-span development of individuals, family development, healthy family relationships, and social policy for the benefit of families.

Evolution of Family Theories

What does history have to do with family theories? Nearly everything! In tracing the evolution of various family theories, one discovers that the historical context influences the assumptions, concepts, and topics of the theories. Further, the streams of thought that have culminated in today's family theories originated in the rather independent disciplines of sociology, psychology, and communications. Although scholars were all influenced by the same historic, political, scientific, and cultural context of their day, they theorized through the lenses of their particular disciplines. Sociologists conceptualized families as the *smallest* unit of analysis within society and a critical training ground for socializing future generations of citizens. Psychologists made implicit assumptions about families in the attempt to understand the individual's psyche and behavior, but had no explicit theory of family until late in the twentieth century. For psychologists, family is a *large* unit of analysis that influences individuals.

In the following two sections—the impact of historical periods on family theory and the snapshots of theories—we mention many developments and major contributors to them. Further information and references to published works are available in Boss, Doherty, LaRossa, Schumm, and Steinmetz (1993); Braithwaite and Baxter (2006); Ingoldsby, Smith, and Miller (2004); Howard (1981), and White and Klein (2007).

Impact of Historical Periods

1859–1900

Bringing the roots of an ecological paradigm to scientific thinking, Darwin shocked the western world with his theory of evolution, which includes the *adaptation* of animals (including humans) to their environments. When "survival of the fittest" is applied to humans, the theory of social Darwinism becomes a way of explaining the social hierarchy of humans as natural, alleviating the socially powerful from responsibility for poverty. This thinking, coupled with the unbridled capitalism of the American Industrial Revolution of the late nineteenth century, created horrible living conditions for the hundreds of thousands of immigrant and rural American families who were enticed to migrate to cities and *adapt* to life in crowded tenements. Fortunately, some people were concerned about how these families, and especially the children, were adapting to their new environments in American cities. These activists created "charity organization societies" like the Children's Aid Society, and "settlement houses" to help these families integrate into society. The most famous of these activists was sociologist Jane Addams, who founded Hull House in Chicago; consequently she is labeled the mother of social work. Consistent with Addams' goals of ameliorating social problems through social reform based on applied research, Hull House became a site where activists worked together with scholars interested in human development from the University of Chicago's fledgling department of sociology. However, by 1900 academic social scientists broke away from the social reformers, causing a scientist-professional breach that would not be healed until family studies departments brought them back together in the 1970s.

Meanwhile, in New England, Ellen Swallow Richards, a Massachusetts Institute of Technology chemist, was also concerned about the effects of the living conditions caused by the Industrial Revolution on human development. She sought social reform through a *science of the home and family environment*, which focused on the relationships between behavior, health, and the environment. Her focus on women and the home was holistic and multidisciplinary. When she attempted to create a new science of "Oekology" (an early version of the word "ecology"), her efforts were rejected, probably because she was a woman and her focus was women and their domain – the home. However, she successfully founded the new discipline of "Home Economics" in 1902. Nearly 70 years later these departments evolved into family studies departments.

1900–1930

During the early 1900s, American social scientists continued to turn away from the nineteenth-century tradition of trying to understand the world by studying history through the writings of philosophers, and embraced "modernism," science, pragmatism, and empirically tested theories, with a focus on functional analysis and microanalysis. Psychology was trying to understand "the mind," particularly children's minds, from a scientific perspective. Developmental psychologists discovered that children learn to classify patterns of interpersonal relating (now called schemas or internal working models) that are used in relationships, including family relationships.

As evidenced in the works of Ernest Burgess and Kurt Lewin, an appreciation for the usefulness of ecological principles pervaded the physical and social sciences, including conceptualizing human social organizations in this paradigm. In contrast to the historical conceptualization of family as basically a legal institution, sociologists began to focus on the family as a "living being" – a social group that is embedded in the community and in the larger social and cultural context. Early family sociologists also focused on how children acquired a self-concept and how family members acquired an understanding of family roles and the relationships between family members. These sociologists hypothesized that family members' daily verbal and non-verbal interactions socialized children into the culture and conditioned family members into patterns of behavior that we call family roles. Decades later, Herbert Blumer named this theory symbolic interactionism. The focus on process (interactions) determining a sense of self was an alternative to the radical behaviorism in psychology and the structural-functional conceptualization of family in sociology.

In 1917 the first academic course on families was taught at the University of Chicago by Ernest Burgess, who is credited as being the father of family studies. His seminal 1926 paper, "The Family as a Unity of Interacting Personalities," used a symbolic interaction perspective to describe how families are living, changing entities, based on changes in interactions in families over time. He hypothesized that, after the changes, the family created new patterns of relating and a new equilibrium (a key concept in family systems theory and family stress theory). It is interesting to note that many of the sociologists' concepts were similar to concepts in psychology at the time or later. For example, the way in which symbolic interactionism is hypothesized to manipulate one's behavior into a social or family role, based on others' behaviors toward one, is similar to early psychologist's "social images" and current social learning theory. It also is prescient to the schema theory of cognitive psychology.

Meanwhile, academic psychology continued to focus on child development by studying mother–child interactions. John Watson claimed that child behavior was completely under parental control through conditioning, while Arnold Gesell observed bidirectional influence and reciprocal feedback between parent and child. In the arena of mental illness, psychoanalysts were breaking away from medicine and forming their own discipline of psychiatry, because drugs were not curing the mental illnesses of their patients. Psychiatrists were searching for a different paradigm in which to work. Perhaps the earliest psychiatrist to notice the influence of family members' behavior on the mentally ill patient was Harry Stack Sullivan. When observing the communication patterns of schizophrenics' families, he noticed that it was not acceptable for the patient to express his true feelings. Instead, the patient had to state feelings that were acceptable to powerful family members. In this way, the pathology (a breakdown in the consistency between thoughts, feelings, and actions) was adaptive in keeping the patient safe from punishment.

1930s

The Depression Era brought a renewed concern for the welfare of children and families and a split in sociology into two paradigms – the ecological or structural (macrolevel) and the social psychological (microlevel). The ecological perspective studied the welfare of families within their communities. Social psychologists used symbolic interactionism to study married couples' interpersonal relationships, attempting to identify interactions between spouses that would promote personal satisfaction with one's family, and marital and family happiness. In 1938, the National Council on Family Relations was founded by sociologists and practitioners to provide a home for family scientists and professionals from all disciplines to share theory and knowledge about families.

It is ironic that the seeds of family systems theory, the theoretical basis of family psychology and family therapy, were planted by a cultural anthropologist, Gregory Bateson. Combining his knowledge of social anthropology, ecology, biology, and psychoanalysis, Bateson observed how symmetry (i.e., actions that mirror each other) and complementarity (e.g., give and take) in social interactions and relational processes can create both stability and change. Later, he integrated the theory of cybernetics (i.e., systems are regulated by feedback loops) to create the idea of circular interaction processes, the basis of family therapy theories (see Chapter 1, this volume). However, it was a psychiatrist, Nathan Ackerman, who founded the first child guidance clinic in 1938, and by the mid-1940s, was working with the whole family as a group. Thus the modern family therapy movement began (see Chapter 2, this volume).

1940s and 1950s

World War II and its fallout dominated the social science scene in the 1940s and 1950s. In response to the social chaos in Europe and the stress on American families, including work outside the home for many wives during World War II, family development theory was created. It delineated and idealized the stages of traditional family life as lived by the White, middle-class, nuclear families who were migrating to the newly created sub-urbs. Supposedly, the prescriptive nature of the theory gave a sense of stability and normality to returning soldiers' families and to society in general. It included a return to "normal" gender roles, with husband as head of household and breadwinner and wife as homemaker. The Department of Defense hired sociologist Reuben Hill to help the families of return-ing soldiers with their adjustment to post-war life. Building on Burgess' process model of family as a group of interacting personalities, Hill created family stress theory, expressed as an ABCX model. "A" denotes the stressor; "B" denotes resources available to cope with the stressor; "C" denotes a symbolic interactionism approach to the perceptions and mean-ings the family makes of "A"; "X" denotes bonadaptation or maladaptation.

Taking a more macro approach to promoting stability in families, Talcott Parsons and Robert Bales created a structural-functional theory of families. They hypothesized that as a social institution, each family must be structured such that it is functional to society and to its own stability. The theory can be viewed as prescriptive and conformist. It is based on consensus regarding traditional sex roles and cooperation between husbands and wives. Wives perform expressive roles in the family while husbands perform instru-mental roles. Similar to family development theory, it was in part a reaction to the chaos of Fascism, World War II, and Communism.

Meanwhile, developments were flourishing in psychology and psychiatry. The 1930s had brought to America an influx of intellectuals who were fleeing the Nazis in Europe. Among them were Kurt Lewin and Sigmund Freud. Trained in biology and Gestalt psychology, which assumed a contextual (ecological) approach, Lewin saw psychology as a natural science. He studied children in their actual, holistic situations (their social and physical environments), unlike the behaviorists, who were studying people in reductionistic ways in laboratories. Later, influenced by physics, Lewin created a reciprocal model of social development, hypothesizing feedback loops between the person and the *perceived* environment, ideas that culminated in his field theory of driving and restraining forces in social relationships. His application of field theory to families was displaced within social psychology by a post-war focus on the horrors of World War II, specifically inter-group relations and prejudice.

1960s and 1970s

The social unrest of this era challenged all social institutions, including dating norms, marriage, and family. This influenced family theory in major ways. The sexual revolu-tion and "free love," along with the dramatic increase in divorce, challenged theories of "normal" family formation and development. The civil rights movement created oppor-tunities for ethnic minority scholars to work in mainstream universities and bring their perspectives of ethnic minority families into family scholarship. Similarly, the feminist movement opened doors for women in academia. Feminists brought constructs like power to the forefront of family theorizing, and challenged theories, such as structural-functionalism, that assumed patriarchy and prescribed gender roles in families.

Meanwhile a major development in family sociology was the attempt to formalize theoretical frameworks in order to guide empirical research and to articulate teachable methods of theory construction – to inspire future generations of scholars to value theorizing from a deductive, logical, positivistic perspective. This development generated the annual Theory Construction and Research Methodology Workshop, which has continually met prior to the annual conference of the National Council on Family Relations since 1971.

Combining sociology's Symbolic interactionism and psychology's family systems theory, University of Chicago scholars studied families as psychosocial groups, focusing on interpersonal interactions, trying to understand how each family constructs its own reality. In California the synergy of adding communications theories and general systems theory to anthropology and psychiatry culminated at the Mental Research Institute. The goal was to research abnormal family communication as a source of mental illness. To share their discoveries, Nathan Ackerman and Don Jackson founded *Family Process* in 1961. In this era, many psychiatrists created their own versions of family theories and therapies, by applying the research on family process. This period started the heyday of family therapy. However, the fundamental assumptions of family systems theories began to be challenged by feminist scholars.

In behavioral psychology the divorce rate inspired a focus on conflict in couples. On the basis of cognitive-behavioral and social learning theories, researchers developed therapies to help couples with conflict and also parents with acting-out children. In developmental psychology the integration of ecological theory expanded the context of development beyond the mother–child dyad to include how relationships between social systems impact human development.

This era witnessed the beginning of two new family disciplines: family communications combined sociology's symbolic interactionism, cognitive psychology, family systems, and communication theories to study couple communication. Perhaps most important, the discipline of family studies integrated family sociology and developmental and behavioral psychology. Family studies also integrated science and practice, which had been split since the 1890s.

1980s to the Present

Dramatic increases in the number of single-parent families and stepfamilies, the visibility of gay families, and immigrant and cross-national families further challenged the formalization movement of the previous period. After 100 years of dominating family theories, sociology relinquished its hegemony, giving in to increasing theoretical eclecticism and the creation of integrative, interdisciplinary theories. Further, this post-positivistic era of constructivist theories based on phenomenological experiences of family members included a shift from structural to transactional models of family, focusing on processes and social cognitions within cultural contexts.

Feminist and other interpretive theorists became mainstream, and they tended to emphasize narrative stories over formal logic, desiring to bring previously marginalized or silent "voices" into theory construction. Feminist, gay, and ethnic minority scholars crusaded to understand family from each family member's perspective using postmodern, constructivist paradigms as opposed to logical positivism. It is no accident that as family theorists became more demographically diverse, so did family theories. Also, traditional theories were adapted to reflect the experiences of ethnic minority, gay, and post-divorce families.

In related disciplines important developments occurred. In communications, psychology's information processing was partnered with schemas and cognition to form "relational dialectics." The first text on family communication was published in 1982. Developmental psychology applied attachment styles to parent–sibling triads and adult love relationships. Finally, on the horizon was socio-biological theory, based on the burgeoning genetics literature.

Current Family Theories

The following are snapshots of current family theories from various disciplines. Some perspectives cut across disciplines. In each snapshot we include concepts, assumptions, uses, an example, and limitations. They are ordered roughly chronologically from oldest to newest.

Ecological theory of families.   ETF addresses the connections between a unit of analysis and its environment. The family is one crucial environment for every person. Families are embedded in neighborhoods, communities, cultures, societies, and natural environments. One key assumption in ETF is adaptation–that is, families respond to their environments by adapting to them. ETF identifies levels – microsystems, mesosystems, exosystems, and macrosystems – of environments, each having a distinct impact. *Example: New parents' behaviors adapt to the demands of family (microsystem) and workplace (microsystem) within the norms of the society (macrosystem).* ETF does not explain *how* the larger systems impact families and individuals.

Symbolic interaction theory.   SIT addresses meanings, perceptions, definitions of the situation, communication, and the social basis of people's sense of self and identity. SIT assumes that people work together to process information, and that they strive to make sense of the world and their place in it. Meaningfulness requires shared understandings, or the confirmation of personal beliefs by significant others. SIT is particularly useful in the family sciences to describe the ways that people explain their own actions or the actions of others. Attribution theory is largely compatible. SIT is most applicable when researchers and practitioners collect narratives from study participants or clients. *Example: In order to learn about "problems" in families, one finds out how the involved family members define the situation, its origins, and it consequences.* SIT does not specify how one symbol becomes favored over another, or how one way of interacting becomes favored over another.

Family development theory.   FDT addresses the ways that families change over time, usually from the marriage of a couple to the couple's dissolution by the death of a partner. Key concepts include stages, transitions, timing norms, and sequencing norms. Transitions between stages involve changes in family structure and operation that are expected but potentially disruptive. Developmentalists assume that families cannot be fully under-stood without taking into account the period of development they are undergoing and the prior changes they have experienced. FDT explains the timing of transitions and the process of adjustment to changes over time. *Example: The extent to which the transition to parenthood is stressful is influenced by such factors as the degree to which it is planned and the economic resources that the prospective parents bring to the situation.* The develop-mental analysis of families is complicated by the fact that families differ in the stages they experience and the lack of social norms for some transitions.

Structural-functional theory.   SFT addresses prevalent social patterns in families (e.g., why most couples get married, why they limit their number of children). SFT employs the idea of *telos*, or purposefulness, to explain such patterns. So, we could argue that some-thing is common because it serves a useful purpose or function. SFT usually argues that social norms arise to promote certain practices. When a social arrangement or practice stops being functional, it declines in frequency. Functionalism at the level of social institutions is parallel to behavioral reinforcement at the level of the individual. SFT is most useful when the phenomenon to be explained is very common. *Example: Laws against polygamy or same-sex marriage may be explained on the basis of the widespread belief that neither practice optimally leads to the reproduction and socialization of young children.* SFT fails to fully deal with changes in functionality. For example, how common does non-marital cohabitation have to be for it to become functional?

Family systems theory.   FST addresses the organization of families to deal with internal and external challenges. A family is viewed as being analogous to an organism or a machine, with subsystems, interconnected parts, and a semi-permeable boundary with the envir-onment. Families input various kinds of resources, process them, and send the results back into the environment. Connections between parts of the family system entail feed-back loops, such that each family tends toward equilibrium. *Example: Families with closed boundaries may be brittle or inflexible in the face of changing external circumstances. They are also relatively impervious to interventions designed to help them adapt to environmental changes.* FST provides a description of how things work rather than an explanation of why they work. FST is the basis of many therapeutic applications in this volume.

Social exchange theory.   SET places a utilitarian economic view into a cognitive-behavioral and social psychology perspective to conceptualize family members as units that exchange goods, services, status, and love to meet each individual's needs. When exchanges are seen as fair, the relationship is stable. SET has integrated cultural norms, expectations for a relationship, attraction, and interdependence into the study of exchanges within couples. Key concepts include rewards, costs, resources, needs, power, comparison level, reciprocity, fairness, norms, and relationship satisfaction. SET assumes that social relationships are interdependent and that humans use rational thought to conduct cost–benefit analyses for individual gain, such that an individual will seek rewards and avoid punishments. This sometimes implies an individualistic, capitalistic, or hedonistic view of the world. SET has been used to study mate selection, the effect of women's movement into the labor force on couples, spouse abuse, divorce, and extra-marital affairs. *Example: Partner A will cook a gourmet meal if Partner B will take the child to the park.* Limitations of SET are similar to the limitations of behaviorism in general. It is reductionistic and does not account well for trust, commitment, or altruistic behavior in families. Therapeutic applications are included in Chapter 15 of this volume.

Social conflict theory.   SCT addresses ways in which interpersonal disputes among family members arise and are resolved in either a constructive or destructive manner. SCT assumes that disagreements are natural in social life and therefore explains how conflict is managed, not how harmony is achieved. Outcomes depend on such factors as the relative resources of participants and the existence of rules about dealing with disputes. *Example: Conflict tactics intended to diminish the self-worth of the opponent rarely lead to constructive outcomes.* SCT does not deal effectively with families who experience few conflicts.

Attachment theory and ecological theory of development.   Currently two theoretical forces within developmental psychology – attachment theory and ecological theory of development (ETD) – address family (particularly parent–child) relationships, and implicitly create theories of family functioning through the assumptions inherent in these theories. *Attachment theory* focuses on the psychological development of children and the intergenerational transmission of styles of relating in close relationships. Concepts include internal working models of self and "other," attachment style, and intergenerational transmission. A parent's attachment style will predict how that parent relates to his child, thus creating the transmission of attachment styles across generations. *Example: If the parental caregiver responds appropriately to the child, the child learns a positive self-concept (she is worthy and competent) and that relationships are positive and safe. Ultimately the child develops a secure attachment style. Depending upon how the parenting may be deficient, the child acquires one of four types of insecure attachment styles. The child's internal working model about close relationships becomes a template (like the schema concept in cognitive theory) for future close relationships throughout the life span.* Assumptions include: one primary caregiver; bidirectionality of development (children also affect their parents' development); plasticity of the working model decreasing with age; parental behaviors being cognitively processed by the child; and, therefore, the same parental behavior possibly having different meanings based on culture, social class, sex, and the child's age. Limitations include lack of attention to the influences on a child's development of other family members besides the primary caregiver, the family environment, genetic predispositions, and contextual factors like neighborhood. See Chapters 16 and 27, this volume, for therapeutic applications.

ETD answers some of the limitations in attachment theory by focusing on more macrolevel constructs. It explains (un)healthy child development by placing the child in the context of a variety of proximal and distal environments, ranging from the family environment (a microsystem) to the society (macrosystem), with a focus on the relationships *between* the environments (mesosystems) in which the developing child lives. ETD applies the concepts of ecological theory of family (above), but adds the chronosystem. *Example: An immigrant child's family microsystem may value family time more than individual achievement. Therefore, the child may go to school (another microsystem) without homework being completed, because his grandparents, were visiting his home, and he was expected to put family first. The child's teacher, a dominant-culture American (macrosystem), has inter-nalized the value of individual achievement, and scolds the child for not completing home-work. The mesosystem between the two microsystems has a conflict of values and messages conveyed to the child, affecting the child's development negatively.* ETD is unable to explain *how* families function in the home, or exactly how children and other family members deal behaviorally, cognitively, or emotionally with conflicts between any of the systems. See Chapter 24, this volume, for therapeutic application.

Social-cognitive-behavioral family theory. SCBFT originates in the behavioral psycho-logy paradigm and explains family processes, as opposed to structure. Concepts include behavior, stimulus, response, reinforcement or reward, punishment, observational learning, cognitive mediation, cognitions (attributions, schemas), modeling, role model, and environment. Assumptions underlying the theory include: behavior is learned; normal humans act rationally to meet their physical, psychological, and emotional needs, seeking rewards and avoiding punishment; and family members influence each others' cognitions and behaviors through interactions. SCBFT is relatively culture-free and value-free. It is useful in understanding and explaining how a family member's behavior evolved into the current patterns, and in changing the patterns of behavior for one or more family members. *Example: A 3-year-old is not speaking yet, because he observes that every time his adolescent brother tries to speak with their alcoholic father, their father yells, "Nobody asked you." Through observational or vicarious learning, the child learns to anticipate punishment if he speaks, so he avoids punishment by not speaking. These brothers are learning a nega-tive schema for "father."* The theory's limitations include downplaying genetic and other biological factors (temperament) and not accounting for altruistic and sacrificing behavior common in families. See Chapters 15 and 26, this volume, for therapeutic applications.

Family communication theory. FCT combines symbolic interactionism, systems theory, information processing aspects of cognitive psychology, and a dialectic perspective to focus on verbal, non-verbal, and emotional communication between family members. Concepts include: verbal and non-verbal symbols, encoding, decoding, meaning-making, schemas, and patterns of communication acts. FCT assumes a transactional (as opposed to a structural) definition of family. That is, family is defined by interactional commun-ication patterns (who communicates with whom) regardless of place of residence, legal relationship, etc. FCT assumes that the meanings given to communication behaviors depend upon the immediate context (e.g., other words in a sentence, tone of voice, other events occurring concurrently) and the cultural context. Family members are motivated to under-stand each other's communication and clarify their roles and relationships. Acts of communication function on two levels: the meaning of verbal and non-verbal behaviors, and the maintenance of the structure of family relationships through patterns of com-munication acts. *Example: If a 15-year-old challenges his mother's authority for the first time by saying angrily, "I will come home when I want to," his father may stand very close to the teen in an intimidating way and shout, "Children do not speak to their parents like that in this family; go to your room." This reasserts the family's power relations and also demonstrates solidarity within the parental subsystem, as well as giving a command to the teen.* In these ways, family members make meaning of each other's communication behaviors, and they can negotiate their relationships as they change over time. Repeated patterns of communication function to define and create cognitive schemas for the individual's family role, dyadic family relationships, and the family as a group, regardless of family structure. Relationship schemas are composed of the self-schema or self-concept, the other-schema, and the interpersonal scripts between self and other (e.g., schema for marriage). Further, communication scholars have identified types of marital communication styles. This perspective does not address contextual variables, however.

Feminist family theory.   FFT has roots in critical theory, cultural studies, philosophy, and sociology. It emerged from the women's movement of the 1970s. It deconstructs the family, challenging all of the assumptions about family structure and family roles that are based on the family member's sex, age, or any other demographic characteristic. It values equal power between males and females, and equal value of the labor that is performed by males and females in families. FFT brought topics salient to women (e.g., housework) and the processes (from inside and outside the family) that maintain family patriarchy into the discourse and research on families. Concepts include: patriarchy, hierarchy, power, sex roles, gender, family labor, and social construction and deconstruction. FFT assumes that family roles are socially constructed – that there is nothing "correct" or "true" about traditional sex roles in families. It is useful in helping men and women become consciously aware of the family roles that are being played out, freeing them to construct fairer roles for all family members. *Example: It is well documented that women perform the vast majority of childcare and eldercare in families, which usually interferes with their earning power. In heterosexual couples this loss of income reduces a wife's decision-making power.* FFT shows the inequality in this situation and would argue for a fairer arrangement. FFT does not guide family members in making such changes at the interpersonal level. Nevertheless, it has applied feminist thought to helping female and male clients *deconstruct* their family roles and processes, and other social environments, as a way of understanding and improving their lives.

Sociobiological theory.   SBT addresses the ways in which biology (nature) interacts with the social environment (nurture) to produce observable behaviors. While principles of evolution and genetic predispositions are important, sociobiological theorists do not argue that biology is destiny. SBT is useful for explaining a variety of family variables, including mate preferences, fertility rates, and parenting strategies. *Example: Neglect of stepchildren is more prevalent than neglect of biological children, who carry the parent's genes.* SBT does not account for altruistic behaviors that do not have survival value.

Theoretical eclecticism.   Various theoretical traditions interact in multiple ways. Some theories have historically influenced others. For example, early ecological theory helped to shape structural-functional theory, systems theory, child development theory, and sociobiological theory. Scholars sometimes eclectically draw upon insights from two or more traditions to attempt a more comprehensive picture. For example, family development theory has drawn insights from theories about the development of individual persons, and from both symbolic interaction and structural-functionalism. Sometimes, two theoretical traditions may be placed in a competitive confrontation, the objective being to see which one provides the more persuasive account of a particular phenomenon. One example has been the challenge to structural-functionalism by feminism.

The Future of Family Theory

As has been the case in the past, theorists in the future will revisit standard topics like mate selection, fatherhood, and couple satisfaction in light of contemporary social changes. We also will tackle relatively new topics that emerge (e.g., family interaction with technology). We will attend to evolving understandings of diversity (gender, race, social class, immigration status, and sexual orientation).

As more demographically diverse scholars enter family disciplines, we predict increased diversity of theoretical perspectives and possibly even new paradigms. Further, we will recognize more global perspectives. Theorists will expand conceptualizations of family, including fictive kin, godparents, extended family, and close friends. We will make mainstream theories more applicable to families who are not dominant-culture and middle-class, by integrating marginalized groups' perspectives. For example, a family headed by an interracial lesbian couple may live in a working-class urban neighborhood, be part of their gay and lesbian social network, visit extended family in China and in an African American community, as well as interact closely with the child's biological father in an affluent, dominant-culture suburb. This structurally, financially, psychologically, and emotionally complex family deals with multiple cultural contexts, each including sets of norms for family roles and relationships; this requires new theoretical constructs. We do not intend to overemphasize the influence of cultural diversity on family theories; good theories can incorporate variation. It remains unclear whether or not cultural variation demands different theories. We also predict an increased integration of theories across disciplines. Given the complexities of many families, using a combination of psychological (micro) and sociological (macro) theories may best explain research findings.

Ultimately, we must advance theory through research. We can conduct studies that test rival theories (Crosbie-Burnett et al., 2005). Qualitative studies can generate new theories that reflect better the reality of today's families, particularly marginalized families. Also, mixed-method studies (i.e., qualitative and quantitative) can help us understand how each of two or more theories makes meaning of quantitative results.

Judging from comprehensive works like Bengtson, Acock, Allen, Dilworth-Anderson, and Klein (2005), much new family theorizing in the future will be driven by topical interests rather than by pre-existing theories. Scholars still care most about specific topics, and topical interest is what most influences research projects and their funding. The motivation to theorize has been largely a reactive response to large amounts of data seeking a coherent interpretation.

One thing is certain. The impact of changes on families will create endless challenges for family theorists in our ongoing attempt to understand and help families.

Resources

Theory Construction and Research Methodology Workshop, www.ncfr.org/conf/TCRM.asp.

Almeida, R. (ed.) (1994). *Expansions of Feminist Family Theory through Diversity.* New York: Routledge.

Blieszner, R., & Bedford, V. (Eds.). (1994). *Aging and the family: theory and research.* Westport, CT: Praeger.

Carr, A., & VanLeeuwen, M. (Eds.). (1996). *Religion, feminism, and the family.* Louisville, KY: Westminster John Knox Press.

Coontz, S. (1999). *American families: A multicultural reader.* New York: Routledge.

Demo, D., Allen, K., & Fine, M. (2000). *Handbook of family diversity.* New York: Oxford.

Ingoldsby, B., & Smith, S. (2006). *Families in global and multicultural perspective* (2nd ed.). Thousand Oaks, CA: Sage.

McAdoo, H. (2007). *Black families* (4th ed.). Thousand Oaks, CA: Sage.

Trask, B., & Hamon, R. (2007). *Cultural diversity and families: Expanding perspectives.* Thousand Oaks, CA: Sage.

References

Adams, B., & Trost, J. (2005). *Handbook of world families.* Thousand Oaks, CA: Sage.

Bengtson, V., Acock, A., Allen, K., Dilworth-Anderson, P., & Klein, D. (Eds.). (2005). *Sourcebook of family theory and research.* Thousand Oaks, CA: Sage.

Boss P., Doherty, W., LaRossa, R., Schumm, W., & Steinmetz, S. (Eds.). (1993). *Sourcebook of family theories and methods: A contextual approach.* New York: Plenum.

Braithwaite, D., & Baxter, L. (Eds.). (2006). *Engaging theories in family communication: Multiple perspectives.* Thousand Oaks, CA: Sage.

Crosbie-Burnett, M., Lewis, E., Sullivan, S., Podolsky, J., Mantilla, R., & Mitrani, V. (2005). Advancing theory through research: The case of extrusion in stepfamilies. In V. Bengtson, A. Acock, K. Allen, P. Dilworth-Anderson, & D. Klein (Eds.), *Sourcebook of family theory and research* (pp. 213–238). Thousand Oaks, CA: Sage.

Howard, R. L. (1981). *A social history of American family sociology, 1865–1940.* Westport, CT: Greenwood Press.

Ingoldsby, B., Smith, S., & Miller, J. (2004). *Exploring family theories.* Los Angeles: Roxbury.

Pequegnat, W., & Bray, J. H. (1997). Families and HIV/AIDS: Introduction to the special section. *Journal of Family Psychology, 11,* 3–10.

White, J., & Klein, D. (2007). *Family theories.* Thousand Oaks, CA: Sage.

4

Changing Landscape of American Family Life

Kay Pasley and Spencer B. Olmstead

Even the uninformed observer has some awareness that American family life has changed. For scholars, taking notice of these changes and placing them within the broader social context is important for understanding families and their complex and multiple relationships. In this chapter, we identify and discuss the key changes families have undergone in our more recent past and attempt to place the notable changes within the broader social and economic contexts of our society. We also speculate about what this means for the future of families and those who assume the challenge of gleaning insight into family processes and interaction and elect to work with families in clinical practice.

Changes in the Broader Context in Which Families Are Embedded

A valuable way of gaining insights into the changing nature of American families is to examine the broader sociodemographic context in which they are embedded. Looking at this context reveals that the general population has grown and diversified. The population more than tripled from 76 million in 1990 to 281 million in 2000 (Hobbs & Stoop, 2002). Estimates also suggest that the population is expected to almost double by 2040 (U.S. Census Bureau, 2004a).

In addition to the population growth, we increasingly reside in metropolitan areas (from only 28% in 1910 to 80% in 2000), and much of this increase resulted from the development and movement toward the suburbs. In fact, those living in suburbs accounted for half of the population in 2000 (Hobbs & Stoop, 2002).

We also have become and will continue to become more racially diverse. Specifically, all estimates suggest that by 2050, "White alone, not Hispanic" will no longer represent the majority race, whereas in 2000 this category of persons made up 69.4% of the population (U.S. Census Bureau, 2004b). Between 1980 and 2000, the Hispanic population more than doubled, and minorities made up the majority in three states (California, Hawaii, and New Mexico) and the District of Columbia (Hobbs & Stoop, 2002); Texas now makes a fourth such state. Hispanics (of any race) are expected to grow dramatically from 12.6% in 2000 to 24.4% in 2050 compared with other racial groups (U.S. Census Bureau, 2004b).

Another change in the broader social context is that of age and gender distribution. People are living longer, and older adults will make up an increasing portion of the population. Those 65 years and older represent the biggest change; they made up 10.4% of the population in 2000 and are expected to grow to 18.2% in 2040 and then level off (U.S. Census Bureau, 2004a). Regarding gender, at all ages, there will continue to be more females than males with the overall percentages being 51% to 49% respectively. This difference becomes more dramatic with age, as the number of females will exceed males, especially among those 45 years and older. Estimates through 2050 suggest that this trend is expected to hold (U.S. Census Bureau, 2004a).

A final change in the social context is one of shifting social norms as reported in attitude studies. Scholars suggest that behaviors that were once acceptable and proper only within marriage, such as sexual activity, childbearing and childrearing, and sharing a home, are more acceptable outside of marriage (Thornton & Young-DeMarco, 2001). Still people report valuing marriage (Thornton & Young-DeMarco, 2001; Edin & Reed, 2005) and most expect to marry (Lichter, Batson, & Brown, 2004).

Changes in the Formation and Nature of Relationships

Two of the most prominent changes in American family life are changes in marriage (i.e., delay of marriage, divorce and remarriage/repartnering) and relationship formation (i.e. cohabitation), which remain strongly linked. Between 1970 and 1990 there was a growing awareness and concern stemming from the dramatic increase in cohabitation (Bramlett & Mosher, 2002), an increase in age of marriage (U.S. Census Bureau, 2008a), a decrease in marriage (Fields, 2004), and an increase in divorce and remarriages following divorce (Kreider, 2005). We discuss "the delay in marriage" (age and cohabitation) and the effects of both on marriage, divorce, and repartnering.

Delaying marriage

Since 1970 there has been an increase in the number of people who marry for the first time at a later age, and this change is especially dramatic for those of childbearing age. For example, in 1970, about 55% of men ages 20–24 had never married, and by 2000 this figure had increased to almost 84%. For women of the same ages in 1970, almost 34% had never married compared with almost 73% in 2000. These same comparisons for men ages 25–29 years who had never married were 19% in 1970 and almost 52% in 2000. For women of the same ages in 1970 almost 11% had never married, and by 2000 this had grown to 39%. For those ages 30–34 years, only 9% of men and 6% of women had never married in 1970, but by 2000 30% of men and almost 22% of women had never married (U.S. Census Bureau, 2001). Thus, we see an increase in the median age at first marriage to the current all-time high of 27.5 for men and 25.5 for women in 2006 (U.S. Census Bureau, 2008a).

Cohabitation – an unexpected popular choice

Cherlin (2004) noted that in the 1970s few scholars "foresaw the greatly increased role of cohabitation in the adult life course" (p. 849), thinking that it would remain common amongst the poor and a short-term situation for those who would quickly marry. We realize that we were wrong, and we now recognize the growing prevalence, acceptance, and complexity of cohabitation.

Our most recent estimates show that almost 4.6 million households in the US reflect heterosexual cohabitating couples, up from .4 million in 1960 (Seltzer, 2004). There is some additional indication that another half million same-sex couples were cohabiting in 2000 (Simmons & O'Connell, 2003). Not only has the incidence of cohabitation increased over time, but we now are able to estimate the prevalence of cohabitation among heterosexual and same-sex couples. Also, the increase is common across all education levels and racial groups (Bumpass & Lu, 2000), as well as those with children (Seltzer, 2004). Over 40% of heterosexual cohabiting couples had children under 18 living in their home, and 22% of homosexual couples and 34% of lesbian couples resided with children (Simmons & O'Connell, 2003).

We know that cohabitation is most common among those who have yet to marry, followed by those who are between marriages. Further, cohabitation occurs among those who are younger (under 39 years of age) rather than older (Seltzer, 2004). Racial differences are also noted. Bramlett and Mosher (2002) examined first unions and reported that compared with White women, Black women are more likely to cohabit rather than marry, and they are less likely to formalize cohabitation through marriage. However, if we look beyond first unions only and ask whether a woman has ever cohabited, the data show greater racial similarity than differences. For example, estimates show that 40–45% of both White and Black women have cohabitated at some point in their lives, although fewer Hispanic women have done so (see Bramlett & Mosher, 2002; Bumpass & Lu, 2000).

Although the prevalence of cohabitation has increased across all education levels, Bumpass and Lu (2000) showed that women with higher levels of education are less likely to cohabit than are women with lower levels of education. About 60% of those lacking a high school degree had cohabited at some time, whereas about 39% of those with at least some college had done so.

Clearly, the evidence suggests that some types of cohabitation are more common among those with fewer resources, while simultaneously there has been an overall increase across all groups (Seltzer, 2004). This may suggest that for some, but not all, cohabitation is a viable alternative to marriage, whereas for others it represents a step toward marriage.

The link between cohabitation and marriage has been recently described as a "retreat from marriage," especially among low-income families (Gibson-Davis, Edin, & McLanahan, 2005). Smock and Gupta (2002) presented evidence suggesting a weakening link between these two relationship statuses. These researchers reported that 60% of all cohabiting couples in the 1970s had married within three years, whereas only 33% had done so in the 1990s. Cherlin (2004) interpreted these findings in two ways, suggesting that "fewer cohabitating unions were trial marriages (or that fewer trial marriages were succeeding)" (p. 850). Further, Seltzer (2004) documented that these unions did not last. About half of them ended within 1 year and 1 out of 10 lasted only 5 years. The probability that a first premarital cohabitation will end is higher among Black women than Hispanics or Whites, and especially higher among younger than older White women. Further, cohabiting women who "live in communities with higher male unemployment, lower median family income and higher rates of poverty and receipt of welfare" are more likely to end their union (Bramlett & Mosher, 2002, p. 2). Cohabiting after divorce is also less common for Black women than other groups.

Marriage

Marriage remains the overwhelming choice of the majority of Americans, as 80–90% of men and women age 15 in 1996 were projected to marry at some time (Kreider & Fields, 2002). However, the dominance of marriage has decreased ever so gradually since the 1960s (Cherlin, 2004). Recent estimates show that in 1970, 70.6% of households (including non-family [e.g., women living alone] and family [e.g., married couples, grandparent households]) included married couples; this had dropped to 51.5% in 2003 (Fields, 2004). Of course, during this same period we saw an increase in cohabitation which offsets the decrease in marriage. Moreover, the trend reflects a general increase then stabilizing in the number of marriages that dissolve.

Cherlin (2004) argued convincingly that the meaning of marriage has changed and this is reflected in the decline of marriage. Starting in the 1960s the companionate marriage "lost ground . . . as the cultural ideal" (p. 852), being taken over by dual-employment marriages and the behavioral changes around spousal roles. These changes resulted in the growing prominence of individualistic marriages that emphasized self-development, role flexibility, and communication and openness in confronting problems. Because the context was then characterized by greater latitude for personal choices, the social acceptability of alternatives to marriage, and the desire for personal growth and gaining intimacy through open communication, Cherlin argued that marriage might be unable to meet these expectations. However, even with greater demands on marriage, 78% of high school seniors expected to marry at some point (Thornton & Young-DeMarco, 2001), an expectation that has remained high over the last two decades (Popenoe, 2005). In fact, Manning, Longmore, and Giordano (2007) found that more seniors expect to marry than cohabit.

Much of recent evidence shows that marriage and marriage outcomes are linked to indicators of economic security (Smock, 2004; Smock, Manning, & Porter, 2005). For example, race differentiates patterns of relationship formation, marriage, divorce, and re-marriage. Lifetime marriage rates declined more dramatically for Black women (25%) than White women (5%) (Goldstein & Kenney, 2001). As one ages, this difference grows (Gibson-Davis et al., 2005). Further, once married, Black women are also more likely to experience marital disruption (separation or divorce) and not remarry (see Bramlett & Mosher, 2002). Other evidence shows that low-resource couples and those from working- and middle-income groups hold similar expectations for meeting financial goals before marriage (Smock, 2004). Such financial goals include: demonstrating financial respons-ibility, having substantial backup (money in the bank, established credit), and having a house, car, and other things typical of the middle class (Gibson-Davis et al., 2005).

Divorce and remarriage

Divorce remains a common occurrence in American family life. Our best estimates sug-gest that 40–50% of all first marriages will end in divorce, and 43% will divorce before the fifteenth anniversary when young children are still in the home (Kreider, 2005; Kreider & Fields, 2002). Data from 2004 (U.S. Census Bureau, 2008b) show that the median duration of first marriages that end in divorce is 8 years, although couples who divorce separate and remain separated for about 1 year prior to divorce. For those who go on to remarry (estimates suggest about 75% do so), the median duration between first divorce and remarriage is 3.5 years. These figures are similar for men and women. However, there is a notable gender difference for median duration of second marriages that ends in divorce: men = 8.6 years and women = 7.2 years. This suggests that for about half of all first married persons and half of all those in remarriages, the duration of those unions are about the same, a finding that was true in a similar analysis for 2001 data (Kreider, 2005).

Divorce and remarriage are associated with certain individual characteristics, includ-ing race and social class. Divorce is more common among Blacks than Whites, although remarriage is less common among Blacks (Kreider, 2005). Further, some scholars sug-gest that certain characteristics predispose persons to divorce (selectivity hypothesis; e.g., parental divorce in one's family of origin), whereas others argue that divorce is the outcome of a series of interactions that occur in a marriage over time (see Amato, 2003). There is growing evidence that multiple transitions are associated with divorce (e.g., children and adults changing residence, schools, churches, friendship networks, etc.), and they are also associated with challenges in adjustment over time. Importantly, most of the results from longitudinal studies show that over time the majority of children of divorce adjust well (Ahrons, 2007; Amato, 2003).

Commonly women retain physical custody of young children after divorce. Although there has been a slight increase in the number of single fathers whose children reside with them (1.1% in 1970 compared to 3.2% in 2004), the majority of children in single-parent homes reside with their mothers (23.2% of children; Kreider, 2008); there are no reliable data available differentiating single fathers from divorced single fathers.

Also, recent evidence (Kreider, 2005) shows that of all marriages in 2001, 69.8% were a first marriage for both spouses; 17% were a remarriage for only one; and 13.3% were remarriages for both spouses. Our best estimates suggest that about 65% of all remarriages include children from the prior union. This means that many remarriages form stepfamilies. Remarriages in general dissolve at a slightly higher rate than first marriages, but remarriages that include stepchildren do so more quickly than do first marriages with only biological children (Kreider, 2005). Clearly, children and stepchildren complicate the adjustment to remarriage and are associated with a higher probability that the remarriage will end (Bramlett & Mosher, 2002).

Changes in Childbearing and Childrearing

Among more recent cohorts of adults, fertility has declined, parenthood is being postponed, and childbearing outside of marriage is more common and less stigmatized (Martin et al., 2006; Cherlin, 2004). For example, 1957 was the high point in fertility with 3.6 children per woman, which dropped to 1.7 in 1976; the rate rose and has remained about 2.0 since then (Hamilton, Martin, & Ventura, 2007; U.S. Census Bureau, 2008c). Further, births to adolescents declined 34% between the peak in 1991 and 2005 (Martin et al., 2007); however, preliminary data from 2006 (Hamilton et al., 2007) show a 3% increase. The lowest rate of births to youth 14–19 years ever recorded in the 65 years during which such data were available was in 2005, and the most dramatic decrease was among Black teens. Yet, increases in childbearing are seen in women in their early 20s or in their 30s and 40s, with the greatest increase in Hispanic women. Increases are most notable among unmarried women in general; during 2002–2005 there was an overall 12% increase to women 15–44 years (Martin et al., 2006). Among these women, there is some variation by age, such that over four in five births were to adolescents; over half of births were to women 20–24 years; and almost 3 in 10 were to women 25–29 years.

Childrearing occurs within different family forms. Census data on type of household show a consistent decline in the number of married couples with children and an increase in the number of "other" family households, including single-parent family households and households with no parent(s) present (Fields, 2003, 2004; Kreider, 2008). For example, married couples with children declined from 40.3% of all households in 1970 to 23.3% in 2003, while "other" family households increased from 10.6% to 16.4%. Data also show that in 2004, 70% of children lived with two parents (86% were children living with two biological/adoptive parents), 23.4% lived with only their mothers, 3.2% lived with only their fathers, and 3.9% lived in households absent both parents (56% were with a grandparent) (Kreider, 2008). Thus, not only are fewer children living with two parents, but grandparents play an increasingly important role in childrearing and the growth of multigenerational households.

Further, many children who live with a single parent actually reside with a parent and his or her unmarried partner. For example, Kreider (2008) reported that in 2004, of the 17 million children living with an unmarried parent, 18% of them lived with a mother and her unmarried partner, and 53% lived with a father and his unmarried partner. Thus, children living with a single father were more likely to be living also with his unmarried partner than those living with a single mother.

Children's living arrangements also vary by race (Kreider, 2008). Of Black children, only 38% lived with two parents, whereas 78% of White, 87% of Asian, and 68% of Hispanic children did so. Regarding single parents, 54% of Black children lived with a single parent compared with 20% of non-Hispanic White children and 28% of Hispanic children.

Many young adult children continue to reside with their parents, which represents a change in family life. Data from 2006 show that of those 18–24 years, 53.7% of men and 46.7% of women lived with parents; of those 25–34 years, another 14.3% of men and 8.8% of women lived with parents (U.S. Census Bureau, 2008d). Thus, for many young adults, economic independence, as one indicator of adulthood, has yet to be achieved.

Economics of Family Life

In addressing the economic realities facing American families, we focus on changes in employment and median family income, the effects of family structure and employment trends, and the implications of such changes for child wellbeing. The reality of family life is that most parents are employed outside the home regardless of the structure of the family (AmeriStat, 2003). For example, 66% of children in two-parent households had two working parents, and in 89% of father-only and 77% of mother-only households the lone parent was working (Fields, 2003). Changes in median family income using 2005 comparisons show an overall increase of 30.8% (all races) over a 35-year period, from $42,958 in 1970 to $56,194 in 2005. Race makes a difference in income, as comparisons between non-Hispanic Whites and Blacks for a similar period reflect dramatic differences. Specifically, for non-Hispanic Whites the change in median income was from $47,292 in 1972 to $63,156 in 2005, an increase of 33.5%. For Blacks the change was from $27,759 to $35,464, an increase of 31.3% (U.S. Census Bureau, 2007a). Clearly, income has risen for all groups; however, it remains much lower for non-Whites, which means that those of color have reduced access to financial resources.

In addition, there are notable differences in median income by family structure. For example, married-couple families are economically advantaged over those without a spouse present, and this advantage has increased since 1970. The median family income for married couples increased from $40,407 to $65,906 (63.7% increase over 35 years), compared with male, no spouse present, from $36,359 to $41,111 (13.1% increase), and with female, no spouse present, from $22,174 to $27,224 (22.9% increase) (U.S. Census Bureau, 2007b). These data show that both historically and currently economic disadvantage accompanies a single householder (no spouse present) in overall income and increases in income over time. Most glaring are the gender differences: women start and finish with lower incomes than men. However, their percent of increase over this period was greater than that of males. Further, when race is considered, those of color (i.e., Blacks and Hispanics) are at greatest risk for inadequate income (Page & Stevens, 2005). Black single mothers with children are at the greatest economic disadvantage, because they experience more barriers to employment, have less human capital (e.g., skills, knowledge; Jackson, Tienda, & Huang, 2001), and at all ages, are much less likely to marry (Martin, 2006) than all other racial groups. Those who do marry are also less likely to remain married.

Data from the Fragile Families and Child Well Being Study demonstrate that single mothers, including those who are cohabiting, report that the fathers of their children provide cash assistance. How much and from which sources (employment or "underground" economy; Norland, 2001) remain unsubstantiated. Thus, there are some data to suggest that fathers, even in the most challenging of circumstances (e.g., non-resident, low income), do provide some financial support. Further, evidence shows that children in low-income single-mother families are economically advantaged when their mother cohabitates. The potential for two incomes makes a difference in the quality of children's lives (DeNavas-Walt, Proctor, & Smith, 2007).

Forecasting the Future – Better or Worse or Somewhere In Between?

This chapter outlines some of the key changes in American family life and takes a cautionary stance toward the data (see Appendix). As other scholars have noted, families change over time. We believe that an expectation for a return to the companionate model of marriage (our becoming less individualistic) or a dramatic increase in the number of marriages that endure is unrealistic. Instead, we agree with Seltzer's (2004) observation that "children learn about cohabitation firsthand" (p. 925). We believe this holds true for all relationships to which children are exposed – they learn about relationships first-hand through their exposure. This exposure has a lasting effect on the nature of the unions they will form as adults (Amato & Booth, 1997), so marriage becomes only one of a number of acceptable contexts for childrearing (Cherlin, 2004). Some contexts provide more effective skills training than do others; some provide greater relationship stability than do others; and some provide models of "intergenerational feedback mechanisms as children witness and experience the family and marital careers of their parents, relatives, others in their milieus, and society at large" (Cherlin, 2004, p. 967).

Taken together, we suggest that people will continue to be attracted to marriage, although for some groups (e.g., Black women) cohabitation may provide the most viable form of partnering because of the barriers to other forms (e.g., availability of attractive marriage partners; Gibson-Davis et al., 2005). Because of the link between education, marriage, and economic stability, we suggest that greater support be provided to ensure educational achievement of those with the fewest resources, regardless of marital status.

Moreover, we were encouraged by the recent data showing that median duration of remarriages that end in divorce is similar to that of first marriages. We hope this signifies that individuals are making stronger commitments to do the necessary marriage work that fosters longevity in relationships, are becoming better informed about the complexities of remarried family life, and are applying this information to their own unions. However, we do not anticipate that divorce will become less popular; instead, we see it as remaining a viable alternative.

What we find most alarming are two changes: non-marital childbearing and childrearing within the economic reality in which families are situated. If the current trend reflects the future, then children will continue to be disadvantaged by both trends. We believe, as do other scholars, that children reared in single-parent families often, but not always, grow up in a context that is potentially void of models for healthy relationships and are disadvantaged overall (Amato, 2005; Amato & Maynard, 2007). They may lack the necessary skills as they begin to form their own romantic relationships, which sets the stage for repeating patterns (Amato, 2006), and their lone parent often experiences more stress, which affects the quality of their parenting. When two loving and nurturing parents are available for childrearing, children are advantaged. When two parents are available, but there is high conflict or other conditions (parental depression) which negatively affect children, living with two parents, married or not, fails to provide a healthy context for growth.

Regarding the economic realities of families, we believe that families who are most disadvantaged will continue to remain disadvantaged. Federal programs such as Temporary Assistance for Needy Families (TANF) are designed to assist families in greatest need. Unfortunately, some of the associated stipulations and requirements create something of a double bind for families where employment is concerned. Specifically, mothers who remain on TANF experience greater economic disadvantage than those who successfully leave by obtaining employment, and mothers who remain on welfare are also more financially disadvantaged than those who were never on welfare. Further, mothers who experience a time expiration under the current TANF stipulations and never obtain employment are the most economically disadvantaged (Moffitt, Cherlin, Burton, King, & Roff, 2007). This last group of families lack income from either government support or employment, which affects the wellbeing of their children.

Recall that married-couple families experience the least economic disadvantage compared with other family forms. This is potentially due to the fact that married-couple families can pool resources from two working spouses. This also may be true of cohabiting couples who choose to combine incomes. Single-mother families likely have trouble meeting their family's financial needs due to a lack of resources associated with not having a spouse present (Jackson et al., 2001). Access to this additional income is of greater import for Black mothers, because Black children experience greater economic gains with their mother's marriage than do White children (Page & Stevens, 2005). Despite the potential assistance that spousal income could bring to Black single-mother families, the number of children in Black married-couple families has declined (Iceland, 2003) – while there was a concomitant increase in children residing with a single mother. One reason for this increase in children residing with a single mother is the high incarceration and death rates of Black men, leaving fewer Black men available to marry and more Black families fatherless and absent the crucial income of a second spouse (McLanahan & Carlson, 2004).

Importantly, despite the many difficulties that low-income families experience, particularly single-mother families, we would be remiss if we failed to point out that these families continue to demonstrate resilience, coping, and reliance on personal strength and problem-solving skills to ease them through difficult times (Orthner, Jones-Sanpei, & Williamson, 2004). Indeed, when times are difficult, single mothers, particularly those on welfare, use personal strengths and resources to access the support necessary to ensure that needs are met (Edin & Lein, 1997). Thus, in spite of the adversities and challenges of low-income families, they continue to strive for economic equilibrium and hold similar expectations to those facing fewer challenges (Gibson-Davis et al., 2005).

Implications for Clinical Practice

Several clinical implications can be gleaned from an examination of the changing landscape of American families. One important implication is that clinicians must be prepared to address multiple family forms. Families can no longer be viewed monolithically. As family forms evolve, couple and family therapists should be arming themselves with the ability to treat a variety of families, not just married heterosexual families. Therapists must become familiar with treating gay and lesbian couples, cohabiting couples, cohabiting families, single-parent families, and divorced and remarried families. Each of these family forms includes complex issues and potential problems which therapists should be educated and trained to treat.

A second critical implication is the growing need for clinicians who are considered culturally competent. As suggested in this chapter, the racial and cultural diversity of families is increasing in the US. With this diversity, clientele will also likely become more diverse, and therapists must become familiar with clinically oriented research devoted to racially and culturally diverse families (e.g., Bean, Perry, & Bedell, 2002; Carter & McGoldrick, 2005; Constantine, Juby, & Liang, 2001; Hall, 2001; Kim, Bean, & Harper, 2004).

We noted the increasing acceptability of cohabitation either prior to marriage or as a substitute for marriage. As such, it is critical that therapists be knowledgeable about the complex issues facing these families. For example, therapists should be prepared to address parenting issues when one cohabiting partner attempts to parent her or his partner's biological children. Also, because the pooling of resources is one important reason couples and families cohabit, therapists should be ready to address issues related to finance and resource management and allocation.

Married heterosexual couples that come for treatment do not resemble those couples in the past. As men and women delay marriage to pursue additional education or job security, they move from more traditional gender roles to more egalitarian gender relationships. This is also true of those marriages where both partners are employed outside the home. Clinicians must be prepared not only to address presenting problems related to conflicting employment requirements, spending less time together as a couple and spending more time working to make ends meet, and competing gender-role expectations, but also to educate couples about reducing individual stress and couple strain resulting from the competing demands of work and family.

As the divorce rate remains high, yet stable, family therapists must have the skills necessary to help married and cohabiting couples, heterosexual, gay, or lesbian, dissolve their relationships in an amicable manner (Ahrons, 1998; Emery & Sbarra, 2002). This is particularly important when children are involved. In addition, therapists should be ready to treat and educate single parents (divorced or never married) regarding the difficulties associated with parenting children alone and often the financial strains that accompany this status.

As families and family circumstances change, we urge therapists to continue to remain on the cutting edge of related research, including clinical research specifically, so as to continue to grow in knowledge, experience, and effective treatment of diverse family structures. Only in this way can therapists become clinically flexible to better meet the needs of families. Ultimately, therapists must develop a heightened awareness of the contextual factors accompanying all individuals, couples, and families that enter their offices. Those who neglect the multiplicity of contextual factors that influence today's families will likely miss important components essential to successful therapeutic treatment.

Appendix: A Cautionary Note About the Data Reported Here

One of the challenges facing any attempt to outline the nature of changes in American family life is making sense of the available data, in part because of the way that families are defined in various data sources. Teachman, Tedrow, and Crowder (2000) argued that caution was needed when commenting on data from the U.S. Census Bureau; these data do not provide information that permits tracking of different family forms (e.g., two-parent, cohabiting couples, gay and lesbian families) nor regarding valuable sociodemographic characteristics such as race and class. For example, it is easy to ignore the fact that in census data a family is defined as "a group of two persons or more (one of whom is the householder) related by birth, marriage or adoption and residing together" (U.S. Census Bureau, 2001, p. 4). Because a married couple is defined as a husband and wife, an unmarried couple is defined as "two unrelated adults of the opposite sex (one of whom is the householder) who share a housing unit with or without the presence of children under 15 years old" (p. 22). Given these definitions, it is easy to see how entire groups of people are excluded, resulting in undercounting. Specifically, families include couples of the same sex with adopted children, but these same couples are excluded from counts of married couples. "Married couples" also exclude those who cohabit, even when they are of the opposite sex, as well as (a) those whose children are over 15 years of age and, most certainly, (b) any family relationships that extend across households, as is the case in divorce where children reside in two households composed of their single or repartnered/remarried parents.

We see this latter exclusion as especially egregious, because of the large number of families who experience or are expected to experience divorce and repartnering of some form (cohabitation or remarriage). In fact, the census definition of stepfamily is "a married couple family household with at least one child under the age of 18 who is a stepchild (i.e., a son or daughter through marriage, but not by birth) of the householder" (U.S. Census Bureau, 2001, p. 22). The Census Bureau admits that this undercounts the number of stepfamilies, because families are only counted when there is a stepchild of the householder present. If the spouse is not the designated householder ("the person in whose name the housing unit is owned or rented," and in the case of "owned or rented jointly by a married couple, the householder may be either spouse" but not both spouses), then his or her stepchild does not qualify the family as a stepfamily or the child as a stepchild. Also, this ignores the reality that many stepchildren reside with a single parent but remain a regular part of the family life of their other parent who is remarried. Excluded from these counts are stepfamilies where children are older than 18 years, who may or may not reside in the home. (The census definition of children includes only those younger than 18 years of age residing in the household.)

Another area in which official statistics are limited is our data on divorce and remarriage. By their own admission, the Center for Disease Control (CDC), which was responsible for collecting "Information on the total number and rates of marriage/remarriages and divorces at the national and state levels" (p. 1) that were published in the *National Vital Statistics Reports*, suspended the collection of detailed data beginning January 1996 (CDC, 1996). This decision was due to "limitations in the information collected by the States" (p. 1) and budgetary constraints. Thus, our most recent detailed information dates to 1989–1990. For individuals interested in studying the demographic characteristics of those who divorce and remarry, it is more difficult to obtain such information (e.g., number of first marriages that are remarriages and for whom).

Contributing to our understanding of family racial and ethnic diversity, Teachman et al. (2000) also reported the limited past information on some of the subgroups in our population. For example, not until 1989 could persons self-identify in detailed subgroups (e.g., Mexican, Puerto Rican, Cuban, Central or South American) of the Hispanic race. Similarly, the race category of Asian, as of 1997, included Asian Indian, Chinese, Filipino, Japanese, Korean, Vietnamese, Cambodian, Hmong, Laotian, Thai, and "other." Thus, we are unable to address historical trends for many subgroups. As of the 2000 census, persons were able to self-identify with more than one race and ethnic group.

References

Ahrons, C. A. (1998). *The good divorce* (2nd ed.). New York: HarperCollins.

Ahrons, C. A. (2007). Family ties after divorce: Long-term implications for children. *Family Process, 46*, 53–65.

Amato, P. R. (2003). Reconciling divergent perspectives: Judith Wallerstein, quantitative family research, and children of divorce. *Family Relations, 52*, 332–339.

Amato, P. R. (2005). The impact of family formation change on the cognitive, social, and emotional well-being of the next generation. *The Future of Children, 15*, 75–96.

Amato, P. R. (2006). Marital discord, divorce, and children's well-being: Results from a 20-year longitudinal study of two generations. In A. Clarke-Stewart & J. Dunn (Eds.), *Families count:*

Effects on child and adolescent development (pp. 179–202). New York: Cambridge University Press.

Amato, P. R., & Booth, A. C. (1997). *A generation at risk: Growing up in an era of family upheaval.* Cambridge, MA: Harvard University Press.

Amato, P. R., & Maynard, R. (2007). Decreasing nonmarital births and strengthening marriage to reduce poverty. *The Future of Children, 17,* 117–142.

AmeriStat (2003). *Traditional families account for only 7 percent of U.S. households.* Retrieved March 3, 2003, from http://www.ameristat.org.

Bean, R. A., Perry, B. J., & Bedell, T. M. (2002). Developing culturally competent marriage and family therapists: Treatment guidelines for non-African-American therapists working with African-American families. *Journal of Marital and Family Therapy, 28,* 153–164.

Bramlett, M. D., & Mosher, W. D. (2002). Cohabitation, marriage, divorce and remarriage in the United States. *Vital and Health Statistics,* Series 23 (No. 22). Washington, DC: National Center for Health Statistics.

Bumpass, L. L., & Lu, H. H. (2000). Trends in cohabitation and implications for children's family contexts in the United States. *Population Studies, 54,* 19–41.

Carter, B., & McGoldrick, M. (Eds.). (2005). *The expanded family life cycle: Individual, family, and social perspectives* (3rd ed.). Boston: Allyn & Bacon.

CDC (Center for Disease Control). (1996). Change in the reporting of marriage and divorce statistics, NCHS 1996 Fact Sheet. Retrieved June 23, 2003, from http://www.cdc.gov/nchs/releases/96facts/mardiv/htm.

Cherlin, A. J. (2004). The deinstitutionalization of American marriage. *Journal of Marriage and Family, 66,* 848–861.

Constantine, M. G., Juby, H. L., & Liang, J. (2001). Examining multicultural counseling competence and race-related attitudes among White marital and family therapists. *Journal of Marital and Family Therapy, 27,* 353–362.

DeNavas-Walt, C., Proctor, B. D., & Smith, J. (2007). *Income, poverty, and health insurance coverage in the United States: 2006.* Current Population Reports, P60–233. Washington, DC: U.S. Government Printing Office.

Edin, K., & Lein, L. (1997). Work, welfare, and single mothers' economic survival strategies. *American Sociological Review, 62,* 253–267.

Edin, K., & Reed, J. M. (2005). Why don't they just get married? Barriers to marriage among the disadvantaged. *The Future of Children, 15,* 117–137.

Emery, R. E., & Sbarra, D. A. (2002). Addressing separation and divorce during and after couple therapy. In A. S. Gurman & N. S. Jacobson (Eds.), *Clinical handbook of couple therapy* (3rd ed., pp. 508–530). New York: Guilford Press.

Fields, J. (2003). *Children's living arrangements and characteristics: March 2002.* Current Population Reports, P20–547. Washington, DC: U.S. Census Bureau.

Fields, J. (2004). *America's families and living arrangements: 2003.* Current Population Reports, P20–533. Washington, DC: U.S. Census Bureau.

Gibson-Davis, C. M., Edin, K., & McLanahan, S. (2005). High hopes but even higher expectations: The retreat from marriage among low-income couples. *Journal of Marriage and Family, 67,* 1301–1312.

Goldstein, J. R., & Kenney, C. T. (2001). Marriage delayed or marriage forgone? New cohort forecasts of first marriage for U.S. women. *American Sociological Review, 66,* 506–519.

Hall, G. C. N. (2001). Psychotherapy research with ethnic minorities: Empirical, ethical, and conceptual issues. *Journal of Consulting and Clinical Psychology, 69,* 502–510.

Hamilton, B. E., Martin, J. A., & Ventura, S. J. (2007). Births: Preliminary data for 2006. *National Vital Statistics Report, 56(7).*

Hobbs, F., & Stoop, N. (2002). *Demographic trends in the 20th century.* U.S. Census Bureau, Census 2000 Special Reports, Series CENSR-4. Washington, DC: U.S. Government Printing Office.

Iceland, J. (2003). Why poverty remains high: The role of income growth, economic inequality, and changes in family structure, 1949–1999. *Demography, 40,* 499–519.

Jackson, A. P., Tienda, M., & Huang, C. (2001). Capabilities and employabilities of unwed mothers. *Children and Youth Services Review, 23,* 327–351.

Kim, E. Y., Bean, R. A., & Harper, J. M. (2004). Do general treatment guidelines for Asian American families have application to specific ethnic groups? The case of culturally-competent therapy with Korean Americans. *Journal of Marital and Family Therapy, 30,* 359–372.

Kreider, R. M. (2005). *Number, timing and duration of marriage and divorces: 2001.* Current Population Reports, P70–97. Washington, DC: U.S. Census Bureau.

Kreider, R. M. (2008). *Living arrangements of children: 2004.* Current Population Reports, P70–114. Washington, DC: U.S. Census Bureau.

Kreider, R. M., & Fields, J. (2002). *Number, timing and duration of marriages and divorces: 1996.* Current Population Reports, P70–80. Washington, DC: U.S. Census Bureau.

Lichter, D. T., Batson, C. D., & Brown, J. B. (2004). Welfare reform and marriage promotion: The marital expectations and desires of single and cohabiting mothers. *Social Service Review, 78,* 2–25.

Manning, W. D., Longmore, M. A., & Giordano, P. C. (2007). The changing institution of marriage: Adolescents' expectations to cohabit and to marry. *Journal of Marriage and Family, 69,* 559–575.

Martin, J. A. (2006). Family structure and income inequality in families with children, 1976 to 2000. *Demography, 43,* 421–445.

Martin, J. A., Hamilton, B. E., Sutton, P. D., Ventura, S. J., Menacker, F., & Kimeyer, S. (2006). *Births: Final data for 2004. National Vital Statistics Report, 55(1).*

Martin, J. A., Hamilton, B. E., Sutton, P. D., Ventura, S. J., Menacker, F., Kimeyer, S., & Mundson, M. L. (2007). Births: Final data for 2005. *National Vital Statistics Report, 56(6).*

McLanahan, S., & Carlson, M. S. (2004). Fathers in fragile families. In M. E. Lamb (Ed.), *The role of the father in child development* (4th ed., pp. 368–396). Hoboken, NJ: Wiley.

Moffitt, R., Cherlin, A., Burton, L., King, M., & Roff, J. (2007). *The characteristics of families remaining on welfare.* Policy Brief 02–2.

Norland, C. (2001). Unwed fathers, the underground economy, and child support policy. *Fragile Families Research Brief.*

Orthner, D. K., Jones-Sanpei, H., & Williamson, S. (2004). The resilience and strengths of low-income families. *Family Relations, 53,* 159–167.

Page, M. E., & Stevens, A. H. (2005). Understanding racial difference in the economic costs of growing up in a single-parent family. *Demography, 42,* 72–90.

Popenoe, D. (2005). *The state of unions 2005: The social health of marriage in America.* Piscataway, NJ: National Marriage Project.

Seltzer, J. A. (2004). Cohabitation in the United States and Britain: Demography, kinship, and the future. *Journal of Marriage and Family, 66,* 921–928.

Simmons, T., & O'Connell, M. (2003). *Married-couple and unmarried partner households: 2000.* Census Special Report CENSR-5. Washington, DC: U.S. Census Bureau.

Smock, P. J. (2004). The wax and wane of marriage: Prospects for marriage in the 21st century. *Journal of Marriage and Family, 66,* 966–973.

Smock, P. J., & Gupta, S. (2002). Cohabitation in contemporary North America. In A. Booth & A. C. Crouter (Eds.), *Just living together: Implications of cohabitation on families, children and social policy* (pp. 53–84). Mahwah, NJ: Erlbaum.

Smock, P. J., Manning, W. D., & Porter, M. (2005). Everything's there except money: How money shapes decisions to marry among cohabitors. *Journal of Marriage and Family, 67,* 680–696.

Teachman, J. D., Tedrow, L. M., & Crowder, K. D. (2000). The changing demography of America's families. *Journal of Marriage and the Family, 62,* 1234–1246.

Thornton, A., & Young-DeMarco, L. (2001). Four decades of trends in attitudes toward family issues in the United States: The 1960s through the 1990s. *Journal of Marriage and Family, 63,* 1009–1037.

U.S. Census Bureau. (2001). Current Population Survey (CPS), Definitions and explanations. Retrieved February 18, 2001, from http://census.gov/populations.www.cps.cpsdef.html.

U.S. Census Bureau. (2004a). Projected population of the United States by age and sex: Table 2a. Retrieved August 31, 2007, from http://www.census.gov/ipc/www/usinterimproj.

U.S. Census Bureau. (2004b). Projected population of the United States by race and Hispanic origin: Table 1a. Retrieved August 31, 2007, from http://www.census.gov/ipc/www/usinterimproj.

U.S. Census Bureau. (2007a). Historical income tables – Families, Table F-5. Retrieved November 20, 2007, from http://www.census.gov/hhes/www/income/hitinc/f05ar.html.

U.S. Census Bureau. (2007b). Historical income tables – Families, Table F-7. Retrieved November 20, 2007, from http://www.census.gov/hhes/www/income/hitinc/f07ar.html.

U.S. Census Bureau. (2008a). Estimated median age at first marriage, by sex: 1890 to the present, Table MS-2. Retrieved February 23, 2008, from http://www.census.gov/population/www/socdemo/hh-fam.html#history.

U.S. Census Bureau. (2008b). Number, timing, and duration of marriages and divorces: 2004, Table 6. Retrieved February 23, 2008, from http://www.census.gov/population/www/socdemo/mar-div.html.

U.S. Census Bureau. (2008c). Household size: 1960 to present, Table HH-5. Retrieved February 23, 2008, from http://www.census.gov/population/www/socdemo/hh-fam.html#history.

U.S. Census Bureau. (2008d). Young adults at home: 1960 to present, Table AD-1. Retrieved February 23, 2008, from http://www.census.gov/population/www/socdemo/hh-fam.html.

5

Family Diversity

George K. Hong

Diversity, as used in the field of psychology, has a wide range of meanings. Oftentimes, it is used synonymously with *multiculturalism* to refer to racial, cultural, or ethnic minority groups. It is also used in a broader context to refer to characteristics of any group that differs from the majority population in some significant way that is not addressed by psychological theories and practice developed or based on the mainstream population. These characteristics or factors, for example, may include age, gender, sexual orientation, gender identity, physical or mental disability, social or economic class, education, religion or spiritual orientation, etc. (American Psychological Association [APA], 2002a; Atkinson & Hackett, 2004). In fact, the APA *Guidelines on Multicultural Education, Training, Research, Practice, and Organizational Change for Psychologists* explains that these factors may be considered as cultural dimensions that are parts of a person's racial, ethnic, and personal identity (APA, 2002a).

Typically, groups included in the term *diversity* share common characteristics such as being overlooked, underserved, oppressed, marginalized, or disenfranchised (APA, 2002a; Atkinson & Hackett, 2004). They are minority groups in the sense of power and social opportunities, and oftentimes in terms of numbers. A person or a family may hold multiple identities as members of two or more minority groups. For example, one may be an ethnic minority person, belong to a disadvantaged socioeconomic class, and be gay/lesbian. Given that minority groups are underserved and disenfranchised, it is crucial for family psychologists to take an active role in both research and practice to develop better understanding of these populations and to provide appropriate services for them. APA's Ethics Code urges psychologists to be aware of all aspects of diversity, to respect these differences, and to consider them when working with members of diverse groups (APA, 2002b).

In the context of family psychology, in addition to families from racial, cultural, or ethnic minority groups, diversity also includes bi- or multi-racial/cultural families, gay and lesbian families, and families with members with disabilities, as well as families with other non-traditional compositions that result in disadvantages or discrimination, or whose needs are not addressed by majority institutions. Various forms of diverse families are covered in different chapters of this Handbook. This chapter will focus on families from racial, cultural, or ethnic minority groups in contemporary U.S. society.

Race, Culture, Ethnicity

The terms *race, culture,* and *ethnicity* are sometimes used interchangeably, and may overlap in meaning in the mass media. While there is still debate on the implications and usage of these terms, the following is a synopsis of their meanings (APA, 2002a). *Race* is typically defined on the basis of physical characteristics of people, such as color of skin, and other features. It is a controversial topic, and many authors have cautioned that the criteria for categorizing races are simply socially constructed rather than biologically based. *Culture* involves a worldview, a set of beliefs, values, norms, practices, and social institutions, as well as a way of life that is transmitted within a group. *Ethnicity* refers to a group of people having a shared sense of belonging to it, and acceptance of a group's culture or way of living.

The U.S. Census uses the term *racial groups* in its reports. However, *culture* and *ethnicity* are more meaningful in the present discussion of families from these racial groups, as they refer to their worldviews and ways of living. Hence the preference is to use these two terms rather than *race* to describe families in this chapter. The terms *race* and *racial groups* are used mainly in reference to Census data.

Cultural/Ethnic Diversity in United States

Census 2000 uses six major racial categories in its reports: (1) White, (2) Black/African American, (3) Hispanic/Latino, (4) American Indian/Alaska Native, (5) Asian, and (6) Native Hawaiian/Other Pacific Islander. Asians and Pacific Islanders were combined under one single category in Census data prior to Census 2000. This led to the prevalent use of the term API or Asian Pacific Islanders in publications. The Census also includes data on people from "Some Other Race" and "Two or More Races." The assignment of race is by self-identification of the respondent rather than by any external or objective criteria. In May 2007, the U.S. Census Bureau announced that the number of racial minorities has reached a milestone at 100.7 million, or about 30% of the total U.S. population (U.S. Census Bureau, 2007a). Hispanic/Latino Americans are the largest group, and Black/African Americans are a close second. Asian Americans are the third, followed by American Indians/Alaska Natives and Native Hawaiians/Other Pacific Islanders, respectively.

Obviously, the racial categories used in the U.S. Census are very broad. In the seminal work *Ethnicity and Family Therapy* (3rd edition) (McGoldrick, Giordano, & Garcia-Preto, 2005), the authors discussed families from over 40 ethnic groups in the

United States, categorizing them in the nine sections of the book as: (1) American Indian families and Pacific Islander families, (2) Families of African origin, (3) Latino families, (4) Asian families, (5) Asian Indian and Pakistani families, (6) Middle Eastern families, (7) Families of European origin, (8) Jewish families, and (9) Slavic families. In fact, while using the six major racial categories to summarize data in its reports, Census 2000 also identified close to 100 ethnic origins or ancestries with 100,000 or more people in the U.S. (U.S. Census Bureau, 2004a).

Keeping in mind the complexity of cultures and subcultures, the pitfall of overgeneralization, and the limitations of Census racial categories, this chapter will examine the demographics of the minority groups reported in the Census, as well as the salient sociocultural considerations for working with these groups. It is critical to caution that this discussion is simply a very concise synopsis of certain selected issues for the major Census racial minority groups. There is no way to represent the richness and intricacy of every culture. Readers are referred to specific literature on each ethnic group in developing their desired cultural competency. Demographics on some ethnic groups are also discussed in Chapter 4, this volume.

Black/African Americans

In 2006, the Black/African American population was estimated to be about 40.2 million (U.S. Census Bureau, 2007a). According to Census 2000 data, 12.9% of the total U.S. population, or 36.2 million people, are Black/African Americans (U.S. Census Bureau, 2005a). Of this number, about 1.9 million indicated that they were Black in combination with another race(s). The following data are based on those who reported themselves to be Black/African American alone.

Marriage and families/households

Census 2000 data indicate that Black/African Americans tend to have a lower marriage rate than the total U.S. population. About 41% of Black/African Americans age 15 and older have never been married, compared with 27% of the total U.S. population (U.S. Census Bureau, 2005a). About 36% of Black/African Americans are married, as compared to 54% of the total population. Approximately 5% of Black/African Americans are separated; 7% are widowed; and 11% are divorced. These rates are higher than the corresponding rates of 2.2%, 6.6%, and 9.7% of the total population.

The average family size of Black/African Americans is 3.33 members, compared with 3.14 in the total population (U.S. Census Bureau, 2000a). Similar to the total population, about 68% of Black/African American households are family households (i.e., consisting of a householder and one or more people who are related to the householder by birth, marriage, or adoption) (U.S. Census Bureau, 2005a). However, the composition of households tends to be different. For example, 32% of Black/African American households are maintained by married-couple families, as compared to 53% of households in the total population. About 30% of Black/African American households are maintained by women with no spouse present, and about 6% by men with no spouse present, as compared to 12% and 4% respectively in total population households.

Education and economic attainment

About 72% of Black/African Americans age 25 and older have high school or more education, and 14% have bachelor's degree or more education; compared with 80% and 24% respectively of the total population (U.S. Census Bureau, 2005a). About 15% of Black/African American women and 13% of Black/African American men have at least a bachelor's degree. In comparison, 23% of women versus 26% of men in the total population have at least a bachelor's degree.

In 1999, the median income of Black/African American families ($33,300) was lower than that of families in the total population ($50,000); and 24.9% of Black/African Americans were in poverty, about double that of the total population (12.4%) (U.S. Census Bureau, 2005a). Among Black/African Americans, married-couple families tended to fare much better than single-parent families. The former had an annual median income of about $50,700, which was much higher than that of families maintained by women with no husband present ($20,600), or maintained by men with no wife present ($19,300). Overall, an increasing number of Black/African Americans are moving into the middle class. Census 2000 indicated that 33.3% of all Black/African American families were middle-class, as compared to 11.4% in 1970 (McGoldrick et al., 2005).

Sociocultural considerations

One of the major issues discussed in the psychology literature on Black/African Americans is the importance of the extended kinship system, which may assume important roles in caring for one's family (Axelson, 1999; McGoldrick et al., 2005; Sue & Sue, 2003). For example, grandparents or uncles and aunts, as well as family friends and community members, may share in the rearing of children or care of family members. Black/African American families have more role flexibility than mainstream White American families. An older child may take on parental roles, and a mother may assume the role of the father. This role flexibility and the involvement of the extended kinship and the community are important assets for the family. However, clinicians must also be sensitive to the possible stress experienced by family members assuming multiple roles.

Another observation is the importance of religion and spirituality (Axelson, 1999; McGoldrick et al., 2005; Sue & Sue, 2003). Most African Americans are Christians and may belong to various Black/African American denominations as well as mainstream denominations. They may also belong to other religious groups, such as Islam, which has a significant presence. Spiritual values may affect the way a family perceives a problem and its resolution, and clinicians need to take them into consideration. The churches in the African American community often function as a support system for the family, offering social activities and services for members of different age groups, or for individuals with various needs. In times of adversity, the church can provide important socioemotional support as well as physical or material assistance. Collaboration with the churches in the community can be a useful way for service providers to reach out to families.

When working with Black/African American families, one should be aware of the legacy of slavery and racial discrimination (Axelson, 1999; McGoldrick et al., 2005; Sue & Sue, 2003). At times this may manifest as distrust or even hostility toward mainstream society, or a service provider being perceived as belonging to the oppressive class or racial group. One must be sensitive to the sociopolitical and psychoemotional underpinnings of this resentment. Noting the limitations of Eurocentric psychological approaches, some African American psychologists have called for the development of an African-centered psychology and new conceptual paradigms (Parham, 2002). In therapy, cultur-ally meaningful rituals, music, poetry, and prose could be used to connect with clients with African cultural orientation. It has also been cautioned that much of the literature on Black/African Americans is based on the lower socioeconomic group, and more attention needs to be paid to the increasing number of Black/African Americans who are middle-class or higher (Sue & Sue, 2003).

Hispanic/Latino Americans

Hispanic/Latino is defined as a person of Mexican, Puerto Rican, or Cuban descent, or belonging to other Spanish cultures in South or Central America, or some other Hispanic origin regardless of race (U.S. Census Bureau, 2004b). As such, Hispanics/Latinos may be of any race, and the Census data for this group overlap with data for the other racial groups. Hispanic/Latino Americans are presently the largest minority group. In 2006, they reached 44.3 million, or 14.8% of the total U.S. population (U.S. Census Bureau, 2007a). According to Census 2000 data, the three largest groups are Mexicans, Puerto Ricans, and Cubans. They number 20.9 million, 3.4 million, and 1.2 million, or 59%, 9.7%, and 3.4% respectively of the U.S. Hispanic/Latino population (U.S. Census Bureau, 2004b).

Hispanics/Latino Americans are one of the fastest growing minority groups, with a 61% increase between the 1990 and 2000 Censuses, as compared to an increase of 13% in the general U.S. population during the same period. This increase is mainly the result of immigration. About 40% of Hispanics/Latino Americans are foreign born, and about 70% of Hispanics/Latinos residing in the United States are either native or naturalized citizens. Over 75% of Hispanic/Latino Americans speak a language other than English (i.e., Spanish) at home.

Marriage and families/households

About 51% of the Hispanic/Latino American population age 15 and older are married (U.S. Census Bureau, 2004b). This rate is similar to that of the total U.S. population (54%). However, 34% of Hispanics/Latinos age 15 and older are never married, compared with 27% of the total population. About 14% of Hispanics/Latinos are separated, widowed, or divorced, compared with 19% of the total population.

The average family size of Hispanic/Latino Americans is 3.93 members, which is higher than families in the total population (3.14 members) (U.S. Census Bureau, 2000a). The Hispanic/Latino population also has a greater proportion (81%) of family households than the total population (68%) (U.S. Census Bureau, 2004b). However, there are similar proportions of married-couple families in Hispanic/Latino households (55%) and total population households (53%). About 17% of Hispanic/Latino households are maintained by a woman with no spouse present, and 8% by a man with no spouse present, as compared to 12% and 4% respectively of total population households.

Education and economic attainment

About 52% of Hispanic/Latino Americans age 25 and over have at least a high school diploma, and 10% have a bachelor's degree or more (U.S. Census Bureau, 2004b). This is lower than the 80% and 24% respectively in the total population. Education attainment varies among the different Hispanic/Latino groups. For example, about 8% of Mexicans, 13% of Puerto Ricans, and 21% of Cubans have attained at least a bachelor's degree; and about 46% of Mexicans, 63% of Puerto Ricans, and 63% of Cubans have at least a high school diploma.

In 1999, the median family income for Hispanic/Latino Americans was $34,400, which was lower than the $50,000 for total population families (U.S. Census Bureau, 2004b). The median income was $33,500 for Mexican American families, $32,800 for Puerto Rican American families, and $42,600 for Cuban American families. About 22.6% of the Hispanic/Latino American population were in poverty, compared with 12.4% of the total population. Among Latino groups, the poverty rates ranged from 23.5% for Mexicans and 25.8% for Puerto Ricans to 14.6% for Cubans.

Sociocultural considerations

The major cultural characteristics identified in the psychology literature on Hispanic/ Latino Americans include: *familismo, personalismo*, and spirituality/religion (Axelson, 1999; McGoldrick et al., 2005; Santiago-Rivera, Arredondo, & Gallardo-Cooper, 2002; Sue & Sue, 2003). *Familismo* refers to a strong familistic and collectivistic cultural orientation that values close relationships. Interdependence, cohesiveness, and cooperation among family members are valued. The family focus goes beyond the nuclear family to include extended kin such as grandparents, uncles and aunts, cousins, and close friends. *Los compadres* (godparents) are also important members of the family. This extended family system shares a sense of responsibility for the wellbeing of the family, such as child care, and providing financial and emotional support. *Personalismo* refers to the value on building and maintaining interpersonal relationships. High importance is given to positive social skills, and to warmth and friendliness in interpersonal interactions. Clinicians need

to be sensitive to this cultural value and be aware of the negative impact of the impersonal and formal atmosphere often present in public clinics or service agencies. At times,
personalismo may even oblige a clinician to attend family events (e.g., baptisms). Here,
one must ascertain the therapeutic value for each individual situation, and be careful to
maintain the fine line between culturally appropriate practice and infringement of
boundaries or ethical improprieties.

The vast majority of Hispanic/Latino Americans are Roman Catholics while some belong
to other Christian denominations. Spiritual beliefs are deeply ingrained in their worldviews, and for many, religious practices and cultural practices are closely intertwined.
Baptisms, weddings, and major feast days are all occasions of celebrations in church, at
home, and/or in the community. The cultural value of *Marianismo* (referring to the Virgin
Mary) exhorts women to be virtuous, pious, nurturing, and strong. For men, *machismo*
refers to their duty to provide and care for the family.

Language is another major consideration in psychological services for Hispanic/Latino
Americans. As stated earlier, about 40% of this population are foreign born, and a large
proportion speak Spanish at home. Hence bilingual/bicultural services are often needed
for providing adequate services in the Hispanic/Latino American communities. It is important to note that while Hispanic/Latino Americans share a common language and the
Spanish influence, they are very diverse in many other aspects. Besides different countries of origin, their histories of migration to the U.S. may be different. Some families
have been in the U.S. for many generations, while others are recent immigrants. Some
have come to the U.S. as refugees, such as many Cuban Americans as well as others
coming from Central America. Some immigrants are documented, while others are not.
Family psychologists need to be sensitive to the diversity among this population.

Asian Americans

In the U.S. Census, Asian refers to people having origins in the Far East, Southeast Asia,
or the Indian subcontinent. This term includes nationalities as well as ethnicities.
Census 2000 identified 11 Asian groups plus an "Other Asian" category: Asian Indian,
Cambodian, Chinese, Filipino, Hmong, Japanese, Korean, Laotian, Pakistani, Thai, and
Vietnamese (U.S. Census Bureau, 2004c). Each of these groups comprises at least 1%
of the total Asian American population. In discussing Asian Americans, it should be emphasized that this population includes diverse groups with different languages/dialects,
cultures, and histories of migration to the U.S.

The Asian American population reached 14.4 million in 2005, or about 5% of the
total United States population (U.S. Census Bureau, 2007b). Among Asians, about 22.9%
(3.3 million) are Chinese, 19.4% (2.8 million) are Filipino, and 17.4% (2.5 million) are
Asian Indian. This is followed by Vietnamese (10.4% or 1.5 million), Koreans (9.7% or
1.4 million) and Japanese (8.3% or 1.2 million). Between Census 1990 and 2000, the
Asian American population grew by 63%, from 7.27 million to 11.9 million, matching
the Hispanic/Latino American population as one of the fastest growing groups (Hong
& Ham 2001; U.S. Census Bureau, 2004c). In Census 2000, 10.2 million people

indicated that they were Asian alone, and 1.7 million indicated that they were Asian and another race(s) (U.S. Census Bureau, 2004c). The data discussed here are based on those who reported themselves to be Asian alone.

Immigration is a major factor contributing to the rapid growth of the Asian American population. About 69% of Asian Americans are foreign born. Approximately 31% of Asian Americans are U.S. citizens by birth, and another 34% are naturalized citizens. About 79% of Asian Americans age 5 and over speak a language other than English at home. The rate is over 90% for some newer immigrant groups, such as Cambodians, Hmong, Laotians, Pakistanis, and Vietnamese. Japanese Americans are the only group with a majority (53%) speaking only English at home.

Marriage and families/households

About 60% of Asian Americans age 15 and older are married, as compared to 54% of the total population (U.S. Census Bureau, 2004c). About 9.8% of Asian Americans are separated, widowed, or divorced, as compared to 19% of the total population.

The average family size of Asian Americans is 3.61 members, which is higher than total population families (3.14 members) (U.S. Census Bureau, 2000a). About 75% of Asian households are family households, compared with 68% of total population households (U.S. Census Bureau, 2004c). About 62% of Asian households are maintained by married couples, as compared to 53% of total population households. About 8.8% of Asian family households are maintained by women with no spouse present, and 4.5% by men with no spouse present. In comparison, the corresponding rates are 12% and 4% in total population households.

Education and economic attainment

The proportion of Asian Americans age 25 and older having at least a high school education is about 80%, which is similar to the total population (U.S. Census Bureau, 2004c). However, 44% of Asians have earned at least a bachelor's degree, which is much higher than that of the total population (24%). Among Asian Americans, Asian Indians have the highest proportion (64%) with a bachelor's degree or more, followed by Pakistanis (54%), and Chinese (48%). In contrast, about 60% of Hmongs, 53% of Cambodians, and 50% of Laotians have less than a high school education. This is likely related to the refugee background of these groups.

In 1999, the median income of Asian American families was $59,300, which was higher than that for total population families ($50,000) (U.S. Census Bureau, 2004c). Among Asian Americans, Asian Indian and Japanese families' median incomes were the highest, both at about $71,000; while Hmong and Cambodian families were the lowest ($32,400 and $35,600, respectively). About 12.6% of Asian Americans lived in poverty, similar to the total population (12.4%) (U.S. Census Bureau, 2004c). The poverty rates ranged from a low of 6.3% for Filipinos, 9.7% for Asian Indians, and 9.8% for Japanese; to a high of 37.8% for Hmongs and 29.3% for Cambodians.

Sociocultural considerations

Asian Americans come from different countries in Asia and speak different languages. Sometimes, they speak different dialects even when they are from the same country. In terms of culture, they can be grouped into East Asian (Chinese, Japanese, and Koreans), which historically shared a strong Chinese cultural influence, and South Asian (Asian Indian and Pakistani), which historically shared the Indian cultural heritage (Hong & Ham, 2001). Cultures in Southeast Asia (Cambodian, Filipino, Hmong, Laotian, Thai, and Vietnamese) were historically influenced by either one or both of these cultures depending on geographical proximity and historical interactions. In East Asian cultures, the dominant philosophies and/or religions are Confucianism, Taoism, and Buddhism. In South Asian cultures, Hinduism and Islam are the major traditional religions and philosophies. The Philippines, because of its location on the seafaring route and colonization by Spain, had been strongly influenced by Spanish culture as well as Chinese culture. It is the only Asian country where Catholicism is the majority religion.

Keeping in mind the diversity among Asian Americans, several cultural characteristics they share are discussed in the psychology literature. Familism, as opposed to individualism, is the cultural orientation (Axelson, 1999; Hong & Ham, 2001; McGoldrick et al., 2005; Sue & Sue, 2003). The focus is on the welfare of the family rather than on the individual. The extended kinship network is considered an important part of the family system and is a crucial support network in daily life and in time of need. However, since many Asian Americans are immigrants, they often do not have the extensive support network available in their pre-migration environment. The Asian family hierarchy is clearly defined, and is less egalitarian than the mainstream U.S. family. Also, concern for the family name inhibits one from disclosing shameful family matters (e.g., major disputes or mental disorders) to outsiders, such as a therapist. Clients may often feel awkward or hesitant when they have to discuss intimate family matters or family conflicts.

Other salient cultural values include the emphasis on interpersonal harmony and non-aggression. Open disagreements are to be avoided in polite settings. The expression of anger or negative emotions is often controlled, toned down, or done indirectly. These social etiquettes often lead to the perception that Asian Americans are non-assertive, non-expressive, or sometimes, passive aggressive. Clinicians must be alert to these misperceptions.

While the majority of Asian Americans are immigrants, they may differ in their reasons for migration and the process of migration. Some came to the U.S. voluntarily in a pre-planned manner to work or to study (and stayed on to work). Others came to join their families already here. There are some who had to leave their homeland under dire situations, such as Southeast Asians who came as refugees in the aftermath of the Vietnam War. Thus, there are great differences in Asian American immigrants' social, emotional, and physical needs and in their adaptation to life in the U.S. Also, recall that many Asian Americans speak a language other than English at home. As such, bilingual and bicultural services are often necessary. However, since Asian Americans speak different languages and dialects, the provision of linguistically and culturally appropriate services is a major challenge for mental health professionals.

Pacific Islander Americans

In the U.S. Census, the term "Pacific Islanders" refers to Native Hawaiian, Samoan, Guamanian or Chamorro, Fijian, Tongan, Marshallese, and an "Other Pacific Islander" group. In the Census data, this population is also referred to as "Native Hawaiian and Other Pacific Islanders" (NHPI). In 2006, the number of people reporting to be NHPI alone or in combination with (an)other group(s) reached about 1 million, or about 0.3% of the total U.S. population (U.S. Census Bureau, 2007a). In Census 2000, 44% of the NHPI population, or about 378,000 people, identified themselves to be NHPI alone, and another 482,000 (56%) indicated that they were NHPI in combination with (an)other group(s) (U.S. Census Bureau, 2005b). The data discussed here are based on those who reported themselves to be NHPI alone. The three largest groups of NHPI are Native Hawaiian, Samoan, and Guamanian. They make up about 37%, 23%, and 15% of the NHPI American population.

Around 80% of NHPI Americans are native U.S. citizens, since people born in American Samoa, Guam, or Hawaii are citizens by definition. However, about 44% of the NHPI American population speak a language other than English at home. This percentage varies among different groups; for example, 64% for Samoans, 44% for Guamanians, and 17% for Native Hawaiians.

Marriage and families/households

Approximately 51% of all NHPI Americans age 15 and older are married, about the same as the total population (54%) (U.S. Census Bureau, 2005b). Around 14% of NHPI are separated, widowed, or divorced, compared with 19% for the total population.

The average family size of all NHPI Americans is 4.05 members, which is higher than total population families (3.14 members) (U.S. Census Bureau, 2000a). About 79% of NHPI households are family households, compared with 68% of total population households (U.S. Census Bureau, 2005b). About 56% of NHPI households are maintained by married couples, as compared to 53% of total population households. About 15.4% of NHPI family households are maintained by women with no spouse present, and 7.4% by men with no spouse present. In comparison, the corresponding numbers are about 12% and 4% in total population households.

Education & economic attainment

About 78% of NHPI Americans age 25 and older have at least a high school education, which is similar to the total population (80%) (U.S. Census Bureau, 2005b). However, only 14% of NHPI have a bachelor's degree or more, which is lower than the total population (24%). Among the NHPI American groups, 15% of Native Hawaiians, 11%

of Samoans, and 14% of Guamanians have a bachelor's degree or more. In comparison, the groups having the largest percentage with less than a high school education are Tongian (35%), Fijian (33%), and Marshallese (32%).

In 1999, the median income of NHPI American families was $45,900, which was lower than that for total population families ($50,000). There was variation among different groups, with median income of $49,700 for Native Hawaiian families, $49,100 for Guamanian families, and $41,100 for Samoan families. About 17.7% of the NHPI population lived in poverty, compared with 12.4% of the total population.

Sociocultural considerations

Pacific Islanders are people whose native homelands are islands that are mostly (but not exclusively) located over a large area in the Pacific Ocean known as Polynesia (Spickard, Rondilla, & Wright, 2002). They share many cultural elements, but are also diverse in other aspects. Since it is impossible to describe all these groups here, this discussion will point out some commonalities, and then focus on Native Hawaiians, the largest group among Pacific Islanders in the U.S.

One common observation is the collectivistic orientation of the cultures of Pacific Islanders, where the family and the extended kinship system have a central role (McGoldrick et al., 2005; Phenice, 1999; Spickard, 1994; Spickard et al., 2002). However, for Pacific Islanders who have moved to the U.S. mainland, such an extensive social network may not be available. For Native Hawaiians, *o'hana* means family, and that includes both the nuclear family and the extended family. It also includes individuals who are not related by blood or marriage, but are simply considered as a part of the family by their close association and cooperative interactions with others in the family (McGoldrick et al., 2005; Phenice, 1999). The *Hanai* system is the practice of giving one's children to relatives or friends who have no children. A family may also willingly take in another child to ensure that he or she has a warm and affectionate home (Phenice, 1999). Family psychologists need to be attuned to these family compositions.

Core Native Hawaiian cultural values include harmony with nature and with other people in the family, in the community, and in society in general (McGoldrick et al., 2005; Phenice, 1999). These are reflected in values such as *aloha* – love and affinity, *malama* – care, *kokua* – help, *lokahi* – connection or unity, and *ha'aha'a* – humility, etc. Decency and generosity are expected in interpersonal interactions. Traditionally, the elderly are respected for their experiences and knowledge. They play an important role in helping to resolve disputes. One indigenous way of mediating conflicts is *ho'oponopono*, which means to have a frank discussion to make things right. This process is grounded in spirituality and is traditionally led by a respected family elder (*kupuna*). Presently, *ho'oponopono* is also used in clinical settings to resolve family conflicts for those who are identified with their indigenous culture. It is facilitated by a clinician trained in this method and chosen by consensus of the family members. Other common traditional healing practices include prayers, use of herbs, and physical treatments including *lomilomi* – massage. Clinicians should be cognizant of these practices and consider using them as possible adjuncts to therapy as needed.

American Indians and Alaskan Natives

In 2006, the number of people reporting themselves to be American Indian and Alaska Native alone or in combination with another group was about 4.5 million, or about 1.5% of the total U.S. population (U.S. Census Bureau, 2007a). Census 2000 reported on 10 major American Indian tribal groups, with Cherokee and Navaho being the largest (U.S. Census Bureau, 2006). Four Alaskan Native tribal groups are identified in the data, with Eskimo being the largest. Of the 4.3 million who reported themselves to be American Indian and Alaska Native (AIAN) in Census 2000, about 2.4 million indicated they were AIAN alone, with the rest reporting AIAN in combination with (an)other group(s). The data discussed here are based on those reported to be AIAN alone. About 28% of AIAN speak a language other than English at home. This percentage varies among different groups, ranging from 68% of Navajos and 47% of Eskimos to only 9% of Cherokees.

Marriage and families/households

Approximately 44% of AIAN age 15 and older are married, compared with 54% of the total population (U.S. Census Bureau, 2000b). Around 20.5% of AIAN are separated, widowed, or divorced. This is similar to the total population (19%).

The average family size of AIAN is 3.58 members, which is higher than the total population (3.14 members) (U.S. Census Bureau, 2000a). About 73% of AIAN house-holds are family households, compared with 68% of total population households (U.S. Census Bureau, 2006). About 45% of AIAN households are maintained by married couples, as compared to 53% of households in the total population. About 20.7% of AIAN family households are maintained by women with no spouse present, and 7.5% by men with no spouse present. These percentages are much higher than the corresponding 12% and 4% in total population households.

Education and economic attainment

About 71% of AIAN age 25 and older have at least a high school education, and 11.5% have at least a bachelor's degree; compared with 80% and 24% respectively of the total population (U.S. Census Bureau, 2006). The percentages of Cherokees, Navahos, and Eskimos having a high school education or better are 77%, 63%, and 70% respectively; and having a bachelor's degree or more are 16%, 7%, and 6% respectively.

The median income of AIAN families was about $33,144 in 1999, which was lower than that for total population families ($50,000) (U.S. Census Bureau, 2000c). About

25.7% of the AIAN population lived in poverty, almost double that of the total population (12.4%) (U.S. Census Bureau, 2006).

Sociocultural considerations

AIAN are a diverse group of people from over 500 federally recognized tribes, nations, bands, or communities (Axelson, 1999; McGoldrick et al., 2005; Sue & Sue, 2003). Ethnogeographically, they may be grouped into Peoples of the Far North, Tribes of the Eastern Woodlands, Tribes of the Plains, Tribes of the Southwest, and Tribes of the Northwest (Axleson, 1999). They speak many different languages and there are also differences in their customs and values. Thus one has to be careful about overgeneralization when discussing this group.

Overall, AIAN cultures are collectivistic. The welfare of the extended family and the tribe takes precedence over the individual (Garrett, 2004; Sue & Sue, 2003). The extended family, with at least three generations, is the typical basic unit. Children are often raised by extended family members such as aunts, uncles, or grandparents. Family members may not even be linked by blood. It is common practice to claim and welcome a person into the family as a relative, and the person becomes a relative, for all purposes, in the context of Indian culture and society. While many tribes/nations are matriarchal, they may be matrilineal or patrilineal. There are also some that are patriarchal. Elders hold positions of honor and respect as "wisdom keepers" because of their life experiences (Garrett, 2004). Family psychologists must be sensitive to the family configurations and roles when working with native populations.

Spirituality is another common cultural characteristic. There is a general belief in the connectedness of the spirit, the mind, and the body (Garrett, 2004; McGoldrick et al., 2005; Sue & Sue, 2003). Wellness is harmony among these elements. Each person should be attuned to self, relations, and environment to achieve wellness. Traditional healing rituals are aimed at restoring harmony. Harmonious interpersonal relationship, generosity, and sharing are emphasized in daily life. Salient cultural values and norms also include humility, patience, preference for non-verbal communication over verbal communication, and respect for authority figures (Garrett, 2004; Herring, 1999; Juntunen, 2004; McGoldrick et al., 2005; Sue & Sue, 2003). In a therapy session, these qualities may be manifested as silence, moderation in speech, and avoidance of direct eye contact with the therapist. Clinicians must be attuned to these cultural preferences. Clients who are identified with their native cultures could be encouraged to participate in traditional ceremonies and rituals to facilitate their healing (McGoldrick et al., 2005). Creative art media in native cultures, such as pottery, blankets, masks, sand painting, storytelling, poetry, folktales, etc., can also be effective in therapy (Herring, 1999).

Finally, clinicians must be cognizant of the long history of oppression of the native peoples, including extermination, land seizures, and the forced removal of children from their families under the misguided notion of providing them with a better life. This legacy may create mistrust between the clients and clinicians who are perceived as agents of the government. Family psychologists must take special care to address such sentiments.

Diversity: A Cultural and Social Environmental Framework

In approaching the issue of culture, one needs to be aware that individuals and families may have different degrees of identification with their culture of origin and mainstream U.S. culture. For example, immigrants and those who left their ethnic or tribal communities to live in mainstream U.S. areas may follow a blending of cultures rather than their home culture. Even for people in a specific cultural community, there is still the consideration of *traditional* culture versus *modernized* versions of their culture. Culture is not stationary and may evolve and change over time. Besides culture, individuals and families live under different social environmental conditions that affect their psychoemotional and physical wellbeing. The diversity factors or characteristics mentioned earlier are part of this social environmental consideration. The *cultural and social environmental (CASE)* model (Hong & Ham, 2001) offers a useful conceptual framework for understanding diversity in this broad context (Figure 5.1).

The first factor in the *CASE* model is the *cultural context.* This refers to the cultural identification of the person or the family (keeping in mind possible differences among family members). An ethnic minority person may be highly identified with his or her culture of origin or may be totally acculturated into mainstream society, i.e., highly identified with mainstream culture. There are also individuals who are proficient in both cultures and embrace both effectively (adaptively bicultural). Then there are those who are marginalized, feeling disconnected from their culture of origin and from mainstream culture (maladaptively bicultural). These four major cultural orientations are depicted on the top or horizontal part of Figure 5.1. The arrows emphasize that cultural identification is a continuum, rather than dichotomous as high/low. For individuals who are multiracial or multiethnic, their identification with each culture can be conceptualized in a similar manner. Cultural identification is not static. It may change over a person's life span as a result of socialization and life events. Also, immigrant families often experience a cultural gap within the family, i.e., parents and children may have different degrees of cultural identification with culture of origin and mainstream culture, because they have different degrees of exposure to these cultures in their upbringing. This cultural gap could lead to family discord or complicate other conflicts.

The second factor in the *CASE* model is the *social environmental context.* This is depicted on the vertical part of Figure 5.1. It refers to life problems and barriers a person or a family encounters in daily living as an individual, as a family, as a group, or as a community. Examples include financial hardships, educational problems, occupational concerns, etc. The problems may be on a personal level, pertaining to the specific individual or the specific family. They may also be on the societal level, pertaining to entire communities or groups, such as socioeconomic disadvantages and lack of resources in certain ethnic communities or inner-city areas, social barriers to achievement, racism, sexism, or discrimination toward particular groups such as people with disabilities, gays and lesbians, the elderly, etc. Individuals and families may be on any point of a continuum on the dimension of social environmental problems regardless of their ethnic identification or perceived racial group. However, there may also be interactions between

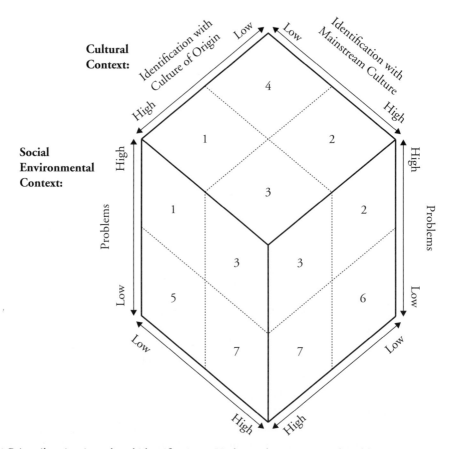

1 Primarily minority cultural identification – High social environmental problems
2 Primarily mainstream cultural identification – High social environmental problems
3 Adaptively bicultural – High social environmental problems
4 Marginal/maladaptively bicultural – High social environmental problems
5 Primarily minority cultural identification – Low social environmental problems
6 Primarily mainstream cultural identification – Low social environmental problems
7 Adaptively bicultural – Low social environmental problems
8 Marginal/maladaptively bicultural – Low social environmental problems (not shown in figure)

Figure 5.1   Cultural and social environmental model (CASE)
Adapted from Hong and Ham (2001).

the cultural context and the social environmental context. For example, being a member of an ethnic minority group may by itself result in barriers and hardships in daily life because of racial prejudice that still exists in mainstream society.

For simplicity in illustrating the *CASE* model, Figure 5.1 identifies eight different combinations based on the high/low distinctions on these two factors. There are actually infinite combinations since each factor is on a continuum rather than dichotomous. The combination of cultural and social environmental factors offers a more complete picture of diversity. For example, a family indicates they are Chinese American, but with which culture does each member really identify? Does their ethnicity as perceived by others lead to blatant or subtle forms of prejudice in their daily life, including institutional racism? What does it mean to have a disability, to be gay/lesbian, to be a single parent, or to be elderly family members in their minority cultural context and in the mainstream cultural context? How does socioeconomic class impact the situation? Are they facing a double or multiple minority status that brings additional hardships or discrimination? These are issues that family psychologists need to consider rather than using a single-dimensional approach to diversity.

Concluding Remarks

The United States is becoming ever more diverse in every sense of the word. Families from different cultural or ethnic groups, different religions or belief systems, and families with non-traditional configurations or membership are fast increasing. This chapter has highlighted demographics and salient issues in the hope of sensitizing readers to the complexity of the subject, as well as the importance of developing better understanding and services to diverse families through research and practice.

References

American Psychological Association. (2002a). *Guidelines on multicultural education, training, research, practice, and organizational change for psychologists.* Washington, DC: American Psychological Association.
American Psychological Association. (2002b). *Ethical principles of psychologists and code of conduct.* Washington, DC: American Psychological Association.
Atkinson, D. R., & Hackett, G. (2004). *Counseling diverse populations* (3rd ed.). Boston: McGraw-Hill.
Axelson, J. A. (1999). *Counseling and development in a multicultural society* (3rd ed.). Pacific Grove, CA: Brooks/Cole.
Garrett, M. L. (2004). Profile of Native Americans. In D. R. Atkinson (Ed.), *Counseling American minorities* (6th ed., pp. 147–170). Boston: McGraw-Hill.
Herring, R. (1999). *Counseling with Native American Indians and Alaska Natives: Strategies for helping professionals.* Thousand Oaks, CA: Sage.
Hong, G. K., & Ham, M. D. (2001). *Psychotherapy and counseling with Asian American clients: A practical guide.* Thousand Oaks, CA: Sage.
Juntunen, C. L. (2004). Treatment issues for Native Americans: An overview. In D. R. Atkinson, *Counseling American minorities* (6th ed., pp. 193–213). Boston, MA: McGraw-Hill.
McGoldrick, M., Giordano, J., & Garcia-Preto, N. (Eds.). (2005). *Ethnicity and family therapy* (3rd ed., pp. 77–86). New York: Guilford Press.
Parham, T. A. (2002). *Counseling persons of African descent: Raising the bar of practitioner competence.* Thousand Oaks, CA: Sage.

Phenice, L. A. (1999). Native Hawaiian families. In H. P. McAdoo (Ed.), *Family ethnicity: Strength in diversity* (2nd ed., pp. 107–118). Thousand Oaks, CA: Sage.

Santiago-Rivera, A. L., Arredondo, P., & Gallardo-Cooper, M. (2002). *Counseling Latinos and la familia: A practical guide.* Thousand Oaks, CA: Sage.

Spickard, P. (Ed.). (1994). *Pacific Island peoples in Hawaii.* Honolulu, HI: Dept of Sociology, University of Hawaii at Manoa.

Spickard, P., Rondilla, J. L., & Wright, D. H. (Eds.). (2002). *Pacific diaspora: Island peoples in the United States and across the Pacific.* Honolulu, HI: University of Hawai'i Press.

Sue, D. W., & Sue, D. (2003). *Counseling the culturally diverse: Theory and practice* (4th ed.). New York: Wiley.

U.S. Census Bureau. (2000a). Average family size. U.S. Census Bureau data set: Census 2000 Summary File 2 (SF 2) 100-Percent Data. Retrieved May 30, 2007, from http://factfinder. census.gov

U.S. Census Bureau. (2000b). Dp-2. Profile of selected social characteristics: 2000; American Indian and Alaska Native alone (300, A01-R99). U.S. Census Bureau data set: Census 2000 American Indian and Alaska Native Summary File (AIANSF) – Sample Data. Retrieved October 13, 2007, from http://factfinder.census.gov

U.S. Census Bureau. (2000c). Census 2000 demographic profile highlights: Selected population group: American Indian and Alaska Native alone. U.S. Census Bureau data set: Summary File 2 (SF 2) and Summary File 4 (SF 4). Retrieved May 29, 2007, from http://factfinder.census.gov

U.S. Census Bureau. (2004a). Ancestry: 2000. Census 2000 brief, C2KBR-35, issued June 2004. Retrieved April 18, 2007, from http://www.census.gov/population/www/cen2000/briefs.html

U.S. Census Bureau. (2004b). *We the people: Hispanics in the United States.* Census 2000 special reports, CENSR-25, issued December 2004. Retrieved April 18, 2007, from http://www. census.gov/population/www/cen2000/briefs.html

U.S. Census Bureau. (2004c). *We the people: Asians in the United States.* Census 2000 special reports, CENSR-25, issued December 2004. Retrieved April 18, 2007, from http://www.census.gov/ population/www/cen2000/briefs.html

U.S. Census Bureau. (2005a). *We the people: Blacks in the United States.* Census 2000 special reports, CENSR-25, issued August 2005. Retrieved April 18, 2007, from http://www.census.gov/ population/www/cen2000/briefs.html

U.S. Census Bureau. (2005b). *We the people: Pacific Islanders in the United States.* Census 2000 special reports, CENSR-25, issued August 2005. Retrieved April 18, 2007, from http:// www.census.gov/population/www/cen2000/briefs.html

U.S. Census Bureau. (2006). *We the people: American Indians and Alaska Natives in the United States.* Census 2000 special reports, CENSR-25, issued February 2006. Retrieved April 18, 2007, from http://www.census.gov/population/www/cen2000/briefs.html

U.S. Census Bureau. (2007a). Minority tops 100 million. U.S. Census Bureau News, CB07-70, released: May 17, 2007. Retrieved May 30, 2007, from http://www.census.gov/Press-Release/ www/releases/archives/population/010048.html

U.S. Census Bureau. (2007b). Asian/Pacific American Heritage Month: May 2007. U.S. Census Bureau News, CB07-FF.05, released: March 1, 2007. Retrieved May 19, 2007, from http:// www.census.gov/Press-Release/www/releases/archives

6

Qualitative Research and Family Psychology

Jane F. Gilgun

Qualitative approaches have much to offer family psychology. They are useful for theory construction and testing, for the development of descriptions of lived experiences, model and concept development, the delineation of social processes, the development of typologies, and the creation of items for surveys, assessment instruments, and evaluation tools among many others. These approaches are particularly useful for understanding meanings that human beings attribute to events in their lives and, through discourse analysis, can aid in understanding the intersections of cultural themes and practices and individual lives. Qualitative methods can be used in basic, applied, and evaluation research.

Qualitative approaches are not useful for establishing prevalence and incidence. Although they can inform researchers about the contexts of experiments and quasi-experiments, how and what treatments were implemented, and subjects' responses to the treatment, they will not yield an effect size or any other quantified outcome. Because of the volume of data generated, they are difficult to use in large-scale surveys. They will not show a mathematical relationship between variables, but they can provide the model to be tested, the hypotheses that compose the model, and the items of instruments that represent the hypotheses.

Despite the usefulness of the products of qualitative research to social science, many researchers steeped in logico-deductive, mathematical approaches are wary. Several issues block a serious consideration of qualitative approaches. Among these are questions about rigor, generalizability, and subjectivity.

The purposes of this chapter are to describe uses for qualitative methods and to examine common concerns that block some researchers from doing qualitative research. The intended audience is other researchers trained in logico-deductive methods and who are interested in exploring whether qualitative approaches can help them answer their research questions. This chapter provides descriptions of procedures that lead to these products and discusses alternative ways of understanding aspects of qualitative approaches that some researchers view as problematic. The chapter will not address the many complex and interesting philosophies of science issues connected to qualitative approaches. (See authors such as Denzin & Lincoln, 2005; Freeman, 2007; McMullen, 2002; O'Neill, 2002 for discussions.) As important as these are, by doing qualitative research, researchers will learn through their own experience how philosophical ideas are relevant to their work. In this chapter, considerations of philosophical issues are linked to procedures of research.

Definitions and Other Fundamentals

Models are defined as a set of interrelated hypotheses that account for significant social phenomena, typically how something works, such as how persons overcome adversities or how family members enact family rituals. Hypotheses are statements of relationships among concepts or variables. Concepts are the components of hypotheses and thus are also part of theories and models. In my work, theories are composed of hypotheses that have been tested qualitatively and/or quantitatively but are always subject to further testing and revision. A set of interrelated theories becomes a model when the theories together are thought to account for how something works. Models may not have undergone tests beyond those that researchers conducted to formulate them in the first place.

In qualitative research, there are two general sources of models: those whose components are drawn from analysis of qualitative data only and those that integrate these analyses with related research and theory that enhance, amplify, and lend significance to the results of the analysis. In addition, researchers often build personal and professional experience into their models of how things work (Gilgun, 2005, 2006; Meleis, 1985).

Data collection methods in qualitative research are interviews, observations, and document analysis. Videotapes, audiotapes, and cameras can provide some of the documents that compose the texts that are analyzed. Other kinds of texts are archived narrative material such as oral histories, photographs and other graphic materials, and case records. The term *text* rather than *data* is used, as *text* fits more closely with the author's philosophy of science, which is realist (the world outside of me exists independently of me), combined with constructivism (the world as I know it is a construction that I share with others to various degrees), and also infused with poststructural thought (what I perceive outside of me and even within me are signs with multiple meanings in the sense that various people can interpret them in various ways; signs are texts to be read, that is, interpreted). See Chapter 20 for further discussion of these issues in therapy.

In terms of their philosophical base, qualitative researchers focus most often on what it means to be human and the meanings that human beings attribute to the events in their lives. We want to understand the everyday meanings and interpretations that individuals make out of their lives. When we report results, we are concerned with fidelity – that is, do we understand what informants are telling us in words and in actions? How well do we represent informants' points of view?

Issues of reliability and validity are important, but most of us prefer not to use these terms because they connote distance from meanings and lived experience. Instead, most qualitative researchers use the term *trustworthiness*, which requires transparency, meaning that researchers demonstrate how they arrived at their analysis and conclusions and that these procedures lead to trustworthy representations.

We also are concerned with application: how can these findings be used in other settings with other persons? We assume that we have to test our findings for their fit in these other settings. Many of us are concerned with social justice and fostering social change and use our research to advocate for policy changes and program development, although we set aside, to the extent possible, our advocacy positions while we do the research.

There are other fundamental issues, such as the recognition that the texts (e.g., data) we produce are co-creations in that how informants represent themselves is in response to how they perceive researchers; they might have presented themselves differently with different researchers under different conditions at different times. We recognize the tentative nature of knowledge, enjoy it in fact, and look forward to undermining our own findings in the hope that we can come up with something even more useful and representative of the lived experiences of research informants.

The remainder of this chapter discusses the three main products of qualitative research, procedures for doing three main types of qualitative research, and the ways that qualitative approaches can work in concert with surveys and other forms of quantitative research. The chapter ends with an examination of common concerns about qualitative research.

The Products of Qualitative Research

Theory-building and model-testing

Family scholars have a long-term interest in theory-building. Qualitative methods can make unique contributions to the identification, development, testing, refinement, and reformulation of concepts, hypotheses, and theoretical models of family processes. One approach is *deductive qualitative analysis* (DQA) (Gilgun, 2004c, 2005, 2008). DQA begins with a conceptual model for the purpose of testing it, refining it, or refuting it and coming up with a better set of concepts and hypotheses. "Better" means the concepts and hypotheses produced are based upon research evidence and have implications for theory, research, policy, and practice. A second approach is *grounded theory* (Charmaz, 2006; Clarke, 2003; Glaser, 1978; Glaser & Strauss, 1967; Strauss & Corbin, 1998), which involves entering the field with an open mind and trusting that a research focus will emerge. The goal of grounded theory is to identify and develop concepts and hypotheses that elucidate social processes and that are linked to data, an idea that builds on Lazarfeld's (1959) concept-indicator model. DQA and grounded theory can contribute to the refinement and reformulation of existing theory and lead to the creation of new theory in overlooked areas.

Deductive qualitative analysis (DQA).   Researchers trained in logico-deductive approaches prefer to begin their studies with conceptual models and use these models to guide research and also to derive hypotheses from these models in order to test them (see Bell et al., 2007). Many researchers assume that to do qualitative studies, they have to forsake well-formulated conceptual models and hypothesis-testing and begin their research in an open-ended way (see Kidd, 2002, as one example). This widespread impression stems from the procedures of grounded theory, to be discussed later, that are designed for researchers who want to identify research problems through preliminary studies and whose goals typically are to develop theories and understandings in areas where there is little clarity. Yet researchers interested in particular theoretical models cannot, and should not be expected to, start anew, or act as if they do not already know something about their areas of interest. Furthermore, dissertation committees are unlikely to approve studies that do not build on what is already known, and funders are not inclined to commit money to such studies.

DQA recognizes these issues and provides guidelines for doing qualitative research that begins with an initial conceptualization that can range from a parsimonious theory to a rather loose set of ideas that guide and focus the research. The term *deductive qualitative analysis* is one I coined. The idea of theory-driven qualitative research is not new (Haverkamp & Young, 2007), but with the prominence of grounded theory's emphasis on "discovery" and its suspicion of "received theory" there is a need for clarity about how prior research and theory can be used in qualitative work.

This approach is based on procedures of DQA from earlier work on analytic induction (Cressey, 1953; Gilgun, 1995; Lindesmith, 1947; Znaniecki, 1934) and the thinking of philosophers John Dewey (1910) and Karl Popper (1969). For Dewey, hypotheses are always open to modification when researchers identify new evidence. Popper's thought provides a rationale for negative case analysis, a sampling strategy in analytic induction that involves actively searching for cases that will modify, amplify, or undermine developing theory and descriptive material.

Coding, analysis, and interpretation in DQA can be done any number of ways, such as the generic three-level codes described in Strauss (1987) and Strauss and Corbin (1998), or the levels of analysis associated with interpretive phenomenology (Benner, 1994). Team analysis of texts is recommended to test emerging understandings against the interpretations of others who have different life experiences, training, knowledge, and other preconceptions. Crist and Tanner (2003) provided an overview of group analysis using a phenomenological approach.

In DQA, the initial conceptual model with which researchers begin their studies may range from tightly defined to rough and unfocused. One possible type of initial conceptual model is highly abstract and parsimonious and is based on previous research and theory. A second type of conceptual model is composed of a loose set of ideas and concepts derived from one or more sources, such as previous research and theory, professional experience, and personal experience.

Researchers can put this model to many different uses, such as developing open-ended hypotheses that bring some focus to the study, using the model to do pattern matching, or drawing on the theory as a guide in exploring new areas of understanding. An example is my use of theory-testing in a study of the moral discourse of incest perpetrators (Gilgun, 1995) where I developed hypotheses derived from theories of feminist moral development.

I tested the hypotheses on a series of cases where incest perpetrators talked about the incest that they had perpetrated. The words of perpetrators provided evidence that led to changes in the initial hypotheses. The study ended with revised hypotheses. Readers who are familiar with theory-guided quantitative research will find these procedures familiar, but they are not familiar to most qualitative researchers. Most qualitative researchers avoid theory-testing and many do not think they are supposed to do theory-guided research.

An example of theory-guided research is the analysis of Abrams (2003) on young women's gender identity negotiations with their male partners. Abrams used a loose conceptual framework to illuminate and interpret her analysis and showed how her research contributed to theory. Again, this type of theory-guided research already is familiar to quantitative researchers, but qualitative researchers frequently must be reminded of the importance of theory-guided research because of many researchers' assumption that qualitative research is for the "discovery" of theory.

A third type of DQA begins with roughly formulated ideas and hunches, sometimes based on professional and/or personal experience. The guidance that this type of DQA provides is that of a general orientation or framework. Elizabeth Bott's (1957) work on family social networks is a classic example, where she used Lewin's ecology theory as her initial general framework, had no hypotheses to test, and ended with a richly described social network theory, and where she shared her processes of theorizing in some detail. Undoubtedly, there are many other ways to use conceptual models at the onset of qualitative research, and there are probably more to be developed. In psychology, as in many other fields, examples of qualitative research are relatively rare, but because of their potential for theory and model-building and their capacities for in-depth examinations of social processes their presence will grow rapidly.

Grounded theory approaches.   The purposes of grounded theory, according to Strauss & Corbin (1998), are "to build rather than test theory" and to "identify, develop and relate the concepts that are the building blocks of theory" (p. 13). A key idea is the *emergence* of the research problem as a result of immersion in the field, which literally means the research settings. Immersion in the research material – which can be interviews, observations, document analysis, and analysis of quantitative data – also is required for an in-depth understanding and analysis (Glaser & Strauss, 1967; Strauss & Corbin, 1998).

To generate grounded theory, researchers enter the field, according to Glaser (1992), with "an open mind to the emergence of the subjects' problem" (p. 23), a trust that the central problem will emerge, and a commitment "not to know" until it does (p. 24). Many influences "core out" the central problem, such as the researchers' training, the location of the study, the nature of the research participants, and funding, among others. Both Strauss and Glaser maintained a career-long interest in basic social processes, derived from Lazarfeld's (1959) elaboration analysis and symbolic interaction theory (Glaser, 1978, 1992; Glaser & Strauss, 1967; Strauss, 1987; Strauss & Corbin, 1998). Thus, *emergence* might not be an accurate term because as trained researchers, we have a tendency to see in texts what we have already been sensitized to see; our own favored theories and other coring-out influences shape our interpretations of texts. Nonetheless, the point here is to make every effort to understand and theorize informants' points of views.

Sampling in grounded theory is theoretical, which means that sampling depends on what researchers want to know next, and this usually involves a principle of comparison within and across cases (Glaser & Strauss, 1967; Strauss & Corbin, 1998). Theoretical sampling and negative case analysis have common assumptions in that for both types, researchers have a reason, based on emerging findings, to choose the next case. In practice, there is little difference between the two. Rarely is there reason to do random or convenience sampling in grounded theory, although descriptive qualitative researchers make use of these methods. In doing theoretical sampling, researchers select a homogeneous sample on which to focus. They continue interviewing and/or observing this sample until they find that they are learning little or nothing that adds to their emerging understanding, thus reaching the point of theoretical saturation. Researchers then reflect on what comparisons they need to make next to deepen their understanding. These reflections lead to a decision on which kind of sample to recruit next. Strauss and colleagues' coding scheme is a set of generic procedures that can be used in research other than grounded theory such as oral histories and other narrative approaches. For example, they originated a coding scheme consisting of open, axial, and selective coding (Glaser, 1978; Glaser & Strauss, 1967; Strauss & Corbin, 1998). The first level consists of open coding, which attaches labels to concrete instances of phenomena identified in texts. These labels are the codes. The second level consists of axial coding, which happens after researchers have tentatively chosen the concepts on which they want to focus. In axial coding, researchers seek to identify the connections between various codes and decisions about which codes might be "core concepts" that are central to understanding social phenomena. Selective coding occurs after axial coding and involves additional documentation of core concepts through re-reading and re-analyzing data.

The hypotheses that Strauss & Corbin (1998) and other qualitative researchers use are statements of relationships that link two or more concepts, as stated earlier. For example, in evaluating the moral discourse of incest perpetrators, Gilgun (1995) examined the hypothesis that incest perpetrators have special regard for themselves and do not have regard for the impact of incest on their victims. Persons unfamiliar with qualitative methods might not recognize this as a hypothesis at all.

Summary.   Although theirs is widely thought of as an approach that rejects the formulation of conceptual frameworks prior to entering the field, contemporary grounded theorists at least entertain this formulation as a possibility. DQA is an attempt to encourage researchers to test, refine, reformulate, refute, and replace theoretical models qualitatively. This approach acknowledges the importance of logico-deductive methods, but includes variations based on qualitative approaches. Qualitative thinking underlies all science (Cook & Campbell, 1979), and qualitative analysis in the end, regardless of whether it begins with a conceptual model, is a way of thinking qualitatively.

Grounded theory is a far more detailed set of procedures for coding and analysis than DQA. What DQA adds is an invitation to do deductive research, suggestions for several different types of deductive qualitative research, guidelines for ensuring that researchers do not impose preconceptions onto their findings (search for negative evidence/

conjectures and refutations), and guidelines for ensuring that findings account for diversities (negative case analysis).

Many of the notions and procedures of grounded theory fit well with DQA, including the coding scheme that grounded theory encourages, the notions of core concepts and their dimensions, definitions of hypotheses, commitment to identifying and representing the points of view of informants, and open-mindedness as to how researchers present their findings, among many others. The notions of processes, contexts, and consequences are embedded within grounded theory, and although researchers may not use these terms, much qualitative research involves these ideas.

Descriptions of lived experiences

Qualitative researchers in general seek to understand subjective human experience. Researchers might want to know: what is it like to fall in love? How do widows experience the influence of God in their lives? How does living in the United States affect the gender role negotiations of Liberian refugee couples? Open-ended questions such as these lead to new analyses that can be used in a variety of ways, both theoretical and applied. An example of descriptive qualitative research is the work of Padgett, Hawkins, Abrams, and Davis (2006) on how formerly homeless women with mental illness construct their experiences with trauma and substance abuse. Sensitivity to research participants' situations and points of view on the part of interviewers is required to elicit such personal material. Many types of qualitative research build on lived experience, such as oral histories (Martin, 1995; Ritchie, 2003), portraiture (Lawrence-Lightfoot & Davis, 1997), narrative analysis (Wodak, 2001), life histories (Gilgun & McLeod, 1999; Padgett et al., 2006), and interpretive phenomenology (Benner, 1994; Leonard, 1994; Nehls, 2000).

Typologies.   Descriptive research lends itself to the development of typologies, a strategy for organizing findings that show similarities, differences, and overlaps between and within classes of phenomena. Typologies often are a step along the way to developing theory. They are particularly helpful in educational and clinical settings, where practitioners are confronted with complex human behaviors. Often interventions, such as medication, educational strategies, and forms of therapy, are linked to classifications that typologies can provide. Robinson, Prest, Susman, Rouse, & Crabtree (2001) used observations of family physicians' responses to patients' emotional distress and developed a four-quadrant typology: the technician, the friend, the detective, and the healer. They noted that this typology can contribute to physician training, and it can also provide direction to future research that asks such questions as whether physician style is linked to outcome and whether patients select physicians who suit their personal preferences. A classic example of the use of typologies is Frazier's (1932) *The Negro Family in Chicago*, in which African Americans living in Chicago during the early part of the nineteenth century were classified as migrants, old settlers, and *nouveaux riches*.

Theoretical analyses of texts

Theoretical analysis of texts is a hybrid, composed of both theoretical analyses (e.g., DQA) and description. The analysis involves using a theoretical framework or model on case material in order to illuminate aspects of human lives and to demonstrate the relevance of particular theories to particular life stories. For example, Gilgun and Abrams (2005) presented two case studies involving a woman and a man who perpetrated violence. The theoretical model on the development of violent behaviors was presented and it was then shown how the model worked with these two cases.

Some forms of cultural studies involve close analyses of texts. Cultural studies is a multi-disciplinary field, practiced in sociology, social work, and the humanities. Researchers in this tradition often build on lived experience in their quest to critique culturally based power structures in a wide range of social institutions, such as scouting, the mass media, and families (Schulman, 1993).

Critical discourse analysis (CDA) is an important tool of cultural studies. CDA, broadly defined, involves an analysis of language, where researchers recognize that language does more than communicate information (Gee, 2005); it embodies and maintains social inequalities that include status, power, domination, discrimination, and control (Wodak, 2001).

Using Qualitative Methods with Quantitative Methods

Hypotheses that can be tested on large samples

Because qualitative studies rarely have large samples, questions about the generality of findings often arise. How widespread are the findings from a qualitative study? Will there be similar findings with a large sample using a survey? Surveys are a logical way to test this wider applicability. Therefore, qualitative research can produce hypotheses that researchers test through surveys with large samples. The hypotheses can then be tested through statistical analysis. For example, Gilgun (1996, 1999c) used qualitative methods to develop hypotheses regarding factors associated with overcoming risks for violence, such as sharing personal problems and finding that it helped, and feeling loved and connected to family and friends. Gilgun, Klein, and Pranis (2000) then used survey methodology to test these hypotheses and found that indeed these factors did generalize to a large survey sample.

Items for surveys, standardized instruments, and clinical tools

Concepts from qualitative research are composed of concrete indicators. Therefore, qualitative data are rich sources of items for both research instruments and clinical assessment tools. Items developed from this kind of qualitative research focus on the perspectives of informants, and the language of the items will be at the appropriate level of abstraction.

The survey instrument used in the inmate study mentioned earlier (Gilgun et al., 2000) was informed by my life history case studies as well as my knowledge of related research on developmental psychopathology.

The findings of qualitative research are readily amenable to the construction of clinical rating scales. The CASPARS (Clinical Assessment Package for Assessing Risks and Strengths) (Gilgun, 1999a, 2004a, 2004b; Gilgun, Keskinen, Marti, & Rice, 1999) represents the core concepts that appear to distinguish at-risk persons who demonstrate resilience from those who are imprisoned for felony-level violence. The CASPARS has excellent psychometric properties, including coefficient alphas above .9 for each of the five scales. Another set of clinical instruments based upon qualitative research is the 4-D, which also has excellent psychometric properties (Gilgun, 2004d). In summarizing her decades-long research on women who had experienced miscarriages, Swanson (1999) provided another example of the continuity between descriptive qualitative research, theory-building in qualitative research, and the development of valid, reliable instruments.

Multiple-method research

Multiple-method research is yet another kind of research where qualitative methods can provide important information. Known more commonly today as mixed-method research, multiple-method research is as old as social research, extending back in time to the research of Frederic LePlay (1855) on European families and Charles Booth's (1891) studies of the London poor (Gilgun, 1999d). These studies used surveys, in-depth interviews, participant observation, document analysis, and analysis of demographic data. Multiple-method research crossed the Atlantic and took root in the United States early in the twentieth century.

A common mix is the use of surveys with qualitative cases studies. The statistical analysis of survey data provides an understanding of the distributions and relationships among a limited number of variables in large samples. Yet these results do not account for the deeper meanings, the subjective dimensions of the phenomena under investigation, and the complexity of contexts and influences on individual activities. For example, Seccombe's (1999) research includes a statistical portrait of women on welfare as well as the results of 47 in-depth interviews that undermine the stereotype of the "welfare queen." Multiple-method research has received a great deal of attention recently (Hanson, Creswell, Clark, Petska, & Creswell, 2005) and is becoming expected in projects that the federal government funds (Morse, 2005).

Some Common Concerns

Analytic and probabilistic generalizability

Researchers accustomed to think in terms of probability theory find it difficult to understand how the results of qualitative research can be generalized. Qualitative approaches rarely have random samples or even randomized assignment to groups. The samples can be composed of few participants and therefore are case studies, sometimes single case studies. In general, case studies are useful for studying a phenomenon in depth so as to develop a comprehensive understanding and to identify key processes, concepts, and hypotheses (Gilgun, 1994; Stake, 1995; Yin, 2002). What researchers learn from the particularities of a case can be used for many different purposes, such as (a) feedback to the individuals, families, or institutions studied; (b) as part of a strategy that compares case material to what theory tells us, so that we can enlarge understandings; or (c) as a source of concepts and hypotheses that can be tested and implemented in other settings for research purposes or practical applications. Finally, case studies can provide the foundation for theoretical analyses and theory development.

Generalizability has several different meanings, and only one of them is probabilistic and dependent on random samples. As Cronbach (1975) observed many years ago in his presidential address to the American Psychological Association, all findings, regardless of how they are derived, are working hypotheses when applied to new settings. Some well-established philosophies of science depend upon detailed studies of individual cases, such as work done on chaos and complexity theory, genetics, astrophysics, and the work of early behaviorists.

The usefulness of case study findings depends on their analytic generalizability, meaning whether they shed new light on phenomena of interest. In the social sciences, the concern is whether the findings can make contributions to theory, policies, programs, and interventions.

Subjectivity

Qualitative research typically involves the immersion of researchers in the field, which means that researchers seek to understand persons and their cultures in great detail and from many points of view (Gilgun, 1992, 1999b, 2001a, 2001b). Geertz (1973) calls this "thick description." To develop thick descriptions requires that researchers make personal connections to those they research. Otherwise, informants might not trust them enough to reveal details important to understanding.

Researcher self-awareness is important in emotion-laden situations. Academic integrity requires fair presentations of informants' experiences. Knowing the difference between one's own responses and the views of informants is central to the interpretation of research material. Informants too have emotional reactions to being part of a research projects. Especially when working in emotionally sensitive areas, researchers are bound ethically to ensure that no harm comes to participants.

While informants – also known as subjects or research participants – have the power to define researchers as well as to choose what to withhold and to share, researchers have the power to represent informants in research reports and public presentations. Attention to issues such as how researchers represent informants, how and whether researchers influence informants, and how to account for any such influences improves the quality of the research.

How researchers perceive themselves in relationship to informants is a topic worthy of serious consideration. For example, in my research, I am a woman who talks to men about their violence toward women. Do I have a point of view on men who commit violence? Do I have a point of view of myself as a member of a class of persons oppressed by male violence? Certainly, I do. How I manage these issues greatly affects what the informants say to me. Can I shape and manage my own reflexivity so that my representation of these men is balanced? There are no easy answers.

Subjectivity, then, provides many opportunities for the development of rich and deep data, but subjective reactions can also result in researchers' losing their analytic thread. As a result we can fall back on stereotypes, biases, and familiar ways of thinking that do not fit the phenomena we want to understand.

Group analysis of data helps researchers to avoid or work themselves out of emotional reactions that are disconnected from analytic thinking. Members of the group have not been immersed in the field and thus are not affected emotionally, as researchers may be. Also, as discussed earlier, members of the group have perspectives that differ from those of researchers who have been in the field. Thus, group members can help researchers engage in conjectures, refutations, and reformulations. These strategies help qualitative researchers represent informants and their cultures in ways that reflect the perspectives of informants more than they reflect the biases of researchers. These are enduring issues in social research, not only qualitative research.

Discussion

Qualitative approaches have much to offer family psychologists, including theory-building and hypothesis-testing, rich descriptions of family phenomena, close analyses of texts, and items for various types of measurement tools and surveys, and may constitute an important component of multi-method social research. DQA in particular invites researchers trained in logico-deductive methods to develop theory and to test hypotheses. Skills required to do qualitative theory-building and model-testing are (a) capacities to draw detailed descriptions of phenomena of interest from respondents, from observations of settings, and from documents of various types; (b) capacities for conceptual thinking, that is, the ability to conceptualize social phenomena and identify them in data; (c) capacities for flexible thinking, where researchers are willing to challenge and undermine their own preconceptions and favorite theories, some of which may be out of their awareness; and (d) the discipline to answer questions such as "How do my findings add to, modify, transform, or undermine what is already known?" For many researchers, qualitative research is a way of thinking.

Increasingly, funding agencies encourage researchers to conduct studies that combine qualitative and quantitative research. For example, the document *Qualitative Methods in Health Research* (http://obssr.od.nih.gov/publications/qualitative.pdf) provides guidance on proposal writing that fulfills the requirements of the U.S. National Institutes of Health (NIH). Developed by a working group of 12 qualitative researchers who are recipients of NIH funding and/or served as NIH reviewers, this document helps qualitative researchers interpret the instructions in Public Health Service Grant Application PHS 398, which is used for proposals submitted to NIH for funding (Gilgun, 2002).

In the long run, many forces lead to increased interest in qualitative research methods. Books, journal articles, and new journals devoted to qualitative research are appearing at a growing rate. The first issue of the journal *Qualitative Research in Psychology* was published in the United Kingdom in January 2004. No approach or sets of approaches will resolve the many pressing issues with which family psychologists contend. However, qualitative approaches can add to the social science repertoire of research methods by increasing capacities for constructing knowledge that has promise of relevance to both application and theory development.

Note

This is a revised version of Gilgun, Jane F. (2005). Qualitative research and family psychology. *Journal of Family Psychology, 19(1)*, 40–50.

References

Abrams, L. S. (2003). Contextual variations in young women's gender identity negotiations. *Psychology of Women Quarterly, 27*, 64–74.

Bell, L., Goulet, C., Tribble, D. S., Paul, D., Boisclair, A., & Tronick, E. Z. (2007). Mothers' and fathers' views of the interdependence of their relationships with their infant: A systems perspective on early family relationships. *Journal of Family Nursing, 13(2)*, 179–200.

Benner, P. (Ed.). (1994). *Interpretive phenomenology*. Thousand Oaks, CA: Sage.

Booth, C. (1891). *Labour and life of the people: London* (Vols. 1 & 2). London: Williams & Norgate.

Bott, E. (1957). *Family and social network*. New York: Free Press.

Charmaz, K. (2006). *Constructing grounded theory: A practical guide through qualitative analysis*. Thousand Oaks, CA: Sage.

Clarke, A. E. (2003). Situational analyses: Ground theory mapping after the postmodern turn. *Symbolic Interaction, 26*, 553–576.

Cook, T. D., & Campbell, D. T. (1979). *Quasi-experimentation: Design and analysis for field settings*. Boston: Houghton Mifflin.

Cressey, D. (1953). *Other people's money*. Belmont, CA: Wadsworth.

Crist, J. D., & Tanner, C. A. (2003). Interpretation/analysis methods in hermeneutic interpretive phenomenology. *Nursing Research, 52*, 202–205.

Cronbach, L. (1975). Beyond the two disciplines of scientific psychology. *American Psychologist, 30*, 116–127.

Denzin, N. K., & Lincoln, Y. S. (Eds.). (2005). *Handbook of qualitative research* (3rd ed.). Thousand Oaks, CA: Sage.

Dewey, J. (1910). *How we think*. Amherst, NY: Prometheus.

Frazier, E. F. (1932). *The Negro family in Chicago*. Chicago: University of Chicago Press.

Freeman, M. (2007). Performing the event of understanding hermeneutic conversations with narrative texts. *Qualitative Inquiry, 13(7),* 925–944.

Gee, J. P. (2005). *An introduction to discourse analysis: Theory and method* (2nd ed.) New York: Routledge.

Geertz, C. (1973). *The interpretation of culture.* New York: Basic Books.

Gilgun, J. F. (1992). Definitions, methodologies, and methods in qualitative family research. In J. F. Gilgun, K. Daly, & G. Handel (Eds.), *Qualitative methods in family research* (pp. 22–39). Newbury Park, CA: Sage.

Gilgun, J. F. (1994). A case for case studies in social work research. *Social Work, 39,* 371–380.

Gilgun, J. F. (1995). We shared something special: The moral discourse of incest perpetrators. *Journal of Marriage and the Family, 57,* 265–281.

Gilgun, J. F. (1996). Human development and adversity in ecological perspective: Pt. 2. Three patterns. *Families in Society, 77,* 459–576.

Gilgun, J. F. (1999a). CASPARS: New tools for assessing client risks and strengths. *Families in Society, 80,* 450–459. (Tools available at http://ssw.che.umn.edu/Faculty_Profiles/Gilgun_Jane/ Gilgun_pubs.html)

Gilgun, J. F. (1999b). Fingernails painted red: A feminist, semiotic analysis of "hot" text. *Qualitative Inquiry, 5,* 181–207.

Gilgun, J. F. (1999c). Mapping resilience as process among adults maltreated in childhood. In H. I. McCubbin, E. A. Thompson, A. I. Thompson, & J. A. Futrell (Eds.), *The dynamics of resilient families* (pp. 41–70). Thousand Oaks, CA: Sage.

Gilgun, J. F. (1999d). Methodological pluralism and qualitative family research. In S. K. Steinmetz, M. B. Sussman, & G. W. Peterson (Eds.), *Handbook of marriage and the family* (2nd ed., pp. 219–261). New York: Plenum.

Gilgun, J. F. (2001a, November). *Case study research, analytic induction, and theory development: The future and the past.* Paper presented at the 31st Preconference Workshop on Theory Construction and Research Methodology at the annual National Conference on Family Relations, Rochester, NY.

Gilgun, J. F. (2001b). Grounded theory, other inductive methods, and social work methods. In B. Thyer (Ed.), *Handbook of social work research* (pp. 345–364). Thousand Oaks, CA: Sage.

Gilgun, J. F. (2002). Conjectures and refutations: Governmental funding and qualitative research. *Qualitative Social Work, 1,* 359–375.

Gilgun, J. F. (2004a). Qualitative methods and the development of clinical assessment tools. *Qualitative Health Research, 14,* 1008–1019.

Gilgun, J. F. (2004b). A strengths-based approach to child and family assessment. In D. R. Catheral (Ed.), *Handbook of stress, trauma and the family* (pp. 307–324). New York: Brunner-Routledge.

Gilgun, J. F. (2004c). Deductive qualitative analysis and family theory-building. In V. Bengston, P. Dillworth Anderson, K. Allen, A. Acock, & D. Klein (Eds.), *Sourcebook of family theory and methods.* Thousand Oaks, CA: Sage.

Gilgun, J. F. (2004d). The 4-D: Strengths-based assessments for youth who have experienced adversities. *Journal of Human Behavior in the Social Environment, 10(4),* 51–73.

Gilgun, J. F. (2005). The four cornerstones of evidence-based practice in social work. *Research on Social Work Practice, 15(1),* 52–61.

Gilgun, J. F. (2006). The four cornerstones of qualitative research. *Qualitative Health Research, 16(3),* 436–443.

Gilgun, J. F. (2008). *On being a shit: Unkind deeds and cover-ups in everyday life.* Morrisville, NC: Lulu.

Gilgun, J. F., & Abrams, L. S. (2005). Gendered adaptations, resilience, and the perpetration of violence. In M. Ungar (Ed.), *Handbook for working with children and youth: Pathways to resilience across cultures and context* (pp. 57–70). Toronto: University of Toronto Press.

Gilgun, J. F., Keskinen, S., Marti, D. J., & Rice, K. (1999). Clinical applications of the CASPARS instruments: Boys who act out sexually. *Families in Society, 80,* 629–641.

Gilgun, J. F., Klein, C., & Pranis, K. (2000). The significance of resources in models of risk. *Journal of Interpersonal Violence, 14,* 627–646.

Gilgun, J. F., & McLeod, L. (1999). Gendering violence. *Studies in Symbolic Interaction, 22,* 167–193.

Glaser, B. (1978). *Theoretical sensitivity.* Mill Valley, CA: Sociology Press.

Glaser, B. (1992). *Basics of grounded theory analysis: Emergence vs. forcing.* Mill Valley, CA: Sociology Press.

Glaser, B., & Strauss, A. (1967). *The discovery of grounded theory.* Chicago: Aldine.

Hanson, W. E., Creswell, J. W., Clark, V. L. P., Petska, K. S., & Creswell, J. D. (2005). Mixed methods research designs in counseling psychology. *Journal of Counseling Psychology, 52(2),* 224–235.

Haverkamp, B. E., & Young, R. A. (2007). Paradigms, purposes, and the role of the literature: Formulating a rationale for qualitative investigations. *The Counseling Psychologist, 35(2),* 265–294.

Kidd, S. A. (2002). The role of qualitative research in psychological journals. *Psychological Methods, 7,* 126–138.

Lawrence-Lightfoot, S., & Davis, J. H. (1997). *The art and science of portraiture.* San Francisco: Jossey-Bass.

Lazarfeld, P. F. (1959). Problems in methodology. In R. K. Merton, L. Broom, & L. S. Cottrell, Jr. (Eds.), *Sociology today* (pp. 47–67). New York: Basic Books.

Leonard, V. W. (1994). A Heideggerian phenomenological perspective on the concept of person. In P. Benner (Ed.), *Interpretive phenomenology: Embodiment, caring, and ethics in health and illness* (pp. 43–63). Thousand Oaks, CA: Sage.

LePlay, F. (1855). *Les ouvriers européens.* Tours, France: Alfred Mame.

Lindesmith, A. R. (1947). *Opiate addiction.* Bloomington, IN: Principia.

Martin, R. R. (1995). *Oral history in social work: Research, assessment, and intervention.* Thousand Oaks, CA: Sage.

McMullen, L. U. (2002). Learning the language of research: Transcending illiteracy and indifference. *Canadian Psychology, 43,* 195–204.

Meleis, A. I. (1985). *Theoretical nursing: Development and progress.* Philadelphia: Lippincott.

Morse, J. M. (2005). Editorial: Evolving trends in qualitative research: Advances in mixed-methods designs. *Qualitative Health Research, 15(5),* 583–586.

Nehls, N. (2000). Recovering: A process of empowerment. *Advances in Nursing Science, 22(4),* 62–70.

O'Neill, P. (2002). Tectonic change: The qualitative paradigm in psychology. *Canadian Psychology, 43,* 190–194.

Padgett, D. K., Hawkins, R. L., Abrams, C., & Davis, A. (2006). In their own words: Trauma and substance abuse in the lives of formerly homeless women with serious mental illness. *American Journal of Orthopsychiatry, 76(4),* 461–467.

Popper, K. R. (1969). *Conjectures and refutations: The growth of scientific knowledge.* London: Routledge & Kegan Paul.

Ritchie, D. A. (2003). *Doing oral history: A practical guide.* Oxford: Oxford University Press.

Robinson, W. D., Prest, L. A., Susman, J. L., Rouse, J., & Crabtree, B. F. (2001). Technician, friend, detective, and healer: Family physicians' responses to emotional distress. *Journal of Family Practice, 50*, 864–870.

Schulman, N. (1993). Conditions of their own making: An intellectual history of the Centre for Contemporary Cultural Studies at the University of Birmingham. *Canadian Journal of Communication, 18*. Retrieved from http://cjc-online.ca

Seccombe, K. (1999). *"So you think I drive a Cadillac?" Welfare recipients' perspectives on the system and its reform.* Boston: Allyn & Bacon.

Stake, R. E. (1995). *The art of case study research.* Thousand Oaks, CA: Sage.

Strauss, A., & Corbin, J. (1998). *Basics of qualitative research: Techniques and procedures for developing grounded theory* (2nd ed.). Thousand Oaks, CA: Sage.

Strauss, A. L. (1987). *Qualitative analysis for social scientists.* New York: Cambridge University Press.

Swanson, K. M. (1999). Research-based practice with women who have had miscarriages. *Image: The Journal of Nursing Scholarship, 31*, 399–345.

Wodak, R. (2001). What CDA is about – a summary of its history, important concepts and its development. In R. Wodak & M. Meyer (Eds.), *Methods of critical discourse analysis* (pp. 1–13). Thousand Oaks, CA: Sage.

Yin, R. K. (2002). *Case study research: Design and methods* (3rd ed.). Thousand Oaks, CA: Sage.

Znaniecki, F. (1934). *The method of sociology.* New York: Farrar & Rinehart.

7

Systemic Research Controversies and Challenges

Danielle A. Black and Jay Lebow

The chasm between research and practice in family psychology is similar to couple dynamics in a failing long-term marriage. The relationship between the two is characterized by poor communication skills, perceived lack of shared values, and different worldviews. Perhaps the key to improving the relationship between these seemingly different entities rests within understanding the narrative of this relationship.

Many of the first family therapy theorists were both researchers and clinicians (e.g., Murray Bowen, Gregory Bateson, Don Jackson, etc.; Nichols & Schwartz, 1995). They created a narrative emphasizing science; indeed, their principal theory, general systems theory, is a theory based on not only social science but physical science as well. However, the research methods of these pioneers were far from today's state-of-the-art randomized clinical trial research. As the field developed, family researchers began to adopt more rigorous methodologies, and the clinical implications of such research became less clear and perhaps also, ironically, less convincing to practicing clinicians than earlier, simpler research methods (Nichols & Schwartz, 1995).

The goals of the emerging fields of family research and family therapy quickly moved in quite different directions. Family researchers sought to first understand family dynamics and family patterns, believing that to create effective methods of intervention such patterns needed to be identified. In contrast, clinicians, given their needs in practice, sought to develop and disseminate effective interventions. Furthermore, research appeared too reductionistic to clinicians to capture the complex dynamics of families; thus, family research came to be viewed as inapplicable to the real world of family therapy (Tomm, 1986). The academy of researchers came to be highly critical of the application of methods that had limited empirical support.

An additional factor in the development of this problem has been theoretical orientation. Those family psychologists trained in the cognitive-behavioral tradition have typically treated evidence as a strong input into their treatments. Those associated with the "family therapy" field and such approaches as structural, strategic, and psychoanalytic family therapy have found little room for empirical research. Given the way psychologists are socialized into academia, many of the most productive researchers have cognitive-behavioral orientations. It is a sad development in the broad field of family therapy that cognitive-behavioral family therapists and the broader community of family therapists functioned almost wholly independently until the beginning of the twenty-first century.

The relationship narrative between family psychology practice and research is a story of a relationship once close with common goals, but that over time became characterized by growing distance. It is time for the field of family psychology to re-author the story of the relationship between research and practice from an either/or approach to a both/and approach. In this chapter, we review some of the barriers to bridging the gap between research and practice, summarize the pros and cons of different research methods, and describe the controversy between positivist and postmodern methods.

The Myth of Lack of Shared Values and Goals

Why is it important to improve the relationship between researchers and practitioners? If their goals are distinct and divergent, why spend the time trying to improve such a relationship? We contend the goals between clinical researchers and practitioners are ultimately the same – to provide the most effective family interventions possible. The view that clinicians and researchers differ in their ultimate goals is a misperception.

The common goal between researchers and clinicians has in part been obscured by the slow process of science. An example from the research literature will illustrate this point. Many clinicians are aware of John Gottman's work (Gottman & Silver, 1999), and it is often applied in clinical settings that treat couples. We often hear clinicians at our clinic citing Gottman and the "four horsemen" that predict marital dissolution (i.e., criticism, contempt, defensiveness, and stonewalling) when discussing cases at grand rounds and during supervision. If you ask these clinicians about the usefulness of Gottman's work, they would emphatically tell you they use it in their everyday practice. Further, these same clinicians would agree that Gottman's goals are similar to their own. Yet Gottman's clinical suggestions emerge from a base of over 30 years of empirical research. He has published hundreds of research articles that inform his principles of effective therapy. However, if one were to read any one of Gottman's research articles in isolation, it might not be evident that his goal was to create effective interventions. In fact, several might strike the practicing clinician as dull and irrelevant, focusing on fine points of methodology and statistics. To look at the sorts of questions in which Gottman has been interested, this was precisely the sort of work that needed to be done. The importance of the "four horsemen" did not emerge from simply asking couples whether they felt contempt for one another (in fact, most people wouldn't even share a common idea of what contempt means), but required the development of subtle measures of these concepts.

As in this telling example, the stated goal of any one particular research article is not necessarily representative of the long-term goals of a researcher. The slow progress of research is due to the epistemology that guides it. In order to provide evidence for a particular relationship, a researcher must follow a set of guidelines that entail years of work. For example, in order to provide evidence that stonewalling predicts marital discord and/or divorce, a researcher must establish the validity of his or her measures, rule out that this relationship is the product of other variables, and replicate the same finding in multiple samples. Gottman's work has become well known to practitioners because, after establishing such a base of research, he made a resourceful effort to communicate to clinicians via books, trainings, and websites (Gottman, 1993, 1994, 1998) in bridging research and practice.

Gottman's ability to relate science to practice illuminates by contrast one of the main problems between practitioners and scientists – poor communication. If Gottman's work is an example of a successful relationship between practitioners and scientists emanating from good communication by a researcher to clinicians, there are innumerable other examples of poor communication. Such poor communication between scientists and clinicians is partly due to the means by which scientist communicate their findings. Most scientists publish in scientific journals to which therapists rarely subscribe and which are steeped in the arcane language of the researcher, such as the *Journal of Family Psychology*. For example, that journal has a circulation of 2,307 (www.apa.org); clinicians are more likely to subscribe to the *Family Therapy Networker*, which has over 50,000 subscribers (Gladding, 2007).

When scientists and practitioners do communicate, there may be a lack of respect for each other's viewpoint. Like a distressed couple, each party has a valid point of view, but their different ways of perceiving the world can cause a breakdown in communication. Gottman's work stands out as a positive model for how this chasm can be negotiated. His work became more influential with therapists after he wrote several popular-press books (e.g., *The Seven Principles for Making Marriage Work*, Gottman & Silver, 1999) and started conducting workshops for clinicians. Further, the mode of communication also made the bridge between science and practice successful. Gottman found a way to boil down some of his very complex findings into clinicians' language.

Different Worldviews

One reason for the divide between researchers and practitioners lies in the different emphasis placed on ways of knowing the "truth." There are several different methods by which we can know the truth, but the most common ways of knowing can be divided into two categories: subjective (intuition, experience) and objective (science, authority). Psychotherapy is an art and a science blending together both subjective and objective ways of knowing. However, the culture of academia and academic research places a premium on only objective ways of knowing; and so researchers place more credence on these. Clinicians practicing every day use both subjective and objective ways of knowing to help clients.

The Value of the Research Viewpoint

There are many reasons for clinicians to value research. First, research helps justify the use of family therapy as a legitimate and effective treatment for many different problems. For example, empirical research has helped establish family therapy as an effective treatment for adolescent substance abuse (see Chapters 22, 23, and 25, this volume), conduct disorder (Patterson, 1974), schizophrenia (Barrowclough & Lobban, 2008), and child anxiety disorder (Wood, Piacentini, Southam-Gerow, Chu, & Sigman, 2006). Similarly, couples therapy is an effective treatment for substance abuse (see Chapter 26, this volume), and depression (see Chapter 46, this volume). Providing such evidence of couple and family therapy's efficacy helps legitimize it to other clinicians, clients, and managed care (see Chapter 2 this volume).

Ignoring research findings can also lead to ineffective treatments and even iatrogenic effects for clients. Put simply, it is just plain good practice to base one's interventions on research. There have been several classic examples of the likely negative effects from earlier methods of treatment uncovered by research (Lebow, 2006). For example, the experiential approach of Carl Whitaker (1958; Keeney, 1986) of arousing confrontation and enactments to treat families with schizophrenic members increased expressed emotion within these families. Expressed emotion is a reliable predictor of relapse for schizophrenia (Butzlaff & Hooley, 1998). Although Whitaker's approach may have been beneficial for specific types of problems and families, from the expressed emotion research that has emerged, this approach would be expected to be counterproductive for families with a member suffering from schizophrenia.

The Palo Alto model for family therapy (Watzlawick, Weakland, & Fisch, 1974) represents another example of a therapy that is inconsistent with available research. This model of family therapy radically challenged the importance of building therapeutic alliances with clients, ignoring the large body of research that establishes the crucial importance of the therapeutic alliance for treatment success (Horvath & Symonds, 1991; Martin, Garske, & Davis, 2000).

Yet another example of the negative impact that some therapies can have on clients is illustrated by group treatment for juvenile delinquents. Although group treatment is clearly helpful in some populations, the research assessing group treatment for juvenile delinquents indicates this mode of treatment frequently creates iatrogenic effects. For example, Dishion and Dodge (2005) found that group therapy increased deviant behavior. Thus, many new forms of treatment for juvenile delinquency avoid using group formats in their treatment (e.g., Henggeler, Schoenwald, Borduin, Rowland, & Cunningham, 1998; see also Chapter 25, this volume).

The researcher's objective way of "knowing" offers many advantages to the clinician. Research provides support for family therapy as a legitimate form of therapy to other clinicians, clients, and managed care. Research can also guide clinicians and serves to help clinicians provide the best possible treatment for clients. However, the scientific method which is based on an objective way of "knowing" has intrinsic limits as well. The controversy over the push for empirically valid treatments highlights the flaws in applying research too rigorously in clinical practice.

Too Much of a Good Thing?

Nowhere is the clash between researchers and therapists more evident than in the debate regarding empirically supported treatments (ESTs). Academic researchers have criticized clinicians for practicing treatments that lack empirical support. Clinicians, in turn, criticize the limited scope of the thinking of these researchers (Lilienfeld, 2002). The "four horsemen" are evident in what often passes for dialogue about ESTs between clinicians and researchers.

The clinical researchers that started the EST movement did not intend to dictate treatment and stifle creativity (Chambless, 1996). Their intent was to help research inform practice (Chambless, 1996; Chambless et al., 1996). The spirit of the movement was to help practitioners provide clients with sound effective clinical treatment. Yet the way that this debate emerged first stifled the flow of knowledge before it enabled it.

More recently, there have been several positive developments with regard to ESTs in family psychology. Treatments are being developed that build on family therapy methods such as functional family therapy and multidimensional family therapy, and which are also successfully being disseminated to clinicians (see Chapter 21, this volume, for a thorough description of the development of evidence-based practices in family psychology). The field is also exploring and expanding the definition of evidence-based practice. For example, Beutler and Castonguay (2006) have sought to establish evidence-based principles of practice rather than simply provide a lengthy list of approaches supported by empirical evidence. The value of the EST debate is that it helped the field start to discuss, investigate, and develop principles for evidence-based practice.

Evidence-Based Practice

Research is becoming an important input into clinical practice. However, restricting practice to a "list" of approved treatments may hinder the effectiveness of treatment. A more balanced way of blending research and practice without being too restrictive is what we call evidence-based practice (EBP). This incorporates clinical wisdom and research-informed decision-making. There are some treatments that have been found to be so especially effective for specific populations, such as cognitive behavioral therapy for panic disorder, that they are the clear treatment of choice (see Chapter 15, this volume). However, for many problems there is not a clear treatment of choice. Other factors, such as common ones relevant to all treatments and broad, evidence-based principles of practice, may be more important than specific techniques. Lambert and Barley (2001), in a highly regarded and widely disseminated article, reviewed the psychotherapy outcome literature and found that specific techniques accounted for no more than 15% of the variance in treatment outcomes. In contrast, these researchers found that common factors (such as the therapeutic alliance) accounted for 30% of therapeutic outcome.

An evidence-based approach to therapy incorporates research and clinical decision-making by taking into account what is best for the specific case. Many clinical cases in the real world do not fit into a neat category that translates into a specific EBP. There are different means through which one can incorporate research into practice. One lies in broadly using the results of empirical research to guide practice. Lebow (2006) outlines a set of research principles to guide practice that can be applied across theoretical disciplines and modalities. Transforming research findings into clear clinical guidelines can help clinicians to practice on the basis of empirically sound decisions.

Another means of incorporating research into practice is for clinicians to collect outcome and process data on their cases. This type of idiographic research can be done simply by using brief questionnaires relevant to the clinical outcomes important to the particular case. At our clinic, clinicians collect data on every session using the Systemic Therapy Inventory of Change (STIC®; Pinsof et al., 2005; see also Chapter 29, this volume). The STIC is a relatively brief measure that requires 15 minutes for the client to complete the assessment. The STIC measures some basic clinical outcomes at the individual, couple, and family levels, as well as the therapeutic alliance. Information from the STIC can be used to tailor treatments or change them on the basis of client feedback. For example, a drop in the therapeutic alliance scale would alert the clinician to working on the therapeutic alliance in the next session rather than staying the course. The value of such information is an immediate feedback system between the client and therapist as well as collecting objective information regarding treatment progress.

The Value of the Clinician's Viewpoint

The clinician worldview based on subjective knowledge is an essential source in the development of innovative and effective psychotherapies. Most EBPs originated in clinicians' subjective ways of knowing long before the slow pace of science could provide evidence for their efficacy. Many clinical researchers used their own experiences and intuition in order to develop these treatments. For example, the empirical evidence for the efficacy of mindfulness interventions has proliferated since the late 1990s. Mindfulness-based interventions have been found to be helpful for preventing relapse for depression (Teasdale et al., 2000), decreasing suicide and parasuicidal behaviors in borderline personality disorder (Linehan, 1999), and increasing coping among a variety of chronically ill patients (Kabat-Zinn et al., 1992). All of the developers of these mindfulness-based interventions based them on their own personal experience with mindfulness, a set of techniques and methods that have been part of eastern traditions for centuries. Marsha Linehan (developer of dialectic behavior therapy), John Kabat-Zinn (developer of the mindfulness-based stress reduction program), and John Teasdale (developer of mindfulness-based cognitive therapy for depression) practiced mindfulness for years before they developed formal models of therapy (Kabat-Zinn, 2005). Their subjective experience with mindfulness influenced the development of their therapies.

Similar innovations in family psychology have stemmed from resourceful family clinicians developing methods that only later have become supported by evidence and parts of empirically supported therapies. For example, what we now know as communication training has long been a part of marital counseling, and reframing first gained prominence in the work of Watzlawick and others. Only later was an empirical base for the impact of such techniques established in the slow evolution of research.

It also is our observation that the supposed contrast between hard-headed researchers and less structured clinicians often is overstated. Clinicians often display the same sort of hypothesis-driven testing of their ideas about what may be useful in a case that the researcher brings to a formal study. Stricker and Trierweiler (1995) have referred to this as the work of the local clinical scientist. Clinicians frequently present their "study" at case conferences using methodology remarkably similar to what in the research world is known as n of 1 studies.

Logical Positivist versus Postmodern Epistemology

Some of the origins for the difficulties in dialogue between researcher and clinician can be found in the history of the development of family therapy. Systemic models of therapy developed as a reaction to traditional individualistic models of psychotherapy. The earliest narratives in family psychology and family therapy were about challenging the status quo. The most prominent early theorists were considered mavericks in the broader worlds of psychiatry and psychology, rebels establishing a new way of thinking and approaching therapy. These theories focused on the influence of social context on problems rather than focusing on problems residing within the individual (for a historical review, see Chapter 2, this volume; Becvar & Becvar, 1996).

Although many family theories proliferated during the early developmental years, they all incorporated a systemic and cybernetic epistemology. Cybernetic epistemology rejected many of the longstanding assumptions of previous individual theories of psychotherapy. Additionally, as a part of its core worldview, cybernetic epistemology challenged logical positivism, the epistemology on which our current scientific method of inquiry is based. Specifically, logical positivism postulates that the only way of "knowing" reality is through observations that can be empirically verified. Cybernetics counters some of logical positivism's basic assumptions on the basis of its own assumption of contextualism. From this viewpoint, we can never be fully objective because we are part of the system we are studying. At the extreme of this view is the idea that research based on the philosophy of logical positivism is inherently flawed and cannot be trusted, and therefore that all empirical research should be rejected as biased and distorted.

More recently, a variation on this epistemology emerged, post-cybernetic or second-order cybernetics, which came to dominate the philosophy of a certain portion of the family therapy community (Gladding, 2007). Post-cybernetic epistemology criticized the cybernetic movement for being too mechanical and insufficient to deal with human systems, especially families (Anderson & Goolishian, 1990). This new epistemology questions the role of anyone as expert in relation to the system. Such a viewpoint sees even less value than the earlier cybernetic view in traditional methods of empirical research. Radical tomes written from this point of view have discouraged even attending to research, let alone utilizing such findings in relation to practice.

Strikingly, in postmodern epistemology there remains a role for research but with a quite different method. Qualitative methodology is viewed as superior in providing the raw data of the voices of all the participants.

We contend that a both/and approach needs to be utilized regarding quantitative versus qualitative research. Many advances have been made in quantitative methodology, allowing for techniques which are more in line with systemic thinking (Bray, Maxwell, & Cole, 1995). First, new statistical techniques have been developed, allowing tests of non-linear relationships and multiple dependent variables, such as structural equation modeling. Further, many of the assumptions of traditional statistical techniques were not able to handle dependent data (e.g., such as parents and children's data, which would be considered dependent upon one another). Thus, these older techniques would need to analyze results by subsystems rather than analyzing the whole system. However, newer statistical techniques such as hierarchical linear modeling allow for nested data, which are more consistent with the systemic view of families (e.g., children are nested in the parent subsystem; the parent subsystem is nested within a larger extended family; and so on). Ultimately, without quantitative methodology we are left without the sorts of data that can distinguish levels of treatment impact, and which are most salient to third party funders of services.

On the other hand, qualitative research is often criticized for lacking scientific rigor. Critics contend qualitative methodology increases the likelihood of researcher bias as well as being difficult to replicate (even as postmodern critics say this of the work of the quantitative researchers themselves who espouse this criticism). However, many techniques have been developed over the years to reduce researcher bias and increase the reproducibility of methods (for a review see Mays & Pope, 1995; see also Chapter 6, this volume). Further, the philosophical underpinnings of qualitative research, such as phenomenology, emphasize the meaning of the subjective experiences of the researcher. The researcher's experience is considered part of the method. Thus, rather than viewing researcher bias as a flaw, this perspective views the researcher's view as part of the methodology (Patton, 1987). Qualitative methods uniquely tap into the narratives of subjects in a way that quantitative measures cannot. Qualitative methods parallel clinical practice in some ways by attempting to understand the experiences of families through the client's narrative.

Both qualitative and quantitative research methodologies offer opportunities to expand family psychology knowledge. Both methodologies have their strengths and weaknesses. A more balanced understanding of these two methodologies views them as complements rather than opposites or adversaries. The two research methods can be combined to compensate for each other's weaknesses. At the beginning stages of research, qualitative research can allow the flexibility for hypothesis generation and developing research questions. Quantitative research can be used at later stages of research to test and refine theories, with subsequent qualitative research that enhances that body of work by providing insight into subjects' or clients' narratives. These two methodologies can be used in a circular fashion to continue expanding knowledge (Bray, 1995).

Impact of Epistemology Debates on Couple and Family Psychology

The epistemological debates over the decades have created confusion within the family field. The result for the field has been the devaluing of research in practice rather than developing a more evolved view of research and practice. Many programs emphasize the development of clinical skills, and research-informed practice is ignored or underrepresented. The epistemological problem described above is only one reason for this trend. There are many practical barriers to a scientist-practitioner model within programs.

For example, Crane, Wampler, Sprenkle, Sandberg, and Hovestadt (2002) outlined the most common barriers to implementing a scientist-practitioner model in marital and family therapy (MFT) programs. They suggest these barriers include MFT culture not supporting research, lack of research role models within the discipline, inadequate course coverage of research and research-informed practice, and lack of communication between researchers and MFT clinicians. Further, the degree requirements of MFT programs make it difficult to support students interested in conducting research. MFT programs require 500 client clinical hours and 100 hours of supervision per year (Hodgson, Johnson, Ketring, Wampler, & Lamson, 2005). The large clinical load makes it difficult to devote any time to a research project. Experience with research during graduate school increases the likelihood of MFTs using research in their clinical practice (Johnson, Sandberg, & Miller, 1999). Further, many practicing MFT clinicians experience barriers to research involvement and using clinical research in their practice. Sandberg, Johnson, Robila, and Miller (2002) investigated the most common barriers to practicing MFTs participating in research and use of research in practice. MFTs reported several barriers to participating in research such as time, money, lack of a supportive research environment, client concerns (e.g., research may be harmful to clients or to the therapeutic relationship), and lack of understanding of the research study. MFTs also identified the barriers to applying clinical research to their practice, such as time (e.g., time to read studies), lack of relevant research (e.g., research must be relevant to their clinical work), and workplace barriers (e.g., lack of support from work for using research in practice). Finally, MFTs indicated that the ways in which researchers communicate to clinicians prevent them from using research in practice. MFTs expressed a need for shorter articles, better writing styles, less statistics, and more narrative examples of research.

There is a quite different tradition in family psychology. Teachers, practitioners, and trainees in the cognitive-behavioral tradition link research and practice. Furthermore, such integrative models as multidimensional family therapy, emotion-focused couple therapy, and multisystemic family therapy build on a confluence of research informing practice and practice informing research (see Chapters 23, 25, and 27, this volume). Yet, even though such examples exist and although the gap between research and practice is less pronounced among family psychologists than other family therapists, a considerable gap remains.

The take-home message applicable to all disciplines here is clear. The notion of EBP needs to be presented to trainees and clinicians in a way that puts it at the core of training, where it is understood and seen as a resource rather than a threat. Trainees and students don't need to become expert in the nuances of research statistics but do need to understand research findings and fully grasp the value of evidence. They also need time and mentors to help them master how to incorporate research into practice. There are several ways family psychology programs can engender an understanding of empirically driven practice. Classes such as research methods or intervention could include teachings on how to base interventions on evidence. Programs can strive to develop practicum sites or in-house clinics that provide training and supervision in EBP. We find that involving trainees in progress research where they see the value of data in helping make clinical decisions is immeasurably helpful in this regard.

Conclusion

In this chapter we reviewed some of the controversies faced by the field of family psychology. The development of family therapy as a reaction to individualized theories helped create the field's identity as a maverick, challenging the status quo. The strengths of such an identity created a fertile environment for questioning and challenging the norm. Thus, the field challenges conventional thinking, allowing for the development of new ideas and improvements on existing methods. The weakness of such an identity is challenging and negating principles and thoughts which may advance the field. The narrative of the field needs to be re-authored from one of a discordant relationship between researchers and clinicians to a marriage that is mutually beneficial. Further, the debates and controversies regarding epistemology seem similar to an adolescent child's rebelling against his or her parents. It is time for the field to mature by developing a both/and approach to research, epistemologies, and methodologies, rather than a reactionary either/or approach. Researchers and clinicians need to each appreciate the complexities of the task of the other and learn from one another. Neither will ever be fully the possessor of the "truth" about such complex activities as couple and family therapy. This proposed future narrative will include room for all views, allowing for greater advancement of family psychology.

Clinicians and researchers have much to offer one another. Clients are served best when clinicians are able to synthesize both research and subjective ways of knowing into practice. The synthesis is much like the improvisation of jazz music. Jazz has a melody that repeats, but in between the melody the musicians improvise, such that the piece moves back and forth between melody (the structure) and improvisation (which changes depending on the interaction between the musicians). Research provides the melody for therapy, and the art is the improvisation (the interaction between the client and the therapist) we use in order to provide the best fit for our clients.

Resources

Lebow, J. (2006) *Research for the psychotherapist: From science to practice.* New York: Routledge.

References

Anderson, H., & Goolishian, H. (1990). Beyond cybernetics: Comments on Atkinson and Heath's "Further thoughts on second-order family therapy." *Family Process, 229*, 157–163.

Barrowclough, C., & Lobban, F. (2008). Family intervention. In K. T. Mueser (Ed.), *Clinical handbook of schizophrenia* (pp. 214–225). New York: Guilford Press.

Becvar, D. S., & Becvar, R. J. (1996). *Family therapy: A Systemic Integration* (3rd ed.). Needham Heights, MA: Allyn & Bacon.

Beutler, L., & Castonguay, L. (2006). *Principles of therapeutic change that work.* New York: Oxford University Press.

Bray, J. H. (1995). Methodological advances in family psychology. *Journal of Family Psychology, 9*, 107–109.

Bray, J. H., Maxwell, S. E., & Cole, D. (1995). Multivariate statistics for family psychology research. *Journal of Family Psychology, 9*, 144–160.

Butzlaff, R. L., & Hooley, J. M. (1998). Expressed emotion and psychiatric relapse. *Archives of General Psychiatry, 55*, 547–552.

Chambless, D. L. (1996). In defense of dissemination of empirically supported psychological interventions. *Clinical Psychology: Science and Practice, 3*, 230–235.

Chambless, D. L., Sanderson, W. C., Shoham, V., Bennett Johnson, S., Pope, K. S., Crits-Christoph, P., et al. (1996). An update on empirically validated therapies. *Clinical Psychology, 49*, 5–18.

Crane, D. R., Wampler, K. S., Sprenkle, D. H., Sandberg, J. G., & Hovestadt, A. J. (2002). The scientist-practitioner model in marriage and family therapy doctoral programs: Current status. *Journal of Marital and Family Therapy, 28*, 75–83.

Dishion, T. J., & Dodge, K. A. (2005). Peer contagion in interventions for children and adolescents: Moving towards an understanding of the ecology and dynamics of change. *Journal of Abnormal Child Psychology, 33*, 395–400.

Gladding, S. T. (2007). *Family therapy: History, theory, and practice* (4th ed.). Upper Saddle River, NJ: Pearson Education.

Gottman, J. M. (1993). A theory of marital dissolution and stability. *Journal of Family Psychology, 7(1)*, 57–75.

Gottman, J. M. (1994). *What predicts divorce? The relationship between marital processes and marital outcomes.* Hillsdale, NJ: Erlbaum.

Gottman, J. M. (1998). Psychology and the study of the marital processes. *Annual Review of Psychology, 49*, 169–197.

Gottman, J. M., & Silver, N. (1999). *The seven principles for making marriage work: A practical guide from the country's foremost relationship expert.* New York: Three Rivers Press.

Henggeler, S. W., Schoenwald, S. K., Borduin, C. M., Rowland, M. D., & Cunningham, P. B. (1998). *Multisystemic treatment of antisocial behavior in children and adolescents.* New York: Guilford Press.

Hodgson, J. L., Johnson, L. N., Ketring, S. A., Wampler, R. S., & Lamson, A. L. (2005). Integrating research and clinical training in marriage and family training programs. *Journal of Marriage and Family Therapy, 31*, 75–88.

Horvath, A. O., & Symonds, B. D. (1991). Relation between working alliance and outcome in psychotherapy: A meta-analysis. *Journal of Counseling Psychology, 38*, 139–149.

Johnson, L. N., Sandberg, J. G., & Miller, R. B. (1999). Research practices of marriage and family therapists. *American Journal of Family Therapy, 27*, 239–249.

Kabat-Zinn, J., Massion, A. O., Kristeller, J., Peterson, L. G., Fletcher, K., Pbert, L., et al. (1992). Effectiveness of a meditation-based stress reduction program in the treatment of anxiety disorders. *American Journal of Psychiatry, 149*, 936–943.

Kabat-Zinn, J. (2005). *Full catastrophe living: Using the wisdom of your body and mind to face stress, pain, and illness.* New York: Bantam Dell.

Keeney, B. P. (1986). Cybernetics of the absurd: A tribute to Carl Whitaker. *Journal of Strategic and Systemic Therapies, 5*, 20–28.

Lambert, M. J., & Barley, D. E. (2001). Research summary on the therapeutic relationship and psychotherapy outcome. *Psychotherapy: Theory, Research, Practice, Training, 38*, 357–361.

Lebow, J. (2006). *Research for the psychotherapist: From science to practice.* New York: Routledge.

Lilienfeld, S. O. (2002). The scientific review of mental health practice: Our raison d'etre. *Scientific Review of Mental Health Practice, 1*, 5–10.

Linehan, M. M. (1999). Standard protocol for assessing and treating suicidal behaviors for patients in treatment. In D. G. Jacobs (Ed.), *The Harvard Medical School guide to suicide assessment and intervention* (pp. 146–187). San Francisco: Jossey-Bass.

Martin, D. J., Garske, J. P., & Davis, M. K. (2000). Relation of the therapeutic alliance with outcome and other variables: A meta-analytic review. *Journal of Consulting and Clinical Psychology, 68*, 438–450.

Mays, N., & Pope, C. (1995). Qualitative research: Rigour and qualitative research. *British Medical Journal, 311*, 109–112.

Nichols, M. P., & Schwartz, R. C. (1995). *Family therapy: Concepts and methods.* Needham Heights, MA: Allyn & Bacon.

Patterson, G. R. (1974). Interventions for boys with conduct problems: Multiple settings, treatment and criteria. *Journal of Consulting and Clinical Psychology, 42*, 471–481.

Patton, M. Q. (1987). *How to use qualitative methods in evaluation* (2nd ed.). London: Sage.

Pinsof, W. M., Lebow, J. L., Mann, B., Knobloch-Fedders, L., Freidman, G., Karam, E., et al. (2005). *STIC.* Evanston, IL. Family Institute at Northwestern University.

Sandberg, J. G., Johnson, L. N., Robila, M., & Miller, R. B. (2002). Clinician identified barriers to clinical research. *Journal of Marital and Family Therapy, 28*, 61–67.

Strickler, G., & Trierweiler, S. J. (1995). The local clinical scientist: A bridge between science and practice. *American Psychologist, 50*, 995–1002.

Teasdale, J. D., Segal, Z. V., Williams, J. M. G., Ridgway, V. A., Soulsby, J. M., & Lau, M. A. (2000). Prevention of relapse/recurrence in major depression by mindfulness-based cognitive therapy. *Journal of Consulting and Clinical Psychology, 68*, 615–623.

Tomm, K. (1986). On incorporating the therapist in a scientific theory of family therapy. *Journal of Marriage and Family Therapy, 12*, 373–378.

Watzlawick, P., Weakland, J. H., & Fisch, R. (1974). *Change: Principles of problem formation and problem resolution.* Oxford: Norton.

Whitaker, C. A. (1958). *Psychotherapy of chronic schizophrenic patients.* Boston: Little, Brown.

Wood, J. J., Piacentini, J. C., Southam-Gerow, M., Chu, B. C., & Sigman, M. (2006). Family cognitive behavioral therapy for child anxiety disorders. *Journal of the American Academy of Child and Adolescent Psychiatry, 45*, 314–321.

8

Training in Family Psychology: A Competencies-Based Approach

Nadine J. Kaslow, Marianne P. Celano, and Mark Stanton

Family psychologists are influenced by major trends in psychology, such as the emphasis on competency-based education, clinical training, and credentialing (Kaslow, 2004; Kaslow et al., 2004). Thus, we believe that the time is ripe to extend the core competencies in professional psychology to include family-related elements consistent with systems theory. The extant organizations devoted to promoting family psychology need to take the lead in the identification, education and training, and credentialing of family psychologists in accordance with the core competencies.

Core Competencies in Professional Psychology

A competency-based approach emphasizes the ability to apply knowledge and skills in the real world and uses performance outcomes as criteria for evaluating learners and training programs. This approach offers an explicit framework to initiate, develop, implement, and evaluate the processes and outcomes of training. The competency-based movement in psychology took center stage in 2002 at the Competencies Conference: Future Directions in Education and Training in Professional Psychology (Kaslow, 2004; Kaslow et al., 2004). Building upon prior work, eight core competencies were named:

- application of scientific knowledge to practice
- psychological assessment
- psychological intervention
- consultation and interprofessional collaboration
- supervision
- professional development

- ethics and legal issues
- individual and cultural diversity

The last two competencies were viewed as relevant to all competency domains. This conference underscored conceptualizing the training of core competencies from a developmental perspective. Training in each competency domain will vary according to the student's professional stage of development, and the level of competence expected within each domain depends on whether one is a beginning or advanced graduate student, pre-doctoral intern, post-doctoral fellow, licensed psychologist, or applicant for board certification in family psychology.

Family psychologists are cognizant of the need to delineate developmental outcome markers of competencies. The Commission for Recognition of Specialties and Proficiencies in Professional Psychology (CRSPPP) petition initiated this process. A competency-based perspective will facilitate American Psychological Association Commission on Accreditation review of programs with an emphasis or specialty in family psychology. These efforts are consistent with work being done by other disciplines that have identified core competency requirements for work with families (Heru, 2004; www.aamft.org).

Increasing attention has been paid to effectively assessing competence (Kaslow, 2004). Assessment should determine what a trainee knows, if one knows how, if one shows how, how one does, how accurately one evaluates what one knows and does, and how much one cares about what one does. Assessment takes into account developmental factors by ascertaining which competencies should be mastered and when (Kaslow, 2004; Kaslow et al., 2004). Assessments are most effective if they integrate formative (i.e., corrective feedback for further development) and summative (i.e., conclusive evaluations for progression and gatekeeping purposes) evaluations, which are mutually informative. Increasingly, psychologists utilize a multi-trait, multi-method, multi-informant process of evaluating knowledge, skills, and attitudes. They attend to work samples (e.g., videotape recordings, assessment or therapy reports, research portfolios) and direct observation.

Training in Competencies in Family Psychology

Application of scientific knowledge to practice

Consistent with the focus in professional psychology to prepare students to be scientifically minded psychologists (Bieschke, Fouad, Collins, & Halonen, 2004), training within family psychology requires a familiarity with systemic epistemology. This epistemology, which is not a core component of most psychology curricula, often entails a paradigm shift toward conceptualizing human behavior in a fashion that integrates intra-individual, interpersonal, environmental, and macrosystemic elements (Liddle, Santisteban, Levant, & Bray, 2002; Stanton, 1999). It promotes an awareness of ecological context and environmental factors and their impact on individual, social, and group behavior (Robbins, Mayorga, & Szapocznik, 2003; Stanton, 1999). Trainees should be encouraged to conceptualize, assess, and intervene on the basis of these criteria (Liddle et al., 2002). They must learn evidence-based models of systemic assessment, intervention, and consultation, and methodological and statistical approaches consistent with a systemic approach. They should study the application of systemic theory and practice to individual, couples, and families in primary healthcare, school–family relations, organizations, and other larger social systems (McDaniel, Lusterman, & Philpot, 2001).

Psychological assessment

Consistent with an overall emphasis on assessment within professional psychology (Krishnamurthy et al., 2004), we think that students and trainees should be taught to administer, interpret, and apply established systemic assessment measures and procedures. Some examples are self-report measures of personal and relationship functioning, genogram assessment (McGoldrick, Gerson, & Shellenberger, 1999), and observational methodologies (Gottman & Notarius, 2000; Kerig & Lindahl, 2001). We think that they should also receive training in the effective use of personality tests (e.g., Minnesota Multiphasic Personality Inventories, Millon Clinical Multiaxial Inventories, 16PF, Rorschach Inkblot Test, Kinetic Family Drawing) with individuals in couples and family therapy (Nurse, 1999), along with training in standard couples and families measures (e.g., Dyadic Adjustment Scale, Marital Satisfaction Inventory-Revised, Family Adaptability and Cohesion Evaluation Scales, Family Assessment Device). It is imperative that students learn to ascertain the advantages and disadvantages of assessment approaches (Snyder, Cavell, Heffer, & Mangrum, 1995). Students should be trained to link family assessment and evaluation data with clinical interventions (Carlson, Sperry, & Lewis, 1997; Kocahalka & L'Abate, 1997), and to assess the clinical outcomes of their interventions (Sperry, 2004).

Psychological intervention

Training in family psychology interventions has developed in the context of the movement toward evidence-based practice (Chambless & Hollon, 1998) and evidence-based relationships (Norcross, 2002). Students must be taught an intervention science that highlights functional and dysfunctional relationships and processes within couples and families; how these processes impact the adjustment of constituent members; and the complex interplay between interventions, psychological disorders, and health problems (Liddle et al., 2002). We support the shift in the training from theory-driven approaches founded by charismatic leaders with sparse empirical data toward well-developed, comprehensive, evidence-based couples and family interventions (Liddle, 2003; Liddle et al., 2002). In addition to learning traditional theory-based interventions, we concur that psychology students and trainees should be taught family-oriented intervention models that have substantial evidence for their effectiveness (Liddle et al., 2002; Sexton & Alexander, 2002) such as behavioral couples therapy (Epstein & McCrady, 2002; Fals-Stewart & O'Farrell, 2003; Gottman & Silver, 1999; Winters, Fals-Stewart, O'Farrell, Birchler, & Kelley, 2002), insight-oriented marital therapy (Johnson & Talitman, 1997), functional family therapy (Alexander & Sexton, 2002), multidimensional family therapy (Liddle et al., 2002), multisystemic therapy (Curtis, Ronan, & Borduin, 2004; Henggeler, Schoenwald, Borduin, Rowland, & Cunningham, 1998), and parent–child interaction therapy (Eyberg & Boggs, 1998; Herschell, Calzada, Eyberg, & McNeil, 2002). They should learn empirically supported partner–family-assisted interventions, disorder-specific parent–family interventions, more general couple–family interventions, and parent–child-oriented interventions (Baucom, Shoham, Mueser, Daiuto, & Stickle, 1998; Diamond, Serrano, Dickey, & Sonis, 1995; Estrada & Pinsof, 1995).

Trainees must learn the value of outcome data from well-designed efficacy studies (Baucom et al., 1998; Campbell, 2003; Diamond et al., 1995; Dunn & Schwebel, 1995; Estrada & Pinsof, 1995; Pinsof, Wynne, & Hambright, 1996), as well as the limitations in applying data from efficacy trials to clinical practice (Levant, 2004). We firmly believe that our training programs must also highlight clinical judgment and patient values as part of an evidence-based approach, and underscore the importance of integrating empirical data with clinical experience and skill (American Psychological Association, 2002a; Institute of Medicine, 2001; Levant, 2004; Liddle et al., 2002).

In addition to teaching about efficacy research, it is important to train students about process variables key to intervention success and to help them learn to track changes and shape interventions through feedback during therapy (Pinsof, 2004). Family psychology trainees also need to be challenged to learn from and conduct effectiveness trials, which are more applicable to the real world of clinical practice (Liddle, 2003). They need to discover the mixed results of dissemination research (McGovern, Fox, Xie, & Drake, 2004), and learn about integrated models for achieving successful dissemination of empirically supported psychotherapies (Stirman, Crits-Christoph, & DeRubeis, 2004).

Consultation and interprofessional collaboration

Systemic training often entails instruction and supervised practice with families embedded within various systems (e.g., medical, school, businesses) (McDaniel, Belar, Schroeder, Hargrove, & Freeman, 2002). As a result, training should focus on collaboration among all parties to develop a constructive solution in the best interests of the family. We recommend that family psychologist educators train students to consult to the multiple systems that influence and are influenced by the family.

One domain of consultation and interprofessional collaboration in which students can benefit from training is in healthcare settings. To work effectively in such contexts, trainees must learn to conduct relationship-centered care in accord with a collaborative family healthcare approach (Frank, McDaniel, Bray, & Heldring, 2003; McDaniel & Campbell, 1996). For individuals interested in consultation with families of medically ill youth, skills in family assessment, family support, disease management, and interdisciplinary teamwork must be taught (Kazak, Rourke, & Crump, 2003). For example, by the end of a post-doctoral fellowship in pediatric psychology from a family systems perspective, the trainee should be able to: engage the medically ill child and his or her family as full partners in healthcare; attend to collaborative values with the family and the healthcare team; maintain accountability for use of resources; negotiate issues related to communication and shared power among and between professionals, medically ill youth, and their families; attend to issues of diversity and spirituality; bolster the competencies of all concerned parties; recognize and accept their own limits and the limits of others; and evidence the capacity for self-reflection and an investment in personal growth (McDaniel & Campbell, 1996).

We also need to teach our students how to utilize a systemic-ecological framework to consult in school settings (McDowell, 1999). Training in family–school intervention should familiarize students with the school culture, principles of organizational consultation, and empirically supported school-based programming (Weissberg, Kumpfer, & Seligman, 2003). Trainees should be taught to help family members and school personnel to work together to resolve family–school problems and maximize children's social and academic competence (Christenson & Sheridan, 2001).

Supervision

We recommend that family psychology supervisors ground their supervisory efforts in an integration of diverse theoretical frameworks (Fraenkel & Pinsof, 2001; Lee & Everett, 2004). Supervision from an integrative framework may be based on (a) theoretical eclecticism, in which students are taught multiple theories and a framework for selecting which theoretical approach to use when and with whom; or (b) assimilative integration, in which students are introduced to multiple theories and techniques while being allowed to maintain a secure base in one (Fraenkel & Pinsof, 2001). Just as an integrative therapist systematically combines multiple theoretical perspectives, the integrative supervisor must incorporate and adapt supervisory practices from myriad conceptual models.

When interacting with our supervisees we use contracting and a balancing of collaborative and hierarchical modes of interaction (Prouty, Thomas, Johnson, & Long, 2001). We pay considerable attention to such contextual variables as gender, ethnicity, race, socio-economic class, sexual orientation, religion, and spirituality in terms of their impact on the supervisory process and work being supervised (Roberts, 1991; Todd & Storm, 2002; Walsh, 1999). We integrate a feminist perspective by encouraging our trainees to help families develop greater role flexibility, equality, and choices for all family members (Silverstein & Goodrich, 2003; Weingarten & Bograd, 1996). In addition, our supervisory encounters address power hierarchies, oppression, conceptualization of information in an historical and current context, self-empowerment, and personal reflection (Silverstein & Goodrich, 2003). We use the concept of isomorphism to understand and discuss interactional patterns that are replicated across subsystem boundaries (White & Russell, 1997) – that is, we consider the parallel processes between the supervisory relationship and the therapy that is unfolding.

In general, consistent with our family psychology colleagues, we conduct supervisions using fairly standard supervisory techniques: case presentation, audiotapes or videotapes, live supervision, and co-therapy (Sprenkle & Wilkie, 1996). We have a particular preference for live supervision and co-therapy approaches for the purposes of modeling, gaining greater access to richer clinical data in order to offer more meaningful supervisory input, and forming a more collaborative partnership with the trainee and the family being served. We recognize that supervisory formats and structures typically depend upon the theoretical preferences of the participants, the learning goals of the supervisees, and the professional setting in which the supervision takes place (Storm, Todd, Sprenkle, & Morgan, 2001). Unfortunately, with few exceptions, little attention has been paid to supervision of family treatments in novel contexts, such as in homes and community settings (Boyd-Franklin & Bry, 2000; Henggeler & Schoenwald, 1998).

In keeping with the emphasis on evidenced-based practice, there is a greater need to provide supervision in assessment and intervention protocols with empirical support (Webster, 2002). Evidenced-based interventions guided by treatment manuals pose advantages and disadvantages to the supervisory process (Liddle, Becker, & Diamond, 1997). These manual-based therapies clarify how to structure the approach and note specific therapist behaviors that are proscribed or not recommended. Such approaches may be most acceptable to beginning family psychology trainees, and thus it is not surprising that they are more commonly employed in graduate programs. However, supervision of manual-based interventions that target specific populations often are experienced by the supervisor and/or the supervisee as limiting creativity and as not applicable to diverse populations, problems, and treatment contexts. While we find the use of such manuals to be helpful for some families and beneficial for trainees early in the course of their training, we do not support rigid adherence to such manuals. We find the principles and techniques included in these manuals to be useful when incorporated into the context of a well-conceptualized treatment plan tailored to a particular family. Unfortunately, many manuals have not been created for culturally diverse populations and thus their applicability to some training and clinical settings is limited. Some manuals do offer more flexibility and cultural relevance and thus have greater applicability across families and settings.

There is a need for more controlled research on supervision of family assessment, intervention, and research within psychology, as the level of empirical investigation regarding family therapy supervision has not kept pace with broader developments in theory, research, and practice. More psychometrically sound measures need to be developed to ascertain change in supervisees' knowledge, skills, and values. Greater attention needs to be paid to evaluating gender sensitivity and cultural competence in family therapy supervision and supervisees (Guanipa, 2002). More comprehensive, multi-informant evaluations of training programs need to be conducted (Perlesz, Stolk, & Firestone, 1990). More attention needs to be paid to developmentally informed training for advanced family psychologists to become effective family therapy supervisors (Todd & Storm, 2002).

Professional development

Self-awareness, central to the professional development of psychologists (Elman, Illfelder-Kaye, & Robiner, in press), has been focal in education and training programs. However, the most recent Ethical Principles of Psychologists and Code of Conduct (Ethics Code) (American Psychological Association, 2002b) states that:

> Psychologists do not require students or supervisees to disclose personal information in course- or program-related activities, either orally or in writing, regarding sexual history, history of abuse and neglect, psychological treatment, and relationships with parents, peers, and spouses or significant others except if: (1) the program or training facility has clearly identified this requirement in its admissions and program materials, or (2) the information is necessary to evaluate or obtain assistance for students whose personal problems could reasonably be judged to be preventing them from performing their training- or professionally related activities in a competent manner or posing a threat to the students or others (7.04).

This principle poses challenges for trainers who value the trainee's process of self- and family disclosure in the service of personal growth and better clinical practice (Lee & Everett, 2004). One vehicle that has been used as a tool for gaining greater awareness of self and family relationship patterns has been the personal genogram (McGoldrick et al., 1999; Todd & Storm, 2002). There have been adaptations of the genogram (e.g., cultural genogram) that take into account contextual factors, which have been utilized effectively in training programs (Keiley et al., 2002). We personally believe that self- and family-of-origin-awareness is critical to effective functioning as a family therapist and, as a result, we continue to recommend that trainees engage in self-exploration using supervisory dialogue, the genogram, and entering personal psychotherapy. However, in accord with our Ethics Code, we publicly inform prospective trainees in writing that the self-of-the-therapist is a focus of our supervisory activities, and we protect trainees' confidentiality by delegating the in-depth genogram work to an adjunct faculty member who has no direct supervisory or evaluative role.

One aspect of professional development that we place considerable emphasis upon is the capacity for accurate self-assessment, which is crucial to the conduct of ethical practice and to improving quality of care (Belar, 2004; Belar et al., 2001). As trainers, we must routinely model self-assessment and facilitate actively our students' efforts to engage in accurate self-assessment.

Developing a professional identity as a family psychologist for trainees is complicated for a number of reasons. First, APA's Committee on Accreditation only accredits specialty programs at the post-doctoral level. As such, family training at the graduate school level is integrated with general training in psychology (clinical, counseling, school, combination), rather than being the core identity of the training program. At the internship level, family training is only one component of a broad and general training curriculum. Students and trainees wishing to become family psychologists often must go beyond the required curriculum and practicum experiences to obtain more in-depth family therapy training and supervision. Trainees at advanced levels seek continuing professional education training in family psychology because of the limited emphasis on couples and family work in their training programs.

Second, few training programs have more than a limited number of interested and qualified teachers and supervisors due to previously noted recruitment challenges, lack of commitment to a systemic perspective, and limited institutional support for the development of an identity as a family psychologist. Those who want to become identified as family psychologists need to be biculturally competent, to speak the dominant theoretical language of their psychology department and the systemic language, and often to seek more comprehensive training via supervision upon licensure.

Third, as many psychology graduate programs increasingly train students in empirically supported treatment models, often cognitive-behavioral in orientation, there is less emphasis on historical family therapy interventions, which have not kept pace with this evidence-based practice movement. Exceptions to this practice include but are not limited to psychoeducational approaches for families with a loved one with a major mental illness (Schaub, 2002). In a related vein, systemic theoretical models are not well grounded empirically and thus are accorded, by some, less status within the profession. Evidence-based couples and family interventions may be considered too labor intensive or costly to implement in graduate training programs, internships, and post-doctoral training programs because they have not developed dissemination processes, or they are unknown to psychologists who teach and practice from an individual orientation.

Despite the myriad challenges in developing an identity as a family psychologist, growing numbers of students at the graduate, internship, and post-doctoral levels express enthusiasm about doing so. We believe that students need a firm grounding in the broad and general competencies of professional psychology before they become specialized in family psychology. However, we also think that from the outset of their training forward they should receive course work, practicum experiences, research opportunities, and mentoring in family psychology in order to develop a core identity as a family psychologist.

Ethics and legal issues

Family psychology trainees are taught to perform all professional activities in a manner consistent with the Ethics Code (American Psychological Association, 2002b). However, since systemic issues and processes are not covered as thoroughly as single-person processes in the Ethics Code, trainers should use other resources to help trainees identify and resolve ethical dilemmas in family assessment, intervention, consultation, and research. Training in ethical issues must occur in formal courses, in seminars, in supervision, through modeling, and in continuing professional education programs. The provision of guidance regarding ethical behavior is most effective when it occurs in the context of models for ethical decision-making (Fly, van Bark, Weinman, Kitchener, & Lang, 1997; Kitchener, 1984; Rest, 1986).

Trainers must work with their students to understand ethical issues unique to the treatment of couples and families, including definition of the patient, nature of the relationship that the psychologist will have with each person in the family, confidentiality and its limits, therapeutic neutrality, handling of multiple relationships, informed consent, and live supervision complications (American Psychological Association, 2002b; Gladding, Remley, & Huber, 2000; Gottlieb, 1995; Woody & Woody, 2001). Students also must be helped to appreciate the ethical complexities (e.g., confidentiality, responsibility, multiple roles of the therapist, risks) inherent in changing intervention formats

(Gottlieb, 1995). Trainees should be afforded the opportunity to address ethical quandaries associated with specific family dynamics, patterns, and transitions such as divorce, family violence, and end-of-life decisions. This training also should provide information about relevant guidelines for family-based practice, such as child custody evaluations. Finally, trainers must convey the importance of representing their professional competence as family psychologists in an accurate fashion and in accord with current specialty guidelines and credentialing processes (Patterson, 1995).

Individual and cultural diversity

APA has passed guidelines related to multicultural education, training, research, practice, and organizational change for psychologists (American Psychological Association, 2002c), psychotherapy with lesbian, gay, and bisexual clients (Division 44, 2000), and psychological practice (American Psychological Association, 2004). APA's Ethics Code (American Psychological Association, 2002b) underscores the importance of competence in the domain of individual and cultural diversity, which includes attention to age, gender, gender identity, race, ethnicity, culture, national origin, religion, spirituality, sexual orientation, disability, language, and socioeconomic status. We concur with the delegates at the Competencies Conference who emphasized the value of psychologists' self-awareness and knowledge with regard to racism, homophobia, and ageism in all aspects of psychological practice (Daniel, Roysircar, Abeles, & Boyd, 2004) and believe these must be a focus of training for family psychology trainees. Despite the burgeoning interest in contextually sensitive family interventions and culturally competent family research, it is unfortunate that contextually sensitive supervision models are less well developed within family psychology (Todd & Storm, 2002). Thus, new approaches must be co-created by supervisors and trainees. Indeed, efforts are in place to ensure that family psychology trainees receive culturally competent training that includes sensitization, didactic training, personal contact, supervised clinical experience, and consultation (Davis-Russell, 2002). Such an approach must create a safe environment for discussions of all aspects of diversity; focus on the trainee's own sociocultural context; and pay attention to the trainee's cultural values and beliefs as these impact assessments, interventions, and research with couples and families. Again, we firmly believe that such exploration is critical to the process of becoming a culturally competent family psychologist; trainees should be informed that this type of exploration is an expected part of training. Coursework and supervision should provide a knowledge base, grounded in the empirical literature, about myriad cultural groups, cultural variations in normal family processes, relational patterns, and life-cycle transitions; cultural idioms of distress; and the family's relationship to the larger ecological system (Celano & Kaslow, 2000; Imber-Black, 1997; McGoldrick, Giordano, & Pearce, 1996).

There has been considerable debate about the optimal training approach for incorporating issues about individual and cultural diversity into training programs, and a growing consensus has emerged that the integration model is the most effective (Davis-Russell, 2002). We share this view. Rather than relegating information about diversity to a separate course or an area of concentration, this model aims to integrate a focus on diversity throughout the curriculum and supervised clinical experience in a seamless fashion. This model may be particularly efficacious if training in concepts of family and cultural diversity is "front ended" in the training programs, such that psychology students' awareness of the role of culture and context is emphasized from the outset of training (Fraenkel & Pinsof, 2001). Culturally competent psychology educators must recognize and model that cultural competence in work with families is both a value and process and underscore the importance of becoming familiar with one's own culture as well as the culture of the families with whom they work (Lee & Everett, 2004).

One training tool that some family psychology programs and supervisors use to promote cultural awareness and sensitivity is the cultural genogram (Hardy & Laszloffy, 1995; Keiley et al., 2002). We have found that constructing and using a cultural genogram enables students to explore their personal cultural issues, become more cognizant of their culturally constructed realities, and heighten their awareness of the ways in which their own cultural biases are deeply embedded in their families of origin and creation.

Consistent with feminist family therapy training and supervision approaches, our work has focused on gender-related power dynamics and oppression. More recently, our training efforts have expanded to examine the interrelationships among multiple forms of oppression associated with gender, as well as the impact of gender relations on men. The gender meta-framework perspective (Breunlin, Schwartz, & Mac Kune-Karrer, 1997), a developmentally informed approach to teaching trainees to conceptualize gender issues in family therapy, has received increasing attention in the training community (Silverstein & Goodrich, 2003) and has been increasingly informative of our work. Utilizing this framework in supervision, attention is paid to collaboration in the supervisory relationship, as well as between the student-therapist and the family. At the outset of supervision (i.e., baseline assessment), supervisors ascertain the trainee's awareness of the ways in which the families with whom they work identify gender imbalance in their relationships, as well as the therapist's comfort in raising issues of gender imbalance with families. Attention also is paid to the student's expectations regarding learning a feminist approach. Mutual learning objectives are developed in a way that respects different learning styles and stages of professional development. Finally, attention is paid in the supervisory process to connecting therapeutic themes at the intrapsychic, interactional, and sociocultural levels.

Consistent with the APA's Ethics Code (American Psychological Association, 2002b), we support focusing on sexual orientation when indicated and its implications for the supervisory process (Long, 2002). The supervisor must convey respect for and acceptance of diverse sexual orientations and encourage the same on the part of the trainee. Supervision must attend to the sexual orientation of the family members being seen in therapy, and, when appropriate, to the sexual orientation of the therapist, and possibly that of the supervisor. Supervision attuned to sexual orientation creates a safe environment for disclosure of sexual orientation; provides information about sexual orientation issues as they impact family life; ensures that supervisees have the knowledge and skills to work with gay men, lesbian women, and bisexual persons in couples and family therapy; and addresses and corrects heterosexist bias in the clinical work (Long, 1996). It also focuses on heterosexism as it impacts the supervisory process.

We have found that much less attention has been paid in psychology to issues of training and supervision for working with couples and families where one or more member has a disability (Olkin, 1999). We recommend that supervision assist trainees, who in turn can assist family members, in developing an awareness of the major models of disability (moral, medical, social) and appropriate language to describe people with disabilities; becoming knowledgeable about types of disabilities and associated psychosocial experiences; learning about the medical, developmental, psychological, familial, sociocultural, ethnic, cultural, political, and spiritual contexts of disabilities and the effects on the person and family; understanding the impact of the political, social, and physical environment of persons with disabilities; recognizing the stigma, prejudice, and discrimination affecting, and role and status of, persons with disabilities in our society; and collaborating with an interdisciplinary team of colleagues involved in services to families with disabilities (Olkin, 1999, 2002). This supervision also should provide a safe context for students to talk about their reactions to working with people with disabilities and to help them appreciate disability status as a social construct.

Only recently has spirituality become a subject of discourse in professional psychology (Richards & Bergin, 1999; Sperry & Sharfranske, 2004). This is consistent with the growing surge of interest in spirituality by family therapists, including family psychologists (Walsh, 1999). We must educate our students about effective ways of attending to spirituality in clinical assessment and intervention, as well as family-oriented research. Sometimes this training focuses on the use of the spiritual genogram and spiritual ecomap in conducting couples and family therapy (Frame, 2000; Hodge, 2000). More attention to spirituality in family therapy courses and supervision will enable trainees to feel competent in understanding spiritual sources of distress and to help the family use their spiritual resources to aid their healing (Walsh, 1999). It also enhances their comfort in collaborating with clergy and other spiritual leaders to help a family in distress (Wendel, 2003). Although little effort has been paid to ascertaining the extent to which supervision focuses on spirituality, in the future, family psychology trainers may want to assess this dimension of supervision via such measures as the Spiritual Issues in Supervision Scale (Miller, Korinek, & Ivey, 2004).

Conclusion

Family psychology training needs to be more formally organized in accord with the core competencies outlined above. This coordinated effort will result in more competent family psychologists, and will facilitate the acceptance of the specialty of family psychology. Although there is some research into the training of family therapists (Gurman & Kniskern, 1992; Liddle, 1991; Street, 1997), very little empirical attention has been paid to the training of family psychologists.

With their educators and trainers as role models, trainees with an interest in family psychology need to learn to advocate for their craft. Such advocacy efforts should be directed toward insurance carriers in an effort to increase reimbursement for couples and family therapy. These efforts also should target local, state, and federal government agencies involved in program development and implementation in the public sector. Further, advocacy endeavors should be focused on the leadership of the National Institutes of Health and other public and private funding agencies to increase support and initiatives for family research. Finally, students may become most invested in engaging in advocacy efforts geared toward public awareness of the community at large regarding the value of family prevention and intervention services.

Note

This chapter is an edited version of an article by the same title published in 2005 in *Family Process*. Reprinted by permission of Blackwell Publishing and the authors.

References

Alexander, J., & Sexton, T. (2002). Functional family therapy. In F. W. Kaslow (Ed.), *Comprehensive handbook of psychotherapy: Integrative/eclectic (Vol. 4)* (pp. 111–132). New York: Wiley.

American Psychological Association. (2002a). *Criteria for evaluating treatment guidelines*. Washington, DC: American Psychological Association.

American Psychological Association. (2002b). Ethical principles of psychologists and code of conduct. *American Psychologist, 57*, 1060–1073.

American Psychological Association. (2002c). *Guidelines on multicultural education, training, research, practice, and organizational change for psychologists*. Washington, DC: American Psychological Association.

American Psychological Association. (2004). Guidelines for psychological practice with older adults. *American Psychologist, 59*, 236–260.

Baucom, D. H., Shoham, V., Mueser, K. T., Daiuto, A. D., & Stickle, T. R. (1998). Empirically supported couple and family interventions for marital distress and adult mental health problems. *Journal of Consulting and Clinical Psychology, 66*, 53–88.

Belar, C. D. (2004). The future of education and training in academic health centers. *Journal of Clinical Psychology in Medical Settings, 11*, 77–82.

Belar, C. D., Brown, R. A., Hersch, L. E., Hornyak, L. M., Rozensky, R. H., Sheridan, E. P., et al. (2001). Self-assessment in clinical health psychology: A model for ethical expansion of practice. *Professional Psychology: Research and Practice, 32*, 135–141.

Bieschke, K. J., Fouad, N. A., Collins, F. L., & Halonen, J. S. (2004). The scientifically-minded psychologist: Science as a core competency. *Journal of Clinical Psychology, 80*, 713–724.

Boyd-Franklin, N., & Bry, B. H. (2000). *Reaching out in family therapy: Home-based, school, and community interventions*. New York: Guilford Press.

Breunlin, D. C., Schwartz, R. C., & Mac Kune-Karrer, B. M. (1997). *Metaframeworks: Transcending the models of family therapy*. San Francisco: Jossey-Bass.

Campbell, T. L. (2003). The effectiveness of family interventions for physical disorders. *Journal of Marital and Family Therapy, 29*, 263–281.

Carlson, J., Sperry, L., & Lewis, J. A. (1997). *Family therapy: Ensuring treatment efficacy*. Pacific Grove, CA: Brooks/Cole.

Celano, M. P., & Kaslow, N. J. (2000). Culturally competent family interventions: Review and case illustrations. *American Journal of Family Therapy, 28,* 217–228.

Chambless, D. L., & Hollon, S. D. (1998). Defining empirically supported therapies. *Journal of Consulting and Clinical Psychology, 66,* 7–18.

Christensen, S. L., & Sheridan, S. M. (2001). *Schools and families: Creating essential connections for learning.* New York: Guilford Press.

Curtis, N., Ronan, K., & Borduin, C. (2004). Multisystemic treatment: A meta-analysis of outcome studies. *Journal of Family Psychology, 18,* 411–419.

Daniel, J. H., Roysircar, G., Abeles, N., & Boyd, C. (2004). Individual and cultural diversity competency: Focus on the therapist. *Journal of Clinical Psychology, 80,* 755–770.

Davis-Russell, E. (Ed.). (2002). *The California School of Professional Psychology handbook of multicultural education, research, intervention, and training.* San Francisco: Jossey-Bass.

Diamond, G. S., Serrano, A. C., Dickey, M., & Sonis, W. A. (1995). Current status of family-based outcome and process research. *Journal of the American Academy of Child and Adolescent Psychiatry, 35,* 6–16.

Division 44. (2000). Guidelines for psychotherapy with lesbian, gay, and bisexual clients. *American Psychologist, 55,* 1440–1451.

Dunn, R. L., & Schwebel, A. I. (1995). Meta-analytic review of marital therapy outcome research. *Journal of Family Psychology, 9,* 58–68.

Elman, N., Illfelder-Kaye, J., & Robiner, W. (in press). Professional development: A foundation for psychologist competence. *Professional Psychology: Research and Practice.*

Epstein, E. E., & McCrady, B. S. (2002). Couple therapy in the treatment of alcohol problems. In A. S. Gurman & N. S. Jacobson (Eds.), *Clinical handbook of couple therapy* (pp. 597–628). New York: Guilford Press.

Estrada, A. U., & Pinsof, W. M. (1995). The effectiveness of family therapies for selected behavioral disorders in childhood. *Journal of Marital and Family Therapy, 21,* 403–440.

Eyberg, S. M., & Boggs, S. R. (1998). Parent–child interaction therapy for oppositional preschoolers. In C. E. Schaefer & J. M. Briesmeister (Eds.), *Handbook of parent training: Parents as co-therapists for children's behavior problems* (2nd ed., pp. 61–97). New York: Wiley.

Fals-Stewart, W., & O'Farrell, T. J. (2003). Behavioral family counseling and naltrexone for opiod-dependent patients. *Journal of Consulting and Clinical Psychology, 71,* 432–442.

Fly, B. J., van Bark, W. P., Weinman, L., Kitchener, K. S., & Lang, P. R. (1997). Ethical transgressions of psychology graduate students: Critical incidents with implications for training. *Professional Psychology: Research and Practice, 28,* 492–495.

Fraenkel, P., & Pinsof, W. M. (2001). Teaching family therapy-centered integration: Assimilation and beyond. *Journal of Psychotherapy Integration, 11,* 59–85.

Frame, M. W. (2000). The spiritual genogram in family therapy. *Journal of Marital and Family Therapy, 26,* 211–216.

Frank, R. G., McDaniel, S. H., Bray, J. H., & Heldring, M. (Eds.). (2003). *Primary care psychology.* Washington, DC: American Psychological Association.

Gladding, S. T., Remley, T. D., & Huber, C. H. (2000). *Ethical, legal, and professional issues in the practices of marriage and family therapy* (3rd ed.). Englewood Cliffs, NJ: Prentice Hall.

Gottlieb, M. (1995). Ethical dilemmas in change of format and live supervision. In R. Mikesell, D.-D. Lusterman, & S. McDaniel (Eds.), *Integrating family therapy: Handbook of family psychology and systems theory* (pp. 561–569). Washington, DC: American Psychological Association.

Gottman, J. M., & Notarius, C. I. (2000). Decade review: Observing marital interaction. *Journal of Marriage and the Family, 62,* 927–947.

Gottman, J. M., & Silver, N. (1999). *The seven principles for making marriage work: A practical guide from the country's foremost relationship expert.* New York: Three Rivers Press.

Guanipa, C. (2002). A preliminary instrument to evaluate multicultural issues in marriage and family therapy supervision. *Clinical Supervisor, 21,* 59–75.

Gurman, A. S., & Kniskern, D. P. (1992). The future of marital and family therapy. *Psychotherapy: Theory, Research, & Practice, 29,* 65–71.

Hardy, K. V., & Laszloffy, T. A. (1995). The cultural genogram: Key to training culturally competent family therapists. *Journal of Marital and Family Therapy, 21,* 227–237.

Henggeler, S. W., & Schoenwald, S. K. (1998). *Multisystemic therapy supervisory manual: Promoting quality assurance at the clinical level.* Charleston, SC: MST Institute.

Henggeler, S. W., Schoenwald, S. K., Borduin, C. M., Rowland, M. D., & Cunningham, P. B. (1998). *Multisystemic treatment of antisocial behavior in children and adolescents.* New York: Guilford Press.

Herschell, A. D., Calzada, E. J., Eyberg, S. M., & McNeil, C. B. (2002). Parent–child interaction therapy: New directions in research. *Cognitive and Behavioral Practice, 9,* 9–15.

Heru, A. M. (2004). Basic family skills for an inpatient psychiatrist: Meeting Accreditation Council for Graduate Medical Education core competency requirements. *Families, Systems, and Health, 22,* 216–227.

Hodge, D. R. (2000). Spiritual ecomaps: A new diagrammatic tool for assessing marital and family spirituality. *Journal of Marital and Family Therapy, 26,* 217–228.

Imber-Black, E. (1997). Developing cultural competence: Contributions from recent family therapy literature. *American Journal of Psychotherapy, 51,* 607–610.

Institute of Medicine. (2001). *Crossing the quality chasms: A new health system for the 21st century.* Washington, DC: National Academy Press.

Johnson, S., & Talitman, E. (1997). Predictors of outcome in emotionally focused marital therapy. *Journal of Marital and Family Therapy, 23,* 135–152.

Kaslow, N. J. (2004). Competencies in professional psychology. *American Psychologist, 59,* 774–781.

Kaslow, N. J., Borden, K. A., Collins, F. L., Forrest, L., Illfelder-Kaye, J., Nelson, P. D., et al. (2004). Competencies Conference: Future directions in education and credentialing in professional psychology. *Journal of Clinical Psychology, 80,* 699–712.

Kazak, A. E., Rourke, M. T., & Crump, T. A. (2003). Families and other systems in pediatric psychology. In M. C. Roberts (Ed.), *Handbook of pediatric psychology* (3rd ed., pp. 159–175). New York: Guilford Press.

Keiley, M. K., Dolbin, M., Hill, J., Karuppaswamy, N., Liu, T., Natrajan, R., et al. (2002). The cultural genogram: Experiences from within a marriage and family therapy training program. *Journal of Marital and Family Therapy, 28,* 165–178.

Kerig, P. K., & Lindahl, K. M. (2001). *Family observational coding systems: Resources for systemic research.* Mahwah, NJ: Erlbaum.

Kitchener, K. S. (1984). Intuition, critical evaluation, and ethical principles: The foundation for ethical decisions in counseling psychology. *The Counseling Psychologist, 12,* 43–56.

Kocahalka, J. A., & L'Abate, L. (1997). Linking evaluation with structured enrichment: The Family Profile Form. *American Journal of Family Therapy, 25,* 361–374.

Krishnamurthy, R., Vandecreek, L., Kaslow, N. J., Tazeau, Y. N., Milville, M. L., Kerns, R., et al. (2004). Achieving competency in psychological assessment: Directions for education and training. *Journal of Clinical Psychology, 80,* 725–740.

Lee, R. E., & Everett, C. A. (2004). *The integrative family therapy supervisor: A primer.* New York: Brunner-Routledge.

Levant, R. (2004). The empirically validated treatments movement: A practitioner/educator perspective. *Clinical Psychology: Science and Practice, 11*, 219–224.

Liddle, H. (2003). Graduate training: The next frontier in bridging the research–practice divide. *The Family Psychologist, 19*, 35–40.

Liddle, H., Santisteban, D., Levant, R., & Bray, J. (Eds.). (2002). *Family psychology: Science-based interventions.* Washington, DC: American Psychological Association.

Liddle, H. A. (1991). Training and supervision in family therapy: A comprehensive and critical analysis. In A. S. Gurman & D. P. Kniskern (Eds.), *Handbook of family therarpy (Vol. II)* (2nd ed., pp. 638–697). New York: Brunner/Mazel.

Liddle, H. A., Becker, D., & Diamond, G. M. (1997). Family therapy supervision. In J. C. E. Watkins (Ed.), *Handbook of psychotherapy supervision* (pp. 400–418). New York: Wiley.

Long, J. K. (1996). Working with lesbians, gays, and bisexuals: Addressing heterosexism in supervision. *Family Process, 35*, 377–388.

Long, J. K. (2002). Sexual orientation: Implications for the supervisory process. In T. C. Todd & C. L. Storm (Eds.), *The complete systemic supervisor: Context, philosophy, and pragmatics* (pp. 59–71). New York: Authors Choice Press.

McDaniel, S. H., Belar, C. D., Schroeder, C. S., Hargrove, D. S., & Freeman, E. L. (2002). A training curriculum for professional psychologists in primary care. *Professional Psychology: Research and Practice, 33*, 65–72.

McDaniel, S. H., & Campbell, T. L. (1996). Training for collaborative family healthcare. *Families, Systems, and Health, 14*, 147–150.

McDaniel, S. H., Lusterman, D.-D., & Philpot, C. L. (2001). Introduction to integrative ecosystemic family therapy. In S. McDaniel, D.-D. Lusterman, & C. Philpot (Eds.), *Casebook for integrating family therapy* (pp. 3–17). Washington, DC: American Psychological Association.

McDowell, T. (1999). Systems consultation and Head Start: An alternative to traditional family therapy. *Journal of Marital and Family Therapy, 25*, 155–168.

McGoldrick, M., Gerson, R., & Shellenberger, S. (1999). *Genograms: Assessment and intervention* (2nd ed.). New York: Norton.

McGoldrick, M., Giordano, J., & Pearce, J. K. (Eds.). (1996). *Ethnicity and family therapy* (2nd ed.). New York: Guilford Press.

McGovern, M., Fox, T., Xie, H., & Drake, R. (2004). A survey of clinical practices and readiness to adopt evidence-based practices: Dissemination research in an addiction treatment system. *Journal of Substance Abuse Treatment, 26*, 305–312.

Miller, M. M., Korinek, A., & Ivey, D. C. (2004). Spirituality in MFT training: Development of the Spiritual Issues in Supervision Scale. *Contemporary Family Therapy, 26*, 71–81.

Norcross, J. C. (Ed.). (2002). *Psychotherapy relationships that work: Therapist contributions and responsiveness to patients.* New York: Oxford University Press.

Nurse, A. R. (1999). *Family assessment: Effective uses of personality tests with couples and families.* New York: Wiley.

Olkin, R. (1999). *What psychotherapists should know about disability.* New York: Guilford Press.

Olkin, R. (2002). Could you hold the door for me? Including disability in diversity. *Cultural Diversity and Ethnic Minority Psychology, 8*, 130–137.

Patterson, T. (1995). Macro-ethics: The current state of the family field. *The Family Psychologist, 11*, 19–20.

Perlesz, A. J., Stolk, Y., & Firestone, A. F. (1990). Patterns of learning in family therapy training. *Family Process, 29*, 29–44.

Pinsof, W. M. (2004). Progress research: Toward empirically informed systems therapy. *The Family Psychologist, 20*, 29–32.

Pinsof, W. M., Wynne, L. C., & Hambright, A. B. (1996). The outcomes of couple and family therapy: Findings, conclusions, and recommendations. *Psychotherapy: Theory, Research, Practice, Training, 33*, 321–331.

Prouty, A. M., Thomas, V., Johnson, S., & Long, J. K. (2001). Methods of feminist family therapy supervision. *Journal of Marital and Family Therapy, 27*, 85–97.

Rest, J. R. (1986). *Moral development: Advances in research and theory.* New York: Praeger.

Richards, P. S., & Bergin, A. E. (Eds.). (1999). *Handbook of psychotherapy and religious diversity.* Washington, DC: American Psychological Association.

Robbins, M., Mayorga, C., & Szapocznik, J. (2003). The ecosystemic "lens" to understanding family functioning. In T. Sexton, G. Weeks, & M. Robbins (Eds.), *Handbook of family therapy: The science and practice of working with families and couples* (pp. 21–36). New York: Brunner-Routledge.

Roberts, J. M. (1991). Sugar and spice, toads and mice: Gender issues in family therapy training. *Journal of Marital and Family Therapy, 17*, 121–132.

Schaub, A. (Ed.). (2002). *New family interventions and associated research in psychiatric disorders.* New York: Springer.

Sexton, T., & Alexander, J. (2002). Family-based empirically supported interventions. *The Counseling Psychologist, 30*, 238–261.

Silverstein, L. B., & Goodrich, T. J. (Eds.). (2003). *Feminist family therapy: Empowerment in social context.* Washington, DC: American Psychological Association.

Snyder, D. K., Cavell, T. A., Heffer, R. W., & Mangrum, L. F. (1995). Marital and family assessment: A multifaceted, multilevel approach. In R. H. Mikesell, D.-D. Lusterman, & S. H. McDaniel (Eds.), *Integrating family therapy: Handbook of family psychology and systems theory* (pp. 163–182). Washington, DC: American Psychological Association.

Sperry, L. (2004). Ethical dilemmas in the assessment of clinical outcomes. *Psychiatric Annals, 34*, 107–113.

Sperry, L., & Sharfranske, E. P. (Eds.). (2004). *Spiritually oriented psychotherapy.* Washington, DC: American Psychological Association.

Sprenkle, D. H., & Wilkie, S. G. (1996). Supervision and training. In F. P. Piercy, D. H. Sprenkle, & J. L. Wetchler (Eds.), *Family therapy sourcebook* (2nd ed., pp. 350–391). New York: Guilford Press.

Stanton, M. (1999). Family psychology. In D. Benner & P. Hill (Eds.), *Baker encyclopedia of psychology and counseling* (pp. 438–439). Grand Rapids: Baker.

Stirman, S. W., Crits-Christoph, P., & DeRubeis, R. J. (2004). Achieving successful dissemination of empirically supported psychotherapies: A synthesis of dissemination theory. *Clinical Psychology: Science and Practice, 11*, 343–359.

Storm, C. L., Todd, T. C., Sprenkle, D. H., & Morgan, M. M. (2001). Gaps between MFT supervision assumptions and common practice: Suggested best practices. *Journal of Marital and Family Therapy, 27*, 227–239.

Street, E. (1997). Family therapy training research: An updating review. *Journal of Family Therapy, 19*, 89–111.

Todd, T. C., & Storm, C. L. (Eds.). (2002). *The complete systemic supervisor: Context, philosophy, and pragmatics.* Lincoln: Authors Choice Press.

Walsh, F. (Ed.). (1999). *Spiritual resources in family therapy.* New York: Guilford Press.

Webster, J. (2002). Family therapy and workforce planning. *Journal of Family Therapy, 24*, 134–149.

Weingarten, K., & Bograd, M. L. (Eds.). (1996). *Reflections on feminist family therapy training.* New York: Haworth Press.

Weissberg, R. P., Kumpfer, K. L., & Seligman, M. E. P. (2003). Prevention that works for children and youth. *American Psychologist, 58*, 425–432.

Wendel, R. (2003). Lived religion and family therapy: What does spirituality have to do with it? *Family Process, 42*, 165–179.

White, M. B., & Russell, C. S. (1997). Examining the multifaceted notion of isomorphism in marriage and family therapy supervision: A quest for conceptual clarity. *Journal of Marital and Family Therapy, 23*, 315–333.

Winters, J., Fals-Stewart, W., O'Farrell, T. J., Birchler, G. R., & Kelley, M. L. (2002). Behavioral couples therapy for female substance-abusing patients: Effects on substance use and relationship adjustment. *Journal of Consulting and Clinical Psychology, 70*, 344–355.

Woody, R. H., & Woody, J. D. (2001). *Ethics in marriage and family therapy.* Washington, DC: American Association of Marriage and Family Therapy.

9

Education in Family Psychology

Mark Stanton, Michele Harway, and Arlene Vetere

Martina Sanchez just graduated from the university with a bachelor's degree in psychology and she is investigating graduate programs in psychology (American Psychological Association, 2003). Because of the strong emphasis on family in her cultural heritage, she is looking for programs that will prepare her to work with couples, families, and the larger social system with which they interact. It is not easy; *Graduate Study in Psychology* (American Psychological Association, 2007) primarily identifies clinical, counseling, and school psychology programs, as well as some emphases in those programs, but it is hard to tell exactly what kind of education and training in family psychology she will receive.

Education in family psychology is evolving from its roots in post-doctoral institutes to a wider range of teaching–learning venues that include doctoral programs with an emphasis in family psychology; pre-doctoral internships with concentrations in couple and/or family psychotherapy; and post-doctoral internships, continuing education seminars, and institute training in the specialty. However, there is still ambiguity regarding education and training venues. This chapter provides an overview of current educational pathways related to family psychology in the United States (US) and the United Kingdom (UK).

There continues to be some confusion between the specialty of family psychology and the practice of family therapy in both countries (Nutt & Stanton, 2008). Some psychologists are unaware of the broad and general nature of family psychology, considering it only an appellation for clinical practice with couples or families. The primary distinction of family psychology is its adoption of a systemic orientation to human behavior while maintaining the characteristics of the discipline of psychology (Nutt & Stanton, 2008; Stanton & Harway, 2007). Family psychology and family therapy have evolved as separate guilds with different accrediting bodies in the US (the American Psychological Association Commission on Accreditation [APA CoA] vs. the American Association for Marital and Family Therapy [AAMFT] Commission on Accreditation for Marriage and

Family Therapy Education [COAMFTE]) and separate certifications (e.g., board certification in family psychology vs. clinical member or approved supervisor status with the AAMFT). This chapter focuses on education and training in family psychology with the recognition that the "modal form of family psychology training in all but a handful of doctoral programs in the US still appears to be limited to a one-semester three-unit introductory course in family therapy" (Green, 2005, p. 8), yet some programs provide a more substantial elective track and a few programs provide a thorough emphasis in the specialty.

Family Psychology Graduate Education in the United States

The development of family psychologists requires an epistemological transformation and the achievement of core systemic competencies by following one of several pathways to achieve the knowledge, attitudes, and skills necessary to identify oneself ethically as a family psychologist and to achieve specialty board certification.

Epistemological transformation. Family psychology is a broad-based specialty that includes working with individuals, couples, and families in psychotherapy and also working within other systemic contexts (school systems, primary healthcare, the justice system, and family businesses) to provide direct and indirect service. Family psychologists provide assessment and treatment services to children, adults, couples, and families. They provide supervision and leadership to various individuals and organizations and support effective program development and implementation through evaluative or basic research.

The discipline represents a paradigm change in the field of psychology. Traditional psychology has long focused almost exclusively on the individual's functioning. Often this focus has virtually ignored the impact of the various systems within which that individual is embedded. By contrast, family psychology requires that psychologists focus on the relational and contextual nature of the individual's functioning. Moreover, by studying how small and large systems intersect, family psychologists gain a broad understanding of human behavior. In addition to the individual, family psychologists look at the interactional system (the couple), the intergenerational system (the family), the community system (including cultural groups), and other larger organizational and societal systems. However, regardless of the number of clients being treated, the family psychologist conceptualizes problems in terms of systems. Psychological problems are conceptualized in terms of the context in which the symptom was created, maintained, and influenced by others with whom the individual relates and interacts. The context includes the external social context and the internal meaning of the context within family members.

Systems views of individuals, families, and relationships have a rich history drawing upon traditional psychological theory as well as the multi-disciplinary field of family therapy (see Chapter 2, this volume). Psychologists who use systems thinking are not considering different aspects of human behavior than other psychologists. Rather it is the epistemic perspective of the systems thinker that differentiates him or her from other psychologists. The systemic thinker has made a paradigm shift to considering all aspects of human behavior within the multiplicity of contexts within which they occur. This provides a more expansive view than traditional psychological approaches.

Consider how systems thinking would apply to a clinical example. Imagine a woman who learns she has breast cancer. Any psychologist is likely to focus on her illness, her feelings about her own mortality, psychological consequences of the diagnosis (e.g., depression), and impact of the physical changes due to the illness on her body image and self-esteem. Approaching the same case systemically would involve the above-listed items, plus:

1 Examining the impact of her illness on her family. Her diagnosis may affect her relationship with her husband as he adjusts to new demands placed upon him to be caretaker, to take on chores his wife previously performed, and possible changes in the couple's sexual and affective relationship. Her diagnosis and illness may also affect her relationship with her children and extended family. How each member of the family reacts to the changes, in turn, will affect her functioning. See Chapter 11, this volume, for further examples of a systems perspective in diagnoses and assessment.
2 Examining the impact of her illness on other systems within which she is embedded and how those systems' response to her illness further affect her (e.g., medical system, labor force).

When first introduced to family psychology and systems thinking, many individually trained psychologists worry that they must forego an individual theoretical orientation (for example psychodynamic or behavioral) in order to be systemic. In fact, systems thinking can be superimposed upon any already existing understanding of human behavior; for that reason, systems theory is often said to be a theory of theories or a metatheory.

Family psychology was approved as a specialty in 2002 by the APA Commission for the Recognition of Specialties and Proficiencies in Professional Psychology (CRSPPP). Being recognized as a specialty includes an understanding that family psychology represents a fundamental orientation to psychology that is broad and general.

Family psychology competencies. Contemporary graduate education in psychology in the US is focused on the development of core outcome competencies considered essential for the practice of professional psychology: application of scientific knowledge to practice, psychological assessment, psychological intervention, consultation and interpersonal collaboration, supervision, professional development, ethics and legal issues, and individual and cultural diversity (Kaslow, 2004; Kaslow et al., 2004). Graduate education in family psychology extends these competencies by ensuring a thorough inclusion of the entire system (individual factors, interpersonal factors, and macrosystemic/ environmental factors; Stanton, 1999; and see Chapter 1, this volume) that interact reciprocally as the context for psychological understanding, assessment, and intervention (Kaslow, Celano, & Stanton, 2005). The best education and training in family psychology will systemically develop student outcome competencies informed by a systemic epistemology.

Developmental pathways.   Stanton and Nurse (2005) created a flowchart that depicts the pathways by which a psychologist may achieve education and training in the specialty of family psychology. It details five steps for development of the competency:

1   Foundation: family psychologists must have a broad and general education in professional psychology, in accord with the APA CoA Guidelines and Principles of Accreditation (G&P; American Psychological Association, 2005). Some receive this education in doctoral programs with an emphasis or track in family psychology, while others receive traditional psychology education and training without family psychology education.
2   Development of core competencies specifically applied to family psychology.
3   Post-doctoral education and training to enhance competency in the specialty, especially if the doctoral program did not provide a thorough family psychology emphasis. This may occur in an institute or in other venues (e.g., continuing education or supervision) that develop specialty competencies.
4   Independent clinical, counseling, or school psychology practice as a licensed psychologist, in which the knowledge, skills, and attitudes of the competencies are matured.
5   Examination of competency in family psychology by the American Board of Couple and Family Psychology (ABCFP), a constituent board of the American Board of Professional Psychology (ABPP).

Ethics of identification as family psychologist.   Labeling oneself as a family psychologist requires that one has received the formal education and training necessary to develop the specialty competencies for professional practice with individuals, couples, families, and larger social systems from a systemic perspective (Stanton & Nurse, 2005).

Green (2005) notes the disconnect between common presenting issues for psychotherapy (two sorts of relationship problems are the top two reasons cited in recent surveys he summarizes, and couple problems are listed much more frequently than mood or anxiety disorders for pursuit of therapy) and graduate education that often provides only one course in family therapy and none in couple therapy. He suggests that professional psychology is not preparing clinicians to perform needed services in a competent and ethical manner. Norcross, Hedges, and Castle (2002) conducted a survey of APA Division 29 (Psychotherapy) members and found that 78% conduct marital or couples therapy and 38% conduct family therapy.

Nichols (2005) indicates that "attempting" to treat couples or families without specialized training may cause harm and violates the standard of competence. Stanton (2005a) observes that many specialties (e.g., clinical health psychology, clinical child psychology, rehabilitation, geropsychology, primary care, and family psychology) are struggling to determine the core preparation necessary for ethical practice. Patterson (Chapter 12, this volume) indicates that current standards are too vague and he presents an argument that standards are needed to clearly delineate the preparation and competencies needed for practice in this specialty area. He concludes that it is not enough to simply state that one can provide systemic therapy or to cite one's own prior practice as evidence of competency. Board certification in couple and family psychology by ABPP provides external validation of preparation and competency.

Doctoral education

Despite the fact that many doctoral programs offer only one course in family psychology-related areas, interest in doctoral training in family psychology has increased (Stanton, 2005b) and studies have reflected the interest in this specialty. A 2004 survey of APA-accredited program directors in clinical psychology indicated that approximately one-fifth of clinical psychology faculty members in PsyD and practice or practice-research PhD programs cited systems or family systems as their theoretical orientation, making it the third most widely embraced orientation (Norcross, Castle, Sayette, & Mayne, 2004). A study of doctoral psychology programs that include a strong emphasis in family psychology identified 12 programs that have specialty faculty, several courses in family psychology, and clinical training in family psychology (Stanton, Harway, & Eaton, 2006). Many other programs have a selection of elective courses in the specialty, and additional programs are moving to add the specialty training. These are the programs that students desiring family psychology education and training need to find. They are currently being catalogued and organized by the Graduate Education Special Interest Group of APA Division 43.

Recommendations for doctoral education.   In order for doctoral programs in psychology to receive accreditation by the APA CoA, they must meet certain criteria that have been laid out in the G&P. To assist doctoral programs that provide thorough instruction in family psychology, Stanton and Harway (2007) developed a set of recommendations for doctoral education and training in family psychology that closely parallel the CoA G&P. These recommendations have been endorsed by all the family psychology constituent groups, notably the Family Psychology Division of APA (Division 43), the Academy of Family Psychology (AFP), the ABPP constituent board in Family Psychology (formerly ABFamP, now known as the ABCFP), and the Family Psychology Specialty Council (FPSC). The recommendations have been approved by the Council of Specialties and forwarded to the CoA. Select material from these recommendations is provided below.

Family psychology doctoral programs that are deemed to be accreditable in this specialty area are seen as preparing students for the science and practice of professional psychology within the specialty field of family psychology. The systemic training provided in these programs allows professional activity in a wide variety of contexts and settings, such as mental health agencies, in both clinical and administrative positions; independent practice with individuals, couples, and families; healthcare organizations (e.g., rehabilitation facilities, hospitals, and other health settings, in collaboration with physicians; Holleman, Bray, Davis, & Holleman, 2004); legal and judicial settings (e.g., forensic assessment; family forensic psychology); school settings (e.g., consultants to the family or the school); organizations (e.g., consultation, group/team dynamics); universities and colleges in academic or training positions; or public policy or public service domains (e.g., advocates, clinicians, or administrators). Programs in family psychology may be housed in departments of psychology; in departments located within schools or colleges of education; or in schools of medicine or psychiatry.

To demonstrate that a program is clearly within the parameters of family psychology, the program's education and training model and its curriculum plan should be consistent with key aspects of the articulated family psychology philosophy, including the following:

- There is a paradigm shift from an intrapsychic and individual conceptualization to a systemic conceptualization.
- There is a systemic conceptualization: a focus on individuals, couples, families, and other systems as they operate within the various systems in which they are embedded.
- Patterned interactions within and among these systems are identified in order to gain a comprehensive understanding of human functioning.
- The client may be defined as an individual (whose presenting problems are considered within the larger systemic perspective) or any larger system (whether it is a couple, family, organization, or other type of system).
- The types of problems being treated may not be different from those treated by other professional psychologists. What differs is the conceptualization of the problem. Psychological problems are conceptualized from a systems perspective that incorporates systemic/contextual/interactional contributions to the etiology and maintenance of the symptom and how these problems are embedded in and reciprocally influence the relational system of the client.
- Family psychologists are competent to treat the full spectrum of mental disorders, but they do so with special attention to the relational context of the disorders and the reciprocity between disorders and interpersonal contexts, whether clients are being treated individually or in couple, family, or group contexts.
- The skills needed to be a family psychologist include systemic case conceptualization, systemic assessment, and systemic intervention approaches and techniques in individual psychotherapy, sex therapy, couples and marital therapy, family therapy, and divorce therapy. Family psychologists have knowledge, skill, and experience in assessment approaches and instruments that measure individual, couple, family, and broader system functioning.
- Systemic conceptualizations also require special attention to ethical issues which must be dealt with somewhat differently than with more intrapersonal approaches.

The competencies expected of family psychology graduates must be consistent with the philosophy of family psychology. Systemic competencies are based upon the principles and concepts of systems theory (Bertalanffy, 1974). Systems theory suggests that to understand human behavior adequately in real-life contexts, one must pay attention to the variety of factors that influence life in a system and the interaction between those factors. A systemic epistemology provides a framework for conceptualizing, assessing, structuring a professional relationship, and intervening in a variety of psychological circumstances.

Coursework in the core areas of psychology is a necessary component of any family psychology training program. However, the specialty of family psychology requires that training programs incorporate a systemic perspective into the core content areas of psychology. A course in biological bases of behavior, for example, would emphasize "understanding the principles of anatomy and physiology and the interaction between the biological and environmental (social) variables as determinants of behavior . . . Specific areas . . . most relevant to family psychology would be the effects of drugs and neuropsychological problems on family interactions, developmental disabilities, and organically-based psychological problems" (Weeks & Nixon, 1991, p. 15). So, while addressing typical broad and general core content areas, family psychology program content interacts with the relevant interpersonal and relational contexts.

Other examples of how family psychology programs approach the teaching of the core areas of psychology follow:

- Content in history and systems of psychology includes the history of family and systemic thinking and the development of the field of family psychology.
- Content on life-span human development considers both individual and family life-cycle development.
- Because multicultural and diversity issues strongly affect not only the individual but the systems within which she or he is embedded, the program offers content in multicultural issues and diversity, including each area of diversity defined in the G&P, such as gender and sexual orientation. Ideally, multiculturalism and diversity themes are reflected in each of the core and advanced content areas.
- Ethical and legal issues are studied and the special ethical and legal challenges which systemic work engenders are addressed (e.g., confidentiality considerations in couple and family therapy).
- Psychological measurement includes family and relational assessment along with more traditional psychological assessment tools.
- Content on research methodology considers the methodological approaches best suited to the study of systems. Because qualitative approaches are particularly well suited to the study of systems, the program includes qualitative research and qualitative data analysis strategies in any content areas on research methodology.

In addition to broad training as a psychologist, family psychologists are expected to receive targeted training which focuses on the key areas of the discipline of family psychology. The content areas listed below are intended to delineate the basic fund of information that a family psychologist should possess. Individual programs may present the content listed in separate courses or provide a more integrated curriculum featuring knowledge in the listed areas.

- History of family psychology, including its relationship to major systems of thought and practice in the discipline of psychology and related fields. Such coursework is important because most students of psychology are not acquainted with the historical roots of family psychology and where it fits in the context of the larger field.
- Family life cycle. Traditional approaches to developmental theories seldom consider the developmental stages through which a family goes and ignore the intersection between individual development and the life cycle of the family.

- Couple and family systems theory, including family dynamics, structures, and functioning. A thorough understanding of the multiple "schools" of family therapy and their common factors should be supplemented by an understanding of the functioning of different family forms, in accordance with current social demographics.
- Couple and family intervention skills and strategies. Understanding the functioning of couples and families from an ecosystemic perspective (considering the multiple interlocking systems within which these couples and families are embedded) is crucial. Couples and families present particular challenges to clinicians that differ significantly from those presented by individual therapy. Developing the ability to conceptualize multiple simultaneous dynamics and conduct effective interventions in complex couple and family systems is critical. Knowledge of evidence-based practices in couple and family interventions and the competency to implement these interventions is needed (Lebow, 2005).
- Assessment issues in family psychology. These include clinical interview formats suitable for use with systems, family assessment instruments, semi-structured approaches such as genograms, and lifestyle analyses and traditional psychological assessments applied when multiple individuals present for treatment.
- Special factors affecting family functioning, including divorce and remarriage, blended families, sexual dysfunction, adjustment to serious, chronic or terminal illness, injury to or death of a child, infidelity, loss of employment, financial conflicts, and other traumatic life events. Families and larger systems have become increasingly complex in their composition and functioning.
- Larger systems, including an understanding of family functioning within larger systems and the application of a systems perspective to understanding the functioning of larger systems. Family psychologists are likely to be employed in larger systems (e.g., groups, social organizations, businesses, agencies, etc.) and called upon to address organizational problems, either as consultants or in administrative roles, and to apply systems principles to those larger systems. When working with families, psychologists will encounter issues that center on larger systems which intersect with family functioning, such as the impact upon families of racism, socioeconomic status, access to resources, culture, and immigration/assimilation.
- Sex therapy. Family psychologists should be knowledgeable about and skilled in working within the normal range of sexual functioning as well as with sexual dysfunctions.
- Family law, including issues having to do with custody, parental competency, visitation, child maltreatment, termination of parental rights, and family forensic consulting.
- Family research. Researching the functioning and dynamics of relationships and interactional systems presents particular methodological challenges. This content area should include study of traditional methodologies suitable for understanding individual behavior and those suitable to examining dyadic and larger group interaction.
- Educational interventions, including psychoeducational strategies for intervening with families. This involves developing competence in the clear communication of complex scientific understanding of human behavior to clients and families to better equip them to become managers of their own emotional and physical health. Psychoeducational approaches are used with a wide range of clinical issues, including

schizophrenia, bipolar disorder, and other major mental disorders, substance abuse disorders, couples conflict, parenting behavior, disordered children, and dealing with medical illness, as well as with non-clinical issues including leadership training, marriage preparation, and marriage enrichment.

- Legal and ethical issues in family psychology. Working with families and larger systems requires a reexamination of legal and ethical issues of the mainstream discipline. This includes clear identification of the client when multiple individuals are involved in treatment; limits of confidentiality when working with couples, families, and groups; modifications of the working alliance and therapeutic contract in couple or family treatment; and legal constraints in working with families.

- Supervision and consultation in family psychology. Special issues conducting supervision in family psychology treatment and the means for consultation from a systemic perspective are addressed. In the consultation area, for example, family psychologists are uniquely suited to providing organizational consultation (from a systemic perspective) or working with family-owned businesses.

In addition to academic training, a family psychology doctoral program requires that its students receive adequate and appropriate practicum experiences in family psychology. Students should be placed in practicum sites that provide a wide range of training experiences under the supervision of a sufficient number of family psychologists to ensure quality of training. The practicum experiences must be integrated into the doctoral program and there must be sufficient opportunity for discussion of the practicum in the educational program.

The family psychology core faculty function as role models for students in the specialty area and they socialize students into the discipline of family psychology. The specialty of family psychology recognizes the centrality of issues of diversity in the training of professional psychologists. Our increasingly diverse society requires that students be trained to understand the multiplicity of cultural factors that impact individuals, families, and other systems. The multisystemic approach of family psychology puts culture in the forefront, and students in family psychology are taught to consider cultural and individual differences within the larger systems within which they are embedded. Students are specifically taught to consider the cultural and systemic issues that may affect assessment and intervention strategies offered to families and their members. The impact of the family and of larger systems on issues of culture, ethnicity, gender, sexual orientation, socioeconomic status, and physical ability are emphasized in both academic and training activities throughout the degree program. Furthermore, an emphasis is placed on understanding the role of culture and diversity on the development of individual and family belief systems which guide the work of the professional psychologist.

Models of family psychology programs

Stanton et al. (2006) conducted a survey of programs identified as having course content in family psychology. These fell into three general categories: (a) *programs with an emphasis*, that is, multiple courses in family psychology (both required and electives; median number of required family psychology courses is 6) and clinical training in family; (b) *programs with a track*, that is, those offering 3–4 courses in family psychology, often as an elective concentration; and (c) *programs with one or two required courses in couples or family psychology*.

These categories seem to encapsulate the range of offerings in family psychology provided across APA-accredited doctoral programs. Programs with an emphasis on family psychology provide a thorough education and training in the specialty, and graduates of those programs receive much of the preparation needed to pursue board certification in family psychology following graduation and licensed experience. They have faculty who identify as family psychologists, perhaps with board certification in family psychology, as well as providing a strong theoretical foundation in a systemic epistemology, several population-specific courses (child therapy, adolescent therapy, gerontology, couples therapy, family therapy, etc.), clinical training in the specialty, and opportunities for dissertation research in family psychology. There are 12–15 of these programs identified in the United States at this time (see APA Division 43 website). Programs with a track in family psychology usually provide some foundation in systems theory as well as three or four population-specific courses. Many programs provide such family psychology tracks, but they may be taught by one core faculty member and/or adjunct faculty. Graduates of these programs may need to complete additional postgraduate education or supervised experience in family psychology in order to pursue board certification in family psychology. Programs that fall into the third category do not provide sufficient education or training to be considered as family psychology programs. One course may spark interest in the specialty, but further education and clinical training opportunities will be needed to develop competencies.

Curriculum. Family psychology courses offered in doctoral programs are most often entitled couple and family therapy, family therapy, family systems theory, or family psychology. Some of these courses provide the epistemological foundation of systems theory, while others focus on specific population issues from a systemic perspective.

Clinical training. Programs with an emphasis in family psychology often provide clinical training opportunities at practicum sites consistent with the specialty (e.g., school-based programs where students interact with teachers, parents, and students; community clinics that provide child, adolescent, couple, and family therapy).

Post-doctoral education and training

Historically, most family psychology education and training was accomplished in family institutes that were affiliated with the major founders of various models of family therapy. Few of these remain, sometimes diminishing or terminating at the death of the founder, but those that do continue to provide significant training opportunities (e.g., Bowen Center for the Study of the Family at Georgetown University).

Alternatively, there is a variety of continuing education programs that provide specialty training. ABPP occasionally sponsors workshops, sometimes in conjunction with the APA convention. The Family Psychology Specialty Council is developing a model of continuing education to meet the needs of individuals who desire board certification in the specialty but did not receive such education in their doctoral programs.

Post-doctoral board certification

Post-doctoral board certification in family psychology is the next step for individuals who have the graduate education and clinical experience to qualify for the diplomate. Family psychology was recognized as a specialty in 1990 by ABPP, and the ABCFP is the specialty board within ABPP that conducts examinations and awards board certification in family psychology. The process requires certification of credentials, evaluation of preparation, presentation of theoretical orientation and case materials, and an oral examination.

Family Psychology Education in the United Kingdom

The teaching of family psychology at graduate and postgraduate level within the UK has a complex and somewhat disconnected history. Family psychology is not a recognized academic discipline in the UK in the same way as it is in the US. This section will explore the two parallel developments within the UK that at times remain strangely disconnected and at other times are mutually informing. One development is the fragmented field of family psychology, with more of a connection to the field of family sociology in some UK universities. The other development is the field of systemic psychotherapy and systemic practice within the UK that draws on family systems theories amongst other theories of human development across the life span.

Family psychology

Writing in 1987, Tony Gale and Arlene Vetere call for the teaching of family psychology at undergraduate level (Vetere & Gale, 1987). They argue that family life is the cradle and web of human social and emotional development across the life span, and believe that the neglect of family psychology at undergraduate level leaves applied psychology practice oddly decontextualized. The British empirical tradition of teaching psychology focuses almost exclusively on the individual. Developmental psychology has moved into considering the relationship between children and their main caregivers, usually the mother, and more recently fathers and sibling relationships are coming into focus. Historically, social psychology has researched group interaction with laboratory groups formed of strangers, rather than focusing on naturally occurring social groups, such as families. Writing later, one of the same researchers found the situation at undergraduate level had not changed much (Vetere & Dallos, 2003), with the focus largely on individual process and functioning.

Academic psychologists have individually pioneered the teaching of family psychology as a specialist seminar option during the final year of undergraduate study, for example Andy Treacher at Bristol University, Tony Gale at Southampton University, Neil Frude at Cardiff University, Peter Stratton at Leeds University, and Arlene Vetere at Reading University. But the commitment ends there, it seems, because when these pioneers leave their posts or retire, the department does not keep a commitment to family psychology within the curriculum. The British Psychological Society (BPS) accreditation process does not require this area of study for graduate registration with the BPS.

Final year undergraduate courses in psychology are usually seminar-based, rather than lecture courses. This means that reading of theory and research papers is prescribed at the start of the course, and the students are required to present their reading of the appropriate papers for group discussion. Topics within family process seminar courses might include the following: feminist critiques of family interaction research; difference and diversity within family life; family interaction studies; major theories of family functioning; mental health, wellbeing and resilience in families; the impact of divorce and separation; and so on.

The situation for master's/doctorate-level teaching and training of applied psychologists is somewhat different. For example, master's-level health psychology, forensic and occupational psychology, and doctorate-level educational, clinical, and counseling and psychotherapeutic psychology do include family psychology and systemic practice within their academic curricula and offer training placements in systemic theory and practice. The master's/doctoral level of applied psychology training in the UK provides the interface for the integration of family psychology and systemic theory and practice teaching. For instance, the research carried out by (usually) North American family psychologists finds its way into curricula under other headings, such as child development, working with older people, life-span development, and so on. Most applied psychology trainings at postgraduate level within the UK would include discussion of the family as the context for development, and with some consideration of family-based interventions, but primarily the family finds its way into the curriculum as the context for understanding individual development, with the main focus on intervention at an individual level, whether it be formal psychotherapy, or a behavioral intervention within a team or residence. Within adult mental health teaching and practice, across a variety of social and healthcare settings, families are often not included in the work because of a medical model approach to patient confidentiality. And therein lies the rub, because if teaching about the importance of family relationships to individual and community wellbeing is not included at undergraduate level, then graduates will be unfamiliar with the particular theoretical, ethical, and methodological issues needed to research and practice with family groups.

Staying with this discussion of applied psychology practice in the context of mental health for a while longer, we may note that many applied psychologists are trained in the major schools of psychotherapy. Recent government initiatives within the UK have promoted evidence-based practice for psychological distress, based on the medical model of intervention. The National Institute for Health and Clinical Excellence provides guidelines on the treatment of psychological/psychiatric conditions, so diagnosed. This emphasis on modern, evidence-based psychotherapies has offered some opportunities for the recommendation of family therapy/systemic psychotherapy, for example with children and depression, with early onset eating disorders, with a diagnosis of schizophrenia, and so on. However, we should note that the major randomized clinical trials of family therapy have been conducted by a range of professionals, for example, psychologists, psychiatrists, and social workers, and very few family therapists themselves.

Family therapy, systemic psychotherapy, and systemic practice

In contrast to the patchy and disappointing development of family psychology, the rise of family therapy education in the UK has been meteoric. Family therapy found its way into child, adolescent, and family mental health settings in the UK during the 1970s, largely inspired by the work of North American systemic pioneers, such as Bateson, Haley, Minuchin, Watzlawick, Jackson, and so on, and the feminist-informed therapists, such as Walters, Goldner, Hare-Mustin, Papp and Silverstein, and so on. Robyn Skynner, John Howells, and John Byng-Hall were early leaders, followed by Allen Cooklin, Gill Gorell Barnes, Hugh Jenkins, and Arnon Bentovim (Kaslow, 2000). During the 1980s the work of the Milan team became more prominent, followed by the work of Tom Andersen on the reflecting teams, and the more recent turn to narrative practice. British family therapists form a small but influential community and over four decades have made a substantial contribution to the development of theory and practice, at home and abroad. Currently, family therapy and systemic practice is flourishing across National Health Service (NHS) mental health communities, in the social services, and in the private and voluntary sector of healthcare.

Family therapy training in the UK is part time, over four years: (a) introductory level; (b) intermediate level; and (c) master's level over two years. Training is offered by family therapy training institutes. The curriculum includes the work of family psychologists and family systems thinking and research. Their training programs are validated by UK university partners and accredited by the professional association, the UK Association for Family Therapy and Systemic Practice. The required hours of theory and supervised practice are in line with European standards set within the European Association of Psychotherapy, i.e., 7 years' training in total, to include 3 years as an undergraduate, and 4 years as a postgraduate. Different European countries manage the training and practice of the psychotherapies according to country-specific laws or practices without any consistency across countries. For example, countries such as Italy and the Netherlands limit the practice of systemic psychotherapy to psychiatrists and psychologists within their public health services. In Germany, only the behavioral and psychodynamic psychotherapies are reimbursed through their public health insurance systems. This means that the public can only access systemic psychotherapy through private practice. Family therapy and systemic practice in Europe is organized, developed, and supported through the European Family Therapy Association (EFTA), which awards the Euro-Certificate in Psychotherapy for family therapy, through its membership of the European Association for Psychotherapy (EAP). EFTA consists of three chambers: the national family therapy organizations (27 countries); the training institutes chamber (160 institute members); and the chamber of individual members (1,400 members).

Many mental healthcare and social care professional workers train in systemic practice to either introductory or intermediate level, as they wish to influence and contextualize their work using systemic ideas. Fewer go on to complete the master's training. Admission to the master's programs requires a previous relevant professional training, such as social work, clinical psychology, psychiatry, or mental health nursing, that gives a grounding in developmental psychology and mental health practice. Training to master's level is carried out over four years on a part-time basis. Introductory courses are theoretical in content, covering the main theories of family therapy with more recent innovations, such as narrative therapies. Intermediate courses further develop theoretical understanding, and participants are required to have a professional practice base, so their current therapeutic work can be consulted to within the program. Both introductory and intermediate programs are assessed through written assignments. Master's programs include a major research project, a program of personal and professional development, and an examination of the application of systemic work in diverse settings with diverse populations, including both therapy and consultation. Therapeutic practice is supervised live within a supervision group, by an accredited trainer.

The profession of family therapist was established in the UK during the 1990s, largely due to the initiatives within the professional association (AFT). Most family therapists in post work for the NHS. The current pay scales reflect the postgraduate status of the profession. The family therapy training institutes in the UK work collaboratively through CONFETTI (the Confederation of Family Therapy Training Institutes). A CONFETTI representative has a place on the board of the AFT, which ensures good communication and liaison between the institutes and the professional association.

Psychotherapy training and practice in the UK are regulated through a voluntary register, managed by the United Kingdom Council for Psychotherapy (UKCP). AFT is a member of the UKCP and registers its members through their Registration Committee. Panelists scrutinize professional and academic qualifications. NHS-based family therapists are required to hold UKCP registration as a guarantee of the quality of their training. Currently the UKCP is working toward statutory registration of psychotherapists and protection of the title.

The UKCP is made up of sections, which include the main psychotherapy professional associations and training institutes. The BPS, which accredits the training of clinical psychologists, but not of psychotherapists, and the Royal College of Psychiatrists are corresponding members of the UKCP, but not section members. So, for example, if a clinical psychologist is also a trained family therapist, they may register with the UKCP, whilst also holding clinical psychology chartered status with the BPS. This gives double jeopardy in the case of complaints, of course. This situation shows well the confusion amongst professions, professional associations, as to how psychotherapy fits with the traditional disciplines of clinical and applied psychology and psychiatry in the UK. This situation is further complicated by the present government initiative to expand and increase access to the psychological psychotherapies, some of which are informed by the work of the family psychologists.

Potential future developments

Family therapy and systemic practice are developing fast in the UK, with areas of practice opening up to training, consultation, supervision, and providing services for couples and families where previously individualized approaches had pertained, for example in psychiatric rehabilitation, adult mental health services, services for older people, and physical health services. Systemic practice finds its application within areas of specialist practice, such as domestic violence, addictions, eating disorders, child protection, and brain injury rehabilitation. Similarly the individual psychotherapies as practiced within UK public sector services are more attuned to people's relationships and cultural contexts, so although the relationship itself might not be the focus of the intervention, certainly interpersonal factors now feature within formulation and service evaluation.

Theoretical development also continues apace, with many practicing family therapists influenced by social constructionist critiques and the recent turn to narrative. The field could be described as mature in that the different schools of family therapy promote integrative practice and look to theories developed outside the field, such as the recent interest in attachment theory. Such integration of theory and practice offers couples and families more choice in our public sector services. However, we cannot afford to rest as the UK Department of Health wishes to fund only modern, evidence-based psychotherapies. Family therapists and systemic practitioners need to constantly develop their practice base, thus contributing hypotheses and approaches for the future of the evidence base.

Conclusion

Family psychology is not yet mainstream in either the UK or the US. In the UK, change will come through government approval of systemic approaches to treatment. The most significant issue for the future of graduate education in family psychology in the United States is accreditation by the APA CoA. Most APA-accredited programs that include a strong emphasis on family psychology today are accredited as clinical, counseling, or school psychology programs with an emphasis on family psychology. Historical attitudes toward the three main categories of programs are difficult to change and many programs find it easier to pursue accreditation within those categories and build the emphasis into the program. It remains to be seen how many programs will take up the challenge to demonstrate that family psychology is broad and general in orientation and able to stand on its own for accreditation.

In the meantime, it is essential that more doctoral programs provide additional coursework and clinical training in the areas where their graduates will actually be providing psychological services. It is unconscionable that we know that most psychologists provide couple and/or family therapy yet receive little or no doctoral preparation to do so. It is important that all graduate education in psychology include systems theory and evidence-based family psychology interventions in the curriculum.

Note

Some material in this chapter is adapted from Stanton & Harway (2007).

Resources

Posted on the APA Division 43 website: (a) compendium of family psychology course syllabi, (b) "Recommendations for doctoral education and training in family psychology" (Stanton & Harway, 2007), and (c) list of current doctoral programs emphasizing family psychology (http://www.apa.org/divisions/div43).

Qualification criteria and applications for board certification in family psychology are available at the ABPP website (http://www.abpp.org/).

References

American Psychological Association. (2003). Demographic shifts in psychology. Retrieved August 9, 2007, from http://research.apa.org/demoshifts.html

American Psychological Association. (2005). *Guidelines and principles for accreditation of programs in professional psychology.* Washington, DC: American Psychological Association.

American Psychological Association. (2007). *Graduate study in psychology: 2008 edition.* Washington, DC: American Psychological Association.

Bertalanffy, L. V. (1974). The unified theory for psychiatry and the behavioral sciences. *Adolescent Psychiatry, 3,* 43–48.

Green, R.-J. (2005). The shallowness and narrowness of graduate education in family psychology: Are we providing ethical training and supervision? *The Family Psychologist, 21,* 8–45.

Holleman, W. L., Bray, J. H., Davis, L., & Holleman, M. C. (2004). Innovative ways to address the mental health and medical needs of marginalized patients: Collaborations between family physicians, family therapists, and family psychologists. *American Journal of Orthopsychiatry, 74(3),* 242–252.

Kaslow, F. (2000). History of family therapy: Evolution outside of the U.S.A. *Journal of Family Psychotherapy, 11(4),* 1–34.

Kaslow, N. J. (2004). Competencies in professional psychology. *American Psychologist, 59(8),* 774–781.

Kaslow, N. J., Borden, K., Collins, F., Forrest, L., Illfelder-Kaye, J., Nelson, P., et al. (2004). Competencies conference: Future directions in education and credentialing in professional psychology. *Journal of Clinical Psychology, 60(7),* 699–712.

Kaslow, N. J., Celano, M., & Stanton, M. (2005). Training in family psychology: A competencies-based approach. *Family Process, 44(3),* 337–353.

Lebow, J. (Ed.). (2005). *Handbook of clinical family therapy.* Hoboken, NJ: Wiley.

Nichols, W. C. (2005). Ethical issues in practice with couples and families. *The Family Psychologist, 21,* 4–7.

Norcross, J. C., Castle, P., Sayette, M., & Mayne, T. (2004). The PsyD: Heterogeneity in practitioner training. *Professional Psychology: Research and Practice, 35,* 412–419.

Norcross, J. C., Hedges, M., & Castle, P. H. (2002). Psychologists conducting psychotherapy in 2001: A study of the Division 29 membership. *Psychotherapy: Theory, Research, Practice, Training, 39(1)*, 97–102.

Nutt, R., & Stanton, M. (2008). Family psychology specialty practice. *Professional Psychology: Research and Practice, 39*, 519–528.

Stanton, M. (1999). Family psychology. In D. Benner & P. Hill (Eds.), *Baker encyclopedia of psychology and counseling* (2nd ed., pp. 438–439). Grand Rapids: Baker.

Stanton, M. (2005a). Ethical considerations in identification as a family psychologist. *The Family Psychologist, 21(3)*, 1, 46.

Stanton, M. (2005b). The evolving state of family psychology in graduate education in psychology. *The Family Psychologist, 21(1)*, 11–12.

Stanton, M., & Harway, M. (2007). Recommendations for doctoral education and training in family psychology. *The Family Psychologist, 23*, 4–10.

Stanton, M., Harway, M., & Eaton, H. (2006, August). *Comparison of doctoral programs with an emphasis in family psychology.* Paper presented at the American Psychological Association Annual Convention.

Stanton, M., & Nurse, R. (2005). The development of family psychologists: An annotated flowchart. *The Family Psychologist, 21(4)*, 4–5.

Vetere, A., & Dallos, R. (2003). *Working systemically with families: Formulation, intervention, and evaluation.* London: Karnac.

Vetere, A., & Gale, A. (1987). *Ecological studies of family life.* Chichester: Wiley.

Weeks, G. R., & Nixon, G. F. (1991). Family psychology: The specialty statement of an evolving field. *The Family Psychologist, 7(4)*, 9–18.

Part II

Clinical Family Psychology

Introduction

The professional practice of family psychology has progressed significantly from the early days when treatment models were based on the work of charismatic leaders, often in reaction to individualistic mainstream psychological models (see Chapter 2, this volume). Contemporary family psychology practice interacts with the wider psychology environment and is increasingly cognizant of the need for scientific evidence to support professional interventions.

This part of the Handbook presents an introduction to family psychology practice through chapters on systemic assessment, the current status of couple and family processes in the revision of the *Diagnostic and Statistical Manual* (American Psychiatric Association, 1994), an overview of legal and ethical issues in professional practice that focuses especially on the important issue of competence to provide services to couples and families, and an introduction to important issues in professional practice.

This part proceeds to provide introductions to many well-known and evidence-supported models for the systemic treatment of individuals, couples, families, and larger social systems. These chapters are written by practitioners and researcher-practitioners who use the approaches regularly. Almost all include a case study or illustrations that unpack the model in a descriptive manner. We hope that clinicians and students will enjoy these examples, as they reflect the real-life use of the models.

This part concludes with a chapter on the cutting-edge process of incorporating active feedback into the therapeutic process in order to enhance effectiveness. This model reflects the increasing desire to ensure positive treatment outcomes and it demonstrates one way to incorporate outcome evaluation into ongoing treatment instead of waiting until the conclusion of treatment.

Finally, several chapters in this part include a list of resources for further exploration of the chapter subject in a box inset at the end of the chapter. Many authors noted websites, videos, and additional written materials that will allow interested readers to pursue the topic further.

Reference

American Psychiatric Association. (1994). *Diagnostic and statistical manual of mental disorders* (4th ed.). Washington, DC: American Psychiatric Association.

10

Couple and Family Assessment

James H. Bray

Accurate assessment of family relationships and functioning is an important issue in evaluating and treating couples and families (Bray, 1995a, 1995b; Bray & Frugé, 2000; Heffer, Lane, & Snyder, 2003; Mash & Foster, 2001). In family interventions, just like in individual psychotherapy, the success of a treatment plan often depends on accurate assessment of the nature of the problem and the potential for solutions (Heffer et al., 2003). This chapter discusses issues and methods for assessing couples and families.

Characteristics of Family Functioning

Efforts to capture the complexity of family relationships, their natural processes, and the influences on family members over time have led to a variety of assessment strategies (Bray, 1995b; Bray & Frugé, 2000; Grotevant & Carlson, 1989; Jacob & Tennenbaum, 1988; Olson, 2000; Snyder, Heyman, & Haynes, 2005). There are no gold-standard measures for couple and family assessments. A diversity of perspectives is useful to reflect the uniqueness of each family and variety of family dynamics. There are six types of family characteristics that are frequently assessed in research and clinical evaluation of families: family structure and composition, family process, relationship patterns, family affect, family organization, and family diversity. These characteristics come from couple and family research and are useful in treatment as well, as many of them have been linked to individual and family outcomes (Bray, 1995a; Fisher, 1976; Grotevant & Carlson, 1989). Family diversity interacts among all of these factors (Fine, 1993; Sciarra, 2001).

Family structure and composition include family membership (e.g., couple only, couple with children, single-parent family) and structure of the family (e.g., cohabitating couple, first-marriage family, divorced family, stepfamily). Family structure and composition are key markers for other aspects of family functioning. For example, children in single-parent families and stepfamilies often have more behavior problems than children in first-marriage families, and parenting practices often differ as well.

Family process factors include interactions and transactions among family members that characterize patterns of behavioral exchanges between family members and the function or outcomes associated with these interactions. Process measures reflect core features of transactional behavior such as conflict, communication, and problem solving. Family process is distinguished from content. Family process is the transactions between family members without regard to content. For example, if a wife says to a husband, "You never help me get our daughter ready for school," the content is chores. However, the process "You never help me" could easily apply to any content area other than chores. In this regard, process also refers to the message or metacommunication "I do not feel supported by you" (Watzlawick, Weakland, & Fisch, 1974). Process can also refer to transactional patterns. For instance, if a husband says to his wife, "Let's go make love now," and the wife responds by saying, "when I am finished cleaning the kitchen," the function of "cleaning the kitchen" may be to avoid discussion or action on the husband's request to make love. The same words (content) depending on their context could have very different functions (process). In this case, what is reflected may be part of a *pattern* in which an emotionally laden request receives a response that changes the topic of conversation.

Relationship patterns refer to sequences of couple or family interactions that develop over time and are related to specific outcomes. For example, Gottman (1993, 1994) identified a sequence of interactions in marital relationships that is highly predictive of divorce. Couples that are happy have a different rate of positive and negative interactions than do unhappy couples. Happy couples have five positive statements to every one negative statement. In unhappy couples, there is one positive to every one negative statement. The relationship sequence is criticism, contempt, defensiveness, stonewalling. Couples start with being overly critical of each other. The next step is couples feeling and exhibiting contempt for each other. Non-verbal facial expressions and reactions are often displayed between the couple. Following this couples becoming defensive and often do not hear each other. There is more focus on how a spouse is going to respond to their partner, rather than listening to what their partner is saying. The last step is for couples to stonewall and shut down their interactions with each other. At this point, many couples recast their relationship as totally negative, which is highly predictive of divorce. These types of relationship patterns may develop over time or may be present in the early stages of a relationship. Gottman's research is based on observational, interview, and self-reported assessments.

Family affect relates to the nature of the emotional expression among family members. The emotional tone and volume of interactions are important aspects of the context of family processes and greatly affect how family members experience or interpret communications. Measures of expressed emotion between family members, particularly negative emotion, offer some of the most reliable predictors of outcome in studies of chronic problems such as schizophrenia, mood disorders, divorce, alcoholism, and antisocial adolescents (Gottman, 1994; O'Farrell, Hooley, Fals-Stewart, & Cutter, 1998; Robbins, Hervis, Mitrani, & Szapocznik, 2001).

There is a broad range of affective qualities that must be considered in determining the character of expression of affect, and it is often related to culture and ethnicity (Bray &

Frugé, 2000; Olson, 2000). Expression of affect includes the variability in the ability to express affect and the appropriateness of the expressed affect (Miller, Ryan, Keitner, Bishop, & Epstein, 2000). Affect ranges from loving, supportive, and nurturing to negative, hostile, and sarcastic. In addition, the level or volume of affective tone is also important and may range from families in which there is little affect, or affect is over-controlled, to families in which the volume of either positive or negative affect is very high. Negative affect at high volume is usually disruptive of family life. Hence, there is widespread accept-ance that negative affect is undesirable and in need of therapeutic intervention.

Family organization factors are the roles and rules (spoken and unspoken) within the family. This also refers to expectations for behavior that contribute to family function-ing. These factors include aspects such as (1) boundaries, (2) decision-making hierarchy, and (3) the distribution of labor and emotional support functions. Boundaries refer to the emotional and psychological closeness or distance between family members and between the family and the external world (Carter & McGoldrick, 1998). Functional boundaries need to be permeable to permit interaction across them. However, appropriate bound-aries change with the developmental stage of the family. Families with an infant, for example, naturally have strong boundaries around the mother and infant. As the infant grows, the boundary between mother and infant becomes more flexible and eventually, when the child and siblings are developmentally at a similar stage, the boundaries among siblings may be stronger than the boundary around the mother and child.

Another interesting boundary issue occurs in the relation of nuclear and extended family/kin networks. In some cultures, boundaries around the nuclear family are inflex-ible, whereas in other cultures boundaries between the nuclear family and their extended or kinship network are open and fluid. Culture is an important defining feature of families, which will prescribe the nature of the family interactions that are acceptable. What is acceptable may change considerably from family to family and from culture to culture (Olson, 2000).

Family diversity includes ethnicity, sexual orientation, socioeconomic status, and religion. Family diversity contributes significant variations within and across the factors presented above. For example, family process may be quite different for various family composi-tions in diverse ethnic groups at different developmental stages; and these differences may result in important disparities in individual functioning for family members in different family roles (Bray, 1995a, 1995b; Fine, 1993; Szapocznik & Kurtines, 1993; Whaley & Davis, 2007). Families are also dynamic rather than static systems. Relationships between factors noted at one point may change in form over time. Thus, as families develop and family members move into different family roles (i.e., infant grows and begins school; children leave the home) the nature of family composition, process, affect, and organ-ization will all be affected by these important developmental transitions.

Issues in Assessing Families

In choosing a couple or family assessment strategy, clinicians should first determine what aspects of family functioning are most likely to be relevant to the goals of prevention and treatment that are of most interest (Floyd, Weinand, & Cimmarusti, 1989; Heyman, 2001). This involves several dimensions: (1) the members of the family who are being evaluated; (2) the methods of the assessment that have been selected; and (3) the methods of examining the family system by using all these sources of information (Dakof, 1996; Davidson, Quinn, & Josephson, 2001; Heyman, 2001). It is also important in assessing interpersonal interactions to distinguish between properties of the relationship (e.g., conflict, cohesion) and feelings or attitudes (e.g., anger, positivity–negativity) that individuals have about the relationship (Thompson & Walker, 1982).

Insights have emerged from family research that can be useful for clinical applications (Heyman, 2001; Mash & Foster, 2001; Olson, 2000; Pequegnat & Szapocznik, 2000; Roberts, 2001; Snyder et al., 2005). For example, family research measures are often based on self-report data from individual family members describing their own perceptions of the family, rather than reports from multiple family members or direct observations of families in interaction (Bray, 1995a, 1995b; Fisher, Kokes, Ransom, Phillips, & Rudd, 1985). Most surveys and assessments of individual family members utilize this type of information, with the assumption that self-report information represents valid and complete information on family functioning.

There is unresolved controversy in both the research and clinical literatures about the necessity to assess the entire family (Bray, 1995b; Mash & Foster, 2001; Roberts, 2001). Examining the interactions of various family dyads (e.g., a couple within the family) and triads (e.g., two parents and a child) may be more useful than examining the family as a whole (Bray, 1995a; Cole & Jordan, 1989; Cook & Kenny, 2004; Dickstein et al., 1998; Hetherington & Clingempeel, 1992; Hetherington & Kelly, 2002). Sometimes, information from smaller family subgroups can lead to more focused treatment plans. Changing the behavior of a few members of a family will ultimately lead to shifts in the entire family (Szapocznik & Kurtines, 1989). This marks a shift from viewing and discussing the family exclusively as a coherent whole.

In recognizing that many critical aspects of family functioning are reflected in specific processes and interactions between particular family members (e.g., the couple), the arena of family assessment and intervention has become more differentiated – recognizing that sometimes individual perceptions are most useful, while other times contrast in individual perceptions, measures of full family functioning, or the functioning of family subsystems may be most useful. More recent efforts include assessments of the entire family, important subsets, and individual characteristics (Gaughan, 1995; Hayden et al., 1998; Heffer et al., 2003; Miller et al., 2000; Skinner, Steinhauer, & Sitarenios, 2000; Watson & McDaniel, 1998; Wilkinson, 2000).

Without a consensus on what constitutes a "gold standard" in family measurement (Bray, 1995a), researchers and clinicians usually rely on more than one method for assessing family process (how the family interacts) and outcomes (whether the family successfully achieves its goals). The two most common measurement methods in family assessment are the use of self-report instruments and behavioral observations of family interactions (Bray, 1995b). It is important to understand that the information obtained by these methods does not always agree (Cole & McPherson, 1993; Cook & Kenny, 2004; Kolevzon et al., 1988; Markman & Notarius, 1987), but may be combined to provide significant overlap and consensus (Hetheringon & Clingempeel, 1992; Jacob & Windle, 1999).

Self-report methods

Self-reports of family functioning are probably the most common means of assessing family relations and processes in research contexts (Bray, 1995b) and there are hundreds of published self-report measures of family functioning (Forman, Aronson, & Combs, 2003; Touliatos, Perlmutter, Straus, & Holden, 2001). Self-report measures include perceptions of the family by individual family members, ratings by family members of other family members' behavior or relationships, and self-reports of affect and emotions while engaging in certain interactions (Bray, 1995b). The reader is referred to Forman et al. (2003), Fredman and Sherman (1987), Grotevant & Carlson (1989), Jordan (2003), and Touliatos et al. (2001) for reviews of many of the couple and family measures.

There are many benefits to self-report instruments of family functioning (Bray, 1995b). Foremost, self-reports are usually economical, easy to collect in a clinic setting, and can be administered in repeated sessions to document changes within the family. Self-report measures thus can be a convenient gauge for changes in outcomes as a result of a preventive or treatment intervention. To measure changes over time, however, the clinician must be careful to select measures that reflect the kinds of changes that are likely to occur in the prevention or treatment program rather than a measure of stable family or individual characteristics (Jacob, 1995). It is also wise to select more specific measures of family functioning with reasonable theoretical or empirical linkages to the prevention or treatment interventions being evaluated, in addition to global reports on family functioning. For example, to assess the effectiveness of an intervention that is trying to improve marital communication one should use a specific measure for this rather than a global measure of marital satisfaction.

Family research reveals that information obtained from an individual may or may not accurately reflect the functioning of the entire couple or family (Fisher et al., 1985; Hayden et al., 1998; Jacob & Windle, 1999; Ransom, Fisher, Phillips, Kokes, & Weiss, 1990). Several studies have found statistically significant and clinically important differences among family members' reports of family functioning (Cole & McPherson, 1993; Cook & Kenny, 2004; Stevenson-Hinde & Akister, 1995). For instance, research on the breakup of relationships indicates that there are frequently significant differences reported by the partners in satisfaction (His and Her marriages) with the relationship and why it is ending (Gottman, 1994; Hetherington & Kelly, 2002). The examination of the differences in perceptions between individual family members can be useful for prevention and treatment efforts. For example, examining the self-reported differences in marital satisfaction within a couple may reveal important areas for future work. Clinical practice suggests that bridging these differences in perception can have therapeutic value for improving the quality of relationships (Bray, 1995a).

While the assessment of an individual's perceptions is suitable for evaluating certain aspects of the family system (e.g., differentiation within the family of origin), these assessments are not truly measures of the family system as a whole. Information obtained from individuals within a family can be transformed into relational measures by various means that are beyond the scope of this chapter (Bray, 1995a; Cole & McPherson, 1993; Cook & Kenny, 2004; Fisher et al., 1985; Kolevzon et al., 1988; Ransom et al., 1990). Family-level measures can be developed from averaged or weighted responses of individual family members. This provides an overall evaluation of the family that may be helpful if it provides information about how distressed this family is in comparison to other families with whom the practitioner has successfully worked (Olson, 1977). Self-reports of individual family members can also be compared to other members of the family to see how much agreement there may be on issues that are likely to be important in prevention or treatment programs.

Observational methods

Observations of families can range from qualitative measures, such as narrative descriptions of family relations, to very quantitative approaches, such as the specific coding of interactional sequences (e.g., microanalytic coding; Carlson & Grotevant, 1987; Gottman, 1994; Ransom et al., 1990). Qualitative approaches may include experiential activities that help engage the family and serve as the beginning of the change process (Deacon & Piercy, 2001). Coding of observational measures attempts to assess the real-time patterning of family interactions that are of interest to family researchers and clinicians.

In contrast to self-report measures, observational assessments also represent an *outsider's* view of the family. These assessments involve judgments by a trained professional about family interactions. However, family members can also make ratings and observations about family interactions, as exemplified by Gottman's work on marital relationships (Gottman, 1993, 1994).

There are three dimensions of standardized observations: (1) what is observed (i.e., what task family members are asked to perform); (2) where it is observed (i.e., home, office); and (3) how it is observed (i.e., the coding system employed) (Bray, 1995b; Bray & Frugé, 2000). To facilitate comparisons between families, it is desirable to establish a specific task to be performed by each family (e.g., plan a menu). The task chosen often reflects common problematic situations in average family life (e.g., discussing how to solve a discipline problem with a child). Alternatively, the specific task may be designed to stimulate dimensions of interaction that are thought to be particularly relevant to the problem being investigated (e.g., discussing who is going to have custody of a child after a divorce). These types of observations can be analogue situations, as in the case of family laboratories, or of typical family settings, such as in the home during dinner (Mash & Foster, 2001; Roberts, 2001).

Observation tasks.   Problem-solving tasks, where family members are asked to identify a common problem, discuss it, and attempt to develop a solution to the problem, are widely used (Bray, 1995b; Markman & Notarius, 1987; Mash & Foster, 2001; Roberts, 2001). These tasks are engaging and often revealing of typical patterns of family interactions. They can elicit discord, creativity, and a family's usual style or pattern of conflict resolution. Problems selected may be identified as internal to the family or couple versus external. There are also standardized games, such as the Simulated Family Activity Measurement (SIMFAM; Straus & Tallman, 1971), which can be used as the catalyst for a problem-solving task. Other types of tasks include providing emotional support or encouragement for a family member, planning pleasant events (e.g., a family trip or vacation), describing qualities of the family, making up stories to standardized pictures (e.g., the Thematic Apperception Test), putting together puzzles or games, and talking about what happened during the day (Grotevant & Carlson, 1989).

Each type of task tends to elicit different types of family interactions. For example, the task of discussing differences in individual views asks family members to defend their position on certain ideas and values and can reflect issues of power, group pressure, and autonomy, whereas the planning tasks may be more likely to elicit positive interactions and role relationships. In all family assessments, it is important to sample various content domains to ensure that one obtains a picture of how the family functions across a variety of meaningful domains.

Context of observation.   The contexts in which families are observed may impact how families behave. Therefore, we may see different family relationships and interactions depending on the context in which the family is observed and what the family is asked to do (i.e., discussing a family problem versus planning a family vacation). For example, in a clinic, a family may be on their best behavior, but in their own dining room, they may interact in a more typical way that includes more negative interactions and affect. Direct observation of family interaction usually occurs in a clinic due to financial and logistical constraints. The observations can also be set in more natural settings such as the home (e.g., dinner-table conversations) or school (e.g., classroom). Research indicates that families show little reactivity to observation per se (Jacob, Tennenbaum, Seilhamer, Bargiel, & Sharon, 1994), and to exposure to standardized tasks, although different types of behavior may be exhibited in different settings. Thus, the setting used for observation should be selected for the purpose of the assessment and chosen to maximize the chances for a relevant sample of behavior. For example, if parenting for child behavior problems is the target then a home observation may be particularly useful. If the base rate of a particular behavior is low, such as temper tantrums or abusive behaviors, then the use of more naturalistic and longer-term observational approaches may be required.

Observational coding systems.   Family interactions can be used to obtain global ratings (e.g., positive to negative quality of interaction), on the one hand, or highly specific frequency counts of a particular behavior (e.g., how many times did a parent criticize a child), on the other (Bray, 1995b). The latter type of observation can be very useful for identifying linked patterns of behaviors (Gottman, 1993; Markman & Notarius, 1987). For example, what follows a parental criticism of a child? Is a critical parental behavior followed by an adolescent compliant or rebellious behavior? In some families, parental criticism of an adolescent may result in adolescent compliant response, while in another family it may result in adolescent rebellious response. The reader is referred to Grotevant and Carlson (1989) and Markman and Notarius (1987) for reviews of various behavioral observation systems, and other examples (Robbins et al., 2001; Szapocznik et al., 1991).

Clinician rating methods

Clinician ratings are one form of observational methods. Clinician ratings of family inter-actions provide clinicians with systematic methods for coding and observing family inter-actions. Clinician rating systems can be used in clinical interviews that are standardized or unstandardized (Carlson & Grotevant, 1987). Floyd et al. (1989) provide good examples of how clinicians can utilize behavioral observations and ratings in a clinical context.

A useful clinical method for assessing families is the genogram, a standard format for recording information about family relationships over at least three generations (McGoldrick, Gerson, & Petry, 2008). Genograms are recommended widely from family therapy settings to family medicine settings. McGoldrick et al. (2008) and Rogers and colleagues (Like, Rogers, & McGoldrick, 1987; Rogers & Rohrbaugh, 1991) have developed systematic methods for using and interpreting genograms in clinical practice. However, there is limited research that the use of genograms impacts how problems are conceptualized or addressed (Rogers & Rohrbaugh, 1991).

Factors that influence observations of family functioning

Context plays a critical role in influencing families (Bray & Frugé, 2000). Context includes both the observable interactions and settings for family interactions and the meanings and interpretations of those interactions by individual family members. Another example of the context of family is consideration of how the stage of a family's life cycle may influence the behavior of a family. Family life-cycle theory teaches us that most families progress through a definable set of stages each of which is characterized by an inter-related set of developmental tasks and dynamics (e.g., caring for young children). Life-cycle theory suggests that the ways families adapt to both predictable and unpredictable challenges and changes are greatly influenced by the life-cycle stage of the family (Carter & McGoldrick, 1998).

Yet a third example of context is the consideration of the broader cultural and ethnic attributes that may specifically define and influence family life-cycle stages and the characteristic behaviors of certain groups of families (Whaley & Davis, 2007). Thus, the appraisal of family functioning, and in particular the definition of "normality," should be considered in the context of the specific life-cycle stages as well as in the context of cultural/ethnic dimensions (Olson, 2000; Walsh, 2003).

Most of the current models of family relationships and functioning are based on White, middle-class families that do not necessarily reflect variations that may be typical for families from different cultural and ethnic backgrounds (Bray, 1995b; Fine, 1993). Indeed, most family measures, with a few exceptions (e.g., Friedmann, Astedt-Kurki, & Paavilainen, 2003; Shek, 1998, 2002; Szapocznik & Kurtines, 1993; Szapocznik et al., 1991), are based on these models and have not been validated with families from diverse ethnic backgrounds (Aarons, McDonald, Connelly, & Newton, 2007; Baer & Bray, 1999; Bray, 1995b; Hampson, Beavers, & Hulgus, 1990; Morris, 1990). Researchers and clinicians are cautioned to keep this limitation in mind when using measures and instruments developed on one ethnic group to assess the health and dysfunction of families from other ethnic and cultural backgrounds (Fine, 1993; Whaley & Davis, 2007).

However, standardized family measures can still be useful in providing information about the family at several different points using the same assessment ruler. Self-report measures can then be interpreted in the broader context of what is known about the life and culture of the family. Hence, although many measures have not been used with a particular cultural group, the practitioner can nevertheless use the measure across a sample of ethnically specific families, and establish her or his own sense of how families compare with each other on a particular measure. Further, environmental context in terms of community and interactions between family and community may provide a wider framework for assessing the needs and conditions of children and adolescents (cf. Gray, 2001). This approach is intended to encourage practitioners to try out family measures that have not been developed for their population and see what the measures tell them about the specific cultural group served in their practice setting.

Clinical Application of Family Assessments

There are many reasons for clinicians to use formal, standardized methods for assessing families (Bray, 1995b). However, family-oriented practitioners frequently do not use formal family assessments in their practices (Boughner, Hayes, Bubenzer, & West, 1994; Bray, 1995b; Floyd et al., 1989; Mash & Foster, 2001; Snyder et al., 2005). Evaluations conducted before prevention or treatment intervention begins can provide a rich source of information about the family and can be used to develop initial hypotheses about problem areas, causes of problems, and potential areas of strengths. Assessment also insures that a broad range of routine information is collected to make certain that important areas are not overlooked. By using a battery of self-report methods, a substantial amount of information can be ascertained with minimal clinician time. In addition, given that most clients and family members initially view the presenting problem as within an individual, completing family assessment instruments begins to redefine the problem as a family systems issue (Bray, 1995b). A thorough assessment is part of ethical treatment (see chapter 12, this volume).

Many of the available family measures and methods have been developed for research contexts and have not been specifically applied to clinical practice. Consequently, many instruments do not provide either the instructions or clinically relevant norms and comparisons necessary for use in practice settings. However, more recent work in couple and family assessment has integrated research findings into clinically relevant and useful methods (Gottman 1994, 1996; Hayden et al., 1998; Heffer et al., 2003; Mash & Foster, 2001; Miller et al., 2000; Skinner et al., 2000; Snyder et al., 2005; Szapocznik & Kurtines, 1989; Watson & McDaniel, 1998; Wilkinson, 2000).

Using a standard battery of instruments also facilitates comparisons between a family's current functioning and published normative data. Given the limitations of family assessment, it is probably wise to view the normative data as suggestive rather than as defining pathology. Likewise, clinicians and researchers need to be cognizant of different norms for various family structures (e.g., nuclear, single-parent, stepparent) and ethnic backgrounds (Bray, 1995b). In addition, initial assessments can be compared to post-treatment assessments to document intervention-related changes. With the changes in healthcare reimbursement and the demand for the demonstration of treatment efficacy, formal assessments that document positive change are becoming a central part of the therapeutic process. The use of measures will make it easier for clinicians to compare families and gain insights that may be applicable to future client families.

It is clear that more attention is needed to develop methods that can capture the complex phenomena of family relationships. There are a number of new and promising methods that are being developed in other areas of family research that may provide clinicians with innovative ways of assessing family relationships and outcomes. These types of innovations will facilitate the further development of effective family prevention and treatment interventions.

Note

This chapter is an updated version of Bray (1995; Bray & Frugé, 2000).

Resources

Cierpka, M., Thomas, V., & Sprenkle, D. H. (Eds.). (2005). *Family assessment: Integrating multiple perspectives.* Cambridge, MA: Hogrefe.

Sperry, L. (Ed.). (2004). *Assessment of couples and families: Contemporary and cutting-edge strategies.* New York: Brunner-Routledge.

References

Aarons, G. A., McDonald, E. J., Connelly, C. D., & Newton, R. R. (2007). Assessment of family functioning in Caucasian and Hispanic Americans: Reliability, validity and factor structure of the Family Assessment Device. *Family Process, 46,* 557–569.

Baer, P. E., & Bray, J. H. (1999). Adolescent individuation and alcohol usage. *Journal of Studies on Alcohol, 13,* 52–62.

Boughner, S. R., Hayes, S. F., Bubenzer, D. L., & West, J. D. (1994). Use of standardized assessment instruments by marital and family therapists: A survey. *Journal of Marital and Family Therapy, 20,* 69–75.

Bray, J. H. (1995a). Assessment of family health and distress: An intergenerational-systems perspective. In J. C. Conoley & E. Werth (Eds.), *Family assessment* (pp. 67–102). Lincoln, NE: Buros Institute of Mental Measurement.

Bray, J. H. (1995b). Family assessment: Current issues in evaluating families. *Family Relations, 44,* 469–477.

Bray, J. H., & Frugé, E. F. (2000). Assessment and evaluation of families with HIV/AIDS: Application to prevention and care. In W. Pequegnat & J. Szapocznik (Eds.), *Working with families in the era of HIV/AIDS* (pp. 27–43). Thousand Oaks, CA: Sage.

Carlson, C. I., & Grotevant, H. D. (1987). A comparative review of family rating scales: Guidelines for clinicians and researchers. *Journal of Family Psychology, 1*, 23–47.

Carter, E. A., & McGoldrick, M. (Eds.). (1998). *The expanded family life cycle: Individual, family, and social perspectives* (3rd ed.). New York: Allyn & Bacon.

Cole, D. A., & Jordan, A. E. (1989). Assessment of cohesion and adaptability in component family dyads: A question of convergent and discriminant validity. *Journal of Counseling Psychology, 36*, 456–463.

Cole, D. A., & McPherson, A. E. (1993). Relation of family subsystems to adolescent depression: Implementing a new family assessment strategy. *Journal of Family Psychology, 7*, 119–133.

Cook, W. L., & Kenny, D. A. (2004). Application of the social relations model to family assessment. *Journal of Family Psychology, 18*, 361–371.

Dakof, G. A. (1996). Meaning and measurement of family: Comment on Gorman-Smith et al. (1996). *Journal of Family Psychology, 10*, 142–146.

Davidson, B., Quinn, W. H., & Josephson, A. M. (2001). Assessment of the family: Systemic and developmental perspectives. *Child and Adolescent Psychiatric Clinics of North America, 10*, 415–429.

Deacon, S. A., & Piercy, F. (2001). Qualitative methods in family evaluation: Creative assessment techniques. *American Journal of Family Therapy, 29*, 355–373.

Dickstein, S., Seifer, R., Hayden, L. C., Schiller, M., Sameroff, A. J., Keitner, G., et al. (1998). Levels of family assessment: II. Impact of maternal psychopathology on family functioning. *Journal of Family Psychology, 12*, 23–40.

Fine, M. A. (Ed.). (1993). Family diversity (Special issue). *Family Relations, 42(3)*.

Fisher, L. (1976). Dimensions of family assessment: A critical review. *Journal of Marriage and Family Counseling, 2*, 367–382.

Fisher, L., Kokes, R. F., Ransom, D. C., Phillips, S. L., & Rudd, P. (1985). Alternative strategies for creating "relational" family data. *Family Process, 24*, 213–224.

Floyd, F. J., Weinand, J. W., & Cimmarusti, R. A. (1989). Clinical family assessment: Applying structured measurement procedures in treatment settings. *Journal of Marital and Family Therapy, 15*, 271–288.

Forman, D. D., Aronson, J., & Combs, M. P. (2003). Family assessment. In G. Sholevar Pirooz (Ed.), *Textbook of family and couples therapy: Clinical applications* (pp. 277–302). Washington, DC: American Psychiatric Publishing.

Fredman, N., & Sherman, R. (1987). *Handbook of measurements for marriage and family therapy.* New York: Brunner/Mazel.

Friedmann, M. L., Astedt-Kurki P., & Paavilainen, E. (2003). Development of a family assessment instrument for transcultural use. *Journal of Transcultural Nursing, 14*, 90–99.

Gaughan, E. (1995). Family assessment in psychoeducational evaluations: Case studies with the Family Adaptability and Cohesion Evaluation Scales. *Journal of School Psychology, 33*, 7–28.

Gottman, J. M. (1993). A theory of marital dissolution and stability. *Journal of Family Psychology, 7*, 57–75.

Gottman, J. M. (1994). *What predicts divorce? The relationship between marital processes and marital outcomes.* Hillsdale, NJ: Erlbaum.

Gottman, J. M. (1996). *What predicts divorce? The measures.* New York: Erlbaum.

Gray, J. (2001). The framework for the assessment of children in need and their families. *Child Psychology and Psychiatry Review, 6*, 4–10.

Grotevant, H. D., & Carlson, C. I. (1989). *Family assessment: A guide to methods and measures.* New York: Guilford Press.

Hampson, R. B., Beavers, W. R., & Hulgus, Y. (1990). Cross-ethnic family differences: Interactional assessment of White, Black, and Mexican-American families. *Journal of Marital and Family Therapy, 16*, 307–319.

Hayden, L. C., Schiller, M., Dickstein, S., Seifer, R., Sameroff, S., Miller, I., et al. (1998). Levels of family assessment: I. Family marital and parent–child interaction. *Journal of Family Psychology, 12*, 7–22.

Heffer, R. W., Lane, M. M., & Snyder, D. K. (2003). Therapeutic family assessment: A systems approach. In K. Jorday (Ed.), *Handbook of couple and family assessment* (pp. 21–47). Hauppauge, NY: Nova Science.

Hetherington, E. M., & Clingempeel, W. G. (1992). Coping with marital transitions: A family systems perspective. *Monographs of the Society for Research in Child Development, 57*, Nos. 2–3, Serial No. 227.

Hetherington, E. M., & Kelly, J. (2002). *For better or for worse: Divorce reconsidered.* New York: Norton.

Heyman, R. E. (2001). Observation of couple conflicts: Clinical assessment application, stubborn truths, and shaky foundations. *Psychological Assessment, 13*, 5–35.

Jacob, T. (1995). The role of time frame in the assessment of family functioning. *Journal of Marital and Family Therapy, 21*, 281–288.

Jacob, T., & Tennenbaum, D. L. (1988). *Family assessment: Rationale, methods, and future directions.* New York: Plenum.

Jacob, T., Tennenbaum, D., Seilhamer, R. A., Bargiel, K., & Sharon, T. (1994). Reactivity effects during naturalistic observation of distressed and nondistressed families. *Journal of Family Psychology, 8*, 354–363.

Jacob, T., & Windle, M. (1999). Family assessment: Instrument dimensionality and correspondence across family reporters. *Journal of Family Psychology, 13*, 339–354.

Jordan, K. (2003). *Handbook of couple and family assessment.* Hauppauge, NY: Nova Science.

Kolevzon, M. S., Green, R. G., Fortune, A. E., & Vosler, N. R. (1988). Evaluating family therapy: Divergent methods, divergent findings. *Journal of Marital and Family Therapy, 14*, 277–286.

Like, R. C., Rogers, J. C., & McGoldrick, M. (1987). Reading and interpreting genograms: A systematic approach. *The Journal of Family Practice, 26*, 407–412.

Markman, H. J., & Notarius, C. I. (1987). Coding marital and family interaction: Current status. In T. Jacob (Ed.), *Family interaction and psychopathology: Theories, methods, and findings* (pp. 329–390). New York: Plenum.

Mash, E. J., & Foster, S. L. (2001). Exporting analogue behavioral observation from research to clinical practice: Useful or cost-defective? *Psychological Assessment, 13*, 86–98.

McGoldrick, M., Gerson, R., & Petry, S. (2008). *Genograms: Assessment and Intervention* (3rd ed.). New York: Norton.

Miller, I. W., Ryan, C. E., Keitner, G. I., Bishop, D. S., & Epstein, N. B. (2000). The McMaster approach to families: Theory, assessment, treatment and research. *Journal of Family Therapy, 22*, 168–189.

Morris, T. M. (1990). Culturally sensitive family assessment: An evaluation of the Family Assessment Device used with Hawaiian-American and Japanese-American families. *Family Process, 29*, 105–116.

O'Farrell, T. J., Hooley, J., Fals-Stewart, W., & Cutter, H. S. G. (1998). Expressed emotion and relapse in alcoholic patients. *Journal of Consulting and Clinical Psychology, 66*, 744–752.

Olson, D. H. (1977). Insiders' and outsiders' view of relationships: Research strategies. In G. Levinger & H. Raush (Eds.), *Close relationships* (pp. 115–135). Amherst: University of Massachusetts Press.

Olson, D. H. (2000). Circumplex model of marital and family systems. *Journal of Family Therapy, 22,* 144–167.

Pequegnat, W., & Szapocznik, J. (2000). *Working with families in the era of HIV/AIDS.* Thousand Oaks, CA: Sage.

Ransom, D. C., Fisher, L., Phillips, S., Kokes, R. F., & Weiss, R. (1990). The logic of measurement in family research. In T. W. Draper & A. C. Marcus (Eds.), *Family variables: Conceptualization, measurement, and use* (pp. 48–66). Newbury Park, CA: Sage.

Robbins, M. S., Hervis, O., Mitrani, V. B., & Szapocznik, J. (2001). Assessing changes in family interaction: The Structural Family Systems Ratings. In P. K. Kerig and K. M. Lindahl (Eds.), *Family observational coding systems: Resources for systemic research* (pp. 207–224). Hillsdale, NJ: Erlbaum.

Roberts, M. W. (2001). Clinic observations of structured parent–child interaction designed to evaluate externalizing disorders. *Psychological Assessment, 13,* 46–58.

Rogers, J. C., & Rohrbaugh, M. (1991). The SAGE-PAGE trial: Do family genograms make a difference? *Journal of the American Board of Family Practice, 4,* 319–326.

Sciarra, D. T. (2001). Assessment of diverse family systems. In L. A. Suzuki, J. G. Ponterotto, & P. J. Meller (Eds.), *Handbook of multicultural assessment: Clinical, psychological and educational applications* (2nd ed., pp. 135–168). San Francisco: Jossey-Bass.

Shek, D. T. L. (1998). The Chinese version of the Self-Report Family Inventory: Does culture make a difference? *Research on Social Work Practice, 8,* 315–329.

Shek, D. T. L. (2002). Assessment of family functioning in Chinese adolescents: The Chinese version of the Family Assessment Device. *Research on Social Work Practice, 12,* 502–524.

Skinner, H., Steinhauer, P., & Sitarenios, G. (2000). Family Assessment Measure (FAM) and process model of family functioning. *Journal of Family Therapy, 22,* 190–210.

Snyder, D. K., Heyman, R. E., & Haynes, S. N. (2005). Evidence-based approaches to assessing couple distress. *Psychological Assessment, 17,* 288–307.

Stevenson-Hinde, J., & Akister, J. (1995). The McMaster Model of Family Functioning: Observer and parental ratings in a nonclinical sample. *Family Process, 34,* 337–347.

Straus, M. A., & Tallman, I. (1971). SIMFAM: A technique for observational measurement and experimental study of families. In J. Aldous (Ed.), *Family problem-solving* (pp. 381–438). Hinsdale, IL: Dryden Press.

Szapocznik, J., Hervis, O., Rio, A. T., Mitrani, V. B., et al. (1991). Assessing change in family functioning as a result of treatment: The Structural Family Systems Rating scale (SFSR). *Journal of Marital and Family Therapy, 17,* 295–310.

Szapocznik, J., & Kurtines, W. M. (1993). Family psychology and cultural diversity: Opportunities for the theory, research and application. *American Psychologist, 48,* 400–407.

Thompson, L., & Walker, A. (1982). The dyad as the unit of analysis: Conceptual and methodological issues. *Journal of Marriage and the Family, 44,* 889–900.

Touliatos, J., Perlmutter, B. F., Straus, M. A., & Holden, G. W. (Eds.). (2001). *Handbook of family measurement techniques (vols. 1–3).* Thousand Oaks, CA: Sage.

Walsh, F. (2003). *Normal family processes: Growing diversity and complexity* (3rd ed.). New York: Guilford Press.

Watson, W. H., & McDaniel, S. H. (1998). Assessment in transitional family therapy: The importance of context. In J. W. Barron (Ed.), *Making diagnosis meaningful: Enhancing evaluation and treatment of psychological disorders.* (pp. 161–195). Washington, DC: American Psychological Association.

Watzlawick, P., Weakland, J., & Fisch, R. (1974). *Change: Principles of problem formation and problem resolution.* New York: Norton.

Whaley, A. L., & Davis, K. E. (2007). Cultural competence and evidence-based practice in mental health services: A complementary perspective. *American Psychologist, 62,* 563–574.

Wilkinson, I. (2000). The Darlington Family Assessment System: Clinical guidelines for practitioners. *Journal of Family Therapy, 22,* 211–224.

11

Couple and Family Processes in DSM-V: Moving Beyond Relational Disorders

Erika Lawrence, Steven R. H. Beach, and Brian D. Doss

Although clinicians and researchers generally do not discuss them as such, we suspect that most professionals who work with distressed marriages have some internal criteria for certain categories of relationship dysfunction. For example, couples experiencing marital distress (somewhat arbitrarily categorized as such by having a score on the Dyadic Adjustment Scale [DAS; Spanier, 1979] of 97 or lower) are often subdivided into couples with and without intimate partner violence and whether or not they have certain communication problems (e.g., demand–withdraw communication) or other difficulties (e.g., affairs, sexual problems). On the basis of these categories, different modes and methods of intervention are recommended. The question that currently faces the field of clinical couple and family psychology is whether some of these informal categories should be operationalized into formal diagnoses or identified as discrete syndromes.

In clinical psychology, the dominant classification system of diagnosis is the Diagnostic and Statistical Manual (DSM-IV-TR; American Psychiatric Association [ApA], 1994). The DSM has at least three primary and explicit goals: (a) to provide a structure for understanding the etiology of mental disorders; (b) to provide a common language to describe and diagnose mental disorders; and (c) to inform clinical treatment of those disorders. For the last two decades, couple and family psychologists have been working to include a consideration of couple and family processes in the DSM. (See Kaslow & Patterson, 2006, for a review of these efforts.) However, even in the most recent edition, DSM-IV, the role of relationships is only tangentially addressed. DSM-IV incorporates relational processes in four ways. Perhaps the most visible mention of relational processes in DSM-IV is the inclusion of partner relational and parent–child V-codes on Axis I, which recognizes that some clinical interventions may be targeted specifically at couple and family processes. Indeed, it is this recognition that forms the basis for one of the primary recommendations described below. Second, DSM-IV also recognizes that family and relational processes provide an important context in which to consider Axis I and Axis II individual disorders by allowing for inclusion of contextual descriptors on Axis IV. Third, the Global Assessment of Relational Functioning (GARF) scale, a parallel to the Global Assessment of Functioning (GAF) scale, is presented in "Appendix B: Criteria Sets and Axes Provided for Further Study." Fourth, Volume 3 of the DSM-IV Source Book reviews important relational processes omitted from the body of DSM-IV. The DSM-IV task force stated that the GARF and other relational content were placed in supplemental resources, rather than integrated into the body of DSM-IV, because "there was insufficient information to warrant inclusion . . . as official categories or axes in DSM-IV" (ApA, 1994, p. 703). However, since the publication of DSM-IV, there have been notable gains in the research on dysfunctional relationships, which we review below.

The future of relational diagnosis

Despite these additional resources, we believe relational diagnoses will not be incorporated into the larger field's conceptualization of disordered functioning until the DSM further develops and expands its presentation of dysfunctional relationships. Fortunately, the importance of dysfunctional relationships is beginning to be recognized by both psychiatrists and psychologists. In the early stages of planning for the DSM-V, the ApA commissioned a series of six research-planning work groups, one of which was tasked to explore important gaps in the DSM-IV. Along with the categorical conceptualization of personality disorders, this group identified the lack of relational disorders as one of "the most important gaps in the current DSM-IV" (First et al., 2002, p. 123).

Despite the extensive empirical support that can be used to buttress the idea that relational processes are essential to understanding, preventing, and treating many psychological disorders, it is likely that relational processes will be largely excluded from the DSM-V unless they can be shown to be consistent with the zeitgeist of the ApA and their efforts in crafting the DSM-V. What role do relational processes have to play within that framework? Although it is true that relational processes do not fit within a traditional medical and individually focused model of mental illness, we believe that empirical evidence is encouraging both psychiatrists and psychologists to adopt an integrative, biopsychosocial model of mental and behavioral health problems and dysfunction. Within this broader framework, relational factors can be integrated with genetic, neurobiological, environmental, and cultural factors contributing to the etiology, maintenance, exacerbation, and burden of mental illness. Additionally, it becomes possible to move away from an exclusive focus on mental illness and toward incorporation of health-maintaining and health-promoting factors. (Although the reciprocal role of relational and other factors in disordered functioning is too extensive to review here, interested readers should consult the text of *Relational Processes and DSM-V* [Beach, Wamboldt, Kaslow, Heyman, First, et al., 2006] or the 2006 special section of *Journal of Family Psychology* [Beach, Wamboldt, Kaslow, Heyman, & Reiss, 2006].)

In the remainder of the chapter, we present three possible ways that disordered relationships could be productively included in the DSM. Although these possibilities are certainly not an exhaustive list, we believe they illustrate the rich potential for further development. To further illustrate these three ways of including relational processes in DSM, we conclude the chapter with a clinical example of how conceptualization and diagnoses of these disordered relationships could progress and inform subsequent treatment.

Relational Syndromes

Relational syndromes include well-defined, established patterns of interaction between or among members of a relational unit that are associated with either (a) clinically significant impairment in functioning, or (b) symptoms among one or more members of the relational unit, or (c) impairment in the functioning of the relational unit itself. These problems may exacerbate or complicate the management of a mental disorder or a general medical condition, may exist independent of concurrent medical conditions, or may occur in the absence of any other condition. First et al. (2002) described relational syndromes as "serious behavioral disturbances that can lead to major impairments in physical health and psychological adjustment" (p. 159). They are "persistent and painful patterns of feelings, behavior and perceptions involving two or more partners in an important personal relationship . . . [and are] marked by distinctive, maladaptive patterns that show little change despite a great variety of challenges and circumstances" (p. 161). First et al. (2002) also provided a definition to distinguish normal fluctuations in relationship functioning from true relational syndromes.

> There is little flexibility or change in . . . [relational syndromes], and the dyad responds to a range of stresses and challenges with the same distinctive and maladaptive patterns . . . [T]he patterns are of long standing and are not a response to a recent stressful event . . . [T]he corrosive patterns of the relationship are unresponsive to supportive features that may occur naturally in the social environment. (pp. 161–162)

Development of relational syndromes. There is growing evidence that the development of relational syndromes involves both biological and psychosocial factors. However, in contrast with the wealth of research documenting the psychosocial factors influencing the development of relational syndromes (see Beach, Wamboldt, Kaslow, Heyman, First, et al., 2006; Beach, Wamboldt, Kaslow, Heyman, & Reiss, 2006), far less is known about the emerging evidence of biological influences on these syndromes. For example, researchers have demonstrated familial patterns of parenting and marital difficulties, suggesting the presence of at least some genetic influence in relational syndromes (e.g., Kendler, 1996; Reiss, Neiderhiser, Heterington, & Plomin, 2000). Published studies of spouses' autonomic responses during marital conflict also help elucidate the biological factors involved in the development and persistence of relational syndromes (e.g., Gottman, Jacobson, Rushe, & Wu Shortt, 1995). Further research on the biological etiologies of relational syndromes, such as those in *Relational Processes and DSM-V* (Beach, Wamboldt, Kaslow, Heyman, First, et al., 2006), are critical for making a sound, empirically supported argument for incorporating such syndromes into DSM-V.

Assessment of relational syndromes.   There is also accumulating empirical evidence supporting a distinction between normal fluctuations in dyadic functioning and relational syndromes. Standardized instruments have been developed and used to demonstrate distinct features for classification (e.g., Beach, Fincham, Amir, & Leonard, 2005; Heyman & Smith Slep, 2006; Messer & Reiss, 2000). Beach and colleagues (2005) have demonstrated the possibility of moving from arbitrary cutoffs (e.g., a 97 on the DAS; Spanier, 1979) to taxonomic approaches that identify natural points of rarity to establish cutoffs for some relational syndromes. Researchers have documented the clinical course of couple discord using longitudinal designs, including studies establishing specific early risk factors for marital dissolution (e.g., Karney & Bradbury, 1995).

Treatment of relational syndromes.   An important strength of the close relationship literature is our establishment of empirically supported treatments for relational syndromes. Multiple specific treatments have been subjected to the rigors of controlled, clinical trials and have demonstrated the efficacy of specific therapies for what we tentatively label partner relational dysfunction syndrome (e.g., see Snyder, Castellani, & Whisman, 2006, for a review) and intimate partner violence syndrome (e.g., O'Leary, Heyman, & Neidig, 1999). We also have evidence of specific, empirically supported intervention programs that have been shown to effectively *prevent* relational syndromes (e.g., Prevention and Relationship Enhancement Program; Markman, Renick, Floyd, Stanley, & Clements, 1993).

Central Relational Processes

The category of central relational processes is an expansion of the DSM code V61.9 "Relational Problem Related to a Mental Disorder or General Medical Condition." Central relational processes need not be distressing in and of themselves but may modify the course of mental illness. They are generally not associated with functional impairment in general, but rather in the context of an ongoing mental disorder or medical condition. However, like relational syndromes, their assessment may provide important and clinically useful information. We conceptualize central relational processes as being useful when the focus of clinical attention is on the impaired interaction pattern that may influence the longitudinal course of the disorder, the pattern of remission, or the likelihood of relapse following treatment. For example, for patients suffering from schizophrenia, mood disorders, and a broad range of other psychiatric conditions, family environments that are characterized by critical, hostile, or emotionally overinvolved or intrusive attitudes (high expressed emotion [EE] families) create significantly elevated risk of early relapse (Butzlaff & Hooley, 1998; Leff & Vaughn, 1985). These processes also provide guidance regarding key dimensions of relationship functioning that may influence the course of treatment, maintenance of gains, and/or relapse. There are at least two central relational processes with strong and consistent empirical support: maladaptive attachment styles and EE. Given space considerations, and the current advantages of EE in providing an example of a central relationship process, we focus on EE in the remainder of this section.

Impact of central relational processes. EE defines a cluster of beliefs and behaviors, with criticism a salient component of the cluster, that are not routinely associated with distress or functional impairment in the absence of a co-existing psychiatric diagnosis, but may be associated with problematic outcomes when psychiatric conditions are present. One attractive feature of EE as a central relational process worthy of DSM inclusion is that it is a highly reliable psychosocial predictor of psychiatric relapse across a number of different disorders. Patients suffering from a broad range of other psychiatric conditions who live in family environments characterized by critical, hostile, or emotionally overinvolved or intrusive attitudes (that is, in high EE families) are at significantly elevated risk of early relapse compared to patients who do not live in such family environments (Hooley, Miklowitz, & Beach, 2006). For example, an association between high EE and risk for relapse has been established for schizophrenia, affective disorders, eating disorders, anxiety disorders, and substance use disorders (Butzlaff & Hooley, 1998; Chambless, Bryan, & Aiken, 2001; O'Farrell, Hooley, Fals-Stewart, & Cutter, 1998). This is important in the context of DSM-V, because it suggests that a single set of assessment guidelines could allow enhanced prediction of course of illness for several different disorders. Likewise, the similarities between measures of communication deviance developed by Wynne (1981) and the construct of EE suggest the potential for including observational measures in these assessment guidelines that may parallel the assessments used to measure EE.

It is important to note that high levels of EE are relatively benign in many family contexts, and in others it may be elicited by the presence of physical and mental health problems. For example, chronic health conditions in childhood may set the stage for maladaptive changes in family functioning that would not have been manifested if the illness had never occurred. Likewise, parents or partners of the severely mentally ill may find themselves confronted with situations for which they are poorly prepared, and as a result, their behavior may change in problematic ways (Hooley & Gotlib, 2000), leading to high EE. Or, confronted with unusual behavior, family members may misapply strategies that would have been relatively benign in the absence of severe mental illness in a family member, again resulting in high EE. Taken together, these findings suggest that EE has both trait-like and state-like properties. Thus, some relatives may be temperamentally predisposed to high-EE attitudes and the onset of the patient's symptoms may be sufficient to push them across the threshold for high EE (Hooley & Gotlib, 2000), with enduring negative consequences. If so, measurement of EE has the potential to be more than an indirect assessment of degree of family burden. Rather, it can help identify a constellation of attitudes and behaviors that can be addressed therapeutically with positive effects on patient adjustment (Miklowitz, et al., 2007).

Assessment of central relational processes. The criterion measure of EE, the Camberwell Family Interview (CFI), is generally viewed as being rather long and cumbersome for many clinical settings, particularly those with limited staffing. To be used as a routine assessment, the average time taken by the CFI interview is somewhat long: 1.5 hours to administer and an additional 2–3 hours to be rated by raters who have received rather extensive training (typically 40–80 hours). In addition, training in rating EE is currently expensive and difficult to obtain for those in clinical settings. So, although the CFI is likely to remain the "gold standard" for EE assessment, the need for "practical" assessment alternatives in the context of DSM-V forces consideration of briefer assessment methods for measuring EE. Two such assessments are described in more detail in the clinical example below.

Treatment of central relational processes.   When clinicians are alerted to the presence of family processes predictive of rapid relapse and rehospitalization, it may prompt them to utilize family interventions where these are available. The range of family and couple interventions that can reduce EE is not yet known. However, there is growing evidence of the effectiveness of several specific approaches to family intervention. For example, the combination of family-focused therapy (FFT) and pharmacotherapy delays relapses and reduces symptom severity among patients followed over the course of 1 to 2 years (see Miklowitz, 2007, for a review). Likewise, there is initial evidence that family-based interventions provided in the prodrome of a disorder may help alleviate its severity. For example, McFarlane (2006) examined the role of biological and socioenvironmental factors in the early and later prodromal phases of psychosis among at-risk persons. The design involved an open trial of community-based family-aided intervention and low-dose atypical antipsychotic medications. At 12-month follow-up, McFarlane and colleagues observed low rates of conversion to full-blown schizophrenia when at-risk persons received comprehensive family intervention in addition to pharmacological treatment. These results suggest that in addition to providing useful information about course of illness and relapse, EE may increasingly supply indications for family intervention that may positively impact treatment.

Relational Specifiers and Embedded Relational Criteria

Even when relational processes are not the primary focus of diagnosis or treatment, they have much to offer future editions of the DSM. In particular, we anticipate that the integration of relational processes into existing individual disorders will advance the mental health field. In particular, we suggest that integration of relational specifiers of certain disorders (e.g., peer group influence in conduct disorder) and embedded relational criteria (e.g., coercive parenting in conduct disorder) within the diagnoses of existing individual disorders be added to future conceptualizations of individual disorders.

There are several advantages to integrating relational processes into the diagnosis of individual disorders. First, inclusion of relational processes can improve our understanding of the etiology, diagnosis, and treatments for individual disorders. Depending on the specifics of the particular disorder, relationship processes may be incorporated into specifiers, disorder symptoms, or a combination of the two. Second, the identification of important relationship components may improve treatment success and decrease the likelihood of relapse. Third, inclusion of relationship processes in the etiology, description, or treatment of individual disorders would encourage clinicians and researchers to assess relationship domains. In this way, broadening our conceptualization of "individual" disorders will strengthen our research and clinical knowledge base regarding the role of relationships in individual disorders. Indeed, potential changes to the future diagnosis of individual disorders would serve to further strengthen future investigations on the critical overlap between individual and relationship distress.

Impact of relational specifiers and embedded relational criteria. Since the development of the DSM-IV, there have been numerous studies demonstrating strong associations between individual disorders and distressed relationship processes (cf. Whisman & Uebelacker, 2003). For example, in a population-based sample involving over 2,500 individuals, marital distress was strongly associated with 10 of the 11 individual disorders examined including substance use, anxiety, and depression. In each case, marital distress increased the likelihood of psychological disorders; these associations ranged from a 1.8-fold increase for alcohol use disorders to a 5.7-fold increase for dysthymia (Whisman, 1999; Uebelacker & Whisman, 2006).

Moreover, there is evidence that marital distress predicts the development of subsequent individual disorders even after controlling for relevant demographic variables and previous history of individual disorders. Specifically, marital discord at baseline has been shown to predict a 2.7-fold increase in the likelihood of developing a major depressive episode (Whisman & Bruce, 1999) and a 3.7-fold increase in the likelihood of developing an alcohol use disorder (Whisman, Uebelacker, & Bruce, 2006). Over shorter periods of time, the association between marital distress and depression is reciprocal (Davila, Karney, Hall, & Bradbury, 2003); this pattern may also hold for other individual disorders. Because marital discord appears to be a critical risk factor for many, if not most, psychiatric disorders, integrating these research findings into the description and symptomatology of DSM-V disorders would be an important step forward in our ability to diagnose and understand individual psychopathology.

Assessment of relational specifiers and embedded relational criteria. Inclusion of relationship distress as specifiers of individual disorders can also serve to structure our description of individual disorders and clarify important subtypes or symptoms. For example, in the DSM-IV category "Feeding Disorder of Infancy or Early Childhood," there are no subtypes included even though difficulties may arise from physical digestion difficulties versus from an intrusive feeding style on the part of the caregiver (Chatoor, Hirsch, Ganiban, Persinger, & Hamburger, 1998). Thus, inclusion of parent–child relationship factors would seem to highlight important descriptive differences in subtypes or specifiers of feeding disorders. Even without identifying different subtypes, inclusion of relationship difficulties in the symptoms of a disorder can clarify the construct of that disorder. For example, although a hostile, coercive, and punitive parenting style is associated with conduct disorder (Stoolmiller, 2001), and interrupting this style is an efficacious treatment for conduct disorder, dysfunctional parent–child interactions are not included in the diagnostic criteria for conduct disorder (Beach, Wamboldt, Kaslow, Heyman, & Reiss, 2006).

Treatment of individual disorders with relational specifiers or relational criteria.   Relationship discord is strongly associated with treatment effectiveness for individual disorders. Individually based psychological and pharmacological treatments for depression are less effective when individuals are experiencing marital distress at the beginning of treatment (e.g., Hickie & Parker, 1992; Hooley & Teasdale, 1989). Further, marital distress at the end of treatment appears to have an even larger impact on subsequent depression outcomes (e.g., Whisman, 2001). Additionally, several studies have identified marital distress as increasing the likelihood of relapse following treatment for alcohol disorders (e.g., Maisto, McKay, & O'Farrell, 1998; O'Farrell et al., 1998) and poorer outcomes following treatment for panic disorder with agoraphobia (e.g., Marcaurelle, Belanger, & Marchand, 2003). Further, there are several lines of research that point to the added benefits of involving spouses in treatment for disorders that have typically been treated using only individual treatments, such as alcohol dependence (e.g., Fals-Stewart, Klostermann, Yates, O'Farrell, & Birchler, 2005) and bipolar disorder (e.g., Rea et al., 2003). In sum, there is strong and consistent evidence of the utility of incorporating couple therapies into our treatments for a variety of individual disorders.

Clinical Example

As an example of how the availability of relational syndromes, central relational processes, relational specifiers, and embedded relational criteria might enhance a clinician's ability to assess, diagnose, and successfully treat clients, we present the fictitious case of Sharon, a 38-year-old woman who presents for individual therapy. At the first session, she indicates that she is depressed, is having trouble functioning, and can't seem to "snap out of it." She also reports that her depression is affecting her productivity at work and her relationship with her husband Jack. First we present the typical assessment protocol, diagnosis and treatment plan that would likely be implemented for Sharon without consideration of a relational component. Then we present alternative assessment protocols, diagnostic conclusions, and treatment recommendations that would be useful if Sharon were to meet criteria for a relational syndrome, central relational process, or relational specifier, respectively.

Assessment, diagnosis, and treatment without a relational component

Using the DSM-IV as our guide, we conduct an individual psychodiagnostic assessment. Specifically, we conduct a clinical interview to get a history and present level of functioning across multiple domains (e.g., educational and occupational functioning, family history, developmental and medical history, psychological history, social functioning). We also administer a variety of self-report questionnaires and a structured clinical interview to determine whether or not to formally diagnose Sharon with an affective disorder, and to rule in or rule out other comorbid disorders (e.g., anxiety disorders). We learn that Sharon has been struggling with multiple symptoms of depression for approximately six months. She demonstrates vegetative symptoms (hypersomnia, loss of appetite, psychomotor retardation). Her affect is flat at times and sad at times. She cries easily and when appropriate to content. She demonstrates social withdrawal, anhedonia, and apathy as well. Finally, she demonstrates cognitive features of depression, including thinking of herself as worthless and of her situation as hopeless. She is experiencing difficulties functioning in her marital relationship, at work, and in her social life.

Upon completion of our assessment protocol, we conclude that Sharon meets criteria for major depressive disorder, current. She does not meet criteria for any other Axis I disorders. Under Axis IV, we note "marital problems and distress." We do not include a V-code on Axis I for partner relational problem because we conceptualize Sharon's marital problems as one example of the global functional impairment caused by her depression. We refer Sharon to a psychiatrist for a medication evaluation, and we begin individual treatment to treat her depression. For example, we might implement behavior activation strategies, cognitive behavioral therapy, interpersonal psychotherapy, or acceptance and commitment therapy to treat her depression.

This plan represents a strong, sound approach to clinical work. However, it is based on an assumption that (a) Sharon's marital problems are secondary to her depression and (b) treating Sharon's depression will alleviate her marital problems. What if the depression is secondary to her marital problems? What if we would be more effective at treating both the marital distress and the depression if we treated the marital problems first?

Assessment, diagnosis, and treatment incorporating relational syndromes

Another possibility is that Sharon and Jack are experiencing partner relational dysfunction, one example of a relational syndrome. Specific criteria have been already been proposed to determine whether a couple meets specifications for this syndrome, and the criteria comprise four key domains: relationship dissatisfaction, relationship conflict/communication, intentions, and relationship efficacy.

Assessment. A comprehensive assessment of a relational syndrome, just like an assessment for any DSM diagnosis, should be multi-method in nature. Thus, if initial brief screening procedures suggest it, we strongly recommend that a more comprehensive set of self-report questionnaires, semi-structured clinical interviews, and objectively coded, behaviorally observed dyadic interactions be utilized to guide clinical decision-making about the presence of this relational syndrome in Sharon and Jack's marriage. A variety of published, psychometrically strong questionnaires exists to assess relationship dissatisfaction, relationship conflict, psychological and physical violence partner-specific attributions. Structured clinical interviews to assess partner relational dysfunction have been developed and validated. To collect behavioral observation data, standardized

Table 11.1 Resources for Relationship Assessment

Relational syndromes

Recommended measures of partner distress/conflict/violence

Relationship satisfaction and adjustment:
- Dyadic Adjustment Scale[a]: Spanier (1979)
- Quality of Marriage Index: Norton (1983)
- Couples Satisfaction Index: Funk and Rogge (2007)
- Structured Diagnostic Interview for Marital Distress and Partner Aggression: Heyman et al. (2001)

Conflict management/problem-solving skills:
- Marital Satisfaction Inventory-Revised[a]: Snyder and Aikman (1999)
- Communication Skills Test (CST): Floyd (2004)
- 10-minute problem solving interaction task coded for positive and negative behaviors and/or affect[b]: Specific Affect Coding System; Shapiro and Gottman (2004); Rapid Marital Interaction Coding System; Heyman (2004)
- Areas of Change Questionnaire: Weiss and Birchler (1975)

Interpartner support skills:
- Support in Romantic Relationships Scale (SIRRS): Dehle, Larsen, and Landers (2001)
- 10-minute social support interaction task coded for positive and negative support provision and solicitation behaviors[b]: Social Support Interaction Coding System; Pasch, Harris, Sullivan, & Bradbury (2004); Support Behavior Code; Suhr, Cutrona, Krebs, & Jensen (2004)

Emotional intimacy/disengagement:
- Romantic Disengagement Scale (RDS): Barry, Lawrence, and Langer (2008)

Forgiveness:
- Dispositional forgiveness: Fincham and Beach (2002)
- Event forgiveness: Fincham, Beach, and Davila (2004)

Commitment:
- Commitment Inventory: Stanley and Markman (1992)

Psychological, emotional, and physical aggression:
- Mulitidimensional Emotional Abuse Scale: Murphy and Hoover (1999)
- Conflict Tactics Scales – 2nd Version: Physical Assault Scale and Injury and Consequences Scale[a]: Straus, Hamby, Boney-McCoy, and Sugarman (1996)
- Structured Diagnostic Interview for Marital Distress and Partner Aggression: Heyman, Feldbau-Kohn, Ehrensaft, Langhinrichsen-Rohling, and O'Leary (2001)

Recommended measure of family functioning
- Parenting Alliance Inventory: Abidin and Brunner (1995)
- Parenting Stress Index[a]: Abidin (1995)
- Childcare responsibility: Cowan and Cowan (1990)

Table 11.1 *(cont'd)*

Central relational processes

Recommended measures of expressed emotion (EE)
- Perceived Criticism Scale: Hooley and Teasdale (1989)
- The Five Minute Speech Sample (FMSS): Magana et al. (1986)
- The Family Attitude Scale: Kavanagh et al. (1997)

Recommended measures of maladaptive attachment
- Relationship Scales Questionnaire: Griffin and Bartholomew (1994)
- The Berkeley Adult Attachment Interview: George, Kaplan, and Main (1985)

Notes. [a] Measure is not free to the public. [b] Although there exist standardized, psychometrically sound interaction protocols to assess couples' transactions with established coding systems, there is no network at present that can readily and conveniently code these interactions and provide results in a timely manner. However, as the importance of these assessments becomes increasingly clear, we hope that there will be corresponding developments.

dyadic interaction protocols exist to assess couples' conflict-management/problem-solving skills, with established coding systems to quantify partners' positive and negative affect and/or behaviors. There are also standardized interaction protocols to assess couples' support transactions with established coding systems. Recommendations for specific, empirically supported assessments are presented in Table 11.1.

Diagnosis and treatment. Assuming that we conclude that Sharon and Jack meet criteria for partner relational dysfunction as a relational syndrome, it may be appropriate to proceed with any of the empirically supported couple therapies (see Snyder et al., 2006, for a review) so long as they are modified to take into account the special needs of couples with a depressed member (Beach, Dreifus, Franklin, Kamen, & Gabriel, 2008). If the couple did not meet criteria for a relational syndrome, or the relational syndrome were found to be secondary to the particular episode of depression, individual treatment for depression would be appropriate (Beach et al., 2008). Likewise, treatment of the relational syndrome might be added to supplement the use of pharmacological treatment for depression.

Assessment, diagnosis, and treatment incorporating central relational processes

Another possibility is that the couple does not meet criteria for a relational syndrome. Perhaps Jack is highly critical of Sharon, and we conclude that much of Jack's criticism is in reaction to his view of Sharon's problems. In this case, we might suspect that Jack is contributing to a high EE family environment, one example of a central relational process. Central relational processes such as EE have been shown to increase risk of relapse of depression. The weighted mean effect size for the EE–relapse association across six studies of major mood disorder was .39–.45 (r statistic), slightly higher than the mean effect size for Schizophrenia ($r = .31$; see Butzlaff & Hooley, 1998). Further supporting its clinical importance as a family context, EE is associated with greater *reciprocal negativity* (Hooley, 1990; Simoneau, Miklowitz, & Saleem, 1998) and higher levels of physiological arousal during interactions with high EE than low EE relatives (see Tarrier & Turpin, 1992). In sum, if Jack exhibits high EE behaviors, there may be an important source of chronic family stress exacerbating Sharon's depression and/or increasing her risk of relapse after successful individual therapy for her depression.

Assessment.   There are at least two clinically relevant and practical options for assessing EE. First, in the Five Minute Speech Sample (FMSS; Magana et al., 1986), we would have Jack talk about his thoughts and feelings about Sharon for five uninterrupted minutes. We would record his speech and later code it for the overall level of EE, criticism, and emotional overinvolvement. Supporting clinical use of the FMSS in Sharon's case is evidence that it is associated with worse clinical outcomes in mood disorders among children (Asarnow, Goldstein, Tompson, & Guthrie, 1993), depressed outpatients (Uehara, Yokoyama, Goto, & Ihda, 1996) and depressive symptoms among patients with bipolar I disorder (Yan, Hammen, Cohen, Daley, & Henry, 2004). Second, we could administer the Perceived Criticism (PC) measure (Hooley & Teasdale, 1989). Specifically, we would ask Sharon to rate how critical she thinks Jack is of her; we would also ask her how upset she gets in these situations and how critical she thinks she is toward Jack. The PC demonstrates good predictive validity not only for unipolar depression, but also for anxiety disorders, obsessive compulsive disorder, and substance abuse problems. (For more detail on brief assessments for EE, see Hooley et al., 2006.)

Diagnosis and treatment.   Let's assume that, upon completion of the assessment phase, we still conclude that Sharon meets criteria for major depressive disorder, current. However, we also determine that her marital relationship meets criteria for being classified as a high EE family environment, a central relational process that can increase her risk of depression relapse. Thus, our primary diagnosis is still depression, but our additional identification of a central relational process indicates that some dyadic work could be helpful in preventing Sharon from having a relapse after successful individual treatment for her depression. We might proceed with the same plan we described earlier to treat Sharon's depression; however, we might also implement couple or family therapy to treat the high EE that increases Sharon's risk of relapse. There is empirical evidence that introducing family therapy for high EE decreases the risk of relapse and improves symptomatic outcomes (Miklowitz, 2007; McFarlane, 2006).

Assessment, diagnosis, and treatment incorporating relational specifiers

Relatively benign relational processes such as partner support have been shown to increase vulnerability to, worsen the course of, and increase the risk of relapse for depression. For example, spousal support has been linked to depression vulnerability such that the presence of a supportive marital relationship decreases vulnerability to depression and a lack of support in marriage increases vulnerability (Browne & Harris, 1978; Jacobson, Fruzzetti, Dobson, Whisman, & Hops, 1993; Taylor & Lynch, 2004). Katz and Beach (1997) found that one type of esteem support provision – partner self-verifying feedback – intensifies the effect of level of self-esteem on depression. This type of support appears to be beneficial for women with high self-esteem because high levels of support of self-esteem reinforce positive self-views and may provide a buffer against depressive symptoms. Conversely, self-verifying partner support appears detrimental for women with low self-esteem because low levels of support of self-esteem reinforce negative self-evaluations and may lead to higher levels of depressive symptoms (Katz & Beach, 1997).

Assessment.   If we wanted to assess Sharon for depression with a relational specifier of low partner support provision, we would administer the same assessment protocol we described above to diagnose depression. In addition, we would conduct a multi-method assessment of low support provision. There exist multiple psychometrically sound self-report measures of perceptions of partner support provision and the adequacy of that support. We would likely also administer measures of self-esteem and relationship satisfaction, given their moderating and mediating effects on the link between support provision and depression (e.g., Katz & Beach, 1997). Interview measures are currently being developed and validated for these purposes as well. To collect behavioral observation data, standardized dyadic interaction protocols exist to assess couples' support provision and support solicitation skills with established coding systems.

Diagnosis and treatment.   Let's assume that, upon completion of the assessment phase, we continue to conclude that Sharon meets criteria for major depressive disorder, current. Additionally, she meets criteria for low support provision in depression, a proposed relational specifier for major depressive disorder. Thus, our primary diagnosis is still depression, but the relational specifier indicates that some couple therapy focused on support provision will need to be implemented in order to lower Sharon's risk of relapse following successful treatment. Thus, we might proceed with the same plan we described earlier to treat Sharon's depression; however, we might also implement an abbreviated form of couple therapy to treat the low support that worsens the depression.

Conclusion

We believe this is an exciting time in the intimate relationships field. Since the publication of DSM-IV in 1994, there have been important advances in the understanding of the biopsychosocial etiology, impact, prevention, and treatment of dysfunctional relationships. Furthermore, there is now a solid body of literature demonstrating the impact of relational functioning on the development, expression, treatment, and outcome of individual mental health disorders. As discussions of the structure and content of DSM-V progress, it will be important for couple and family psychologists to be involved to help guide revisions using this solid foundation of existing research. In this chapter, we have presented three potential ways in which relational processes could be productively incorporated into our diagnostic system. First, relational syndromes that are maladaptive in their own right (e.g., partner relational dysfunction) could be included as a focus of clinical attention. Second, central relational processes that are pervasive but only harmful in the presence of an individual mental or physical disorder (e.g., expressed emotion) could be added as important contextual factors to consider. Finally, relational processes could be integrated into individual disorders when those processes are important to the diagnosis or treatment of the disorder (e.g., low social support provision in the context of depression). On the basis of the growing body of empirical research in support of the importance of relational processes, we believe it a question of how, not whether, relational processes should be more extensively included in the next edition of the DSM.

References

Abidin, R. R. (1995). *Parenting Stress Index (PSI) manual* (3rd ed.). Charlottesville, VA: Pediatric Psychology Press.

American Psychiatric Association. (1994). *Diagnostic and statistical manual of mental disorders* (4th ed.). Washington, DC: American Psychiatric Association.

Asarnow, J. R., Goldstein, M. J., Tompson, M., & Guthrie, D. (1993). One-year outcomes of depressive disorders in child psychiatric in-patients: Evaluation of the prognostic power of a brief measure of expressed emotion. *Journal of Child Psychology and Psychiatry, 34,* 129–137.

Barry, R. A., Lawrence, E., & Langer, A. (2008). Conceptualization and assessment of disengagement in romantic relationships. *Personal Relationships, 15,* 297–315.

Beach, S. R. H., Dreifus, J. A., Franklin, K. J., Kamen, C., & Gabriel, B. (2008). Couple therapy and the treatment of depression. In A. S. Gurman (Ed.), *Clinical handbook of couple therapy* (4th ed., pp. 545–566). New York: Guilford Press.

Beach, S. R. H., Fincham, F. D., Amir, N., & Leonard, K. E. (2005). The taxometrics of marriage: Is marital discord categorical? *Journal of Family Psychology, 19,* 276–285.

Beach, S. R. H., Wamboldt, M. Z., Kaslow, N. J., Heyman, R. E., First, M. B., Underwood, L. G., et al. (Eds.). (2006). *Relational processes and DSM-V: Neuroscience, assessment, prevention and treatment.* Washington, DC: American Psychiatric Association.

Beach, S. R. H., Wamboldt, M. Z., Kaslow, N. J., Heyman, R. E., & Reiss, D. (2006). Describing relationship problems in DSM-V: Toward better guidance for research and clinical practice. *Journal of Family Psychology, 20,* 359–368.

Browne, G. W., & Harris, T. (1978). *Social origins of depression: A study of psychiatric disorders in women.* New York: Free Press.

Butzlaff, R. L., & Hooley, J. M. (1998). Expressed emotion and psychiatric relapse. *Archives of General Psychiatry, 55,* 547–552.

Chambless, D. L., Bryan, A. D., & Aiken, L. S. (2001). Predicting expressed emotion: A study with families of obsessive-compulsive and agoraphobic outpatients. *Journal of Family Psychology, 15,* 225–40.

Chatoor, I., Hirsch, R., Ganiban, J., Persinger, M., & Hamburger, E. (1998). Diagnosing infantile anorexia: The observation of mother–infant interactions. *Journal of the American Academy of Child & Adolescent Psychiatry, 37,* 959–967.

Cowan, C. P., & Cowan, P. A. (1990). Who does what? In J. Touliatos, B. Perlmutter, & M. Straus (Eds.), *Handbook of family measurement techniques* (pp. 447–448). Thousand Oaks, CA: Sage.

Davila, J., Karney, B. R., Hall, T. W., & Bradbury, T. N. (2003). Depressive symptoms and marital satisfaction: Within-subject associations and the moderating effects of gender and neuroticism. *Journal of Family Psychology, 17,* 557–570.

Dehle, C., Larsen, D., & Landers, J. E. (2001). Social support in marriage. *American Journal of Family Therapy, 29,* 307–324.

Fals-Stewart, W., Klostermann, K., Yates, B. T., O'Farrell, T. J., & Birchler, G. R. (2005). Brief relationship therapy for alcoholism: A randomized clinical trial examining clinical efficacy and cost-effectiveness. *Psychology of Addictive Behaviors, 19,* 363–371.

Fincham, F. D., & Beach, S. R. (2002). Forgiveness in marriage: Implications for psychological aggression and constructive communication. *Personal Relationships, 9,* 239–251.

Fincham, F. D., Beach, S. R., & Davila, J. (2004). Forgiveness and conflict resolution in marriage. *Journal of Family Psychology, 18,* 72–81.

First, M. B., Bell, C. C., Cuthbert, B., Krystal, J. H., Malison, R., Offord, D. R., et al. (2002). Personality disorders and relational disorders: A research agenda for addressing crucial gaps in DSM. In D. J. Kupfer, M. B. First, & D. A. Regier (Eds.), *A research agenda for DSM-V* (pp. 123–199). Washington, DC: American Psychiatric Association.

Floyd, F. J. (2004). Communication Skills Test (CST): Observational system for couples' problem-solving skills. In P. K. Kerig & D. H. Baucom (Eds.), *Couple observational coding systems* (pp. 143–158). Mahwah, NJ: Erlbaum

Funk, J. L., & Rogge, R. D. (2007). Testing the ruler with item response theory: Increasing precision of measurement for relationship satisfaction with the Couples Satisfaction Index. *Journal of Family Psychology, 21,* 572–583.

George, C., Kaplan, N., & Main, M. (1985). *The Berkeley Adult Attachment Interview.* Unpublished protocol, University of California, Berkeley.

Gottman, J. M., Jacobson, N. S., Rushe, R. H., & Wu Shortt, J. (1995). The relationship between heart rate reactivity, emotionally aggressive behavior and general violence in batterers. *Journal of Family Psychology, 9,* 227–248.

Griffin, D. W., & Bartholomew, K. (1994). The metaphysics of measurement: The case of adult attachment. In K. Bartholomew & D. Perlman (Eds.), *Attachment processes in adulthood: Advances in personal relationships* (pp. 17–52). Philadelphia, PA: Jessica Kingsley.

Heyman, R. E. (2004). Rapid Marital Interaction Coding System. In P. K. Kerig & D. H. Baucom (Eds.), *Couple observational coding systems* (pp. 67–94). New York: Routledge.

Heyman, R. E., Feldbau-Kohn, S. R., Ehrensaft, M. K., Langhinrichsen-Rohling, J., & O'Leary, K. D. (2001). Can questionnaire reports correctly classify relationship distress and partner physical abuse? *Journal of Family Psychology, 15,* 334–346.

Heyman, R. E., & Smith Slep, A. M. (2006). Relational diagnoses: From reliable rationally-derived criteria to testable taxonic hypotheses. In S. R. H. Beach, M. Z. Wamboldt, N. J. Kaslow, R. E. Heyman, M. B. First, L. G. Underwood, et al. (Eds.), *Relational processes and DSM-V: Neuroscience, assessment, prevention, and treatment* (pp. 139–155). Washington, DC: American Psychiatric Association.

Hickie, I., & Parker, G. (1992). The impact of an uncaring partner on improvement in non-melancholic depression. *Journal of Affective Disorders, 25,* 147–160.

Hooley, J. M. (1990). Expressed emotion and depression. In G. I. Keitner (Ed.), *Depression and families* (pp. 31–54). Washington, DC: American Psychiatric Press.

Hooley, J. M., & Gotlib, I. H. (2000). A diathesis-stress conceptualization of expressed emotion and clinical outcome. *Journal of Applied and Preventive Psychology, 9,* 135–151.

Hooley, J. M., Miklowitz, D. J., & Beach, S. R. H. (2006). Expressed emotion and the DSM-V. In S. R. H. Beach, M. Z. Wamboldt, N. J. Kaslow, R. E. Heyman, M. B. First, L. G. Underwood, et al. (Eds.), *Relational processes and DSM-V: From neuroscience to assessment and treatment* (pp. 175–191). Washington, DC: American Psychiatric Association.

Hooley, J. M., & Teasdale, J. D. (1989). Predictors of relapse in unipolar depressives: Expressed emotion, marital distress, and perceived criticism. *Journal of Abnormal Psychology, 98,* 229–235.

Jacobson, N. S., Fruzzetti, A. E., Dobson, K., Whisman, M., & Hops, H. (1993). Couple therapy as a treatment for depression: II. The effects of relationship quality and therapy on depressive relapse. *Journal of Consulting and Clinical Psychology, 61,* 516–519.

Karney, B. R., & Bradbury, T. N. (1995). The longitudinal course of marital quality and stability: A review of theory, method and research. *Psychological Bulletin, 118,* 3–34.

Kaslow, F., & Patterson, T. (2006). Relational diagnosis: A brief historical overview: Comment on the Special Section. *Journal of Family Psychology, 20,* 428–431.

Katz, J., & Beach, S. R. H. (1997). Self-verification and depressive symptoms in marriage and courtship: A multiple pathway model. *Journal of Marriage and the Family, 59,* 903–914.

Kavanagh, D. J., O'Halloran, P., Manicavasagar, V., Clark, D., Piatkowska, O., Tennant, C., et al. (1997). The Family Attitude Scale: Reliability and validity of a new scale for measuring the emotional climate of families. *Psychiatry Research, 70,* 185–195.

Kendler, K. S. (1996). Parenting: A genetic-epidemiological perspective. *American Journal of Psychiatry, 153,* 11–20.

Leff, J., & Vaughn, C. (1985). *Expressed emotion in families: Its significance for mental illness.* New York: Guilford Press.

Magana, A. B., Goldstein, J. M., Karno, M., Miklowitz, D. J., Jenkins, J., & Falloon, I. R. (1986). A brief method for assessing expressed emotion in relatives of psychiatric patients. *Psychiatry Research, 17,* 203–212.

Maisto, S. A., McKay, J. R., & O'Farrell, T. J. (1998). Twelve-month abstinence from alcohol and long-term drinking and marital outcomes in men with severe alcohol problems. *Journal of Studies on Alcohol, 59,* 591–598.

Marcaurelle, R., Belanger, C., & Marchand, A. (2003). Marital relationship and the treatment of panic disorder with agoraphobia: A critical review. *Clinical Psychology Review, 23,* 247–276.

Markman, H. J., Renick, M. J., Floyd, F. J., Stanley, S., & Clements, M. (1993). Preventing marital distress through communication and conflict management training: A 4- and 5-year follow-up. *Journal of Consulting and Clinical Psychology, 61,* 70–77.

McFarlane, W. R. (2006). Family expressed emotion prior to onset of psychosis. In S. R. H. Beach, M. Z. Wamboldt, N. J. Kaslow, R. E. Heyman, & M. B. First (Eds.), *Relational processes and DSM-V: Neuroscience, assessment, prevention, and treatment* (pp. 77–87). Washington, DC: American Psychiatric Association.

Messer, S. C., & Reiss, D. (2000). Family and relational issues. In A. J. Rush, H. A. Pincus, M. First, D. Blacker, J. Endicott, S. J. Keith, et al. (Eds.), *ApA handbook of psychiatric measures* (pp. 239–260). Washington, DC: American Psychiatric Association.

Miklowitz, D. J., Otto, M. W., Frank, E., Reilly-Harnngton, N., Wisniewski, S. R., Kogan, J. N., et al. (2007). Psychosocial treatments for bipolar depression. *Archives of General Psychiatry, 64,* 419–427.

Murphy, C. M., & Hoover, S. A. (1999). Measuring emotional abuse in dating relationships as a multifactorial construct. *Violence and Victims, 14,* 39–53.

Norton, R. (1983). Measuring marital quality: A critical look at the dependent variable. *Journal of Marriage and the Family, 45,* 141–151.

O'Farrell, T. J., Hooley, J. M., Fals-Stewart, W., & Cutter, H. S. G. (1998). Expressed emotion and relapse in alcoholic patients. *Journal of Consulting and Clinical Psychology, 66*, 744–752.

O'Leary, K. D., Heyman, R. E., & Neidig, P. H. (1999). Treatment of wife abuse: A comparison of gender-specific and conjoint approaches. *Behavior Therapy, 30*, 475–505.

Pasch, L. A., Harris, K. W., Sullivan, K. T., & Bradbury, T. N. (2004). The Social Support Interaction Coding System. In P. K. Kerig & D. H. Baucom (Eds.), *Couple observational coding systems* (pp. 319–334). New York: Routledge.

Rea, M. M., Tompson, M. C., Miklowitz, D. J., Goldstein, M. J., Hwang, S., & Mintz, J. (2003). Family-focused treatment versus individual treatment for bipolar disorder: Results of a randomized clinical trial. *Journal of Consulting and Clinical Psychology, 71*, 482–492.

Reiss, D., Neiderhiser, J., Heterington, E. M., & Plomin, R. (2000). *The relationship code: Deciphering genetic and social patterns in adolescent development.* Cambridge, MA: Harvard University Press.

Shapiro, A. F., & Gottman, J. M. (2004). The Specific Affect Coding System. In P. K. Kerig & D. H. Baucom (Eds.), *Couple observational coding systems* (pp. 191–208). New York: Routledge.

Simoneau, T. L., Miklowitz, D. J. & Saleem, R. (1998). Expressed emotion and interactional patterns in the families of bipolar patients. *Journal of Abnormal Psychology, 107(3)*, 497–507.

Snyder, D. K., & Aikman, G. G. (1999). Marital Satisfaction Inventory-Revised. In M. E. Maruish (Ed.), *The use of psychological testing for treatment planning and outcomes assessment* (2nd ed., pp. 1173–1210). Mahwah, NJ: Erlbaum.

Snyder, D. K., Castellani, A. M., & Whisman, M. A. (2006). Current status and future directions in couple therapy. *Annual Review of Psychology, 57*, 317–344.

Spanier, G. B. (1979). The measurement of marital quality. *Journal of Sex and Marital Therapy, 5*, 288–300.

Stanley, S. M., & Markman, H. J. (1992). Assessing commitment in personal relationships. *Journal of Marriage and the Family, 54*, 595–608.

Stoolmiller, M. (2001). Synergistic interaction of child manageability problems and parent-discipline tactics in predicting future growth in externalizing behavior for boys. *Developmental Psychology, 37*, 814–825.

Straus, M. A., Hamby, S. L., Boney-McCoy, S., & Sugarman, D. B. (1996). The revised Conflict Tactics Scales (CTS2). *Journal of Family Issues, 17*, 283–316.

Suhr, J. A., Cutrona, C. E., Krebs, K. K., & Jensen, S. L. (2004). The Social Support Behavior Code. In P. K. Kerig & D. H. Baucom (Eds.), *Couple observational coding systems* (pp. 311–318). New York: Routledge.

Tarrier, N., & Turpin, G. (1992). Psychosocial factors, arousal, and schizophrenia relapse: The psychophysiological data. *British Journal of Psychiatry, 161*, 3–11.

Taylor, M. G., & Lynch, S. M. (2004). Trajectories of impairment, social support, and depressive symptoms in later life. *Journals of Gerontology Series B – Psychological Sciences and Social Sciences, 59*, S238–S246.

Uebelacker, L., & Whisman, M. (2006). Moderators of the association between relationship discord and major depression in a national population-based sample. *Journal of Family Psychology, 20(1)*, 40–46.

Uehara, T., Yokoyama, T., Goto, M., & Ihda, S. (1996). Expressed emotion and short-term treatment outcome of outpatients with major depression. *Comprehensive Psychiatry, 37*, 299–304.

Weiss, R. L., & Birchler, G. R. (1975). *Areas of Change Questionnaire.* Unpublished manuscript, University of Oregon, Marital Studies Program, Eugene, OR, http://darkwing.uoregon.edu/~rlweiss/#Assess

Whisman, M. A. (1999). Marital dissatisfaction and psychiatric disorders: Results from the National Comorbidity Study. *Journal of Abnormal Psychology, 108*, 701–706.

Whisman, M. A. (2001). Marital adjustment and outcome following treatments for depression. *Journal of Consulting and Clinical Psychology, 69*, 125–129.

Whisman, M. A., & Bruce, M. L. (1999). Marital distress and incidence of major depressive episode in a community sample. *Journal of Abnormal Psychology, 108*, 674–678.

Whisman, M. A., & Uebelacker, L. A. (2003). Comorbidity of relationship distress and mental and physical health problems. In D. K. Snyder and M. A. Whisman (Eds.), *Treating difficult couples: Helping clients with coexisting mental and relationship disorders* (pp. 3–26). New York: Guilford Press.

Whisman, M. A., Uebelacker, L. A., & Bruce, M. L. (2006). Longitudinal association between marital dissatisfaction and alcohol use disorders in a community sample. *Journal of Family Psychology, 20*, 164–167.

Wynne, L. C. (1981). Current concepts about schizophrenics and family relationships. *Journal of Nervous and Mental Disease, 169*, 82–89.

Yan, L. J., Hammen, C., Cohen, A. N., Daley, S. E., & Henry, R. M. (2004). Expressed emotion versus relationship quality variables in the prediction of recurrence in bipolar patients. *Journal of Affective Disorders, 83*, 199–206.

12

Ethical and Legal Considerations in Family Psychology: The Special Issue of Competence

Terence Patterson

This chapter considers specific ethical and legal issues related to the practice of family psychology, focusing first on the special issue of competency for identification as a family psychologist and proceeding to introduce clinical factors from a legal and ethical perspective.

Competence in Family Psychology

Family psychology has been viewed as a distinct field since the inception of APA Division 43, and although its practitioners in psychology proudly identify with its distinctiveness, it is often difficult for others to distinguish it from the larger "family field." The latter includes the profession of family therapy (as embodied in the American Association for Marriage and Family Therapy [AAMFT]), the modality of family therapy as practiced by other mental health professionals (social work, professional counseling, nursing, and psychiatry), and others in areas such as family life education, research, and sociology. There is, of course, much overlap, and just as a psychiatrist doing family therapy may be indistinguishable from a social worker practicing a specific type of family therapy, a psychologist trained in a family psychology post-doctoral fellowship may practice in comprehensive areas within the field very similarly to a PhD trained in an AAMFT family therapy program. Nonetheless, advances have been made in defining the specific realm of family psychology, and guidelines and certification actively identify competent family psychology specialists.

What, then, is distinctive about ethical practice in family psychology? As in all ethical considerations, it is important to begin with applicable ethics codes, legal guidelines, and common standards of practice. The American Psychological Association (APA) identifies competence in specialty areas, and state regulations and case laws regarding licensure, mandated reporting, protection of clients, and prevailing practices among competent professionals in a specific area provide guidance for mental health practice. The APA, through its Council of Specialties, also provides separate specialty guidelines that elaborate upon standards for specialties to follow, and related groups such as APA divisions, American Board of Professional Psychology (ABPP) specialty boards and academies, and accrediting bodies offer additional details to further define a given area of practice. Of course, all of these standards apply directly only to those who are members of those organizations. However, there is considerable ambiguity in the profession regarding competence to practice in many specialty areas. Even where guidelines exist, they are often considered to be optimal, not enforceable standards, and many people practice without specialty training or certification.

To add further to this vagueness, terms such as *systemic, contextual,* and *interactional* are often used to describe the basic concepts in family psychology. To underscore the synchronicity of these three terms, the Commission for the Recognition of Specialties and Proficiencies in Professional Psychology (CRSPP) recommended that the specialty be identified as "systems psychology," but the name "family psychology" was finally established. Even though the term "systems psychology" may be a more accurate descriptor, "family psychology" is better understood by both professionals and the general public.

Similarities and differences between fields in preparation for couple and family therapy

It may seem simple to define a specialty, but there is much inconsistency among the mental health professions in distinguishing general from specialty competence. Medicine has pioneered board certification, and psychology has followed suit, with a clear procedure for obtaining a diplomate in family psychology. However, many psychologists practice family therapy without the diplomate, and they are practicing ethically as long as they can demonstrate competence. A brief review of licensed therapists who may perform couple and family psychotherapy may demonstrate the current difficulty in family psychology. Licensed professional counselors in some states have a procedure for certifying competence in couple and family therapy, involving coursework and live supervision, and certification programs exist in some universities and private institutes. The AAMFT offers an Approved Supervisor status, and the AAMFT and licensure boards in 50 states identify MFT as a separate profession, with a wide scope of practice that includes general psychotherapy in a relational context. However, despite their title, many MFTs today have no specialty training to demonstrate competence for couple or family therapy. A large number prefer to treat only individual adults or children. Many in the field are indifferent to this kind of ambiguity, but it raises significant issues, such as how the general public or a referring professional knows whether a therapist is competent in family therapy or any other modality. This is a significant question for psychologists who cannot demonstrate specialty training in the field.

Selma Halicki, PsyD, is a recent graduate of a professional school where she took the "couple and family track," consisting of two courses in each area and a 400-hour practicum supervised by a competent specialist. In her internship and post-doctoral training, she worked in both inpatient and outpatient community mental health centers, and saw a handful of couples and families under the supervision of a community psychologist and a psychoanalyst. Dr. Halicki would like to open a private practice specializing in couple and family therapy.

- Is she competent to do so?
- What further training and experience might she pursue in order to demonstrate competence?
- What standards exist in the field to guide her?

Dr. Halicki would qualify as competent at an intermediate or B level (please refer to the guidelines for A-, B-, and C-level certification at the end of this chapter). We would suggest, however, that every psychologist must determine how her or his own education and training relate to the standards for practice in the specialty. These standards are delineated below.

Ethical, legal, and professional standards for the practice of family psychology

APA Ethical Principles and Code of Conduct.   The APA standards, similar to those of other professional organizations, apply generally to all members and in specific ways to family psychologists. The APA code is the only one of its kind that outlines optimal, ideal principles and minimal, enforceable codes or standards. Both apply to psychologists in general, but Standards 2: Competence, 4: Privacy and confidentiality, 6: Record keeping and fees, 7: Education and training, 9: Assessment, and 10: Therapy have specific implications for family psychologists. The competence standard is described here.

Standard 2.1(a.): Boundaries of competence is especially relevant here: "Psychologists provide services, teach, and conduct research with populations and in areas only within the boundaries of their competence, based on their education, training, supervised experience, consultation, study, or professional experience" (APA, 2002). Ample evidence exists that family psychology is a distinct specialty area, and other guidelines will be listed in the following sections.

American Board of Professional Psychology.   Although board certification in professional psychology has existed for 60 years, it has not met with widespread acceptance as the standard by most practicing psychologists. Board certification currently appears to be considered an add-on, or a "nice-to-have" credential in some academic and agency settings. The military and Veterans Administration have periodically offered special "proficiency pay" to ABPP psychologists. However, the percentage of psychologists board certified in family psychology is very small compared to the number of licensed psychologists who engage in couple or family therapy. Many advertise expertise in couple or family therapy without having demonstrated competence through the ABPP certification process.

One can speculate as to how many psychologists who engage in couple or family therapy, or who advertise that they practice it as a specialty, are actually competent. The general requirements for certification are:

- completion of a recognized internship;
- a recognized post-doctoral residency program in family psychology, *or*
- at least one post-doctoral year of supervised practice in family psychology and two graduate family practicum courses or equivalent and 40 hours of continuing education (CE) in family psychology or closely related activities. CE requirements must be within the last 5 years (American Board of Couple and Family Psychology, 2006).

APA Division of Family Psychology (43).   Although the Division 43 and APA recognize family psychology as a specialty, it has not established criteria for identifying oneself as a family psychologist. The closest it came was in a 1993 draft, which could be further developed to be an official set of criteria, along with the ABPP requirements. The *Specialty Guidelines for the Delivery of Services by Family Psychologists* (Division 43 APA, 1993) are aspirational and describe the specialty and its scope, confidentiality, and related aspects. They indicate the need for a contextual perspective, systemic assessment, and cultural competence, and quote the APA standards regarding the need for specialized training to demonstrate competence, but do not stipulate any additional requirements for becoming a competent family psychologist.

Commission for the Recognition of Specialties and Proficiencies in Professional Psychology.   The Commission (CRSPPP) defines a specialty as follows:

> A specialty is a defined area of psychological practice that requires advanced knowledge and skills acquired through an organized sequence of education and training. The advanced knowledge and skills specific to a specialty are obtained subsequent to the acquisition of core scientific and professional foundations in psychology. (CRSPPP, 1995)

In similar fashion, CRSPPP was established to coordinate specialization in professional psychology, upon petition by organizations in the field. Of the 12 specialties, family psychology was recognized in 2002. CRSPPP makes a clear distinction between a comprehensive area of practice obtained at the postgraduate level (a specialty), and a technique or proficiency. This relates to this author's delineation as set forth in an article differentiating theories and techniques (Patterson, 1998). In essence, theoretical foundations provide a framework to guide the clinician's basic philosophy of human growth and change, and the modalities involved in treatment planning, assessment, and selection of techniques. The specific *tools* (techniques) employed must be consistent with the theory base, and many techniques can be used across theories. For example, Bowenian family therapy is based on psychodynamic theory, while a key technique, the genogram, is useful in all forms of family therapy. On the other hand, psychodynamic orientations do not generally view the behavior exchange and problem-solving techniques of behavior couple therapy as appropriate.

APA Commission on Accreditation. The Commission on Accreditation (CoA) now accredits doctoral graduate programs and pre- and post-doctoral internships in (a) clinical, (b) counseling, (c) school psychology, (d) other developed practice areas, and (e) combinations of two or three of those areas (CoA, 2008). To date, the CoA has not recognized family psychology as a domain of accreditation, although it can qualify within the fourth category above, or be an emphasis within the first three categories.

Allied clinical standards and research

It should be clear by now that neither research nor prevailing practice in the profession has provided much information or experience to establish clarity on the question of competence in family psychology or most other specialty areas in the field. Various standards described above show that family psychology has progressed in all of its modalities to an advanced level, and the experience of both trainees and advanced clinicians can attest to the complexity and skill involved in effectively implementing valid approaches and techniques. It remains imperative for family psychologists to remain abreast of empirical studies and best practices in the field (see Alexander, Holtzworth-Munroe, & Jameson, 1993; Liddle, Santisteban, Levant, & Bray, 2002; and many chapters in this volume). Ultimately, aside from a summons to provide information to a licensing board or ethics committee, or a court order, it is up to the psychologist's conscience to fulfill the ethical mandate to be competent when engaging in the modalities of family psychology.

Legal statutes and community standards

State psychology licensees are variously designated, generally as "psychologist," with some states allowing the use of the term "clinical" or "counseling." Generally, state licensure guidelines do not provide any more specific criteria for competence than ethics codes, nor do most professional associations, and both describe competence in specialties as a necessity that must be demonstrated when the clinician is called upon to do so. While 50 states license marriage and family counselors, 49 (the exception is California) license professional counselors (with a few allowing for a specialty designation), and all states license psychologists almost exclusively at the doctoral level (Vermont is one exception allowing master's licensees). Thus, licensure regulations in all of the mental health professions include couple and family therapy within their scope of practice; it is up to the clinician to demonstrate competence. This is a floating standard that is generally enforced only when clear harm results from incompetence.

> *Margarita Yousaffa is a licensed psychologist who has been a practicing clinician for 10 years. Her state licensing statutes designate only the title "psychologist" with a broad scope of practice, and indicate that competence must be demonstrated. She had two couple and two family therapy courses in her doctoral program, and a few cases with supervision and some in-service training in couple therapy in her internship and post-doctoral training. She takes at least one*

third of her continuing education courses in couple therapy and participates in a bimonthly peer consultation group with some ABPP family psychologists. Although she does not consider herself a specialist, she treats couples periodically. Is Dr. Yousaffa practicing couple therapy ethically?

(Please see proposed competence levels at end of chapter. These are intended to help the reader render a judgment regarding competence in these vignettes.)

Training and experience

Most doctoral programs today offer one to four courses which may constitute a "track" in family psychology, along with accompanying practica (see Chapter 9, this volume, for a thorough review of doctoral education in family psychology). These programs can be affiliated with internships that offer specialized family psychology training, although APA accreditation does not yet extend to such pre-doctoral or internship programs as family specializations per se. Externships, private institutes, and other continuing education programs have traditionally offered specialized training in family therapy, but they are fading rapidly. Settings such as these and a few master's and doctoral programs that provide progressive, comprehensive training are the best current models for training and certifying competence in the field. In addition to this type of intensive training, expert supervision, periodic consultation, and focused continuing education are means by which clinicians can develop and maintain competence.

Summary of criteria for competence in family psychology

To date, there is no formal requirement for competence or certification based on training and experience for family psychologists, except for the ABPP. In reality, psychologists who practice family psychology and do not hold the ABPP may not meet recognized standards for competency; in other words, they "just do it." In summary:

1 Sufficient clear criteria exist to indicate that family psychology is indeed a specialty area within the domains of clinical, school, and counseling psychology.
2 "Tracks" in family psychology and degrees in marriage and family therapy require specific, concentrated coursework and experience.
3 Numerous subtheories and techniques in the field indicate the need for extensive knowledge and an integrated method for applying them.
4 The experience of trainees and clinicians in treating the turmoil and confusion that often accompany couple and family cases points to a "reasonable standard" that a demonstrated level of competence is required to practice ethically in the family field.
5 The APA code and state regulations require demonstrated competence in all areas in which a member practices.

Brenda Staples, PhD, earned her degree in clinical psychology from a major APA-accredited clinical psychology program in 1975. She is known for her teaching and practice of behavior therapy, has directed programs in behavioral medicine and developmental disabilities, and has maintained an independent psychotherapy practice. When asked by a family psychologist if she works with couples, she says "I always have," and when asked where she trained replies that she relies on her experience and general theoretical foundation to guide her. Is Dr Staples competent to provide couple therapy?

Dr Staples, with no training in couple therapy, should refrain from all except the most basic, brief cases in which behavior therapy techniques can be used. If her experience can be reviewed and competence demonstrated, she should take continuing education and join a peer consultation group or obtain supervision.

It should be clear at this point that even without mandatory specialty criteria at all levels, "just doing it" because one has always done so, or because many others do the same, is not adequate justification for practicing without relevant training and experience in family psychology.

Unique Ethical Issues in Family Psychology Practice

The unique ethical issues that arise in clinical practice with couples and families will be discussed in this section, assuming that the practitioner has addressed the issue of competence as indicated above. Special issues involving bias, neutrality, change of format, informed consent, responsibility to clients, records, and secrets will be highlighted.

The role of values and culture

Values.   Couple and family therapy may require a much higher degree of openness and freedom from bias than other specialties. Narrow gender perspectives may have significant impact on our alignment and advocacy for one partner over another, and our views on childrearing may have a direct influence on the ways we work and the recommendations we make. At any given moment in therapy, we might appropriately align with one family member on an issue and leave others feeling misunderstood or even angry. Through the use of co-therapy and consultation involving complementary roles, varied backgrounds, and shared observation, we can decrease potential bias.

Universal values vs. personal biases.   The detrimental effects of imposing personal values around highly sensitive, personal, life-changing, and controversial issues are obvious. To the extent that clinicians have influence with clients, direct recommendations regarding issues such as separation and divorce, birth control and pregnancy, religious dogma and personal autonomy, traditional family loyalties and individuation, to name a few, can harm clients and result in lawsuits and ethics charges. Subtle biases in the form of disclosing personal experiences inappropriately, discussing specific options without considering others, and allowing a more verbal family member to dominate by advocating a belief or certain course of action may be equally damaging. For more on self-disclosure, see Alden (1989).

Family psychologists share universal values with all clinicians, which are especially salient in treating couples and families. These values are based on principles of autonomy, justice, and fidelity, among others, which are embodied in professional ethics codes (Beauchamp and Childress, 2001, Knapp and VandeCreek, 2006) and also serve as foundations for human rights, equality, and freedom of conscience throughout the world (Universal Declaration of Human Rights, 1997).

Integrity requires that a degree of honesty, forthrightness, and lack of deception characterize psychotherapy, consultation, teaching, and research. This principle requires adherence to full informed consent, consistency, and "doing what we say and saying what we do" as service providers. Honesty in disclosing credentials and experience, timeliness in keeping appointments, and fulfilling agreements with clients are fundamental to maintaining integrity. For clients it involves keeping agreements and providing accurate details in assessment and information disclosure in order for services to be effective. For instance, when clients withhold information about affairs or details of substance abuse, clinical intervention is sabotaged. Family and couple clinicians must then appeal to equality in sharing essential information that others need to know, and at times must terminate services when maximum benefit has been reached. A therapist who is dishonest in billing for Axis I (major DSM-IV) disorders while actually treating family dysfunction (e.g., diagnosing one family member with major depression when the criteria are not fully met) may be undermining therapy just as a client who provides false information in a child custody dispute may do. Thus, integrity becomes a *sine qua non* value for effective, ethical outcomes to occur.

Similarly, *autonomy and freedom of thought and choice* are essential for effective family psychology services to be effective. A dogmatic set of beliefs requiring individuals to follow a certain path that causes significant distress for them may be incompatible with psychotherapy principles and processes. Religions and cultures that prescribe and prohibit specific practices regarding sexuality and gender roles, cultures that require mutilation or physical punishment, and traditions that prohibit freedom of choice in selecting spouses or careers may be incompatible with therapy objectives. Our clinical skills are highly challenged when we see immigrant family members who wish to move away from home, leave the family business, and select their own marriage partners when family traditions are in conflict. Such situations may arise even when the most culturally competent therapist treats a family in which parents expect to select marriage partners for their children, and the younger generation has been acculturated into the western value of individual choice. The clinician's role is to foster clear communication and understanding, to elucidate the issues involved, and to facilitate an accommodation that is suitable for both parties. It is not the therapist's prerogative to impose or condone any specific cultural practice.

Equality and *justice* are related to the two principles above, yet have distinct implications in themselves. As family psychologists, we need to be certain that all family members have equal opportunities for expression and development of their abilities. Children need to be seen *and heard*, both men and women should be able to explore flexible gender roles, and the disabled, seniors, and all others should be assisted not only in assuming roles of which they are capable, but also in letting go of functions they need or wish to relinquish. The feminist literature informs family psychologists on the need for equality in intimate relationships and the dysfunction that can occur with inflexibility and dominance (see Rabin & Shapell, 1996).

Cultural conflicts.   Section 201 (b) of the Ethical Principles of Psychologists and Code of Conduct (APA, 2002) requires psychologists to be culturally competent. "Culture," considered in the broadest possible sense to include gender, race, ethnicity, sexual orientation, geography, socioeconomic status, disability, religion, age, immigration status, and regional affiliation, has profound implications for assessment, treatment planning, and intervention. Assessment needs to include a careful exploration of culture, and the couple or family's own perceptions of their cultural identification and assimilation into the larger society. Issues such as traditional vs. flexible gender roles, patriarchal or matriarchal authority within a family, individuation, religion as a dominating influence, and other factors have a direct bearing on the role of the therapist and the clients' motivation and capacity for change in therapy.

   Of course, respect for other cultures does not always change decisions regarding critical issues that have legal or life-changing implications, such as partner violence, child abuse, affairs, or medical matters. When these issues surface, the clinician needs to focus on safety, prevention, and crisis management while maintaining a therapeutic stance. Thus, competent couple and family therapy requires particular attention to assessment, self-awareness, objectivity, and relevant knowledge of specific subcultures.

Assessment as an ethical obligation

The requirement to conduct a thorough assessment as an ethical mandate can be accomplished through interviews, history and records reviews, tests and inventories, and observation. With multiple members involved in couple and family therapy, the use of structured forms and inventories makes this process more comprehensive and efficient. Rather than clinicians spending hours asking tedious questions or ignoring vital areas of development, history, functioning, and demographic details, these tools can assist in developing a comprehensive view of a couple or family in a short time. For a comprehensive description of couple, family, and parent–child assessment tools, see Patterson (1999), Tomlinson (2007), and Chapter 10, this volume. Family psychologists are strongly urged to use at least one form of structured assessment with couples and families, if for no other reason than to gather the most information in an efficient manner from multiple individuals, and to develop a treatment plan that adheres to high standards of competence.

Selection of treatment modality and change of format

Competent assessment and treatment planning are an integral part of ethical practice, and specialized training in family psychology is essential to be able to make such decisions.

A significant body of empirical information has been obtained from research on the need for adjunctive or separate treatment when individual clinical disorders are identified in couples or families. The question often arises regarding which treatment modality is best when co-morbid conditions exist, such as depression and couple conflict or child conduct disorder and family dysfunction (see Chapter 46, this volume). Does depression cause marital discord or do marital problems cause partners to be depressed? The answer seems to be that the relationship between problems may be bidirectional, and clinicians treating couples need to be aware of the research that informs such issues. Options may include conjoint couple therapy with a few individual sessions for informational purposes, individual therapy as an adjunct to conjoint treatment for one or both individuals, family therapy with the extended family, individual therapy for one or both partners, or no therapy at all. Decisions regarding these alternatives are based on a thorough assessment, availability of services, motivation, and the resources of the clients, and are referred to as *selection and change of format* (Gottlieb, 1995). Clinicians monitoring the progress of therapy need to be attuned to the need for shifts to another format as the need arises and to involve clients in making appropriate choices. This is a critical aspect of competence to practice ethically.

When problems related to children are presented, individually oriented therapists may select individual child therapy as the preferred treatment. There is considerable evidence that family therapy is effective with a variety of child behavior and emotional problems. Pioneers in areas such as juvenile delinquency and conduct disorders (see Chapter 22, this volume) have developed models that have been successfully implemented in a variety of settings. An underused treatment modality in family psychology is parent–child therapy, in which the primary parental figure is engaged with the child for problem-focused assessment and intervention. From a best practices perspective, it is difficult for anyone to make the argument that individual child therapy should automatically be the treatment of choice in light of the contextual variables that are always involved in the emotional and behavioral problems of children.

Couple and family therapy have also been used extensively to assess and treat substance abuse (see Chapters 26 and 45, this volume), eating disorders (see Chapter 38, this volume), and health-related issues such as cancer (Carlson, Bultz, Speca, & St-Pierre, 2000). Family psychologists can act most ethically by being aware of the research in specific areas, determining their level of competence to treat these issues, and making appropriate referrals.

Record-keeping

In light of confidentiality and in order to protect information obtained in an individual interview during conjoint therapy, separate records for each person interviewed are advised in order to prevent a spouse or another person involved in conjoint sessions from asserting his or her privilege to obtain treatment records. While there are separate considerations for Health Information Privacy and Portability Act (HIPPA) records, "commingled" or combined records do not allow for the same level of confidentiality and legal protection that individual records afford. In the event of a commingled record being subpoenaed as part of a contested divorce proceeding, discovery of such events as a terminated affair or a child conceived with another person can create crises and expose the therapist to undue risk. It is therefore advised that separate case records be kept when sessions are held with individuals as part of couple or family therapy. For a complete guide to record-keeping in family psychology, see Patterson (1998).

Full informed consent

The requirement for informed consent has regularly been emphasized in ethical and clinical forums, and family psychology deserves special consideration in this area. Ethics codes and regulatory statutes require that informed consent be given at the outset of treatment for clients to make decisions regarding their treatment. The maxim "If it isn't written, it didn't happen" is a useful guideline that applies to the need for complete documentation of services. This section discusses the aspects of informed consent that apply particularly to family psychology practice (see Bray, Shepherd, & Hays, 1985).

Systemic perspective. Informed consent guidelines recommend that clinicians provide information about their theoretical model, and include the requirement that information be provided regarding individual and family development, general functioning, and problems in a relational context. Thus, others who are directly involved in a client's relational network may be asked to be included for assessment and/or treatment, and informed consent is required for all adults and recommended for minors.

Confidentiality and secrets. Involving other individuals in treatment creates potential confidentiality dilemmas. The legal concept of *privilege* may not apply when a third party is present, as there is no guarantee that one party will keep the other client's information confidential. When individual interviews are used as adjunctive methods in assessment (as this author does regularly), it is important to assure confidentiality if relevant information is to be obtained. Disclosed critical issues such as partner violence, child abuse, affairs, secret spending or addictions, and significant history are all areas that must be dealt with sensitively by the therapist. Mandated reporting issues are necessarily excluded from confidentiality, and the therapist incurs a legal obligation as required by state law.

Some therapists take the position that they will not keep secrets and will tell the partner or other family members involved. This places the therapist at great risk for causing emotional harm and perhaps losing the case, while the potential for civil litigation looms. Anticipating situations that may arise with couples and families by stating the therapist's procedures in the informed consent is much more effective in protecting clients and minimizing risks for the therapist. A common situation is when one partner informs the couple therapist that he or she is having a current affair. This poses a dilemma, in that open communication, mutual trust, and integrity will be compromised in the couple therapy if the affair continues. The therapist who keeps the secret colludes with the client and jeopardizes the process, while disclosing it puts the therapist at risk legally and ethically. A competent therapeutic stance is to work with the client to disclose it and to facilitate discussion according to current clinical standards (see Lusterman, 1998).

Feedback, advice, and directiveness

More than in individual therapy, conjoint therapy commonly involves active methods of intervention and the perception of specific advice giving that may have unanticipated effects. Providing feedback to a couple on such issues as differences, past history, and commitment may be an important aspect of treatment, yet can also induce conflict that may have been previously stifled. Allowing a couple to argue in sessions for the purpose of observation and assessment can trigger violence or increased alienation if "cooler" emotions are not reached by the end of the hour. Intensifying emotions through Gestalt or other techniques may intimidate partners or exacerbate depression or violence, and can be especially harmful if a couple terminates therapy prematurely. Feedback offered perceptively, taking into account the emotional and cognitive states of family members, can bring awareness of difficult issues to the forefront. Sensitive questions can help clients take ownership, deflect blame from the therapist, and keep in check a directive therapist's tendency to offer solutions inappropriately or precipitously.

Referrals

Family psychologists must understand the need for referrals of individuals to a host of other providers and agencies. Some aspects of referral are mentioned in the earlier section on *change of format*, and clinicians need to refer for treatments or services they may not be competent to offer, such as sex therapy, milieu therapy, or testing. Another reason to refer clients is the need to maintain neutrality and objectivity. It may also become clear that given the resources and priorities of a family, referral with an adolescent exhibiting school behavior problems to a community multi-service agency may be more beneficial than family therapy (see Chapter 34, this volume). A community agency offering parenting classes, peer groups, tutoring, and recreational activities can provide primary support for a family, along with periodic consultation sessions with the therapist. Making relevant, timely referrals embodies the elements of competent assessment and systemic intervention that are inherent in family psychology and serves families most effectively.

Conclusion: Future Trends and Prospects

To all fellow psychologists and clinicians: imagine a professional world in which the "family field" (family psychology and family therapy) is recognized as a distinct specialty by all disciplines and professions, and common standards of competency exist. In fact, there is little disagreement at present concerning ethical and legal procedures on the basic *clinical* aspects of practice; variations are based on theoretical orientation and geography rather than professional identification (e.g., Huber, 1994). On the other hand, agreement within and among the professions on standards for competence remains elusive.

The basic foundation for competence would be a graduate degree and license in psychology, social work, counseling, psychiatry, or mental health nursing. Graduate programs would offer a "track" providing a concentration in family systems, and internships, private institutes, continuing education, and postgraduate programs would offer a certificate of specialization recognized by state licensing boards. The professions, the specialty, and consumers would designate which practitioners were qualified to provide these critical services. The field would thrive, and the need for interdisciplinary turf battles among family specialists would decline. Competency standards could be adopted without any adverse effects on any individual profession. A three-tiered set of standards similar to the following for determining competence to practice couple or family therapy in the mental health disciplines would set standards for all the professional associations to follow.

Level A: Specialists who identify as couple and family therapists or psychologists with relevant graduate coursework and supervised experience, and have a significant amount of postgraduate training and supervision in the field that would be equivalent to specialty designation as either an ABPP- or AAMFT-approved supervisor, or are certified as a family or couple therapist by state licensing boards. Continuing education would include concentrated advanced training in the field.

Level B: Clinicians who regularly see couples or families conjointly, and in addition to graduate coursework in the field obtain at least 12 hours of continuing education courses and obtain consultation specifically focused in this area each renewal period.

Level C: Practitioners who occasionally see couples or families conjointly for relatively common problems and short duration, obtain some continuing education each licensure renewal period and in focused consultation as needed, and have had some graduate-level training in the field.

A system such as this would allow the professions and the general public to identify the specific level at which a clinician practices couple or family therapy and would make it clear who meets none of these criteria. Most licensed clinicians could qualify for Level C at a minimum, and licensing boards and professional associations could specify reasonable equivalencies. The prospects for this relatively simple measure being adopted depend upon all practitioners recognizing the uniqueness of the field, and the desire for the greater good to supersede individual or disciplinary concerns.

Quong Li, PhD, has graduated from an APA-accredited clinical psychology program with a family track. He has completed 24 semester units in family psychology, 400 hours of practicum, and an internship in family psychology. He has accepted a post-doctoral APA fellowship in health psychology in family medicine, and is concurrently obtaining supervision and training to become an AAMFT-approved supervisor. His state licensure allows designation as a family specialist, and he plans to apply for the Diplomate in Couple and Family Psychology within five years, while taking 24 of his (e.g., 36 in CA) required continuing education courses in the field. His social work and counseling colleagues at the community mental health center where he is employed have pursued similar paths in their respective professions. (Dr. Li would qualify as a Level-A specialist.)

Research, theory integration, and clinical practice have provided the basis for this type of collaboration and advancement, and family psychologists are well positioned to lead the way. Family psychology and family therapy have reached an advanced level of practice, and as a specialty, licensing regulations and ethics codes require evidence of competency. Although standards exist, adherence and enforcement vary greatly. Psychologists who engage in any form of family psychology practice are encouraged to familiarize themselves with current guidelines, seek continuing education, obtain certification, and adhere to practices that will not only serve the best interests of clients, but also maintain the integrity of the profession and the specialty.

Resources

References highlighted with an asterisk* are recommended for additional reading.

References

Alden, L. E. (1989). Review of enhancing marital intimacy through facilitating cognitive self-disclosure. *Canadian Psychology/Psychologie Canadienne, 30(4),* 695–697.

*Alexander, J. F., Holtzworth-Munroe, A., & Jameson, P. B. (1993). Research on the process and outcome of marital and family therapy. In A. E. Bergin & S. L. Garfield (Eds.), *Handbook of psychotherapy and behavioral change* (4th ed., pp. 595–630). New York: Wiley.

American Board of Couple and Family Psychology. (2006). *Specialty certification in couple and family psychology.* Unpublished manuscript.

American Psychological Association. (2002). Ethical principles of psychologists and code of conduct. *American Psychologist, 57,* 1060–1073.

Beauchamp, T. L., & Childress, J. F. (2001). *Principles of biomedical ethics* (5th ed.). New York: Oxford University Press.

*Bray, J. H., Shepherd, J. N., & Hays, J. R. (1985). Legal and ethical issues in informed consent to psychotherapy. *American Journal of Family Therapy, 13,* 50–60.

Carlson, L., Bultz, B., Speca, M., & St. Pierre, M. (2000). Partners of cancer patients: I. Impact, adjustment, and coping across the illness trajectory. *Journal of Psychosocial Oncology, 18(2),* 39–63.

Commission for the Recognition of Specialties and Proficiencies in Professional Psychology (CRSPPP). (1995). *Principles for the recognition of specialties in professional psychology.* American Psychological Association. Retrieved November 21, 2007, from http://www.apa.org/crsppp/specprinciples.html

Commission on Accreditation. (2008). *Guidelines and principles for the accreditation of programs in professional psychology.* American Psychological Association. Retrieved November 21, 2007, from http://www.apa.org/ed/accreditation/G&P0522.pdf

Division 43 APA. (1993). *Specialty guidelines for the delivery of services by family psychologists.* Unpublished manuscript.

*Gottlieb, M. C. (1995). Ethical dilemmas in change of format and live supervision. In R. H. Mikesell, D. Lusterman, & S. H. McDaniel (Eds.), *Integrating family therapy: Handbook of family psychology and systems therapy* (pp. 561–570). Washington, DC: American Psychological Association.

*Huber, C. H. (1994). *Ethical, legal, and professional issues in the practice of marriage and family therapy* (2nd ed.). New York: Merrill.

Knapp, S., & VandeCreek, L. (2006). *Practical ethics for psychologists: A positive approach.* Washington, DC: American Psychological Association.

Liddle, H., Santisteban, D., Levant, R., & Bray, J. (2002). *Family psychology: Science-based interventions.* Washington, DC: American Psychological Association.

*Lusterman, D.-D. (1998). *Infidelity: A survival guide.* Oakland, CA: New Harbinger.

*Patterson, T. E. (1998). Theoretical unity and technical eclecticism: Pathways to coherence in family therapy. *American Journal of Family Therapy, 25(2),* 97–109.

*Patterson, T. E. (1999). *The couple and family clinical documentation sourcebook.* New York: Wiley.

Rabin, C. L., & Shapell, B. (1996). *Equal partners – good friends: Empowering couples through therapy.* Florence, KY: Taylor & Francis/Routledge.

Tomlinson, B. (2007). *Family assessment handbook.* Belmont, CA: Thomson Brooks/Cole.

Universal Declaration of Human Rights. (1997). *British Medical Journal, 315(7120),* 1455–1456.

13

Clinical Practice in Family Psychology

John Thoburn, Gwynith Hoffman-Robinson, Lauren J. Shelly, and Ashly J. Hagen

The Parminters presented for therapy as a family; Avery Parminter, Caucasian, age 44, and his wife, Celeste, Caucasian, age 42, and their two children: Heather, age 16, and Richie, age 14. Avery was a Certified Public Accountant for a large manufacturing company and Celeste worked in the communications department of a technology company. Richie was in the eighth grade and Heather was a junior in high school. Richie was referred for therapy by his school counselor for poor grades and a defiant attitude toward school authorities.

The Parminters are a typical family that might present for family psychological treatment and will be used in this chapter to illustrate how family psychologists work with individuals, couples, and families while embracing a systemic perspective in theory, research, and practice (see Chapter 1, this volume).

Introduction

Clinicians draw upon relevant research and theory to ensure the best in client-system care, and the practitioner acts as a clinical scientist where outcome determines scientific treatment efficacy (Goodheart, Kazdin, & Sternberg, 2006). A systems paradigm naturally flows to recursive biopsychosocial treatment, where intake, assessment, and diagnosis generate hypotheses that are shaped, interpreted, and reshaped in light of new information. Hypothesis generation occurs throughout the course of therapy, making family psychology distinctly scientific in its approach to the human condition. The Parminters' family psychologist will draw upon objective testing, clinical assessment data, and adjunctive school and medical and/or developmental data in generating hypotheses for diagnosis and treatment planning.

Family psychology recognizes the importance of therapeutic intervention in the client system at multiple entry points, engendering a sense of inclusivity about the discipline. Inclusivity leads family psychology to champion a multi-team, multi-disciplinary approach to treatment which seeks to impact the family at both the intrapersonal and interpersonal levels. Intrapersonal factors include development, personality, psychopathology, and personal strengths, while interpersonal factors include the type of communication used in relationships and the way in which communication is carried out in relationships. Traditionally, psychology has focused on intrapersonal factors to affect change outcome, but research indicates interpersonal or relationship factors consistently explain a significant percentage of variance in change (Baucom, Gordon, Snyder, Atkins, & Christensen, 2006).

When dysfunctional relationships lead to significant impairment in individual or family functioning, therapy may be required. Research indicates that family psychology tends to yield positive outcomes, and therapy, regardless of modality, is preferable to no therapy (Lebow, 2000; Snyder & Wills, 1989). Treatment in family psychology consists of referral, intake, assessment, diagnosis, treatment, and ethical considerations. These factors, their uniqueness in family psychology and how they are managed, will be considered in the following pages, with continued use of the Parminter vignette to illustrate the concepts of family psychology clinical practice.

Managing Referrals

Two important aspects of referral in family psychology are obtaining and managing referrals. The prevailing wisdom for generating referrals is to network, network, and network some more. Networking generally has the tenor of meet and greet, as therapists go into the healthcare community and seek meetings (i.e., coffee meetings) with as many therapists, healthcare providers, attorneys, case workers, managed care representatives, and spiritual figures or religious leaders as possible. Therapists also set up websites, take out advertising in the Yellow Pages, and hold open houses. While none of these attempts to generate referrals is problematic, they do not tend to represent the most efficient use of time, and they may actually contravene core principles of family psychology, that relationships form around knowing someone, not simply knowing about someone.

First, the best, and most lasting, referral sources arise not simply out of reputation, but out of relationships that foster reputation. When a therapist obtains a referral from a family physician, a school counselor, or an attorney, he or she should not write a simple thank you note, but rather, obtain a release from the client system and send a brief note of introduction, indicating the commencement of psychotherapy for the client system, and the request for collaborative input from the collateral professional that might bring greater clarity and perspective to client-system issues. Referral sources tend to respond to inclusive collegiality and often contribute useful information toward assessment and diagnosis. With the formal agreement of the client system (e.g., a signed release of consent or assent by each family member), the psychologist should continue to offer periodic reports on the status and progress of psychotherapy. Consequently, it is likely the referral source(s) will come to trust the psychologist because she or he has been committed to communication and collegiality (Patterson, Williams, Grauf-Grounds, & Chamow, 1998).

Second, a referral should be managed appropriately. Simply meeting a potential referral source will not have much affect on the likelihood of a referral in the future; however, offering to perform a service for the referral source will. For example, primary care physicians have caseloads which consist of approximately 20% psychosomatic patients who make constant demands on their limited time (Sayre, 2002). The family psychologist can provide a workshop for patients on stress reduction or pain management, thereby reducing the time the physician spends with this population. The family psychologist can also offer to consult with the physician on avoiding triangulation into family dynamics (Thoburn, Hoffman-Robinson, Shelly, & Sayre, 2008). Another example of a service the family psychologist can offer is to do an in-service for teachers on how and when to refer a child for therapy. The Parminter case offers an example:

> *The school counselor referred Richie Parminter to the family psychologist after attending a school district in-service on how to manage oppositional defiant students, given by the family psychologist. The school counselor had subsequently consulted with the psychologist regarding several of her students and had come to trust the psychologist's perspective and recommendations.*

Part of managing a referral includes recognizing the unique and inherent emphasis of family psychology on working with multi-disciplinary teams. Such teams are especially useful when working with the family court system, the school system, family medicine, or particular disorders. For example, an eating disordered client is likely to require many services:

> The most effective treatment is a multi-team approach with appropriate coordination of care, usually by a physician. Care giving team members include, but are not limited to: possible inpatient care, treating psychiatrist, individual and/or family psychologist or social worker, family therapist, nutritionist, teacher(s), school nurse, spiritual advisor, and parents. There is a need for communication between all parties working with the eating disordered individual, especially with regard to matters of referral, evaluation, diagnosis and treatment. (Thoburn & Hammond-Meyer, 2004, p. 165)

Determining the Client System

The family psychologist must make an initial determination about whether therapy is to be with an individual, couple, or family. In addition, if family therapy is the treatment modality of choice, which family members should be invited to the initial intake session? In some instances, the family unit is considered to be the client or patient (often called the client system); in other instances, an individual family member will be the client, with the other family members there to provide support for treatment. Generally, if the psychologist can get the entire family of origin to come to the first session, then she or he can organize family members according to hierarchy of importance in attendance for subsequent sessions.

It should be noted that when a family is referred by a professional, as opposed to having come to therapy on their own, the family may be resistant to the therapeutic process (Hanna & Brown, 2004). It is not uncommon for people to have ambivalent feelings about psychotherapy (i.e., fears regarding stigma, concerns about psychotherapy's efficacy, and/or denial of personal responsibility for the state of individual family members or relationships). The family psychologist may need to use motivational techniques during the referral process to heighten the felt need for psychotherapy on the part of all members of the family, insuring a greater likelihood that they will enter psychotherapy as participants and not merely observers. The clinician's goals in the initial contact are not only to motivate the family to come in for treatment, but also to acquire highly important information about the identified patient in the family. This information includes the nature of the perceived issues, the family members most involved, and what other professionals might be involved in the family's care (e.g., legal, medical, or educational). The Parminter case highlights an effective use of a family psychology intervention to draw in the identified patient, Richie, as well as other members of the family.

> During the initial phone conversation with the Parminters, the psychologist discovered that Richie was reluctant to come to therapy. The psychologist suggested that the entire family come for the first couple of sessions in order to ease Richie into the therapeutic process. The psychologist then informed the family that this would allow him to assess the entire family and determine whether Richie's issues were solely his own, or if there might be family dynamics at play as well.

In addition to identifying the client and motivating the client to come in for treatment, the family psychologist should ascertain the services for which she or he is being retained. Often the client or client system is not sure what it is they want, especially if they are acting on a professional's suggestion or a requirement from court. The psychologist should clarify these details in order to make sure that he or she is competent to perform the necessary treatment. For example, a psychologist may not be adequately trained in custody evaluation procedures and may need to refer the family to another therapist who is competent in the specified area of need. Managing such concerns is illustrated in the case example.

> The psychologist sought to ascertain what service the Parminters wanted, such as formal assessment for Richie or psychotherapy (which might include family psychotherapy). The Parminters weren't sure; they simply had acted on the school counselor's recommendation that Richie get some help. As a result, the psychologist recommended at least one family session to get a better idea about the presenting problem, any other family issues that might be contributing to the presenting problem, and any potential need for formal assessment.

Intake

The intake session is designed to provide order and structure to ongoing psychotherapy. The initial telephone contact, intake forms, clinical interview, and any objective testing should lead to comprehensive individual and family assessment. This assessment should culminate in a diagnosis for pertinent individuals and the family as a whole, providing the foundation for a cohesive treatment plan. A primary focus should be on creating a safe place where each family member can share his or her experiences in the family as transparently as possible. Because of power differentials among family members, the psychologist needs to have family members contract with one another regarding what is said in therapy, such that everyone agrees there are no recriminations when the family leaves the therapy office and returns home. The psychologist should make it clear, however, both verbally and in writing in the informed consent that she or he cannot guarantee that material presented in session will not result in recriminations outside the therapy office.

Clinical intake forms should be constructed so information for individuals and family members can be easily gathered. For example, intake forms are often constructed for individuals, but if you have a couple or family, the psychologist needs information on each person, i.e. intake information on the individual and the relationships pertinent to the presenting problem (Patterson et al., 1998). Intake forms should be designed to obtain information such as client contact information, medical history, demographics, symptoms, and psychosocial history for each family member. Signatures of consent or assent should be obtained from each family member presenting, on both the client disclosure form and the release of information form.

Assessment

There are two kinds of psychotherapy assessment: formal objective assessment and subjective clinical observation. Objective assessment in family psychology tends to include self-report measures or direct observations coded for behaviors that seek to measure generalized factors creating interpersonal profiles in contrast to a normed sample (see Chapter 10, this volume). Subjective clinical observation tends to get at the unique aspects of a particular family by focusing on specific relational patterns and interactions. Objective and subjective assessment should together create a three-dimensional, and bio-psychosocial, diagnostic picture of the family.

In family psychology, a biopychosocial assessment approaches family psychotherapy with a "gradual linking of specific types of family communication patterns to the occurrence of specific individual psychiatric disorders" (Miklowitz & Clarkin, 2003, p. 357). Additionally, biopsychosocial assessment will uncover family members' individual strengths and family resources, which may be capitalized upon in treatment. Assessment should occur at multiple levels of the family system (Grovetant & Carlson, 1989; Snyder, Cavell, & Heffer, 1995). Snyder et al. suggest approaching family assessment from the perspective of levels of systems: individual, dyadic, nuclear, and extended family systems. These systems should not be treated modally, but in concert, recognizing the recursive nature of sociality, with each subsystem affected by and affecting the others.

Assessment of individual family members should first entail an assessment of the safety of each family member and taking appropriate action where necessary to insure the safety of any member who might be in imminent danger of harm to self or others. Assessment of individual family members should also include the assessment of possible neurosis, personality disorder, or psychosis that might affect the functioning of the family as a whole. Research indicates individual family members manifesting neurosis can "pass on" the neurosis to other family members (Katz, Beach, & Joiner, 1999). Additionally, the psychologists should assess for relational conflicts between family members that affect the psychological wellbeing of individual family members. Once the psychologist has gathered developmental, psychosocial information, and information about relational conflicts between family members, the data may warrant further individual objective assessment.

A perusal of Richie's report cards through the years and speaking with his teachers indicated a pattern consistent with ADHD, suggesting that a formal ADHD assessment might be useful. The results of the assessment seemed to rule out ADHD, but did indicate elevated levels of trait anxiety and highly elevated levels of state anxiety. The psychologist began to look for family dynamics that might be contributing to anxiety in Richie's life and quickly settled on what appeared to be a strained relationship between his parents.

The next level of assessment is among dyads (such as parents) or alliances (such as one parent and a child) in the family. The therapist must assess for dysfunctional patterns of communication in dyads, such as high expressed emotion or skewed emotion; alliances dyads in the family; emotional, verbal, and/or physical aggression; amount of anxiety and avoidance in dyad attachment; positive and/or negative filters in dyad relating; conflict resolution skills; the degree of criticalness and withdrawal between dyad members; and the strengths that members bring to dyadic relationships, such as empathy, caring, and forgiveness. Dyads should also be assessed for their ability to tolerate what is unlikely to change (Gottman, 1999; Gurman & Jacobson, 2002). Objective measures used at the level of the dyad include the Marital Satisfaction Inventory (Snyder, 1981), Parenting Stress Index (Abidin, 1995), Sexual Functioning Inventory (Derogatis & Melisaratos, 1979), Child's Report of Parental Behavior Inventory (Schaefer, 1965), and Dyadic Adjustment Scale (Spanier, 1976).

The relationship between Avery and Celeste appeared to be distant and strained. Celeste frequently rolled her eyes when Avery spoke (Heather appeared to mirror her mother's contempt). At one point Richie angrily stated he thought his parents should get divorced. Avery interjected that the kids should not be concerned or involved in his relationship with Celeste. Richie retorted, "Well, tell Mom that. She's the one who told me she can't stand you and would leave if it wasn't for us kids. Don't do us any favors, OK!"

The next level of assessment of the nuclear system involves the examination of "networks of interlocking dyadic relationships" (Snyder et al., 1995, p. 171) that comprise the family. The psychologist assesses family alliances, boundaries, parenting styles, boundaries between generations, family hierarchy, roles in the family, and decision-making in the family. The family's social network also needs to be assessed. A dense, supportive social network can serve as a prophylactic against individual, dyadic, and family pathology, and a strong social network can be a repository for coping resources (Han, Kim, Lee, Pistulka, & Kim, 2007; Perry, 2006;). Equally, a family's social network can draw resources away from the family, creating heightened stress and conflict. For example, church or school activities may be perceived as sources of strength for the family, but they may require responsibilities and commitments that take members away from family life, becoming a greater source of family stress and burden, and thus creating a net loss of resources to the family. The extended system may be the source of coalitions and alliances that work for or against a family's life (Hartman, 1995).

> *Celeste often spent an hour or more on the phone with her mother every night, which was a source of irritation to Avery, who characterized his mother-in-law as a parasite on their family. While Celeste did spend a lot of time listening to her mother's complaints (mostly about her father), she was also able to complain about Avery to her mother, who would often wistfully commiserate, "why don't we just dump these two fellas, take the kids, and move to California?"*

Extended systems may be analyzed through the ecomap and genogram, offered as pictorial representations, providing measures of family and community factors that may be construed as assets or liabilities to family life. Using the ecomap or genogram, the psychologist should assess the impact on family life of multigenerational family dynamics, the school system, religious obligations, outside programs, such as sports, as well as the legal and medical systems where pertinent (McGoldrick, Gerson, & Petry, 2008).

First session assessment material

Psychosocial history of the family.   The psychosocial history provides the family psychologist with an overview of family patterns of interaction and functioning over three generations. The family psychologist looks for the major players in the family over the course of three generations: where the family lived with concomitant moves, what family members do or did for a living, any religious heritage, any major physical or psychological illnesses, any history of alcohol or substance abuse (or other compulsive behavioral patterns), any history of physical or sexual abuse, how family members died, and, most importantly, how family members get or got along with each other. The psychologist gleans information on family patterns of communication, family alliances, and specific family conflicts. Information becomes more detailed as the history moves to the present generation's relationships. The psychologist should obtain information on current members of the family: who is living at or away from home, current and previous marriages, and divorces and blended family issues if applicable. It may also be useful to have family members share specific stories about their lives, providing diagnostic value through the identification of personal life or corporate family themes. For example, having a couple describe how they met and became committed can have diagnostic value in determining the likelihood for success in couples therapy (Gottman, 1999; Mosak & Pietro, 2006; Stone & Hoffman, 2005).

Psychiatric, developmental, and medical history of the family.   The psychologist will want to obtain information on developmental issues, medical conditions, or psychiatric history that might be pertinent to treatment. For example, if the case involves behavior problems, the psychologist will want to know if there were any pertinent developmental issues such as an abnormal birth, childhood head trauma, etc. Collateral information (e.g., report cards, medical records, and/or custody reports) can be useful in fleshing out the assessment picture. Additionally, notation of previous outpatient or inpatient mental health services and the past or current use of any psychotropic medications will be helpful. Finally, as stated earlier, it is crucial to assess for suicidal or homicidal ideation.

Diagnosis

The family psychologist takes the accumulated information and synthesizes it into a cohesive diagnostic picture of the family, assigning a diagnosis for relevant individuals in the family, and a relational diagnosis for the family as a whole. The diagnosis should reflect the etiology of the disorder(s) and pathogenesis, or course of development (Maxmen & Ward, 1995). Gottlieb (1996) suggests the need for a relational diagnosis alongside personal diagnoses "when there is a dysfunctional pattern of interaction between two or more people within a system that leads to a reduced level of functioning for at least one member of the system" (p. 19). Patterson et al. (1998) have noted that "the practical, ethical, and logistical dilemmas of using both individual and family diagnosis have never been clearly delineated" (p. 173). In their argument on how to manage diagnosis, they propose the psychologist focus both on the individual diagnosis of the identified patient and on relating family processes and symptoms important to family functioning. They conclude the exigencies of third party payers frequently require individual diagnosis (e.g., treatment authorization and reimbursement); and, therefore, family psychologists must be knowledgeable about and assess for individual diagnosis. However, a contextual approach to family psychology will help family psychologists assess individual diagnosis while taking into consideration the family and its problems as a whole (Patterson et al., 1998). (See Chapter 11, this volume, for the most recent information on couple and family processes and DSM diagnosis.)

Concluding the intake.   The psychologist should take all the information gathered through objective and subjective assessment and (a) explore other, more manageable ways than those the family has used to describe or define the issues at play, (b) offer the family an initial assessment and recommendation for treatment, and (c) devise an evidence based treatment plan (goals and interventions) that treats the family's presenting problem(s) and also treats the issues derived from the family diagnosis (Hanna & Brown, 2004).

Assessment should end with the psychologist informing the client system about his or her findings. For many couples and families, entering psychotherapy is an enterprise of last resort, that is, they have most likely already tried other avenues for change and have failed (Miller, Duncan, & Hubble, 1997). Thirty to forty percent of couples do not return for second sessions with their therapists (Nichols, 1987). Waters and Lawrence (1993) point out the troubling reality in therapy that "too often we map our clients' prison, but not their escape" (p. 53); therefore the session should offer hope and end on a positive note giving the couple or family concrete tasks to accomplish, while making some plans for future sessions.

Treatment

The development of the therapeutic alliance, both with individual family members and with the family as a whole, is an important initial process that begins during assessment and continues throughout treatment. It is important to be allied with persons in the family while at the same time remaining neutral about the problems that emerge in therapy. Perlmutter (1996) suggests the psychologist take the role of a participant observer, where she or he is "both involved and objective at the same time" (p. 13). Gardner's (2000) research found that the presence of an observer does not necessarily distort the nature of family interactions, and so the psychologist can gain accurate information about the family while remaining neutral. Scaturo and McPeak (1998) defined neutrality as follows: "the psychotherapist maintains sufficient objectivity so as to not take sides with respect to the patient's internal conflict" (p. 8), and suggest that psychologists must effectively manage therapeutic boundaries. The psychologist, while a part of the inter-action in family sessions, should try to avoid siding with family members and colluding with the targeting of the identified patient. Consequently, the psychologist may need to be more directive than he or she would be in individual therapy. All of these methods help create a healthy therapeutic boundary. Additionally, the psychologist can use his or her position as participant observer to track interactional sequences and foster bonds between family members (Hanna & Brown, 2004; Kaslow, 2001).

Difference between individual and family treatment.   It should be noted that there are significant differences between individual and family treatment. While the development of a therapeutic alliance, with concomitant transference and counter-transference, is import-ant, there will be a difference when family members are actually present in the session. There will be a greater focus on the transference and counter-transference that take place between family members, rather than between the individual and the psychologist. Thus, the emphasis of treatment becomes how family members might treat each other in more healthful ways.

In individual treatment, the client is generally focused on his or her own need for change; however, in family treatment, the initial focus of family members tends to be on the need for other members to change. One of the goals of family psychology is to change this focus to one of personal responsibility. In individual therapy, the psycholo-gist must make inferences regarding family dynamics from the client's description (which is going to be biased). On the other hand, in family psychology, the psychologist can directly observe functional and dysfunctional patterns of interpersonal exchange, and the impact of family members on each other. In individual psychology, the client therapist relationship is at the heart of the talking cure; and while absent family members may influence the therapy session through the client's transference or counter-transference, they remain "ghosts" involved behind the scene (Nichols, 1987). However, in family psychology, relational dynamics increase exponentially with multiple family members in the therapy office and can easily lead to the psychologist feeling overwhelmed (Patterson et al., 1998). The family psychologist must be more directive than the individual therapist because he or she typically deals with a more emotionally charged atmosphere due to the greater number of people and alliances in the room.

> *At the psychologist's request, each of the Parminters shared why they believed they were there and what they hoped to get from being in therapy. Avery and Celeste indicated they were concerned about Richie's grades. Celeste expressed chagrin at Richie's oppositional behavior, while Avery did not seem very concerned; in fact, Avery seemed somewhat proud that Richie was "taking on" school officials. Celeste appeared annoyed by Avery's "cavalier" attitude about Richie's behavior, and after she finished castigating him for encouraging Richie's behavior, there was an uncomfortable silence. Heather shared that she thought that Richie was just going through a phase and would grow out of his present behavior. "He's a good guy," she said. Avery interjected jokingly, "No, you're the angel and Richie is the devil – we made you that way." Heather glanced at him with something akin to contempt and kept talking to the therapist. When the therapist inquired about her look and feelings about her father and what he said, she flatly stated, "You can't take anything Dad says seriously." The psychologist suggested, "Why don't you tell your dad what you just said to me?"*

The corrective emotional experience. All therapy, including family therapy, should lead to cognitive restructuring, greater affective processing and regulation, behavioral change, increased communication and intimacy, and differentiation of self for all family members, including the identified patient. When a client system is distorting reality, simple exposure to a healthy or realistic environment is not by itself an adequate remedy. To change, a couple or family must be exposed to a corrective emotional experience, not simply a description of one. The psychologist can use the therapy sessions to guide the family toward the corrective emotional experience. To begin the corrective emotional experience, psychologists use probes, clarification, modeling, reframing, softening, and interpretation in uncovering and explaining difficult-to-access feelings, beliefs, and expectations contributing to current observable client-system difficulties (Snyder & Wills, 1989). The psychologist seeks to make overt that which is covert. Specifically, the psychologist seeks to make thoughts, feelings, and beliefs that are either totally or partially beyond awareness overt, so that these can be restructured or renegotiated at a conscious level. Emphasis is placed on working through or processing those difficulties at behavioral, cognitive, affective, and relational levels (Snyder & Wills, 1989). A number of specific, evidence-based approaches to treatment are detailed in the subsequent chapters of this Handbook. Exploring client experiences allows all family members the opportunity to explain their thoughts, feelings, actions, and intentions, described as "interactional sequences of each person's perception of the problem over time" (Hanna & Brown, 2004, p. 136).

The therapist was able to gently point out to the family that Richie's behavior problems and decline in grades were due in part to his being placed in the position of the "devil" child juxtaposed over and against Heather's role as the "angel". The therapist facilitated functional emotional confrontation between Richie and his parents, where he broke down and indicated that he felt trapped in a no-win role. His parents expressed remorse to both Richie and his sister. The children were also able to express their fears about their parents' relationship, and all were surprised to realize how much the fear of a breakup occupied their thoughts.

Ethics

There are ethical issues and dilemmas unique to family psychology. The family psychologist must truly embrace the American Psychological Association's aspirational principles as well as the relevant codes in order to make ethical decisions when working with a client system on issues such as determining the client system, confidentiality, and disclosure. We will comment briefly on two ethical issues we experience most frequently in the practice of family psychology (see Chapter 12, this volume, for a comprehensive discussion of family psychology ethics).

Determining the client.   The family psychologist must have a clear sense of how he or she personally views systemic therapy prior to entering into a therapeutic alliance with the familial unit or each individual within the familial unit. The American Psychological Association's 2002 Ethics Code states,

> When psychologists agree to provide services to several persons who have a relationship (such as spouses, significant others, or parents and children), they take reasonable steps to clarify at the outset (1) which of the individuals are clients/patients and (2) the relationship the psychologist will have with each person. (p. 15)

At the very least, the therapist must make sure that improvement in one family member does not occur at the expense of another family member (Snyder & Doss, 2005).

Snyder and Doss (2005) suggest four approaches a psychologist can take in order to prevent ethical dilemmas when determining who exactly constitutes the client. First, the psychologist can treat each family member as if he or she were being treated as an individual, a stance that would best serve the interests of each family member individually. Second, the psychologist could view only the marital or familial system as the client and consequently refuse to form an alliance with any single individual, as the focus would be on the marital relationship or familial relationships for treatment. Third, the psychologist has the option of shifting her or his alliances between individuals and the relationships on the basis of his or her judgment. A final option that the psychologist could utilize is to strictly follow the family's or couple's goals and formulate a treatment plan based on those specific goals. The family psychologist must make it clear to the client(s) if the psychologist decides to switch his or her view of who constitutes the client during the course of treatment.

Secrets.   There is perhaps no greater ethical dilemma faced by family psychologists than how to deal with the disclosure of family secrets during the course of therapy. Snyder and Doss (2005) suggest four different methods for dealing with confidentiality within couple and family therapy. First, the psychologist can decide to treat all information disclosed individually as confidential. A second approach is to consider no information, regardless of whether shared individually or in the course of joint therapy, as confidential. Another alternative is for the therapist to keep certain information confidential as a matter of privacy due to the sensitive nature of the disclosure. A final approach to confidentiality is for the psychologist and the client(s) to agree to keep certain information confidential until a later date. In order to avoid ethical dilemmas, the psychologist must inform the client system of how he or she will handle confidential disclosures.

Conclusion

The family psychologist may see individuals, couples, or families, but all work is done utilizing a systems paradigm. Referral, assessment, and diagnosis are made with a biopsychosocial attitude, recognizing the utility of engaging the entire client system in therapy. Treatment embraces a multi-team and multi-discipline approach (i.e., the psychologist recognizes that she or he is embedded in a healthcare context and utilizes the full resources of that context in the pursuit of health and wholeness for clients).

Resources

Fischer, J., & Corcoran, K. (2007). *Measures for clinical practice and research: A sourcebook two-volume set.* Oxford: Oxford University Press.
Fredman, N., & Sherman, R. (1987). *Handbook of measurements for marriage and family therapy.* Philadelphia: Brunner/Mazel.
Genopro. *Introduction to the genogram.* http://www.genopro.com/genogram
Smart Draw. *Genogram & Ecomap.* http://www.smartdraw.com/specials/genogram.htm
Snyder, D. K. *Marital Satisfaction Inventory, Revised (MSI-R).* Los Angeles: Western Psychological Services. http://portal.wpspublish.com/portal/page?_pageid=53,103808&_dad=portal&_schema=PORTAL

References

Abidin, R. R. (1995). *Parenting Stress Index* (3rd ed.). Lutz, FL: Psychological Assessment Resources.
American Psychological Association. (2002). Ethical principles of psychologists and code of conduct. *American Psychologist, 57,* 1060–1073.

Baucom, D. H., Gordon, K. C., Snyder, D. K., Atkins, D. C., & Christensen, A. (2006). Treating affair couples: Clinical considerations and initial findings. *Journal of Cognitive Psychotherapy: An International Quarterly, 20,* 375–392.

Derogatis, L. R., & Melisaratos, N. (1979). The DSFI: A multidimensional measure of sexual functioning. *Journal of Sex and Marital Therapy, 5,* 244–281.

Gardner, F. (2000). Methodological issues in the direct observation of parent–child interaction: Do observational findings reflect the natural behavior of participants? *Clinical Child and Family Psychology Review, 3,* 185–198.

Goodheart, C. D., Kazdin, A. E., & Sternberg, R. J. (2006). *Evidence-based psychotherapy: Where theory and practice meet.* Washington, DC: American Psychological Association.

Gottlieb, M. C. (1996). Some ethical implications of relational diagnoses. In F. W. Kaslow (Ed.), *Handbook of relational diagnosis and dysfunctional family patterns* (pp. 19–34). Oxford: Wiley.

Gottman, J. M. (1999). *The marriage clinic: A scientifically based marital therapy.* New York: Norton.

Grovetant, H. D., & Carlson, C. I. (1989). *Family assessment: A guide to methods and measures.* New York: Guilford Press.

Gurman, A. S., & Jacobson, N. S. (2002). *Clinical handbook of couple therapy* (3rd ed.). New York: Guilford Press.

Han, H. R., Kim, M., Lee, H. B., Pistulka, G., & Kim, K. B. (2007). Correlates of depression in the Korean American elderly: Focusing on personal resources of social support. *Journal of Cross-Cultural Gerontology, 22,* 115–127.

Hanna, S. M., & Brown, J. H. (2004). *The practice of family therapy* (3rd ed.). Belmont, CA: Brooks/Cole-Thomson Learning.

Hartman, A. (1995). Diagrammatic assessment of family relationships. *Families in Society, 76,* 111–122.

Kaslow, F. W. (2001). Whither countertransference in couples and family therapy? A systemic perspective. *Journal of Clinical Psychology, 57,* 1029–1040.

Katz, J., Beach, S., R. H., & Joiner, T. E. (1999). Contagious depression in dating couples. *Journal of Social and Clinical Psychology, 18,* 1–13.

Lebow, J. (2000). What does the research tell us about couple and family therapies? *Journal of Clinical Psychology, 56,* 1083–1094.

Maxmen, J. S., & Ward, N. G. (1995). *Essential psychopathology and its treatment.* New York: Norton.

McGoldrick, M., Gerson, R., & Petry, S. (2008). *Genograms: Assessment and intervention.* New York: Norton.

Miklowitz, D. J., & Clarkin, J. F. (2003). Diagnosis of family relational disorders. In G. Sholevar & L. D. Schwoeri (Eds.), *Textbook of family and couples therapy* (pp. 341–363). Washington, DC: American Psychiatric Publishing.

Miller, S. D., Duncan, B. L., & Hubble, M. A. (1997). *Escape from Babel: Toward a unifying language for psychotherapy practice.* New York: Norton.

Mosak, H. H., & Pietro, R. D. (2006) *Early recollections: Interpretative method and application.* New York: Routledge.

Nichols, M. P. (1987). *The self in the system: Expanding the limits of family therapy.* New York: Brunner/Mazel.

Patterson, J., Williams, L., Grauf-Grounds, C., & Chamow, L. (1998). *Essential skills in family therapy: From the first interview to termination.* New York: Guilford Press.

Perlmutter, R. A. (1996). *A family approach to psychiatric disorders.* Washington, DC: American Psychiatric Press.

Perry, B. L. (2006). Understanding social network disruption: The case of youth in foster care. *Social Problems, 53,* 371–391.

Sayre, G. (2002). *The psychosomatic marriage: An empirical study.* Unpublished dissertation, Seattle Pacific University.

Scaturo, D. J., & McPeak, W. R. (1998). Clinical dilemmas in contemporary psychotherapy: The search for clinical wisdom. *Psychotherapy, 35,* 1–12.

Schaefer, E. S. (1965). Children's reports of parental behavior: An inventory. *Child Development, 32,* 413–424.

Snyder, D. K. (1981). *Marital satisfaction inventory.* Los Angeles: Western Psychological Services.

Snyder, D. K., Cavell, T. A., & Heffer, R. W. (1995). Marital and family assessment: A multi-faceted, multilevel approach. In R. H. Mikesell, D-D. Lusterman, & S. H. McDaniel (Eds.), *Integrating family therapy: Handbook of family psychology and systems theory* (pp. 163–182). Washington, DC: American Psychological Association.

Snyder, D. K., & Doss, B. D. (2005). Treating infidelity: Clinical and ethical directions. *Journal of Clinical Psychology, 61,* 1453–1465.

Snyder, D. K., & Wills, R. M. (1989). Behavioral versus insight-oriented marital therapy: Effects on individual and interspousal functioning. *Journal of Consulting and Clinical Psychology, 57,* 39–46.

Spanier, G. B. (1976). Measuring dyadic adjustment: New scales for assessing the quality of marriage and similar dyads. *Journal of Marriage and the Family, 38,* 15–28.

Stone, M. H., & Hoffman, N. M. (2005). Borderline states and individual psychology. In A. Freeman, M. H. Stone, & D. Martin (Eds.), *Comparative treatments for borderline personality disorder* (pp. 133–149). New York: Springer.

Thoburn, J., & Hammond-Meyer, A. (2004). Eating disorders. In F. M. Kline & L. B. Silver (Eds.), *The educator's guide to mental health issues in the classroom* (pp. 141–170). Baltimore, MD: Paul Brooks.

Thoburn, J., Hoffman-Robinson, G., Shelly, L., & Sayre, G. (2008). *Collaborative treatment for the psychosomatic couple.* Manuscript submitted for publication. Seattle Pacific University.

Waters, D. B., & Lawrence, E. C. (1993). *Competence, courage, and change: An approach to family therapy.* New York: Norton.

14

Solution-Focused Brief Therapy

Stephen Cheung

Solution-focused brief therapy (SFBT) has been one of the most popular approaches in the current managed care environment because of its emphasis on a non-pathological view of individuals, its focus on brief treatment, and its easily teachable skills. In contrast to traditional therapies, SFBT stresses an egalitarian relationship between the therapist and the client that truly empowers the client. It further posits that language is the primary vehicle for change, and therefore engages the client in a therapeutic conversation from the beginning of therapy to help the client to explore and construct new meanings in his life. Because it provides a clear and concrete guideline for treatment, SFBT has been widely well received by clinicians (Becvar & Becvar, 2006; Cheung, 2005; Goldenberg & Goldenberg, 2008; Nichols & Schwartz, 2008). The rapid increase in the number of therapists that practice SFBT is evidenced by the websites of the Solution Focused Brief Therapy Association (www.sfbta.org) and the European Brief Therapy Association (www.ebta.nu) (see Resources below).

The leading figures of SFBT were Steve de Shazer (1985, 1988, 1991, 1994) and Insoo Kim Berg (1994), a husband-and-wife team, who were the main proponents of this approach from the mid-1980s. They co-founded the Brief Family Therapy Center (BFTC) in Milwaukee, Wisconsin, where they researched and developed SFBT and trained many national and international clinicians in this approach. Unfortunately de Shazer passed away in September, 2005, and Berg in January, 2007. Other proponents and prolific writers of SFBT include Scott Miller (1994), Michele Weiner-Davis (1993), Eve Lipchik (1993, 2002), and Bill O'Hanlon (1993a, 1993b). The first three individuals were at one time or another affiliated with the BFTC. Scott Miller continues to direct alcohol and drug treatment there and practices in Chicago. Michele Weiner-Davis, after leaving the BFTC, continues to practice SFBT in Woodstock, Illinois. Eve Lipchik has discussed and advocated the importance of affect in SFBT and continues to practice in Milwaukee. Bill O'Hanlon, who co-authored with Michele Weiner-Davis an influential book titled *In search of solutions* (2003), used to call his approach solution-oriented therapy, but renamed it possibility therapy. He maintains his practice in Santa Fe, New Mexico (Goldenberg & Goldenberg, 2008; O'Hanlon & Weiner-Davis, 2003).

With the aforementioned proponents and many others, SFBT fits well with, and contributes much to, family psychology for several reasons. First, espousing the epistemology of social constructionism, SFBT focuses on co-constructing meaning and solutions with one's client in her contexts, and therefore moves family psychology along in the postmodern era. Second, it focuses on the reciprocal relationship between the client and her interpersonal contexts by asking questions that address the recursive interactions and perceptions between the client and her intimates; it is therefore amendable to not only individual, but also couples and family therapy. Third, because it is parsimonious and pragmatic in its theorizing and clinical applications, it is highly effective and efficient in helping the client with her presenting problems.

This chapter will first review briefly the existing theoretical, clinical, and research literature on SFBT. Then it will discuss the clinical applications of SFBT, with an illustrative example of a couple. The chapter will conclude with recommendations for future research, theory-building, and clinical applications of SFBT. Helpful resources will be highlighted in the clinical resource box at the end of the chapter.

Review of Theoretical, Clinical, and Research Literature on SFBT

SFBT was first influenced by the brief therapy model of the Mental Research Institute (MRI) and Milton Erickson's strategic therapy, and subsequently by social constructionism.

Theoretical literature: worldviews, assumptions, and key concepts

SFBT was formulated in the context of western cultural worldviews of individualism and emphasizes heavily the wellbeing of the individual. In stark contrast to most deficit therapeutic models, SFBT begins with some refreshing assumptions: (a) individuals are healthy and competent; (b) they have the innate capacity to construct solutions and meanings that can enhance their lives; (c) nonetheless, they have lost sight of these abilities because their problems appear so large to them that their strengths are crowded out of the picture. According to de Shazer (1985, 1991), individuals do not resist change; they in fact want to change.

Originally trained in the MRI brief therapy model to focus on the interactional sequence of the problem and solutions, de Shazer decided to depart from it as he evolved as a theoretician and clinician. He helped clients to concentrate exclusively on solutions that have worked in the past or will work in the future, as opposed to MRI therapists' attempts at zooming in on the interactional context of the client's presenting problems with an eye on discovering problematic attempted solutions.

Although he was influenced by Milton Erickson's strategic therapy, de Shazer decided not to adhere to structuralism, which claims that symptoms are a sign of some underlying problem and imply a cause-and-effect relationship between the underlying problem and symptoms. Instead, he became a poststructuralist and introduced the concept that the solution does not need to have any relationship to the problem; in other words, the set of variables that contribute to the formation of a problem can be totally different from the set of variables that will help to solve the problem. The notion that the solution of a problem can be non-problem-specific liberates the therapist and the client from the rigid thinking that one has to find the cause of the problem in order to solve the problem. Consequently, the therapist and the client can be more creative and client-directed in their search for problem resolution.

As he evolved, de Shazer was influenced by social constructionism. Social construc-tivism expands on constructivism, which argues that we cannot perceive true objective reality and that what is perceived is influenced by the assumptions we make about the world around us, including other people, objects, events, and our relationship with them. Social constructionism further asserts that the reality we construct "is mediated through language, and is socially determined through our relationships with others and the culture's shared set of assumptions" (Goldenberg & Goldenberg, 2008. p. 21). There are several implications of social constructionism for a therapist. First, the therapist and his client both bring their assumptive framework to analyze and interpret a situation; the therapist should not confuse it with the way the situation really is. Second, he should not regard what he sees in a family as existing in the family, but should understand it is the product of his own assumptions about people, problems, and families as well as his interactions with them. Third, the client knows her life the best and is its expert; her therapy should therefore be directed by her.

Because de Shazer believed that the client already has the ability and knows what she needs to do to solve the problem, the main treatment goal of SFBT is to help the client construct a new use of her existing abilities and resources. The way to achieve this is to help the client to start the solution-building process. De Shazer maintains that one can-not change one's past, but one can change one's goals. Better goals can get one out of one's stuck places and can lead one into a more fulfilling future. Much of the work for SFBT lies in the negotiation of well-formed and achievable therapeutic goals. Rather than changing personality and psychopathology types, SFB therapists help clients construct well-formed goals (Berg & de Shazer, 1993; de Shazer, 1991). Well-formed therapeutic goals have the following characteristics:

1   The goal is important to the client.
2   The goal can be stated in interactional terms. For example, the goal would include what difference others will notice about the client as she moves toward her thera-peutic goal.
3   The goal should not be too global, but should specify a targeted context (e.g., place and setting).
4   The goal should specify some desirable behaviors rather than the absence of problems.
5   The goal will state a beginning step rather than the final result.

6 The client recognizes a role for herself.
7 The goal will be stated in concrete, behavioral, and measurable terms.
8 The goal is realistic and achievable.
9 The goal will be a challenge to the client. (De Jong & Berg, 2008, pp. 77–83)

De Shazer and his associates decided to not just use highly clever and well-designed interventions; instead, they chose to stay with the client in discovering his innate resources and successful solutions. They believe that a simple shift in focus from what is not going well to what the client is already doing that works can remind him, and expand the use, of his resources (Berg & Miller, 1992; de Shazer, 1985, 1988, 1991, 1994). To be client-driven, de Shazer and his associates focus only on the complaints clients themselves present, remain "not knowing," and help the clients reexamine the ways they describe themselves and their problems.

Before a review of the clinical literature on SFBT, it is expedient to highlight several crucial theoretical principles. First, although there are clear guidelines for treatment, the philosophy of co-constructing solutions and reality with their clients inherently propels what the SFB therapist does in a therapy session. Without fully embracing this philosophy, the many ingenious and powerful techniques will be ineffective. Second, while change of perception and cognition has remained the major focus of SFBT since its inception, the emphasis on emotions has recently been articulated and accentuated (Lipchik, 2002). Rather than being formulaic and adhering rigidly to the therapeutic procedures of SFBT, it is advocated that the therapist be in tune with the client's feelings, empathizing and validating them in the sessions. Third, it was proposed that the problem talk by the client be shifted as soon as possible to solution talk. However, Cheung cautioned not to shift from problem talk to solution talk too quickly because this can be construed as minimizing the client's suffering and disrespecting the client (2001, 2005).

Clinical literature: Therapeutic goals, content, process, and techniques

The goals and contents of SFBT therapy revolve around resolution of the client's presenting complaints. SFBT begins by understanding the presenting complaints from the client's perspective. Then the SFB therapist helps the client construct his or her solutions.

The process of solution-building involves these stages: (1) describing the problem; (2) developing well-formed goals; (3) exploring for exceptions; (4) formulating and delivering feedback to clients; and (5) measuring and amplifying client progress. First, in the stage of describing the problem, the therapist asks, "How can I be useful to you?" and listens respectfully to the client's problem talk. Second, the therapist elicits descriptions of what will be different in the client's life when his or her problems are solved in the stage of developing well-formed goals. Third, in the stage of exploring for exceptions, the therapist inquires about the times in the client's life when his problems are not happening or are less severe. Here the therapist asks for specific information such as who did what to whom to make the exception happen. Fourth, the therapist constructs and delivers a message to the client that includes compliments and some suggestions in the stage of end-of-session feedback. Last, in the stage of evaluating client progress, the therapist asks the client to rate his progress on a scale of 0 to 10. This is done regularly throughout the course of therapy (De Jong & Berg, 2008, pp. 17–19).

Pre-session change.   Sometimes, setting an appointment may itself facilitate change. To capitalize on the client's existing strengths and resources, a question like this is asked:

> It is our experience that many people notice that things are better between the time they set up an appointment and the time they come in for the first session. Have you noticed such changes in your situation? (Berg & Miller, 1992, p. 72)

This question sets up an expectation and assumption that it is quite normal and expected that their serious problems may have eased a bit since they made the appointment. Rather than rigidly adhering to the format of immediately asking a direct question about any pre-session changes in the beginning of the first session, this question, like any useful question, should be asked judiciously.

Description of solution-building interview.   In the first session the SFB therapist clarifies the role of the team and that the team may interrupt by inputting their ideas to the therapist via intercom or computer monitor during the session. Then she explains the structure of the therapy, which includes the first half of the interview, an intermission, and a feedback section at the end of the session. The explication of the interview process is aimed at abating client anxiety and providing informed consent. The therapist asks about the client's concern or problem and expresses a wish to help. Listening to the client's description of problems and concerns is of paramount importance. The client's perception and feelings of the problems are acknowledged, empathized with, and validated. Then, to formulate treatment goals, a question is asked: "What would have to be different as a result of our meeting today for you to say that our talking was worthwhile?" (De Jong & Berg, 2008, p. 352).

The purpose of this question is to elicit specific description of a therapeutic goal from the client. The therapist asks follow-up questions to make the goal more specific, concrete, interactional, and behaviorally measurable. To further help the client to specify the goal, a miracle question is asked:

> Suppose that, when you are sleeping tonight, a miracle happens. The miracle is that the problem which brought you here today is solved. Only you don't know that it is solved because you are asleep. What difference will you notice tomorrow morning that will tell you that a miracle has happened? What else will you notice? (De Jong & Berg, 2008, p. 354)

After the client has answered the questions above, the therapist focuses on what differences the client's significant others will notice when the miracle happens. She further amplifies the client's perception around the client's system of relationships by asking the following questions:

When your husband (children, best friend, co-workers, teachers, etc.) notice _____ (the difference that the client mentions), what will your husband (they) do differently? What else? And when he does that, what will you do? And when you do that, what else will be different? (De Jong & Berg, 2008, p. 355)

All the questions asked above are intended to elicit the client's detailed description of perceptions and actions about the future goal wherein the problem is solved. The purpose of this kind of questioning is to help the client to form some small, specific, concrete, and behavioral therapeutic goals that involve "the beginning/presence of something different/better" (De Jong & Berg, 2008, p. 354). Moreover, this helps the client focus on future goals, engenders hope, and empowers him to face the future. For more details on how to ask these questions and problem solve when the client cannot work with the miracle question, please refer to the appendix on Solution-Building Tools (pp. 351–356) of De Jong and Berg's (2008) book *Interviewing for solutions.*

In some situations, a scaling question is asked to invite the client to put observations, impressions, and predictions on a scale from 0 to 10. It can be used to access the client's perception of many things, including "self-esteem, presession change, self-confidence, prioritizing of problems to be solved, perception of hopefulness, and evaluation of progress" (Berg, 1994, p. 107). For instance:

I'd like you to put some things on a scale for me, on a scale from 0 to 10. First, on a scale from 0 through 10, where 0 equals the worst your problems have been and 10 means the problems we have been talking about are solved, where are you today on that scale? (De Jong & Berg, 2008, p. 15)

After 30–40 minutes of interview, there is an intermission of 10–20 minutes. During the intermission, the therapist consults the team and comes up with feedback for the client. This typically includes compliments and bridges to suggestions. Certainly, the type of feedback depends on the client's motivation, the problems brought into the session, and the relationship with the therapist. There are guidelines and a protocol for formulating feedback to different types of clients (De Jong & Berg, 2008, pp. 125–126, 357). Furthermore, there are several categories of common end-of-session feedback messages (De Jong & Berg, 2008, pp. 126–138, 358–361). When the client perceives a problem and can identify exceptions that are due to someone else doing something different, but does not find a role for herself in a solution, one common feedback messages is:

Alice, pay attention to those times when your boss is more reasonable and open. Besides paying attention to what's different about those times, pay attention to what he might notice you doing that helps him to be more polite, reasonable, and open toward you. Keep track of those things and come back and tell me what's better.

A variation adds the element of prediction:

Alice, I agree with you; there clearly seem to be days when your boss is more reasonable and open and days when he is not. So, between now and the next time that we meet, I suggest the following: Each night before you go to bed, predict whether or not tomorrow will be a day when he acts reasonable and open and polite to you. Then, at the end of the day, before you make your prediction for the next day, think about whether or not your prediction for that day came true. Account for any differences between your prediction and the way the day went and keep track of your observations so that you can come back and tell me about them. (de Shazer, 1988, pp. 179–183)

The subsequent sessions focus on what is happening that is better and continue with the solution-building process. The therapist proceeds with EARS, an acronym for the following activities:

Elicit more information from your client about what is happening that is better
Amplify the successes/solutions by asking "how does that happen?" or "What do you do to make that happen?"
Reinforce/compliment the client: "Not everyone could have said or done _____. So you're the kind of person who is/does/ believes _____?"
This is to highlight the client's success and future possibility.
Start again: "What else is better?"

In addition to these themes for exploration, the therapist can encourage the client to do more of what makes things better by asking:

"What will it take to do _____ again? To do it more often?" Furthermore, if nothing is better, the therapist can ask: "How are you coping? How do you make it? How come things aren't even worse?" (De Jong & Berg, 2008, p. 364)

Finally, SFB therapists have five practical guides to therapeutic choices for the therapist and the client:

1 If it works, don't fix it. Choose to do more of it.
2 If nothing seems to be working, choose to experiment, including imagining miracles.
3 Keep the intervention simple.
4 Choose to approach each session as if it were the last. Change starts now, not next week.
5 There is no failure, only feedback. (Walter & Peller, 1992, pp. 37–41)

It is reported that SFBT has been applied to various populations in divergent settings with success in the past two decades (De Jong & Berg, 2008; Miller, Hubble, & Duncan, 1996). Research support for the efficaciousness of the SFBT will be reviewed in the next section.

Research literature on the efficacy of SFBT

De Jong and Berg (2008) concisely summarized the research on the efficacy of SFBT to date. There are preliminary research data to support the effectiveness of SFBT

(Gingerich & Eisengart, 2000, 2001; McKeel, 1996, 1999). Nevertheless, some of the critiques include the fact that very few studies have used comparison groups, random assignment to treatment conditions, and strong and varied outcome measures (Franklin, 2006; Franklin & Streeter, 2006; McKeel, 1999).

One of the challenges of conducting well-controlled research is the need for a manualized description of SFBT to ensure that clinicians in the research study are adhering to the generally accepted practice standard of SFBT. As of this writing, members of the European Brief Therapy Association and the Solution Focused Brief Therapy Association are creating a manual for solution-focused therapy for use in future research.

Mckeel (1996, 1999) made several research recommendations that include more collaboration between researchers and clinicians because research will inform and validate practice. Second, he recommended more process research that investigates the relationship between positive outcomes and specific SFBT techniques. He also recommended more qualitative research in SFBT; in fact, he stated: "Using both the qualitative and quantitative research strategies . . . will allow the consumer of research to benefit from the rich qualitative description as well as to gain the information about generalizability that quantitative studies provide" (p. 266).

Diversity in SFBT

As summarized above, SFBT has been reportedly applied to a myriad of populations with success. Research has shown some preliminary support of its effectiveness when it is applied to clients who come from the same cultural context as the SFBT, but its effective application to culturally diverse populations has yet to be determined. On a theoretical level, because the approach is so rooted in individualistic cultural worldviews, one may query how applicable SFBT is to people that come from different cultural backgrounds, such as those who espouse collectivistic cultural worldviews. At first glance, SFBT seems to be very appealing to people from collectivistic cultures because of its brevity in treatment, focus on change of cognition and perception, action orientation, and upbeat tone of the treatment process. Nonetheless, its emphasis on therapeutic conversations, egalitarian relationship, and solution orientation may go counter to the cultural expectations of therapy for some cultural groups. For instance, Asian Americans, who have their cultural identity in Asian American collectivistic worldviews, would see the therapist as the expert, and expect the therapist to give advice and/or directives to solve their problems instead of engaging in long conversations of co-constructing solutions. The rather quick shift from problem talk to solution talk in the SFBT may also be interpreted as dismissing the gravity of their problems and invalidating their experience. It is therefore proposed that the therapist acquire multicultural awareness, knowledge, and skills as he adapts SFBT to culturally diverse populations (Ivey, D'Andrea, Ivey, & Simek-Morgan, 2007; Pedersen, 1991; Pedersen, Draguns, Lonner, & Trimble, 2002; Sue & Sue, 2008). For example, he may spend more time to establish the therapeutic relationship with a person with cultural identity in Asian American or Latino cultural worldviews, and stay problem-focused longer so as to validate and empathize with his client's dilemma and suffering. He may even give some appropriate suggestions and directives in order to meet his client's cultural expectations for therapy before he helps the client to build her own solutions (Cheung, 2001, 2005).

Clinical Applications of SFBT

SFBT has been applied to a wide range of populations and settings including children, adolescents, couples, families, psychiatric patients, and mandated involuntary clients in hospital, outpatient, schools, and community counseling settings (De Jong & Berg, 2008; Miller et al., 1996). For the applications of SFBT to children, adolescents, and families, please refer to De Jong and Berg (2008, pp. 176–201) and Berg and Steiner (2003).

Case illustration

Amy, a 46-year-old Caucasian female homemaker, called to present with symptoms of dysphoric mood, difficulty concentrating and falling asleep, and loss of appetite, weight, and interest in her favorite activities. She reported that she used to enjoy gardening, reading, and watching TV in her leisure, but had lost interest in them in the past year or so. She is currently living with her husband, John. She admitted to experiencing loneliness and emptiness in her life as she had found nothing worth doing. She added that she could not communicate well with her husband either. In fact, when they talked, they either had not much in common to talk about, or they ended up in "arguments" about differences in spending time together or managing money.

Amy and John have been married for 24 years. They have two sons: Paul, age 22, is a computer engineer and is working in Boston; Matt, 19, is a sophomore in a pre-med program in a liberal arts college on the east coast. John is a well-established lawyer, who has been spending about 50–60 hours a week at work most of his career. Before marriage and up until 4 years into their marriage, Amy worked as an executive secretary in a shipping company. When the two children were young, John was always the busy breadwinner and Amy was the homemaker, but they managed to have a family vacation once a year. However, Amy felt that she and John had drifted apart from each other over time.

After a brief screening conversation over the phone, the therapist invited Amy and John to meet for a conjoint couple session. In the first session, the therapist greeted Amy and John individually and made small talk with each of them. Then he started the session by clarifying his role and the structure of the session, including the intermission and feedback at the end of the session. He then asked Amy and John what would have to be different as a result of seeing him that would indicate to them that coming to see him was worthwhile. To this question, Amy said, "I don't want to be depressed and I want to be my old self again." When asked to specify what her old self was like before, she replied that she used to have a purpose and was happy each day to take care of things at home, but things seemed to have changed about a year and a half ago. She was asked further what changed a year and a half ago, and she replied that all she could think of was that her youngest son, Matt, left home and began college about two years ago. She admitted to feeling sad, depressed, lonely, and irritated easily about things at home, after her two sons had left home for work and for college. She was empathized, validated, and normalized about her feelings. When asked further what she wanted to be different, she said that she would like to have fewer arguments with John and be close to him. Then the therapist turned to John and asked him the same question; that is, what he wanted to be different. To this John responded that he wanted Amy to be rid of depression and be her usual self. John was further asked, "Instead of seeing depression in Amy, what would you want to see happening?" John replied that he would like to see Amy full of energy, taking care of things, and being "less sensitive and grouchy." The impact of the change in Amy's mood on Amy and John was then explored. First, Amy stated that she did not know why she had changed, but she did not like the change because every day had been "a chore for her." Then, John said that he had lost his wife and "felt kind of down sometimes." Again their feelings about the impact of the change were empathized, normalized, and validated.

The therapist then prepared the couple for the miracle question: "I'd like to ask you to ask a question that requires some imagination. Is it OK?" With the couple's affirmative answer, he asked the miracle question. It was interesting to note their responses:

AMY: I'll notice that I'm full of energy and excited to start a new day. I'll quickly fix breakfast for John and me in the morning. We'll have pleasant conversations around the breakfast table and talk about our next trip to Europe.

THERAPIST: What will John notice about the difference in you?

AMY: He will see the same thing . . . I'm less grouchy and much happier . . . like I used to be.

THERAPIST: John, what will you notice when a miracle happened?

JOHN: Amy is full of energy and more cheerful.

THERAPIST: What will you see Amy do differently when the miracle happened?

JOHN: She will put some make up on and look very beautiful. She will smile a lot and won't take little things I said personally.

THERAPIST: What do you mean by "taking little things you said personally"? Would you give me an example?

JOHN: Like she felt I was criticizing her, when I said, "We need to do the dishes" or something.

THERAPIST: After the miracle has happened, what would she do differently?

JOHN: She will either do the dishes herself, or she will ask if I can do them. Most likely, she will do them herself.

THERAPIST: Amy, when your husband sees you do that, what will he do?

AMY: He will offer help in mowing the lawn or doing something else around the house.

The brief interchange between the therapist and the couple illustrates how to engage the couple in specifying their future goals when the presenting problem is solved. Next, the therapist asked the couple to think of exceptions to their current problem: "John and Amy, can you think of a time in which Amy was not depressed and grouchy?" After a little thinking, John replied that Amy was not depressed when their two sons were home for Christmas and some of their extended family members came to join them. Amy agreed on the same event, but added that she also felt good when they went to a nice restaurant to have dinner about two weeks ago. The therapist then asked more detailed questions about what took place and the impact of the series of events on them. Amy replied that she really enjoyed the one-on-one attention she received from John, when he took the time to make the dinner reservation and spend the evening talking nothing about work or the children, but about her and the fun things they could do together. The therapist asked the couple what it would take for them to do that more often. They responded by saying that it would take a little time to plan and actually do it. The therapist then validated their efforts and plan as well as encouraged them to do more of that in the future.

In the middle of the session, Amy brought up the fact that she and John did not communicate or understand each other well and wanted some suggestions from the therapist. The therapist explored her concerns together with John respectfully and then asked what they wanted to be different in a fairly detailed fashion. Again, he explored with the couple the occasions on which they communicated well with each other (i.e., exceptions) and built on their past successes. The rest of the session was devoted to exploring and expanding on the couple's resources and already successful solutions. At the end of the session, on the basis of the couple's motivation and ability to identify their goals and exceptions as well as see their roles in the solutions, the following feedback message was delivered:

> John and Amy, you both care not only about Amy's wellbeing, but also about each other very much. You both are hard working: John at work and Amy at home. You mentioned about Amy's feelings of depression and loneliness in the past while and yet you have found ways to combat them. For example, you, John, have tried to spend more time with Amy and take her out for a nice dinner and have a get-together with your family at Christmas. You also said that you sometimes could not understand each other and felt frustrated with each other. You seemed to have found a good solution of time out. When both of you calmed down and were ready to talk again, you got back together and tried to listen harder and resolve the differences, and this has worked on several occasions. Because you are so motivated and capable to solve your two major problems, I'd encourage you to do more of what's worked and also observe what you each do when Amy is less depressed and when you're communicating well with each other. I want you to write down the details and tell me about them next week when we meet.

Case discussion.   The case above exemplifies several seminal features of a SFBT first session. First, the therapist conducted a solution-building interview with the two foci of developing well-formed goals and developing solutions based on exceptions. He used the technique of the miracle question, exception-finding questions, and follow-up questions to highlight the resources and future possibilities in the couple. Instead of focusing too much attention on their problems, the session balanced this well with an emphasis on the strengths of the couple. Second, when Amy asked for solutions for their communication problems from the therapist, he resisted the temptation to give advice or solutions, but instead respectfully listened, empathized, and asked for times when they had communicated well. Third, he adapted his feedback message in accordance with the couple's motivation, awareness, and ability to identify goals, exceptions, and roles in building their solution.

Conclusion

SFBT has enjoyed increasing popularity in the past two decades because of its non-pathological view of individuals, "not-knowing" therapeutic stance, brief therapy model, and teachable skills. SFBT has in the past decade incorporated the importance of affect and therapeutic relationship into its theory-building and practice and has therefore made it a more versatile and powerful treatment approach. Although treatment efficacy has been reported when it is applied to clientele that are from the same individualistic culture as SFBT, research has yet to be conducted to demonstrate its effectiveness with culturally diverse populations. At this point, it behooves the therapist to acquire multicultural competency in self-awareness, knowledge, and skills when she adapts SFBT to culturally diverse clientele. Rather than totally "not knowing," it would be expedient to modify her therapeutic stance to "not knowing and some knowing" when working with diverse populations, who would expect some concrete benefits from the therapist (e.g., her expert recommendations). Certainly the optimum mixture of these two therapeutic stances depends on the myriad of client variables, therapist variables, and relationship variables between the client and the therapist. To further inform, sharpen, and refine this popular and powerful therapy approach, a stronger reciprocal relationship among research, theory-building, and clinical practice is recommended. In other words, as researchers, theoreticians, and practitioners come together more often to confer and collaborate, they can inform each other and improve each other's work and therefore serve clients better.

Resources

Interviewing for solutions DVD (ISBN: 0-495-09882-5; De Jong & Berg 2008) for skills training and examples of interventions
Solution Focused Brief Therapy Association (www.sfbta.org)
European Brief Therapy Association (www.ebta.nu)

Berg, I. K., & Dolan, Y. (2001). *Tales of solutions: A collection of hope-inspiring stories.* New York: Norton.
Berg, I. K., & Steiner, T. (2003). *Children's solution work.* New York: Norton.
De Jong, P., & Berg, I. K. (2008). *Interviewing for solutions* (3rd ed.). Belmont, CA: Thomson Higher Education.

References

Becvar, D. S., & Becvar, R. J. (2006). *Family therapy: A systemic integration* (6th ed.). Boston: Allyn & Bacon.

Berg, I. K. (1994). *Family based services: A solution-focused approach.* New York: Norton.

Berg, I. K., & de Shazer, S. (1993). Making numbers talk: Language in therapy. In S. Friedman (Ed.), *The new language of change* (pp. 5–24). New York: Guilford Press.

Berg, I. K., & Miller, S. D. (1992). *Working with the problem drinker.* New York: Norton.

Berg, I. K., & Steiner, T. (2003). *Children's solution work.* New York: Norton.

Cheung, S. (2001). Problem-solving and solution-focused therapy for Chinese: Recent developments. *Asian Journal of Counselling, 8(2)*, 111–128.

Cheung, S. (2005). Strategic and solution-focused couples therapy. In M. Harway (Ed.), *Handbook of couples therapy* (pp. 194–210). New York: Wiley.

De Jong, P., & Berg, I. K. (2008). *Interviewing for solutions* (3rd ed.). Belmont, CA; Thomson Higher Education.

de Shazer, S. (1985). *Keys to solutions in brief therapy.* New York: Norton.

de Shazer, S. (1988). *Clues: Investigating solutions in brief therapy.* New York: Norton.

de Shazer, S. (1991). *Putting difference to work.* New York: Norton.

de Shazer, S. (1994). *Words are originally magic.* New York: Norton.

Franklin, C. (2006). Outcome studies on solution-focused therapy. Retrieved February 17, 2008, from http://www.utexas.edu/courses/franklin

Franklin, C., & Streeter, C. L. (2006). Solution-focused accountability schools for the twenty-first century: A training manual for Gonzalo Garza Independence High School. Retrieved February 17, 2008, from http://www.utexas.edu/courses/franklin

Gingerich, W. J., & Eisengart, S. (2000). Solution-focused brief therapy: A review of the outcome research. *Family Process, 39*, 477–498.

Gingerich, W. J., & Eisengart, S. (2001). Solution-focused brief therapy outcome studies. Retrieved February 17, 2008, from http://www.gingerich.net/SFBT/research/Default.htm

Goldenberg, H., & Goldenberg, I. (2008). *Family therapy: An overview.* Belmont, CA: Thomson Higher Education.

Ivey, A. E., D'Andrea, M., Ivey, M. B., & Simek-Morgan, L. (2007). *Theories of counseling and psychotherapy: A multicultural perspective* (6th ed.). Boston: Allyn & Bacon.

Lipchik, E. (1993). "Both/and" solution. In S. Friedman (Ed.), *The new language of change: Constructive collaboration in psychotherapy* (pp. 25–49). New York: Guilford Press.

Lipchik, E. (2002). *Beyond technique in solution-focused therapy: Working with emotions and the therapeutic relationship.* New York: Guilford Press.

McKeel, A. J. (1996). A clinician's guide to research on solution-focused brief therapy. In S. D. Miller, M. A. Hubble, & B. L. Duncan (Eds.), *Handbook of solution-focused brief therapy* (pp. 251–271). San Francisco: Jossey-Bass.

McKeel, A. J. (1999). A selected review of research of solution-focused brief therapy. Retrieved February 17, 2008, from http://www.ebta.nu

Miller, S. D. (1994). The solution-conspiracy: A mystery in three installments. *Journal of Systemic Therapies, 13(1)*, 18–37.

Miller, S. D., Hubble, M. A., & Duncan, B. L. (Eds.). (1996). *Handbook of solution-focused brief therapy.* San Francisco: Jossey-Bass.

Nichols, M. P., & Schwartz, R. C. (2008). *Family therapy: Concepts and methods* (8th ed.). Boston: Allyn & Bacon.

O'Hanlon, W. H. (1993a). Possibility therapy: From iatrogenic injury to iatrogenic healing. In S. Gilligan & R. Price (Eds.), *Therapeutic conversations* (pp. 258–271). New York: Norton.

O'Hanlon, W. H. (1993b). Take two people and call them in the morning: Brief solution oriented therapy with depression. In S. Friedman (Ed.), *The new language of change: Constructive collaboration in psychotherapy* (pp. 50–84). New York: Guilford Press.

O'Hanlon, W. H., & Weiner-Davis, M. (2003). *In search of solutions: A new direction in psychotherapy.* New York: Norton.

Pedersen, P. B. (Ed.). (1991). Multiculturalism as a fourth force in counseling. *Journal of Counseling and Development, 70* [Special issue]

Pedersen, P. B., Draguns, J. G., Lonner, W. J., & Trimble, J. E. (Eds.). (2002). *Counseling across cultures* (5th ed.). Thousand Oaks, CA: Sage.

Sue, D. W., & Sue, D. (2008). *Counseling the culturally diverse* (5th ed.). New York: Wiley.

Walter, J., & Peller, J. (1992). *Becoming solution-focused in brief therapy.* New York: Brunner/Mazel.

Weiner-Davis, M. (1993). Pro-constructed realities. In S. Gilligan & R. Price (Eds.), *Therapeutic conversations* (pp. 149–157). New York: Norton.

15

Behavioral and Cognitive-Behavioral Therapies

Kristina Coop Gordon, Lee J. Dixon, Jennifer M. Willett, and Farrah M. Hughes

Although many treatments co-exist under the umbrella of behavioral and cognitive-behavioral couple and family therapy, these therapies all share roots in social-learning theories; consequently, they tend to be predicated on similar fundamental premises. As with most systemic theories, a basic assumption underlying these treatments is that behaviors exhibited in family relationships are multiply determined and reciprocal. Thus, although traditionally behavioral couple and family therapy has primarily focused on changing behaviors, once the contingencies of a situation are altered via these new behaviors, significant changes in cognition and affect throughout the family system are expected to follow. Cognitive-behavioral treatments tend to incorporate many of the existing behavioral interventions, yet they also place a greater emphasis on exploring how couples and families understand their interactions in an attempt to more directly intervene on problematic cognitions. Still further, the newer generations of treatments have expanded to attend to family-of-origin issues and to more directly elicit and affect emotional experiences.

These treatments also share an assumption that the family psychologist's role is part educator and part coach, as he or she interrupts destructive interactions during therapy sessions, educates the couple about the impact of cognitions and behavior on relationship satisfaction, increases the partners' awareness of their own behavioral patterns, and teaches them how to use specific relational skills. Typically, the family psychologist provides concrete instructions about how to use a skill, models the desired behavior, coaches the partners as they rehearse the skills in the therapy office, provides feedback on communication processes, and helps the couple plan how and when they will apply the skills at home.

Behavioral and cognitive-behavioral psychologists tend to approach therapy in a collaborative manner; for example, they arrive at the specific formulations, goals, and procedures of treatment through open discussions with their clients. Clients are usually given homework assignments that are jointly generated out of the work accomplished in their sessions, and the following session usually begins with a review of the homework to see what the couple learned from the experience and "trouble-shoot" any problems that they had in carrying it out. The emphasis is on teaching couples and family members a number of skills that they can apply on their own. Thus, therapy does not necessarily end when the clients are "problem-free"; rather, the therapy ends when they are judged to have the ability to use their new skills and understandings to arrive at their own solutions to their problems. Consequently the task of the family psychologist is to provide a great deal of modeling and shaping during the early part of treatment, and then remove those supports gradually until the couple and/or family can move forward on their own.

However, despite these fundamental similarities, each cognitive-behavioral approach has its own unique perspective on the mechanisms of change in therapy, and, similarly, each has its own unique interventions and contributions to the field. Below, we outline several of the major approaches to couple and then family treatments.

Overview of Behavioral and Cognitive-Behavioral Couples Therapy Models

Overview of the general models

Traditional behavioral couples therapy.   Traditional behavioral couples therapy (BCT), also known as behavioral marital therapy (BMT; e.g., Jacobson & Margolin, 1979), was developed from the theoretical models of social exchange theory (Thibaut & Kelley, 1959) and social learning theory (Bandura, 1977; Rotter, 1954). These models suggest that satisfaction in a relationship is influenced by the ratio of positive to negative experiences in the dyad (i.e., a matter of benefits to costs), and that members of a dyad shape each other's behavior through their responses to each other's actions. As a result, behavioral couple therapists attempt to alter a couple's unbalanced cost–benefit ratios by using behavior-exchange procedures to increase positive experiences between the partners; an example of this technique would be "caring days" (Stuart, 1980), in which each partner agrees to enact on particular days some positive behaviors requested by his or her partner.

Another technique used by traditional behavioral couple therapists to increase positive experiences is to coach couples in creating behavioral contracts, in which each person agrees to behave in specific ways desired by the partner during a specific trial period of time, such as the following week. These contracts can be set up as *quid pro quo* (where the partners' responses are contingent on the other person also following through on his or her side of the agreement) or as "good faith" agreements (in which each person agrees to engage in the positive behaviors desired by the partner, even if the partner does not reciprocate). Consistent with their behavioral approach, behavior therapists also teach couples specific skills for expressing thoughts and feelings, active empathic listening, and problem solving. The classic training manuals by Jacobson and Margolin (1979) and Stuart (1980) provide more complete details on these interventions; however, these models have been largely eclipsed by the newer generations of BCT.

Cognitive-behavioral couple therapy.   Cognitive-behavioral couple therapy (CBCT, also know as cognitive-behavioral marital therapy or CBMT; e.g., Baucom & Epstein, 1990) was the next step in the evolution of behavioral couples approaches. These therapies retained many of the interventions central to BMT, but they also focused more on how the couples cognitively processed and understood their relationships, their partners, and themselves. Thus, CBCT addresses behavioral, cognitive, and affective factors influencing the quality of couples' relationships. CBCT is similar to BMT, particularly in its use of interventions, such as skills training for expressing thoughts and feelings, actively listening and responding constructively, and problem solving, and in its attention to increasing positive couple behaviors to provide more pleasure in the relationship.

However, the basic assumption behind these therapies is that behavior, cognition, and affect are *mutually* influential; therefore these behavioral interventions do not just change couples' interaction patterns but also are likely to alter the ways in which partners process their interactions and affectively experience these interactions. Consequently, the cognitive-behavioral couple therapist carefully attends to how partners are cognitively processing their relationships. Common techniques to assess partners' cognitions concerning their relationships are self-report questionnaires, interviews, and observations of couples' behavioral interactions in which the partners spontaneously verbalize their thoughts about each other or exhibit emotional and behavioral reactions to particular types of situations (e.g., one partner becomes angry whenever the other disagrees with him or her). The therapist then explores how the partners are interpreting their interactions and what meanings they are attaching to behaviors (e.g., "When she interrupts me, it means she doesn't respect me"). During this exploration, the therapist is careful to use non-directive, open-ended questions to reduce the likelihood of shaping the client's reported experience according to the therapist's own beliefs or views of the situation.

Once the relevant cognitions have been uncovered, examples of standard cognitive restructuring strategies would include: (a) helping an individual to generate alternative attributions for a partner's negative behavior, (b) asking an individual to conduct daily "experiments" to assess the accuracy of a negative perception concerning his or her partner (e.g., that the partner always disagrees with requests for help), and (c) examining costs and benefits of expecting one's relationship to live up to an extreme standard. As the therapist engages in the more "behavioral" communication skills training, the changes effected as the couples engage in more positive, skillful interactions can alter how the partners perceive each other. For example, if a wife observes her husband struggling to inhibit his tendency to interrupt and to communicate more effectively, this observation might challenge her view that he does not care about her or the relationship. Consequently, she may become less hostile toward him and strive to become less attacking in her own communication.

A more recent version of cognitive-behavioral therapy is the enhanced CBT model (Epstein & Baucom, 2002). The enhanced CBT model extends traditional CBCT by focusing on intrapersonal characteristics, individual and relational needs, contextual influences, and developmental influences of both the individuals and the life cycle of the relationship. The model also strives to acknowledge and build upon couples' strengths, rather than focusing solely on relationship problems, and also strongly emphasizes the importance of emotion in impacting relationship functioning. Epstein and Baucom (2002) provide a more thorough discussion of these enhanced CBMT interventions.

Schema-focused couple therapy.   Schema-focused couple therapy (e.g., Dattilio, 2006; Whisman & Uebelacker, 2007) is similar to other cognitive-behavioral therapies in its assumption that the way couples process and understand their interactions has a major influence on their subsequent behavior and affective experiences. However, it has a more central focus on how ingrained belief systems about self, partner, and relationships in general developed over long periods of time (i.e., schemata) can play a crucial role in understanding couple distress. These therapies believe that exploring individuals' experiences in their family of origin is critical to unlocking couples' current enmeshment in rigid, negative interactions.

Consequently, a key intervention in this group of therapies is to conduct a developmental exploration with each partner regarding their earlier relational experiences in their families of origin. These explorations tend to be targeted toward issues that are currently problematic for the couples; for example, if the couple is having difficulties regarding how they express affection for one another, these explorations look carefully at how affection was shown in their families of origin, in hopes of uncovering for the partners what beliefs and "rules" they developed about this issue from watching their parents' modeling of this behavior. Typically, these sessions are conducted with both partners present, but they focus on one partner at a time with the other partner listening in. The idea behind this structure is to expose the listening partner to this information about their partners' histories in order to foster more understanding and empathy with their partners' experiences. As these belief systems are gradually revealed, the therapist helps the couple to evaluate their schemas in light of their current situations and to ask themselves what parts of these schemas they are willing to change to improve their relationships, as well as what parts they are unwilling to give up. The therapist also might structure homework assignments that help the clients to act in opposition to schemas that they identify as problematic, in an effort to give them a new platform from which to view their schemas and to aid them in identifying and enacting new behavioral choices in their interactions with their partners. Dattilio (2006) and Whisman and Uebelacker (2007) provide a more complete description of schema therapy with couples.

Integrative behavioral couple therapy.   Another iteration of behavioral couple therapy, integrative behavioral couple therapy (IBCT; Jacobson & Christensen, 1996) evolved to address the fact that couples face many issues that are unlikely to change (e.g., differences in firmly held worldviews, basic personality traits, or differing desires about having children). Thus, IBCT promotes behavior change when it is possible *and* mutual acceptance in situations in which it is not. Similarly to traditional behavioral couple therapy, this therapy employs behavior exchange procedures, as described above, but these behaviors are usually self-selected rather than requested by the other partner, in order to increase the individual's freedom of choice when they engage in new behavior. As a result, their choice is more likely to be interpreted as motivated by positive feelings toward the relationship by both partners. Other change strategies employed in IBCT are traditional communication and problem-solving skills training to decrease negative interactions and increase positive ones.

However, IBCT also focuses on balancing these interventions with acceptance strategies when needed. For example, one strategy, "empathic joining," helps couples to view prob-lematic interactions as almost inevitable given their different personalities, histories, and worldviews. Thus, the therapist creates empathy between the partners by (a) reformu-lating their views of each other's displeasing behavior (e.g., as socially learned ways of coping with distress about normal differences), (b) helping the partners to disclose more vulnerable feelings (e.g., sadness and hurt about a partner's withdrawal) rather than accusations and angry responses, and (c) specific training in communication skills for expressing and listening to thoughts and emotions.

A second strategy used to promote acceptance is role-playing negative behaviors during therapy sessions, which helps the couple to anticipate future occurrences of those negative behaviors, and increases their ability to tolerate and accept them. Yet another intervention used in integrative couple therapy to promote acceptance is highlighting positive features of negative behavior. Jacobson and Christensen (1996) note that this strategy is similar to the use of "positive connotation" in systems approaches, but differs from it by continuing to acknowledge the negative aspects of the behavior rather than creating a totally positive reframe. Acceptance-enhancing strategies, such as the therapist refor-mulating a couple's problem in a manner that increases each person's empathy for the other's pain and normalizes the couple's differences, are intended to increase a sense of intimacy and satisfaction; i.e., an emotional shift. These interventions are described in more detail in their treatment manual, *Integrative Couple Therapy* (Jacobson & Christensen, 1996).

Overview of Behavioral and Cognitive-Behavioral Family Therapy Models

There are many functions of behavioral family therapy (BFT), but its primary goal always has been to enhance the efficiency of family functioning (Falloon, 2003). A basic premise for BFT is that in order for there to be significant change in a person's life, even when someone is presenting with a traditionally "individual" disorder, there must be a change in the behaviors of the people within the social system in which this person finds himself or herself. Tharp and Wetzel (1969) pointed out that our siblings, parents, and spouses typically make up the social system that is our family (although it has been suggested that this definition of family can be expanded to include those who provide us with emotional support on an everyday basis; Falloon, 2003). The family behavioral therapist does not view interactions between family members as coincidental; instead, they are guided by each family member's best, most cost-effective efforts to resolve presenting problems (Thibaut & Kelley, 1959). Thus, even when the responses made by family members appear to be relationally destructive, they are believed to be the most rewarding of the family members' available response options. Consequently, the goal of changing the response patterns of individuals must include increasing the rewards gained from responding in a more constructive manner, reducing the costs associated with this response, and working to alter the contingencies within the family system that elicit a particular response pattern. Each of these basic behavioral principles can be identified in the BFT approaches to different mental disorders that are outlined below.

Additionally, many behavioral approaches to family therapy have integrated the use of cognitive techniques, such as educating families about the nature of their psychological illnesses and their management (Falloon & Lillie, 1988). As cognitive techniques have become more empirically supported, particularly within the marital domain, their use has become more widespread, particularly in the treatment of disorders in which cognitive distortions are thought to be the culprits for maladaptive behaviors (e.g., eating disorders, anxiety disorders, etc.). Below, we describe examples of applications of BFT to a variety of problems (for an example of how to use BFT to treat eating disorders see Chapter 38, this volume).

Schizophrenia and bipolar disorder

The presence of a psychiatric illness such as schizophrenia or bipolar disorder can place a significant strain on family relationships (Mueser, 2001). For example, those who care for and maintain a close relationship with someone who suffers from either of these disorders find that it is an emotionally draining task (Hatfield & Lefley, 1987, 1993). This task can be made even more strenuous for family members if they do not understand the characteristics of the illness, which can lead to unwarranted blaming and frustration being directed toward those who suffer from these illnesses. Unfortunately, research has shown that high levels of familial stress and expressed emotion increase the risk of relapse and re-hospitalization for family members who suffer from either schizophrenia or bipolar disorder (e.g., Butzlaff & Hooley, 1998). Most models of family therapy make an effort to reduce familial stress through educating family members about the illness and its treatment and through teaching communication skills and problem solving to the family to better negotiate these stressors (e.g., Falloon, Boyd, & McGill, 1984).

The most widely studied family intervention for both schizophrenia and bipolar disorder is BFT. Falloon and colleagues (1984) have written a detailed manual for this approach, and empirical investigation of this method has demonstrated that it is successful in reducing relapse in patients suffering from schizophrenia (e.g., Falloon & Pederson, 1985). Additionally, Mueser and Glynn (1999) also have published a manual that describes how to use BFT in treating schizophrenia, along with myriad other severe mental illnesses, including bipolar disorder. Mueser (2001) describes BFT for psychiatric illnesses such as bipolar disorder as "an intervention that combines education with social learning strategies designed to better equip families with the knowledge and skills necessary to manage psychiatric illness in a family member, [including] skills for effective communication and problem solving" (p. 60).

Childhood anxiety disorders

Empirical research has demonstrated that cognitive-behavioral family-based interventions can improve anxiety symptoms, along with other externalizing symptoms and overall functioning in children (e.g., Barrett, Dadds, & Rapee, 1996). In family-based cognitive-behavioral treatment (FCBT; Barrett & Shortt, 2003), distorted cognitions are believed to be responsible for children's subsequent emotions and behavior, and, thus, are the target of these approaches. However, FCBT sees the family as "the optimal environment for effecting change in the child's dysfunctional cognition" (Barrett & Shortt, 2003, p. 103). This approach emphasizes rewarding coping behavior, extinguishing excessive anxious behavior, and developing family communication and problem-solving skills. Additionally, FCBT prompts parents to manage their own anxiety through cognitive-behavioral techniques so that they can be better models for their children.

Attention deficit hyperactivity disorder

Attention deficit hyperactivity disorder (ADHD) is one of the most cited reasons for referral to school personnel, pediatricians, and mental health professionals, which is not surprising given that it occurs in 5–7% of the general child population (Barkley, 1998). Having ADHD heightens individuals' risk for a broad array of psychosocial difficulties, not only in youth, but throughout life (Anastopoulos & Shelton, 2001). Furthermore, ADHD can have negative consequences for the family members of a child who suffers from this disorder: children with ADHD are more likely to interact aggressively with their siblings; parents of a child with ADHD are more likely to become negative in their parenting style and to view themselves as a parent in a more negative light; parents may also become depressed and suffer from marital discord (Barkley, 1998; Anastopoulos & Farley, 2003).

Although stimulant medication is considered by most experts to be the unimodal treatment of choice for ADHD (Northey, Wells, Silverman, & Bailey, 2003), research has found the combination of psychosocial treatment and medication to be more effective than medication alone (Klein & Abikoff, 1997). One psychosocial treatment that can be combined with medication is parent training (PT), which involves teaching parents specialized child-management techniques that include positive reinforcement, establishing home rules, and giving effective commands. Some forms of PT also incorporate additional techniques that target the management of mood, anger, and stress in parents, along with teaching parents the necessary skills to become advocates for their child within the school system (for a detailed outline of this method see Barkley, 1998, and Wells et al., 2000). PT has been extensively researched and been found to be effective in reducing ADHD symptoms and improving parenting skills (e.g., Anastopoulos, Shelton, DuPaul, & Guevrement, 1993).

Diversity in Behavioral and Cognitive-Behavioral Couple and Family Therapy

Behavioral and cognitive-behavioral couple and family therapy has so far been limited in its adaptation to ethnic and racial minority populations, most likely because it is often employed with a "color-blind" approach that does not attend to cultural and societal influences upon individual and couples behavior (LaTaillade, 2006). For both couple and family behavioral and cognitive-behavioral approaches, additional research is needed to further explore the impact of race and ethnicity upon couple and family relationships and therapy, and diversity issues such as race and socioeconomic status should be addressed both in therapy and in future research (Kelly & Iwamasa, 2005). Racial minorities often have noticeable differences in family structure from those of White, middle-class families, such as emphasizing parent–child bonds over the marital bond, living in an intergenerational household, and having flexible boundaries between generations. The family values and economic decisions underlying these culturally influenced family arrangements should be acknowledged and incorporated into therapy for the clients to be fully understood (Leslie, 1995).

Additionally, couple and family therapy clinicians have been criticized for largely tending to ignore gay, lesbian, and bisexual issues (e.g., Martell, Safren, & Prince, 2004). These authors suggest that it is particularly important to develop behavioral and cognitive-behavioral therapies tailored to gay and lesbian families because of the unique and often difficult situations they face in daily life, politics, and family formation (see Chapter 40, this volume). Lesbians and gay men often do not share the sexual orientation of their families, and thus often instead create "families of choice" to have social support networks (Hancock, 2003); they also face legal roadblocks that make marital relationship benefits difficult, if not impossible, to obtain. Behavioral and cognitive-behavioral therapies should be cognizant of these unique family constellations and legal difficulties in order to successfully help same-sex couples navigate the inevitable obstacles of leading an alternative lifestyle in today's society (Martell et al., 2004).

Behavioral and cognitive-behavioral couple and family therapy clearly has a long way to go in terms of addressing the many diversity issues facing today's families. However, many properties of behavioral and cognitive-behavioral couple and family therapy are likely to be compatible with diverse couples and families. For example, behavioral couple therapy incorporates multi-method assessment data that tailor the therapy to each couple's unique needs, using functional analysis and skills building to meet their specific goals (Kelly & Iwamasa, 2005). Similarly, behavioral and cognitive-behavioral therapies have a collaborative nature that encourages an atmosphere of mutual respect through discussion in establishing treatment goals and choice of interventions, allowing couples to become skilled enough to become "co-therapists" in their ongoing quest to better their relationship, and thus giving them the freedom to incorporate their own cultural beliefs, economic difficulties, or issues unique to same-sex relationships into their therapies (Kelly, 2006). Recent advances in behavioral and cognitive-behavioral approaches have adopted a more integrative focus that incorporates multiple successful treatments, such as structural, strategic, solution-focused, and emotionally focused couple therapy, that greatly widen cognitive-behavioral therapy's scope of effectiveness with diverse populations (Kelly & Iwamasa, 2005). For example, enhanced cognitive-behavioral therapy (Epstein & Baucom, 2002) recognizes the environment's influence upon the couple, including family systems, community supports, stressors, and life circumstances. Similarly, IBCT (Jacobson & Christensen, 1996) emphasizes a contextual focus and examines unifying themes underlying individuals' cognitions, behaviors, and emotional responses (LaTaillade, 2006). The utility of expanding these approaches to address multicultural and contextual factors is illustrated in the case example below.

Case Study

The case presented below is necessarily brief due to space limitations; however, it illustrates some of the key concepts and interventions employed in enhanced cognitive-behavioral therapy (Epstein & Baucom, 2002).

Background.   The therapist conducted an assessment that included one conjoint and two individual sessions as well as self-report measures that assessed the couple's individual and relational functioning. James and LeAnn were each 45 years old when they presented for therapy and had been married for two years. James was Latino and LeAnn was Caucasian. They had no children. They presented for therapy because they "argued all the time." LeAnn described James as "overly emotional" during their disagreements, and she perceived him as being aloof the rest of the time. James reported that LeAnn probed him too much about his feelings, and he perceived her as domineering. In addition, James's retail business had recently gone bankrupt, which had increased their stress and fueled worries about their financial future. LeAnn worked as a freelance writer.

James was the oldest of five children; his parents emigrated from Mexico two years before he was born. They both were legal immigrants and were able to secure blue-collar jobs. He described his mother as "melodramatic" and unpredictable, sometimes exhibiting violence and displaying erratic behavior. Given the chaos in the family, he wondered why his father remained married to her. Currently, his father was very ill and unemployed; thus James, as the oldest male child, felt responsible for his entire family. James had been married once before; he reported that that marriage lasted 15 years and dissolved due to financial struggles and his wife's alcohol abuse.

LeAnn was the younger of two sisters. She had never been married before but reported having two long-term relationships prior to meeting James. LeAnn reported that her mother moved LeAnn's family to another state to flee from LeAnn's father, who was physically aggressive toward her mother. LeAnn described her older sister as angry and abusive and reported that her mother did not intervene in their arguments or protect LeAnn from her sister, which led her to feel abandoned by her mother in this regard.

James and LeAnn met via a mutual friend. They immediately fell in love and James proposed one year after they met. Soon thereafter, James realized that his older brother had embezzled several thousand dollars from him while they were running their business together. He was reluctant to confront his brother but did so at LeAnn's urging. James and his brother "had it out" but none of the money could be recovered. They both believe that this stressor triggered their recent problems.

Case formulation.   James and LeAnn's marital functioning was influenced by many individual, relationship, and environmental factors. Most strikingly, they were affected greatly by interpersonal dynamics learned in their families of origin and in their previous relationship experiences. For example, neither partner's family had modeled appropriate strategies for managing conflict; rather, they had both been exposed to angry, violent interchanges growing up. LeAnn's feelings of abandonment by her mother in the past created intense fears of future abandonment by her husband when conflict arose, which made it difficult for her disengage whenever their fights seriously escalated. However, James's previous marital experience included intense arguments exacerbated by his wife's alcohol abuse, which led him to avoid conflict at all costs. Thus, James and LeAnn had developed a *demand–withdraw* pattern of interaction (Christensen & Heavey, 1993) in which LeAnn would pursue James, and he would become angry and attempt to flee from what he perceived as emotionally charged exchanges. Consequently, both partners felt alone and dissatisfied in the relationship, and problems were rarely resolved. However, despite these problems, both partners also reported that they valued their relationship a great deal when they were not fighting and would work very hard to make their marriage successful.

Contextually, James and LeAnn reported experiencing several stressors that were impacting their relationship. First, their finances were unstable due to the recent failure of James's business and the loss of money to James's brother. In addition, LeAnn's monthly income was inconsistent. Because of James's previous experiences with financial stress impacting his first marriage, he was fearful that financial stress also would be the undoing of this marriage, which made him anxious whenever the topic arose. Second, neither partner reported having positive relationships with family members, so they lacked a stable support network and potential source of emotional and financial assistance. Additionally, James's cultural values of *machismo* and *familismo* dictated that he needed to support his extended family financially and be their caretaker while his father was ill; at the same time, he had his own financial struggles, and LeAnn was furious when he gave his family money when the couple could not pay their own bills. However, despite their problems with their family systems, one of their strengths was that they had developed supportive friendships with several other couples, which gave them an outlet for having positive experiences together.

Interventions.   An initial behavioral intervention for James and LeAnn involved communication training. Both of them usually were able to communicate appropriately with a wide variety of people; however, they experienced a breakdown in communication in their own emotionally charged discussions. Therefore, the therapist gave them guidelines to help each partner to focus on such things as speaking in paragraphs and taking turns "having the floor," sharing positive emotions when also sharing negative ones, trying to understand the speaker's perspective, and responding with empathy. The therapist then led James and LeAnn through practice discussions, starting with relatively mild topics and progressing into the more emotionally charged subjects that James typically avoided. The therapist also taught them structured problem-solving skills to help them resolve some of their daily arguments. One of the goals of this training was to slow down their interactions and to give James a sense of efficacy regarding conflict situations. The other goal was to set the stage for more intimacy-enhancing interactions.

To enhance the effectiveness of the behavioral interventions, the therapist also used cognitive and affective interventions. To address the partners' maladaptive cognitions, the therapist helped them to identify and challenge "hot thoughts" as they occurred during their discussions. As an example, the therapist addressed LeAnn's attributions that James's avoidance of intense discussions, particularly those involving their childhoods, was because he did not care and was uninterested in her. The therapist asked LeAnn to consider evidence both for and against those attributions. She was able to list many ways that James showed his love for her, including cooking her breakfast, giving her back-rubs, and telling her, "I love you." She then became more curious about his experiences during emotionally laden discussions, such as their childhood experiences or financial topics, which opened the floor for James to explore his feelings about those topics.

James's discovery that he avoided difficult discussions as a way of avoiding emotional pain, such as those discussions that reminded him of his pain during childhood, facilitated affective interventions that focused on, for example, accessing and heightening those feelings that James had been avoiding, such as fear and sadness. The therapist helped James to "sit with" those feelings of fear and sadness. His withdrawal and avoidance were reactions to those painful, vulnerable emotions that were very anxiety-provoking for him. The therapist helped LeAnn create a safe place for James to explore those previously avoided emotions by helping her use her new skills to validate his feelings, listen, and express support and empathy; the use of structured couple discussions further enhanced LeAnn's ability to create safety for him. James's withdrawal decreased, and he became increasingly able to engage in a dialogue about their childhood experiences, which helped LeAnn feel close to James. Both partners reported that they felt greater intimacy now that they could engage in these discussions. At the same time, this new understanding and reframe of James's withdrawal helped LeAnn to allow him some space when it was clear that he was not comfortable talking about some issues.

The couple was then able to use this new closeness and communication skill to address their other difficult issue of family and finances. During this discussion, they were able to talk about their differing cultural beliefs and how that influenced their reactions when this topic was raised. LeAnn was finally able to understand just how complicated this issue was for James, and how his financial struggles both made him feel less of a "man" and compelled to care for his extended family even against his own best interests. With this understanding, and with their new sense of efficacy regarding conflict, they were able to discuss some compromises that would allow James to help his family, but also protect his relationship with LeAnn.

James and LeAnn were in couple therapy for 23 sessions, which was longer than usual due to LeAnn's characterological difficulty with emotion regulation. The therapist helped them to generalize the progress that they had made by using the strategies they had learned to discuss a wide variety of difficult topics and to problem solve issues that might arise in the future. The therapist prepared them for setbacks, which are inevitable for any couple, and helped them develop strategies for dealing with those setbacks appropriately, including coming in for a "booster session" if they so desired. They both reported feeling more hopeful about their future and greater intimacy between them at the end of therapy. At the end of treatment, the frequency of their conflicts had decreased, and although they still experienced some degree of conflict about once per week, they felt they were better equipped to address these problems.

Conclusions

As has been mentioned throughout this chapter, evidence that demonstrates the efficacy of behavioral and cognitive-behavioral family therapy continues to mount. Not only are these types of therapy beneficial in promoting better familial and couple relationships, they are also useful for treating specific individual difficulties within the context of couple and family therapy. However, there is still more work that needs to be done in this area. For example, approximately 50% of couples do not experience clinically significant change in treatment, and many of these couples who do still relapse post-treatment (Epstein & Baucom, 2002). Additionally, mechanisms of change still need to be explored further in order to enhance the efficacy of treatment. Finally, these therapies all need a great deal more evaluation of their effectiveness with diverse populations and settings.

Resources

Epstein, N. B., & Baucom, D. H. (2002). *Enhanced cognitive-behavioral therapy for couples: A contextual approach.* Washington, DC: American Psychological Association.

Jacobson, N. S., & Christensen, A. (1996). *Integrative couple therapy: Promoting acceptance and change.* New York: Norton.

Mueser, K. T., & Glynn, S. M. (1999). *Behavioral family therapy for psychiatric disorders.* Oakland, CA: New Harbinger.

References

Anastopoulos, A. D., & Farley, S. E. (2003). A cognitive-behavioral training program for parents of children with attention-deficit/hyperactivity disorder. In J. R. Weisz & A. E. Kazdin (Eds.), *Evidence based psychotherapies for children and adolescents* (pp. 187–203). New York: Guilford Press.

Anastopoulos, A. D., & Shelton, T. L. (2001). *Assessing attention-deficit/hyperactivity disorder.* New York: Kluwer Academic and Plenum.

Anastopoulos, A. D., Shelton, T. L., DuPaul, G. J., & Guevremont, D. C. (1993). Parent training for attention-deficit hyperactivity disorder: Its impact on parent functioning. *Journal of Abnormal Child Psychology, 21*, 581–596.

Bandura, A. (1977). *Social learning theory.* Oxford: Prentice Hall.

Barkley, R. A. (1998). *Attention-deficit hyperactivity disorder: A handbook for diagnosis and treatment* (2nd ed.). New York: Guilford Press.

Barrett, P. M., Dadds, M. R., & Rapee, R. M. (1996). Family treatment of childhood anxiety: A controlled trial. *Journal of Consulting and Clinical Psychology, 64*, 333–342.

Barrett, P. M., & Shortt, A. L. (2003). Parental involvement in the treatment of anxious children. In J. R. Weisz & A. E. Kazdin (Eds.), *Evidence based psychotherapies for children and adolescents* (pp. 101–119). New York: Guilford Press.

Baucom, D. H., & Epstein, N. (1990). *Cognitive-behavioral marital therapy.* Philadelphia: Brunner/Mazel.

Butzlaff, R. L., & Hooley, J. M. (1998). Expressed emotion and psychiatric relapse. *Archives of General Psychiatry, 55*, 547–552.

Christensen, A., & Heavey, C. L. (1993). Gender differences in marital conflict: The demand/withdraw interaction pattern. In S. Oskamp & M. Costanzo (Eds.), *Gender issues in contemporary society: Claremont Symposium on Applied Social Psychology, Vol. 6* (pp. 113–141). Thousand Oaks, CA: Sage.

Dattilio, F. D. (2006). Restructuring schemata from family of origin in couple therapy. *Journal of Cognitive Therapy, 20*, 359–375.

Epstein, N. B., & Baucom, D. H. (2002). *Enhanced cognitive-behavioral therapy for couples: A contextual approach.* Washington, DC: American Psychological Association.

Falloon, I. R. (2003). Behavioral family therapy. In G. P. Sholevar (Ed.), *Textbook of family and couples therapy: Clinical applications* (pp. 147–172). Washington, DC: American Psychiatric Publishing.

Falloon, I. R., Boyd, J. L., & McGill, C. W. (1984). *Family care of schizophrenia: A problem-solving approach to the treatment of mental illness.* New York: Guilford Press.

Falloon, I. R., & Lillie, F. J. (1988). Behavioral family therapy: An overview. In I. R. Falloon (Ed.), *Handbook of behavioral family therapy* (pp. 3–26). New York: Guilford Press.

Falloon, I. R., & Pederson, J. (1985). Family management in the prevention of morbidity of schizophrenia: The adjustment of the family unit. *British Journal of Psychiatry, 147*, 156–163.

Hancock, K. A. (2003). Lesbian, gay, and bisexual psychology: Past, present, and future directions. In J. S. Mio & G. Y. Iwamasa (Eds.), *Culturally diverse mental health: The challenges of research and resistance* (pp. 289–308). New York: Brunner-Routledge.

Hatfield, A. B., & Lefley, H. P. (1987). *Families of the mentally ill: Coping and adaptation.* New York: Guilford Press.

Hatfield, A. B., & Lefley, H. P. (1993). *Surviving mental illness: Stress, coping, and adaptation.* New York: Guilford Press.

Jacobson, N. S., & Christensen, A. (1996). *Integrative couple therapy: Promoting acceptance and change.* New York: Norton.

Jacobson, N. S., & Margolin, G. (1979). *Marital therapy: Strategies based on social learning and behavior exchange principles.* New York: Brunner/Mazel.

Kelly, S. (2006). Cognitive behavioral therapy with African Americans. In P. A. Hays & G. Y. Iwamasa (Eds.), *Culturally responsive cognitive-behavioral therapy: Assessment, practice, and supervision* (pp. 97–116). Washington, DC: American Psychological Association.

Kelly, S., & Iwamasa, G. Y. (2005). Enhancing behavioral couple therapy: Addressing the therapeutic alliance, hope, and diversity. *Cognitive and Behavioral Practice, 12*, 102–112.

Klein, R. G., & Abikoff, H. (1997). Behavior therapy and methylphenidate in the treatment of children with ADHD. *Journal of Attention Disorders, 2,* 89–114.

LaTaillade, J. J. (2006). Considerations for treatment of African American couple relationships. *Journal of Cognitive Psychotherapy, 20,* 341–358.

Leslie, L. A. (1995). The evolving treatment of gender, ethnicity, and sexual orientation in marital and family therapy. *Family Relations, 44,* 359–367.

Martell, C. R., Safren, S. A., & Prince, S. E. (2004). *Cognitive-behavioral therapies with lesbian, gay, and bisexual clients.* New York: Guilford Press.

Mueser, K. T. (2001). Family treatment of schizophrenia and bipolar disorder. In M. M. MacFarlane (Ed.), *Family therapy and mental health: Innovations in theory and practice* (pp. 57–81). Binghamton, NY: Haworth Clinical Practice Press.

Mueser, K. T., & Glynn, S. M. (1999). *Behavioral family therapy for psychiatric disorders.* Oakland, CA: New Harbinger.

Northey, J. W. F., Wells, K. C., Silverman, W. K., & Bailey, C. E. (2003). Childhood behavioral and emotional disorders. *Journal of Marital and Family Therapy, 29,* 523–545.

Rotter, J. B. (1954). *Social learning and clinical psychology.* Englewood Cliffs, NJ: Prentice Hall.

Stuart, R. B. (1980). *Helping couples change: A social learning approach to marital therapy.* New York: Guilford Press.

Tharp, R. G., & Wetzel, R. J. (1969). *Behavior modification in the natural environment.* New York: Academic Press.

Thibaut, J. W., & Kelley, H. H. (1959). *The social psychology of groups.* New Brunswick, NJ: Transaction.

Wells, K. C., Pelham, W. E., Jr., Kotkin, R. A., Hoza, B., Abikoff, H. B., Abramowitz, A., et al. (2000). Psychosocial treatment strategies in the MTA study: Rationale, methods, and critical issues in design and implementation. *Journal of Abnormal Child Psychology, 28,* 483–505.

Whisman, M. A., & Uebelacker, L. A. (2007). Maladaptive schemas and core beliefs in treatment and research with couples. In D. J. Stein, J. E. Young, L. P. Riso, & P. L. du Toit (Eds.), *Cognitive schemas and core beliefs in psychological problems: A scientist-practitioner guide* (pp. 199–220). Washington, DC: American Psychological Association.

16

Psychodynamic Family Psychotherapy: Toward Unified Relational Systematics

Jeffrey J. Magnavita

This chapter presents an evolving model of relational psychodynamic family psycho-therapy that is strongly embedded in personality systematics and relational science. Early versions of this model have been previously published (Magnavita, 2000, 2002). Psycho-dynamic psychotherapy has expanded in its domain of operation from primarily an *intrapsychic-biological* model, originated by Freud, to one that is embedded in the relational matrix and personality systematics (Magnavita, 2006). There are other earlier versions of psychodynamic and relational approaches that share many features of this model but are beyond the scope of this chapter to review (Magnavita, 2007). One such model representing a significant advance is Wachtel's (1977) "cyclical psychodynamic" model that initially integrated both psychodynamic and behavioral approaches and later was expanded to include a systemic component, further broadening its application and theoretical explanatory power.

New ideas emerge and are *differentiated* from existing ones and then inexorably *integrated* and absorbed into the mainstream. This dialectic process has allowed the field of psychodynamics to evolve into a theoretical and clinical approach that main-tains some of the more robust constructs of affective-defensive operations, the power of unconscious processing, and transference-schematic representational systems which guide interpersonal relationships. This has been shaped by a number of disciplines such as neuroscience, system theory, developmental psychopathology, attachment theory, and affective science. The advancements in system theory[1] (von Bertalanffy, 1969) and ecolo-gical theory (Bronfenbrenner, 1979) have enveloped psychodynamics in a new, unified theoretical approach that depicts interrelated domains that can account for the spec-trum of psychopathological-dysfunctional adaptations at the individual, dyadic, triadic, and sociocultural level (Magnavita, 2005a, 2005b, 2006).

An Emphasis on Clinical Utility

A relational psychodynamic model offers the family psychologist the flexibility to move between the microscopic lens of the intrapsychic model, the wider lens of the interpersonal/triadic, and, finally, the widest magnification of the total ecological system. This enables the clinician to intervene at various fulcrum points in a subsystem, shifting the focus of intervention among individual, dyadic, triadic, and larger systems. Relational psychodynamics uses new, powerful, and cost-effective tools such as audiovisual recording and physiological measurements, galvanic skin response, heart-rate variability, and other forms of bio- and neuro-feedback to enhance treatment efficacy and range (McCraty & Tomasino, 2006).

Emphasizing the Personality System as the Mode of Operation: Personality Theory, Psychopathology, and Psychotherapy

Psychodynamic theory in its origins was primarily concerned with the character development and fixations of individuals. Psychopathological adaptations, as they express themselves in symptom constellations, were understood as emerging from the dynamic movement of impulses–defense–anxiety subsystems, the result of tension among the intrapsychic agencies, the id, ego, and superego. Culture and family were not seen as central components of theory and practice, as were intrapsychic-biological components of Freudian metapsychology. Psychoanalysis rested on an instinctual-biological drive impulse framework. Although it was accepted that the evolution of these intrapsychic structures was shaped by the sociopolitical and cultural systems, scant attention was paid to these until later theorists began to explore these domains, which psychoanalysis often integrated, and new perspectives emerged. The search for unifying principles of psychotherapy, which includes psychodynamics, has begun and is solidly based in systematics and "interdisciplinarity – breadth and general knowledge, integration, and synthesis – [which are] ancient" (Klein, 2004, p. 2). Psychodynamics offers a well-developed and useful way to understand primarily biological-intrapsychic and secondarily interpersonal processes, but this is only a portion of what constitutes human nature, consciousness, and psychopathology. As useful as many of the constructs are to conceptualizing and treating psychopathology, other domain levels require attention, and a solid basis in systematics is necessary.

A New Era for Unification: Von Bertalanffy's General System Theory

System theory emerged post-World War II when computers were beginning to be developed, cognitive science was emerging from behaviorism, and mechanistic, reductionistic models of science were challenged by a new approach that highlighted the importance of processes and principles that organize and set the parameters for how complex systems function (von Bertalanffy, 1969). These innovative ways of understanding complex phenomena were applied to biological and social sciences. In the clinical sciences, individuals such as Gregory Bateson (1972), Murray Bowen (1978), and many others began applying these principles to understanding and treating families, thus breaking away from emphasis on the individual. Gottman, Ryan, Carere, & Erley (2002) wrote of this remarkable advance that system theory ushered in, and the clinical utility and explanatory power of system theory in its application to couples and marital transactions and communication.. Gottman states: "This change in thinking was a major breakthrough in the study of marriage because it focused not on the individuals, but on the temporal patterns they created when they are together, much as one focuses on the harmonies of a jazz quartet" (p. 165).

Personality Systematics and Ecological Domains

Continuing with the work of many of the pioneering figures from the last century, personality systematics attempts to further evolve a holistically based systemic model for how the personality system operates throughout all levels of human ecology, from the microscopic to the macroscopic. Any system of relational dysfunction and psychopathology, as well as health, must account for the interrelatedness of these various levels in the nested structure of human functioning. Extending Bronfenbrenner's (1979) nested structure of human ecology allows us to organize all the domain areas of human functioning.

To understand the complex and abstract phenomena that determine personality and relational functioning, we need to categorize the system levels and domains they encompass. Bronfenbrenner (1979) established the system levels in his conceptualization of human development. He viewed the entire ecological system of human functioning in systemic terms, analyzing basic units such as dyad and triadic configuration as they are embedded in larger interpersonal subsystems.

Bronfenbrenner organizes the total ecological system of the individual from the microscopic to the ecological sphere in such a way as to allow us to continually change our perspective. What Bronfenbrenner underscores in his work is the fundamental importance of relational systems in human development and functioning. The building blocks of relational systems are individuals, dyads, and triads that in a sense are *relational molecules*, forming family units, social systems, and culture. Psychodynamics offers useful perspectives for how these relational molecules are bound by affective charges in relational configurations that create convergence points (i.e., attachment patterns, symptom expressions, and dysfunctional patterns). Affect appears to be one of the central dynamic forces, like gravity in physics. Affect creates valences that attract, repel, and otherwise orient us and allow us to adapt to and respond to the complex stimulus features in our environment.

Contemporary Relational Psychodynamics as a Component of Unified Clinical Science

Psychodynamics has proved to have a significant place in the theoretical and clinical domains of unified psychotherapy and clinical science. Conscious and unconscious affect–anxiety–defense processes can be observed at the triadic, family, and cultural levels. Emotional dysregulation is a common phenomenon seen in most forms of psychopathology (Gross, 2007) and represents an emotional system that is highly charged. This relational psychodynamic approach is congruent and grounded in developmental psychopathology, as well as a family-oriented model of psychology. With the creation of system and complexity theory it is clear that psychodynamics cannot exist in a vacuum that ignores other findings from related fields. Interdisciplinarity is essential in unifying the clinical, social sciences, and humanities. Just as early psychoanalytic theory emphasized character functions, contemporary relational psychodynamics orients itself to the personality functioning as it is expressed in various levels of human nature. Even when one chooses to operate within one domain or subsystem, it behooves clinicians, researchers, and theorists to be cognizant of the multiple interacting domains that exert mutual influence. It is the hope of the author that single-domain systems, regardless of type, will recede as more scientific evidence allows us to construct a truly unified relation science grounded in system and complexity theory, as well as personality systematics and psychodynamics. This, then, is not a traditional perspective of psychodynamic family psychotherapy but an evolving, unified one based on empirical and clinical findings from a variety of scientific disciplines.

Organizing the Multiple Domains of Human Functioning into Four Nested Domains based on Twentieth-Century Theoretical Developments

The domains of human functioning can be divided in a seemingly infinite number of ways, which is not helpful to clinicians, who seek parsimony in utilizing templates for pattern recognition with the array of clinical symptoms, personality dysfunction, and relational disturbances that are the focus of practice. Based on an extensive review of the dominant theoretical systems of the past century, it seemed that one way in which to carve nature at her joints was to incorporate aspects of the "best" systems developed to organize data at various theoretical levels. What became apparent in this process was that many clinical theorists utilize triangular configurations as a method of depicting process among various components of a system. Among the many, Malan's (1979) arrangement of two triangular figures in psychodynamic theory (see Figure 16.1, Level I: intrapsychic-biological triangle and Level II: interpersonal-dyadic triangle) and Bowen's (1978) triangular matrix (see Figure 16.1, Level III: relational-triadic matrix) in systemic theory remain among the most recognized, although there are quite a few others. Triangles are excellent symbols for depicting geometric relationships that can alter their shape as

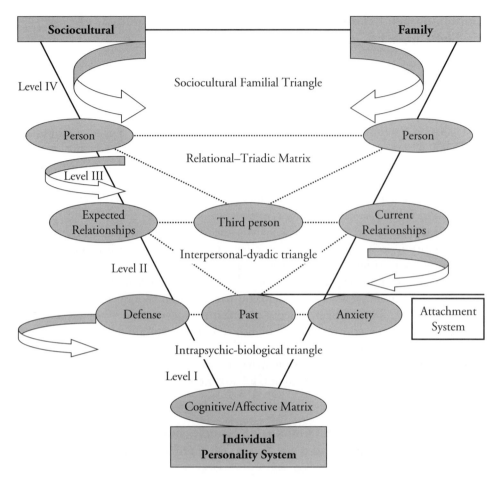

Figure 16.1 Diagram of the four nested triangular subdomains

attraction among the three corners is intensified or relaxed. Any impact on any corner of a triangle impacts the remaining corners. Thus, triangles can denote synergistic relationships. Relational psychodynamics combines these and a fourth which depicts the interplay among the individual personality system, sociocultural structures/process, and the family (see Figure 16.1, Level IV: sociocultural-familial triangle). Readers who are interested in understanding this in greater depth can refer to the references provided.

Part–whole relationships characterizing human functioning at all domain levels

In addition to expanding the domains of operation it is essential that the interrelationships, mutual influence, and co-construction among these components are understood as fundamental assumptions of a systemically based theory of relational psychodynamics. Parts do not exist as isolated elements but in the context in which they are observed and in which they operate. When dealing with complex phenomena, it is unrealistic to separate parts from their networks and not to expect that there will be a loss of explanatory power (see Chapter 1, this volume). Human beings are embedded in multiple nested structures/networks that offer differing perspectives of phenomena.

It is important, especially in the context of this volume devoted to the field of family psychology, to locate psychodynamic theory and practice in an overall unified system, and not as an isolated, one-person psychology. Various authors in this volume will emphasize in more depth the structure and process of these other domains (see Chapters 19 and 24, this volume), so they will not be recapitulated here. In previous publications a unified model is depicted using four embedded domain subsystem that account for the overall ecosystem of human functioning (see Figure 16.1). These include (I) *intrapsychic-biological*, (II) *interpersonal-dyadic*, (III) *relational-triadic*, and (IV) *sociocultural-familial* (Magnavita, 2005a, 2005b, 2006). Classic psychodynamics primarily is concerned with microlevel processes that occur mainly at the first and second domain levels. Initially, psychoanalytic theory was most concerned with intrapsychic operations and structures and later, with the ground-breaking work of Sullivan (1953), expanded its domains to the interpersonal-dyadic (Magnavita, 2007). Although there have been exceptions, such as the work of Scharff and Scharff (1991), very few psychodynamic theorists fully embraced system theory, although many family therapy pioneers were originally trained in psychoanalytic technique.

The Four Nested Triangular Subsystems: Their Operating Principles, Processes, and Structures

In this section each of the four levels of a unified framework will be presented. It is important to note that separations in the various levels do not represent independently functioning subsystems, but are made for heuristic purposes so that clinicians and researchers have a map with which to orient their modes of examination and operation. We begin at the microlevel of process and then increasingly widen our perspective to the macrolevel.

Level I: Intrapsychic-biological triangle (individual system)

The intrapsychic-biological triangle depicts the interrelationships among the cognitive/affective matrix at the bottom of the triangle, anxiety at the top right, and defense at the top left. These include neurobiological process-structures, affective-defense functions, cognitive schemas, and temperamental predispositions. On the basis of genetic, temperamental, and neurobiological structures, each individual's intrapsychic structure is shaped by the attachment-relational system. The bottom corner of the triangle can be depicted as the cognitive schemas (templates of self–other) and affective system primed by quality of attachment experience and shaped by traumatic events and developmental challenges. Feeling that has not been processed (i.e., identified, experienced, and contextualized in a narrative) is activated in later attachment experiences and gives rise to anxiety, (located at the upper-right corner), which is modulated by defenses on the upper-left side. Various constellations of defenses are used at the intrapsychic level depending upon developmental stage and progression of personality development. The more primitive the defenses and reactive the affective system, the higher the level of dysfunction present in this subsystem. When this subsystem lacks differentiation, emotions are not experienced, resulting in unmanageable anxiety, which requires overutilization of defenses; this can undermine adaptive functioning. In this case, the individual may follow two primary courses regarding affect. He or she may be emotionally under-regulated or over-regulated, that is, emotionally over-reactive or constricted.

Level II: Interpersonal-dyadic triangle (two-person system)

This triangle depicts the dyadic configuration and accounts for processes that occur between two people, in regulating the tension between intimacy and separateness. The dyadic relationship is the primary architect of the mind (intrapsychic system), shaping, through interpersonal interaction, the activation, kindling, and pruning of neuronal networks. The primary attachment system is the maternal–infant dyad, which is the foundational dyad that begins to shape the emergent self (intrapsychic structures/processes) from the genetic and temperamental substrate. Attachment systems develop and are codified, in the rich nutrient of attunement, regulation, and repair, and become robust predictors of adult interpersonal styles (Schore, 2003). The interpersonal matrix offers a window into the early attachment experiences that are recreated in relationships with others and in the therapeutic relationship. Attachment experiences build the capacity for and interest in intimacy as development progresses. Intimacy is necessary for our family and social relationship and is the building block of empathy for others.

The lower corner of the triangle represents *past relationships* and the encoded relational schemas and attachment patterns that are recapitulated in *current relationships* (upper-right corner) and *expected relationships* (i.e., therapeutic relationship or entering any new relationship; upper-left corner). All current and expected relationships are influenced by internalized relational schemas based on attachment experiences and shaped by family, extrafamilial relationships, and cultural forces.

There are four main findings emerging from psychodynamic theory that summarize the implications for family psychotherapists and relational researchers, emphasizing the interrelationship among self, affect, and relationships (Anderson, Reznik, & Glassman, 2005):

1 Significant-other representations are activated automatically in transference.
2 Affect arises relatively automatically in transference when the significant-other representation is activated.

3 The relational self is activated relatively automatically when the significant-other representation is activated.
4 Some self-regulatory processes in the relational self are evoked in the response to "threat" (e.g., negative cues) in transference and may be automatic. (p. 423)

Robust evidence from convergent lines of research provides support for the notion that human beings use templates for relationships when approaching others to serve a pattern-recognition function. Psychotherapy capitalizes on these processes by allowing the family psychologist to experience and witness how these unfold in dyads. Before proceeding with the remainder of the model it is worthwhile to present the summary of empirical findings concerning these psychodynamic matrices (Westen & Gabbard, 1999):

1 Much of mental life is unconscious, including thoughts, feelings, and motives.
2 Mental processes, including affective and motivational processes, operate in parallel, so that individuals can have conflicting feelings toward the same person or situation that motivate them in opposing ways and often lead to compromise solutions.
3 Stable personality patterns play an important role in personality development, particularly in shaping the ways people form later social relationships.
4 Mental representations of the self, others, and relationships guide people's interactions with others and influence the ways they become psychologically symptomatic.
5 Personality development involves not only learning to regulate sexual and aggressive feelings but also moving from an immature, socially dependent state to a mature, interdependent one. (p. 74)

We can also broaden our perspective by widening our lens, observing the third domain level and yet another relational molecule: triadic configurations. With this transition we leave behind what have been the traditional realms of psychodynamic operation. There is a loss of flexibility when failing to take the next two domains into account in our model. Expanding the range requires a broader system that includes family processes.

Level III: Relational-triadic configuration (three-person matrix)

This triangular configuration represents the relations among a primary dyad and a third person. The dyad is essentially unstable and seeks stabilization by deflecting anxiety to a third person, often a child or another adult as in an extramarital affair. An unstable dyad has more anxiety than the individual affect-defense system of the individual and the intimacy-closeness capacity of the couple can effectively manage. The lower level of differentiation that exists at the emotional or self–other level increases the likelihood that triangulation will occur in a dyad (Bowen, 1976). Again, the processes can be depicted using a triangle. At the bottom of the triangle a third (triangulated) person is depicted and the top two corners represent two people in a dyad. An unstable dyad is one in which each member is relatively undifferentiated, which refers to both emotional differentiation, or what has been termed emotional intelligence, and self–other differentiation, which refers to flexible boundaries in two individuals with a coherent, integrated sense of themselves. Within this triad is a dyad that does not effectively maintain intimacy and closeness in a regulated way – they tend to try to fuse/merge or are overly distant, or that fluctuates wildly between the two poles – they tend to spill their emotions into third parties in an attempt to stabilize the dyad. According to Guerin, Fogarty, Fay, & Kautto (1996), "a person emotionally entrapped in a triangle is likely, by virtue of being trapped, to suffer some loss of function" (p. 31). This is particularly evident in clinical practice when there are natural transition periods in the family life cycle, such as when an adolescent goes off to college and then for a variety of reasons ends up coming home in defeat. Triangles are in a sense anxiety-management defense operations that can allow a relationship to continue with minimal change required, at the cost of emotional maturity and capacity for intimacy and closeness.

Level IV: Sociocultural-familial triangle (mesosystem)
This triangle depicts the synergy among three corners: the individual personality system, the family system, and the cultural system (see Figure 16.1, largest triangle). The interaction of these three corners exerts a major impact on the development of personality by shaping how genetic predispositions and vulnerabilities will be expressed. This triangle accounts for the often neglected sociocultural aspects of psychopathology and relational dysfunction. For example, an in-depth understanding of eating disorders requires acknowledging the impact of popular culture on body type, as well as dynamic and familial pressures and expectations.

The sociocultural-familial matrix is the entire mesosystem representing the most macrolevel of operation of the biopsychoecosphere. It includes the individual, couples, families, groups, culture, and their operating systems that mutually shape and influence each other. The primary mode of operation is language and non-verbal modes of communication that, through a multigenerational transmission process, transmit memes (social units) (Dawkins, 1976) just as genes transport genetic codes.

Culture confers identity and is linked bidirectionally to all four levels in terms of operating systems and structures both intrapsychic and relational schemas. Culture adapts to environmental and human forces, transmitting values, parenting styles, modes of preferred communication, intimacy rituals, etc. (Prager, 1995).

Application of Model to Treatment of Complex Clinical Syndromes, Personality Dysfunction, and Relational Disturbances

Treating complex clinical syndromes is the ultimate test of any model of treatment. Complex disorders are multi-pathway phenomena where co-morbid disorders (anxiety, depression, substance abuse, PTSD, and so forth) usually exist in the context of a personality system that is dysfunctional at the intrapsychic level, and also in various relational configurations such as dyadic, triadic, family, and societal. Determining the domain level to focus clinical attention on in a complex system is not a simple task even for experienced clinicians. The disruption of the equilibrium of the various personality subsystems reverberates throughout the entire personality system. When individual, dyadic, triadic, familial, and cultural systems are chronically stressed, or deficient in basic processes, dysfunction will occur at the various diathesis points; vulnerability of the neurobiological system might emerge as depression when a family member loses economic standing or endures a relationship loss. Over the course of time, dysfunction in the family system may result in marital discord or child behavioral problems that mutually affect the other. Left untreated, there may be a cascading chain of events over generations leading to greater personality dysfunction in the family members. Change can also result from perturbations in any domain of the system that can potentially reverberate at any level, setting into motion a wave of cascading change.

The centrality of the family system

The family is the primary unit for shaping personality and thus is a critical component of a unified system of relational psychodynamics. Humans are born into family systems and shaped by the attachment experiences and family processes that are unique to every one. When chronic dysfunction exists, personality development and function in the members of these family systems can be adversely affected. Important functions such as emotional regulation, pro-social behavior, and capacity for intimacy and closeness are derailed and then, through a process of modeling and learning, passed on to the following generation. Family psychotherapy broadly conceptualized, whether practiced at the individual, dyadic, or familial level, takes into consideration these forces and seeks to stop the multigenerational transmission process evident in dysfunctional personologic systems. They are defined as follows:

- A dysfunctional family system in which a preponderance of individuals have personality pathology, often observable over generations.
- A lineage of certain types of personality pathology associated with central family themes, dynamics, and triangles. (Magnavita, 2000, p. 4)

Features of dysfunctional personologic systems.   These features can be defined as:

- Impermeable external boundaries that separate the family system from others.
- Poor boundaries among family members.
- Disturbed level of communication and over-reliance on primitive defenses.
- Reversal of the parent–child relationship.
- Need for family to revolve around a narcissistic parent.
- Poor emotional differentiation and regulation.
- Emotional malnourishment.
- Financial instability.
- Multigenerational transmission process. (Magnavita, 2000, p. 54)

Returning to our conceptual schema, we can see that embedded in the various domains are important functions that are central to healthy emotional development at the various levels of the system. Each of these areas should be assessed and functional deficiencies mended by restructuring the subsystem. Next, each of the four domains and treatment implications for navigating these is presented.

Micro and Macro-Processes and Structures in Operation

In the following section we will shift our perspective from the microlevel to the macrolevel and examine some of the processes and suggestions for clinical intervention. At each of the four levels various strategies, methods, and techniques of psychotherapy can be utilized. The family psychologist must be trained in the full spectrum of evidence-based techniques in order to practice unified psychotherapy. In order to illustrate the way in which a unified approach helps the family psychologists organize multilevel interventions, a brief case example is presented and strategies at each of the four levels of operation are discussed.

Case example.   A married couple in their early forties consults with the family psychologist because of marital distress that has brought them to the brink of divorce. They are both in their first marriage of 13 years and have three children. The marital distress was worsened a year ago when the husband experienced a major setback in his business and investigation by state regulators.

Intrapsychic-biological substrate

When the intrapsychic system (microsystem) of the individual is chronically dysfunctional, capacities for operating within the complex relational world are limited. Clinical syndromes will emerge over time as an expression of a system in distress. Over time a system that is not evolving, reorganizing, and restructuring itself is generally in serious distress. Human personality systems are self-organizing and respond to demands placed upon them when optimally functioning. When the intrapsychic system is exposed to various traumas, developmental insufficiencies, neurobiological insult, or other bionegativity, the system may show signs of dysfunction. There are various general guidelines for clinically navigating this level of the operating system.

Suggestions for clinical practice: Pattern recognition and subsystem navigation.

- Catalogue the defenses of all the members of a system you are seeing by observing their static-state defenses (low anxiety) and higher-state defenses (higher anxiety). If individuals shift rapidly to lower levels of functioning, the system is fragile. If, on the other hand, they can withstand some anxiety, the system is more stable.

- Assess whether defenses are developmentally appropriate and educate parents and adults about adaptive viability.
- Identify cognitive and relational schemas that maintain a coherent sense of self, and restructure when maladaptive.
- Notice how anxiety is experienced and channeled. Does it go into symptoms, clinical syndromes, behavior disorder, relational disturbances, or somatic experience, or is it expressed in character or personality, for example grandiosity, passivity, lack of empathy?
- Investigate system vulnerabilities such as temperament, neurobiological, and intrapsychic.
- Assess capacity for affective regulation. Is affect directed inward (such as internalizing conditions, avoidant, dependent, or obsessive-compulsive), or is it externalized or spilling out (borderline conditions, histrionic, antisocial), or does it derail cognition (schizotypal, schizoid, and paranoid conditions)?

Case discussion. An evaluation of each of the marital dyad revealed important information concerning each of their intrapsychic levels of functioning. The husband was suffering from anxiety and depression. His defensive constellation primarily consisted of intellectual, rationalization, detachment, withdrawal, and avoidance. The wife was angry and anxious. She felt deceived by her husband's business decisions, which she felt demonstrated poor judgment and put their family at risk. Her defense constellation primarily included arguing, denial, complaining, and sarcasm. As their distress intensified both began to become more fixed in their response patterns. His sense of self was based on his capacity to be a good provider and hers on maintaining family connection. In each case they were feeling massively disappointed in themselves and each other. He felt abandoned in his time of need and she felt angry about his distancing.

Interpersonal-dyadic substrate

In this matrix we focus our attention on the operating system that accounts for processes that occur between two people. The interpersonal domain offers a window into the rich tapestry of attachment experiences that are re-created in relationships with others and in therapeutic relationships. Attachment capacity forms the parameters for interest in and tolerance for intimacy. Our past relationships with our primary and secondary attachment figures shape our internal relational schemas. Beginning with our earliest attachment experience we build an internal representation of self and others. If there are traumatic experiences such as losses, parental neglect or abuse, and so forth the personality system can show a cascading sequence of rebounding social, neurobiological, and emotional circuits.

Our current relational capacities are based on overall system integrity. The capacity to form and maintain intimate relationships is highly influenced by our level of self–other differentiation. Our current relationships are an excellent window on recurring patterns, and afford the patient and psychotherapist a unique opportunity to learn what the internal schemas are and how they can be restructured at a higher level of adaptation.

Suggestions for clinical practice: Pattern recognition and subsystem navigation.

- Observe the dyadic process between family members and assess the level of self–other differentiation (e.g., look for fused, enmeshed, or disengaged relationships and observe the capacity to tell a coherent narrative while remaining emotionally present and engaged with another person).
- Identify repetitive or recurrent interpersonal patterns and explore multigenerational connections (e.g., history of trauma, neglect, conflicted parental dyad, etc.).
- Explore the themes of recurrent patterns and assist in finding more adaptive and functional patterns (e.g., improved communication, enhanced differentiation).
- Encourage non-reactive emotional communication processes. If the level of reactivity is too high, bring anxiety down to a tolerable level.
- Seek to enhance emotional capacity by assisting in emotional experiencing and expression.
- Identify interpersonal preferences and styles and provide psychoeducation that enhances acceptance of stylistic differences (e.g., individuals often vary in their interpersonal tempo and style).

Case discussion.   In the marital session, witnessing the process of transaction and communication in the dyad was revealing. There was a high level of reactivity. Each partner was blaming the other for the marital problems and reacting with moderate defensiveness. They had become so distant that they were unable to participate in a process of conflict resolution and repair. As the wife expressed her anger the husband became more withdrawn, and his anxiety escalated to the point where he wasn't able to be rational. As a child he reported he was left with his actively alcoholic mother, whom he learned to take care of and protect. This he realized was now an important part of his self-concept that he felt that he was no longer being validated for fueling his distancing and non-communication with his wife. This distancing furthered the wife's feeling of abandonment and rage. She realized that she never really fully trusted any man because her father, who was an alcoholic, could not be depended upon. Her solution was to make it clear to him that he was not important as a father. Overall the level of intimacy/closeness was dangerously low and the beginnings of contempt were emerging, a negative indicator for the survival of the marriage.

Relational-triadic substrate

When unstable dyads are unstable by virtue of their low level of emotional capacity and ability to communicate their internal states' experience, too high a level of anxiety problems ensues. Children, by virtue of their developmentally appropriate lack of differentiation, often become anxious, and this can overtax their intrapsychic operating system. Their symptoms may serve multiple functions, one of which is to stabilize the parental dyad. Triangular configurations are ubiquitous in human relationships. They commonly shift and reconfigure, but when fixed may over time interfere with optimal growth and development.

Suggestions for clinical practice: Pattern recognition and subsystem navigation.

- Consider a symptomatic child or adolescent a possible navigational pointer to a highly conflicted dyad. These children may be like the proverbial canary in the mine, in being the first signal of a dysfunctional dyad. These dyads can exist across generational boundaries (e.g., between grandmother and an adult child).
- When there are chronic symptoms of personality dysfunction in a child or adolescent, evaluate the family to determine whether there is evidence of a dysfunctional personologic system, and if possible initiate multimodal treatment to address multiple levels of the system.
- Encourage self-focus in treatment modalities to enhance relational and self–other capacities.
- Where possible increase tension in the dyad and block channeling to the triangulated third person.
- Observe that fixed triangles are more pathogenic of personality dysfunction and initiate treatment to address the personality disturbance where possible.

Case discussion.   With the low level of intimacy/closeness and high level of distress, the couple was intensifying triangulation in order to maintain stability. The husband's mother was becoming an increasingly hostile point of conflict. She was in a position where, because of her own needs for control, she was undermining the marital dyad. The wife was becoming furious and feeling even more abandoned by her husband, who she felt sided with his mother. He felt caught in between two important people in his life both of whom he wanted to please. His solution was to become less disclosing of his activities with his mother, further engaging his wife. A review of the situation showed that the children were not being pulled in to the conflict.

Sociocultural-familial substrate

The influence of the macrosystem on all levels presented is powerful. Contextualism allows us to understand how the individual, dyadic, family, and larger social units are affected by social and cultural pathologies such as poverty, racism, discrimination, and so forth, which create bionegativity. The individual personality system, which we have discussed, has been the basic unit of psychodynamic operation, which is shaped and nurtured by the family and cultural systems that support or prove to be an impediment to optimal development.

Suggestions for clinical practice: Pattern recognition and subsystem navigation.

- Look for obvious signs of dysfunction that are affecting family cohesion, stability, and functions, such as poverty, discrimination, or cultural expectations not consistent with current context.

- Familiarize yourself with the cultural, ethnic, social, political, and economic forces that represent the ecological system of the family and individuals being assessed and treated.
- Educate families about the impact of contemporary popular culture and some of the toxic effects of excessive television viewing and internet usage on child and adolescent obesity and aggression.
- Understand the themes of significant sociopolitical forces on successive generations and explore the meaning to children who were raised by Holocaust survivors or fled their country because of genocide or the effects of war.

Case discussion.   The father was an Irish immigrant and in his cultural experience things like grandparents sharing a bed with their grandchildren was acceptable. However, to the wife this was entirely unacceptable. She felt that the grandmother would continue to do this even if they asked her not to. The wife's upbringing was more traditional for New England Caucasians, where privacy was highly respected. Another important cultural difference was in the ways their extended families operated. His was what we might describe as highly enmeshed, with multiple generations interacting in what her background made her feel were intrusive and inconsiderate ways. These issues had to be identified and understood, and compromises agreed upon.

Expanding the Realm of Psychodynamics

Incorporating psychodynamics into a unified relational approach allows family psychologists to expand their realm of operation by utilizing some of the robust findings from the past century concerning personality adaptations and the emergence of clinical syndromes and relational disturbances from these. A systemic approach allows a greater degree of flexibility about where and how to intervene and what modalities of treatment can be utilized. Human systems are best characterized by a complexity theory that is one of non-linearity, and thus they are prone to disruption and self-organization often with small perturbations. Conceptualizing human functioning and dysfunction as a unified system allows many paths to addressing dysfunction. Techniques and methods of various schools of psychotherapy that are evidence based can be incorporated in the treatment package. Unlike technical eclecticism, this allows the family psychologist to navigate the complex relational system using theory as a navigation tool.

Psychodynamic Family Psychotherapy

A full presentation of the range, techniques, and processes of psychodynamic family psychotherapy is beyond the scope of what can be covered in a single chapter. Distilling the basic constructs by adopting a unified psychodynamic framework that is systemically grounded allows clinicians maximum flexibility of movement within the relational subsystems. The psychodynamic operating systems most important for the clinician operate at the dyadic level when working in individual psychotherapy and couples psychotherapy, as well as at the dyadic and triadic when conducting group and family psychotherapy. Arguably the most useful operating subsystems for family psycho-therapists are the *anxiety–defense–emotion* and *intimacy/closeness processes*, as well as the *past–current–expected relationships* ones. These processes can be viewed in individuals, couples, and families when affective experience is increased and defensive operations are activated. There is a clear relationship between capacity for intimacy and closeness based on early attachment schemas and the emotion/anxiety/defense matrix. When the capa-city is low for intimacy and closeness, as individuals approach intimacy non-metabolized emotional constellations can be activated and anxiety can ensue, leading to an exacer-bation of defensive responding. In couples this can result in a downward spiraling pattern whereby each member of the dyad becomes increasingly dysregulated, thus becoming anxious and setting in motion a pattern of increasingly primitive or regressive defenses. Concomitantly, there may be a decrease in perceptual clarity and cognitive dys-regulation. Behaviorally, this may then manifest in screaming, yelling, cursing, blaming, stonewalling, or paranoid reactions. Low states of coherence and emotional dysregulation can then be communicated from limbic system to limbic system, creating a dyadic state of dysregulation such as researchers observe in disorganized maternal–infant attach-ments (Beebe & Lachmann, 2002). Psychodynamics offers clinicians guidelines for identifying the unique defense constellation of each person in a system and using this information to calibrate tolerance for rise in anxiety (Magnavita, 1997; Blackman, 2004). Psychodynamics also offers useful constructs that are evidence based (PDM Task Force, 2006) for assessing the integrity of the intrapsychic and interpersonal system of both children and adults. This is essential information for all family psychotherapists to learn and master to enhance diagnostic ability and treatment efficacy.

Summary

The family psychologist now has an array of treatment strategies and interventions from various schools of psychotherapy on which to draw. Each system is unique and requires the development of a holistic treatment plan. Relational psychodynamics emerges from multiple scientific and clinical disciplines and is unified in its conceptualization, process, and psychotherapeutics. Solidly basing psychodynamics on a systemic framework creates the ability to view multiple perspectives of the system at various domain levels. Thus, when not constrained to one or two levels of operation, there is greater flexibility to create a treatment package that is highly individualized and can respond to the needs of individual and family members over the course of their life span, as the family life cycle produces the stress and strain of differentiation and integration which is the hallmark of complex systems as they evolve and adapt.

Note

1   In von Bertalanffy's original volume he used the term "system theory." Later theorists often used the plural "systems theory."

Resources

Blackman, J. S. (2004). *101 defenses: How the mind shields itself.* New York: Brunner-Rutledge.

Magnavita, J. J. (2005). *Personality-guided relational therapy: A unified approach.* Washington, DC: American Psychological Association.

Magnavita, J. J. (2006). *Treating personality disorders* [American Psychological Association videotape]. Washington, DC: American Psychological Association.

Magnavita, J. J. (in process). *Personality-guided psychotherapy over time* [six-session DVD]. Washington, DC: American Psychological Association.

Millon, T. (with Grossman, S., Meagher, S., Millon, C., & Everly, G.). (1999). *Personality-guided therapy.* Hoboken, NJ: Wiley.

PDM Task Force. (2006). *Psychodynamic diagnostic manual.* Silver Springs, MD: Alliance of Psychoanalytic Organizations.

References

Anderson, S. M., Reznik, I., & Glassman, N. S. (2005). The unconscious relational self. In R. R. Hansen, J. S. Uleman, & J. A. Bargh (Eds.), *The new unconscious* (pp. 421–481). New York: Oxford University Press.

Bateson, G. (1972). *Steps to an ecology of mind: Collected essays in anthropology, psychiatry, evolution, and epistemology.* Chicago: University of Chicago Press.

Beebe, B., & Lachmann, F. M. (2002). *Infants and adults in treatment.* Hillsdale, NJ: Analytic Press.

Blackman, J. S. (2004). *101 defenses: How the mind shields itself.* New York: Brunner-Rutledge.

Bowen, M. (1976). Theory and practice of family therapy. In P. J. Guerin, Jr. (Ed.), *Family therapy: Theory and practice* (pp. 42–90). New York: Gardner Press.

Bowen, M. (1978). *Family therapy in clinical practice.* New York: Aronson.

Bronfenbrenner, U. (1979). *The ecology of human development : Experiments by nature and design.* Cambridge, MA: Harvard University Press.

Dawkins, R. (1976). *The selfish gene.* New York: Oxford University Press.

Gottman, J. M., Ryan, K. D., Carere, S., & Erley, A. M. (2002). Toward a scientifically based marital therapy. In H. Liddle, D. Santiseban, R. Levant, & J. H. Bray (Eds.), *Family psychology: Science-based interventions* (pp. 147–174). Washington, DC: American Psychological Association.

Gross, J. J. (Ed.). (2007). *Handbook of emotion regulation.* New York: Guilford Press.

Guerin, P. J., Fogarty, T. F., Fay, L. F., & Kautto, J. G. (1996). *Working with relational triangles: The one-two-three of psychotherapy.* New York: Guilford Press.

Klein, J. T. (2004). Interdisciplinarity and complexity: An evolving relationship. *Emergence: Complexity and Organization, 6,* 2–10.

Magnavita, J. J. (1997). *Restructuring personality disorders: A short-term dynamic approach.* New York: Guilford Press.

Magnavita, J. J. (2000). *Relational therapy for personality disorders.* Hoboken, NJ: Wiley.

Magnavita, J. J. (2002). Relational psychodynamics for complex clinical syndromes. In F. W. Kaslow & J. J. Magnavita (Eds.), *Comprehensive handbook of psychotherapy: Psychodynamic/object relations: Vol. 1.* (pp. 435–453). Hoboken, NJ: Wiley.

Magnavita, J. J. (2005a). *Personality-guided relational therapy: A unified approach.* Washington, DC: American Psychological Association.

Magnavita, J. J. (2005b). Systems theory foundations of personality, psychopathology, and psychotherapy. In S. Strack (Ed.), *Handbook of personology and psychopathology* (pp.140–163). Hoboken, NJ: Wiley.

Magnavita, J. J. (2006). In search of the unifying principles of psychotherapy: Conceptual, empirical, and clinical convergence. *American Psychologist, 61(8),* 882–892.

Magnavita, J. J. (2007). A systemic family perspective on child and adolescent personality disorders. In A. Freeman & M. A. Reinecke (Eds.), *Personality disorders in childhood and adolescence* (pp. 131–181). Hoboken, NJ: Wiley.

Magnavita, J. J. (2008). Psychoanalytic psychotherapy. In J. Lebow (Ed.), *Twenty-first century psychotherapies: Contemporary approaches to theory and practice* (pp. 206–236). Hoboken, NJ: Wiley.

Malan, D. H. (1979). *Individual psychotherapy and the science of psychodynamics.* London: Butterworth.

McCraty, R., & Tomasino, D. (2006). Coherence-building techniques and heart rate rhythm coherence feedback: New tools for stress reduction, disease prevention and rehabilitation. In E. Molinari, A. Compare, & G. Paran (Eds.), *Clinical psychology and heart disease.* New York: Springer.

PDM Task Force. (2006). *Psychodynamic diagnostic manual.* Silver Springs, MD: Alliance of Psychoanalytic Organizations.

Prager, K. J. (1995). *The psychology of intimacy.* New York: Guilford Press.

Scharff, D. E., & Scharff, J. S. (1991). *Object relations family therapy.* Northvale, NJ: Aronson.

Schore, A. N. (2003). *Affect regulation and the repair of the self.* New York: Norton.

Sullivan, H. S. (1953). *The interpersonal theory of psychiatry.* New York: Norton.

von Bertalanffy, L. (1969). *General system theory.* New York: Braziller.

Wachtel, P. L. (1977). *Psychoanalysis and behavior therapy. New York: Basic Books.*

Westen, D., & Gabbard, G. O. (1999). Psychoanalytic approaches to personality. In L. A. Pervin & O. P. John (Eds.), *Handbook of personality: Theory and research* (2nd Ed., pp. 57–101). New York: Guilford Press.

17

Personality-Guided Couples Psychotherapy

Mark Stanton and A. Rodney Nurse

The thesis of this chapter is that couple therapy may be enhanced by attention to the interactive personality dynamics in the couple relationship. Personality-guided couple psychotherapy (PGCP) may focus specifically on individual personality or the personality interaction, or it may incorporate personality dynamics to attend to relational or psychological disorders. This chapter focuses specifically on two instruments developed by Theodore Millon (Millon & Bloom, 2008); other assessment devices may be used within the general principles described here.

Role of Personality in Couple Relationships

Individual personality manifests itself in intimate couple relationships (Magnavita, 2005). Couple relationships often are formed around complementary personality dynamics. Millon's model of personality (Davis & Millon, 1997) notes three bipolarities (pleasure–pain, active–passive, and self–other) on which individual personality is grounded, but it is common for couples to balance each other on these polarities. Consider, for instance, the magnetic attraction experienced between the self-centered person with narcissistic traits and the other-centered person with dependent traits. The narcissist seeks admiration and obedience and the dependent submits to receive rewards; both feel they have found their match.

Initial positive attraction may degenerate over time. The differences that originally attracted may now irritate and annoy. This is especially true if the complementarity is extreme (i.e., couples with complementary traits may find it easier to co-exist than couples with complementary personality disorders). Patterns of interaction based on personality may be difficult to modify, even if they are not effective for the relationship. In addition, these patterns may be complicated further by the presence of other psychological disorders. "There are documented connections between relational processes and the etiology, maintenance, relapse, and optimal treatment of many disorders" (Beach, Wamboldt, Kaslow, & Heyman, 2006).

Individual perceptions of quality and satisfaction in a marital relationship are related to the personalities of the partners (Spotts et al., 2005). Research finds that individual personality explains a substantial amount of the satisfaction in a relationship.

These findings suggest that couple therapy focused on improving interpersonal personality adjustment may help to alleviate relationship distress, improve perceptions of quality in the relationship, and connect to treatment of psychological disorders.

Personality within a Systemic Epistemology

Personality is an individual factor within the interactive systemic model (Stanton, Chapter 1, this volume) of individual, interpersonal, and environmental-macrosystemic factors. As such, its etiology is first understood within the context of individual development. Personality derives from the complex evolutionary interaction of heritable and biologic elements with social influences and the wider ecology (Bronfenbrenner, 1979; Magnavita, 2005). Although it is often understood as intrapsychic, personality is fundamentally relational in its origins and manifests itself in the way one perceives, thinks, feels, and behaves toward others.

Magnavita and MacFarlane (2004) note that relationship adversity and family dysfunction influence the etiology of personality disorders and the impact of personality-disordered individuals on family members. They suggest that "personality-disordered individuals demonstrate disturbances in the relational matrix" (p. 27), and they recommend including family members, such as spouses or partners, in treatment and the need to adopt a systemic perspective to address the complex, multifaceted nature of personality disorders.

It is important to recognize that personality demonstrates itself automatically in interpersonal relations. A couple relationship is the composite of two personalities interacting with each other in reciprocal fashion; each person influences and is influenced by the other, so that various personality characteristics are either minimized or exacerbated in the relationship. Over time each person may become even more polarized with the partner than with other people in their life. Consider the woman who is aggressive and dominating with her passive, submissive husband. He is convinced that she will never back down, and she criticizes him for his failure to say what is on his mind. Over time, the polarization increases between them and the pattern becomes deeply entrenched. At work, however, more assertive people stand up to the woman's aggressive style and she may learn to moderate her approach with those individuals. So the social surround (e.g., extended family, friendship network, and work relations) provides an alternative context for personality exploration and modification. In fact, couple treatment may be facilitated by encouraging a partner to rebalance an individual personality characteristic in an extended relationship first, to demonstrate success and convince the individual that it is possible to change his or her style of interaction in the couple relationship (e.g., the passive man may learn assertion in the less threatening environment at work and then transfer that behavior to the couple relationship).

The couple relationship also is set within the context of the wider environment and the macrosystemic elements with which it interacts regularly. Cultural convictions, religious beliefs, socioeconomic influences, geographic traditions, and media depictions may normalize or undermine certain personality traits. For instance, some cultures value female submission and passivity, while other cultures have very different gender prescriptions. A couple will interact with these macrosystemic influences to find their unique style of living within their system. PGCP pays attention to the complex, interactive nature of these systemic factors while focusing specifically on the dyadic relationship.

Assessing Personality

PGCP can be assisted by utilizing one of the two personality questionnaires by Millon and colleagues for assessing personality: The Millon Clinical Multiaxial Inventory-III (MCMI-III; Millon, 2006) and the Millon Index of Personality Styles Revised (MIPS; Millon, 2004). The MCMI-III is a 175-item inventory with statements in a true/false format designed for use with clinical populations. It provides scores on 14 personality dimensions (e.g., Dependent, Narcissistic, Antisocial, Borderline), as well as 10 clinical syndromes (e.g., Anxiety, Dysthymia, Major Depression); the categories are similar to those in the *Diagnostic and Statistical Manual of Mental Disorders* (DSM-IV) (American Psychiatric Association, 1994). Since the categories parallel those known and understood by most psychologists, it is possible to adopt use of the instrument fairly readily.

By contrast, the MIPS, with its 180-item format, provides assessment data based on a non-clinical sample approximating the US population on key variables. The MIPS is particularly appropriate for a couple whose overt individual psychopathology appears minimal, with any problems seeming to focus on life transitions (e.g., marriage, remarriage, divorce). The MIPS may help the partners individually and together work to enhance their personality strengths, rather than focusing on psychopathology.

Both inventories provide interpretive reports, but only the MIPS report is to be shown and given to the client. These inventories should be utilized only by clinicians with appropriate education, training, and experience. Other personality instruments may be used within the general model described here.

Personality-Guided Couple Psychotherapy

This section describes a format for conducting PGCP (Nurse & Stanton, 2008). It begins with the common psychotherapeutic process of creating a therapeutic alliance and conducting an intake evaluation of the presenting issues. Careful consideration of the couple interactions in the first session around identified concerns allow the personality-guided therapist to generate initial impressions regarding individual personality attributes and to consider the focus of treatment (e.g., relational problems, relationship problems associated with individual disorders, or individual disorder(s) strongly influenced by relationship factors; Reiss, 1996). PGCP may evolve from individual treatment when individual problems are so inexorably bound to a relationship that couple therapy may be more appropriate, or occur when a couple seek conjoint treatment for relational problems.

Toward the end of the first session, it is usually possible to summarize an understanding of the concerns that have been presented by the couple and to introduce the idea that individual personality characteristics may interact reciprocally with these issues. In our experience, a brief explanation of personality and personality-guided treatment allows couples to appreciate the value of completing a personality assessment device. At that point, we recommend the MCMI-III or the MIPS.

Interpreting MCMI-III results

The MCMI-III provides assessment information parallel with DSM-IV. Computerized scoring of the MCMI-III generates an interpretive report that includes a profile of the base rate scores on the modifying indices (e.g., disclosure, desirability, debasement), clinical and severe personality scales (e.g., Avoidant, Histrionic, etc., parallel to Axis II), and the basic and severe clinical syndromes scales (symptomatic difficulties). Millon suggests that Axis II provides the context "in which the Axis I symptoms derive their meaning" (2006, p. 138), so emphasis is placed on the personality scales. Grossman Facet Scale (Grossman, 2005) scores are now included in the report for the top three personality scales. These refine the personality patterns by identifying which major aspects of the personality drive up those scores. For instance, if a person's score on Antisocial was elevated, the Grossman scales would indicate which facets of Antisocial personality are high (e.g., expressively impulsive, acting-out mechanism, and/or interpersonally irresponsible).

The MCMI-III is interpreted in three broad steps: (1) evaluating the validity of the inventory profile; (2) making single-scale diagnostic decisions; and (3) assessing overall functioning on the basis of the profile pattern while carefully reading the interpreted print-out with its diagnostic and treatment plan suggestions. Other interpretive approaches are available to supplement the report (Craig, 2005; Millon & Davis, 1996). The MCMI-III Manual (Millon, 2006) provides summaries of each personality type and charts with terminology and depictions by type that may be used in couple therapy to facilitate understanding of the particular individual style of each partner. Primary treatment attention is given to balancing the polarities of pain–pleasure, active–passive, and self–other for improved individual and interpersonal functioning (Millon & Davis, 1996).

Due to the conjoint nature of the assessment, Bagby and Marshall (2005) suggest that response styles on the modifying indices of the MCMI (e.g., disclosure, desirability, debasement) may reflect some response bias. Some individuals may disclose less or more than their partner, while others might "fake good" in order to focus attention on the partner at the initiation of treatment. Some people are so distressed by relationship problems that they respond to inventory items in an extreme fashion. In couple assessment, it is important to compare desirability vs. debasement score differences between the partners; if one partner evidences a significantly higher desirability score while the other evidences a debasement score, that difference should be factored into the couple interpretation. It may also suggest the need for individual sessions to discuss results before sharing them as a couple.

By taking these progressive steps the clinician has an ordered way to view the individual profile in the context of the patient's background and living context (e.g., socioeconomic status, family-of-origin relationships, and immediate reasons for seeking help).

MCMI-III couple patterns and presenting issues

There are several common couple personality interaction patterns and they should be considered as a basis for explaining potential couple dynamics (Nurse & Stanton, 2008). It is common for couples to evidence complementary styles on the personality polarities (pain–pleasure; active–passive; self–other). A number of classic patterns may be observed in clinical practice, including: (a) Narcissist – Dependent, (b) Compulsive – Histrionic, (c) Narcissist – Histrionic, (d) Compulsive – Dependent, (e) Histrionic – Schizoid or Avoidant, (f) Antisocial or Sadistic – Histrionic or Dependent, (g) Compulsive – Negativistic, and those involving a personality disorder on the clinical personality scales combining with a strong style or disorder on the severe personality pathology scales (e.g., Narcissist – Borderline). Awareness of these combinations may allow psychotherapy to focus on strengthening the weaker polarity of a partner while simultaneously moderating the polarity between the two partners. For example, therapy may encourage the dependent spouse ("other" polarity) to develop more assertiveness skills, but it is most successful when done while rebalancing the couple dynamic, so that the narcissistic spouse ("self" polarity) is concurrently working on increasing empathy and decreasing self-centered behaviors.

It is important to integrate individual personality and couple interactive patterns conceptually with the presenting issues that brought the couple into psychotherapy. Treatment may address these problems through the lens of the personality dynamic. PGCP emphasizes the same basic elements as other couple treatment models, including the need to establish a solid therapeutic alliance and the ability to convey, and model, accurate empathy for both individuals (Norcross, 2002).

Interpreting the MIPS with a couple

The MIPS is based on Millon's contention that "principles that guide the deduction of pathological personality traits should be the same as those which explicate personalities in the normal range" (2004, p. ix). The profile is organized as Motivating Styles, Thinking Styles, and Behaving Styles. Motivating Style scales attend to the three evolutionary foundation dimensions of Millon's theory. Four pairs of Thinking Style scales focus on how a person cognitively processes, while five Behavior Style scales assess a person's style of relating to others. We recommend that clinicians appraise the MIPS results carefully prior to meeting with the spouses to discuss results. First check the validity scores, then consider the individual profile scores, noting patterns, and finally read the interpretive printout. Because the questionnaire provides descriptions based on a normative sample and personality results are presented in non-technical language, a copy of the results printout may be given to clients.

Providing results

Assessment results may be provided in individual or conjoint sessions (Nurse & Stanton, 2008). Each has its advantages and disadvantages. Individual sessions allow greater freedom to discuss sensitive elements in the results and to focus on the individual apart from the relationship and without direct spousal influence, but they require clear agreement about how confidentiality issues will be handled between individual and conjoint sessions (see Chapters 12 and 13, this volume, for different perspectives on this ethical issue). This may be crucial in high-conflict situations to provide the safety needed to discuss results without generating defensive postures or providing ammunition for one partner against another. This may also allow an opportunity to process individual issues that are impacting the couple relationship, such as childhood abuse. This approach is especially useful for enmeshed spouses and reinforces healthy boundaries.

Conjoint sessions start the therapeutic process of understanding each other's personality immediately but require agreement on ground rules, such as not using terms or ideas against the partner. In conjoint sessions it is possible for the family psychologist to model understanding and empathy for each partner, noting the strengths of each style, as well as the opportunities for growth and rebalancing. The individual and the partner are invited to share examples of perceptions, thoughts, feelings, and behaviors based on the individual personality in a manner that facilitates understanding and empathy between the partners. Couples frequently begin to spontaneously link personality style to the presenting issues. The family psychologist must manage this process to ensure that it is positive and constructive, but it often opens the door to introduce the idea of personality interaction in the dyad and to describe ensuing steps in treatment. If using the MIPS, the family psychologist may hand clients their profiles to read in the couples session with additional interpretive information provided by the psychologist.

Treatment process

The first goal of PGCP is to increase the knowledge and awareness by each individual of personality dynamics in the relationship. Couples are asked to note personality-driven behaviors during their daily life and document examples of personality that they recognize in the relationship. For example, a Sadistic wife may become more aware of her need to dominate her husband in an abrasive manner, even in minor encounters, while the Dependent husband may see how he backs away too quickly from discussions without expressing his feelings or concerns because he is afraid of conflict. Increased insight into perceptions, thoughts, feelings, and behaviors driven by personality brings them out of the unconscious, automatic realm into a place where they may be managed or modified.

Treatment then attempts to increase each person's empathy for the partner's personality. As each individual begins to understand the subconscious motivations and drives of the other, some of the personality-driven thoughts, feelings, and behaviors start to make more sense to the partner. This may require opportunities to transfer one's self-awareness that he or she is compelled toward certain actions to understanding the other; the personality-guided therapist may explain that "he (or she) isn't doing this to you deliberately, just as you don't plan some of the things you do toward him (or her)." Once each person recognizes this personality motivation process, it is easier to step back from negative interactions and deconstruct them.

The therapist may then promote efforts to minimize or manage personality-driven behaviors that offend the partner. Even small efforts by a partner to move away from actions that bother the other can shift a negative dynamic toward positive interaction. For example, if the Sadistic partner resists the desire to criticize, dominate, or attack in the early stages of a discussion, the Dependent partner may find the psychological space to remain present and speak up more, which is exactly what the Sadistic partner wants. Both benefit and feel more positive toward the other and the relationship.

This positive interaction may be amplified by decreased negative reactions to the partner's personality-driven behaviors. Some ability to detach from offensive actions diminishes the need for a polarizing rejoinder. The partner who experiences the controlling behavior of the Compulsive person may learn to "let it go" without getting upset or reacting once they realize that it is driven by the other's personality, instead of being a conscious or deliberate negative act.

This provides the context to teach conjoint problem solving that includes personality management. Couples are asked to work on issues that arise in daily life and to seek to resolve them together, factoring in the personality interaction. As each rebalances the polarities at the individual and couple level, they often find it easier to address concerns that have grown over the years of the relationship. From a therapeutic standpoint, successfully solving one, two, or three of these issues in session provides a foundation for the couple to address other problems alone at home.

Ultimately, the outcome goal is renewed appreciation of the partner's style as counterbalance to one's own personality (which was often the unconscious initial attraction) and improved ability to function together as a couple.

Case Example Using the MCMI-III

Marcia and Ruben[1] were referred to therapy by a friend. They had both just turned 40 years old and had been married 15 years. Marcia was a nurse working part-time and

Ruben was an artist whose work required regular travel to art shows in other cities. Marcia had given birth to a daughter (Amy) about 10 months ago. They presented for treatment because Marcia recently discovered that Ruben had been having an affair. She stumbled on the affair when she answered Ruben's cell phone and was surprised to see a picture of a vagina on the screensaver. It shocked her so much that she explored the stored photos in the phone and found several nude pictures of another woman, some with Ruben. She was hurt and angry, in part because of the brazen display of sexual pictures on Ruben's cell phone. Ruben, on the other hand, reported that he had "no guilt," since they had not had sex in the marriage since the early stages of Marcia's pregnancy.

Marcia appeared professional, conservative, and careful in her social demeanor. She was polite and she chose her words judiciously as she explained her thoughts and feelings. Ruben, however, was quite different. He wore designer jeans, a tight-fitting T-shirt with a Quixote phrase on the front, and his hair was long. It was no surprise to discover that he was an artist. In addition, he spoke spontaneously, and at length, about his thoughts and ideas. He put no restrictions on his choice of vocabulary, including the use of several terms for female body parts that are often considered crude or inappropriate in most social environments.

I (M. S.) completed a brief couple genogram (McGoldrick, Gerson, & Petry, 2008) during the intake session, providing information about individual development in the family of origin. Marcia was the oldest child of an alcoholic, "controlling" father, and a flirtatious mother who had two affairs before the marriage ended in divorce. Ruben was the middle child of an abusive father who had multiple affairs and a mother who was a "bulldozer" with "poor boundaries" and pack-rat tendencies. The couple described their own marriage as primarily positive (each claimed the other as "best friend") despite communication problems and disagreements around household responsibilities and use of space in the home (e.g., Ruben required a room for a studio, often retreating there for hours at a time requesting not to be disturbed) until the pregnancy. Ruben had resisted parenthood throughout the marriage, but finally acceded to Marcia's desire for a baby. The relationship worsened during her pregnancy as she gained weight and sexual relations slowed and then ceased. The deterioration exacerbated following the baby's birth when Ruben declined to help with the baby or the expanded household chores. Sexual relations were non-existent, complicated by the particular infant-rearing regimen Marcia had chosen. Ruben got involved with a woman he met while out of town at an art show and this precipitated the crisis in the relationship.

When I suggested that their differences in personality might contribute to the issues between them and to their ability to resolve the effects of the affair, both readily agreed. They were open to the idea of securing a more detailed analysis of the way their individual personalities meshed in the relationship. I recommended that they complete the MCMI-III and they were able to stay for the additional half-hour it required for them to complete it that day.

Once scored, I noted that Marcia's profile showed a significant Desirability score. In contrast, her Debasement score was zero, suggesting that she presented herself in a favorable light. Regardless, she had two high clinical personality scales, Histrionic and Compulsive. Grossman Facets Scales indicated that "gregarious self-image" and "expressively dramatic" facets were most important on the Histrionic scale while the "cognitively constricted" facet was much higher than other facets on the Compulsive scale. There were no elevations on clinical scales.

Ruben had moderate scores on all three modifying indices. No clinical scales were elevated, but he did have an elevated score on the Schizotypal scale in the severe personality pathology section, joined by an elevated Avoidant scale among the clinical personality patterns. This combination of Avoidant and Schizotypal styles accords with Millon's circumplex of typical personality alignments (Millon, 2006).

These results characterized the marital relationship. Ruben often kept most people at a distance and withdrew into his artwork. He functioned at art shows by focusing on his work, even while interacting with others. He had a close relationship with Marcia ("best friend") and valued sexual intimacy with her; in fact, frequent sexual relations were desired to provide the sense of connection he needed. Ruben did not want to be a parent, fearing what would happen to the marital relationship. When he finally relented and agreed to have a child, he was quite disturbed when Marcia gained weight, lost interest in sex (although she was willing to meet his needs, it "was not the same"), and began to expect more from him around the home. He avoided household responsibilities, believing Marcia was too demanding and particular. This was exacerbated after the baby was born. He withdrew into his art studio for large blocks of time, uncommunicative and sullen, leaving Marcia alone to deal with the baby. Marcia, on her part, felt a combination of moral indignation and rejection; indignation that Ruben was not stepping up to the demands of parenting and rejection in that he withdrew from her and did not seem attracted to her. She knew the relationship was troubled for some time, but she internally neutralized her distress because she did not know what to do about it. She experienced a variety of somatic complaints that suggested underlying tension and she would occasionally erupt in fits of anger and resentment when she could not contain it any longer.

Meanwhile, an art dealer at one of his shows flirted with Ruben, acting toward him in a forward manner that made it easy for him to connect with her, much as Marcia had done years ago (e.g., an apparently Histrionic style). Ruben felt accepted and responded to her overtures, leading to a sexual relationship. He enjoyed the closeness and the sexual intimacy, taking pictures of her naked so that he could look at them while they were apart. It didn't seem odd to him to use one of them as his screensaver on his phone so that he could look at it regularly. The relationship continued over a period of months as they met at different art shows.

It was clear to me that personality dynamics contributed to the presenting complaints and to their desire to resolve the effects of the affair. By the time they came to therapy the affair was already terminated (the woman backed away as she discovered more about Ruben) and both expressed a strong desire to rekindle the marriage. Marcia had lost weight and sexual relations resumed, but significant hurt, anger, and distrust remained on both sides.

In this case, I determined that it was appropriate to provide assessment results in a conjoint session. I believed that discussing the results together might facilitate their understanding of each other's personality style, which is one of the first treatment goals. I felt like I had joined with them as individuals and as a couple sufficiently to be able to speak openly and clearly to both of them together. In the conjoint session I described the results, first for Marcia, then for Ruben. I encouraged each of them to provide examples or validation of the results for themselves and for their partner. Marcia readily identified with the Histrionic and Compulsive categories and Ruben took the opportunity to point out how strong and controlling she could be when stating her desires for his behavior. It was a little tough for her to hear, but she nodded her understanding that he might feel that way when she tried to tell him what she thought he should know already in a somewhat moralistic manner. The real breakthrough, though, came as we discussed Ruben's Schizotypal-Avoidant personality style. Marcia was very surprised as we discussed typical Schizotypal traits; she had always known that he was different, but she had attributed it to artistic style without considering the psychological underpinnings of his peculiar attitudes, beliefs, dress, and behavior. A light bulb came on that allowed her to re-interpret some of her thoughts and beliefs about Ruben and his behavior. Ruben laughed when we discussed the atypical nature of his ideation and his unusual "lectures" on various subjects that could go on "forever" (in Marcia's words). It became a joke between us all when we would reflect on the interesting array of T-shirt logos and quirky sayings that he wore to sessions, all reflecting his taste for the peculiar. He would cite obscure movie characters and enigmatic quotations as points of reference for his ideas, further revealing his personality. Marcia recognized that her Histrionic style appreciated the constant novelty and interesting ideas Ruben brought to the relationship.

We were able to amplify this understanding through consideration of particular events and circumstances in the marriage. Of course, the affair, with all the feelings and dynamics involved, was front and center in this discussion. It was helpful to each of them to discuss the relational deterioration that preceded the affair, clarifying the different perceptions, thoughts, and feelings on both sides that gave new meaning to the behavior. This understanding allowed Marcia to back away from her compulsive judgments toward a sense of mutual responsibility for the relationship deterioration. Ruben began to understand Marcia's compulsive traits in a more accepting manner, recognizing that she was not deliberately controlling. As empathy for the other's style increased, each was reminded of how those traits attracted them to the other in the beginning of the relationship. Ruben took responsibility for the affair, noting that he needed to be able to express his distress more directly to Marcia. Marcia realized that she needed to be more careful about the way she expressed herself, to avoid the perception that she was moralizing. Ruben admitted that perhaps his ideas were a little "out there" and that he might need to moderate his tendency to talk non-stop about esoteric subjects. These efforts to manage personality-driven behaviors that were offending the other person resulted in increased satisfaction with the relationship. In addition, both were managing their negative reactions to the other's personality and letting go of small behaviors that had previously become major irritants.

The photo on the phone was a crucial issue, since it really hurt Marcia that he had placed it there. Ruben, however, vehemently denied that it was a passive-aggressive attempt to reveal the affair, noting simply that he "liked looking at it." His attitudes toward sex and sexual material were discussed. It was clear that he was more on the fringe than Marcia in this area, expressing desires and practices that contrasted with the more mainstream attitudes she held. Although he did not like having to discuss his attitudes, it became clear that shared expectations were needed in this area. Understanding, increased empathy, and compromise resulted in agreements that both could feel good about for the marriage. Sexual frequency increased as some of the marital tensions decreased, to the point that both expressed satisfaction.

Other lifestyle issues were raised and processed in light of the mix of individual personalities. We discussed how to present problems for mutual discussion in a manner that avoided the roadblocks they typically encountered. Marcia worked on lowering her Histrionic reactions while Ruben worked on increasing his willingness to hear and understand her viewpoint. They were able to successfully discuss and resolve problems around household chores and space usage in the home. Interestingly, Ruben became more attached to his daughter as the marriage improved and began to provide more child care. He noted with surprise that he had "real feelings" for Amy and no longer resented her presence. This was a major breakthrough and boded well for the future. By the conclusion of our brief intervention (less than 10 sessions), both partners expressed increased marital satisfaction, sufficient resolution of the issues related to the affair that caused them to initiate therapy, and greater appreciation of each other's personality style.

Case Example Using the MIPS

Harry, 50 years of age, married, with a teenage daughter, came to therapy stirred by his depressive feelings, although he described his problems as centered on lack of interest and energy at home and his boredom at work as a mid-level corporate manager. He told me (A. R. N.) that he needed help to figure out how to manage his life more effectively. Almost as an afterthought he added that this might help at home. After the evaluative interview, I suggested that a few sessions might help him become more in touch with his feelings. Harry, although very agreeable, personable, and oriented toward being in relationships with others, lacked much conscious awareness of his feelings and had difficulty identifying them despite often acting on them.

After a series of cognitively-emotionally focused sessions he gradually became more in contact with his feelings and expanded his vocabulary to describe them. As this occurred he talked more and more about his marriage. He viewed it as a technical project, as if to say "I need to get the right formula and apply it." He seemed to think that I (as the therapist) might have the formula. I demurred, but proposed that Harry's wife come in for an evaluative interview with a female colleague to tackle the relationship problem directly. He appreciated this specificity and prevailed upon her to come in, indicating to me that she would, but she stated that she had no need for therapy.

Sally, 45, came to the interview with the female therapist and agreed to participate in couple sessions with Harry to explore with both therapists whether undertaking a longer series of couple sessions seemed appropriate. In the first session, both agreed to take the MIPS as a way to learn more about themselves, their relationship, and as a basis for goal-setting. Each MIPS was to be discussed in individual session with each individual's couple therapist, and each spouse was given a copy of the printout interpretation.

When the co-therapist and I looked at the MIPS profiles together prior to the individual interpretation discussions, we found several striking differences that would be critical to face in their relationship. Within the Motivating Styles section, we were struck by the contrast between Harry's fundamental propensity to nurture others and in turn expect nurturance and Sally's lack of need to nurture and be nurtured. While Harry had little impetus to focus on himself, Sally's focus was on self to the extent of considerable self-absorption. These different styles meant Harry's energy moved primarily in a world of relationships, while Sally's energy was spent mostly in the life of the mind – her mind.

Not surprisingly, Harry's thinking style was externally focused. With his technical background he was grounded in concrete phenomena, ready to set goals and innovatively negotiate crises in concert with others (who at work undoubtedly appreciated this style). Sally, by expected contrast, was very internally conceptually focused, imaginative/intuitive, and not at all innovation-seeking like Harry; she preferred control of her behavior and careful application of new knowledge to situations while maintaining a proper, conventional, often distant exterior.

With Sally's energy focused interiorly and because of her intuitive style, to anyone observing her she could appear asocial/withdrawn and overly unsure, although overtly going along in a cooperative way. Harry would be viewed as overly agreeable, yet principled and constantly oriented toward more team or couple decisions than independent action.

My co-therapist and I guessed that each might have wanted some of the other's qualities when they met. Perhaps for him, she was an attractive challenge. It may have been that she appreciated his stability and was initially attracted to his strong, persistent, reaching-out qualities, present even when she was more withdrawn. We further concluded that these same originally attracting qualities were now at the heart of their problems, particularly from his standpoint, since she evidenced little dissatisfaction except when he failed to meet her inner standard of expectations (even though she had not verbalized them).

After the separate discussions with each partner, we held a four-way meeting in which they shared with each other what was most important that they took from the MIPS findings. As we facilitated this process, we discussed with them the possible implications for their relationship. We agreed on meeting for couples sessions, punctuated as needed by individual therapy, depending on what transpired in the four-way sessions.

By combining individual and conjoint therapy Harry came to terms with the reality that he desired emotional interrelationships, and that strength was not Sally's. They could still have moments with each other, however, and share warmth as they parented their daughter. With the help of my co-therapist, Sally was able to go toward Harry more emotionally on occasion, but Sally made it clear to Harry that she must have major time for herself. She also was willing to work on communicating her expectations more clearly for him. As they thrashed this dynamic through in couples sessions, progress was made. For example, on vacation they agreed that he could go exploring by himself, while she could remain in a hotel reading. As of the end of treatment they had both separately decided to stay together, having formed a more compatible life. Harry could take more active enjoyment interpersonally at work, while usually managing more emotional isolation at home than he might prefer. Sally, experiencing less pressure to be close, was able to move with more feeling toward him. When one or both of them retreated to old, non-accepting behaviors, we were able to point back to the MIPS profiles, providing more distance for both, and resulting in less personalizing by Sally and self-blaming by Harry. One bonus for Harry was that as he understood himself more he was more self-reliant. This discovery also helped him at work.

Conclusion

This chapter provides a brief overview of PGCP. When family psychologists work with couples, we recommend that personality-guided processes may augment other therapeutic approaches or stand alone as a treatment modality.

Anecdotal evidences suggests that PGCP is beneficial to couples and that it may be employed successfully with a range of couple problems or included as an aspect of treatment for psychological disorders that interact with couple functioning. PGCP may integrate into evidence-based couple treatments for relational problems or individual psychological disorders. For example, Epstein and Baucom (2002) suggest that taking account of individual attributes of the partners may enhance cognitive-behavioral couples therapy. Further research is needed to establish PGCP as an evidence-based practice.

Note

1   Here and in the second case example, pseudonyms have been used and some identifying material altered to protect the identity of the individuals.

Resources

Pearson Assessments (www.pearsonassessments.com): Sample MCMI-III and MIPS interpretive reports may be downloaded; free independent study training program for the MCMI-III.

References

American Psychiatric Association. (1994). *Diagnostic and statistical manual of mental disorders* (4th ed.). Washington, DC: American Psychiatric Association.

Bagby, R., & Marshall, M. (2005). Assessing response bias with the MCMI modifying indices. In R. Craig (Ed.), *New directions in interpreting the Millon Clinical Multiaxial Inventory-III* (pp. 227–247). Hoboken, NJ: Wiley.

Beach, S. R. H., Wamboldt, M., Kaslow, N., & Heyman, R. (2006). Describing relational problems in DSM-V: Toward better guidance for research and clinical practice. *Journal of Family Psychology, 20,* 359–368.

Bronfenbrenner, U. (1979). *The ecology of human development.* Cambridge, MA: Harvard University Press.

Craig, R. (Ed.). (2005). *New directions in interpreting the Millon Clinical Multiaxial Inventory-III (MCMI-III).* Hoboken, NJ: Wiley.

Davis, R., & Millon, T. (1997). The Millon inventories: Present and future directions. In T. Millon (Ed.), *The Millon inventories: Clinical and personality assessment* (pp. 525–537). New York: Guilford Press.

Epstein, N., & Baucom, D. (2002). Why couples are the way they are: Individual influences. In N. Epstein & D. Baucom (Eds.), *Enhanced cognitive-behavioral therapy for couples: A contextual approach* (pp. 105–143). Washington, DC: American Psychological Association.

Grossman, S. (2005). The MCMI-III Facet Subscales. In R. Craig (Ed.), *New directions in interpreting the Millon Clinical Multiaxial Inventory-III* (pp. 3–31). Hoboken, NJ: Wiley.

Magnavita, J. (2005). *Personality-guided relational psychotherapy.* Washington, DC: American Psychological Association.

Magnavita, J., & MacFarlane, M. (2004). Family treatment of personality disorders: Historical overview and current perspectives. In M. MacFarlane (Ed.), *Family treatment of personality disorders: Advances in clinical practice* (pp. 3–39). New York: Haworth Press.

McGoldrick, M., Gerson, R., & Petry, S. (2008). *Genograms: Assessment and intervention.* New York: Norton.

Millon, T. (2004). *MIPS-R (Millon Index of Personality Styles Revised) manual.* Minneapolis, MN: Pearson Assessments.

Millon, T. (2006). *Millon Clinical Multiaxial Inventory-III: Manual* (3rd ed.). Minneapolis: Pearson Assessments.

Millon, T., & Bloom, C. (2008). *The Millon inventories: A practitioner's guide to personalized clinical assessment.* New York: Guilford Press.

Millon, T., & Davis, R. (1996). *Disorders of personality: DSM-IV and beyond* (2nd ed.). New York: Wiley.

Norcross, J. C. (2002). Empirically supported therapy relationships. In J. C. Norcross (Ed.), *Psychotherapy relationships that work: Therapist contributions and responsiveness to patients* (pp. 3–16). New York: Oxford University Press.

Nurse, A. R., & Stanton, M. (2008). Using the MCMI-III in treating couples. In T. Millon & C. Bloom (Eds.), *The Millon inventories: A practitioner's guide to personalized clinical assessment* (pp. 347–368). New York: Guilford Press.

Reiss, D. (1996). Foreword. In F. Kaslow (Ed.), *Handbook of relational diagnosis and dysfunctional family patterns* (pp. ix–xv). New York: Wiley.

Spotts, E., Lichtenstein, P., Pedersen, N., Neiderhiser, J., Hansson, K., Cederblad, M., et al. (2005). Personality and marital satisfaction: A behavioural genetic analysis. *European Journal of Personality, 19,* 205–227.

18

Intensive Family-of-Origin Consultation: An Intergenerational Approach

Timothy Weber and Cheryl Cebula

The intergenerational family is an emotionally charged force field in which we are deeply embedded and from which we inherit messages, usually covert, that shape, influence, and compel us to certain destinies for better and for worse. Although we are not passive puppets manipulated by our familial histories, the emotional forces constituting this high-voltage system are profound and deep, demanding and unyielding, laden with blessings and curses that infiltrate our ordinary, everyday lives. Framo (1992, p. 7) describes the wide and deep range of family life:

> Families can provide the deepest satisfaction of living: unreserved and unconditional love; gratifying bonding; measureless sacrifice; enduring dependability; compassionate belonging; the joys and warmth of family holidays; the fun and play; the give and take . . . Still, the hurts and damage that family members can inflict upon one another are infinite: scapegoating; humiliation and shaming; parentification; crazymaking; physical, sexual, and psychological abuse; cruel rejections; lies and deceit; and the manifold outrages against the human spirit.

This power of the intergenerational force field has been at the center of many historic family therapy models (e.g., Boszormenyi-Nagy & Krasner, 1986; Bowen, 1978; Framo, 1992; Framo, Weber, & Levine, 2003; Kerr & Bowen, 1988; Satir & Baldwin, 1983; Whitaker, 1989; Williamson, 1991; Williamson & Bray, 1985). However, over the last couple of decades, attention to the intergenerational perspective as a primary therapeutic resource seems to have waned, eclipsed by growing attention to therapeutic orientations driven more by solutions, results, brevity, and evidence-based support. Intergenerational approaches to marriage and family therapy have faded and have been cast as long-term, more laborious, cost-ineffective, insight-oriented, and often impractical, considering the frequent need to involve other family-of-origin members.

Interestingly, in spite of the paucity of attention given to the intergenerational approach in the literature, a family-of-origin perspective regarding the etiology and development of problems seems to be a core factor across different therapeutic models of couple and family therapy (Davis & Piercy, 2007a, 2007b). The family-of-origin framework also has been helpful in the training of therapists, especially with greater attention being paid to the "self of the therapist" in training programs (e.g., Aponte, 1992).

Sometimes therapists integrate intergenerational techniques and methods into their ongoing therapy. The genogram may be used to enhance insight into one's family-of-origin dynamics (McGoldrick, Gerson, & Petry, 2008). Attention to family-of-origin dynamics from the "then and there" may help illuminate snags and loyalties in the "here and now" (e.g., strong reactivity to a boss's suggestions is linked to a parent who ruled by demand). A therapist might coach a client to interview family-of-origin members as a way of humanizing the other and lessening the tendency to imprison family members on the basis of one's internal imagination and prejudice. Certain family-of-origin members may be incorporated into a client's ongoing therapy as different issues emerge (e.g., bringing in a sibling to enhance greater understanding and connection). Family reconstruction, using non-family surrogates in live enactments of family-of-origin dramas, has been used to heighten intergenerational learning (Nerin, 1986; Satir, 1972). The Bowenian tradition (Bowen, 1978; Gilbert, 2006) emphasizes the therapist as a "coach" helping the client to develop a more differentiated self in journeys within the family of origin. Williamson (1991) has utilized this coaching format within a group setting. Framo (1992; Framo et al., 2003) and Whitaker (1989) gathered family-of-origin members for several hours over two or three days for direct conversations about their history and relationships.

This chapter proposes a model of intergenerational intervention with the whole family of origin that can serve as a stand-alone consultation or as an adjunctive resource for clients in individual or couple therapy. The intervention is a "consultation" because of the brief contact and limited history the consultants may have with the entire family (Wynne, McDaniel, & Weber, 1986). We will outline our model of intensive family-of-origin consultation – "intensive" in the compressed three-day consultation and in the depth and intensity of the conversation; "extensive" in the pre- and post-consultation interactions we have with the family; and "brief" in the punctuated impact we have on an intergenerational system within a compressed framework. As Framo put it, family-of-origin therapy is the major heart surgery of family therapy (Framo, 1992).

Review of Intergenerational Theory

We are all embedded within a deep history across the generations called the "family of origin," comprised of both biological and non-biological members who define themselves as "family." We are usually aware of only a small fragment of our intergenerational history as a few stories, anecdotes, maxims, rituals, and memorabilia cross our paths. How we live within this intergenerational force field builds the foundation of the health of our attachments, our capacity for self-definition and compassion, our desires and despairs, what appears in our world and what lies hidden, our resources and restraints, our visions of what might be and what cannot be, our gifts and our handicaps, our drives and retreats across our life span. We are not determined by our family of origin; but we most certainly are blessed, cursed, and spoken to through the invisible whispers of our family history.

The unaddressed and unresolved relationships within the family may unconsciously go "underground" within the self and emerge in disguised and camouflaged forms in our body, our sense of self, and our interpersonal life in a process known as "projective identification" (Scharff & Scharff, 1987). The inner conflicts of the self, couple problems, parenting challenges (Siegel & Hartzell, 2003), and our behavior within organizations may often stem from reparative efforts to heal, redo, replicate, repair, defend, attach, or hide from conflicts and relationships in the family of origin (Framo, 1992, Framo et al., 2003). While our family-of-origin relationships certainly may yield gifts in strengthening our adaptability, the unresolved and unaddressed relationships within the family of origin snag us in our life with others as they are mindlessly "recruited" to help us deal with our history. But these "surrogates" (partners, children, friends, and colleagues) are not the real thing and thus, while they might serve as resources for emotional healing, they cannot ultimately resolve our family work. Direct address with the real family members opens new vistas and possibilities that are impossible with surrogates. Even if family members are deceased, their energy lives on in the living, and they too can be addressed in conversations with other family members and at the graveside (Williamson, 1991). Death ends a life, not a relationship (Anderson, 1970).

In spite of the arguments supporting an intergenerational consultation, a more frequent response to the idea of bringing family members together for authentic conversations is some form of protest – intense fear, disgust, opposition, numbed disinterest, sometimes curiosity, and most often a decline of the invitation. Examples of retorts may include: "I don't want to disturb things"; "My parents are too old, and I don't want to upset them"; "It wouldn't do any good because they'll never change"; "What does a family meeting have to do with my own problems?"; "All that is in the past" (Framo, 1992, p. 16). The anxiety is pitched high. The oppositional stance toward these kinds of meetings makes sense in families where there has been a distressing history of destructive abuse along with a defensive and impervious block to dialogue. However, the initial protests and concerns by clients, often reinforced by anxious therapists, are understandable reactions toward the "high-voltage system" of the family and are better understood as developmental anxieties on the way to considering a family-of-origin consultation a real possibility.

Core Factors in the Consultation Process

The following are 10 core factors that are instrumental in the practice of family-of-origin consultation.

1 *Pre- and post-consultation phases.*   Our consultation model includes a thorough preparation phase with each family member. Family connections are made, therapeutic bridges

are built, concerns are surfaced and addressed early on, family themes are identified, individual goals are elucidated, coaching commences, and the overall therapeutic system is being co-created before the first family meeting, expanding the possibilities of a good beginning. All family members are interviewed, not just the initiator or protagonist as in Framo's (1992) model. Post-consultation contact with family members includes a summary letter solidifying the key learnings and family commitments, and reinforcing the embodiment of the family consultation.

2 *Psychoeducational perspective.*   Clients appear to benefit from having a model of human behavior which enhances their understanding of healthy functioning, how problems develop over time, and what might be done to resolve or at least evolve these problems so they might be more manageable (Davis & Piercy, 2007a, 2007b). Repeatedly, we identify and explain interpersonal and intergenerational constructs as they unfold in the moment (e.g., triangles, loyalty, family secrets, boundaries, parentification, gender disparities, fairness and equity, differentiation, attunement).

3 *Direct address.*   Direct address describes the basic process between family members that increases intimacy and builds trust. Typically, family members talk *about* other family members (with therapists or other third parties), talk *around* family members (indirect, obtuse verbal and non-verbal behavior), or *avoid* family members altogether. One of our most important roles is to host a safe and secure context of responsiveness and accessibility between family members – to help direct the difficult conversations of direct address (Johnson, 2004; and see Chapter 27, this volume).

4 *Immediacy.*   The most riveting and fluid opportunities come in the immediate encounters between family members, *in the moment,* when the stories are experientially enacted, coming alive in the room (e.g., a son defends and rescues a passive mother in the face of a father's disengaged authority; a sister's fragility is her only expressed voice in the midst of a family dominated by male power; a father lectures his son and daughters in support of their growth without blessing them for their good efforts and past accomplishments). We seize the moments of immediacy, amplifying the conversations into what we call "a guided crisis." These are the "birthquakes" of the consultation when family dynamics appear in living color. Embedded in these real-time interactions are all the stories – stories of attachment and attachment injuries, stories of fairness and justice, stories of loss, life, and loyalty. As the stories take on flesh and spirit, much more is malleable as we help family members toward greater awareness and coach them in small steps toward change in the present.

5 *Learning.*   Learning is the thread that ties together the family consultations. We often ask "What are you learning about yourself, other family members, your family as a group?"; "What are your hunches, hypotheses of what happened, what just happened?"; "How do you want to check out your hunch?" Any event in a family's experience is redeemable when framed with the learning question: "What did you learn from that and how can your learning serve you as a resource in the future?"

6 *Relational integrity.*   We define "relational integrity" as wholeness when one is atten-tive and responsive, moment by moment, to the dialectic between self and other. We argue that differentiation alone is inadequate as the primary construct in describing a healthy interpersonal process. Differentiation must be integrated with attunement to the other (inquiry, curiosity, empathy, compassion, openness to being influenced, etc.), with the core dialectic of life being the ever-present attention to fairness and justice, the balance of giving and receiving in the self–other dialectic (Boszormenyi-Nagy & Krasner, 1986; Johnson, 2004; Williamson, 1991; see also Chapter 27, this volume).

7 *Creativity.*   Langer (1997) describes how mindful learning is oriented toward creative, unconventional, and novel approaches to stuck issues. We cultivate creativity as we expand our conversations to include free associations, metaphors, and images as we promote a more open system of play and experiment. For example, a more deferring mother reported that she wore a red dress somewhat defiantly at her wedding years ago. In the sub-sequent conversations we referred to the "red dress" as a symbol of her courage and creativity which she was attempting to amplify in renegotiating her life and marriage. The creative theme also includes attention to contributions. Typically and sadly, families under-attend to the contributions their family members have made within the family. We will model making "micro-credits" – quick acknowledgments of something that some-one does well in the moment. We will steadily punctuate individual and collective strengths (e.g., tenacity, sacrifice, compassion, dedication).

8 *Truth speaking and seeking.*   Speaking the truth (differentiation) and seeking the truth (attunement) especially in the midst of a tense emotional field are primary processes of relational integrity that build family trust. Trust is less about resolution and more often related to the hospitality of creating space to speak and to having one's experience, one's truth, simply acknowledged. We differentiate between truth and transparency (immedi-ate reactions) and support tenacity and inquiry in the face of anxiety, working to unpack the layers of truth within the multiple realities of family members so that a greater, more collaborative truth emerges. Family secrets (often critical things known but not discussed openly) bind the family within a web of anxiety that saps energy for creative intimacy.

A commitment to truth also means expanding the elasticity of the self and the family toward giving space for those thoughts, feelings, and questions deemed taboo and forbidden, toward making room for the shadow side of family life. True intimacy puts us eyeball to eyeball with the experience that all of us are "mixed bags" – composites of the good, the bad, the ugly, and the beautiful.

Truth also means being open to the often unsettling and surprising experience of feedback from others that may confirm or disconfirm what we think we know. Our con-sultations are replete with challenges to family members both to give feedback and to be open to feedback from others, whether or not it seems to fit.

9 *Relationship renegotiation.*   We promote action-oriented change within the family by coaching family members to renegotiate explicitly and behaviorally their life together in terms of specific requests and offers, commitments and contracts. We want family

members (in the spirit of relational integrity) to be clear about what they want and to consider fairly the requests of others as they discern what they might offer as they practice both differentiation and attunement. However, sometimes collaborative *contracting* gets stuck. Therefore, we also accent the power of *commitments* – unilateral declarations of what one will do, where the self is headed, the differentiated "I will . . ." Family trust is increased as promises (commitments and contracts) are made and reliably kept.

10 *Co-consulting.*   Although the first author conducted family-of-origin consultations solo for years, the co-consulting format deeply enriches the entire process and increases the emotional latitude and perspective of the consultant. It takes two consultants to adequately marshal the energy required to engage with multiple family members in intense conversations in a brief period of time. Options for building relational bridges in the family and entertaining diverse perspectives are amplified with two consultants. Cultural and gender diversity are elevated with our female–male team. Our co-consulting with each other between the two-hour family meetings helps stimulate a more enriched point of view and facilitates sharper self-correction. Sometimes we gossip about the family as the family listens. We hope to perturb, stimulate, support, and model relational integrity as our differences are blended with fair consideration of the other. The co-consulting team models a relationship in which curiosity, humor and teasing, collaboration, disagreement and negotiation, fondness and respect are all part of the relationship dance.

The Method of Intensive Family-of-Origin Consultation

We will now describe the structure and method of intensive family-of-origin consultation, which includes three phases: the pre-consultation, the consultation, and the post-consultation. While the consultation phase occurs for 12 hours in 2-hour segments over three days, the pre-consultation phase may begin in earnest anywhere from three to six months in advance of the consultation, and the active post-consultation phase may extend six months beyond the consultation.

Pre-consultation phase: Contacting, contracting, connecting

Contacting.   The initiation of an intensive family-of-origin consultation may begin when a client approaches us or when one of the consultants suggests to a client that, given the current issues or possible impasses in the therapy process, she or he might benefit from a family-of-origin consultation, addressing issues directly with family members. For instance, a client may be working relational issues of fairness and justice with his spouse that largely belong with the original family. Or a client may be unable to make healthy choices clearly for her life because of issues of loyalty to a parent who is developmentally stalled or under-functioning. Sibling conflicts regarding family business, inheritance, care for aging parents, or unresolved family history have also prompted desires for a family-of-origin consultation. In many cases, however, there is no clear and present crisis. Families simply want to be closer and find new ways of being with each other as the life-span changes, such as marriages, births, deaths, divorces, grandchildren, retirement, geographical distance, and competing commitments, swirl about (Pipher, 1999). The aging of parents, the anticipation of parental death, and the overall mounting awareness of the brevity of life often serve as the spoken stimulus for the consultation.

One of us may have a brief phone consultation with the client upon the initial inquiry. We refer clients to our website (http://www.familyoforigintherapy.com), and to the first author's co-authored volume on family-of-origin therapy, *Coming Home Again* (Framo et al., 2003), for further information. The client may request coaching on how to recruit family members, since we require that all family-of-origin members attend the consultation. Chapter 2 in *Coming Home Again* is especially helpful in addressing recruitment strategies. Frequently, the recruitment of all family members is not easily done due to everything from lack of interest and time to active triangles and deflection from hot family issues. The proposal of a family-of-origin consultation may activate old snags around issues of power, support, money, attention, compassion, family secrets, and so on. The process "work" in the family begins at this stage as the anxiety begins to amplify. This is why we want to allow plenty of time for this pre-consultation phase; the ripe possibility for change is in the air and we don't want to short-circuit the process.

Strategies of engagement include the following: inviting family members to participate in order to help the protagonist with a particular goal or with moving beyond a challenging issue; inviting others to address some specific concerns within the family (e.g., aging of parents, inheritance) or some general themes (sibling caught in parental triangles, distance between family members); and suggesting a consultation to help the family deal with some upcoming issues which would require the resources of family members (e.g., the illness of a family member). It may become evident in conversations with the client that another family member has the ability to influence reluctant members; we would coach the client on how to enlist that member's assistance. If the client has been unable to get full attendance, we may put the consultation on hold while the family does its work. We also may consult further with the client and try to discover what might be contributing to the reluctance of the family member. There may be a concern that the consultation is a set-up for an ambush by one or both of the parents. Sometimes we have invited other family members to call us if there are any questions. We also have a brief "Q and A" on intensive family-of-origin consultation that family members may receive to help frame the purpose and process of this work.

Contracting.   After family members have agreed to go ahead with the consultation, dates are chosen and a location is agreed upon (some consultations have occurred during family reunions and in distant cities). The client is sent a contract which specifies the above, and includes the fee for the consultation and any charges for travel, lodging, meals, and adjustments made for travel time. The contract also includes statements on confidentiality, a commitment to attend the entire consultation, and a requirement that all family members attending the consultation sign the contract.

Connecting.   Once the contract is signed, a common letter is sent to each family member. The letter gives a brief introduction to the consultants, describes the purpose and process of the consultation, and includes 11 questions that orient the family to some of the foci of the consultation. The questions help set a tone of inquiry and self-reflection, emphasize intentionality, direct attention to strengths and challenges, and evoke personal interest and initiative. We let the family know we are available for questions about the consultation format, and that we will be calling each family member in several weeks for a personal interview of about 30–45 minutes to help prepare better for the consultation.

We want the anticipation of the consultation to percolate and perturb the system, using the energy of anxiety and curiosity to help loosen fixed positions and open new possibilities. We divide family members between us so that one of us calls each family member about the letter. The questions and the letter are a starting place, helping us all weave together the web of connectedness and elicit family members' interest and commitment to the consultation. These phone calls help us get an early "reading" of the kinds of concerns individuals have, what kinds of "snags" we might encounter, what themes are alive in the family, and how we might support individuals on the basis of their goals and appraisal of their own strengths and liabilities. We want to tap into their deepest hopes and expectations as well as into their most anxious fears. We underscore that there might be a range of outcomes – some individuals gaining a lot from the consultation, others maybe learning a thing or two, and still others disappointed at not getting enough. Still, we reiterate our belief that these meetings require courage, dedication, and good will, and we respect their desire to move forward.

Consultation phase: Opening (hours 1–3), middle (hours 4–10), closing (hours 11–12)

The 12 hours of the consultation are typically scheduled over three days in six 2-hour sessions with two sessions per day. We have found that the intensity of these conversations requires good rest, a reasonable pacing, and time for the learning to percolate within individuals as they reflect and converse with each other between the sessions. We usually have our first two sessions on Friday afternoon and Friday evening, followed by two sessions on Saturday, and the last two sessions on Sunday morning and early Sunday afternoon. The intense scheduling keeps family members "in the fire" and allows the consultants to deepen the conversations more quickly.

Opening (hours 1–3).   We begin the consultation with a welcoming and orientation to the three days, introducing ourselves and inviting each family member to introduce himself or herself. We discuss how the family was invited to the consultation, why they accepted the invitation, and the specifics of their hopes and fears. We ask them about their specific goals and what they imagine a good outcome would include. The work begins immediately in this "family overture" as these questions spark a variety of provocative and engaging responses.

We then have a brief "tutorial" on how the family can best use their time together, how they might optimize their chances for success, and how they can also squander this opportunity. We encourage family members to "go for what matters" – grasp the opportunity and take the initiative. We want family members to get clear, to take stands and risks, and to be open to learning and to surprise. We point out that the success of the consultation is ultimately in their hands. We want them to get clear about what each wants to state and to ask and with whom, and to think about requests (what you want) and offers (what you are willing to give), and from whom and to whom. We identify "intimacy" in life as including the commitment to enter and stay with difficult conversations with the goal of at least "evolving vs. resolving" difficulties with other family members. Our goal is to help normalize much of what many people consider unwelcome aberrations in family life, including experiencing the normal abrasions and opportunities of multiple realities in one family. We talk about the typical fears they may have already or might encounter: that someone will die, that the consultants won't be entertained and the family will be too boring, that someone will leave (maybe for good), that the family – and particularly the parents – will be fractured beyond repair, and ultimately that life will be worse, not better. We identify ourselves as available resources in their collaborative learning.

The other focus of the opening hours is our exploration and elaboration of the family's developmental history using a three-generational genogram and timeline of nodal events. We begin to identify the relationship history across the generations and the stories that explain and reinforce these relationship patterns: the closeness and distance, attachment, unhealed attachment injuries, issues of fairness and justice, secrets, legacies of honor and dishonor, success and failure, love and distain. These intergenerational stories may be known, but frequently there are new "spins" and fragments of the stories that are added by other family members evoking surprise. As important as all this history might be to the family, rarely if ever has the family sat together and discussed these stories with all family members present. This moment is usually the first collective conversation about the family's history and the emotional meanings of those stories. The genogram is drawn on a large scale, and often the visual impact of the family story on paper has a deep and profound effect. We refer to the genogram throughout the consultation as we "unpack" family stories and begin to enlarge the contextual lens of relationships and events. We also draw a chronological timeline of the nodal events in the family's life, noting correlations of those events and relationship issues (e.g., the collapse of a start-up business after moving away from a supportive family, and the relationship hypotheses associated with this correlation). This contextualizing of the stories can broaden the understanding of people and events which had previously seemed mysterious or even capricious.

With the family in the spirit of mutual inquiry, we begin to build intergenerational hypotheses as we note themes and patterns across the generations, linking these hypotheses to what we have come to learn about the family through our interviews. This begins to soften the tendency to "devilfy and deify" family members, and to enhance the understanding of personality attributes and family judgments in the context of a profound relationship history. The consultants lead the family in the braided processes of unpacking stories, highlighting the meaning made, inviting alternative explanations, and reframing intentions and purposes. It is not uncommon at this point for some family member to disclose a family secret or some tender and avoided relationship – to launch a trial balloon – as if to check: "Can we really talk about these things?" Issues raised include abandonment, adoption, abortion, homosexuality, sexual abuse, neglect, infidelity, alcoholism, and violence. Feelings of hurt and shame, yearning for more closeness, anger and forgiveness, unmet desires, the load of responsibility and obligation, the distribution of burdens and benefits – all these feelings are "lifted" out of these discussions of family history.

This is the overture where the family themes are illuminated and connected to the deep history that surrounds this family. The overture begins to set the tone and direction of the ensuing hours, usually opening up possibilities, surprises, and mysteries never before considered. It may seem that we are simply getting "background information," but this is the entry point into a world that is high voltage and reinforced with strongly fixed and unchecked assumptions about people and the rules of life. If we start out in the spirit of all being "seekers," we begin to open doors. We are welcoming the possibility of these stories changing in the moment, in the metamorphosis of conversation.

Middle (hours 4–10).   Because we dedicate three hours to an incisive examination of family history and relationships, we are well underway by the time we get to the fourth hour of the consultation, our last hour on Friday night. The generation of family energy has usually been triggered multiple times in the review of the family's history. Bridges to this middle phase have already been built. We may begin this fourth hour by asking, "What was it like growing up in this family?" Whatever the content of the conversation, we are active in guiding the process that is built on the core factors discussed earlier: psychoeducation, direct address, immediacy, truth speaking and seeking, integrity, learning, creativity, relationship renegotiation, and co-consulting modeling. Real-time interactions are used to heighten family strengths and challenges. We believe that the experiential expression, elaboration, reorganizing, and renegotiating of relationships *in the moment* constitute one of the most curative aspects of the consultation.

These evolving conversations may focus on both the content issues of the family's life and the dynamic processes which have maintained them. The stories may include: family secrets (known and unknown); triangles; cutoffs; rules and roles, including limitations and constrictions of gender; the distribution of benefits and burdens in family life; loyalty and destructive entitlement; strengths of the family and individual members and unvoiced appreciations; unperceived or unacknowledged changes and developmental advances; unresolved resentments; unresolved or unvoiced regrets; unexamined critical incidents in the family history; repeat and repair efforts of successive generations; the aging and death of parents; money, inheritance, and allocation of family resources; and individual and family losses and grief.

The focus on family process may include, for example, noting and observing redundant patterns such as under-/over-functioning or pursuer/distancer dances; deepening emotional experience and response in the moment; promoting inquiry and curiosity of self and other; exploring the dynamics of tenderness and affection and sexuality; and facilitating apologies and reparations.

We will often include action-oriented, structural changes in order to vary the total group conversation. For example, we often use a "fish bowl" methodology where a subsystem of the family (e.g., siblings) is in the small circle in the center of the room, focusing exclusively on their own sibling relationships, while the parents listen on the outside. After this "fish bowl" conversation, we will turn to the parents and ask them to give feedback to their sons and daughters on the impact of what they heard. We vary our work like this in order to shift attention and create different feedback loops.

As we conclude each 2-hour session, we may summarize the themes and learnings from the session, soliciting from family members their learnings and responses, and inviting/challenging them to prepare in specific ways for the next session. Sometimes we consultants will turn and talk about the family with each other, usually to help turn the work in the family in a particular direction.

Closing (hours 11–12).   Family members are asked to come to the final session having done some "homework" around key questions: "What have you learned?"; "What do you want and from whom (requests)?"; "What are you willing to give and to whom (offers)?"; "What contracts do you want to make (bilateral agreements with other family members)?"; "What commitments do you want to make (unilateral declarations non-contingent on other family members)?" We may quote Aristotle, who declared that "character" is defined not by what we think, what we say, what we value, but "by what we repeatedly do." We like that emphasis on the commitment toward action, while we underscore that one of the greatest disappointments of these meetings is when family members make promises that they do not keep in action. These conversations begin to put the question of integrity on the table as the family consultation moves toward closure.

As we begin hour 11, family members tie together loose ends and finish enough of their work so that they can move toward closure. Previously, we have announced to the family that in hour 12, extended family members are invited to attend if the family desires their inclusion. In the final hour, the homework assignments are discussed, deals are made, and declarations are announced. If present, extended family members (usually partners of the sons and daughters) are invited to comment on what they have seen and heard in the last hour. We have heard apologies from family members to extended family members for how they were treated that dramatically change the emotional field of the family. We may offer additional suggestions for family members to consider. For example, we might suggest consultation with a psychiatrist for a member who reports depressive symptoms, or suggest couples work for the parents or siblings. We review the consultation process with the family, soliciting their feedback. We conclude by reminding the family that we will be sending a letter with a synopsis of the consultation within four weeks, and that we can be a resource for them in the future. Sometimes we have had follow-up meetings with the entire family, subsystems of the family, or individual members.

Post-consultation phase: The letter

After the consultation, the consultants consolidate their observations into a letter which is sent to the family members within a month of the consultation. Included in this synopsis are the major concerns of the family, the primary themes explored, the critical events that occurred during the consultation itself, the strengths in individuals and in the family, the summary of key learnings identified by family members and the consultants, and an outline of the family's commitments and contracts. Recommendations for further treatment or next steps are included.

We have begun calling family members six months after the consultation to check for changes, surprises, and unfolding effects in the evolution of individual and family life. We do this follow-up also as an anecdotal way of gathering "outcome data" on the impact of the consultation across the lives of individual family members and in the family as a group. We are also interested in what Framo (1992) called "the spreading effect," the impact of this consultation on relationships and issues far beyond the immediate dynamics of the family of origin.

Cautions, Contraindications, and Challenges

Every presentation of a model of therapy should also include a statement of caveats and contraindications – what the limits of this model are and when a family-of-origin consultation is not advised. We would refuse a consultation if the purpose of the meeting were to ambush and confront other family members regarding a noxious behavior (e.g., "Dad, we all now want to deal with your various affairs"). Challenge is one thing; a confronting coalition is quite another phenomenon. Another contraindication is not mere ambivalence (usually the common mode of entry), but partial attendance by a family member who has "competing commitments" elsewhere. Sporadic attendance impedes the process and endangers a good outcome. We have already noted that we require all family members to attend the full 12 hours unless there are extraordinary circumstances (e.g., incarceration, threat of physical danger). All members are important. We typically include all family members who might have a physical, emotional, or mental handicap regardless of their family cohorts (e.g., "She won't understand"; "He won't be able to take it . . . it will be too much"). We invite and require all members to attend and will make adjustments, if necessary, based on our experience. The anxiety generated by anticipating the family coming together in direct address for conversations of love and truth serves as a powerful stimulus for family members not to attend or for others to block their participation.

We meet with families where there have been divorces, remarriages, and a combination of biological and stepchildren. Depending on the particular history of the family, we divide the total hours into subparts with different membership. For example, in a family where the mother had been married twice, we dedicated some time to the family group with the biological father and some hours to the family and the stepfather, and then spent some concluding hours with everyone in the room.

In cases of multiple remarriages and divorces, an assessment of interfamily cohesion and commitment would be a critical antecedent to an intensive consultation. The complexity of these family formations and relations and the varying levels of family "glue" may either require additional time to work with the various subsystems, or may simply be inappropriate for this type of intervention in a family's life.

Violence, recent or ongoing, may also be a contraindication. Given the nature of the conversations and the importance of truth telling and truth hearing, it is counter-therapeutic to invite family members to engage in a process where there might be physical threats or retribution. There may be options for preliminary meetings with the individual who has been violent to assess their resilience and capacity to be engaged in the consultation.

Working with the family of origin is always a challenging adventure that feels more like an eloquent epic unfolding in the family – the first time this group has gathered in an intensive and extensive conversation together about the things that deeply matter with the people that matter. This is no small thing! Deep emotional currents are pervasive. Ancient stories unfold with new twists and fresh feelings. New commitments intersect with entrenched loyalties. The vigilant fears that guard these conversations begin to give way before advancing hope and possibility. The anecdotal data we gather in post-consultation interviews appear to lend strong validation to this intergenerational work. A more evidence-based analysis is the next step.

References

Anderson, R. (1970). *I never sang for my father.* New York: Signet.

Aponte, H. (1992). Training the person of the therapist in structural family therapy. *Journal of Marital and Family Therapy, 18,* 269–281.

Boszormenyi-Nagy, I., & Krasner, B. R. (1986). *Between give and take: A clinical guide to contextual therapy.* New York: Brunner/Mazel.

Bowen, M. (1978). *Family therapy in clinical practice.* New York: Aronson.

Davis, S. D., & Piercy, F. P. (2007a). What clients of couple therapy model developers and their former students say about change. Part I: Model dependent common factors across three models. *Journal of Marital and Family Therapy, 33,* 318–343.

Davis, S. D., & Piercy, F. P. (2007b). What clients of couple therapy model developers and their former students say about change. Part II: Model independent common factors and an integrative framework. *Journal of Marital and Family Therapy, 33,* 344–363.

Framo, J. L. (1992). *Family-of-origin therapy: An intergenerational approach.* New York: Brunner/Mazel.

Framo, J. L., Weber, T. T., & Levine, F. (2003). *Coming home again: A family-of-origin consultation.* New York: Brunner-Routledge.

Gilbert, R. M. (2006). *Extraordinary leadership: Thinking systems, making a difference.* Falls Church, VA: Leading Systems Press.

Johnson, S. M. (2004). *The practice of emotionally focused couple therapy.* New York: Brunner-Routledge.

Kerr, M. E., & Bowen, M. (1988). *Family evaluation.* New York: Norton.

Langer, E. J. (1997). *The power of mindful learning.* New York: Addison-Wesley.

McGoldrick, M., Gerson, R., & Petry, S. (2008). *Genograms: Assessment and Intervention* (3rd ed.). New York: Norton.

Nerin, W. F. (1986). *Family reconstruction: Long day's journey into light.* New York: Norton.

Pipher, M. (1999). *Another country: Navigating the emotional terrain of our elders.* New York: Riverhead Books.

Satir, V. (1972). *Peoplemaking.* Palo Alto, CA: Science & Behavior Books.

Satir, V., & Baldwin, M. (1983). *Satir step by step: A guide to creating change in families.* Palo Alto, CA: Science & Behavior Books.

Scharff, D. E., & Scharff, J. S. (1987). *Object relations family therapy.* New York: Aronson.

Siegel, D. J., & Hartzell, M. (2003). *Parenting from the inside out.* New York. Penguin.

Whitaker, C. A. (1989). *Midnight musings of a family therapist.* New York: Norton.

Williamson, D. S. (1991). *The intimacy paradox.* New York: Guilford Press.

Williamson, D. S., & Bray, J. H. (1985). The intergenerational view. In S. Henao & N. Grose (Eds.), *Principles of family systems in family medicine* (pp. 90–110). New York: Brunner/Mazel.

Wynne, L. C., McDaniel, S. H., & Weber, T. T. (1986). *Systems consultation: A new perspective for family therapy.* New York: Guilford Press.

19

Psychotherapy Based on Bowen Family Systems Theory

David S. Hargrove

This chapter describes the process of psychotherapy from the perspective of Bowen family systems theory (Bowen, 1971, 1978, 1988). The first section is a brief historical account of the development of Bowen theory to identify its place in the larger context of family therapies. Second is a description of the eight concepts of Bowen theory to establish the theoretical position from which the therapist operates. This section also may clarify some similarities and distinctions between Bowen theory and other approaches and applications, though that is not its intent. The third section describes the management of anxiety in Bowen theory. The fourth section is a discussion of some common dimensions of psychotherapy from the perspective of Bowen theory. Embedded in this section are clinical examples to illustrate the principles of psychotherapy based on Bowen theory. The chapter concludes with a brief comment on empirical research on Bowen theory.

Bowen theory is distinctive among other family therapies as well as psychotherapy in general in the importance placed on theory in the application to clinical situation. A working knowledge of theory to test hypotheses about human behavior and relationships is a foundation on which Bowen's work developed. The theory guides the work of psychotherapy; the work of psychotherapy continues to test and refine the theory. Kerr underscores its importance in the training of psychotherapists at the Georgetown Family Center that was founded by Bowen: "At Georgetown, therapy and technique have always been viewed as logical extensions of theory and have received, therefore, secondary emphasis in the training programs" (1981, p. 226). Perhaps the simplest statement of the power of that underlying principle is by Roberta Gilbert (2004, p. 3), "If you know theory you can use it. If you don't you can't."

Techniques and procedures of psychotherapy based on Bowen family systems theory are driven by the therapist's beliefs and understanding of the theory. The therapist's level of functioning in his or her own life and the fundamental beliefs that support clinical practice are the bedrock for what is done in psychotherapy. The importance of "theory driving therapy" cannot be overemphasized.

Historical Perspective of Bowen Theory

Murray Bowen was a psychiatrist, family researcher, and one of the pioneers of the family psychotherapy movement in the 1940s and 1950s. Bowen's interest in the family as a system to understand human behavior began when he was at the Menninger Clinic in Topeka. Particularly interested in schizophrenia, he observed the importance of the symbiotic relationship between the child and the mother in the disorder. This observation led him to a "systems" theory of emotional disorder based on relationships within families. He moved his work to the National Institute of Mental Health, where, for a brief period, he hospitalized entire families in research units to gather data to further understand the schizophrenic process in its larger context. Here he expanded his thinking to include the father and his role in the family emotional process. Bowen soon expanded this idea to include the entire family, both nuclear and extended. Later he moved to the Department of Psychiatry at the Georgetown University Medical School in Washington, where he founded the Georgetown Family Center, now the Bowen Center for the Study of the Family. By this time, Bowen thought of the family as a system and recognized the importance of the functioning of each part.

Bowen was one of several early theorists who emphasized the importance of the system, particularly the family, as the unit of analysis to understand human behavior. In other parts of the country, other systems theorists were moving in similar directions. They began to share their perspectives with one another in the 1950s. Guerin (1976) has a particularly poignant description of this development (see also Chapter 2, this volume).

An important aspect of the development of Bowen theory was his concern that psychiatry and the mental health professions be based on facts, not inferences or other subjective phenomena. While deeply appreciative of Freud's work in his own psychoanalytic effort, Bowen believed that psychiatry should be rooted in facts. A driving force throughout his entire career was to identify these facts, put them in a framework to understand human functioning, and relate them to what is known about other forms of life. As a result, Bowen relied upon the natural sciences, particularly the work of Darwin, Freud, Paul McLean, John Calhoun, E. O. Wilson, and others. His effort toward a firmer scientific base for psychiatry and the mental health disciplines is chronicled in the epilogue of Kerr and Bowen (1988).

Bowen believed that the human was not qualitatively different from other species of animals but had evolved adaptive capabilities that were different and, perhaps, unique. His study of science and his observation of human activity taught him that humans functioned in systems of relationships. This functioning was not "cause-and-effect" but reciprocal. Functioning in systems is circular, not linear; influences run in several directions. For that reason, it was and continues to be difficult to demonstrate the impact of an action on a particular object. His application of systems theory to the human led him to the prototype human system: the family. Bowen was, essentially, a family researcher.

Bowen theory is transgenerational. Anxiety moves across generations within families to influence styles of management and symptom development. An individual's knowledge of the transgenerational characteristics of anxiety is an important asset in resolving the impact of anxiety on the person's functioning. As a result, the Bowentrained psychotherapist almost always uses a family diagram as a part of the diagnostic and treatment process. Family diagrams are means of presenting important facts about family structure as well as suggesting influences in family dynamics. Behavior, in Bowen theory, always is interpreted within the context of both nuclear and transgenerational family systems.

Eight Concepts of Bowen Theory

Bowen theory consists of eight interrelated core concepts: the nuclear family emotional system, differentiation of self scale, triangles, emotional cutoff, family projection process, multigenerational transmission process, sibling position, and emotional process in society. The core concepts are in the context of two sets of drives and they provide a basis on which to understand the therapeutic process that emerges from them. This order of presentation of the core concepts of Bowen's theory is influenced by Gilbert's thinking (personal communication, 2003). She selected the nuclear family emotional system as the first concept to be presented because it established the "emotional unit" which "changes the way one thinks about everything relational" (p. 5). Papero (1990) wrote, "The concept of differentiation of self is the core of Bowen Family Systems Theory. No other concept in Bowen Family Systems Theory is so often discussed and associated with Bowen's work: (p. 45). But he further wrote, "It is difficult, if not impossible, to understand the concept of differentiation of self without seeing the family as an emotional unit" (p. 45). The order of presentation may change over time, depending on circumstances.

Nuclear family emotional system

Since the foundation of Bowen theory lies in its systems – rather than individual – orientation, it is reasonable that the cornerstone concept of Bowen theory is the nuclear family emotional system. This concept is based on the fused, or closely bound, relationships within family systems. The system, rather than the individual organism, is the level of analysis. The meaning of behavior is found in the network of relationships in which all the components of a system are related to one another. Change in one aspect of the system results in change in other parts of the system. The marriage is the foundation for relationships within the nuclear family emotional system.

Bowen (1978) noted four potential responses to increasing anxiety in a marriage. People can have conflict with one another; they can distance from one another; one person can offer a lower level of functioning to avoid threatening the relationship; or they can project anxiety onto one or more of the children in the family as a means of preserving harmony in the couple. Each of these possibilities deserves attention.

Marital conflict, in one sense, enables the relationship to maintain stability. Complaining, accusations, and other expressions of conflict provide a focus for the energy of the marital partners, frequently preventing more maladaptive consequences of the stress. Of course, if the conflict is carried to an extreme, maladaptive consequences can occur.

Emotional distance in a relationship is an avoidance reaction to stress in the system. Individuals will avoid certain topics of conversation, certain situations, or even being in the physical presence of the other. This is frequently heard in the consulting room when people complain that they have "grown apart." The distance is an adaptive response of the system to the individuals' noxious relationship with one another.

Emotional distance as a response to anxiety is an automatic reaction to an intense emotional process. "What people are avoiding with emotional distance is their own emotional reactivity to each other," writes Kerr (1981, p. 242). "The other person can seem like the problem, but the problem exists equally in both people." Marital tension, then, is reduced by avoidance.

A third means of managing marital stress is for one partner to "give in" to the other, compromising a level of functioning to calm the anxiety. When one's level of functioning is compromised, an individual is said to be "under-functioning." The person is not maintaining his or her responsibility in the relationship and the under-functioning can result in physical, mental, or social (acting out) dysfunction.

An under-functioning person in a relationship requires an over-functioning person. Because of the reciprocity in the relationship, the under-functioner needs the over-functioner to maintain a needed level of activity. Of course individuals engaged in over- and under-functioning typically blame the other person for either being over-controlling (over-functioning) or too weak and dependent (under-functioning). In extreme cases, under-functioning partners in a marriage become sufficiently impaired to require intense medical or psychological intervention. This intensifies the over-/under-functioning reciprocity, reinforcing these role patterns in the family.

A fourth way to manage anxiety is to focus on the impairment of children. This is an example of a triangle in the family. Excessive attention to children, either a selected one or several, can result from tension in the marital relationship. The child who receives the focus becomes sensitized to the turbulence of the couple and becomes vulnerable to a range of problems.

Focus on a child frequently is seen when a couple seeks psychological assistance. Attention remains on the child since the couple brings the child for professional assistance with the expectation that the child can be "fixed." The further expectation is that the "problems" of the child are caused by some internal condition or response to some environmental circumstance that does not include the family.

Differentiation of self scale

Differentiation of self is the means by which Bowen explains differences between people. People differ in the degree to which they take positions that are consistent with or different from the emotional processes of their families. A person who always acts consistently with the family emotional process is said to be fused within that family system and functioning at a lower level of differentiation of self. The person who balances emotional reactivity and thinking without regard to the family's emotional process is thought to be functioning at a higher level of differentiation of self. Differentiation of self is a means of defining the position that the individual takes toward the system, whether the family or some other social system of which the person is a part.

Bowen (1978) referred to the differentiation of self scale. This scale is a heuristic device, not a psychometric instrument, to gauge the levels of differentiation at which individuals function. The scale expresses the degrees of influence over behavior that come from a balance of emotion or thinking. As individuals move toward the extremes of emotion or thinking, expressing an imbalance between the two, they are thought to be functioning more poorly.

Levels of differentiation are determined by the degree to which a person has a choice of emotional and intellectual responsiveness to stress. Persons who function at the extremes of the continua of emotional and intellectual reactivity are not high on the scale of differentiation of self.

Differentiation of self is roughly equated with maturity. A mature person lives within a balance of the emotional and cognitive dimensions of life, able to stay connected with persons in the system of relationships while distinguishing self from others. The extremes of attachment and detachment are moderated in adaptive ways.

Triangles

The three-person relationship is the smallest stable unit of an emotional system. Two-person units are stable until there is sufficient stress that results in the introduction of a third person. The third person is brought in to calm the anxiety by distributing it among more people. If calm is not reached with the third person, another person is brought in, constituting an interlocking triangle. A useful analogy for the triangle is the three-legged stool. If the legs are cut perfectly flat and the floor is perfectly flat, the stool, theoretically, can stand on two legs. But the slightest stress to any part of the stool will cause it to tip. Human relationships are much the same way. As long as harmony is maintained, two-person relationships work well. In the face of stress, however, a third person is brought in to distribute the anxiety among more people.

Interlocking triangles provide the structure by which anxiety is communicated in the emotional process of a family. This may take place across generations (multigenerational transmission) or within a nuclear family (nuclear family projection process).

Emotional cutoff

Emotional cutoff is a means by which individuals may manage the transmission of anxiety across generations. It is a process of removal of one's self from the parental family and denying its importance. Cutoff does not reduce the amount of influence of the parental family, because of the intensity of the relationship and the extreme measure of coping with it. Cutoff is demonstrated by the physical or psychological removal of a person from the interpersonal environment of the family.

Family projection process

The family projection process is the emotional triangle operating in a single family, consisting of a father, mother, and at least one child. As anxiety increases between the father and mother, it may be projected onto a child, manifest as excessive attention to the child (termed "child-focus"). This is a triangle operating in the specific nuclear family. The child, in turn, may become symptomatic, as expressed in behavioral, medical, or social manifestations.

Multigenerational transmission process

This is the operation of the nuclear family emotional system across generations. As anxiety increases in a given nuclear family, it may result in distance between the spouses, conflict between the spouses, over- and under-functioning in the marital relationship, or projection onto a child. Typically, more than one of these processes is activated in the face of heightened anxiety in the system.

Sibling position

Bowen (1978) draws upon the work of Walter Toman (1976) to incorporate birth order into the theoretical framework. Toman postulated that birth order played an important role in understanding the dynamics of families and that there were predictable characteristics based there. He identified 11 positions in birth order, including oldest brother of brothers, youngest brother of brothers, oldest brother of sisters, youngest brother of sisters, male only child, oldest sister of sisters, youngest sister of sisters, female only child, and twins. He did not list middle children, believing that they would adopt one of the above positions depending on to whom they were closest in years. While birth order is not in and of itself a meaningful predictor of behavior, it provides a rich source of material for the understanding of family emotional process.

Emotional process in society

The eighth core concept is the application of emotional process in larger groups, including social groups, business, governmental agencies, and other systems. The larger-scale application is important in psychotherapy because it broadens the environment of stressors in which an individual's work on differentiation may occur.

Anxiety Management

Bowen theory posits two sets of drives that relate to the management of anxiety, expressed in polar concepts. Those principles are detachment and togetherness, and emotionality and rationality. Under conditions of high anxiety, most people will move toward one of the extremes of those polar concepts. For example, in conditions of high anxiety, some people will make strong moves toward other people and some will detach completely from others. Similarly, some people under conditions of high anxiety become emotionally reactive and others absolve themselves of emotion in a "stone-cold," or shut-down, mode.

Bowen believed that symptoms were signs of distress that result from imbalances of biological and psychological processes that are under stress. Symptoms are not located in a person's character, but develop as an aspect of the struggle of the system to adapt to stressful conditions. It is important to maintain a consistent perspective of symptom development as being a consequence of stress in the system, not a personality characteristic of the individual who absorbs the anxiety for the system. This important principle differentiates systems thinking from individual thinking. It is particularly important as it concerns the therapist's anxiety. The pressure for individual diagnosis, struggle to understand behavior within the systems context, and demand to develop a specific plan of intervention for apparently obvious problematic behaviors place mounting strain on a clinician. The temptation to resort to individual thinking by assigning a specific diagnosis to a particular individual that results in a clear treatment strategy may be a function of the anxiety of the larger provider system as well as the anxiety of the clinician. Practically, the clinician must work within the health and mental systems. Clinicians are left to determine for themselves how work within a systems perspective may be done in their context. A significant first step is to differentiate one's own anxiety from that of the larger system to ameliorate the effect of that anxiety on one's own functioning.

Bowen believed that the two polar concepts of togetherness–detachment and emotion–intellect were characteristic of human life and provided a context for the development of the theory. The individuality and togetherness forces are rooted in instinctual needs that characterize all relationships and operate outside the awareness of the individuals in the relationships. Kerr writes, "The individuality force is rooted in an instinctual drive to be a self-contained, independent organism, an individual in one's own right. The togetherness force is rooted in an instinctual need for others, a sense of being connected to the group or another person" (Kerr 1981, p. 236). The interplay of individuality and togetherness is dynamic, changing subtly in response to levels of anxiety in relationships. Clearly exaggerated response to either of these forces can be the basis for problematic behavior that represents the system's maladaptive response to stress. Homeostasis or a balance of responsiveness to these forces leads to greater adaptation.

Bowen Psychotherapy

Bowen systems theory provides a context for psychotherapy for individuals, couples, or families. Psychotherapy within a system, however, requires a different understanding of several dimensions of the process. These include the therapeutic relationship, the roles of the therapist and patient, the structure of therapy, specific techniques of psychotherapy, the goals of psychotherapy, and the process of psychotherapy.

The therapeutic relationship

Bowen changed his perspective of the therapeutic relationship from the intensity of the transference early in his career to functioning as a coach, attempting to remain outside the emotional field in which the patient lived. The most important work is done by the patient in relationship to his or her family and not in relationship to the therapist. Bowen attempted to be as neutral in his relationship to the patient as possible, understanding that it is impossible to be completely objective.

The effort is to enable the patient to be as objective as possible about his or her own situation, focusing on the nuclear family and the family of origin as the prototypical relationships. Work in the consulting room is designed to gain objectivity about the system and one's part in it. This defines the therapist's role as one of neutrality, staying out of the emotional process of the patient.

One particularly poignant example of this is found with a 44-year-old female who sought help for depression. She complained that she was undervalued in her home and had not developed a career outside the home. She was further concerned that her daughter would "inherit" the same predicament. She was asked to diagram her family as a part of the diagnostic process and to help her become more objective about her family. The therapist explained to her that a part of drawing the diagram involved gathering information in conversations with people in her family. After several weeks' work on the diagram, she discovered that strong women had provided the stability for her extended family for four generations. This knowledge strengthened her perspective of herself, improved her relationship with her daughter and husband, and energized her participation in her own family.

Roles of therapist and patient

Bowen's focus on the importance of the relationship between the patient and the family changed the roles of the therapist and patient from conventional psychotherapy. In conventional psychotherapy, the power of the process is found in the healing properties of the transference relationship as it influences the learning of the patient to generalize from psychotherapy to other domains of life. In psychotherapy based on Bowen theory, the patient develops or changes relationships with both nuclear and extended family by making changes in the self. This is done within a coaching rather than healing relationship. The therapist takes on the role of coach by clarifying, making suggestions from the perspective of theory, and assisting the patient in the evaluation of the effectiveness of the efforts.

The therapist also functions as a teacher of the theory of human behavior that governs the therapeutic enterprise. Understanding the theory of behavior change is an important aspect of the therapeutic process.

In the example above, the therapist explained the influence of the extended family and taught the patient how to do the diagram. This was a means of helping her become more objective about her family, enabling her to define herself in the emotional process. It also sent her to her mother, grandmother, and several aunts who had lived in close proximity. The common belief among these women was that women in her family were dependent, serving only roles of service to the men. The facts were, however, that women provided the stability that carried the family for four generations. These facts were revealed in a systematic attempt to understand the emotional process of the family. They demonstrated that the women played stronger roles and managed the daily life of the family. The men played more socially prominent roles, frequently taking them away from the family. The patient had never realized this before the conversations and making the diagram of the family.

The role of the therapist was to provide a perspective and to encourage the patient to initiate the conversations and record them in a systematic way. As she discussed her findings with the therapist, she made her own interpretations from the facts. This particular case supported Papero's idea of therapy based on Bowen theory being "self help therapy – almost" (2005).

An important aspect of the therapist's role is to manage the implicit triangle in the therapy process. Individual manifestations of anxiety in symptom development are expressions of distance or conflict in the family system. Psychotherapeutic assistance for these symptoms constitutes a triangle between those in the system and the therapist. The therapist's management of his or her role in this therapeutic triangle requires major effort. The therapist's intent is to take a calm, neutral position amid anxious relationships to assist patients to maintain calm in the process. In the case described above, the woman initially sought a "psychotherapeutic relationship" in which she could explore the sources of the depression, using the term "self-exploration." She clearly was moving toward a dependent relationship with the therapist. By taking the outside position in a triangle of the woman and her husband, the therapist maintained sufficient neutrality to encourage the woman to engage her family, particularly her husband, as a means of alleviating the depression.

The patient is a co-researcher in understanding the management of anxiety and the way it functions in the extended and nuclear family. Papero's suggestion about "self-help therapy – almost" is relevant in this case because the patient took prime responsibility in making changes.

Structure of therapy

Structure involves who is present in the consulting room. It evolved with the development of the theory. For example, psychoanalyst Bowen struggled in the NIMH years (mid-1950s) to move away from individual psychotherapy that consisted of the analysis of the transference relationship. This was difficult and included several stages. Kerr points out,

> At that time, he made a distinction in his own practice between family therapy, individual psychotherapy and psychoanalysis and had some patients in each category. He was calling it "family" only when two or more family members were seen together in sessions. The technical effort was to analyze the already existing emotional process between family members, keeping himself emotionally disengaged, or what he called "staying out of the transference." (1981, p. 231)

Bowen moved through this stage to embrace whoever in the family was motivated to pursue the needed change, but getting to this point was a slow, tedious process.

Bowen's later position on parents who brought apparently troubled children for therapy is among the most interesting and controversial. He worked with the most motivated people, typically one or both parents, to understand the emotional process, particularly the projection process, to enable the parents to reach homeostasis of the family system. He rarely thought seeing the child in therapy was of value and focused his efforts on assisting the parents to change.

An elderly couple, Walter and Esther, sought the assistance of a psychologist in determining what to do about their 44-year-old daughter who was diagnosed with bipolar disorder. She had been hospitalized several times but appeared to be in remission. She was employed and lived with her boyfriend in a small duplex in a nearby city. The parents became disturbed when they found the place in considerable disarray, with stacks of magazines and clothes filling the duplex. The couple appeared to be unconcerned. The parents decided that they should increase the frequency and intensity of their visits, showing their daughter how to keep a clean house.

A description of Esther's mother revealed that she was a rigid housekeeper who believed that "cleanliness was next to godliness," demanding that order be maintained in the household or there would be serious consequences. She frequently visited her adult children, correcting their housekeeping habits. The recognition of this similarity was startling to Esther, whose husband agreed, and they decided to keep their distance on this matter. The anxiety about the daughter calmed.

Techniques of therapy

Bowen was not particularly impressed with specific therapeutic techniques. It is important to point out that he was first a researcher who sought to establish a "science of human behavior" before he developed therapeutic procedures. Therapeutic technique took a back seat to the development of theory. Bowen demonstrated more interest in the functioning, or level of differentiation of self, of the therapist in the system.

The techniques of therapy emerge from the theory. For example, the theory places a heavy emphasis on objectivity. One of the ways in which objectivity is gained is through the family diagram. The diagram enables both the therapist and the patient to gain a degree of objectivity about family history and dynamics. One purpose of creating the diagram is to become factual about the family, then enabling the patient to move toward greater objectivity about the family.

Other techniques of self-regulation may be utilized. Biofeedback, for example, is used by some therapists to enable patients to control biological responsiveness to stress. Friesen (personal communication, 2003) discusses the use of biofeedback and neurofeedback for the purpose of self-regulation. Self-regulation in this context is in the service of differentiation of self.

Goals of psychotherapy

Ideally, the goals of psychotherapy are to improve differentiation of self and the functioning of the family. Increases in the functional levels of persons in the system result in the system itself becoming more adaptive. This goal suggests that individuals in the system can become less emotionally reactive and more balanced in response to various levels of anxiety in the system.

It is important to point out again the common tenet that change in one part of the system results in change in other parts of the system. One individual making substantial change in self can result in others functioning at higher levels.

It is possible, however, for positive individual change to occur without the entire system becoming more adaptive. For instance, "When someone attempts to be more of a self in a relationship system, the absolutely predictable response from important others is, 'You are wrong; change back; if you don't, these are the consequences'" (Kerr & Bowen, 1988, pp. 107–8). In this situation, the individual demonstrates growth in defining a self but the system has not yet incorporated the new position. Systems do not respond to change easily and the struggle for both individual and systems change may be long and arduous.

Process of psychotherapy

The process of psychotherapy is influenced by the structure and dynamics of the family, the functioning of the person who is motivated to seek change, the degree with which the therapist connects with the emotional level of the family, and the intensity of the anxiety for which assistance is sought. The process includes embracing a theory of human functioning that enables a person to define a self in relation to the larger system.

From within the theory, psychotherapy may be thought of as managing triangles. The therapist focuses on the process by which the triangle was formed, suggesting a consideration of the parts each person in the triangle is playing in that process. This requires the therapist to maintain an acute awareness of his or her own role in the triangle and the ability to help the others see their roles.

Of course, managing these therapeutic triangles is much easier said than done. Recognizing triangles of which one is a part is difficult enough. Managing one's own behavior and observing the behavior of others is even more challenging. Since the triangle is the means by which anxiety is transmitted within a group and it flows with electrical fluency, the only way to inhibit the flow of anxiety is to recognize the part that a given individual plays, usually one's self, and adjust one's level of functioning in a thoughtful, calm process. Triangles occur both within and across generations of families, requiring the interested individual to work at understanding both nuclear and extended families. This work includes observing the interactions and flow of anxiety in the group, especially one's own contribution to it. This perspective of functioning of the family can help the individual define himself or herself within the group, allowing a more objective perspective to emerge and form the basis of new behavior.

Meyer (1998) describes four phases of therapy based on Bowen theory. Phase one consists of the observation of the family of origin. The presentation of thorough, clear information about the family of origin in a diagram enables the family or patient to become more objective about the family of origin and to identify patterns that occur and re-occur over time. Becoming more objective about the family of origin enables individuals to understand the role that each one plays in the system. Meyer writes, "When phase one is vigorously pursued, most individuals will automatically begin to focus on self, making comments such as 'the more I see the pattern of cutoff in my family, the more I see the very same pattern within myself'" (Meyer, p. 77). It is essential in this phase to understand the importance of being connected to the family of origin and to the nuclear family, participating in the family's events and celebrations, while maintaining a self within this context. Meyer's second phase considers the functional patterns of the individual in the system. Working within the framework of phase one, greater understanding of the family system, the movement toward an individual's accepting responsibility for self in the family and its history involves a person accurately assessing the roles he or she may have played in the development of problems. It is important that the individual not accept more responsibility for problems (victim) or less responsibility (blaming) than is due.

The recognition of one's own part in the problems sets the stage for the third phase of the therapeutic process, which is the "formulation of a strategy for personal change" (Meyer, 1998, p. 80). The strategy is determined by the nature of the problem, characteristically involving extensive data collection about the person's family and the rediscovery of a person's deeply held principles for life. This third stage of the therapeutic process is the design of a strategy that enables the person to engage the family in an objective manner to assess the nature of relationships, and to determine how change in one's self can take place. Meyer writes,

> The formulation of a strategy for change is a completely different process than "technique," which is a specific action for a specific situation. Strategy is a plan of action based on life principles that *guide* an individual to think, decide, and act. These principles can provide

guidelines throughout an individual's life. *How* a specific decision is carried is a *technical* question; *what* decision is appropriate is a *theoretical* question. (author's italics; p. 80)

Such strategies likely involve attendance at family events, remaining in contact with the family, thinking objectively about the family, and rediscovery of one's principles that are uniquely characteristic of the self.

Meyer's fourth phase, the work of changing self, involves the person employing the objective view of the family and his or her own participation. It is to understand the role that the individual plays in the emotional process of the family and make the changes necessary to increase the individual's level of functioning. For example, a man may discover in phases two and three that he is reactive to many of the females in the family in a way that is predicated on his own reactivity to his mother. Working on himself in the system involves increasing awareness of his relationship to females in the system to alter his level of functioning in these relationships. This requires him to become aware of his emotional reactivity and increase his effort to remain calm in these intense relationships. The calm is attained as he realizes that his reactivity is in relationship to his mother and has little if anything to do with other females in his environment. The psychotherapy process encourages him to establish his own position in relation to his mother, decreasing his emotional reactivity as he maintains the contact.

Being aware of one's own family emotional process enables therapists to assist patients in the therapeutic work of managing the emotional process of which they are a part. This includes learning the multigenerational emotional process and the dynamics of the nuclear family, and assistance toward differentiation of self. The therapist's management of self in this process frees the patient to do the same. Finally, Bowen's avoidance of the development of techniques requires each therapist to develop his or her own procedures for the management and resolution of anxiety.

Research Findings

While it is not the intent of this chapter to review empirical research in Bowen theory, it is important to point out that it has stimulated considerable empirical investigation. The results have been mixed and controversial (Miller, Anderson, & Keala, 2004). Some of the constructs of Bowen theory have been supported while others remain at the level of a theoretical postulation.

Significant research has supported Bowen's concept of differentiation of self, and two scales have been developed to measure it. Skowron's Differentiation of Self Inventory (Skowron & Friedlander, 1998) appears to be the most frequently used scale in a number of studies in which differentiation of self is an important variable. Haber (1993) reports the usefulness of a differentiation of self scale but it does not appear to have been extensively utilized. Bartle-Haring and her colleagues (2002) have utilized the Behavioral and Emotional Reactivity Index to assess differentiation of self and have found interesting results in relationship to other significant variables.

Limited empirical support for the multigenerational transmission of anxiety has been reported. Bowen's specific ideas about triangles are rarely tested, if ever (Miller et al., 2004). Sibling position has been widely studied and little, if any, meaningful support for it has been reported.

Bowen theory offers a fertile field for empirical research. Care must be taken to gain construct validity for the measures as well as to assure that a systems perspective of the investigation be maintained.

References

Bartle-Haring, S., Rosen, K. H., & Stith, S. M. (2002). Emotional reactivity and psychological distress. *Journal of Adolescent Research, 17(6)*, 568–585.

Bowen, M. (1971). Family therapy and family group therapy. In H. Kaplan & B. Sadock (Eds.), *Comprehensive group psychotherapy* (pp. 384–421). Baltimore, MD: Williams & Wilkins.

Bowen, M. (1978). *Family therapy in clinical practice.* New York: Aronson.

Bowen, M. (1988). An odyssey toward science. In M. E. Kerr & M. Bowen (Eds.), *Family evaluation* (pp. 339–386). New York: Norton.

Gilbert, R. M. (2004). *The eight concepts of Bowen theory: A new way of thinking about the individual and the group.* Falls Church, VA: Leading Systems Press.

Guerin, P. J. (1976). Family therapy: The first twenty-five years. In P. J. Guerin (Ed.), *Family therapy: Theory and practice* (pp. 2–22). New York: Gardner Press.

Haber, J. E. (1993). A construct validity study of a differentiation of self scale. *Scholarly Inquiry for Nursing Practice, 7*, 165–178.

Kerr, M. E. (1981). Family systems theory and therapy. In A. S. Gurman & David Kniskern (Eds.), *Handbook of family therapy: Vol. 1* (pp. 226–264). New York: Brunner/Mazel.

Kerr, M. E., & Bowen, M. (1988). *Family evaluation: An approach based on Bowen theory.* New York: Norton.

Meyer, P. H. (1998). Bowen theory as a basis for therapy. In P. Titelman (Ed.), *Clinical applications of Bowen family systems theory* (pp. 69–116). Binghamton, NY: Haworth Press.

Miller, R. B., Anderson, S., & Keala, D. K. (2004). Is Bowen theory valid? A review of basic research. *Journal of Marital and Family Therapy, 30(4)*, 453–466.

Papero, D. V. (1990). *Bowen family systems theory.* Needham Heights, MA: Allyn & Bacon.

Papero, D. V. (2005). The clinical process: "A do-it-yourself therapy – almost." Symposium conducted at the meeting of the Bowen Center for the Study of the Family, Georgetown Family Center, Washington, DC.

Skowron, E. A., & Friedlander, M. L. (1998). The Differentiation of Self Inventory: Development and initial validation. *Journal of Counseling Psychology, 45*, 235–246.

Toman, W. (1976). *Family constellation* (3rd ed.). Oxford: Springer.

20

Collaborative Practice: Relationships and Conversations that Make a Difference

Harlene Anderson

"How can our practices have relevance for people's everyday lives in our fast changing world, what is this relevance, and who determines it?" are persistent questions for collaborative practitioners. This chapter presents *one* response to these questions.

The landscape of collaborative practice is our ever-changing world that is characterized by social, cultural, political, and economic transformations as well as the influence of the internet and media on the decentralization of information, knowledge, and expertise. A new international spotlight is coincidentally being placed on democracy, social justice, and human rights; the importance of the people's voice, singular or plural; and the need for collaboration. People increasingly want input into what affects their lives; they have lost faith in rigid institutions and practices in which being treated as numbers and categories ignores their humanity or, worse yet, violates it. People demand systems and services that are more flexible and respectful. These contemporary global and local shifts, the unavoidable complexities inherent in them, and the effects they have on our individual and communal lives and on our world press family psychologists to reassess how we understand the world around us, our clients, and our roles as practitioners. Collaborative practice is a response that shares common ground with a growing international community of practitioners and clinical scholars including Tom Andersen, Vivien Burr, John Cromby, Kenneth Gergen, Mary Gergen, Lynn Hoffman, Lois Holzman, Imelda McCarthy, Susan McDaniel, Sheila McNamee, Robert Neimeyer, David Nightingale, Peggy Penn, Sallyann Roth, Jaakko Seikkula, John Shotter, Lois Shawver, and Michael White.

Collaborative practice, as described in this chapter, has evolved over time with its roots tracing back to the 1950s multiple impact therapy project in Galveston, Texas (MacGregor et al., 1964). Its evolution over the years has been continually influenced by the reflexive nature of theory and practice (Anderson, 1997; Anderson & Gehart, 2007; Anderson & Goolishian, 1988, 1992). Because the Galveston team's clinical and consultation practice then – and that of the Houston Galveston Institute afterwards – included a large percentage of people referred for whom previous treatments were not successful, we were always curious about why the client thought that the helpers had not been helpful, what we could learn from their described previous therapy experiences, and how our therapy could be more relevant and effective. This ambition and curiosity has led to lessons learned from over 25 years of inquiry into client's experiences, descriptions of the nature of successful and unsuccessful therapy, and the advice that clients – the true experts – have had for therapists and particularly family psychologists (Anderson, 1997; Anderson & Goolishian, 1992).

Assumptions of Collaborative Practice: A Tapestry

Your attitude towards your life will be different according to which understanding you have.
(Suzuki, *Zen Mind, Beginner's Mind*)

Collaborative practice has grown from assumptions in the broader postmodern movement in the social and human sciences, as well as from related assumptions regarding social construction and dialogue theories (Bahktin, 1986; Gadamer, 1975; Gergen, 1999; Hacking, 1999; Lyotard, 1984; Shotter, 1984, 2005; Vygotsky, 1986). Common among postmodern, social construction, and dialogue assumptions is the centrality of knowledge and language as social and communal processes; they are relational and generative and therefore inherently transforming. (I more fully discuss these assumptions below.) These assumptions inform the way the family psychologist conceptualizes and approaches therapy, and apply regardless of the designated system or the number of people involved in it. This book is about family psychology. Notably absent from collaborative family psychology practice is a distinction between therapy designations such as individual, couple, or based on family or numbers of people in the therapy room or their relationships (Anderson, 1997, 2006; Anderson & Goolishian, 1988). As well, a collaborative family psychologist works with a variety of systems from the same set of assumptions, including systems such as education, research, and combinations of people called organizations and communities.

I use *postmodern* as an umbrella term for my guiding assumptions. As there is no single definition of *postmodern*, I refer to the set of abstract assumptions that inform collaborative practice as a "postmodern tapestry." These assumptions – the threads of the tapestry – challenge our inherited traditions of knowledge and language, and provide a contemporary alternative (see Chapter 1, this volume, for a description of the epistemological evolution). The central challenge is to reexamine these traditions of knowledge as fundamental and definitive, the top-down nature of knowledge systems, language as descriptive and representational, and the stability of meaning. For the purposes of this chapter I identify six assumptions.

Maintaining skepticism.   Postmodernism asserts the importance of holding a critical and questioning attitude about knowledge as somehow fundamental and definitive. This includes knowledge of inherited and established dominant discourses, metanarratives, universal truths, or rules. We are born, live, and are educated within knowledge traditions that we mostly take for granted. A postmodern perspective suggests that unwittingly buying into and reproducing institutionalized knowledge can lead to forms of practice that risk being out of sync with our contemporary societies and possibly alien to humanity as well. This is not to suggest that we abandon our inherited knowledge or discourses (e.g., psychological theories, a priori criteria), or that these can be discarded for that matter. Any and all knowledge can be useful. Nor is it suggested that postmodernism is a metaknowledge narrative. The invitation is simply to question any discourse's claim to truth, including that of the postmodern discourse itself.

Eluding generalization.   The probability that dominant discourses, metanarratives, and universal truths can be generalized and applied across all peoples, cultures, situations, or problems is suspect. Thinking in terms of ahead-of-time knowledge (e.g., theoretical scripts, predetermined rules) can create categories, types, and classes (e.g., people, problems, solutions) that inhibit our ability to learn about the uniqueness and novelty of each person or group of people. Instead, we might learn about the distinctiveness of others and their lives directly from them and see the familiar or what we take for granted in an unfamiliar or fresh way. We are accustomed to viewing, wittingly or unwittingly, many people and the events of their lives encountered in therapy as familiar rather than exceptional. Familiarity tempts us to fill in the gaps and proceed from our assumptions about these gaps; this knowing can put us at risk of depersonalizing the client and preventing us from learning about their specialness – limiting our and the client's possibilities.

Knowledge as an interactive social process.   Embedded as it is in culture, history, and language, knowledge is a product of social discourse. The creation of knowledge (e.g., theories, ideas, truths, beliefs, or how to) is an interactive interpretive process in which all parties contribute to its creation, sustainability, and change. Knowledge is not fundamental or definitive; it is not fixed or discovered. Instead, it is fluid and changeable. So, instructive interaction is not possible; knowledge cannot literally be transmitted from the head of one person to another.

Privileging local knowledge.   Local knowledge – the knowledge, expertise, truths, values, conventions, narratives, etc. – that is created within a community of persons (e.g., family, classroom, board room) who have first-hand knowledge (i.e., unique meanings and understandings from personal experience) of themselves and their situation is important. Since knowledge is formulated within a community it will have more relevance, be more pragmatic, and be sustainable. Local knowledge, of course, always develops against the background of dominant discourses, metanarratives, and universal truths and is influenced by these conditions. This cannot be, nor is it suggested that it should be, avoided.

Language as a creative social process.   Language in its broadest sense – any means by which we try to articulate, express, or communicate with ourselves verbally or otherwise and with others – is the medium through which we create knowledge. Language, like knowledge, is viewed as active and creative rather than as static and representational. Words for instance are not meaning-mirrors; they gain meaning as we use them and in the way that we use them. This includes a number of things such as context, why we use them, and how we use them, involving our tone, our glances, and our gestures. Language and words are relational. As Bakhtin (1986) suggests, "No utterance in general can be attributed to the speaker exclusively; it is the *product of the interaction of the interlocutors*, and broadly speaking, the product of the whole complex *social situation* in which it has occurred" (p. 30). He further suggests that we do not own our words: "The word in language is half someone else's. The word becomes 'one's own' only when the speaker populates it with his own intention . . . the word does not exist in a neutral and impersonal language . . . but it exists in other people's mouths, in other people's contexts" (1986, pp. 293–4).

Knowledge and language as transforming.   Knowledge and language are relational and generative, and therefore intrinsically transforming. Transformation – whether in the form of a shift, modification, difference, movement, clarity, etc. – is inherent in the fluid and creative aspects of knowledge and language. That is, when engaged in the use of language and in the creation of knowledge one is involved in a living activity (i.e., dialogue with oneself or another) and cannot remain unchanged.

To reiterate, these assumptions do not suggest that postmodernism is an oppositional perspective calling for the abandonment of our inherited knowledge or any discourse, or that these can be discarded, for that matter. Nor do these assumptions suggest that postmodernism is a metanarrative or metaperspective, since self-critique is essential to postmodernism itself. Nor does postmodern define a school of therapy. It offers a different language or set of assumptions, or as Wittgenstein suggests, a different language game (Amscombe & Amscombe, 2001).[1]

Implications for Clinical Practice

> *All understanding is dialogical.*
>
> (Bahktin, *Speech, Genre and Other Late Essays*)

The question is "How does this different language or language game influence the way that I think about the goal of therapy and its process, including the client's role and my role?"

First, they inform what I call a *philosophical stance*: *a way of being.* And second, particular kinds of relationships and conversations naturally develop from this philosophical stance.

The philosophical stance is *the heart and spirit* of the collaborative approach: *a way of being.* It is a posture, an attitude, and a tone that communicate to another the special importance that they hold for me, that they are a unique human being and not a category of people, and that they are recognized, are appreciated, and have something to say worthy of hearing. This stance invites and encourages the other to participate on a more equitable basis. It reflects a way of being *with* people, including ways of thinking with, talking with, acting with, and responding with them. The significant word here is *with*: a "withness" process of orienting and re-orienting oneself to the other person (Hoffman, 2002; Shotter, 2004, 2005). Hoffman (2002) refers to this kind of relationship withness as one that is as communal and collective as it is intimate, witness that requires us to "jump, like Alice, into the pool of tears with the other creatures" (p. 66). *Witness* therapy relationships and conversations become more participatory and mutual and less hierarchical and dualistic.

With this belief *connecting, collaborating*, and *constructing* with others become authentic and natural performances, not techniques. I call these performances *collaborative relationships* and *dialogical conversations*, and although I address them separately below, they are intrinsically interrelated. The philosophical stance becomes an expression of a value, a belief, and a worldview that does not separate professional from personal. Before elaborating on the philosophical stance, I will briefly discuss collaborative relationship and dialogical conversation.

Collaborative relationship and dialogical conversation

Collaborative relationship refers to the way in which we orient ourselves to be, act, and respond "with" another person so the other joins a therapeutic shared engagement and joint action that I call a *shared inquiry* (I discuss shared inquiry in the next section). Shotter (1984) suggests that all living beings exist in joint action – in meeting and interacting with one another in mutually responsive ways. That is, we are relational beings who mutually influence and are mutually influenced by each other. As relational beings our "selves" cannot be separated from the relationship systems which we are, have been, and will be a part of. As well, though we are always speaking an ambiguous and different language than the other, as Bahktin (1986) suggests, our speaking and our language always includes others' intentions and meanings.

Here I want to highlight "respond." We are always responding: there is no such thing as a "no response" or "lack of response." There is simply one kind of response which, as with any response, the "receiver" interprets, and decides whether this action is hearable or visible or not. Our responses to the other are critical to the development and quality of the relationship. They create the framework, the parameter, and the opportunity for the relationship. Collaborative practitioners value *partnerships* characterized by joint action or *social activity* in which each member develops a sense of participation, belonging, and co-ownership. The family psychologist is the catalyst for this partnership and its process. I am talking about their response to the client, yet responding is an interactive two-way process.

Dialogical conversation refers to talk in which participants engage "with" each other (out loud) and "with" themselves (silently) – in words, signs, symbols, gestures, etc. – in a mutual or shared inquiry: jointly responding (e.g., commenting, examining, questioning, wondering, reflecting, nodding, gazing, etc.) as they talk about the issues at hand.

Drawing on Bakhtin's (1986) definition, dialogue is a form of verbal interaction; it is communication between people that takes place in the form of an exchange of utterances. Dialogue, however, is not limited to spoken words; it also includes the silent way (inner talk and physical expressions) in which we talk with ourselves and others.

Dialogue involves a process of *trying to understand the other person from their perspective, not ours.*[2] Dialogical understanding is not a search for facts or details but an orientation. It is an (inter)*active process*, not a passive one, that requires participation through responding to *connect* and *learn* about the other, rather than to pre-know and understand them and their words from a theory. In relation to therapy, dialogue is invited through the process of the family psychologist's learning about the other, especially about their uniqueness and noticing the not-yet-noticed. Through the process of trying to understand, *local understandings* develop from within the conversation. Dialogue is an always *becoming, never-ending,* and *immeasurable* process. As Bakhtin (Holmquest, 1981) said, dialogue is the condition for the emergence of new meaning and other newness.

I assume that when people have a space and process for collaborative relationships and dialogic conversations, they begin to talk with themselves, each other, and others in a *new* way. Through these conversations newness develops and can express itself in an infinite variety of forms, such as enhanced self-agency and freeing self-identities; different ways to understand themselves, their life events, and the people in their lives; as well as new options to respond to the challenges and dilemmas of the circumstances and situations in their lives.

I ask, "How can practitioners invite and facilitate the condition and the metaphorical space for dialogue?" I return to the philosophical stance.

Philosophical Stance

> *. . . not to solve what had been seen as a problem, but to develop from our new reactions new socially intelligible ways forward, in which the old problems become irrelevant.*
> (Shotter, *Social Accountability and Selfhood*)

> *Problems are not solved but dissolved in language.*
> (Anderson and Goolishian, "Human systems as linguistic systems")

The philosophical stance expresses the assumptions of collaborative practice. It has seven distinctive, interrelated features that are guiding ideas for the family psychologist; together they inform how the family psychologist thinks about the relationship and the conversation with the client, and helps create and foster a metaphorical "space" for these. Despite guiding ideas, collaborative practice is not replicable, but creatively invented and customized each time a family psychologist meets a client. In other words, though the stance has common identifiable features, their expression is unique to each family psychologist, each client, and each human system and to the circumstances and desires of each. It acts as a philosophy of collaborative practice, a conceptual guide, and not a formula.

Mutually inquiring partnership

Attracting and engaging another into a collaborative relationship and dialogic conversation entails inviting them through the family psychologist's way of being, a way that communicates to the client, as mentioned above, that they and their situation hold a special importance for the family psychologist, that their views are respected, and that what they have to say is valued without judgment. This begins a partnership relationship and process characterized by a joint activity that I refer to as *shared or mutual inquiry*. It is an in-there-together process in which two or more people (one of whom can be yourself) put their heads together to puzzle over and address something.

The family psychologist invites the client into this mutual inquiry by taking a *learning position*, through:

- making room for and giving the client the choice of telling their story in their own manner and at their own pace;
- being genuinely interested in and curious about the client's story;
- listening and responding attentively and carefully;
- responding to better understand the client's perspective or sense-making map;
- trying to respond to what the client is saying (not what the family psychologist thinks they should be saying);
- noticing how the other person responds before continuing;
- paying attention to their words and their non-words;
- checking out through comments, questions, and alternative words whether you have heard what the other wants you to hear;
- pausing and allowing silences for listening and reflecting spaces; and
- allowing each person to choose to respond to what piques their interest and in their own way.

A host/guest metaphor.   As Derrida (Bennington, 2003) suggests, the invitation requires *unconditional hospitality*. With my students I sometimes use a host/guest metaphor to highlight the importance of unconditional hospitality, as well as the subtleties and nuances of greetings and meetings and how they begin to shape the tone, the quality, and the possibilities of the relationship and the conversation, and consequently its potential (Anderson, 1997, 2006). I emphasize that the family psychologist is the host and is, at the same time, a temporary guest in the client's life.

> it is as if the therapist is a host who meets and greets the client as a guest while simultaneously the family psychologist is a guest in the client's life. I ask my students to think about how they like to be received as a guest. What does the host do that makes them feel welcomed or not, at ease or not, and special or not? What did the quality of the

meeting and greeting feel like? These are not rhetorical questions. I do not expect specific answers. Instead, I want the students to think about the sense of their experience in the relationship and conversation and what it communicated to them. (Anderson, 2006, p. 45)

A storyball metaphor. I also use a "storyball" metaphor to discuss the learning position and mutual inquiry with my students. When I first meet a client and they begin to talk, it's as if they gesture to hand a storyball to me – a ball of intertwined threads of their life narratives and their current circumstance. I respond (Anderson, 2006):

> As they put the ball toward me, and while their hands are still on it, I gently place my hands on it but I do not take it from them. I begin to participate with them in the story telling, as I slowly look at/listen to the aspect that they are showing me. I try to learn about and understand their story by responding to them: I am curious, I pose questions, I make comments, and I gesture. In my experience, I find that this therapist learning position acts to spontaneously engage the client as a co-learner; it is as if the therapist's curiosity is contagious. In other words, what begins as one-way learning becomes a two-way, back-and-forth process of mutual learning as client and therapist co-explore the familiar and co-develop the new, shifting to a mutual inquiry of examining, questioning, wondering, and reflecting with each other. (p. 47)

My responses – whatever form they may take, whether questions, comments, gestures, etc. – are informed by and come from inside the conversation itself; they relate to what the client has just said or done. They are not informed by my "truth" about the client: what I think the client should be talking about, is really thinking, or should be doing. My responses are my way of participating in the conversation from a continually learning position and to insure that I understand as best I can, all to encourage the back-and-forth process that I call mutual inquiry and to engage the client in a new curiosity about themselves. Through the process of mutual inquiry the client begins to develop meanings for themselves and for the people and events that permit addressing the circumstances in their lives for which they sought consultation, as well as other possibilities with far-reaching effects. In other words, the newness comes from within the dialogical process. These possibilities or the newness, as mentioned above, may take infinite forms.

Through this joint activity, the client–family psychologist relationship and conversation begin to determine the process or method of inquiry; the process or method does not define the relationship and the conversation. That is, client and family psychologist create from *within* the present relationship and conversation in the moment as each moment unfolds, not from outside it or ahead of time. The family psychologist does not control the direction of the conversation or storytelling but participates in it. Together, client and family psychologist shape the storytelling, the re-telling, and the new telling, yielding a richness of novel, freshly seen possibilities and previously unimagined futures.

When working with a family I think of each member as coming with his or her own storyball. I want to make room for and show the importance I place on each one. It is not unusual for members to have different and sometimes competing story versions. These are part of the collective storytelling. I am interested in understanding each version;

I do not strive for consensus. I have found that the differences are important and that possibilities emerge from these differences as we engage with each other in the tellings and re-tellings.

Regardless of the number of people in the therapy room, an in-there-together connection and activity begin in which people talk with, not to, each other. Each member develops a sense of *belonging* which invites *participation*, which in turn invites *ownership* and a sense of *shared responsibility.*

I tend to talk with one person at a time, listening intensely to their story, and conveying with words and actions the importance for me of what they are saying. I respond with questions, comments, etc. that are informed by what they have just said, not by what I think they should be saying. My listening and responding are not modeling a way for family members to talk and interact with each other outside the therapy. Though they may do so, my intent is to help me listen, and importantly *hear*, their story and what is important to them. I want my responses to be congruent and not inadvertently steer the conversation in a different direction. In my response to the client and theirs to mine, meanings and understandings begin to be clarified, expanded, and altered. As one member of a family talks and the others listen, all parties begin to experience a difference in the story tellings and re-tellings. When a speaker has the room to fully express himself or herself without interruption and the others have equally full room for listening, all begin to have a different experience of each other and what is said and heard. When you are able to fully listen without sitting on the edge of your chair preparing a corrective response, you begin to hear and understand things in other ways.

Relational expertise

Both client and family psychologist bring expertise to the encounter. The client is an expert on themselves and their world; the family psychologist is an expert on a process and space for collaborative relationships and dialogical conversations. The focus on the expertise of the client does not deny the expertise of the family psychologist. It calls our attention to the client's wealth of know-how on his or her life and cautions us not to value, privilege, and worship the family psychologist as a better knower than the client. Again, I do not suggest that a professional lacks or pretends a lack of expertise. Of course, family psychologists have expertise, though from a collaborative perspective it is a different kind of expertise: it is a "know-how" in inviting and maintaining a space and process for collaborative relationships and dialogical conversations.

Not-knowing

Not-knowing refers to how a family psychologist thinks about the construction of knowledge and the intent and manner with which it is introduced into the therapy. It is a humble attitude about what the family psychologist thinks he or she might know and a belief that he or she does not have access to privileged information, can never fully understand another person, and always needs to learn more about what has been said or not said.

A collaborative family psychologist keeps the emphasis on knowing *with* another instead of knowing another person, their circumstances, or the preferred outcome better than the person or beforehand. A collaborative family psychologist is aware of the risk that these knowings can place people in problem categories or identify them as members of a type of person. Such knowing can interfere with the family psychologist's ability to be interested in and learn about the uniqueness of that person and the novelty of their life. Knowing *with* is crucial to the dialogical process.

A not-knowing position does not mean the family psychologist does not know anything or can discard or not use what she or he knows (e.g., theoretical knowledge, clinical experience, life experience). Rather, the emphasis is on the intent, the manner, and the timing with which the family psychologist's knowing is introduced. The introduction of a family psychologist's knowledge is simply a way of participating in the conversation, offering food for thought and dialogue, and offering a way to continue to talk about what is already being addressed. Following the client's response, including being able to let go if the client is not interested, and refraining from private interpretations regarding the response are important.

Being public

Family psychologists also have private thoughts – whether in the form of professionally, personally, theoretically, or experientially informed understandings (such as diagnoses, judgments, or hypotheses). These thoughts influence how the family psychologist listens and hears, and inform his or her responses. From a collaborative stance, the family psychologist is open and generous with his or her invisible thoughts, making them visible, or what I call *being public*. Being public does not refer to what we traditionally think of as self-disclosure. Instead it has to do with the inner conversations that family psychologists have with themselves about the client and the therapy. Being public is offering food for thought and dialogue, putting forward possibilities of things to talk about or ways to talk about them. It is one way for the family psychologist to contribute to the conversation. I want to highlight the notion of *participate*; the intent is to *take part in* an unbiased manner and not to unduly steer the conversation or promote an idea or opinion.

When talking about their experiences of successful and unsuccessful therapy, I have consistently heard clients comment that they always wondered what the family psychologist really thought of them. They always wondered what was "behind" the family psychologist's questions. They felt that there was a private conversation about them that they were not part of.

Elsewhere I have articulated two grounds for making private thoughts public (Anderson, 2006). One, making private thoughts public invites what Bahktin (1986) refers to as responsive understanding. He suggests that, "A passive understanding of linguistic meaning is not understanding at all" (p. 281). Shotter (1984, 2004), influenced by

Wittgenstein, suggests a relational-responsive kind of understanding. In other words, understanding cannot take place unless both the speaker-listener and the listener-speaker are responsive to each other. An unresponsive inner conversation is in danger of leading to missed understanding or understanding that does not fit with that of the speaker or their intent (e.g., the client's).

Two, putting private inner talk or thoughts into spoken words produces something other than the thought or understanding itself. The expression of the thought organizes and re-forms it; therefore, it is altered in the process of articulation. The presence of the client and the context, along with other things, affect the words chosen and the manner in which they are presented. As well, the client then has the opportunity to respond to the family psychologist's inner thought. The response – in the many forms that it may take, such as expressing interest, confirming, questioning, or disregarding – will affect it.

Both put the family psychologist at risk for their inner talk becoming a monologue and contributing to the creation or maintenance of family psychologist–client monologue. By monologue I mean the same thought, like a tune in one's head that plays over and over again. When this happens, family psychologist and client side by side both sing their individual tunes and the conversation breaks down.

Living with uncertainty

Therapy conversations are more like natural talk in which each person's response informs and invites the other's response. The conversations are not guided by structured maps as to how the conversation should look or unfold; for instance, the pace or the sequence of what is talked about. Nor are they guided by pre-structured questions or other strategies. Conversations are a spontaneous activity in which client and family psychologist together create the paths and determine the destination. What is created is different from, and more than, what could have been created by one without the other.

When client and family psychologist engage in this kind of spontaneous endeavor, there is always an uncertainty about where they are headed and how they will get there. This does not ignore the fact that clients may come in with a pre-defined problem and a destination as well as expectations about how you will help them. They often do. It is not unlikely, however, that these will change through the course of the therapy conversations. As conversational partners, client and family psychologist coordinate their actions as they respond, making their path and destination unpredictable. What the path looks like, the detours along the way, and the final destination will vary from client to client, from family psychologist to family psychologist, and from situation to situation.

Put another way, no one knows how a story will unfold, how newness in it will emerge, or what the newness will look like when engaged in a collaborative relationship and dialogical conversation. Though there is nothing wrong with having an idea and comfort about where you are headed and how you will get there, surprises in the endless shifts and possibilities (e.g., thoughts, actions, meanings) of conversations emerge from the process. Trusting uncertainty involves taking a risk and being open to unforeseen change.

Mutually transforming

I have been trying to stress the mutuality of the therapy encounter. In this kind of *withness* relational process, each party is under the influence of the other(s) and hence each party, including the family psychologist, is as much at risk for change as any other. It is not a one-sided, family-psychologist-driven process, nor is the family psychologist passive and receptive. The family psychologist is actively involved in a complex interactive process of continuous response with the client, as well as with his or her own inner talk and experience. In other words, as conversational partners we continually coordinate our actions with each other as we respond with each other. And each of us is continuously influenced by the other. Therapy is an active process for both the client and the family psychologist.

Orienting toward everyday, ordinary life

Over my years of practicing, teaching, and consulting in various contexts and countries I saw that therapy, like all of life, is a social event. Though it takes place in a particular context with a particular agenda, therapy does not need to be a sacred event with high priests and commoners. It can resemble the way we interact and talk in everyday life, or the "naturally occurring interactional talk . . . through which people live their lives and conduct their everyday business" (Edwards, 2005, p. 257). As in everyday life, we search for how to know our "way about" and how to "go on." In therapy, participants strive for ways to move forward and carry on with their lives.

I have found it helpful to have a positive outlook regarding the people who consult me, regardless of their histories and circumstances. This includes a belief that the human species is naturally resilient and desires healthy relationships and qualities of life. I have also found it helpful not to be constrained by discourses of pathology and dysfunction. As I mentioned earlier, I do not think in terms of categories of people or kinds of problems, though of course if I looked for similarities across the board they could be found. This does not mean that I think diagnoses, for instance, should be thrown out the window, but rather I keep in mind that they, like other deficit discourses, can pose limits to possibilities. Instead, I have found it helpful to create more conventional frameworks of understanding *with* my clients that are less confining, more likely to yield an increased sense of personal agency, and more likely to hold the promise of different futures. I think of each person and each family I meet as one I have not met before. I am interested in learning about them and their distinctive circumstances from their perspective, and creating with them a unique response to what they are seeking consultation about. This is not to say that commonalities cannot be found if looked for or that I would never bring them into the discussion. Foremost is the intent with which I would do so, being open with the client about my intent, and open to being questioned about it as well. For instance, if I were seeing a client who wanted to use their insurance, I would be respectful of the insurance company's need for a diagnosis. I would have a discussion with the client regarding the need for a diagnosis and involve them in the designation.

Conclusion

If a family psychologist assumes the philosophical stance described here, they will naturally and spontaneously create a space that invites and encourages conversations and relationships in which clients and family psychologists "connect, collaborate, and construct" with each other (Anderson, 1997), and where each member will have a sense of participation, belonging, and ownership. All combine to promote effective outcomes and their sustainability. Because the philosophical stance becomes a natural and spontaneous way of being as a collaborative family psychologist, theory is not put into practice and techniques and skills are not employed as we usually think of them. Instead, the stance stems from a set of philosophical assumptions that inform a *way of being* in relationships and conversations that are collaborative and dialogical. In other words, the philosophical stance *is* a way of being that, as suggested above, sets the "tone" for the way in which we orient ourselves to be, respond, and act *with* another person. It invites them into shared engagement, mutual inquiry, and joint action – the process of generative and transforming dialogue (Anderson, 1997, 2001) – making collaborative therapy and other collaborative endeavors *withness insider* practices.

Notes

1 In discussing Wittgenstein's language game psychologist Lois Shawver (1995) quotes him as follows: "the term 'language game' is meant to bring into prominence the fact that the 'speaking' of language is part of an activity, or form of life." Continuing, she suggests that *language game* "refers to models of primitive language that Wittgenstein invents to clarify the working of language in general . . . The idea is that if we think in terms of language games, that is, if we ask how our language games are taught and how they are used, then we will begin to see past certain myths in our culture that trap us in misleading pictures of language processes and communication. Getting past these pictures will enable us to see human psychology with fresh eyes, but what we see with fresh eyes is not predetermined. Wittgenstein does not tell us what we will see. He simply helps us see past these ancient pictures because, quoting Wittgenstein, a 'picture' held us captive. And we could not get outside it, for it lay in our language and language seemed to repeat it to us inexorably."

2 Are there similarities between the notion of dialogue and Carl Rogers' notions of empathy and unconditional positive regard? Dialogue places emphasis on the relational and interactive aspects of understanding, while humanism has historically "been oriented to the individual" (Hoffman, 2002, p. 181). From a dialogical perspective neither is viewed as an internal therapist attribute but rather as a product of social interaction, the relationship (Anderson, 2001).

Resources

Houston Galveston Institute. http://www.talkhgi.com
Postmodern Therapy News: http://users.california.com/~rathbone/pmth.htm
Taos Institute. http://www.taosinstitute.net

References

Anderson, H. (1997). *Conversation, language and possibilities: A postmodern approach to therapy.* New York: Basic Books.

Anderson, H. (2001). Postmodern collaborative and person-centered therapies: What would Carl Rogers say? *Journal of Family Therapy, 23,* 339–360.

Anderson, H., & Gehart, D. (Eds.). (2007). *Collaborative therapy: Relationships and conversations that make a difference.* New York: Routledge.

Anderson, H., & Goolishian, H. (1988). Human systems as linguistic systems: Evolving ideas about the implications for theory and practice. *Family Process, 27,* 371–393.

Anderson, H., & Goolishian, H. (1992). The client is the expert. In K. Gergen & S. McNamee (Eds.), *Therapy as social construction.* Thousand Oaks, CA: Sage.

Anderson, H., & Jensen, P. (Eds.). (2007). *Innovations in the reflecting process: The inspiration of Tom Andersen.* London: Karnac Books.

Anscombe, G. E. M., & Anscombe, E. (2001). *Philosophical investigations: The German text with a revised English translation. 50th anniversary commemorative edition.* Malden, MA: Blackwell.

Bakhtin, M. (1986). *Speech, genre and other late essays* (W. McGee, Trans.). Austin: University of Texas Press.

Bennington, G. (2003). *Politics and friendship: A discussion with Jacques Derrida.* Retrieved November 24, 2007, from http://www.hydra.umn.edu:80/derrida/pol+fr.html

Edwards, D. (2005). Discursive psychology. In K. L. Fitch & R. E. Sanders (Eds.), *Handbook of language and social interaction* (pp. 257–273). Mahwah, NJ: Erlbaum.

Gadamer, H.-G. (1975). *Truth and method.* New York: Seabury.

Gergen, K. J. (1999). *An invitation to social construction.* Thousand Oaks, CA: Sage.

Hacking, I. (1999). *The social construction of what?* Cambridge, MA: Harvard University Press.

Hoffman, L. (2002). *Family therapy: An intimate history.* New York: Norton.

Holmquest, M. (1981). *The dialogic imagination: Four essays by M. M. Bakhtin* (C. Emerson & M. Holquist, Trans.). Austin: University of Texas Press.

Lyotard, J.-F. (1984). *The postmodern condition: A report on knowledge.* Minneapolis: University of Minnesota Press.

MacGregor, R., Ritchie, A. M., Serrano, A. C., Schuster, F. P., McDanald, E. C., & Goolishian, H. A. (1964). *Multiple impact therapy with families.* New York: McGraw-Hill.

Shawver, L. (1995). On Wittgenstein's concept of a language game. Retrieved March 1, 2008, from http://users.california.com/~rathbone/word.html

Shotter, J. (1984). *Social accountability and selfhood.* Oxford: Blackwell.

Shotter, J. (2004). *On the edge of social constructionism: "'Withness'"-thinking versus "'aboutness'"-thinking.* London: KCC Foundation.

Shotter, J. (2005). *Wittgenstein in practice: His philosophy of beginnings, and beginnings, and beginnings.* London: KCC Foundation.

Vygotsky, L. (1986). *Thought and language* (Alex Kozulin, Trans. and Rev.). Cambridge, MA: MIT Press.

21

Science, Practice, and Evidence-Based Treatments in the Clinical Practice of Family Psychology

Thomas L. Sexton and Kristina Coop Gordon

One of the biggest challenges in any type of clinical practice is to choose the best treatment for each client given the problem they present, the context in which they live, and their unique individual characteristics. This challenge presents itself at many levels. For the clinical practitioner the challenge is to identify and then tailor a specific intervention or treatment protocol to clients. For program administrators and policy makers, the difficulty is choosing which types of treatments to support in their agency or practice in order to achieve the highest likelihood of positive outcome for the broadest range of clients. For professional educators and professional organizations, the burden is to develop sound policy and relevant current clinical curricula based on the best available practices. As in all other areas of psychotherapy, family psychology has two major domains to consider in decisions like these. The profession has a vast store of clinical experience and practice-based theory that has been developed over the years. At the same time, there is a robust and systematic array of clinically focused research to guide practice in family psychology. Inconveniently, these two domains do not always point in the same direction. The dilemma is how to integrate relevant science, clinical experience, and theory in such a way that it can improve practices and lead to the best treatments.

Evidence-based practices (EBP) and treatment guidelines have not developed without significant controversy, and both continue to be viewed with great skepticism and uncertainty among prevention and treatment professionals (Westen, Novotny, & Thompson-Brenner, 2004). For some, EBP raise questions concerning the validity of clinical research given the complexities of clinical practice (i.e., client and therapist) factors that may mediate positive or negative clinical outcome. For others, however, EBP represent major steps forward in describing, defining, and systematically attempting to evaluate treatments.

We suggest that given our current level of theory development, base of research knowledge, and sophistication of clinical practices, EBP have an important place in the clinical practice of family psychology. We also suggest that EBP are important in family psychology because they can build on the existing research evidence in a way that goes beyond the "common factors" inherent in any good psychological intervention, by providing both a comprehensive conceptual model and well-defined clinical interventions for clients with specific clinical problems. At the same time, we acknowledge that this approach is complex, and that many issues need to be considered before the field is fully ready to adopt EBP. To be clinically useful, practice guidelines regarding EBP would need to be more than "lists" of what is and what is not evidence-based. Instead, the nature of EBP guidelines should allow for the consideration of evidence in a *dynamic* way: using "levels of evidence" to provide evidence-based decision-making such that the quality and quantity of the research evidence are considered depending on the decision to be made.

Our goal in this chapter is to consider both evidence-based treatments and treatment guidelines as an approach to integrating research into the clinical practice of family psychology. To do so, we first consider the nature of evidence-based treatments, the evolution of efforts to identify evidence-based treatments, and the benefits and difficulties inherent in this process. These issues provide a context for integrating evidence in family psychology. Next, we focus on the essential ingredients of EBP and definition of the terms associated with them. We focus these issues on family psychology through a discussion of the recommendations for evidence-based treatment in family psychology recently developed by the American Psychological Association (APA) Division 43 (Family Psychology) Task Force on Evidence-Based Treatments (Sexton et al. 2007). These recommendations, in combination with the Division 43 (Family Psychology) Evidence-Based Treatment Guidelines, provide a conceptual scheme for integrating research into clinical decision-making. In a case study, we use these guidelines as a model to demonstrate how they might be used in a dynamic, decision-making manner. In conclusion, we review the future directions, challenges, and next steps in the integration of science, practice, and evidence-based treatments in family psychology.

Evolution of Evidence-Based Practices

EBP are those practices that integrate the best research evidence with clinical experiences, the most current and clinically relevant psychological theory, and patient values (Institute of Medicine, 2001). In family psychology, the movement to incorporate EBP into clinical decision-making mirrors efforts in other fields of clinical practice where the goal is improving clinical effectiveness through "the conscientious, explicit and judicious use of current best evidence in making decisions about the care of individual patients" (Sackett, Rosenberg, Gray, Haynes, & Richardson, 1996). Whether they refer to a specific intervention or a comprehensive treatment program, the core philosophical principles of EBP are not different from those of any healthcare practice: every individual has the right to the most effective services available at the time (Hyde, Falls, Morris, & Schoenwald,

2003). What is unique to the EBP movement is that treatment decisions are based on *scientific* evidence to create a standard of quality and reliability that allows the best care possible (Sexton, Gilman, & Johnson, 2005).

Most recently, the APA's Task Force on Evidence-Based Practice (2006) made a major statement regarding EBP, which essentially established the official policy regarding evidence-based practices for its member psychologists. The Task Force suggested that best treatments are a combination of the best available research evidence, the judgment and experience of the clinician, and the applicability of the intervention to the patient's values and goals. The inclusion of the latter two criteria represented an important emphasis on empirical evidence, clinical decision-making, and client input.

The evolution of evidence-based and evidence-informed treatment programs and interventions fits within a broader movement of evidence-based model development in medicine, psychology, and other social services. Interest in identifying empirically supported treatment initially arose from a movement in Great Britain known as evidence-based medicine, which was primarily interested in enhancing patient care and improving busy clinicians' knowledge of evolving best practices (Sackett, Richardson, Rosenberg, & Haynes, 1997). Even though this movement began in medicine, many healthcare professionals saw that its basic goal, to utilize scientific research findings and/or methods of assessing therapy process and outcome in some way to inform clinical practice, was applicable to other forms of treatment as well. In synchrony with theses goals, in 1993 Division 12 (Clinical Psychology) of the APA established the Task Force on Promotion and Dissemination of Psychological Procedures. The Division 12 Task Force developed a set of guidelines to evaluate existing treatments based upon their existing empirical evidence and, in 1998, the Division 12 Task Force published their findings and a list of validated treatments in a special issue of *The Clinical Psychologist* (1995). There have been a number of other similar efforts. For example, in 1996 Division 17 (Society for Counseling Psychology) developed a set of principles to use for evaluating the empirical status of psychosocial interventions for the purposes of informing counseling psychologists, training pre-doctoral and post-doctoral students, and informing the public about the value of services offered by counseling psychologists. In contrast to the Division 12 Task Force, Division 17 did not produce a *list* of empirically supported treatments, but instead produced and endorsed seven principles of empirically supported interventions (PESI) to serve as guidance in reviewing research evidence about a particular treatment approach (Wampold, Lichtenburg, & Waehler, 2002). APA Division 29 (Psychotherapy)'s Task Force focused on identifying empirically supported therapeutic relationships, while APA Division 53: Society of Clinical Child and Adolescent Psychology's Task Force considered the principles involved in implementing and identifying supported treatments of childhood and adolescent disorders.

What are Evidence-Based Treatments?

There are a number of terms used to represent treatments that "work." To be considered *efficacious*, treatments must demonstrate at least two good between-group design experiments or a large series of case studies (more than nine) demonstrating efficacy in one of more of the following ways: (a) superiority to pill or psychological placebo, (b) equivalence to an already established treatment in experiments with adequate sample size, and/or (c) favorable comparison to another psychological intervention. These studies also must demonstrate good experimental design (e.g., well-specified target population, clearly specified treatment interventions and manual, adequate sample size to demonstrate results, etc.) and have demonstrated results in at least two different studies with two different research teams to control for allegiance effects. A more complete description of these criteria can be found in Chambless and Hollon (1998).

After demonstrating *efficacy*, the next aim is demonstrating whether these treatments can work in the less-controlled environments found in most community mental health settings. In other words, this kind of research answers questions about whether the treatments are *effective*. Effectiveness is demonstrated through transportability studies, demonstrating that treatments can be taken out of the laboratory and applied in natural circumstances and with a less carefully selected population.

There is a range of terms and associated parameters used to describe research-based treatments. *Empirically supported treatments* (EST) "clearly [specify] psychological treatments shown to be efficacious in controlled research with a delineated population (Chambless & Hollon, 1998, p. 7)." *EBP* have a broader focus than the criteria specified by EST's. EBP do not rely solely upon controlled research in clinical decision-making; rather, they also take clinical experience and characteristics of the particular patient into account as well.

Regardless of the specific term, both are built on specification of the treatment and the desired clinical outcome. For example, Alexander, Holtzworth-Monroe, & Jameson (1994) defined a research-based clinical intervention program as one that targets clinically meaningful syndromes or situations with a coherent conceptual framework underlying the clinical intervention, described in sufficient detail to explain the specific interventions and therapist qualities necessary to implement them. Wampold, Mondin, Moody, Stich, Benson, & Ahn (1997) defined a "bona fide" treatment as one in which those providing the program do so within a therapeutic relationship, using a treatment that is both tailored to the client and systematically described with clearly identified psychological change mechanisms. Furthermore, the active ingredients of the treatment are to be articulated and contained within a clinical manual that is used to guide administration of the treatment (Wampold et al., 1997). Whether an intervention or treatment program, EBP include both theoretical *principles* that explain clients, therapy, and change, as well as a systematic *clinical protocol* followed by the therapist (Sexton & Alexander, 2002a).

Research or Practice: The Emerging Debate

The development and identification of treatment guidelines and practice recommendations that are based on research evidence has stirred considerable controversy in psychology (Westen et al., 2004). The controversy has added to the already growing gap between research and practice in the field. In some contexts, establishing EBP has become a "flash point" in the debate about the future direction of clinical practice.

Those who support EBP suggest that working according to clear protocols has convincing evidence for positive impact on their clients. Furthermore, the supporters of EBP emphasize that evidence for these claims does not solely rest in the charisma of the treatment developer, the common sense or rationality of the treatment, or the potential marketing of the treatment. Manualized therapies are specifically tailored to certain diagnoses and/or populations, making clear for whom these treatments work. When clearly described by a manual, therapies can become widely disseminated for consistent delivery among other clinicians. Considering that many evidence-based treatments have been shown to work with difficult and severe disorders, clinicians are potentially empowered by manualized treatments to navigate the therapeutic process with otherwise overwhelming client cases. Examples of these types of treatments include integrated, family-based psychoeducation, medication, and individual skills-training treatments for clients with schizophrenia (Simoneau, Miklowitz, Goldstein, Nuechterlein, & Richards, 1996); family therapy interventions for conduct disordered adolescents (Henggeler & Lee, 2003; Sexton & Alexander, 2002b; see Chapter 22, this volume); dialectical behavior therapy for borderline personality disorder (Lynch, Trost, Salsman, & Linehan, 2007); and cognitive behavioral treatments for severe forms of panic disorder and obsessive compulsive disorder (e.g., Barlow, 2007).

Those opposing model-specific practices identify a number of problems inherent in identifying empirically supported treatments. Some suggest these treatments address only the diagnoses found in the APA's *Diagnostic and Statistical Manual* (DSM). A logical argument is that such a focus does not address the reasons why most individuals enter psychotherapy, such as general life dissatisfaction, problems in relationships, or familial distress (Westen et al., 2004). In community settings, moreover, clients often have multiple problems, and the randomized controlled clinical trials that typically provide the base of evidence for EBP often exclude individuals with multiple problems for reasons of internal validity. Another potential issue is that the kinds of research used to verify treatments is weighted in the direction of traditional treatment–outcome projects that in turn favor those treatments with very particular outcomes (e.g., cognitive-behavioral treatments), thus limiting other treatment approaches' ability to validate their treatments. Even considering these legitimate arguments, some of these same critics of EST also admit that the dearth of research on these other approaches to treatment is due to a fundamental worldview that often does not value empirical endeavors. Finally, many therapists complain, and probably rightly so, that there are too many therapies to learn, that it is impossible to learn the "correct" EST for each disorder and clinical problem that they face, and that, even if they were so disposed, access to training in all of these EST is often limited (Westen et al., 2004).

We suggest that the controversies and issues surrounding EBP represent a tension marked by the pull between the differing roles that research and clinical experience play in clinical decision-making. The emergence of guidelines and treatment recommendations that may limit and direct practice through either funding or the support of professional organizations has even further escalated the importance of these issues for the field. The potential limitations of EBP noted above are important and must be considered if research is to move more into the mainstream of practice. Unfortunately, this division between research and practice is often marked by "either/or" types of debates. It seems clear that both research and clinical experience are necessary to provide good clinical service. We suggest that scientific evidence can never change clinical practice until a way of integrating both is developed that can systematically value both the reliability and validity of research-based evidence and the necessary input of clinical experience. Sexton, Alexander, & Mease (2004) suggested that the gap can be best overcome not through "either/or" conclusions, but instead by considering research and practice in a more "dialectical way." In other words, both empirical and clinical data are necessary, yet neither is sufficient when it comes to determining the best treatment for a client. What is needed is a conceptual model that integrates both in a dynamic way.

EBP in Family Psychology

Research by early pioneers in family psychology focused on systemically studying the outcome and process of couple and family therapy, thereby establishing family and couple therapy as effective and clinically useful practice. In the ensuing decades, the research agenda of early family therapy broadened from answering initial questions of outcome (i.e., establishing whether it works in general) to assessing more specific applications of family practice with specific clinical problems in specific settings. The result of these decades of research is a strong, scientific evidence base for the effectiveness of both couple and family therapies (Lebow & Gurman, 1995; Sexton & Alexander, 2002b; Sexton et al., 2004). Outcome research for couple and family therapy has drawn from meta-analyses that combine results across large client groups, and individual studies that have been evaluated in local communities with diverse clients in realistic clinical settings. In addition to these outcome-research efforts, studies have identified the change mechanisms that *underlie* positive clinical outcomes (i.e., process research) and that are both common across methods and specific to certain approaches. Consequently, family psychologists now have at their disposal a vast array of both general and specific studies of interventions, treatments, and clinical processes for both couples and families. Even so, that evidence is complex, dispersed across many publications, and not easily available to integrate into clinical practice. However, successfully moving empirical work into clinical practice requires more than just a summary of results or a list of which treatments may work.

Sexton et al. (2004) suggested a "levels of evidence" approach as a way of bringing together the research and practice in clinically relevant ways, particularly in the diverse field of family psychology. A "levels of evidence" approach takes a dynamic view of the research evidence, considering evidence as both varied and evolving. At the same time, research needs to be reliable and valid in the practice contexts for particular areas of practice. Therefore, not all research should be equally weighted. For example, the question of interest (be it a policy question, a broad treatment program decision, or a specific clinical implementation question) should match the research strategy used to answer the question, if evidence is to be used as a logical argument. Policy questions, often asked by organizations and large systems, are probably best answered through systematic research reviews (e.g., meta-analysis). Intervention and prevention program adoption decisions are probably best made by looking at the cumulative efficacy and effectiveness research over time. Individual clinical decisions are best made by the process research that identifies the operative mechanisms of change. One example of this approach is contained in the recommendations for evidence-based treatments in family and couple psychology completed by the Task Force for Evidence-Based Treatment of Division 43 (Family Psychology) of the APA (Sexton et al. 2007).

The Task Force for Evidence-Based Treatments in Couple and Family Therapy

The Task Force for Evidence-Based Treatments in Couple and Family Psychology was commissioned by the Family Psychology Division of APA (Division 43) to develop a set of evidence-based practice guidelines relevant to the research and practice of family psychology, and to use the guidelines to systematically review the literature to identify clinical practices that have the greatest potential to help diverse clients in diverse settings. The task force consists of a group of researchers, practitioners, trainers, supervisors, and treatment-model developers; it also has a similarly diverse panel of advisory members who provide initial feedback on the task force's product. The task force developed a set of guidelines and then systematically presented these guidelines in public forums at major conferences involving family researchers and practitioners, such as APA, AFTA/IFTA, AAMFT, and ABCT. The task force then revised the guidelines on the basis of feedback received at these meetings. The task force sought to use the principles discussed earlier as the basis for developing recommendations identifying research-based treatments for family psychologists in an attempt to overcome some of the issues inherent in treatment guidelines noted above.

The work of the task force was based on the assumption that different issues and, therefore, different types of research knowledge are important in different settings; thus it is impossible to create a single, ecologically valid hierarchy of what research is "best" or what approaches might ultimately be "best." In fact, no treatment or intervention will likely have evidence that is relevant to every domain of clinical practice. However, the extent to which evidence exists in these domains is important in determining if, when, and how to use a treatment model. Thus, our approach is one that focuses on two criteria: reliability ("What is the level of reliable evidence for this program?") and utility in context ("Whom does this work for, in what contexts is it effective, and what are the critical change mechanisms?"). The primary goal of the task force was to help direct clinical practice toward the most effective practices, in a way that recognized the complexity of the clinical process and the breadth and depth of the clinical research.

The Task Force Report provides a detailed description of the model as well as its assumptions, definitions, and founding principles (Sexton et al., 2007). In brief, the guidelines propose three *levels*, expressed as a levels-of-evidence-based scale. The three levels of increasing evidence provide a hierarchical index of confidence that the intervention/treatment model works. The task force concluded that, while helpful, a simple hierarchical system could not adequately capture the complexity of clinical decision-making. Thus, in the third level, programs must have evidence that demonstrates their effectiveness in differing settings and with specific populations. This final level is intended to further identify and note programs with significant clinical relevance.

Level I: Evidence-informed interventions/treatments are those that are informed by psychological research or research on therapeutic common factors. At this level evidence is based on the explicitly identified pre-existing empirical or research-based evidence, or to portions of an already validated evidence-based treatment model, to suggest that they have an evidence base.

Level II: Promising interventions/treatments are those that have either preliminary results, evaluation outcomes, or only comparison-level studies of high quality. These results have not been replicated in another setting or evaluated for specific outcomes with specific populations.

Level III: Evidence-based treatments are specific and comprehensive treatment intervention programs that have systematic high-quality evidence demonstrating that they work with the clinical problems they are designed to impact. At a minimal level, such evidence should include multiple outcome studies to show that the program can reliably demonstrate that the treatment program produces outcomes greater than gained from the normal improvement process typical in that treatment population.

Thus, within the evidence-based treatments (Level III) are four additional categories of evidence that demonstrate the breadth of a treatment model in regard to model-specific change mechanisms, improved change when compared to other viable treatment options, and generalizability to broad clinical settings and populations.

Category 1: Absolute efficacy. This category suggests that this intervention/treatment program is a clinically reliable treatment for a specific class of clinical problems, because it has absolute efficacy/effectiveness evidence. This type of evidence demonstrates that the specific treatment intervention program produces reliably improved, clinically relevant outcomes when compared to the typical improvement rates for natural recovery of given clinical problems.

Category 2: Relative efficacy. This category suggests that this intervention/treatment program is a clinically reliable treatment for a specific class of clinical problems. This type of evidence emphasizes relative efficacy studies showing that the specific treatment intervention program produces reliably improved, clinically relevant outcomes when compared to an alternative or viable treatment.

Category 3: Verified mechanisms. This category would suggest that the treatment program is clinically reliable for a class of clinical problems and operates through the described mechanisms to produce the demonstrated outcomes. Efficacious models with verified mechanisms show evidence that the model-specific change mechanisms operating within the specific treatment models are linked to relevant identifiable outcomes, as theoretically expected.

Category 4: Effectiveness. This category suggests not only that the program produces change, but that the outcomes are effective for specific client populations, with specific clinical problems, and is successful in specific service delivery systems, which make up the context within which the program must work. The evidence can demonstrate the degree to which the intervention model might be matched with the needs of a community.

Levels of Evidence in Clinical Practice: A Case Study

To date, there are few "real-life" examples of such a comprehensive application of a levels -of-evidence-based approach to integrating research into practice. We use an example of a state system that took on the difficult problem of identifying effective treatments for youth behavior problems. In our example, we consider three perspectives – the treatment system, a community-based treatment provider/organization, and an individual practitioner – in addition to the unique decision to be made by each in integrating research into practice. Each level of the broader system (system, organization, and individual practitioner) was responsible for different decisions and therefore needed to turn to different levels of evidence in order to implement EBP. As an illustration we link the levels and category system of the Division 43 EBP model to this example.

In 1998 the State of Washington decided to take a research-based approach to the problems of youth behavior and mental health. In the decade prior, the state had witnessed rising costs, increased incidents of youth with serious behavior problems, and a seeming inability in existing treatments to engage and ultimately reduce the incidences of behavior problems. Uniquely, the emphasis was on finding what "works" to reduce youth problems, help families, and eventually reduce costs with the juvenile justice and adolescent mental health systems. The Washington State Institute for Public Policy took the lead in taking a research-based approach to this problem. At that time treatment guidelines did not exist and the field was only beginning to evaluate evidence-based treatment. As a result, the Institute had to do its own studies to determine how to use the existing research evidence to answer its questions of effective outcome and cost.

In a series of studies, the Institute considered the existing research literature first by conducting a systematic review of the outcome literature. As a broad system, the goal of the Institute's work was to find the level of research evidence that pointed to those programs that had the greatest potential to work across the diverse youth and communities in the state. Thus, the type of evidence (Level III, Category 1) that was initially most useful was outcome-based studies that could provide an indication of the size of the potential effect of the various treatments (effect sizes). Since the larger goal was treatments that worked and treatments that could be implemented, the Institute considered both the traditionally valued randomized clinical trails and quasi-experimental designs in an attempt to determine both efficacy and effectiveness. Studies were weighted by effect size and an analysis was published as a first step in integrating new treatments into the system. From their analysis, a range of intervention programs was identified (multisystemic therapy, functional family therapy, and aggression replacement training). The approaches were put forward into a series of community discussions and legislative actions, which created funding to support the implementation of these programs.

For community agencies working with youth behavior problems, the work of the Institute posed an interesting set of issues. Each agency in the state system had existing programs in place to serve youth and their families. These programs were familiar and fit into the culture of the agency. The work of the Institute for Public Policy required that agencies reconsider the treatments they used and their level of effectiveness in helping youth. For agencies, the decision to implement particular practices is complex and requires considering the skills of the staff, the culture of the agency, the mission and goals of the agency, and the client population they serve. Unlike the broader state goal of finding 'what works," community agencies needed to find what works within their context and the community setting in which they practice (Level: III, Categories 2 and 3). The staff and agencies had a more specific understanding of the clients' and community's needs. Thus, their decision about "what works" was more specific and more ideographic.

On the basis of the broad findings of the Institute, community agencies were encouraged to begin a process of investigation into the principles of the most effective practices noted in the outcome reports. By considering the theoretical and conceptual principles of research-based programs, agencies could find a fit with the culture, goals, and aspirations of the individual agency. In addition, agencies were particularly interested in a more specific review of the research, particularly in regard to "what works with whom." Thus, agencies looked to see what fit them and what approaches had evidence that might suggest the likelihood of success for the types of clients in their practices and the types of communities in which they worked. In collaboration with the Institute, a series of discussions and presentations of treatment models identified within the Institute's outcome report was organized. These forums provided additional information for agencies to use in deciding on which practices to implement.

The Washington story also illustrates ways in which a levels-of-evidence-based approach can aid the EBP decisions of practitioners and the agencies within which they work. From the broad outcome analysis provide by the Institute for Public Policy, local service agencies needed to consider a different type of evidence when considering which, if any, EBP to use. Broad outcomes were certainly a consideration – "Does the treatment program work?" However, agencies have specific treatment goals and serve particular populations. As a result, a different level of evidence was needed; specifically, the agencies needed to investigate "with whom and under what conditions" the programs might work. For some of the treatment programs with positive outcomes with youth behavior problems, there was additional research that considered specific client groups (age, ethnicity, gender, and presenting problem, among others). When that evidence was available, agencies could use it to guide a choice. For other models, that evidence was not yet available. In that case agencies had to decide whether, given the nature of the treatment model, there was reason to believe it might work. In sum, a more specific level of evidence was needed to guide individual agency decisions.

The individual therapists in agencies were also faced with decisions – "how it works" – that required a different type of evidence: what clinical change mechanisms were validated by research to support the clinical interventions and proposed therapist actions within the treatment model (Level III, Category 3). This even more specific level of evidence was necessary for individual clinicians to determine whether the treatment model contained guidance for when they were faced with the myriad of clinical decisions when working with a client. Certainly, those models with process research supporting theoretical change mechanisms were more helpful for a clinician in deciding to implement a treatment model, because they helped specifically identify what needs to be done with the clients at the level of individual therapist behaviors and what kinds of changes in clients are most likely to lead to positive outcomes. When that level of research was not available, clinicians were forced to look to see whether the principles of a particular model might guide clinical decisions. Clearly, the greater the specificity of the evidence to the context of services that was available, the more the choice and use of the treatment model were facilitated.

Conclusions

Any kind of system that involves classifying and evaluating treatments presents both potential benefits and potential dangers. From the benefits perspective, the evaluation and classification system helps to organize a vast and overwhelming array of clinical information and make clear to the busy researcher/practitioner where the field has made progress and where the gaps still lie. It also distills this literature into an understandable list of treatments for which the field can have most confidence in their ability to effectively address clients' problems. Thus, these guidelines are intended to serve as a method to quickly identify the areas of research knowledge that exist and those that are missing, directing the researcher to the appropriate level of evidence that may answer the question at hand, and directing the clinician to the treatments with the greatest amount of existing evidence with respect to the context in which they deliver services.

However, naturally these guidelines also have difficulties. Mirroring the complexity of clinical practice, these guidelines do not necessarily make it simple to clearly determine the appropriate placement for every intervention or treatment program. Furthermore, these types of systems can only address and classify the treatments and problems for which there is research. Such a system may be frequently less directive for decision-making in the couple and family therapy field, in which there are numerous widely practiced treatments that have not been subject to empirical evaluation.

We wish to note that an absence of evidence for an approach does not mean that that approach is ineffective; however, it does indicate that there is no present evidence for such an approach, and until such evidence emerges, *caveat emptor*. Furthermore, existing research will not be able to answer all treatment questions. For example, few treatments have been applied across multiple cultures and populations, despite the best efforts of those doing treatment research. Similarly, many of these treatments have been conducted in more controlled settings and may not address the multi-layered issues that clients present when they appear before a clinician. Consequently, the techniques described in these treatments will almost always require creative application and adaptation by the therapist.

Thus, we want to be clear that this set of guidelines should not be taken to trivialize the role of the therapist in delivering treatment. Moreover, if evidence-based assessment schemas such as the one proposed here are to positively influence clinical practice, they can do so only via the therapist. Again, one of the underlying principles of our system is that the best practice is an evolving interaction between our increasing empirical knowledge base, the clinical experience of the therapist, and the particular idiosyncrasies of the client. Practice at its peak efficacy is a dialectical and integrative effort that is constantly changing to accommodate new information and understandings of psychological functioning.

Classification systems of this kind can be enormously helpful in pointing to effective treatments, but, if not carefully understood, they can also unwittingly promote problems. Therefore, we are concerned that lists of the kind described here should not serve to limit the generation of improvements in these treatments because they have already "made the list." We must come to terms with a way of incorporating the best standards for evidence (which must emphasize a core consistency in treatments across studies for a treatment to qualify as a member of a class) and the natural tendency for treatments to evolve and improve. Research as described here provides the consumer with the relative degree of confidence that treatments might provide the best possible outcomes. It is our hope that this classification system will motivate those scientist-practitioners associated with treatments they believe to be effective to research further the impact and outcomes of those treatments. It also is our hope that this system of classification can help sort out the non-specific and somewhat random research process into a relevant, clinically useful knowledge base.

References

Alexander, J. F., Holtzworth-Monroe, A., & Jameson, P. (1994). The process and outcome of marital and family therapy: Research review and evaluation. In A. E. Bergin & S. L. Garfield (Eds.), *Handbook of psychotherapy and behavior change* (pp. 594–630). New York: Wiley.

APA Presidential Task Force on Evidence-Based Practice. (2006). *Evidence-based practice in psychology. American Psychologist, 61*, 271–283.

Barlow, D. (2007). The case of Hope: "Evidence-based practice" (EBT) in action. *Pragmatic Case Studies in Psychotherapy, 3(4)*, 50–62.

Chambless, L. L., & Holon, S. D. (1998). Defining empirically supported therapies. *Journal of Consulting and Clinical Psychology, 64*, 497–504.

Henggeler, S. W., & Lee, T. (2003). Multisystemic treatment of serious clinical problems. In A. E. Kazdin & J. R. Weisz (Eds.), *Evidence-based psychotherapies for children and adolescents* (pp. 301–322). New York: Guilford Press.

Hyde, P. S., Falls, K., Morris, J. A., & Schoenwald, S. K. (2003). *Turning knowledge into practice: A manual for behavioral health administrators and practitioners about understanding and implementing evidence-based practices.* Technical Assistance Collaborative, www.tacinc.org.

Institute of Medicine. (2001). *Crossing the quality chasm: A new health system for the 21st century. (Executive summary).* Washington, DC: National Academy Press.

Lebow, J. L., & Gurman, A. S. (1995). Research assessing couple and family therapy. *Annual Review of Psychology, 46,* 24–57.

Lynch, T., Trost, W., Salsman, N., & Linehan, M. (2007). Dialectical behavior therapy for borderline personality disorder. *Annual Review of Clinical Psychology, 3,* 181–205.

Sackett, D. L., Richardson, W. S., Rosenberg, W., & Haynes, R. B. (1997). *Evidence-based medicine.* New York: Churchill-Livingstone.

Sackett, D. L., Rosenberg, W. M. C., Gray, J. A. M., Haynes, R. B., & Richardson, W. S. (1996). Evidence based medicine: What it is and what it isn't; It's about integrating individual clinical expertise and the best external evidence. *British Medical Journal, 312 (7023),* 71–72.

Sexton, T. L., & Alexander, J. F. (2002a). Functional family therapy for at risk adolescents and their families. In T. Patterson (Ed.), *Comprehensive handbook of psychotherapy Volume II: Cognitive-behavioral approaches* (pp. 117–140). New York: Wiley.

Sexton, T. L., & Alexander, J. F. (2002b). Family-based empirically supported interventions. *The Counseling Psychologist, 30(2),* 238–261.

Sexton, T. L., Alexander, J. F., & Mease, A. L. (2004). Levels of evidence for the models and mechanisms of therapeutic change in family and couple therapy. In M. J. Lambert (Ed.), *Bergin and Garfield's handbook of psychotherapy and behavior change* (5th ed., pp. 590–646). New York: Wiley.

Sexton, T. L., Coop-Gordon, K., Gurman, A. S., Lebow, J. L. Holtzworth-Munroe, A., & Johnson, S. M. (2007). *Task force report recommendations from the Division 43: Family Psychology Task Force on Evaluating Evidence-Based Treatments in Couple and Family Psychology.* San Francisco: Division 43 (American Psychological Association).

Sexton, T. L., Gilman, L., & Johnson, C. (2005). Evidence based practices in the prevention and treatment of adolescent behavior problems. In T. P. Gullotta & A. Gerald (Eds.), *Handbook of adolescent behavioral problems: Evidence-based approaches to prevention* (pp. 101–128). New York: Springer.

Simoneau, T., Miklowitz, D., Goldstein, M., Nuechterlein, K., & Richards, J. (1996). Nonverbal interactional behavior in the families of persons with schizophrenic and bipolar disorders. *Family Process, 35(1),* 83–102.

Task Force on Promotion and Dissemination of Psychological Procedures. (1995). Training in and dissemination of empirically-validated psychological treatments. *The Clinical Psychologist, 48,* 3–23.

Wampold, B. E., Lichtenburg, J. W., & Waehler, C. A. (2002). Principles of empirically supported interventions in counseling psychology. *The Counseling Psychologist, 30 (2),* 197–217.

Wampold, B. E., Mondin, G. W., Moody, M., Stich, F., Benson, K., & Ahn, H. (1997). A meta-analysis of outcome studies comparing bona fide psychotherapies: Empiricially, "all must have prizes." *Psychological Bulletin, 122(3),* 203–215.

Westen, D., Novotny, C. M., & Thompson-Brenner, H. (2004). The empirical status of empirically supported psychotherapies: Assumptions, findings, and reporting in controlled clinical trials. *Psychological Bulletin, 130(4),* 631–663.

22

Functional Family Therapy: Traditional Theory to Evidence-Based Practice

Thomas L. Sexton

Family psychology is rooted in rich traditions of clinical theory and research (Gurman & Kniskern, 1981). Its conceptual and theoretical traditions have evolved from early systemic thinking principles to clinical theories, and more recently to systematic clinical treatment models that integrate clinical theory with models of the etiology and development of clinical problems, research, and specific clinical practice (Sexton, Weeks, & Robbins, 2003). Functional family therapy (FFT) is a clinical model that illustrates the evolving clinical and research practices of family psychology. In many ways FFT's development mirrors the development of family psychology as a field. Initially a clinical theory, yet also built on clinical observation and an early research foundation, FFT integrated new developments in the field and has emerged as one of the major family-based evidence-based practices for troubled youth and their families (Alexander & Sexton, 2002; Elliott, 1998; Kazdin, 1997). In the last decade, FFT has been designated as a "model program" and an evidence-based program in numerous independent reviews in the United States (Alvarado, Kendall, Beesley, & Lee-Cavaness, 2000; Surgeon General: U.S. Public Health Service, 2001).

FFT is a systematic, evidenced-based, manual-driven, family-based treatment program which is successful in treating a wide range of problems affecting youth (including drug use and abuse, conduct disorder, mental health concerns, truancy, and related family problems) and their families in a wide range of multiethnic, multicultural, and geographic contexts (Alexander & Sexton, 2002). As a prevention program, FFT is effective in diverting youth away from entering the mental health and justice systems (Alexander & Sexton, 2002). As a treatment program, FFT works within clinical and home settings focusing on specific and high-risk youth in justice and mental health settings. In both applications FFT is short-term, generally ranging on average from 8 to 12 sessions for mild cases, and up to 30 hours of direct service for more difficult cases. In most treatment systems FFT sessions are spread over a 3–6-month period, and intervention targets youth populations between the ages of 11 and 18, although younger siblings of referred adolescents are also regularly involved. These high-risk youth are often involved with juvenile justice and/or drugs, frequently reflect complex behavioral and mental health issues, and face myriad multisystem risk factors.

FFT represents an interesting niche in the converging fields of family therapy and family psychology, in that it is both a systematic and evidence-based practice (manual-based: Sexton & Alexander, 200), while at the same time being a clinically focused therapy that is highly personal, relational, and focused on "in the room" interactions. As a result, FFT is difficult to categorize as a particular "type" or theoretical orientation of family therapy. FFT has made the step from traditional "theory" to evidence-based practice while maintaining its focus on the therapeutic process, and the individuality and uniqueness of the family. As an individualized treatment program, FFT has attended to culture, the distinctive nature of the family, and the almost magical relational process that unfolds "in the room" during the therapy process. Thus, FFT is a combination of systematic yet flexible, model-focused yet client-responsive, and model-consistent yet relationally focused principles and practices. To date FFT has been used in agencies serving clients who are Chinese Americans, African Americans, Dutch, Moroccan, Russian, Turkish, White-Caucasian, Vietnamese, Jamaican, Cuban, and Central American families, among others. FFT is also provided consistently in eight different languages.

FFT and its clinical theory have been presented in many publications over the last decade (Alexander & Sexton, 2002; Sexton & Alexander, 2002, Sexton et al., 2003). This chapter begins with the history of FFT, emphasizing its dynamic and ever-evolving constructs around a core set of conceptual principles. Second, the clinical theory of FFT is presented, both its model of change and its model of clinical disorders, followed by a brief summary of the research foundation. Finally, a case example is used to illustrate the clinical principles and specific clinical model in context with a multiethnic family.

Functional Family Therapy: A Dynamic Evolution

For many practicing clinicians who have come to know it as one of the current and "new" evidence-based models, it may come as a surprise that FFT is not new at all. Initially developed by Alexander and Parsons in the late 1960s, FFT was first applied to youth in juvenile justice contexts and focused on one of the critical issues of this population: engagement in the treatment process. In addition, FFT was among the first models to do both research and clinical model development by including one of the first treatment process and randomized outcome studies as part of the early development process (Alexander & Parsons, 1973; Parsons & Alexander, 1973). This work resulted in an early version of the FFT clinical model that focused on a two-phase process of therapy (engagement and client motivation) and education (specific behavioral interventions). The first major articulation of the core principles of FFT were developed by Barton and Alexander (1981), and FFT was included as one of the "second generation" of family therapy models in the historic *Handbook of Family Therapy* (Gurman & Kniskern, 1981). Unique in the work of Barton and Alexander (1981) was the introduction of relational functions as a theoretical description regarding the role of individual psychological process in the systematic patterns and relationship among family members. The research focusing on clinical process, particularly the work on gender, and relational negativity and blame contributed to the further understanding of the FFT clinical process.

In the late 1990s FFT entered its most recent evolution with two major developments. First, further developments expanded the clinical model to include three phases, initially labeled the phase task analysis (Sexton & Alexander, 2000). This model was based on the concept that the clinical process was guided by both systematic and consistent treatment, and assessment goals representing successful change (with this population), drawing on the constant and complex relational process that played out within the room, depending on the personal and often circular relational process between the family psychologist and family. Thus, a successful application was described as circular, relational, and individualized as captured by the intense "in the room" dynamics, moving forward through specific and predictable phases where treatment outcomes built on one another, ultimately resulting in positive behavior change. Second, the dissemination and transportation of FFT evolved from a clinical theory to use in a myriad of community settings. Further developments regarding implementation, including a manualized approach to clinical supervision (Sexton et al., 2003) and a computer-based quality assurance/improvement system to promote transportation (Sexton & Alexander, 2000, 2004), as well as a systematic approach to training and community dissemination (Sexton & Alexander, 2004), continued to move FFT forward.

The Clinical Model

The FFT clinical model is based on two interlocking components. First, the theoretical *principles* explain clients' functioning and problem development, therapy process, and clinical change mechanism. *The principles* answer the questions: "How does the client function?" and "What is the nature of change?" Second, a systematic, phasic-based *clinical protocol* details the goals and objectives of early, middle, and late stages of treatment. *The protocol* answers the questions "What actions should I take?" and "When should I take them?"

Theoretical principles

In FFT the primary goal is to try and understand how the problem behavior "functions" in the family system. To do so, the theoretical principle is that current behavior patterns of adolescents and their families are a "holistic package," representing current and past individual, biological, relational, family, socioeconomic, and environmental factors that pose risk and provide protective forces for the family. This pattern represents the "way" the family interacts around the problem behavior. As such, FFT views specific present-ing clinical problems (clinical syndromes) as relational problems – as specific behaviors embedded within enduring patterns of behaviors that are the foundation for stable relational "functions" within family relationships (Alexander & Sexton, 2002; Sexton & Alexander, 2002). From this perspective, FFT views the "referring" and often times individually focused problems as embedded within a "core family relational" pattern. Relying on the notions of systemic relational process, we suggest these patters become very stable and ultimately serve to maintain the problem behavior.

Consequently, family relational patterns, or relational sequences, are central to the daily functioning of the family. Some of these patterns are effective in accomplishing the tasks of the family (e.g., parenting, communicating, supporting) and may protect the family and its members from manifesting specific behavior problems. Other patterns put one or all members of the family at risk for individual symptoms of mental health, drug abuse/use, relational conflict, and externalizing behavior disorders. Regardless of whether the relational patterns represent potential risk or protective factors, they are maintained and supported by the ways in which relationships "*function*" within the family. Thus, relational patterns are usually seen in the descriptions of problems that family members bring to treatment. It is common that these patterns are represented "in the therapy room" by the "problem definitions" (the way family members come to understand what is a problem in their family), and serve as the entryway to understanding how the family functions. Problem definitions represent the natural and normal attempts to understand, through reflection, what is causing the pain and struggle in the family and typically con-tain the attributional (meaning), the emotional, and the related behavioral interactions.

Regardless of their form, the common, repetitive, and highly entrenched behavioral sequences in families lead to consistent relational outcomes or "relational functions" (Barton & Alexander, 1981). Relational functions are conceptualized along two different dimen-sions: relatedness (closeness–distance) and hierarchy (one-up vs. one-down). They are the "outcomes" of relational patterns/sequences and represent the "motivation" that maintains them over time. What makes this notion different in FFT is the ideographic nature of functions. Very different behaviors (e.g., anger and fighting vs. cooperation) can produce the same functional outcomes (e.g., high degree of interconnectedness). Conversely, very similar relational sequences (e.g., clear communication and nurturing behavior) can produce entirely different relational outcomes (e.g., they enhance contact or can increase distance in another relationship). While not the target of change, relational functions are accepted as the unique way in which this individual family functions. In the behavior change of therapy, specific behavioral targets are "matched to" functions, thus promoting an individualized approach to therapy.

These principles of clinical problems have led to four primary principles that guide FFT therapy. *Alliance-based motivation* suggests that the therapeutic change process is one in which the family psychologist is successful in developing an atmosphere of hope, expectation of change, sense of responsibility (internal locus of control), and positive sense of alliance shared by the family. This sense of alliance is not only between each family member and the family psychologist, but among family members as well. *Meaning change through reframing* represents a relationally based way of changing the cognitive and perceptual basis for negative interaction, painful emotions, and unsuccessful change strategies. In FFT, reframing is a relational process that helps create alternative cognitive and attributional perspectives that redefine meaning events, thus reducing the negativity and redirecting the emotionality surrounding the events. *Obtainable change goals* direct FFT therapists to focus on significant yet obtainable behavioral changes, unique for each family, that will have a lasting impact on the family relational patterns. These specific change goals have a major impact on family function because they are targeted to alter the underlying risk and protective patterns that support and maintain other problematic behaviors. Finally, "*matching to*" represents a respectful therapeutic position that asserts that while each family is unique, they all have the potential to function in a positive and adaptive manner. Matching to allows families to maintain their cultural and personal values, while at the same time being led through a systemic process of change.

Clinical protocol: Phases of change in FFT

FFT consists of three specific and distinct phases of clinical intervention: (1) engagement and motivation, (2) behavior change, and (3) generalization. Together, they provide a "map" that details specific goals and strategies for each phase of change, and is intended to guide the family psychologist through the often intense, emotional, and conflicted interactions presented by the family (Sexton & Alexander, 2004). Each of the three phases of FFT has specific therapeutic goals and therapist skills that, when used competently, maximize the likelihood of successful accomplishment of these goals. Each phase also has specific focused and intervention components and desired "proximal" outcomes.

Despite the "structure," it is important to note that the FFT model can only be successfully applied when there is an emphasis on the unique therapeutic nature of the interaction between the family and the family psychologist as the primary mechanism of change. As the family tells "their story," the family psychologist responds in a personal, yet therapeutic way, taking every opportunity to purposefully respond, meeting the phase-based relational goals of the model, and move therapy forward. Thus, to be successful FFT must be conducted in a style that is artful, personal, and relational.

The *engagement and motivation phase* has four primary goals: alliance building, reduction of negativity, reduction of blame, and developing a shared family focus to the presenting problems. Engagement and motivation begin with the first contact between the family psychologist and family, as the family psychologist purposefully attempts to involve the family in the immediate activities (of the session or of an initial phone call) such that they become interested in taking part in and accepting of therapy (engagement). In an active and engaging way, FFT therapists immediately focus on the process goals of the phase – namely reducing between-family member negativity and blame, while trying to develop a family focus to the presented problems by actively reframing and creating a sense of "balanced alliance." The desired outcome of these early interactions is that the family develops motivation by experiencing a sense of support in their position, emotions, and concerns, a sense of hope for change, and a belief that the family psychologist and therapy can help promote those changes. When negativity and blaming are reduced, more positive interactions among family members foster hope. This allows the family psychologist to demonstrate that she is a competent force, capable of guiding the family toward change. An alliance develops where each family member believes that the family psychologist supports and understands his or her position, beliefs, and values.

The primary goal of the *behavior change phase* is to target and change specific behavioral skills of family members, thereby increasing their ability to perform more competently the myriad of tasks (e.g., communication, parenting, supervision, problem solving) that contribute to successful family functioning. Successful behavior change is accomplished by identifying the risk factors that contribute to the specific problem behavior and helping change these in a way that matches the relational functions of the family. This phase emphasizes building protective family skills that will improve the factors that put the family and adolescent at risk. Desired outcomes of this phase are competent performances of the primary activities associated with risk factors, including parenting, rewards and punishments, communication between adolescent and parent, negotiation of limits and rules, and problem solving and conflict management in a developmentally appropriate way, matching the relational capabilities and the culture of the family. Thus, the goal might be to increase competent performance of communication, but approached in a way that matches the relational functions of that particular parent and adolescent.

In the *generalization phase*, the therapeutic goals are generalizing, maintaining, and supporting the changes the family has made throughout the process. Generalization takes place both within the family and between the family and its environment. The focus of attention moves from within-family changes to ways in which the family will interact with the systems around them (e.g., schools, community, extended family), and ways they will respond to similar challenges in the future. As the phase begins, the family psychologist helps the family generalize changes that have occurred in the earlier phases to other areas of family functioning that were not specifically addressed. Then, the family psychologist works to help the family maintain these gains by helping them overcome the natural "roller-coaster" of change. Maintenance of change occurs through using relapse prevention techniques to normalize the typical problems that will inevitably occur, while having confidence that the family's newly acquired skills will work in different situations over time. The goal of supporting change is usually accomplished by bringing the necessary community resources and support to the family. In general, long-term change is accomplished when the family is helped to use their own skills to obtain these changes without the guidance of the family psychologist. The desired outcomes of the generalization stage are to stabilize emotional and cognitive shifts made by the family in engagement and motivation, as well as the specific behavior changes made to alter risk and enhance protective factors. Having the family develop a sense of mastery around their ability "to generalize," or to address future and different situations, does this.

Research Foundation

The cumulative data suggest that FFT is effective on two critical fronts. First, the results indicate that FFT is particularly successful in engaging and retaining families in treatment. Engagement rates in FFT studies range from 78% (Sexton, Ostrom, Bonomo, & Alexander, 2000) to 89.8% (Barnoski, 2003). This outcome is fairly dramatic given the traditionally high rates of dropout (50–75%) in most treatment programs (Kazdin, 1997). Second, FFT reduces recidivism to between 26% and 73% with status offending, moderate, and seriously delinquent youth as compared to both no-treatment and juvenile court probation services (Alexander, Pugh, Parsons, & Sexton, 2000). In a community-based clinical trial using community-based therapists, and working in community service delivery systems with very high-risk youth, FFT resulted in a statistically significant 38% reduction in felony crime and a 50% reduction in violent crime as compared to a randomly selected control group (Barnoski, 2003) when FFT was done as it was designed. These data emphasize that FFT is effective in reducing serious re-offense rates of at-risk adolescents, but only when FFT is delivered as the model was designed (e.g., in a competent fashion according to the national FFT dissemination protocol). Positive outcomes of FFT remain relatively stable at follow-up times as great as five years (Gordon, Arbuthnot, Gustafson, & McGreen, 1988), and the positive impact even affects siblings of the identified adolescent (Klein, Alexander, & Parsons, 1977). More recently, another community-based study of FFT found a statistically and clinically significant 38% reduction in the most serious of crimes, a 50% reduction in violent crimes, and a significant cost savings with FFT as compared to traditional treatment methods (Barnoski, 2003; Sexton, Alexander, & Mease, 2004). In addition, these significant results of FFT hold up when compared to other types of treatments. For example, Lanz (1982) found that recidivism rates for seriously delinquent youth were lower for those youth who received FFT (50% recidivism) than for those who received residential treatment (88% recidivism) or traditional juvenile services (92% recidivism). Alexander and Parsons (1973) found significant differences in recidivism rates when comparing FFT (26% recidivism) to client-centered family groups (47% recidivism) and eclectic psychodynamic family therapy (73% recidivism). In a recent study (Sexton, Turner, & Schuster, in process), FFT was compared to a matched control and alternative family treatment. Results indicate that 1-year post-treatment FFT reduced felony recidivism by 16%, as compared to the matched control (32%) and the alternative treatment (40%).

FFT is also a cost-effective intervention. In the most comprehensive investigation of the economic outcomes of family-based interventions to date, the State of Washington did an economic analysis of the outcome and cost-effectiveness of various approaches to reduce delinquency (Aos & Barnoski, 1998). These researchers calculated average effect size and combined it with the costs of implementing the program, justice system costs averted, crime victim costs avoided if implemented, and years it would take to recover the cost of program implementation, and found a cost-to-return rate of $14 saved for every $1 of treatment and system costs.

Case Study

Alex was a 17-year-old male referred to a forensic psychiatric treatment group in a major European city. He received FFT by the author, who worked with Alex in 11 family sessions over a 6-month time period. Alex was from Suriname and was adopted at the age of 1 year by parents of Dutch descent. At the time of referral and first FFT session, he was in the process of being removed from his home and being placed in residential care. He had been expelled from school 3 years prior, had become a chronic runaway and a frequent legal offender often involving the police (i.e., theft, fighting, habitual drug use, and interpersonal violence). In fact, both he and his parents referred to him as a "street kid." FFT was considered the final option before residential placement. During the initial assessment period at the Forensic Psychiatric Center, Alex had been diagnosed with conduct disorder and depression, and the psychiatric staff was contemplating a diagnosis of bipolar disorder.

Engagement and motivation phase

The first two sessions of FFT were conducted in the first week of treatment. Going into the session, the primary aim was to engage the family in treatment and build motivation to change by focusing on the goals of the initial phase of treatment: reduce the within-family negativity and blame, create a family focus for the presenting problem, and build therapist-to-family alliance and family-to-family alliance through reframing. After a brief introduction the first session quickly moved to meeting the phasic goals. Alex came to the session wearing traditional Surinamese clothes. The family psychologist took this opportunity to ask about the clothes and engaged him in a brief discussion about his coat. According to Alex, this coat made him unique among other street kids because it identified him as of Surinamese descent; it was one of his most prized possessions. The exchange was brief, but a purposeful attempt to engage Alex on his terms. The family psychologist then quickly moved from this brief engagement discussion to a focus on the family and their presenting problems by directly asking, "I have been told that all of you were very reluctant to come today, and that you are considering having Alex live somewhere else. Can you help me understand what goes on between the three of you that ends up in this level of discouragement?" While subtle, this initial question represented an important core principle of FFT: problems are embedded in the family's relational patterns. Without placing blame, the question directly addressed issues known to the family psychologist, and casts them within a family focus.

As is common in an FFT session, the parents (and the youth) all responded with their perception of the presenting clinical issue (or problem definitions). For the father the problem was that Alex didn't follow the "rules," and was "rude" and "disrespectful." For the mother the issue was the violent fights erupting between her and Alex, "because he explodes" whenever she asked him to do anything. As he listened to these descriptions, Alex said nothing. In this case, both parents attributed the problems to Alex (blaming), but in ways that lacked high levels of negativity (emotional or behavioral). The early focus in this phase was on problem definitions presented by each family member, specifically on changing the external attributions from blame on Alex to identifying parental contributions to the problem. Thus, the response to these opening blame statements was to engage each family member in a discussion concerning their role in the problem, building a more complex, family-focused definition.

By means of reframing, the family psychologist began by acknowledging the father's attention to detail and his dedication to his son's wellbeing despite the clear discouragement he expressed earlier. The family psychologist went on to acknowledge the father's struggle to understand why such a smart and resourceful young man as Alex struggled to follow simple rules. Though angry on the surface, the father seemed hurt underneath. Through a series of interchanges the family psychologist attempted to introduce this "theme" of hurt into the conversation. Likewise, the family psychologist and the mother discussed the hurt behind her anger. Though expressed through angry fights, this hurt came from an invested mother who was devastated because she could not seem to "reach" her son. When she spoke of exploding, Alex laughed. From his perspective, his mother yelled, and when people yelled at him he became "crazy." Reframing, the family psychologist began by acknowledging his assertiveness, a necessary trait to possess on the street where he was the "man" among his peers. It was reframed so that the focus shifted to emphasize his difficulty in hearing his mother as a parent, and her anger as pain, and to her not knowing what else to do except yell. For him the struggle seemed to be the transition between his street self and his home self. Realizing his dissonance, he began to cry. He continued to cry as he explained that he had lost one mother (his biological mother in Suriname) and he was not now going to lose another, and that his parents saw him as a "bad" guy but inside he was a boy with a heart. He described other kids on the street speaking of their mothers in derogatory terms, and how, while he loved his mother, he often got caught up in their escalations.

The intent of these early reframing interventions was not to take away the responsibility of the bad behavior from Alex or any other family member, but to expand the "problem" to include everyone. In addition, the goal was to build an alliance between the family psychologist and each family member. For the parents, the family psychologist was sensitive and understanding in framing the meaning of their behavior and emotion to a cause (the theme) that, while not always helpful, was understandable and guided by good intention. The non-blaming and supportive way of discussing "their part" in the problem helped build the alliance and created a purposeful, safe environment where important issues were directly discussed in a supportive manner.

While the conversation focused on reframing and the relational process, the family psychologist also gathered information concerning the relational patterns in which the delinquent behavior was embedded. In addition, the family psychologist began to hypothesize about the relational functions or outcomes of these patterns for each family member. Clearly, the central pattern was one of escalation between Alex and his mother. Occasionally the father would step in to support either mother ("Alex has to follow the simple rules") or Alex ("we need to be patient and understand him"). This pattern was essential to their interaction sequence regardless of the specific "content" issue (staying out too late, etc.).

Behavior change phase

The decision to move to the behavior change phase is based on the family psychologist's assessment of the degree of achievement regarding the engagement/motivation goals. In this case, blame and negativity were significantly reduced, alliance was high, and there emerged a family-focused theme/problem redefinition shared by both the family psychologist and the family. To successfully move into behavior change the family psychologist must have identified specific behavior change targets and made a relational assessment. The targets of behavior change are those specific behavioral competencies that, if adopted by the family, would serve a protective function for the family. In the case of externalizing behavior-disordered adolescents, the targets tend to be related to the broad areas of communication, problem solving/negotiating, conflict management, and parenting. Like the earlier engagement and motivation phase, behavior change requires a high level of creativity on the part of the family psychologist. The family psychologist must identify relevant targets and construct a way of implementing those new behavior change competencies within the unique family system.

Within the central behavior patterns or problem sequences of any family therapy, many different and potentially useful behavior change targets can be identified, some preventive and some remedial. Regardless, the more specifically the target is linked to the problem sequences, the more relevant and meaningful the potential change. In this case, the initial focus of behavior change was on the escalating altercations that ensued when Alex came home. This was a salient issue for the family as it is clearly illustrated a struggle amongst family members. The family psychologist noted two specific competencies that could prove beneficial: first, proposing a new means of negotiation regarding the rules of Alex's movement between home and the "street," and second, addressing the process of conflict management when these rules were disregarded (e.g., coming home late). Given the organizing theme developed during engagement and motivation, these goals were logical and accepted by the family.

In the fourth session, the family arrived to therapy upset about a recent incident. Alex had been late, neglected to inform them, and when he returned home a typical "volcano explosion" erupted between him and his mother. The father stepped in to lecture Alex about rules and help the mother become more patient. From the family psychologist's perspective, this sequence of events represented a common relational pattern in this family. Rather than focus on reframing, the family psychologist focused on teaching a new skill. It was designed to give the family the tools to solve this situation. The family psychologist said,

> I think this is a common struggle between the three of you. I want to ask you to try something different in your discussion of this event. First, it seems that when you (Alex) are late it is an opportunity for you and your parents to negotiate a time to come home so that they are not worried and scared. In addition, negotiation might help you find a different way to identify a common set of rules that might serve as a basis of what you can expect to occur. So, here are the steps in negotiating . . .

A guided discussion followed, describing how negotiating might take place: requests that are concrete and specific, presented as a set of alternatives, followed by a joint discussion of one alternative, and a contract identifying the option that was agreed upon.

It is important to note that the specific nature of the negotiated agreement is much less important than helping the family follow a *process* of negotiating that helps develop and build a competency. It is not uncommon in this phase for the family psychologist to serve as a teacher, coach, and director of relational processes rather than a mediator and a problem-solver for the family. The goal is not to help "find the middle" or come up with an acceptable agreement to both sides. Instead, the desired outcome is to have the family learn how to negotiate. In addition, the introduction of behavior change requires in-session practice using the struggles the family brings in as the content through which specific skills are developed. The challenge for the family psychologist is to focus on the specific phase goals of competency building in ways that match the relational functions of the family.

In the three behavior change sessions with this family, the family psychologist took the most salient presenting issue brought to each session and structured the conversation in a way that allowed the family to practice the negotiation and conflict-management strategies. In the end it was a collaborative effort between the family psychologist and the family to tailor the competencies to fit the unique family. The focus was on providing a framework to successfully replicate the new skills in different situations. The remaining two sessions of behavior change focused on applying the negotiation and conflict-management skills to many problem situations raised by the family.

Generalization phase

As with behavior change, it is the family psychologist who moves the therapy discussion into the generalization phase. In this case, the family had multiple successes in utilizing the skills of negotiation and conflict management. They demonstrated their ability to handle situations that previously would have resulted in highly emotive conflicts and threatened Alex's removal from the home. However, it should be noted not all specified problems in Alex's family were solved in the three behavior change sessions. In addition, the school and learning issues associated with his attention problems had yet to be systematically addressed. Nevertheless, the family was feeling better, and actually cancelled a session. In this phase, the family psychologist faced many challenges common in FFT: generalizing the changes made in the behavior change phase to other areas, building motivation within the family to continue with therapy even when they felt better, helping prepare the family for future problems and relapses, and identifying other services or resources that might be needed.

The family psychologist began session 7 with a discussion about an additional challenge they all had to face. "The good news is that you are feeling better, the bad news is that there is yet another problem you as a family have yet to face." Puzzled, the family inquired about the meaning of this statement. "While you have had great success, there will be additional problems you will face." Alex was quick to say, "I have really learned that the way we had been working together will not work, so I know I won't do what I did before." Likewise, the father suggested that he was now convinced that Alex had learned and that they were now able to work things out. The subsequent discussion focused on the many ways in which the strong emotion generated by their "volcano" reaction was likely to pull them into old, comfortable patterns.

In the two sessions that followed, the family experienced additional struggles. The family psychologist responded by reframing the discouragement as normal, and identifying the challenge as an opportunity to utilize their newly discovered skills. In addition, other areas of concern surfaced, particularly around Alex's drug use. Rather than initiating a new behavior change strategy, the family psychologist helped the family generalize the same negotiation skill to this specific problem. For the family psychologist the primary concern was helping the family generalize existing skills and systematically helping the family learn and practice relapse prevention, rather than returning to behavior change. The goal was to empower the family to use their skills to solve current and future problems on their own.

It was also important to help the family support the changes they had made by utilizing outside resources. The family psychologist began a conversation about Alex's school and learning struggles. Because of the between-family member alliance, the family took this as a shared problem to be solved as a family. The parents quickly moved to utilize the resources of the mental health center and accessed a psychiatric consultation. This resulted in a diagnosis of Alex's attention-deficit problems and medication. In addition, the psychiatric consultation revealed that no further treatment was required for his bipolar disorder, as symptoms had subsided. In addition, the family identified a contained classroom (operated by the mental health center) and Alex enrolled in classes. The goal was to empower the family to support the changes they had made by accessing relevant community resources. In FFT it is important for the family psychologist to encourage the family to access these resources on their own, rather than making the arrangements for the family.

Conclusions

FFT is a systematic, evidence-based, manual-driven therapy, as well as a clinically responsive and sensitive relational model of therapy. As a "therapy" its focus is on the clinical model providing a "map" to follow and the theoretical principles providing a consistent basis for thinking about clients, problems, and therapy. Having both principles and a specific protocol allows the family psychologist to be both systematic (helping the family move ahead) and client-centered and personal (using the most important and relevant issues of the family as the content to move the change process forward). As a dissemination model, FFT combines this clinical model with a systematic, model-focused supervision approach (Sexton et al., 2004), and a training and quality assurance system designed to aid learning, monitor quality, and enhance therapeutic outcomes.

Resources

Clinical Training Manual: Sexton & Alexander (2004).
FFT Supervision Manual: Sexton, Alexander, & Gilman (2004).
General FFT Information: FFT Blueprints Manual (www.colorado.edu/cspv/blueprints)
www.functionalfamilytherapy.com
www.fftinc.com

References

Alexander, J. F., & Parsons, B. V. (1973). Short term behavioral intervention with delinquent families: Impact on family process and recidivism. *Journal of Abnormal Psychology, 81*, 219–225.

Alexander, J. F., Pugh, C., Parsons, B. F., & Sexton, T. (2000). Functional family therapy. In D. S. Elliott (Series Ed.), *Blueprints for violence prevention* (2nd ed.). University of Colorado, Center for the Study and Prevention of Violence. Golden, CO: Venture.

Alexander, J. F., & Sexton, T. L. (2002). Functional family therapy: A model for treating high-risk, acting out youth. In J. Lebow (Ed.), *Comprehensive handbook of psychotherapy: Vol. 4. Integrative/eclectic.* New York: Wiley.

Alvarado, R., Kendall, K., Beesley, S., & Lee-Cavaness, C. (2000). *Strengthening America's families: Model family program for substance abuse and delinquency prevention.* Washington, DC: Office of Juvenile Justice and Delinquency Prevention.

Aos, S., & Barnoski, R. (1998). *Watching the bottom line: Cost-effective interventions for reducing crime in Washington.* Washington State Institute for Public Policy: RCW 13.40.500.

Barnoski, R. (2003). *Outcome evaluation of Washington State's research-based programs for juvenile offenders.* Washington State Institute for Public Policy, www.wsipp.wa.gov

Barton, C., & Alexander, J. F. (1981). Functional family therapy. In A. S. Gurman & D. P. Kniskern (Eds.), *Handbook of family therapy* (pp. 403–443). New York: Brunner/Mazel.

Elliot, D. S. (Series Ed.). (1998). *Blueprints for violence prevention.* University of Colorado, Center for the Study and Prevention of Violence. Golden, CO: Venture.

Gordon, D. A., Arbuthnot, J., Gustafson, K., & McGreen, P. (1988). Home-based behavioral systems family therapy with disadvantaged juvenile delinquents. *American Journal of Family Therapy, 16*, 243–255.

Gurman, A. S., & Kniskern, D. P. (Eds.). (1981). *Handbook of family therapy.* New York: Brunner/Mazel.

Kazdin, A. E. (1997). Practitioner review: Psychosocial treatments for conduct disorder in children, *Journal of Child Psychology and Psychiatry, 38*, 161–178.

Klein, N., Alexander, J. F., & Parsons, B. V. (1977). Impact of family systems intervention on recidivism and sibling delinquency: A model of primary prevention and program evaluation. *Journal of Consulting and Clinical Psychology, 45*, 469–474.

Lanz, B. (1982). Preventing adolescent placement through functional family therapy and tracking. Utah Department of Social Services, West Valley Social Services, District 2K, Kearns, UT 84118. Grant3CDP 1070 UT 83-0128020 87-6000-545-W.

Parsons, B. V., & Alexander, J. F. (1973). Short-term family intervention: A therapy outcome study. *Journal of Consulting and Clinical Psychology, 10*, 28–34.

Sexton, T. L., & Alexander, J. F. (2000). Functional family therapy. *Juvenile Justice Bulletin*, Office of Juvenile Justice and Delinquency Prevention. Washington, DC: Department of Justice.

Sexton, T. L., & Alexander, J. F. (2002). FBEST: Family-based empirically supported treatment interventions. *The Counseling Psychologist, 30*, 238–261.

Sexton, T. L., & Alexander, J. F. (2004). *Functional family therapy clinical training manual.* Seattle, WA: Annie E. Casey Foundation.

Sexton, T. L., Alexander, J. F., & Gilman, L. (2004). *Functional family therapy clinical supervision manual.* Seattle, WA: Annie E. Casey Foundation.

Sexton, T. L., Alexander, J. F., & Mease, A. L. (2004). Levels of evidence for the models and mechanism of therapeutic change in couple and family therapy. In M. Lambert (Ed). *Handbook of psychotherapy and behavior change* (5th ed., pp. 590–646). New York: Wiley.

Sexton, T. L., Ostrom, N., Bonomo, J., & Alexander, J. F. (2000). *Functional family therapy in a multicultural, multiethnic urban setting.* Paper presented at the annual conference of the American Association of Marriage and Family Therapy, Denver, CO.

Sexton, T. L., Turner, C., & Schuster, R. (in process). *The role of client gender in the outcomes of functional family therapy.*

Sexton, T. L., Weeks, G. R., & Robbins, M. S. (2003). *Handbook of family therapy: The science and practice of working with families.* New York: Brunner-Routledge.

Surgeon General: U.S. Public Health Service. (2001). *Youth violence: A report of the Surgeon General.* Washington, DC: DHHS.

23

Multidimensional Family Therapy: A Science-Based Treatment System for Adolescent Drug Abuse

Howard A. Liddle

Formulated first in clinical and therapist training settings, multidimensional family therapy (MDFT) connects to the structural-strategic family therapy tradition (Liddle, 1984). The MDFT research program began in 1985 with National Institute on Drug Abuse (NIDA) funding that continues to the present day. MDFT is an empirically supported, family-based intervention for adolescent substance abuse and associated mental health and behavioral problems (Liddle, 2002a; Liddle, Dakof, & Diamond, 1991). The developmental psychology/psychopathology research knowledge base guides assessment, specifies change targets, and informs outcome evaluation. Integrative in several ways, MDFT uses an ecological or contextual conceptual framework to understand development. Research-derived knowledge about risk and protective factors, and proximal causes, correlates, and contributors to adolescent drug and related problems, inform clinical thinking and interventions with every case.

MDFT assesses and intervenes in four domains: (1) the adolescent as an individual *and* a member of a family and peer network; (2) the parent(s), both as individual adults and each in his or her role as mother, father, or caregiver; (3) the family environment and family relationships, as manifested in day-to-day family transactional patterns; and (4) extrafamilial sources of influence such as peers, school, and juvenile justice. Interventions are coordinated across domains. Progress in one area has implications for use in others. Individual meetings with parent(s) and teen set the stage for family sessions, and family meetings may offer content and new outcomes that need to be brought to extrafamily meetings with juvenile justice or school personnel. To maximize transportability, MDFT was developed and tested as a *treatment system* rather than a one-size-fits-all approach. A treatment system offers different versions of a clinical model that vary according to factors such as clinical sample characteristics (older versus younger adolescents, juvenile justice involved versus no involvement in juvenile justice systems) and treatment parameters (type of clinical setting and treatment dose). Overall our treatment development strategy has been to create a clinically and cost-effective approach for teen substance abuse and delinquency that can be used in a range of clinical settings.

Adolescent Substance Abuse

Considerable scientific progress has been made in our knowledge about the causes and correlates of adolescent alcohol and drug problems (Liddle & Rowe, 2006). We know a great deal about the ingredients, sequence, and interactions that predict initial and increased drug involvement. Adolescent substance abuse can progress along various and intersecting developmental pathways, hence its designation as a multidimensional and multidetermined phenomenon requiring a multiple systems strategy and interventions that target different contexts and domains of functioning (Hawkins, Catalano, & Miller, 1992).

Drug problems are understood through the filters of multiple theoretical lenses. Social-cognitive factors; psychological functioning; personality and temperament; values and beliefs; family factors; peer relationships; environmental influences, such as school and neighborhood/community; and sociocultural factors, such as media influences, all have links to the development and maintenance of teen drug abuse. Responding to longitudinal and cross-sectional findings that have illuminated how drug problems develop, remit, or worsen over time, adolescent drug treatments have changed dramatically over the years. Systems-oriented family-based therapies are the most researched teen drug misuse intervention (Liddle, 2004); and for some, these interventions are referred to as the treatment of choice (Stanton & Shadish, 1997; Williams & Chang, 2000).

Knowledge about risk and protective forces, at multiple system levels and in different domains of individual and family functioning, guides treatment. Intrapersonal factors (e.g., identity, self-competence), interpersonal factors (family and peer relationships), and contextual and environmental factors (school support and community influences) are all included in case conceptualization, treatment planning, and intervention delivery. As a developmental disorder, adolescent drug abuse is a deleterious deviation from healthy, adaptive development (Cicchetti & Rogosch, 2002; Guo, Hill, Hawkins, Catalano, & Abbott, 2002). By working with individual, family, and extrafamilial system levels and targeting interactional change in these systems and at these system intersections, MDFT aims to reorient the adolescent and family toward a more functional developmental trajectory.

Principles of MDFT

1   *Adolescent drug abuse is a multidimensional phenomenon.* MDFT clinical work is guided by an ecological and developmental perspective and corresponding research. Adolescent drug abuse problems are understood intrapersonally, interpersonally, and contextually as well, in terms of the interaction of multiple systems and levels of influence.

2   *Problem situations provide important assessment information and change oppor-*
tunities. Current symptoms of the adolescent or other family members, as well as crises
pertaining to the adolescent and family, provide critical information as well as valuable change
opportunities. Therapists analyze the organizational features and process dimensions of
these rich situations, support existing competence and good intentions, and use the stress
and distress of these situations to build the case that change is needed.

3   *Change is multidetermined and multifaceted.* Multidimensional problems require
multidimensional solutions. Change emerges out of the synergistic effects of interaction
among different systems and levels of systems, different people, domains of functioning,
time periods, and intrapersonal and interpersonal processes. Assessment and interventions themselves give indications about the timing, routes, or kinds of change that are
accessible and potentially efficacious at particular times.

4   *Motivation is malleable.* Motivation to enter treatment or to change may not be
present with adolescents or their parents. Treatment receptivity and motivation vary across
individual family members and extrafamilial others. Behaviors typically defined as resistance are not immutable, they communicate a great deal about the barriers to successful
treatment implementation, and they point to important processes requiring therapeutic
focus.

5   *Working relationships are fundamental.* The therapist makes treatment possible
through non-judgmental but outcome-focused working relationships with family
members and extrafamilial supports, and the facilitation and working through of personally meaningful relationship and life themes. These therapeutic themes emerge from
discussions about generic individual and family developmental tasks and the case-specific
aspects of the adolescent's and family's development.

6   *Interventions are individualized.* Although they have generic aspects (e.g., promoting competence of adolescent or parent inside and outside of the family), interventions
are customized according to each family, family member, and the family's environmental circumstances. Interventions target known etiologic risk behaviors and circumstances related to drug abuse and problem behaviors, and promote protective and
development-enhancing personal and interpersonal processes.

7   *Planning and flexibility are two sides of the same therapeutic coin.* Case formulations
are practically oriented, prescriptive blueprints that guide the therapist throughout
the therapeutic process. Formulations are revised on the basis of new information, in-
treatment experiences, and feedback. In collaboration with family members and relevant
extrafamilial others, therapists continually evaluate the results of all interventions and
alter the intervention plan according to intervention results on a session-by-session and
week-by-week basis.

8   *Treatment is phasic.* MDFT relies on research-based knowledge about the laws
governing the unfolding of human development. Similarly, finding and focusing
relevant therapeutic content and theme development, intervention plans and implementation,
and the overall therapy process organize and unfold in stages. Progress in one area (therapeutic relationships with different family members and relevant extrafamilial persons,
for instance), lays the foundation for the next steps in the change process – action steps
and change strategies with multiple persons inside and outside of the family.

9   *Therapist responsibility is emphasized.* Therapists accept responsibility for promoting participation and enhancing motivation of all involved individuals; creating a workable agenda and clinical focus; devising multidimensional and multisystemic alternatives; providing thematic focus and consistency throughout treatment; prompting behavior change; evaluating the ongoing success of interventions; and revising the interventions as needed according to the outcomes of the interventions.

10   *Therapist attitude and skill are fundamental to success.* Therapists advocate for both the adolescent and the parent. Extreme positions as either "child savers" or proponents of the "tough love" philosophy are avoided. Therapists are optimistic but not naïve about change. They understand that their own ability to remain positive, committed, creative, and energetic in joining with all family members and important extrafamilial persons is instrumental to therapeutic success.

The Interdependence of Assessment and Intervention

Multidimensional assessment

Assessment creates a therapeutic blueprint. This blueprint directs therapists as to where to intervene in the multiple domains of the teen's life. A comprehensive, multidimensional assessment process involves identifying risk and protective factors in all relevant areas and then targeting specific areas for change. Information about functioning in each target area comes through individual and family interviews, observations of both spontaneous and directed family interactions, and observation of family member interactions with influential others outside of the family as well (see Chapter 10, this volume). The approach has four target areas: (1) adolescent, (2) parent, (3) family interaction, and (4) extrafamilial social systems. In their investigation of the target areas, therapists explore life details and current functioning on the basis of research-derived knowledge about the multifaceted development of adolescent substance abuse and related problems. We attend to deficits and hidden areas of strength, so as to obtain a complete clinical picture of the unique combination of assets and weaknesses in the adolescent, family, and ecosystem. A full picture of the adolescent and family includes a formulation of how the current situation and behaviors are understandable, given the adolescent's and family's developmental history and current risk and protection profile. Interventions aim to decrease risk processes known to be related to dysfunction development or progression, and enhance protection, first within what the therapist finds to be the most accessible and malleable domains. An ongoing process rather than a single event, assessment continues throughout therapy as new information comes forward.

Family assessment.   The assessment process typically begins with a meeting that includes the entire family. Therapists observe family interaction and note how individuals contribute differentially to the adolescent's life and current circumstances. We meet individually with the adolescent, the parent(s), and other members of the family within the first session or two. Individual meetings clarify the unique perspective of each family member, their different views of the current problems, how things have gone wrong (e.g., legal and drug problems, neighborhood and peer influences, school and family relationship difficulties), what they have done to address the problems, and what they believe needs to see change with the youth and family.

Adolescent assessment. Therapists elicit the adolescent's life story, an important assessment and intervention strategy, during early individual sessions. Sharing their life experiences contributes to the teen's engagement. It provides a detailed picture of the severity and nature of the teen's drug use and circumstances and trajectory of drug use over time, family history, peer relationships, school and legal problems, and important life events. One useful technique involves asking the adolescent to draw an ecomap that represents his or her current life space. This would include the neighborhood, indicating where the teen hangs or goes to buy and use drugs, where friends live, the location of school or work, and, in general, where the action is in his or her environment. Therapists inquire about the adolescent's health and lifestyle issues, including sexual behavior (Marvel, Rowe, Colon, DiClemente & Liddle, 2009). The presence and severity of comorbid mental health problems is determined through the review of previous records and reports, the clinical interview process, and psychiatric evaluations. Particular adolescent substance abuse screening devices are psychometrically sound and clinically useful. They can be invaluable in one's quest to obtain a comprehensive picture of the teen's and family's circumstances.

Assessment with the parent(s). Assessment with the parent(s) includes their functioning both as parents and as individual adults, with an individual, unique history and concerns. We assess the parents' strengths and weaknesses in terms of parenting knowledge, skills, and general parenting style, as well as parenting beliefs and emotional connection to their child. In assessing parenting knowledge and competencies, the therapist inquires in detail about parenting practices and observes and takes part in parent–teen discussions, looking for things like supportive expressions and communication skills in their ways of relating with the adolescent. In discussing parenting style and beliefs, the therapist asks parents about their own experiences, including their family life when they were growing up. Considerable attention is paid to the parent's commitment and emotional investment to the adolescent. If parental abdication exists, therapists work diligently to elicit and rekindle even modest degrees of hope about helping their teen get back on track. Parents need to be responsive to having a role in facilitating the needed changes. A parent's mental health problems and substance abuse are also evaluated as potential obstacles to parenting, and, when indicated, referrals for individual treatment of drug or alcohol abuse or serious mental health problems are appropriate and sometimes used in MDFT.

Assessment of relevant social systems. Finally, assessment of extrafamilial influences involves gathering information from all relevant sources. This information is combined with the adolescent's and family's reports in order to compile the fullest possible picture of each individual's and the family's functioning relative to external systems and current circumstances. The adolescent's educational/vocational placement is assessed thoroughly. Alternatives are generated in order to create workable alternatives to drug use and to build bridges to a productive lifestyle. Therapists build relationships and work closely and collaboratively with the juvenile court and probation officers in relation to the youth's legal charges and probation requirements. They focus the parents on the potential harm of continued negative or deepening legal outcomes, and, using a non-punitive tone, they strive to help teens face and deal with their legal situation. Assessment of peer networks involves encouraging the adolescent to talk about peers, school, and neighborhood contexts in an honest and detailed manner, and this is used to craft focal treatment areas. The creation of concrete alternatives that provide pro-social, developmentally enhancing, day-to-day activities using family, community, or other resources is a driving force for the extrafamilial domain, and of course, of MDFT generally.

Multidimensional interventions facilitate adolescent, parent, and family development

A multidimensional perspective suggests that symptom reduction and enhancement of pro-social and appropriate developmental functions occur by facilitating adaptive, risk-combating processes in important functional domains. We target behaviors, emotions, and thinking patterns implicated in substance use and abuse, as well as the complementary aspects of behaviors, emotions, and thought patterns associated with development-enhancing intrapersonal and familial functioning (Hawkins et al., 1992).

Change targets are prioritized. The focus for change begins in certain areas first, and then changes in these areas are used as departure points for the next, usually more difficult, working areas for change. All roads must lead to changing drug use and abuse and related problem areas. When development-enhancing interventions are effective, they create everyday outcomes that are incompatible with previous drug-using behaviors and ways of moving through life. New developmental competencies emerge, sponsoring progress toward completing previously compromised developmental tasks.

We assess and intervene in four interdependent and mutually influencing subsystems with each case. While other family-based interventions might address parenting practices by working alone with the parent for much of the therapy, MDFT is unique in its way of not only working with the parents alone but also focusing significantly on the teen alone, apart from the parent sessions, and apart from the family sessions. These individual sessions have enormous strategic, substantive, and relationship-building value. They provide vital point-of-view information and reveal feeling states and historical events that are not always forthcoming in family sessions. The individual meetings establish one-on-one relationships with each family member. Family-based treatment means establishing multiple therapeutic relationships rather than single therapeutic alliances, as is the case in individual treatment. They actualize the kinds of therapeutic processes from which positive clinical outcomes emerge. A therapist's relationships with different people in the mosaic that forms the teen's and family's lives are the starting place for inviting and instigating change attempts. There is a leveraging that occurs in the individual sessions as they are worked to create content, motivation, and readiness to address other family members in joint sessions.

Interventions with the adolescent.   Establishing a therapeutic alliance and relationship with the teenager, distinct from but related to identical efforts with the parent, builds an essential foundation (Diamond, Liddle, Hogue, & Dakof, 1999). We conceptualize and apply alliance-building techniques, called adolescent engagement interventions (AEI), sequentially. They present therapy as a collaborative process, define therapeutic goals that are personally meaningful to the adolescent, generate hope, and attend to the youth's experience and evaluation of his or her life. We aim to have treatment attend to these "big picture" dimensions. Problem solving, elimination of drug use and a drug-taking lifestyle, and all of these remediation efforts should exist in the context of work that connects to a teen's conception of his or her own life, its direction, and its meaning. Success in one's alliance with the teenager does not go unnoticed by most parents. We find that parents both expect and like the fact that the therapist reaches out to and assertively tries to form a distinct relationship and therapeutic focus with the teen. Considerable work occurs in individual sessions with parents and teens to prepare them to come together to discuss matters that need to be faced, improved, or resolved.

Interventions with the parent.   We focus on reaching the teen's caregiver(s) as both adults each with her or his own needs and issues, and in their position as a parent who may have lost motivation or faith in their ability to raise and influence their adolescent. Parental reconnection interventions (Liddle, Rowe, Dakof, & Lyke, 1998) include such things as enhancing feelings of parental love and emotional connection, validating parents' past efforts, acknowledging difficult past and present circumstances, and generating hope. When parents enter into, think and talk about, and experience these processes, their emotional and behavioral investment in their adolescent grows. And this process, the expansion of a parent's commitment and investment to their child and his or her welfare, is basic to the MDFT change model. These thoughts, feelings, and behaviors on the parent's part are fundamental and necessary developmental/therapeutic tasks that must be actualized before mid-therapy and are fundamental ingredients for later changes to occur and be sustained. These interventions take the first step toward change, and grow parents' motivation and, gradually, their willingness to address relationship improvement and parenting strategies. Increasing parental involvement with the adolescent (e.g., showing an interest, initiating conversations, creating a new interpersonal environment in day-to-day transactions) provides a new foundation for behavioral and attitudinal change in parenting strategy. Parenting competency is fostered by teaching and coaching about normative characteristics of parent–adolescent relationships, consistent and age-appropriate limit setting, monitoring, and emotional support – all research established parental behaviors that enhance relationships and individual and family development.

Interventions to change the parent–adolescent interaction.   Family therapy originally articulated a theory and technology about changing particular dysfunctional family transactional patterns that connect to the development of problem behaviors. Following in this tradition, MDFT interventions also change development-retarding transactions. Direct, in-session changes in the parent–adolescent relationship are made through the structural family therapy technique of enactment (Minuchin, 1974). Typically, enactment involves elicitation, in a family session, of topics or themes that are important in the everyday life of the family, and preparing and/or assisting family members to discuss and try to solve problems in new ways (Liddle, 1999). The method actively guides, coaches, and shapes increasingly positive and constructive family interactions. In order for discussions between parent and adolescent to involve problem solving and relationship healing, parents and adolescents must be able to communicate without excessive blame, defensiveness, or recrimination (Diamond & Liddle, 1996). We help teens and parents to steer clear of extreme, inflexible stances as these actions create poor problem solving, hurt feelings, and erode motivation and hope for change. Skilled therapists direct and focus in-session conversations on important topics in a patient, sensitive way (Diamond & Liddle, 1999). Although success in individual and interaction work with the adolescent and parent(s) is central to changing the teen's drug use, other family members can also be important in the change process. Thus, we include siblings, adult friends of parents, or extended family members in the assessment and interventions. These individuals are invited to be a part of the family sessions, and meetings are held with them alone as well per MDFT session composition guidelines. Cooperation with the involved adults is achieved and motivation is grown by underscoring the serious, often life-threatening circumstances of the youth's life, and establishing an overt, discussable connection between that caregiver's involvement in treatment and the creation of behavioral and relational alternatives for the adolescent. This follows the general procedure used with the parents – the attempt to promote caring and connection through several means, first through an intense focusing and detailing of the youth's difficult and sometimes dire circumstances and the need for his or her family to help.

Interventions with social systems external to the family.   MDFT also facilitates changes in the ways that the family and adolescent interact with systems outside the family. Success or failure in negotiating these systems has considerable impact on the teen's and parent's life course. Close collaboration with the school, legal, employment, mental health, and health systems influencing the youth's life is critical for initial and durable change. For an overwhelmed parent, help in dealing with complex bureaucracies or in obtaining needed adjunctive services not only increases engagement, but also improves his or her ability to parent effectively by reducing stress and burden. Therapists help to set up meetings at school or with juvenile probation officers. They regularly prepare the family for and attend youth's juvenile justice disposition hearings, understanding that successful compliance with the juvenile justice supervision requirements is a core therapeutic focus and task. School or job placements are also basic aspects of the therapeutic program since they represent real-world settings in which the youth can develop competence, succeed, and build a pathway away from deviant peers, drugs, and antisocial behavior. In some cases, medical or immigration issues or financial problems may be obvious and urgent areas of need and stress. Our approach understands the interconnection of all of these life circumstances to the improvement of family life, parenting, and a teen's reclaiming of his or her life from the perils of the streets. Not all multisystem problems can be solved, but in every case, our rule of thumb is to assess all of them, make priorities, and as much as possible work actively and directively to help the family achieve better day-to-day outcomes relative to the most consequential and malleable areas.

Using drug screens

We integrate the drug urine screening procedure and the results of the drug screen directly into the therapeutic context of parent–teen sessions (Liddle, 2002b). Results from weekly urinalyses are shared with both the adolescent and the family, creating an atmosphere of openness and honesty about drug use from the beginning of therapy. The MDFT therapist, as a part of ongoing work with the youth, will often say, "So, tell me what the (drug screen) results are going to be" prior to conducting the urine screen. This context shift sets the stage for a teen's forthright communication with parents and others. When the teen produces a drug-free urinalysis, this outcome creates a context for adolescents and parents to communicate differently. Parents may rediscover hope and believe that their lives may begin to be less disrupted by drug use and its consequences. With the therapist's help, family agreements about restrictions and privileges, as well as shifts in emotional interactions, occur.

When teens do not want to complete the drug test, it may be a sign that their drug use persists. The therapist may ask, "Are you afraid of what the results might be?" The therapist discusses a positive drug test from a non-punitive stance: "What we're doing isn't working and we're not helping you enough. What do we have to do to avoid continued use?" This process begins by eliciting the critical details of the social context of use, as well as the teen's intrapersonal functioning prior to and after drug use: "Can you talk about what happened; when did you use; what time and place; how much and what did you use; how many times; what were your thoughts and feelings before, during, and after using; which friends were present; could that use episode have been prevented?" These details help the therapist determine the next steps.

While parents want the problem fixed, therapists help parents to understand that, given the nature of the adolescent's problems, recovery from serious drug use can be a roller-coaster ride, not problem-free continuous progress. The therapist's work is to shift the parents' fear to a developmental perspective of their adolescent, where they understand that the teen has several areas of impairment needing attention, and that the development of a drug-free, more adaptive lifestyle takes time, and depends on several areas of progress meeting and reinforcing each other (individual outcomes, parent outcomes, family changes, school improvement, juvenile justice involvement decreased or stabilized).

Decision rules about individual, family, or extrafamilial sessions

MDFT is a therapy of subsystems. Treatment consists of working with parts (subsystems) to larger wholes (systems) and then from wholes (family unit) back down to smaller units (individuals). Systematic decision rules specify how to constitute any given session or piece of therapeutic work. Session composition is usually not random or at the discretion of the family or extrafamilial others, although sometimes this is the case. When therapists are new to MDFT, one of their main questions is, "When is it appropriate to meet with the adolescent alone, the parent alone, or the parent and the adolescent together?" Clinicians want to know about the inclusion of extrafamilial people in treatment as well. Composition of sessions (i.e., who attends/is included in that meeting) depends on the goals of that particular piece of therapeutic work, the stage of treatment, and the goals of that particular session. Goals may exist in one or more categories. For example, there may be strategic goals at any given point that dictate or suggest who should be present for all or part of an interview. The first session, for example, from a strategic and information-gathering point of view, suggests that all family members and even important people outside of the family be present, at least for a large part of the session. Later in treatment, individual meetings with parents and the teen may be needed because of estrangement or high conflict. The individual sessions build relationships, acquire information, and also prepare for joint sessions (working parts to a larger whole). Session composition may be dictated by therapeutic needs pertaining to certain kinds of therapeutically essential information. Individual sessions are often required to uncover aspects of relationships or circumstances that may be impossible to learn about in joint interviews. Therapeutic goals about working a particular relationship theme in vivo, via enactment for instance, may be another compelling rationale for decisions about session composition.

If decisions about session composition flow from therapeutic goals, it should be emphasized that not all goals are set a priori. For instance, some goals are at smaller operational levels than an objective such as increase of parental competence. Therapeutic feedback from any and all parts of the therapeutic system and environment is sought and used constantly to answer the following core questions:

- How is this therapy going?
- What have I accomplished in terms of addressing and successfully attending to MDFT's core areas of work – the four domains of focus? (For example do I know the teen's hopes and dreams? Do I know the parents' burdens? What am I working on extrafamilially – in the natural environment of the teen and family?)
- What are we working on and is this content and focus meaningful?
- Are we getting results, progressing reasonably?

Thus, while core pieces of work in MDFT, such as engagement of the teen and working on parent issues (e.g., parenting practices, the shaping of the parent–teen relationship through the interpersonally and behaviorally oriented technique of enactment), may dictate session composition and participation because of the obvious nature of their work, other aspects of therapy, such as working a given therapy theme, may require feedback to be read before session composition can be determined or decided. A therapist's realization that his relationship with the adolescent is slipping after a rough session or negative outside-of-therapy event (e.g., a tense court hearing where a decision went against the adolescent) must be used quickly (i.e., reading of feedback) to right the therapeutic course. An individual meeting, in the clinic, in the home, at school, or at a restaurant, is needed, and it is in the therapist's best interest to act quickly in relation to feedback of this type. The therapist's ongoing and naturally occurring assessments of multiple domains of functioning always provide a trustworthy answer to where he or she needs to go and what needs to be focused on.

Research Evidence

Four types of MDFT studies have been conducted: (1) efficacy/effectiveness controlled trials, (2) process studies that identify ingredients and therapeutic processes related to clinical progress and outcomes, (3) economic analyses, and (4) implementation or transportation studies that test the transfer of the approach to community settings. Independent reviews support MDFT's scientific soundness (Austin, Macgowan, & Wagner, 2005; Vaughn & Howard, 2004; Waldron & Turner, 2008) and identify it as a model program and evidence-based practice (SAMHSA, 2005).

MDFT has been developed and tested primarily in NIDA and other federally funded research projects since 1985. This research program has accumulated considerable evidence in support of the intervention's effectiveness for adolescent substance abuse and delinquency. The studies have been conducted at sites across the United States, among diverse samples of adolescents (African American, Hispanic/Latino, and White youth between the ages of 11 and 18) of varying socioeconomic backgrounds. Internationally, a five-country, multisite trial of MDFT, funded by the health ministries of Germany, France, Switzerland, Belgium, and the Netherlands, is nearly complete. In MDFT studies, all research participants met diagnostic criteria for adolescent substance abuse disorder. Generally, most samples had significant co-occurring problems as well, most commonly delinquency, and secondarily, depression and anxiety.

Randomized controlled trials

Seven completed randomized controlled trials have tested MDFT against a variety of comparison adolescent drug abuse therapies. MDFT has demonstrated superior outcomes to several other state-of-the-art, active treatments, including a psychoeducational multi-family group intervention, peer group treatment, individual cognitive-behavioral therapy (CBT), and residential treatment. These studies have included samples of teens with serious drug abuse (i.e., heavy marijuana users, with alcohol, cocaine, and other drug use) and serious delinquency problems. Next we briefly identify some key areas in which MDFT has yielded favorable clinical outcomes.

Substance use is significantly reduced in MDFT to a greater extent than comparison treatments investigated in the controlled clinical trials (examples include 41% to 82% reduction from intake to discharge). Additionally, substance-abuse-related problems (e.g., antisocial, delinquent, externalizing behaviors) are significantly reduced in MDFT to a greater extent than in comparison interventions.

Youth receiving MDFT often abstain from drug use. During the treatment process and at the 12-month follow-up, youth receiving MDFT had higher rates of abstinence from substance use than those in comparison treatment. The majority of MDFT youth report abstinence from all illegal substances at 12 months post-intake (64% and 93% respectively). Comparison treatments reported abstinence rates of 44% for CBT and 67% for peer group treatment. And, MDFT's changes are durable. MDFT clients continue to decrease substance use after termination up to 12-month follow-up (58% reduction of marijuana use at 12 months; 56% abstinent of all substances, and 64% abstinent or using only once per month). Other areas of favorable outcome include school functioning (MDFT improves school bonding and school performance, including grades improvements and decreases in disruptive behaviors), family functioning (reductions of family conflict and increases in family cohesion), psychological functioning (psychiatric symptoms show greater reductions during treatment in MDFT than in comparison treatments), including superior improvement for drug-abusing teens with co-occurring disorders, and reductions in high-risk sexual behavior and HIV and STD risk (MDFT reduces HIV risk behaviors and, importantly, laboratory-confirmed STDs).

Economic advantages. The average weekly costs of treatment are significantly less for MDFT ($164) than for community-based outpatient treatment ($365). An intensive version of MDFT designed as an alternative to residential treatment provides superior clinical outcomes at significantly less cost (average weekly costs of $384 versus $1,068).

MDFT also has studies on the therapeutic process and mechanisms of change, and implementation studies. (See Resources section for website address. A more complete research summary is available from the author.)

Summary

MDFT is an empirically validated, family-based treatment for adolescent drug abuse and delinquency. Its core ideas relied first on family therapy, systems concepts, and eventually family psychology, and other areas of psychology including the community, cognitive, behavioral, and humanistic psychology traditions. Developed first in clinical service and therapist training settings, and then refined, manualized, and tested in rigorous, state-of-the-science clinical trials, MDFT has been included in the national registries of empirically based therapies. It has been evaluated as a therapy of distinction by independent reviews and national entities involved in the science-based therapy movement. Stimulated by opportunity (i.e., federal government focus on adolescent drug problems and the need for new treatments over two decades ago), justified criticism ("Yes, I have heard about family psychotherapy – but opinions are no substitute for data"; Garfield, 1982), professional interest, and normal developmental process (Liddle, 2004; White, Dennis, & Tims, 2002), family-based, drug-abuse-focused therapies have entered a new period of transition. As part of this stage, MDFT continues its clinical expansion into new client groups and clinical phenomena (e.g., trauma-related clinical problems and trauma-based interventions, brief therapy, adult women at risk of losing their children to child welfare systems, and alcohol problems of youth). At the same time, another burgeoning area of work for MDFT concerns its transportation to non-research clinical settings, and developing effective, efficient, and cost-conscious training for new practitioner groups to do MDFT with competence and fidelity. The challenges in the implementation area are formidable. Despite all of the progress in the family-based treatment area, significant problems exist in the extent to which most regular care settings fail to use evidence-based therapies. The treatment research area has expanded, and given the urgent need to transport effective interventions into non-research settings, it seems destined to continue to grow in complexity, scope, and mission.

Resources

Center for Treatment Research on Adolescent Drug Abuse: http://www.miami.edu/ctrada

Liddle, H. A. (2008). *Multidimensional family therapy DVD*. Washington, DC: American Psychological Association.

Liddle, H. A. (2009). *Multidimensional family therapy for adolescent drug abuse: Clinician's manual and DVD*. Centercity, MN: Hazelden.

References

Austin, A. M., Macgowan, M. J., & Wagner, E. F. (2005). Effective family-based interventions for adolescents with substance use problems: A systematic review. *Research on Social Work Practice, 15*, 67–83.

Cicchetti, D., & Rogosch, F. A. (2002). A developmental psychopathology perspective on adolescence. *Journal of Consulting and Clinical Psychology, 70*, 6–20.

Diamond, G. S., & Liddle, H. A. (1996). Resolving a therapeutic impasse between parents and adolescents in multidimensional family therapy. *Journal of Consulting and Clinical Psychology, 64*, 481–488.

Diamond, G. S., & Liddle, H. A. (1999). Transforming negative parent–adolescent interactions: From impasse to dialogue. *Family Process, 38*, 5–26.

Diamond, G. M., Liddle, H. A., Hogue, A., & Dakof, G. A. (1999). Alliance-building interventions with adolescents in family therapy: A process study. *Psychotherapy: Theory, Research, Practice, and Training, 36*, 355–368.

Garfield, S. L. (1982). Yes, I have heard about family psychotherapy – but opinions are no substitute for data. *American Psychologist, 37(1)*, 99–100.

Guo, J., Hill, K. G., Hawkins, J. D., Catalano, R. F., & Abbott, R. D. (2002). A developmental analysis of sociodemographic, family and peer effects on adolescent illicit drug initiation. *Journal of the American Academy of Child and Adolescent Psychiatry, 41(7)*, 838–845.

Hawkins, J. D., Catalano, R. F., & Miller, J. Y. (1992). Risk and protective factors for alcohol and other drug problems in adolescence and early adulthood: Implications for substance abuse prevention. *Psychological Bulletin, 112*, 64–105.

Liddle, H. A. (1984). Toward a dialectical-contextual co-evolutionary translation of structural strategic therapy. *Journal of Strategic and Systemic Therapies, 3(3),* 66–79.

Liddle, H. A. (1999). Theory development in a family-based therapy for adolescent drug abuse. *Journal of Clinical Child Psychology, 28,* 521–532.

Liddle, H. A. (2002a). Advances in family-based therapy for adolescent substance abuse: Findings from the multidimensional family therapy research program. In L. S. Harris (Ed.), *Problems of drug dependence 2001: Proceedings of the 63rd annual scientific meeting* (NIDA Research Monograph No. 182, pp. 113–115). Bethesda, MD: NIDA.

Liddle, H. A. (2002b). *Multidimensional family therapy for adolescent cannabis users. Cannabis Youth Treatment (CYT) Series: Vol. 5.* Rockville, MD: Center for Substance Abuse Treatment, Substance Abuse and Mental Health Services Administration.

Liddle, H. A. (2004). Family-based therapies for adolescent alcohol and drug use: Research contributions and future research needs. *Addiction, 99* (Suppl. 2), 76–92.

Liddle, H. A., Dakof, G. A., & Diamond, G. (1991). Adolescent substance abuse: Multidimensional family therapy in action. In E. Kaufman and P. Kaufmann (Eds.), *Family therapy of drug and alcohol abuse* (2nd ed., pp. 120–171). Needham Heights, MA: Allyn & Bacon.

Liddle, H. A., & Rowe, C. L. (Eds.). (2006). *Adolescent substance abuse: Research and clinical advances.* London: Cambridge University Press.

Liddle, H. A., Rowe, C., Dakof, G., & Lyke, J. (1998). Translating parenting research into clinical interventions for families of adolescents [Special issue]. *Clinical Child Psychology and Psychiatry, 3,* 419–443.

Marvel, F. A., Rowe, C. R., Colon, L., DiClemente, R., & Liddle, H. A. (2009). Multidimensional family therapy HIV/STD risk-reduction intervention: An integrative family-based model for drug-involved juvenile offenders. *Family Process, 48,* 69–84.

Minuchin, S. (1974). *Families and family therapy.* Cambridge, MA: Harvard University Press.

SAMHSA (Substance Abuse and Mental Health Services Administration). (2005). Multidimensional family therapy certified as a model program. Washington, DC: Center for Substance Abuse Prevention. Retrieved from www.modelprograms.samhsa.gov

Stanton, M. D., & Shadish, W. R. (1997). Outcome, attrition, and family – couples treatment for drug abuse: a metaanalysis and review of the controlled, comparative studies. *Psychological Bulletin, 122,* 170–191.

Vaughn, M. G., & Howard, M. O. (2004). Adolescent substance abuse treatment: A synthesis of controlled evaluations. *Research on Social Work Practice, 14,* 325–335.

Waldron, H. B., & Turner, C. W. (2008). Evidence-based psychological treatments for adolescent substance abuse. *Journal of Clinical Child and Adolescent Psychology, 37,* 238–261.

White, W. L., Dennis, M., & Tims, F. (2002). Adolescent treatment: Its history and current renaissance. *Counselor Magazine, 3(2),* 20–25.

Williams, R. J., & Chang, S. Y. (2000). A comprehensive and comparative review of adolescent substance abuse and treatment outcome. *Clinical Psychology: Science and Practice,* 138–166.

24

Structural Ecosystems Therapy (SET) for Women with HIV/AIDS

Victoria B. Mitrani, Carleen Robinson, and José Szapocznik

Structural ecosystems therapy (SET) is a family-ecosystemic intervention that focuses on improving the family and social environment to improve the health of HIV+ women. SET combines two approaches: structural/systemic family therapy (Haley, 1987; Minuchin & Fishman, 1981; Szapocznik & Kurtines, 1989) and Bronfenbrenner's ecosystemic model (1979, 1986). SET is also strongly influenced by the work of Nancy Boyd-Franklin (Boyd-Franklin, Steiner, & Boland, 1995) and Judith Landau (Landau-Stanton & Clements, 1993). As a structural/strategic treatment, SET aims to transform interactions within the family in the "here and now" of the therapy session to maximize adaptive family processes and minimize problematic interactions. SET's ecosystemic focus is designed to help the woman and family to skillfully interact with service systems, and to capitalize upon and enhance the tradition of strong social supports in minority communities.

The basic intervention components of SET are as follows:

- *Joining* is the process whereby the therapist builds the therapeutic alliance with all therapy participants, as individuals and as part of their system.
- *Diagnosis* refers to identifying interactional patterns (structures) that are contributing to the problems experienced by the woman. SET's diagnostic framework includes five dimensions of functioning: structure (leadership, alliances, communication), developmental stage, resonance (enmeshment and disengagement), identified patienthood (negativity toward the woman), and conflict resolution.
- *Restructuring* involves orchestrating opportunities for individuals within the system to interact in new ways and includes three categories of techniques: working in the present (i.e., enactments), reframing (re-labeling), and shifting boundaries (bringing people closer together or pulling them further apart).

SET is intended as a time-limited treatment (typically 4–8 months), with a taper-ing of sessions toward the end of treatment. Weekly sessions with the woman and members of her family and/or other systems can take place at whatever location provides access to critical participants. Additional sessions and telephone calls can be offered during the week as needed or when there are special opportunities for change or outreach.

Although SET is not a structured treatment modality, it is useful to think of it as consisting of initiation, treatment, and termination phases. All of the SET techniques are conducted in every phase, but each phase has a different emphasis and goal. During initiation, the therapist forms the therapeutic alliance, begins to diagnose the ecosystem, and sets initial treatment goals. The treatment phase is when the major restructur-ing interventions take place as the therapist puts the treatment plan into action. The termination phase is a period of testing to see if the interactional changes have taken hold.

Women with HIV/AIDS face numerous hurdles in their daily lives that can seriously jeopardize their physical and emotional health. In our work in Miami, we have encoun-tered a wide range of functioning among women living with HIV, most of whom are African American and burdened with the difficulties endemic to urban inner-city living. They have access to reservoirs of strength in themselves, their families, and their com-munities that are often unrecognized and untapped by the institutions designed to serve them. This chapter illustrates SET with the case of Emily J., an educated HIV activist, in denial about her drug problem, and raising a teenage son who has HIV and a serious criminal charge. Emily J.'s case is based on that of an actual SET client, whose name and other case details have been disguised.

Case of Emily J.: Initiation Phase

Establishing that therapy sessions will include the family

The first clinical contact in SET is conducted by telephone with the woman alone. The goals of this contact are to begin to build rapport, learn some key facts that the therapist should know before meeting with the family (e.g., is anyone unaware of the woman's HIV status?), and plan for a first family session (e.g., who is most immediately accessible?). This first contact is conducted by phone to help establish the norm that in-person therapy sessions are to be family sessions. SET therapists work with the woman on developing a plan for getting others involved in the treatment by identifying potential participants, coaching and rehearsing ways to invite them, and offering out-reach as needed.

In the first telephone contact, the therapist learned that Emily J. was a 43-year-old African American divorced mother of two: 24-year-old Faith, and 14-year-old Michael. Michael lived with Emily and acquired the HIV perinatally. Michael periodically spent weekends with his biological father, who provided financial support. Emily had a boyfriend who did not live with her. The family had lived in a historically African American inner-city neighborhood of Miami for several generations. Emily was enrolled full-time in a nursing certification program. She was in recovery for crack cocaine as well as alcohol dependence, and reported that she is not completely abstinent. Emily was not involved in any drug recovery services. Both Emily and Michael received medical care at the university-affiliated hospital. Michael was enrolled in an HIV medication protocol but Emily reported that getting Michael to take his medications lately had been causing friction between them. She reported her own medication adherence as excellent.

Collaborating with the client to set initial treatment goals

SET is not a structured intervention with pre-determined content. Rather, it provides a theoretical and practical framework for conducting a treatment tailored to the needs of each client. The woman and therapist work together on goals that are important to the woman and that the therapist deems relevant to the woman's health. At the first clinical contact, Emily identified improving Michael's adherence as a goal that was important to her. Her desire to work on this with Michael was an important first step toward building the therapeutic alliance. The therapist and Emily agreed on a first family session with Emily and Michael at their home.

The process of structural change as the heart of SET

While clients typically define treatment goals along content domains (such as getting a teenager to take his medications), the therapist uses these content goals as a vehicle for changing problematic interactions. Therefore, Emily's goal of getting Michael to co-operate in taking his medications was seen as an opportunity to more broadly improve Emily's effectiveness as the parent of a newly emerging adolescent who seemed to be seeking autonomy. By working on *content* goals, the therapist alleviates the woman's presenting complaints and builds the therapeutic alliance; by working on *process* goals, the therapist helps to build the woman's and family's skills, roles, and support network in a way that can help alleviate or prevent other health-related problems.

SET's strategic side

While structural change (i.e., change in interactional patterns of behavior) is the goal of SET, strategy is the means toward that goal. SET is problem-focused, planful, and directive. Therapists select and sequence their targets of intervention strategically, first aiming at those interactional patterns that are relatively accessible to change (e.g., where there is high motivation/readiness for change; where existing strengths and flexibility are apparent) because success in one area will prime the therapeutic system for further success. In Emily's case, the most immediately apparent maladaptive behavior was her drug use and denial of its consequences. However, the therapist determined that Emily was not yet prepared to work on this issue. The therapist did not press further in the first conversation but determined that it would be important to establish an alliance with Emily on addressing the drug use later.

The focus on strengths as a cornerstone of SET

All human systems have structural strengths and contain the ingredients for better functioning, and it is the SET therapist's job to unearth these underutilized resources and put them to work. Throughout the therapy, therapists actively search for, comment upon, and build from the relational strengths that exist in every family. Pre-existing strengths are the foundation from which more adaptive interactions are built. In transforming interactions, therapist are not "creating" something new, but merely widening the range of behavior that people use in a particular relationship. Clients are responsive to an intervention that capitalizes on existing strengths because they gain confidence that changes are within reach, since they already possess the basic building blocks. It was not difficult to identify considerable strengths in Emily during the telephone contact. She was well-spoken and related calmly and confidently to the therapist. A key strength was Emily's knowledge about health and commitment to her own and Michael's healthcare. In addition, she belonged to a family network with long-standing ties to the neighborhood.

Gaining entry into the family

Because the "identified patient" is an adult, the context of treatment is considerably different from pediatric-focused structural/strategic therapies. First, the woman is not brought to treatment by concerned parents seeking help for their child; the momentum for seeking treatment and bringing in the family relies almost solely on the woman herself. Second, women are wary about giving strangers access to their family business and about having family deeply involved in their personal affairs. Therefore, gaining entry to the family requires a gradual and carefully considered approach. Third, women are not just dealing with their own issues; they are deeply involved in their roles as mother, wife/girlfriend, daughter, etc. Like most women, those with HIV/AIDS do not have the luxury of focusing primarily on themselves, and their health is usually not even high on their priority list. Therefore, getting women to be able to focus on their own health sometimes requires that the therapist first attend to goals that are centered on the needs of others who are important to the woman. This pattern of focusing on others was evident in Emily's initial treatment goals, which were centered on Michael, and would become even more apparent in the coming weeks.

Emily and her family were not immediately engaged in treatment. After the initial telephone contact she cancelled the scheduled appointment and a game of telephone tag ensued. By persisting in communicating with Emily by telephone, the therapist soon learned that Emily was not accessible for therapy because she was busy and emotionally preoccupied with a legal problem that Michael was facing, related to horse-play at school that resulted in the injury of a younger child and a charge of assault for Michael. At the court hearing, the therapist was able to offer both emotional and instrumental support. The therapist also briefly interacted with Michael and other family members who were present at the hearing. By the end of the day in court, the therapist had gained entry into the family as a friendly helper, and the first family session occurred within a week. This episode illustrates that joining requires the therapist to find opportunities to demonstrate her relevance, helpfulness, and a friendly, non-judgmental attitude.

The first family sessions were attended by Emily, Michael, and Emily's maternal grand-mother, who Emily felt comfortable including from the beginning of treatment. Unfortunately, like many people who have been involved in drug treatment, Emily had expected family therapy to be confrontational and therefore was initially reluctant to include her daughter and mother, two people with whom she had contentious relationships. HIV+ women and their families live high-stress lives and therefore they are not interested in adding a taxing or tense treatment to their lives. One of the therapist's first tasks is establishing soothing and positive expectations about the therapeutic experience by transforming negative interactions and highlighting strengths in the family and individuals.

Although the tone of SET sessions is generally conversational and non-confrontational, sessions cannot merely be pleasant get-togethers. Family members need to see from the start that they have something to gain from participating in therapy sessions. Some of the gains experienced by Emily's family in the first sessions included instrumental assistance (the therapist imparted information about the juvenile justice system), emotional support (an interaction in which Emily's grandmother felt validated by Emily and Michael), and addressing a family problem (a family discussion in which Emily supported her grandmother's decision that Michael should complete his homework before starting to watch television when he came to his great-grandmother's home after school).

Case of Emily J.: Treatment Phase

The therapist parlayed her initial joining with Emily and her family to gain entry into other family relationships and to work on sensitive issues that were not initially open for discussion. Over a period of 6 months there were 10 conjoint sessions with members of the family and 3 individual sessions with Emily. Family sessions were typically held at the grandmother's home, which was identified early on as a natural (and neutral) gathering place for the family. Emily preferred to come to our clinic for her individual sessions.

After two sessions with Michael and her grandmother, Emily agreed to an expansion of the therapeutic system to also include Emily's mother and daughter. Soon, the therapist identified Emily's cousin as an important source of support and encouraged Emily to invite her to a session. The therapist even had two sessions in which Emily did not participate: one to reach out to Emily's mother, who was convalescing at home from a hospitalization and was in danger of becoming disengaged from therapy, and one with Michael and his great-grandmother to help to strengthen their bond without Emily having to be central in their interactions.

Diagnosis: Mapping and Evaluating the Ecosystem

All individuals are part of many social systems, the family being the most proximal and influential. SET focuses on the entire ecosystem that has or can have an influence on the family, because extra-familial systems can be helpful resources and can also wield tremendous influence, particularly in the lives of poor families confronting HIV/AIDS. As such, the woman's friends, neighborhood, church, medical providers, social service providers, etc., are all considered to have (or potentially have) an impact on her psychosocial functioning. Diagnosis of the family is primarily based on observing interactions that occur in vivo, while diagnosis of extrafamilial systems typically rely on information that is told to the therapist.

Emily J.'s microsystems: The extended family

Emily J.'s extended family is shown in the genogram in Figure 24.1.

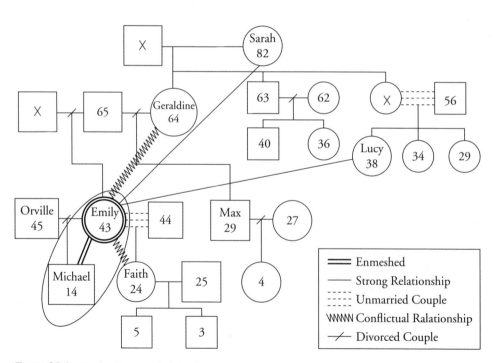

Figure 24.1 Emily J.'s extended family genogram

The women in Emily's family were relatively cohesive. Although not all members could be described as close, they could generally count on each other's assistance in times of trouble and weathered even serious conflicts without permanent cutoffs. Family members had suffered losses due to addiction and therefore were potentially important allies in confronting Emily's drug use, but they believed in staying out of each other's private business. Emily's family members were aware that she and Michael were HIV+ and were proud of Emily's activism and supportive of the need for her to take care of their health. The family members who were most central to Emily's wellbeing are described below.

Emily's maternal grandmother, Sarah, was an independent 82-year-old who lived alone and had raised three children, one of whom had died subsequent to drug addiction, and seven grandchildren. She was a central figure in the family and assertive about her role in providing emotional, spiritual, and financial support. Sarah was fully aware of the family dynamics, including the specific types of behaviors each member was involved in and whether they were doing the "right thing." Family members respected her, even though Sarah felt they sometimes abused her generous nature (e.g., not paying back loans) and did not fully appreciate her and provide her with adequate attention. Because of Sarah's leadership role in the family, her buy-in to therapy was crucial. Sessions took place at Sarah's home as a sign of respect, and the therapist aligned herself strongly with Sarah and deferred to her as a co-leader of the therapeutic system. If Sarah sanctioned therapeutic work on a difficult issue (e.g., Emily's drug use or the conflict between Emily and her mother), then it was open to discussion.

Emily's mother, Geraldine, was a 64-year-old divorced mother of two children, Emily and Emily's 29-year-old brother, Max, who lived with Geraldine. Geraldine worked full-time and had her own health problems, so she did not have regular contact with Emily and Michael. Besides, Emily and Geraldine had a difficult relationship marked by serious verbal and physical confrontations over the years, so they tended to stay away from each other. Emily desired a closer relationship with Geraldine for its own sake. In addition, Geraldine was close to Emily's daughter, Faith, and the two were joined in a coalition that was negative toward Emily. Therefore, Geraldine was a central figure in Emily's desire to patch up her relationship with Faith.

Emily's daughter, Faith, was the single mother of two small boys. She and her sons lived with Geraldine, who raised Faith. Faith felt that while she was growing up Emily did not have time for her because she was too busy "doing drugs, partying and having fun." Faith considered Geraldine to be her main maternal figure and they were very close. Faith was occupied with raising her children and was not as concerned about her relationship with Emily. However, Faith did acknowledge that her sons might benefit from a relationship with Emily, their grandmother. Faith also gave credit to Emily for the positive lifestyle changes she had made, especially in reducing her drug use and being a good mother to Michael. Emily agreed to invite Faith to the family sessions. But despite her efforts and outreach from the therapist and the support of the other female participants, Faith declined to join in. Emily's relationship with Faith was eventually addressed through enlisting the support of Geraldine in helping to bring the two together at a family dinner.

Emily's son, Michael, behaved like a child who was younger than his 14 years. He was socially awkward and made poor choices, especially with other children. Emily reported that she and his teachers would frequently admonish Michael about his acting up in class by clowning around or displaying other attention-seeking behaviors, such as not turning in his homework and making a joke about it.. Michael's response was that he wanted to be considered "normal" by his classmates. Unfortunately, during one of his playful moments a more serious situation developed that resulted in intervention by the juvenile justice system. In contrast to Emily's relationship with her daughter, which was disengaged, Emily and Michaels's relationship was enmeshed. A good amount of the therapy was focused on Emily's parenting of Michael.

Emily's cousin, Lucy, was a 38-year-old former crack abuser who had been in recovery for about one year. Lucy and Emily maintained a very close and supportive relationship. Lucy worked full-time and was actively involved in aftercare support groups through Narcotics Anonymous (NA). Lucy was a no-nonsense type of person who offered the family the "plain and simple facts." The therapist saw her as an important ally for addressing Emily's drug use.

Emily J.'s other microsystems

Emily J.'s ecosystem is represented in Figure 24.2. Each "petal" of the "flower" represents a microsystem (Bronfenbrenner, 1979). Emily's ties to her healthcare system were strong and functional. Beyond her own and Michael's healthcare, Emily participated in community social-political advocacy groups for those infected with HIV. She was very

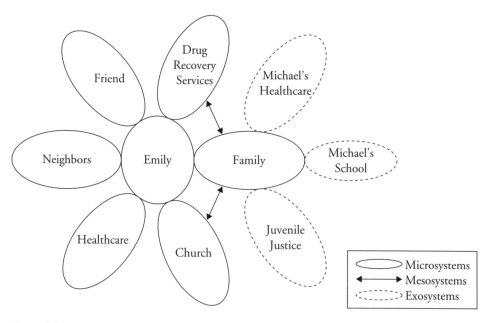

Figure 24.2   Emily J.'s ecosystem

knowledgeable about HIV and the various laws and rights of those afflicted by this disease. Emily was a member of the same church as her grandmother Sarah, but did not attend regularly, and strengthening this tie was seen as a potential source of support for both Emily and Michael and a way of getting both of them involved with pro-social activities and peers. Emily was not connected with any type of drug recovery or after-care support group, therefore strengthening her engagement in this microsystem was an important therapeutic goal.

Emily's ties to one peer, her drug-using boyfriend, were problematic. Besides the drug use, Lucy mentioned a violent incident between Emily and the boyfriend. SET uses two general approaches to addressing a woman's connection to a drug-abusing partner: (1) attempt to help both the woman and her partner to reduce their drug use (best in cases of strong or long-standing relationships); or (2) attempt to build a boundary between the woman and the partner (best when the bond between the woman and partner is tenuous). The therapist assessed the strength of the bond between Emily and her boyfriend by offering couples therapy as a treatment option. She also phoned the boyfriend (with Emily's consent) to invite him to attend a session with Emily and Michael. He refused both offers, and even after the therapeutic alliance was well developed, Emily seemed unenthusiastic about involving him in therapy. She was reluctant to discuss her boyfriend beyond a superficial level but did state that he provided financial assistance. It seemed clear that she was ambivalent about this relationship and the therapist concluded that it would be possible to work on building the boundary between Emily and the boyfriend. However, this is a potentially therapy-killing route, so it had to be navigated delicately.

Emily J.'s mesosystems

Emily J.'s mesosystems (Bronfenbrenner, 1979) are shown in the arrows between the "petals" in Figure 24.2. Some mesosystems that were the focus of treatment included the relationship between the family and the church, and the connection between the family (Lucy) and drug recovery services. While Emily was only marginally involved in the church, both Sarah and Geraldine attended regularly. Sarah also participated in several church ministries and fundraising activities, and desired more attendance and participation by Emily and Michael in the church. Emily agreed that she was interested in getting Michael more involved in church youth activities. Her family's ties to the church were seen as a bridge for bringing Emily closer to this important resource. Lucy's ties to drug recovery services served as an important link to get Emily more connected to this important system. Lucy was very expressive in her desire to get Emily to attend NA meetings with her.

Emily J.'s exosystems

Emily J.'s exosystems (Bronfenbrenner, 1979) were focused on Michael's wellbeing: the juvenile justice system, his healthcare system, and the school system. Emily was well connected with Michael's school and his healthcare providers, but, like most parents, needed help navigating the juvenile justice system.

Treatment Planning

Once the ecosystem is evaluated, the therapist identifies which maladaptive interaction patterns can be corrected to result in functioning that would benefit the woman's wellbeing. By focusing on patterns of interaction rather than specific problematic behaviors or symptoms, the diagnostic process leads naturally to a treatment plan. This does not mean that the therapist evaluates the entire ecosystem before moving on to re-structuring, but identification of a particular problematic pattern precedes restructuring on that problem. The therapist also identifies the strengths upon which the treatment will be built.

The SET therapist found much strength in Emily and her family beyond what was readily apparent at the initial clinical contact. The first strength was the family's flexibility and the ease with which it adapted to therapeutic change (e.g., opening up the therapeutic system to admit Geraldine and responding to enactments). Second, there was respect for the family hierarchy and Sarah was a strong leader. Third, there was a collective sense of spiritual power and guidance in directing the family toward a sense of purpose, hope, and fulfillment in life. Fourth, despite tension between certain family members, family members cared for each other and tended to rally in times of crisis (e.g., Michael's court case). Finally, there was the family's connection with community and service resources (e.g., church and drug services) and their desire to draw Emily into the realm of these helpful institutions.

Problematic interaction patterns that were identified and targeted for change included:

1 Emily's drug use, which was maintained by her relationship with a drug-using boyfriend, her detachment from drug recovery supports, and her family's "respectful" stance of staying out of her business. In addition to the deleterious effects of the drug use on Emily's wellbeing, Michael's exposure to the drug use also had negative consequences for his development.
2 Weak direct communication and cooperation between family members. This reduced support and cohesion, and occasionally resulted in explosive altercations, par-ticularly between Emily and Geraldine, further distancing Emily from the support of her family.
3 Emotional and physical enmeshment between Emily and Michael. This included Emily treating Michael below his age level, which prevented Michael from taking respons-ibility for his behavior, and which caused Emily to behave overly emotional when correcting Michael's behavior.
4 A pattern of conflict avoidance in much of the family (which was not Emily's usual manner of dealing with conflict outside of the family).

Restructuring: Changing Interactional Patterns

Working in the present

SET is a directive approach. While respect for the autonomy of women and their families is a fundamental value in SET, there is also a pragmatic belief that change requires direct guidance and intervention. Changing interactions primarily involves facilitating direct contact between members of systems in the presence of the therapist; this is a basic technique of structural family therapy that is known as *enactment* (Minuchin & Fishman, 1981). Enactments involve asking system members to interact in the presence of the therapist (e.g., "Please talk together about what Michael should do when he comes home from school"), including sustaining an interaction after it would normally come to an end ("You've stopped talking because you are unhappy about what your mom just said, but I'd like you to try to tell her what you heard her say to you"), or bringing a problem sequence into the therapy room ("Show me what you do when Geraldine comes over after work tired and irritated"), so that the therapist can observe and coach participants to change them.

Enactments were used liberally throughout Emily's family sessions. Early in treatment the enactments were used to facilitate joining by actively engaging each family member in the session and intensifying the family's relationship with the therapist. Enactments also were useful for diagnosis by exposing system strengths and weaknesses (e.g., Emily would intervene for Michael when the therapist asked him to talk to Sarah) and for treatment planning by gauging the family's level of responsiveness to the enactments and therefore its readiness for change. The J. family was very responsive to the therapist's suggestions that they talk together in sessions, and once the therapist was well accepted by the family, they were also willing to go along with enactments that were used to open up communication and re-shape interactions between Emily and Geraldine.

Enactments were also instrumental in addressing Emily's drug use, which was partly maintained by her family's reticence on this issue. Lucy confronted Emily's drug use in a supportive but straightforward manner, and helped Emily admit to her family that she sometimes used drugs with her boyfriend on the weekend. The fact that Michael had sometimes been present when Emily used drugs provided an entry point for breaking the family's silence and Emily's denial that her drug use was a problem.

Once a new interaction has been established through an enactment, the therapist may ask the family to practice it outside of the therapy session, and check at the next session on how it went. For example, the J. family discussed ways they could communicate more often and agreed on a system of meeting at Sarah's once a week. Another "homework" assignment included Michael showing his school work to Emily every day without having to be asked.

Reframing

Sometimes the emotional terrain needs some preparation before people can behave differently with each other, particularly when negativity is high. *Reframes* (Minuchin & Fishman,

1981) shake up the emotional tone in a relationship by offering a different perspective about a situation, a person's motivation, or an emotion that is being expressed. Reframes typically focus on positive aspects of the relationship and individuals, or changing motivational explanations for a person's behavior. Some of the reframes that the therapist used with Emily's family were "stubbornness or hard-headedness" as "clear-mindedness or sense of direction," and "insensitivity" as "telling it like it is." The therapist knew that her reframes had taken hold when the family started using the reframes themselves to describe what was behind someone's behavior. Geraldine even provided her own reframe for the root cause of some of her confrontations with Emily when she stated that sometime she got involved in Emily's personal business because she "just wanted to help" all of her children the best way she could.

Shifting boundaries and alliances

If a treatment goal is to move people closer together or further apart, the therapist realigns or *shifts boundaries* by regulating the distance or proximity between system members. Boundaries can be regulated by manipulating space in the session or by excluding persons from a session. Greater proximity can be achieved by directing disengaged system members to do an activity together or facilitating direct contact between them.

There were several boundary-related goals in Emily's case, including achieving more age-appropriate separation between Emily and Michael, bringing Emily closer to her mother and daughter, bringing Emily closer to extrafamilial resources (drug recovery and church), and achieving separation between Emily and her boyfriend (or at least from his drug use).

Several techniques were used to address Emily's enmeshment with Michael. These included choreographing opportunities for Michael to have meaningful interactions with other adults in his life. For example, the therapist sought permission to contact Michael's father, and via a telephone "session" that was then reinforced by Emily, spurred the father to increase his contact with Michael (which resulted in his father teaching him to ride a scooter, an experience that was rewarding for Michael and presumably for his father too). Emily also enrolled Michael in more youth activities. Another method for building a more age-appropriate boundary between Emily and Michael involved in-session enactments to help them negotiate Michael's extracurricular activities, school work, and medication in a manner that highlighted Michael's competence and Emily's confidence.

Emily was brought closer to Geraldine by having other family members help them to talk together about some of the painful incidents that had occurred between them. The therapist also highlighted similarities such as their shared history of not being as present as they would have wanted in their daughters' upbringing, their shared concern for Michael, Faith, and Sarah, and common values. Once Geraldine and Emily were on better terms, Geraldine was willing to serve as a bridge to increase contact between Faith and Emily.

Emily was brought closer to the church through Sarah, who was one of the oldest and most active church members and was interested in seeing her legacy continue. Emily had stopped attending the church after a minister made an announcement from the pulpit about HIV that Emily felt was insensitive. However, with some coaching by the therapist

Sarah was able to get Emily re-connected to the church. Sarah began by telling Emily how many of the congregants missed her and Michael, and that there was a special appeal to youth to join the choir and spoken word ministries. Emily thought this would be a positive social activity for Michael, especially because one of his interests was in writing poetry. Along with the warm reception they received from church members, this served as the impetus for Emily's return to her home church, and the connection took hold when Michael joined the youth choir.

To bring Emily to drug treatment services, the therapist encouraged Lucy to talk to Emily about the different events held by her recovery group and invite her to attend. These recovery activities included weekend prayers, special speaker meetings, and other theme-oriented social gatherings (e.g., women's night, dinners, picnics, etc.). Finally, Lucy had her one-year anniversary of being sober, and this was the event that Emily agreed to attend and that she felt was a positive and enlightening experience that made it worth her considering future participation.

Building the boundary between Emily and her boyfriend entailed a gradual process of supportive family discussions about the implications of drug use and violence on the health and emotional wellbeing of Emily and Michael, and safety planning. Emily steadfastly remained in a state of denial about the dangers of her relationship and of the drug use for most of the treatment. Finally, toward the end of treatment Emily and Michael moved in with Sarah, and remained until Emily found a permanent housing arrangement that her boyfriend was not allowed to enter.

Case of Emily J.: Termination Phase

Although we have defined the termination phase as taking place at the end of treatment, in actuality termination begins with the very first contact. The therapist's job is to work herself out of a job, and every intervention is directed at developing interactions that will continue beyond the duration of the therapy. In this regard, an important indicator of readiness for termination involves the manner in which the woman and relevant ecosystems resolve crises that arise. Such a crisis took place when Emily and Geraldine had an altercation which resulted in Geraldine ejecting Emily from her home. In the past, such an incident would have resulted in a prolonged period of each not speaking to the other, and Faith taking sides with her grandmother. To Faith's credit, she declared herself neutral and Emily took the initiative in reaching out to Geraldine to patch things up. Further, Emily had reduced her drug and alcohol use and achieved a more balanced relationship with Michael. Thus, the therapist, in collaboration with Emily, started to guide the treatment toward a termination point.

During this phase, sessions were conducted less frequently and tended to focus on a particular issue that Emily wanted to work on. It's notable that these issues continued to be centered on Michael, showing that to the end, Emily was concentrated on her role as mother. Michael fared well from all of this attention throughout therapy. By termination, he had joined an acceptable peer group that Emily felt comfortable with, won a poetry award at his school, where his teachers reported that he had greatly improved his classroom behavior, joined an adolescent HIV support group, begun attending church regularly, participated in the church choir, and even sung a solo. Michael's legal case was adjudicated with what Emily considered to be a fair outcome.

Despite Emily's stated focus on Michael throughout treatment, she also made some significant gains in terms of her relationships with family members, her confidence in her parenting, letting go of a destructive relationship, and engaging with pro-social institutions. It could be said that the focus on Michael's wellbeing was the impetus for much of Emily's own progress, such as rejoining the church and recognizing that her drug use and relationship with her boyfriend were problematic. Emily dropped in at the therapist's office one day after a medical appointment about four months post-termination and the gains seemed to be holding up.

The Evidence for SET's Effectiveness

Our program of research on SET for HIV+ women began about 20 years ago in response to the dramatically increased prevalence of HIV/AIDS among minority women. Miami was the epicenter of this phenomenon and home to seminal clinical research to reduce perinatal transmission of HIV. We learned that HIV/AIDS was not a major focus of concern for the women because of so many other basic needs and problems. Outside of the research realm, our clinical experience in working with a primary care service for women with HIV/AIDS taught us about some problematic interaction patterns between women, their families, and service providers. For example, we found that some well-intentioned case managers tended to breed dependence and did not recognize the strengths of families. These case managers saw their jobs as rescue operations and sometimes inundated women with services in a manner that was not well coordinated, and then were baffled when the women did not use the services to their best advantage.

Armed with this knowledge, we adapted our family therapy model for behavior problem adolescents, brief strategic family therapy (BSFT™; Szapocznik & Kurtines, 1989), for HIV+ women and began a major study that first developed a SET treatment manual and then tested SET in a randomized trial with HIV+ African American mothers. SET was compared with an individual person-centered treatment and with the usual services available to women with HIV/AIDS. Intent-to-treat analyses found that SET was more efficacious for reducing psychological distress and family hassles than were the other two conditions (Szapocznik et al., 2004). In the middle of the trial an assessment of HIV medication adherence was added and intent-to-treat analysis found that women in SET experienced greater reductions in missed medications than did women in the other conditions. Secondary analyses also show that SET was superior to the person-centered treatment for reducing relapse among the 68% of women in the trial who had a history of alcohol and/or drug abuse. While the results of one randomized trial do not qualify as empirically validating SET, they do point to its promise.

SET continues to evolve. We have ongoing research on issues of treatment engagement and retention (Mitrani, Prado, Feaster, Robinson-Batista, & Szapocznik, 2003;

Prado et al., 2002). We are also working on adaptations of SET for new populations such as HIV+ women in drug recovery and HIV+ women in prenatal care, and for delivering SET from within a primary care setting. Our work in SET has been predominantly with African Americans, and some of the themes and engagement and intervention strategies that have worked well with African Americans might not be well suited for other cultural groups. We strongly believe in the need for culturally tailored interventions and are examining how to adapt SET for use with Hispanics. Finally, we are highly concerned with issues of transportability of SET, particularly how best to train SET therapists and supervisors.

Resources

Mitrani, V. B., Robison, C., & Szapocznik, J. (2005), *Structural ecosystems therapy for women with HIV/AIDS: Treatment manual.* Unpublished resource, available at no charge from the first author at v.mitrani@miami.edu.

References

Boyd-Franklin, N., Steiner, G. L., & Boland, M. G. (Eds.). (1995). *Children, families, and HIV/AIDS.* New York: Guilford Press.

Bronfenbrenner, U. (1979). *The ecology of human development: Experiments by nature and design.* Cambridge, MA: Harvard University Press.

Bronfenbrenner, U. (1986). Ecology of the family as a context for human development: Research perspectives. *Developmental Psychology, 22,* 723–742.

Haley, J. (1987). *Problem-solving therapy* (2nd ed.). San Francisco: Jossey-Bass.

Landau-Stanton, J., & Clements, C. D. (1993). *AIDS, health, and mental health: A primary sourcebook.* Philadelphia, PA: Brunner/Mazel.

Minuchin, S., & Fishman, H. C. (1981). *Family therapy techniques.* Cambridge, MA: Harvard University Press.

Mitrani, V. B., Prado, G., Feaster, D. J., Robinson-Batista, C., & Szapocznik, J. (2003). Relational factors and family treatment engagement among low-income, HIV-positive African American mothers. *Family Process, 42(1),* 31–45.

Prado, G., Szapocznik, J., Mitrani, V. B., Mauer, M. H., Smith, L., & Feaster, D. J. (2002). Factors influencing engagement into interventions for adaptation to HIV in African American women. *AIDS and Behavior, 6(2),* 141–151.

Szapocznik, J., Feaster, D. J., Mitrani, V. B., Prado, G., Smith, L., & Robinson-Batista, C. (2004). Structural ecosystems therapy for HIV-seropositive African-American women: Effects on psychological distress, family hassles, and family support. *Journal of Consulting and Clinical Psychology, 72,* 288–303.

Szapocznik, J., & Kurtines, W. M. (1989). *Breakthroughs in family therapy with drug abusing problem youth.* New York: Springer.

25

Multisystemic Therapy (MST)

Scott W. Henggeler, Ashli J. Sheidow, and Terry Lee

Multisystemic therapy (MST; Henggeler, Schoenwald, Borduin, Rowland, & Cunningham, 1998) is an intensive family- and community-based treatment that has been applied to a wide range of serious clinical problems presented by youths, including chronic and violent criminal behavior, substance abuse, sexual offending, psychiatric emergencies, and, recently, serious healthcare problems. Youths with these types of serious clinical problems present significant personal and societal (e.g., crime victimization) costs, and due to their high rates of expensive out-of-home placements, consume a grossly dispro-portionate share of the nation's mental health treatment resources. Across these clinical populations, the overarching goals of MST programs are to decrease rates of antisocial behavior and other clinical problems, improve functioning (e.g., family relations, school performance), and reduce use of out-of-home placements (e.g., incarceration, residential treatment, hospitalization).

Theoretical Framework

With roots in social ecological (Bronfenbrenner, 1979) and family systems (Haley, 1976; Minuchen, 1974) theories, MST views youths as embedded within multiple intercon-nected systems, including the nuclear family, extended family, peers, school, neighbor-hood, and community (e.g., juvenile justice, child welfare, and mental health systems). In assessing the major determinants of identified problems, the clinician considers the reciprocal and bidirectional nature of the influences between a youth and his or her family and social network as well as the indirect effects of more distal influences (e.g., parental workplace; see Chapter 1, this volume).

Conceptual assumptions

Several assumptions are critical to the design and implementation of MST interventions.

Multidetermined nature of serious clinical problems. The social ecological theoretical model is supported by decades of correlational and longitudinal research in the area of youth antisocial behavior. This behavior is multidetermined from the reciprocal interplay of individual, family, peer, school, and community factors. As such, MST interventions assess and address these potential risk factors in a comprehensive, yet individualized, fashion.

Caregivers as key to long-term positive outcomes. Ideally the caregiver is a parent, but another adult (e.g., grandparent, aunt, uncle, sibling) with an enduring emotional tie to the youth can serve in this role. Caregivers are viewed as the key to long-term positive outcomes because they are in a position to provide ongoing nurturance and guidance to the youths, and to monitor and support the youths' relations with other pivotal contexts such as peers and school. By focusing clinical attention on developing the caregiver's ability to parent effectively and strengthening the family's indigenous support system, treatment gains are more likely to be maintained.

Integration of evidence-based practices. MST incorporates empirically based treatments insofar as they exist. Thus, MST programs include cognitive behavioral approaches, the behavior therapies, behavioral parent training, pragmatic family therapies, and certain pharmacological interventions that have a reasonable evidence base (Kazdin & Weisz, 2003). As suggested by other assumptions noted in this section, however, these treatments are delivered in a considerably different context than usual. For example, consistent with the view that the caregiver is key to achieving long-term outcomes, a MST cognitive-behavioral problem-solving intervention would ideally be delivered by the caregiver under the coaching of the therapist. Although the caregiver might not be as proficient as the therapist in delivering this intervention, treatment gains are more likely to be sustained as the caregiver is empowered to support the youth's problem-solving efforts in the future.

Intensive services that overcome barriers to service access. In light of the serious clinical problems presented by youths and their families in MST programs (i.e., referral criteria include high risk of out-of-home placement) and the high dropout rates of such youths and families in traditional treatment programs, clinicians provide intensive services with a commitment to overcoming barriers to service access. The home-based model of service delivery used by MST facilitates the provision of intensive services and overcomes barriers to service access, as described subsequently.

Rigorous quality assurance system. Treatment fidelity is needed to achieve desired clinical outcomes. Intensive quality assurance protocols are built into all MST programs, differentiating MST from most mental health practices. The quality assurance system, which includes training and monitoring components, is outlined subsequently.

Together, these quality assurance components aim to enhance clinical outcomes through promoting treatment fidelity.

Characteristics of MST Interventions

Treatment principles

The complexity of serious clinical problems presented by adolescents and their families requires considerable flexibility in the design and delivery of interventions. As such, MST is operationalized through adherence to nine core treatment principles that guide treatment planning (see Table 25.1).

Table 25.1   MST Treatment Principles

Principle	Description
1 Finding the fit	The primary purpose of assessment is to understand the "fit" between identified problems and their broader systemic context and how identified problems "make sense" in the context of the youth's social ecology.
2 Positive and strength-focused	Therapeutic contacts emphasize the positive and use systemic strengths as levers for positive change.
3 Increasing responsibility	Interventions are designed to promote responsible behavior and decrease irresponsible behavior among family members.
4 Present-focused, action-oriented, and well-defined	Interventions are present-focused and action-oriented, targeting specific and well-defined problems.
5 Targeting sequences	Interventions target sequences of behavior within and between multiple systems that maintain the identified problems.
6 Developmentally appropriate	Interventions are developmentally appropriate and fit the developmental needs of the youth.
7 Continuous effort	Interventions are designed to require daily or weekly effort by family members, presenting youth and family frequent opportunities to demonstrate their commitment.
8 Evaluation and accountability	Intervention effectiveness is evaluated continuously from multiple perspectives, with MST team members assuming accountability for overcoming barriers to successful outcomes.
9 Generalization	Interventions are designed to promote treatment generalization and long-term maintenance of therapeutic change by empowering caregivers to address family members' needs across multiple systemic contexts.

Treatment format

MST works with youth, family members, and all pertinent systems in which the youth is involved including peers, school, extended family, family supports, the neighborhood, community groups, and other involved agencies such as child welfare or juvenile justice. Early in treatment, specific, measurable, overarching goals and functionally meaningful outcomes are set in collaboration with the family and, as appropriate, other stakeholders. MST overarching goals are broken down into measurable weekly goals. Any person or agency that might influence attainment of these goals is engaged by the therapist and caregiver with specific interventions designed to encourage actions that will facilitate goal achievement.

Model of service delivery

MST is provided via a home-based model of service delivery, and the use of such a model has been crucial to the high engagement and low dropout rates obtained in MST outcome studies (e.g., Henggeler, Pickrel, Brondino, & Crouch, 1996). The critical service delivery characteristics utilized in MST include:

1 *Low caseloads* to allow intensive services. An MST team consists of 2–4 full-time therapists, a half-time supervisor per team, and appropriate organizational support. Each therapist works with 4–6 families at a time.
2 *Delivery of services in community settings* (e.g., home, school, neighborhood center) to overcome barriers to service access, facilitate family engagement in the clinical process, and provide more valid assessment and outcome data.
3 *Time-limited duration of treatment* (3–5 months) to promote efficiency, self-sufficiency, and cost-effectiveness.
4 *24-hour-a-day and 7-day-a-week availability of therapists* to provide services when needed and to respond to crises.

Cultural competence

As described in Huey and Polo's (2008) recent review of evidence-based psychosocial treatments for ethnic minority youth, MST is one of the few interventions that has demonstrated favorable outcomes for the behavioral and emotional problems of African American and multiracial Hawaiian youth. The cultural effectiveness of MST is likely due to its inherent flexibility (i.e., interventions are adapted to family ecologies), strength focus, emphasis on pursuing family-defined goals, commitment to removing barriers to service access, and provision of services in the natural ecologies of youth and their families.

Skills and achievements emphasized in treatment

Interventions are designed to be consistent with the nine core principles of MST, to be empirically based whenever possible, and to emphasize behavior change in the youth's natural environment that empowers caregivers and youth. A more extensive description of the range of problems addressed and clinical procedures used in MST can be found in the MST treatment manuals (Henggeler et al., 1998; Henggeler, Schoenwald, Rowland, & Cunningham, 2002).

Family interventions.   A frequent goal of treatment at the family level is to enhance caregivers' capacity to effectively monitor adolescent behavior and whereabouts, and to support responsible youth behavior and apply sanctions to irresponsible behavior. Hence, the therapist will often help the caregivers to develop increased family structure, operationalize desired youth behavior, and identify natural reinforcers to be linked with desired behavior. Importantly, the therapist also identifies barriers to the effective implementation of these new rules and consequences. Such barriers might include caregiver substance abuse, caregiver mental health difficulties, high levels of family stress, and so forth. The therapist then helps to design interventions to overcome these barriers, understanding that new family rules and contingencies cannot be implemented effectively or consistently until barriers are removed. In addition, family-based interventions often focus on enhancing the positive affective aspects of family relations that are important to family harmony and the favorable social development of children.

Peer interventions.   At the peer level, a frequent goal of treatment is to decrease the youth's involvement with delinquent and drug-using peers and to increase his or her association with pro-social peers. Interventions for this purpose are optimally conducted by the youth's caregivers, with the guidance of the therapist, and might consist of active support and encouragement of associations with non-problem peers (e.g., providing transportation and increased privileges) and substantive discouragement of associations with deviant peers (e.g., applying significant sanctions). Caregivers are encouraged to use indigenous opportunities for youths to develop relations with pro-social peers under adult supervision. Such opportunities include church youth groups, after-school activities, and community recreational resources.

School interventions.   With guidance from the therapist, the caregivers develop strategies to monitor and promote the youth's school performance and/or vocational functioning. Typically included in this domain are strategies for opening and maintaining positive communication lines with teachers and for restructuring after-school hours to promote academic efforts. Emphasis is placed on developing a collaborative relationship between the parents and school personnel.

Individually oriented interventions.   Whether for youth or caregivers, MST individually oriented interventions always occur in the context of a larger systemic treatment plan.

Cognitive-behavioral therapy (CBT) (e.g., Kendall, 2005) is an evidence-based individual treatment approach that frequently is used in MST individual interventions for addressing problems such as anxiety and depression.

Interventions for increasing family social supports.   A major goal of MST is to develop and maintain social supports for the youth and family to promote sustainability of treatment gains. The preference is to develop more proximal informal supports, as these are likely to be more responsive, accessible, and maintained over time. To maintain long-term informal social supports, families who receive support must reciprocate. For example, a neighbor might be enlisted to help monitor the after-school time of a problem adolescent with working parents; and in return, the youth might cut the neighbor's lawn each week. Even with strong indigenous support, however, family needs can sometimes overwhelm the informal support system, necessitating the use of more formal supports. Hence, the MST treatment team should have a good understanding of the available formal supports in the community.

Quality assurance system

Considerable resources have been devoted to the development of quality assurance mechanisms aimed at enhancing MST treatment fidelity, and this has taken place for two primary reasons. First, considerable research supports the link between therapist adherence to MST treatment principles and youth outcomes (e.g., Henggeler, Melton, Brondino, Scherer, & Hanley, 1997; Henggeler, 1999; Huey, Henggeler, Brondino, & Pickrel, 2000; Schoenwald, Henggeler, Brondino, & Rowland, 2000). Hence, the development and testing of a strong quality assurance system is critical to optimize youth and family outcomes. Second, with the transport of MST programs to community settings, which began in the mid-1990s and has expanded to include programs in more than 30 states and 10 nations treating approximately 15,000 youths annually, quality assurance procedures to support the effective implementation of MST in distal sites became critical. As such, MST sites are licensed through MST Services, Inc. (www.mstservices.com), which has the exclusive license for the transport of MST technology and intellectual property through the Medical University of South Carolina.

Schoenwald (2008) has summarized the validation of the MST quality assurance system across numerous studies. The therapist's interactions with the family are viewed as primary because of their critical role in achieving outcomes. Several structures and processes are used to support therapist adherence to MST when interacting with families. These include manualization of key components of the MST program, ongoing training of clinical and supervisory staff, ongoing feedback to the therapist from the supervisor and MST expert consultant, objective feedback from caregivers on a standardized adherence questionnaire, and organizational consultation. By providing multiple layers of clinical and programmatic support and ongoing feedback from several sources, the system aims to optimize favorable clinical outcomes through therapist support and adherence.

Evidence for Effectiveness of Treatment

Federal entities such as the Surgeon General (U.S. DHHS, 1999; U.S. Public Health Service, 2001), National Institute on Drug Abuse (1999), National Institutes of Health (2006), Center for Substance Abuse Prevention (2001), and President's New Freedom Commission on Mental Health (2003); leading reviewers (e.g., Elliott, 1998; Kazdin & Weisz, 1998; Waldron & Turner, 2008); and consumer organizations (e.g., National Alliance for the Mentally Ill, 2003; National Mental Health Association, 2004) have identified MST as either demonstrating or showing considerable promise in the treatment of youth criminal behavior, substance abuse, and emotional disturbance. These conclusions are based on the findings from 15 published outcome studies (13 randomized, 2 quasi-experimental) with youths presenting serious clinical problems and their families. As presented in Table 25.2, these studies included more than 1,600 families. Findings from these studies are summarized next, according to the defining characteristics of the study sample and the primary types of outcomes targeted. Copies of all published MST outcome studies can be requested at www.musc.edu/fsrc.

Juvenile justice outcomes

The vast majority of MST outcome studies have focused on adolescents presenting serious antisocial behavior, usually serious juvenile offenders, and their families. Following favorable psychosocial outcomes (e.g., decreased behavior problems, improved family relations) achieved in the first MST delinquency study (Henggeler et al., 1986), which used a quasi-experimental design, three randomized trials of MST with violent and chronic juvenile offenders were conducted in the 1990s (Borduin et al., 1995; Henggeler, Melton, et al., 1997; Henggeler, Melton, & Smith, 1992). As summarized in Table 25.2, these studies provided important support for the effectiveness of the MST model, with significant improvements in family relations as well as substantive decreases in re-arrests and out-of-home placements that extended for as long as 14 years post-treatment (Schaeffer & Borduin, 2005).

The transport of MST programs to community settings began in the mid-1990s and provided an opportunity for independent evaluations of the effectiveness of MST in treating adolescent antisocial behavior. Two of these replications have been published. Ogden's (Ogden & Hagen, 2006; Ogden & Halliday-Boykins, 2004) 4-site randomized trial with seriously antisocial adolescents in Norway (Norway does not have a juvenile justice system) showed that initial MST effects on out-of-home placements and youth internalizing and externalizing problems were maintained at a 2-year follow-up. Importantly, analyses also demonstrated differential site effects – the one site with problematic adherence to the MST intervention protocols had the worst outcomes. In the United States, Timmons-Mitchell and her colleagues (Timmons-Mitchell, Bender, Kishna, & Mitchell, 2006) also provided an independent replication of MST effectiveness with juvenile offenders in community settings. At 6 months post-recruitment, youths

Table 25.2 Published MST Outcome Studies

Study	Population	Comparison	Follow-up	MST outcomes
Henggeler et al. (1986) N = 57[a]	Delinquents	Diversion services	Post-treatment	Improved family relations Decreased behavior problems Decreased association with deviant peers
Brunk, Henggeler, & Whelan (1987) N = 33	Maltreating families	Behavioral parent training	Post-treatment	Improved parent–child interactions
Borduin, Henggeler, Blaske, & Stein (1990) N = 16	Adolescent sexual offenders	Individual counseling	3 years	Reduced sexual offending Reduced other criminal offending
Henggeler et al. (1991)[b]	Serious juvenile offenders	Individual counseling Usual community services	3 years	Reduced alcohol and marijuana use Decreased drug-related arrests
Henggeler, Melton, & Smith (1992) N = 84	Violent and chronic juvenile offenders	Usual community services – high rates of incarceration	59 weeks	Improved family relations Improved peer relations Decreased recidivism (43%) Decreased out-of-home placement (64%)
Henggeler, Melton, Smith, Schoenwald, & Hanley (1993)	Same sample		2.4 years	Decreased recidivism (doubled survival rate)
Borduin et al. (1995) N = 176	Violent and chronic juvenile offenders	Individual counseling	4 years	Improved family relations Decreased psychiatric symptomatology Decreased recidivism (69%)

Table 25.2 (cont'd)

Study	Population	Comparison	Follow-up	MST outcomes
Schaeffer & Borduin (2005)	Same sample		13.7 years	Decreased rearrests (54%) Decreased days incarcerated (57%)
Henggeler, Melton, et al. (1997) N = 155	Violent and chronic juvenile offenders	Juvenile probation services – high rates of incarceration	1.7 years	Decreased psychiatric symptomatology Decreased days in out-of-home placement (50%) Decreased recidivism (26%, non-significant) Treatment adherence linked with long-term outcomes
Henggeler, Rowland, et al. (1999) N = 116 (Final sample = 156)	Youths presenting psychiatric emergencies	Psychiatric hospitalization	4 months post-recruitment	Decreased externalizing problems (CBCL) Improved family relations Increased school attendance Higher consumer satisfaction
Schoenwald, Ward, Henggeler, & Rowland (2000)	Same sample		4 months post-recruitment	75% reduction in days hospitalized 50% reduction in days in other out-of-home placements
Huey et al. (2004)	Same sample		16 months post-recruitment	Decreased rates of attempted suicide
Henggeler, Rowland, et al. (2003)	Same sample		16 months post-recruitment	Favorable 4-month outcomes, noted above, dissipated
Sheidow et al. (2004)	Same sample		16 months post-recruitment	MST cost benefits at 4 months, but equivalent costs at 16 months
Henggeler, Pickrel, & Brondino (1999) N = 118	Substance abusing and dependent delinquents	Usual community services	1 year	Decreased drug use at post-treatment Decreased days in out-of-home placement (50%) Decreased recidivism (26%, non-significant) Treatment adherence linked with decreased drug use

Study	Sample	Follow-up	Outcomes
Schoenwald, Ward, Henggeler, Pickrel, & Patel (1996)	Same sample	1 year	Incremental cost of MST nearly offset by between-groups differences in out-of-home placement
Brown, Henggeler, Schoenwald, Brondino, & Pickrel (1999)	Same sample	6 months	Increased attendance in regular school settings
Henggeler, Clingempeel, Brondino, & Pickrel (2002)	Same sample	4 years	Decreased violent crime Increased marijuana abstinence
Borduin & Schaeffer (2001) – preliminary N = 48	Juvenile sex offenders	8 years	Decreased behavior problems and symptoms Improved family relations Decreased sex-offender recidivism (70%) Decreased recidivism for other crimes (53%) Decreased days incarcerated (62%)
Ogden & Halliday-Boykins (2004) N = 100	Norwegian youths with serious antisocial behavior	6 months post-recruitment	Decreased externalizing and internalizing symptoms Decreased out-of-home placements Increased social competence Increased consumer satisfaction
Ogden & Hagen (2006)	Same sample	24 months post-recruitment	Decreased externalizing and internalizing symptoms Decreased out-of-home placements
Ellis, Frey, et al. (2005a, 2005b) N = 127	Inner-city adolescents with chronically poorly controlled type 1 diabetes	7 months post-recruitment	Increased blood glucose testing Decreased inpatient admissions Improved metabolic control
Ellis, Naar-King, et al. (2005)	Same sample	7 months post-recruitment	Decreased medical charges and direct care costs

Table 25.2 (cont'd)

Study	Population	Comparison	Follow-up	MST outcomes
Ellis, Frey, Naar-King, et al. (2005a, 2005b)	Same sample		7 months post-recruitment	Decreased diabetes stress
Ellis, Templin, et al. (2007)	Same sample		13 months post-recruitment	Decreased inpatient admissions sustained Favorable metabolic control outcomes dissipated
Rowland et al. (2005) N = 31	Youths with serious emotional disturbance	Hawaii's intensive Continuum of Care	6 months post-recruitment	Decreased symptoms Decreased minor crimes Decreased days in out-of-home placement (68%)
Timmons-Mitchell, Bender, Kishna, & Mitchell (2006) N = 93	Juvenile offenders (felons) at imminent risk of placement	Usual community services	18-month follow-up	Improved youth functioning Decreased substance use problems Decreased rearrests (37%)
Henggeler et al. (2006) N = 161	Substance abusing and dependent juvenile offenders in drug court	Four treatment conditions, including family court with usual services and drug court with usual services	12 months post-recruitment	MST enhanced substance use outcomes Drug court was more effective than family court at decreasing self-reported substance use and criminal activity
Stambaugh et al. (2007)[a] N = 267	Youths with serious emotional disturbance at risk for out-of-home placement	Wraparound	18-month follow-up	Decreased symptoms Decreased out-of-home placements (54%)

Notes. [a]Quasi-experimental design (groups matched on demographic characteristics); all other studies are randomized. [b]Based on participants in Henggeler et al. (1992) and Borduin et al. (1995).

in the MST condition evidenced significantly improved functioning in several areas and had significantly fewer re-arrests than comparison counterparts at 18-month follow-up. These studies are important for demonstrating the effective transport of MST to distal community settings.

In summary, across several trials with violent and chronic juvenile offenders, MST produced 26% to 69% decreases in long-term rates of re-arrest, and 47% to 64% decreases in long-term rates of days in out-of-home placements. A recent meta-analysis that included most of these studies (Curtis, Ronan, & Borduin, 2004) indicated that the average MST effect size for both arrests and days incarcerated was .55, with efficacy (e.g., under ideal implementation contexts) studies having stronger effects than effectiveness (e.g., in real-world, community-based contexts) studies.

Substance use outcomes

Sheidow and Henggeler (in press) provide a comprehensive overview of MST substance-related research. As shown in Table 25.2, favorable substance-related outcomes were obtained in two of the early randomized trials of MST with violent and chronic juvenile offenders (Borduin et al., 1995; Henggeler et al., 1992), and these findings were published in a single report (Henggeler et al., 1991). Subsequently, the effectiveness and transportability of MST were examined in a study with juvenile offenders meeting DSM-III-R criteria for substance abuse or dependence and their families (Henggeler, Pickrel, et al., 1999). In comparison with usual community substance abuse services, MST was significantly more effective at reducing self-reported alcohol and marijuana use at post-treatment, decreased days incarcerated by 46% at the 6-month follow-up, decreased total days in out-of-home placement by 50% at 6-month follow-up (Schoenwald et al., 1996), and increased youth attendance in regular school settings (Brown, Henggeler, Schoenwald, Brondino, & Pickrel, 1999). Moreover, the incremental cost of MST was offset by the reduced placement (i.e., incarceration, hospitalization, and residential treatment) of youths in the MST condition (Schoenwald et al., 1996), and a 4-year follow-up (Henggeler, Clingempeel, et al., 2002) demonstrated significantly higher rates of drug abstinence and reduced crime for MST participants. More recently, Henggeler and colleagues (Henggeler et al., 2006) showed that MST substance-related outcomes for substance-abusing juvenile offenders in juvenile drug court were enhanced by integrating contingency management (Petry, 2000) interventions into MST treatment protocols. Favorable MST substance-related outcomes have also been reported in the aforementioned independent replication conducted by Timmons-Mitchell (Timmons-Mitchell et al., 2006).

Sex-offending outcomes

With the exception of higher rates of internalizing symptoms and deficient relations with same-age peers, research suggests that adolescent sexual offenders may have more in common with other delinquents than is generally assumed (e.g., Blaske, Borduin, Henggeler,

& Mann, 1989). Such findings suggest that effective treatments for delinquency hold promise in treating juvenile sexual offenders. This proposition was first tested and supported (see Table 25.2) in a small randomized trial conducted by Borduin and his colleagues (Borduin, Henggeler, Blaske, & Stein, 1990) and subsequently replicated in a larger study (preliminary findings reported in Borduin & Schaeffer, 2001). Importantly, in the latter study an 8-year follow-up showed that MST was significantly more effective at preventing sexual offending, other criminal offending, and incarceration. The promising results from these two efficacy trials (i.e., doctoral students as therapists, Borduin as the clinical supervisor) formed the foundation for a larger effectiveness trial using community-based practitioners that has recently been completed. Preliminary results are providing further support for the effectiveness of MST with juvenile sex offenders.

Mental health outcomes

In light of the favorable decreases in psychiatric symptoms in three MST studies with juvenile offenders (Borduin et al., 1995; Henggeler et al., 1997; Henggeler et al., 1986) and the lack of evidence for the effectiveness of inpatient psychiatric hospitalization, a randomized clinical trial was conducted to examine the viability of MST as an alternative to the inpatient treatment of youths presenting psychiatric emergencies (e.g., suicidal, homicidal, psychotic). As described in the corresponding treatment manual (Henggeler, Schoenwald, et al., 2002), several clinical adaptations were made to the basic MST model to better address the needs of youths presenting psychiatric emergencies and their families (MST-Mental Health [MST-MH]). As shown in Table 25.2, clinical and service outcomes at 4-months post-study entry strongly favored MST-MH (Henggeler et al., 1999), but the favorable short-term clinical, school, and placement results dissipated at 16-month follow-up (Henggeler et al., 2003). The favorable short-term findings in the alternative to hospitalization study have been replicated by Rowland et al. (2005) in a study with Hawaii's Felix Class Youths as well as in a recent independent evaluation comparing MST and wraparound in the treatment of youths with serious emotional disturbance at risk for out-of-home placement (Stambaugh et al., 2007). Together, these studies provide strong support for the capacity of MST-MH to produce favorable short-term clinical and service outcomes for youths presenting serious mental health problems.

Maltreatment outcomes

In the first randomized MST trial that was ever conducted, Brunk, Henggeler, and Whelan (1987) examined the efficacy of MST with maltreating families. Families in the MST condition changed in ways that reflected the use of more favorable parenting strategies. More recently, Swenson and her colleagues (Swenson, Saldana, Joyner, & Henggeler, 2006) have completed a randomized effectiveness trial of MST adapted for maltreatment (MST-Child Abuse and Neglect [MST-CAN]) compared with an evidence-based behavioral parent training condition. The results from this study are currently being prepared for publication.

Pediatric healthcare outcomes

Researchers at Wayne State University have taken the lead in adapting and evaluating the use of MST for improving the health outcomes of youths with challenging and costly healthcare problems (MST-Health Care [MST-HC]). MST was selected as the platform for this work because of its capacity to overcome barriers to service access and to address the multidetermined nature of difficulties in following complex medical adherence regimens. Ellis, Naar-King, and their colleagues evaluated the capacity of MST-HC to improve the health status of adolescents with type 1 diabetes who had chronically poor metabolic control, and significant findings favoring the MST-HC condition emerged for several key outcomes (Ellis, Frey et al., 2005a, 2005b). Youths in the MST-HC condition, in comparison with counterparts receiving standard care alone, had improved metabolic control, engaged in blood testing more frequently, reported less diabetes-related stress, and had fewer diabetes-related inpatient hospitalizations, which led to significantly lower medical charges and direct care costs (Ellis, Naar-King, et al., 2005). In light of these promising outcomes for youths with poorly controlled diabetes, this research group has also successfully pilot-tested adaptations of the MST model for other challenging health problems such as HIV (Cunningham, Naar-King, Ellis, Pejuan, & Secord, 2006; Ellis, Naar-King, Cunningham, & Secord, 2006). This research team is clearly forging new ground in the extension and adaptation of MST for challenging and costly healthcare problems, and their commitment to rigorous research is exemplary.

Summary and Conclusions

MST is a family- and community-based treatment for youths presenting serious clinical problems including criminal behavior and violence, substance abuse, serious emotional disturbance, and healthcare challenges. The evidence base for MST, especially in treating serious antisocial behavior in adolescents, is relatively strong, with several published randomized trials with violent and chronic juvenile offenders showing reductions in recidivism and out-of-home placement. On the strength of this record, MST programs focusing on adolescent antisocial behavior have been adopted by provider organizations in more than 30 states and 10 nations. Importantly, multisite transportability research is examining the capacity of MST programs in community-based settings to achieve outcomes comparable to those attained in clinical trials.

Note

Portions of this chapter were published previously in Kazdin and Weisz (2003). We greatly appreciate the permission from Guilford Press to reprint this material. In addition, revisions of this chapter were supported by grants K23DA015658, R01DA019708, R01DA017487, and R01DA013066 from the National Institute on Drug Abuse; grant R01MH65414 from the National Institute of Mental Health; and the Annie E. Casey Foundation.

Resources

Henggeler, S. W., Schoenwald, S. K., Borduin, C. M., Rowland, M. D., & Cunningham, P. B. (1998). *Multisystemic treatment of antisocial behavior in children and adolescents.* New York: Guilford Press.

For MST-related research: http://www.musc.edu/fsrc

For information on the development of MST programs: http://www.mstservices.com

---

References

Blaske, D. M., Borduin, C. M., Henggeler, S. W., & Mann, B. J. (1989). Individual, family, and peer characteristics of adolescent sex offenders and assaultive adolescents. *Developmental Psychology, 25,* 846–855.

Borduin, C. M., Henggeler, S. W., Blaske, D. M., & Stein, R. (1990). Multisystemic treatment of adolescent sexual offenders. *International Journal of Offender Therapy and Comparative Criminology, 35,* 105–114.

Borduin, C. M., Mann, B. J., Cone, L. T., Henggeler, S. W., Fucci, B. R., Blaske, D. M., et al. (1995). Multisystemic treatment of serious juvenile offenders: Long-term prevention of criminality and violence. *Journal of Consulting and Clinical Psychology, 63,* 569–578.

Borduin, C. M., & Schaeffer, C. M. (2001). Multisystemic treatment of juvenile sexual offenders: A progress report. *Journal of Psychology & Human Sexuality, 13,* 25–42.

Bronfenbrenner, U. (1979). *The ecology of human development: Experiments by design and nature.* Cambridge, MA: Harvard University Press.

Brown, T. L., Henggeler, S. W., Schoenwald, S. K., Brondino, M. J., & Pickrel, S. G. (1999). Multisystemic treatment of substance abusing and dependent juvenile delinquents: Effects on school attendance at posttreatment and 6-month follow-up. *Children's Services: Social Policy, Research, and Practice, 2,* 81–93.

Brunk, M., Henggeler, S. W., & Whelan, J. P. (1987). A comparison of multisystemic therapy and parent training in the brief treatment of child abuse and neglect. *Journal of Consulting and Clinical Psychology, 55,* 311–318.

Center for Substance Abuse Prevention (CSAP). (2001). *Strengthening America's families: Model family programs for substance abuse and delinquency prevention.* Salt Lake City: Department of Health Promotion and Education, University of Utah.

Cunningham, P. B., Naar-King, S., Ellis, D. A., Pejuan, S., & Secord, E. (2006). Achieving adherence to antiretroviral medications for pediatric HIV disease using an empirically supported treatment: A case report. *Journal of Developmental and Behavioral Pediatrics, 27,* 44–50.

Curtis, N. M., Ronan, K. R., & Borduin, C. M. (2004). Multisystemic treatment: A meta-analysis of outcome studies. *Journal of Family Psychology, 18,* 411–419.

Elliott, D. S. (Series Ed.). (1998). *Blueprints for violence prevention.* University of Colorado, Center for the Study and Prevention of Violence. Boulder, CO: Blueprints Publications.

Ellis, D. A., Frey, M. A., Naar-King, S., Templin, T., Cunningham, P. B., & Cakan, N. (2005a). Use of multisystemic therapy to improve regimen adherence among adolescents with type 1 diabetes in chronic poor metabolic control: A randomized controlled trial. *Diabetes Care, 28,* 1604–1610.

Ellis, D. A., Frey, M. A., Naar-King, S., Templin, T., Cunningham, P. B., & Cakan, N. (2005b). The effects of multisystemic therapy on diabetes stress in adolescents with chronically poorly controlled type 1 diabetes: Findings from a randomized controlled trial. *Pediatrics, 116,* e826–e832.

Ellis, D. A., Naar-King, S., Cunningham, P. B., & Secord, E. (2006). Use of multisystemic therapy to improve antiretroviral adherence and health outcomes in HIV-infected pediatric patients: Evaluation of a pilot program. *AIDS, Patient Care, and STDs, 20,* 112–121.

Ellis, D. A., Naar-King, S., Frey, M. A., Templin, T., Rowland, M., & Cakan, N. (2005). Multisystemic treatment of poorly controlled type 1 diabetes: Effects on medical resource utilization. *Journal of Pediatric Psychology, 30,* 656–666.

Ellis, D. A., Templin, T., Naar-King, S., Frey, M. A., Cunningham, P. B., Podolski, C., et al. (2007). Multisystemic therapy for adolescents with poorly controlled type I diabetes: Stability of treatment effects in a randomized controlled trial. *Journal of Consulting and Clinical Psychology, 75,* 168–174.

Haley, J. (1976). *Problem solving therapy.* San Francisco: Jossey-Bass.

Henggeler, S. W. (1999). Multisystemic therapy: An overview of clinical procedures, outcomes, and policy implications. *Child Psychology & Psychiatry Review, 4,* 2–10.

Henggeler, S. W., Borduin, C. M., Melton, G. B., Mann, B. J., Smith, L., Hall, J. A., et al. (1991). Effects of multisystemic therapy on drug use and abuse in serious juvenile offenders: A progress report from two outcome studies. *Family Dynamics of Addiction Quarterly, 1,* 40–51.

Henggeler, S. W., Clingempeel, W. G., Brondino, M. J., & Pickrel, S. G. (2002). Four-year follow-up of multisystemic therapy with substance abusing and dependent juvenile offenders. *Journal of the American Academy of Child & Adolescent Psychiatry, 41,* 868–874.

Henggeler, S. W., Halliday-Boykins, C. A., Cunningham, P. B., Randall, J., Shapiro, S. B., & Chapman, J. E. (2006). Juvenile drug court: Enhancing outcomes by integrating evidence-based treatments. *Journal of Consulting and Clinical Psychology, 74,* 42–54.

Henggeler, S. W., Melton, G. B., Brondino, M. J., Scherer, D. G., & Hanley, J. H. (1997). Multisystemic therapy with violent and chronic juvenile offenders and their families: The role of treatment fidelity in successful dissemination. *Journal of Consulting and Clinical Psychology, 65,* 821–833.

Henggeler, S. W., Melton, G. B., & Smith, L. A. (1992). Family preservation using multi-systemic therapy: An effective alternative to incarcerating serious juvenile offenders. *Journal of Consulting and Clinical Psychology, 60,* 953–961.

Henggeler, S. W., Melton, G. B., Smith, L. A., Schoenwald, S. K., & Hanley, J. H. (1993). Family preservation using multisystemic treatment: Long-term follow-up to a clinical trial with serious juvenile offenders. *Journal of Child and Family Studies, 2,* 283–293.

Henggeler, S. W., Pickrel, S. G., & Brondino, M. J. (1999). Multisystemic treatment of substance abusing and dependent delinquents: Outcomes, treatment fidelity, and transportability. *Mental Health Services Research, 1,* 171–184.

Henggeler, S. W., Pickrel, S. G., Brondino, M. J., & Crouch, J. L. (1996). Eliminating (almost) treatment dropout of substance abusing or dependent delinquents through home-based multi-systemic therapy. *American Journal of Psychiatry, 153,* 427–428.

Henggeler, S. W., Rodick, J. D., Borduin, C. M., Hanson, C. L., Watson, S. M., & Urey, J. R. (1986). Multisystemic treatment of juvenile offenders: Effects on adolescent behavior and family interactions. *Developmental Psychology, 22,* 132–141.

Henggeler, S. W., Rowland, M. D., Halliday-Boykins, C., Sheidow, A. J., Ward, D. M., Randall, J., et al. (2003). One-year follow-up of multisystemic therapy as an alternative to the hospitalization of youths in psychiatric crisis. *Journal of the American Academy of Child & Adolescent Psychiatry, 42*, 543–551.

Henggeler, S. W., Rowland, M. R., Randall, J., Ward, D., Pickrel, S. G., Cunningham, P. B., et al. (1999). Home-based multisystemic therapy as an alternative to the hospitalization of youth in psychiatric crisis: Clinical outcomes. *Journal of the American Academy of Child & Adolescent Psychiatry, 38*, 1331–1339.

Henggeler, S. W., Schoenwald, S. K., Borduin, C. M., Rowland, M. D., & Cunningham, P. B. (1998). *Multisystemic treatment of antisocial behavior in children and adolescents.* New York: Guilford Press.

Henggeler, S. W., Schoenwald, S. K., Rowland, M. D., & Cunningham, P. B. (2002). *Serious emotional disturbance in children and adolescents: Multisystemic therapy.* New York: Guilford Press.

Huey, S. J., Henggeler, S. W., Brondino, M. J., & Pickrel, S. G. (2000). Mechanisms of change in multisystemic therapy: Reducing delinquent behavior through therapist adherence and improved family and peer functioning. *Journal of Consulting and Clinical Psychology, 68*, 451–467.

Huey, S. J. Jr., Henggeler, S. W., Rowland, M. D., Halliday-Boykins, C. A., Cunningham, P. B., Pickrel, S. G., et al. (2004). Multisystemic therapy effects on attempted suicide by youth presenting psychiatric emergencies. *Journal of the American Academy of Child & Adolescent Psychiatry, 43*, 183–190.

Huey, S. J. Jr., & Polo, A. J. (2008). Evidence-based psychosocial treatments for ethnic minority youth. *Journal of Clinical Child & Adolescent Psychology, 37*, 262–301.

Kazdin, A. E., & Weisz, J. R. (1998). Identifying and developing empirically supported child and adolescent treatments. *Journal of Consulting and Clinical Psychology, 66*, 19–36.

Kazdin, A. E., & Weisz, J. R. (Eds.). (2003). *Evidence-based psychotherapies for children and adolescents.* New York: Guilford Press.

Kendall, P. C. (Ed.). (2005). *Child and adolescent therapy: Cognitive-behavioral procedures.* New York: Guilford Press.

Minuchin, S. (1974). *Families and family therapy.* Cambridge, MA: Harvard University Press.

National Alliance for the Mentally Ill. (2003, Fall). *NAMI beginnings.* Arlington, VA: National Alliance for the Mentally Ill.

National Institute on Drug Abuse. (1999). *Principles of drug addiction treatment: A research-based guide.* NIH Publication No. 99–4180.

National Institutes of Health. (2006). National Institutes of Health state-of-the-science conference statement: Preventing violence and related health-risking, social behaviors in adolescent, October 13–15, 2004. *Journal of Abnormal Child Psychology, 34*, 457–470.

National Mental Health Association. (2004). *Mental health treatment for youth in the juvenile justice system: A compendium of promising practices.* Alexandria, VA: National Mental Health Association.

Ogden, T., & Hagen, K. A. (2006). Multisystemic therapy of serious behaviour problems in youth: Sustainability of therapy effectiveness two years after intake. *Journal of Child and Adolescent Mental Health, 11*, 142–149.

Ogden, T., & Halliday-Boykins, C. A. (2004). Multisystemic treatment of antisocial adolescents in Norway: Replication of clinical outcomes outside of the US. *Child & Adolescent Mental Health, 9(2)*, 77–83.

Petry, N. M. (2000). A comprehensive guide to the application of contingency management procedures in clinical settings. *Drug & Alcohol Dependence, 58(1–2)*, 9–25.

President's New Freedom Commission on Mental Health. (2003). *Achieving the promise: Transforming mental health care in America – Final report.* Rockville, MD: DHHS.

Rowland, M. R., Halliday-Boykins, C. A., Henggeler, S. W., Cunningham, P. B., Lee, T. G., Kruesi, M. J. P., et al. (2005). A randomized trial of multisystemic therapy with Hawaii's Felix Class youths. *Journal of Emotional and Behavioral Disorders, 13*, 13–23.

Schaeffer, C. M., & Borduin, C. M. (2005). Long-term follow-up to a randomized clinical trial of multisystemic therapy with serious and violent juvenile offenders. *Journal of Consulting and Clinical Psychology, 73(3)*, 445–453.

Schoenwald, S. K. (2008). Toward evidence-based transport of evidence-based treatments: MST as an example. *Journal of Child and Adolescent Substance Abuse, 17*, 69–91.

Schoenwald, S. K., Henggeler, S. W., Brondino, M. J., & Rowland, M. D. (2000). Multisystemic therapy: Monitoring treatment fidelity *Family Process, 39*, 83–103.

Schoenwald, S. K., Ward, D. M., Henggeler, S. W., Pickrel, S. G., & Patel, H. (1996). MST treatment of substance abusing or dependent adolescent offenders: Costs of reducing incarceration, inpatient, and residential placement. *Journal of Child and Family Studies, 5*, 431–444.

Schoenwald, S. K., Ward, D. M., Henggeler, S. W., & Rowland, M. D. (2000). MST vs. hospitalization for crisis stabilization of youth: Placement outcomes 4 months post-referral. *Mental Health Services Research, 2*, 3–12.

Sheidow, A. J., Bradford, W. D., Henggeler, S. W., Rowland, M. D., Halliday-Boykins, C., Schoenwald, S. K., et al. (2004). Treatment costs for youths in psychiatric crisis: Multisystemic therapy versus hospitalization. *Psychiatric Services, 55*, 548–554.

Sheidow, A. J., & Henggeler, S. W. (in press). Multisystemic therapy with substance using adolescents: A synthesis of research. In N. Jainchill (Ed.), *Understanding and treating adolescent substance use disorders*. Kingston, NJ: Civic Research Institute.

Stambaugh, L. F., Mustillo, S. A., Burns, B. J., Stephens, R. L., Baxter, B., Edwards, D., et al. (2007). Outcomes from wraparound and multisystemic therapy in a center for mental health services system-of-care demonstration site. *Journal of Emotional and Behavioral Disorders, 15*, 143–155.

Swenson, C. C., Saldana, L., Joyner, C. D., & Henggeler, S. W. (2006). Ecological treatment for parent to child violence. In A. F. Lieberman & R. DeMartino (Eds.), *Interventions for children exposed to violence* (pp. 155–185). New Brunswick, NJ: Johnson & Johnson Pediatric Institute.

Timmons-Mitchell, J., Bender, M. B., Kishna, M. A., & Mitchell, C. C. (2006). An independent effectiveness trial of multisystemic therapy with juvenile justice youth. *Journal of Clinical Child and Adolescent Psychology, 35*, 227–236.

U.S. DHHS (Department of Health and Human Services). (1999). *Mental health: A report of the Surgeon General*. Rockville, MD: U.S. Department of Health and Human Services, National Institutes of Health, National Institute of Mental Health.

U.S. Public Health Service. (2001). *Youth violence: A report of the Surgeon General*. Washington, DC: U.S. Public Health Service.

Waldron, H. B., & Turner, C. W. (2008). Evidence-based psychosocial treatments for adolescent substance abuse. *Journal of Clinical Child and Adolescent Psychology, 37*, 238–261.

26

Behavioral Couples Therapy for Alcoholism and Drug Abuse

William Fals-Stewart, Timothy J. O'Farrell, Gary R. Birchler, and Wendy (K. K.) Lam

For much of the last century, there has been a longstanding and largely unchallenged position held by providers in the substance abuse treatment community, as well as by the public more generally, that alcoholism and drug abuse are fundamentally problems of the individual and are thus most appropriately addressed on an individual basis. More recently, however, awareness of family members' potentially crucial roles in addictive behavior has grown. As understanding has evolved as to how family interaction and dynamics influence substance abuse etiology, maintenance, relapse, and recovery, treatment providers and researchers alike have placed increased emphasis on viewing drinking and drug use from a systemic perspective and, in turn, on treating the family as an approach to addressing members' substance abuse. This is now reflected in different elements of how substance abuse treatment is conceptualized and delivered in contemporary community practice. For example, the Joint Commission on Accreditation of Health Care Organizations (JCAHO) standard for accrediting substance abuse treatment programs in the United States now requires that an adult family member who lives with an identified substance-abusing patient be included at least in the initial assessment (Brown, O'Farrell, Maisto, Boies, & Suchinsky, 1997).

Of the various family-based intervention approaches that have been developed and used by providers to treat substance abuse by adults, partner-involved therapies have received the most attention. Indeed, among the various psychosocial interventions presently available to treat alcoholism and substance abuse, it could be reasonably argued that partner-involved treatments are the most broadly efficacious. There is not only substantial empirical support for the use of couple-based treatments in terms of improvements in primary targeted outcomes such as substance use and relationship adjustment, but also in other areas that are of clear public health significance, including intimate partner violence, children's adjustment, and cost-benefit and cost-effectiveness.

Behavioral couples therapy (BCT) currently has the strongest empirical support for its effectiveness (e.g., Fals-Stewart, O'Farrell, Birchler, Cordova, & Kelley, 2005). In this chapter, we will (a) provide a conceptual rationale as to why couples therapy for substance-abusing patients may be particularly appealing compared to more traditional individual-based approaches; (b) describe theoretical and practical considerations when implementing couples therapy with these patients; (c) examine available evidence as to the efficacy of couples therapy with alcoholic and drug-abusing patients; and (d) discuss future directions with respect to partner-involved therapies with these patients.

The Use of Couples Therapy to Treat Substance Use Disorders: Conceptual and Practical Considerations

Theoretical rationale

The relationship between substance use and couple dysfunction is complex and appears to constitute a type of "reciprocal causality." For example, compared to well-functioning dyads, couples in which one of the partners abuses drugs or alcohol usually have extensive relationship problems, often characterized by comparatively high levels of relationship dissatisfaction, instability (i.e., partners taking significant steps toward separation or divorce), high prevalence and frequency of verbal and physical aggression (e.g., Fals-Stewart, Birchler, & O'Farrell, 1999), significant sexual problems (O'Farrell, Choquette, Cutter, & Birchler, 1997), and often significant levels of psychological distress in both partners and other family members, such as children (e.g., Kelley & Fals-Stewart, 2002; Moos & Billings, 1982).

Although chronic substance use is correlated with reduced marital satisfaction for both spouses, relationship dysfunction also is associated with increased problematic substance use and is related to relapse among alcoholics and drug abusers after treatment (e.g., Maisto et al., 1988). Thus, the relationship between substance use and marital problems is not unidirectional, with one consistently causing the other, but rather each can serve as a precursor to the other, creating a "vicious cycle" from which couples that include a partner who abuses drugs or alcohol often have difficulty escaping.

There are several relationship-based antecedent conditions and reinforcing consequences of substance use. Marital and family problems (e.g., poor communication and problem solving, arguing, financial stressors) often serve as precursors to excessive drinking or drug use, and unfortunately, resulting family interactions can inadvertently help to facilitate continued drinking or drug use once these behaviors have developed. For example, substance abuse often provides more subtle adaptive consequences for the couple, such as facilitating the expression of emotion and affection (e.g., caretaking when a partner is suffering from a hangover). Finally, even when recovery from the alcohol or drug problem has begun, marital and family conflicts can, and very often do, precipitate relapses.

Taken as a whole, the strong interrelationship between substance use and family interaction would suggest that interventions addressing the behavior of only one member of

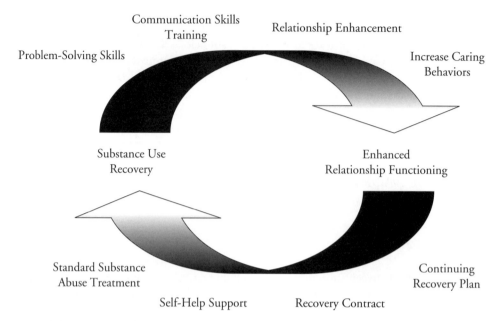

Figure 26.1   "Virtuous cycle" illustrating concurrent treatment for substance use and relationship functioning

the family, in isolation from the family system, would be less than optimal. However, standard treatments for substance abuse, which focus largely on the individual substance-abusing patient, usually do just that. In contrast, BCT (and, for that matter, family-based treatments for substance abuse in general) have two primary objectives that evolve from a recognition of the interrelationship between substance use and family interaction: (a) eliminate abusive drinking and drug use and harness the support of the family to support positively the patients' efforts to change, and, relatedly, (b) alter dyadic and family interaction patterns to promote a family environment that is more conducive to long-term stable abstinence. As depicted in Figure 26.1, the goal of BCT is to create a "virtuous cycle" between substance-use recovery and relationship functioning by using interventions designed to address both sets of issues concurrently.

Appropriate candidates

Before reviewing the core elements of the standard BCT intervention, it is important to note that BCT is not a suitable intervention for all substance-abusing individuals involved in intimate relationships. Because BCT attempts to harness the influence of the dyadic system to promote abstinence, some evidence of relationship commitment is an important prerequisite. Thus, one general criterion is that the partners are married or, if not married, have been cohabiting in a stable relationship for at least 1 year. Consistent with other behaviorally oriented treatments, BCT is skill-based and thus relies heavily on participants' abilities to receive and integrate new information, complete assignments, practice skills, and so forth. Thus, neither partner can have conditions, such as gross cognitive impairment or psychosis, which would significantly interfere with these abilities.

Couples are also excluded from participation in BCT if there is evidence that the relationship is significantly destructive or harmful to one or both partners. In particular, BCT is contraindicated for couples in which there is an extensive history of severe partner physical aggression. In such circumstances, partners would be referred for domestic violence treatment in conjunction with the substance-abusing partner receiving counseling for his or her drinking or drug-use problem.

Element of BCT intervention for substance abuse

When delivering BCT to a married or cohabiting alcoholic or drug-abusing patient, a therapist treats the substance-abusing patient with his or her intimate partner and works to build support from within the dyadic system for abstinence. The therapist, with extensive input from the partners, develops and has the partners enter into a *Recovery Contract* (which is also referred to as a *Sobriety Contract*). As part of the contract, partners agree to engage in a daily *Sobriety Trust Discussion*, in which the substance-abusing partner states his or her intent not to drink or use drugs that day. In turn, the non-substance-abusing partner verbally expresses positive support for the patient's efforts to remain sober. For substance-abusing patients who are medically cleared and willing, daily ingestion of medications designed to support abstinence (e.g., naltrexone, disulfiram), witnessed and verbally reinforced by the non-substance-abusing partner, is often a component of and occurs during the daily Sobriety Trust Discussion. The non-substance-abusing partner records the performance of the Sobriety Trust Discussion (and consumption of medication, if applicable) on a daily calendar provided by the therapist. As a condition of the Recovery Contract, both partners agree not to discuss past drinking or drug use or fears of future substance use when at home (i.e., between scheduled BCT sessions) during the course of couples treatment. This agreement is put in place to reduce the likelihood of substance-related conflicts occurring outside the confines of the therapy sessions, which can trigger relapses. Partners are asked to reserve such discussions for the BCT therapy sessions, which can then be monitored and, if needed, mediated by the therapist. Many contracts also include specific provisions for partners' regular attendance at self-help meetings (e.g., Alcoholics Anonymous [AA] meetings), which are also marked on the provided calendar during the course of treatment.

At the start of a typical BCT session, the therapist reviews the calendar to ascertain overall compliance with different components of the contract. The calendar provides an ongoing record of progress that is rewarded verbally by the therapist at each session; it also provides a visual (and temporal) record of problems with adherence that can be addressed each week. When possible, the partners perform behaviors that are aspects of their Recovery Contract (e.g., Sobriety Trust Discussion, consumption of abstinence-supporting medication) in each scheduled BCT session to highlight its importance and to allow the therapist to observe the behaviors of the partners, providing corrective feedback as needed.

Through the use of standard couple-based behavioral assignments, BCT also seeks to increase positive feelings, shared activities, and constructive communication; these relationship factors are viewed as conducive to sobriety. *Catch Your Partner Doing Something Nice* (Turner, 1972) has each of the partners notice and acknowledge one pleasing behavior performed by their partner each day. In the *Caring Day* assignment (e.g., Liberman, Wheeler, deVisser, Kuehnel, & Kuehnel, 1980), each partner plans ahead to surprise their significant other with a day when they do some special things to show their caring. Planning and engaging in mutually agreed-upon *Shared Rewarding Activities* (e.g., O'Farrell & Cutter, 1984) is important because many substance abusers' families have ceased engaging in shared pleasing activities; participating in such activities has been associated with positive recovery outcomes. Each activity must involve both partners, either as a couple only or with their children or other adults, and can be performed at or away from home. Teaching *Communication Skills* (e.g., Gottman, Notarious, Gonso, & Markman, 1976) such as paraphrasing, empathizing, and validating, can help the substance-abusing patient and his or her partner better address stressors in their relationship and in their lives as they arise, which also is viewed as reducing the risk of relapses. Relapse-prevention planning occurs in the final stages of BCT. At the end of weekly BCT sessions, each couple completes a *Continuing Recovery Plan*. This written plan provides an overview of the couples' ongoing post-BCT activities to promote stable sobriety (e.g., continuation of the daily Sobriety Trust Discussion, attending self-help support meetings) and contingency plans if relapses occur (e.g., re-contacting the therapist, re-engaging in self-help support meetings).

During initial sessions, BCT therapists focus on decreasing negative feelings and interactions about past and possible future drinking or drug use and increasing positive behavioral exchanges between partners. Later sessions move to engage partners in communication skills training, problem-solving strategies, and negotiating behavior-change agreements.

Traditionally, the substance-abusing patient and his or her partner are seen together in BCT, typically for 15–20 outpatient couple sessions over 5–6 months. However, with increased pressures of cost containment for mental health services influencing providers and researchers alike, other formats for BCT are now available and being practiced. These include variations that are delivered (a) in a multicouple group therapy context (Fals-Stewart, Birchler, & O'Farrell, 2002), (b) in a significantly reduced number of sessions (Fals-Stewart, Birchler, & Kelley, 2006), and (c) to only one member of the partner (Morgan-Lopez & Fals-Stewart, 2007).

Empirical Support

BCT as a treatment for alcoholism

A series of studies has compared drinking and relationship outcomes for alcoholic clients treated with BCT or individual alcoholism counseling. Outcomes have been measured at 6-months follow-up in earlier studies and at 18–24 months after treatment in more recent studies. The studies show a fairly consistent pattern of more abstinence and fewer alcohol-related problems, happier relationships, and lower risk of marital separation for alcoholic clients who receive BCT than for clients who receive only individual treatment (Azrin, Sisson, Meyers, & Godley, 1982; McCrady, Stout, Noel, Abrams, & Nelson, 1991). Domestic violence, with more than 60% prevalence among alcoholic couples before entering BCT, decreased significantly in the 2 years after BCT and was nearly eliminated with abstinence (e.g., O'Farrell & Murphy, 1995). Cost outcomes in small-scale studies show that reduced hospital and jail days after BCT save more than five times the cost of delivering BCT for alcoholic clients and their partners (O'Farrell et al., 1996). Finally, for male alcoholic clients, BCT improves the psychosocial adjustment of couples' children more than does individual-based treatment (Kelley & Fals-Stewart, 2002), even though children are not directly treated in either intervention. Thus, there may be a "trickle-down" effect of the communication skills training used as part of BCT, with improved methods of interacting permeating the entire family system. An abbreviated form of BCT (which requires roughly half the number of sessions and places proportionally more emphasis on substance-use reduction than standard BCT) appears to be as effective as the standard variant across a number of important areas of adjustment (e.g., drinking behavior, relationship satisfaction), but is far less costly to deliver (Fals-Stewart, Yates, Klostermann, O'Farrell, & Birchler, 2005). Lastly, although most studies of BCT for alcoholism have focused on male patients, results of a recent trial revealed that BCT was more effective than other alternatives for female alcoholic patients (Fals-Stewart, Birchler, & Kelley, 2006).

Research on BCT as a treatment for drug abuse

Although research on BCT for alcoholism has been ongoing for several decades, the years since the mid-1990s have seen several studies of BCT with drug-abusing patients and their partners appear in the empirical literature. Fals-Stewart, Birchler, and O'Farrell (1996) conducted the first randomized study of BCT with drug-abusing clients, comparing BCT plus individual treatment to an equally intensive individual-based treatment. Clinical outcomes in the year after treatment favored the group that received BCT on both drug use and relationship outcomes. Compared to those who participated in individual-based treatment only (i.e., 12-step facilitation, cognitive-behavioral treatment, depending on the study), BCT participants had significantly fewer cases that relapsed, fewer days of drug use, fewer drug-related arrests and hospitalizations, and longer time to relapse. Couples in BCT also had more positive relationship adjustment on multiple measures and fewer days separated due to relationship discord than couples whose partners received individual-based treatment only. Cost-benefit and cost-effectiveness in this study also favor BCT over individual treatment (Fals-Stewart, O'Farrell, & Birchler, 1997). Finally, domestic violence outcomes in this same study also favored BCT (Fals-Stewart, Kashdan, O'Farrell, & Birchler, 2002). Although nearly half of the couples reported male-to-female violence in the year before treatment, the number reporting violence in the year after treatment was significantly lower for BCT (17%) than for individual treatment (42%).

In another randomized study of BCT with drug-abusing clients (Fals-Stewart, O'Farrell, & Birchler, 2001), 30 married or cohabiting male clients in a methadone maintenance program were randomly assigned to individual treatment only or to BCT plus individual treatment. The individual treatment was standard outpatient drug-abuse counseling for the drug-abusing partner. Results during the 6 months of treatment favored the group that received BCT on both drug-use and relationship outcomes. Fals-Stewart and O'Farrell (2003) conducted a clinical trial in which 80 married or cohabiting men with opioid addiction were randomly assigned to equally intensive naltrexone-involved treatments, either (a) BCT plus individual treatment (i.e., the client had both individual and couple sessions and took naltrexone daily in the presence of his spouse) or (b) individual treatment only (i.e., the counselor asked the client about naltrexone compliance but there was no spouse involvement or compliance contract). In the year after treatment, those who received BCT had significantly more days abstinent from opioids and other drugs, longer time before relapse, and fewer drug-related legal and family problems than did those who received individual treatment only.

As with alcoholism, nearly all studies of BCT for drug abuse have focused on male patients. However, a randomized clinical trial of BCT with drug-abusing female patients revealed it to be more effective than individual-based treatment in terms of substance use reduction and other outcomes of interest (Winters, Fals-Stewart, O'Farrell, Birchler, & Kelley, 2002).

Barriers to dissemination of BCT into community-based programs

Although BCT has very strong research support for its efficacy, it is not yet widely used in community-based alcoholism and drug-abuse treatment settings. Fals-Stewart and Birchler (2001) conducted a national survey of 398 randomly selected U.S. substance abuse treatment programs. In general, BCT was viewed as too costly to deliver and requiring too many sessions in its standard form. In addition, most BCT studies used master's-level therapists as treatment providers, but most community-based treatment Alcohol and Other Drug Abuse (AODA) programs employ counselors with less formal education or clinical training. A series of more recently completed studies addressed each of these concerns. First, Fals-Stewart, Yates, et al. (2005) evaluated the efficacy of an abbreviated version of BCT and found it to be as effective as the standard version, in terms of reductions in drinking and improvements in dyadic adjustment of participants. Second, Fals-Stewart, Birchler, et al. (2002) demonstrated that combined with 12 sessions of group drug counseling for the substance abuser, BCT delivered in a 12-session, small-group format versus the standard 12-session, individual-couple format was equally effective and, again, more effective than 24 sessions of group drug counseling (GDC) for the substance abuser alone in reducing substance use and improving relationship outcomes during a 12-month post-treatment follow-up period. Third, Fals-Stewart and Birchler (2002) examined the differential effect of BCT based on counselors' educational background, comparing outcomes of couples that received BCT who were randomly assigned to either a bachelor's- or master's-level counselor. Results showed that, in comparison to those treated by master's-level counselors, those treated by bachelor's-level counselors obtained equivalent positive outcomes.

Case Illustration

To illustrate some of the procedures we have described thus far, a case example is provided, based on a couple treated by a therapist under the supervision of the first author. Although selected background data have been altered to mask the identities of the participating partners to protect their confidentiality, the methods used and results obtained have not been changed.

Steve was a 44-year-old African American male who was referred to outpatient substance abuse treatment by his clergyman after multiple problems resulting from excessive alcohol and other drug use (e.g., two recent job losses, conviction for driving while intoxicated). During a psychosocial assessment, Steve reported that, by his early 20s, he drank nearly every day, usually consuming a six-pack of beer daily. By his mid-20s, he began drinking greater quantities of alcohol on weekends (i.e., two six-packs on Fridays and Saturdays, as well as on holidays and during sporting events) and experienced occasional blackouts. He began experimenting with cocaine in his mid-20s, but was not a regular user; however, and during the last 3 years, he had begun snorting it 3–4 times per week.

Steve had previously been treated in an inpatient drug-abuse treatment program about 10 years ago, but quickly relapsed after discharge. He said he had prolonged sobriety (2–4 weeks) on five different occasions in the last 3 years in an effort to "prove" to himself and his wife he could control his use. He noted each of these periods of abstinence ended after verbal altercations with his wife, who he said always brought up his past use and would "never let me forget what I had done."

Steve reported that his drinking and cocaine use had gotten progressively worse in the last 3 months, with daily use of one or both substances. He reported he was on the verge of losing his current job due to excessive absences, which was causing regular conflict with his wife along with clear financial strain in the family. A diagnostic interview confirmed that Steve met criteria for both alcohol and cocaine dependence.

Steve was asked if he was willing to participate in relationship assessment with his wife, Kathy. He was very reluctant, emphasizing that his wife was hypercritical and that he felt his drug problem was "my problem" not "our problem." It was explained that the purpose of seeing him and his wife together was not to allow the assessment to become a forum for criticism, but rather for assessing how his marriage might be contributing to his use and how it might help in his recovery. It was also emphasized that early sessions were only for assessment; he, his wife, and the therapist were not engaging in or committing to entering formal treatment. With this explanation, he agreed to participate in the assessment.

Steve attended Kathy's initial session; the assessment procedures to be used were described to the partners. It was again emphasized to both partners that this was only an assessment and that participation in this evaluation did not commit either the couple or the therapist to a course of treatment. Both partners agreed to complete the assessment.

The therapist collected background data from Kathy and information about the partners' marriage. Kathy was a 40-year-old African American female who was employed part-time as an accounts payable clerk for a property management firm. She reported she had never abused alcohol or used other drugs. Steve and Kathy married after a 2-year courtship after she discovered she was pregnant with their first (and only) child, Aaron; they have been married for 10 years. Kathy said she knew Steve drank "way too much" but was not aware of the extent of his drinking or that he used cocaine until his recent admissions to her. She saw his drinking and drug use as "his weakness and lack of discipline."

Both partners described their relationship as unstable and reported they had been discussing the possibility of getting separated and ultimately divorced. Steve said the only reason he stayed in the relationship "and take all of this s**t" was for his son. Steve's primary complaint was that Kathy was "always bitching, as if that hearing that for the millionth time is going to make me stop" and "is never satisfied." Kathy described Steve as "irresponsible. When we met he was a lovable loser; now he is just a loser!"

As part of the assessment, the partners completed a communication sample. The topic the partners chose was "financial problems." As part of this conflict-resolution task, the partners were asked to describe the problem and work toward a solution. The following is a partial transcript of their discussion:

W(IFE):   You are such a f**king liar; you are never clean and sober. You use all of our money to ignore our problems. Can't you see that it is causing the problems? I want to help you but you won't let me; you're such a loser!

H(USBAND):   We get nowhere. If I use, you rant. If I don't use, you rant because I didn't stop earlier. When do you put down the f**king cross? When is it enough?

W: I'll let you know when it is enough.

H: Is it enough when Aaron gets hurt? You shove all this up my ass and he gets it too, ya know . . .

W: Don't lay that on me; you're the drunk. He has seen enough . . . for a lifetime!

H: He has seen enough from you, too. It is not just me.

W: Right . . . I yell at his father for being a drug addict and a drunk . . . and it is me, too? You have fooled no one; I know you will be back out there screwing up the minute you think everyone is fooled. Just know, I won't be fooled.

H: Why the hell did you agree to come here then?

W: You think I like all of this? I hate it! I just want to stop all of this. Please, please . . . try to stop. You can be mad at me, but Aaron never bargained for this life . . . never!

H: (whispers) Leave him out of this . . . (long pause).

W: He is in it; that is the point. You know, we have not saved dime one for college; he is a great student. You are f**king up his future, your future, our future . . . just to get loaded.

H: It's a disease; it is a disease . . .

w: No, don't run from what you have done. I get it . . . the bills, the school, the shame. You are going to lose your job for the third time this year and then we are greased in the ass. Then what is the plan, Einstein?

H: What plan?

w: You know, the one where you get us out of this hole you have shoveled us in.

H: The start of the plan is now. That is why I am here. But you have to get off your high horse over here and think life is perfect. It is not perfect. You are not blameless . . .

w: That is just such bulls**t! I AM the victim here. Everyone and everything around you is a victim. The only ones who aren't are the boys; you have been hanging out with those losers since high school. When do you grow up; when does it change?

H: It is all I have. You have it all. I have nothing.

w: Well, that is convenient. You have responsibilities and Aaron is one – to be an involved parent.

H: I want my friends, too . . .

w: So what? When Aaron came along, you were supposed to be a Dad. What the hell are you? You ignore him. I am the mother and the father.

This exchange, along with other assessment data from the paper-and-pencil interviews and the clinical interviews, revealed multiple problem areas. The discussion above not only revealed significant deficits in these partners' communication patterns, but also a lack of mutual caring and a general level of interpersonal antagonism. The approach the couple used for conflict resolution can best be described as "kitchen sinking"; although the agreed topic was "financial problems," they introduced several other conflict areas without addressing the problem at hand. The partners described clear deficits in commitment, noting on a few occasions that they were only staying together for the sake of their only child. Lastly, the communication sample revealed a contract problem. Kathy thought Steve would be involved as a parent once Aaron was born; Steve believed it should not have changed his lifestyle very much.

The partners agreed to participate in couples therapy. Steve realized that conflict and distrust were making it difficult for him to maintain abstinence. Kathy agreed to participate, hoping that she would get a better understanding of why Steve drank and used drugs, as well as find ways to help him stay sober.

Early sessions involved introducing and following through with a negotiated Recovery Contract. The contract included five primary components: (a) Steve agreed to take Antabuse (for which he was medically evaluated) while being observed by Kathy; (b) the couple agreed to a positive verbal exchange (i.e., a Sobriety Trust Discussion) at the time when Steve took the Antabuse (i.e., Steve reporting he had stayed abstinent from alcohol and drugs during the last day and promising to remain abstinent for the ensuing day and Kathy thanking him for remaining sober); (c) Kathy agreed not to bring up negative past events concerning Steve's drinking and drug use; (d) Steve agreed to attend AA meetings daily; (e) the partners would not threaten to divorce or separate while at home and would, for the time being, bring these thoughts into the sessions; and (f) Steve would provide urine samples each week at sessions to determine if any cocaine or other drug use had occurred.

Kathy reported that Steve's willingness to take Antabuse while she watched gave her great comfort because she knew that, when he was taking it, he was not drinking. The positive verbal exchange between the partners made the daily Sobriety Trust Discussion a caring behavior rather than a "checking-up" procedure. Steve said there was less stress in the home because Kathy did not bring up his past drinking very often (although there were occasions when Kathy lapsed into bringing up the past). Steve's AA involvement provided him with a support network that did not include friends with whom he drank or used drugs. Urine screens were negative for all drugs tested, which was consistent with Steve's reports that he was clean and sober.

Communication skills training focused on slowing down the partners' verbal exchanges, with an emphasis on staying on a single topic. Session time was also spent training partners to make positive specific requests and use "I" statements as a way to express and own their feelings rather than attributing how they felt to their spouse.

Later sessions addressed relationship problems. Assignments such as Catch Your Partner Doing Something Nice and Shared Rewarding Activities served to increase positive verbal exchanges and mutual caring, along with re-establishing a long-term commitment to the relationship. Toward the end of therapy, the partners reported that participation in BCT helped them learn to "enjoy their marriage again."

During the latter phase of treatment, the focus shifted toward Steve's parenting and toward working with Kathy to allow her to let Steve play a more active role in Aaron's life. Since Kathy had been doing most of the parenting for the last few years, it was difficult for her to relinquish any control to Steve even after extended sobriety. Steve and Kathy agreed to allow Steve to do separate recreational activities with Aaron that did not include Kathy. This issue remained a longstanding, on-going struggle for the partners both during and after treatment.

During the 2-year post-treatment follow-up interviews, Steve reported that he had remained sober, except for a 1-week relapse with alcohol during the first year. However, he contacted his sponsor, returned to AA, and re-established abstinence. Both partners reported they made a point of doing something fun together at least once per week. Steve was attending AA meetings 5–6 times weekly. Although the partners continued to have money problems, Kathy received a work promotion, which helped to alleviate some of the stress.

Conclusions and Future Directions

In the early 1970s, partner-involved therapies were seen as holding great promise as interventions for substance abuse (e.g., Keller, 1974). Since that time, that promise has, in many important respects, been realized; BCT has been shown to be very effective across various outcomes (e.g., substance use, children's adjustment, partner violence) and different patient populations (e.g., alcohol-dependent men and women, drug-abusing men and women, patients being maintained on methadone).

Indeed, BCT has come a very long way in 30 or so years, but it clearly has a very long way to go. Future directions for BCT can be thought of in terms of *how*, *who*, and *where*. First, although BCT appears to work, very little research has been conducted to determine *how* it works. In other words, what are the mechanisms of action that make BCT curative? If these factors can be identified, then BCT can be modified to maximize its efficiency and effectiveness. Second, BCT has been used with different patient populations in terms of drug of abuse (i.e., primary alcohol, primary illicit drug abuse) and gender (i.e., men, women), but no published research has examined *who* BCT may be effective for in terms of racial and ethnic diversity. More specifically, more research is needed to determine how the BCT intervention package for substance abuse might need to be modified to address the unique needs of patients (and their families) that are from underrepresented minority groups.

Third, and perhaps most importantly, far more research is needed as to *where* BCT is practiced. Despite its clear demonstrated efficacy, BCT has not been widely adopted in community practice. Examination of barriers to the dissemination of BCT to treatment providers, and methods to overcome them, is a critical next step in this programmatic line of research. Because BCT has been shown to be efficacious across a number of different formats (one-person couples treatment, abbreviated formats, multicouple group therapy, standard conjoint format), BCT is an intervention that might be a strong candidate for a stepped care approach (e.g., Sobell & Sobell, 2000), moving from least to most intensive as treatment response dictates. Thus, married or cohabiting patients entering treatment can enter a therapy group, without the participation of their partners, which focuses on relationship issues. Patients for whom it is clinically indicated can then move to a multicouple group format which would include their partners. Those couples who require more conjoint treatment can participate in a planned abbreviated BCT; if that is insufficient, then patients and their partners can participate in the standard BCT, which is the most intensive and requires the most time and commitment by both providers and partners. There is some suggestion that such an approach may be the most acceptable to providers and patients (Fals-Stewart, Logsdon, & Birchler, 2004).

Resources

Addiction and Family Research Group, www.addictionandfamily.org. Training materials, therapy manuals, articles, and videotape examples.

Fals-Stewart, W., O'Farrell, T. G., Birchler, G. R., Cordova, J., & Kelley, M. L. (2005). Behavioral couples therapy for alcoholism and drug abuse: Where we've been, where we are, and where we're going. *Journal of Cognitive Psychotherapy, 19*, 231–249. Detailed review of the empirical literature supporting BCT.

O'Farrell, T. J., & Fals-Stewart, W. (2006). *Behavioral couples therapy for alcoholism and drug abuse.* New York: Guilford Press. Comprehensive overview of the theory and empirical literature supporting BCT as well as a step-by-step guide (including handouts and other materials) for practice.

References

Azrin, N. H., Sisson, R.W., Meyers, R., & Godley, M. (1982). Alcoholism treatment by disulfiram and community reinforcement therapy. *Journal of Behavior Therapy and Experimental Psychiatry, 13*, 105–112.

Brown, E. D., O'Farrell, T. J., Maisto, S. A., Boies, K., & Suchinsky, R. (Eds.). (1997). *Accreditation guide for substance abuse treatment programs.* Newbury Park, CA: Sage.

Fals-Stewart, W., & Birchler, G. R. (2001). A national survey of the use of couples therapy in substance abuse treatment. *Journal of Substance Abuse Treatment, 20*, 277–283.

Fals-Stewart, W., & Birchler, G. R. (2002). Behavioral couples therapy for alcoholic men and their intimate partners: The comparative effectiveness of master's- and bachelor's-level counselors. *Behavior Therapy, 33*, 123–147.

Fals-Stewart, W., Birchler, G. R., & Kelley, M. L. (2006). Learning sobriety together: A randomized clinical trial examining behavioral couples therapy with female alcoholic patients. *Journal of Consulting and Clinical Psychology, 74*, 579–591.

Fals-Stewart, W., Birchler, G. R., & O'Farrell, T. J. (1996). Behavioral couples therapy for male substance-abusing patients: Effects on relationship adjustment and drug-using behavior. *Journal of Consulting and Clinical Psychology, 64*, 959–972.

Fals-Stewart, W., Birchler, G. R., & O'Farrell, T. J. (1999). Drug-abusing patients and their partners: Dyadic adjustment, relationship stability and substance use. *Journal of Abnormal Psychology, 108*, 11–23.

Fals-Stewart, W., Birchler, G. R., & O'Farrell, T. J. (2002, November). *Behavioral couples therapy for drug-abusing men and their intimate partners: Group therapy versus conjoint therapy formats.* In D. C. Atkins (Chair), *Affairs, abuse, drugs, and depression: The promises and pitfalls of couple therapy.* Symposium conducted at the 36th Annual Meeting of the Association for the Advancement of Behavior Therapy, Reno, NV.

Fals-Stewart, W., Kashdan, T. B., O'Farrell, T. J., & Birchler, G. R. (2002). Behavioral couples therapy for drug-abusing patients: Effects on partner violence. *Journal of Substance Abuse Treatment, 22*, 87–96.

Fals-Stewart, W., Logsdon, T., & Birchler, G. R. (2004). Diffusion of an empirically supported treatment for substance abuse: An organization autopsy of technology transfer success and failure. *Clinical Psychology: Science and Practice, 11*, 177–182.

Fals-Stewart, W., & O'Farrell, T. J. (2003). Behavioral family counseling and naltrexone for male opioid-dependent patients. *Journal of Consulting and Clinical Psychology, 71*, 432–442.

Fals-Stewart, W., O'Farrell, T. J., & Birchler, G. R. (1997). Behavioral couples therapy for male substance-abusing patients: A cost outcomes analysis. *Journal of Consulting and Clinical Psychology, 65*, 789–802.

Fals-Stewart, W., O'Farrell, T. J., & Birchler, G. R. (2001). Behavioral couples therapy for male methadone maintenance patients: Effects on drug-using behavior and relationship adjustment. *Behavior Therapy, 32*, 391–411.

Fals-Stewart, W., O'Farrell, T. J., Birchler, G. R., Cordova, J., & Kelley, M. L. (2005). Behavioral couples therapy for alcoholism and drug abuse: Where we've been, where we are, and where we're going. *Journal of Cognitive Psychotherapy, 19*, 231–249.

Fals-Stewart, W., Yates, B., Klostermann, K., O'Farrell, T. J., & Birchler, G. R. (2005). Brief relationship therapy for alcoholism: Clinical and cost outcomes. *Psychology of Addictive Behaviors, 19*, 363–371.

Gottman, J., Notarius, C., Gonso, J., & Markman, H. (1976). *A couple's guide to communication.* Champaign, IL: Research Press.

Keller, M. (Ed.). (1974). Trends in treatment of alcoholism. In *Second special report to the U.S. Congress on alcohol and health* (pp. 145–167). Washington, DC: Department of Health, Education, and Welfare.

Kelley, M. L., & Fals-Stewart, W. (2002). Couples- versus individual-based therapy for alcoholism and drug abuse: Effects on children's psychosocial functioning. *Journal of Consulting and Clinical Psychology, 70*, 417–427.

Liberman, R. P., Wheeler, E. G., deVisser, L. A., Kuehnel, J., & Kuehnel, T. (1980). *Handbook of marital therapy: A positive approach to helping troubled relationships.* New York: Plenum.

Maisto, S. A., O'Farrell, T. J., McKay, J., Connors, G. J., & Pelcovitz, M. A. (1988). Alcoholics' attributions of factors affecting their relapse to drinking and reasons for terminating relapse events. *Addictive Behaviors, 13*, 79–82.

McCrady, B., Stout, R., Noel, N., Abrams, D., & Nelson, H. (1991). Comparative effectiveness of three types of spouse involved alcohol treatment: Outcomes 18 months after treatment. *British Journal of Addiction, 86*, 1415–1424.

Moos, R. H., & Billings, A. G. (1982). Children of alcoholics during the recovery phase: Alcoholic and matched control families. *Addictive Behavior, 7*, 155–163.

Morgan-Lopez, A., & Fals-Stewart, W. (2007). Analytic methods for modeling longitudinal data from rolling therapy groups with membership turnover. *Journal of Consulting and Clinical Psychology, 75*, 580–593.

O'Farrell, T. J., Choquette, K. A., Cutter, H. S. G., & Birchler, G. R. (1997). Sexual satisfaction and dysfunction in marriages of male alcoholics: Comparison with nonalcoholic maritally conflicted and nonconflicted couples. *Journal of Studies on Alcohol, 58*, 91–99.

O'Farrell, T. J., Choquette, K. A., Cutter, H. S. G., Floyd, F. J., Bayog, R. D., Brown, E. D., et al. (1996). Cost-benefit and cost-effectiveness analyses of behavioral marital therapy as an addition to outpatient alcoholism treatment. *Journal of Substance Abuse, 8*, 145–166.

O'Farrell, T. J., & Cutter, H. S. G. (1984). Behavioral marital therapy couples groups for male alcoholics and their wives. *Journal of Substance Abuse Treatment, 1*, 191–204.

O'Farrell, T. J., & Fals-Stewart, W. (2006). *Behavioral couples therapy for alcoholism and drug abuse.* New York: Guilford Press.

O'Farrell, T. J., & Murphy, C. M. (1995). Marital violence before and after alcoholism treatment. *Journal of Consulting and Clinical Psychology, 63*, 256–262.

Sobell, M. B., & Sobell, L. C. (2000). Stepped care as a heuristic approach to the treatment of alcohol problems. *Journal of Consulting and Clinical Psychology, 68*, 573–579.

Turner, J. (1972, October). *Couple and group treatment of marital discord.* Paper presented at the Sixth Annual Meeting of the Association for Advancement of Behavior Therapy, New York.

Winters, J., Fals-Stewart, W., O'Farrell, T. J., Birchler, G. R., & Kelley, M. L. (2002). Behavioral couples therapy for female substance-abusing patients: Effects on substance use and relationship adjustment. *Journal of Consulting and Clinical Psychology, 70*, 344–355.

27

Emotionally Focused Couple Therapy: Creating Loving Relationships

Sue Johnson and Brent Bradley

Emotionally focused therapy for couples (EFT; Johnson, 2004) offers therapists a powerful approach to treatment that is empirically informed on many levels. First, EFT is one of only two empirically supported approaches to couples therapy (Johnson & Lebow, 2000), with a research base that continues to grow. Its focus and goals are consonant with research on the nature of couple distress and satisfaction (Gottman, 1994). EFT is anchored in change process research – a type of research scholars are strongly advocating in addition to empirical outcome studies (Bradley & Johnson, 2005; Johnson, 2003; Sprenkle, 2002; see also Chapter 29, this volume). EFT is based on attachment theory (Johnson, 1986, 2008a), a systematic and well-researched theory of personality development within the context of close relationships. According to attachment theorists, the most basic human need is for safe emotional engagement with precious others on whom we can depend and to whom we are precious (Bowlby, 1969, 1988). Humans have a healthy need for secure emotional connections *first* and *foremost*. Recent research with adults supports the most basic tenets of attachment theory. We've learned, for example, that accepting dependence and being able to reach for others promotes independence and autonomy rather than enmeshment (Feeney, 2007). We've learned that emotional responsiveness, the essence of secure attachment, is the key ingredient in defining couple relationships (Huston, Caughlin, Houts, Smith & George, 2001). Recent neuroscience research utilizing brain imaging is also now able to demonstrate that attachment responses, such as holding the hand of a loved one with whom we have a secure bond, mitigate the human response to stress and threat (Coan, Schaefer, & Davidson, 2006). As Bowlby (1969, 1988) suggested, emotional isolation is inherently traumatizing for humans.

Empirical Studies

EFT is now recognized as both an empirically supported treatment (EST; Baucom, Shoham, Mueser, Daiuto, & Stickle, 1998) and a meta-analytically supported treatment (MAST; Sprenkle, 2002). EFT has also demonstrated efficacy when studied by independent researchers, not only the originators of the approach (Denton, Burleson, Clark, Rodriguez, & Hobbs, 2000). A meta-analysis of the four most rigorous EFT outcome studies yielded a 70% to 73% recovery rate for relationship distress and a 90% significant improvement over controls (Johnson, Hunsley, Greenberg, & Schindler, 1999). Positive changes made in treatment also appear to be stable even in high-risk couples, with little evidence of relapse (Clothier, Manion, Gordon Walker, & Johnson, 2002).

Process research studies exist on both client and therapist behaviors relating to successful change in EFT. Johnson and Greenberg (1988) examined the process of change in EFT sessions by rating clients' performance specific to the partner's depth of experiencing and the quality of interpersonal interactions. They found that high levels of emotional experiencing, the presence of disclosing and affirming interactions, and the creation of powerful enactments where attachment needs and fears were shared were distinctive elements in "best sessions" of successful EFT treatment and predicted recovery from couple distress in EFT.

More recently, Bradley and Furrow (2004) examined *therapist* content themes and interventions utilized in the facilitation of successful change events termed "blamer softening." The EFT softening event is defined as when the more-blaming partner softens and reaches to their now responsive partner for support and reassurance, sharing their attachment needs and fears. Important content themes during softenings are processing fears of reaching to the other, and the negative views of self and other that tend to keep partners stuck and unable to risk reaching for comfort and support.

Diverse Applications

Recent research involves the application of EFT to different populations such as trauma survivors (MacIntosh & Johnson, 2008) and cancer victims (Naaman & Johnson, in press), as well as therapeutic processes such as the creation of forgiveness and the renewal of trust after emotional injurious events (Makinen & Johnson, 2006). EFT is also used with couples suffering from trauma (Johnson, 2002), depression (Dessaulles, Johnson, & Denton, 2003; Whiffen & Johnson, 1998), and chronic illness such as heart disease (Kowal, Johnson, & Lee, 2003). It is used with older (Bradley & Palmer, 2003), and gay couples (Josephson, 2003). The approach has been integrated within feminist (Vatcher & Bogo, 2001) and life-cycle (Dankoski, 2001) perspectives. EFT's collaborative and reassuring stance makes it especially well suited to working within the spiritual beliefs and values of clients (Bradley, 2001). EFT is also used with generally distressed families (EFFT; Johnson, 2004; Johnson et al. 2005) and families with a bulimic child

(Johnson, Maddeaux, & Blouin, 1998). Additionally, an individual modality of EFT has been repeatedly tested, and is now empirically validated (Elliot & Greenberg, 2001).

Attachment Theory

John Bowlby (1969, 1988) taught that the attachment system is an active relational guidance system "from cradle to grave." Similar to the adult–child attachment relationship, the core of the adult–adult attachment relationship is the necessity for emotional accessibility and responsiveness (Hazan & Shaver, 1987). Regardless of age, when an attachment figure is not responding to attachment wants and needs – and is perceived as inaccessible and unresponsive – a set of predictable attachment behaviors is activated. In adult–child and couple relationships these include angry protest, clinging, despair, and last, detachment. Over time, ways of interacting with loved ones when attachment needs arise become patterned; they become "self maintaining patterns of social interaction and emotion regulation strategies" (Shaver & Clarke, 1994, p. 119).

Four attachment styles have been identified: secure, preoccupied or anxious, dismissive, and fearful avoidant (Bartholomew & Horowitz (1991). These information-processing styles are constantly filtering current and meaningful relationship experiences through a grid of: "Am I really lovable – worthy of love and care?" (i.e., view of self); and "Can I count on significant others in times of real emotional distress and need?" (i.e., views of others). Views of self and other are not one-dimensional cognitive schemas. On the contrary, they are immersed in emotion and translate into procedural scripts for how to create relatedness with others. Attachment theory offers the couple therapist a systematic guide to the key emotions, conflicts, and motivational states that define close relationships.

Attachment protest at the loss of safe emotional connection and the use of anxious clinging or defensive dismissal strategies are viewed as the basic scaffolding of relationship distress in EFT. This perspective fits very well with recent research on the nature of relationship distress as elaborated in the work of Gottman and colleagues (Gottman, 1994; Gottman, Coan, Carrere, & Swanson, 1998), and also that of Pasch and Bradbury (1998). This research stresses the power of emotional cues, such as facial expression, to organize key sequences of interactions in close relationships. Generally, positive emotion appears to be the best predictor of couple satisfaction and stability (Gottman et al., 1998). Facial expressions of negative emotion, specifically fear on the face of the husband and angry contempt on the face of the wife, have been found to be powerful predictors of the negative future trajectory of couple relationships (Gottman, 1994). Habitual interactions centered on negative absorbing affect states organize "stuck" patterns of relating in distressed relationships (Gottman, Driver, & Tabares, 2002; Heavey, Christensen, & Malamuth, 1995). These patterns become self-reinforcing, often taking the form of critical pursuit followed by distance and defensiveness. This pattern in particular is a powerful predictor of divorce (Gottman, 1994).

Attachment theorists suggest that sexual behavior connects adult partners as holding connects parent and child (Hazan & Zeifman, 1994). In EFT, negative interactional patterns are understood within an attachment context of separation distress and an insecure bond. In attachment terms, a bond refers to an emotional tie, i.e., a set of attachment behaviors to create and manage physical and emotional proximity to attachment figures. The emotional accessibility and responsiveness of attachment figures are necessary to a feeling of personal security and should then be the ultimate goal of couple therapy, rather than the dampening of conflict or negotiations concerning personal differences. In a secure bond, differences are not inherently threatening and can be accepted and conflict managed. Lasting change is then based on creating new levels of secure emotional engagement that create a corrective emotional experience of connection for the couple.

Emotion

According to Bowlby (1991), the main function of emotion is to communicate our attachment needs, motives, and priorities to ourselves and others. Similarly, in EFT, when emotion is no longer overwhelming or dismissed, but can be accessed, ordered, and integrated, it focuses partners on vital needs and motivates them to heed these calls for action – most often action toward reconciliation and reconnection. Emotions are relational compasses, guiding us to attend to them for personal growth and relational health. Attachment theory and EFT see emotion as essentially adaptive and compelling, as organizing core cognitions and responses to others. Both subscribe to the central belief that *impaired affect regulation is the core issue underlying most constricted responses seen in therapy*. Recent research (Panksepp, 2004) supports Bowlby's understanding that emotional disconnection from an attachment figure elicits a primal panic that has to be regulated effectively in order to formulate needs and send clear signals that can bring a loved one closer.

The Practice of Emotionally Focused Couples Therapy

Rather than list the steps and interventions of EFT or describe this model in detail (Johnson 2004, 2008b; Johnson et al., 2005), we will focus on the three stages of change and present pivotal elements within each. The three stages of change in EFT are: de-escalation of negative cycles and stabilization; creation of new stances and patterns of interaction that foster open responsiveness and more secure bonding; and consolidation and integration.

Stage I: De-escalation of negative cycles and stabilization

The first three sessions of EFT are highly focused on assessment. Key areas of assessment include: gaining an understanding of the couple's interactional cycle, positions taken (who pursues more, who eventually withdraws; who attacks more, who defends); each partner's secondary reactive emotion, such as anger or numbing; and primary underlying *attachment-related* emotion (loneliness, fears of being abandoned or rejected or fears of failing the other, etc.). The therapist works to create an egalitarian, transparent, and empathic alliance with each partner and takes the stance of a process consultant to the couple's relationship.

A case study.   John and Felicia came to couple therapy complaining of "too much fighting" and "too often being in different worlds." In attachment terms, the couple described John as operating mainly from a fearful-avoidant attachment style with Felicia, in which he at times got angry and then "clingy," while other times got angry and removed himself from contact with her for "one or two days." The couple described Felicia in terms of a secure attachment style with John. Both partners agreed she was "the healthy and stable one" of the two, with John declaring, "She is consistently there for me. Stable. I seem to be the one that overreacts and gets us into horrible fights most of the time."
   In session 2 John divulged:

J: I don't know what to do. I love her, but I get hurt so badly too.
T: You obviously love her deeply. And with that comes a deep hurt when things go roughly. *(Validation, Reflecting Underlying Emotions)*
J: Absolutely. (begins to tear up, head goes down) I can only take so much. I want this to work. But sometimes the pain is overwhelming. Love is a bitch man.
T: You really love her. You really care for her. I can see how you begin to tear up just sharing that with me. *(Validation, Reflecting Underlying Emotion; focus on present experiencing)*
J: I really do care for her. I am crazy about her.
T: You really want it to work. It just hurts to badly when you two fight, am I hearing you correctly? *(Validation, Reflecting Underlying Emotion)*

   In session 3, John's anger when Felicia is late arriving home from work (a common point of conflict) was framed as a normal response stemming from attachment anxiety. This attachment protest alerted the therapist to slow down and process John's "real-time" emotional experience, asking evocative questions such as: "What's it like for you when her arrival time passes and she's not there? In the second before the anger overtakes you, what happens inside of you that Felicia does not see?" When a partner often responds from a fearful-avoidant attachment style, it is vitally important to slow the process down and help them to begin to touch their emotions, and make contact with their experience.
   The following vignette exemplifies work focused on John's partner, Felicia, in session 4. The therapist focuses on tracking and helping her experience her inner emotional processing, but the context is always her *relationship* with John.

F: It's terrible. I find myself in that place of hearing his anger and disappointment all of the time. (she gets softer, eyes tear-up) I get caught there. I hate it.
T: It's awful. You say, "I hate it."
(Heightening Emotion and use of First-Person Stance when reflecting)

F: I do. I really do. I just feel defeated, like "Here we go again." (sighs deeply)

T: You sigh deeply as you say that. What's happening inside right now?

(Therapist notes and reflects bodily-felt immediate experience, uses Evocative Responding to continue the emotional processing. This is a good example of the client's emotional processing leading the way.)

F: I am feeling it now. I feel defeated right now.

T: Share with me about feeling defeated . . .

(Note the non-expert stance of the therapist. The attachment-related emotions give the meaning and motivation for movement. The therapist helps the client access and process them.)

The therapist keenly focuses on the cycle and underlying emotions in the ensuing sessions. The couple is asked to notice when the cycle starts to happen outside of session, and to bring that information back to the therapist. More importantly to lasting change, it is the growing experiential awareness of each partner's *own* attachment-related affect *and* that of their spouse's that begins to soften the negative cycle and create the space for a new kind of contact. EFT is a bottom-up therapy – integrating experience as it happens rather than teaching per se, which is more top-down. The therapist often summarizes and validates key emotional experiences and risks taken by each partner before concluding sessions, and this may involve normalizing and reframing couple responses in the context of attachment theory.

As couples increasingly talk in terms of their cycle, and how they are fighting against it, at times defeating it, the tide begins to change in EFT. Couples often show more affection to each other, and begin making love more often. Fights occur less often, and are less intense in duration and tone. Once the couple can effectively de-escalate their negative cycle they can enter Stage II of EFT and begin to create positive cycles of reaching and responsiveness.

Stage II: Creation of new stances and patterns of interaction that foster open responsiveness and more secure bonding

The two change events in Stage II of EFT are withdrawer re-engagement and blamer softening.

Withdrawer re-engagement process.   The therapist explores the internal drama that is expressed by Felicia's distancing and helps her shape her emotional reality into a coherent whole that can then be deeply felt and congruently expressed to John. The therapist provides safety, helping Felicia engage with difficult emotions and helping John tolerate and process them without lapsing into negative responses. As attachment emotions become more explicit, the meanings and needs they reflect become clear (Bradley & Johnson, 2004).

F: I just get so overwhelmed when he gets angry at me. I get so tense, like we've said before.

T: You get tense when you hear his anger. It's just overwhelming.

F: There's nothing for me to do. It always leads to us being apart. I can't stop the train. You know?

T: Hmm. It's like this big train, right? This big train that has one direction and one track, and that track leads only to loneliness, to being apart from each other . . . to not understanding each other.

(Therapist goes with the client's metaphor, heightening the attachment affect of loneliness)

F: That train just leads to pain. Me alone in my pain.

T: Yeah, it's really painful for you. Not only that, it's painful and lonely. A powerful combination.

(Heightening)

F: (Head down, tearing up)

T: What's happening for you now, Felicia? What's it like to find yourself in this painful, lonely place over and over again? What's it like to be a wife in this situation?

(Evocative Responding; helping Felicia feel the impact of being in her current situation)

F: It feels hopeless. (cries harder) How did this happen to us? Where did I go wrong?

T: You go to a place that says, "How in the world did we get here, to this painful place? What did I do?" Tell me more.

(Reflecting Underlying Emotion; Evocative Responding)

F: I don't know. I seem to vacillate between blaming myself and then blaming him. On one hand, I think he's being unreasonable, and that's his own stuff!! On the other hand, I think there must be something I am doing to upset him so. Why can't I stop? Will this pain and distance between us ever go away? (cries again)

T: There's a part of you that blames him. That says he is just caught up in his own baggage. (she nods) And then there's this other part that says, "Hey, what am I doing so wrong here? Why do I upset him so?"

(Reflecting, Heightening. The therapist uses "parts" language" to further refine and understand her emotional experience. Therapist also speaks from a "first-person" stance, which serves to heighten.)

F: Yes. And I think that if I upset him so then maybe I am not the right person for him. Maybe I just can't do things correctly enough for him.

T: Help me; is that a scary place to be?

(Therapist uses empathic conjecture to help aid the client in taking one step forward in her experience.)

F: Oh yes it is. It's really scary. That's when I get so afraid that I shut it off. I don't want to go down that road!

T: You say, "Don't go down that road. It's too scary!" Help me, but, I wonder if a part of you says, "If I go down that road and I am right, we might not make it." And that's just too scary to handle. Is that somewhat close?

(Heightening; Empathic Conjecture/Interpretation. Note again how the therapist uses "parts" language and takes a "first-person" stance when reflecting. This is very effective in heightening experience.)

F: (Cries more) Yes. That's right. I don't want to lose him. I don't want to lose "us." I love him. I love "us."

T: It's like you're saying, "I love John. I love John and me. I don't want to lose us." Right? (she nods) But there is this other voice, this other part, help me out here, but this other part says something like, "I can't stand being stuck in this pain, and being alone in this pain. It hurts too much! I begin to feel hopeless." *(Heightening)*

F: Yes. He's got to come off his anger. I can't live being trapped like an animal just out of the blue. I can't live with that fear. I can't live feeling alone and hopeless.

(Felicia is now clear that she can no longer live with the status quo. She is no longer withdrawn.)

T: This anger is too much for you. It paralyses you . . . leaves you confused, alone. Could you begin to tell him directly about this fear now? Could you please let him in just a bit now, in your own words?

(Restructuring Interactions; Therapist has engaging withdrawer begin to share fears directly with her partner.)

As this process continues the EFT therapist moves to the other partner's response. "John, did you know that Felicia gets trapped in your anger, and that she feels hopeless and alone? What's it like for you right now to hear how she wants desperately to be close with you, and yet ends up so afraid . . . so far removed from you. What happens inside as you see this?" These are powerful sessions for each partner, as often neither partner has heard or shared their attachment fears, needs, and wants in such authentic fashion.

The next step with the engaging withdrawer often comes quite naturally for the couple. The specific attachment-anchored processing itself moves the engaging withdrawer to clearly realize and ask for their attachment needs and wants. With Felicia this unfolded as follows:

F: (to therapist) I need him to be more gentle with me. More understanding. I need him to take responsibility for blaming me, and getting angry at me. It makes me feel like I am crazy or something. I can't take it anymore. I know I am to blame for things too, and I am ready to step up and take responsibility for the things that I do that drive him nuts too. But I can't take the blame and anger at this level anymore. These fights kill me. They just wear me out. Exhaust me. Like I feel now!!!! (laughs)

T: Let me be sure I heard you correctly, because I think this is very important for both of you. You're saying that you just can't take the fighting, and separation, and hopelessness that ensues anymore. That's a scary place for you. But you went there just now. And what came out of that it seemed to me was this honest *yearning* for a better way for the two of you. You need him to be more gentle with you, and to work on these things with you. Is that close?

(Therapist uses Empathic Conjecture/Interpretation informed by attachment theory to help Felicia take one step further into her experience.)

F: (crying again) Yes. Yes that's it. I need a gentle companion. A lover. A sup-
     porter – not someone who I am battling with. (Looks directly at John) I don't
     want to do battle with you anymore.

J: I don't either. I am sorry. I don't know what's wrong with me.

*(John clearly indicates that he will respond positively to Felicia's attachment needs and
wants. But he starts to go into his own negative view of self. The therapist wants to
keep the current focus on Felicia and her attachment processing.)*

T: Felicia, it's really good what you are doing. You are being very clear about what
     you really need from John to be safe and loving in this relationship. Would you
     please, right now, turn and share this directly with John? I think he wants to
     hear from you directly, and that he is ready. Can you open up directly with him
     now about your fears and desires please? *(Validation, Restructuring Interactions)*

In EFT it is vital that Felicia *directly asks John* for her own attachment needs to be
heard and cherished. The therapist helps the couple navigate through this process. The
withdrawer engagement process with each partner has been delineated in greater detail
elsewhere (Johnson et al., 2005), but it involves a similar pattern of inner and between
work to that presented here.

Blamer-softening process.   The blamer-softening process has been delineated into content
themes and distinct interventions in a process research study (Bradley & Furrow, 2004,
2007). It seems clear that the therapist needs to fully process the more-blaming partner's
fears and anxieties associated with reaching to the other for attachment needs to be met.
These fears are centered on negative views of the other as unavailable or unloving, and
negative views of self as unlovable, unworthy, and/or full of shame. In some of the cases
studied there the therapist processed fears associated with both – negative views of self
and negative views of other. These findings align with attachment theory's emphasis on
internal working models, and the fears that block bids for attachment (Bowlby, 1988).
More in-session time was usually spent in the "fears of reaching" category, in fact, than
in all the other categories combined.

Key moments in John's softening process follow:

- John let himself deeply feel the "sinking emptiness" when he and Felicia were emotionally separated and feuding.
- John described these times as "life threatening," adding "I get so afraid and so
  panicked that I actually think that I may come out of the bedroom and she will be
  gone. She will have left me."
- Felicia did not believe this at first. "You really feel like that?" she said to John. "I find
  that so hard to believe. I just had NO idea. You really go through this kind of pain?"
  (The therapist helped Felicia make sense of John's emerging emotional awareness of
  the depth of his fears of losing her, and his ensuing panic.)
- The therapist also helped both partners process John's negative views of self, which
  manifested typically as, "I wouldn't blame her if she did leave. I am a worthless piece
  of rubbish anyway. Just look at me. Who could love me?"

- Finally, the therapist helped John reach to his partner while experiencing his despair, all the while boldly seeking her love and reassurance. John's "softening reach" was: "Honey, I know that I've put us through hell. I know that my upbringing is screwed up in comparison to yours. I guess I just need your help in reassuring me that I am OK, and that you really want me. That you really do love me. And that you aren't leaving."

The nature of the transforming emotional connection between partners that occurs in these change events, a connection that predicts recovery from distress at the end of treatment, is perhaps more understandable in light of recent findings in neuroscience, specifically the work on mirror neurons (Gallese, 2001) and the cuddle hormone oxytocin (Carter, 1998; Uvnas-Moberg, 1998), and writings on the concept of inter-subjectivity (Stern, 2004; Trevarthen, 1980). In brief, mirror neurons fire when we are emotionally engaged and watching another's actions, allowing us to feel within our bodies the actions of the other. This appears to be the basis of empathic responsiveness. It has been noted in forgiveness studies in EFT that showing non-verbal signs that an offending partner can feel an injured partner's pain, a felt sense that the pain of the injured one "hurts" the other, is key to effective apologies. When monogamous mammals move into close connection with a mate, there is evidence that oxytocin is released in the brain, resulting in a state of calm contentment and joy. Oxytocin is also released at orgasm and at times such as when a mother is breastfeeding a child. This research seems to explain the emotional power, the "high," of key moments of connection and the power such moments seem to have to redefine a relationship. Finally, the concept of intersubjectivity captures the moments of exquisite coordination, of synchrony in pacing, intention, and emotional state, that are observed between emotionally engaged attached individuals, whether lovers or mother and child.

All of this new research and conceptualization has great implications for the couple therapist. It implies that "mental life is co-created" (Stern, 2004, p. 77), and that lovers are the hidden regulators of each other's physiology. The EFT therapist attempts in key change events to create a new neural duet (Goleman, 2006) that restructures the inner emotional experience of connection, and the steps in the interpersonal dance.

Stage III: Consolidation/integration

The goals of Stage III include aiding the couple in finding new solutions to old problems, and consolidating new positive interactional cycles and the new positions each partner has taken in the relationship. Past arguments that would send the couple into panic, such as extended work hours, money, extended family visits, house duties, and so forth, may still bring disagreements or have relapses, but now the couple is able to stand together on relationally safe ground to face these and other challenges hand in hand. In this stage the therapists helps them stay connected and on track as they walk through these issues that were once minefields. Some key issues for John and Felicia were:

- Felicia had wanted John to finish staining the deck for over a year. While she had continued doing more than her share of the housework, he had not done the deck, which was the agreement they had. Felicia was able to share with John how this made her feel unappreciated and a bit used.
- John was able to hear Felicia's vulnerability now, and he responded in kind, "The last thing I want is for you feel unappreciated and used. Before I just heard you nagging and indirectly calling me unfit or unworthy. I will start on that deck this weekend. It will be done, I promise." The deck was completed that weekend – although it took John a full 12 hours and 2 days!

The therapist helps the couple further consolidate the newly acquired and still-forming secure base between them by reflecting and summarizing the couple's journey. This helps cement a coherent narrative of their relationship transformation that empowers partners on the basis of their own emotional bonding experiences in and out of therapy.

EFT offers the couple therapist a clear conceptualization of couple relationships that fits with recent research on couple distress, adult attachment, and neuroscience. The targets of the change process are clear, and the process of intervention has been delineated, manualized, and tested. EFT is increasingly being applied to many different couple populations and DSM diagnoses. The repair of adult intimate relationships is no longer a mystery, but an increasingly lit road where the couple therapist can guide and support couples in their struggle for a more secure bond.

Resources

Professionals offer EFT training around North America and the world. There is an EFT training/certification process for those wanting to become more proficient in the approach. The first step in this advanced training in EFT is a 30-hour, 4-day externship. Certification in EFT is not necessary to use the approach, however.

The following are helpful websites that provide many services for those seeking to better learn EFT. These sites are kept updated to note upcoming presentations, supervision opportunities, 1-day workshops, 30-hour training externships, core skills 2-day trainings, listserves, helpful video-clips, and more. Please see www.eft.ca and www.theeftzone.com.

Hold me tight (Johnson, 2008a) is a new book for couples themselves to read. Therapists are also using this book with their couples. See www.holdmetight.net.

References

Bartholomew, K., & Howowitz, L. M. (1991). Attachment styles among young adults: A test of a four-category model. *Journal of Personality and Social Psychology, 61,* 226–244.

Baucom, D., Shoham, V., Mueser, K., Daiuto, A., & Stickle, T. (1998). Empirically supported couple and family interventions for marital distress and mental health problems. *Journal of Consulting and Clinical Psychology, 66,* 53–88.

Bowlby, J. (1969). *Attachment and loss: Vol. 1. Attachment.* New York. Basic Books.

Bowlby, J. (1988). *A secure base.* New York, Basic Books.

Bowlby, J. (1991). Postscript. In C. M. Parkes, J. Stevenson, R. Hinde, & P. Morris (Eds.), *Attachment across the life cycle* (pp. 293–297). London: Routledge.

Bradley, B., & Furrow, J. L. (2004). Toward a mini-theory of the blamer softening event: Tracking the moment by moment process. *Journal of Marital and Family Therapy, 30,* 233–246.

Bradley, B., & Furrow, J. L. (2007). Inside blamer softening: Maps and missteps. *Journal of Systemic Therapies, 26,* 25–43.

Bradley, B., & Johnson, S. M. (2004). Emotionally focused couples therapy: An integrative contemporary approach. In M. Haraway (Ed.), *Handbook of couple therapy* (pp. 179–193). New York: Wiley.

Bradley, B., & Johnson, S. M. (2005). Task analysis of couple and family change events. In D. Sprenkle & F. Piercy (Eds.), *Research methods in family therapy* (2nd ed., pp. 254–271). New York, Guilford Press.

Bradley, B. A. (2001). An intimate look into emotionally focused therapy: An interview with Susan M. Johnson. *Marriage and Family: A Christian Journal, 4,* 117–124.

Bradley, M. J., & Palmer, G. (2003). Attachment in later life: Implications for intervention with older adults. In S. M. Johnson & V. Whiffen (Eds.), *Attachment processes in couple and family therapy* (pp. 281–299). New York: Guilford Press.

Carter, S. (1998). Neuroendocrine perspectives on social attachment and love. *Psychoendocrinology, 23,* 779–818.

Clothier, P. F., Manion, I., Gordon Walker, J., & Johnson, S. M. (2002). Emotionally focused interventions for couples with chronically ill children: A two year follow-up. *Journal of Marital and Family Therapy, 28,* 391–398.

Coan, J., Schaefer, H., and Davidson, R. (2006). Lending a hand. *Psychological Science, 17,* 1–8.

Dankoski, M. E. (2001). Pulling on the heart strings: An emotionally focused approach to family life cycle transitions. *Journal of Marital and Family Therapy, 27,* 177–187.

Denton, W. H., Burleson, B. R., Clark, T. E., Rodriguez, C. P., & Hobbs, B. V. (2000). A randomized trial of emotion focused therapy for couples in a training clinic. *Journal of Marital and Family Therapy, 26,* 65–78.

Dessaulles, A., Johnson, S. M., & Denton, W. H. (2003). Emotion-focused therapy for couples in the treatment of depression: A pilot study. *American Journal of Family Therapy, 31,* 345–353.

Elliot, R., & Greenberg, L. S. (2001). Process-experiential psychotherapy. In D. J. Cain (Ed.), *Humanistic psychotherapies: Handbook of research and practice* (pp. 279–306). Washington, DC: American Psychological Association.

Feeney, B. C. (2007). The dependency paradox in close relationships: Accepting dependence promotes independence. *Journal of Personality and Social Psychology, 92,* 268–285.

Gallese, V. (2001). The shared manifold hypothesis: From mirror neurons to empathy. *Journal of Consciousness Studies, 8,* 33–50.

Goleman, D. (2006). *Emotional intelligence: The new science of human relationships.* New York: Bantam Press.

Gottman, J. (1994). *What predicts divorce?* Hillsdale, NJ: Erlbaum.

Gottman, J., Coan, J., Carrere, S., & Swanson, C. (1998). Predicting marital happiness and stability from newly wed interactions. *Journal of Marriage and the Family, 60,* 5–22.

Gottman, J. M., Driver, J., & Tabares, A. (2002). Building the sound marital house: An empirically derived couple therapy. In A. S. Gurman & N. S. Jacobson (Eds.), *Clinical handbook of couple therapy* (pp. 373–399). New York: Guilford Press.

Hazan, C., & Shaver, P. (1987). Conceptualizing romantic love as an attachment process. *Journal of Personality and Social Psychology, 52,* 511–524.

Hazan, C., & Zeifman, D. (1994). Sex and the psychological tether. In K. Bartholomew & D. Perlman (Eds.), *Attachment processes in adulthood* (pp. 151–180). London, PA: Jessica Kingsley.

Heavey, C. L., Christensen, A., & Malamuth, N. M. (1995). The longitudinal impact of demand and withdrawal during marital conflict. *Journal of Consulting and Clinical Psychology, 63,* 797–801.

Huston, T. L., Caughlin, J. P., Houts, R. M., Smith, S. E., & George, L. J. (2001). The connubial crucible: Newly-wed years as predictors of delight, distress and divorce. *Journal of Personality and Social Psychology, 80,* 237–252.

Johnson, S. M. (1986). Bonds or bargains: Relationship paradigms and their significance for marital therapy. *Journal of Marital and Family Therapy, 12,* 259–267.

Johnson, S. M. (2002). *Emotionally focused couple therapy with trauma survivors: Strengthening attachment bonds.* New York: Guilford Press.

Johnson, S. M. (2003). The revolution in couple therapy: A practitioner-scientist perspective. *Journal of Marital and Family Therapy, 29,* 365–384.

Johnson, S. M. (2004). *The practice of emotionally focused couples therapy: Creating connection.* New York: Brunner-Routledge.

Johnson, S. M. (2008a). *Hold me tight: Seven conversations for a lifetime of love.* New York: Little, Brown.

Johnson, S. M. (2008b). Attachment and emotionally focused therapy: Perfect partners. In J. Obegi & E. Berant (Eds.), *Clinical applications of adult attachment.* New York: Guilford Press.

Johnson, S. M., Bradley, B., Furrow, J., Lee, A., Palmer, G., Tilley, D., et al. (2005). *Becoming an emotionally focused couples therapist: A workbook.* New York Brunner-Routledge.

Johnson, S. M., & Greenberg, L. S. (1988). Relating process to outcome in marital therapy. *Journal of Marital and Family Therapy, 14,* 175–183.

Johnson, S. M., Hunsley, J., Greenberg, L., & Schindler, D. (1999). Emotionally focused couples therapy: Status and challenges. *Clinical Psychology: Science and Practice, 6,* 67–79.

Johnson, S. M., & Lebow, J. (2000). The "coming of age" of couple therapy: A decade review. *Journal of Marital and Family Therapy, 26,* 23–38.

Johnson, S. M., Maddeaux, C., & Blouin, J. (1998). Emotionally focused family therapy for bulimia: Changing attachment patterns. *Psychotherapy, 35,* 238–247.

Josephson, G. (2003). Using an attachment based intervention with same sex couples. In S. Johnson & V. Whiffen (Eds.), *Attachment processes in couple and family therapy* (pp. 300–320). New York: Guilford Press.

Kowal, J., Johnson, S. M., & Lee, A. (2003). Chronic illness in couples: A case for emotionally focused therapy. *Journal of Marital and Family Therapy, 29,* 299–310.

MacIntosh, H., & Johnson, S. (2008). Emotionally focused therapy for couples and childhood sexual abuse survivors. *Journal of Marital and Family Therapy, 34,* 298–315.

Makinen, J., & Johnson, S. (2006). Resolving attachment injuries in couples using EFT: Steps towards forgiveness and reconciliation. *Journal of Consulting and Clinical Psychology, 74,* 1055–1064.

Naaman, S., & Johnson, S. (in press). The clinical efficacy of emotionally focused therapy on psychological adjustment of couples facing early breast cancer. *Journal of Marital and Family Therapy.*

Panksepp, J. (2004). *Affective neuroscience: The foundations of human and animal emotions.* New York: Oxford University Press.

Pasch, L. A., & Bradbury, T. N. (1998). Social support, conflict and the development of marital discord. *Journal of Consulting & Clinical Psychology, 66,* 219–230.

Shaver, P., & Clarke, C. L. (1994). The psychodynamics of adult romantic attachment. In J. Masling & R. Borstein (Eds.), *Empirical perspectives on object relations theory* (pp. 105–156). Washington, DC: American Psychological Association.

Sprenkle, D. H. (2002). Editor's introduction. In D. H. Sprenkle (Ed.), *Effectiveness research in marriage and family therapy* (pp. 9–25). Alexandria, VA: AAMFT.

Stern, D. (2004). *The present moment in psychotherapy and everyday life.* New York: Norton.

Trevarthen, C. (1980). The foundation of intersubjectivity. In D. Olson (Ed.), *The social foundation of language and thought* (pp. 316–342). New York: Norton.

Uvnas-Moberg, K. (1998). Oxytocin may mediate the benefits of positive social interaction and emotions. *Psychneuroendocrinology, 23,* 819–835.

Vatcher, C. A. & Bogo, M. (2001). The feminist/emotionally focused therapy practice model: An integrated approach for couple therapy. *Journal of Marital and Family Therapy, 27,* 69–84.

Whiffen, V., & Johnson, S. M. (1998). An attachment theory framework for the treatment of childbearing depression. *Clinical Psychology, Science & Practice, 5,* 478–493.

28

Brief Strategic Family Therapy™ for Adolescents with Behavior Problems

Michael S. Robbins, José Szapocznik, and Viviana E. Horigian

Brief strategic family therapy™ (BSFT; Szapocznik, Hervis, & Schwartz, 2003; Szapocznik & Kurtines, 1989) is a systemic treatment that was developed in a program of theory development, clinical practice, and research spanning more than three decades. BSFT combines structural and strategic theory and intervention techniques to address systemic/relational interactions that are associated with behavior problems. The structural components of BSFT draw on the work of Minuchin (Minuchin & Fishman, 1981), and the strategic aspects of BSFT were influenced by Haley (1976) and Madanes (1981).

Evolution of BSFT

BSFT was developed in response to the increased number of Hispanic adolescents in Miami with behavior problems in the early 1970s. To address this problem, the Spanish Family Guidance Center (now Center for Family Studies) was established at the University of Miami, Florida, to serve the Hispanic community. The first goal of the program of clinical research was to develop a culturally appropriate treatment for behavior-problem Cuban youths. We launched a series of studies to examine the values of the Cuban population and identify a culturally acceptable intervention. From these studies, we determined that a family approach was particularly relevant for this population (Szapocznik, Scopetta, Aranalde, & Kurtines, 1978).

In reviewing the extant clinical and research literature, we were impressed by the ground-breaking advances of the work of Salvador Minuchin and colleagues at the Philadelphia Child Guidance Center. The fact that this work was being conducted with inner-city, minority families was particularly relevant to our goal of providing services to the Hispanic population in Miami. It was not long until we determined that a systemic approach to family therapy was particularly well suited for this population (Szapocznik, Scopetta, & King (Hervis), 1978), and structural family therapy (cf. Minuchin & Fishman, 1981) was adopted as the Center's core approach. Structural theory and therapy have provided the foundation for every clinical development and innovation of the Center's work in culturally diverse contexts (Szapocznik, Scopetta, & King (Hervis), 1978; Szapocznik & Williams, 2000). Over time, we systematically integrated treatment methods that are both strategic (i.e., problem-focused and pragmatic) and time-limited (Haley, 1976; Madanes, 1981).

Theoretical Principles

Systems

BSFT is first and foremost a "systems" approach. Families are viewed as whole organisms rather than merely as the composite sum of individuals. This systems view is evident in the following assumptions: (a) the family is comprised of interdependent/interrelated parts; (b) each family member's behavior influences the family and the family influences each of its members; (c) the behaviors of family members can only be understood by examining the family context in which they occur; and (d) interventions must be implemented at the family level to address complex relationships within the family system. Interventions also attend to the social context of the family as well as to the unique characteristics of individual family members.

Structure

BSFT draws most heavily from structural family theory (Minuchin & Fishman, 1981) to provide an organizational framework for explaining patterns of behaviors among family members. In BSFT, structure is defined as the linked behavioral interactions among individual family members that tend to recur and become manifested in stable patterns of interaction among family members. This view of structure assumes that repetitive patterns of interactions occur in any family and are either successful or unsuccessful in achieving the goals of the family or its individual members.

Strategy

The inclusion of strategic principles (Haley, 1976; Madanes, 1981) was influenced by our explicit focus on developing an intervention that was quick and effective in eliminating symptoms. This strategic influence is most notable in the following assumptions:

- Interventions are practical. That is, BSFT interventions are tailored to the unique characteristics of families and their needs, and are sensitive to the abilities of each family member.
- Interventions are problem-focused. A problem-focused approach targets first those patterns of interactions that most directly influence the youth's drug use and problem behaviors.
- Interventions are well planned, meaning that the therapist determines what seem to be the maladaptive interactions, determines which of these are most amenable to change, and establishes a treatment plan to help the family develop more successful patterns of interaction.

The problem-focused aspect of BSFT refers to targeting family interaction patterns that are the most directly relevant to the symptomatic behavior. Although families with behavior-problem youth usually have multiple problems, targeting mainly those patterns of interactions linked to the development and maintenance of the symptomatic behavior contributes to the brevity of the intervention.

Process and relational focus

BSFT is a process and relational focused intervention. At all times the therapist is focused on the family. This process focus is manifested in a present-oriented, "here-and-now" approach in which the therapist facilitates interactions between family members in the session. Early in treatment, these in-session family interactions are useful for entering the family system and diagnosing strengths and weaknesses in family relationships; while later in treatment, these in-session interactions create an opportunity to bring about new relational patterns.

BSFT tracks (elicits and acknowledges) interactions between family members as well as the content that individuals bring to family therapy sessions. Tracking content helps therapists understand what is important to each family member and to tailor interventions to the unique personal characteristics of individual family members. Tracking content, however, is not intended for use in individually based interventions. Content is only used to serve relational goals. For example, obtaining information about history (e.g., a separation between parents and children, the difficulty adjusting to a divorce) or current events outside of the session (e.g., a recent arrest, a parent's loss of job) is used to connect with individuals and to create a motivational context for family members to change their behaviors in the present therapeutic context. Information about individual family members, important events, and key behaviors is strategically highlighted to create a relational focus. For example, as a therapist listens to a parent's anger about their child's behavior, the therapist looks for opportunities to move beyond simply acknowledging the parent's frustration ("I can hear how frustrating this is for you") by highlighting relational aspects that are evident (directly or inferred) in the parents' statements ("This is even more difficult for you because you have so many dreams about what you want your child to become").

Intervention Strategies

Joining individual family members and the family system

Joining occurs at two levels. At the individual level, joining involves establishing a relationship with each participating family member. At the family level, joining involves entering the family to create a new system, the therapeutic system. Joining thus requires sensitivity and the ability to respond to the unique characteristics of individuals as well as the ability to quickly discern and become part of the family's governing processes.

At the individual level, joining involves seeking the opinions of, validating, and respecting each family member. Therapists must balance their connection with individual family members, particularly with family members who are in overt conflict. For example, in prior research on BSFT with Hispanic families (Robbins et al., 2008), we demonstrated that the greater the unbalance in mother and adolescent alliances with therapists, the more risk there is for the family to drop out of treatment. To obtain this balance, therapists must include all family members in treatment, validate one family member's perspective without disagreeing with another, and expand the family's frame to move from negative, conflicted views to highlight positive, appropriate connections.

At the family level, the goal is to form a new system that includes the therapist as both a member and a leader. There are a number of specific techniques that can be used in establishing this therapeutic system, including maintenance, tracking, and mimesis. Maintenance involves supporting the family's structure and entering the system by accepting its rules. Maintenance also involves supporting areas of family strength, rewarding or affiliating with a family member, and supporting an individual member who feels threatened by therapy. Tracking involves adopting the content of family communications or utilizing the nature of family interactions (process) to join with the family. In tracking, the therapist uses the content and process of the session to move the family's process from what it is to what we would like it to be. Mimesis is directed at the family's style and affect, and involves therapist attempts to match the tempo, mood, and style of family member interactions as a way of blending in with the family.

Diagnosis and assessment

Diagnosis refers to identifying those family patterns (structure) that are allowing or encouraging the youth's behavior problems. To derive complex diagnoses of the family, therapists examine family interactions along five interactional dimensions: (1) organization or structure, (2) resonance, (3) developmental stage, (4) identified patienthood, and, (5) conflict resolution (see Table 28.1). Diagnosis is based on what families do in the therapy sessions, not what they report they do at home. Therapists must create a therapeutic context where family members are free to interact in their typical style. These "enactments" permit the therapist to directly observe how the family behaves at home and are critical for accurately identifying the family's characteristic pattern of interaction.

Table 28.1   Family Interaction Domains

Structure	Resonance	Developmental stage	Identified patienthood (IP)	Conflict resolution
Leadership a. Hierarchy b. Behavior control c. Guidance *Subsystem organization* a. Alliances b. Triangulations c. Subsystems *Communication flow* a. Directness b. Gatekeeper c. Switchboard operator d. Spokesperson	*Differentiation* a. Undifferentiated b. Semi-differentiated c. Differentiated *Enmeshment* a. Mind readings b. Personal control c. Joint affective reactions d. Simultaneous speeches e. Interruptions f. Continuations g. Loss of distance *Disengagement* a. Absence of communication b. Absence of affective relating c. Absence of alliances d. Absence of participation	a. Parenting roles and tasks b. Child/sibling roles and tasks c. Extended family roles and tasks	a. Negativity about IP b. IP centrality c. Overprotection of IPhood d. Nurturance of IPhood e. Denial of other problems	a. Denial b. Avoidance c. Diffusion d. Emergence without resolution e. Emergence with resolution

Therapists use the domains noted above to characterize the family's typical manner of relating to one another. The next step is to integrate the information obtained through assessment into larger molar processes that characterize the family's interactions. In BSFT, this process of clinical formulation is necessary to explain the presenting symptom in relationship to the family's characteristic patterns of interaction. A variety of factors influence clinical formulation. Although not included in the assessment, information that can help contextualize family interactions is required for clinical formulation. For example, in assessment the appropriateness of each family member's developmental level is evaluated. Also important to clinical formulation is the chronicity of the patterns encountered and the family's flexibility in adapting to internal or external changes. The more chronic the problem and the more inflexible the family, the greater the level of intervention that will be required to bring about changes in the family system.

Restructuring family interactions

The ultimate goal of treatment is to move the family from their current set of maladaptive interactions to a more effective and adaptive set of interactions. Those interventions aimed at helping the family change maladaptive interactions are called restructuring. In restructuring, therapists orchestrate opportunities for families to interact in new ways by using a range of techniques that fall within three broad categories: (a) working in the present, (b) reframing (creating a context for change), and (c) working with boundaries and alliances.

Working in the present. BSFT focuses on present interactions that are observable. Enactments are a critical feature of BSFT. Enactments are therapist interventions that are intended to encourage, help, and/or allow family members to behave or interact as they would if the therapist were not present. Very frequently, family members will spontaneously behave in their typical way when they fight, interrupt, or criticize one another. However, when families become rigidly focused on speaking to the therapist, the therapist must stimulate an enactment by systematically redirecting communication to encourage interactions between family members. For example, instead of acknowledging a parent's frustration or anger, the therapist may springboard the comment to another family member to get their reaction. In doing so, the therapist explicitly asks the other family member to respond directly to the parent.

Enactments provide therapists with the opportunity to directly restructure family interactions. Specifically, interactions are transformed when the therapist allows family members to interact and then intervenes in the midst of these interactions to facilitate the occurrence or emergence of a different, more positive set of interactions. Two such intervention techniques follow.

Reframing. Reframes give family members the opportunity to perceive their interactions or situation from a different perspective. Reframing serves two functions. First, it is a tool for changing negative and apparently "uncaring" emotions into positive and caring interactions. This is achieved, for example, by redefining anger and frustration as the bonds that tie a family together. The other important function is to create the opportunity for the family to behave in new, more constructive ways. Reframing interventions often transform negative, maladaptive sequences and help the family interact in new, more positive ways.

Working with boundaries and alliances. Boundaries are the social "walls" that exist around groups of people who are allied with one another and that stand between individuals and groups who are not allied with one another. Shifting boundaries refers to changing the patterns of alliance. A common situation of drug-using youth is a strong alliance with only one parent. The resulting alliance may cross generational lines and work against the importance of having differential hierarchy across generations. A frequently occurring interaction pattern in Hispanic families with behavior-problem boys is that there is a strong bond between a youth and one parent figure. Whenever the youth is punished by the other parent figure for inappropriate behavior, the youth may solicit sympathy and support from the allied parent figure to undermine the non-allied parent figure's authority and remove the sanction. Shifting of boundaries involves (a) creating a more solid bond between the parents so they will make executive decisions together, and (b) removing inappropriate parent–child alliances and replacing them with an appropriate alliance between both parents and the youth that meets the youth's needs for support and nurturance.

Treatment Parameters

Treatment population

BSFT has been implemented with a variety of populations. Families are generally of low to moderate income, and the target youth is between 6 and 18 years of age. In studies of younger children, presenting problems have included behavioral disturbances at home or school; in studies of adolescents, presenting problems include conduct problems, delinquent behavior, association with antisocial friends, and alcohol and drug use. Early research on BSFT was conducted at a time when the Hispanic population in Miami was almost exclusively of Cuban origin (e.g., Szapocznik et al., 1989). In more recent studies (e.g., Santisteban et al., 2003; Santisteban, Szapocznik, Perez-Vidal, Kurtines, Murray, & Laperriere, 1996), families have been from more varied Hispanic backgrounds, including Nicaraguans, Colombians, Hondurans, and Puerto Ricans. At present, we are conducting a study that includes an ethnically diverse sample of White/non-Hispanic, Hispanic, and African American adolescents and families representing many regional variations across the USA. Beyond the ongoing randomized clinical trial, our BSFT Training Institute has a history of training and supervising the implementation of BSFT in community agencies across the country with an ethnically and geographically (rural to inner-city) diverse population of adolescents and families.

In conducting work with diverse populations, therapists are challenged to address issues that are culturally relevant to the "local" population. This relevance is not simply defined as sensitivity to client race/ethnicity; for example, therapists in rural settings often encounter challenges that therapists in inner-city contexts do not (and vice versa). Nonetheless, racial/ethnic differences have always been a prominent issue that we have addressed as we implemented BSFT in new populations (both non-Hispanic and Hispanic) across the country. For example, in working with African American families, we have stressed the importance of attending to issues such as racism, rage, disenfranchisement, and cultural mistrust as part of the "content" of sessions. This focus on getting meaningful content "on the table" adds complexity to treatment and makes sessions more relevant to family members. However, this does not require an adaptation or change in the clinical model. Maladaptive patterns of interaction are still defined for each family in a manner that is attuned to whether or not relational sequences are successful in helping a family to achieve its goals. Also, specific strategies for joining and restructuring interactions are not changed; however, these techniques are implemented in a flexible manner to match the variability in individual and family behaviors, attitudes, and beliefs (which may be related to issues of race and ethnicity) that is always present in clinical practice.

Who is seen and in what format

BSFT sessions typically occur once per week for 8–16 weeks. Sessions run 1 to $1^{1}/_{2}$ hours. Treatment often requires ongoing re-engagement efforts to maintain continuity, frequently extending the 8–16 sessions across 6 months. For severe cases, treatment may require more sessions. Also, we do recommend increasing the frequency of sessions during times of crises because these are opportune moments for change. There are also regular phone contacts to re-engage, coach, support, and acknowledge the gains that the family is making in treatment. Early in treatment, we train therapists to have at least 5 contacts per case per week to ensure that at least one session is conducted each week.

Location of treatment

Most of our work with behavior-problem children has occurred in our clinic. However, in our treatment with behavior-problem adolescents and their families, we have often found it necessary to conduct treatment in the family's home. Although some of these youth and their families quickly engage in treatment, it is more common for us to encounter difficulties if we follow standard clinic-based procedure when engaging and treating these families. We do not believe that home-based treatment is absolutely required. However, with more severe cases, given the level of family disruption and chaos that characterizes these families, home-based sessions are often necessary. Our philosophy about home-based versus office-based sessions is that therapists should never allow location of treatment to become an obstacle in treatment delivery.

Training program

The Center for Family Studies at the University of Miami has a dedicated institute for training therapists to provide BSFT. The training program consists of approximately 150 hours of direct contact, including 12 days of face-to-face workshops and weekly group supervision sessions. To date, hundreds of individuals from community agencies (nationally and internationally) have participated in this rigorous training program. The program also includes a model for training supervisors. The supervisor training program is dedicated to building leadership in family therapy services within community agencies and is intended to facilitate the maintenance of high-quality family services beyond the conclusion of the intensive training period.

BSFT Case Example

The Pérez family, mother, stepfather, and 14- and 17-year-old sons, were referred to family therapy from the juvenile justice system following the arrest of the 14-year-old (identified patient, IP) for marijuana possession. The therapist assigned to the case contacted the mother via telephone to schedule a first visit to their home, explaining that the first session should take place at a time when every member of the family could participate. Upon hearing this, Mrs Pérez expressed concern that she would not be able to convince her two sons and her husband to be present. She sounded overwhelmed and frustrated. The therapist explored strategies for presenting "therapy" to her boys and husband. Her anxiety abated and she expressed confidence that she would be successful in getting everyone to the session.

The therapist arrived at the home of the Pérez family and was greeted by Mrs Pérez, who was visibly upset. She explained that her husband was working and would not attend the session, and that her older son had agreed to participate but had not come home yet. The IP was in his room, and according to his mother, he was angry at having to stay home for therapy. The therapist introduced himself to the IP and thanked him for making the effort to attend their first session. The therapist began the joining process by having an open discussion with mother and IP about the reasons that brought the family to therapy and the importance of making sure that everyone was present for all sessions. Working with Mrs Pérez, the therapist explored difference strategies to get her husband and older son into the session. Consistently, she attempted to focus the session on complaints about her son's drug use, association with negative peers, lack of respect, and verbal attacks toward her. IP interrupted his mother frequently, angrily rebutting her complaints and blaming her for being too "naggy" and constantly angry. The therapist joined with the family system by acknowledging mother's concerns and focusing the conversation on the loss that each of them had experienced in their relationship over time. After establishing this theme, the therapist returned to developing strategies to engage the non-attending family members. Clearly frustrated, Mrs Pérez explained that the discipline of her children was her responsibility and that her husband worked too hard to have to come home to family therapy. IP added to her comments by saying that his stepfather was not his father and thus had no place in the conversation. The therapist stressed the importance of having everyone present in the sessions so that they could all work together to improve communication and relationships within the family. The therapist then asked Mrs Pérez for permission to speak to her husband directly, and encouraged her to do everything she could to bring her older son to the following sessions.

The following day, the therapist called Mr Pérez to join with him and attempt to engage him in the family sessions. Mr Pérez was polite and surprisingly talkative. He described his family as "chaotic" due to his wife's inability to control the behavior of her children, especially IP, and said that whenever he had tried to intervene he ended up fighting with everyone. The therapist was able to convince Mr Pérez that he had something to gain by participating in the family sessions, as his involvement was necessary to support his wife in managing the behavior of the boys and thus regain a peaceful family life. He agreed to come to the next session and make sure his older son was also present.

Over the course of the next few family sessions, the therapist gathered the following diagnostic impressions about the Pérez family:

Organization: The family's hierarchy and leadership were problematic, mainly due to lack of collaboration in the parental subsystem. IP triangulated between mother and stepfather and thus held a great deal of power.

Resonance: IP and mother were enmeshed, and the quality of their enmeshment was conflictive and hostile. At the same time, mother and stepfather were disengaged to the point of not being able to support one another, and thus stepfather remained isolated from the rest of the family system.

Developmental stage: Mrs Pérez was overwhelmed by her parental responsibilities, and her frustrated attempts to control her children made her angry and conflictive.

Identified patient: The family system was organized around the IP's problem behaviors. Communications between family members occurred in a negativistic and critical tone and were usually centered on the IP's drug use.

Conflict resolution: Conflicts arose frequently and were never resolved because family members would typically complain about several different things at the same time (diffusion) and/or blame each other until there was no room for agreement or compromise (emergence without resolution).

Having effectively engaged the stepfather and older son in therapy, one of the therapist's first interventions was to bring Mrs and Mr Pérez closer together as parents by creating a dialogue between them about how to support one another as leaders of the family, highlighting their mutual concern for the wellbeing of the boys and the need for Mr Pérez to participate as a parent, even if only in a supportive type of role. Facilitating direct dialogue in the parental subsystem also allowed the therapist to strengthen the boundaries between mother and IP. Feeling supported by her husband, Mrs Pérez was able to begin to regain control as a parent and avoid unproductive arguments with her son. She also began supporting her husband as an authority figure within the family. Next, the therapist intervened to strengthen the sibling subsystem by fostering an alliance between the IP and his older brother, which also helped to reduce the over-involved relationship between IP and mother. Lastly, the therapist coached the mother and stepfather to agree upon rules and consequences for the IP's behavior, encouraging negotiation of such rules with the IP when appropriate. In parallel to this, the therapist helped the family acquire new conflict-resolution skills by highlighting attempts by family members to diffuse and avoid conflict, coaching them to direct their focus to the task at hand without losing sight of agreed-upon goals. Ultimately, Mr and Mrs Pérez were able to work together to set consistent, reasonable limits to the IP, whose behavior improved in response to a more balanced and supportive family structure.

Research Findings

The evolution of BSFT and the development of our research program were deeply intertwined. From our earliest studies, we have maintained a consistent focus on refining the model through a rigorous program of research. Our research studies have thus not only tested aspects of the efficacy and effectiveness of BSFT, but also been critical for identifying what intervention strategies work or do not work; which, in turn, has led to the modification of unsuccessful strategies and the integration of successful strategies into the clinical model.

As noted, the first challenge we encountered was to identify and develop a culturally appropriate and acceptable treatment intervention for Cuban adolescents with behavior problems. Our initial clinical work with drug-using adolescents in Miami revealed that failure to include families in treatment led to failure to retain the youth in treatment (Szapocznik, Scopetta, & King (Hervis), 1978) and that therapists that adopted an active, directive, present-oriented leadership role that attended to family hierarchy matched the values and expectations of the population (Szapocznik, Scopetta, Arnalde, et al., 1978).

From our earliest work with Cuban youth and their families to our extensive work with Central and South American families, it became evident that the youths and parents had become adversaries around a struggle that was culturally flavored: Americanism vs. Hispanicism (Szapocznik, Kurtines, & Hanna, 1979). We suggested that the youths' problem behaviors needed to be examined in the context of immigrant Hispanic families that had been immersed in mainstream culture (Szapocznik, Scopetta, Arnalde, et al., 1978; Szapocznik, Scopetta, & King (Hervis), 1978). Our focus was consistent with a movement within psychology that suggests that behavior is best understood in the social and cultural context in which it occurs (Bronfenbrenner, 1986). We thus became interested both in the family as the immediate social context of the youth, and in the cultural streams which were differentially affecting the youths and their parents (Szapocznik & Kurtines, 1993).

Although the majority of families successfully manage in bicultural contexts, many families experience conflict as normal developmental family processes, such as an adolescent becoming more independent, clash with parents maintaining a strong and central focus on the family. This clash often occurs when there are intergenerational differences in the acculturation process. For a Hispanic immigrant family in a bicultural context, two interdependent processes converged to create acculturative conflict: the adolescent's normal striving for independence combined with the adolescent's powerful acculturation to the American cultural value of individualism (cf. Szapocznik, Santisteban, et al., 1986), on the one hand; and the parent's normal tendency to preserve family integrity and adherence to the Hispanic traditional cultural value of strong family cohesion and parental control, on the other. The additive effects of intergenerational (adolescent seeks autonomy; parent(s) seek(s) family integrity) and cultural differences (American individualism; Hispanic parental control) produce an exacerbated and intensified intrafamilial conflict in which parents and adolescents feel alienated from each other.

In our early clinical experience, we found that a family approach that integrated these intrafamilial themes was particularly effective with Hispanic families (Scopetta et al., 1977). Additionally, we demonstrated that family psychoeducational interventions rich with cultural content that utilized strategic methods (i.e., shifting blame to cultural conflict) to achieve structural goals could produce results as strong as family therapy (Szapocznik, Santisteban, et al., 1986).

Research evidence

We have documented the efficacy of BSFT with children and adolescents with behavior problems, including reductions in conduct problems, association with antisocial peers, and drug use, and improvements in family functioning. In a study with 6- to 11-year-old boys with disruptive behavior problems (Szapocznik et al., 1989), we compared the efficacy of BSFT to an individual psychodynamic child-centered psychotherapy, and a recreational control condition. The results of this study revealed several important findings. First, the recreational control condition was significantly less effective in retaining cases than the two treatment conditions, with over two thirds of all dropouts occurring in the control condition. Second, both BSFT and individual psychodynamic child therapy were more effective than the recreational control group in reducing behavior problems as well as improving child psychodynamic functioning, and no significant differences between the two intervention groups were observed on these variables. Third, BSFT was significantly more effective than individual child psychodynamic therapy in protecting family functioning at the 1-year follow-up. In particular, in the individual psychodynamic child therapy condition, a significant deterioration of family functioning was observed at the 1-year post-termination follow-up. In contrast, a significant improvement in family functioning at the 1-year follow-up was observed in BSFT.

In another study with Hispanic adolescents (13 and 17 years old) with externalizing problems (e.g., violent or disruptive behavior, drug use, trouble with the law), we examined the efficacy of BSFT versus a group therapy control condition (Santisteban et al., 2003). Results indicated that adolescents in the BSFT condition showed significantly greater reductions in measures of conduct disorder, delinquency in the company of peers, and marijuana use than youth in the group control condition. An analysis of clinically significant change indicated that a substantially and significantly larger proportion of BSFT than group cases demonstrated clinically significant improvement. Also, analyses of changes in family functioning showed that BSFT was more effective than group therapy in improving family functioning for families that entered the study with poor family functioning, and protecting family functioning for families that entered with good family functioning.

BSFT with specialized engagement strategies

Engaging adolescents and their families in treatment has been a challenge for the drug treatment field. To address this challenge, BSFT has developed, evaluated, and integrated specific engagement and retention strategies. In separate studies, the effectiveness of specialized BSFT engagement strategies has been demonstrated.

Our early work in this area focused extensively on developing strategies for working with one family member to engage other family members in treatment and facilitate improvements in family interaction. Our work with one-person family interventions (Szapocznik, Kurtines, Perez-Vidal, Hervis, & Foote, 1990) capitalized on the systemic concept of complementarity, which suggests that when one family member changes, the rest of the system responds by either restoring the family process to its old ways or adapting to the new changes (Minuchin & Fishman, 1981). As in family therapy, family patterns remain the focus of treatment, not the individual family member. The goal is to facilitate changes by addressing those family interactions that include the individual family member. These changes often create a family crisis as the family attempts to return to its old ways. We use the opportunity created by crises to engage reluctant family members. In a clinical trial study with Hispanic families with a drug-abusing adolescent, we demonstrated that our one-person family approach was as potent as conjoint therapy in facilitating improvements in family functioning and reducing adolescent drug use (Szapocznik, Kurtines, Foote, Perez-Vidal, & Hervis, 1983, 1986).

Building on the success of these early studies, we developed a more sophisticated tool for engaging and retaining adolescents and family members in treatment. These engagement interventions were heavily influenced by the theoretical principles of our one-person approach, in which conceptualized "resistance" to participation was viewed in family relational terms rather than individual terms. In a series of studies, we evaluated the efficacy of these engagement strategies.

The first study (Szapocznik et al., 1988) compared the efficacy of BSFT with specialized engagement strategies to BSFT with engagement-as-usual strategies in a sample of drug-using Hispanic youth (ages 12–21). With successful engagement defined as completion of an intake appointment, 92.9% of families in the BSFT specialized engagement condition were successfully engaged, as compared to 42.3% of the families in the engagement-as-usual condition. Continuing to use the same specialized engagement strategies to retain cases in treatment in the experimental conditions, 77% of families in the BSFT specialized engagement condition successfully completed a full dose of therapy (approximately 8 sessions), compared to 25% of families in the engagement-as-usual condition. Santisteban and colleagues (1996) replicated and extended the findings of the initial engagement study, by including a more stringent criteria for successful engagement (i.e., intake assessment plus first therapy session), a second control group (group treatment with engagement as usual), and a more culturally diverse sample (i.e., a larger percentage of non-Cuban Hispanics), and Coatsworth, Santisteban, McBride, & Szapocznik (2001) established the superiority of these engagement techniques to a community control condition.

Ongoing research on BSFT

Currently, we are conducting a multisite randomized controlled clinical trial to examine the effectiveness of BSFT compared to treatment as usual in reducing adolescent drug use, conduct problems, and sexually risky behavior, and in improving family functioning. This study, launched within the U.S. National Institute on Drug Abuse-funded National Drug Abuse Treatment Clinical Trials Network, is being conducted at eight community agencies located across the USA with 480 drug-using adolescents and their families (a total of over 2,000 adolescents and family members).

Conclusion

BSFT is a structural and strategic approach that has evolved through a continuous interplay between clinical theory, clinical practice, and research. The theoretical underpinnings and interventions strategies of BSFT share much with other structural and strategic family approaches. However, BSFT is unique in its specificity in addressing relationships that are particularly relevant for adolescents with behavior problems. The efficacy of this approach has been established in numerous research studies, and at present, a major emphasis of work in BSFT is on training community practitioners and evaluating the effectiveness of BSFT in real-world settings.

Notes

This work was supported by the National Institute on Drug Abuse (Grant No. U10-DA13720, José Szapocznik, Principal Investigator).

BSFT is pending approval for trademark.

References

Bronfenbrenner, U. (1986). Ecology of the family as a context for human development: Research perspectives. *Developmental Psychology, 22,* 723–742.

Coatsworth, J. D., Santisteban, D. A., McBride, C. K., & Szapocznik, J. (2001). Brief strategic family therapy versus community control: Engagement, retention, and an exploration of the moderating role of adolescent symptom severity. *Family Process, 40,* 313–332.

Haley, J. (1976). *Problem solving therapy.* San Francisco: Jossey-Bass.

Madanes, C. (1981). *Strategic family therapy.* San Francisco: Jossey-Bass.

Minuchin, S., & Fishman, H. C. (1981). *Family therapy techniques.* Cambridge, MA: Harvard University Press.

Robbins, M. S., Turner, C. W., Mayorga, C. C., Alexander, J. F., Mitrani, V. B., & Szapocznik, J. (2008). Adolescent and parent alliances with therapists in brief strategic family therapy with drug using Hispanic adolescents. *Journal of Marital and Family Therapy, 34,* 316–328.

Santisteban, D., Coatsworth, J. D., Perez-Vidal, A., Kurtines, W. M., Schwartz, S. J., LaPerriere, A., et al. (2003). The efficacy of brief strategic family therapy in modifying Hispanic adolescent behavior problems and substance use. *Journal of Family Psychology, 17,* 121–133.

Santisteban, D. A., Szapocznik, J., Perez-Vidal, A., Kurtines, W. M., Murray, E. J., & Laperriere, A. (1996). Efficacy of intervention for engaging youth and families into treatment and some variables that may contribute to differential effectiveness. *Journal of Family Psychology, 10,* 35–44.

Scopetta, M. A., Szapocznik, J., King (Hervis), O. E., Ladner, R., Alegre, C., & Tillman, W. S. (1977). The Spanish drug rehabilitation research project: Final report to NIDA Grant No. H81 DA 01696-03. Miami, FL: University of Miami.

Szapocznik, J., Hervis, O. E., & Schwartz, S. (2003). *Brief strategic family therapy manual* [NIDA *Therapy manuals for drug addiction* Series]. Rockville, MD: National Institute on Drug Abuse.

Szapocznik, J., & Kurtines, W. (1989). *Breakthroughs in family therapy with drug abusing problem youth.* New York: Springer.

Szapocznik, J., & Kurtines, W. M. (1993). Family psychology and cultural diversity: Opportunities for theory, research, and application. *American Psychologist, 48(4),* 400–407.

Szapocznik, J., Kurtines, W. M., & Hanna, N. (1979). Comparison of Cuban and Anglo-American cultural values in a clinical population. *Journal of Consulting and Clinical Psychology, 47,* 623–624.

Szapocznik, J., Kurtines, W. M., Foote, F., Perez-Vidal, A., & Hervis, O. E. (1983). Conjoint versus one-person family therapy: Some evidence for effectiveness of conducting family therapy through one person. *Journal of Consulting and Clinical Psychology, 51,* 889–899.

Szapocznik, J., Kurtines, W. M., Foote, F., Perez-Vidal, A., & Hervis, O. E. (1986). Conjoint versus one-person family therapy: Further evidence for the effectiveness of conducting family therapy through one person with drug-abusing adolescents. *Journal of Consulting and Clinical Psychology, 54,* 395–397.

Szapocznik, J., Kurtines, W. M., Perez-Vidal, A., Hervis, O. E., & Foote, F. (1990). One-person family therapy. In R. A. Wells & V. J. Giannetti (Eds.), *Handbook of the brief psychotherapies* (pp. 493–510). New York: Plenum.

Szapocznik, J., Perez-Vidal, A., Brickman, A., Foote, F. H., Santisteban, D. A., Hervis, O. E., et al. (1988). Engaging adolescent drug abusers and their families into treatment: A strategic structural systems approach. *Journal of Consulting and Clinical Psychology, 56,* 552–557.

Szapocznik, J., Rio, A. T., Murray, E., Cohen, R., Scopetta, M. A., Rivas-Vasquez, A., et al. (1989). Structural family versus psychodynamic child therapy for problematic Hispanic boys. *Journal of Consulting and Clinical Psychology, 57,* 571–578.

Szapocznik, J., Santisteban, D., Rio, A., Perez-Vidal, A., & Kurtines, W. M. (1986). Family effectiveness training for Hispanic families: Strategic structural systems intervention for the prevention of drug abuse. In H. P. Lefley & P. B. Pedersen (Eds.), *Cross cultural training for mental health professionals.* Springfield, IL: Charles C. Thomas.

Szapocznik, J., Scopetta, M., Arnalde, M., & Kurtines, W. (1978). Cuban value structure: Treatment implications. *Journal of Consulting and Clinical Psychology, 46,* 961–970.

Szapocznik, J., Scopetta, M. A., & King (Hervis), O. E. (1978). Theory and practice in matching treatment to the special characteristics and problems of Cuban immigrants. *Journal of Community Psychology, 6,* 112–122.

Szapocznik, J., & Williams, R. A. (2000). Brief strategic family therapy: Twenty-five years of interplay among theory, research and practice in adolescent behavior problems and drug abuse. *Clinical Child and Family Psychology Review, 3,* 117–134.

29

Empirically Informed Systemic Psychotherapy: Tracking Client Change and Therapist Behavior During Therapy

William M. Pinsof and Anthony L. Chambers

An empirical imperative confronts psychotherapeutic practice which asserts that it must be informed and guided by empirical or scientific information. The American Psychological Association has interpreted this imperative to mean that therapists should practice empirically validated treatments – manualized treatments that have been shown, in randomized clinical trials, to be statistically more effective than no treatment or treatment as usual. As this volume testifies, family psychology has responded to this imperative with a growing number of empirically validated treatments.

Client-focused research

A number of individual therapy researchers (Barkham et al., 2001; Howard, Moras, Brill, Martinovich, & Lutz, 1996; Lambert, Hansen, & Finch, 2001) have developed another strategy for addressing this imperative – client-focused or progress research. It provides therapeutic stakeholders (e.g., therapists, supervisors, care managers, and clients) with scientific information about client change throughout therapy. Among this approach's many benefits (i.e., risk and outcomes management, quality assurance, etc.), the use of scientific information to influence clinical decision-making during therapy remains primary.

The psychotherapies have been characterized by a yawning gap between research and practice, particularly family therapy. Family therapists have been slow to integrate scientific data into practice. Beyond "normal" therapist resistance to research, family therapists have been hampered by a misguided epistemological notion that using quantitative data is incompatible with a systemic perspective. Scientific data have been incorrectly viewed as reductionistic, separating the parts from the whole. We view quantitative data as just another source of information that minimizes the likelihood of our lying to each other. In this sense, they are not at all incompatible with a systemic perspective (Pinsof & Lebow, 2005).

Empirically informed therapy

Empirically informed therapy bridges research and practice. It provides therapists with ongoing quantitative information that illuminates and enriches practice. It provides critical information in real time about specific clients and their therapy that can influence the subsequent behavior of the therapist and the course of therapy.

Psychotherapy and particularly family therapy have struggled with the "medical model." The reality is that psychotherapeutic practice and medical practice are kin, empirically grounded clinical arts that work with the same principles of human problem solving. Medical practice has been progressively informed by the two empirical traditions articulated above. Intervention choice is guided by knowledge about empirically validated drugs and procedures. Subsequently, utilization of drugs and procedures is guided by scientific data (blood tests, radiography, etc.) that are sought at critical points to inform decision-making throughout treatment. As psychotherapeutic practice matures, the artful integration of these two empirical traditions becomes the new imperative.

Research on empirically informed treatment has occurred exclusively within individual psychotherapy. Systems for tracking and feeding back client data have been developed and are being increasingly utilized. However, family therapy and family psychology have yet to develop systems for tracking and feeding back information about client change. Furthermore, family psychologists and therapists have not brought a systemic perspective to the individual therapy change process (Pinsof & Wynne, 2000).

The Psychotherapy Change Project

In the mid-1990s the Psychotherapy Change Project at the Family Institute at Northwestern University was created to study change in family, couple, and individual therapy from a multisystemic and multidimensional perspective.[1] The project had five objectives: (1) to develop a system for quantitatively tracking client change in family, couple, and individual therapy from a multisystemic and multidimensional perspective; (2) to create a user-friendly internet system for feeding back client change information throughout treatment to therapeutic stakeholders; (3) to develop a system for tracking in-session therapist behaviors and client responses during therapy from an integrative and generic perspective that transcends, yet still differentiates, strategies and techniques from specific schools of therapy; (4) to create an internet system to provide therapists and supervisors with feedback about therapist behavior and key therapeutic processes throughout therapy; and (5) to link the two feedback systems to simultaneously provide client change and therapist–client session behavior information.

The first three objectives have been addressed to date. The Systemic Inventory of Change (STIC®) was developed to quantitatively delineate the process of client change from a multisystemic and multidimensional perspective. The methodological properties of the STIC have begun to be explored (Pinsof et al., in press). An on-demand internet feedback system has been developed (sticfeedback.com) that provides client change information to therapists (and others) over the course of therapy. This system is being used by therapists and supervisors at the Family Institute and partner institutions. The Integrative Therapy Session Report (ITSR) has been developed to quantitatively delineate in-session therapist behaviors and client responses over the course of therapy from an integrative and generic perspective. After multiple revisions, the ITSR manual and rating form have been finalized and reliability and validity testing is underway). The creation of the ITSR feedback system will follow (Objective 4). This chapter focuses on the STIC and the STIC feedback system.

The STIC®

The STIC system consists of two client-report questionnaires: the *INITIAL STIC* and the *INTERSESSION STIC*. Clients fill out the INITIAL STIC before the first session. It contains a demographic questionnaire and five "system" scales. The first, *Individual Problems and Strengths (IPS)*, measures individual functioning. The second, *Family of Origin (FOO)*, assesses clients' perspectives on their family of origin when they were growing up. The third scale, *Relationship with Partner (RWP)*, addresses clients' perspectives on their marriage or relationship with a significant other. The *Family/Household (FH)* scale measures client's experience of their current family. The last scale, *Child Problems and Strengths (CPS)*, taps adult clients' perspectives on one of their children between the ages of 4 to 18. If there is more than one child, parents select the child about whom they have the most concerns.

The INTERSESSION STIC is a briefer version of the INITIAL that clients fill out sometime in the 24 hours before every session after the first. It includes questions from four of the INITIAL system scales – IPS, RWP, FH, and CPS. The FOO scale is not in the INTERSESSION STIC, because we did not expect it to change over the course of therapy and its status as an outcome variable is questionable. It is in the INITIAL as a predictor of client's response to therapy. The INTERSESSION STIC also includes short-form versions of the revised Integrative Psychotherapy Alliance Scales (Pinsof, 1994; Pinsof & Catherall, 1986): the *Individual Therapy Alliance Scale revised–short form (ITASr-SF)*, the *Couple Therapy Alliance Scale (CTASr-SF)*, and the *Family Therapy Alliance Scale (FTASr-SF)*.

With both the INITIAL and the INTERSESSION STIC, demographics determine which system scales are filled out, not the type of therapy. A married client in individual therapy living with at least one child between 4 and 18 fills out all of the INITIAL and INTERSESSION system scales. In contrast, a married adult with no children only fills out the IPS, the FOO, and the RWP scales on the INITIAL and the IPS and the

RWP scales on the INTERSESSION. The only exception to this "demographic" rule is that clients only fill out the alliance scale that fits their type of therapy. A client in couple therapy only fills out the CTASr-SF.

STIC questions are in plain, simple language accessible to most people over the age of 12 with basic reading skills. The question format is a statement like "I love my partner," which clients rate on a five-point Likert scale ranging from completely disagree to completely agree. For a married adult with children it takes about 45 minutes to complete the INITIAL and about 5–8 minutes to complete the INTERSESSION STIC.

Creating the STIC Scales

Core development principles

Four core principles guided the creation of the STIC.

Intensive measurement.   Both our research agenda, studying change, and our clinical agenda, creating an empirically informed therapy in which therapists receive feedback on client change throughout therapy, required intensive measurement. The most rigorous, yet reasonable strategy that we could envision was to measure change before the beginning of therapy (to get a baseline) and before every subsequent session.

This strategy derived from our desire to study and provide feedback about two relevant clinical phenomena. The first derived from Bordin's (1980) dual hypothesis that the therapeutic alliance could be ruptured and repaired, and that the rupture and repair process constituted a critical therapeutic event. We believe that this rupture and repair process takes place over a two-to-three session interval, and that usually, if the alliance is not repaired within that interval, the therapy is moribund. The second phenomenon was documented by Tang and DeRubeis (1999), who found that many successful cases in individual cognitive behavior therapy had a "sudden" and lasting gain that took place over a two-session interval. Measuring change every session also derived from our belief that it is easier to train clients to provide and therapists to collect data every session than at periodic points over the course of therapy.

Client self-report.   The second core principle, to rely on client self-report, derived from two considerations. First, we wanted to establish a large data base with thousands of cases that would permit delineating projected and actual change trajectories for a particular case by finding its "nearest neighbors" within that base (Lutz et al., 2005). For research on this scale, collecting observational data would be impossibly expensive.

Second, we believe that the client's experience of being helped and changing is the therapeutic bottom line and that the best strategy for measuring client experience is asking the client directly. This links to our belief (Pinsof & Catherall, 1986; Pinsof, Zinbarg, & Knobloch-Fedders, 2008) that the client's experience of the psychotherapeutic alliance is also a therapeutic bottom line. This is not to deny the utility of observational data in measuring change or the alliance, but rather to clarify the primacy of self-report data in this project and our approach to the alliance.

Multisystemic diagnosis and evaluation.   The third development principle is that psychotherapeutic change must be viewed from a multisystemic perspective, regardless of the type of therapy. We view psychotherapy as the interaction of two systems – a client system and a therapist system, which together comprise the therapy system (Pinsof, 1995, 2005). For brevity's sake we confine our comments to the client system, which consists of all of the people who are or may be involved in maintaining and/or resolving the presenting problem. The client system contains the direct and indirect subsystems. The direct subsystem includes members of the client system directly involved in therapy; the indirect subsystem includes members of the client system not directly involved in therapy. For us the only difference between individual and family therapy is the location of the boundary between direct and indirect client subsystems.

The STIC operationalizes this systemic view of psychotherapy by measuring change within multiple systems that comprise most of the client system. The STIC targets four client subsystems in which changes can occur: individual, couple, family-household, and child. The STIC also targets the therapy system with the alliance scales.

Multidimensional diagnosis and evaluation.   The fourth development principle was our belief (hypothesis) that client system assessment should primarily be multidimensional rather than categorical. For many years clinical psychology has debated the relative virtues of categorical versus dimensional diagnosis (Widiger & Trull, 2007). We created the STIC to help clinicians focus treatment on critical problem areas and facilitate tracking progress in these areas. The problem with categorical diagnostic systems is that they are not clinically rich and do not directly translate into relevant and focused interventions. With a clinically rich dimensional assessment, the problematic dimensions become the intervention targets. Also, as a comprehensive assessment and treatment evaluation system, the STIC needed to cover a wide variety of dimensions and problems, given that different client systems would present with different problems. Thus, we created the STIC to yield a multidimensional profile of each client's experience of each of the relevant systems. Furthermore, we created the STIC feedback system to track the problem dimensions within each case's profile over the course of therapy.

The development process

The development process of the STIC and its scales is detailed in two other publications (Pinsof et al., 2008; Pinsof et al., in press). The core of this process was a series of confirmatory factor analyses (CFA) for each scale on a set of clients at the Family Institute that resulted in the final system and alliance scales for the INITIAL STIC. For the INTERSESSION Scales, we took the items in the INITIAL that loaded most highly on each dimensional factor for each scale in the CFA and used one or two of them.

The STIC Scales, Dimensions and Exemplary Items

Tables 29.1 through 29.8 present the dimensions or factors, exemplary items, and the number of items on each version (INITIAL AND INTERSESSION) for each STIC scale.

Client system scales

Table 29.1 presents the eight factors that emerged from the CFA for the 25-item INITIAL *Individual Problems and Strengths (IPS) Scale.* The Negative Affect dimension

Table 29.1   STIC Individual Problems and Strengths (IPS) Scale

Factor/Dimension	Subdimension	INITIAL items (INTERSESSION)
Negative Affect		**8 (5)**
	Depression *Ex: Felt sad most of the day.*	4 (2)
	Anxiety *Ex: Felt tense or anxious.*	2 (1)
	Well-Being *Ex: How well have you been getting along emotionally these days?*	2 (2)
Disinhibition *Ex: Had urges or impulses you could not control.*		**3 (2)**
Life Functioning *Ex: Managing day-to-day life.*		**2 (1)**
Open Expression *Ex: I can speak up for myself when the situation calls for it.*		**3 (2)**
Flexibility/Resilience *Ex: When I get upset, I find healthy ways to make myself feel better.*		**3 (1)**
Self Understanding *Ex: I don't understand why I do the things I do.*		**2 (1)**
Substance Abuse *Ex: Drank too much alcohol.*		**2 (1)**
Self-Acceptance *Ex: I am comfortable with who I am.*		**2 (2)**

Table 29.2 STIC Family of Origin (FOO) Scale

Factor/Dimension	INITIAL items
Positivity *Ex: I knew I was loved in my family.*	5
Negativity *Ex: I felt like nobody really understood me.*	5
Mutuality of Expectations (Clear Expectations) *Ex: I knew the right thing to do in my family.*	2
Family Pride *Ex: I was proud of my family.*	1
Intrusiveness *Ex: You could be pretty sure that if you needed to be alone, someone in my family was going to bother you.*	2
Physical Abuse *Ex: Someone in my family pushed people around physically to get his or her way.*	1
Sexual Abuse *Ex: There was inappropriate sexual behavior between some of the members of my family.*	1
Abusive Climate *Ex: I was afraid of someone in my family.*	1
Substance Use *Ex: Someone in my family thought that I drank alcohol too much.*	4

includes three subdimensions that were not distinct in the CFA – Depression, Anxiety, and Well-Being. We included them as subscales because of their clinical relevance and our hope that they will emerge as distinct in subsequent CFAs with larger samples. The INTERSESSION IPS scale contains 15 items. Table 29.2 presents the nine dimensional factors that emerged from the CFA of the 22-item *Family of Origin (FOO)* Scale.

The CFA of the 24-item INITIAL *Relationship with Partner (RWP) Scale* produced the eight factors in Table 29.3. The largest factor was Positivity, which contained four subdimensions (Fun, Love, Communication, and Intimacy) that did not emerge as distinct in the CFA. We included these subdimensions for the reasons specified above for the IPS scale. The INTERSESSION RWP scale has 12.

Table 29.4 presents the nine factors supported by the CFA of the 32-item INITIAL *Family/Household (FH) Scale*. The two largest factors, Positivity and Negativity, respectively contain five and four subdimensions that did not emerge as distinct in the CFA, but are included for the above-mentioned reasons. The INTERSESSION FH scale contains 10 items.

Table 29.3   STIC Relationship with Partner (RP) Scale

Factor/Dimension	Subdimension	INITIAL Items (INTERSESSION)
Positivity		**9 (5)**
	Fun *Ex: We enjoy doing things together.*	2 (1)
	Love *Ex: I love my partner.*	2 (1)
	Communication *Ex: My partner really listens to me when we discuss things.*	3 (2)
	Intimacy *Ex: We are each other's best friend.*	2 (1)
Trust/Betrayal *Ex: I feel betrayed by my partner.*		**3 (1)**
Commitment *Ex: I am sure we will make it as a couple.*		**2 (1)**
Inequity *Ex: I am expected to do too much.*		**2 (1)**
Anger/Contempt *Ex: I am filled with anger toward my partner.*		**2 (1)**
Sexual Satisfaction *Ex: I am sexually frustrated in this relationship.*		**2 (1)**
Physical Abuse *Ex: We get into shoving or hitting each other when we fight.*		**2 (2)**
Substance Abuse *Ex: My partner uses drugs or alcohol too much.*		**2 (0)**

The CFA of the 29-item INITIAL *Child Problems and Strengths (CPS) Scale* produced the nine factors in Table 29.5. The factors included one macro factor, Antisocial, that contained three clinically relevant subdimensions that did not emerge as distinct in the CFA. The INTERSESSION CPS scale has 9 items.

Table 29.4 STIC Family Household (FH) Scale

Factor/Dimension	Subdimension	INITIAL items (INTERSESSION)
Physical Abuse *Ex: Someone in my family is physically abusive to other family members.*		**2 (1)**
Abusive Climate *Ex: I feel abused by someone in my family.*		**2 (1)**
Sexual Abuse *Ex: There is someone in my family who is sexually abusive to other family members.*		**2 (0)**
Positivity		**10 (3)**
	Respect/Differentiation *Ex: People in my family respect each other's feelings and thoughts.*	2 (0)
	Nurturance/Affection *Ex: We feel loved and supported by each other.*	2 (1)
	Fun/Good Times *Ex: We know how to have fun together.*	2 (1)
	Loyalty/Commitment *Ex: I know my family will be there for me.*	2 (0)
	Good Communication *Ex: People in my family are honest with each other.*	2 (1)
Decision Making *Ex: Everyone has a say in my family.*		**2 (1)**
Negativity		**8 (2)**
	Bad Conflict *Ex: Talking together as a family is a nightmare.*	2 (0)
	Nastiness/Coercion *Ex: If people in my family know what you are really feeling, they use it against you.*	2 (1)
	Trapped/Oppressed *Ex: I feel like a prisoner in my family.*	2 (0)
	Intrusiveness *Ex: My family is too much in my business.*	2 (1)
Boundary Clarity *Ex: I know the right thing to do in my family.*		**2 (1)**
Feeling Misunderstood *Ex: I feel like nobody in my family really understands me.*		**2 (1)**
Family Pride *Ex: I'm proud of my family.*		**2 (0)**

Table 29.5   STIC Child Problems and Strengths (CPS) Scale

Factor/Dimension	Subdimension	INITIAL items (INTERSESSION)
Depression *Ex: My child is sad.*		**3 (2)**
Anxiety *Ex: My child worries.*		**3 (1)**
Antisocial		**6 (1)**
	Anger/Aggression *Ex: My child starts physical fights.*	2 (1)
	Defiance/Oppositionality *Ex: My child blames others for his/her problems.*	2 (0)
	Delinquency *Ex: My child lies.*	2 (0)
Self Control/ Impulsivity *Ex: My child has difficulty controlling his/her reactions.*		**4 (1)**
Substance Abuse *Ex: My child uses marijuana or other illegal drugs.*		**2 (1)**
Parent-Child Alliance *Ex: My child enjoys spending time with his/her parents.*		**2 (0)**
Prosocial *Ex: My child is thoughtful and caring toward others.*		**3 (1)**
Food/ Weight *Ex: I am concerned about my child's attitude about food.*		**2 (0)**
Social/Academic *Ex: My child does well at school.*		**4 (2)**

On certain scales (FH and CPS particularly) there is a substantial difference between the number of items representing some INITIAL scale dimensions and the number representing them on the INTERSESSION. In all cases the INTERSESSION items loaded highly on the INITIAL dimension and represented well the other items not included in the INTERSESSION. We worked to keep the INTERSESSION as brief, but as representative of the scale dimensions, as possible.

Therapeutic alliance scales

The CFA with the Revised Integrative Therapy Alliance Scales had two goals. The first tested the original theoretical factor structure of the Revised Integrative Psychotherapy Alliance Model. The second was to reduce the number of items in the three Revised Scales to 15 or fewer to fit within the INTERSESSION STIC.

The theoretical model of the Integrative Psychotherapy Alliance consists of two large dimensional domains – Content and Interpersonal System. Content includes three dimensions – Tasks, Goals, and Bonds. *Tasks* refers to how much the therapist and the client agree about their tasks in the therapy. *Goals* addresses how much the therapist and the client agree about the client's goals in therapy. *Bonds* refers how much the client feels bonded to the therapist (i.e., trusting, cared for, attached, etc.). Bordin (1979) originally articulated and subsequently Horvath (1982) operationalized these dimensions in the Working Alliance Inventory, a leading individual therapy alliance measure.

Pinsof and Catherall (1986) added the Interpersonal System Domain to alliance theory to bring a systemic perspective to the alliance in couple and family therapy as well as individual therapy. The first Interpersonal dimension, *Self*, refers to the alliance (Tasks, Goals, and Bonds) between the therapist and client. The second, *Other*, addresses the client's perception of the alliance between the therapist and relevant others in the client's life (e.g., "my partner" in couple therapy, the "other people in my family" in family therapy, and "the people who are important to me" in individual therapy). The third dimension, *Group*, targets the client's perception of the alliance between the therapist and the client's "key group," including the client ("us" as a couple or family in couple and family therapy and "my important relationships" in individual therapy). Pinsof (1994) added the last Interpersonal dimension, *Within*, creating the revised alliance scales. It refers to the alliance between the client and their "relevant other(s)" and does not include the therapist.

The Integrative Psychotherapy Alliance revised model forms a 3 × 4 matrix in which the Interpersonal dimensions cut across the Content dimensions. Items for the three revised alliance scales fall in the 12 cells of the matrix. The CFA of the Individual Therapy Alliance Scale revised (ITASr) supported the seven-factor model. The ITASr-SF consists of 22 items spread over the seven factors in Table 29.6. Each item theoretically loads on a Content and Interpersonal factor.

In the CFA, however, most items primarily loaded on a Content or Interpersonal factor, which is indicated by the cell indicator column. Pinsof et al. (2008) found that Other, Within, and Bonds correlated with progress over eight sessions in individual therapy. Other also predicted eighth-session continuation.

With the Couple Therapy Alliance Scale revised, the CFA did not support the seven-factor model. As illustrated by Table 29.7, for the CTASr-SF only three factors emerged covering 12 items. The largest factor (6 items) merged Self ("the therapist and I") and Group ("we and the therapist"). The other two factors were Other and Within. Pinsof et al. (in press) found that Other and Within correlated with progress in couple therapy. Within also predicted eighth-session continuation.

Table 29.6   The Individual Therapy Alliance Scale Revised – Short Form (ITASr-SF)

Factors	Example items	Cell indicator	Factor items in STIC
Tasks	Some of the people who are important to me would not be pleased with what I am doing in this therapy.	Tasks/Within	2
Goals	The therapist and I are not in agreement about the goals for this therapy.	Goals/Self	4
Bonds	Some of the people who are important to me would not trust that this therapy is good for my relationships with them.	Bonds/Within	4
Self	I do not feel accepted by the therapist.	Bonds/Self	4
Other	The people who are important to me would not approve of the way the therapy is being conducted.	Tasks/Other	2
Group	The therapist is helping me with my important relationships.	Tasks/Group	3
Within	The people who are important to me would understand my goals in this therapy.	Goals/Within	3

Table 29.7   The Couple Therapy Alliance Scale Revised Short Form (CTASr-SF)

Factors	Example items	Cell indicator	Factor items in STIC
Self/Group	The therapist cares about me as a person.	Bonds/Self	6
	The therapist does not understand the relationship between my partner and myself.	Tasks/Group	
Other	The therapist understands my partner's goals for this therapy.	Goals/Other	3
Within	My partner and I are not pleased with the things that each of us does in this therapy.	Tasks/Within	3

Table 29.8 shows the same pattern of findings from the CFA of the Family Therapy Alliance Scale revised. For the FTASr-SF the same three factors emerged covering 12 items. An insufficient number of clients precluded testing the link between these factors and progress or continuation.

It is noteworthy that the Interpersonal dimensions were empirically supported in all three CFAs, including the Individual Therapy Alliance Scale. Additionally, the interpersonal dimensions were associated with continuation and progress in individual and

Table 29.8   The Family Therapy Alliance Scale Revised – Short Form (FTASr-SF)

Factors	Example items	Cell indicator	Factor items in STIC
Self/Group	The therapist does not understand me.	Tasks/Self	6
	The therapist cares about my family.	Bonds/Group	
Other	The therapist understands the goals that all the other members of my family have for this therapy.	Goals/Other	3
Within	Some of the other members of my family and I do not feel safe with each other in this therapy.	Bonds/Within	3

couple therapy. This pattern of findings empirically supports including the Interpersonal domain and a multisystemic perspective in alliance, theory, research, and practice, regardless of the type of therapy.

The STIC feedback system

The STIC feedback system uses the internet to provide users with graphical, quantitative feedback about the initial status and changes on all of the dimensions in all of the appropriate systems for each client directly involved in a case. A thorough presentation of the system exceeds this chapter's scope. We highlight some of its main features.

Initial diagnosis.   In regard to the initial status of a case, the feedback system provides users with a bar graph analysis of each scale as well as the dimensions (factors) within each scale. With an actual couple, whom we will call Sally and Tom,[2] Tom initiated the referral. The feedback system provides a bar graph of each client's INITIAL total scale score (average of all answers) on each of the five client system scales. All of the client system scales and dimensions are on five-point scales. A higher score is always better than a lower score. Therapists focus initially on the lowest dimensions, which constitute the problem *areas for a case*. With Tom and Sally all of their INITIAL scale total scores ranged from the high threes to the mid-fours, except Tom's RWP score, which was below three. Sally's RWP score was four. Although we are just determining norms for the STIC scales and dimensions (see Future Projects below), scores in the high-three to mid-four range generally reflect a lack of serious problems. The INITIAL scale bar graphs indicate that Tom is unhappy about his marriage and that Sally does not share his distress.

In addition to the INITIAL scale total scores, the feedback system provides INITIAL subscale or dimensional scores. Beyond focusing on low dimensional scores, therapists focus on dimensions in which there is a large discrepancy *between clients' scores*. With Tom and Sally, there were large discrepancies between their scores on three dimensions

– Positivity (S4/T2), Commitment (S4.5/T3), and Trust (S4.6/T3). These differences further corroborated that they were not on the same marital page – he was dissatisfied and she was oblivious.

Ongoing evaluation.   With Tom and Sally, the therapist initially focused on these discrepancies, revealing that Tom was so unhappy he was considering leaving the marriage. This shocked Sally. Over the first five sessions, as the therapist facilitated communication, Sally's scores decreased – Positivity 4 to 3.3 and Commitment 4.5 to 3, while Tom's Positivity increased by 2 to 3.2. Tom's Commitment score remained stable throughout therapy at 3. These changes reflected Sally's growing discomfort as she became aware of Tom's marital dissatisfaction. In contrast, Tom's increased Positivity reflects his encouragement that Sally understood his feelings. However, as she progressively returned to her pre-therapy levels of Positivity about the marriage he became discouraged, returning almost to the level at which he started. After nine sessions Tom and Sally mutually decided to stop therapy. He decided that she would never understand him and that he would leave well enough alone until the children left home. She wanted to stop because she hated "bad news" and hoped that things might spontaneously improve in the future.

Alliance tracking.   In addition to tracking client system change, the STIC feedback system tracks alliance change. In contrast to the five-point client system scales, the alliance scales cover seven points. With another couple, whom we will call Arnie and Mary, their graphs clearly depicted rupture and repair episodes. Specifically, Arnie's Self/Group and Within graphs showed a large V-shaped depression between the sixth and eighth sessions, which depicted a tear–repair episode in which Arnie's Self/Group ("the therapist and I/the therapist and us") score plunged from over 5 before session six to below 2 before session seven. His Within ("my partner and I") score fell from a high of 6 before session four to below 2 before session seven. Both tears were repaired by session eight. His graphs also depicted another, less severe four-session tear–repair episode between sessions 24 and 28, in which Arnie's Self/Group score goes from over 6 to 4 and then back to the 6 range.

In both episodes, Arnie felt the therapist was more empathic and supportive to Mary about her "right" to say "No" when she did not want to have sex than he was to Arnie about his feelings of frustration and rejection. In both tear and repair episodes, the therapist's repair included apologizing and actively empathizing with Arnie's experience of dual rejection by his wife sexually and by the therapist empathically. It is noteworthy that the tears in the client–therapist alliance (as well as in the husband–wife alliance) got less severe over time, suggesting growth in the strength and resilience of Arnie's alliance with the therapist and his wife.

The feedback findings presented above for Tom and Sally and Arnie and Mary can be seen online at the STIC Feedback Example on the Family Institute website at wwwfamilyinstitute.org.

Feedback summary.   The STIC feedback system provides a multisystemic and multidimensional assessment of clients' lives and tracks change over the course of therapy on problematic dimensions. It also provides an ongoing assessment of the therapeutic alliance for each client and depicts alliance rupture–repair episodes. It gives therapists the flexibility to focus on the most relevant dimensions for each case.

Future Projects

Three major hurdles lie ahead. The first concerns norming the STIC. In concert with the National Opinion Research Center (NORC) at the University of Chicago we sent 2,500 STICs to a random and representative sample of the U.S. population. We received 1,400 back and are currently determining the "normal" and "clinical" range on each dimension on each client system scale. We aim to provide an initial profile of the dimensions on which each case is in the clinical range at the beginning of therapy (the "clinical diagnosis") as well as continual feedback about progress on those dimensions.

The second hurdle is finishing and preliminarily testing the Integrative Therapy Session Report (ITSR). After finalizing the measure with feedback from a panel of nationally renowned experts, we intend to test the ITSR's ability to significantly discriminate sessions from expert therapists from different orientations and modalities. Additionally, we must show that therapists can use the ITSR to reliably and validly characterize their sessions.

The third hurdle, assuming positive results from the ITSR studies, is to create an ITSR feedback system that integrates with the STIC system. We ultimately want to provide an integrated picture of client change, the therapeutic alliance, and therapist behavior over the course of therapy. This achievement will create the scientific and technological platform for an empirically informed systemic of psychotherapy that uses quantitative feedback to guide clinical evaluation and decision-making throughout therapy.

Notes

1 The staff of the Psychotherapy Change Project are Anthony Chambers, Emily Durbin, Jacob Goldsmith, Eli Karam, Lynne Knobloch-Fedders, Tara Latta, Jay Lebow, Bill Pinsof (director), and Rick Zinbarg. At various times Greg Friedman, Bart Mann, and Emma Sterrett were also project staff members. Ken Howard (deceased) played a critical role in the inception of the project and our work is dedicated to his memory.
2 All information about the cases, except the graphs and patient gender, have been changed to protect the anonymity of the patients.

References

Barkham, M., Margison, F., Leach, C., Lucock, M., Mellor-Clark, J., Evans, C., et al. (2001). Service profiling and outcomes benchmarking using the CORE-OM: Toward practice-based evidence in the psychological therapies. *Journal of Consulting and Clinical Psychology, 69,* 184–196.

Bordin, E. S. (1979). The generalizability of the psychoanalytic concept of the working alliance. *Psychotherapy: Theory, Research, and Practice, 16,* 252–260.

Bordin, E. S. (1980). *New developments in psychotherapy research.* Presidential address. Annual Conference of the Society for Psychotherapy Research, Asilomar, CA.

Horvath, A. O. (1982). *The Working Alliance Inventory (Revised).* (Instructional. Psychology Research Group, 82). Burnaby, Canada: Simon Fraser University.

Howard, K. L., Moras, K., Brill, P. L., Martinovich, Z., & Lutz, W. (1996). Evaluation of psychotherapy: Efficacy, effectiveness and client progress. *American Psychologist, 51,* 1059–1064.

Lambert, M. J., Hansen, N. B., & Finch, A. E. (2001). Patient-focused research: Using patient outcome data to enhance treatment effects. *Journal of Consulting and Clinical Psychology, 69,* 159–172.

Lutz, W., Leach, C., Barkham, M., Lucock, M., Stiles, W. B., Evans, C., et al. (2005). Predicting change for individual psychotherapy clients on the basis of their nearest neighbors. *Journal of Consulting and Clinical Psychology, 73,* 904–913.

Pinsof, W. M. (1994). An integrative systems perspective on the therapeutic alliance: Theoretical, clinical and research implications. In A. Horvath & L. Greenberg (Eds.), *The working alliance: Theory, research and practice* (pp. 173–195). New York: Wiley.

Pinsof, W. M. (1995). *Integrative problem centered therapy: A synthesis of biological, individual and family therapies.* New York: Basic Books.

Pinsof, W. M. (2005). Integrative problem centered therapy. In J. C. Norcross & M. R. Goldfried (Eds.), *Handbook of psychotherapy integration* (2nd ed., pp. 382–402). New York: Oxford University Press.

Pinsof, W. M., & Catherall, D. R. (1986). The integrative psychotherapy alliance: Family, couple and individual therapy scales. *Journal of Marital and Family Therapy, 12,* 137–151.

Pinsof, W. M., & Lebow, J. (2005). A scientific paradigm for family psychology. In W. M. Pinsof & J. Lebow (Eds.), *Family psychology: The art of the science* (pp. 3–22). New York: Oxford University Press.

Pinsof, W. M., & Wynne, L. C. (2000). Toward progress research: Closing the gap between family therapy practice and research. *Journal of Marital and Family Therapy, 26,* 1–8.

Pinsof, W. M., Zinbarg, R. E., & Knobloch-Fedders, L. M. (2008). Factorial and construct validity of the revised short form integrative psychotherapy alliance scales for family, couple, and individual therapy. *Family Process, 47(3),* 281–301.

Pinsof, W. M., Zinbarg, R., Lebow, J., Knobloch-Fedders, L. M., Durbin, K. E., Chambers, A., et al. (in press). Laying the foundation for progress research in family, couple and individual therapy: The development and psychometric features of the INITIAL Systemic Therapy Inventory of Change (STIC). *Psychotherapy Research.*

Tang, T. Z., & DeRubeis, R. J. (1999). Sudden gains and critical sessions in cognitive behavioral therapy for depression. *Journal of Consulting and Clinical Psychology, 67,* 894–904.

Widiger, T. A., & Trull, T. J. (2007). Plate tectonics in the classification of personality disorder: Shifting to a dimensional model. *American Psychologist, 62,* 71–83.

Part III

Dimensions of Family Psychology

Introduction

The application of family psychology has grown tremendously as the field has expanded from the early days in which general theories and techniques were developed to more sophisticated and specialized applications. This part of the Handbook discusses applications of family psychology to a variety of special populations and settings. These chapters are written by either the senior leaders of the area or rising stars who are contributing new and innovative ideas and methods. These chapters provide excellent resources for discussions about special populations and settings.

This part of the Handbook includes chapters that reflect the changing demographics in families, such as premarital interventions; single-parent, divorced, and stepfamilies; gay and lesbian families; and the special needs of recent immigrant families. In addition, this part has chapters on special populations, such as pediatric issues, family psychology in healthcare, substance abuse, depression, and eating disorders. Most of these chapters provide clinical examples of the application of family psychology in these areas.

The part proceeds to provide overviews of family psychology in different settings. These include schools, the legal system, religious settings, and work settings. We hope that clinicians and students will enjoy these examples as they reflect the real-life applications of family psychology theories and applications.

The part concludes with chapters on family policy considerations and on international perspectives on family psychology. Chapter 47 describes how federal policies impact families and some ideas about the development of family friendly legislative policies. Chapter 49 gives the reader a broad overview of the many developments of family psychology throughout the world.

Many of the chapters in this part include a list of resources for further exploration of the chapter subject in a box inset at the end of the chapter. Many authors have noted websites, videos, and additional written materials that will allow interested readers to pursue the topic further.

30

Relationship Education Programs: Current Trends and Future Directions

Erica P. Ragan, Lindsey A. Einhorn, Galena K. Rhoades, Howard J. Markman, and Scott M. Stanley

Many people desire a long-term, loving relationship, and for most, this desire means that they will one day marry. Research indicates that close relationships are a crucial part of wellbeing, in part because they provide a stable source of emotional and social support (Baumeister & Leary, 1995; Waite & Gallagher, 2000). Moreover, research indicates that a happy marriage is linked with better health, greater happiness, and living longer (Glenn et al., 2002).

Marital distress is related to a number of poor outcomes, including higher rates of mental illness (Fincham, 2002), more depressive symptoms (Whisman & Bruce, 1999), alcoholism (see Chapter 26, this volume), poorer cardiovascular and immunological functioning (Kiecolt-Glaser, McGuire, Robles, & Glaser, 2002), and greater economic instability, especially for men (Forthofer, Markman, Cox, Stanley, & Kessler, 1996). Low-quality marriages reduce life satisfaction, have the potential to harm relationships with family and friends, and can interfere with career satisfaction (Hawkins & Booth, 2005). When marriages end, partners are at risk for experiencing even poorer health, more psychological distress, less happiness, and poorer wellbeing (see Amato, 2001, for a review). Unstable and unhealthy marriages affect children, too. Marital conflict is associated with withdrawn parenting and poor child adjustment (Grych & Fincham, 2001). More specifically, conflict is associated with a greater risk for childhood mental illness (Coie et al., 1993), including conduct problems and depression (Essex, Klein, Cho, & Kraemer, 2003).

Given the benefits of healthy relationships and the costs of unhealthy relationships, understanding who is at risk for poorer marital outcomes is key for developing relationship education programs. Known risk factors include parental divorce, marrying at a young age, having a courtship that is either too short or too long, cohabiting before marriage, poor communication and conflict management skills, and having children before marrying (Halford, Markman, Kline, & Stanley, 2003). Protective factors include good communication skills; having skills related to being good at fun, friendship, and romance; having parents who have a good relationship with one another; having realistic expectations for healthy relationships; being a committed and dedicated person; and being able to handle conflict in a non–violent manner (Bray & Jouriles, 1995; Halford et al., 2003). Some of these factors are static in that they cannot be altered easily (e.g., parental divorce), but others are dynamic and could be changed (e.g., communication skills; Markman, Stanley, & Kline, 2003; Stanley, 2001). Most relationship education programs are designed to decrease couple-based dynamic risk factors (e.g., poor conflict resolution) and increase couple-oriented protective factors (e.g., fun and friendship).

The rationale for the development, evaluation, and dissemination of research-based relationship education programs is derived in part from the fact that the divorce rate in the United States is 40–45% for first marriages (U.S. Census Bureau, 2002) and even higher for second marriages (Cherlin, 1992). Relationship education programs generally aim to prevent distress and divorce. Disseminating them is important because, of couples who divorce, 80% never seek traditional mental health services (Glenn et al., 2002; Johnson et al., 2002). Of couples who do seek counseling, many seek it at a time when negative patterns have likely already eroded many of the positive connections (Doss, Rhoades, Stanley, & Markman, 2008). Thus, many relationship education programs are delivered before marriage, when a couple is still happy and before negative patterns have formed.

Research demonstrates that relationship education can improve couples' skills and reduce their risk for future marital distress and divorce (Carroll & Doherty, 2003; Hawkins, Blanchard, Baldwin, & Fawcett, 2008). In addition, relationship education is associated with greater marital satisfaction, lower levels of conflict, higher levels of dedication to partner, and lower odds of divorce, with such effects being consistent across income, education, and racial backgrounds of recipients (Bray & Jouriles, 1995; Markman, Stanley, Jenkins, Petrella, & Wadsworth, 2006; Stanley, Amato, Johnson, & Markman, 2006). We next review several relationship education programs and then discuss future directions for this field.

Evidence-Based Relationship Education Programs

Following are examples of evidence-based relationship education programs that help couples by teaching skills and providing education about relationships, such as about the roles of expectations and commitment.

Minnesota Couples Communication Program

The Minnesota Couples Communication Program (MCCP; Nunnally, Miller, & Wackman, 1975) was developed with a focus on increasing awareness of self, others, and interactions, and on teaching couples good communication skills so that they can deal effectively with natural changes in relationships, such as shifting priorities after the birth of a child. MCCP is a 12-hour program, typically delivered to small groups of couples. In the first session, participants learn how to be more self-aware and how to communicate this awareness effectively. In the second session, participants learn listening skills and how to help a partner self-disclose. The third session focuses on verbal metacommunication, which allows the couple to talk about how they negotiate a problem. In the final session, couples are taught the differences between skills and styles, focusing on identifying actions and behaviors that affect either partner's self-esteem. Couples practice the skills both in the group and at home. MCCP group leaders are highly trained and undergo a certification process, but they do not need to possess a professional degree. MCCP leads to more effective communication and a greater relationship satisfaction (Butler & Wampler, 1999; Wampler, 1982). It has been implemented in a variety of contexts, including universities, churches, and YMCAs. For more information on MCCP, see their website (www.couplecommunication.com).

Relationship Enhancement Program

The Relationship Enhancement Program (RE; Guerney, 1977) is a widely used program in which couples are taught how to communicate their feelings, the behaviors associated with these feelings, and to stop blaming others for relationship problems. RE strives to create an environment in which partners can express sensitive issues effectively (Ridley & Sladeczek, 1992). Communication skills are divided into four components: Expressor Mode, Empathic Responder Mode, Switching Mode, and the Facilitator Mode. In the Expressor Mode, couples are taught how to clearly express their feelings, needs, and desires with the use of an "I" statement that directly links feelings with behaviors. When one is in the Empathic Responder Mode, his or her role is to elicit self-disclosure from their partner and to gain a better understanding of the partner's thoughts and feelings. The Empathic Responder uses paraphrasing and reflective listening. In the Switching Mode, partners learn to identify which behavior to use, speaking or listening. Finally, the Facilitator Mode allows one to help others in the RE group by providing feedback as couples use these skills (Guerney, 1977). Ridley and Sladeczek (1992) found that RE was more effective than a lecture or discussion group in helping partners identify their needs for affection, inclusion, and control as well as increasing the amount of affection between partners. For the latest information on RE, please visit the National Institute of Relationship Enhancement website (www.nire.org).

Couple Commitment and Relationship Enhancement

The Couple Commitment and Relationship Enhancement program (Couple CARE; Halford, 2004) is based on existing programs including the Prevention and Relationship Enhancement Program (PREP; Markman, Stanley, & Blumberg, 1994) and Self-PREP

(Halford, Sanders, & Behrens, 2001). Couple CARE was developed to address the need for programs that do not need to be delivered face to face and that can be completed in couples' own time. Similar to PREP, Couple CARE is a skills-based program focused on couples' communication, relationship expectations, and commitment. The program includes six units: Self-Change, Communication, Intimacy and Caring, Managing Differences, Sexuality, and Adaptation to Change. Couples watch a 12–15-minute video at the beginning of each unit that explains key concepts and provides examples of the skills. Next, partners complete tasks both separately and together for approximately 50 minutes from a guidebook. Tasks encourage partners to relate what they are learning to their own relationship, set goals for the relationship, and initiate change. After each unit, the couple has a 45-minute conversation with a family psychologist who reviews the unit's concepts and helps them create a change plan.

In a study evaluating the effectiveness of Couple CARE, Halford, Moore, Wilson, Farrugia, and Dyer (2004) found that most couples completed all of the tasks (96%) and reported high satisfaction with the program. Couples completing the program had greater relationship satisfaction and stability, though the effect for stability was small. Somewhat surprisingly, Couple CARE did not reduce negative communication patterns; most couples in the study had low initial levels of negative communication, so this finding may represent a floor effect (Halford et al., 2004).

Prevention and Relationship Enhancement Program

The Prevention and Relationship Enhancement Program (PREP) was developed in 1980 to help couples diminish dynamic risk factors and protect the positives in their relationships (Markman et al., 1994; Markman, Stanley, Blumberg, Jenkins, & Whaley, 2004; Stanley, Blumberg, & Markman, 1999). PREP uses a skills-based model and is influenced by behavioral marital therapy and family systems theory and interventions. PREP relies on the assumption that couples can change behavior by learning new skills and cognitive sets that help them protect the quality of their relationship and prevent deterioration. A great strength of the PREP approach is that it is based on empirical research and is regularly updated as new research is published (Stanley et al., 1999). PREP has four major goals: (1) to teach better communication and conflict management strategies; (2) to help couples understand and evaluate their relationship expectations; (3) to increase under-standing of commitment and their choices reflecting commitment; and (4) to enhance the bonding that comes from spending time as friends and having fun. We next describe the methods used to achieve these goals.

PREP addresses relationship risk by teaching couples how to manage conflict as a team without damaging closeness. Poor communication and ineffective conflict resolution can have a lasting negative impact on couples. In addition to their causing distress, couples with these communication patterns may be at risk for associating their partner with the pain and frustration that results from such interactions (Markman, Stanley, & Blumberg, 1994). In time, negative interpretations are made about the partner, and a "you versus me" attitude can emerge (Baucom & Epstein, 1990). This pattern, as well as poor conflict management, begins to erode attachment (Fincham, 2001). Patterns of escalation, conflict, and negative interpretations are corrosive to marital quality. PREP works to ameliorate these negative effects by helping couples learn to control when problems are discussed, such as at a weekly couples meeting, and by structuring the conversation to help manage conflict. Couples are taught the Speaker–Listener technique, which makes it harder to slide into patterns of negative interaction, what PREP calls Communication Danger Signs. The technique promotes basic elements of healthy communication such as turn-taking, listening, and the importance of speaking up, making it safer for partners to connect. When using the technique, one person, the Speaker, has "the floor." The Speaker is only allowed to talk about their thoughts, feelings, and needs. The Listener's job is to focus on the Speaker's words and to paraphrase what he or she has heard. After the Speaker has shared several thoughts, the floor is then passed to the Listener and the roles are reversed (Stanley et al., 1999). Sometimes couples become too upset or angry to effectively use the Speaker–Listener technique. When this happens, couples are instructed to take a Time Out, which is a period to cool down, relax, and prevent further escalation. Once both partners are calm, they can continue the discussion (Stanley et al., 1999).

In addition to learning how to manage conflict more constructively, couples are also taught to prevent risk by examining their relationship expectations in PREP. Many people have "core belief systems" (Markman et al., 1994), which are sometimes related to religious beliefs or other value systems. When partners do not understand one another's beliefs, conflict can arise. In PREP, couples discover and discuss their expectations through a series of structured exercises (Stanley et al., 1999).

While reducing risk factors in couples' relationships, PREP also aims to increase and maintain the positive connection between partners by helping them understand their attitudes and choices regarding commitment. Couples are taught the importance of having a sense of safety about a future together. PREP uses a series of exercises to emphasize the importance of having a long-term view of marriage and to help partners articulate their dreams, goals, and aspirations. The exercises are also used to help couples understand how life choices and priorities can either help or hinder commitment (Markman et al., 2004; Stanley et al., 1999).

PREP also teaches couples about the importance of maintaining a positive connection through fun, friendship, and sensuality. Many couples have a strong positive connection before marriage, but it can decline with time, as it is either eroded by conflict or becomes downgraded on the list of priorities. PREP uses behavioral strategies to help preserve these important elements (Markman et. al., 2003; Stanley et al., 1999).

PREP can be administered to couples at any point in their relationship. Both happy and distressed couples seem to benefit from PREP, which is usually delivered by educational, service-oriented institutions such as places of worship, mental health centers, or HMOs. The typical program lasts 12 hours and can be delivered as a weekend workshop or spread out over several evenings. The program is designed to be delivered by both mental health professionals and religious and lay leaders. Leaders deliver the lectures and monitor coaches who work directly with couples as they practice skills such as the Speaker–Listener technique (Stanley et al., 1999). PREP's efficacy has been demonstrated by a number of studies both in the United States and abroad; it produces both short-term and long-term positive changes in couples' relationship satisfaction, communication skills, and conflict management skills (Hahlweg, Markman, Thurmaier, Engl, & Eckert, 1998; Laurenceau, Stanley, Olmos-Gallo, Baucom, & Markman, 2004; Markman, Floyd, Stanley, & Storaasli, 1988; Markman, Silvern, Clements, & Kraft-Hanak, 1993; Stanley et al., 2001; Stanley, Markman, St. Peters, & Leber, 1995).

To date, much of the research on programs such as MCCP, RE, Couple CARE, and PREP has been conducted only with samples of primarily White and middle-class couples. We next discuss how relationship education programs are being adapted to work with other populations.

Diversity in Premarital Education Programs

Until recently, minimal work had been done with specific populations such as families in poverty or non-traditional families (e.g., foster parents) and even less had been done to evaluate the effectiveness of programs used with these populations. Over the past decade, adapted versions of PREP have been implemented in the military (see Stanley, Allen, et al., 2005), in correctional facilities (see Einhorn, Williams, Stanley, Wunderlin, & Markman, 2008), in faith-based organizations (see Stanley et al., 2001), and with couples who have low income levels. Relationship education services have also been disseminated through the internet and to foster parents and stepfamilies. Additionally, there is a new focus on relationship education with individuals rather than couples, including youth in schools. Because of their circumstances, some of these diverse populations may be more at risk for relationship stress than the samples typically used in relationship education research, thus future research in this area is very important. Next, we review several of these new arenas for relationship education and provide up-to-date information on progress within them.

PREP for Strong and Ready Families

Building Strong and Ready Families (BSRF) is an adapted version of PREP currently used in the United States Armed Forces. BSRF includes the traditional PREP program as well as material specific to the needs of Army couples at a time of high stress and frequent deployments, such as skills for stress management and tools for successfully navigating reintegration. The program is available to couples in which one or both partners are active-duty Army personnel and is delivered by Army chaplains. BSRF has been evaluated in two samples of Army couples. Both samples reported positive impact from the program and significant improvement on a range of relationship variables. These effects were shown for both men and women, for ethnically diverse couples, and for those with lower incomes (Stanley, Allen, et al., 2005). A longer-term, large-scale, randomized trial of BSRF is currently being conducted.

PREP Inside and Out

An adapted version of PREP (PREP Inside and Out) has been implemented by trained chaplains with prison populations in Oklahoma correctional facilities. Along with the traditional PREP skills, PREP Inside and Out includes additional communication skills training, models how to do homework assignments, and provides examples, videos, and movies that are specific to inmates' lives and current situations. The short-term effects of PREP Inside and Out were evaluated with 254 inmates. Significant differences from pre to post were observed for all relationship variables (i.e., satisfaction with relationship, dedication, confidence, communication skills) regardless of gender and racial/ethnic background (Einhorn et al., 2008).

Christian PREP

Christian PREP is a version of PREP that integrates Christian principles and research on marriage and relationships (Stanley, Trathen, McCain, & Bryan, 1998). The program uses Biblical themes and Christian theology on marriage along with the skills-based strategies of PREP in order to help Christian couples who are interested in this specific approach to strengthen and maintain their marriages in a context tailored to their beliefs. Christian PREP is commonly used in churches. The incorporation of Christian principles is very attractive and helpful for some couples, though there are no published studies on its effectiveness.

Within Our Reach

Within Our Reach (WOR) is a 36-hour, newly developed curriculum based on the PREP approach designed to meet the needs of lower-income and higher-risk couples (Stanley, Markman, et al., 2006). The curriculum adaptations include new emphases such as helping couples meet their goals, discovering new ways to cope with the specific stressors of economic strain, and units designed to foster parenting skills, community connection and involvement, and thinking about the future. WOR also incorporates more activities, discussions, and practice time than classic PREP.

Researchers at the University of Denver are conducting a randomized controlled trial to evaluate an adapted version of WOR called Fatherhood, Relationship, and Marriage Education (FRAME). This study is using a 16-hour version of the 36-hour program and is offered to groups of couples, groups of men, and groups of women. The 16-hour version omits certain modules and activities from WOR, reduces time on lectures, decreases redundant material, and shortens practice times. The same materials and skills are presented and practiced in the couple and individual groups, just in a slightly different manner. For example, both groups are taught the Speaker–Listener technique. However, participants in the couple group practice the skill by discussing a relationship issue with their partner, while participants in the individual groups pair up with another group member. Members of the male and female groups are instructed to talk with their partners about what they learned in the session. Preliminary data reveal satisfaction with WOR (Markman, Rhoades, Delaney, White, & Pacifici, 2007); outcome data will be available in the near future.

Within My Reach

Within My Reach (WMR) is a 15-hour curriculum based on PREP that is designed for individuals (regardless of whether they are currently in a relationship), rather than couples (Pearson, Stanley, & Kline, 2005). WMR is part of a growing trend toward individually oriented relationship education services that take advantage of the multiple opportunities in schools and public service settings to help individuals reach their aspirations for life-long love (Stanley, Pearson, & Kline, 2005). WMR aims to improve the odds that participants will choose, remain in, or develop healthy relationships, and where possible, develop those relationships into sustainable and healthy marriages that benefit the individual and his or her children. Individuals are taught evidence-based information on healthy relationships, models for how to think about expectations and values in partner choices, relationship skills for managing and understanding communication, conflict, commitment, and forgiveness, and tools for thinking about and planning for overcoming barriers to healthy relationships. One quantitative and one qualitative evaluation of WMR are underway with other studies in the planning stages.

ePREP

Relationship education services have also been disseminated through the internet and to foster parents, stepfamilies, and youth in schools. Braithwaite and Fincham (2007) were the first to offer an internet version of PREP, which was modified to make PREP appropriate for a college dating population and for computerized administration. Their study consisted of a group that received ePREP, a group that received cognitive behavioral psychotherapy, and a control group. Participants who received ePREP reported significantly fewer depressive and anxiety symptoms and significant improvements in relationship distress compared to controls. However, improvements for the ePREP group were not significantly different than gains made by a comparison cognitive behavioral psychotherapy group (Braithwaite & Fincham, 2007).

Foster and adoptive parents

An internet version of PREP has also been created and disseminated for foster and adoptive parents (Markman et al., 2007). This program consists of an overview of marriage education today and of why marriage education is important, and teaches the key PREP skills (e.g., Communication Danger Signs, the Speaker–Listener technique, Time Out). This service delivery model also includes interactional questions and answers with animated foster parents and adoptive couples. Participants view couples learning and practicing skills while being coached by animated versions of PREP facilitators. Participants also listen to mini-lectures of the PREP material. A pilot study revealed significant gains in knowledge of the PREP content and increased confidence in handling future problems and in handling spousal conflict for the intervention group, though there were not significant decreases in negative communication (Markman et al., 2007).

Stepfamilies

There are several programs for use with stepfamilies, such as Designing Dynamic Stepfamilies (www.designingdynamicstepfamilies.com) and Smart Steps for Stepfamilies (www.stepfamilies.info/SmartSteps.php) (see also Chapter 33, this volume, and Whitton, Nicholson, & Markman, 2008). Designing Dynamic Stepfamilies is an eight-part video and study-guide series designed to teach communication skills, stepparenting discipline approaches, and how to create meaningful stepfamily bonds through presentations, exercises, and group discussions. Couples can participate in workshops or use the videos and study guide on their own. Smart Steps for Stepfamilies is a 12-hour educational program designed to build couple and family strengths by focusing on understanding stepfamily development, defining roles and rules, developing stepparenting strategies, and navigating healthy co-parenting relationships.

Relationship education with youth

Relationship education programs have also been implemented with youth in schools. Connections and Love U2 are two programs that incorporate PREP material and are used with young populations. Connections teaches teens skills for successful dating relationships and marriage preparation (http://www.dibblefund.org/connections.htm). The various skills taught include self-understanding, how relationships work, managing emotions, dating, effective communication, and what to expect from dating and marriage. The program incorporates lectures, group activities, games, role-plays, and brainstorming. The Connections curriculum has been evaluated in 10 ethnically diverse high schools across the United States with over 500 students.

Love U2 is designed for use in schools and youth organizations (http://www.dibblefund.org/love_u2.htm). It focuses on teaching skills for healthy relationships, addressing issues such as attraction, rejection, dating, falling in love, breaking up, and building healthy, sound relationships. The program also includes training in communication skills that is based on PREP.

Conclusion

Relationships benefit when couples are able to effectively communicate and manage conflict. Effective communication and conflict management predict relationship satisfaction and decrease risk of divorce (Clements, Cordova, Markman, & Laurenceau, 1997; Karney & Bradbury, 1995). Moreover, research shows that through relationship education couples can successfully be taught these kinds of skills (Halford et al., 2003). Despite high rates of divorce and relationship distress, life-long love is an aspiration of most adults. People are generally open to receiving education of varying sorts that enhances their opportunities to achieve their aspirations, in areas such as education, careers, or finances. People are increasingly open to receiving educational help in the area of romantic relationships, as well. This includes our primary focus here – preventive education services designed to help couples preserve lasting love – as well as a growing interest in services designed to help individuals make better partner choices in the first place. In the past few decades, the field of preventive relationship education (premarital and otherwise) has grown significantly in terms of types of approaches, research on outcomes, models of change, and use with groups beyond merely middle-class, college-educated couples. Despite the advances in this field, there remains a clear need for ongoing research in order to gain knowledge about mechanisms of effect, moderation of effects, and best practices adaptations of approaches for different groups. Such efforts will not only inform ongoing practice of preventive relationship education, but will fuel new theories and knowledge about couples, marriages, and families.

Resources

http://www.healthymarriageinfo.org
www.couplecommunication.com
www.nire.org
http://www.okmarriage.org
http://www.prepinc.com
http://www.loveyourrelationship.com
www.designingdynamicstepfamilies.com
www.stepfamilies.info/SmartSteps.php
http://www.dibblefund.org/connections.htm
http://www.dibblefund.org/love_u2.htm
http://www.fosterparentcollege.com

References

Amato, P. R. (2001). Children of divorce in the 1990s: An update of the Amato and Keith (1991) meta-analysis. *Family Psychology, 15,* 355–370.

Baucom, D. H., & Epstein, N. (1990). *Cognitive-behavioral marital therapy.* Philadelphia, PA: Brunner/Mazel.

Baumeister, R. F., & Leary, M. R. (1995). The need to belong: Desire for interpersonal attachments as a fundamental human motivation. *Psychological Bulletin, 117,* 497–529.

Braithwaite, S. R., & Fincham, F. D. (2007). ePREP: Computer based prevention of relationship dysfunction, depression and anxiety. *Journal of Social & Clinical Psychology, 26,* 609–622.

Bray, J. H., & Jouriles, E. (1995). Treatment of marital conflict and prevention of divorce. *Journal of Marital and Family Therapy, 21,* 461–473.

Butler, M., & Wampler, K. (1999). A meta-analytical update of research on the couple communication program. *American Journal of Family Therapy, 27,* 223–237.

Carroll, J. S., & Doherty, W. J. (2003). Evaluating the effectiveness of premarital prevention programs: A meta-analytic review of outcome research. *Family Relations, 52(2),* 105–118.

Cherlin, A. J. (1992). *Marriage, divorce, remarriage.* Cambridge, MA: Harvard University Press.

Clements, M. L., Cordova, A. D., Markman, H. J., & Laurenceau, J. P. (1997). The erosion of marital satisfaction over time and how to prevent it. In R. J. Sternberg & M. Hojjat (Eds.), *Satisfaction in close relationships* (pp. 335–355). New York: Guilford Press.

Coie, J. D., Watt, N. F., West, S. G., Hawkins, J. D., Asarnow, J. R., Markman, H. J., et al. (1993). The science of prevention: A conceptual framework and some directions for a national research program. *American Psychologist, 48,* 1013–1022.

Doss, B. D., Rhoades, G. K., Stanley, S. M., & Markman, H. J. (2008). Marital therapy, retreats, and books: The who, what, when and why of relationship help-seeking behaviors. *Journal of Marital and Family Therapy, 34,* 527–538.

Einhorn, L. A., Williams, T., Stanley, S. M., Wunderlin, N. K., & Markman, H. J. (2008). *PREP Inside and Out: Marriage education for inmates. Family Process, 47,* 341–356..

Essex, M. J., Klein, M. H., Cho, E., & Kraemer, H. C. (2003). Exposure to maternal depression and marital conflict: Gender differences in children's later mental health symptoms. *Journal of the American Academy of Child and Adolescent Psychiatry, 42,* 728–737.

Fincham, F. D. (2001). Attributions and close relationships: From balkanization to integration. In G. J. Fletcher & M. Clark (Eds.), *Blackwell handbook of social psychology.* (pp. 3–31). Oxford: Blackwell.

Fincham, F. D. (2002). Child abuse: An attribution perspective. *Child Maltreatment, 7,* 77–81.

Forthofer, M. S., Markman, H. J., Cox, M., Stanley, S., & Kessler, R. C. (1996). Associations between marital distress and work loss in a national sample. *Journal of Marriage and Family, 58,* 597–605.

Glenn, N. D., Nock, S., Waite, L., Doherty, W., Gottman, J., Makey, B., et al. (2002). Why marriage matters: Twenty-one conclusions from the social sciences. *American Experiment Quarterly, 5,* 34–44.

Grych, J. H., & Fincham, F. D. (2001). *Interparental conflict and child development: Theory, research, and applications.* New York: Cambridge University Press.

Guerney, B. G., Jr. (1977). *Relationship enhancement: Skill training programs for therapy, problem prevention, and enrichment.* San Francisco: Jossey-Bass.

Hahlweg, K., Markman, H. J., Thurmaier, F., Engl, J., & Eckert, V. (1998). Prevention of marital distress: Results of a German prospective longitudinal study. *Journal of Family Psychology, 12,* 543–556.

Halford, W. K. (2004). The future of couple relationship education: Suggestions on how it can make a difference. *Family Relations, 53,* 559–566.

Halford, W. K., Markman, H. J., Kline, G. H., & Stanley, S. M. (2003). Best practice in couple relationship education. *Journal of Marital and Family Therapy, 29,* 385–406.

Halford, W. K., Moore, E., Wilson, K. L., Farrugia, C., & Dyer, C. (2004). Benefits of flexible delivery relationship education: An evaluation of the Couple CARE Program. *Family Relations, 53*, 469–476.

Halford, W. K., Sanders, M. R., & Behrens, B. C. (2001). Can skills training prevent relationship problems in at-risk couples? Four-year effects of a behavioral relationship education program. *Journal of Family Psychology, 15*, 750–768.

Hawkins, A. J., Blanchard, V. L., Baldwin, S. A., & Fawcett, E. B. (2008). Does marriage and relationship education work? A meta-analytic study. *Journal of Consulting and Clinical Psychology, 76*, 723–734.

Hawkins, D. N., & Booth, A. (2005). Unhappily ever after: Effects of long-term, low-quality marriages on well-being. *Social Forces, 84*, 451–471.

Johnson, C. A., Stanley, S. M., Glenn, N. D., Amato, P., Nock, S. L., Markman, H. J., et al. (2002). *Marriage in Oklahoma: 2001 baseline statewide survey on marriage and divorce (S02096OKDHS)*. Oklahoma City: Oklahoma Department of Human Services.

Karney, B. R., & Bradbury, T. N. (1995). The longitudinal course of marital quality and stability: A review of theory, methods, and research. *Psychological Bulletin, 118*, 3–34.

Kiecolt-Glaser, J. K., McGuire, L., Robles, T. F., & Glaser, R. (2002). Psychoneuroimmunology: Psychological influences on immune function and health. *Journal of Consulting and Clinical Psychology, 70*, 537–547.

Laurenceau, J.-P., Stanley, S. M., Olmos-Gallo, A., Baucom, B., & Markman, H. J. (2004). Community-based prevention of marital dysfunction: Multilevel modeling of a randomized effectiveness study. *Journal of Consulting and Clinical Psychology, 72*, 933–943.

Markman, H. J., Floyd, F., J., Stanley, S. M., & Storaasli, R. D. (1988). Prevention of marital distress: A longitudinal investigation. *Journal of Consulting and Clinical Psychology, 56*, 210–217.

Markman, H. J., Rhoades, G. K., Delaney, R., White, L., & Pacifici, C. (2007, September). *Extending the reach of research-based couples intervention: The role of marriage education.* Paper presented at the Klaus-Grawe Think-Tank Meeting, Zuoz, Switzerland.

Markman, H. J., Silvern, L., Clements, M., & Kraft-Hanak, S. (1993). Men and women dealing with conflict in heterosexual relationships. *Journal of Social Issues, 49*, 107–125.

Markman, H. J., Stanley, S. M., & Blumberg, S. L. (1994). *Fighting for your marriage.* San Francisco: Jossey-Bass.

Markman, H., Stanley, S., Blumberg, S., Jenkins, N., & Whaley, C. (2004). *Twelve hours to a great marriage.* San Francisco: Jossey-Bass.

Markman, H. J., Stanley, S. M., Jenkins, N. H., Petrella, J. N., & Wadsworth, M. E. (2006). Preventive education: Distinctives and directions. *Journal of Cognitive Psychotherapy, 20*, 411–433.

Markman, H. J., Stanley, S. M., & Kline, G. H. (2003). Why marriage education can work and how government can be involved: Illustrations from the PREP approach. In W. D. Allen & L. L. Eiklenborg (Eds.), *Vision 2003: Contemporary family issues.* Minneapolis, MN: National Council on Family Relations.

Nunnally, E. W., Miller, S., & Wackman, D. B. (1975). The Minnesota Couples Communication Program. *Small Group Behavior, 6*, 57–71.

Pearson, M., Stanley, S. M., & Kline, G. H. (2005). *Within My Reach leader manual.* Denver: PREP for Individuals.

Ridley, C. A., & Sladeczek, I. E. (1992). Premarital relationship enhancement: Its effects on needs to relate to others. *Family Relations, 41*, 148–153.

Stanley, S. M. (2001). Making a case for premarital education. *Family Relations, 50*, 272–280.

Stanley, S. M., Allen, E. S., Markman, H. J., Saiz, C. C., Bloomstrom, G., Thomas, R., et al. (2005). Dissemination and evaluation of marriage education in the Army. *Family Process, 44,* 187–201.

Stanley, S. M., Amato, P. R., Johnson, C. A., & Markman, H. J. (2006). Premarital education, marital quality, and marital stability: Findings from a large, random household survey. *Journal of Family Psychology, 20,* 117–126.

Stanley, S. M., Blumberg, S. L., & Markman, H. J. (1999). Helping couples fight for their marriage: The PREP approach. In R. Berger & M. T. Hannah (Eds.), *Preventive approaches in couples therapy* (pp. 279–303). Philadelphia, PA: Brunner/Mazel.

Stanley, S. M., Markman, H. J., Jenkins, N., Rhoades, G. K., Noll, L., & Ramos, L. (2006). *Within Our Reach leader manual.* Denver, CO: PREP.

Stanley, S. M., Markman, H. J., Prado, L. M., Olmos-Gallo, P. A., Tonelli, L., St. Peters, M., et al. (2001). Community-based premarital prevention: Clergy and lay leaders on the front lines. *Family Relations, 50(1),* 67–76.

Stanley, S. M., Markman, H. J., St. Peters, M., & Leber, B. D. (1995). Strengthening marriages and preventing divorce: New directions in prevention research. *Family Relations, 44,* 392–401.

Stanley, S. M., Pearson, M., & Kline, G. H. (2005, November). *The development of relationship education for low income individuals: Lessons from research and experience.* Paper presented at the meeting of the Association for Public Policy Analysis and Management, Washington, DC.

Stanley, S., Trathen, D., McCain, S., & Bryan, M. (1998). *A lasting promise.* San Francisco: Jossey-Bass.

U.S. Census Bureau. (2002). *Number, timing, and duration of marriages and divorces: 1996.* Washington, DC: U.S. Census Bureau.

Waite, L. J., & Gallagher, M. (2000). *The case for marriage: Why married people are happier, healthier, and better off financially.* New York: Random House.

Wampler, K. (1982). Bringing the review of literature into the age of quantification: Meta-analysis as a strategy for integrating research findings in family studies. *Journal of Marriage and the Family, 44,* 1009–1023.

Whisman, M. A., & Bruce, M. L. (1999). Marital dissatisfaction and incidence of major depressive episode in a community sample. *Journal of Abnormal Psychology, 108,* 674–678.Whitton, S. W., Nicholson, J. M., & Markman, H. J. (2008). Research on interventions for stepfamily couples: The state of the field. In J. Pryor (Ed.), *The international handbook of stepfamilies: Policy and practice in legal, research, and clinical spheres* (pp. 455–484). Wiley.

31

Children of Divorce: New Trends and Ongoing Dilemmas

Marsha Kline Pruett and Ryan Barker

Currently, and for the foreseeable future, divorce occupies a persistent place in the social structure as a family transition that substantially impacts all members, not least are the children. In this child-centered chapter we will describe three major aspects of family relationships that exacerbate children's problematic development or shield them from the potentially more pernicious effects of divorce: (1) the child's relationship with the residential parent; (2) the amount and type of conflict between parents; and (3) the quality of access and relationship the child has with the non-residential, or less seen parent, typically the father. We will then introduce some of the new concepts and dilemmas mental health and legal professionals have encountered in recent years: parenting plans for young children, parent relocation cases, and child alienation from one parent.

Divorce as a Stressful Transition in Family Life

Divorce creates a number of stressors for family members (Clarke-Stewart & Brentano, 2006), and it is thus a potent risk factor for children. As compared to children with married parents, children with divorced parents have poorer academic achievement and higher school dropout rates, more behavioral and emotional problems, lower self-esteem, and more difficulties with interpersonal relationships (Amato, 1993, 2000; Kelly, 2000). Qualitative reports on the emotional costs children experience detail painful feelings and memories, and longing for more contact with fathers, over the course of childhood (Emery, 2004; Marquadt, 2006; Wallerstein, Lewis, & Blakeslee, 2000).

Despite these risks, most children face 2–3 years of destabilization before adapting to the divorce, with few lasting detrimental effects (Hetherington & Kelly, 2002). While almost all children experience distress from divorce, only 20–25% are at risk for developing emotional problems such as mood disorders, anxiety disorders, and conduct disorders (Emery, 2004). Thus, divorce does not condemn children to a life of problems and hardship but does elevate risk factors that are cause for concern (Clarke-Stewart & Brentano, 2006).

Age Differences in Adjustment

When parents ask at what age it is least harmful to their children to separate, the answer from existent research points to different risks at different ages, and the divorcing process and family relationships before and after divorce hold more weight than age and developmental stage in and of themselves.

Infancy and early childhood

Research examining the impact of divorce on young children, under 6 years of age, remains consistent in the types of difficulties portrayed for children, but inconclusive in the longevity of those difficulties. Since infancy through preschool is a sensitive and rapid time for cognitive development, young children may be at greater risk of developing a negative self-image, behavioral problems, and an inability to form positive attachments and rela-tionships. Changes in the amount of time an infant spends with her or his parents, changes in her or his living environment and schedule, and changes in her or his primary caretaker(s)' emotional wellbeing may interfere with the infant's emotional development and ability to form and maintain secure attachments. For example, both Solomon and George (1999) and Clarke-Stewart et al. (2000) described infant–mother attachment prob-lems in separated and divorced families, though both studies attributed the problems to other factors – parental conflict and the economic and emotional wellbeing of the mother – rather than the divorce itself.

Consistent with their developmental proclivities toward autonomy and regression demands, toddlers with divorced parents show greater fear of abandonment, regressive behaviors (often around toilet habits), distrust in others, frequency and immensity of tantrums, and a tendency to blame themselves (Clarke-Stewart & Brentano, 2006; Hermon & Bretherton, 2001). Pruett and Pruett (1999) found that children under the age of 6 often had inaccurate or vague information concerning the nature of the divorce and expressed concern about their relationships with both parents. Still in an egocentric stage of cognitive development, they were likely to think that their behavior caused the separation and clung to hopes that their parents would reunite.

Middle childhood

Children ranging in age from 6 to 12 experience stress in academic and social as well as emotional domains. Approximately one third of children who experience divorce tend to suffer academically (Amato, 2001), particularly in reading, spelling, and math (Bisnaire, Firestone, & Rynard, 1990). Further, school-age children of divorce demonstrate more aggressive conduct than their peers from two-parent households, particularly within the first 2 years after parental separation (e.g., Hoyt, Cowen, Pedro-Carroll, & Alpert-Gillis, 1990). As the development of loyalty and passions for following the "rules of the game" are important characteristics of this age group, so these children may be especially prone to allying with one parent against the other (Johnston & Roseby, 1997). Though statistical group differences are modest (Amato, 2001), children may feel depressed even when functioning well in the outer world (Kliewer & Sandler, 1993). School-based interventions and group therapy tend to be the most accessible and relied-on methods of treatment for this age.

Adolescence

While older adolescents experiencing parental divorce have a more intimate understanding of what is happening between their parents, they may also feel frustrated and powerless to make things better, turning to alcohol, drugs, and premature sexual activity, along with aggressive and delinquent behaviors, to express their upset (Clarke-Stewart and Brentano, 2006; Kirby, 2002). Boundaries may blur with children becoming confidantes to their parents as the parents openly criticize their ex-spouse, discuss their own personal struggles, and consult their teenagers about parenting issues of younger children and household expenses while issuing the teens increased responsibilities in household duties and child care. Although maternal disclosure is more often associated with mother–daughter relationships, Koerner, Wallace, Lehman, Lee, & Escalante (2004) found a significant correlation between maternal disclosure and psychological distress for both sons and daughters.

Overall, studies show that adolescents experiencing parental divorce are more likely to have greater psychological distress and poorer self-esteem than adolescents from two-parent households (Amato, 2001; Hetherington & Kelly, 2002), including difficulty trusting and higher conflict in their romantic relationships (Ross & Mirowsky, 1999; Jacquet & Surra, 2000), and a greater likelihood of divorcing themselves in adulthood (Ross & Mirowsky, 1999). While a meta-analysis of relevant studies indicates that emotional problems manifest more strongly for older children, compared to academic problems for younger children (Amato, 2001), the academic problems that surface for adolescents may be compounded due to the more serious turn that schooling takes in older years, with concomitant risks for school dropout (Lansford, Malone, & Castellino, 2006; Simons & Associates, 1996).

Gender Differences in Adjustment

Early divorce research found that boys at various ages showed greater difficulty adjusting to divorce than girls in a variety of areas. More recent research with methodological improvements is less clear about differing gender effects: there is modest support for boys' greater vulnerability, yet both genders show difficulties across various domains (Amato, 2001). Among younger children, boys exhibit more negative effects, for example, while among adolescents, girls seem to bear the brunt of the parental divorce (Hetherington & Stanley-Hagan, 1999). Further, Pruett, Ebling, & Insabella (2004) found that overnights with fathers, inconsistent parenting plan schedules, and having more caretakers were more difficult adjustments to make for toddler boys than for girls. Also, Johnston (1993) found that boys were more vulnerable to becoming embroiled in parental conflict than girls. It seems clear that gender differences in adjustment may favor one gender or the other depending on the age of the child and the involvement status of both parents; however, it should be noted that only a cluster of girls from divorced families show the development of exceptional competence following divorce (Hetherington, 1999), and it is girls who seem to actually benefit from overnights with their fathers at an early age (Pruett et al., 2004). Thus, being a girl may have some protective functions for younger children of divorce.

Relationship with the Residential Parent

For many adults, divorce is a period of personal identity reformation and rapid change in many aspects of their lives. The resulting parental disequilibrium may be manifested in temporary despondency or the longer-term development of alcoholism, drug abuse, and depression (Kelly & Emery, 2003; Williams & Dunne-Bryant, 2006). These symptoms are generally most intense during the first year post-separation, in which parents must learn to negotiate the economic, social, and emotional adjustments that divorce entails.

Throughout the transition, the primary or residential parent's mental health is of particular concern for the child. If the residential parent is experiencing mental health symptoms, other pre-existing risk factors may be stirred up, decreasing the healthier family functions that serve a protective function during and after divorce (Cowan, Cowan, Cohen, Pruett, & Pruett, 2008), exposing children to further risks and complications. Mental health problems may also exacerbate conflict with the nonresidential parent (Whiteside & Becker, 2000).

The mental health and stability of both parents are a central ingredient in the maintenance of quality parenting, which is, in turn, one of the strongest protective factors for children of divorce, with evidence pointing particularly to the salience of the custodial or residential parent's relationship with the child (Forgatch, Patterson, & Ray, 1995; Hetherington, 1999). A strong and consistent link exists between authoritative parenting and positive child adjustment, a parenting style that involves consistent discipline, parental monitoring, and engaging in warm and open communication with children (Kelly, 2000; Krishnakumar & Buehler, 2000). In addition to psychological stressors, the need for many residential parents to work outside of the home more hours than previously, and a lowered economic status of the family (especially among female-headed households), contribute to parents' decreased availability and effectiveness. Conditions outside of the nuclear family also impact parenting quality after divorce, notably extended family involvement and conflict, and legal conditions such as the family's engagement in the adversarial court system versus alternative dispute resolution (Kelly & Emery, 2003).

Parental Cooperation and Conflict

Parent conflict is widely recognized as a key risk factor for poorer overall development for children post-divorce (Laumann-Billings & Emery, 2000). While the majority of parents reduce their levels of dispute within 2–3 years, 8–20% of parents may continue to display high levels of conflict for a greater period of time (Hetherington, 1999; Kelly, 2006), exposing their children to attitudes and behaviors that undermine childhood development. Frequent or continuous conflict, especially that which places children as the central focus, occurs in the children's presence, or encourages children to declare their loyalty to one parent over the other, is associated with academic, behavioral, relational, and emotional problems during childhood and into adulthood (Amato & Afifi, 2006; Grych, 2005; Johnston & Roseby, 1997). Parental conflict may also have indirect effects that negatively impact the family system, including the development of gatekeeping behaviors, often manifested in divorcing families as the residential parent's efforts to restrict the non-residential parent's access to and involvement with the children after divorce (Pruett, Arthur, & Ebling, 2007). It is important to note, however, that if parents are able to keep their children out of their conflicts, children are more likely to have levels of functioning that are similar to those of children whose parents had very little or no conflict (Grych, 2005). Even when parents engage in conflict, a child's relationship with a warm and caring extended family member or adult outside of the family, such as a neighbor, coach, or teacher, can help mitigate the negative effects of parental strife (Hetherington, 1999).

Some parents can cooperate on a child's behalf even when they disagree on major issues or values. Such cooperation facilitates the child's adaptation to the divorce, especially when making transitions between homes or activities. Such cooperation is especially important for positive paternal involvement since mothers are usually primary caretakers of the children after divorce, as described below (Pruett et al., 2007).

Non-Residential Parent–Child Contact and Relationship

Despite a general trend toward increased father involvement over the past generation (Cowan et al., 2008), the traditional structure of primary child custody and residence with the mother continues to prevail in the majority of divorce situations. The corresponding reduction in father involvement, interest, and economic support over time (Baum, 2006; Kelly, 2006), and the lack of clarity surrounding paternal roles and responsibilities after divorce (Madden-Derdich & Leonard, 2000; Minton & Paisley, 1996), may even result in a complete loss of contact with fathers, viewed as one of the more negative effects of divorce (Fabricius & Hall, 2000; Johnston, 1993; Kelly & Emery, 2003).

Early research on the relationship between father–child contact and children's post-divorce adjustment focused on the frequency of contact as the critical determinant of the relationship and revealed only equivocal effects (Amato & Gilbreth, 1999). Yet as researchers began to explore the quality (rather than quantity) of father–child contact and involvement, studies consistently indicated that when fathers are attuned to and active in their children's lives, children experience more positive psychological and social adjustment and perform better academically (Pruett, 2000). A healthy relationship between fathers and children could actually counteract some of the effects of parental conflict. Fabricius and Luecken (2007) found that children who spent more time with their fathers post-divorce had better long-term relationships with them, even in families with high levels of conflict. Moreover, as time spent with fathers increases, especially in shared residential arrangements, parent conflict can decrease (Fabricius & Luecken, 2007; Bauserman, 2002).

A cautionary note must be added: father involvement in children's lives is not always healthy or desirable. In situations of severe mental health problems, drug or alcohol abuse, family domestic violence, or child abuse, father access may be limited, supervised, or suspended as deemed appropriate in the child's best interests.

While non-residential parents, as recently as 1980, often lost all relationship with their children post-divorce, the percentage of children who lose contact with their fathers 2–3 years after divorce dropped to 18–25% by the late 1990s (Furstenberg, Nord, Peterson, & Zill, 1983; Kelly, 2006). This trend has been aided by the development of a variety of alternative dispute resolution (ADR) procedures and post-divorce interventions supported and/or mandated in the legal system (Schepard, 2004). Mediation is one intervention widely implemented and researched with positive results (Beck, Sales, & Emery, 2004). Gradually, divorce and court-related interventions such as the Collaborative Divorce Project (Pruett, Insabella, & Gustafson, 2005) are incorporating the interests and needs of fathers. These interventions typically are designed to encourage fathers to remain active in childrearing after divorce, to increase parenting skills and motivation, and to decrease parental conflict (also see Cookston, Braver, Griffin, deLusé, & Miles, 2007; Mincy & Pouncy, 2002).

Newer Issues of Which We Know Little Empirically

Parenting plans for young children

Along with the growth and expansion of joint custody statutes and litigation, attitudes and parenting practices have undergone a shift in favor of more varied patterns of custody and access. Parenting plans are the medium through which custody labels get operationalized into actual schedules regarding all decisions, including time spent with each parent. Parenting plans for young children are highly disputed (Pruett, 2005; Pruett et al., 2004) and quietly contested in the offices of therapists and mediators. Dilemmas include at what age a child should begin regular overnights with a non-residential parent, how many transitions per week a child should reasonably be able to manage, and whether young children can split their time near equally in two households, to name a few. While little research exists in this area, available data suggest that a young child's adjustment to spending overnights in both homes will be a function of child characteristics and parents' ability to respond to their child's needs sensitively and collaboratively (Pruett et al., 2004; Solomon & Biringen, 2001).

Relocation/move-aways

In relocation cases, children who have experienced care and nurturance from two involved parents are faced with the loss of regular contact with one parent when the other one initiates a residential move in order to secure a better job, support a new romantic relationship, or live closer to extended family. In such situations, parents – and often a judge – weigh the potential attenuation in the non-residential parent–child relationship against the potential gains in life circumstances and satisfactions for the residential parent, and consider how the risks and benefits would trickle down to the child.

State laws on relocation vary widely, with some states declaring a presumption permitting relocation and others declaring a presumption that precludes it (Braver, Ellman, & Fabricius, 2003). Currently, the majority of states favor a "best interests of the child" standard, with no presumptions attached (Elrod, 2006), though this direction is of little comfort to mental health professionals who work with the courts to determine the best interests of a particular child in a particular case.

Little to nothing is currently known about the effects of parental moves on the wellbeing of parents and children after divorce. Family relocations generally can have a negative impact on children's emotional adjustment and school performance, and there are indications that relocations are more difficult for children in divorcing than intact families (Austin, 2000), but research in this area is sorely needed to understand the impact on children of varying ages and their families.

Parental alienation

Parental alienation is a phenomenon associated with high-conflict divorce and custody disagreements. In this process, the child becomes hostile to one parent while strongly allying with the other parent, with alienation implying that the aligned parent intentionally created a wedge between the child and her or his other parent. While alignments are common in disputing families, such alignments cross over into alienation when the child's hatred of and/or withdrawal from the parent is unremitting and out of proportion to the parent's behavior (Kelly & Johnston, 2001).

Research suggests that all family members make contributions to family dynamics that result in alienation of a parent (Johnston, Walters, & Friedlander, 2001). The goals of interventions targeting alienated children and their parents are to take the child's mutually exclusive views of each parent as "bad" or "good," and help the child cope with distressing feelings and appraise their parents and the situation more realistically, while addressing relationships between all family members, treating the family system as well as the disenfranchised parent. Successful interventions combine strict contracts with families and support from the legal system for residential arrangements, enforcement of contact, and monitoring the wellbeing and safety of the child (Sullivan & Kelly, 2001).

Conclusions

No matter how normative divorce has become, the decision for parents to separate and divorce places children and their families at risk for both short- and long-term suffering. The field of psychology has made great strides in understanding what makes divorce difficult for children of all ages, and how to support family adaptation through various models of intervention. In addition to divorce counseling, psychotherapy, and family evaluation conducted separately from or in adjunction to legal actions, systemic policies and practices that support family adaptation have been developed, researched, and implemented in courts, schools, and communities throughout the western world. Some of the most common of these include: (1) school-based groups and interventions that help students stay on track educationally and socially (e.g., O'Halloran & Carr, 2000; Wolchik et al., 2002); (2) parent education that helps parents become aware of what their children need during divorce, and enhances parental communication, conflict management, and problem-solving skills (Cookston, Braver, Sandler, & Genalo, 2002; Pedro-Carroll, Nakhnikian, & Montes, 2001); (3) alternative dispute resolution strategies such as mediation that aim to maximize parental cooperation, minimize conflict, and reduce the financial costs of protracted and intensive involvement in the legal system (Pruett & Johnston, 2004; Schepard, 2004); and (4) quasi-judicial services such as parenting coordination in which mental health professionals mediate or arbitrate parental disputes related to day-to-day issues (Coates, Deutsch, Starnes, Sullivan, & Sydlik, 2004). The goals of these practices are to promote parent self-determination and child stability and adaptation during this family transition.

However, a great deal remains in terms of the development of mental health practices related to some of the newer, distressing trends in divorce law and social policy. Parenting plans for vulnerable children, relocation, and parental alienation are but a few of these lesser-understood areas. We have much to learn, and much work to do, to sustain the children and families for whom this transition will be one of life's critical tests, and support their capacity to rise above the pain toward greater self-understanding and relational competence.

References

Amato, P. R. (1993). Children's adjustment to divorce: Theories, hypotheses, and empirical support. *Journal of Marriage and the Family, 55,* 23–38.

Amato, P. R. (2000). The consequences of divorce for adults and children. *Journal of Marriage and the Family, 62,* 1269–1287.

Amato, P. R. (2001). Children of divorce in the 1990s: An update of the Amato and Keith (1991) meta-analysis. *Journal of Family Psychology, 15,* 355–370.

Amato, P. R., & Afifi, T. D. (2006). Feeling caught between parents: Adult children's relations with parents and subjective well-being. *Journal of Marriage and Family, 68,* 222–235.

Amato, P. R., & Gilbreth, J. G. (1999). Nonresident fathers and children's well-being: A metaanalysis. *Journal of Marriage and Family, 61,* 557–573.

Austin, W. G. (2000). A forensic psychology model of risk assessment for child custody relocation law. *Family and Conciliation Courts Review, 38,* 192–207.

Baum, N. (2006). Postdivorce paternal disengagement: Failed mourning and role fusion. *Journal of Marital and Family Therapy, 32,* 245–254.

Bauserman, R. (2002). Child adjustment in joint-custody versus sole-custody arrangements: A meta-analytic review. *Journal of Family Psychology, 16,* 91–102.

Beck, C. J. A., Sales, B. D., & Emery, R. E. (2004). Research on the impact of family mediation. In J. Folberg, A. L. Milne, & P. Salem (Eds.), *Divorce and family mediation* (pp. 447–482). New York: Guilford Press.

Bisnaire, L. M., Firestone, P., & Rynard, D. (1990). Factors associated with academic achievement in children following parental separation. *Journal of Orthopsychiatry, 60,* 67–76.

Braver, S. L., Ellman, I. M., & Fabricius, W. V. (2003). Relocation of children after divorce and children's best interests: New evidence and legal considerations. *Journal of Family Psychology, 17,* 206–219.

Clarke-Stewart, A., & Brentano, C. (2006). *Divorce: Causes and consequences.* New Haven: Yale University Press.

Clarke-Stewart, K. A., Vandall, D. L., McCartney, K., Owen, M. T., & Booth, C. (2000). Effects of parental separation and divorce on very young children. *Journal of Family Psychology, 14,* 304–326.

Coates, C. A., Deutsch, R., Starnes, H., Sullivan, M. J., & Sydlik, B. (2004). Parenting coordination for high-conflict families. *Family Court Review, 42,* 246–262.

Cookston, J. T., Braver, S. L., Griffin, W., deLusé, S. R., & Miles, J. C. (2007). Effects of the Dads for Life intervention on interparental conflict and co-parenting in the two years after divorce. *Family Process, 46,* 123–137.

Cookston, J. T., Braver, S. L., Sandler, I. N., & Genalo, M. T. (2002). Prospects for expanded parent education services for divorcing families with children. *Family Court Review, 40,* 190–203.

Cowan, P. A., Cowan, C. P., Cohen, N., Pruett, M. K., & Pruett, K. D. (2008). Supporting fathers' involvement with kids. In J. D. Berrick & N. Gilbert (Eds.), *Raising children: Emerging needs, modern risks, and social responses* (pp. 44–80). New York: Oxford University Press.

Elrod, L. D. (2006). A move in the right direction? Best interests of the child emerging as the standard for relocation cases. *Journal of Child Custody, 3,* 29–61.

Emery, R. E. (2004). *The truth about children and divorce.* New York: Viking Press.

Fabricius, W. V., & Hall, J. (2000). Young adults' perspectives on divorce: Living arrangements. *Family and Conciliation Courts Review, 38,* 446–461.

Fabricius, W. V., & Luecken, L. J. (2007). Postdivorce living arrangements, parent conflict, and long-term physical health correlates for children of divorce. *Journal of Family Psychology, 21,* 195–205.

Forgatch, M. S., Patterson, G. R., & Ray, J. A. (1995). Divorce and boys' adjustment problems: Two paths with a single model. In E. M. Hetherington & E. A. Blechman (Eds.), *Stress, coping and resiliency in children and families* (pp. 67–105). Mahwah, NJ: Erlbaum.

Furstenberg, F. F., Jr., Nord, C. W., Peterson, J. L., & Zill, N. (1983). The life course of children of divorce: Marital disruption and parental contact. *American Sociological Review, 48(6),* 656–668.

Grych, J. H. (2005). Interparental conflict as a risk factor for child maladjustment: Implications for the development of prevention programs. *Family Court Review, 43,* 97–108.

Hermon, P., & Bretherton, I. (2001). "He was the best daddy": Postdivorce preschoolers' representation of loss and family life. In A. Goencue & E. L. Kline (Eds.), *Children in play, story, and school* (pp. 177–203). New York: Guilford Press.

Hetherington, E. M. (1999). Should we stay together for the sake of the children? In E. M. Hetherington (Ed.), *Coping with divorce, single parenting and remarriage: A risk and resiliency perspective* (pp. 93–116). Mahwah, NJ: Erlbaum.

Hetherington, E. M., & Kelly, J. (2002). *For better or for worse: Divorce reconsidered.* New York: Norton.

Hetherington, E. M., & Stanley-Hagan, M. (1999). The adjustment of children with divorced parents: A risk and resiliency perspective. *Journal of Child Psychology and Psychiatry, 40,* 129–140.

Hoyt, L. A., Cowen, E. L., Pedro-Carroll, J. L., & Alpert-Gillis, L. J. (1990). Anxiety and depression in young children of divorce. *Journal of Clinical Child Psychology, 19,* 26–32.

Jacquet, S. E., & Surra, C. A. (2000). Parental divorce and premarital couples: Commitment and other relationship characteristics. *Journal of Marriage and Family, 63,* 627–638.

Johnston, J. R. (1993). Children of divorce who refuse visitation. In C. E. Depner & J. H. Bray (Eds.), *Nonresidential parenting: New vistas in family living* (pp. 109–135). Newbury Park, CA: Sage.

Johnston, J. R., & Roseby, V. (1997). *In the name of the child: A developmental approach to understanding and helping children of conflicted and violent families.* New York: Free Press.

Johnston, J. R., Walters, M. G., & Friedlander, S. (2001). Therapeutic work with alienated children and their families. *Family Court Review, 39(3),* 316–333.

Kelly, J. B. (2000). Children's adjustment in conflicted marriage and divorce: A decade review of research. *Journal of American Academy of Child and Adolescent Psychiatry, 39(8),* 963–973.

Kelly, J. B. (2006). Children's living arrangements following separation and divorce: Insights from empirical and clinical research. *Family Process, 46,* 35–52.

Kelly, J., & Emery, R. (2003). Children's adjustment following divorce: Risk and resilience perspectives. *Family Relations, 52,* 352–362.

Kelly, J. B., & Johnston, J. R. (2001). The alienated child: A reformulation of parental alienation syndrome. *Family Court Review, 39(3),* 249–266.

Kirby, J. B. (2002). The influence of parental separation on smoking initiation in adolescents. *Journal of Health and Social Behavior, 43,* 56–71.

Kliewer, W., & Sandler, I. N. (1993). Social competence and coping among children of divorce. *American Journal of Orthopsychiatry, 63,* 432–440.

Koerner, S. S., Wallace, S., Lehman, S. J., Lee, S., & Escalante, K. A. (2004). Sensitive mother-to-adolescent disclosures after divorce: Is the experience of sons different from that of daughters? *Journal of Family Psychology, 18,* 46–57.

Krishnakumar, A. & Buehler, C. (2000). Interparental conflict and parenting behaviors: A meta-analytic review. *Family Relationships, 49,* 25–44.

Lansford, J. E., Malone, P. S., & Castellino, D. R. (2006). Trajectories of internalizing, externalizing, and grades for children who have and have not experienced their parents' divorce or separation. *Journal of Family Psychology, 20,* 292–301.

Laumann-Billings, L., & Emery, R. E. (2000). Distress among young adults from divorced families. *Journal of Family Psychology, 14,* 671–687.

Madden-Derdich, D. A., & Leonard, S. A. (2000). Parental role identity and father's involvement in coparental interaction after divorce: Father's perspectives. *Family Relations, 49*, 311–318.

Marquadt, E. (2006). *Between two worlds: The inner lives of children of divorce.* New York: Crown.

Mincy, R., & Pouncy, H. (2002). The responsible fatherhood field: Evolution and goals. In C. S. Tamis-LeMonda & N. J. Cabrera (Eds.), *Handbook of father involvement: Multidisciplinary perspectives* (pp. 555–597). Mahwah, NJ: Erlbaum.

Minton, C., & Pasley, K. (1996). Fathers' parenting role identity and father involvement: A comparison of nondivorced and divorced, nonresident fathers. *Journal of Family Issues, 17*, 26–45.

O'Halloran, M., & Carr, A. (2000). Adjustment to parental separation and divorce. In A. C. Carr (Ed.), *What works for children and adolescents: A critical review of interventions with children, adolescents, and their families* (pp. 280–299). New York: Routledge.

Pedro-Carroll, J. L., Nakhnikian, E., & Montes, G. (2001). Court affiliated parent education: Assisting children through transition: Helping parents protect their children from the toxic effects of ongoing conflict in the aftermath of divorce. *Family Court Review, 39*, 377–392.

Pruett, K. D. (2000). *Fatherneed: Why father care is as essential as mother care for your child.* New York: Free Press.

Pruett, M. K. (2005). Applications of attachment theory and child development research to young children's overnights in separated and divorced families. *Overnights and Young Children: Essays from the Family Court Review*, 5–12.

Pruett, M. K., Arthur, L., & Ebling, R. (2007). The hand that rocks the cradle: Maternal gatekeeping after divorce. *Pace University Law Review, 27*, 709–739.

Pruett, M. K., Ebling, R., & Insabella, G. (2004). Critical aspects of parenting plans for young children. *Family Court Review, 42*, 39–59.

Pruett, M. K., Insabella, G. M., & Gustafson, K. (2005). The collaborative divorce project: A court-based intervention for separating parents with young children. *Family Court Review, 43*, 38–51.

Pruett, M. K., & Johnston, J. R. (2004). Therapeutic mediation with high-conflict parents: Effective models and strategies. In J. Folberg, A. L. Milne, & P. Salem (Eds.), *Divorce and family mediation: Models, techniques, and applications* (pp. 92–111). New York: Guilford Press.

Pruett, K. D., & Pruett, M. K. (1999). "Only God decides": Young children's perception of divorce and the legal system. *Journal of the American Academy of Child and Adolescent Psychiatry, 38*, 1544–1550.

Ross, C. E., & Mirowsky, J. (1999). Parental divorce, life-course disruption, and adult depression. *Journal of Marriage and Family, 61*, 1034–1045.

Schepard, A. (2004). *Children, courts, and custody: Interdisciplinary models for divorcing families.* Cambridge and New York: Cambridge University Press.

Simons, R. L., & Associates. (1996). *Understanding differences between divorced and intact families: Stress, interaction, and child outcomes.* Thousand Oaks, CA: Sage.

Solomon, J., & Biringen, Z. (2001). Another look at the developmental research: Commentary on Kelly and Lamb's, "Using child development research to make appropriate custody and access decisions for young children." *Family Court Review, 39*, 355–364.

Solomon, J., & George, C. (1999). The development of attachment in separated and divorced families: Effects of overnight visitation, parent and couple variables. *Attachment and Human Development, 1*, 2–33.

Sullivan, M. J., & Kelly, J. B. (2001). Legal and psychological management of cases with an alienated child. *Family Court Review, 39(3)*, 299–315.

Wallerstein, J. S., Lewis, J. M., & Blakeslee, S. (2000). *The unexpected legacy of divorce: A 25 year landmark study.* New York: Hyperion.

Whiteside, M. F., & Becker, B. J. (2000). Parental factors and young child's postdivorce adjustment: A meta-analysis with implications for parenting arrangement. *Journal of Family Psychology, 14,* 5–26.

Williams, K., & Dunne-Bryant, A. (2006). Divorce and adult psychological well-being: Clarifying the role of gender and child age. *Journal of Marriage and the Family, 68,* 1178–1196.

Wolchik, S. A., Sandler, I. N., Millsap, R. E., Plummer, B. A., Greene, S. M., Anderson, E. R., et al. (2002). Six-year follow-up of preventive interventions for children of divorce: A randomized controlled trial. *Journal of the American Medical Association, 288(15),* 1874–1881.

32

Collaborative Divorce: A Family-Centered Process

A. Rodney Nurse and Peggy Thompson

Collaborative divorce (CD) is a family-centered, non-adversarial, interdisciplinary-based, interprofessional process for divorcing. CD addresses divorce as a family reorganization process occurring over time, consisting of interpersonal, legal, and financial components. Still evolving from its beginning only a decade ago, CD is now available in all large cities in the USA and Canada. CD is spreading over the UK, continental Europe, Australia, and New Zealand.

This chapter by two of CD's originators sketches the origins of CD in the San Francisco/Bay Area and Minneapolis. Five assumptions underlying the CD process are delineated, followed by a description of CD's interdisciplinary-based professional team and the local practice group. The chapter then presents the phases of CD: Phase 1, Contracting and initiating team/family relationships; Phase 2, Individually focused preparation of parents and children – beginning; Phase 2, Relationship integration, legal/financial factors, and reaching agreements – concluding; and Phase 3, Following through post-agreement. The chapter concludes with brief sections on the essential role of family psychology for the development of CD and the future of CD.

Origins of Collaborative Divorce

During the 1980s we (the authors) conducted many child custody evaluations in northern California, worked as special masters/parent coordinators, and served as divorce therapists. One of us (A. R. N.) worked nationally on an interdisciplinary team investigating child sexual abuse allegations, and had taught mental health professionals how to conduct child custody evaluations.

What struck us most forcefully (and continues to) is that the adversarial divorcing system further polarizes already struggling, pained parents, and has a negative impact on their children. Divorce is framed as a *dispute* between two *parties* rather than as one (statistically) normal transition occurring to almost half of families. The media reinforces the societal view of divorce as a battle. However, as legal scholar Janet Weinstein comments disdainfully, "a process which pits family members against each other is not conducive to relationships" (1997, p. 87).

In reaction to the destructiveness of the adversarial system we found ourselves repeatedly saying that "there must be a better way to divorce." We looked and could find none. So one of us (P. T.) pulled together a small group of lawyers and mental health professionals (later adding a financial specialist), all experienced in and disturbed by the destructiveness of the divorcing system. These colleagues joined with us in forming a small think tank which met for many months to attempt the development of a new, workable divorcing system.

At about the same time in Minneapolis a family lawyer, Stuart G. Webb (see Webb & Ousky, 2006), decided that he would no longer represent divorcing parties in court. He was available to work with any other lawyer willing to sign an agreement with clients that if the clients could not reach good faith agreements with the help of two attorneys and wanted to take the matter to court, the couple would have to use other lawyers. With this agreement focusing all energy on finding solutions, the new process of *collaborative law* (CL) was born. Through a referral to a San Francisco/Bay Area attorney, our group learned of this new legal development and realized that by joining together we could have a complete team approach for divorce.

Our group developed a new interdisciplinary-based professional divorce system and put together a small book describing the new divorce process for the public (Fagerstrom et al., 1997). The two of us (A. R. N. and P. T.) published articles on CD in *The Family Psychologist* (1997) and the *American Journal of Family Law* (1999), plus a chapter in *Innovations in Clinical Practice: A Source Book* (2000).

This blend of the legal and the psychology systems propelled the spread of CD. A new interprofessional organization was formed, the International Academy of Collaborative Professionals (IACP), led by attorney Pauline Tesler (1999) and one of us (P.T.), who became the first presidents of IACP. Less than a decade in existence, IACP now has over 3,000 members and 170 practice groups, as well as its own professional journal and an executive director. The Family Law section of the American Bar Association published Pauline Tesler's professional book, *Collaborative Law* (2001), which she is presently revising. HarperCollins published for the public *Collaborative Divorce* (Tesler & Thompson, 2006). The two authors of this chapter are presently completing *Collaborative divorce: A family centered approach*, for publication by the American Psychological Association (Nurse & Thompson, in press). We are convinced that this new divorce process is an idea whose time has come.

Assumptions of Collaborative Divorce

There are at least five major assumptions underlying CD.

Just as couples marry because of feelings, couples divorce because of feelings. Couples with children must not only manage painful feelings about the couple separation and the end of their attachment actuality and dreams, they must also forge a new, ongoing co-parenting relationship with each other in order to care for their children under the new conditions of living their separate adult lives emotionally while living geographically apart.

Conceptualizing divorce as a family process rather than as a legal event fits the reality of the family members' experience of divorce. This paradigm shift, underscored by critical research on divorcing families, is fundamental for planning and taking action in the CD process.

The divorce process for family members extends well past reaching the post-divorce agreement. Research on divorce consistently finds that the most emotionally taxing and behaviorally disruptive time for families is during the months immediately *after* concluding the divorce agreement, with the disruption reaching a peak at the end of the first year post-agreement, receding the second, followed by ripples of divorce-related problems up to five years post-divorce agreement (Hetherington & Kelly, 2002; Kelly & Emery, 2003).

While the divorcing experience is painful (Schwartz & Kaslow, 1997) *and often difficult to navigate, defining divorce as a change in family relationships carries optimistic overtones.* Hetherington and Kelly write: "Marital transitions offer great opportunities for personal growth and change. As families are reorganized, and old relationships and roles between husbands and wives, parents and children, and siblings that sustain our notions of who we are and what is important in our lives alter or are peeled away, a window of change opens" (2002, p. 276).

Beyond avoiding difficulties, we believe *flourishing* is possible ultimately for many persons and their reorganized family relationships. The concept of *flourishing* is adapted from the work-related research of B. L. Frederickson and M. F. Losada (2005). CD positive expectation is consistent with what Constance Ahrons found in her follow-up divorce study sample: "The good news is that twenty years after divorce the majority of the adult children felt that their (divorced) parents had relationships that were relatively free of conflict, and they enjoyed the benefits of sharing special times as a family" (2004, p.174).

The three aspects of divorce (the family relationships, the legal structure/process, and the financial sorting out) are best addressed by experts in each area. Relevant knowledge about each aspect has expanded significantly together with the continued development of concomitant expertise. This has resulted in increased professional specialization in each area of divorce work, whether it is the psychology of families (as attested to in this Handbook) or increased understanding of the impact of divorce family law (Tesler, 2001, pp. 967–971).

The Professional Team and the Local Practice Group

The professional helping team consists of a divorce coach (family psychologist or other family mental health professional) for each spouse; a child specialist (family-systems-oriented child psychologist usually); a family lawyer for each spouse; and a financial specialist. All go through special education and training on how to function in their respective CD roles and how to work together as an interprofessional team. Team members provide divorce-related information while working to assist parents in making informed choices.

Well-developed team working relationships add significantly to the effectiveness of a CD team. The importance of the team is emphasized especially by three principles:

1   In CD a team's impact is greater than simply the additive value of the different professionals on the team (Laughlin, Hatch, Silver, & Boh, 2006).
2   Three-person groupings (e.g., coaches and child specialist; lawyers and financial analyst; lawyer, coach, and client) are consistently useful combinations for coordinated work, surpassing the work effectiveness of similar individual efforts (Kozlowski & Ilgen, 2007).
3   Total team or smaller grouping communication is best face to face, superior to phone or email (Kozlowski & Ilgen, 2007).

Teams are formed from local interdisciplinary *practice groups*, whose members benefit particularly when they attend CD trainings together. Members also continually learn from each other and with each other through regularly scheduled meetings.

The overall intent of the team is to assist clients to make educated and informed choices (psychological, legal, and financial) as they make the major life transition of divorce. Team members focus on providing necessary information and assist in developing options addressing the needs of all family members. The family psychologist's work described in the remainder of this chapter is paralleled by that of the lawyers and financial specialist.

The Three Phases of Collaborative Divorce

The process of CD is comprised of three phases: (1) contracting and initiating team/family relationships; (2) assisting a family through interpersonal, legal, and financial steps to reach the divorce agreement; and (3) following through with the family post-divorce agreement process.

Phase 1: Contracting and initiating team/family relationships

While a divorcing couple may begin a CD with any trained divorce professional (regardless of profession), a couple more typically follows the historically conditioned tradition of starting with a family lawyer. The clients are encouraged to form their own team with the guidance of the initial professional. The couple and their team members sign the disqualification agreement noted earlier, and a transparency agreement that specifies that team members may share family information among themselves that is judged by them to be potentially helpful for the couple's divorcing process.

Phase 2: Individually focused preparation of parents and children – beginning

In the beginning of this phase the team gathers and shares information that is critical for the team and important for informed decision-making by clients. As team members share information and professional observations they work together to develop family-specific strategies and revise their formulations as they increasingly understand the family interpersonally, together with their attendant legal and financial aspects.

Preparing spouses separately to work together. As in Phase 1, coaches continue in the beginning of Phase 2 to be responsible for providing divorce-related information and to help the couple with family crises. Now, however, each coach focuses more on preparing each spouse separately to work together later. This preparation takes a spouse through seven overlapping tasks: (1) managing feelings and behaviors; (2) broadening the marriage story; (3) becoming aware of external influences on the CD process; (4) adapting to differences between spouses in timing of the decision to divorce; (5) expanding self-knowledge; (6) envisioning the family's future; and (7) communicating in a more complete way. The remaining subsection addresses preparing the child for family reorganization.

Managing feelings and behaviors. A coach adapts already-acquired therapeutic skills to express warmth, be authentic, and respond empathetically in developing an alliance with a spouse, yet provides structure to the CD process. The coach may help a spouse, often by using cognitive strategies, to further effective self-management of feelings and behavior; this step is crucial for the success of subsequent coach/couple dyad meetings and team contact, and for the divorcing spouses.

Broadening the marriage story. Because of the pain, disappointment, and other difficult feelings when a relationship has soured, the newly divorced more likely focus on the negative (Schacter, 2001). A coach, borrowing from the narrative approach, listens for positive experiences to begin a fuller construction of the marriage/divorce story (Winslade & Monk, 2000). Establishing the relationship narrative (articulating connected meanings or themes) assists binding emotions and thoughts formerly fragmented, and processes them so that a parent can manage practical tasks during the entire course of the divorce.

Becoming aware of external influences on the CD process. External influences include talking with close friends or relatives, an individual therapist, a couple or family therapist, and, of course, the impact of the spouses' continuing discussions. By ascertaining the weight of these influences early, a coach can balance them if they are extremely one-sided or correct misperceptions of the collaborative process. Otherwise the collaborative process can be undercut despite the best of intentions.

Adapting to differences between spouses in timing of the decision to divorce. Often one spouse has struggled to reach a divorce decision and privately mourned the marriage loss significantly earlier than his or her partner. By being clear about different timing, the team members can facilitate the mourning of the delayed partner and help the early decider to recognize and slow down in the best interests of the long-term aims of the couple.

Expanding self-knowledge. In addition to using family data collection forms, three specific questionnaires may be useful: the Millon Index of Personality Styles–Revised (MIPS; Millon, 2004); the Signature Strengths Survey (Seligman, 2002, pp. 134–161), and selected questionnaires from the Behavior Assessment System for Children, Second Edition (BASC-2; Reynolds & Kamphaus, 2004). Approaches for interpreting these questionnaires to divorcing spouses may be adapted from several test interpretation resources (e.g., Finn & Tonsager, 1997; Fischer, 1985; Nurse, 1999, pp. 185–194).

The MIPS, a true/false questionnaire standardized on a representative normal sample and processed on a coach's computer, provides a client-friendly, balanced personality printout based on fundamental, thinking, and interpersonal personality dimensions. The MIPS results serve as a positive base for discussing each adult client's personality style, and later exploring how spouses' styles together may impact co-parenting.

Each spouse takes (for no fee) the Signature Strengths Survey on line at the Authentic Happiness website, University of Pennsylvania (www.authentichappiness.sas.upenn.edu). This tool supplies a printout of a client's major strengths. This document provides a further, objective base for discussion and strengthening the coach–spouse alliance.

The third procedure, the BASC-2, provides an expanded understanding of the children and their needs. The BASC-2 is a nationally standardized, school-oriented questionnaire that allows for comparison of the description of a child by each parent, useful for both coach–parent discussions and for child specialist consideration. Results can later enrich subsequent co-parenting discussions, including those comprised of parents, coaches, and the child specialist.

Envisioning the family's future.   Each spouse ordinarily has some ideas about the future of the family. These can be honed first with a coach, subsequently discussed in coaches'/spouses' meetings later in this phase, and modified still more as information from the child specialist is addressed. One basis for the discussions consists of forms filled out early on which ask each spouse to rank-order short-term goals, and then long-term goals. With these results a coach assists a spouse to fill out a vision of what the spouse would want for all family members. Later in Phase 2 spouses and coaches will put together a paragraph (or more) reflecting what the divorcing couple envisions for themselves and their children coupled with related principles and specific goals. This jointly developed document can be referenced by team members as well as the spouses to ensure planning is guided by a couple's vision of what they want for the future.

Communicating in a more complete way.   Couples typically cite difficulties in communication in marriage. Even if communication is not at the top of the difficulties list, co-parenting communication is different because parents have dispensed with intimacy as a goal, they have separate adult lives, and their only contact usually relates to co-parenting collaboration. More structure planning and execution are needed for a reasonable degree of communication success to occur.

Practice groups and teams may adopt different communication models to help parents. We have found useful the Couple Communication System (Miller & Miller, 1997), with its underpinning of research (Wampler, 1990). The system provides a way to focus communication into defining an issue, delineating the data making for an issue, differentiating feelings, differentiating thoughts, demarking "wants," and clearly separating past, present, and anticipated future actions.

Preparing the child for family reorganization. Just as parents have coaches to assist them through the personal and interpersonal process of a CD, children have their own professional person – the child mental health specialist. Having a child specialist on the team is an attempt to remedy at least three important omissions in the traditional divorce (Hetherington & Kelly, 2002, pp. 145–146; Kelly & Emery, 2003, pp. 353–354). Children have been typically:

- inadequately prepared for or informed about the divorce at the time of parents' separation;
- less adequately parented during the pre-divorce agreement *and* after;
- not empowered by the divorce process, but more usually left feel helpless.

In addition to remedying these omissions, the presence of the child specialist makes possible the (age-appropriate) active inclusion in this family reorganization process that affects the child so significantly. In CD the number of sessions the child is seen by the child specialist is a combination of several factors, including age, need, and coach-child specialist-parent collaboration.

Along with listening empathetically, the child specialist works to help the child understand what is happening in his or her life and what the future will look like. The specialist addresses how well the child is coping with what are usually difficult divorce-related changes. Often children have misconceptions to be corrected about divorce based on classmates' comments and TV shows. Because a child may try to protect a parent by not sharing worries, a child specialist can both give credit to the loving, concerned child and help take the burden off the child.

Having knowledge of child development, the specialist can estimate whether a child is within normal developmental ranges, has regressed, or has symptoms that are likely associated directly with the anxiety of the unknown future for the child in the family (Emery, 1999; Johnson & Roseby, 1997). With the younger child especially, the specialist can make a judgment about what behavior to anticipate within the usual acute time frame of the divorce (approximately the first 2 years). The child specialist can share later in the Phase 2 with the parents and their coaches.

The child specialist serves as a support for the child and as a professional bringing the child's needs to the attention of the parents and the team. Adolescents need information and support, whether or not they admit it. *Emerging adults*, 18–25+ years of age (Arnett, 2000), should not be overlooked. Even a phone call with these older children from the specialist can be helpful because parental divorce affects them in this time of change, and they also can be helpful to the rest of the family, particularly if they understand CD.

Phase 2: Relationship integration, legal/financial factors, and reaching agreements – concluding

Coaches meet with parents. In four-way working meetings the clients are helped by the coaches to develop a unified vision of how they want the family post-divorce life to be, along with specifying major supporting principles and specific goals. Coaches teach the particular couple how to use the new communication by addressing immediate difficulties and looking at long-range difficulties. The coaches continue to assist the spouses in managing strong feelings that may accompany their work with lawyers and the finance specialist.

The child specialist provides feedback to the parents/coaches working on a draft of the plan for co-parenting.   The child specialist provides professional observations of the child in a meeting with parents and coaches, and may speak for the child, or the child may join the meeting to speak. This input permits the parents, assisted by the coaches in subsequent meetings, to hone a draft of a co-parenting plan which the parents later discuss with lawyers.

Legal and financial factors worked through for the divorce agreement.   During Phase 2 collaborative lawyers have been providing the formal legal structure and containment for the collaborative process. They organize and put in context information being gathered by other team members and utilize additional client-generated information. Unlike traditional adversarial law, the collaborative approach seeks to expand the possibilities of possible solutions to the issues faced by the divorcing spouses. While the lawyers may provide their clients with the default position of the specific laws in their state and local area, they encourage the clients to consider the deeper personal values and needs as they move toward seeking solutions. This collection of information considered in this personal context makes possible the interest-based interaction and negotiation which increase through the second phase, and are focused on in concluding Phase 2, reaching the divorce agreement.

Every divorce has financial issues as a family makes the transition from one household to two. With many couples one person manages most of the finances, and as a result usually knows much more about the family's financial situation than their spouse. In addition, couples often have differences in their attitudes toward money, its meaning, and its uses. These factors are sources of misunderstandings and suspicion, which easily become more pronounced during the divorce process.

The specially educated financial specialist helps the couple identify what financial information is needed and assists in gathering, clarifying, and organizing the information. The specialist often financially educates the less knowledgeable spouse. Working in concert with the collaborative lawyers and the clients, the financial specialist looks carefully at the long-term effects of different divisions of property, and in doing so can maximize the number of possible solutions to reach equitable and needs-based division of property. The work of the financial specialist is particularly intense during the beginning of Phase 2, attenuating during the concluding aspects, while at the same time remaining available to lawyers and spouses at key junctures in later-stage negotiations. The financial specialist holds the only psychologically neutral position on the team.

The financial specialist completes information needed by the parents and lawyers for negotiation.   That specialist remains available for assisting the parents and lawyers.

Parents meet with lawyers to develop the divorce agreement.   Parents meet with the lawyers, who have discussed and organized information from all other team members and the parents. Collaborative lawyers focus during this ending of Phase 2 on negotiations, but do not negotiate for the spouses without the spouses being present, unlike what can occur in the traditional divorce process. This grouping of lawyers and parents works to develop the divorce agreement, supported by all other team members as needed.

Phase 3: Following through post-agreement

After signing the divorce agreement, family emotional and behavioral difficulties escalate during the first year post-agreement, only to recede in year 2, at least with the traditional, adversarial divorce, as we mentioned earlier. We hope that this painful disruption is less with all families going through the CD process, as seems to be the case with our client families.

All collaborative team members have signed on with the concept in mind that divorce is a family change, a reorganization, rather than a legal event. Basing our work on this conceptualization and being aware of the peaking post-divorce of emotional and behavioral problems (in at least traditional divorce), we believe that we have the obligation to the family to not only help prepare them for this time period, but also be available through the immediate post-agreement period of their divorce. For the mental health professionals especially, having established emotional bonds working intensively with the family, our value is that it is very important for these professionals to be actively available post-divorce. To do otherwise could result in some families experiencing feeling abandoned, a potentially harmful outcome.

Simply referring family members to therapists for continued divorce work may result in disruption of the divorce process because therapists work more broadly with the individual, family, or subgroupings within the family and do not have the history of the divorce process with the family (of course this stance should not interfere with referring to therapists as needed for broad psychotherapeutic work).

A Composite Case Study

Because Jeff, 39, a business systems programmer, and Emily, 37, a high school English teacher, had read *For Better or for Worse* (Hetherington & Kelly, 2002) and *Collaborative Divorce* (Tesler & Thompson, 2006), they chose their CD team expeditiously (Phase 1). Married 15 years, they had two children, Janice, 13, and Ed, 7.

The couple and team met for an orientation (beginning Phase 2). Psychologist coaches next discussed meeting structure with the couple before holding separate coach–spouse meetings, where tasks included identifying short- and long-range goals along with reinforcing self-management skills. Unsurprisingly, their goals were similar: to successfully co-parent their children, ameliorate old habits, and develop individual adult lives.

Responding, coaches helped each spouse identify personal strengths and apply these to parenting, especially important for Ed, who had done less. Coaches then taught the couple a "business-like" communication pattern.

Meanwhile, the financial specialist helped the couple organize financial information, separately instructing Emily (formerly financially uninterested) in money management. The couple met with lawyers, learning that the legal system sets limits, leaving great latitude for decision-making by parents. Lawyers (enriched by team meetings) began discussing the implications of information from specialists for constructing the divorce agreement.

The couple's improving communication, facilitated by team members' collaboration, proved especially helpful when the child specialist described their children, supposedly "unaffected" by the divorce. Janice was furious with her mother as the divorce initiator, and Ed was withdrawn, feeling needy for mother. Both had overheard nasty parental arguments. Spousal blaming was blocked by coaches, capitalizing on this opportunity to further parents' applying new communication approaches. Acknowledging upset, they subsequently talked with their children. Team members, informed in their meeting, responded to the broader context by a momentary cooling of couple energy in sessions.

When Jeff's temper flared on learning of Emily's evolving emotional relationship with another teacher, his coach (aware of Jeff's sensitivity to abandonment) helped him manage. Coaches worked through the couple's feelings of emotional emptiness in their marriage and helped them mourn the loss of their marriage dream, stressing that each was likely to develop relationships requiring adjustments.

Being relieved of some of the emotional pressure within the family and having developed beginning practical, logistical plans to meet family members' needs facilitated the parents' collaboration with their attorneys as they negotiated their divorce agreement (ending Phase 2). The (now) ex-spouses experienced reassurance at continued team availability (Phase 3), avoiding (for Jeff particularly) experiences of abandonment.

Caveat: Actions may seem to flow, but typically represent a year-plus of struggle.

The Future of Collaborative Divorce

The accelerating development of CD during the 2000s attests to its filling a need in society for an improved divorce process. CD's growth is facilitated by the growing recognition that divorce is fundamentally a family reorganization process, not solely a legal event (Hetherington & Kelly, 2002; Kelly & Emery, 2003).

CD emerged in response to destructive behavior within divorcing families aggravated by families going through an outdated divorce system that has been inadvertently destructive. The new divorcing system has been constructed to avoid or at least work to mitigate this destructiveness. CD offers assistance for building positively toward a flourishing future, rather than focusing energy on the elimination of psychopathological appearing behavior (Fredrickson & Losada, 2005; Keyes, 2007).

This change offers a new, made to order, opportunity for family psychologists. The family psychologist practitioner/scholar can provide direct mental health services in the

CD system while also explicating, modifying, theorizing, and stimulating studies of CD designed to understand and improve this interprofessional, interdisciplinary process. CD has matured sufficiently to benefit from the work of the family psychologist, who is able to conduct specifically defined studies and broader research programs aimed at teasing out elements in CD that both further the humane managing of a difficult family transition and can lead toward flourishing lives post-divorce.

References

Ahrons, C. (2004). *We're still family: What grown children have to say about their parents' divorce.* New York: HarperCollins.

Arnett, J. J. (2000). Emerging adulthood: A theory of development from the late teens through the twenties. *American Psychologist, 5,* 469–480.

Emery, R. E. (1999). *Marriage, divorce, and children's adjustment* (2nd ed.). Thousand Oaks, CA: Sage.

Fagerstrom, K., Kalish, M., Nurse, A. R., Ross, N., Thompson, P., Wilde, D., et al. (1997). *A problem to be solved not a battle to be fought.* Orinda, CA: Brookwood.

Finn, S. E., & Tonsager, M. E. (1997). Information gathering and therapeutic models of assessment. *Psychological Assessment, 9,* 374–385.

Fischer, C. T. (1985). *Individualizing psychological assessment.* Monterey, CA: Brooks/Cole.

Fredrickson, B. L., & Losada, M. F. (2005). Positive affect and the complex dynamics of human flourishing. *American Psychologist, 60(7),* 678–686.

Hetherington, E. M., & Kelly, J. (2002). *For better or for worse: Divorce reconsidered.* New York: Norton.

Johnson, J. R., & Roseby, V. (1997). *In the name of the child.* New York: Free Press.

Kelly, J., & Emery, R. E. (2003). Children's adjustment following divorce: Risk and resilience perspectives. *Family Relations, 52,* 352–362.

Keyes, C. M. (2007). Promoting and protecting mental health as flourishing: A complementary strategy for improving national mental health. *American Psychologist, 62(2),* 95–108.

Kozlowski, S. W. J., & Ilgen, D. R. (2007). The science of team success. *Scientific American Mind, 6/7,* 54–61.

Laughlin, P., Hatch, E., Silver, J., & Boh, L. (2006). Groups perform better than the best individuals on letters-to-numbers problems: Effects of group size. *Journal of Personality and Social Psychology, 90(4),* 644–651.

Miller, S., & Miller, P. A. (1997). *Core communication: Skills and processes.* Littleton, CO: Interpersonal Communications Programs.

Millon, T. (2004). *MIPS-R (Millon Index of Personality Styles Revised) manual.* Minneapolis, MN: Pearson Assessments.

Nurse, A. (1999). *Family assessment: Effective uses of personality tests with couples and families.* Hoboken, NJ: Wiley.

Nurse, A. R., & Thompson, P. (1997). Collaborative divorce: Oxymoron or a new process? *The Family Psychologist, 13(2),* 21, 25.

Nurse, A. R., & Thompson, P. (1999). Collaborative divorce: A new, interdisciplinary process. *American Journal of Family Law, 13,* 226–234.

Nurse, A. R., & Thompson, P. (2000). Collaborative divorce: A humane, interdisciplinary approach. In L. VandeCreek (Ed.), *Innovations in clinical practice: A source book: Vol. 18* (pp. 169–184). Sarasota, FL: Professional Resource Press.

Nurse, A. R., & Thompson, P. (in press). *Collaborative divorce: A family centered approach.* Washington, DC: APA Books.

Reynolds, C. R., & Kamphaus, R. W. (2004). *BASC-2: Behavior Assessment System for Children manual* (2nd ed.). Circle Pines, MN: AGS.

Schacter, D. L. (2001). *The seven sins of memory: How the mind forgets and remembers.* New York: Houghton Mifflin.

Schwartz, L. L., & Kaslow, F. W. (1997). *Painful partings: Divorce and its aftermath.* New York: Wiley.

Seligman, M. E. P. (2002). *Authentic happiness: Using the new positive psychology to realize your potential for lasting fulfillment.* New York: Free Press.

Tesler, P. H. (1999). Collaborative law: A new paradigm for divorce lawyers. *Psychology, Public Policy, and Law, 5(4)*, 966–1000.

Tesler, P. H. (2001). *Collaborative law: Achieving effective resolution in divorce without litigation.* Chicago: Section of Family Law, American Bar Association.

Tesler, P. H., & Thompson, P. (2006). *Collaborative divorce: The revolutionary way to restructure your family, resolve legal issues, and move on with your life.* New York: HarperCollins.

Wampler, K. S. (1990). An update of research on the Couple Communication Program. *Family Science Review, 3(1)*, 21–40.

Webb, S. G., & Ousky, R. D. (2006). *The collaborative way to divorce: The revolutionary method that results in less stress, lower costs, and happier kids without going to court.* New York: Hudson Street.

Weinstein, J. (1997). And never the twain shall meet: The best interests of children and the adversary system. *University of Miami Law Review, 52*, 79–175.

Winslade, J., & Monk, G. (2000). *Narrative mediation: A new approach to conflict resolution.* San Francisco: Jossey-Bass.

33

Treating Stepfamilies:
A Subsystems-Based Approach

Scott Browning and James H. Bray

Stepfamilies are a unique and challenging group to work with. There are an estimated 15 to 20 million stepfamilies in the USA and the number is projected to increase (Bramlett & Mosher, 2001, 2002; Robertson, Adler-Baeder, Collins, DeMarco, & Fein, 2006). There are not exact estimates of the number of stepfamilies because the 2000 U.S. Census did not include information about marital status and many states no longer report information about marriage and divorce. Stepfamilies are linked to major demographic changes: increases in cohabitation and childbearing outside marriage, high divorce rates, and high remarriage rates (Bramlett & Mosher, 2001, 2002; Bray, 1999; Kreider, 2005). The divorce rate for second and subsequent marriages is higher (5–10%) than for first marriages and has been partially attributed to the presence of children from previous relationships (Bramlett & Mosher, 2001). If the remarriage makes it through the first year, then the probability of divorce drops to that of first marriages. It is estimated that 65–75% of women and 75–85% of men will eventually remarry. Black women are less likely to remarry than White and Hispanic women (Smock, 1990). The percentages vary because younger people are more likely to remarry, while older adults are less likely to remarry.

Problems presented clinically by stepfamilies frequently seem to match, in tone and nature, problems from first-marriage families. However, attempting to address these problems by incorporating a traditional family therapy approach only reminds the clinician of the unique dilemmas experienced by most stepfamilies. Therapeutic impasse is not uncommon when the distinction between the stepfamily and first-marriage family is ignored (Bray, 2001; Browning, 1994).

Therapies and interventions specifically designed for stepfamilies are less common than general family therapy approaches. The writings of Emily and John Visher (1979, 1988, 1991), Patricia Papernow (1993), and Bray and colleagues (Bray, 1992, 2001, 2005; Bray & Berger, 1993; Bray & Harvey, 1995; Bray & Kelly, 1998) are examples of sophisticated and useful clinical models. The Vishers laid out specific challenges that stepfamily members could expect (boundary problems, insider/outsider status and loyalty conflicts), whereas Papernow created a comprehensive model of stepfamily development, with clear clinical suggestions on how to address families within each stage of growth. Bray and colleagues utilized an extensive research study to garner a clear understanding of the developmental issues for stepfamilies and the importance of addressing parenting issues, family relationships, and dealing with non-residential parents.

Research on the efficacy of specific interventions with stepfamilies is minimal (Bray & Easling, 2005). Pasley, Rhoden, Visher, and Visher (1996) provided useful information from their survey of stepfamilies that had received therapy. Along with the importance of emotional connection between therapist and client, improved communication skills, and problem resolution, stepfamilies clearly stated that they benefited from therapy when the therapist was aware of the unique nature and issues present in stepfamilies.

The approach that is articulated in this chapter is informed by theory and the research literature on stepfamilies. In order for one to work effectively with stepfamilies the clinician should approach the stepfamily with a specific plan, a familiarity with the relevant research, and clinical interventions beneficial for stepfamilies (see Bray, 1999; Bray & Easling, 2005; Coleman, Ganong, & Fine, 2000; Ganong & Coleman, 2004; Hetherington & Clingempeel, 1992; Hetherington, Henderson, & Reiss, 1999; and Robertson et al., 2006, for reviews of research on stepfamilies). A 10-step approach is offered as a method to approach stepfamilies that enter therapy.

Ten Steps to Utilize in Understanding and Treating Stepfamilies

Diagnostic steps

1   Recognize the structure of the stepfamily (e.g., simple stepfather family, simple stepmother family, complex stepfamily where both adults are stepparents) and look for systemic similarities within the context of extant research literature.

Once the therapist becomes aware of the specific structure of the family, then an awareness of particular concerns will emerge. Using genograms to map the family structure and relationships is a useful method in the diagnostic phase (McGoldrick, Gerson, & Shellenberger, 1999).

Stepfamilies, although individually unique, share certain dynamic truisms with other stepfamilies that are structurally similar. For example, the experiences of a stepmother family in which the biological mother is deceased will usually have distinct similarities with other bereaved families with a new stepmother. Stepfamilies are often concerned that the therapist, especially one that has not resided in a stepfamily, may not understand their needs. This perception is exacerbated by the fact that many of these families are having a difficult enough time understanding how they transitioned so quickly from newlyweds to therapy clients.

2 Clarify the distinct subsystems in the stepfamily and utilize this to provide a direction for clinical treatment. Determine the membership of the first session – usually the marital dyad – and further delineate the unique concerns of the stepfamily presenting for treatment.

The underlying premise in stepfamily therapy must be viewed as a treatment of a collection of subsystems with the end goal of proceeding toward stepfamily integration. The term "blended" will be conspicuously absent from this chapter because generally, "stepfamilies do not blend." Blending, as a cooking term, refers to a process whereby the two products being blended become a completely unique product, with no way of determining the individual characteristics any longer. A stepfamily does not become an entirely new family, with no memory of the past attachments. It is an extended family, with all the advantages and stressors that increased complexity implies. Over time, this collective is capable of being as fully viable and positive as a first-marriage family can be.

The notion of viewing a stepfamily, or any family, as a collection of subsystems is not new, but this therapeutic approach to treating a stepfamily views the stepfamily as a collection of subsystems that enter an "initial period of disequilibrium" following the creation of the stepfamily (Hetherington & Clingempeel, 1992). Each subsystem is actually less viable following the remarriage. While the couple may be in love, their relationship becomes impacted not only by the inevitable difference in how they view their roles and parenting obligations within the home, but also by the complicating emergence of additional extended family members (Hetherington & Clingempeel, 1992). Secondly, the biological parent and child(ren) often experience a reduction in their bond, especially as reported by the child(ren) (Browning, 1987). The third subsystem, already weakly connected, is the relationship between the stepparent and stepchild(ren), especially if the children are pre-adolescent or adolescent (Bray & Berger, 1993; Hetherington & Clingempeel, 1992).

The couple enters remarriage not necessarily naïve about the possible difficulties experienced by many stepfamilies, but rather, lulled into a sense of safety from the dating period. While dating, most people, and future stepparents in particular, do not present themselves as they will be following the remarriage. These people are not trying to fool anyone, but rather, the effect of context and structural change should not be underestimated (Hetherington & Stanley-Hagen, 1995).

Unfortunately, many stepfamilies attempt to integrate and become a complete new family too quickly. The drive for this effort is simple to understand; both the parent and stepparent would like to affirm the stability of the stepfamily for everyone's sake. Living as a collection of subsystems is unnatural to those who have previously lived in either a first-marriage family or a divorced home. Until the natural process of building a relationship with new people and stabilizing all subsystems occurs, the stepfamily is not an integrated whole. Trying to force that integration often has the contradictory effect of pushing people apart (Bray & Kelly, 1998).

A parent and child will almost always be closer than a child and stepparent. Often, however, the parent, stepparent, or both greatly desire that members of this new stepfamily spend time together to get to know each other and grow in fondness toward each other. Interestingly, in the stepfamily, when a child reacts negatively to the pressure to be close to a stepparent, that reaction is perceived as a rejection of the stepparent (which it may be). However, it is also commonly due to a fear that the child has less connection to their biological parent (Papernow, 1993). The great irony is that the parent is frequently frustrated by her or his child's anger at the stepparent and does not see her or his own role in the tension. As pressure continues to build between the stepparent and the child, the biological parent is caught in the middle, often feeling unable to offer any solution to the growing disharmony. The approach articulated in this chapter hypothesizes that by stabilizing the different subsystems, the tension is alleviated and the impasse can be resolved.

The list of potential subsystems is extensive; there are six that are typically considered when planning ongoing stepfamily therapy. These six most likely subsystems are: (1) the remarried couple, (2) the custodial parent and child, (3) the sibling, (4) the stepparent–stepchild, (5) the stepfamily, and (6) the extended "bi-nuclear" family. While the couple is the most frequent subsystem to be invited into treatment for the initial session, the other five subsystems listed here are suggestions of who might be invited in as therapy progresses. While the order presented is the most common sequence, there can be great variability based on the specific case. Some cases may never involve the "bi-nuclear" family, or there may only be one child, so a sibling subsystem is not applicable. However, by examining the six common subsystems, the therapist is pushed to consider the different advantages of seeing various collections of people. Clearly, subsystems can include many people who have not been noted in these common six scenarios. Grandparents and other relatives may be completely appropriate to invite into treatment; however, it is best to avoid an exhaustive list until you have the actual stepfamily in front of you.

Therapy with stepfamilies requires clear communication and all clinical decisions should be discussed openly with the stepfamily. This does not mean that the therapist is without power, but rather, the power held by the therapist comes from gaining the client's trust. Trust is gained when one conducts therapy with no explicit agenda other than to fully understand the stepfamily's predicament. The stepfamily will be open to the process if they feel that the therapist understands their situation and has a method by which she or he proceeds.

In keeping with openness between the clients and therapist, the question of who to invite into therapy and when to involve them is one that is openly discussed. The question that the therapist must answer is: what subsystem would most benefit from being seen together? Secondarily, the ramification of meeting with any subsystem must be assessed as to how the overall stepfamily is affected. Although no one can perfectly predict how each session will evolve, the couple will comment on various benefits or detriments of any particular meeting.

As stated above, the most frequent subsystem invited into the initial session is the remarried couple. This is not a pro forma decision, however; this subsystem appears to be the best clinical foundation for further progress, especially under the following conditions: (1) the couple does not see "eye to eye" in how they describe the behavior and/or discipline of the stepchild, and (2) an initial session with the remarried couple and any stepchildren/children would predictably involve a "blow-up" between either the stepparent and stepchild, or the remarried couple.

The justification for seeing the remarried couple first is simple. Faulty communications, anger, and confusion are often the result of misperceptions. The new stepfamily is usually experiencing intense emotions that become more complicated in the therapist's office if additional people are added to the interview (Rhoden & Pasley, 2000).

When a mother is in an initial session with her new husband and her two biological children, she will be editing her comments in order not to displease anyone, and in so doing, she will not be sharing her true thoughts and feelings; or she may tailor her comments depending on which member she believes is strongest or most vulnerable. In other words, if the therapist asks a question of the mother/remarried wife, she will need to examine the potential effect of her response on her husband and child if both are present. An example such as this highlights a difference between the stepfamily and the first-marriage family. Generally, in a first-marriage family, of all the potential conflicts that may make such work difficult, annoyance directed toward a woman for loving both her husband and child is not a common problem. Therefore, the couple by themselves, although still potentially vulnerable, is often better able to explain their concerns without an audience of children.

One might believe that the emphasis on seeing the couple first is a rejection of systemic thinking in regard to the stepfamily. The approach articulated in this chapter is clearly systemic, but the therapist needs to be aware of the primitive emotions that are generated both within and between subsystems in a recently formed stepfamily. Just as Murray Bowen (1978) brilliantly understood that most psychological healing occurs in a dyadic form, this does not lessen the importance of understanding the systemic dynamics of the entire system. In much the same way, addressing the issues of all primary subsystems in the stepfamily eventually assists the entire stepfamily to be secure.

The remarried couple presents with a dynamic that is often quite distinct from the first-marriage couple. Typically, in first-marriage families with children, the couples who cannot agree on parenting issues may be experiencing marital difficulties as well. Whereas the remarried couple is often in disagreement about some aspect of the child's behavior or attitude, they are usually still romantically in love during the early months and years, but stressed about co-parenting. The other great irony is that many stepparents enter into such a relationship with a great willingness to assist in the parenting and welfare of the children to whom they now serve as an additional parent. The stepparent is often the "unsung hero," providing financial stability, emotional support, and structure to the stepfamily (Pasley, personal communication, June 6, 2000).

Clinical interventions

3   Using a psychoeducation approach, consider the research findings that normalize the experience of the stepfamily and introduce them where appropriate and meaningful (Bray, 2001).

Knowledge of the research literature is a foundation for treating stepfamilies. The awareness of any population assists clinicians in being more empathic and conversant with any family. However, the tremendous need for clinicians to be familiar with the research literature is particularly true in those populations for which "normal" or "typical" is difficult to summarize. Stepfamilies are one such population. It is common for stepfamilies to question the pace of their development and the stability of this new stepfamily. Therefore, the research literature assists both the clinician and the stepfamily members in assessing what strengths exist and what challenges need to be addressed. For example, a stepfamily that approaches treatment, caught up in an impasse between the remarried couple regarding how to discipline, is looking for some benchmarks to place their concern in the context of stepfamilies, in general. It is the psychological and sociological research literature that provides these benchmarks.

Continuing with the example cited above, the clinician will offer to the stepfamily that it is quite typical to have a stepfather become an authority figure prior to the family being prepared for his role to be so powerful (Bray, 1988). Power and authority usually generate less interpersonal volatility as the relationships mature. Although the age of a child is certainly an influential factor in determining the level of authority that can be assumed without a previous relationship, it is rarely helpful to evaluate anyone's authority in a stepfamily without the building blocks of some mutual respect (Bray, 1988). Information, such as this, presented to the stepfamily creates an opportunity whereby each person can re-evaluate the reason that they do what they do. This perspective assists the stepfamily in placing their behaviors, feelings, and dilemmas within the context of other stepfamilies, rather than comparing themselves to first-marriage families.

Two unique issues that present often to remarried couples are the differences in expectations and rules of the home. The expectation of the roles played by each person (stepmother, stepfather, or parent) is not often discussed overtly (Bentley, 2001; Bray, Berger, & Boethel, 1994). This confusion over what a stepmother, for example, is expected to do can cause tremendous confusion and upset. Similarly, the rules of a home are often assumed to be more shared than they turn out to be when children begin to find that their parent and stepparent view transgressions and punishments differently. In the early months after remarriage, having the stepparent play an indirect parental role and provide additional parental monitoring is an effective method for integrating the stepparent into the parental role (Bray & Berger, 1993; Bray & Harvey, 1995). Therefore, it is very common for these two topics to be highlighted and addressed early in treatment.

4   Actively assess and assist in the recognition of empathy when present and increase the empathic experience between stepfamily members and subsystems.

The next likely intervention will both establish if each member of the couple has an empathic understanding of the other's view and enable the therapist to forward the idea that these two people will not view the child in question from the same perspective. If one or both members of this couple cannot summon even a rudimentary empathic understanding of the other's view the treatment will be less effective. This intervention is the nucleus of an early session with a couple and therefore must be approached only after some rapport has begun to build.

It is this intervention, in particular, that mandates that the therapist see the couple first in working from this perspective. It is almost impossible for the parent to show an empathic understanding of their spouse's view in front of the child in question. Such an exercise in the presence of the child, early in the development of a stepfamily, can feel like betrayal. Most parents are very aware of the balancing act they are forced into between the needs of both their child and their new spouse.

The empathic intervention proceeds in a stepwise fashion. The first step is to determine the thoughts and feelings of each member of the couple in regard to a child in question. The therapist looks for clear evidence that the stepparent appears, at some level, interested in the welfare of the child. The stepparent does not need to be effusive in his or her concern; however, some indication that he or she wants the child to do well in the world is an important foundation. It is important to note that stepparents and stepchildren often value different kinds of affection and concern. From stepparents, stepchildren are more interested in verbal expressions of affection than physical ones (Bray, 1988; Bray & Berger, 1993).

Both members of the couple must be confident that each person cares for the welfare of the child, even though their approaches may be different. In a later part of the intervention, the therapist will need to clarify and corroborate this distinction. If the therapist hears no statement from the stepparent that can be honestly reframed as a desire for the welfare of the child, this intervention is not recommended. If, however, as is most often the case, the stepparent does have an interest in the child's welfare then the intervention is often quite helpful.

When a stepparent holds a concern for the welfare of the child, that interest need not come strictly from a position of unconditional love. While it may be that the stepparent's commitment is primarily in order to ensure that this stepchild will not be living in the home at age 22, the desire for that child to succeed remains far more important than the current rationale for that stance. Too often, a person's concern is invalidated because the origin of the feeling is considered selfish. Clinically it is important to support the concern and steer the questioning away from challenging the basis of such a feeling. Therapists must be willing to take a stand to support that a client is concerned about another family member without the emphasis being placed on the intention or origin of that concern. In other words, when "Bill," the stepfather, says that he is, in fact, worried about the grades received by his stepchild, the therapist supports that position rather than endorsing the view of "Sally's," the mother, when she says, "he is just looking for her not to be any trouble at all." "Sally" will often look to the therapist at this point and say, "But shouldn't he just care about her?" The recommended response is,

> It is rare to have uncomplicated feelings. As a parent, your love for your child dominates your hopes for that child. Bill comes to his feelings having probably examined a number of angles. It is far more important, at this time, for you to accept that Bill *does* want Chelsea (Sally's daughter) to do well, rather than focus on his motivation.

Commonly, the biological parent will ask whether it isn't natural to want her new spouse to be motivated by a love for the child, a question to which the therapist should respond. It is important for the therapist to seek out all invitations for love that are put out by any stepfamily member. The response to such a question will allow the therapist to support the parent's desire for their spouse to be motivated by love, followed by the realistic fact that an expression of concern is still preferable to a lack of concern. If this stance can be agreed upon, the therapist continues in the next step of the empathic intervention.

The second step of the empathic intervention is for the therapist to use professional judgment as to which member of the couple would be best able to empathically describe the experience of her or his spouse in relation to the child in question. When both members of the couple have expressed the view of the other and have had that view confirmed as being *accurate* or close to correct, the therapist completes the intervention. The therapist then asks each, one at a time, "Do you feel that there is anything your spouse could do or say that would cause you to abandon your perspective and embrace completely the view of the other?" Most often each states that understanding what the other believes does not alter his or her own belief. The therapist then asks,

> Then why do you both spend so much energy trying to prove that your own view of Chelsea is the correct perspective? The two of you will never see Chelsea as if through the same lens. Bill, no matter how long you are her stepfather and no matter how deeply you grow to care about her, you will never have had the experience of being with her when she was a baby, and also seeing her suffer during the divorce. Sally, you see that Bill holds a less sentimental view of Chelsea. Sentiment exists in established relationships, and Bill and Chelsea's relationship is only in early formation. Therefore, for you to try to picture Chelsea without the fuller contextual picture of the past twelve years is impossible. Neither view of her is the correct perspective; you see her through two different lenses.

When this intervention goes well, the tension in the therapy room drops. The couple realizes that they have become embroiled in a debate with neither emerging as the victor. The debate has become repetitive and oppressive because of how intractable each person's perspective has become. They are each staking out a position, which forces them to view the identified child in certain ways. Each may still disagree on the nature of the interactions between the other and the child, but usually, following this intervention, less energy is expended trying to prove one's own perspective.

5   Determine unreasonable expectations and discuss the creation of "house rules" (rules and consequences that apply to all children in the home). The age of the child certainly changes particular responses by the parent or stepparent.

Expectations need to be examined as they will determine responses to the children. Developing an explicit set of household rules helps the parent and stepparent develop a clear parenting plan and work together in parenting the children.

6   Identify and challenge unhelpful beliefs and specific miscommunication circulating in the stepfamily – the role of labels.

The beliefs held by stepfamily members, especially unhelpful beliefs, are more difficult to discern; nevertheless it is important to do so. Such beliefs can be particularly insidious in the functioning of a stepfamily because they can cause rigid interactions between members over time (Visher & Visher, 1988).

In first-marriage families, most people are cautious in assigning a negative attribute to a loved one. Over time, if a family member consistently lets you down, the trust in that person erodes. However, there are many second, third, and fourth chances between members of first families. In the stepfamily, the steeper learning curve makes it more difficult for mistakes to be offset by successful or caring efforts. Therefore, it can be easy to slip into a belief that will profoundly affect how you act and interact with the other. Due to the relative newness of the stepfamily, there are many ways for an inaccurate and unhelpful belief to take root and close down communication and different avenues to growth for the stepfamily. Often an unhelpful belief is not totally inaccurate, but because it is drawn from a limited pool of expressed beliefs or from stereotypes, it becomes more likely to be embraced.

7   Support the naturally connected subsystem (parent and child) and confirm that they are capable of expressing mutual concern.

The subsystems that have received the least attention in the clinical literature have been parent–child relationships and sibling relationships. Although these "original" sub-systems are usually formed through biological connections, long-term adoptions are also included in this category. The original subsystem that usually needs some attention is the parent–child relationship. The dynamics that place the parent between one's own child and one's new spouse force many people to pull away from their child simply to reduce the pressure of being "stuck" between two people that they love.

Due to the higher distress usually evident in other subsystems throughout the stepfamily, these original subsystems are frequently overlooked because they are perceived as permanent, and therefore, more stable. While they may be more stable, they may not be functioning well. Because they are identified less often as a subsystem in jeopardy, the members of these subsystems are generally seen either in individual sessions or with the whole family.

8   Teach the family about its own systemic functioning.

Another important clinical intervention is teaching people about the stepfamily's systemic function through psychoeducation (Nelson & Levant, 1991). Increasing people's under-standing of the manner in which systems function does not relieve each person of respons-ibility for individual actions; rather, it elucidates to them how individuals effect and are affected by the system (or stepfamily).

The therapist assists the couple in understanding the effect that increased commit-ment between them brings. This increased clarity on the shifts in the relationship may not in turn lessen each person's frustration with the growing pains of the developing stepfamily; however, what it does tend to do is help the couple see that the circumstances are more powerful than any one person. As one begins to see that their own willpower cannot, in and of itself, force the personal dynamics of each member of the stepfamily in a particular direction, the seeds of true systemic understanding are sown.

These interventions usually involve a specific description of the stepfamily's actions and how these actions can be understood as interrelated. In other words, the therapist might say, "While mom sees the logic in her husband's comments, as well as the comments of her son, she is unable to make either person feel supported due to her precarious position balanced between these two people, both of whom she deeply cares about and who want her loyalty." The importance of interventions that highlight the systemic functions of a stepfamily is that frequently such an intervention propels each individual to expand their understanding of the situation to beyond their own perspective. Once behaviors are interlocked, the notion that one stepfamily member is guilty, while the other is innocent, becomes increasingly rare.

Stepfamily integration

9   Assist in co-parental work between any and all involved parental figures.

In the later steps of stepfamily treatment the therapist pursues the integration of the now more stable subsystems into a more coherent and satisfied whole stepfamily. The therapist will invite the entire residential stepfamily into the session in order to observe their interaction with one another, and to address those concerns that still exist, but can now be discussed in front of all involved.

At this stage of the stepfamily treatment, the therapist is going to determine if any subsystem that has begun to make progress when being treated as a separate entity is also able to function well in the context of the entire stepfamily. Is there a subsystem (e.g., stepparent and stepchild) that when seen together as a subsystem alone appeared stable, but when thrust into the full stepfamily is destabilized by pressures and stressors?

10   Increase communication between all stepfamily members available, possibly involving the entire bi-nuclear family system, and move toward integrating the various subsystems into a functioning and satisfied stepfamily.

Having entire families in therapy has always been important because having everyone in the room permits the therapist the clearest picture of those issues or relationships that seemed most conflict-centered. This view of the stepfamily was avoided early in treatment due to the stepfamily's vulnerability, but now resilience has increased due to the strengthening of selected subsystems.

Conclusions

This chapter has presented an approach for treating stepfamilies. While the work with stepfamilies will always be somewhat different from that with first-marriage families, the unique needs of stepfamilies must be the focus of early treatment, in order for the stepfamilies to feel understood and supported. This approach emphasizes the subsystems that constitute the entire stepfamily, supporting each subsystem, in order to move toward integration and stability.

References

Bentley, A. (2001). *Expectations of the stepmother's role*. Unpublished doctoral dissertation, Chestnut Hill College, Philadelphia, PA.

Bowen, M. (1978). *Family therapy in clinical practice*. New York: Aronson.

Bramlett, M. D., & Mosher, W. D. (2001). *First marriage dissolution, divorce, and remarriage: United States* (Advance Data from Vital and Health Statistics No. 323). Hyattsville, MD: National Center for Health Statistics.

Bramlett, M. D., & Mosher, W. D. (2002). *Cohabitation, marriage, divorce, and remarriage in the United States* (Vital and Health Statistics, Series 23, No. 22). Hyattsville, MD: National Center for Health Statistics.

Bray, J. H. (1988). Children's development during early remarriage. In E. M. Hetherington & J. Arasteh (Eds.), *The impact of divorce, single-parenting and step-parenting on children* (pp. 279–298). Hillsdale, NJ: Erlbaum.

Bray, J. H. (1992). Family relationships and children's adjustment in clinical and nonclinical stepfather families. *Journal of Family Psychology, 6*, 60–68.

Bray, J. H. (1999). From marriage to remarriage and beyond: Findings from the Developmental Issues in Stepfamilies Research Project. In E. M. Hetherington (Ed.), *Coping with divorce, single-parenting and remarriage: A risk and resiliency perspective* (pp. 253–271). Hillsdale, NJ: Erlbaum.

Bray, J. H. (2001). Therapy with stepfamilies: A developmental systems approach. In D. D. Lusterman, S. H. McDaniel, & C. Philpot (Eds.), *Integrating family therapy: A casebook* (pp. 127–140). Washington, DC: American Psychological Association.

Bray, J. H. (2005). Family therapy with stepfamilies. In J. Lebow (Ed.), *Handbook of clinical family therapy* (pp. 497–515). New York: Wiley.

Bray, J. H., & Berger, S. H. (1993). Developmental Issues in Stepfamilies Research Project: Family relationships and parent–child interactions. *Journal of Family Psychology, 7*, 76–90.

Bray, J. H., Berger, S. H., & Boethel, C. L. (1994). Role integration and marital adjustment in stepfather families. In K. Pasley & M. Ihinger-Tallman (Eds.), *Stepfamilies: Issues in research, theory, and practice* (pp. 69–86). New York: Greenwood Press.

Bray, J. H., & Easling, I. (2005). Remarriage and stepfamilies. In W. Pinsof and J. Lebow (Eds.), *Family psychology: State of the art* (pp. 267–294). Oxford: Oxford University Press.

Bray, J. H., & Harvey, D. M. (1995). Adolescents in stepfamilies: Developmental and family interventions. *Psychotherapy, 32*, 122–130.

Bray, J. H., & Kelly, J. (1998). *Stepfamilies: Love, marriage, and parenting in the first decade*. New York: Broadway Books.

Browning, S. (1994). Treating stepfamilies: Alternatives to traditional family therapy. In K. Pasley & M. Ihinger-Tallman (Eds.), *Remarriage and stepparenting: Current research and therapy* (pp. 175–198). New York: Guilford Press.

Browning, S. W. (1987). Preference prediction, empathy and personal similarity as variables of family satisfaction in intact and stepfather families. *Dissertation Abstracts International, 47 (11-B)*, 4642–4643.

Coleman, M., Ganong, L., & Fine, M. A. (2000). Reinvestigating remarriage: Another decade of progress. *Journal of Marriage and the Family, 62,* 1288–1307.

Ganong, L. H., & Coleman, M. (2004). *Stepfamily relationships: Development, dynamics, and interventions.* New York: Kluwer.

Hetherington, E. M., & Clingempeel, W. G. (1992). Coping with marital transitions: A family systems perspective. *Monographs of the Society for Research in Child Development, 57,* Nos. 2–3, Serial No. 227.

Hetherington, E. M., Henderson, S., & Reiss, D. (1999). *Adolescent siblings in stepfamilies: Family functioning and adolescent adjustment.* Malden, MA: Blackwell.

Hetherington, E. M., & Stanley-Hagan, M. (1995). Parenting in divorced and remarried families. In M. Bornstein (Ed.), *Handbook of parenting* (pp. 233–255). Hillsdale, NJ: Erlbaum.

Kreider, R. M. (2005). *Number, timing, and duration of marriages and divorces: 2001.* Current Population Reports, P70–97. Washington, DC: U.S. Census Bureau.

McGoldrick, M., Gerson, R., & Shellenberger, S. (1999). *Genograms: Assessment and intervention.* New York: Norton.

National Stepfamily Resource Center. (2007). A division of Auburn University's Center for Children, Youth, and Families. Retrieved May 21, 2007, from http://www.stepfamilies.info

Nelson, W. P., & Levant, R. F. (1991). An evaluation of a skills training program for parents in stepfamilies. *Family Relations, 40,* 291–296.

Papernow, P. (1993). *Becoming a stepfamily: Patterns of development in remarried families.* San Francisco: Jossey-Bass.

Pasley, K., Rhoden, L., Visher, E. B., & Visher, J. S. (1996). Successful stepfamily therapy: Clients' perspectives. *Journal of Marital & Family Therapy, 22,* 343–357.

Rhoden, J. L., & Pasley, K. (2000). Factors affecting the perceived helpfulness of therapy with stepfamilies: A closer look at gender issues. *Journal of Divorce & Remarriage, 34,* 77–93.

Robertson, A., Adler-Baeder, F., Collins, A., DeMarco, D., & Fein, D. (2006). *Marriage education services for economically disadvantaged stepfamilies.* Report for Office of Planning, Research and Evaluation, Administration for Children and Families, Washington, DC.

Smock, P. J. (1990). Remarriage patterns of Black and White women: Reassessing the role of educational attainment. *Demography, 27,* 467–473.

Visher, E., & Visher, J. (1979). *Stepfamilies.* New York: Brunner/Mazel.

Visher, E. B., & Visher, J. S. (1988). *Old loyalties, new ties: Therapeutic strategies with stepfamilies.* New York: Brunner/Mazel.

Visher, E. B., & Visher, J. S. (1991). *How to win as a stepfamily* (2nd ed.). New York: Brunner-Routledge.

34

A Family-Centered Intervention Strategy for Public Middle Schools

Thomas J. Dishion and Elizabeth Stormshak

Students' disruptive behavior at school can be a serious problem for teachers, parents, and society. Youth who show problem behavior at school often have a variety of related concerns, including poor achievement, low attendance, depression, anxiety, and substance use. Many problem behaviors can be managed with school-based programs through the use of carefully designed behavior management systems such as positive behavior support (Sugai, Horner, & Sprague, 1999). However, a subset (5–10%) of school-age children requires intensive intervention and treatment in the school context. These youth are best served with a multifocused intervention that targets behavior across contexts, at home and at school (Dishion & Kavanagh, 2003).

Numerous school-based programs and curricula have been developed to prevent problem behavior. The majority of these programs focus on individual child skills and outcomes, such as problem solving, coping, and anger management, and they are typically delivered in classrooms by teachers or by behavior support specialists in the schools. Many are delivered with limited success at impacting long-term adjustment because they do not target parents and families in the home. Best practice suggests that it is advisable to design interventions for children that motivate parents to engage in family management practices to improve student behavior at home and school (Forgatch, Bullock, & DeGarmo, 2003; Kazdin, 2002). These family-centered interventions must be realistic with respect to professionals' available time and must be coordinated with efforts by the school to promote the students' success (Dishion & Stormshak, 2007). In addition, it is important that the intervention model be amenable for implementation with a set of skills familiar to existing school professionals such as special educators, school counselors, and school psychologists.

This chapter provides an overview of an ecological approach to family intervention and treatment that can be implemented in schools: the EcoFIT model. EcoFIT has seven unique features, briefly described below. For a more in-depth discussion of these principles, see Dishion and Stormshak (2007).

1   EcoFIT is *based on an empirically derived developmental model* of child and adolescent psychopathology in general and behavior problems in particular (e.g., Dishion & Patterson, 2006; Patterson, Reid, & Dishion, 1992). Longitudinal studies on the etiology of problem behavior repeatedly indicate that parenting practices in general and family management in particular are highly correlated with the degree of child and adolescent problem behavior (e.g., Loeber & Dishion, 1983). Family management, therefore, is central to effective ecological intervention with children and families.

2   EcoFIT is *family centered.* The premise that family-centered strategies are effective for reducing child and adolescent problem behavior is strongly supported by treatment outcome research (e.g., Borduin & Henggeler, 1990; Dishion & Patterson, 1992; Eddy & Chamberlain, 2000; Webster-Stratton, 1990) and prevention science literatures (e.g., Conduct Problems Prevention Research Prevention Group, 2002). See the evidence-based models section of this volume for further references and summaries of the most recent models.

Family-centered interventions have undergone a critical shift in the past 20 or so years, having moved from a treatment model that is delivered to clients in clinic settings to an intervention model involving proactive recruitment of parents to engage in interventions in community settings such as schools (Stormshak, Dishion, Light, & Yasui, 2005). The approach described in this volume is potentially applicable to implementation in several service settings, including preschools and welfare programs' family services (Shaw, Dishion, Supplee, Gardner, & Arnds, 2006), and is especially designed for public school settings (Dishion & Kavanagh, 2003).

3   EcoFIT is *assessment driven* in that the intervention is based on a comprehensive, objective, and psychological assessment of the child, his or her family, and other relevant environments. Direct observations are a critical component of this assessment process. An ecological assessment can complement clinical impressions and increase the reliability and validity of the case conceptualization that underlies clinical judgment, and therefore it can improve the design of an effective intervention.

4   EcoFIT emphasizes *addressing social interactions* in which children's mental health problems are embedded. Developmental psychology has made tremendous progress during the past 30 years by more precisely identifying and measuring the functional dynamics of family and peer relationships that lead to psychopathology in children and adolescents (Dishion & Patterson, 2006). In particular, coercive parent–child interactions are related to antisocial behavior (e.g., Patterson et al., 1992), and targeting these interactions reduces problem behavior (Dishion, Patterson, & Kavanagh, 1992; Forgatch, 1991; Forgatch & DeGarmo, 2002). Recent work examines the role of family interaction in adolescent depression, with the aim of targeting these family interactions during the course of interventions to reduce adolescent depression (Connell & Dishion, in preparation). From an ecological perspective, individual adjustment is relevant to relationship dynamics, so interventions to improve mental health must necessarily assess social interactions and motivate change in order to reduce or alleviate problem behavior and improve emotional adjustment.

5   EcoFIT explicitly addresses *parental motivation to change* parenting behaviors and the interaction between children and parents. Research on readiness to change and methods of increasing internal motivation shows that motivational interviewing is an effective incentive (Miller & Rollnick, 2002; Prochaska & Norcross, 1999). Giving feedback to families about their assessments in a supportive, non-confrontational fashion is a critical component of motivational interviewing. In the EcoFIT model, we adapted this strategy to engage caregivers in a relevant intervention service at home and at school, which we refer to as the family check-up (FCU; Dishion & Kavanagh, 2003). The FCU is central to our ecological approach to child and family interventions.

6   EcoFIT works within a *health maintenance framework* (Stormshak & Dishion, 2002). This is a radical departure from conventional approaches to child and to adult clinical and counseling psychology, which focus on "treating" mental health disorders as if there were a permanent cure. If one assumes an interaction between biological and environmental factors in mental health (see Rutter et al., 1997), then one accepts that some individuals are more vulnerable to environmental stress than are others, in terms of both initial manifestations of disorder and recurrence (Monroe & Harkness, 2005). Given variation in vulnerability to environmental stress, periodic assessments and interventions are necessary to prevent, treat, or reduce harm associated with problem behavior and emotional distress. Integrating family interventions in the public school environment fits well with the health maintenance framework in that there are clear time points that naturally occur when it is desirable and feasible to evaluate a student's school adjustment (academic, behavioral, and emotional) and to make adjustments to the school or family environments.

7   EcoFIT is based on a *developmental–ecological model*, and therefore is sensitive to both cultural variations and contextual factors that have an impact on service delivery. In a family-centered intervention, it is critical to appreciate and be sensitive to the variety and strengths of parenting patterns across cultures. EcoFIT can be adapted to meet the needs of various cultural groups and families because of its tailored approach to intervention.

EcoFIT in Public Schools

Overview

In the United States, the vast majority of children attend school up to age 18, with dropout rates increasing dramatically as youth enter late adolescence. Many of the behavioral problems that define the risk trajectory for serious delinquency and early-onset substance use are apparent in early childhood as they emerge in the context of public schools (Dishion & Patterson, 1993; Loeber & Dishion, 1983). In addition, schools are the key setting where youth aggregate into peer groups, some of which exacerbate risk for problem behavior (Dishion, Duncan, Eddy, Fagot, & Fetrow, 1994). As such, schools have become the ideal setting for the implementation of interventions to reduce problem behavior (Trickett & Birman, 1989).

Enhancing communication and cooperation between parents and school staff can significantly enhance parents' potential for monitoring, limit setting, and supporting academic progress (Gottfredson, Gottfredson, & Hybl, 1993; Reid, 1993). Regularly providing parents with specific information about their child's attendance, homework, and class behavior results in improved monitoring and support for the academic and social success of children at risk (Blechman, Taylor, & Schrader, 1981; Heller & Fantuzzo, 1993). The problem is that many schools find it difficult to administer these activities to all students. Students with low attendance and high rates of behavior problems often "fall through the cracks" and receive less support in the form of communication with parents.

To implement family-centered interventions in the public school setting, it is necessary to create a context within the host environment. Leaders in public schools can take a variety of steps to facilitate home–school collaboration. The first step is to create a physical space that is appropriate for meetings with families and parents. The second is to have a trained parent consultant available to work as a parents' ally when responding to problem behavior and emotional difficulties of individual students. This staff-person can be identified by the school and may be the school counselor, vice-principal, or other support person within the school. Parents can then be recruited early to help effectively remediate the problem. Third, a less tangible step is for the principal and vice-principal to acknowledge daily that collaborating with families and supporting their involvement is central to the education of students. It is important for staff at every school to ask themselves, "What changes could we make to increase parental involvement?" Clearly, successful implementation of prevention programs in schools is based on both support from the school leadership (e.g., principals) and successful implementation of the program by school staff (Kam, Greenberg, & Walls, 2003).

Family resource center

The first step for establishing family-based services in a school setting is to create a family resource center (FRC). FRC goals are to (a) establish an infrastructure for collaboration between school staff and parents, (b) provide a vehicle through which a program of specific family-centered interventions can be implemented and coordinated with educational services in the school, and (c) promote norms and strategies for empirically validated family management practices. Some examples are the FCU, parent management training, and follow-up academic monitoring services to parents.

Positive behavior support (PBS) systems in public school provide an excellent potential for universal family-centered interventions. The PBS system should provide clear communication about school rules and expectations and a mechanism for periodic feedback to parents regarding student compliance with school expectations. Dishion & Kavanagh (2003) recommended an ABC report that can be sent to parents on a daily (very high-risk students), weekly (at-risk students), or monthly/quarterly basis (all students). A refers to *attendance* (excused and unexcused, tardiness), B refers to *behavior* (referrals and teacher reports of a student's compliance with behavioral expectations), and C refers to *completion* of academic tasks. This level of process information is extremely important for establishing a collaborative communication link between parents and schools.

It is critical for the FRC's trained parent consultants to be school staff who are knowledgeable in constructively collaborating with parents to make relevant changes in family management to improve school and home behavior. Changing one's parenting practices can be a difficult and emotional journey that requires the skills of professionals who know how to use effective interventions and can work with resistance to change (e.g., Patterson & Forgatch, 1985). Parent consultants will know how to use a variety of strategies to engage caregivers at various stages in the continuum of risk, all of which serve to establish rapport and collaboration in the best interest of the student (Henggeler, Schoenwald, Borduin, Rowland, & Cunningham, 1998; Szapocznik & Kurtines, 1989).

Home visits

If you want to work effectively with parents, you must visit them in their own home (Szapocznik & Kurtines, 1989). We have repeatedly found that initial engagement of parents in either parent groups or the FCU requires that the parent first meet the parent consultant. We found that about 20% of the parents who initially agreed to participate in groups actually attended the group meeting. Among a new group of parents, however, a brief home visit pushed the attendance rate to more than 75%.

An important consideration when implementing school interventions is how to effectively identify the families needing support. Thus, we designed a cost-effective screening, called the *multiple gating strategy* (Dishion & Patterson, 1993; Loeber & Dishion, 1987; Loeber, Dishion, & Patterson, 1984), to proactively identify students most in need of additional support in the public school environment. The key concept is that decisions about children's level of risk are largely based on systematically collected data and less on day-to-day reactions of school staff to students' behavior. This approach has been adopted and found to be quite feasible in public schools (Feil, Walker, & Severson, 1995).

In general, we found that comprehensive teacher ratings of behavioral risk can be an inexpensive way to identify families who need interventions and who are likely to engage. Paradoxically, when analyzing the long-term results of our intervention program, we found that the families at highest risk were the most likely to engage in the intervention, and also the most likely to benefit. That is, six years later, compared with their randomly assigned controls, children at high risk who were proactively identified and whose families engaged in the intervention were least likely to increase drug use or be arrested by the police (Connell, Dishion, Yasui, & Kavanagh, 2007).

The family check-up

The FCU is a selected intervention that offers family assessment, professional support, and motivation to change. As described by Dishion and Stormshak (2007), the FCU's

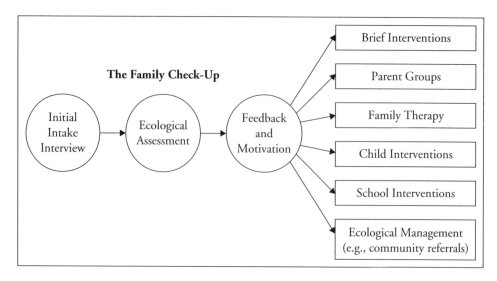

Figure 34.1 An overview of the ecological strategy

method elicits parents' accurate appraisal of their child's risk status and leads to a range of empirically supported interventions. This brief family intervention has been effective for reducing risk factors and promoting adjustment, and is feasible to implement in a public school setting. An overview of the EcoFIT model linking the FCU with a set of interventions is summarized in Figure 34.1.

The FCU, which is based on motivational interviewing (Miller & Rollnick, 2002), is a three-session intervention that consists of (a) an initial interview; (b) a comprehensive, multi-agent, multi-method assessment; and (c) a family feedback session. It uses motivational techniques to encourage maintenance of current positive practices and change of disruptive practices.

The formal integration of diverse perspectives in developing motivation to change is the underpinning of EcoFIT in general and the FCU in particular. Outpatient clinics commonly use unstructured interviews and questionnaires and rely almost exclusively on parent report to guide their judgment about diagnosis and treatment. In contrast, we obtain structured reports from parents, teachers, and the child and then compare the reports using normative standards. In addition, we directly observe family interactions. These diverse data sources provide the parent consultant with a "family-centered perspective"; that is, one that is inclusive but not overly reliant on any one reporting agent. Collecting multiple reports also allows us to coordinate the data across reporters and to provide feedback for parents that is comprehensive and strength-based. Caregivers who may not be actively involved in the child's life (such as stepparents or biological parents who are living outside the home) are actively engaged in this process to create links between family members and begin a collaborative process toward changing behavior.

Feedback

Data are critical to motivational interviewing and change. They help parents reconsider "issues" (e.g., violent behavior) as serious problems that require attention and change, and also guide the tailoring of the intervention to fit the school setting and individual family. Thus, a fundamental step of the feedback journey is sharing data with the parent and other involved caregivers; especially useful are data that come from other sources such as teachers and direct observation. Providing feedback to parents from the findings of psychological assessments is conducive to change (Sanders & Lawton, 1993). The critical feature of such feedback is that it be presented in a supportive and motivating manner with a focus on strengths and areas of growth.

Motivation

The FCU uses motivational interviewing and assessment information to help parents identify appropriate services and reasonable change strategies. This step usually occurs when parents come to the FRC because of concerns about their child's adjustment at home or at school. When parents are notified of discipline problems in the school, it provides an opportunity to link school staff with families and provide feedback to parents. FRC staff should strive to catch problems early and make recommendations for family intervention in addition to the typical child interventions common in schools.

Intervention menu

Our approach allows us to target one aspect of parenting behavior and work directly on that problem in the context of the larger issue. For example, a parent who is aware of his or her student's performance and knows only to criticize failures would benefit tremendously from a tailored intervention about positive reinforcement. The FCU would have identified this need, as well as parenting strengths, and the motivational interviewing would be targeted to encourage the caregiver in the process of providing positive reinforcement.

The presumption underlying the menu of family intervention services is that a variety of family-centered interventions can be equally effective for reducing problem behavior (Webster-Stratton, Kolpacoff, & Hollingsworth, 1988). The indicated intervention menu typically includes three levels of intervention sessions (Dishion & Stormshak, 2007). The first level provides motivation, support, and problem solving of relatively minor problems and adjustment issues. Following the FCU, many parents request only follow-up telephone calls from the parent consultant, often referred to as *phone check-ins*. These calls are used to check in about a problem behavior and provide immediate brief consultation.

The second type of indicated intervention is what we refer to as *skill-building interventions*. They involve actively working with parents to improve their family management skills and closely following the principles of parental management training

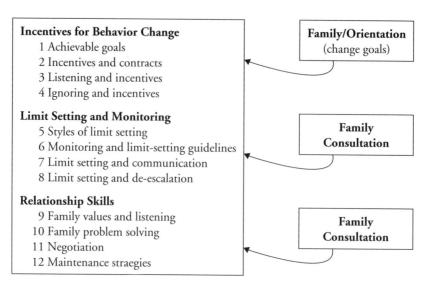

Figure 34.2   Family management curriculum

(Forgatch, Patterson, & DeGarmo, 2005). The skills include setting limits, proactive parenting, positive reinforcement, monitoring, problem solving, and communication. We either conduct these sessions individually with parents, such as in behavioral family therapy, or we may work with parents in groups. The Family Management Curriculum, derived from more than 30 years of research at the Oregon Social Learning Center, serves as the manual for these interventions (Dishion, Kavanagh, et al., 2003). See Figure 34.2 for a description of the family management curriculum.

Working with multiproblem families is often challenging with respect to addressing severe life stressors, potential abuse, and family disruption such as divorce and remarriage, which can create a volatile, emotionally dysregulated atmosphere that is not conducive to caregiver PBS. Family adaptation and coping interventions are designed to reduce emotional dysregulation, support the parents' attention on family-centered issues, and provide support for positive, realistic coping that is within the parents' skill set and control.

As shown in Figure 34.3, these sessions address two interrelated client responses to severe stress and crises: the emotional response and self-efficacy for coping with the stress.

Emotional response to stress can overwhelm parents, and they may become distracted or engage in maladaptive coping and parenting. Erratic actions such as moving suddenly or demonstrating violent behavior can have long-lasting implications for a student's achievement and development in an educational setting. For example, when a parent discovers his partner is having an affair, his response to this information may have more severe implications for the children than does the actual stressor, as traumatic as it may seem. Violence to the partner, suddenly moving to another location, and quitting work can have long-term disruptive effects on children and adolescents. Thus, a timely intervention during this crisis would support the father in coping with emotional reactions

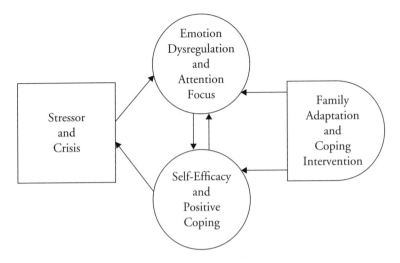

Figure 34.3   Family adaptation and coping interventions to reduce disruption in crises

without acting them out, and refocus attention on issues of parenting and the long-term interests of the children in general.

The second helpful service that can be provided in the context of adaptive coping sessions is to provide the parent with improved self-efficacy, primarily by guiding parents to actions that are within their control, immediately beneficial, and minimally harmful to others. For example, interventions during an episode of domestic violence could involve (a) removal of the mother and children to a safe shelter, (b) a court-ordered restraining order, and (c) structured communication with the abusing partner regarding communications during the next week. Thus, the caregiver is able to ensure the safety of herself and her children and is placed in a supportive social context that enables problem solving the immediate and long-term future of the family.

One of the EcoFIT goals is to facilitate family engagement in community resources that will best fit the family's long-term needs. EcoFIT encourages collaborations with community agencies designed to support children and families. For example, when one is working with a mother in recovery from methamphetamine abuse, it is wise to respond to crises by reinforcing her involvement in services designed to keep her in recovery. When a breach in services occurs, the parent consultant can support the caregiver in taking steps to reengage in services.

There are a variety of barriers to effective parenting: some are historical (e.g., past abuse and trauma, history of discrimination and oppression), some are contextual (e.g., poverty, low resources in communities), and others are chronic (e.g., long-term disabilities, health problems). In these circumstances a key role of the parent consultant is to support caregivers in the course of coping, problem solving, and making efforts to reduce harm to the youth. At times, this requires guiding the caregiver into services that are more appropriate to recovery or safety. Thus, providing a parent with the insight and motivation to seek realistic levels of support to make family changes and to adapt to the stressor is a pivotal function of the parent consultant during the FCU and beyond.

Given its flexible approach to delivery and tailored assessment, the FCU can be easily adapted to diverse families and cultural groups. Each family has its own parenting values. Some of these values are based on cultural experiences and beliefs, and others are grounded in a history of parenting and a skill base. It is imperative for the parent consultant to work within a family's cultural beliefs and values, while at the same time differentiating culturally based parenting from parenting that is ineffective. For example, parents may spank their child because they were spanked as a child, and that is one of their few parenting skills. Another parent may use spanking because physical punishment is valued in their culture and family. Spanking in the context of warmth and support may be effective in some cultures, whereas spanking in other cultures may lead to child problem behavior (Deater-Deckard, Dodge, Bates, & Pettit, 1996). In each case, the FCU can be used to tailor feedback to the family by teaching new skills and supporting parenting that is effective within that cultural context. Outcomes of the parenting skill (e.g., child aggressive behavior) are assessed during the assessment phase, and feedback about the link between parenting strategies and the child's behavior is given to the family. In this way, a parent's own behavior is linked to child outcomes and is viewed in the context of both cultural values and parenting skills.

Structured interventions

In summary, the FRC delivers a variety of specific interventions and addresses student and family needs in terms of the full range of the risk continuum. The FCU is the cornerstone of the service delivery system. This brief intervention ideally would be provided to families every year, as is the case in prevention trials. We offer a variety of structured interventions following the FCU. The most common are:

1   Brief parenting interventions. This service focuses primarily on motivation, but also includes problem solving solutions to parenting challenges that may be transient (e.g., improving grades).
2   School interventions. A daily, weekly, or biweekly report to parents about their student's attendance, behavior in school, and completion of homework is set up and delivered. This service is contingent on working with parents on positive reinforcement for meeting goals.
3   Family management skill support. This set of services includes more intensive support for family management practices known to reduce rates of emergence and growth of problem behavior in children and adolescents.
4   Support in crises and family disruption. This service focuses primarily on the parents' immediate response to acute crises and family disruption in the context of sessions that emphasize adaptation and coping.
5   Community referrals. Key to the EcoFIT model is its collaborative design that can be adjusted from community to community. As such, referrals to services may vary depending on resources and cultural values.

Outcomes

Overview

During the 2000s, we have engaged in two randomized prevention trials in which half of the sixth-grade population of metropolitan middle schools were randomly assigned at the individual level to the FRC versus public middle school as usual. Each parent consultant was assigned to a school where they attempted to engage parents of youth who were identified as at risk by teachers. Services were provided primarily in the seventh and eighth grades of three middle schools.

Engagement

In the first project, we actively engaged 25% of the families in the FCU during the two years of service, across the three schools. We had contact with an additional 25% of the families, but did not conduct an FCU with them. By and large, we found that the families at highest risk were the most likely to participate in the FCU. Connell, Dishion, and Deater-Deckard (2006) found that single-parent families, those with students involved in a deviant peer group, and those rated by teachers as at high risk were the most likely to engage in the FCU. In the second project (which is currently ongoing), we have actively engaged 40% of families in the FCU intervention across the three participating schools. Interestingly, the average hours of contact per family total about 6, with the contact time increasing as student risk increases (Dishion, Kavanagh, Schneiger, Nelson, & Kaufman, 2002).

We conducted an effectiveness trial of the EcoFIT model in another set of four public middle schools. In this study we also carefully counted the minutes of contact with parents of students. Parent consultants were creative in engaging parents. In one middle school, the parent consultant established a coffee cart for parents and would meet them as they dropped off their middle school child and picked up coffee. In this study, we found that the number of parent contacts in Grades 6, 7, and 8 was associated with reductions in growth in teacher ratings of risk (Stormshak et al., 2005).

Randomized intervention effects

Several reports have been published about FRC intervention effects on adolescent substance use. The first revealed that randomization to the FRC in sixth grade was associated with reductions in substance use (Dishion, Kavanagh, et al., 2002) and in deviant peer involvement (Dishion, Bullock, & Granic, 2002). We found that for the youth at highest risk, reductions in drug use were mediated by changes in observed parental monitoring practices (Dishion, Nelson, & Kavanagh, 2003).

Our recent analyses concur with these findings, suggesting that the most dramatic effects of EcoFIT are with sixth-grade students who are most severely problematic and whose

Table 34.1 Five-Year Intervention Effects

Eleventh-grade outcomes	Engagers (intervention)	Engagers (control)	Declined (all)
Percent arrested at least one time	15	100	5
Frequency of marijuana use, previous month	1	5	3
Days absent from school	13	32	12

families are most in need of services (Connell et al., 2007). Assessment of outcomes to age 17 are modest. However, if one considers the level at which a family was engaged in the intervention, compared with that of control subjects who would also have likely engaged in the FCU intervention, the effects are quite dramatic.

In our analysis of problem behavior, we found a marked reduction in the percentage of youth arrested at least once in the "engager" group (15% had been arrested) who actually received the FCU compared with the control (100% had been arrested). Thus, sixth-grade students at high risk were six times more likely to be arrested within the next 5 years if they were not offered the FCU. Similarly, they used marijuana five times more frequently during a 1-month period than did the intervention group. These findings were extended to marijuana and tobacco dependence by age 18 as well. These analyses revealed that random assignment to the EcoFIT intervention reliably reduced substance use, antisocial behavior, and the probability of arrest (Connell et al., 2006).

Table 34.1 reveals that random assignment to the intervention resulted in a 50% reduction in days absent from high school from sixth through the eleventh grade. Control engagers missed an average of 32 days during the school year, and intervention youth missed only 13 (Stormshak, Connell, & Dishion, 2008).

Another trend is particularly important to consider when inspecting Table 34.1. Although it is often said that family-based services offered in the school will be received only by families that are at low or no risk, we did not find this to be the case. Our proactive approach to offering the FCU suggested that in fact, the families who declined participation were those who were at the lowest risk of all. In other words, these parents accurately assessed their young adolescents' risk status and did not feel the need to receive information or support on behavior management strategies. This is an optimistic finding indeed, because it suggests that if we have the appropriate outreach and engagement strategies in place for caregivers of the highest-risk students, we are likely to reduce their long-term risk by supporting their use of PBS strategies and coordinating with school staff in supporting student success.

Summary

This chapter provides an overview of the ecological approach to family intervention and treatment within the school setting (EcoFIT). Over 20 years ago (Dishion, Reid, & Patterson,

1988) we set out to translate a developmental model of problem behavior into an effective intervention for reducing the emerging risks associated with childhood and adolescence. Although the developmental model included constructs such as parental monitoring and deviant peer involvement, we had not yet linked the model to effective interventions. At the time, we referred to this model as the Adolescent Transitions Program (ATP). The ATP was refined through research on positive family management outcomes (Dishion & Andrews, 1995; Dishion et al., 1992) and on negative outcomes related to deviant peer involvement (e.g., Dishion, McCord, & Poulin, 1999). Today we are reluctant to refer to ATP as a stand-alone program, but instead prefer to think of the approach as a general set of principles for prevention and treatment of adjustment problems in children and families.

Until recently, family-based interventions have been difficult to integrate with a prevention model primarily because of the expense of the service, but also because of the challenge of reaching families in need. Implementation of family intervention in a school setting, however, addresses these cost issues. Our data indicate that we are averaging 6 hours of contact over 2 years for the families at highest risk. These data suggest that even students who are in the highest range of problem behavior can benefit from relatively little intervention time, making this approach very inexpensive and feasible for delivery in schools and other community agencies.

Integrating family-centered interventions into the public school system would undoubtedly generate public health benefits for children and adolescents. As such, we can continue to import programs such as EcoFIT into the school context, which would require intensive training, monitoring, accountability, and organization of change agents outside the system. Alternatively, we can change our graduate training of school counselors and psychologists, as well as of school principals, to provide these services as a customary component of their professional role in the school context. The latter approach is a more promising long-term strategy for improving the education of children both in academic competencies and for meeting the social and emotional demands of living in the twenty-first century.

Note

This project was supported by grant DA16110, grant DA07031, and grant 018374, all from the National Institutes of Health. This work benefits especially from the contributions of the following colleagues at the Child and Family Center: Arin Connell, Kate Kavanagh, Peggy Veltman, and Charlotte Winter. Cheryl Mikkola is gratefully acknowledged for her help with this manuscript. The Portland Public Schools and the Project Alliance youth and families are appreciated for their participation in this research.

Resources

Please see our resource information located on our website at cfc.uoregon.edu.

References

Blechman, E. A., Taylor, C. J., & Schrader, S. M. (1981). Family problem solving versus home notes as early intervention with high-risk children. *Journal of Consulting and Clinical Psychology, 49*, 919–926.

Borduin, C. M., & Henggeler, S. W. (1990). A multisystemic approach to the treatment of delinquent behavior. In R. J. McMahon & R. D. Peters (Eds.), *Behavior disorders of adolescence: Research, intervention and policy in clinical and school settings* (pp. 63–80). New York: Haworth Press.

Conduct Problems Prevention Research Group. (2002). Evaluation of the first 3 years of the Fast Track Prevention Trial with children at high risk for adolescent conduct problems. *Journal of Abnormal Child Psychology, 30*, 19–35.

Connell, A., & Dishion, T. J. (in preparation). Self-regulation and depression: Buffering the effects of exposure to stressful events in adolescence.

Connell, A., Dishion, T. J., & Deater-Deckard, K. (2006). Variable- and person-centered approaches to the analysis of early adolescent substance use: Linking peer, family, and intervention effects with developmental trajectories. *Merrill-Palmer Quarterly, 52(3)*, 421–448.

Connell, A., Dishion, T. J., Yasui, M., & Kavanagh, K. (2007). An adaptive approach to family intervention: Linking engagement in family-centered intervention to reductions in adolescent problem behavior. *Journal of Consulting and Clinical Psychology, 75*, 568–579.

Deater-Deckard, K., Dodge, K. A., Bates, J. E., & Pettit, G. S. (1996). Physical discipline among African-American and European-American mothers: Links to children's externalizing behaviors. *Developmental Psychology, 32*, 1065–1072.

Dishion, T. J., & Andrews, D. W. (1995). Preventing escalation in problem behaviors with high-risk young adolescents: Immediate and 1-year outcomes. *Journal of Consulting and Clinical Psychology, 63*, 538–548.

Dishion, T. J., Bullock, B. M., & Granic, I. (2002). Pragmatism in modeling peer influence: Dynamics, outcomes, and change processes.. *Development and Psychopathology, 14*, 995–1009.

Dishion, T. J., Duncan, T. E., Eddy, J. M., Fagot, B. I., & Fetrow, R. A. (1994). The world of parents and peers: Coercive exchanges and children's social adaptation. *Social Development, 3*, 255–268.

Dishion, T. J., & Kavanagh, K. (2003). *Intervening in adolescent problem behavior: A family-centered approach.* New York: Guilford Press.

Dishion, T. J., Kavanagh, K., Schneiger, A., Nelson, S. E., & Kaufman, N. (2002). Preventing early adolescent substance use: A family-centered strategy for the public middle school ecology. *Prevention Science, 3*, 191–201.

Dishion, T. J., Kavanagh, K., Veltman, M., McCartney, T., Soberman, L., & Stormshak, E. A. (2003). *Family Management Curriculum V.2.0: Leader's guide.* Eugene, OR: Child and Family Center Publications (http://cfc.uoregon.edu).

Dishion, T. J., McCord, J., & Poulin, F. (1999). When interventions harm: Peer groups and problem behavior. *American Psychologist, 54*, 755–764.

Dishion, T. J., Nelson, S. E., & Kavanagh, K. (2003). The FCU for high-risk adolescents: Preventing early-onset substance use by parent monitoring. *Behavior Therapy, 34*, 553–571.

Dishion, T. J., & Patterson, G. R. (1992). Age effects in parent training outcome. *Behavior Therapy, 23*, 719–729.

Dishion, T. J., & Patterson, G. R. (1993). Childhood screening for early adolescent problem behavior: A multiple gating strategy. In M. Singer, L. Singer, & T. M. Anglin (Eds.), *Handbook for screening adolescents at psychosocial risk* (pp. 375–399). New York: Lexington.

Dishion, T. J., & Patterson, G. R. (2006). The development and ecology of antisocial behavior in children and adolescents. In D. Cicchetti & D. J. Cohen (Eds.), *Developmental psychopathology: Vol. 3. Risk, disorder, and adaptation* (pp. 503–541). New York: Wiley.

Dishion, T. J., Patterson, G. R., & Kavanagh, K. (1992). An experimental test of the coercion model: Linking theory, measurement, and intervention. In J. McCord & R. E. Tremblay (Eds.), *The interaction of theory and practice: Experimental studies of interventions* (pp. 253–282). New York: Guilford Press.

Dishion, T. J., Reid, J. B., & Patterson, G. R. (1988). Empirical guidelines for the development of a treatment for early adolescent substance use. In R. E. Coombs (Ed.), *The family context of adolescent drug use* (pp. 189–224). New York: Haworth Press.

Dishion, T. J., & Stormshak, E. (2007). *Intervening in children's lives: An ecological, family-centered approach to mental health care.* Washington, DC: APA Books.

Eddy, J. M., & Chamberlain, P. (2000). Family management and deviant peer association as mediators of the impact of treatment condition on youth antisocial behavior. *Journal of Child Clinical Psychology, 5,* 857–863.

Feil, E. G., Walker, H. M., & Severson, H. H. (1995). The Early Screening Project for young children with behavior problems. *Journal of Emotional and Behavioral Disorders, 3(4),* 194–202.

Forgatch, M. (1991). The clinical science vortex: Developing a theory for antisocial behavior. In D. J. Pepler & K. H. Rubin (Eds.), *The development and treatment of childhood aggression* (pp. 291–315). Hillsdale, NJ: Erlbaum.

Forgatch, M. S., Bullock, B. M., & DeGarmo, D. S. (2003). *Parenting through change: An experimental test of the parent management training model for stepfamilies.* Manuscript in preparation.

Forgatch, M. S., & DeGarmo, D. S. (2002). Extending and testing the social interaction learning model with divorce samples. In J. B. Reid & G. R. Patterson (Eds.), *Antisocial behavior in children and adolescents: A developmental analysis and model for intervention* (pp. 235–238). Washington, DC: American Psychological Association.

Forgatch, M. S., Patterson, G. R., & DeGarmo, D. S. (2005). Evaluating fidelity: Predictive validity for a measure of competent adherence to the Oregon Model of Parent Management Training. *Behavior Therapy, 36(1),* 3–13.

Gottfredson, D. C., Gottfredson, G. D., & Hybl, L. G. (1993). Managing adolescent behavior: A multiyear, multischool study. *American Educational Research Journal, 30,* 179–215.

Heller, L. R., & Fantuzzo, J. W. (1993). Reciprocal peer tutoring and parent partnership: Does parent involvement make a difference? *School Psychology Review, 22,* 517–534.

Henggeler, S. W., Schoenwald, S. K., Borduin, C. M., Rowland, M. D., & Cunningham, P. B. (1998). *Multisystemic treatment of antisocial behavior in children and adolescents.* New York: Guilford Press.

Kam, C., Greenberg, M. T., & Walls, C. T. (2003). Examining the role of implementation quality in school-based prevention using the PATHS curriculum. *Prevention Science, 4,* 55–63.

Kazdin, A. E. (2002). Psychosocial treatments for conduct disorder in children and adolescents. In P. E. Nathan & J. M. Gorman (Eds.), *A guide to treatments that work* (2nd ed., pp. 57–85). London: Oxford University Press.

Loeber, R., & Dishion, T. J. (1983). Early predictors of male delinquency: A review. *Psychological Bulletin, 94,* 68–99.

Loeber, R., & Dishion, T. J. (1987). Antisocial and delinquent youths: Methods for their early identification. In J. D. Burchard & S. N. Burchard (Eds.), *Prevention of delinquent behavior* (pp. 75–89). Newbury Park, CA: Sage.

Loeber, R., Dishion, T. J., & Patterson, G. R. (1984). Multiple gating: A multistage assessment procedure for identifying youths at risk for delinquency. *Journal of Research in Crime and Delinquency, 21,* 7–32.

Miller, W. R., & Rollnick, S. (2002). *Motivational interviewing: Preparing people for change* (2nd ed.). New York: Guilford Press.

Monroe, S. M., & Harkness, K. L. (2005). Life stress, the "Kindling" hypothesis, and the recurrence of depression: Considerations from a life stress perspective. *Psychological Review, 112,* 417–445.

Patterson, G. R., & Forgatch, M. S. (1985). Therapist behavior as a determinant for client resistance: A paradox for the behavior modifier. *Journal of Consulting and Clinical Psychology, 53,* 846–851.

Patterson, G. R., Reid, J. B., & Dishion, T. J. (1992). *Antisocial boys.* Eugene, OR: Castalia.

Prochaska, J. O., & Norcross, J. G. (1999). *Systems of psychotherapy.* Pacific Grove, CA: Brooks/Cole.

Reid, J. B. (1993). Prevention of conduct disorder before and after school entry: Relating interventions to development findings. *Journal of Development and Psychopathology, 5,* 243–262.

Rutter, M., Dunn, J., Simonoff, G., Pickles, A., Maughn, B., Ormel, J., et al. (1997). Integrating nature and nurture: Implications of person–environment correlations and interactions for developmental psychopathology. *Development and Psychopathology, 9,* 335–364.

Sanders, N. R., & Lawton, J. M. (1993). Discussing assessment findings with families: A guided participation model of information transfer. *Child and Family Behavior Therapy, 15,* 5–33.

Shaw, D. S., Dishion, T. J., Supplee, L., Gardner, F., & Arnds, K. (2006). Randomized trial of a family-centered approach to the prevention of early conduct problems: Two-year effects of the FCU in early childhood. *Journal of Consulting and Clinical Psychology, 74,* 1–9.

Stormshak, E. A., Connell, A., & Dishion, T. J. (2008). *An adaptive approach to family-centered intervention in schools: Linking intervention engagement to academic outcomes in middle and high school.* Manuscript submitted for publication.

Stormshak, E. A., & Dishion, T. J. (2002). An ecological approach to child and family clinical and counseling psychology. *Clinical Child and Family Psychology Review, 5,* 197–215.

Stormshak, E. A., Dishion, T. J., Light, J., & Yasui, M. (2005). Implementing family-centered interventions within the public middle school: Linking service delivery change to change in problem behavior. *Journal of Abnormal Child Psychology, 33,* 723–733.

Sugai, G., Horner, R. H., & Sprague, J. R. (1999). Functional-assessment-based behavior support planning: Research to practice to research. *Behavior Disorders, 24,* 253–257.

Szapocznik, J., & Kurtines, W. M. (1989). *Breakthroughs in family therapy with drug-abusing and problem youth.* New York: Springer.

Trickett, E. J., & Birman, D. (1989). Taking ecology seriously: A community development approach to individually based preventive interventions in schools. In L. A. Bond & B. E. Compas (Eds.), *Primary prevention and promotion in the schools: Primary prevention of psychopathology: Vol. 12* (pp. 361–390). Newbury Park, CA: Sage.

Webster-Stratton, C. (1990). Long-term follow-up of families with young conduct problem children: From preschool to grade school. *Journal of Clinical Child Psychology, 19,* 144–149.

Webster-Stratton, C., Kolpacoff, M., & Hollingsworth, T. (1988). Self-administered videotape therapy for families with conduct-problem children: Comparison with two cost-effective treatments and a control group. *Journal of Consulting and Clinical Psychology, 56,* 558–566.

35

Families and Schools

Cindy Carlson, Catherine L. Funk, and KimHoang T. Nguyen

The family and school represent two of the most important socialization environments of children. The importance of the family to child development is ubiquitous in theory, research, policy, and practice (Masten & Shaffer, 2006). Parents serve as regulators of emotion, teachers and conveyers of culture, and providers of social and economic resources. The family also serves as a source of genetic and behavioral risk or resilience. The importance of the family to children's academic success has been viewed as so central we may argue that it is the family that sits in the classroom each day.

Schools are also significant socialization agents of children. Child academic motivation is impacted by a variety of school-level characteristics and classroom practices (Wigfield, Eccles, Schiefele, Roeser, & Davis-Kean, 2006). A school culture that is structured, values academic performance, and has high expectations for children's learning promotes achievement. Positive teacher–student relationships and a sense of belonging at the classroom level improve behavior and performance. Structured schools and caring teachers may serve as important sources of support and guidance that buffer the impact of family and neighborhood stress (Hetherington, Cox, & Cox, 1985; Rutter, 1985a, 1985b). Poorly functioning schools, like dysfunctional families, may increase child risk and vulnerability.

The quality of the home–school relationship is a third dimension that impacts the success of children in school. Regardless of income or background, when parents are involved in their children's education, youth are more likely to earn higher grades and test scores, pass their classes and be promoted, attend school regularly and graduate, and engage in more socially skilled school behavior (Henderson & Mapp, 2002). White, middle-class families tend to be more involved in schools than families that are economically disadvantaged or cultural minorities. Nearly 40% of the public school population in 2000, however, was non-White (Swick, Head-Reeves, & Barbarin, 2006). Engaging parents in partnership regarding children's learning is viewed by educators as a key strategy for reducing the minority–majority achievement gap; however, schools face numerous barriers in establishing and maintaining effective partnerships with diverse families (Henderson & Mapp, 2002).

The importance of family–school relations is theoretically rooted in Bronfenbrenner's (1979; and see Chapter 1, this volume) ecological systems theory, which proposed that the developmental outcomes of children are affected not only by their social interactions within the primary socialization settings in which they live, but also by the quality of the relations between these settings. Consistent with systems theory, Bronfenbrenner viewed the family and school as functioning synergistically on the development of the child; that is, their joint operation produces an effect that is greater than the sum of the individual effects. The joint operation of the family and the school may be considered the home–school relationship, a broad term that encompasses attitudes and beliefs, communication, parent involvement, home–school collaboration and home–school–community partnership.

In this chapter we briefly review research on the impact of the family environment, the school environment, and the home–school relationship on children's academic success. We then examine home–school interventions with an emphasis on evidence-based practice. A case study illustrates the use of school-based family counseling in response to academic failure. Throughout the chapter we pay particular attention to the home–school relationship needs of diverse families.

Developmental Influence of Family and School

Impact of the family on children's behavior and learning

Research that examines the impact of the family on children's school behavior and learning is rooted in the socialization theory tradition of child development. Socialization refers to the "process by which parents shape a child's behaviors, attitudes, and social skills so that the child will be able to function as a member of society"; academic socialization includes the "variety of parental beliefs and behaviors that influence children's school-related development" (Taylor, Clayton, & Rowley, 2004, p. 163). Parental influences on children's school-related development are best understood when parenting styles and parenting practices are independently examined (Darling & Steinberg, 1993). Parenting style reflects the emotional environment in which parents raise their children, and it is commonly differentiated orthogonally along the dimensions of *responsiveness* and *demandingness*, resulting in four parenting style categories: authoritative, authoritarian, permissive/indulgent, and neglectful. Parenting practices are the specific behaviors parents apply to socialize their children. Parenting practices relevant to academic socialization include involvement in school, monitoring of children's behavior, and the creation of a home learning environment (Spera, 2005).

Parenting style and academic achievement.   Numerous studies have examined the link between parenting style and school achievement. The consensus is that the authoritative parenting style, characterized by the combination of high levels of responsiveness, demandingness, and warmth with low levels of negativity and conflict, provides an environment most conducive to positive child academic and social outcomes (Taylor et al., 2004). Non-authoritative parenting styles are consistently associated with comparatively lower levels of psychosocial competence and school achievement, as well as higher levels of internal distress and problem behaviors among children and adolescents (Darling & Steinberg, 1993).

The positive effects of the authoritative parenting style are robust across different family structures but not different ethnic groups (Spera, 2005). Whereas authoritative parenting is positively associated with grade point average (GPA) and school engagement for European American and Hispanic adolescents, the authoritarian parenting style, which is characterized by high *demandingness* and low *responsivensss*, is more strongly related to positive academic outcomes for African American and Asian American adolescents (Darling & Steinberg, 1993; Taylor et al., 2004). Different parenting styles may be optimal for different social ecological niches. Culture may also impact the validity and generalizability of existing parenting style measures.

Parent practices and academic achievement.　A number of parent behaviors have been found to foster academic achievement. Parental use of language-stimulating behaviors shapes young children's vocabulary, reading, and academic skills (Taylor et al., 2004). Parental monitoring of children's after-school activities, including homework completion and activities with peers, is associated with higher academic achievement and lower substance use among adolescents; parental help with homework, attendance at school conferences and functions, and provision of a supportive home learning environment inversely relate to school dropout (Bray, Adams, Getz, & Baer, 2001; Spera, 2005; see also Chapter 34, this volume).

Parent behaviors that support children's academic achievement may be broadly categorized as *parent involvement* in schooling. The most widely cited contemporary definition of parent involvement is one based on a typology proposed by Epstein (Epstein & Dauber, 1991) that includes six specific types of activities: parenting, communicating with the school, learning at home, volunteering and/or attending school activities, decision-making (participating in school governance), and engaging in community connections that foster education. Parent involvement is positively related to children's school achievement, attendance, adaptability, and classroom behavior (Epstein & Dauber, 1991), and a review of studies concluded the academic benefits to students of parent involvement holds across families of all economic, racial/ethnic, and educational backgrounds, and for students of all ages (Henderson & Mapp, 2002).

One criticism of the research on parent involvement, however, has been the multi-dimensional nature of the construct, making it difficult to determine which parent behaviors relate to specific components of school success. In a large-scale study based on data from the National Education Longitudinal Study, Ho Sui-Chu and Willms (1996) found home discussions about school-related topics have the strongest relationship with academic achievement. The initiation of home discussions about school communicates to their children parental academic values, expectations and aspirations, which are associated with children's academic goal-setting, persistence in school, intellectual accomplishments, and enrollment in postsecondary education (Spera, 2005).

Socioeconomic status (SES) and ethnicity influence parent involvement in education (Spera, 2005). Parents are more likely to volunteer or attend school functions when their children attend a high SES school (Ho Sui-Chu & Willms, 1996). White, middle-class families are more involved at school, whereas low-income, ethnic minority, and immigrant families engage in activities at home that support their children's education (Boethel, 2003). Barriers to school involvement noted by low-income minority families included time constraints, child-care needs, transportation problems, language differences, cultural beliefs, and lack of knowledge or understanding of the educational processes in the United States.

The family context.   Relatively few studies examine the impact on children's learning of sibling or spousal relationships. In young children, positive sibling relationships (joint attention activities, discussion of thoughts and feelings with younger siblings) are associated with greater social cognitive skill development (Howe & Ross, 1990). Survey data from a large, multiethnic sample of middle school students indicated that in high-risk families perceived support from one's older sister or brother related positively to school adaptation and achievement; in low-risk families, older brother support was related to achievement and a positive school attitude for boys in Hispanic families (Milevsky & Levitt, 2005). Not surprisingly, high levels of marital conflict and family disruption are linked to social, emotional, behavioral, and academic problems in children (Hoglund & Leadbeater, 2004). Given the potential positive impact of supportive sibling relationships, it is unfortunate that marital conflict is also associated with sibling conflict at home and with peer, social, and academic problems in school (Stocker & Youngblade, 1999).

School effects on children and families

Schools influence children's attitudes about self and achievement. As children start formal schooling, and their work and behavior are evaluated by teachers and classmates, they develop a sense of self that is no longer singularly dependent on the mirror provided by family members (Wigfield et al., 2006). A warm classroom environment, in conjunction with clear student expectations and administrative policies, can have a particularly positive impact on at-risk children (Arnold & Doctoroff, 2003). Hetherington et al. (1985) found that post-divorce children who were in authoritative classrooms were more likely to maintain pre-divorce levels of achievement and behavior in school and home; the protective effect was most marked for boys, children with difficult temperaments, and children exposed to multiple stressful life events. Authoritative teachers and schools moderate the negative impact on children of family disruption and dysfunction.

The authors could locate only one study that examined directly the impact of the school environment on the family system. Results of the study, based on child reports, suggested a circular negative process in which academic failure experienced by the child at school increased the probability of child perceptions of parent disapproval at home later in the day, which, in turn, increased the child's propensity to perceive rejections and failures at school the following day (Repetti, 1996). The results of this study are provocative. Research that examines the reciprocal inter-setting impact of home and school on children, parents, and teachers is sorely needed.

Home–School Partnership

Although a home–school relationship characterized by parent involvement, frequent communication, and collaboration between caregivers and teachers enhances the academic performance and behavioral conduct of children and adolescents in schools regardless of race, ethnicity, or SES, a genuine, co-equal partnership can be difficult to achieve. In this section we examine some of the challenges to home–school collaboration, and highlight the evidence-based practices that build bridges between diverse families and schools.

Parent involvement programs

Schools vary in their ability to foster parent participation. This is a particular concern in conditions where there is a difference between the cultures of the family and the school. Public schools are rooted in European American, middle-class culture. If home and school do not share the same cultural construction of socialization goals (e.g., independence), parents, as well as their children, may be confused and fail to follow expected rules (Harry, 2002). Schools that seek to establish a relationship with diverse families from their majority sociocultural perspective may inadvertently devalue the parents of their students, resulting in lower parent involvement (Sosa, 1997).

Studies confirm that teachers and parents in economically disadvantaged schools do not share similar views of parental involvement. Whereas teachers believe parent involvement should start in the school (e.g., attending meetings, volunteering) and then branch out to the home, parents view their involvement priority to be within the community (e.g., keeping children off the streets) and secondarily within the school (e.g., chaperoning school trips; Lawson, 2003). The parent involvement behaviors of economically disadvantaged minority families are consistent with their view that their primary role is to support their child's education through home activities. Thus, the involvement of culturally diverse families in the schooling of their children may be invisible to teachers, lending support to their view that parents do not care.

Evidence for the effectiveness of school-based parent involvement programs is weak. In contrast with the conclusions reached by most descriptive reviews, when the methodological soundness of studies is considered, there is little evidence that systematic school-based parent involvement programs enhance either the academic or social competence of children (Fishel & Ramirez, 2005; Mattingly, Prislin, McKenzie, Rodriguez, & Kayzar, 2002). In contrast with the lack of evidence for the broad, multicomponent programs that are common in schools, evidence is promising for programs that focus on engaging parents as tutors at home to prevent or improve a single academic problem (mathematics or reading) among elementary school-aged children (see Table 35.1; see

Table 35.1 Evidence-Based Family–School Intervention Models Across Six Program Types

Intervention(s) with preliminary support	Representative reference(s)
Family–school interventions with preschool children	
Incredible Years Training Series	Webster-Stratton, Reid, & Hammond (2001)
PARTNERS Parent Education Program	Webster-Stratton (1998)
Parent Child Interaction Therapy (PCIT)	Funderbunk, Eyberg, Newcomb, McNeil, Hembree-Kigin, & Capage (1998)
	Hembree-Kigin & McNeil (1995)
	McNeil, Eyberg, Eisenstadt, Newcomb, & Funderbunk (1991)
Dialogic Reading	Lonigan & Whitehurst (1998)
	Whitehurst, Arnold, Epstein, Angell, Smith, & Fischel (1994)
Parent consultation	
Behavioral Consultation	Sheridan, Eagle, Cowan, & Mickelson (2001)
	Sheridan, Kratochwill, & Bergan (1996)
	Weiner, Sheridan, & Jenson (1998)
Parent Behavioral Consultation	Cavell & Hughes (2000)
	Rhoades & Kratochwill (1998)
Parent education, parent training, and family interventions	
Aware Parenting	Bronstein, Duncan, Clauson, Abrams, Yannett, Ginsberg, & Milne (1998)
Problem-Solving Skills Training (PSST)	Kazdin, Esveldt-Dawson, French, & Unis (1987)
plus Parent Management Training (PMT)	Kazdin, Seigel, & Bass (1992)
Social Learning Family Therapy (SLFT)	Sayger, Horne, Walker, & Passmore (1988)
Adolescent Transitions Project (ATP)	Dishion & Kavanagh (2000)
Family–school collaboration	
School-Home Notes and Family Problem Solving Game	Blechman, Taylor, & Schrader (1981)
School-Based/Family Literacy Program	Morrow & Young (1997)
Parent–Teacher Action Research (PTAR) Teams plus Social Skills Instruction	McConaughy, Kay, & Fitzgerald (1999)
Parent involvement	
Parent Tutoring	Duvall, Delquadri, Elliott, & Hall (1992)
	Hook & DuPaul (1999)
Parents Encourage Pupils (PEP)	Shuck, Ulsh, & Platt (1983)
Reciprocal Peer Tutoring with Parent Involvement	Heller & Fantuzzo (1993)

Note. References available in Carlson & Christenson (2005).

also Fishel & Ramirez, 2005). Several large-scale studies of diverse families also find that enhancing learning at home, with such activities as monitoring homework, reading, and expressing high expectations for achievement, is more predictive of success in school at both the elementary and secondary levels than are school-based parent involvement activities (Henderson & Mapp, 2002). Thus schools that focus parent involvement efforts on helping "hard-to-reach" parents assist their children at home are most likely to enhance the academic achievement of children in diverse families. For example, in a school serving a large immigrant population, students and teachers created a video that explained the school's curriculum and offered suggestions for how parents could be supportive of their children's learning through activities in the home (Calabrese, 2006). Parents enjoyed watching the video with their children and found the ideas helpful.

When schools do manage to overcome barriers to parent involvement (e.g., language differences and low education or reading levels of parents), student performance on achievement tests is significantly higher (Sheldon, 2003). Schools that succeed in engaging families from diverse backgrounds engage in three key practices: (a) they build trusting collaborative relationships among teachers, families, and community members; (b) they recognize, respect, and address families' needs, as well as class and cultural differences; and (c) they embrace a philosophy of partnership, where power and responsibility are shared (Henderson & Mapp, 2002). Successful schools, for example, invite parents into the classroom, consider parent schedules when planning meetings, provide child care during meetings, and offer specific suggestions for learning activities parents can do at home with their children (Henderson & Mapp, 2002). Parent involvement among working-class and ethnic minority families is also higher when teachers and administrators keep parents informed frequently about their children's education (Sheldon, 2003).

Home–school communication

Both parents and teachers identify home–school communication as a primary way to enhance trust and improve partnership (Christenson & Sheridan, 2001). Two-way home–school communication is an opportunity for *shared learning* between the parent and teacher (Swick et al., 2006). Studies of parent–teacher conferences, however, indicate these are largely characterized by one-way communication from teachers to parents, and both parties report feelings of anxiety that interfere with the open exchange of communication (Minke & Anderson, 2003).

A recent study compared the differential effectiveness of the traditional parent–teacher conference style with an alternative collaborative model (CORE) grounded in systems theory (Minke & Anderson, 2003). The CORE model was implemented through a family–school conference (FSC) that included the child in the customary annual meeting between the parent(s) and teacher. The FSC, compared with the traditional conference style, improved communication, increased learning about one another, and enhanced a sense of shared responsibility. Parents and teachers also reported valuing the opportunity to observe the other interact with the child in the conference.

The CORE approach to parent–teacher conferencing builds on efforts decades earlier to apply systems principles and techniques to communication between the home and school. Aponte (1976) pioneered this approach with his ecostructural family–school interview, an "experiment" in conducting a joint initial interview at the school with the family and school staff present in school-referred clinic cases. The Family–School Collaboration Project at the Ackerman Institute in the 1980s was a programmatic inter-vention to enhance collaborative problem-solving partnerships between families and schools that was incorporated into the traditional parent–teacher conference and family–school meetings related to child problems (Weiss & Edwards, 1992). Parents and adolescents rated a solution-oriented adaptation of the joint family–school collaborative problem-solving meeting as an unexpectedly positive experience and the intervention strategy that emerged as an effective solution to the presenting problem; however, teachers were less optimistic than parents and adolescents that the problem would, in fact, be resolved (Carlson, Hickman, & Burrows-Horton, 1992).

Home–school collaboration

Despite 25 years of effort developing and piloting mechanisms that promote co-equal, collaborative partnerships between family and school, there is no indication in the pub-lished literature that these collaborations, once introduced to the schools, are sustained. The failure to sustain collaborative family–school and parent–teacher communication highlights endemic historical, psychological, and structural challenges. Home and school have been viewed as autonomous functioning systems with clear, and possibly rigid, bound-aries in roles and responsibilities (Christenson & Sheridan, 2001). The communication framework between home and school is shaped by underlying attitudes held by parents and teachers about themselves and the other as partners in education and problem solving (Swick et al., 2006). Teachers can state clearly their expectations for families, and they are quick to blame parents for the academic and behavioral problems of children; however, they are less articulate about their responsibility to families and commonly view the home to be supplemental, not a true partner, in the education of children (Christenson & Sheridan, 2001). The strong role identification with the professional culture may also impair the ability of teachers to engage in collaborative communication with working-class parents; reciprocally, parents who do not share the professional culture of the school may not feel empowered in their role as collaborators in the educa-tion of their children (Harry, 2002). Parents often wait to be directed by the school on ways to help their child be more successful, remain passive recipients of information in meetings, and are more likely to become involved only after their child is having difficulty. Collaboration between home and school, especially in economically disadvant-aged neighborhoods, is further challenged by demanding and conflicting work schedules, lack of access or freedom to use communication systems, and language differences.

The difficulty establishing co-equal family–school collaborations as routine in schools is unfortunate because interventions that not only engage families in the solutions to their children's problems, but also treat them as equal partners, produce the largest effect sizes in changing both the academic and behavioral performance of children (Cox, 2005). Evidence-based models and methods of family–school collaboration and interventions have been identified (Carlson & Christenson, 2005) and appear on Table 35.1. Several existing family therapy models also show promise in changing school behavior (Carlson, 2006). The following case provides an illustration.

Case Example

This case illustrates the effective use of brief, school-based family therapy in conjunction with academic intervention to improve the declining performance of a 10-year-old, Hispanic girl (Raffy) who is in the fourth grade of a minority–majority elementary school that serves an economically disadvantaged population.

Raffy started off her academic year as a strong student, earning straight As consistent with her previous year's performance. Her teacher noted concern as Raffy's grades began to drop; also Raffy's seat was changed because she was getting into trouble in the classroom. The teacher contacted Raffy's mother to discuss her concerns. The mother shared that since her recent divorce from Raffy's father, her daughter seemed withdrawn, got easily frustrated with homework, and gave up quickly instead of displaying her usual determination to work through difficult assignments.

Consistent with contemporary education policy, Raffy's school relies extensively on continuous assessment of academic progress, evidence-based curriculum, and the Response to Intervention (RTI) model to treatment. In the RTI model when a child is struggling academically, data are collected and curriculum adjusted over time until the child succeeds. RTI typically includes three or four "tiers" of instruction with more intensive instructional help provided at each tier.

At Tier 1, the teachers modified instruction and closely monitored Raffy's progress. A school-based team of teachers, administrators, and special education professionals, along with Raffy's mother, met to analyze the data. Since Raffy was not showing improvement, she was referred to Tier II, in which she received additional instructional support that included individual tutoring and a mental health screening by the school psychologist. On a commonly used child behavioral checklist, Raffy's mother rated her child in the clinical range for Hyperactivity, Depression, Atypicality, and Anxiety and at-risk for Somatization, Attention Problems, Withdrawal, and Adaptive Skills; the teacher concurred with the mother's ratings for several domains. Given that Raffy's academic decline was proximal to significant family disruption, the mother was informed about the availability of family counseling at the school.

The family, including the mother, Raffy, and one younger sister (7 years old, second grade), completed five sessions that included an adaptation of the Family Check-Up (see Chapter 34, this volume) and several sessions of counseling. Significant family stressors included the recent departure of the father, the impending divorce, and resulting financial strain that required the sale of their home and a move into the home of a family friend where the three of them currently shared a bedroom. Consistent with traditional

Hispanic cultural values, the mother reported the father had been the disciplinarian in the home, and she was struggling with the demands of single parenting. Evaluation of individual and family assessment measures confirmed a family challenged by disruption with both children exhibiting internalizing and externalizing symptoms, and the mother reporting stress related to ineffective parenting.

Treatment initially focused on enhancing the mother's functioning as an authoritative parent. The mother learned to provide clear commands, to notice compliance, and to establish and carry through with reasonable consequences for non-compliance. Assessment feedback in session three alerted the mother to her daughters' anxiety, opening the door for the family therapist to engage the mother in developing a firmer parent–child boundary related to information about adult issues. Following three treatment sessions, the family discontinued therapy due to an impending move out of the city to be closer to the mother's family, which was necessitated by the lack of affordable housing in the local area. Although a formal post-treatment assessment was not possible within the time frame, several indicators pointed to an effective intervention: the mother was observed to engage in significantly improved parenting; she reported better communication and less fighting among the children at home; she reported high levels of satisfaction with treatment on a follow-up questionnaire; and a follow-up with Raffy's teacher indicated there had been almost immediate improvement in Raffy's classroom behavior with the onset of family therapy.

Conclusion

This chapter highlighted the extensive body of research that demonstrates the impact of parenting on children's success in school, the modest body of research that demonstrates the impact of the school on the family, and the limited but promising evidence base to support the efficacy of home–school collaboration in improving the academic and behavioral performance of students. Largely ignored in research is the effect on children's academic success of family relationships beyond parenting quality and the effect of reciprocally determined processes between home and school. Family psychologists, with their commitment to understanding and intervening at the levels of the system, relationships, and the circular, complementary processes that characterize these levels, bring a unique and essential perspective to the school-referred problems of children.

Resources

Wrightslaw: http://www.wrightslaw.com
Website contains accurate and reliable information about special education law, education law, and advocacy for children with disabilities.
Future of School Psychology Task Force on Family–School Partnerships: http://fsp.unl.edu
Website presents the work of the task force and includes training modules in evidence-based family–school interventions for use by professionals.

References

Aponte, H. J. (1976). The family–school interview: an eco-structural approach. *Family Process*, *15*, 303–312.

Arnold, D. H., & Doctoroff, G. L. (2003). The early education of socioeconomically disadvantaged children. *Annual Review of Psychology*, 54, 517–545.

Boethel, M. (2003) *Diversity: School, family, and communication connections: Annual synthesis*. Retrieved August 20, 2007, from http://www.sedl.org/connections/resources/diversity-synthesis.pdf

Bray, J. H., Adams, G., Getz, J. G., & Baer, P. E. (2001). Developmental, family, and ethnic influences on adolescent alcohol usage: A growth curve approach. *Journal of Family Psychology*, *15*, 301–314.

Bronfenbrenner, U. (1979). *The ecology of human development*. Cambridge, MA: Harvard University Press.

Calabrese, N. M. (2006). Video technology: A vehicle for educators to enhance relationships with families. *Education, 127(1)*, 155–160.

Carlson, C. (2006). Best models of family therapy. In C. Franklin, M. Harris, & P. Allen-Meares (Eds.), *The school services sourcebook: A guide for school-based professionals* (pp. 663–670). Oxford: Oxford University Press.

Carlson, C., & Christenson, S. (Eds.) (2005). Evidence-based parent and family interventions in school psychology [Special issue]. *School Psychology Quarterly, 20(4)*.

Carlson, C. I., Hickman, J., & Burrows-Horton, C. (1992). From blame to solutions: Solution-oriented family–school consultation. In S. L. Christenson & J. C. Conoley (Eds.), *Home–school collaboration: Enhancing children's academic and social competence* (pp. 193–214). Washington, DC: National Association of School Psychologists Publications.

Christenson, S. L., & Sheridan, S. M. (2001). *Schools and families: Creating essential connections for learning*. New York: Guilford Press.

Cox, D. (2005). Evidence-based interventions using home–school collaboration. *School Psychology Quarterly, 20(4)*, 473–497.

Darling, N., & Steinberg, L. (1993). Parenting style as context: An integrative model. *Psychological Bulletin, 113*, 487–496.

Epstein, J. L., & Dauber, S. L. (1991). School programs and teacher practices of parent involvement in inner-city elementary and middle schools. *The Elementary School Journal, 91(3)*, 289–305.

Fishel, M., & Ramirez, L. (2005). Evidence-based parent involvement interventions with school-age children. *School Psychology Quarterly, 20(4)*, 371–402.

Harry, B. (2002). Trends and issues in serving culturally diverse families of children with disabilities. *Journal of Special Education, 36(3)*, 131–138.

Henderson, A. T., & Mapp, K. L. (2002). *A new wave of evidence: The impact of school, family, and community connections on student achievement*. Retrieved August 20, 2007, from http://www.sedl.org/connections/resources/evidence.pdf

Hetherington, E. M., Cox, M., & Cox, R. (1985). Long-term effects of divorce and remarriage on the adjustment of children. *Journal of the American Academy of Child Psychiatry, 24*, 518–530.

Hoglund, W., & Leadbeater, B. (2004). The effects of family, school, and classroom ecologies on changes in children's social competence and emotional and behavioral problems in first grade. *Developmental Psychology, 40*, 533–544.

Ho Sui-Chu, E., & Willms, D. (1996) Effects of parental involvement on eighth-grade achievement. *Sociology of Education, 69(2)*, 126–141.

Howe, N., & Ross, H. (1990). Socialization, perspective-taking, and the sibling relationship. *Developmental Psychology, 26(1),* 160–165.

Lawson, M. (2003). School–family relations in context: Parent and teacher perceptions of parent involvement. *Urban Education, 38(1),* 77–133.

Masten, A. S., & Shaffer, A. (2006). How families matter in child development: reflections from research on risk and resilience. In A. Clarke-Stewart & J. Dunn (Eds.), *Families count* (pp. 5–25). New York: Cambridge University Press.

Mattingly, D., Prislin, R., McKenzie, T., Rodriguez, J., & Kayzar, B. (2002). Evaluating evaluations: The case of parent involvement programs. *Review of Educational Research, 72(4),* 549–576.

Milevsky, A., & Levitt, M. (2005). Sibling support in early adolescence: buffering and compensation across relationships. *European Journal of Developmental Psychology, 2(3),* 299–320.

Minke, K. M., & Anderson, K. J. (2003). Restructuring routine parent–teacher conferences: The family–school conference model. *The Elementary School Journal, 104(1),* 49–69.

Repetti, R. L. (1996). The effects of perceived daily social and academic failure experiences on school-age children's subsequent interactions with parents. *Child Development, 67,* 1467–1482.

Rutter, M. (1985a). Family and school influences on cognitive development. *Journal of Child Psychiatry and Psychology, 26(5),* 683–704.

Rutter, M. (1985b). Family and school influences on behavioural development. *Journal of Child Psychiatry and Psychology, 26(3),* 349–368.

Sheldon, S. B. (2003). Linking school–family–community partnerships in urban elementary schools to student achievement on state tests. *The Urban Review, 35(2),* 149–165.

Spera, C. (2005). A review of the relationship among parenting practices, parenting styles, and adolescent school achievement. *Educational Psychology Review, 17,* 125–146.

Sosa, A. (1997). Involving Hispanic parents in educational activities through collaborative relationships. *Bilingual Research Journal, 21(2),* 103–111.

Stocker, C., & Youngblade, L. (1999). Marital conflict and parental hostility: Links with children's sibling and peer relationships. *Journal of Family Psychology, 13,* 598–609.

Swick, D., Head-Reeves, D., & Barbarin, O. (2006). Building relationships between diverse families and school personnel. In C. Franklin, M. Harris, & P. Allen-Meares (Eds.), *The school services sourcebook: A guide for school-based professionals* (pp. 793–802). Oxford: Oxford University Press.

Taylor, L., Clayton, J., & Rowley, S. (2004). Academic socialization: Understanding parental influences on children's school-related development in the early years. *Review of General Psychology, 8,* 163–178.

Weiss, H. M., & Edwards, M. E. (1992). The family–school collaboration project: Systemic interventions for school improvement. In S. L. Christenson & J. C. Conoley (Eds.), *Home–school collaboration: Enhancing children's academic and social competence* (pp. 215–244). Silver Spring, MD: National Association of School Psychologists.

Wigfield, A., Eccles, J., Schiefele, U., Roeser, R., & Davis-Kean, P. (2006). Development of achievement motivation. In N. Eisenberg, W. Damon, & R. Lerner (Eds.), *Handbook of child psychology: Vol. 3. Social, emotional, and personality development* (6th ed., pp. 933–1002), Hoboken, NJ: Wiley.

36

Family Psychology in the Context of Pediatric Medical Conditions

Melissa A. Alderfer and Mary T. Rourke

Psychologists have long recognized the important role families play in pediatric medical conditions. Families provide the context in which child health and illness are managed and either contribute to positive outcomes or place the child at risk for adverse ones (Weihs, Fisher, & Baird, 2002). Stable, secure family environments support behaviors needed for appropriate management of disease, buffer negative emotional reactions to illness and treatment, and insure that normative developmental goals are accomplished for the family and its members. Pediatric illness also has an impact on the family. The diagnosis may be distressing and treatment may necessitate shifts in family roles and responsibilities. The purpose of this chapter is to introduce family-based models of adjustment to child-hood illness, provide a case study illustrating the clinical application of these principles, and review empirical evidence of family-based interventions within the context of pediatric medical conditions.

Models of Family Adjustment to Pediatric Medical Conditions

Three models of family adaptation are presented below to introduce important family constructs within the context of childhood illness.

The circumplex model of marital and family systems

The circumplex model (Olson & Gorall, 2003; Olson, Russel, & Sprenkle, 1983) characterizes families on two orthogonal dimensions: cohesion and flexibility. *Cohesion* refers to the emotional bonds between family members. *Flexibility* refers to the amount of change occurring in a family's leadership, roles, and relationship rules. Well-functioning families tend to fall in the mid-range on these dimensions, but do shift along the continuum in predicted ways across the family life cycle. A third component of the model – *communication* – allows the family to adapt to meet changing needs (Olson et al., 1983).

When confronted with an illness, the family is postulated to pull together emotionally and make dramatic shifts in daily routines to accommodate treatment. In the terminology of this model, the family becomes more enmeshed and chaotic. After the crisis phase resolves, the family may remain enmeshed, but now the routine of treatment organizes the family and they may become rigid in their patterns. After mastering disease management, the family becomes balanced again, but perhaps more cohesive and structured. In short, in response to illness a well-functioning family is hypothesized to move toward the extremes and become similar to less well-functioning family types, but then returns to near baseline. An unbalanced, poorly functioning family, however, would remain entrenched in their family pattern and have difficulty adapting to the illness.

Family systems health model

The family systems health model (e.g., Rolland, 1987, 2003) highlights the complex mutual interactions between illness and the family and conceptualizes adaptation as a developmental process. The model stresses family competence and strength and the "goodness of fit" between family style and the demands of disease over time. *Illness attributes* (i.e., onset, course, outcomes, uncertainty) contribute to the magnitude and type of psychosocial challenge faced by the family. The family's *prior experiences* with illness, loss, and crisis, *health and illness beliefs*, and *developmental phase* affect their response to illness.

In this model, serious illnesses are postulated to cause a *centripetal* force, focusing the family inward, pulling them together, and weakening boundaries to allow for more effective teamwork. This force causes different strains on the family depending upon their current life-cycle phase. If illness arises during a *centrifugal* period when family members are being pushed apart to allow for family structure shifts and accommodation of family members' goals outside of the family (e.g., a child moving into high school), it may derail development. If it coincides with a centripetal period (e.g., birth of a baby) it can prolong this period. In short, reactions to illness must be considered within the context of the family's current developmental phase, their previous experiences and beliefs, and the characteristics of the illness itself.

Family stress theory

Various stress and coping models, such as Hill's ABC-X model (Hill, 1949), the double ABCX model of family stress (McCubbin & Patterson, 1983), and the family adjustment and adaptation model (Patterson, 1988), have been applied to families facing pediatric medical conditions and fall under the umbrella term "family stress theory" (e.g.,

Hobfoll & Spielberger, 1992; see Chapter 3, this volume). These models have three basic elements: (a) the stressor; (b) family resources; and (c) family perceptions and meaning.

The stressor is defined as an environmental influence that threatens the family's well-being, such as a childhood illness. Family resources are strengths of individual members and the family system and may be psychological (e.g., self-esteem), social (e.g., social support), interpersonal (e.g., communication), and/or material (e.g., income). They are used to meet the demands of the stressor. The family system also has resources such as flexibility, cohesiveness, and problem-solving skills. Resources can be pre-existing, thus reducing vulnerability to stressors, or may develop in response to stress. Family perceptions and meaning are the third component and refer to the family's conceptualization of both the stressor and the resources they have to cope with it.

During a crisis, the family copes by fitting resources to the demands of the stressor, seeking more resources, removing some of the demands, and/or changing their perception of the circumstance. Families are hypothesized to repeatedly cycle through stable adjustment, crisis, and adaptation. Some cycles occur naturally as part of the family life cycle. Others, like coping with illness in a family member, are less typical.

Summary

These models propose that childhood illness will cause expected family turmoil. The following family-level constructs emerge as important: cohesion (e.g., involvement and close-ness), adaptability (e.g., flexibility in roles and responsibilities), communication (e.g., clarity of expression and directness), the affective environment (e.g., expression of feelings and conflict), problem-solving ability (e.g., goal-directed negotiation and task accomplishment), and organization (e.g., roles, leadership). Also, the individual and shared beliefs and perceptions of family members, the developmental stage of the family and its members, and specific characteristics of the illness are important determinants of how the family responds to illness and mobilizes to manage it. These models accept that adaptation to illness is a process that unfolds and shifts over time and with development. To illustrate these and other important components of family-based intervention when a child has an illness, we provide the following case example.

A Case Example: Kate's family

Kate is an 11-year-old girl with multiple medical complications related to premature birth, cerebral palsy, and history of cancer treatment. She lives at home with both parents and a healthy twin brother, Timmy. Kate was referred to treatment for anger, withdrawal, and frequent crying spells. She reported feeling frustrated with her physical limitations, the way her family "babies" her, and her "perfect" brother. Mom indicated feeling angry with Kate for not managing her illness better, and furious at herself for having these feelings. Mom and Dad coped differently with Kate's situation; Mom kept trying harder to fix the things that upset Kate, while Dad, believing this was futile, spent more time at work, away from the family. Kate's mother explained that everyone in the family was unhappy, and that Kate's frustrations and "graceless" way of managing her distress were upsetting the family's balance. These issues consumed the family's time, and everyone was emotionally depleted.

Although Kate reported symptoms of depression, psychopathology was not seen as the most helpful conceptualization. Instead, the family's distress was seen as a result of the misalignment of the family's developmental course and the developmental course of the illness.

Family organization.   This family had been mobilized for medical emergency since the premature birth of the children. Mom focused on Kate's medical issues, while Dad, worried about finances and maintaining medical insurance, worked as many hours as possible. As Kate grew, her relationship with her mother increased in intensity – many of their routine interactions revolved around what were perceived to be life-and-death care decisions. Over the years, the central dyad of the family evolved to be Kate-and-Mom, with Dad taking on an ancillary role of provider. All family decisions, including Timmy's participation in age-appropriate activities, were made on the basis of whether Kate-and-Mom's routine would allow time. While such family organization is frequently necessary during medical crisis, sustaining it during years of sub-acute medical management had become impractical and painful.

Cohesion.   The family's patterns of involvement and closeness did not match their developmental stage. Mom and Kate's closeness stunted Kate's ability to develop independence. As an example, Mom home-schooled the children because she believed the school would not meet Kate's needs. Kate's immersion inside the home limited her ability to develop activities of daily living within her capability (e.g., working on a schedule, organizing herself). At the parent level, while Mom and Dad remained committed to each other, they were emotionally distant. Dad resented Mom's over-involvement in Kate's life, while Mom resented that Dad had "checked out" of the medical management. Further, Mom felt she was the only one who cared, so needed to be hyper-vigilant. Dad felt that because of Mom's hyper-vigilant worry, he had to provide the children with a more worry-free, normative experience.

Adaptability.   This family remained rigidly adherent to routines most appropriate for early in the disease process, and had not figured out a way to manage more flexibly so that all family members could continue to grow. For example, Mom continued to insist on home-schooling, although it became clear that Timmy needed more stimulation, and Kate's cognitive difficulties were frustrating both Mom and Kate. The children had few play dates, because it was difficult for the family to plan ahead. "You never know what could happen," Mom explained.

Communication and problem-solving processes.   Both communication and problem-solving processes in the family were constrained by the rigid family organization.

Communication was strained; Mom felt urgency about all issues, while Dad was increasingly mystified about this. Problem solving was limited by the rigidity as well, and by the lack of parent concordance on which issues were significant and needed action.

Affective environment. Their rigid roles and routines did not allow anyone in the family to process or express their own sadness at their true losses. They were resentful of each other and unable to count on each other's support, leading them to feel alone and isolated. The affective environment was strained, and everyone was irritable and short-tempered. No one's needs were being met.

Treatment. A top priority for treatment was to re-instate a family structure that was more consistent with the family's and the illness's developmental stage. First, the parent dyad was rebuilt as the central decision-making dyad in the family. Parents structured time alone together daily to discuss family management and longer-term planning. To realign cohesion, they instituted a "date night" every week to enjoy each other's company. Considerable time in treatment was spent addressing barriers to implementing these practices and supporting the parents as central decision-makers. In-session time was also spent trying to construct a different emotional environment for the family. Family members were coached on identifying and expressing their feelings; this became easier as the new family organization evolved, with a strong parenting unit that could handle intense emotion.

The family "reorganization" also needed to account for managing the medical issues that Kate faced. To this end, Kate was encouraged to take more responsibility for tracking her medical care. She made a chart of daily medical management issues, and was to review it daily with a parent. To reduce the intensity of the Kate-and-Mom dyad and to rebalance parental division of labor, Dad reviewed the chart with Kate at least 4 out of 7 days.

As the family introduced more flexibility into daily routines, they began to tolerate the discomfort in considering educational alternatives. Over time, they could discuss pros and cons of different options and delineated what they would need to do to make a transition back to school (e.g., updating assessments, building school relationships). Eventually, as the family problem-solved the difficulties moving back to school, they became more comfortable taking other risks, like allowing the children to have overnight play dates, and attend summer camp.

As the family began to successfully navigate developmentally appropriate transitions, and to support each other through a flexible problem-solving process when they encountered barriers, all members of the family reported less distress. The parents reported renewed intimacy in their marriage, while both children attended school, did well, and built friendships with other children. Kate's medical management became somewhat more independent, although she still needed to rely on her parents – both of them, now – for assistance with some issues. After about a year of maintaining these changes, Mom explored going back to school, and enrolled in a master's degree program. As she began to work, Dad changed jobs, and began spending more time at home.

The Empirical Base

Research regarding family interventions in the context of pediatric medical disorders is growing and a range of examples is available. These interventions seek to improve or maintain adaptive family functioning and relationships, restore the emotional adjustment of family members, and enhance disease management, quality of physical functioning, and health. Below, interventions involving multiple family members and those targeting aspects of family functioning are introduced within the context of the medical condition in which they have been developed or applied.

Diabetes

Type I diabetes, typically diagnosed in childhood, requires a life-long treatment regimen including multiple daily blood glucose tests and insulin injections, a prescribed meal plan, and regular physical exercise. During adolescence, when the normative developmental process is one of individuation and increased self-reliance for the child, diabetes management becomes challenging and treatment adherence and metabolic control decline. Parent–adolescent communication, conflict resolution skills, and conjoint problem solving have been suggested as important contributors to effective diabetes management (Wysocki et al., 2000).

Behavioral family systems therapy (BFST; see Chapters 16 and 22, this volume) has been applied to families of adolescents with diabetes by Wysocki and his colleagues (Wysocki, Greco, Harris, Bubb, & White 2001; Wysocki et al., 2000). This intervention involves: (a) training in communication and problem-solving skills; (b) cognitive restructuring to address counterproductive beliefs, attributions, and assumptions regarding one another's behaviors; and (c) systemic family therapy techniques to strengthen appropriate boundaries, roles, and relationships. One large randomized clinical trial (RCT) demonstrated that BFST leads to greater improvements in parent–teen relations and reductions in diabetes-specific conflict at 3, 6, and 12 months post-intervention and improved adherence at 6 and 12 months post-intervention than do standard care and an educational support group (Wysocki et al., 2001; Wysocki et al., 2000). A recent revision of the intervention includes more rigorous diabetes management training components (e.g., behavioral contracting around adherence, clinical algorithms for modifying insulin injections on the basis of glucose levels, parental simulation of living with diabetes for one week) and has been found to produce the previously noted gains plus improvement in HbA1c, a marker of diabetes control (Wysocki et al., 2006).

A brief family teamwork intervention (Anderson, Brackett, Ho, & Laffel, 2000) has also been developed and evaluated. It focuses on the importance of sharing diabetes management tasks among parents and teens and ways to avoid conflicts that undermine teamwork. This intervention includes written educational materials about diabetes and ways parents and teens can work together effectively (i.e., without blaming or shaming).

A plan of shared responsibility is tailored to each family and the plan is reviewed, reinforced, and/or renegotiated as part of routine medical visits. When compared to treatment as usual and an attention control group in an RCT, the teamwork intervention group demonstrated maintenance of or increases in parental involvement in diabetes care without increases in parent–child conflict or decreases in adolescent quality of life (Anderson, Brackett, Ho, & Laffel, 1999; Laffel et al., 2003).

In addition to these reports, a small RCT demonstrated that a non-manualized structural/strategic family intervention based upon the work of Minuchin produced improved diabetic control in 8 out of 9 families, whereas, over the same time period, only 2 out of 9 families receiving standard care showed improvement (Ryden et al., 1994). As a final example, in another small study, families were randomized to a multifamily group, a multifamily group plus parental simulation of diabetes, or no intervention. The groups met for six 90–minute sessions focusing on how diabetes has impacted the family and how the family can work together to improve disease management through effective problem solving, communication, and realistic expectations. The intervention groups showed greater improvements on indices of diabetes control than did the control group, but no differences were found in family functioning (Satin, La Greca, Zigo, & Skylar, 1989).

Cystic fibrosis

Cystic fibrosis (CF) is a genetic disease that leads to the production of thick, sticky mucus in several organs. In the lungs, this mucus can cause infection and damage and in the pancreas it can lead to problems with digestion and absorption of food. Treatment, including aerosol medications and chest physiotherapy, is required two to four times a day and the child's diet must be high in caloric value and consistently supplemented with replacement enzymes. Because of the progressive and variable course of CF, management typically increases in complexity across time. Because CF is diagnosed early in the child's life, parents assume early responsibility for the treatment, with this shifting toward the adolescent over time. As in diabetes management, adherence to treatment for CF is more problematic as the child gets older (Ricker, Delamater, & Hsu, 1998). Research indicates that more emotional expressiveness and organization (Patterson, Goetz, Budd, & Warwick, 1993) and higher quality of relationships (i.e., open communication, low conflict) within the family predict adherence to CF treatment (DeLambo, Ievers-Landis, Drotar, & Quittner, 2004).

Despite the apparent important role of the family in management of CF and the possible toll the disease can take on the family, relatively little family intervention research exists in this area. The Cystic Fibrosis Family Education Program (Bartholomew et al., 1997) and the Multi-Family Psychoeducational Program for Cystic Fibrosis (Goldbeck & Babka, 2001) both focus primarily on education regarding CF (e.g., respiratory care, nutrition, physical symptoms), but psychosocial issues, communication, and coping are also addressed. Each program was designed for families of children with CF across a broad age range with developmentally appropriate activities for children school-age and older. The CF Family Education Program was evaluated against a non-randomized control group and showed significantly greater improvements in self-efficacy, CF knowledge, disease management, and some health outcomes, but no significantly greater changes in family functioning. A small investigation of the Multi-Family Psychoeducational Program indicated that only those participants with poor family functioning and adherence at pretest showed improvements after the program. A large, three-armed RCT comparing the Family Education Program, a CF-tailored version of BFST, and standard medical care is currently underway (Quittner, Drotar, Ievers-Landis, Seidner, Slocum & Jacobsen, 2000).

Asthma

Asthma is the most common chronic disease of childhood, characterized by airway hyper-reactivity and episodes of respiratory disease, wheezing and coughing. Treatment consists of avoidance of personal triggers (e.g., allergens, exercise, or stress), use of bronchodilator drugs during attacks, and long-term prophylactic therapy (inhaled or oral medication) for chronic and more severe cases. Attacks can be life-threatening and emotionally difficult for family members. Family psychology has had a long history in the conceptualization and treatment of asthma (Celano, 2001; Renne & Creer, 1985). Currently, family relational patterns such as structure (boundaries), communication, conflict, and rigidity of routines (Fiese & Wamboldt, 2000; Masterson, 1985) are targeted to improve the course and management of pediatric asthma.

More than 30 years ago, great success was reported in a case study of structural/strategic family therapy with a family of a child with asthma (Liebman, Minuchin, & Baker, 1974). Small RCTs conducted in the following years showed some similar benefits. In Lask and Matthew (1979), the 18 children in the experimental family therapy group showed statistically greater improvements on two of five medical outcome measures compared to a control group. Gustafsson, Kjellman, & Cederblad (1986) also demonstrated positive effects with family therapy. A greater percentage of the 12 families in their experimental group showed gains in terms of reduced reliance on inhalers, less functional impairment, and overall reduction in the severity and frequency of symptoms and impairment than in the standard treatment group. In a more recent report (Onnis et al., 2001), 10 families receiving family therapy showed significantly greater improvements in medical outcomes than did a treatment-as-usual control group, and also showed improvements in relational patterns (i.e., less enmeshment, rigidity, conflict avoidance, and overprotectiveness) from pre- to post-therapy.

Psychoeducational programs have also been used in the management of pediatric asthma symptoms (Bernard-Bonnin, Stachenko, Bonin, Charette, & Rousseau, 1995). Only a few of these programs include family-based components, but those that do tend to show improved family management and medical outcomes and/or improved family functioning in case studies or when compared to standard care (e.g., Tal, Gil-Spielberg, Antonovsky, Tal, & Moaz, 1990; von Schlippe, Theiling, Lob-Corzilius, & Szczepanski, 2001; Weinstein, Chenkin, & Faust, 1997).

Recurrent abdominal pain

Recurrent abdominal pain (RAP) is a common pediatric complaint, defined as recurring episodes of abdominal pain with no identifiable organic pathology, severe enough to interfere with functioning. These children frequently access healthcare services and the disorder often generates considerable parental anxiety and uncertainty about how to respond (Walker & Greene, 1989). Abnormal physiological processes, child psychological factors, and family functioning have all been proposed as important components in the etiology and maintenance of RAP (e.g., Barr, Green, & Watkins, 1987; Logan & Scharff, 2005).

Two cognitive-behavioral family interventions have been developed for families of children with RAP. Each of these provides an explanation of recurrent pain and instruction regarding active management of and adaptive responses to pain episodes. The first study demonstrated that those receiving such intervention compared to those in standard care showed greater rates of complete elimination of pain and significantly lower rates of relapse at 6 and 12 months post-treatment, but no significant differences in number of pain episodes or child psychological outcomes (Sanders, Shepherd, Cleghorn & Woolford, 1994). The second investigation indicated that those receiving intervention showed greater improvements than those receiving standard care on both parent- and child-reported abdominal pain and these effects were sustained 6 to 12 months later. No differences, however, were found on indices of functional disability or somatization (Robins, Smith, Glutting, & Bishop, 2005).

Conclusions

There are many similar theoretical models suggesting that families affect children's well-being and children's health affects family functioning. The constructs delineated in these models are valuable to consider in the clinical context, as illustrated in the presented case study. The empirical base for such family interventions is currently growing. In addition to the disorders discussed in this chapter, family-based interventions are emerging as part of medical care for obesity (e.g., Kitzman & Beech, 2006), traumatic brain injury (e.g., Wade, Carey, & Wolfe, 2006a, 2006b), sickle cell disease (e.g., Kaslow, 2000), and procedural distress (Barrera, 2000; Kazak et al., 1996). Interventions to improve psychological distress among families of children with cancer have also been tested with some success (Hoekstra-Weebers, Heuvel, Jaspers, Kamps, & Klip, 1998; Kazak et al., 2004; Kazak et al., 2005). Across all of the family intervention research in pediatric psychology, findings are promising. Unfortunately, many of the available research studies suffer from methodological shortcomings, including small, heterogeneous samples and reliance on self-report measures that may not be sensitive to actual changes in relational patterns (Wood, 2005). Despite these drawbacks, it is important for researchers and clinicians to continue to study, use, and refine family interventions within pediatric medical care.

Note

The authors thank Lauren Bradley for her assistance preparing this chapter and the American Cancer Society (MRSG05213) for providing support to the first author.

References

Anderson, B. J., Brackett, J., Ho, J., & Laffel, L. M. (1999). An office-based intervention to main-tain parent–adolescent teamwork in diabetes management. *Diabetes Care, 22*, 713–721.

Anderson, B. J., Brackett, J., Ho, J., & Laffel, L. M. B. (2000). An intervention to promote family teamwork in diabetes management tasks. In D. Drotar (Ed.), *Promoting adherence to medical treatment in chronic childhood illness: Concepts, methods, and interventions* (pp. 347–365). Malwah, NJ: Erlbaum.

Barr, R. B., Green, M., & Watkins, J. B. (1987). *Recurrent abdominal pain.* Great Neck, NY: Medical Information Systems.

Barrera, M. (2000). Brief clinical report: Procedural pain and anxiety management with mother and sibling as co-therapists. *Journal of Pediatric Psychology, 25*, 117–121.

Bartholomew, L. K., Czyzewski, D. I., Parcel, G. S., Swank, P. R., Sockrider, M. M., Mariotto, M. J., et al. (1997). Self-management of cystic fibrosis: Short-term outcomes of the Cystic Fibrosis Family Education Program. *Health Education & Behavior, 24*, 652–666.

Bernard-Bonnin, A. C., Stachenko, S., Bonin, D., Charette, C., & Rousseau, E. (1995). Self-management teaching programs and morbidity of pediatric asthma: a meta-analysis. *Journal of Allergy and Clinical Immunology, 95*, 34–41.

Celano, M. P. (2001). Family systems treatment for pediatric asthma: Back to the future. *Families, Systems & Health, 19*, 285–289.

DeLambo, K. E., Ievers-Landis, C. E., Drotar, D., & Quittner, A. L. (2004). Association of observed family relationship quality and problem-solving skills with treatment adherence in older children and adolescents with cystic fibrosis. *Journal of Pediatric Psychology, 29*, 343–353.

Fiese, B. H., & Wamboldt, F. S. (2000). Family routines, rituals, and asthma management: A proposal for family-based strategies to increase treatment adherence. *Families, Systems, & Health, 18*, 405–415.

Goldbeck, L., & Babka, C. (2001). Development and evaluation of a multi-family psychoeduca-tional program for cystic fibrosis. *Patient Education and Counseling, 44*, 187–192.

Gustafsson, P. A., Kjellman, N. I., & Cederblad, M. (1986). Family therapy in the treatment of severe childhood asthma. *Journal of Psychosomatic Research, 30*, 369–374.

Hill, R. (1949). *Families under stress.* New York: Harper & Bros.

Hobfoll, S. E., & Spielberger, C. D. (1992). Family stress: Integrating theory and measurement. *Journal of Family Psychology, 6*, 99–112.

Hoekstra-Weebers, J. E. M., Heuvel, F., Jaspers, J. P. C., Kamps, W. A., & Klip, E. C. (1998). Brief report: An intervention program for parents of pediatric cancer patients: A randomized controlled trial. *Journal of Pediatric Psychology, 23*, 207–214.

Kaslow, N. J. (2000). The efficacy of a pilot family psychoeducational intervention for pediatric sickle cell disease. *Families, Systems & Health, 18*, 381–404.

Kazak, A. E., Alderfer, M. A., Streisand, R., Simms, S., Rourke, M. T., Barakat, L. P., et al. (2004). Treatment of posttraumatic stress symptoms in adolescent survivors of childhood cancer and their families: A randomized clinical trial. *Journal of Family Psychology, 18*, 493–504.

Kazak, A. E., Penati, B., Boyer, B. A., Himelstein, B., Brophy, P., Waibel, M. K., et al. (1996). A randomized controlled prospective outcome study of a psychological and pharmacological intervention protocol for procedural distress in pediatric leukemia. *Journal of Pediatric Psychology, 21*, 615–631.

Kazak, A. E., Simms, S., Alderfer, M. A., Rourke, M. T., Crump, T., McClure, K., et al. (2005). Feasibility and preliminary outcomes from a pilot study of a brief psychological intervention for families of children newly diagnosed with cancer. *Journal of Pediatric Psychology, 30*, 644–655.

Kitzman, K. M., & Beech, B. M. (2006). Family-based interventions for pediatric obesity. *Journal of Family Psychology, 20*, 175–189.

Laffel, L. M., Vangsness, L., Connell, A., Goebel-Fabbri, A., Butler, D., & Anderson, B. J. (2003). Impact of ambulatory, family-focused teamwork intervention on glycemic control in youth with type I diabetes. *Journal of Pediatrics, 142*, 409–416.

Lask, B., & Matthew, D. (1979). Childhood asthma: A controlled trial of family psychotherapy. *Archives of Disease in Childhood, 54*, 116–119.

Liebman, R., Minuchin, S., & Baker, L. (1974). The use of structured family therapy in the treatment of intractable asthma. *American Journal of Psychiatry, 131*, 535–540.

Logan, D. E., & Scharff, L. (2005). Relationships between family and parent characteristics and functional abilities in children with recurrent pain syndromes. *Journal of Pediatric Psychology, 30*, 698–707.

Masterson, J. (1985). Family assessment of the child with intractable asthma. *Journal of Developmental & Behavioral Pediatrics, 6*, 244–251.

McCubbin, H. I., & Patterson, J. M. (1983). The family stress process: The double ABCX model of adjustment and adaptation. *Marriage & Family Review, 6*, 7–37.

Olson, D. H., & Gorall, D. M. (2003). Circumplex model of marital and family systems. In F. Walsh (Ed.), *Normal family processes* (3rd ed., pp. 514–548). New York: Guilford Press.

Olson, D. H., Russel, C. S., & Sprenkle, D. H. (1983). Circumplex model of marital and family systems: VI. Theoretical update. *Family Process, 22*, 69–83.

Onnis, L., Di Gennaro, A., Cespa, G., Dentale, R. C., Beneditti, P., Forato, F., et al. (2001). Prevention of chronicity in psychosomatic illness: A systemic research study into the treatment of childhood asthma. *Families, Systems, & Health, 19(3)*, 237–250.

Patterson, J. M. (1988). Families experiencing stress: I. The family adjustment and adaptation response model: II. Applying the FAAR model to health-related issues for intervention and research. *Family Systems Medicine, 6*, 202–237.

Patterson, J. M., Goetz, D., Budd, J., & Warwick, W. J. (1993). Family correlates of a 10-year pulmonary health trend in cystic fibrosis. *Pediatrics, 9*, 383–389.

Quittner, A. L., Drotar, D., Ievers-Landis, C., Seidner, D., Slocum, N., & Jacobsen, J. (2000). Adherence to medical treatments in adolescents with cystic fibrosis: The development and evaluation of family-based interventions. In D. Drotar (Ed.), *Promoting adherence to medical treatment in childhood chronic illness: Interventions and methods* (pp. 383–407). Hillsdale, NJ: Erlbaum.

Renne, C. M., & Creer, T. L. (1985). Asthmatic children and their families. In M. L. Wolraich & D. L. Routh (Eds.), *Advances in developmental and behavioral pediatrics: Vol. 6.* (pp. 41–81). Greenwich, CT: JAI Press.

Ricker, J. H., Delamater, A. M., & Hsu, J. (1998). Correlates of regimen adherence in cystic fibrosis. *Journal of Clinical Psychology in Medical Settings, 5*, 159–172.

Robins, P. M., Smith, S. M., Glutting, J. J., & Bishop, C. T. (2005). A randomized controlled trial of a cognitive-behavioral family intervention for pediatric recurrent abdominal pain. *Journal of Pediatric Psychology, 30*, 397–408.

Rolland, J. S. (1987). Chronic illness and the life cycle: A conceptual framework. *Family Process,* *26,* 203–221.

Rolland, J. S. (2003). Mastering family challenges in illness and disability. In F. Walsh (Ed.), *Normal family processes* (3rd ed., pp. 460–489). New York: Guilford Press.

Ryden, O., Nevander, L., Johnsson, P., Hansson, K., Kronvall, P., Sjoblad, S., et al. (1994). Family therapy in poorly controlled juvenile IDDM. *Acta Paediatrica, 83,* 285–291.

Sanders, M. R., Shepherd, R. W., Cleghorn, G., & Woolford, H. (1994). The treatment of recurrent abdominal pain in children: A controlled comparison of cognitive-behavioral family intervention and standard pediatric care. *Journal of Consulting and Clinical Psychology, 62,* 306–314.

Satin, W., La Greca, A. M., Zigo, M. A. & Skylar, J. S. (1989). Diabetes in adolescence: Effects of multifamily group intervention and parent simulation of diabetes. *Journal of Pediatric Psychology, 14,* 259–275.

Tal, D., Gil-Spielberg, R., Antonovsky, H., Tal, A., & Moaz, B. (1990). Teaching families to cope with childhood asthma. *Family Systems Medicine, 8,* 135–144.

von Schlippe, A., Theiling, S., Lob-Corzilius, T., & Szczepanski, R. (2001). The "Luftikurs:" Innovative family focused training of children with asthma in Germany. *Families, Systems, & Health, 19,* 263–284.

Wade, S. L., Carey, J., & Wolfe, C. R. (2006a). An online family intervention to reduce parental distress following pediatric brain injury. *Journal of Consulting and Clinical Psychology, 74,* 445–454.

Wade, S. L., Carey, J., & Wolfe, C. R. (2006b). The efficacy of an online cognitive-behavioral family intervention in improving child behavior and social competence following pediatric brain injury. *Rehabilitation Psychology, 51,* 179–189.

Walker, L. S., & Greene, J. W. (1989). Children with recurrent abdominal pain and their parents. *Journal of Pediatric Psychology, 14,* 231–243.

Weihs, K., Fisher, L., & Baird, M. (2002). Families, health, and behavior. A section of the commissioned report by the Committee on Health and Behavior. Research, Practice, and Policy Division of Neuroscience and Behavioral Health and Division of Health Promotion and Disease Prevention Institute of Medicine, National Academy of Sciences. *Families, Systems, & Health, 20,* 7–46.

Weinstein, A. G., Chenkin, C., & Faust, D. (1997). Caring for the severely asthmatic child and family. I. The rationale for psychological treatment. *Journal of Asthma, 34,* 345–352.

Wood, B. L. (2005). Commentary: Is it time for family-based interventions in pediatric psychology? *Journal of Pediatric Psychology, 30,* 694–697.

Wysocki, T., Greco, P., Harris, M. A., Bubb, J., & White, N. H. (2001). Behavior therapy for families of adolescents with diabetes. *Diabetes Care, 24,* 441–446.

Wysocki, T., Harris, M. A., Buckloh, L. M., Mertlich, D., Lochrie, A. S., Taylor, A., et al. (2006). Effects of behavioral family systems therapy for diabetes on adolescents' family relationships, treatment adherence, and metabolic control. *Journal of Pediatric Psychology, 31,* 928–938.

Wysocki, T., Greco, P., Harris, M. A., Bubb, J., Danda, C. E., Harvey, L. M., et al. (2000). Randomized, controlled trial of behavior therapy for families of adolescents with insulin-dependent diabetes mellitus. *Journal of Pediatric Psychology, 25,* 22–33.

37

Families and Health: An Attachment Perspective

Tziporah Rosenberg and William Watson

Julia, a 27-year-old Latina, was referred to me (T. R.) by her primary care physician for difficulties related to management of her type 1 diabetes. She had been diagnosed over 10 years prior, and had never demonstrated adequate control of the illness. From her physician's perspective, she had also failed to demonstrate adequate adherence to the treatment regimen, including a strict schedule of blood glucose testing, insulin injections, regular and carefully measured meals and snacks, and appointments with various specialists with whom she was scheduled to meet every two to three months. Julia was also being treated with antidepressant medications; she apparently denied suicidal ideation, though her medical providers felt her poor decision-making with her health indicated some latent wish to end her life. She was perhaps the oldest-appearing 27-year-old woman I had ever worked with; at our initial meeting, she appeared fatigued and worn out, slumped in a wheelchair and in obvious physical discomfort. Her mother and daughter sat close to her but seemed at the same time to be someplace far away.

During the course of our initial interview, I began to learn about Julia, her family, and how diabetes and its complications had come to play such a critical role in how they functioned. She was one of three adult children born to her mother, who had raised them on her own; she was the only one of them still living at home. Her other siblings had moved out, secured employment, and built homes and families of their own. Julia, herself, had one child, a 12-year-old daughter who was born soon after Julia's diagnosis with diabetes. Julia's mother worked full time to support their three-generation household. The severity of Julia's complications from diabetes and her chronic pain precluded her from working; she remained home most days, tending to the home and her daughter when she was well enough to do so. The role of diabetes was an interesting one. While many may consider diabetes a treatable and manageable illness, when it became unmanaged in this family it seemed to draw on the physical, emotional, and financial resources of virtually all of its members. Julia's mother called several times a day to check in on her from work, rushed home when Julia's glucose was out of control, and often missed work to attend to her. Julia's daughter often found it difficult to concentrate on her school work when her mother was ill, and seemed to feel guilty when she was not worrying; when I attempted to explore this further with her, she denied any difficulties of her own and insisted that "everything's fine." Julia smiled proudly at her daughter's independence.

As this case[1] illustrates, the realms of physical, emotional, and relational health in individuals and families are inextricably intertwined. This premise is the foundation for George Engel's (1980) biopsychosocial model. "A person has the illness, and that person is embedded within a network of people who are also affected by the illness. Their families interact with larger societal organizations to assist and cope with illness in one of their members" (McDaniel, Doherty, & Hepworth, 1992, p. 16).

Findings on Families and Health

Research consistently demonstrates the prevalence of psychosocial and family influences on common, and uncommon, medical presentations (Bray & Campbell, 2007). For example, relational factors have been clearly associated with resulting changes in immune functioning (Barrera, 1986; Cohen, 1988; Kiecolt-Glaser et al., 1993), parental depression and poor family cohesion are associated with more health problems among children with rheumatic disease (Daniels, Moos, Billings, & Miller, 1987), and families of patients with psychogenic seizures have been shown to have higher levels of distress than families of patients with epilepsy (Wood, McDaniel, Burchfiel, & Erba, 1998).

How is it that families affect health? There are several possible pathways. First, the direct effects of genetic or environmental factors can mean that members of the same family are at higher health risk just by virtue of being related (Campbell, 2003). For example, those living in a household with a member who smokes may be more susceptible to developing pulmonary symptoms or asthma.

Second, families tend to set the standards by which members operate around health behaviors. The impact of social context on health was recently demonstrated by a study that showed that the chances of an individual's becoming obese is related to the obesity of friends, partners, and siblings (Christakis & Fowler, 2007).

Third, research has verified a connection between physiology, relationships and individual psychology (Campbell, 2003). Family therapy pioneer Salvador Minuchin (1974) showed that family stress and tension can actually produce changes in children's ability to fight infection or prevent deleterious effects of poor glucose control. In this same vein, Kiecolt-Glaser and colleagues (2002) found that exposure to chronic stressors, particularly those perceived as uncontrollable and unpredictable, is associated with elevated stress hormone levels. These stress hormone levels, in turn, increase the risk for immune dysregulation and negative changes in health status. Interestingly, they note that family caregivers of patients with Alzheimer's disease are at particular risk for such changes in their own health status, and that these changes persist even after the responsibilities of caregiving end (Kiecolt-Glaser et al., 2002). Other evidence has linked marital hostility during conflict discussion with persistently elevated blood pressure (Kiecolt-Glaser et al., 1993), couple distress with worsened prognosis in cardiovascular disease (Orth-Gomér et al., 2000), and disease-related parent–child conflict with poorer glycemic control among children with early onset diabetes (Anderson et al., 2002).

Fourth, the family environment has the potential to mediate physiological changes in a member with acute or chronic illness. It is well established that family and social support can shorten recovery time from heart attacks, can shorten healing time from infection, and is generally health promoting (Berkman, 2000; Campbell, 2003). Fisher and Weihs (2000) note in particular that some physiologic mechanisms can be influenced by the calming effects of secure attachments among family members, and by the disruptive effects of family hostility and criticism.

Fifth, the emotional context of families affected by illness also impacts the degree of self-care practiced by its members. Given the numerous demands and relational stress many chronic diseases bring, family members have the choice to accommodate those demands, thus encouraging self-care, or undermine this process through behavior that isolates the patient, inhibits cooperation with medical regimens, or obstructs self-care (Mahler & Heika, 1993). The negative effects of high expressed emotion in families (high criticism, low warmth) outweigh the positive effects of less critical and warmer communication when it comes to health outcomes (Campbell, 2003), though family support continues to be a protective factor against disease complications (Kiecolt-Glaser & Newton, 2001). In sum, the matrix of interpersonal family functioning and physiological process affects short-term outcomes (e.g., poor glucose control or poorly controlled hypertension) as well as those that evolve over the long term (e.g., complications from ongoing poorly managed disease process) (Bray & Campbell, 2007).

Just as families affect health and the course of illness, so too does illness affect the family. For example, it is widely understood that childhood chronic illness greatly increases both child and parental emotional distress and behavioral problems (Goldberg et al., 1997; Pless & Nolan, 1991; Quittner et al., 1998). Several studies have demonstrated that illness changes family dynamics by provoking changes in the emotional climate of the family (Wamboldt & Wamboldt, 2000). In the case of childhood diabetes, for example, Seiffge-Krenke (1998) discovered that families with an ill child become more routinized, more structured, and less emotionally warm and stimulating. This is not to say, however, that illness precludes families from being satisfied or "functional"; rather, illness requires families to change in order to accommodate the new reality illness brings.

Additional factors such as socioeconomic status, age, gender, race/ethnicity, and religious or spiritual beliefs can account for differences among groups in terms of how they respond to illness. For example, a terminal illness in a child is apt to generate a different kind of distress in the family than such illness in a grandparent (Rolland, 1987). Family beliefs about illness, healing, suffering, and health are informed by cultural prescriptions and ethnic narratives (McCubbin, Thompson, Thompson, McCubbin, & Kaston, 1993), including religious or spiritual faith traditions (Koenig, Larson, & Larson, 2001). It is important to keep these factors in mind when assessing family response to illness.

Wayne Katon and colleagues (1990) found that the top 10% of all utilizers of medical services account for more than 30% of outpatient and over 50% of inpatient healthcare costs; half of those 10% also carry mental health diagnoses. The majority of visits in primary care are related to behavioral health needs but not to identified mental health disorders. Kroenke and Mangelsdorff (1989) reported that fewer than 20% of patient visits to primary care physicians are for symptoms with discoverable organic causes. The vast majority of mental health diagnoses are made by primary care medical providers, who often represent the front door to mental health treatment (Seaburn, Lorenz, Gawinski, & Gunn, 1996). The need for medical systems to offer and integrate services provided by mental health professionals has been well established (Blount et al., 2007).

Medical Family Therapy

The field of medical family therapy (McDaniel, Hepworth, & Doherty, 1992) was born out of a conviction that a biopsychosocial systems approach to caring for families would improve adjustment to illness. Its primary goals are to increase agency and communion in the family. Agency refers to a family's ability to act rather than be acted upon, to make personal choices around the demands of illness and treatment, to advocate for and actively protect itself. Communion refers to a family's ability to maintain a sense of connectedness and community. Medical family therapy seeks to enhance families' sense of agency and communion in coping with illness and facilitate a collaborative process between families and healthcare professionals.

Medical family therapy shares with health and primary care psychology a focus on emotional processes and illness (Frank, McDaniel, Bray, & Heldring, 2004). However, while health psychology seeks to identify behaviors that promote health in individuals and society, medical family therapy and primary care psychology pays particular attention to the systemic processes involved in the illness experience as it impacts the family and the patient–family–healthcare system matrix.

Roles for the Family Psychologist in Healthcare

Family psychologists function in a variety of roles and contexts in caring for families dealing with physical illness. Clinical care of such families has traditionally occurred in a location separate from the rest of the medical team. However, there has been increasing recognition of the advantages of having family psychologists at the medical site itself to provide co-located care or integrated (co-provided) care (Blount et al., 2007; Bray, Frank, McDaniel, & Heldring, 2004; Bray & Rogers, 1995; Haley et al., 1998). Co-located care refers to psychotherapy or consultation provided in the medical context itself. Integration or co-provision of care refers to an active incorporation of psychological and behavioral aspects of care into medical practice, with family psychologists serving as an integrated part of the medical team (cf. Blount, 2003; Frank et al., 2004). In both instances, services provided may well extend beyond traditional psychotherapy and include brief consultation to patients and their families as well as to providers struggling to manage a behaviorally challenging family or seeking to incorporate behavioral health and systems perspectives into their medical treatment (Seaburn et al., 1996). Pediatrics is but one example[2] of a venue where medical and family systems issues routinely intertwine, and where family psychologists have an enormous potential to make important contributions to the process of healthcare. Having family psychologists on site facilitates extension of care to patients and family members who might not otherwise seek mental health consultation or treatment, and significantly enhances collaboration with the patient's medical providers.

An Attachment Perspective on Health and Illness

Attachment theory (Ainsworth, Blehar, Waters, & Wall, 1978; Bowlby, 1969/1982, 1988) offers a useful lens through which to understand the connection between families and health. Attachment theory is a framework of survival, safety, and relationships. It holds that individuals, from the time of infancy, seek proximity to critically important caregivers to ensure that their needs are met, that they remain safe and secure, and that they are seen and valued. At the same time, those caregivers provide a secure base from which to explore the surrounding world and take risks. The infant can return to this secure base as needed for reassurance, rest, and redirection; the reliability and responsiveness of the secure base fosters the development of healthy autonomy and interdependence.

Bowlby (1988, pp. 26–27) defines attachment as "any form of behavior that results in a person attaining or maintaining proximity to some other clearly identified individual who is conceived of as better able to cope with the world." The attachment system evolves slowly throughout the first year of life, from interactive patterns of responsiveness, felt security, and trust between parent and infant. Bowlby posited that these systems of attachment become activated in situations that we perceive as strange or dangerous. That is to say, we are most likely to seek safety and reassurance when we are presented with circumstances that make us feel fearful, unsure of ourselves, or otherwise threatened. Once we perceive that the danger has passed, we can resume our normal activities, and proximity to that attachment figure becomes less critical.

While illness is not always life-threatening, it is often experienced as a strange situation. Bowlby (1988) stated that ill health is likely to activate attachment systems, and that individuals' responses to distressing physical symptoms will differ depending on their attachment style. While it makes intuitive sense that illness can be interpreted as a strange and threatening situation to the patient, we argue that threat can be experienced likewise by entire families. Families are directly affected by the intrusion of illness into their routines, rituals, and long-term plans. The extent of the intrusion, of course, depends largely on the nature of the illness, its onset, acuity, and course, and also on the family's emotional reaction to the experience of illness (Rolland, 1994).

Ainsworth developed a categorical model of attachment based on Bowlby's concept of internalized working models. Her work demonstrated that one's security of attachment is situated in a matrix of beliefs about how valuable one is and how reliable and safe others are. Her categories of attachment style thus derived are secure, preoccupied, avoidant, and fearful. Securely attached individuals generally believe themselves to be worthy of love and care, and believe that supportive others are trustworthy; they experience comfort with both intimacy and autonomy (Feeney, 2000). Those with a preoccupied attachment style also hold others in high regard but themselves in low, insecure regard. They therefore tend to experience feelings of overdependence and desire for extreme closeness with others based on earlier experiences of inconsistent caregiving (Ciechanowski, Walker, Katon, & Russo, 2002). Individuals with an avoidant attachment style display what appears to be a fierce independence resulting from an unwillingness to rely on others, who they experience as untrustworthy or unreliable, and a view of themselves as competent and self-sufficient; they tend to devalue close relationships with others as a result. Finally, those with a fearful attachment style have both low self-regard and simultaneous low expectations that others will be reliable sources of support. When distressed, they are apt to experience themselves as needy, but despair that help will not be found. They tend to distrust others but at the same time long to connect to others and fear rejection by them.

Attachment Perspectives on Adjustment to Illness

While the medical family therapy model addresses general themes of adjustment to illness, it stops short of offering useful typologies of families and patterns of behavior predictive of adjustment. Applying Ainsworth's categorical attachment model to health behavior allows us to develop hypotheses regarding how a given individual and his or her family are likely to react to the "strange situation" of illness based on assessment of their predominant attachment styles.

In families characterized by secure attachment (open communication, trustworthy caregivers, emotional accessibility), the affected member may feel free to express the full range of their thoughts and feelings about their illness because they believe other members will respond appropriately. Believing himself or herself to be a worthy and valuable member of that family, the patient is also likely to attend to the demands of the illness in a way that expresses that positive self-worth. The other family members are likewise apt to openly discuss their fears, hopes, and reactions to the illness when the environment validates and accepts them. Securely attached individuals and families also engage responsibly and deliberately with their healthcare providers. They attend appointments as scheduled, ask questions and accept reassurance, and alert providers to problems as they arise (Ciechanowski et al., 2002).

Families with climates of insecure attachment may face added emotional and physiological difficulties with the onset of an illness by virtue of not having fully developed systems of support, communication, and problem solving. Attachment difficulties get expressed in how the individual and family respond to illness, to the demands it brings, and to providers. Insecurely attached individuals with low self-regard (preoccupied and fearful attachment styles) will be less likely to be proactive with their healthcare needs, less likely to take steps toward better self-management, and less likely to react in a timely and effective way when a health crisis arises. Insecurely attached individuals who experience others as unreliable, untrustworthy, or unresponsive (avoidant and fearful attachment styles) will likely show significantly lower willingness to report illness-related distress (emotional or physical) when it sets in, and an inability to access the proper channels (i.e., regular doctor visits vs. emergency or urgent care) to manage those crises.

Families characterized by the preoccupied and avoidant attachment styles outlined by Ainsworth may have more difficulty negotiating the changes demanded by chronic illness. For example, preoccupied families may in some ways seem enmeshed (Minuchin, Rosman, & Baker, 1978), yet in other ways fail to establish a consistent and predictable response to the demands of the illness. Those with preoccupied or fearful attachment styles typically focus more on negative affect, and consequently report a higher number of physical and health complaints even when medical work-ups remain negative (Costa & McCrae, 1987; Russo et al., 1997). These individuals are likely to be overrepresented among somatizing patients.

Avoidant families may encounter more significant difficulties in acknowledging their thoughts and emotions in reaction the illness. They may choose not to discuss it among themselves, which reduces immediate distress because the topic remains unaddressed, but also makes it that much more difficult to plan for crisis or long-term management of a chronic illness. Avoidantly attached individuals may deny or suppress their distress as a way to further distance themselves from caregivers or attachment figures, and are noted to present as sometimes invulnerable or overly independent, though with more physical symptoms and negative affect (Ciechanowski et al., 2002). They appear self-sufficient and self-reliant, and are more likely to reject help that is offered by a caregiver or significant other. The lack of safe interdependence can generate a sense of loneliness in the avoidantly attached family as its members do not trust others to be available for them when they feel most fearful or in need; these families may demonstrate more difficulty working together around changing routines to accommodate to illness demands, and may be more apt to take an "every man for himself" approach to navigating illness.

Implications for Family Treatment

When taken with the research suggesting more optimal outcomes for individuals with chronic illness who are supported by social networks and warm, communicative families, the attachment perspective suggests an approach to intervention at a family level that can be expected to impact health outcomes on group, individual, and even intra-individual levels. It has been well documented that family-based interventions focusing on specific diseases and their management, ranging from psychoeducation to intensive family psychotherapy, can be effective in improving health outcomes for those with chronic illness (Bray & Campbell, 2007; Campbell, 2003; Fisher & Weihs, 2000). However, family therapy is typically thought to be indicated when the "dysfunction" in the family trumps or otherwise complicates the challenges presented by the illness itself. While we agree that family therapy is often useful in such situations, it is also true that higher-functioning families are frequently in need of family intervention.

The basic tenets of medical family therapy also provide a useful framework for understanding the needs of families confronting illness. Inclusion of an attachment perspective allows the medical family framework to be applied in a more nuanced manner, tailored to the specific needs arising from the attachment style of the family.

Let us revisit the case of Julia, the patient with poorly controlled diabetes, and her family. While the primary presentation of this family is not directly related to difficulties with family attachment, it is evident that the styles adopted individually and collectively generated some difficulties in approaching diabetes and its demands more effectively. Julia and her siblings were raised by a single parent with multiple demands. Qualities of independence and self-sufficiency were highly valued in her family during childhood given the numerous family stresses and challenges. Julia, the middle child and only daughter, was often given added responsibility to help with maintaining their household, organizing meal times, and attending to her brothers, which was especially useful to her mother, who was busy and often quite exhausted. Julia developed closeness with her mother, about whom she often worried.

Julia's perception of her mother as needy and relatively unavailable to her, combined with the family emphasis on self-sufficiency, suggested an avoidant attachment style. Julia's daughter was following this path as well – successful at school and caretaking at home, she functioned in many respects as Julia had done for her mother. In this family, overt expressions of dependency are avoided since there is a low expectation they will be received positively. Independence is emphasized, but it comes at a cost. Because it is difficult to refuel and to have normal dependency needs met, members of this family tended to express their needs for one another indirectly and often in counterproductive ways. Diabetes added an additional stressor that exacerbated this pattern; instead of banding together around the illness, family members found themselves pushed further apart (for example, Julia and her brothers). We suspected that her medical noncompliance over the years could have been Julia's attempt to secure warmth and attention from her mother, who continued to devote much time and energy to her career. The result, however, was that the closeness between Julia and her mother hinged now on Julia's medical needs rather than an unencumbered sense of belonging and connection. In some ways, becoming increasingly sick enabled Julia to receive the care and attention she always needed but did not feel safe requesting. In other ways, her deteriorating health both expressed and confirmed her fears of being unable to care for herself, and now, for her child.

Treatment with this family focused on disease management in the context of healing attachments. We validated and normalized the healthy dependency needs of the members while also respecting and validating their strengths, capabilities, and accomplishments. Balancing and affirming their needs for both autonomy and belonging enabled them to begin to experience each other as reliable and trustworthy supports, and to experience themselves as worthwhile and their needs as legitimate and understandable. After thus bolstering security in the family attachment system, they were able to work together more effectively to put diabetes in its place; Julia showed a new willingness to exercise care in her diabetes management, as being ill was no longer her primary means of seeking care and support from her family. She became better able to identify, legitimize, and express her needs as her family became better able to accept, validate, and respond to them (and vice versa). In turn, her family became less critical and rigidly demanding of her, more able to affirm her healthy autonomy, and more sympathetic and unconditional in their expressions of love and support.

Summary

The following are key points from a family attachment and medical family therapy perspective concerning families facing illness:

1 *Patient and family behavior in response to illness can be understood as an expression of their attachment style, and as an attempt to seek safety.* Behavior that may, at first glance, make no sense can often be made sense of when viewed within an attachment framework. For the family psychologist, this shift can help soften feelings of negative countertransference and deepen empathy.
2 *Understanding the particulars of the predominant attachment style of a family can suggest interventions tailored to their specific needs* (Ciechanowski et al., 2002).
    a Respect for autonomy is important for families with an avoidant attachment style, as they will be made anxious by overt dependency. The family psychologist reaching out with reminder calls and accepting calls between sessions can help dependency-avoidant families feel more confident of the family psychologist's investment and reliability.
    b Families with preoccupied attachment styles are apt to idealize the family psychologist and see themselves as helpless and needy. It is important that the family psychologist resist the allure of being idealized and focus instead on the strengths of the family. Family psychologists should avoid taking more responsibility for change than the family does.
    c Families with a fearful attachment style are at particular risk of delaying treatment or terminating prematurely. They see themselves as needy but fear family psychologist reprisals in response. The family psychologist's ability to maintain an affirming, non-anxious presence helps keep the emotional reactivity in-session under control and helps provide a safe environment, contrary to the family's expectation. Family psychologists should keep intimacy from building too rapidly as it can feel threatening to the family.
3 *Create a temporary secure base until the family can develop its own.* A therapeutic secure base should be able to offer both protection and exploration (Byng-Hall, 1995). Careful collaboration with healthcare providers is particularly important for insecurely attached families as it gives the family a clear sense of its care providers "being on the same team," and assurance that the information and recommendations received will be reliable and consistent.

4   *Help the family manage their current attachments in a way that takes into account all members' attachment needs.* This process of managing attachments involves eliciting the illness story (McDaniel, Doherty, & Hepworth, 1992), understanding how the illness has affected them as a system, and how their response to the illness has been shaped by who they are. Listen not only to the content of the story but to how it is organized (coherent and detailed or vague and unelaborated?) for clues about the attachment schema. The family may also present other, non-illness-related attachment injuries (Johnson, Makinen, & Milliken, 2001); working through these is apt to help them more effectively problem solve and manage the illness-specific issues as well.

Notes

1   This case is a composite based on a variety of clinical experiences in our practices with families coping with chronic illness.
2   Others include family medicine, internal medicine, ob/gyn, cardiology, neurology, anesthesiology (pain treatment), oncology, allergy and immunology (asthma).

Resources

Collaborative Family Healthcare Association: http://www.cfha.net
Family, Systems, & Health [Journal]: http://www.apa.org/journals/fsh
University of Rochester Medical Family Therapy Intensive (week-long training workshop for professionals): http://www.urmc.rochester.edu/smd/Psych/educ_train/family/MFTI.cfm
University of Rochester Postdoctoral Fellowship in Primary Care Family Psychology: http://www.urmc.rochester.edu/smd/psych/educ_train/training/postdoctoral/primarycare_psychology_track.cfm
McDaniel, S. H., *Family therapy with patients having physical health problems* [Video]. APA Psychotherapy Video Series.

References

Ainsworth, M. D. S., Blehar, M. C., Waters, E., & Wall, S. (1978). *Patterns of attachment: A psychological study of the strange situation.* Oxford: Erlbaum.
Anderson, B. J., Vangsness, L., Connell, A., Butler, D., Goebel-Fabbri, A., & Laffel, L. M. B. (2002). Family conflict, adherence, and glycemic control in youth with short duration type 1 diabetes. *Diabetic Medicine, 19*, 635–642.
Barrera, M. (1986). Distinction between social support concepts, measures, and models. *American Journal of Community Psychology, 14*, 147–178.
Berkman, L. F. (2000). Social support, social networks, social cohesion and health. *Social Work in Health Care, 31(2)*, 3–14.
Blount, A. (2003). Integrated primary care: Organizing the evidence. *Families, Systems, & Health, 21*, 121–134.

Blount, A., Schoenbaum, M., Kathol, R., Rollman, B. L., Thomas, M., O'Donohue, W., et al. (2007). The economics of behavioral health services in medical settings: A summary of the evidence. *Professional Psychology: Research and Practice, 38*, 290–297.

Bowlby, J. (1969/1982). *Attachment and loss: Vol. 1. Attachment.* New York: Basic Books.

Bowlby, J. (1988). *A secure base: Parent–child attachment and healthy human development.* New York; Basic Books.

Bray, J. H., & Campbell, T. L. (2007). The family's influence on health. In R. E. Rakel (Ed.), *Textbook of family practice* (7th ed., pp. 25–34). Philadelphia, PA. Saunders.

Bray, J. H., Frank, R. G., McDaniel, S. H., & Heldring, M. (2004). Education, practice and research opportunities for psychologists in primary care. In R. G. Frank, S. H. McDaniel, J. H. Bray, & M. Heldring (Eds.), *Primary care psychology* (pp. 3–21). Washington, DC. American Psychological Association.

Bray, J. H., & Rogers, J. C. (1995). Linking psychologists and family physicians for collaborative practice. *Professional Psychology: Research and Practice, 26*, 132–138.

Byng-Hall, J. (1995). Creating a secure family base: Some implications of attachment theory for family therapy. *Family Process, 34*, 45–58.

Campbell, T. L. (2003). The effectiveness of family interventions for physical disorders. *Journal of Marital and Family Therapy, 29(2)*, 263–281.

Christakis, N. A., & Fowler, J. H. (2007). The spread of obesity in a large social network over 32 years. *New England Journal of Medicine, 357(4)*, 370–379.

Ciechanowski, P. S., Walker, E. A., Katon, W. J., & Russo, J. E. (2002). Attachment theory: A model for health care utilization and somatization. *Psychosomatic Medicine, 64*, 660–667.

Cohen, S. (1988). Psychosocial models of the role of social support in the etiology of physical disease. *Health Psychology, 7*, 269–297.Costa, P. T., & McCrae, R. R. (1987). Neuroticism, somatic complaints, and disease: Is the bark worse than the bite? *Journal of Personality, 55*, 299–316.

Daniels, D., Moos, R. H., Billings, R. H., & Miller, J. J. (1987). Psychosocial risk and resistance factors among children with chronic illness, healthy siblings and healthy controls. *Journal of Abnormal Child Psychology, 15(2)*, 295–308.

Engel, G. L. (1980). The clinical application of the biopsychosocial model. *American Journal of Psychiatry, 137*, 535–544.

Feeney, J. A. (2000). Implications of attachment style for patterns of health and illness. *Child: Care, Health and Development, 26(4)*, 277–288.

Fisher, L., & Weihs, K. L. (2000). Can addressing family relationships improve outcomes in chronic disease? *Journal of Family Practice, 49(6)*, 561–566.

Frank, R. McDaniel, S. H., Bray, J. H., & Heldring, M. (Eds.). (2004). *Primary care psychology.* Washington, DC: American Psychological Association.

Goldberg, S., Janus, M., Washington, J., Simmons, R. J., MacLusky, I., & Fowler, R. S. (1997). Prediction of preschool behavioral problems in healthy and pediatric samples. *Journal of Developmental and Behavioral Pediatrics, 18(5)*, 304–13.

Haley, W. E., McDaniel, S. H., Bray, J. H., Frank, R. G., Heldring, M., Johnson, S. B., et al. (1998). Psychological practice in primary care settings: Practical tips for clinicians. *Professional Psychology: Research and Practice, 29*, 237–244.

Johnson, S. M., Makinen, J. A., & Millikin, J. W. (2001). Attachment injuries in couple relationships: A new perspective on impasses in couples therapy. *Journal of Marital and Family Therapy, 27(2)*, 145–155.

Katon, W., Von Korff, M., Lin, E., Lipscomb, P., Wagner, E., & Polik, E. (1990). Distressed high utilizers of medical care: *DSM-IIIR* diagnosis and treatment needs. *General Hospital Psychiatry, 12*, 355–362.

Kiecolt-Glaser, J. K., Malarkey, W. B., Chee, M., Newton, T., Cacioppo, J. T., Mao, H. Y., et al. (1993). Negative behavior during marital conflict is associated with immunological down-regulation. *Psychosomatic Medicine, 55,* 395–409.

Kiecolt-Glaser, J. K., McGuire, L., Robles, T. F., & Glaser, R. (2002). Psychoneuroimmunology: Psychological influences on immune function and health. *Journal of Consulting and Clinical Psychology, 70,* 537–547.

Kiecolt-Glaser, J. K., & Newton, T. L. (2001). Marriage and health: His and hers. *Psychological Bulletin, 127(4),* 472–503.

Koenig, H. G., Larson, D. B., & Larson, S. S. (2001). Religion and coping with serious medical illness. *Annals of Pharmacotherapy, 35,* 352–359.

Kroenke, K., & Mangelsdorff, A. D. (1989). Common symptoms in ambulatory care: Incidence, evaluation, therapy and outcome. *American Journal of Medicine, 86,* 262–266.

Mahler, J. A., & Heika, A. (1993). Emotional support as a moderator of adjustment and compliance after coronary artery bypass surgery: A longitudinal study. *Journal of Behavioral Medicine, 16,* 45–63.

McCubbin, H. I., Thompson, E. A., Thompson, A. I., McCubbin, M. A., & Kaston, A. J. (1993). Culture, ethnicity, and the family: Critical factors in childhood chronic illnesses and disabilities. *Pediatrics, 91(5),* 1063–1070.

McDaniel, S. H., Doherty, W. J., & Hepworth, J. (1992). *Medical family therapy.* New York: Basic Books.

Minuchin, S. (1974). *Families and family therapy.* Cambridge, MA: Harvard University Press.

Minuchin, S., Rosman, B. L., & Baker, L. (1978). *Psychosomatic families: Anorexia nervosa in context.* Cambridge, MA: Harvard University Press.

Orth-Gomér, K., Wamala, S. P., Horsten, M., Schenck-Gustafsson, K., Schneiderman, N., & Mittleman, M. A. (2000). Marital stress worsens prognosis in women with coronary heart disease. *Journal of the American Medical Association, 284,* 3008–3014.

Pless, I. B., & Nolan, T. (1991). Revision, replication and neglect-Research on maladjustment in chronic illness. *Journal of Child Psychology and Psychiatry, 32(2),* 347–65.

Quittner, A. L., Opipari, L. C., Espelage, D. L., Carter, B., Eid, N., & Eigen, H. (1998). Role strain in couples with and without a child with a chronic illness: Associations with marital satisfaction, intimacy, and daily mood. *Health Psychology, 17(2),* 112–24.

Rolland, J. S. (1987). Chronic illness and the life cycle: A conceptual framework. *Family Process, 26(2),* 203–221.

Rolland, J. S. (1994). *Families, illness, and disability.* New York: Basic Books.

Russo, J., Katon, W., Lin, E., & Von Korff, M. (1997). Neuroticism and extraversion as predictors of health outcomes in depressed primary care patients. *Psychosomatics: Journal of Consultation Liaison Psychiatry, 38,* 339–348.

Seaburn, D. B., Lorenz, A. D., Gawinski, B. A., & Gunn, W. (1996). *Models of collaboration: A guide for family therapists practicing with health care professionals.* New York: Basic Books.

Seiffge-Krenke, I. (1998). The highly structured climate in families of adolescents with diabetes: Functional or dysfunctional for metabolic control? *Journal of Pediatric Psychology, 23(5),* 313–322.

Wamboldt, M. Z., & Wamboldt, F. S. (2000). Role of the family in the onset and outcome of childhood disorders: Selected research findings. *Journal of the American Academy of Child & Adolescent Psychiatry, 39(10),* 1212–1219.

Wood, B. L., McDaniel, S., Burchfiel, K., & Erba, G. (1998). Factors distinguishing families of patients with psychogenic seizures from families of patients with epilepsy. *Epilepsia, 39,* 432–437.

38

Anorexia Nervosa and the Family

Ivan Eisler

Clinical accounts of anorexia nervosa (AN), from the early descriptions by Gull (1874) and Lasèque (1873), have tended to portray the family negatively either as a hindrance to treatment or even as the source of the disorder. The first clearly explicated notion of family relationships playing an etiological role in the development of AN comes from Bruch (1973) describing a particular mother–infant relationship, in which the mother's constant anticipation of the child's needs prevents the development of appropriate internal responses and leads to a pervasive sense of ineffectiveness, a lack of identity, and the need for control. More complex accounts of the family role come from family systems descriptions of AN (Minuchin, Rosman, & Baker, 1978; Selvini-Palazzoli, 1974; Stierlin & Weber, 1989) which generally stress over-close family relationships, blurred intergenerational boundaries, difficulties in dealing with conflict, and rigid interactional patterns as central to the understanding of AN.

These clinical accounts, particularly the psychosomatic family model developed by Minuchin and colleagues (1978), have had an important role in the development of family therapy for AN. Paradoxically, while the research data supporting the efficacy of these treatments are increasingly strong, the empirical support for the theoretical model from which the treatment is derived is unconvincing. This chapter will briefly review the current research evidence and offer an alternative conceptualization for the existing evidence-based approaches.

Evidence for the Effectiveness of Family Therapy for Anorexia Nervosa

There is growing evidence for the effectiveness of family therapy in the treatment of AN, particularly for adolescents. Research at the Maudsley Hospital in London compared family therapy with individual supportive therapy following hospitalization and also compared two forms of outpatient family therapy, demonstrating its efficacy with adolescents (Eisler et al., 2000; Russell, Szmukler, Dare, & Eisler, 1987), with continued improvement post-treatment for up to five years (Eisler et al., 1997; Eisler, Simic, Russell, & Dare, 2007). The research led to a gradual refinement of the treatment (Dare & Eisler, 2000; Dare et al., 1995; Eisler, 2005) from the original structural model described by Minuchin et al. (1978), but it retained as a central feature the empowerment of parents in helping their child tackle her eating problems.[1] Similar results were obtained in the USA by Robin et al. (1999) and Lock and colleagues (Lock, Agras, Bryson, & Kraemer, 2005; Lock, Couturier, & Agras, 2006; Lock, Le Grange, Agras, & Dare, 2001). On the basis of the evidence from these studies several reviewers (e.g., NICE, 2004; Wilson & Fairburn, 1998) have concluded that family therapy is the treatment of choice for adolescent AN.

In spite of this growing consensus a degree of caution is needed. First, the studies to date are all relatively small and a number have methodological limitations. Second, there has been hardly any research comparing family therapy with other treatments, such as cognitive or psychodynamic (Gowers, 2006; Jeammet & Chabert, 1998), which are often used in clinical practice but have not been systematically evaluated with adolescent AN, and their relative merits in comparison with family therapy are not known. The third caveat concerns the fact that nearly all the above studies are of family therapy with a strong "structural flavor" (i.e., they all emphasize the importance of helping the parents to have a strong role in opposing the anorexia – see below). The literature contains many accounts of family therapy for AN drawing on other theoretical orientations. including Milan systemic (Selvini-Palazzoli, 1974), strategic (Madanes, 1981), feminist (Luepnitz, 1988), attachment (Dallos, 2004), solution-focused (Jacob, 2001), and most notably in recent years. narrative (Madigan & Goldner, 1998). Other than Stierlin and Weber's (1987) follow-up study of a Milan-oriented treatment, there is no systematic evaluation or comparisons with these other approaches.

Is There a Link between Particular Type of Family Functioning and Anorexia Nervosa?

It is beyond the scope of this chapter to provide a comprehensive review of research on the links between family functioning and anorexia nervosa (for which see, e.g., Eisler, 1995; Vandereycken, 2002). There have been many cross-sectional studies, mostly based on self-report measures which generally find some area of poorer family functioning in AN (e.g., Steiger, Liquornik, Chapman, & Hussain, 1991; Waller, Calam, & Slade, 1989). However, these studies have considerable limitations. First, many include a significant number of chronically ill patients, making it difficult to know what is cause and what is effect. Community-based studies (e.g., Råstam & Gillberg, 1991) or studies of student samples (McNamara & Loveman, 1990) generally find much smaller differences, and some of these disappear completely when factors such as depression are controlled for (e.g., Blouin, Zuro, & Blouin, 1990). Second, even studies that report differences often find that there is a greater difference between the AN group and other clinical samples than between AN groups and controls (e.g., Scholz, Rix, Scholz, Gantcher, & Thömke, 2005). Third, observational studies, perhaps the most direct test of the psychosomatic family model, have provided contradictory findings. While a number have found differences between AN and controls, the findings differ from study to study (Humphrey, 1989; Kog & Vandereycken, 1989; Røijen, 1992), and even where significant differences are found in mean scores, when families are classified in terms of their functioning, the majority fall within a "normal" range (e.g., Røijen, 1992).

Overall, one has to conclude that the empirical evidence in support of a particular type of family functioning in AN is unconvincing, and at best that while there may be some family risk factors, these do not have the force of an explanatory mechanism identifying necessary conditions for the development of the disorder. Moreover, if such risk factors exist they are probably non-specific, increasing the risk of developing a range of disorders rather than being specific to AN. Clearly, therefore, the existing theoretical models do not provide a good basis for identifying targets of treatment or a model of change.

A Theory for Clinical Practice

Once we accept that AN develops in a variety of family contexts, we are faced with two problems. The first is the apparent similarity of experiences that families have of living with someone suffering from an eating disorder (Whitney & Eisler, 2005); the second is the need to find an alternative model of change underpinning the process of family therapy. The two may in fact be closely connected, as they may both relate to family adaptive mechanisms that normally enable it to find a balance between maintaining stability and accommodating the changing needs of individual family members (Eisler, 2002). The way the family functions changes in the presence of serious and persistent problems such as AN disrupting the adaptive processes, which become increasingly unavailable or in some cases become part of the maintaining mechanism of the illness.

The processes through which families accommodate to serious and enduring problems have been well described in relation to problem drinking (Steinglass, Bennett, Wolin, & Reiss, 1987) and chronic physical illness (Rolland, 1994) and are clearly also relevant to AN. Whatever the family was like before the eating problem, the impact of the illness on the family is immense (Nielsen & Bará-Carril, 2003). Steinglass (1998) described in some detail the process of such family reorganization as an increasing disruption of family routines and family regulatory mechanisms, where day-to-day decision-making becomes more difficult, to the point where the problem becomes the central organizing principle of family life. Family responses will vary depending on the nature of the illness, the type of family organization and interactional style, and the particular life-cycle stage they are at when the illness occurs. What may be less variable is the way in which the centrality of the eating disorder magnifies certain aspects of the family's dynamics and narrows their range of adaptive behaviors. The following are aspects of family reorganization around AN that we have observed in families in treatment.

The central role of the symptom in family life

The high levels of preoccupation with thoughts of food and weight in an individual with anorexia are paralleled by the way that issues around food and eating take centre stage in the family. As time goes on, all relationships in the family seem to revolve around and become defined by the problem. Much of the interaction between family members focuses on food, eating, or weight, either overtly or covertly, as the topics may be avoided even though they are on everyone's mind. Just as the young woman may judge her self-worth by whether she is able to resist eating, so interpersonal relationships revolve around food ("If you understood me, you wouldn't make me eat"; "You are not eating to get at us"; "No one seems to care that I am not eating").

Narrowing of time focus on the here and now

The anxiety engendered by the life-threatening nature of the problem and the intensity of interactions around meals result in the family gradually being unable to focus on anything other than the present. What happens at the next meal, indeed the next mouthful, takes on immense importance. The intense preoccupation with the present makes every failure at a meal time seem overwhelming. Families will often comment that they feel that time has come to a standstill. A concomitant of this narrowing of time focus is a high level of intolerance of uncertainty, which makes it seem impossible to try new ways of tackling the problem.

Inflexibility in daily life patterns

Many theoretical accounts of family functioning highlight the importance of flexibility, particularly in dealing with family life-cycle changes. For the clinician, however, flexibility or rigidity is primarily manifested in moment-to-moment interactions. While flexibility over time and flexibility in the here and now are connected, they are not one and the same. The limited patterns of interaction that may appear as rigidity may simply reflect the narrowing of the family routines. Families will often comment that what they are doing is not working but that they are afraid that doing something different could make things worse.

The amplification of aspects of family function

Faced with the painful and frightening nature of AN, certain aspects of the family organization (in particular those which the family itself may have perceived as unsatisfactory) become more pronounced. Above all, it is probably this that gives rise to the assumption that what we are observing is a manifestation of family dysfunction rather than the family's adjustment to the problem. For instance, there are many families where one parent has a much closer relationship with the children than has the other parent, who may have a more peripheral role in the family. In the context of illness these positions may become more extreme, and may in time be experienced in themselves as part of the problem ("If only my husband was around more I would not have to be so involved with my daughter, but the trouble is he doesn't really understand, and when he does try to do something he just makes things worse"). In some cases this may indeed be a problem in its own right (e.g., marital problems that may pre-date the development of the eating disorder). While it may be important to understand how these problems become intertwined it is equally important to emphasize their separateness (i.e., one is not the cause of the other, and by implication, dealing with one is not the solution to the other).

Diminishing ability to meet family life-cycle needs

The processes described above make it increasingly difficult to attend to the varying needs of different family members, and prevent the family from making the necessary adaptations to allow them to progress through family life-cycle transitions. These disruptions have been described well elsewhere (Carter & McGoldrick, 1989).

The loss of a sense of agency (helplessness)

At the point when families seek treatment for their daughter they invariably feel helpless and despairing. AN has been described as a "disorder of control" (Fairburn, Shafnan, & Cooper, 1999), because of the way that anorexia may give the sufferer the sense that through not eating she can be in control. When talking to families, however, it is clear that everyone in the family feels that they have lost control over their lives. Winning the battle with hunger may give the young person a brief sense of mastery and control, but the battles around food at meal times have the opposite effect, regardless of how successful she may be in resisting her parents' exhortations to eat. Parents will similarly recount that they feel helpless and have no control over what their daughter does. The struggle over control around food also leaves them feeling that they have lost control over everything.

A Model of Treatment

We have previously described the development of our treatment approach in the context of a series of randomized control trials (RCT) (Dare et al., 1995; Eisler, Le Grange, & Asen, 2003), the theoretical and conceptual influences (Dare & Eisler, 1997), and the structure and stages of the treatment (Dare & Eisler, 1995). We have also described the adaptation of the treatment as part of a multiple family day treatment program (Dare & Eisler, 2000; Eisler et al., 2003). The central aim of the approach is to use the adaptive mechanisms of the family to explore ways in which attempts at dealing with the problem may have become part of the maintaining mechanisms, and the role that the symptoms have gradually taken on in the way that the family functions.

Phase 1: Engagement and development of the therapeutic contract

The first phase is similar in many ways to any other engagement of a family in therapy. The therapist makes contact with each family member and identifies the focus for the work ahead. This is followed by an exploration of family perceptions of the problem and a discussion of the effects of the eating problem on the family as a whole. The therapist also tries to make connections with all family members through hearing the narratives that different family members have of the problem, particularly those that are not at the forefront of the family's presentation, and asks questions that may enable or highlight alternative narratives or meanings to the ones that the family automatically presents ("You told me that your father couldn't come today because he was too busy and that in any case he doesn't understand your problems. If he believed that he could help, do you think he would want to come? If it was possible for him to understand you better, would you want that?"). From the earliest part of the treatment, the therapist focuses on exploring the strengths and resources in the family and what gets in the way of these being used to the maximum. Exploring beliefs about the problem and its causes can be useful at this stage, since they will frequently reveal feelings of guilt and blame which are important to address early on.

This phase has several features which are distinctive and characteristic of our approach. From the first contact with the family the therapist displays a lack of interest in the causes of the problem, emphasizing that the primary task is to overcome the daughter's AN. The reason for meeting family members is not because they are seen as the source of the problem but because they are needed to help their daughter to recover.

The main focus for engaging the family is firmly problem-oriented. Assessment of the severity of the problem, its history, and what the family has attempted to do to tackle it is combined with giving information about the effects of starvation, including the physical risks such as osteoporosis (Zipfel, Löwe, & Herzog, 2003), effects on mood and cognitions (Channon & De Silva, 1985), and physiological effects such as delayed gastric emptying (Connan & Stanley, 2003). A detailed medical and risk assessment of the young person is an important part of the engagement, shaping the therapeutic relationship with the therapist and the multidisciplinary team. It contributes to the creation of an environment where the family feels supported and has a sufficient sense of safety to accept responsibility for looking for alternative ways of managing the problem within the family.

Descriptions of AN and other symptoms are responded to with concern and a distinct lack of neutrality. If, as is often the case, the young person with AN denies that there is a problem, the therapist acknowledges the difficulty of her predicament but makes it clear that ensuring her health and safety have to come first, and that AN is too serious a problem to give her the benefit of the doubt.

Owning the expertise that the therapist and the rest of the team have in eating disorders is contrasted from the start with the fact that they do not have the answer as to what any individual family will need to do to overcome the problem. Giving information is also part of the process of labeling AN as a quasi-external force taking over the young woman's life, which she is unable to resist on her own. For instance, describing the effects of starvation on healthy volunteers (Keys, Brozek, Henschel, Mickelsen, & Taylor, 1950), and the many parallels with someone suffering from AN (low mood, preoccupation with food, fear of losing control) can change the perception of the anorexic behaviors as being willful and under the young person's control to something that has taken over and requires the combined efforts of the family to resist. This is reinforced by the use of "externalizing conversations" (White, 1995) or, in the context of multiple family therapy groups, by role-playing of anorexia as an oppressive voice.

There are pitfalls in adopting an expert stance; potential power and control struggles in the therapeutic relationship can undermine the family and reinforce a sense of dependency. The stance can ally the therapist more obviously with the parents, making it more difficult to engage the young person. While it is important to be aware of these pitfalls, one should not assume that they can be avoided by simply adopting a neutral position, since they are as much a product of the nature of the problems as they are of the position adopted by the therapist. An awareness of these issues and a willingness to address them openly with the family is more effective than attempting to avoid them ever occurring.

The problem-focused orientation fits with the here-and-now focus of the family, which is reinforced by the nature of the assessment, the emphasis on physical risk, and the need to implement step-by-step changes to get the eating problem under control. Unlike the family, the therapist also holds a broader time frame (based on the experience of having been through the process of therapy with other people) which extends to the future and includes an expectation of change. The therapist conveys this by describing the nature of treatment being offered and the part families generally play, emphasizing that most families at this stage of treatment do not believe that they can help, and that the therapist and the rest of the team are there to assist them through this difficult time. The overt owning of expertise in the disorder, and the express commitment of embarking with the family on a joint search for the specific solutions that will help them overcome the problem, provide the sense of a "secure base" (Vetere & Dallos, 2008) that facilitates the family's engagement in treatment.

Phase 2: Helping the family to challenge the symptoms

The second phase of treatment is primarily concerned with dealing with symptoms. In some families this happens fairly rapidly and dramatically, but more commonly this is a gradual, step-by-step process. There is a great deal of variability in the way families respond to the idea that parents should have a key role in dealing with the eating problem. For some, particularly if the problem is of short duration, it is reasonably easy to accept that the parents and the adolescent are jointly fighting something that has invaded their lives and, even though the daughter may at times feel cornered and frightened when facing food, she may (outside of meal times) encourage her parents not to back off.

In other families, there may be initial protracted negotiations that may require the therapist to repeatedly question whether the negotiations are with the "anorexic voice" or a discussion with an adolescent about reasonable alternatives of food choices. In such situations parents often rely on the therapist to be the voice of authority of what their daughter needs. In accepting such a role it is helpful to acknowledge openly the intentional aspect of the clinician's expert stance ("I'm sure you know what someone of your daughter's age needs to eat to gain weight, but I am more than happy to give you a diet sheet if it is going to help you not to listen to the anorexic voice speaking for your daughter"). If the problem has been going on for a long time, and particularly if attempts at confronting the anorexia have led to overt criticism, hostility, or even violence, the family may feel paralyzed, frustrated, and angry with the therapist for not helping them to avoid conflictual situations.

Detailed exploration of what happens at meal times and how this might need to change has to be accompanied by challenging beliefs about the impossibility of parental action, exploration of customary parental roles, and how these have been undermined by the eating disorder. At this stage the parents often express their wish for detailed instruction in how they should manage meal times. Such requests are best met by describing a range of things which other families have tried, being clear that what works for one family does not necessarily work for everyone.

Phase 3: Exploring issues of individual and family development

Phase 3 is the least structured and least predictable part of the treatment. It starts at a time when concerns around eating and weight recede. The focus of sessions becomes broader, exploring consequences of recovery on the activities and relationships of the whole family. Initially, parents continue to have anxieties about any changes in eating patterns and may be reluctant to reduce their vigilance at meal times. If they have disagreements or clash with their daughter they may find it difficult to differentiate between "adolescent" and "anorexic" behavior, and the earlier externalization of problems may need to be replaced with "de-externalization" ("How do you tell if it is anorexia shouting at you or just your daughter being irritated with what you are doing?"; "Have you found ways of winding up your parents other than by not eating?").

Parental uncertainty and a reluctance to let go of the safety of control over their daughter's eating and weight are often matched by the daughter's own fears and uncertainties of what life without anorexia is going to be about. The focus shifts to exploring issues of independence, adolescent identity, and self-esteem and addressing issues of how parents meet their own needs. It is important to emphasize again that these issues are not being addressed as somehow representing the dysfunction underlying the eating disorder, but rather that one is talking about normal developmental issues that have been put on hold by AN. As anorexia loses its grip, families may initially tend to look to the past, to a time before anorexia. Looking ahead to the future may feel less certain and requires a degree of self-reflection by the family which, in normal circumstances, they might not have undergone.

Explorations of family background, family values, and the cultural context of the family are useful at this stage, particularly if the focus is clearly on strengths and resilience. It is useful to use interventions that span different time frames. This may include the use of future questioning, getting the adolescent to observe her parents discussing their own experience of growing up or other aspects of their genograms, and so on. Shifting discussions to a different time frame can help when issues emerge that seem too difficult to talk about, because it changes the intensity and immediacy of the feelings aroused and can open up areas that may otherwise be too threatening or guilt-provoking. (In one family, a father was only able to acknowledge his harshness to his children when asked to think what kinds of stories he thought his daughter might tell her own children about him. He was then able to talk about the fact that he had never been able to forgive his own father for beating him as a child, and his hope that this would not happen between him and his daughter.)

At this stage families vary considerably in terms of what they need or want to get out of continuing treatment. For some, there is a relatively brief process of adjusting to life with a well daughter. For others, issues that have been obscured and/or intertwined with AN come to the fore and become a focus of the therapeutic work, either in the context of conjoint family meetings or in individual sessions.

Phase 4: Ending and discussion of future plans

Ending treatment is again variable. For some families, little more is required than a reflection on how far they have come and what they have learned about themselves. For others, ending therapy highlights the parallels between the difficulty parents may have in handing back control of eating to their adolescent and the process of growing up and becoming independent. Ending may become protracted when these processes bring forward the therapist's own wishes to see things through until "all problems have been resolved." Discussions of whose responsibility it would be to do something if eating problems re-emerged and returning to themes of safety and uncertainty may be important at this stage.

Conclusion

While there is good evidence showing the efficacy of family therapy for AN, the theoretical base from which such treatment is derived is flawed. This is due in part to the lack of empirical substantiation of the existing theoretical models, but more importantly because etiological models are not particularly useful as a basis for treatment. Instead we should direct our attention to possible processes that lead to families reorganizing around a developing problem, in a way that may either contribute to the maintenance of the problem and/or prevent the family from being able to use their normal adaptive mechanisms to deal with change.

The treatment model outlined here has evolved in the context of conducting a series of RCTs, and provides a conceptual framework that informs our approach to both individual family therapy and multiple family therapy, although only the former has been described here (for accounts of multiple family therapy for AN see Eisler et al., 2003, or Scholz et al., 2005). Implicit in the model are a number of mechanisms of change which we believe are addressed by the treatment. These have not yet been subject to empirical evaluation, although clearly this would be desirable. While there are no data comparing the outcome and treatment process in individual and multiple family therapy (we are currently completing a large RCT addressing these questions), our clinical experience suggests that there may be specific differences and that different families may benefit more from one or other approach.

Note

1   This chapter uses the female pronoun because the vast majority of diagnosed AN occurs in the female population and most research has been conducted on females.

References

Blouin, A. G., Zuro, C., & Blouin, J. H. (1990). Family environment in bulimia nervosa: The role of depression. *International Journal of Eating Disorders, 9,* 649–658.

Bruch, H. (1973). *Eating disorders: Obesity, anorexia nervosa and the person within.* London: Routledge & Kegan Paul.

Carter, B., & McGoldrick, M. (Eds.) (1989). *The changing family life cycle: A framework for family therapy* (2nd ed.). London: Allyn & Bacon.

Channon, S., & De Silva, W. P. (1985). Psychological correlates of weight gain in patients with anorexia nervosa. *Journal of Psychiatric Research, 19,* 267–271.

Connan, F., & Stanley, S. (2003). Biology of appetite and weight regulation. In J. Treasure, U. Schmidt, & E. van Furth (Eds.), *Handbook of eating disorders: Theory, treatment and research* (2nd ed., pp. 63–87). London: Wiley.

Dallos, R. (2004). Attachment narrative therapy: Integrating ideas from narrative and attachment theory in systemic family therapy with eating disorders. *Journal of Family Therapy, 26,* 40–65.

Dare, C., & Eisler, I. (1995). Family therapy. In G. I. Szmukler, C. Dare, & J. Treasure (Eds.), *Handbook of eating disorders: Theory, treatment and research* (pp. 333–349). London: Wiley.

Dare, C., & Eisler, I. (1997). Family therapy for anorexia nervosa. In D. M. Garner & P. E. Garfinkel (Eds.), *Handbook of treatment for eating disorders* (pp. 307–324). London: Guilford Press.

Dare, C., & Eisler, I. (2000). A multi-family group day treatment programme for adolescent eating disorder. *European Eating Disorders Review, 8,* 4–18.

Dare, C., Eisler, I., Colahan, M., Crowther, C., Senior, R., & Asen, E. (1995). The listening heart and the chi-square: Clinical and empirical perceptions in the family therapy of anorexia nervosa. *Journal of Family Therapy, 17,* 19–45.

Eisler, I. (1995). Family models of eating disorders. In G. I. Szmukler, C. Dare, & J. Treasure (Eds.), *Handbook of eating disorders: Theory, treatment and research* (pp. 155–176). London: Wiley.

Eisler, I. (2002). Family interviewing. Issues of theory and practice. In M. Rutter & E. Taylor (Eds.), *Child and adolescent psychiatry: Modern approaches* (4th ed., pp. 128–140). Oxford: Blackwell.

Eisler, I. (2005). The empirical and theoretical base of family therapy and multiple family day therapy for adolescent anorexia nervosa. *Journal of Family Therapy, 27,* 104–131.

Eisler, I., Dare, C., Hodes, M., Russell, G. F. M., Dodge, E., & Le Grange, D. (2000). Family therapy for adolescent anorexia nervosa: The results of a controlled comparison of two family interventions. *Journal of Child Psychology and Psychiatry, 41,* 727–736.

Eisler, I., Dare, C., Russell, G. F. M., Szmukler, G. I., Le Grange, D., & Dodge, E. (1997). Family and individual therapy in anorexia nervosa. A 5-year followup. *Archives of General Psychiatry, 54,* 1025–1030.

Eisler, I., Le Grange, D., & Asen, K. (2003). Family interventions. In J. Treasure, U. Schmidt, & E. van Furth (Eds.), *Handbook of eating disorders: Theory, treatment and research* (2nd ed., pp. 291–310). London: Wiley.

Eisler, I., Simic, M., Russell, G. F. M., & Dare, C. (2007). A treatment trial of two forms of family therapy for adolescent anorexia nervosa: Five-year follow-up. *Journal of Child Psychology and Psychiatry, 48,* 552–560.

Fairburn, C. G., Shafnan, R., & Cooper, Z. (1999). A cognitive behavioural theory of anorexia nervosa. *Behaviour Research and Therapy, 37,* 1–13.

Gowers, S. G. (2006). Evidence based research in CBT with adolescent eating disorders. *Child and Adolescent Mental Health, 11,* 9–12.

Gull, W. (1874). Anorexia nervosa (apepsia hysteria, anorexia hysteria). *Transactions of the Clinical Society of London, 7,* 222–228.

Humphrey, L. L. (1989). Observed family interactions among subtypes of eating disorders using structural analysis of social behavior. *Journal of Consulting and Clinical Psychology, 57,* 206–214.

Jacob, F. (2001). *Solution focused recovery from eating distress.* London: BT Press.

Jeammet, P., & Chabert, C. (1998). A psychoanalytic approach to eating disorders: The role of dependency. In A. H. Esman (Ed.), *Adolescent psychiatry: Developmental and clinical studies: Vol. 22. Annals of the American Society for Adolescent Psychiatry* (pp. 59–84). Hillsdale: Analytic Press.

Keys, A., Brozek, J., Henschel, A., Mickelsen, O., & Taylor, H. L. (1950). *The biology of human starvation.* Minneapolis: University of Minnesota Press.

Kog, E., & Vandereycken, W. (1989). Family interaction in eating disordered patients and normal controls. *International Journal of Eating Disorders, 8,* 11–23.

Lasèque, E. C. (1873). De l'anorexie hysterique. *Archives Generales de Medecine, 21,* 384–403.

Lock, S., Agras, W. S., Bryson, S., & Kraemer, H. C. (2005). A comparison of short and long term family therapy for adolescent anorexia nervosa. *Journal of American Academy of Child and Adolescent Psychiatry, 44,* 632–639.

Lock, S., Couturier, J., & Agras, W. S. (2006). Comparison of long term outcomes in adolescents with anorexia nervosa treated with family therapy. *Journal of American Academy of Child and Adolescent Psychiatry, 46,* 666–672.

Lock, J., Le Grange, D., Agras, W. S., & Dare, C. (2001). *Treatment manual for anorexia nervosa.* New York: Guilford Press.

Luepnitz, D. A. (1988). *The family interpreted: Psychoanalysis, feminism and family therapy.* New York: Basic Books.

Madanes, C. (1981). *Strategic family therapy.* San Francisco: Jossey-Bass.

Madigan, S. P., & Goldner, E. M. (1998). A narrative approach to anorexia: Discourse, reflexivity & questions. In M. F. Hoyt (Ed.), *The handbook of constructive therapies* (pp. 380–400). San Francisco: Jossey-Bass.

McNamara, K., & Loveman, C. (1990). Differences in family functioning among bulimics, repeat dieters, and non-dieters. *Journal of Clinical Psychology, 46,* 518–523.

Minuchin, S., Rosman, B. L., & Baker, L. (1978). *Psychosomatic families: Anorexia nervosa in context.* Cambridge, MA: Harvard University Press.

NICE. (2004). *Eating disorders: Core interventions in the treatment and management of anorexia nervosa, bulimia nervosa and related eating disorders.* London: National Institute for Health and Clinical Excellence.

Nielsen, S., & Bará-Carril, N. (2003). Family, burden of care and social consequences. In J. Treasure, U. Schmidt, & E. van Furth (Eds.), *Handbook of eating disorders* (2nd ed., pp. 191–206). London: Wiley.

Råstam, M., & Gillberg, C. (1991). The family background in anorexia nervosa: A population-based study. *Journal of American Academy of Child and Adolescent Psychiatry, 30,* 283–289.

Robin, A. L., Siegel, P. T., Moye, A. W., Gilroy, M., Dennis, A. B., & Sikand, A. (1999). A controlled comparison of family versus individual therapy for adolescents with anorexia nervosa. *Journal of American Academy of Child and Adolescent Psychiatry, 38,* 1482–1489.

Røijen, S. (1992). Anorexia nervosa families – a homogeneous group? A case record study. *Acta Psychiatrica Scandinavica, 85,* 196–200.

Rolland, J. S. (1994). *Families, illness, and disability: An integrative treatment model.* New York: Basic Books.

Russell, G. F. M., Szmukler, G. I., Dare, C., & Eisler, I. (1987). An evaluation of family therapy in anorexia nervosa and bulimia nervosa. *Archives of General Psychiatry, 44,* 1047–1056.

Scholz, M., Rix, M., Scholz, K., Gantcher, K., & Thömke, V. (2005). Multiple family group therapy for anorexia nervosa: concepts, experiences and results. *Journal of Family Therapy, 27,* 132–141.

Selvini-Palazzoli, M. (1974). *Self-starvation: From the intrapsychic to the transpersonal approach to anorexia nervosa.* London: Chaucer.

Steiger, H., Liquornik, K., Chapman, J., & Hussain, N. (1991). Personality and family disturbances in eating-disorder patients: Comparison of "restricters" and "bingers" to normal controls. *International Journal of Eating Disorders, 10,* 501–512.

Steinglass, P. (1998). Multiple family discussion groups for patients with chronic medical illness. *Families, Systems and Health, 16,* 55–70.

Steinglass, P., Bennett, L. A., Wolin, S. J., & Reiss, D. (1987). *The alcoholic family.* New York: Basic Books.

Stierlin, H., & Weber, G. (1987). Anorexia nervosa: Lessons from a follow-up study. *Family Systems Medicine, 7,* 120–157.

Stierlin, H., & Weber, G. (1989). *Unlocking the family door.* New York: Brunner/Mazel.

Vandereycken, W. (2002). Families of patients with eating disorders. In C. G. Fairburn & K. D. Brownell (Eds.), *Eating disorders and obesity. A comprehensive handbook* (2nd ed., pp. 215–220). New York: Guilford Press.

Vetere, A., & Dallos, R. (2008). Systemic therapy and attachment narratives. *Journal of Family Therapy, 30,* 374–385.

Waller, G., Calam, R., & Slade, P. (1989). Eating disorders and family interaction. *British Journal of Clinical Psychology, 28,* 285–286.

White, M. (1995). *Re-authoring lives.* Adelaide: Dulwich Centre.

Whitney, J., & Eisler, I. (2005). Theoretical and empirical models around caring for someone with an eating disorder: The reorganization of family life and inter-personal maintenance factors. *Journal of Mental Health, 14,* 575–585.

Wilson, G. T., & Fairburn, C. G. (1998). Treatments for eating disorders. In P. E. Nathan and J. M. Gorman (Eds.), *A guide to treatments that work* (pp. 501–530). New York: Oxford University Press.

Zipfel, S., Löwe, B., & Herzog, W. (2003). Medical complications. In J. Treasure, U. Schmidt, & E. van Furth (Eds.), *Handbook of eating disorders* (2nd ed., pp. 161–190). London: Wiley.

39

Combining Work and Family: From Conflict to Compatible

Diane F. Halpern and Sherylle J. Tan

The prototypical family with two parents, a stay-at-home mother, breadwinning father, and a couple of kids was idealized in the U.S. sitcoms of the 1950s, but this family type is becoming increasingly rare. Almost every aspect of this mythical ideal family has joined the ranks of minority status. One of the most dramatic changes in American families and those in other industrialized countries in the last 40 years is the increased rate of maternal employment, especially among mothers of infants and young children. The proportion of married-couple families with the wife in the paid labor force rose from approximately 43.6% in 1967 to 57.3% in 2005 (U.S. Bureau of Labor Statistics, 2007). As the number of mothers employed outside the home rose, "work and family" emerged as a distinct domain of research (Perry-Jenkins, Repetti, & Crouter, 2000).

Profound changes in the nature of how and where we work and the needs and desires of the contemporary workforce have affected the structure of families, making work–family issues an important topic for employers, families, communities, and public policy makers (Halpern, 2005a, 2005b). Working families are facing new challenges as they struggle to find ways to provide care for children, older adults, and anyone who is sick, while at the same time, employers are concerned with meeting the needs of their employees – a business concern that must be addressed, because no business can remain successful by ignoring dramatic changes in the workforce. A large majority of legislative initiatives are focused on topics at the intersection of work and family. State and national leaders debate topics that include providing medical care for employed and unemployed families, paid family leave so workers can bond with newborn infants or care for sick family members, educational practices that prepare new and continuing workers with necessary workforce skills, and how to make welfare work. Work–family issues are the "hot" topics of our generation.

The Changing Nature of Families

Families are changing. Many more families are living in "non-traditional" family arrangements, thus making the "traditional" nuclear family with heterosexual parents and children, while still the modal family structure, only one among many different types. The number of single parents, cohabitants, same-sex families, and stepfamilies has dramatically increased in the last several decades, and in all industrialized countries, couples are marrying later, having children at older ages, having fewer children, and living longer, especially among the best-educated adults (see Chapter 4, this volume).

Family accommodations

For the first time in U.S. history, women make up close to half of the workforce (Bond, Thompson, Galinsky, & Prottas, 2003). Women are full and equal participants in the formal and informal American economy. Although increasing female employment outside the home may be leveling off, there is no indication that there will be a substantial reversal with women returning to full-time positions in the home. Employers cannot ignore the changes in the workforce or insist that employed mothers fit into a worker mold cast when being employed meant you were male with a wife at home to handle the work of the house and the family. Working families must adapt to new family and workplace structures by rewriting the rules regarding housework and family care when all adults in the household are employed outside the home. Adaptations include increased father involvement in child care and care for other family members (e.g., parental care or sibling care), non-parental child care, work restructuring, and family-friendly work policies (Gottfried & Gottfried, 2008).

Parental participation

With the dramatic rise in dual-earner families, there is concern that parents (especially mothers) are spending less time with their children and that this decrease is detrimental to children's developmental. Working mothers do spend less time with their children overall than do stay-at-home mothers. However, research has shown that working mothers spend about the same amount of time per day in primary care of their children as their stay-at-home counterparts of the 1920s (Bryant & Zick, 1996). Bianchi (2000) concluded, "The increase in female employment outside of the home has occurred with less reallocation of time away from child rearing among parents than would first appear" (p. 402).

Modern women, however, spend *twice* as much time per child on direct child care, primarily because they have fewer children and are better educated, than mothers in the 1920s. Since then, expectations about the role parents should play in their children's lives and the amount of time dedicated to childrearing have risen dramatically. In earlier generations and today in the majority world, women spend more time on fundamental household chores, which includes carrying water long distances, chopping wood, boiling clothes to clean them, churning butter, and so on. The idea that women should dedicate full-time to child care is relatively new and only exists in industrialized countries (Boydston, 1990).

The number of children in a family is an important determinant of the time parents spend on child-care activities. Smaller families may contribute to less adult time invested on children in total; thus the per-child investment time has actually increased because child-time is spread across fewer children (Bryant & Zick, 1996). Although some believe that children of working mothers suffer because of decreased time spent with the mothers, research has not substantiated this claim. In fact, data indicate that working mothers compensate for their absence by the proportion of direct interaction and the amount of time they devote during non-work hours and weekends (Easterbrooks & Goldberg, 1985).

Additionally, families adapt by balancing parental roles. One of the most significant family adaptations is an increase in father participation (Gottfried & Gottfried, 2008). Research has found that fathers spend more time (than in the 1960s) on child-care activities when both parents are employed (Sayer, Bianchi, & Robinson, 2004). Families balance parenting roles in this way to better accommodate the needs of both working parents.

Children benefit by having both parents involved in child-care activities. There are multiple positive child outcomes when fathers are more involved, such as more mature social adjustment and higher academic achievement (Parke, 2002). This is not to say that there is equal division of household chores among men and women; women are still doing more of the housework and child care than men (Bond et al., 2003), but fathers are doing more than their own fathers probably did. In married dual-earner families, 30% of fathers report that they take equal or greater responsibility (Bond et al., 2003). Thus, families have made accommodations so that the total time that children spend with parents has not decreased when mothers are employed; rather the time is more equally distributed among both parents thanks to the increased involvement of fathers.

Child care

When parents work, families must make accommodations for their children's care during their working hours. Child care has become an increasingly critical and controversial issue as a result of the rise in maternal employment and the dual-earner family.

The findings regarding the relation of child care to children's development and behavior problems may seem to be inconclusive and inconsistent. The concern that children might be less attached to their mothers if they were cared for by someone else during the day has not been supported by the research. Findings have maintained that child care is unrelated to the attachment of children to their mothers (National Institute of Child Health & Human Development, 1997). Some studies have reported negative cognitive and social outcomes from the relation with early maternal employment in the child's first year of life (e.g., Belsky & Eggbeen, 1991; Brooks-Gunn, Han, & Waldfogel, 2002). And there are some who still maintain that child care can be a risk factor in children's development and in their attachment to their mother (Belsky, 1988). However, many researchers believe that those findings are weak, that they pertain to a small number of children (i.e., most are doing fine), and that further research is warranted.

The quality of the child care that children receive is positively related to preschool children's developmental outcomes. High-quality child care is related to fewer reports of problem behaviors, higher cognitive performance, higher language ability, and higher levels of school readiness than those for children in low-quality care, and low-income children in home care (Peisner-Feinberg & Burchinal, 1997). Preschool attendance is associated with higher rates of school completion and lower rates of juvenile arrest (Reynolds, Temple, Robertson, & Mann, 2001). Children who participate in good-quality preschool programs perform better on tests of cognitive and social skills, while disadvantaged children receive greater benefits than other children (Peisner-Feinberg & Burchinal, 1997).

However, recent research by the National Institute of Child Health and Human Development Study of Early Child Care and Youth Development (Belsky et al., 2007) found that children who were in day care for long periods of time (i.e., long days or more than 40 hours per week) exhibited slightly more problem behaviors up through sixth grade, but the proportion of children to whom this applies is small. These same children also exhibited higher vocabulary scores when they were in high-quality day-care centers and when parents provided effective care. Thus, positive developmental outcomes, such as enhanced social skills, social-emotional functioning, and reading, math, and vocabulary achievement, are evident when both day care and parenting were higher quality. Positive benefits result from quality day care, and the slight increase in behavioral problems was found only when both day care and parenting were inadequate. Most negative findings tend to be small in size and apply to children who live in poor-quality homes and receive poor-quality child care. This double-whammy of poor quality, not surprisingly, has shown negative effects. The critical effect on children is not whether they are in child care, per se, but the quality of the care they receive – whether they are at home or in child care.

The Changing Nature of the Workplace

With the rise of technology and an increasing globalization of work, employees also need to adjust to changes in the nature of work and the workforce. Technology has redefined the workplace, often blurring the boundary between home and work. The Family and Work Institute's National Study of Changing Workforce (Bond, Thompson, Galinsky, & Prottas, 2002) found that most employees use work computers for personal reasons several times a week, and most employees also use their home computers for work-related reasons. The growing use of computers, e-mail, cell phones, and fax machines has meant that work can be performed almost anywhere, allowing it to become more global (Perry-Jenkins et al., 2000). With the advancement of technology has also come the expectation that a dedicated employee should be readily available and accessible at all times.

Although the proportion of men and women in the workforce is now nearly equal (Bond et al., 2002), many jobs remain segregated by gender, and many other job categories are shifting from primarily male to female (e.g., psychology, law, medicine, and accounting). Many professional and white-collar job categories will change in the near future, as over 60% of all college graduates are women and women now comprise half of medical school and law school graduates and over 75% of veterinary school graduates (U.S. Bureau of the Census, 2000). There are still very few women in the top leadership positions in the corporate world and in governments throughout the world. Fewer women are moving into jobs that require manual labor, and even fewer men are moving into many of the traditionally female jobs such as clerical work and child care, so we can expect sex segregation in many blue-collar job categories to continue.

As working families have changed and continue to change, so have the needs of the workforce. Working mothers, older workers, and other non-traditional employees require flexible working schedules to balance work and family. Yet, despite all the research, employees, especially women who work at lower-level jobs, have little flexibility in their work schedules (McCrate, 2002). In fact, job hours have increased and much of the work has become more demanding (Bond et al., 2002). Single mothers, especially, have rigid schedules, because they cannot afford to hold out for better jobs, while having to balance all the responsibilities of work and family without spousal support.

Family-friendly work policies

As a result of changing workforce demographics, many employers and organizations have created family-friendly policies to help support their employees' family responsibilities. What constitutes family-friendly policies in the workplace varies widely, since there is no uniform definition and offerings differ from employer to employer. Such policies may include dependant care support, flexible work options which can include different starting and ending times for the work day, family leave, telecommuting, and job sharing.

Research shows that family-friendly policies benefit not only employees, but also employers (e.g., Baltes, Briggs, Huff, Wright, & Newman, 1999). Employees afforded more family-friendly policies exhibit higher levels of work commitment, increased job satisfaction, and reduced absenteeism and turnover, which leads to better productivity. A recent study of major employers in the United States found that workplace flexibility is cost-effective to employers because workers miss less time at work and remain more committed to their employer (Corporate Voices, 2005).

Usage of policies.   While there has been an increase in family-friendly policy initiatives among employers and growing recognition that these are employer-friendly as well, employee access to and use of these benefits have been low (Saltzstein, Ting, & Saltzstein, 2001). The decision to use these policies is based on perceptions of the workplace culture. Many employees do not use such policies because they are concerned that the use of family-friendly policies, such as parental leave and flexible work schedules, may be perceived as a lack of job commitment and negatively impact their career advancement (Eaton, 2003;

Rogier & Padgett, 2004). On the other hand, when the workplace culture supports their use, then using these policies is associated with increased productivity and organizational commitment (Eaton, 2003).

Gender is a factor in policy usage decisions because of long-standing gender inequality in the labor market (Catalyst, 2002). Despite the increased involvement of fathers in families, women continue to be the primary caregivers. Thus, family responsibility continues to shape women's work lives and usage of family-friendly policies. However, mothers, more than fathers, are often judged as less committed to employment despite their actual commitment and competency (Fuegen, Biernat, Haines, & Deaux, 2004). Rogier and Padgett (2004) found that female employees on a flexible schedule are perceived as less dedicated and less motivated for job advancement. The traits of an ideal worker are often in contrast to those of a good mother (Halpert, Wilson, & Hickman, 1993).

Family Finances

For many families, a dual-earner household is critical to making ends meet. However, working mothers are often judged negatively. There is a persisting belief that employed mothers are in the workforce to satisfy their desire for extra luxuries. In reality, many American families are unable to support themselves on a single income and often do not have a choice regarding parental employment if they want to maintain a basic standard of living.

Warren and Tyagi (2003) discuss the "two-income trap" and the myth that family spending on frivolous luxuries requires two incomes. They find that families require two incomes to cover the cost of necessities (e.g., health insurance, health care, and mortgage payments), which cost disproportionately more than only a few decades ago, making it difficult to support a family on one salary. The rising cost of homeownership is an issue for many families. Since the mid-1970s, the amount earmarked for the mortgage has increased 69% (adjusted for inflation; Tyagi, 2004). Home prices have risen more than three times as fast for couples with young children because they want homes in the neighborhoods with good schools (Warren & Tyagi, 2003). However, family incomes have not increased at the same pace. In fact, the average father's income (adjusted for inflation) has increased by less than 1%, making it nearly impossible for the average family to live on one income, if they want to purchase a home in desirable neighborhoods (Tyagi, 2004). Thus, for many families, the dual-earner family is not a choice, but a necessity.

The Mommy Wage Gap

Women earn less money than men. The gender wage gap, however, has narrowed, with women earning $76^{1}/_{2}$ cents to every dollar a man earns (Infoplease, 2004). This differential is not entirely about gender; it might be better described as a "mommy gap" (that is, the difference in wages between women with and without children), which continues to widen rather than narrow (Waldfogel, 1998). Working mothers earn 60% of what working fathers earn (Crosby, Williams, & Biernat, 2004) and it is estimated that the wage penalty for motherhood is approximately 7% per child (Budig & England, 2001).

The mommy gap is partly associated with the work patterns of mothers. Men tend to follow a linear path, primarily because they rarely need to take time off for childbirth. Women's work patterns, on the other hand, exhibits significant movement in and out of the workforce, consisting of many starts and stops, interruptions and detours, as they accommodate and adapt to the needs of their family (Hynes & Clarkberg, 2005). When women take time off from paid employment they lose out on promotions and routine pay increases (Barnett & Rivers, 1996). The job interruption that women experience due to childbirth can have long-lasting financial effects (Budig & England, 2001); research suggests that women who maintain employment continuity during childbirth have higher pay than those who do not (Waldfogel, 1997).

Pro-Family Public Policies

Why are work and family the government's business? Most people have parents, friends, neighbors, who function as family, and everyone, at some time, will need care. We need sound policies that are consistent with our values and the bottom line. Despite numerous social changes in how we live and work, public policies have not caught up with the contemporary realities of working families.

Paid family leave

The United States is one of only three major industrialized countries that fail to offer any paid family leave support. In 1993, the U.S. implemented the Family Medical Leave Act (FMLA), which provides employees with 12 weeks of unpaid leave each year to care for a newborn or adopted child or a seriously ill family member, or to recover from an illness while providing job protection. While research on FMLA has been positive for both employees and employers, parental and family care leave is unavailable to most Americans because only about half of all workers are covered by FMLA (fewer than one fifth of mothers; Ruhm, 1997). Furthermore, approximately 64% of parents cannot afford to take unpaid leave (Han & Waldfogel, 2003). Thus, for many families, especially low-income families, unpaid leave is not an option. California became the first state in the nation to offer a paid leave policy in 2004, and other states are following. The California Paid Family Leave program (CPFL) provides eligible workers up to 6 weeks off with partial pay to care for a sick or aging relative, or to bond with a newborn, adopted, or foster child.

Women are more likely to benefit from paid family leave. Because women are often the primary care providers, paid family leave may aid with upward mobility for women, increase their long-term wages (since they are able to stay in the same job instead of leaving employment to care for family members), and help to narrow the wage gap between women and men. When paid leave is available, mothers are more likely to work longer into pregnancy, which is a benefit to company productivity. For California companies, these benefits could result in savings of $89 million under a paid family leave program, which increases employee retention and decreases turnover (Dube & Kaplan, 2002).

Paid leave is a win–win situation for both employers and employees. While employees benefit from paid leave, their employers also have much to gain. Paid family leave allows companies to provide their employees with time to focus on what is important in their lives at that moment and then be fully ready to go back to work and be more productive employees. Employee morale and company loyalty are positively affected when employees are afforded access to different leave options. Furthermore, sick workers who have the choice of using their paid leave are less likely to transfer their sickness to others (Levin-Epstein, 2007), which helps to maintain overall workers' productivity and the wellbeing of customers.

All people experience significant events in life, from the birth of a child to taking care of a loved one with an illness. Paid leave is a necessity for all workers, regardless of age, social class, or gender. The benefits of paid leave exceed implementation costs and make a lasting impact on the equality of men and women in business for years into the future.

Child and elder care as community responsibilities

The number of working adults with significant caregiving responsibilities is expected to rise dramatically. Working adults will not only have to care for their children but many will also care for elderly parents, making child care and elder care important issues in modern society.

Child care. With many mothers in the workforce, working families need affordable and high-quality child care that is convenient to public transportation so that parents can remain employed and families can stay off public assistance. Policies need to coincide with the needs and realities of contemporary families, using evidence provided by our best researchers. Problems with child care are major factors in family stress (Silverstein, 1991) and often interfere with parents' abilities to get and keep a job (Children's Defense Fund, 2003). Low-income families, especially, need reliable, affordable child care to obtain and maintain work that can help them to get out and, most importantly, stay out of poverty (Children's Defense Fund, 2003).

Child care has positive implications in keeping parents employed and off welfare. Mothers are more likely to be employed and stay employed if they use formal child care (Boushey, 2002). Child-care assistance plays a pivotal role in increasing the employment of low-income mothers by assisting families to stay off welfare and allowing them to work (Mezey, 2004). Single mothers with young children who receive child-care assistance are 40% more likely to remain employed after two years than those who do not receive it (Children's Defense Fund, 2003). However, child care, especially quality, formal child care, is expensive (even with the aid of child-care assistance), so many low-income families rely on informal child-care arrangements, such as relative care and family day care, which are not often eligible for child-care assistance (Boushey & Wright, 2004).

Elder care.   People are living longer than ever before and this means that more elderly will need care. It is estimated that almost 1 in 10 Americans will need to take time off work to care for an elderly family member (National Alliance for Caregiving, 2004). Elder care is not a woman's problem or a child-care problem – it is a universal problem that impacts everyone. There are almost 50 million baby boomers approaching retirement in the next decade. An aging population marks an increase in illnesses such as Alzheimer's disease, stroke, and other health problems requiring care. The responsibilities of American workers who care for their elderly parents will affect every segment of society. There are 44.4 million caregivers in the U.S. and many are balancing full- or part-time jobs (National Alliance for Caregiving, 2004).

Not surprisingly, family caregivers often face financial impediments, as well as emotional and physical health problems, as negative consequences of their caregiver roles. What is surprising, however, is the lack of state and federal assistance available to workers who take time off to provide care to a family member. Family caregivers experience a great deal of emotional stress, most evident when caregivers feel that they have had no choice in assuming the role of a caregiver (National Alliance for Caregiving, 2004). Caregivers struggle to meet the demands of their multiple responsibilities and experience physical, emotional, and financial hardships as a result (Halpern, Tan, & Carsten, 2008). Caregivers often have no paid time off, meaning no paid sick leave or vacation time to take off to care for their elderly family members. Many cannot take the time off due to fear of losing their jobs. Time to provide care is penalized with no pay, and some (12%) leave the workforce entirely (National Alliance for Caregiving, 2004). Now, more than ever, there is a need for social policies to address the needs of family caregivers who must balance their dual responsibilities of employment and caregiving.

References

Baltes, B., Briggs, T. E., Huff, J. W., Wright, J. A., & Newman, G. A. (1999). Flexible and compressed workweek schedules: A meta-analysis of their effects on work-related criteria. *Journal of Applied Psychology, 84*, 496–513.

Barnett, R. C., & Rivers, C. (1996). *She works, he works: How two-income families are happy, healthy, and thriving.* Cambridge, MA: Harvard University Press.

Belsky, J. (1988). The "effects" of infant day care reconsidered. *Early Childhood Research Quarterly, 3*, 235–272.

Belsky, J., & Eggbeen, D. (1991). Early and extensive maternal employment and young children's socioemotional development: Children of the National Longitudinal Survey of Youth. *Journal of Marriage and Family, 53*, 1083–1110.

Belsky, J., Vandell, D. L., Burchinal, M., Clarke-Stewart, K. A., McCartney, K., & Owen, M. T. (2007). Are there long-term effects of early child care? *Child Development, 78*, 681–701.

Bianchi, S. M. (2000). Maternal employment and time with children: Dramatic change or surprising continuity? *Demography, 37*, 401–414.

Bond, J. T., Thompson, C., Galinsky, E., & Prottas, D. (2002). *The 2002 national study of the changing workforce*, executive summary. New York: Family and Work Institute.

Bond, J. T., Thompson, C., Galinsky, E., & Prottas, D. (2003). *Highlights of the national study of the changing workforce, No. 3*, executive summary. Retrieved May 5, 2008, from http://www.familiesandwork.org/summary/nscw2002.pdf

Boushey, H. (2002). *Staying employed after welfare: Work supports and job quality vital to employment tenure and wage growth.* Washington, DC: Economic Policy Institute.

Boushey, H., & Wright, J. (2004). *Working moms and child care.* Washington, DC: Center for Economic and Policy Research.

Boydston, J. (1990). *Home and work: Housework, wages, and the ideology of labor in the early republic.* New York: Oxford University Press.

Brooks-Gunn, J., Han, W. J., & Waldfogel, J. (2002). Maternal employment and child cognitive outcomes in the first three years of life: The NICHD Study of Early Child Care. *Child Development, 73*, 1052–1072.

Bryant, W. K., & Zick, C. D. (1996). Are we investing less in the next generation? Historical trends in time spent caring for children. *Journal of Family and Economic Issues, 17*, 365–391.

Budig, M. J., & England, P. (2001). The wage penalty for motherhood. *American Sociological Review, 66*, 207–225.

Catalyst. (2002). *2002 Catalyst census of women corporate officers and top earners in the Fortune 500.* Retrieved March 4, 2007, from http://www.catalystwomen.org/files/fact/COTE%20Factsheet%202002updated.pdf

Children's Defense Fund. (2003). *Key facts: Essential information about child care, early education, and school-age care.* Washington, DC: Children's Defense Fund.

Corporate Voices. (2005, November). *Business impacts of flexibility: A business imperative.* Retrieved September 20, 2006, from http://corporatevoices.org

Crosby, F. J., Williams, J. C., & Biernat, M. (2004). The maternal wall. *Journal of Social Issues, 60*, 675–682.

Dube, A., & Kaplan, E. (2002). *Paid family leave in California: An analysis of costs and benefits.* Retrieved February 23, 2007, from http://www.iies.su.se/~ekaplan/paidfamilyleave.pdf

Easterbrooks, M. A., & Goldberg, W. A. (1985). Effects of early maternal employment on toddlers, mothers, and fathers. *Developmental Psychology, 21*, 774–783.

Eaton, S. C. (2003). If you can use them: Flexibility policies, organizational commitment, and perceived performance. *Industrial Relations, 42*, 145–167.

Fuegen, K., Biernat, M., Haines, E., & Deaux, K. (2004). Mothers and fathers in the workplace: How gender and parental status influence judgments of job-related competence. *Journal of Social Issues, 60*, 737–754.

Gottfried, A. E., & Gottfried, A. W. (2008). The upside of maternal and dual-earner employment: A focus on positive family adaptations, home environments, and child development in the Fullerton Longitudinal Study. In A. Marcus-Newhall, D. F. Halpern, & S. J. Tan (Eds.), *The changing realities of work and family: An interdisciplinary approach* (pp. 25–42). Blackwell.

Halpern, D. F. (2005a). Psychology at the intersection of work and family: Recommendations for employers, working families, and policymakers. *American Psychologist, 60*, 397–409.

Halpern, D. F. (2005b). How time-flexible work policies can reduce stress, improve health, and save money. *Stress and Health, 21*, 157–168.

Halpern, D. F., Tan, S. J., & Carsten, M. (2008). California paid family leave: Is it working for caregivers? In A. Marcus-Newhall, D. F. Halpern, & S. J. Tan (Eds.), *The changing realities of work and family: An interdisciplinary approach* (pp. 159–174). Blackwell.

Halpert, J. A., Wilson, M. L., & Hickman, J. L. (1993). Pregnancy as a source of bias in performance appraisals. *Journal of Organizational Behavior, 14,* 649–663.

Han, W., & Waldfogel, J. (2003). Parental leave: The impact of recent legislation on parents' leave taking. *Demography, 40,* 191–200.

Hynes, K., & Clarkberg, M. (2005). Women's employment patterns during early parenthood: A group-based trajectory analysis. *Journal of Marriage and Family, 67,* 222–240.

Infoplease. (2004). *Women's earnings as a percentage of men's, 1951–2004.* Retrieved October 13, 2006, from http://www.infoplease.com/ipa/A0193820.html

Levin-Epstein, J. (2007, February). Responsive workplaces: The business case for employment that values fairness and families. Retrieved May 8, 2008, from http://www.prospect.org/cs/articles?article=responsive_workplaces

McCrate, E. (2002). *Working mothers in a double bind: Working moms, minorities have the most rigid schedules, and are paid less for the sacrifice.* Washington, DC: Economic Policy Institute.

Mezey, J. (2004, February). *Child care programs help parents find and keep jobs: Funding shortfalls leave many families without assistance.* Retrieved May 8, 2008, from http://www.clasp.org/DMS/Documents/1076435918.03/ CC_shortfall.pdf

National Alliance for Caregiving. (2004, April). *Caregiving in the U.S.* Retrieved May 8, 2008, from http://www.caregiving.org/data/04finalreport.pdf

National Institute of Child Health & Human Development. (1997). The effects of infant child care on infant–mother attachment security: Results of the NICHD Study of Early Child Care. *Child Development, 68,* 860–879.

Parke, R. D. (2002). Fathers and families. In M. H. Bornstein (Ed.), *Handbook of parenting: Vol. 3. Being and becoming a parent* (2nd ed., pp. 27–73). Mahwah, NJ: Erlbaum.

Peisner-Feinberg, E. S., & Burchinal, M. R. (1997). Relations between preschool children's child-care experiences and concurrent development: The Cost, Quality, and Outcomes Study. *Merrill-Palmer Quarterly, 43,* 451–477.

Perry-Jenkins, M., Repetti, R. L., & Crouter, A. C. (2000). Work and families in the 1990s. *Journal of Marriage and Family, 62,* 981–998.

Reynolds, A. J., Temple, J. A., Robertson, D. L., & Mann, E. A. (2001). Long-term effects of an early childhood intervention on educational achievement and juvenile arrest. *Journal of the American Medical Association, 285,* 2339–2346.

Rogier, S. A., & Padgett, M. Y. (2004). The impact of utilizing a flexible work schedule on perceived career advancement potential of women. *Human Resource Development Quarterly, 15,* 89–106.

Ruhm, C. J. (1997). Policy watch: The Family and Medical Leave Act. *Journal of Economic Perspectives, 11,* 175–186.

Saltzstein, A. L., Ting, Y., & Saltzstein, G. H. (2001). Work–family balance and job satisfaction: The impact of family-friendly policies on attitudes of federal government employees. *Public Administrative Review, 61,* 452–467.

Sayer, L. C., Bianchi, S. M., & Robinson, J. P. (2004). Are parents investing less in children? Trends in mothers' and fathers' time with children. *The American Journal of Sociology, 110,* 1–43.

Silverstein, L. (1991). Transforming the debate about child care and maternal employment. *American Psychologist, 46,* 1025–1032.

Tyagi, A. (2004, March 22). Why women need to work [Electronic version]. *Time Magazine, 56.* Retrieved March 23, 2006, from http://www.time.com/time/archive/printout/0,23657,993642,00.html

U.S. Bureau of the Census. (2000). *Statistical abstract of the United States.* Washington, DC: U.S. Government Printing Office.

U.S. Bureau of Labor Statistics. (2007, September). *Women in the labor force: A databook.* Retrieved May 8, 2008, from http://www.bls.gov/cps/wlf-databook-2007.pdf

Waldfogel, J. (1997). The effects of children on women's wages. *American Sociological Review, 62,* 209–217.

Waldfogel, J. (1998). Understanding the "family gap" in pay for women with children. *Journal of Economic Perspectives, 12,* 137–156.

Warren, E., & Tyagi, A. (2003). *The two-income trap: Why middle-class mothers and fathers are going broke.* New York: Basic Books.

40

Lesbian, Gay, and Bisexual Family Psychology: A Systemic, Life-Cycle Perspective

Abbie E. Goldberg

A systemic approach recognizes that individuals are influenced by their families, friends, communities, and workplaces, as well as broader societal institutions and ideologies (Whitechurch & Constantine, 1993; see Chapter 1, this volume). Individuals exist within, are shaped by, and interact with multiple intersecting contexts. Further, these interactions necessarily shift throughout the life cycle as individuals develop, form relationships, and create their own families and communities. A systemic approach is particularly useful in the study of lesbian, gay, and bisexual (LGB) individuals, whose lives and relationships are increasingly visible in society, and yet who continue to be vulnerable to discrimination in many settings (Herek, 2006). This chapter will discuss research on various aspects of LGB people's experiences (coming out, relationship maintenance, the transition to parenthood, and parenting) with special attention to the experiences and contexts, broadly defined, that shape LGB families' development over time.

Coming Out and Disclosure

A process that is unique to the life experience and life cycle of sexual minorities is the process of coming out; or, the process of accepting and disclosing one's sexual orientation to oneself and others. According to the Cass model (1979), individuals move from confusion regarding their feelings of same-sex attraction, to acceptance and tolerance of their sexual orientation, to experiencing a sense of pride and synthesis of their LGB identity. While the coming-out process was initially conceived of as a series of linear and continuous stages, contemporary scholars suggest that coming out is an ongoing process that is often marked by contradiction and change, and both pride and shame (Oswald, 2002). Further, it is important to consider the varied situational and contextual forces that impact decisions to come out. In deciding whether to disclose their sexual orientation, LGB people must consider their immediate social context and potential threats associated with disclosure (e.g., harassment, job loss), how well they know the individual at hand, and the ease of concealment.

Broader contextual factors, such as characteristics of one's family and community, will also influence coming-out processes. Individuals from highly religious and/or politically conservative families may be particularly cautious about coming out for fear of lack of support. Social class and occupation may also impact disclosure. For example, working-class sexual minorities who are employed in male-dominated, blue-collar workplaces (in which heterosexuality is often heavily regulated) may experience less freedom to be "out" at work than their middle-class counterparts (McDermott, 2006). Race and ethnicity may also impact disclosure. For example, Black sexual minorities often experience double discrimination, facing homophobia within their own families and communities and also confronting racism in the gay community (Greene, 2000). Thus, coming out may mean risking the loss of valuable social resources.

The coming-out process may precede or unfold in tandem with the formation of same-sex relationships. While sharing many commonalities with heterosexual relationships, same-sex relationships are characterized by certain unique factors, including the stigmatized nature of the relationship, and, thus, potential barriers to relationship development. Next, the creation and maintenance of same-sex relationships will be discussed.

Creating and Maintaining Relationships

Attitudes about gay rights (e.g., pertaining to marriage and adoption) have become increasingly positive over the past several decades, although negative attitudes about the rights of sexual minorities continue to exist (Herek, 2006). Increased dating opportunities for LGB persons have occurred alongside these changes. Until fairly recently, opportunities for gay men and lesbians to meet and congregate were relatively restricted, and the gay/lesbian bar represented one of the few options for socialization. The growing visibility of LGB persons, however, has led to the development of gay political organizations, gay cruises, gay church groups, and many other opportunities for interaction (James & Murphy, 1998). Sexual minorities (particularly gay men) are also increasingly turning to online dating as a means of meeting potential partners (although, notably, the internet may increase risk for HIV in that it is anonymous and facilitates increased numbers of sexual meetings).

Before turning to a discussion about the nature of committed same-sex relationships, it is important to emphasize that not all same-sex relationships are monogamous. Most lesbians in relationships practice monogamy (e.g., Bryant & Demain, 1994) whereas only about half of gay men in relationships are monogamous (e.g., Solomon, Rothblum,

& Balsam, 2005). As Peplau (2003) points out, the differences between lesbians and gay men regarding sexual exclusivity are at least in part a function of gender: Men *in general* demonstrate higher levels of sexual desire and have more permissive attitudes about sex, whereas women *in general* prefer sex in the context of a committed relationship (Peplau, 2003). These findings may reflect both biological sex differences (men are hormonally predisposed to experience greater sexual arousal) and gender socialization effects (i.e., desire and arousal are socially constructed). Societal discourses also influence couples' sexual relationships. For example, gay men are aware of romance scripts that prescribe sexual exclusivity, but they are also influenced by the attitudes that characterize gay male culture (e.g., sexual consumerism).

Regardless of whether relationships are open or closed, many sexual minorities are in committed, satisfying same-sex relationships (Bryant & Demian, 1994; Mackey, Diemer, & O'Brien, 2004). The fact that so many lesbians and gay men are able to sustain lasting relationships in spite of non-support from family members, the legal system, and society is particularly remarkable. Of interest are the following: (1) (how) do same-sex relationships differ from heterosexual couples, and (2) what factors are associated with relationship quality?

Relationship quality

Many studies have found few differences between same-sex and heterosexual couples in terms of relationship quality and satisfaction (e.g., Kurdek, 1998; Mackey et al., 2004), although some studies have found that lesbian couples report higher relationship quality than heterosexual couples (Kurdek, 2003). This finding may in part reflect the absence of structural barriers that govern heterosexual relationships: That is, the lack of institutionalized barriers to leaving their relationships (e.g., marriage, which confers legal, social, and religious validation and support) may lead couples to end their unions during times of crisis or dissatisfaction. Tentative support for this possibility is provided by the finding that gay and lesbian couples were more likely to separate than were heterosexual married couples with children (i.e., couples with multiple institutionalized barriers to leaving) (Kurdek, 2006).

Psychological intimacy and autonomy

What are the key correlates of relationship quality among same-sex couples? One important aspect of relationship quality in general is intimacy, or the merging of the self and the other. Researchers (e.g., Kurdek, 1998) have hypothesized that because lesbian couples are made up of two women who have been socialized to orient themselves to relationships and to value connection, their relationships should benefit from "a double dose of relationship-enhancing influences" (Kurdek, 1998, p. 554). Some studies have indeed found that lesbians' relationships tend to be characterized by higher levels of psychological intimacy than those of heterosexual partners or gay male partners (e.g.,

Kurdek, 1998); in turn, psychological intimacy is a powerful contributor to relationship satisfaction in all three types of couples (Mackey et al., 2004).

Autonomy, or the degree to which one maintains a sense of self separate from the relationship, is another focus of study. Many theorists have posited that men are socialized to value independence and separateness in their relationships (Gilligan, 1982), which suggests that gay male couples should report greater autonomy because they experience a "double dose of individual-enhancing influences" (Kurdek, 1998, p. 554). Some studies have found that gay male partners have higher levels of autonomy than heterosexual partners (Kurdek, 1998, 2003), although some have also found that lesbian partners have higher levels of autonomy than heterosexual partners (Kurdek, 1998). This finding can perhaps be understood in terms of lesbians' socialization *as lesbians*: that is, women's awareness that they will never be reliant on men to support them may foster emotional and financial independence, which are characteristics of autonomy.

"Too much" intimacy, which may be characteristic of lesbian couples, and "too much" autonomy, which may be characteristic of gay couples, can have detrimental effects. Some theorists argue that high levels of psychological intimacy, combined with lack of support from the outside world, can result in fusion, a state of psychological unity between people in which individual ego boundaries merge (Burch, 1985). Fusion has been blamed for contributing to low sexual desire and infrequent sexual activity in lesbian relationships (Blumstein & Schwarz, 1983). The double dose of autonomous influences that characterizes gay male relationships may have implications for commitment processes (insofar as commitment implies mutual dependence) such that gay male couples demonstrate lower levels than heterosexual couples. Of course, many other factors influence gay men's commitment levels; and, as marriage rights and civil unions become more prominent, it is possible that both gay and lesbian couples will demonstrate higher levels of commitment.

Equality and power

Given their common socialization (e.g., experiences of inequity in contexts such as the workplace), lesbian partners might be especially likely to desire equality in their relationships. Indeed, lesbians tend to highly value equality in their appraisals of "ideal" relationships, and are more likely to perceive equal power in their relationships than are heterosexual couples (Kurdek, 1998) and gay couples (Kurdek, 2003). Higher perceived equality in the relationship has in turn been linked to higher relationship satisfaction among both gay and lesbian couples (Kurdek, 1998).

One important aspect of power is the division of labor. In heterosexual couples, women often perform more unpaid work and men perform more paid work. Given that gay and lesbian couples cannot rely on sex difference as a guide in the division of labor, it is perhaps unsurprising that gay men and lesbians share housework more equitably with their partners than do heterosexual couples (Solomon, Rothblum, & Balsam, 2004; Solomon et al., 2005), although lesbian partners tend to share tasks while gay male partners are more likely to specialize in certain tasks (Kurdek, 1993).

Social support and recognition

The degree of support that same-sex couples receive from their families of origin, their communities, and their state and national governments necessarily impacts their relationships and the families that they create. Lesbian and gay partners perceive less social support from family members than do heterosexual couples (Kurdek, 2003) and may have more contact with friends than family, compared to heterosexual couples (Kurdek, 2006). Whereas research on the relationship between perceived family support and intimate relationship quality is mixed, social support from friends is more consistently linked to relationship quality for gay men and lesbians (Elizur & Mintzer, 2003).

Racial and ethnic minority lesbians and gay men may be especially vulnerable to deficiencies in support from their families and communities. Gay men and lesbians in interracial relationships may also experience low levels of support (Greene, 2000). Interracial relationships among sexual minorities are met with notable challenges, including the heightened visibility of the relationship, antagonism from both families, disapproval within the gay community, and White sexual minorities' inexperience with dealing with racism. Also, gay couples in which one or both partners is diagnosed with HIV/AIDS are vulnerable to the dual stresses of coping with a terminal illness as well as possible rejection by their families of origin.

At a broader level, same-sex relationships are impacted by widespread lack of social and legal recognition. Same-sex couples are denied many of the legal protections and supports that are afforded to heterosexual couples (Herek, 2006); indeed, constitutional amendments that prohibit same-sex civil marriage are currently being pursued in multiple states. Enactment of marriage amendments halts the possibility of obtaining a range of legal and financial rights, including eligibility for public housing, the ability to make medical decisions for an incapacitated partner, and the ability to file joint income tax returns (Pawelski et al., 2006). Such denial of symbolic and legal supports to same-sex couples undermines their mutual commitment to one another and threatens their psychological and relational wellbeing.

A few studies have examined the correlates and consequences of civil unions and marriage for individuals in same-sex relationships. Solomon et al. (2004) found that lesbians in civil unions were more open about their sexual orientation than lesbians not in civil unions, and gay men in civil unions were closer to their families than gay men not in civil unions. Perhaps couples that are more "out" are more oriented toward seeking legal recognition for their relationships; alternatively, obtaining legal recognition may lead to greater visibility. Solomon et al. (2005) found that 54% of same-sex couples reported changes in their love and commitment for each other as a result of having had a civil union, which suggests that the execution of legal documents may have a protective and stabilizing function with regard to relationships (Herek, 2006). Similarly, Alderson (2004) interviewed married gay men and lesbians in Canada and found that many couples felt that marriage brought greater depth and completion to their relationships. Marriage was also perceived as providing couples with a greater sense of security.

The legalization of same-sex marriage is not considered desirable by all sexual minorities. Some gay activists/scholars have questioned whether movements to secure same-sex

marriage rights are assimilationist in nature; others point out that marriage has historically been a vehicle for securing male status and privilege (Peel & Harding, 2004). However,
among gay activists, even those who are the most critical of same-sex marriage agree that
sexual minorities should have access to all of the practical benefits that are conferred on
married heterosexual couples (Peel & Harding, 2004).

Forming Families

Up until the past several decades, the main way that LGB people became parents was
in the context of heterosexual relationships. Advancements in reproductive technology,
in combination with social and political progress, have created a climate in which sexual minorities are aware of a wide range of parenting options, thus facilitating a rise in
the number of intentional LGB parent families.

The most common routes to parenthood (other than heterosexual marriage) are alternative insemination and foster care/adoption. Additionally, some lesbians may engage
in heterosexual sex to become parents. Some lesbians and gay men pursue surrogacy, whereby
a woman carries a baby who will be raised by the couple. Finally, some lesbians and gay
men pursue more complex parenting arrangements (e.g., a single lesbian co-parenting
with gay friend(s)).

The transition to parenthood will unfold somewhat differently depending on what
route LGB couples (or individuals) choose. Lesbians who pursue insemination face a range
of subsequent decisions, including who should carry the child, what type of donor to
use (known/unknown), and desired donor characteristics (Goldberg, 2006). Lesbians and
gay men who pursue adoption must decide what type of adoption to pursue (private
domestic, private international, public), desired or acceptable child characteristics (e.g.,
with respect to drug exposure, race, age), and whether to be "out" during the adoption
process (Goldberg, Downing, & Sauck, 2007).

Regardless of which route they choose, sexual minorities are vulnerable to barriers
throughout the insemination/adoption process. Although social change combined with
the increasing visibility of lesbian mothers has facilitated greater awareness of lesbians
who seek donor insemination, reports of insensitive treatment by healthcare providers
continue to appear in the literature (e.g., Goldberg, 2006). Fertility support services
are often targeted to heterosexual women, clinic forms are often inappropriate for
lesbian/bisexual patients, and healthcare providers often fail to acknowledge the non-
birthing partner (Ross & Steele, 2006). Inseminating couples may also face legal barriers:
Fewer than half of U.S. states have granted second-parent adoptions to sexual minorities
(which allow non-biological mothers to adopt their partners' children without requiring
them to give up their own parental rights) (Pawelski et al., 2006).

Adoptive gay parents also face barriers. Adoption agencies may overtly or covertly
discourage openness about sexual orientation, agency application forms may focus on
heterosexual applicants only, and social workers are sometimes suspected of trying to
match the "least desirable" children with the "least desirable" applicants (i.e., pushing gay

applicants to take the most troubled children) (Goldberg et al., 2007). Further, few states have demonstrated, via judicial ruling, openness to adoption by openly gay/lesbian individuals and couples; thus, many couples must choose one partner to legally adopt, which can create tension in the relationship (Goldberg et al., 2007).

Parenting

What happens when couples become parents? Same-sex couples' parenting experiences are similar to those of heterosexual couples in many ways; however, they are also necessarily shaped by the context of heterosexism, as well as partners' shared gender and the biological and/or legal inequities within the couple. Next, same-sex parenting will be discussed, with attention to several areas that have received the most attention: social support; division of labor; parenting abilities; and child outcomes.

Social support

Several studies suggest that lesbian and gay parents may experience increased support from family members once they become parents. Goldberg (2006) found that lesbians' perceptions of support from their own and their partners' families increased across the transition to parenthood (although women reported the highest levels of support from friends). Gartrell et al. (1999) found that many lesbian mothers felt that having a child had enhanced their relationships with their own parents. Thus, family members may push their feelings about homosexuality aside once a child enters the picture. Family support, however, may depend on the parent's biological and/or legal relationship to their child: Family members of non-biological lesbian mothers appear to be less involved with the child than family members of biological lesbian mothers (Patterson, Hurt, & Mason, 1998).

The division of labor

Despite valuing equality, same-sex couples may find that sharing the division of labor becomes more challenging in the context of parenting: parenthood introduces a new form of labor to be negotiated (child care) which often prompts renegotiation of roles and responsibilities. For example, during early parenthood, lesbian biological mothers tend to perform more child care than non-biological mothers, particularly if they are breastfeeding (Goldberg & Perry-Jenkins, 2007). Similarly, some lesbian couples struggle with issues of jealousy and competitiveness around bonding (Gartrell et al., 1999; Goldberg & Perry-Jenkins, 2007). Such feelings may be especially salient for non-biological lesbian mothers, lesbian stepmothers, and gay stepfathers, whose parental status is particularly undervalued by the broader societal context. As children develop, parents' division of labor may become more equal, and feelings of jealousy may dissipate (Patterson, Sutfin, & Fulcher, 2004) (although at least some research finds that labor continues to be somewhat polarized, with birth mothers performing more child care and non-biological mothers performing more paid work; Bos, van Balen, & van den Boom, 2007).

Parenting abilities and child outcomes

The sexual orientation of gay parents is presumed to negatively affect children in both indirect and direct ways: e.g., via deficiencies in their parenting abilities, via inappropriate "modeling" of their sexual orientation, and via exposing their children to homophobia. The research, however, is consistent in suggesting that sexuality is not relevant to men and women's parenting capacities, thereby challenging stereotypes of gay and lesbian parents as unfit. Studies comparing lesbian and heterosexual mothers have found that the two groups do not differ in terms of parenting skill or parenting stress (Bos et al., 2007; McNeill, Rienzi, & Kposowa, 1998) and studies of lesbian, gay, and heterosexual parents have found few differences in the quality of their parent–child relationships (Bigner & Jacobsen, 1989; Golombok et al., 2003). Some studies have found that sexual minorities may have less conventional parenting values than heterosexual women and men. Lesbian mothers appear to be less interested in fostering conformity in their children (Bos et al., 2007) and tend to have more gender-neutral preferences for their children's play, than do heterosexual mothers (Hoeffer, 1981). These findings may reflect lesbian mothers' greater interest in and acceptance of diversity (Tasker & Golombok, 1997).

Turning to child outcomes, children of LGB parents do not appear to differ from children of heterosexual parents in terms of self-esteem, depression, behavioral problems, or social functioning (Chan, Brooks, Raboy, & Patterson, 1998; Golombok et al., 2003; Tasker & Golombok, 1997). Some research suggests that children tend to demonstrate better adjustment when their lesbian mothers divide child care more equally (Chan et al., 1998), and that adolescents who perceive less stigma in their environments (associated with being a child of lesbian parents) may experience higher self-esteem (Gershon, Tschann, & Jemerin, 1999). Additionally, daughters with lesbian mothers may have higher aspirations to non-traditional gender occupations (Green, Mandel, Hotvedt, & Smith, 1986), and sons of lesbian mothers may behave in less traditionally masculine ways (Golombok, Spencer, & Rutter, 1983), possibly as a function of having two women as parents.

It is unclear whether differences observed between children of LGB parents and children of heterosexual parents are due to the gender of the parent(s), the sexuality of the parent(s), or other factors such as societal heterosexism. For example, it may be that having two female parents specifically frees children from a broad range of traditional gender prescriptions. Alternatively, some differences may be related to the sexual orientation of the parent. For example, as sexual minorities, LGB parents may be more open and affirming with regard to their children's questions about sexuality, which may facilitate greater sexual exploration (Tasker & Golombok, 1997). More research on LGB parents and their children is needed to tease apart potential pathways of influence.

Aging

Aging among LGB adults is understudied but important, in that LGB adults' midlife experiences may differ in certain ways from those of heterosexual adults (Kimmel & Sang, 2003). The work trajectories of lesbians and heterosexual women may diverge in midlife, with lesbians being more likely to continue to work into their older age, out of financial necessity and also because work is a core aspect of their identity (Hall & Gregory, 1991). Furthermore, the LGB community may represent an important source of affiliation as LGB adults age (Kimmel & Sang, 2003), especially for adults who lack support from their families of origin. Involvement in the community, then, may serve a protective function with regard to physical and mental health. Alternatively, of interest is the extent to which gay men, in particular, experience increasing isolation as they age, if they have lost a significant proportion of their social networks to AIDS. Finally, LGB parents' relationships with their own aging parents and with their adult children have rarely been studied. Such research is important in order to more fully map the changing life cycle of LGB adults and their families.

Case Study: A Lesbian Couple Considering Parenthood

Marianna and Evie are a lesbian couple, aged 32 and 35, who have been in a monogamous relationship for six years. Both women describe themselves as highly committed to the relationship. Marianna has been out to her family about her sexual orientation since she was in college whereas Evie came out to her parents five years ago in the context of meeting Marianna; this is her first lesbian relationship. Marianna is employed at the local university as head of residential life, while Evie owns and manages a restaurant.

Marianna and Evie presented for couples therapy because they wanted to have a child together, but had encountered several roadblocks that prevented them from moving forward. First, Evie reported that her family members had responded poorly to her coming out; in turn, she worried how they would respond to news that she was pursuing parenthood with Marianna. Marianna expressed frustration with Evie, urging her to consider the possibility that her family might never fully accept their relationship. Second, both partners were dissatisfied with the level of physical intimacy in their relationship, and worried that this would worsen upon becoming parents. Finally, both partners agreed that Marianna was "best suited" to carry the child, given her greater interest in being pregnant and her more flexible work schedule. But both women were concerned that this decision might carry negative consequences: specifically, Evie did not want to "feel like a dad," but wondered whether the demands of her job and her irregular work hours would keep her from being as involved as Marianna. Further, she worried that her parents would be uninterested in a child that was not biologically related to them.

The therapist, utilizing a systemic approach, was careful to consider the range of contextual forces that were currently impacting both individual and couple functioning. Further, she sought to communicate an authentically affirming stance with regard to this lesbian couple. The therapist began by articulating the couple's mutual and separate concerns. She encouraged Marianna to more fully appreciate Evie's worries about losing her family's support altogether. She also prompted Evie to consider the consequences of her (in)decision: by postponing her desire to become a parent, she maintained her family's low level of support; at the same time, she was resentful of the fact that she was sacrificing her own goals to "keep [her] parents happy." The therapist supported Evie in confronting (and mourning) the possibility of losing her family's support upon announcing her decision to parent with Marianna.

Additionally, she assisted Marianna and Evie in identifying their strengths as a couple (e.g., a strong commitment to the relationship) and as prospective parents, and helping them to recognize the varied resources that they had at their disposal, including a strong community of friends and Marianna's family. She also pushed them to address their intimacy concerns before they became parents, and initiated a series of conversations to help them explore their desires and fears regarding sexual intimacy. Finally, she affirmed their commitment to egalitarianism while acknowledging the potential for inequities to arise in the context of transitioning to parenthood. Relatedly, she encouraged both women to individually and collectively assess their work expectations and goals and to examine how they fit or did not fit with the goal of achieving parenthood.

Conclusions

The current chapter represents an examination of issues encountered by LGB individuals, parents, and families. Effort was made to attend to various contexts that impact the lives and changing life cycle of LGB adults and their families. Researchers and practitioners whose work exposes them to LGB families would benefit from a systemic, life-course approach. Consideration of the multiple contexts that shape the lives and trajectories of LGB adults and their families will enhance our understanding of LGB families specifically and the diversity of family forms in general. Future research should ideally attend to certain life stages (e.g., midlife) and contexts (e.g., the relationship between work and family life) as well as certain populations (e.g., gay fathers) that have received little attention in the study of LGB family psychology.

References

Alderson, K. (2004). A phenomenological investigation of same-sex marriage. *The Canadian Journal of Human Sexuality, 13*, 107–123.

Bigner, J. J., & Jacobsen, R. B. (1989). Parenting behaviors of homosexual and heterosexual fathers. *Journal of Homosexuality, 18*, 173–186.

Blumstein, P., & Schwartz, P. (1983). *American couples: Money, work, sex*. New York: William Morrow.

Bos, H. M. W., van Balen, F., & van den Boom, D. C. (2007). Child adjustment and parenting in planned lesbian-parent families. *American Journal of Orthopsychiatry, 77,* 38–48.

Bryant, A., & Demian (1994). Relationship characteristics of American gay and lesbian couples: Findings from a national survey. *Journal of Gay & Lesbian Social Services, 1,* 101–117.

Burch, B. (1985). Another perspective on merger in lesbian relationships. In L. B. Rosewater & L. E. Walker (Eds.), *Handbook of feminist therapy: Women's issues in psychotherapy* (pp. 100–109). New York: Springer.

Cass, V. C. (1979). Homosexual identity formation: Testing a theoretical model. *Journal of Homosexuality, 4,* 219–235.

Chan, R., Brooks, R., Raboy, B., & Patterson, C. (1998). Division of labor among lesbian and heterosexual parents: Associations with children's adjustment. *Journal of Family Psychology, 12,* 402–419.

Elizur, Y., & Mintzer, A. (2003). Gay males' intimate relationship quality: The roles of attachment security, gay identity, social support, and income. *Personal Relationships, 10,* 411–435.

Gartrell, N., Banks, A., Hamilton, J., Reed, N., Bishop, H., & Rodas, C. (1999). The National Lesbian Family Study: 2. Interviews with mothers of toddlers. *American Journal of Orthopsychiatry, 69,* 362–369.

Gershon, T., Tschann, J., & Jemerin, J. (1999). Stigmatization, self-esteem, and coping among the adolescent children of lesbian mothers. *Journal of Adolescent Health, 24,* 437–445.

Gilligan, C. (1982). *In a different voice: Psychological theory and women's development.* Cambridge, MA: Harvard University Press.

Goldberg, A. E. (2006). The transition to parenthood for lesbian couples. *Journal of GLBT Family Studies, 2,* 13–42.

Goldberg, A. E., Downing, J. B., & Sauck, C. C. (2007). Choices, challenges, and tensions: Perspectives of lesbian prospective adoptive parents. *Adoption Quarterly, 10,* 33–64.

Goldberg, A. E., & Perry-Jenkins, M. (2007). The division of labor and perceptions of parental roles: Lesbian couples across the transition to parenthood. *Journal of Social & Personal Relationships, 24,* 297–318.

Golombok, S., Perry, B., Burston, A., Murray, C., Mooney-Somers, J., Stevens, M., et al. (2003). Children with lesbian parents: A community study. *Developmental Psychology, 39,* 20–33.

Golombok, S., Spencer, A., & Rutter, M. (1983). Children in lesbian and single-parent households: Psychosexual and psychiatric appraisal. *Journal of Child Psychology and Psychiatry, 24,* 551–572.

Green, R., Mandel, J., Hotvedt, J., & Smith, L. (1986). Lesbian mothers and their children: A comparison with solo parent heterosexual mothers and their children. *Archives of Sexual Behavior, 15,* 167–184.

Greene, B. (2000). African American lesbian and bisexual women. *Journal of Social Issues, 56,* 239–249.

Hall, M., & Gregory, A. (1991). Subtle balances: Love and work in lesbian relationships. In B. Sang, J. Warshow, & A. Smith (Eds.), *Lesbians at midlife: The creative transition* (pp. 122–133). San Francisco: Spinsters.

Herek, G. M. (2006). Legal recognition of same-sex relationships in the United States: A social science perspective. *American Psychologist, 61,* 607–621.

Hoeffer, B. (1981). Children's acquisition of sex-role behavior in lesbian-mother families. *American Journal of Orthopsychiatry, 51,* 536–544.

James, S. E., & Murphy, B. C. (1998). Gay and lesbian relationships in a changing social context. In C. J. Patterson. and A. D'Augelli (Eds.), *Lesbian, gay, and bisexual identities in families: Psychological perspectives* (pp. 99–121). New York: Oxford University Press.

Kimmel, D., & Sang, B. (2003). Lesbians and gay men in midlife. In L. Garnets & D. Kimmel (Eds.), *Psychological perspectives on lesbian, gay, and bisexual experiences* (pp. 602–628). New York: Columbia University Press.

Kurdek, L. A. (1993). The allocation of household labor in gay, lesbian, and heterosexual married couples. *Journal of Social Issues, 49,* 127–139.

Kurdek, L. A. (1998). Relationship outcomes and their predictors: Longitudinal evidence from heterosexual married, gay cohabiting, and lesbian cohabiting couples. *Journal of Marriage & the Family, 60,* 553–568.

Kurdek, L. (2003). Differences between gay and lesbian cohabiting couples. *Journal of Social and Personal Relationships, 20,* 411–436.

Kurdek, L. A. (2006). Differences between partners from heterosexual, gay, and lesbian cohabiting couples. *Journal of Marriage and Family, 68,* 509–528.

Mackey, R. A., Diemer, M. A., & O'Brien, B. A. (2004). Relational factors in understanding satisfaction in the lasting relationships of same-sex and heterosexual couples. *Journal of Homosexuality, 47,* 111–136.

McDermott, E. (2006). Surviving in dangerous places: Lesbian identity performances in the workplace, social class, and psychological health. *Feminism & Psychology, 16,* 193–211.

McNeill, K., Rienzi, B., & Kposowa, A. (1998). Families and parenting: A comparison of lesbian and heterosexual mothers. *Psychological Reports, 82,* 59–62.

Oswald, R. (2002). Resilience within the family networks of lesbians and gay men: Intentionality and redefinition. *Journal of Marriage and Family, 64,* 374–383.

Patterson, C. J., Hurt, S., & Mason, C. D. (1998). Families of the lesbian baby boom: Children's contact with grandparents and other adults. *American Journal of Orthopsychiatry, 68,* 390–399.

Patterson, C. J., Sutfin, E. L., & Fulcher, M. (2004). Division of labor among lesbian and heterosexual parenting couples: Correlates of specialized versus shared patterns. *Journal of Adult Development, 11,* 179–189.

Pawelski, J. G., Perrin, E. C., Foy, J. M., Allen, C. E., Crawford, J. E., Del Monte, M., et al. (2006). The effects of marriage, civil union, and. domestic partnership laws on the health and well-being of children. *Pediatrics, 118,* 349–364.

Peel, E., & Harding, R. (2004). Divorcing romance, rights, and radicalism: Beyond pro and anti in the lesbian and gay marriage debate. *Feminism & Psychology, 14,* 588–599.

Peplau, L. A. (2003). Human sexuality: How do men and women differ? *Current Directions in Psychological Science, 12,* 37–40.

Ross, L., & Steele, L. (2006). Lesbian and bisexual women's recommendations for improving the provision of assisted reproductive technology services. *Fertility & Sterility, 86,* 735–738.

Solomon, S. E., Rothblum, E. D., & Balsam, K. (2004). Pioneers in partnership: Lesbian and gay male couples in civil unions compared with those not in civil unions, and married heterosexual siblings. *Journal of Family Psychology, 18,* 275–286.

Solomon, S. E., Rothblum, E. D., & Balsam, K. F. (2005). Money, housework, sex, and conflict: Same-sex couples in civil unions, those not in civil unions, and heterosexual married siblings. *Sex Roles, 52,* 561–575.

Tasker, F. L., & Golombok, S. (1997). *Growing up in a lesbian family: Effects on child development.* London: Guilford Press.

Whitechurch, G. G., & Constantine, L. L. (1993). Systems theory. In P. G. Boss, W. J. Doherty, R. LaRossa, W. R. Schumm, & S. K. Steinmetz (Eds.), *Sourcebook of family theories and methods: A contextual approach* (pp. 325–352). New York: Plenum.

41

The Psychology of Men and Masculinity

Ronald F. Levant and Christine M. Williams

Why Study the Psychology of Men?

Those not familiar with this new work sometimes ask: "Why do we need a psychology of men? Isn't all psychology the psychology of men?" The answer is: yes, males have historically been the focal point of most psychological research, but in studies that viewed males as representative of humanity as a whole. Feminist scholars challenged this traditional viewpoint by arguing for a gender-specific approach, and in the past 40 or so years, have rewritten the canon on the psychology of women. In the same spirit, men's studies scholars over about the past 25 years have begun to examine masculinity not as a proxy for all human behavior, but rather as a complex and problematic construct. In so doing, they have provided a framework for a psychological approach to men and masculinity that questions traditional norms of the male role, such as the emphasis on competition, status, toughness, and emotional stoicism, and views certain male problems (such as aggression and violence, devaluation of women, fear and hatred of homosexuals, detached fathering, and neglect of health needs) as unfortunate but predictable results of the male role socialization process. These scholars have also provided a framework for creating positive new definitions of masculinity that support the optimal development of men, women, and children.

This new psychology of men is both overdue and urgently needed. Men are disproportionately represented among many problem populations – substance abusers, the homeless, perpetrators of family and interpersonal violence, parents estranged from their children, sex addicts and sex offenders, victims of homicide, suicide, and fatal automobile accidents, and victims of lifestyle and stress-related fatal illnesses. A new psychology of men might contribute to the understanding and solution of some of these male problems which have long impacted women, men, children, and society in negative ways.

Moreover, due to long delays in dealing with many of these problems, we are currently experiencing a "crisis of connection" between men and women in the family (Levant, 1996). As a result, the pressures on men to behave in ways that conflict with various aspects of traditional masculinity ideology have never been greater. These new pressures – pressures to commit to relationships, to communicate one's innermost feelings, to nurture children, to share in housework, to integrate sexuality with love, and to curb aggression and violence – have shaken traditional masculinity ideology to such an extent there is now a "masculinity crisis" in which many feel bewildered and confused, and the pride associated with being a man is lower than at any time in the recent past (Levant, 1997). Some men are gravitating to organizations such as the Promise Keepers (Promise Keepers, 1994) and the Fatherhood Initiative (Blankenhorn, 1995), which propose to return the male to his "rightful place" as the "leader of his family" by rolling back the gains of the women's movement. A new psychology of men might help men find solutions to the masculinity crisis and the crisis of connection that enhance rather than inflame gender relations, and provide them with tools for the reconstruction of the traditional male code (Levant & Kopecky, 1995).

The purpose of this chapter is to introduce this field to family psychologists. We will cover the gender role strain paradigm, masculinity ideology, and the three varieties of male gender role strain – discrepancy strain, dysfunction strain, and trauma strain, with a particular emphasis on the trauma of normative emotion socialization.

The Gender Role Strain Paradigm

The new psychology of men views gender roles not as biological or even social "givens," but rather as psychologically and socially constructed entities that bring certain advantages and disadvantages, and, most importantly, can change. This perspective acknowledges the biological differences between men and women, but argues that it is not the biological differences of sex that make for "masculinity" and "femininity." These notions are socially constructed from bits and pieces of biological, psychological, and social experience to serve particular purposes. Western traditional constructions of gender serve patriarchal purposes; other constructions, such as Gilmore (1990) described among the Tahitians and the Semai, serve more equalitarian purposes.

The Gender Role Strain paradigm, originally formulated by Joseph Pleck in *The Myth of Masculinity* (1981), is the forerunner, in the psychology of men, of social constructionism, and of modern critical thinking about masculinity, having been formulated before social constructionism emerged as a new perspective on masculinity (Pleck, 1995). Pleck demonstrated that the paradigm which had dominated the research on masculinity for 50 years (1930–1980) – the Gender Role Identity Paradigm – not only poorly accounts for the observed data, but also promotes the patriarchal bifurcation of society on the basis of stereotyped gender roles. In its place, Pleck proposed the Gender Role Strain Paradigm.

The older Gender Role Identity Paradigm assumed that people have an inner psychological need to have a gender role identity, and that optimal personality development hinged on its formation. The extent to which this "inherent" need is met is determined by how completely a person embraces their traditional gender role. From such a perspective, the development of appropriate gender role identity is viewed as a failure-prone process; and failure for men to achieve a masculine gender role identity is thought to result in homosexuality, negative attitudes toward women, or defensive hypermasculinity. This paradigm springs from the same philosophical roots as the "essentialist" or "nativist" view of sex roles – the notion that (in the case of men) there is a clear masculine "essence" that is historically invariant.

In contrast, the Gender Role Strain Paradigm proposes that contemporary gender roles are contradictory and inconsistent; that the proportion of persons who violate gender roles is high; that violation of gender roles leads to condemnation and negative psychological consequences; that actual or imagined violation of gender roles leads people to over-conform to them; that violating gender roles has more severe consequences for males than for females; and that certain prescribed gender role traits (such as male aggression) are often dysfunctional. In this paradigm, appropriate gender roles are determined by the prevailing gender ideology (which is operationally defined by gender role stereotypes and norms), and are imposed on the developing child by parents, teachers, and peers – the cultural transmitters who subscribe to the prevailing gender ideology. As noted above, this paradigm springs from the same philosophical roots as social constructionism – the perspective that notions of "masculinity" and femininity" are relational, socially constructed, and subject to change.

Masculinity Ideology

Thompson and Pleck (1995) proposed the term "masculinity ideology" to characterize the core construct in the corpus of research assessing attitudes toward men and male roles. Masculinity, or gender, ideology is a very different construct from the older notion of gender orientation. Gender orientation arises out of the Identity Paradigm, and "presumes that masculinity is rooted in actual differences between men and women" (Thompson & Pleck, 1995, p. 130). This approach has attempted to assess the personality *traits* more often associated with men than women, using such instruments as the Bem Sex Role Inventory (Bem, 1974) and the Personal Attributes Questionnaire (Spence & Helmreich, 1978). In contrast, studies of masculinity ideology take a *normative* approach, in which masculinity is viewed as a socially constructed gender ideal for men. Whereas the masculine male in the orientation/trait approach is one who *possesses* particular personality traits, the traditional male in the ideology/normative approach "is one who endorses the ideology that men *should* have sex-specific characteristics (and women should not)" (Thompson & Pleck, 1995, p. 131). Thompson and Pleck (1995) adduced evidence to supports the notion that gender orientation and gender ideologies are independent and have different correlates.

Masculinity ideologies

The Strain Paradigm asserts that there is no single standard for masculinity nor is there an unvarying masculinity ideology. Rather, since masculinity is a social construction, ideals of manhood may differ for men of different social classes, races, ethnic groups, sexual orientations, life stages, and historical eras. Following Brod (1987), we therefore prefer to speak of masculinity ideolog*ies*. To illustrate, consider these brief descriptions of varying male codes among four ethnic-minority groups in the contemporary United States:

> African-American males have adopted distinctive actions and attitudes known as *cool pose* . . . Emphasizing honor, virility, and physical strength, the Latino male adheres to a code of *machismo* . . . The American-Indian male struggles to maintain contact with a way of life and the traditions of elders while faced with economic castration and political trauma . . . Asian-American men resolve uncertainty privately in order to save face and surrender personal autonomy to family obligations and needs. (Lazur & Majors, 1995, p. 338)

Traditional masculinity ideology

Despite the diversity in masculinity ideology in the contemporary USA, Pleck (1995, p. 20) points out that "there is a *particular* constellation of standards and expectations that individually and jointly have various kinds of negative concomitants." It is common to refer to this as "traditional" masculinity ideology, since it was the dominant view prior to the deconstruction of gender that took place beginning in the 1970s.

Traditional masculinity ideology is thought to be a multidimensional construct. Brannon (David & Brannon, 1976) identified four components of traditional masculinity ideology: that men should not be feminine (labeled by Brannon "no sissy stuff"); that men should strive to be respected for successful achievement ("the big wheel"); that men should never show weakness ("the sturdy oak"); and that men should seek adventure and risk, even accepting violence if necessary ("give 'em hell"). These dimensions are assessed by the Brannon Masculinity Scale (Brannon & Juni, 1984).

Later, Levant et al. (1992) developed the Male Role Norms Inventory (MRNI), which defined traditional masculinity ideology in terms of seven dimensions: the requirement to avoid all things feminine; the injunction to restrict one's emotional life; the emphasis on toughness and aggression; the injunction to be self-reliant; the emphasis on achieving status above all else; non-relational, objectifying attitudes toward sexuality; and fear and hatred of homosexuals. A recent review of 15 years of research on the MRNI has shown that gender ideologies vary across a wide range of social location and cultural contextual variables, suggesting that gender roles are not to be regarded as "given," either psychologically or biologically, but rather as socially constructed (Levant & Richmond, 2007).

Types of Male Gender Role Strain

Pleck (1995), in an update on the Gender Role Strain Paradigm, pointed out that his original formulation of the paradigm stimulated research on three varieties of male gender role strain, which he termed "discrepancy-strain," "dysfunction strain," and "trauma strain." Discrepancy strain results when one fails to live up to one's internalized manhood ideal, which, among contemporary adult males, is often a close approximation of the traditional code. Dysfunction strain results even when one fulfills the requirements of the male code, because many of the characteristics viewed as desirable in men can have negative side effects on the men themselves and on those close to them. Trauma strain results from the ordeal of the male role socialization process, which is now recognized as inherently traumatic.

Discrepancy strain

There have been multiple ways to examine discrepancy strain. The first method used a comparison between ratings of the old self and the ideal self, and was not very useful (Pleck, 1995). A more productive approach inquired whether the experience of particular gender discrepancies as conflictual or stressful existed. Two major research programs have used this approach: O'Neil's (O'Neil, Helms, Gable, Davis, & Wrightsman, 1986) work on male gender role conflict, and Eisler and Skidmore's (1987) work on masculine gender role stress.

Male gender role conflict.   The centerpiece of this research program is an empirically derived measure of male gender role conflict, the Gender Role Conflict Scale I (GRCS-I), which is a 37-item scale in which respondents are asked to report the degree to which they agree or disagree with statements, using a 6-point Likert scale. The GRCS-I assesses four domains of gender role conflict in men: (1) Success, Power, and Competition; (2) Restrictive Emotionality; (3) Restrictive Affectionate Behavior Between Men; and (4) Conflict Between Work and Family Relations. O'Neil, Good, and Holmes (1995) summarized the results of 15 years of work on gender role conflict, which included 34 studies using the GRCS-I. The four domains of gender role conflict vary in complex ways with demographic, personality, psychological health, and relational variables. The authors concluded that gender role conflict is a documented area of difficulty for men which is hazardous to their mental health because it is associated with anxiety and depression.

Masculine gender role stress.   Research using the Masculine Gender Role Stress Scale (MGRSS), based on the cognitive stress model (Lazarus & Folkman, 1984), focused on men's health. The MGRSS consists of a 40-item scale in which respondents report on a 6-point scale how stressful various situations would be if they happened to them. Five subscales, derived by factor analysis, assess situations which are common in men's lives, and which are hypothetically more stressful for men than women: (1) Physical Inadequacy; (2) Expressing Emotions; (3) Subordination to Women; (4) Experiencing a Threat to a Male's Intellectual Control; and (5) Performance Failures in Work and Sex. Eisler (1995) summarized the work on the MGRSS, describing the associations between the MGRSS, its component factors, anger, anxiety, health habits, health problems, and emotional expressiveness. The author concluded that there is a significant relationship between masculine gender role stress and cardiovascular reactivity, which suggests that masculinity may play a role in illness. Findings such as this one may play an important role in improving men's cardiovascular health and in reducing their mortality ratesas compared to those for similarly aged women.

Dysfunction strain

Dysfunction strain theory suggests that the fulfillment of the requirements of the male code can be dysfunctional because many of the characteristics viewed as desirable in men can have negative side effects on the men themselves and on those close to them. Pleck's (1995) review of research on dysfunction strain found that is negatively associated with masculine gender-related personality traits on the one hand, and lack of involvement in family roles on the other hand. As examples of the latter, Barnett, Marshall, and Pleck (1991) found that the quality of both men's marital role and their parental role is a significant predictor of men's psychological distress; and Barnett, Davidson, and Marshall (1991) found that the quality of men's parental role, but not that of their marital role, is a significant predictor of men's physical health.

Brooks and Silverstein (1995), in a far-reaching discussion of the "dark side" of masculinity, provide a taxonomy of the problems that result from over-conformity to traditional masculine norms, and thus are examples of dysfunction strain. These are significant social and public health problems that Brooks and Silverstein (1995) argue result from adherence to traditional masculinity. These problems include: (1) violence, including male violence against women in the family, rape and sexual assault, and sexual harassment; (2) sexual excess, including promiscuity, involvement with pornography, and sexual addiction; (3) socially irresponsible behaviors, including chemical dependence, risk-seeking behavior, physical self-abuse, absent fathering, and homelessness/vagrancy; and (4) relationship dysfunctions, including inadequate emotional partnering, non-nurturing fathering, and non-participative household partnering. Brooks and Silverstein's argument has some empirical support. The endorsement of traditional masculinity ideology as measured by the MRNI was found to be associated with a range of problematic individual and relational variables, including reluctance to discuss condom use with partners, fear of intimacy, lower relationship satisfaction, more negative beliefs about the fathers' role and lower paternal participation in child care, negative attitudes toward racial diversity and women's equality, attitudes conducive to sexual harassment, self-reports of sexual aggression, lower forgiveness of racial discrimination, alexithymia and related constructs, and reluctance to seek psychological help (Levant & Richmond, 2007).

Trauma strain

The concept of trauma strain has been applied to certain groups of men whose experiences with gender role strain are thought to be particularly harsh. This includes professional athletes (Messner, 1992), Vietnam veterans (Brooks, 1990), and survivors of child abuse, including sexual abuse (Lisak, 1995). It is also being recognized that gay and bisexual men are traumatized by male gender role strain by virtue of growing up in a heterosexist society (Harrison, 1995). Clinical work with male trauma-strain victims is enhanced by recent analyses of the role of shame in trauma (Krugman, 1995). Beyond the recognition that certain classes of men may experience trauma strain, a perspective on the male role socialization process emerged in the mid-1990s (Levant & Pollack, 1995) that viewed socialization under traditional masculinity ideology as *inherently* traumatic. In this view, contemporary adult men grew up in an era when traditional masculinity ideology held sway. According to the tenets of the Gender Role Strain Paradigm, growing up male under these conditions was an ordeal which had traumatic consequences. We will briefly review the research supporting this perspective, covering gender role socialization using the lens of social learning theory.

Gender role socialization: The ordeal of emotion socialization

Due to biologically based differences, males start out life more emotionally expressive than females. Haviland and Malatesta (1981), reviewing data from 12 studies (11 of which were of neonates), concluded that male infants are more emotionally reactive and expressive than their female counterparts. Boys remain more emotional than girls until at least 6 months of age. Weinberg (1992, p. vii) found that 6-month-old boys exhibited "significantly more joy and anger, more positive vocalizations, fussiness, and crying, [and] more gestural signals directed towards the mother . . . than girls." Despite this initial advantage in emotional expressivity, males learn to tune out, suppress, and channel their emotions, whereas the emotion socialization of females encourages their expressivity. Therefore, infant reactions begin to align with cultural expectations within the first year of life (Malatesta & Haviland, 1982).

How can we account for this "crossover in emotional expression" (Haviland & Malatesta, 1981, p. 16), such that boys start out more emotional than girls, and wind up, as adults, much less so? Using a social learning model, Levant and Kopecky (1995) propose that four socialization influences result in the suppression and channeling of male emotionality:

1   *Mothers* work harder to manage their more excitable and emotional male infants (Garner, Robertson, & Smith, 1997; Haviland & Malatesta, 1981; Kuebli & Fivush, 1992; Malatesta, Culver, Tesman, & Shephard, 1989; Tronick & Cohn, 1989).
2   *Fathers* take an active interest in their children after the thirteenth month of life (Lamb, 1977), and from that point on socialize their toddler sons and daughters along

gender-stereotyped lines (Garner et al., 1997; Greif, Alvarez, & Ulman, 1981; Lamb, Owen, & Chase-Lansdale, 1979; Schell & Gleason, 1989; Siegal, 1987), particularly when the father himself adheres to highly stereotyped beliefs about gender (Plant, Hyde, Keltner, & Divine, 2000).

3   Both parents participate in the gender-differentiated *development of language* for emotions. Parents discourage their son's learning to express vulnerable emotions (such as sadness and fear); and, while they encourage their daughters to learn to express their vulnerable and caring emotions (such as warmth and affection), they discourage their expression of anger and aggression (Brody & Hall, 1993; Casey & Fuller, 1994; Dunn, Bretherton, & Munn, 1987; Eisenberg, Cumberland, & Spinrad, 1998; Fivush, 1989; Fuchs & Thelen, 1988; Greif et al., 1981; Kuebli & Fivush, 1992).

4   Sex-segregated *peer groups* complete the job. Young girls typically play with one or two other girls, and their play consists of maintaining the relationship and telling each other secrets, thus fostering their learning emotional skills of empathy, emotional self-awareness, and emotional expressivity. In contrast, young boys typically play in larger groups in structured games, in which action skills such as learning to play by the rules, teamwork, stoicism, toughness, and competition are learned (Lever, 1976; Maccoby, 1990; Paley, 1984).

The suppression and channeling of male emotionality by mothers, fathers, and peer groups has four major consequences. First, men develop a form of empathy which Levant & Kopecky (1995) referred to as "action empathy," which can be defined as the ability to see things from another person's point of view, and predict what they will *do*. On the other hand men do not develop (as fully as do women) emotional empathy, which can be defined as taking another person's perspective and being able to know how they *feel* (Brody & Hall, 1993; Eisenberg & Lennon, 1983; Hall, 1978). Second, men become strangers to their own emotional life, and many develop at least a mild form of alexithymia (which literally means "without words for emotions") (Allen & Haccoun, 1976; Balswick & Avertt, 1977; Brody & Hall, 1993; Levant & Kopecky, 1995; Stapley & Haviland, 1989). Third, men experience and express more aggression than women (Eagly & Steffen, 1986; Frodi, Macaulay, & Thome, 1977) and also tend to transform their vulnerable emotions into anger which is expressed aggressively (Levant & Kopecky, 1995; Long, 1987). Fourth, men shunt their caring emotions through the channel of sexuality (Brooks, 1995; Hudson & Jacot, 1991; Levant & Kopecky, 1995).

Thus, under the influence of traditional masculinity ideology, the emotion socialization of boys can be an ordeal with traumatic consequences. We will now turn to a discussion of the implications for family psychologists.

Implications for Family Psychologists

This chapter introduced the psychology of men to family psychologists, reviewing the gender role strain paradigm, masculinity ideology, and the three varieties of male gender role strain. It is the authors' hope that this work will open up new areas for assessment, intervention, and applied research, in order to provide improved family psychological services to men that might contribute to the solution of both the contemporary masculinity crisis and the crisis of connection between men and women.

Specifically, the clinician should be aware that some men have learned to measure themselves using the yardstick of traditional masculinity ideology, and as a result may experience discrepancy strain, in either of two forms: gender role conflict, which has been associated with mental health problems such as anxiety and depression; or gender role stress, which has been associated with cardiovascular reactivity, a risk factor for cardiac illness. Patients suspected of suffering from discrepancy strain could be assessed using the available instruments (the GRCS-I or the MGRSS). Treatment of discrepancy strain might include an examination of the standards that the patient holds in measuring himself.

With regard to dysfunction strain, some aspects of traditionally prescribed male role behavior may have negative consequences, which can be categorized under the headings of violence, sexual excess, socially irresponsible behaviors, and relationship dysfunctions. If your patient presents with one or more of these forms of dysfunction strain, treatment might include an examination of the patient's manhood ideals, and the relationship between these internalized standards and the problematic behavior.

Finally, in regard to trauma strain, we have cited work directed toward particular groups of men whose gender role strain is likely to be severe. With regard to the normative trauma of growing up male, psychoeducational techniques have been developed for the treatment of normative male alexithymia (Levant, 1998) that may be useful in the beginning stages of treatment with men who cannot put their feelings into words.

Note

This is an updated version of an earlier publication, Levant, R. (1996). The new psychology of men. *Professional Psychology, 27*, 259–265. Published with permission.

References

Allen, J. G., & Haccoun, D. M. (1976). Sex differences in emotionality: A multidimensional approach. *Human Relations, 29*, 711–722.

Balswick, J., & Avertt, C. P. (1977). Differences in expressiveness: Gender, interpersonal orientation, and perceived parental expressiveness as contributing factors. *Journal of Marriage and the Family, 39*, 121–127.

Barnett, R. C., Davidson, H., & Marshall, N. (1991). Physical symptoms and the interplay of work and family roles. *Health Psychology, 10*, 94–101.

Barnett, R. C., Marshall, N., & Pleck, J. (1991). Men's multiple roles and their relationship to men's psychological distress. *Journal of Marriage and the Family, 54*, 348–367.

Bem, S. L. (1974). The measurement of psychological androgyny. *Journal of Personality and Social Psychology, 42*, 155–162.

Blankenhorn, D. (1995). *Fatherless America: Confronting our most urgent social problem.* New York: Basic Books.

Brannon, R., & Juni, S. (1984). A scale for measuring attitudes about masculinity. *Psychological Documents, 14(1).* (University Microfilms No. 2612).

Brod, H. (1987). *The making of the masculinities: The new men's studies.* Boston: Unwin Hyman.

Brody, L., & Hall, J. (1993). Gender and emotion. In M. Lewis & J. M. Haviland (Eds.), *Handbook of emotions* (pp. 447–460). New York: Guilford Press.

Brooks, G. R. (1990). Post-Vietnam gender role strain: A needed concept? *Professional Psychology: Research and Practice, 21,* 18–25.

Brooks, G. R. (1995). *The centerfold syndrome.* San Francisco: Jossey-Bass.

Brooks, G. R., & Silverstein, L. S. (1995). Understanding the dark side of masculinity: An interactive systems model. In R. F. Levant & W. S. Pollack (Eds.), *A new psychology of men* (pp. 280–333). New York: Basic Books.

Casey, R. J., & Fuller, L. L. (1994). Maternal regulation of children's emotions. *Journal of Nonverbal Behavior, 18,* 57–89.

David, D., & Brannon, R. (Eds.). (1976). *The forty-nine percent majority: The male sex role.* Reading, MA: Addison-Wesley.

Dunn, J., Bretherton, I., & Munn, P. (1987). Conversations about feeling states between mothers and their children. *Developmental Psychology, 23,* 132–139.

Eagly, A. H., & Steffen, V. J. (1986). Gender and aggressive behavior: A meta-analytic review of the social psychological literature. *Psychological Bulletin, 100,* 309–330.

Eisenberg, N., Cumberland, A., & Spinrad, T. L. (1998). Parental socialization of emotion. *Psychological Inquiry, 9,* 241–273.

Eisenberg, N., & Lennon, R. (1983). Sex differences in empathy and related capacities. *Psychological Bulletin, 94,* 100–131.

Eisler, R. M. (1995). The relationship between masculine gender role stress and men's health risk: The validation of a construct. In R. F. Levant & W. S. Pollack (Eds.), *A new psychology of men* (pp. 207–225). New York: Basic Books.

Eisler, R. M., & Skidmore, J. R. (1987). Masculine gender role stress: Scale development and component factors in the appraisal of stressful situations. *Behavior Modification, 11,* 123–136.

Fivush, R. (1989). Exploring sex differences in the emotional content of mother–child conversations about the past. *Sex Roles, 20,* 675–691.

Frodi, A., Macaulay, J., & Thome, P. R. (1977). Are women always less aggressive than men? A review of the experimental literature. *Psychological Bulletin, 84,* 634–660.

Fuchs, D., & Thelen, M. (1988). Children's expected interpersonal consequences of communicating their affective state and reported likelihood of expression. *Child Development, 59,* 1314–1322.

Garner, P. W., Robertson, S., & Smith, G. (1997). Preschool children's emotional expressions with peers: The roles of gender and emotion socialization. *Sex Roles, 36,* 675–691.

Gilmore, D. (1990). *Manhood in the making: Cultural concepts of masculinity.* New Haven: Yale University Press.

Greif, E. B., Alvarez, M., & Ulman, K. (1981, April). *Recognizing emotions in other people: Sex differences in socialization.* Paper presented at meeting of the Society for Research in Child Development, Boston.

Hall, J. A. (1978). Gender effects in decoding nonverbal cues. *Psychological Bulletin, 85,* 845–857.

Harrison, J. (1995). Roles, identities, and sexual orientation: Homosexuality, heterosexuality, and bisexuality. In R. F. Levant & W. S. Pollack (Eds.), *A new psychology of men* (pp. 359–382). New York: Basic Books.

Haviland, J. J., & Malatesta, C. Z. (1981). The development of sex differences in nonverbal signals: Fallacies, facts, and fantasies. In C. Mayo & N. M. Henly (Eds.), *Gender and non-verbal behavior* (pp. 183–208). New York: Springer.

Hudson, L., & Jacot, B. (1991). *The way men think: Intellect, intimacy, and the erotic imagination.* New Haven: Yale University Press.

Krugman, S. (1995). Male development and the transformation of shame. In R. F. Levant & W. S. Pollack (Eds.), *A new psychology of men* (pp. 91–126). New York: Basic Books.

Kuebli, J., & Fivush, R. (1992). Gender differences in parent–child conversations about past emotions. *Sex Roles, 27*, 683–698.

Lamb, M. E. (1977). The development of parental preferences in the first two years of life. *Sex Roles, 3*, 475–497.

Lamb, M. E., Owen, M. J., & Chase-Lansdale, L. (1979). The father–daughter relationship: Past, present, and future. In C. B. Knopp & M. Kirkpatrick (Eds.), *Becoming female* (pp. 89–112). New York: Plenum.

Lazarus, R., & Folkman, S. (1984). *Stress, appraisal, and coping,* New York: Springer.

Lazur, R. F., & Majors, R. (1995). Men of color: Ethnocultural variations of male gender role strain. In R. F. Levant & W. S. Pollack (Eds.), *A new psychology of men* (pp. 337–358). New York: Basic Books.

Levant, R. (1996). The crisis of connection between men and women. *Journal of Men's Studies, 5*, 1–12.

Levant, R. (1997). The masculinity crisis. *Journal of Men's Studies, 5*, 221–231.

Levant, R. (1998). Desperately seeking language: Understanding, assessing and treating normative male alexithymia. In W. Pollack & R. Levant (Eds.), *New psychotherapy for men* (pp. 35–56). New York: Wiley.

Levant, R. F., Hirsch, L., Celentano, E., Cozza, T., Hill, S., MacEachern, M., et al. (1992). The male role: An investigation of norms and stereotypes. *Journal of Mental Health Counseling, 14*, 325–337.

Levant, R. F., & Kopecky, G. (1995). *Masculinity, reconstructed.* New York: Dutton.

Levant, R. F., & Pollack, W. S. (Eds.). (1995). *A new psychology of men.* New York: Basic Books.

Levant, R. F., & Richmond, K. (2007). A review of research on masculinity ideologies using the Male Role Norms Inventory. *Journal of Men's Studies, 15*, 130–146.

Lever, J. (1976). Sex differences in the games children play. *Social Work, 23*, 78–87.

Lisak, D. (1995). *Integrating gender analysis in psychotherapy with male survivors of abuse.* Paper presented at the 103rd Annual Convention of the American Psychological Association, New York.

Long, D. (1987). Working with men who batter. In M. Scher, M. Stevens, G. Good, & G. A. Eichenfield (Eds.), *Handbook of counseling and psychotherapy with men* (pp. 305–320). Newbury Park, CA: Sage.

Maccoby, E. E. (1990). Gender and relationships: A developmental account. *American Psychologist, 45*, 513–520.

Malatesta, C. Z., Culver, C., Tesman, J., & Shephard, B. (1989). The development of emotion expression during the first two years of life. *Monographs of the Society for Research in Child Development, 50* (1–2, Serial No. 219).

Malatesta, C. Z., & Haviland, J. M. (1982). Learning display rules: The socialization of emotion expression in infancy. *Child Development, 53*, 991–1003.

Messner, M. A. (1992). *Power at play: Sports and the problem of masculinity.* Boston: Beacon Press.

O'Neil, J. M., Good, G. E., & Holmes, S. (1995). Fifteen years of theory and research on men's gender role conflict: New paradigms for empirical research. In R. F. Levant & W. S. Pollack (Eds.), *A new psychology of men* (pp. 164–206). New York: Basic Books.

O'Neil, J. M., Helms, B. J., Gable, R. K., David, L., & Wrightsman, L. (1986). Gender Role Conflict Scale: College men's fear of femininity. *Sex Roles, 14,* 335–350.

Paley, V. G. (1984). *Boys and girls: Superheroes in the doll corner.* Chicago: University of Chicago Press.

Plant, E. A., Hyde, J. S., Keltner, D., & Divine, P. G. (2000). The gender stereotyping of emotions. *Psychology of Women Quarterly, 24,* 81–92.

Pleck, J. H. (1981). *The myth of masculinity.* Cambridge, MA: MIT Press.

Pleck, J. H. (1995). The gender role strain paradigm: An update. In R. F. Levant & W. S. Pollack (Eds.), *A new psychology of men* (pp. 11–32). New York: Basic Books.

Promise Keepers. (1994). *Seven promises of a promise keeper.* Colorado Springs, CO: Focus on the Family.

Schell, A., & Gleason, J. B. (1989). *Gender differences in the acquisition of the vocabulary of emotion.* Paper presented at the annual meeting of the American Association of Applied Linguistics, Washington, DC.

Siegal, M. (1987). Are sons and daughters treated more differently by fathers than by mothers? *Developmental Review, 7,* 183–209.

Spence, J. T., & Helmreich, R. L. (1978). *Masculinity and femininity: Their psychological dimensions, correlates, and antecedents.* Austin: University of Texas Press.

Stapley, J. C., & Haviland, J. M. (1989). Beyond depression: Gender differences in normal adolescents' emotional experiences. *Sex Roles, 20,* 295–308.

Thompson, E. H., & Pleck, J. H. (1995). Masculinity ideology: A review of research instrumentation on men and masculinities. In R. F. Levant & W. S. Pollack (Eds.), *A new psychology of men* (pp. 129–163). New York: Basic Books.

Tronick, E. Z., & Cohn, J. F. (1989). Infant–mother face-to-face interaction: Age and gender differences in coordination and the occurrence of miscoordination. *Child Development, 60,* 85–92.

Weinberg, M. K. (1992). *Sex differences in 6-month-old infants' affect and behavior: Impact on maternal caregiving.* Unpublished doctoral dissertation, University of Massachusetts.

42

Religion and Spirituality in Couple and Family Relations

Froma Walsh

Religion and spirituality can be vital resources to strengthen relationships, healing, and resilience. Spiritual distress can increase suffering and block recovery. Yet the spiritual dimension of human experience has been neglected in mental health and healthcare training and services. This chapter addresses the significant influence of religion and spirituality for couples and families over the family life cycle and in light of cultural and religious diversity. Research on spiritual influences in suffering, healing, and resilience is noted. Clinical guidelines are offered to facilitate a bio-psycho-social-spiritual approach to family psychology practice.

Religion and Spirituality

To consider the meaning and significance of religion and spirituality in contemporary family life it is important to clarify our understanding of these terms, which are often used interchangeably. Most research in the USA has focused on religious beliefs, practices, and denominational affiliation (e.g., Gallup & Lindsey, 1999; Pew Forum on Religion & Public Life, 2008) and has been Euro-Christian centered. More recently, attention has been turning to spirituality, a broader and more personal construct, as North Americans, with growing diversity, increasingly shape their own spiritual pathways.

Religion

Religion can be defined as an organized belief system with an institutionalized structure, sacred texts and teachings, rituals and practices, clergy, and congregation. Religious teachings provide a value system that serves as a moral compass to guide actions and relationships. Rituals and ceremonies carry profound significance, connecting family members with their larger community and its history and heritage. Faith communities offer involvement in shared faith practices, as well as pastoral care and congregational support in times of need. For one in three Americans, religion is the most important part of their lives: they receive a great deal of comfort from it and are far more likely to feel close to their families, to find their jobs fulfilling, and to be hopeful about the future (Gallup & Lindsey, 1999).

Spirituality

Spirituality, an overarching construct, is a dimension of human experience involving an active investment in transcendent values and practices. Like culture or ethnicity, spirituality involves streams of experience that flow through all aspects of life, from family and cultural heritage to personal belief systems and practices in everyday life.

Spirituality is the heart and soul of religion (Pargament, 2007). It can also be experienced outside religious affiliation. Many people who do not participate in congregational life are deeply spiritual, viewing their faith as a matter between themselves and God. Personal spiritual resources might include practices of prayer, meditation, or traditional faith-healing rituals. Spiritual nourishment is found in varied ways, even by those who do not consider themselves "religious." Many experience renewal and connection through nature and the creative arts; many find meaning and purpose through secular humanism, service to others, and social activism. Spirituality is expressed most immediately in deep, loving bonds in couple and family relationships.

One simple yet profound definition of spirituality is "that which connects one to all there is" (Griffith & Griffith, 2002). It fosters a sense of meaning, wholeness, harmony, and connection with others – a unity with all life, nature, and the universe. One's spirituality may involve belief in a supreme being, a divine spirit within all living things, or an ultimate human condition toward which we strive. Morality, a related concept, involves the activity of informed conscience orienting lives and judging right or wrong, on the basis of principles of fairness, decency, and compassion (Doherty, 2009; see also Chapter 44, this volume). Spirituality invites an expansion of consciousness, along with responsibility for and beyond oneself, from local to global concerns. It fosters generosity and compassion for the suffering of others, expressed through service to those in need and social activism to improve life conditions or alleviate injustice (Perry & Rolland, 2009). In turn, such actions to benefit others deepen one's spiritual essence.

Spiritual Pluralism: Intertwining of Cultural and Religious Influences

The religious landscape has been changing dramatically over recent decades. While the USA remains primarily Christian, and largely Protestant, membership has been shifting from mainline denominations to evangelical churches. Non-Christians of many faiths increased from 4% in 1900 to over 15% by 2000. Nearly 2% identify as Jewish, varying from orthodox, conservative, and reform movements to secular humanism and cultural bonds. Buddhists, Muslims, and Hindus, each over 1%, are increasing. Only 4% are agnostic or atheist, many of whom practice nature-based spiritualities. Many Americans combine indigenous traditions or eastern teachings, such as Buddhist meditation practices, with Christian or Jewish faiths.

Religion and culture are interwoven in all aspects of spiritual experience and family life. A resurgence of Native American spirituality is reconnecting youth with their cultural and religious heritage (Deloria, 1994). African Americans of all faiths are the most religious of all groups and turn to their congregations for strength in dealing with adversity (Boyd-Franklin & Lockwood, 2009). Latinos, in growing numbers, are reshaping the Catholic church and many are turning to evangelical Christian churches (particularly Pentecostal and Charismatic) for more direct experience of God (Pew Hispanic Project and the Pew Forum on Religion & Public Life, 2007). Recent immigrants, particularly from Latin America, Asia, and Africa, may also draw on traditional spiritual beliefs and healing methods for physical or emotional problems, often alongside western approaches (Falicov, 2009).

It is important not to link ethnicity and religion reflexively. For instance, only one third of Arab Americans are Muslim. Spiritual beliefs and practices also vary with age cohorts, ethnic groups, social classes, and urban or rural settings. Families in impoverished, largely minority communities rely most strongly on their faith, their relationship with God, and their congregational involvement to counter despair at blighted conditions and injustices (Aponte, 2009).

We must also be cautious not to assume that particular individuals or families adhere to all precepts of their religion. Most Americans are very independent in their beliefs and practices. For instance, although the Catholic church condemns abortion, over 60% of Catholics believe that those who have abortions can still be good Catholics (Gallup & Lindsey, 1999). Personal attitudes about social issues vary widely within and across religions. Generational differences can fuel tensions within families.

In our rapidly changing society, religion is less often a given that people are born into and accept unquestioningly. More often, Americans are seeking and shaping their own meaningful spiritual paths within and outside formal religion. With increasing diversity, religious conversion, and interfaith marriage, multifaith families are blending spiritual traditions and creating new ones to fit their lives and relationships.

Spirituality in Family Life

Over recent decades, Americans have been seeking greater meaning, harmony, and connection in their lives. Families have experienced tumultuous social and economic dislocations, as well as disruptive changes in the structure of relationships and households. With the frantic pace of overscheduled lives and the saturation of pop culture and consumerism, some couples and families yearn to share a deeper spiritual fulfillment. In response to major disasters, war, and terrorism, many turn with heightened urgency to their loved ones and to their faith for meaning, consolation, and strength in facing an uncertain future (Walsh, 2003, 2006).

Family process research has found that transcendent spiritual beliefs and practices are key variables in healthy marital and family functioning (Beavers & Hampson, 2003). Just as individuals survive and prosper within significant relationships, families thrive when connected to yet larger systems. A transcendent value system enables members to define their lives and relationships as meaningful and significant.

A system of values and a shared worldview that transcend the limits of personal experience enable family members to better accept the inevitable risks and losses in living and loving fully. Members can view their particular reality, which may be painful, uncertain, and frightening, from a larger perspective that makes some sense of events, fosters hope, and strengthens their bonds and common humanity with all others.

Spirituality Across the Family Life Cycle

Spirituality, intimacy, and family life are deeply intertwined. Faith is inherently relational: from early in life, when the most fundamental meanings about life are shaped within caregiving relationships, convictional faith is forged with others. Caring for and about others sustains lives and infuses them with meaning.

Spirituality involves dynamic processes that ebb and flow over the life course and across the generations (Worthington, 1989). In all religions, the family is central in rites that mark the birth of a new member, entry into the adult community, marriage vows, and the death of a loved one. From the miracle of birth to the mystery of death and afterlife, spiritual matters are at the heart of family relations.

In the family life cycle, marriage often brings religious considerations to the fore. Conflict may arise over the wedding ceremony itself. Even partners of the same faith may differ in how they were raised and expectations for the observance of doctrine and customs in their shared life. Families of origin may exert pressures for wedding plans and future family life in line with their own convictions. This can fuel intergenerational conflict and in-law triangles that reverberate over the years.

Studies have found that when husbands and wives are similar in religious affiliation, beliefs, and practices, they report greater personal wellbeing, more relationship satisfaction, less abuse, and lower likelihood of divorce (Myers, 2006). Couples who find meaning in shared religious practices, such as holiday rituals, report greater marital satisfaction (Fiese & Tomcho, 2001). Strong religious commitment can support fragile marital bonds through times of conflict (Lambert & Dollahite, 2006). A couple's commitment vows as life partners are inherently spiritual, whether or not they conform to religious orthodoxy. Such vows incorporate core values, including honor, respect, loyalty, and trust, found in all faith traditions and in secular humanism. As Victor Frankl (1946/1984) attested, "Love goes very far beyond the physical person of the beloved. It finds its deepest meaning in his spiritual being, his inner self" (pp. 59–60). Loving relationships with "soul mates" infuse lives with meaning and purpose.

Interfaith marriage, traditionally prohibited by many religions, is now widespread. Acceptance has increased with the support of interfaith movements and the blurring of racial and ethnic barriers. However, the high rate of intermarriage by Jews (52%) is of deep concern to their community and may be met with disappointment by families.

Interfaith unions can complicate the issues couples ordinarily bring to any committed relationship. Under stress, tolerance for differences can erode, particularly if one religion is believed to be morally superior. It can matter a great deal whether both families of origin approved of the marriage and attended the wedding. Parental disapproval can have long-lasting ramifications for intergenerational relations and the success or failure of the marriage.

Divorce and remarriage can pose spiritual dilemmas. The Catholic church allows divorce but only sanctions remarriage in cases of annulment. This strict ruling has led many Catholics to leave the church at remarriage. Some couples decide to live together without legal remarriage or religious rites. Others petition the church for annulment of a former marriage when they wish to remarry. Such annulments are commonly granted, even after a long marriage and over objections of a wife and children, who may be deeply wounded that their prior family life and legitimacy are invalidated. It is crucial to explore such conflict-laden issues in clinical practice.

The vast majority of parents want their children to have a religious upbringing. In interfaith marriages, differences that initially attracted partners may over time become contentious in raising children. Couples who have viewed religion as unimportant in their lives may find that one or both partners care deeply about the religious upbringing of their children. Conflicts may arise over such rituals as christening, baptism, or bar/bat mitzvah. The older generation, now as grandparents, may strongly voice their religious preferences. Previous acceptance of their child's non-traditional wedding, an interfaith marriage, or a same-sex commitment may shift when they consider the spiritual development of their grandchildren.

Emerging research finds that family relationships are strengthened by religion in the home, particularly when parents practice what they preach (Marks, 2004). Children most value spiritual practices that are integrated into family life, as in shared daily practices, rituals and holidays, community service, and attendance of worship services. Belief in heaven and guardian angels is comforting for children, particularly in facing the death of a family member. Sometimes children draw parents back to religious roots. It is noteworthy that 95% of adolescents report belief in God and 75% pray when they are alone. Over half report strong interest in discussing life's meaning and moral decisions (Gallup & Lindsey, 1999). Such findings suggest the importance of open communication on spiritual matters between parents and their children.

Young adults – particularly college students – often distance themselves from their religious upbringing. Some simply drift away while others more actively question their family's traditions. Many who are searching for greater meaning and connection in their lives explore other spiritual pathways. One young couple became involved in environmental initiatives and celebrated each season's solstice with their children, meditating together at sunrise on a bluff overlooking the ocean.

Some who choose to convert or marry outside their faith may be seeking to differentiate themselves from their family of origin or to distance themselves from their ethnic or religious background. Parents may perceive such a choice as a rejection of them and all they value, which may not be the case. However, some choices may express a rebellion against religious or parental upbringing that was experienced as oppressive. Such issues should be sensitively explored in clinical practice.

All major faith traditions emphasize the importance of honoring parents and seeking forgiveness and reconciliation of relational wounds. Multigenerational approaches to family therapy share these aims to strengthen bonds, repair injustices, and heal grievances (Boszormenyi-Nagy, 1987; Fishbane, 2009; Hargrave, 1994; Worthington, 2006).

Faith, prayer, and active congregational participation tend to increase over middle and later life. Spirituality comes to the fore as family members increasingly face the illness and death of parents, spouses, and siblings, and as they grapple with questions about the meaning of life and concerns about their own mortality (Walsh, 2009a). The death of a child, even one in adulthood, reverses the natural order in the family life cycle, often generating deep spiritual distress for surviving parents.

With death, relationships do not end, but are transformed from physical presence to spiritual connections, sustained through memory, dreams, rituals, conversations, stories, and legacies (Walsh & McGoldrick, 2004). In some cultures, prayers may be said daily in front of family shrines or photographs of deceased parents or grandparents. Many believe that the spirits of ancestors can be communicated with directly and, if honored appropriately, will confer their blessings and protect their progeny; evil or aggrieved spirits may haunt or cause physical or emotional harm.

The Spiritual Dimension in Suffering, Healing, and Resilience

Spiritual beliefs and practices influence ways of dealing with adversity, the experience of suffering, and the meaning of symptoms. They also influence how people communicate about their problems; beliefs about their causal assumptions and future expectations; their attitudes toward helpers – clergy, physicians, therapists, faith healers; the treatments they seek; and their preferred pathways in recovery. Yet only recently are mainstream mental health and healthcare providers beginning to include the spiritual dimension in clinical assessment and treatment.

A bio-psycho-social-spiritual orientation is required to include spiritual influences in a clinical approach to suffering, healing, and resilience (Walsh, 2009b). Suffering invites us into the spiritual domain (Wright, Watson, & Bell, 1996). To be most helpful to families, we must understand their suffering, and often its injustice or senselessness. Religion and spirituality can offer comfort and meaning beyond comprehension in the face of adversity. Personal faith supports the belief that challenges can be overcome.

Spiritual Sources of Distress

Some individuals and families may seek help for particular spiritual concerns. Many who seek help for physical, emotional, or interpersonal problems are also in spiritual distress.

A spiritual wound or void can block coping, mastery, and the ability to invest life with meaning (Pargament, 2007). Religious beliefs can become harmful if held too narrowly, rigidly, or punitively. One mother's self-destructive drinking was fueled by her belief that her son's death was God's punishment for not having baptized him. A crisis may precipitate a questioning of long-held spiritual beliefs or may launch a quest for a new form or dimension of faith that can be sustaining.

Religious ideas or experiences fostering guilt, shame, or worthlessness may contribute to addictions, destructive behavior, or social isolation. Some religious doctrines and harsh, judgmental convictions can wound the spirit. Patriarchy, a cultural pattern embedded in most religious traditions, has contributed to violence toward women and to abortion and abandonment of baby girls in many parts of the world. In marriage and family life, some take patriarchal religious teachings to justify the abuse of wives and children (Bottoms, Shaver, Goodman, & Qin, 1995). Family psychologists have an ethical responsibility not to condone denigrating or abusive behavior, whether based in family, ethnic, or religious beliefs and traditions. Above all, every religion upholds the core values of respect for others and the dignity and worth of all human beings.

The condemnation of homosexuality in religious doctrine has been a source of deep anguish for those who have felt exiled from traditional faith communities. Some denominations preach the immorality of homosexual practice and opposition to same-sex couples and parenting alongside a loving acceptance of the gay person as a human being created by God. Such a dualistic position nevertheless perpetuates stigma and shame, pathologizing sexual orientation and bonds deemed "unnatural" and sinful. Despite deep schisms in many religious denominations, many faith communities have become more welcoming, and lesbian, gay, bisexual, and transgender (LGBT) persons have been forging more personal spiritual connections. Public attitudes have been moderating toward greater acceptance, particularly in those who have family members who are gay. When the sexual orientation of a family member is a source of pain or cutoff in families that hold more conservative religious views, family therapists can facilitate greater understanding, tolerance of differences, and loving acceptance. Sharing relevant research may allay some concerns, such as the abundant evidence that children raised by gay parents are not damaged, but are as healthy as those in traditional nuclear families (Walsh, 2003).

Spiritual Resources for Healing and Resilience

Life crises, trauma, loss, or a pile-up of stresses can generate emotional symptoms, substance abuse, and interpersonal conflict. They can impact family functioning, with ripple effects for all members and their relationships. Resilience – the ability to rebound from crises and overcome prolonged adversity – is relational, nurtured by family, community, cultural, and spiritual connections (Walsh, 2003, 2006).

A growing body of research documents the powerful influence of faith beliefs, practices, and congregational involvement for (a) physical and psychosocial wellbeing; (b) recovery from trauma and loss; (c) coping and positive growth with serious life challenges; and (d) more meaningful relationships and life pursuits (Koenig, McCullough,

& Larson, 2001; Miller & Thoresen, 2003; Pargament, 2007). Health, healing, and resilience are strengthened by involvement in a faith community, but even more importantly, by a deep faith that is lived out in daily life, interpersonal relationships, and service to others in need.

Prayer and meditation strengthen health and healing by triggering emotions that influence immune, cardiovascular, and neurological systems. Every spiritual orientation values some form of meditative practice, such as chanting or singing, reading scriptures, reciting a rosary or prayer beads, and rituals such as lighting candles or incense. For most, prayer originates in the family and is centered in the home. Almost all pray for their family's health and happiness. Prayer may serve varied functions: to connect with God; to express praise and gratitude; to keep life in perspective; to sustain strength and courage through an ordeal; to find solace and comfort in the face of tragedy; to request help or guidance; or to appeal for a miracle.

Meditative practices foster clarity, emotional tranquility, and more deliberate action. They can ease tension, pain, and suffering (Grossman, Niemann, Schmidt, & Walach, 2004; Kabat-Zinn, 2003). Shared meditative experiences facilitate genuine, empathic communication, reduce defensive reactivity, and deepen couple bonds (Barnes, Brown, Krusemark, Campbell, & Rogge, 2007; Carson, Carson, Gil, & Baucom, 2004). Mindfulness meditation is finding valuable application in clinical intervention and integrative healing approaches (Baer, 2003).

Rituals and ceremonies connect individuals with their families and communities and guide life passage. They facilitate unfamiliar transitions, script family actions, and comfort the dying and the bereaved. Rituals also transcend a particular struggle, suffering, or tragedy, connecting it with the human condition. Rituals are encouraged in family therapy to mark important milestones, reconnect with family heritage, create new patterns, and foster healing (Imber-Black, Roberts, & Whiting, 2003).

Those who are deeply spiritual cope better with stress, having fewer alcohol or drug problems, less depression, and lower rates of suicide than those who are not. What matters most is drawing on the power of faith to find meaning, hope, solace, and strength. Rather than a passive faith, an active faith perspective fuels efforts to take the initiative and persevere in the face of overwhelming challenges (Pargament, 2007).

Resilience involves both active mastery and acceptance of that which cannot be changed, akin to the Serenity Prayer at the heart of recovery movements. An emphasis on spirituality is a key component in 12-step programs, which can be a valuable adjunct to couple or family therapy (see Chapter 46, this volume). In addition to group support, these programs address spiritual issues concerning identity, integrity, an inner life, and interdependence. The steps promote a spiritual awakening that sparks life-altering transformations and strengthens practices for abstinence and greater wellbeing. Connection with a higher power through prayer and meditation facilitates reflection and sustains efforts through troubled times (Leigh, Bowen, & Marlatt, 2005).

Research in the trauma field finds spirituality to be a powerful influence in post-traumatic recovery and growth (Tedeschi & Calhoun, 2004). Beyond coping or surviving trauma, loss, or hardship, this potential for transformation and positive growth can be forged out of adversity (Walsh, 2006). By tapping spiritual resources for resilience, those who have been struggling can emerge stronger and more resourceful in meeting future challenges.

A serious crisis can also be an epiphany, opening lives to a spiritual dimension previously untapped. It can crystallize important matters and spark a reappraisal and redirection of life priorities and pursuits, as well as greater investment in meaningful relationships. Family therapy can facilitate these positive changes and growth in couple and family relations (e.g., Lambert & Dollahite, 2006).

Spirituality can also support the healing of relational wounds from trauma, harm, or injustice. Major faiths encourage forgiveness, rather than holding onto grievances and being bound up in feelings of rage or thoughts of revenge (Hargrave, 1994; Worthington, 2006). Couple and family therapy can facilitate relational repair for those who seek reconciliation and forgiveness by drawing on clients' spiritual resources.

Clinical Guidelines

Family psychologists increasingly are striving to integrate the spiritual dimension of experience in therapeutic practice. In assessment and treatment, the following guidelines are helpful:

- Inquire respectfully about the meaning and significance of religious and/or spiritual beliefs and practices in clients' lives and in relation to presenting problems and coping efforts. Spiritual ecomaps and other assessment tools can be helpful (Hodge, 2005).
- With respect for clients' faith – or non-faith – convictions, explore any spiritual concerns that may be contributing to suffering or blocking healing and problem resolution (e.g., guilt, anger at God; abusive practices; worry about sin or afterlife).
- Facilitate communication, understanding, and mutual respect around religious/ spiritual differences and conflicts in couples and families (e.g., interfaith marriage or conversion).
- Facilitate mutual compassion and possibilities for reconciliation and/or forgiveness in wounded relationships.
- Identify spiritual resources (current, past, or potential) that might contribute to healing and resilience. Encourage clients to draw on or explore those that fit their personal belief systems and preferences, including:
  - prayer, meditation, and rituals;
  - relationship with God or higher power;
  - involvement in faith community;
  - pastoral guidance;
  - communion with nature;
  - expressive/creative arts (e.g., music, poetry, art);
  - service to others; social action.

With growing cultural and spiritual diversity among Americans, it is crucial not to make assumptions about personal beliefs and practices based on client' religious identification or upbringing. It is important to explore the role and meaning of spirituality in their lives and relationships.

When working with conservative families, it is important for clinicians who may be more secular to be respectful of their deeply held religious and cultural values (Delaney, Miller, & Bisono, 2007). Moreover, in a predominantly Christian nation of European origins, we must be cautious not to superimpose the template of western European values on other belief systems and practices that may not be understood in Christian terms. It is crucial not to judge diverse faith approaches as inferior or primitive, particularly those of non-Christian, non-European, and indigenous cultures, such as African, Latin American, or Asian healing traditions. It is also important to respect those who are not religious or may not believe in God.

Caution is required not to impose therapists' own spiritual beliefs (including agnostic or atheist views) on clients. Because all clinicians bring their personal, family-of-origin, and dominant societal values into the therapeutic encounter, therapists need to reflect on their own spiritual journey, examining their spiritual/religious beliefs and issues just as they would their ethnic or other cultural influences (Walsh, 2009b).

There is also growing recognition of the importance of referral, consultation, and collaboration with pastoral care professionals, particularly on spiritual issues beyond a clinician's expertise, and linkage with spiritual resources in the community that fit the faith needs and preferences of the families we serve.

Case Example

One couple, in intense conflict, was referred to couples therapy after the stillbirth of their first child. The anticipation of the birth held special meaning for them and their extended kin network as the first son of the first son in a Greek Orthodox Christian family. When asked if they found comfort in their faith community, the wife said her husband refused to go back. He pounded his fist and shouted that he was too angry at God at the injustice: "How could a loving God take the life of an innocent baby?" He saw no point in coming for therapy because the therapist couldn't solve the problem and bring back their child. Profound distress, such as this, requires compassionate listening, understanding of the meaning of their loss, and facilitation of mutual support in their grief. Consultation with the hospital chaplain helped them with the deeper spiritual aspects of their distress.

Conclusion

In sum, the practice of family psychology, grounded in science, must also be attuned to the spiritual dimension of human suffering and resilience. Strengths-oriented family therapists offer compassion and comfort those who have been wounded or bereaved. Holding a multifaith perspective, we believe in the dignity, worth, and potential of every human being and support their spiritual journey seeking greater meaning, connection, and fulfillment as they move forward in their lives.

Resources

Pargament, K. I. (2007). *Spiritually integrated psychotherapy.* New York: Guilford Press.
Smith, H. (1991). *The world's religions: Our great wisdom traditions* (rev. ed.). New York: HarperCollins.
Walsh, F. (Ed.). (2009). *Spiritual resources in family therapy* (2nd ed.). New York: Guilford Press.

References

Aponte, H. (2009). The stresses of poverty and the comfort of spirituality. In F. Walsh (Ed.), *Spiritual resources in family therapy* (2nd ed., pp. 125–140). New York: Guilford Press.

Baer, R. A. (2003). Mindfulness training as a clinical intervention: A conceptual and empirical review. *Clinical Psychology: Science and Practice, 10,* 125–143.

Barnes, S., Brown, K. W., Krusemark, E., Campbell, W. K., & Rogge, R. D. (2007). The role of mindfulness in romantic relationship satisfaction and responses to relationship stress. *Journal of Marital & Family Therapy, 33(4),* 482–500.

Beavers, W. R., & Hampson, R. B. (2003). Measuring family competence: The Beavers Systems model. In F. Walsh (Ed.), *Normal family processes* (3rd ed., pp. 549–580). New York: Guilford Press.

Boszormenyi-Nagy, I. (1987). *Foundations of contextual family therapy.* New York: Brunner/Mazel.

Bottoms, B. L., Shaver, P. R., Goodman, G. S., & Qin, J. (1995). In the name of God: A profile of religion-related child abuse. *Journal of Social Issues, 51,* 85–111.

Boyd-Franklin, N., & Lockwood, T. W. (2009). Spirituality and religion: Implications for therapy with African American families. In F. Walsh (Ed.), *Spiritual resources in family therapy* (2nd ed., pp. 141–155). New York: Guilford Press.

Carson, J. W., Carson, K. M., Gil, K. M., & Baucom, D. H. (2004). Mindfulness-based relationship enhancement. *Behavior Therapy, 35,* 471–494.

Delaney, H. D., Miller, W. R., & Bisono, A. M. (2007). Religiosity and spirituality among psychologists: A survey of clinician members of the American Psychological Association. *Professional Psychology: Research and Practice, 38(5),* 538–546.

Deloria, V., Jr., (1994). *God is red: A native view of religion* (2nd ed.). Golden, CO: Fulcrum.

Doherty, W. J. (2009). Morality and spirituality in therapy. In F. Walsh (Ed.), *Spiritual resources in family therapy* (2nd ed., pp. 215–228). New York: Guilford Press.

Falicov, C. J. (2009). Religion and spiritual traditions in immigrant families: The therapeutic resources with Latinos. In F. Walsh (Ed.), *Spiritual resources in family therapy* (2nd ed., pp. 156–173). New York: Guilford Press.

Fiese, B. H., & Tomcho, T. J. (2001). Finding meaning in religious practices: The relation between holiday rituals and marital satisfaction. *Journal of Family Psychology, 15(4),* 597–609.

Fishbane, M. (2009). Honor your mother and your father. In F. Walsh (Ed.), *Spiritual resources in family therapy* (2nd ed., pp. 174–193). New York: Guilford Press.

Frankl, V. (1946/1984). *Man's search for meaning.* New York: Simon & Schuster.

Gallup, Jr., G., & Lindsey, D. M. (1999). *Surveying the religious landscape: Trends in U.S. beliefs.* Harrisburg, PA: Morehouse.

Griffith, J., & Griffith, M. (2002). *Encountering the sacred in psychotherapy.* New York: Guilford Press.

Grossman, P., Niemann, L., Schmidt, S., & Walach, H. (2004). Mindfulness-based stress reduction and health benefits: A meta-analysis. *Journal of Psychosomatic Research, 57,* 35–43.

Hargrave, T. (1994). *Families and forgiveness.* New York: Brunner/Mazel.

Hodge, D. R. (2005). Spiritual assessment in marital and family therapy: A methodological framework for selecting from among six qualitative assessment tools. *Journal of Marital and Family Therapy, 31(4),* 341–356.

Imber-Black, E., Roberts, J., & Whiting, R. (Eds.). (2003). *Rituals in families and family therapy* (2nd ed.). New York: Norton.

Kabat-Zinn, J. (2003). Mindfulness-based interventions in context: Past, present, and future. *Clinical Psychology: Science and Practice, 10(2),* 144–156.

Koenig, H., McCullough, M. E., & Larson, D. (Eds.). (2001). *Handbook of religion and health.* New York: Oxford University Press.

Lambert, N. M., & Dollahite, D. C. (2006). How religiosity helps couples prevent, resolve, and overcome marital conflict. *Family Relations, 55,* 439–449.

Leigh, J., Bowen, S., & Marlatt, G. (2005). Spirituality, mindfulness and substance abuse. *Addictive Behaviors, 30(7),* 1335–1341.

Marks, L. (2004). Sacred practices in highly religious families: Christian, Jewish, Mormon and Islamic perspectives. *Family Process, 43,* 217–231.

Miller, W. R., & Thoresen, C. E. (2003). Spirituality, religion, and health. *American Psychologist, 58(1),* 24–35.

Myers, S. (2006). Religious homogamy and marital quality: Historical and generational patterns. *Journal of Marriage and the Family, 68(2),* 292–304.

Pargament, K. I. (2007). *Spiritually integrated psychotherapy.* New York: Guilford Press.

Perry, A. de V., & Rolland, J. S. (2009). Therapeutic benefits of a justice-seeking spirituality: Empowerment, healing, and hope. In F. Walsh (Ed.), *Spiritual resources in family therapy* (2nd ed., pp. 379–396). New York: Guilford Press.

Pew Forum on Religion & Public Life. (2008). *U.S. religious landscape survey.* Retrieved from http://religions.pewforum.org

Pew Hispanic Project and the Pew Forum on Religion & Public Life. (2007, April). *Changing faiths: Latinos and the transformation of American religion.* Retrieved from http://pewresearch.org/pubs/461/religion-hispanic-latino

Tedeschi, R. G., & Calhoun, L. G. (2004). Post-traumatic growth: Conceptual foundations and empirical evidence. *Psychological Inquiry, 15,* 1–18.

Walsh, F. (2003). *Normal family processes: Growing diversity and complexity* (3rd ed.). New York: Guilford Press.

Walsh, F. (2006). *Strengthening family resilience* (2nd ed.). New York: Guilford Press.

Walsh, F. (2009a). Spiritual resources in family adaptation to death and loss. In F. Walsh (Ed.), *Spiritual resources in family therapy* (2nd ed., pp. 81–102). New York: Guilford Press.

Walsh, F. (Ed.). (2009b). *Spiritual resources in family therapy* (2nd ed.). New York: Guilford Press.

Walsh, F., & McGoldrick, M. (2004). *Living beyond loss: Death and the family* (2nd ed.). New York: Norton.

Worthington, E. L., Jr. (1989). Religious faith across the lifespan: Implications for counseling and research. *Counseling Psychologist, 17*, 555–612.

Worthington, E. L., Jr. (2006). *Forgiveness and reconciliation: Theory and application.* New York: Routledge.

Wright, L., Watson, W. L., & Bell, J. M. (1996). *Beliefs: The heart of healing in families and illness.* New York: Basic Books.

43

Moral Identity in the Family

Kevin S. Reimer

Eliana (a pseudonym) is a 15-year-old Latina in the Pico-Union district of Los Angeles, a neighborhood known for drugs, gang violence, and crime. Eliana's family arrived in the United States from El Salvador 12 years prior, making ends meet on less than $10,000 per year. She is revered by local youth workers as a paragon of moral maturity, mainly through her efforts to link peers from high school with elderly patients in a local convalescent hospital. Eliana's "adopt-a-grandparent" program is a neighborhood success, providing infirm seniors with compassion and improved care. Our research interview takes place in her home, a 350-square-foot hotel room shared with her mother and brother. The room is tightly packed with two double beds, clothes, a hot plate, and small television set. During our conversation cockroaches scuttle about the floor and adolescent boys pound the door, making propositions in Spanish and English. The central significance of family in Eliana's moral development is unmistakable:

> *What kind of person would you ideally like to be?*
> I would like to a person like my mom. She doesn't let herself go by what people think of her. She lets herself go by what she thinks of herself and she doesn't do like most people and judge people by what she sees; she judges them by what they think and the way they are. I want to be like her because sometimes I'm picky. I like to judge people without even knowing them, so I think that I would like to be more like by mom. She doesn't judge by just looking at them. She treats them well and talks to them and interacts with them.

Eliana's reflection makes intuitive sense to family practitioners and researchers. Yet her case represents something of a challenge to scholars in the field of moral psychology. The moral literature currently suffers from a paucity of studies on the family. Walker (1999, 2004a) attributes the shortage to historical events associated with competing psychological theories. Cognitive-developmental proposals were drafted to contest powerful psycho-analytic and behaviorist blocs of decades past (Kohlberg, 1969, 1981, 1984; Piaget, 1965). Analytic and behaviorist scholars were unified in their insistence that parents served as the principal source of moral socialization for children. In response, cognitive-developmental researchers emphasized the importance of peer socialization on moral development. Following Lawrence Kohlberg's landmark studies in the 1970s, the cognitive-developmental paradigm became a gold standard for moral research. The few cognitive-developmental studies that did include morality with family underlined the means by which child conscience is shaped through rules and conventions (Eisenberg, 2004; Smetana, 2006).

Eliana's maturity lives outside prevailing psychological definitions of morality. The cognitive-developmental tradition is explicitly rationalist, framing moral development through rules pertaining to *harm, rights*, and *justice* (Helwig & Turiel, 2002; Kohlberg, 1984; Nucci, 2004, 2006; Smetana, 2006; Turiel, 1983, 2006). Despite the utility of this approach, questions persist regarding the extent to which harm, rights, and justice capture the breadth of real-world moral functioning (Campbell & Christopher, 1996; Flanagan, 1991; Haidt, 2001; Narvaez, Lapsley, Hagele, & Lasky, 2007; Walker, 2004b; Walker & Hennig, 2004; Walker & Pitts, 1998; Walker & Reimer, 2005). One influential critique took aim at the close resemblance between cognitive-developmental definitions of moral-ity and liberal ethics typical of the western academic elite (Haidt & Bjorklund, 2008; Haidt, Koller, & Dias, 1993). This led to a spate of cross-cultural studies evaluating the universality of justice reasoning. Heated controversy erupted over findings suggesting that communitarian and religious priorities may supersede justice in the moral reasoning of poor Brazilians and Brahmans from India (Haidt et al., 1993; Shweder, Much, Mahapatra, & Park, 1997; Turiel & Wainryb, 1994). Other concerns surfaced on dis-coveries that individuals with grave injury to the prefrontal cortex of the brain behaved immorally, yet scored in the normal range on moral rationalist inventories (Damasio, 2002). Perhaps most problematic, moral exemplars such as Eliana were found to score no differently than everyday comparisons on the same inventories (Colby & Damon, 1992, 1995; Hart & Fegley, 1995; Matsuba & Walker, 2004).

Eliana showcases the importance of family process in constructing an inclusive account of moral development and maturity. The American social landscape is diverse, particularly in urban regions characterized by multiple and overlapping cultural influ-ences. Children growing up in these environments are exposed to heterogeneous moral influences and colorful family configurations (Halstead, 1999). We might expect an import-ant role for justice reasoning in the parenting of second-generation Hmong immigrants from Southeast Asia, refugees from the Darfur region of Sudan, or newly blended fam-ilies with spouses of differing ethnicities. Yet it is equally reasonable to expect that the same families identify justice as one among many objectives in the moral socialization of their children. The present chapter assumes a broad moral horizon supportive of renewed effort in family research on moral development. Rather than justice reasoning, the foil for this discussion is *moral identity*. Moral identity refers to ethical maturity through com-mitments consistent with a sense of self to actions that promote the welfare of others (Blasi, 1990; Hardy & Carlo, 2005; Hart, Atkins, & Ford, 1999; Reimer, 2005; Reimer & Wade-Stein, 2004). The chapter considers moral identity in family process with addi-tional illustrations provided from Eliana's narrative.

Moral Identity and Family Process

How is family involved in the development of moral identity? Moral identity was initially proposed as a means of integrating self-understanding with social influences in response to the rationalist work of Lawrence Kohlberg (1984). Many readers will be familiar with Kohlberg's moral development scheme, organized as a stage-like maturity framework. Briefly, Kohlberg used abstract dilemmas to understand how children and adolescents make moral decisions through justice reasoning. Responses to dilemmas were catalogued into stage levels that characterized sophistication in reasoning. The framework was validated by other researchers using different sample groups. The result was a six-stage outline for moral rationality that became widely used in psychological and educational circles. An assessment instrument was created for the framework, known as the *moral judgment inventory* (MJI; Kohlberg, 1984). Although Kohlberg makes reference to personality factors and family influences, the burden of his project is placed on individual capacity to apply moral reasoning through dilemmas. Socialization processes related to developing rational ability prioritize peer-to-peer interactions in childhood.

One criticism of this approach is evident in the work of Augusto Blasi (Blasi, 1990, 2005). Blasi proposed a "self model" of moral functioning emphasizing the importance of responsibility in mediating reason with behavior. In the model, fidelity to responsible behavior must be kept consistent with personal goals, values, and beliefs. Beyond harm, rights, and justice, moral functioning is principally reliant upon actions consistent with self-understanding which are gradually incorporated into moral identity. Blasi's argument became influential for work on moral exemplars known for outstanding commitments – persons believed to harbor moral identities. A pioneering example from this literature surveyed nominated exemplars involved in remarkable humanitarian works (Colby & Damon, 1992, 1995). Exemplars were found to be relatively ordinary in terms of intelligence, yet effected great change through service. Exemplars reported that social influences refashioned their personal goals and values related to moral identity. The most powerful social influences came from close relationships where exemplars were challenged to reach and grow. Relationships reflected a spectrum of mentor figures including friends, family members, and religious leaders. Yet influences also arose in unexpected contexts, such as the case of a young elementary school teacher who through her work with dyslexic children became vitally involved in service to the disabled. In the main, relationships galvanized exemplars to confront moral issues that became inextricably associated with self-understanding.

Early studies of moral identity

The Colby and Damon exemplar research was compelling enough to attract the interest of developmental researchers interested in children, adolescents, and family. Hart and Fegley (1995) took up the nominated exemplar paradigm in a study of outstanding adolescents from Camden, New Jersey. The authors reasoned that moral identity would be evident where youth demonstrated exemplary functioning despite living in one of the most underserved urban zones in America. The ethnically and socioeconomically diverse Camden climate required new criteria for exemplar nomination. Focus groups comprised of area social workers, teachers, and youth leaders were asked to provide nomination criteria appropriate to Camden. Criteria were used to nominate 15 Camden adolescents that demonstrated exemplary moral commitments. Exemplar youth took leadership in caring for infirm family members, were stalwart volunteers in service to the local poor, enacted peer-to-peer conflict mediation, and in several instances functioned as surrogate parents to younger siblings. Exemplars were matched on the basis of age, ethnicity, gender, and neighborhood with 15 everyday comparison youth. All were given semi-structured clinical interviews along with Kohlberg's MJI.

Study outcomes provided clues regarding the genesis of attitudes and behaviors associated with moral identity (Hart & Fegley, 1995). Interview responses suggested that exemplar adolescents differed from comparisons in the manner by which they thought about the self, others, and relationships. However, exemplars scored no differently than comparisons on Kohlberg's stage-like framework for moral development. Both exemplars and comparisons were found to function at the stage 3 (conventional) level of moral reasoning. Relative to comparisons, exemplars demonstrated a different pattern of socialization in moral self-understanding. Peers and non-parental adult mentors were prominent in exemplar socialization. Roughly equal weight was afforded to parents and extended kin as sources of moral influence. The methods and small sample size of the study made it difficult to know details of how family was involved in moral socialization. A replication study with exemplar adolescents from diverse urban regions of California found that parental influences were weighted more heavily than peers in exemplar moral identity (Reimer & Wade-Stein, 2004). Exemplars made statements illustrating powerful moral role models in birth parents, stepparents, older siblings, and extended kin.

Findings from the Camden research led to a formal proposal for moral identity development and consolidation. Hart et al. (1999) argued that *personality* and *social influence* are cornerstones of adolescent moral identity, promoting resiliency and community engagement. In the model, personality is manifested through individual capacity to regulate emotions and create effective interactions with others that uphold moral values. Secondarily, personality is related to individual thinking about the self and others. Social influence reflects intentional and pre-conscious moral modeling through relational networks. Such influence might include structural concerns related to social class, an element known to impact moral and social judgment (Hart & Edelstein, 1992). Social influence also points to close relationships loaded with moral currency in the form of shared values and commitments. Consequently, the family is a principal catalyst in the formation of moral identity.

Hart et al. (1999) constructed a developmental test of the moral identity model with the National Longitudinal Survey of Youth (NLSY), including 828 adolescents from across the country. Personality was studied through NLSY items relating to *internalization* or extent to which youth experience self-worth, and *externalization* or extent to which youth interact agreeably with others. Social influences in the family were considered on the basis of (a) family support, (b) joint activities involving parents with children, and (c) parenting styles underscoring autonomy and intimacy toward children. Moral identity was evaluated on the basis of adolescent volunteerism, specifically actions that served the community and did not originate through academic or court-ordered requirements. Results generally supported the model, namely that moral identity flourished in cognitively and relationally nurturing family environments. Adolescent volunteerism was most strongly predicted by a high level of regular activities involving parents and adolescents together. These activities might include volunteer service, weekend shopping trips, or participation in faith communities. Parent–adolescent joint activities were prominent in moral identity formation even controlling for family income, gender, ethnicity, and academic achievement. Personality was also implicated in volunteerism, but at a level that was less statistically robust.

Family influences on moral identity

The central importance of family in the social influence of moral identity formation reflects shared moral priorities structured as expectations for child and adolescent behavior. Expectations might be considered in terms of moral *values* that reflect parental priorities. Along these lines, Pratt, Hunsberger, Pancer, and Alisat (2003) designed a longitudinal study of adolescent moral identity formation considering values together with parenting styles. Six moral values were taken from a study of ethical prototypes (Walker & Pitts, 1998). Values were handled as self-attributions for *trustworthiness, citizenship, honesty, kindness, fairness,* and *integrity.* Moral identity was considered on the basis of self-understanding variables related to community service. Parenting style was assessed on dimensions of *responsiveness* (emotional attentiveness to youth) and *strictness* (boundaries for youth behavior combined with steady reinforcement). Findings suggested that while moral values were related to community service, the pattern indicated moral self-attributions arose as a result of volunteerism rather than as a prerequisite. Moreover, adolescent moral values were successfully integrated into self-understanding where parents provided an *authoritative* (high on responsiveness and strictness) zone of proximal development. Taken together, these results provide an interesting footnote to the Hart et al. (1999) finding that family process emphasizing regular joint activities promotes moral identity formation. Shared activities may provide a stimulus for the articulation and integration of moral values as parental expectations for behavior. Expectations are successfully reinforced in an emotionally responsive and strict family environment. The quality of parent–child relationship appears to play an important role in establishing expectations supportive of moral identity.

A major implication from these studies is that values are best integrated into moral identity where security and trust characterize socialization patterns within the parent–child relationship. Security makes shared experiences morally meaningful prior to becoming established as values expectations for behavior. The consolidation of values into moral identity suggests, from the parent–child vantage, a place for *attachment* in moral maturity. Attachment refers to a behavioral system that evolved to foster adaptive responses to the environment through cognitive models of relationship, foundationally between parents and children (Bowlby, 1969, 1980; Reimer, 2005). Moral identity in the parent–child relationship potentially matures where boundaries for interpersonal behavior are marked by a suite of values. Attachment security mitigates the degree to which those values are consistently reinforced as promoting the security of self and other.

How might this work? Briefly, security and trust are predicated upon attachment styles that reflect emotions organized from experience with early caregivers (Collins & Feeney, 2004; Mikulincer & Shaver, 2007). Attachment styles are believed to reflect variations in *working models* of self and other. Working models integrate knowledge of self and other along with perceived expectations and goals derived from social networks. Working models are generally pre-conscious, reflecting emotional intuitions and habits in behavior. Working models are principally understood on the basis of two dimensions designed to assess external threats. One dimension is characterized in terms of *anxiety*. Children and adolescents with elevated attachment anxiety reflect histories where experiences of parental ambivalence or authoritarianism became firmly established in working models. A second dimension considers the extent to which children and adolescents demonstrate *avoidance* in relationships. Avoidant individuals anticipate rejection or retributive behavior from others.

The link between security and moral identity recalls Piaget's (1965) suggestion that maturity parallels the child's growing emotional understanding. Shame and guilt are emotions that influence the ability of children to integrate parental expectations in a manner enhancing moral identity. When combined with pride, these "moral" emotions are ubiquitous in early attachment relationships, moderating anxiety and avoidance responses through the child's working model of self and other. Where a child experiences appropriate shame, guilt, or pride in morally charged circumstances, he or she learns a framework for regulating the self consonant with parental expectations that maximizes security for self and others. In the event that the child experiences maladaptive shame, guilt, or pride, the same moral situations are endowed with consequences that may enhance insecurity, leading to heightened anxiety, avoidance, or both. Moral ambiguity may result, evident in behavior reflecting an underdeveloped sense of empathy or personal responsibility. This discussion does not mean that securely attached individuals are more ethically mature than those who are insecurely attached. What matters is the extent to which moral emotions are organized in ways that constrain anxiety and avoidance toward security-promoting outcomes. The family is a nexus for this developmental process.

Moral Identity in Color: A Representative Case Narrative

Several years ago I studied adolescent moral exemplars from underserved, ethnically diverse urban regions of California (Balswick, King, & Reimer, 2005; Reimer, 2003; Reimer & Wade-Stein, 2004). The study was a replication of the Camden project, attempting to better understand the nature of social influences articulated in the Hart et al. (1999) model for moral identity with an improved methodology. The study found that relative to comparisons, exemplars prioritized family influences above peer-to-peer networks. In many instances, "family" included extended kin or distant relatives that reflected the realities of dispersal and pressing economic hardship. The majority of exemplar youth did not have two birth parents present in their households. Many were immigrants, reporting difficulties associated with transition to a new and unfamiliar culture. Some had experienced traumatic events such as the murder of a parent or sibling. Despite their circumstances, exemplar youth were nothing short of inspiring. One 16-year-old was nominated for his successful application to a major humanitarian foundation, obtaining a program grant to keep his peers off the street. Exemplar youth were resourceful in taking advantage of family attachments to develop security-promoting moral commitments integrating parental expectations for the good. Many of these themes are evident for Eliana, the urban adolescent introduced at the beginning of this chapter:

What kind of person are you with your mother?
I like to talk with my mom. I like to interact with my mom. I don't hide things from my mom. If I see someone or something that I like, I tell her or I always talk to her.

What kind of person is your mother?
My mother is a person who's straight. If she doesn't like something, she will tell you in a nice way so that you don't feel bad. She's not critical. What I like most about her is she doesn't scream at me like most mothers and they hit you and stuff like that. She makes you feel like even though you did something wrong, it's okay if you learn about the mistake you did. I also like this – she doesn't hit me. Cause instead of hitting me, she talks to me. She makes me feel that I did something bad but that I have to learn not to do it again. Even though sometimes I do it over and over. She still doesn't hit me; she tries to explain to me. She has a lot of patience with me. She's a calm, quiet personality. She doesn't like to be around a big crowd. She has a playful personality. She plays with us, we wrestle, and we ride a bike together. She goes out to the park with us. I can tell her anything without her getting mad. I see a cute guy, I tell her. When I don't understand something, I ask her and she helps me when she can and when she can't, she helps me to get help.

What are her goals?
Well I know my mom would really like me to finish school. She would have like to have her mother or her father [still living in El Salvador] around to help us, to not make a lot of the mistakes that she did.

Can you think of another person you admire?
My aunt. She understands me. I make her laugh and she makes me laugh because of the things she says. Even if my jokes are the lamest or the dumbest, she laughs at them. She makes me feel good. She always goes for me, not anybody else but me. When I'm down and I feel like I'm not special, she makes me feel special.

What kind of person are you with your best friend?
I talk a lot. I help her. She helps me. I tell her everything. I ask her to tell me things. I like to talk to her; she's a shoulder where I can talk and laugh. She knows

most about me. Like sometimes she says, "I know more about you than you know yourself."

What kind of person is your best friend?
She's a quiet person. She's serious. She's more of a person who doesn't like to be involved in big things. She acts more mature than I think most people do. I think because of some of her problems. She mostly doesn't have friends. I'm one of the only friends that she has.

What are her goals?
I really don't know. No, she doesn't like school. She doesn't like very much of anything, I don't know. I only know that one of her goals when we were smaller, she said that she wanted two kids. Like being a teacher or something like that, I don't know.

How did you get to be the way that you are?
My mom helped me a lot to change. She talked to me a lot, because I'm the only girl and one of the youngest, from what I know. I have big brothers from my dad's side, but I don't know any of them. I know that my mom helps me a lot. It's better to talk to your mom, because nobody will tell you things the way they are, but your mom will.

Are there other reasons or other ways that you turned out the way that you did?
I think that it was my environment. Since I was little I've seen a lot of girls that . . . girls who got pregnant. Girls who dropped out of school. Girls who died. Things like that. I always dreamed of not doing what others did. Since I was little I've always said that I don't want to be like the others. I want to be unique.

As a single case, Eliana's responses should not be taken as definitive evidence that moral identity is uniformly dependent upon family influences. Moral socialization in the study sample implicated a variety of figures (Reimer & Wade-Stein, 2004). Moreover, caution is indicated regarding the extent to which Eliana's example informs moral development for all families in every situation. Exemplars are extremely rare, making generalization a tenuous prospect. With these limitations in plain view, Eliana's account traces key elements in the research literature. In the quotation at the beginning of the chapter, she makes unprimed associations between her ideal self and the example of her mother. Eliana provides considerable detail regarding maternally derived values and expectations for behavior. Aspects of this influence are extended to include her aunt. Following empirical findings from the study, the weight of values socialization in this instance seems to favor family process over peers. When asked about her best friend, Eliana recounts a friendship of mutual confidence and intimacy. Yet the relationship is not marked by recognizable values- or other-oriented expectations. Eliana affirms a place for peer-to-peer influence, but indicates that the lion's share of attributions related to moral identity arises within the mother–daughter dyad. The study does not tell us about the developmental particulars of this observation, namely the extent to which family and peer influences are weighted in middle childhood or late adolescence. More work is needed to outline a comprehensive picture of moral identity on the basis of time, place, and role.

Second, despite a multitude of challenges Eliana's family manages to establish a cognitively and relationally nurturing environment associated with optimal moral identity development (Hart et al., 1999). This is evident in joint activities Eliana enjoys with her mother. The costs associated with regular shared activities are more than financial. Eliana's 40-year-old mother suffers from rheumatoid arthritis. Lacking medical insurance, she copes without medication or treatment. At the time of the interview Eliana's mother was only moving with great difficulty. Core values of mutual respect and enjoyment of shared activities together are noteworthy given the magnitude of obstacles to regular family time. Other values are visible in Eliana's account of her mother's impressive ability to resist making superficial judgments of others. Eliana personalizes these values into goals while simultaneously recognizing her own failed efforts. Interestingly, Eliana links the values discussion of social judgment with her mother's parenting style. In stark contrast to her peers, Eliana does not receive harshly punitive or physical discipline. Her mother "explains" matters to her daughter in a lucid example of parental *induction* (inductive reasoning). The combination of induction along with high support suggests that Eliana's mother employs an authoritative parenting style with some consistency. Successful integration of mother's values into Eliana's moral identity happens on the basis of modeling that is authoritative in nature.

Conclusion

Keeping in step with the research literature on family and moral identity, Eliana maintains a secure outlook on her circumstances and relationships. This is remarkable given that adolescence is commonly a period of marked insecurity, particularly for individuals living in a neighborhood as stressful as the Pico-Union. Through her narrative, it seems reasonable to suppose that Eliana's insights into matters of moral self-understanding reflect mature integration of values that successfully promote security for self and others. Anxiety and avoidance are adaptive features of self-regulation for Eliana, aspects that may at times help to save her life. But her core identity is forged on other priorities: to avoid the fate of the girls in her neighborhood, to extend compassion, and to live out her uniqueness as an uncritical leader who is slow to judge others. Eliana has learned adaptive patterns of emotion regulation that permit her to override threat responses in the interest of broadly promoting security for others. Her moral success depends upon the ongoing integration of values into an identity that is a bulwark against an unstable and insecure world. The prominence of her mother as a key influence in this developmental process is unequivocal. The collective decision for mother and daughter to regularly share values, expectations, and simple experiences underscores a noteworthy role for family influence in the development of moral identity. Far from academic debates over the psychological relevance of harm, rights, or justice, Eliana's maturity is fashioned around real-world issues and painful human concerns.

References

Balswick, J., King, P., & Reimer, K. (2005). *The reciprocating self.* Downer's Grove, IL: InterVarsity.

Blasi, A. (1990). How should psychologists define morality? Or, the negative side effects of philosophy's influence on psychology. In T. Wren (Ed.), *The moral domain: Essays in the ongoing discussion between philosophy and the social sciences* (pp. 38–70). Cambridge, MA: MIT Press.

Blasi, A. (2005). Moral character: A psychological approach. In D. Lapsley & F. Power (Eds.), *Character psychology and character education* (pp. 67–100). Notre Dame, IN: University of Notre Dame Press.

Bowlby, J. M. (1969). *Attachment and loss: Vol. 1. Attachment.* New York: Basic Books.

Bowlby, J. M. (1980). *Attachment and loss: Vol. 3. Loss: Sadness and depression.* New York: Basic Books.

Campbell, R. L., & Christopher, J. C. (1996). Moral development theory: A critique of its Kantian assumptions. *Developmental Review, 16,* 1–47.

Colby, A., & Damon, W. (1992). *Some do care: Contemporary lives of moral commitment.* New York: Free Press.

Colby, A., & Damon, W. (1995). The development of extraordinary moral commitment. In M. Killen & D. Hart (Eds.), *Morality in everyday life: Developmental perspectives* (pp. 343–369). New York: Cambridge University Press.

Collins, N. L., & Feeney, B. C. (2004). Working models of attachment shape perceptions of social support: Evidence from experimental and observational studies. *Journal of Personality and Social Psychology, 87,* 363–383.

Damasio, H. (2002). Impairment of interpersonal social behavior caused by acquired brain damage. In S. Post, L. Underwood, J. Schloss, & W. Hurlbut (Eds.), *Altruism and altruistic love: Science, philosophy, and religion in practice* (pp. 264–271). New York: Oxford University Press.

Eisenberg, N. (2004). Prosocial and moral development in the family. In T. Thorkildsen (Ed.), *Nurturing morality* (pp. 119–135). New York: Kluwer.

Flanagan, O. (1991). *Varieties of moral personality: Ethics and psychological realism.* Cambridge, MA: Harvard University Press.

Haidt, J. (2001). The emotional dog and its rational tail: A social intuitionist approach to moral judgment. *Psychological Review, 108,* 814–834.

Haidt, J., & Bjorklund, F. (2008). Social intuitionists answer six questions about moral psychology. In W. Sinnott-Armstrong (Ed.), *Moral psychology: Vol. 3* (pp. 181–217). Cambridge, MA: MIT Press.

Haidt, J., Koller, S., & Dias, M. (1993). Affect, culture, and morality, or is it wrong to eat your dog? *Journal of Personality and Social Psychology, 65,* 613–628.

Halstead, M. (1999). Moral education in family life: The effects of diversity. *Journal of Moral Education, 28,* 265–281.

Hardy, S., & Carlo, G. (2005). Identity as a source of moral motivation. *Human Development, 48,* 232–256.

Hart, D., Atkins, R., & Ford, D. (1999). Family influences on the formation of moral identity in adolescence: Longitudinal analyses. *Journal of Moral Education, 28,* 375–386.

Hart, D., & Edelstein, W. (1992). The relationship of self-understanding to community type, social class, and teacher-rated intellectual and social competence. *Journal of Cross-Cultural Psychology, 23,* 353–365.

Hart, D., & Fegley, S. (1995). Prosocial behavior and caring in adolescence: Relations to self-understanding and social judgment. *Child Development, 66,* 1346–1359.

Helwig, C., & Turiel, E. (2002). Civil liberties, autonomy, and democracy: Children's perspectives. *International Journal of Law and Psychiatry, 25,* 253–270.

Kohlberg, L. (1969). Stage and sequence: The cognitive-developmental approach to socialization. In D. A. Goslin (Ed.), *Handbook of socialization theory and research* (pp. 347–480). Chicago: Rand McNally.

Kohlberg, L. (1981). *Essays on moral development: Vol. 1. The philosophy of moral development.* San Francisco: Harper & Row.

Kohlberg, L. (1984). *Essays on moral development: Vol. 2. The psychology of moral development.* San Francisco: Harper & Row.

Matsuba, M. K., & Walker, L. J. (2004). Extraordinary moral commitment: Young adults working for social organizations. *Journal of Personality, 72,* 413–436.

Mikulincer, M., & Shaver, P. (2007). *Attachment in adulthood: Structure, dynamics, and change.* New York: Guilford Press.

Narvaez, D., Lapsley, D. K., Hagele, S., & Lasky, B. (2007). Moral chronicity and social information processing: Tests of a social cognitive approach to the moral personality. *Journal of Research in Personality, 40,* 966–985.

Nucci, L. (2004). Reflections on the moral self construct. In D. K. Lapsley & D. Narvaez (Eds.), *Moral development, self, and identity* (pp. 111–132). Mahwah, NJ: Erlbaum.

Nucci, L. (2006). Education for moral development. In M. Killen & J. Smetana (Eds.), *Handbook of moral development* (pp. 657–681). Mahwah, NJ: Erlbaum.

Piaget, J. (1965). *The moral judgment of the child.* New York: Free Press.

Pratt, M., Hunsberger, B., Pancer, S., & Alisat, S. (2003). A longitudinal analysis of personal values socialization: Correlates of a moral self-ideal in late adolescence. *Social Development, 12,* 563–585.

Reimer, K. S. (2003). Committed to caring: Transformation in adolescent moral identity. *Applied Developmental Science, 7,* 129–137.

Reimer, K. S. (2005). Revisiting moral attachment: Comment on identity and motivation. *Human Development, 48,* 262–265.

Reimer, K. S., & Wade-Stein, D. (2004). Moral identity in adolescence: Self and other in semantic space. *Identity, 4,* 229–249.

Shweder, R. A., Much, N. C., Mahapatra, M., & Park, L. (1997). The "big three" of morality (autonomy, community, divinity) and the "big three" explanations of suffering. In A. Brandt & P. Rozin (Eds.), *Morality and health* (pp. 119–169). Florence, KY: Taylor & Francis/Routledge.

Smetana, J. (2006). Social-cognitive domain theory: Consistencies and variations in children's moral and social judgments. In M. Killen & J. Smetana (Eds.), *Handbook of moral development* (pp. 119–153). Mahwah, NJ: Erlbaum.

Turiel, E. (1983). *The development of social knowledge: Morality and convention.* Cambridge: Cambridge University Press.

Turiel, E. (2006). The development of morality. In N. Eisenberg, W. Damon, & R. Lerner (Eds.), *Handbook of child psychology: Volume 3. Social, emotional and personality development* (pp. 789–857). Hoboken, NJ: Wiley.

Turiel, E., & Wainryb, C. (1994). Social reasoning and the varieties of social experiences in cultural contexts. In H. Reese (Ed.), *Advances in child development and behavior: Vol. 25* (pp. 289–326). San Diego: Academic Press.

Walker, L. J. (1999). The family context for moral development. *Journal of Moral Education, 28,* 261–264.

Walker, L. J. (2004a). Progress and prospects in the psychology of moral development. *Merrill-Palmer Quarterly, 50*, 546–557.

Walker, L. J. (2004b). Gus in the gap: Bridging the judgment–action gap in moral functioning. In D. Lapsley & D. Narvaez (Eds.), *Moral development, self, and identity* (pp. 1–20). Mahwah, NJ: Erlbaum.

Walker, L. J., & Hennig, K. (2004). Differing conceptions of moral exemplarity: Just, brave, and caring. *Journal of Personality and Social Psychology, 86*, 629–647.

Walker, L. J., & Pitts, R. C. (1998). Naturalistic conceptions of moral maturity. *Developmental Psychology, 34*, 403–419.

Walker, L. J., & Reimer, K. S. (2005). The relationship between moral and spiritual development. In P. Benson, P. King, L. Wagener, & E. Roehlkepartain (Eds.), *The handbook of spiritual development in childhood and adolescence* (pp. 265–301). Newbury Park, CA: Sage.

44

Family Stories and Rituals

Barbara H. Fiese and Marcia A. Winter

I remember a dinnertime when it was Christmas or something like that and mamma would bring out a big turkey, and we would have ham, and beets, and homemade biscuits. And we would sit around and eat. And there was my aunt, uncle, grandmother, grandfather, and cousins, too. I remember my uncle would say a prayer before dinner, bless our food and our family. Or my grandfather might say it, my grandfather was a deacon in the church, and I always loved it when grandfather said the prayer because it was the shortest prayer in the world. Jesus wept. And that was it and we just dove in and that was it. Sometimes there would be other kids over and we would have a little table in the corner and we would eat, the kids, while the adults had the big table to themselves. And I remember that being a 'specially nice time. A lot of laughing, and cutting, and scraping, and eating and talking and all those kinds of good things. (Story told to 5-year-old about her father's meal-time experiences)

One of the challenges in family psychology is capturing how the whole is greater than the sum of its parts. While the subsystems of the family (parent–child, partner–partner, sibling–sibling) are essential to understanding the health and wellbeing of individuals, how the family operates as a group provides an important window into its values, meaning-making process, and affect regulation. Families come together as a group in a variety of ways. They have dinners together, meet for special celebrations, and tell stories to reminisce about memorable events and reinforce collective values. They practice routines to provide order to their lives and create rituals to impart meaning and cement bonds.

Family life is organized on multiple levels, some directly accessible to outsiders through observation and some detectable only through careful interviewing. What can be seen by others is often referred to as the "practicing family"; what is accessed through interviews and closely held beliefs is considered the "representing family" (Fiese &

Spagnola, 2006; Reiss, 1989). These domains are reflected in the study of family stories and rituals.

In this chapter, we provide an overview of family stories and rituals as ways to tap the whole family process, gain access to the "insider's" view of daily life, and access both the practicing and representing families. Stories and rituals therefore have unique potential to show aspects of daily life that are at the heart of family functioning. Indeed, astute clinicians often use stories to connect with families and to understand how they adapt over time (Anderson, 2001). We conclude with a brief discussion of the therapeutic use of family stories and rituals.

Family Stories

For researchers, stories provide a view of family life not readily accessible through questionnaires or even direct observation. Through detailed, and sometimes painstaking, analysis of narrative transcripts it is possible to "get inside" the dynamics of family life. This provides the researcher with a rich accounting of the struggles and joys encountered by families and how they come to make sense out of important challenges. It is this meaning-making process that is illustrative of family resilience under a variety of high-risk conditions (Walsh, 2002). Family stories set an interpretive framework for how members have struggled with, and sometimes resolved, emotionally evocative circumstances. For example, family narratives have been collected about the birth of the first child (Oppenheim, Wamboldt, Gavin, & Renouf, 1996), diagnosis of serious mental illnesses (Stern, Doolan, Staples, Szmukler, & Eisler, 1999), and adoption (Grotevant, Fravel, Gorall, & Piper, 1999). While there is a multitude of ways to define family stories, we consider them verbal accounts of personal experiences that are important to the family, depict rules of interaction, reflect beliefs about the trustworthiness of relationships, and impart values connected to larger social institutions (Fiese et al., 1999; Pratt & Fiese, 2004). Family narratives are typically considered for their thematic content, narrative coherence, and co-constructive features.

Themes inherent in family stories are often related to socialization practices, the formation of intimate relationships, and explanation of personal transgressions. Parents use family stories to teach lessons about growing up. Common themes in stories told to children include close family relationships, role assignment, routines, working hard regardless of the outcome, seeking independence, and risk taking (Fiese & Bickham, 2004). Frequently these themes vary by gender of storyteller and story-listener. For example, fathers are more likely to tell stories about how things work and personal achievement than mothers, and these themes are more likely to be heard by sons than by daughters. Parents also differ in the ways that they reminisce about past experiences. Some parents use rich, elaborative styles when recounting past shared events while others use a more concrete, descriptive style (Fivush, Bohanke, Robertson, & Duke, 2004). These variations are important because they provide clues to how individuals create images not only of themselves but also of their place in the family and larger social world. A son engaged in an elaborate exchange about building a tree house not only learns the nuances of how to use a hammer but also learns about problem solving, teamwork, and perseverance. Over time, these themes have the opportunity to be threaded into his life story.

Moral values are part of family stories, particularly shared across generations. Pratt and colleagues identified themes of justice, care, and kindness in grandparent stories told to grandchildren (Pratt, Arnold, & Hilbers, 1998). One advantage of family stories is that they connect generations across geographic distances, creating an oral heritage (Ryan, Pearce, Anas, & Norris, 2004).

Transgressions are also important variants in family stories – what may be cause for comment in one family may hardly raise an eyebrow in another. The same is true for cultural values imparted through transgression stories. Miller and colleagues found that families in Taiwan and Chicago tell different types of stories about their children's personal transgressions (Miller, Sandel, Liang, & Fung, 2001; Miller, Wiley, Fung, & Liang, 1997). The parents in Chicago would frame the events as sources of personal bravado – even though the 4-year-old had driven the car down the driveway alone! The parents in Taiwan used narratives of personal transgression as teaching opportunities and highlighted misbehavior as the central point of the story in light of social order: "you made your mother lose face." In both instances the child is learning not only about the values of the family but also how the family supports cultural mores.

The formation of intimate ties is another common topic in family stories. Researchers and clinicians interested in the early stages of couple formation and the endurance of satisfactory relationships found family narratives a useful resource. Narrative assessments were used with couples to collect stories about how they met, how they became interested in one another, and what married life is like (Holmberg, Orbuch, & Veroff, 2004; Veroff, Sutherland, Chadiah, & Ortega, 1993). Story content was related to how satisfied couples were with their relationships and how likely they were to remain married years later. For example, couples who described their early days together as chaotic and disappointing were more likely to divorce three years later than couples who focused on the "we-ness" of their early dating relationships (Buehlman, Gottman, & Katz, 1992).

While the thematic focus of family stories is evidenced by an examination of its content, narrative coherence is also important. Coherence refers to the fluidity or organization of the story. A coherent narrative is easy to follow; has a relatively clear beginning, middle, and end; and points are clearly convincing. An incoherent narrative tends to ramble; it is characterized by stops and starts, and the evidence does not fit the overall thread of the story. The relative coherence of a story is proposed as reflecting how the storyteller has resolved an emotionally provocative event (Oppenheim, 2003). The relative coherence of recounting negative experiences may be particularly important, as it calls for processing emotional material that is important to the family. For example, the relative coherence of narratives told about coping with a chronic illness is related to better overall family functioning and problem solving (Fiese & Wamboldt, 2003a).

In addition to adult narratives, child narratives also tap whole family processes and provide unique insight into how the child views his or her interpersonal life. For example, child narratives reflecting high emotional security in the context of challenging events are associated with experiencing a consistency between low family discord and parent communications emphasizing family security (Winter, Davies, Hightower, & Meyer, 2006). Likewise, research indicates that children exposed to more destructive forms of family conflict tend to represent escalating conflict (Grych, Wachsmuth-Schlaefer, & Klockow, 2002) and give more negative portrayals of marital and parent–child interaction (Shamir, Schudlich, & Cummings, 2001).

Stories also need to be told. The act of co-constructing a family narrative reflects the *practicing* aspects of the family. Some families will tell stories of personal experience in a supportive manner, adding to others' comments such that the final tale becomes richer. Other families, however, use this as an opportunity to put each other down, derail the storytelling process through sarcasm and cynicism, or shut off others' opinions through outright denial. Style of co-construction, in turn, is related to marital satisfaction and parent–child relationship quality.

It is possible to consider both the content of the co-constructive process, focusing on the resulting story, and the process by which the family works together (or not) to construct the story (see Table 44.1). These dimensions are related to how the family interacts with itself and are considered a reliable index of family functioning (Dickstein, St. Andre, Sameroff, Seifer, & Schiller, 1999; Fiese & Marjinsky, 1999).

Family stories and health and wellbeing

There is emerging evidence that the stories that families create about critical events in their collective lives are related to important health outcomes. For example, families for whom tales of disease management are marked by clear strategies and a resolution of anxiety over the chronic illness are less likely to use the emergency room one year later and more likely to adhere to medical regimens than families whose family stories are marked by anxiety, worry, and unresolved tension (Fiese & Wamboldt, 2003b). Similarly, narratives of how a mother and daughter cope with their own chronic illnesses are powerful indicators of the interconnectedness of providers, healthcare institutions, and extended family members in supporting health and wellbeing (Weingarten & Weingarten-Worthen, 1997).

Why might this be important? Narratives provide a window into the inner workings of family life and how individuals ascribe meaning to important events. They reflect how the family imparts values (see Chapter 43, this volume), highlight what they hold in esteem, and reflect how they manage emotionally evocative circumstances. The resolution of challenging events can be ascertained by the relative coherence of the story and may reflect how close (or far away) the family is to coming to terms with the diagnosis of an illness, loss of a loved one, or suspected dissolution of a marriage. For clinicians, these are markers that can be used to chart response to treatment and gauge therapeutic movement within sessions. Family storytelling may also be used as a technique to engage families to reveal important aspects of their history. Oftentimes these stories are told in celebratory settings or at regular events such as meal times or weekend gatherings.

Table 44.1 Example of Narrative Coding Scheme

Couple narrative style	*Content and process*
Disengaged	**Content**: There are major disagreements or differences of opinion expressed to the extent that one cannot discern the family's story, only the stories of different individuals. **Process**: Interaction is decidedly cool and distant. There is little affect of any type expressed. Family members' behavior shows disengagement. There may be a few episodes of mild, quickly abated anger/rejection/conflict. No evidence of moderate to severe rejection/conflict.
Conflictual/Disruptive	**Content**: There are major disagreements or differences of opinion expressed, to the extent that one cannot discern the family's story, only the stories of different individuals. **Process**: Interaction is hot and negative. There are several episodes of moderate-to-high-intensity anger/rejection/conflict that linger in the interaction.
Conflictual/Contained	**Content**: Couple produces conjoint story in which there are some discrepancies or differences of opinions. These may or may not be resolved within the narrative, but they are not major disruptions to the story as a whole. **Process**: Interaction is conflictual but socialized. There are a few episodes of mild, quickly abated anger/rejection/conflict, or a few episodes of moderate-to-high-intensity anger/rejection/conflict (e.g., put-downs, character assaults, sarcasm) that linger. However, the couple manages to keep the conflict relatively well contained and continue the narrative.
Cooperative	**Content**: Couple produces a conjoint story that hangs together well, containing similar facts, sequences, perspectives, etc. However, there is little augmentation and expansion, as well as little disagreement or fragmentation of the story. **Process**: Interaction is quite pleasant, with couple being engaged with each other. There may be a few episodes of mild, quickly abated anger/rejection/conflict, such as teases, whines, interruptions, disagreements about facts, etc.
Collaborative	**Content**: The story told conjointly is richer than the one the individuals would have told alone. Family members contribute to different pieces of the story that fit together nicely as an integrated whole. **Process**: Interaction is highly collaborative, with some indicators such as the presence of synthetic, synergistic exchanges in which new words and/or frames of reference are introduced and accepted into the story, thereby improving the overall narrative.

Note. Adapted from Fiese, Sameroff, Grotevant, Wamboldt, and Dickstein (1999).

Family Routines and Rituals

Another way to access the whole family process is through the practice of routines and the meaning ascribed to rituals. Every family has its own set of routines that the family members use to organize daily life. For some families the day is highly scripted, to the extent that hourly calendars are posted on the wall reminding everyone of their respons- ibilities and activities. For other families, however, routines are less deliberate and the day unfolds as a series of unforeseen events. This predictability not only provides a sense of order but comes to define a family identity linked to important developmental transitions and family health outcomes.

There is a developmental quality to family routines. During the childrearing years, creating and maintaining routines is part of daily life (Wolin & Bennett, 1984). Establishing regular routines and predictable rhythms may contribute to parental com- petence and efficacy (Sprunger, Boyce, & Gaines, 1985), provide a sense of enjoyment for parent and child (Kubicek, 2002), and contribute to relational wellbeing (Fiese, Hooker, Kotary, & Schwagler, 1993). Families that practice regular and predictable routines are more likely to have children who perform well in school (Fiese, 2000), including chil- dren in low-income, high-risk neighborhoods (Brody & Flor, 1997). Over time, family routines become better organized and more child-centered. During the adolescent years, family routines become less centered on home activities but their association with well- being and health outcomes remains strong (Fiese, 2006). For example, teens who report more regular meal times with their parents are more mentally healthy and less likely to engage in sexually risky behavior, smoke cigarettes, or consume alcoholic beverages than those teens who do not eat with their parents on a regular basis (Compan, Moreno, Ruiz, & Pascual, 2002; Eisenberg, Olson, Neumark-Sztainer, Story, & Bearinger, 2004). Routines are part of the family climate that includes monitoring, order, and affect regu- lation (Fiese, 2006). While routines overlap with principles of family functioning such as involvement, communication, and shared activities (Epstein, Ryan, Bishop, Miller, & Keitner, 2003), they are also directly accessible to clinicians in providing an avenue for intervention (Fiese & Wamboldt, 2001).

Routines have a protective quality, serving to buffer individuals from some of the mor- bidities associated with chronic health conditions. Bush and Pargament (1997) report that for patients with chronic pain, life was less disrupted and less pain was reported overall when there were more predictable routines in the household. Quality of life and the practice of routines have been associated with children's coping behaviors in the context of severe headaches (Frare, Axia, & Battistella, 2002), reduced length of infant respirat- ory illness (Sprunger et al., 1985), and reduced risk of adolescents developing problematic drinking patterns when raised in households with alcoholic parents (Fiese, 1993).

The mechanism of linking routines to health and wellbeing may be twofold. First, families who are better organized in their daily lives are more likely to follow medical advice and adhere to prescribed protocols (Fiese & Everhart, 2006; Fiese, Wamboldt, & Anbar, 2005). However, organization alone does not account for all the variability in family health. A second dimension, symbolic meaning and affective commitment, is integrally connected to quality of life and the emotional burden experienced for families managing chronic health conditions (Fiese et al., 2005). It is the affective and symbolic aspects of repetitive practices that come to define family rituals.

While it is common to think of family rituals as elaborate affairs such as religious or annual celebrations, most families have their own definitions of rituals that are linked to practices created over time (sometimes over many generations) and have special meaning. Family rituals may be as unique as the child's first haircut or as culturally scripted as Thanksgiving dinner. Key ingredients of family rituals are anticipation and felt absence when they are not practiced. For example, after the death of a family member there is often a re-evaluation of how to carry out annual events (birthdays, holidays, reunions). The subtle alterations in these practices bring to the forefront the absence of the family member and the emotional connections that were made during these collective gatherings.

The meaningful commitment to family rituals is related to a host of positive outcomes for youth and adults. When families report that their family rituals hold special meaning, adolescents are less likely to develop problematic drinking (Fiese, 1993), couples with young children are more satisfied with their marriages (Fiese et al., 1993), and there are smoother transitions post-divorce (Whiteside, 2003). However, while routines and rituals can promote health and wellbeing they can also be disruptive. Routines that are rigid and inflexible do not allow for developmental changes. Strict bedtimes and role expectations for elementary age children will not be appropriate for adolescents. Ritual gatherings can also be used to insult and single out members in non-supportive ways. This may be particularly troublesome for members of marginalized groups such as gay and lesbian family members (Oswald, 2002). We have outlined the supportive and disruptive elements of family routines and rituals in Table 44.2.

Table 44.2   Supportive and Disruptive Elements of Routines and Rituals

Meanings	*Routine activities*	*Ritual*
Supportive	Management strategies	Belonging to the group
	Structure	Emotional containment
	Demarking time	Commitment to the future
	Being supported by others	Emotional lineage
	Planning	Consecration of the past
Disruptive	Being rigid or chaotic	Alienation
	Resentments and obligations	Degradation
	Being pressed for time	Exclusion
	Depletion of energy	Coercion
	Explosive or conflictual interactions	Cutting off emotional expression

Note. From Fiese (2006).

Therapeutic Use of Family Stories and Rituals

Clinicians have long used storytelling as a technique to engage family members. Indeed, much of therapy is creating stories about important life events. There are several resources about narrative therapy used in a family context (see Chapter 20, this volume; Angus & McLeod, 2004). Rather than reiterate those sources, we wish to draw to the readers' attention the possibility of using family stories as an information source as well as a marker of therapeutic change.

As an information source, family stories provide accounts of heroes, rogues, and villains across generations. While these stories can be told to a therapist, the work described here suggests that stories among family members may serve as a source of family heritage. This provides a window onto how family members share information with each other and modulate affect in the telling of sensitive events, and is revealing of what type of information may be shared with one member but not another. Important events to consider in family life may be dealing with transitions (birth, moves, marriage), illness, loss, and celebrations. Our own experience tells us that asking family members to "tell a story about the time" a particular event happened is a meaningful prompt when framed from the perspective that we want to know the story they would tell a neighbor over a cup of coffee.

Telling family stories may also be markers of change during the therapeutic process. As individuals begin to resolve emotional distress, their stories should become more coherent and better organized, and relationships should appear more rewarding. Indeed, there is evidence to suggest that following therapeutic interventions, traumatized children's narratives reveal more positive depictions of relationships (Toth, Cicchetti, Macfie, Maughan, & Vanmeenen, 2000). Clearly, this is an area that deserves further research to identify key markers to guide clinicians.

There is also a long history of using rituals in family therapy. One of the more widely cited resources for the use of rituals in family therapy is the work of Imber-Black and colleagues (Imber-Black, Roberts, & Whiting, 2003). Utilizing five different themes (membership, healing, identity, belief expression, and celebration), rituals are used to assist families making the transition across different parts of the life cycle. Home-based interventions have been used to alter family routines to reduce problematic meal-time and bedtime behaviors (Lucyshyn, Kayser, Irvin, & Blumberg, 2002).

Because families vary considerably in their routine practices, it is important to take into account their previous experiences before implementing interventions. While some families may find it relatively easy to fold a new routine into their daily lives given a relatively ordered lifestyle, others will find it more challenging. For some families, the challenge will come from a lack of experience, perhaps across generations. For others, the challenge will arise because family members disagree about the relative importance of implementing a new routine, a phenomenon often seen in maritally distressed couples. It is for these reasons it is essential to take a careful history of past routine practices and engage in clinical decision-making before implementing routine and ritual interventions (Fiese & Wamboldt, 2000).

Conclusions

Family stories, as windows onto the inner workings of the family and how members ascribe meaning and cope with important events, are often reflective of family health and wellbeing. Likewise, family practice of routines and the meaning ascribed via rituals are associated with a host of markers of family and members' wellbeing. What may appear to be a simple turn of phrase in a story may reveal the family emotional lineage. Commonplace meal-time practices may hold the key to the interior workings of complicated family dynamics. It is up to astute clinicians and researchers to capture how the whole may indeed be greater than the sum of its parts.

References

Anderson, H. (2001). Dreams now and then: Conversations about a family's struggles from a collaborative language systems approach. In S. H. McDaniel, D. Lusterman, & C. L. Philpot (Eds.), *Casebook for integrating family therapy: An ecosystemic approach* (pp. 111–125). Washington, DC: American Psychological Association.

Angus, L. E., & McLeod, J. (Eds.). (2004). *The handbook of narrative and psychotherapy: Practice, theory, and research.* Thousand Oaks, CA: Sage.

Brody, G. H., & Flor, D. L. (1997). Maternal psychological functioning, family processes, and child adjustment in rural, single-parent, African American families. *Developmental Psychology, 33*, 1000–1011.

Buehlman, K. T., Gottman, J. M., & Katz, L. F. (1992). How a couple views their past predicts their future. *Journal of Family Psychology, 5*, 295–318.

Bush, E. G., & Pargament, K. I. (1997). Family coping with chronic pain. *Families, Systems, & Health, 15*, 147–160.

Compan, E., Moreno, J., Ruiz, M. T., & Pascual, E. (2002). Doing things together: Adolescent health and family rituals. *Journal of Epidemiology and Community Health, 56*, 89–94.

Dickstein, S., St. Andre, M., Sameroff, A. J., Seifer, R., & Schiller, M. (1999). Maternal depression, family functioning, and child outcomes: A narrative assessment. In B. H. Fiese, A. J. Sameroff, H. D. Grotevant, F. S. Wamboldt, S. Dickstein, & D. L. Fravel (Eds.), *The stories that families tell: Narrative coherence, narrative interaction, and relationship beliefs. Monographs of the Society for Research in Child Development* (Vol. 64 (2), Serial no. 257, pp. 84–104). Malden, MA: Blackwell.

Eisenberg, M. E., Olson, R. E., Neumark-Sztainer, D., Story, M., & Bearinger, L. H. (2004). Correlations between family meals and psychosocial well-being among adolescents. *Archives Pediatric And Adolescent Medicine, 158*, 792–796.

Epstein, N. B., Ryan, C. E., Bishop, D. S., Miller, I. W., & Keitner, G. I. (2003). The McMaster Model: A view of healthy family functioning. In F. Walsh (Ed.), *Normal family processes* (3rd ed., pp. 581–607). New York: Guilford Press.

Fiese, B. H. (1993). Family rituals in alcoholic and nonalcoholic households: Relation to adolescent health symptomatology and problematic drinking. *Family Relations, 42*, 187–192.

Fiese, B. H. (2000). Family matters: A systems view of family effects on children's cognitive health. In R. J. Sternberg & E. L. Grigorenko (Eds.), *Environmental effects on cognitive abilities* (pp. 39–57). Mahwah, NJ: LEA.

Fiese, B. H. (2006). *Family routines and rituals.* New Haven: Yale University Press.

Fiese, B. H., & Bickham, N. L. (2004). Pincurling grandpa's hair in the comfy chair: Parents' stories of growing up and potential links to socialization in the preschool years. In M. W. Pratt & B. H. Fiese (Eds.), *Family stories across time and generations* (pp. 259–277). Mahwah, NJ: Erlbaum.

Fiese, B. H., & Everhart, R. S. (2006). Medical adherence and childhood chronic illness: Family daily management skills and emotional climate as emerging contributors. *Current Opinions in Pediatrics, 18,* 551–557.

Fiese, B. H., Hooker, K. A., Kotary, L., & Schwagler, J. (1993). Family rituals in the early stages of parenthood. *Journal of Marriage and the Family, 57,* 633–642.

Fiese, B. H., & Marjinsky, K. A. T. (1999). Dinnertime stories: Connecting relationship beliefs and child behavior. In B. H. Fiese, A. J. Sameroff, H. D. Grotevant, F. S. Wamboldt, S. Dickstein, & D. Fravel (Eds.), *The stories that families tell: Narrative coherence, narrative interaction, and relationship beliefs. Monographs of the Society for Research in Child Development* (Vol. 64 (2), Serial no. 257, pp. 52–68). Malden, MA: Blackwell.

Fiese, B. H., Sameroff, A. J., Grotevant, H. D., Wamboldt, F. S., Dickstein, S., & Fravel, D. L. (1999). *The stories that families tell: Narrative coherence, narrative interaction, and relationship beliefs. Monographs of the Society for Research in Child Development* (Vol. 64 (2), Serial no. 257). Malden, MA: Blackwell.

Fiese, B. H., & Spagnola, M. (2006). The interior life of the family: Looking from the inside out and the outside in. In A. Masten (Ed.), *Multilevel dynamics in developmental psychopathology: Pathways to the future* (pp. 119–150). Mahwah, NJ: Erlbaum.

Fiese, B. H., & Wamboldt, F. S. (2000). Family routines, rituals, and asthma management: A proposal for family-based strategies to increase treatment adherence. *Families, Systems & Health, 18,* 405–418.

Fiese, B. H., & Wamboldt, F. S. (2003a). Coherent accounts of coping with a chronic illness: Convergences and divergences in family measurement using a narrative analysis. *Family Process, 42,* 3–15.

Fiese, B. H., & Wamboldt, F. S. (2003b). Tales of pediatric asthma management: Family based strategies related to medical adherence and health care utilization. *Journal of Pediatrics, 143,* 457–462.

Fiese, B. H., Wamboldt, F. S., and Anbar, R. D. (2005). Family asthma management routines: Connections to medical adherence and quality of life. *Journal of Pediatrics, 146,* 171–176.

Fivush, R., Bohanke, J., Robertson, R., & Duke, M. (2004). Family narratives and the development of children's emotional well-being. In M. W. Pratt & B. H. Fiese (Eds.), *Family narratives across time and generations* (pp. 55–76). Mahwah, NJ: Erlbaum.

Frare, M., Axia, G., & Battistella, P. A. (2002). Quality of life, coping strategies, and family routines in children with chronic headache. *Headache, 42,* 953–962.

Grotevant, H. D., Fravel, D. L., Gorall, D., & Piper, J. (1999). Narratives of adoptive parents: Perspectives from individual and couple interviews. In B. H. Fiese, A. J. Sameroff, H. D. Grotevant, F. S. Wamboldt, D. L. Fravel, & S. Dickstein (Eds.), *The stories that families tell: Narrative coherence, narrative interaction, and relationship beliefs. Monographs of the Society for Research in Child Development* (Vol. 64 (2), Serial no. 257, pp. 69–83). Malden, MA: Blackwell.

Grych, J. H., Wachsmuth-Schlaefer, T., & Klockow, L. L. (2002). Interparental aggression and young children's representations of family relationships. *Journal of Family Psychology, 16,* 259–272.

Holmberg, D., Orbuch, T. L., & Veroff, J. (2004). *Thrice-told tales: Married couples tell their stories.* Mawhah, NJ: Erlbaum.

Imber-Black, E., Roberts, J., & Whiting, R. A. (Eds.). (2003). *Rituals in families and family therapy* (2nd ed.). New York: Norton.

Kubicek, L. F. (2002). Fresh perspectives on young children and family routines. *Zero to Three, 22,* 4–9.

Lucyshyn, J. M., Kayser, A. T., Irvin, L. K., & Blumberg, E. R. (2002). Functional assessment and positive behavior support at home with families: Defining effective and contextually appropriate behavior support plans. In J. M. Lucyshyn & G. Dunlap (Eds.), *Families and positive behavior support: Addressing problem behavior in family contexts* (pp. 97–132). Baltimore, MD: Paul H. Brookes.

Miller, P. J., Sandel, T. L., Liang, C., & Fung, H. (2001). Narrating transgressions in Longwood: The discourses, meanings, and paradoxes of an American socializing practice. *Ethos, 29,* 159–186.

Miller, P. J., Wiley, A. R., Fung, H., & Liang, C. (1997). Personal storytelling as a medium of socialization in Chinese and American families. *Child Development, 68,* 557–568.

Oppenheim, D. (2003). Children's emotional resolution of MSSB narratives: Relations with child behavior problems and parental psychological distress. In R. Emde, D. P. Wolf, & D. Oppenheim (Eds.), *Revealing the inner worlds of young children* (pp. 147–162). Oxford: Oxford University Press.

Oppenheim, D., Wamboldt, F. S., Gavin, L. A., & Renouf, A. G. (1996). Couples' co-construction of the story of their child's birth: Associations with marital adaptation. *Journal of Narrative and Life History, 6,* 1–21.

Oswald, R. F. (2002). Inclusion and belonging in the family rituals of gay and lesbian people. *Journal of Family Psychology, 16,* 428–436.

Pratt, M. W., Arnold, M. L., & Hilbers, S. M. (1998). A narrative approach to the study of moral orientation in the family: Tales of kindness and care. In E. E. Aspaas Skoe & A. L. Von der Lippe (Eds.), *Personality development in adolescence: A cross-national and life span perspective* (pp. 61–78). London: Routledge.

Pratt, M. W., & Fiese, B. H. (2004). Families, stories and the life course: An ecological context. In M. W. Pratt & B. H. Fiese (Eds.), *Family stories across time and generations* (pp. 1–26). Mahwah, NJ: Erlbaum.

Reiss, D. (1989). The practicing and representing family. In A. J. Sameroff & R. Emde (Eds.), *Relationship disturbances in early childhood.* (pp. 191–220). New York: Basic Books.

Ryan, E. B., Pearce, K. A., Anas, A. P., & Norris, J. E. (2004). Writing a connection: Intergenerational communication through stories. In M. W. Pratt & B. H. Fiese (Eds.), *Family stories and the life course* (pp. 375–398). Mahwah, NJ: Erlbaum.

Shamir, H., Schudlich, T. D., & Cummings, E. M. (2001). Marital conflict, parenting styles, and children's representations of family relationships. *Parenting: Science and Practice, 1,* 123–151.

Sprunger, L. W., Boyce, W. T., & Gaines, J. A. (1985). Family–infant congruence: Routines and rhythmicity in family adaptations to a young infant. *Child Development, 56,* 564–572.

Stern, S., Doolan, M., Staples, E., Szmukler, G. L., & Eisler, I. (1999). Disruption and reconstruction: Narrative insights into the experience of family members caring for a relative diagnosed with serious mental illness. *Family Process, 38,* 353–369.

Toth, S. L., Cicchetti, D., Macfie, J., Maughan, A., & Vanmeenen, K. (2000). Narrative representations of caregivers and self in maltreated preschoolers. *Attachment and Human Development, 2,* 271–305.

Veroff, J., Sutherland, L., Chadiah, L. A., & Ortega, R. M. (1993). Predicting marital quality with narrative assessments of marital experience. *Journal of Marriage and the Family, 55,* 326–337.

Walsh, F. (2002). A family resilience framework: Innovative practice applications. *Family Relations, 51*, 130–137.

Weingarten, K., & Weingarten Worthen, M. E. (1997). A narrative approach to understanding the illness experience of a mother and daughter. *Families, Systems, & Health, 15*, 41–54.

Whiteside, M. F. (2003). Creation of family identity through ritual performances in early remarriage. In E. Imber-Black, J. Roberts, & R. A. Whiting (Eds.), *Rituals in families and family therapy* (pp. 300–329). New York: Norton.

Winter, M. A., Davies, P. T., Hightower, A. D., & Meyer, S. C. (2006). Relations among family discord, caregiver communication, and children's family representations. *Journal of Family Psychology, 20*, 348–351.

Wolin, S. J., & Bennett, L. A. (1984). Family rituals. *Family Process, 23*, 401–420.

45

Systemic Treatments for Substance Use Disorders

Mark Stanton

Substance use disorders (SUDS) are often considered individual disorders residing solely in the substance abuser. Although substance abuse occurs in the context of social relationships, treatment may exclude concerned significant others (CSOs) or marginalize them to an occasional family group session or a few days at the end of treatment.

This chapter presents an argument for the systemic understanding and the systemic treatment of SUDS.[1] A systemic framework is applied to the initial phase of preparing couples and families for change, to the change process phase itself, and to the final phase of relapse prevention. A clinical example is woven into the text to illustrate systemic treatment processes. It is extrapolated from real cases and represents the generally positive evidence for systemic treatment; any individual case may have additional issues that complicate treatment outcomes. Processes to integrate self-help-group participation into systemic treatment are provided. Diversity issues in treatment are explored from a systemic perspective and the chapter concludes with notation of resources for clinicians and academics.

Many psychologists do not consider the treatment of substance abuse an important part of their practice, yet the prevalence of SUDS in clinical populations, the fact that SUDS interact with the etiology and progression of many psychological disorders, and the availability of evidenced-based psychological treatments for SUDS strongly support the idea that psychologists should assess and treat SUDS (Miller & Brown, 1997). Family psychologists have the opportunity to understand and treat SUDS from a perspective that incorporates the systemic dynamics of addictive behaviors. See Chapter 26, this volume, for a review of arguments supporting couples therapy and the Behavioral Couples Therapy (BCT) intervention for SUDS.

The Systemic Context of Substance Use Disorders

Substance abuse occurs within the systemic interaction between individual, interpersonal, and environmental or macrosystemic factors (see Chapter 1, this volume). Miller and Carroll (2006) summarize recent research in the problematic use of substance, noting principles that focus on all three areas within the system. Individual factors relevant to SUDS may include genetic predispositions and metabolism, individual development and temperament, motivation, choice, behavior, and coping skills. Interpersonal factors comprise family dynamics (i.e., risk differences between individuals who experience family discord and those who have positive family relations; the negative impact of parental drug use; domestic violence) and social relations (close connections with people who are not involved in drug use are a protective factor against the influence of drug-abusing peers). Environmental or macrosystemic factors consist of community dynamics (e.g., crime, poverty), cultural values (about abstinence, moderation, or use), involvement in religion and religious beliefs (protective factor; Humphreys & Gifford, 2006), media influences, and social norms.

Introduction of Clinical Case

Jeff was a 36-year-old president of a mortgage finance company. He was married to Elisa, a 29-year-old Latina he met when she worked for him at a former company. They had a daughter, Alessandra, who was 7 and in the second grade. Their life looked good to those on the outside, but Elisa was upset because Jeff's drinking and drug use were beginning to cause problems in the marriage and on his job.

Preparing Couples and Families for Change

As substance-related problems increase in a relationship, it is common for CSOs to fall into the conflicting response modes of enabling and confronting. When CSOs feel powerless and desire to avoid rocking the boat, they may evidence enabling behaviors, such as taking over responsibilities, lying or making excuses, and even joining in use of substances (Rotunda, West, & O'Farrell, 2004). They believe that such behaviors will minimize or manage the negative consequences of the substance use, but enabling could actually prolong the problem.

When frustration with the addictive behavior increases over time, CSOs may confront the substance abuser, demanding change. Some substance abusers will promise to change, but when the CSOs' anger diminishes, so does the commitment to change. Other substance abusers will defend themselves or pull away during the demand episode, a communication pattern called the demand–withdraw interaction. This pattern is usually associated with low relationship satisfaction, and treatment that mimics the demand for abstinence is likely to result in poor retention of such substance abuse patients (Christensen, Eldridge, Catta-Preta, Lim, & Santagata, 2006). Over time, CSOs may alternate between enabling and demanding, remaining stuck in contradictory dynamics.

At some point, the CSO may enter psychotherapy in order to cope with the challenges of living with a substance abuser. This is an important opportunity for change and it is crucial that the family psychologist provide recommendations that reflect the evidence for systemic interventions.

Clinical case

Elisa called me for an appointment at the recommendation of a friend. She was hurt and upset by her husband's behavior when he was drinking alcohol and abusing prescription medication. She stated that her daughter was beginning to appear tense and anxious and she attributed that condition to the conflict in the home around the substance abuse. She indicated that she had tried to reason with Jeff and that she had threatened him, but nothing worked. We scheduled an appointment to consider her options.

Stages of change

The transtheoretical model of intentional human behavior change (TTM) is a framework for understanding behavior change that shifts the focus from denial and resistance to readiness for change and identifies motivation as a key factor in the implementation of intentional change (Prochaska & DiClemente, 2005). The model indicates that change occurs in progressive stages, from pre-contemplation to contemplation to preparation for action to action to maintenance and/or relapse and recycling. This model has been used in substance abuse treatment to conceptualize treatment engagement and therapeutic progress that accord with natural change (e.g., the relationship of consequences to decision-making; DiClemente, 2006). TTM suggests that identification of the addict's current stage of change may facilitate use of the most appropriate therapeutic method for that stage. For example, DiClemente and Velasquez (2002) suggest that people in the pre-contemplation stage have an aversion to lectures and resist action goals because they are not yet ready to change, and that motivational interviewing is beneficial in the early stages of change.

While TTM is an individually based model, it has been applied to systemic treatment interventions for SUDS, including couple and family models (Vetere & Henley, 2001). A systemic approach recognizes that two or more individuals need to be assessed for readiness to change, and different approaches may be needed for different people in systemic treatment. For instance, a CSO may contemplate change while the substance abuser is still in the pre-contemplation stage (Stanton, 2005a). It may be appropriate to treat one member of the couple or family individually until others are ready to enter treatment. The readiness of one person may influence the readiness of another. Family psychologists who understand the systemic nature of the stages of changes ensure that interventions do not get ahead of the individuals in the social system.

Models for initiation of change

CSOs play an important role in engaging substance abusers in treatment (Meyers, Miller, Smith, & Tonigan, 2002; Pollini, McCall, & Mehta, 2006). Steinberg, Epstein, McCrady, and Hirsch (1997) studied the sources of motivation to seek treatment and found that 53% of male alcoholics cited their partner as a primary source. The greater the severity of dependence and the more social consequences of substance abuse, the more likely it is that CSOs will recommend or demand treatment (Room, Matzger, & Weisner, 2004). One woman brought her husband into therapy when she noted the impact of his addictive behavior on their teenage son. Another was worn down by years of cleaning up after her husband's binge drinking; he never suffered the consequences of his behavior because he always awoke in clean clothes and fresh bed linen until his wife stopped cleaning up after him. It may take years of negative experiences for a CSO to get to the point where she or he will take action to initiate change, but CSOs have more influence than they may believe on substance abuser motivation for treatment.

There are three primary pathways for CSOs: Al-Anon, confrontational intervention, and community reinforcement (Fernandez, Begley, & Marlatt, 2006; Stanton, 2005a). Al-Anon is perhaps the best-known option, but it is not a systemic intervention. It focuses entirely on the non-substance abusing partner or family member; it does not profess any intent to change the addict; and it is less effective than other options in engaging the addict in treatment and effecting change in the addictive behavior (Meyers et al., 2002).

Interventions are guided by a trained professional who prepares family members, friends, and co-workers to confront the unsuspecting substance abuser in order to motivate the person to enter treatment immediately. Uncontrolled research suggests that interventions may result in treatment engagement, but Miller, Meyers, and Tonigan (1999) found that only about 30% of the families who began preparation actually conducted the intervention because most considered it too confrontational. A coercive intervention may be counterproductive in some families (Fernandez et al., 2006).

A third option engages the CSO in psychotherapy using motivational enhancement techniques and behavior change to take personal action that may reduce substance use behavior (e.g., offering positive reinforcement for sobriety, discontinuing positive reinforcement for substance use, developing communication skills, taking precautions against domestic violence, and learning how to invite the substance abuser into therapy). CRAFT (Fernandez et al., 2006) is one model of community reinforcement that provides a thorough framework for screening, assessment, and treatment intended to bring the substance abuser into treatment (see Smith & Meyers, 2004, for a detailed description of the model). CRAFT results in significantly greater engagement of unmotivated alcoholics (64%; Miller, Meyers, & Tonigan, 1999) and drug addicts (CRAFT 58.6%, CRAFT + Aftercare 76.7%; Meyers et al., 2002) in treatment than confrontational intervention or Al-Anon facilitation. CRAFT may engage the substance abuser in treatment within as few as five CSO sessions (Miller, Meyers, & Hiller-Sturmhofel, 1999).

Clinical case

In the in-take session, Elisa expressed frustration and despair. Jeff's drinking and substance use were increasing and she was no longer willing to live with them. She was moving from contemplation to preparation for action (i.e., actively considering what she should do and initiating psychotherapy as her first step). We reviewed her assessment materials and discussed how treatment could enhance her coping skills and concurrently prepare her to invite her husband into treatment. She was open to ideas about her reaction to his substance-related behaviors and she agreed to actively implement changes in her marital relationship.

Facilitating Change in Couples and Families

Once the substance abusing individual is willing to come to psychotherapy, it is important that the therapeutic approach smooth the entry and acceptance of treatment.

Motivational interviewing with couples and families

Motivational interviewing (MI) is a non-confrontational approach that seeks to elicit the motivations of the individual for change (Miller & Rollnick, 2002). MI accepts people wherever they may be in the stages of change and assists them in the change process. MI has demonstrated effectiveness in many formats, including treatment with alcoholic patients within four sessions (Burke, Arkowitz, & Dunn, 2002). There are primary principles that guide the approach: (1) express empathy, (2) develop discrepancy, (3) roll with resistance, and (4) support self-efficacy (Miller & Rollnick, 2002, p. 36). MI focuses on helping the substance abuser to consider the addictive behaviors that brought him or her into treatment by considering the difference between what the person desires and the current conditions. The family psychologist facilitates problem solving by the substance abuser and encourages self-efficacy through active reinforcement of the addict's ability to change. The substance abuser may not commit to abstinence, but any reduction in problematic substance use and/or commitment to positive behaviors is considered success. MI has demonstrated effectiveness as an intervention for at-risk couples, attracting and engaging them without overwhelming them and causing the kind of treatment avoidance typical of couples when problems mount over time (Cordova, Warren, & Gee, 2001).

Although MI is usually considered an individual approach, it has been adapted for use with couples, and research indicates that inclusion of a CSO benefits treatment retention and general treatment outcomes (Burke, Vassilev, Kantchelov, & Zweben, 2002).

Traditional MI does not take the social environment into account, so the positive effects of an MI session may be obviated if the substance abusing individual returns home to a CSO who is stuck in the enabling–demanding cycle.

In sessions, the CSO may enhance the enactment of the MI factors and learn what motivates change and what does not, extending motivational exchanges into the day-to-day relationship. The CSO may assist the family psychologist in developing discrepancy by reporting information about behaviors and consequences that the substance abuser does not provide. It is important that such participation be invited by the substance abuser, but this input can be invaluable. Later, the CSO may be able to support self-efficacy by providing affirmation when the addict handles difficult situations well.

This approach understands the systemic nature of change and employs the social system to enhance change processes. Over time, the couple may build motivation into the fabric of the relationship, perpetuating positive change mechanisms (Burke et al., 2002).

Clinical case

Jeff noticed the changes in Elisa's reactions to him and eventually asked her about psychotherapy. She invited him to come for a session and he grudgingly agreed. I used MI techniques to engage him in the initial conjoint session as we discussed his perspective on his use of alcohol and Vicodin, a prescription pain medication. He admitted that his use negatively impacted his attention span at work and home, but he did not think it was a major problem because "it is prescribed by a doctor" (although we later discovered that he was ordering additional pills over the internet). With his permission, I asked Elisa to share her perceptions, which we had rehearsed in her individual sessions. She said a number of positive things about Jeff and then provided a couple of specific examples of problems she encountered around his drug use. Jeff seemed to receive her comments well and I invited him to continue the conjoint sessions; he agreed to attend "a couple of times."

Systemic models of assessment and diagnosis

The CSO can be an important source of information for assessment and diagnosis. Although MI usually avoids an emphasis on diagnosis, it is sometimes important to determine the amount of substance use, the social conditions (e.g., alone or with others), the topographical characteristics of use (e.g., frequency and delivery system), the common locations of use, and the behavioral symptoms related to use. It is clinically useful to interview the substance abuser and the CSO conjointly to elicit thorough and accurate information about the substance abuse. If the couple is cohabiting and the CSO is regularly exposed to the substance use behavior, the CSO provides a collateral report that enhances the accuracy of the interview (Meyers et al., 2002). Experience suggests that addicts minimize or conceal the amount and frequency of use. For instance, one man reported that he would have only one or two drinks each evening, but his wife clarified that each drink contained the equivalent of three to four shots of alcohol. Caution is needed, however, if it appears that the CSO wants to label the substance abuser for legal benefit (e.g., child custody). A thorough substance use history can promote accurate assessment of the problem and serve as part of the motivational process, if it is conducted in the spirit of MI. It should include discussion of the earliest use, historical and current use patterns, route of administration, environmental conditions, and discussion of the consequences of use that might match diagnostic criteria for abuse or dependence. DSM-IV-TR diagnosis (American Psychiatric Association, 1994) clarifies the extent of a substance use problem and is helpful in treatment planning, even though the diagnosis is not stated or used to pressure the patient. Diagnostic terminology and the substance use history may be beneficial when the patient is at the contemplation, preparation, or change stage, if they are used in a fashion similar to the MI technique termed the "Drinker's Check-Up" to motivate change (Handmaker & Walters, 2002). In addition, a genogram (McGoldrick, Gerson, & Shellenberger, 1999) that notes any problematic use of substances in other family members can assist in recognizing social influences and incorporating them into treatment.

Clinical case

In the second conjoint session, we explored Jeff's history of alcohol and pain medication usage. Jeff had used alcohol throughout his adult life, starting in high school and peaking in college, until the recent increase; he started Vicodin after a motorcycle accident left him with serious leg injury. He had slowly increased his dosage until he was taking 12 pills a day. The mix of alcohol and pain medication often left him moody and irritable and he noted that he was having more negative interactions at work and home. He indicated he needed to cut down on the Vicodin, so I encouraged him to consult his physician. Elisa was encouraged by his openness. He didn't think he had a problem with alcohol, although our assessment indicated he was drinking several beers each evening.

Integrating Self-Help Approaches into Couple and Family Treatment

Twelve-step (TS) group participation is a common stand-alone or adjunct intervention for SUDS. Couple or family treatment may benefit from ancillary involvement in Alcoholics Anonymous or another drug-specific self-help program. TS facilitation (Nowinski, 2002) is a structured process designed to encourage participation in TS meetings because of the beneficial aspects of the program (e.g., social network replacement, sponsors, worldwide meeting locations), increase in therapeutic factors (increased self-efficacy, active coping), and positive outcome measures, such as commitment to abstinence (Morgenstern, Labouvie, McCrady, Kahler, & Frey, 1997). Randomized controlled trials find that active referral to TS groups resulted in greater involvement with TS groups (i.e., service, spiritual awakening, having a sponsor) and better alcohol and drug use outcomes at 6 months (Timko, DeBenedetti, & Billow, 2006).

Two key qualifiers for referral to TS groups are recognition of the mandate for acceptance of the addict label and a commitment to abstinence; TS groups are not a reasonable referral for anyone unwilling to agree with either or both of these conditions. In addition, spirituality is a critical component of the TS model, so it is important to discuss openness to spiritual resources for recovery as part of the referral (Nowinski, 2002). There is evidence for the relationship between religious variables and sobriety (Michalak, Trocki, & Bond, 2007).

A potential conflict between TS participation and systemic treatment is the intense conviction sometimes experienced in TS groups that the addict alone can work the program. This suggests that CSOs play no role in the recovery process, an idea directly contradictory to research findings. In addition, sponsors sometimes mandate practices that conflict with couple and family relationships (e.g., attendance at particular meetings, although this conflicts with family obligations). It is important to balance the demands of active TS participation with family relationships that impact recovery and relapse. On the other hand, TS programs feature many psychosocial components, such as new sober friendships, sober social functions, and couple groups that benefit recovery.

Clinical case

As we continued conjoint sessions, Jeff agreed to lower his alcohol consumption and work with his physician to decrease his Vicodin use until he could switch to another medication with less potential for tolerance and abuse. He was not ready to label himself an addict and he clearly did not want to give up alcohol altogether. Given these conditions, I refrained from referring him to Alcoholics Anonymous, but we discussed the need to monitor his use for any return to higher consumption. He agreed to accept input from Elisa if she noticed any increase.

Dynamic Systems Model of Relapse Prevention

Relapse prevention (RP) is a cognitive-behavioral strategy for identifying and managing situations that present high risk for relapse to SUDS. Witkiewitz and Marlatt (2004) review the tenets of the model (identification of people, places, and events that pose a risk for problematic use; development of adequate coping responses to overcome the risk; questioning beliefs about the positive effects of the substance; and preparing for possible lapses in order to avoid a major relapse), summarize research on the effectiveness of the model ("Several studies have shown sustained main effects for RP, suggesting that RP may provide continued improvement over a longer period of time," p. 225), and introduce a revised dynamic systems model of relapse prevention.

Early models of relapse prevention were linear and presented simple cause–effect relations between factors. Witkiewitz and Marlatt (2004) developed a more complex and dynamic model of relapse that incorporates systemic concepts (e.g., reciprocity, feedback, self-organization) to explain the multidimensional nature of lapse and relapse. The new model recognizes "the utility of non-linear dynamical systems" (p. 231) and unpacks the various intrapersonal (e.g., self-efficacy, outcome expectancies, craving, motivation, coping, and emotional states) and interpersonal (e.g., social support) determinants of relapse. The relapse process is reconceptualized around dealing with multiple influences across time, including distal risks (i.e., "stable predispositions that increase an individual's vulnerability to lapse," p. 229) and proximal risks (i.e., "immediate precipitants that actualize the statistical probability of a lapse," p. 229), and the reciprocal relationship between the various elements of the model (e.g., coping influences use and use influences coping). As illustrated in Figure 45.1, there are tonic processes that reflect chronic vulnerabilities for relapse and phasic responses that incorporate more immediate processes in high-risk situations; these interact in the midst of high-risk situations and predict relapse (p. 230). Clinicians need to gather detailed information about each of the factors in the two arenas in order to determine how they interact in a particular high-risk situation.

Stanton (2005b) welcomes the dynamic systems model of relapse, but notes that while it thoroughly posits intrapersonal elements, it provides inadequate attention to interpersonal factors. Social support is identified as a distal risk (i.e., a stable predisposition), making it a historical artifact similar to family history. He suggests that social support, as a rubric for a variety of interpersonal factors, be included among the phasic responses that occur in the midst of high-risk situations, interacting with intrapersonal factors (see inset in Figure 45.1).

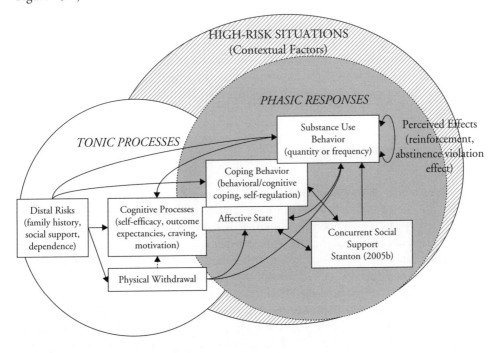

Figure 45.1   Dynamic model of relapse

Witkiewitz & Marlatt (2004), amended by Stanton (2005b)

It is possible to integrate interpersonal factors into the relapse prevention process. For instance, CSOs may help identify high-risk situations, participate in role plays to promote coping, accompany the substance abuser in high-risk situations, and promote self-efficacy by positive comments about coping behaviors. In addition, it is important to recognize that interpersonal conflict may influence the emotional state of the addict and precipitate relapse. Witkiewitz and Marlatt (2005) agreed with the suggestion, although they noted that the interaction between interpersonal factors and treatment outcomes is complex. They suggest that intrapersonal processes mediate the relationship between interpersonal factors and relapse. Further research is needed to understand the dynamic, systemic nature of relapse prevention.

Case Conclusion

We identified the people, places, and events that created the most risk for Jeff to increase his use of alcohol and pain medication. He admitted using Vicodin to cope with people and problems at work that had nothing to do with his physical pain. He also reported that he sometimes reacted to tension at home by increasing his alcohol consumption, although that was less likely now that he and Elissa were in therapy. Elissa verified that a couple of the problem people at work were "jerks," from her interaction with them at various functions, and she suggested some ways to cope with them that Jeff appreciated. We worked on marital communication and discussed ways for Jeff to express himself when he was upset, rather than drinking or using drugs, and ways for Elissa to comment constructively when she recognized a current or upcoming risky situation. Alcohol use was now minimal, usually confined to dinner out or social events, and Jeff was on an antidepressant that helped moderate his pain, so Vicodin abuse was not currently a problem. Jeff gave Elissa permission to comment if she saw him self-medicate.

Diversity Issues in Treatment

The role of ethnic diversity, socioeconomic status, gender, age, religion, and sexual orientation in choice of treatment, treatment engagement, and treatment effectiveness research for SUDS is an important issue that is receiving more attention in the literature. Schmidt, Ye, & Greenfield (2007) found that at higher levels of severity, Hispanics and African Americans were less likely to utilize SUDS services than similar Caucasians. In addition, Hispanics cited more severe alcohol problems than Caucasians, yet they were less likely to have received specialty alcohol treatment, and they were more likely to note financial and logistical barriers to treatment. Increasingly, studies are considering the interaction between multiple diversity issues, such as ethnicity, age, and sexual orientation (Hughes, Wilsnack, & Szalacha, 2006), in order to understand how best to treat segments of the population.

Holder (2006) suggests a community integrated systems model to address ethnic and gender differences for prevention and treatment in a geographical area. He goes against customized treatment programs for each ethnic group to recommend combined prevention and treatment at a community level, addressing the broad spectrum of issues that surround the problematic use of substances (e.g., violence, financial problems, unemployment, crime, child abuse, family discord) in a particular area. He recommends macrosystemic changes in a catchment area to reduce substance abuse, reinforced by microsystemic, group-specific strategies. This results in a systemic intervention to address group differences. SBIRT (screening, brief intervention, and referral to treatment) is an integrated approach to universal screening for substance use disorders that addresses many of these factors in primary care settings and has shown substantial effect (Babor, McRee, & Kassebaum, 2007).

Summary

Despite the effectiveness of many systemic approaches to the treatment of SUDS, these approaches are still not widely known or implemented. Individual approaches continue to dominate the field and many family psychologists are unaware of the opportunity to use systemic approaches for SUDS. This chapter reviews models adapted for therapeutic engagement, motivational interviewing, and relapse prevention to incorporate the system into treatment.

Note

1   This chapter combines information on alcohol and substance abuse or dependence, using the DSM-IV terminology of substance use disorders. Some studies focus specifically on alcohol, others on one or more particular drugs.

Resources

HBO Series on Addiction: see 20-minute presentation of CRAFT
Motivational Interviewing website: http://www.motivationalinterview.org
Project Mainstream: http://www.projectmainstream.net
SAMHSA: http://www.samhsa.gov

References

American Psychiatric Association. (1994). *Diagnostic and statistical manual of mental disorders* (4th ed.). Washington, DC: American Psychiatric Association.

Babor, T. F., McRee, B. G., & Kassebaum, P. A. (2007). Screening, brief intervention, and referral to treatment (SBIRT): Toward a public health approach to the management of substance abuse. *Substance Abuse, 28(3)*, 7–30.

Burke, B., Vassilev, G., Kantchelov, A., & Zweben, A. (2002). Motivational interviewing with couples. In W. Miller & S. Rollnick (Eds.), *Motivational interviewing: Preparing people for change* (2nd ed., pp. 347–361). New York: Guilford Press.

Burke, B. L., Arkowitz, H., & Dunn, C. (2002). The efficacy of motivational interviewing and its adaptations: What we know so far. In W. R. Miller & S. Rollnick (Eds.), *Motivational interviewing: Preparing people for change* (2nd ed., pp. 347–361). New York: Guilford Press.

Christensen, A., Eldridge, K., Catta-Preta, A. B., Lim, V. R., & Santagata, R. (2006). Cross-cultural consistency of the demand/withdraw interaction pattern in couples. *Journal of Marriage and Family, 68*, 1029–1044.

Cordova, J. V., Warren, L. Z., & Gee, C. B. (2001). Motivational interviewing as an intervention for at-risk couples. *Journal of Marital & Family Therapy, 27(3)*, 315–326.

DiClemente, C. C. (2006). Natural change and the troublesome use of substances: A life-course perspective. In W. R. Miller & K. M. Carroll (Eds.), *Rethinking substance abuse: What the science shows, and what we should do about it* (pp. 81–96). New York: Guilford Press.

DiClemente, C. C., & Velasquez, M. M. (2002). Motivational interviewing and the stages of change. In W. R. Miller & S. Rollnick (Eds.), *Motivational interviewing* (2nd ed., pp. 201–216). New York: Guilford Press.

Fernandez, A. C., Begley, E. A., & Marlatt, G. A. (2006). Family and peer interventions for adults: Past approaches and future directions. *Psychology of Addictive Behaviors, 20(2)*, 207–213.

Handmaker, N. S., & Walters, S. T. (2002). Motivational interviewing for initiating change in problem drinking and drug use. In S. G. Hofmann & M. C. Tompson (Eds.), *Treating chronic and severe mental disorders: A handbook of empirically supported interventions* (pp. 215–233). New York: Guilford Press.

Holder, H. D. (2006). Racial and gender differences in substance abuse: What should communities do about them? In W. R. Miller & K. M. Carroll (Eds.), *Rethinking substance abuse: What the science shows, and what we should do about it* (pp. 153–165). New York: Guilford Press.

Hughes, T. L., Wilsnack, S. C., & Szalacha, L. A. (2006). Age and racial/ethnic differences in drinking and drinking-related problems in a community sample of lesbians. *Journal of Studies on Alcohol, 67(4)*, 579–590.

Humphreys, K., & Gifford, E. (2006). Religion, spirituality, and the troublesome use of substances. In W. R. Miller & K. M. Carroll (Eds.), *Rethinking substance abuse: What the science shows, and what we should do about it* (pp. 257–274). New York: Guilford Press.

McGoldrick, M., Gerson, R., & Shellenberger, S. (1999). *Genograms: Assessment and intervention* (2nd ed.). New York: Norton.

Meyers, R. J., Miller, W. R., Smith, J. E., & Tonigan, J. S. (2002). A randomized trial of two methods for engaging treatment-refusing drug users through concerned significant others. *Journal of Consulting and Clinical Psychology, 70*, 1182–1185.

Michalak, L., Trocki, K., & Bond, J. (2007). Religion and alcohol in the U.S. National Alcohol Survey: How important is religion for abstention and drinking? *Drug and Alcohol Dependence, 87(2–3)*, 268–280.

Miller, W. R., & Brown, S. A. (1997). Why psychologists should treat alcohol and drug problems. *American Psychologist, 52*, 1269–1279.

Miller, W. R., & Carroll, K. M. (2006). Drawing the science together: Ten principles, ten recommendations. In W. R. Miller & K. M. Carroll (Eds.), *Rethinking substance abuse: What the science shows, and what we should do about it* (pp. 293–311). New York: Guilford Press.

Miller, W. R., Meyers, R. J., & Hiller-Sturmhofel, S. (1999). The community-reinforcement approach. *Alcohol Research and Health, 23,* 116–121.

Miller, W. R., Meyers, R. J., & Tonigan, J. S. (1999). Engaging the unmotivated in treatment for alcohol problems: A comparison of three strategies for intervention through family members. *Journal of Consulting and Clinical Psychology, 67,* 688–697.

Miller, W. R., & Rollnick, S. (2002). *Motivational interviewing: Preparing people for change* (2nd ed.). New York: Guilford Press.

Morgenstern, J., Labouvie, E., McCrady, B. S., Kahler, C. W., & Frey, R. M. (1997). Affiliation with Alcoholics Anonymous after treatment: A study of its therapeutic effects and mechanisms of action. *Journal of Consulting and Clinical Psychology, 5,* 768–777.

Nowinski, J. (2002). Twelve-step facilitation therapy for alcohol problems. In S. G. Hofmann & M. C. Thompson (Eds.), *Treating chronic and severe mental disorders: A handbook of empirically supported interventions* (pp. 258–276). New York: Guilford Press.

Pollini, R. A., McCall, L., & Mehta, S. H. (2006). Non-fatal overdose and subsequent drug treatment among injection drug users. *Drug and Alcohol Dependence, 83(2),* 104–110.

Prochaska, J. O., & DiClemente, C. C. (2005). The transtheoretical model. In J. C. Norcross & M. R. Goldfried (Eds.), *Handbook of psychotherapy integration* (2nd ed., pp. 147–171). New York: Oxford University Press.

Room, R., Matzger, H., & Weisner, C. (2004). Sources of informal pressure on problematic drinkers to cut down or seek treatment. *Journal of Substance Use, 9(6),* 280–295.

Rotunda, R. J., West, L., & O'Farrell, T. (2004). Enabling behavior in a clinical sample of alcohol-dependent clients and their partners. *Journal of Substance Abuse Treatment, 26,* 269–276.

Schmidt, L. A., Ye, Y., & Greenfield, T. K. (2007). Ethnic disparities in clinical severity and services for alcohol problems: Results from the National Alcohol Survey. *Alcoholism: Clinical and Experimental Research, 31(1),* 48–56.

Smith, J. E., & Meyers, R. J. (2004). *Motivating substance abusers to enter treatment: Working with family members.* New York: Guilford Press.

Stanton, M. (2005a). Couples and addiction. In M. Harway (Ed.), *The handbook of couples therapy* (pp. 313–336). Hoboken, NJ: Wiley.

Stanton, M. (2005b). Relapse prevention needs more emphasis on interpersonal factors. *American Psychologist, 60,* 340–341.

Steinberg, M. L., Epstein, E. E., McCrady, B. S., & Hirsch, L. S. (1997). Sources of motivation in a couples outpatient alcoholism treatment program. *American Journal of Drug and Alcohol Abuse, 23(2),* 191–205.

Timko, C., DeBenedetti, A., & Billow, R. (2006). Intensive referral to 12-step self-help groups and 6-month substance use disorder outcomes. *Addiction, 101(5),* 678–688.

Vetere, A., & Henley, M. (2001). Integrating couples and family therapy into a community alcohol service: A pantheoretical approach. *Journal of Family Therapy, 23,* 85–101.

Witkiewitz, K., & Marlatt, G. A. (2004). Relapse prevention for alcohol and drug problems: That was Zen, this is Tao. *American Psychologist, 59,* 224–235.

Witkiewitz, K., & Marlatt, G. A. (2005). Emphasis on interpersonal factors in a dynamic model of relapse. *American Psychologist, 60,* 341–342.

46

Couples Therapy for Depression

Mark A. Whisman, Valerie E. Whiffen, and Natalie Whiteford

A growing body of research indicates that marital discord is important for understanding the onset, course, and treatment of depression. In this chapter, we provide a selective review of the literature on marital functioning and depression, and a thorough review of the research on the effectiveness of couples therapy in the treatment of depression. Finally, we conclude with suggestions for future research and clinical practice.

Couple Discord and Depression

The quality of close, romantic relationships – most often measured in married couples and labeled as "discord," "distress," or "dissatisfaction" – covaries with depressive symptoms in cross-sectional studies. To provide an overall estimate of the strength of association between marital dissatisfaction and depressive symptoms, Whisman (2001b) conducted a meta-analysis of existing research; a meta-analysis is a summary of previous research that uses quantitative methods to compare outcomes across studies and provide a measure of the magnitude or degree of the association (i.e., an effect size). The weighted mean effect size (r) across 26 studies was .42 for women and .37 for men. The square of the effect size r (i.e., r^2) can be interpreted as the proportion of variance in either of the two variables that may be accounted for by the variance of the other variable. Squaring these effect sizes, therefore, suggests that 18% of the variability in women's and 14% of the men's marital dissatisfaction or depressive symptoms can be accounted for by the other variable. Furthermore, compared to non-depressed individuals, people with diagnosed depressive disorder report greater levels of marital dissatisfaction (Whisman, 2001b). Finally, these effects are not associated with treatment seeking per se, as it has been shown that compared to people who do not have a depressive disorder, marital dissatisfaction is higher in people with either major depression or dysthymia in population-based samples (e.g., Whisman, 1999, 2007).

Cross-sectional studies are limited insofar as they do not address the direction of cause and effect. That is, whereas marital discord may be a consequence of depression in many cases, it also has been suggested as contributing to depression. For example, according to the marital discord model of depression (Beach, Sandeen, & O'Leary, 1990), marital discord contributes to increased risk for depression through the loss of social support and the generation of social stress. Similarly, the interpersonal model advanced by Klerman, Weissman, Rounsaville, and Chevron (1984) proposes that interpersonal conflict, including marital conflict, can act as a precipitating factor in the onset of depression. In support of these perspectives, results from longitudinal studies have shown that marital distress is prospectively associated with increases in depressive symptoms (e.g., Beach, Katz, Kim, & Brody, 2003). Davila, Karney, Hall, and Bradbury (2003) used growth curve analysis in a sample of newlyweds and demonstrated that increases in either marital distress or depressive symptoms were associated with concomitant increases in the other variable. Interestingly, there was no difference in the two effect sizes, which suggests that marital distress is as likely to influence depression as vice versa. Marital functioning at baseline also predicts onset of major depressive episodes at follow-up. For example, in a population-based sample of over 900 married adults who did not meet criteria at baseline for a major depressive episode (MDE) in the past year, a categorical measure of marital distress at baseline was associated with a 2.7-fold increased risk for MDE during the following 12 months (Whisman & Bruce, 1999).

Researchers also have evaluated the association between couple functioning and treatment outcome for depressed individuals. If marital functioning is associated with the maintenance or course of depression, then people in discordant relationships who are in treatments for depression that do not specifically modify relationship functioning may have poorer outcomes than people in better relationships. Generally, the results show that relationship difficulties at the *beginning* of treatment are associated with poorer outcome, both post-treatment (Rounsaville, Weissman, Prusoff, & Herceg-Baron, 1979) and at follow-up (Rounsaville, Prusoff, & Weissman, 1980), and with greater risk for relapse (Hooley & Teasdale, 1989). Similarly, marital functioning at the *end* of treatment is associated with negative outcome at follow-up (Goering, Lancee, & Freeman, 1992). These effects hold regardless of the type of individual treatment. In the NIMH Treatment of Depression Collaborative Research Program (which evaluated the effectiveness of cognitive therapy, interpersonal psychotherapy, pharmacotherapy plus clinical management, or placebo plus clinical management), post-treatment level of marital adjustment (Kung & Elkin, 2000; Whisman, 2001a) and the extent of marital improvement over the course of treatment (Kung & Elkin, 2000) predicted levels of depressive symptoms at follow-up.

In summary, marital discord is a correlate of both depressive symptoms and diagnostic depression. Marital discord predicts subsequent increases in depressive symptoms and the onset of diagnostic depression, and predicts poorer outcome to individual treatments for depression. Such findings have led researchers to consider the possibility that couples therapy may be an effective treatment for depression.

Couples Therapy for Depression

Cognitive-behavioral couples therapy

The approach to couples therapy that has received the most attention from researchers in treating depression is cognitive-behavioral couples therapy (CBCT; Epstein & Baucom, 2002; see Chapter 16, this volume, for a thorough review and case example of CBCT). This treatment usually spans 15 to 20 sessions and uses a combination of behavioral strategies and cognitive restructuring to improve couple's interactions and to decrease discord. Therapy begins by aiming to increase positive behaviors directed toward one's partner, thus enhancing feelings of closeness. Communication skills are then introduced to help partners share their thoughts, feelings, and concerns with each other in increasingly effective ways. Finally, problem-solving skills are taught to help partners negotiate conflict when it does arise. CBCT has been shown to be effective in the treatment of marital discord: a meta-analysis of seven clinical trials comparing CBCT with waiting-list control groups in treating marital discord yielded a mean effect size (d) of .95 (Byrne, Carr, & Clark, 2004). This effect size indicates that the post-treatment mean level of marital satisfaction for people who received treatment was nearly one standard deviation higher than the mean level of marital satisfaction for people who did not receive treatment. This effect size can be interpreted as indicating that the average couple who received CBCT was better off at the end of treatment than 83% of untreated couples.

Several treatment outcome studies have investigated the effectiveness of CBCT as a treatment for depression. Beach and O'Leary (1992) examined the efficacy of CBCT and individual cognitive therapy (CT) relative to a waiting-list control group for couples who were experiencing marital discord and in which the wife met diagnostic criteria for either major depression or dysthymia. CBCT was as effective as CT in reducing wives' depressive symptoms at the end of treatment, and both treatments were more effective than was the waiting-list control condition. In the CBCT condition, wives also experienced a significant increase in marital satisfaction from pre- to post-therapy, and they had significantly higher marital satisfaction scores at post-treatment than wives in CT or the waiting-list control conditions; wives in the other two groups did not demonstrate an increase in satisfaction and they did not differ at post-treatment. At one-year follow-up, improvements in depressive symptoms had been equally maintained in the CBCT and CT groups. However, the CBCT group reported significantly higher marital satisfaction than did the CT group, suggesting that CBCT was a more effective treatment for marital discord than individual CT for these depressed women.

Jacobson, Dobson, Fruzzetti, Schmaling, and Salusky (1991) compared the effectiveness of CBCT and CT, singly and in combination, in the treatment of wives' depression in couples that varied in their level of marital discord. The combined (CO) treatment included some CBT sessions and some CT sessions. All treatment groups were equally successful at alleviating depression. However, level of marital discord had an impact on treatment efficacy such that women who received CT experienced decreases in depression regardless of their level of marital discord, whereas CBCT was more effective in alleviating depression when women were in discordant relationships. Similarly, all groups showed improvements in marital satisfaction, but level of marital discord again played a role in treatment efficacy. In general, non-discordant couples did not show much change in marital satisfaction regardless of treatment type. However, among discordant couples, only CBCT led to significant improvements in marital satisfaction. A one-year follow-up of these couples showed that gains were maintained in all three treatment groups, and CBCT was comparable to CT for couples who were in discordant marriages at the beginning of the study (Jacobson, Fruzzetti, Dobson, Whisman, & Hops, 1993).

In addition to evaluating outcome, these studies examined mediators and moderators of change to begin to address questions about "how" and for "whom" CBCT is effective in treating depression. With regard to mediators of change, Jacobson et al. (1991) reported that improvements in marital satisfaction covaried with decreases in depression in the CBCT condition, but not in the CT or CO conditions, suggesting that treatment effects on depression for people in CBCT, but not CT, may at least in part be due to treatment effect on marital distress. Beach and O'Leary (1992) conducted formal tests of mediation, and found changes in marital adjustment mediated the effects of CBCT on change in depressive symptoms. Taken together, these results suggest that CBCT alleviates depression by improving marital quality, as predicted by the marital discord model of depression.

With regard to moderators of change, Beach and O'Leary (1992) found that the predictor variables they examined were unrelated to outcome for CBCT. However, they found that a better pre-treatment marital environment and more dysfunctional thinking predicted better outcome in CT. In addition, people who believed that marital discord preceded or was the cause of their depression were more likely to experience increases in marital discord following CT than those who felt that depression had preceded their marital problems (O'Leary, Riso, & Beach, 1990). These results support a matching hypothesis, in which CBCT may be a promising treatment choice for depressed individuals who have poorer marriages at the onset of therapy and/or who believe that their marital problems contribute to their depression.

Emanuels-Zuurveen and Emmelkamp (1996) evaluated the efficacy of a slightly modified version of CBCT that initially focused on problems associated with depression that may interfere with marital therapy, before shifting the focus to communication skills. These researchers compared this treatment with CT, and found that both treatments were equally effective in reducing depressive symptoms, depressive behavior, and dysfunctional cognitions. Compared to CT, however, couples therapy resulted in greater improvement in relationship functioning (i.e., greater satisfaction, better communication, and lower levels of expressed emotion). Compared to people who received CT, people in the couples therapy condition were more likely to drop out of treatment (due to marital separation or disappointment that the treatment did not explicitly deal with depression), which may inflate the estimated efficacy of couples therapy. Finally, similar to the results of Jacobson et al. (1991), pre- to post-treatment changes in marital satisfaction covaried with changes in depressive symptoms, consistent with the perspective that the effects of couples therapy on depression may be mediated by improvement in marital quality.

Teichman, Bar-El, Shor, Sirota and Elizur (1995) proposed that interpersonal patterns play a role in maintaining depression, and sought to alter these patterns through couples-based cognitive interventions. Their treatment was compared to individual CT. Results demonstrated that at the end of treatment, individuals in the couples therapy condition had significantly fewer depressive symptoms than individuals in either the CT or waiting-list conditions; individual CT was no more effective than the waiting-list condition. At a 6-month follow-up, however, the rate of recovery was equal between individuals in the couples and CT conditions. With respect to potential mechanisms of change, people in the couples therapy condition improved in their cognitions and emotions, but not in their behaviors (Teichman, Bar-El, Shor, & Elizur, 1998). Also, whereas CT primarily affected the cognitions and emotions of the depressed spouse, couples therapy resulted in more widespread effects on the cognitions and emotions of both spouses.

In summary, the research findings to date on variants of CBCT as a systemic approach to treating depression suggest that: (a) CBCT is as effective as CT in treating depression; (b) CBCT is more effective than CT in improving marital quality; and (c) the effects of CBCT on depression are mediated through treatment effects on marital quality. The limited research on moderators of outcome has not found significant predictors of outcome to CBCT for depression, other than the fact that CBCT appears to be most effective for people that are in discordant relationships.

Emotion-focused couples therapy

To this point in the chapter, we have been discussing the link between marital discord and depression. Another aspect of couple functioning that is important in the development of depression is attachment insecurity. A large body of research suggests that couple relationships can usefully be conceptualized as attachment relationships. Individuals who are securely attached in their couple relationship are more satisfied with their relationships than insecurely attached persons, and they are confident that their partner will be emotionally available to them and responsive to their emotional needs, especially during periods of stress or crisis (Johnson & Whiffen, 1999). Although there is overlap between the concepts of attachment insecurity and marital discord, this correlation is imperfect, and it is possible to be discordant without feeling insecurely attached. One study suggested that marital discord was increasingly associated with depressive symptoms with increasing levels of anxious-ambivalent attachment, which reflects a desire to be closer than the partner seems to want (Scott & Cordova, 2002).

At this time, no comprehensive model of depression exists that explains the link with attachment insecurity. However, we do know that having an emotionally avoidant or unresponsive romantic partner is a risk factor for depression (Whiffen, 2005; Whiffen, Kallos-Lilly, & MacDonald, 2001). Significant life stressors commonly precede episodes of depression (Kessler, 1997), and an unresponsive partner may be particularly problematic when an individual encounters life stress. In a secure couple relationship, partners provide emotional support to one another in the face of life stress (Simpson, Rholes, & Nelligan, 1992). However, mutual support giving is less likely to occur in an insecure couple relationship, which may leave stressed individuals feeling isolated, and hence at risk for depression.

Emotion-focused couples therapy (EFT) is based on adult attachment theory, and the model integrates techniques from the experiential and family systems approaches. In this model, attachment insecurity is the primary target of change rather than marital discord per se (see Chapter 27, this volume, for a thorough review and case example of EFT; Johnson, 1996). For some couples, the relationship never was secure; for other couples, one or both partners experienced an "attachment injury" which damaged the bond (Johnson, Makinen, & Milliken, 2001). Although attachment injuries can arise from many circumstances, common examples include extramarital affairs or one partner's inability to be emotionally supportive of the other partner during a significant life crisis. The goals of EFT are: (a) to identify repetitive negative interaction cycles that are the manifestation of attachment insecurities; (b) to reframe these cycles in terms of the underlying attachment needs; and (c) to facilitate the expression and the acceptance of one another's attachment needs. When specific attachment injuries are identified, the therapist attempts to use emotional processing of these injuries to allow the injured partner to move toward a more secure bond.

Although the target of change in EFT is attachment insecurity, a meta-analysis of seven randomized clinical trials comparing EFT with a waiting-list control group indicated that it also has a positive impact on marital discord, with a mean effect size (d) of 1.27 (Byrne et al., 2004). This effect size can be interpreted as indicating that the average couple who received EFT was better off at the end of treatment than 89% of untreated couples. Furthermore, there is evidence that treatment gains are maintained up to 2 years after the end of treatment, and that, for some couples, the relationship continues to improve after treatment ends (Cloutier, Manion, Walker, & Johnson, 2002).

EFT may be especially effective for the treatment of depression because the therapy targets both marital discord and attachment insecurity. Several case studies have described the use of EFT in the treatment of depressed women (e.g., Whiffen, 2004; Whiffen & Johnson, 1998). Two outcome studies showed EFT to significantly reduce depressive symptoms in couples coping with a chronically ill child (Walker, Johnson, Manion & Cloutier, 1996) and in women with low sexual desire (MacPhee, Johnson, & van der Veer, 1995). One study evaluated treatment outcome in a small sample of clinically depressed women in couples where at least one partner was moderately distressed about the marriage (Dessaulles, Johnson, & Denton, 2003). In this study, EFT was as effective as antidepressants in reducing depressive symptoms.

Other couples therapy approaches

Other couples therapy approaches were developed specifically for the treatment of depression. Because these approaches do not have as firm an empirical foundation as either CBCT or EFT, we review them less extensively.

An early couples therapy that was developed for treating depression is based on interpersonal psychotherapy (IPT; Klerman et al., 1984). This conjoint treatment for depressed patients with marital disputes (IPT-CM) adopts the same basic methods and focuses on the same problem areas as IPT, but differs insofar as the partner is included in each session and that treatment focuses on improving communication and intimacy (Weissman, Markowitz, & Klerman, 2000). In a small pilot study, IPT-CM was compared with individual IPT (Foley, Rounsaville, Weissman, Sholomskas, & Chevron, 1989). People in both treatments improved equally in depression and social functioning, but both partners in IPT-CM reported greater improvements in marital adjustment.

Systemic couples therapy (Jones & Asen, 2000) combines strategic and structural concepts and techniques with feminist, narrative, and social constructionist ideas. This treatment, which consists of three phases spread over 12–20 sessions, focuses on developing new ways of interacting and interrupting problematic cycles of behavior to shift negative attributions (Leff et al., 2000). Interestingly, in developing this treatment, the authors first piloted a treatment that specifically sought to reduce criticism by the partner because perceived and actual criticism predict the course of depression (Hooley & Teasdale, 1989). Techniques to reduce criticism, however, had little impact on depression and therefore were not retained in this approach (Leff et al., 2000). In a randomized controlled trial of systemic couples therapy versus antidepressants for depressed patients who were living with a critical spouse, couples therapy had lower rates of attrition and resulted in lower self-reported depression severity through a 2-year follow-up (Leff et al., 2000). Furthermore, it was found that the reduction in partners' critical comments was similar in the two treatments, and therefore did not account for the improved outcome in the couples therapy condition (Leff et al., 2003). The authors suggest that the better outcome may have been due to a greater reduction in the proportion of patients exposed to partners' hostility in this condition. However, this was largely due a greater number of couples in the couples therapy condition that separated during the study.

Recommendations for the Use of Couples Therapy to Treat Depression

We do not recommend couples therapy as a treatment in all cases of depression. Outcome studies of CBCT suggest that couples therapy is most likely to be effective when depressed individuals are in discordant relationships. In addition, because attributing the onset of depression to relationship distress or recognizing this distress as a factor that maintains it is associated with less improvement in individual treatment, depressed spouses who hold such beliefs may be particularly well suited for couples therapy. Furthermore, because marital discord is more strongly associated with depression among people with elevated anxious-ambivalent attachment (Scott & Cordova, 2002), depressed individuals may benefit most from couples therapy when they also are insecurely attached in that relationship.

In our clinical work, there is an additional condition in which we find couples therapy to be useful: when the depressed individual has recovered from depression, but the couple relationship has not changed sufficiently or in ways that support the changes made in individual therapy. All of us create patterns in the ways we interact with the most important people in our lives. Successful individual therapy changes those patterns, especially in couple relationships. If recovered depressed persons fall back into the same patterns that contributed to the onset of their depression, they will be at risk for subsequent episodes. However, partners do not always perceive the changes made in individual therapy as positive, and they may resist the recovered depressed person's attempts to create new patterns. Couples therapy can be a very helpful adjunct to successful individual treatment when negative patterns in the relationship contributed to the original episode of depression.

Future Directions in Couples Therapy for Depression

One important direction for future research would be to replicate and expand upon studies evaluating the effectiveness of specific approaches to couples therapy. With the exception of CBCT, couples treatments for depression have been evaluated in only one trial, and replication is important, particularly replication conducted by researchers other than those who developed the treatment, to rule out allegiance effects and establish that the intervention is transportable.

Second, relative to the data on overall treatment effectiveness, there is little research on the mediators and moderators of couples therapy for depression. That is, we know relatively little about how couples therapy results in changes in depression. Similarly, we know relatively little about the kinds of couples or individuals that are likely to benefit from couples therapy. It will be important to evaluate not only whether a variable predicts the outcome of couples therapy in general, but also whether it differentially predicts the outcome of one versus another approach to couples therapy or differentially predicts the outcome of couples therapy versus individual treatment. Although differential predictors of outcome may be difficult to identify, such predictors would be particularly helpful in guiding clinical decision-making as to whether couples therapy should be pursued, and if so, which approach is most likely to be beneficial for a particular couple.

A third area for future research is the effectiveness of couples therapy in clinical practice. All the clinical trials conducted to date have been efficacy studies, in which adherence to a protocol has been closely followed by highly trained clinicians working with people who meet detailed inclusion and exclusion criteria. Effectiveness research is needed, therefore, to evaluate the impact of couples therapy in treating depression in routine clinical practice.

The empirical evidence we have reviewed in this chapter is consistent in showing that couples therapy is an efficacious treatment for depression. Our conclusions about the efficacy of couples therapy converge with growing evidence that depression is an emotional disorder that is strongly linked to the interpersonal context in which depressed persons live, particularly depressed women (Whiffen, 2006). Couples therapies inherently address the most significant interpersonal context in a married person's life.

In light of the strength of the empirical evidence, we are concerned that this topic remains relatively neglected both by researchers and in clinical practice. No efficacy study of CBCT for depression has been conducted since the mid-1990s. Although the EFT study was published more recently, the fact that only one study has been published suggests a surprising lack of research on a disorder that is so clearly linked to attachment insecurity. We strongly encourage researchers to pursue this area of research by conducting studies along the lines we described earlier in this section. We also encourage clinicians to consider couples therapy when beginning treatment with any depressed person who is married or in a committed relationship. Administration of a measure of couple discord, such as the Dyadic Adjustment Scale (Spanier, 1976), and a self-report measure of attachment security, such as the Close Relationships Questionnaire (Bartholomew & Horowitz, 1991), would add little time to the assessment, but could quickly identify people who may be better served by couples than individual treatment. More targeted treatment of interpersonal conditions that lead to or exacerbate an individual's depression may prevent the relapse that is so distressingly common in this disorder.

Resources

Beach, S. R. H. (2001). *Marital and family processes in depression: A scientific foundation for clinical practice.* Washington, DC: American Psychological Association.

Beach, S. R. H., Sandeen, E. E., & O'Leary, K. D. (1990). *Depression in marriage: A model for etiology and treatment.* New York: Guilford Press.

Whiffen, V. E. (2006). *A secret sadness: The hidden relationship patterns that make women depressed.* Oakland, CA: New Harbinger.

References

Bartholomew, K., & Horowitz, L. M. (1991). Attachment styles among young adults: A test of a four-category model. *Journal of Personality and Social Psychology, 61,* 226–244.

Beach, S. R., & O'Leary, K. D. (1992). Treating depression in the context of marital discord: Outcome and predictors of response of marital therapy versus cognitive therapy. *Behavior Therapy, 23,* 507–528.

Beach, S. R. H., Katz, J., Kim, S., & Brody, G. H. (2003). Prospective effects of marital satisfaction on depressive symptoms in established marriages: A dyadic model. *Journal of Social and Personal Relationships, 20,* 355–371.

Beach, S. R. H., Sandeen, E. E., & O'Leary, K. D. (1990). *Depression in marriage: A model for etiology and treatment.* New York: Guilford Press.

Byrne, M., Carr, A., & Clark, M. (2004). The efficacy of behavioral couples therapy and emotionally focused therapy for couples distress. *Contemporary Family Therapy, 26,* 361–387.

Cloutier, P. F., Manion, I. G., Walker, J. G., & Johnson, S. M. (2002). Emotionally-focused interventions for couples with chronically ill children: A 2-year follow-up. *Journal of Marital and Family Therapy, 28,* 391–398.

Davila, J., Karney, B. R., Hall, T. W., & Bradbury, T. N. (2003). Depressive symptoms and marital satisfaction: Within-subject associations and the moderating effects of gender and neuroticism. *Journal of Family Psychology, 17*, 557–570.

Dessaulles, A., Johnson, S. M., & Denton, W. H. (2003). Emotion-focused therapy for couples in the treatment of depression: A pilot study. *American Journal of Family Therapy, 31*, 345–353.

Emanuels-Zuurveen, L., & Emmelkamp, P. M. G. (1996). Individual behavioural-cognitive therapy v. marital therapy for depression in maritally distressed couples. *British Journal of Psychiatry, 169*, 181–188.

Epstein, N. B., & Baucom, D. H. (2002). *Enhanced cognitive-behavioral therapy for couples.* Washington, DC: American Psychological Association.

Foley, S. H., Rounsaville, B. J., Weissman, M. M., Sholomskas, D., & Chevron, E. (1989). Individual versus conjoint interpersonal psychotherapy for depressed patients with marital disputes. *International Journal of Family Psychiatry, 10*, 29–42.

Goering, P. N., Lancee, W. J., & Freeman, J. J. (1992). Marital support and recovery from depression. *British Journal of Psychiatry, 160*, 76–82.

Hooley, J. M., & Teasdale, J. D. (1989). Predictors of relapse in unipolar depressives: Expressed emotion, marital distress, and perceived criticism. *Journal of Abnormal Psychology, 98*, 229–235.

Jacobson, N. S., Dobson, K., Fruzzetti, A. E., Schmaling, K. B., & Salusky, S. (1991). Marital therapy as a treatment for depression. *Journal of Consulting and Clinical Psychology, 59*, 547–557.

Jacobson, N. S., Fruzzetti, A. E., Dobson, K., Whisman, M., & Hops, H. (1993). Couple therapy as a treatment for depression: II. The effects of relationship quality and therapy on depressive relapse. *Journal of Consulting and Clinical Psychology, 61*, 516–519.

Johnson, S. M. (1996). *The practice of emotionally focused marital therapy: Creating connection.* Philadelphia: Brunner/Mazel.

Johnson, S. M., Makinen, J., & Millikin, J. W. (2001). Attachment injuries in couples: A new perspective on impasses in couple therapy. *Journal of Marital and Family Therapy, 27*, 145–155.

Johnson, S. M., & Whiffen, V. E. (1999). Made to measure: Adapting emotionally focused couples therapy to partners' attachment styles. *Clinical Psychology: Science and Practice, 6*, 366–381.

Jones, E., & Asen, E. (2000). *Systemic couple therapy and depression.* London: Karnac Books.

Kessler, R. C. (1997). The effects of stressful life events on depression. *Annual Review of Psychology, 48*, 191–214.

Klerman, G. L., Weissman, M. M., Rounsaville, B. J., & Chevron, E. (1984). *Interpersonal psychotherapy of depression.* New York: Basic Books.

Kung, W. W., & Elkin, I. (2000). Marital adjustment as a predictor of outcome in individual treatment of depression. *Psychotherapy Research, 10*, 267–278.

Leff, J., Alexander, B., Asen, E., Brewin, C. R., Dayson, D., Vearnals, S., et al. (2003). Modes of action of family interventions in depression and schizophrenia: The same or different? *Journal of Family Therapy, 25*, 357–370.

Leff, J., Vearnals, S., Brewin, C. R., Wolff, G., Alexander, B., Asen, E., et al. (2000). The London Depression Intervention Trial: Randomised controlled trial of antidepressants v. couple therapy in the treatment and maintenance of people with depression living with a partner: Clinical outcome and costs. *British Journal of Psychiatry, 177*, 95–100.

MacPhee, D. C., Johnson, S. M., & van der Veer, M. M. C. (1995). Low sexual desire in women: The effects of marital therapy. *Journal of Sex & Marital Therapy, 21*, 159–182.

O'Leary, K. D., Riso, L. P., & Beach, S. R. (1990). Attributions about the marital discord/depression link and therapy outcome. *Behavior Therapy, 21*, 413–422.

Rounsaville, B. J., Prusoff, B. A., & Weissman, M. M. (1980). The course of marital disputes in depressed women: A 48-month follow-up study. *Comprehensive Psychiatry, 21*, 111–118.

Rounsaville, B. J., Weissman, M. M., Prusoff, B. A., & Herceg-Baron, R. L. (1979). Marital disputes and treatment outcome in depressed women. *Comprehensive Psychiatry, 20*, 483–490.

Scott, R. L., & Cordova, J. V. (2002). The influence of adult attachment styles on the association between marital adjustment and depressive symptoms. *Journal of Family Psychology, 16*, 199–208.

Simpson, J. A., Rholes, W. S., & Nelligan, J. S. (1992). Support seeking and support giving within couples in an anxiety-provoking situation: The role of attachment styles. *Journal of Personality and Social Psychology, 62*, 434–446.

Spanier, G. B. (1976). Measuring dyadic adjustment: New scales for assessing the quality of marriage and similar dyads. *Journal of Marriage & the Family, 38*, 15–28.

Teichman, Y., Bar-El, Z., Shor, H., & Elizur, A. (1998). Changes in cognitions, emotions, and behaviors in depressed patients and their spouses following marital cognitive therapy, traditional cognitive therapy, pharmacotherapy, and no intervention. *Journal of Psychotherapy Integration, 8*, 27–53.

Teichman, Y., Bar-El, Z., Shor, H., Sirota, P., & Elizur, A. (1995). A comparison of two modalities of cognitive therapy (individual and marital) in treating depression. *Psychiatry, 58*, 136–148.

Walker, J. G., Johnson, S., Manion, I., & Cloutier, P. (1996). Emotionally focused marital intervention for couples with chronically ill children. *Journal of Consulting and Clinical Psychology, 64*, 1029–1036.

Weissman, M. M., Markowitz, J. G., & Klerman, G. L. (2000). *Comprehensive guide to interpersonal psychotherapy*. New York: Basic Books.

Whiffen, V. E. (2004). Myths and mates in childbearing depression. *Women and Therapy, 27*, 151–163.

Whiffen, V. E. (2005). The role of partner characteristics in attachment insecurity and depressive symptoms. *Personal Relationships, 12*, 407–423.

Whiffen, V. E. (2006). *A secret sadness: The hidden relationship patterns that make women depressed*. Oakland, CA: New Harbinger.

Whiffen, V. E., & Johnson, S. M. (1998). An attachment theory framework for the treatment of childbearing depression. *Clinical Psychology: Science & Practice, 5*, 478–493.

Whiffen, V. E., Kallos-Lilly, A. V., & MacDonald, B. J. (2001). Depression and attachment in couples. *Cognitive Therapy and Research, 25*, 577–590.

Whisman, M. A. (1999). Marital dissatisfaction and psychiatric disorders: Results from the National Comorbidity Survey. *Journal of Abnormal Psychology, 108*, 701–706.

Whisman, M. A. (2001a). Marital adjustment and outcome following treatments for depression. *Journal of Consulting and Clinical Psychology, 69*, 125–129.

Whisman, M. A. (2001b). The association between marital dissatisfaction and depression. In S. R. H. Beach (Ed.), *Marital and family processes in depression: A scientific foundation for clinical practice* (pp. 3–24). Washington, DC: American Psychological Association.

Whisman, M. A. (2007). Marital distress and DSM-IV psychiatric disorders in a population-based national survey. *Journal of Abnormal Psychology, 116*, 638–643.

Whisman, M. A., & Bruce, M. L. (1999). Marital distress and incidence of major depressive episode in a community sample. *Journal of Abnormal Psychology, 108*, 674–678.

47

Families and Public Policy

Margaret Heldring

Healthcare costs are rising and the number of uninsured people grows each year. Burdened by the costs of providing healthcare insurance coverage to employees and families, employers are shifting a larger percentage of premium costs to the employee, leaving more employees unable to handle this share and, consequently, declining coverage for themselves and their families. Financial pressures on Medicare, the healthcare program for people 65 years and older and with disabilities, embolden policy makers whose ideology prefers privatization of this social insurance program to attempt to cut payments to providers, means test the benefit, and reduce benefits. Medicare, while clearly an important entitlement for older Americans and disabled ones, has significant benefits beyond provision of healthcare. Poverty rates among older Americans have declined impressively since its 1965 inception, and millions of families have remained employed and productive because they have had the freedom and security of knowing their older family members are protected. The long-term solvency of Social Security is good but not certain, and is best characterized as an inverted triangle where fewer workers pay into the system that must support a growing number of people who retire.

Are there any of these circumstances that do not affect families? The obvious answer is no. In the finite world of most families' resources, rising prices crowd out something else – food, summer camp for a child, and even jobs dependent on use of cars and trucks. A Pittsburgh elementary school teacher admits she does not like to see the school year end in her public school in a low-income neighborhood. "I know many of these kids won't have enough to eat this summer. School is where they get food, not necessarily book learning." Because families are a system, a change in circumstances for one member of the family means a change for all. Yet families are only marginally considered in public policy, if at all.

After more than a decade in public policy and politics, I returned to the practice of psychology with a new view of the field. As health staff to two former U.S. Senators and the director of health policy for a 2000 U.S. presidential campaign, I saw how psychology looks to others and I gained insight about our relation to the policy-making world. These new vantage points allow me to see our professional strengths and liabilities – where we are present and effective as well as where we are absent and ineffective in public policy. Psychology permeates everything. Family psychology is a potentially influential tool for policy making, but not yet as persuasive and potent as it can and should be. There is, however, progress.

The public better understands psychology and mental health now than even a decade ago. Often out of tragedies such as natural and human-made disasters, the public has a more enlightened view of trauma and other psychological conditions that effect individuals, families, or even entire communities. The public resonates to mind–body connection, its intuitive knowledge pre-dating the growing body of scientific evidence that establishes and explains the mechanisms of connection. Both the public and healthcare providers want to act on the U.S. Surgeon General's report (1999) and the President's New Freedom Commission on Mental Health (2003) that stated that mental health is fundamental to health and should flow in the mainstream of healthcare. Psychology has much to offer to the public interest, and recent APA reports, such as *Blueprint for Change: Achieving Integrated Health Care for an Aging Population* (Brehm et al., 2008) and *Psychopharmacological, Psychosocial, and Combined Interventions for Childhood Disorders: Evidence Base, Contextual Factors, and Future Directions* (APA Workgroup on Psychotropic Medications for Children and Adolescents, 2006), are excellent examples of the contributions psychology makes to the public interest and add to public understanding of the field. Each of these is also material for family policies, even while they are presented as population-, age-, or issue-specific.

It is not difficult to establish that family psychology has a vital role to play in public policy. However, it is difficult to bring psychological science to bear on public policy making. This challenge is regrettable, as billions of dollars and millions of lives are misdirected and affected by omission. This dynamic is part of the larger challenge to ensure that any science informs policy. Often, it does not, or is cherry-picked for "facts" that reinforce a particular political point of view and agenda. However, as we focus on families and public policy, and hope to strengthen this connection, we must (1) articulate the rationale for a family view in policy making, (2) review the history of the relation between families and public policy, (3) identify action steps that family psychologists, indeed all psychologists and policy makers, can take to strengthen the relation, and (4) ask three core questions that arise as we explore this area:

- What challenges confront a stronger connection between families and policy making?
- How do gender, culture, race, age, sexual orientation, and ethnicity play out in policies that affect families?
- How can psychology, especially family psychology, help shape positive public policies?

This chapter is a call for greater awareness of how families are affected by U.S. policies on the federal, state, and local levels and a call for greater advocacy on behalf of families (Bogenschneider, 2006). We want to strengthen a family perspective in public policy.

Even a cursory glance at the global and domestic issues confronting people and societies leads us to psychology and families (Bogenschneider, 2006). It leads us to our science, the many professional applications of our science, how we train future psychologists, and to how psychology impacts the public interest. For example, psychology is one of the health and mental health professions working to overcome stigma about mental illness and eliminate discriminatory public policies about it (see Chapter 53, this volume). Neither psychology nor any other mental health profession can eliminate stigma and change the entrenched perceptions of mental illness without significant policy changes. Policies will not change without collaboration among partners and allies who share an agenda for a healthier population and families. Policy changes require leadership, even champions of the cause, and an informed, focused public mandate. As these key ingredients align behind a mission, the chances that policies can change improve. Recent successes in attaining mental health parity on both state and federal levels are casebook examples of alignment and sustained, coordinated, collaborative action.

There is a secondary benefit to collaboration that extends beyond the advocacy of a specific issue, and that is a heightened public understanding of psychology and a stronger, more respected voice in policy making. As we act together in the public interest, we enhance our standing and our power. Collaboration, capturing the wisdom of the crowd and the voices of many, increases chances for new, shared solutions to pressing social problems – whether eliminating racial disparities in health status or changing behavior on a grand scale in order to save the planet. Individual and group behavior and development, person–environment interactions, and systems perspectives are hallmarks of family psychology that stand to enrich solutions to social problems. Because we believe that families are the foundation for stable, healthy people and societies, we must extend our reach beyond our traditional professional boundaries to develop a more mature professional identity and creates new opportunities to shape public policies.

The Place of Family in Public Policy

Families have a legally derived place in U.S. policies, but these policies are insufficiently developed and less respected and influential than they can become. The current legal basis for a family view derives from U.S. P.L. [public law] 105–277, which former U.S. President William Clinton signed into law on October 21, 1998. This law requires that federal agencies assess the impact of proposed agency action on family wellbeing. However, there is no requirement that congressional committees include a family impact statement when reporting out a bill or joint resolution.

The history of this policy starts with Senators Paul Wellstone (D-MN) and Spencer Abraham (R-MI). They each offered amendments to a bill during the close of the 105th Congress. The Wellstone amendment, ultimately deleted, stated that any joint resolution or bill reported by a House or Senate committee and accompanied by a committee without a "detailed analysis of the probable impact of the bill or resolution on family wellbeing and children" would not be in order. The Abraham amendment, ultimately incorporated into final language, was less ambitious and specified only the federal agency requirement. Such family impact statements are not new ideas. As a matter of record, policy makers have considered them periodically and family researchers have tried to develop valid tools and checklists with which to assess impact and define the construct "family wellbeing." Despite attempts, these efforts stall for several reasons.

It is challenging to agree on a definition of family (see Chapter 10, this volume, for more discussion of this issue). It has proven difficult to develop valid measures and consensus about the benefit of such actions. Family impact statements come up against the ambiguous, often tense, intersection of values and policy. Leadership and advocacy for family impact statements have been uneven and have increasingly been caught up in the political rhetoric about family values. We hear more about the need to help America's families during political campaigns than we do during the legislative process, when the public is less tuned in and the ability to reach consensus on definition and import more elusive. In short, there are landmines aplenty in the field of family policy and few legislators know how to traverse this territory. This is where family psychology, indeed all professions working for families, can be of assistance. We could spend several years mapping guiding principles and developing metrics for a valid, sustainable framework for family public policy. This is a worthy aspiration.

As background, family impact statements originated in Scandinavia in the 1960s. In 1973, former Senator Walter Mondale chaired a U.S. Senate Subcommittee on Children and Youth. He and others recognized the changing composition of families, changes they attributed to an increasing divorce rate, a declining number of children in families, and the large-scale entry of women into the workforce. It is time to review these assumptions certainly, but they were the prevailing sociological theories of that time. Mondale held hearings to discuss to what extent government policies are helping or hurting families and called Urie Bronfenbrenner, Margaret Mead, and Edward Zigler to testify. Each recommended family impact statements. Although the hearings brought new legitimacy to family policy, and while the subcommittee endorsed the idea of a family impact statement, it nonetheless determined that additional research was needed before introducing legislation. The Family Impact Seminar (FIS) assumed responsibility for conducting this research (Ooms, 1984). Using environmental impact statements as a model, FIS developed a framework and methodology for conducting family impact statements. FIS is now the Policy Institute or Family Impact Seminars, located at the University of Wisconsin-Madison, and has developed and published a checklist that offers policy makers a framework on which policies that affect families could be developed. This serves as a start for a new roadmap.

The University of Wisconsin Policy Institute's checklist for assessing the impact of policies on families identifies six principles to frame the checklist. Some of the principles strive to be value free and some, the institute acknowledges, may be interpreted as values that may not be universally shared. These principles are:

- family support and responsibilities;
- family membership and stability;
- family involvement and interdependence;

- family partnership and empowerment;
- family diversity;
- support of vulnerable families.

Just reading these words, one grasps their ambiguity and controversy immediately. No wonder any forward progress in finding consensus in a definition of family, shared goals and aspirations, and strategies with which to achieve these stalls quickly. Nonetheless, there is a history of efforts and a rationale for trying again.

In an attempt to move toward a coherent family policy and perhaps family impact statement, Jimmy Carter made family a central theme in his 1976 campaign, stating that, "it is clear that the national government should have a strong pro-family policy, but in fact our nation has no family policy, and that is the same as an anti-family policy." In 1980, the Carter Administration held a White House Conference on Families in three U.S. cities: Baltimore, Minneapolis, and Los Angeles. Issues such as abortion, gay marriage, and the Equal Rights Amendment dominated the debate among delegates. Today only one-fifth of U.S. Senators address family policy on their websites. An encouraging sign is the bipartisan distribution of mention. Two website examples are:

> Ultimately, our national well being – our economic prosperity and our quality of life – depends on the strength of our families. It is a legitimate function of our government to support strong families and make sure parents have the tools they need to protect their children and do what's best for them. (Senator Amy Klobuchar (D-MN); Klobuchar, 2007)

> Strong families are an essential function of society. I believe our government therefore has a duty to promote and protect the family in the policies we create and sustain. (Senator John Thune (R-SD); Thune, 2007)

Again, this highlights the ambiguity of family policy in the United States. Other issues are addressed with much greater frequency: immigration, agriculture, energy, Social Security, Medicare, national security, and transportation. There is less debate that these issues are properly within the domain of government actions. No one would argue that government does not belong in these domains, but there is plenty of disagreement about the merits of considering the family in the formulation and implementation of policies.

There was a trend toward greater specificity in family policies. In 1987, President Ronald Reagan issued an Executive Order that required the Executive Branch to argue how, if at all, government should go about the shared goal of protecting and strengthening families. The Clinton presidential years saw the passage of the Family and Medical Leave Act and several other pieces of legislation with a direct bearing on families. These include the Child Health Insurance Program (S-CHIP), which requires mental health parity, and the Temporary Assistance to Needy Families (TANF), which replaced welfare reform as we knew it. This is not an endorsement of these laws, but a note that new family laws were written. The Big Issues of today and recent years – war, natural disasters, climate change, immigration, economic stability, poverty, healthcare and public health, and education – all bear intensely on families and children.

While there is a legal requirement that family have a place in public policy, its place remains too hidden, minimally effective, and unknown. The struggle to find a place for family in policy has surfaced periodically for some 35 years, but is regularly obstructed by controversial wedge issues. It remains challenging to come together, separate ideology and politics from policy, and actually develop and implement family policy.

Action Steps

There are important actions psychologists can take to advocate for thoughtful, culturally competent, inclusive family policies. On the local, state, and federal levels, family psychologists must raise the profile on this issue. Education efforts to make known the existence of the federal agency requirement to conduct a family impact statement are a good first step. The American Psychological Association can help build a coalition to develop and issue a national report card on how policies are affecting families. Priority must be given to highlighting how the burdens of poverty, unemployment, access to healthcare, education, and even agriculture fall disproportionately across race, class, gender, ethnicity, age, and immigrant and refugee status. Discourse about family policies must be separated from those about family values. While advocating for a national family policy, we should be attuned to life-stage issues and argue for their singularity as much as their commonality. Aging, children, gay and lesbian parenting, fostering and adopting, early family formation, stepfamilies, single-parent families, cross-cultural and biracial families, parenting by grandparents, and caring for family members with chronic health conditions are all unique at the same time that they share experiences within and about family.

Traditionally, the U.S. government aims to support strong families, but falls short on providing the means, tools, protections, and opportunities to make this vision a reality. Serious actions on behalf of families would have a positive ripple effect across many social issues. As Drew Altman, CEO of the Kaiser Family Foundation, commented, "the best health and human services program is a strong family and a good job."

References

APA Workgroup on Psychotropic Medications for Children and Adolescents (2006). *Psychopharmacological, psychosocial and combined interventions for childhood disorders.* Washington, DC: American Psychological Association.

Bogenschneider, K. (2006). *How policymaking affects families and what professionals can do.* Mahwah, NJ: Erlbaum.

Brehm, S. S., Antonucci, T. C., Zeiss, A. M., Hinrichsen, G. A., King, D. A., Lichtenberg, P., et al. (2008). *Blueprint for CHANGE: Achieving integrated health care for an aging population.* Washington, DC: American Psychological Association.

Klobuchar, A. (2007). *Families and children.* Retrieved October 29, 2007, from http://klobuchar.senate.gov/families.cfm

New Freedom Commission on Mental Health (2003). *Achieving the promise: Transforming mental health care in America. Final report.* DHHS Pub. No. SMA-03–3832. Rockville, MD.

Ooms, T. (1984). The necessity of a family perspective. *Journal of Family Issues, 5,* 160–181.

Thune, J. (2007). *Issue statements – family.* Retrieved October 29, 2007, from http://thune.senate.gov/public/index.cfm policy

U.S. Department of Health and Human Services. (1999). *Mental health: A report of the Surgeon General – Executive Summary.* Rockville, MD: U.S. Department of Health and Human Services, Substance Abuse and Mental Health Services Administration, Center for Mental Health Services, National Institutes of Health, National Institute of Mental Health.

48

Family Psychology of Immigrant Mexican and Mexican American Families

Joseph M. Cervantes and Olga L. Mejía

It is difficult to imagine a time when immigration in the United States was not a salient theme of conversation. It is a truism that this country is a nation of immigrants where battles and wars have been fought over who rightly deserves citizenship and who does not (Takaki, 1993). The immigration experience for all documented and undocumented individuals is a complex and often non-validating process that frequently threatens the integrity of the family (Hernandez, Denton, & McCartney, 2007; Ngai, 2004). Immigrating to this country has been an issue for many groups with each having a relevant sociocultural history that highlights specific traditions, economic needs, and reasons for entry into the United States. Although at times there will be references to Latino subgroups in general, this chapter will focus on the Mexican immigrant who historically has had generations of political, economic, and familial presence in the United States (Gonzalez, 2000; Vigil, 1998).

This chapter will offer an overview of issues surrounding immigration with Mexican and Mexican American families. To illustrate salient concepts, two cases are interwoven in the chapter. Each reflects distinct immigration experiences that provide some of the complex challenges for these families.

Terminology

Cultural population referents will be used throughout this chapter. *Immigrant*, synonymous with first-generation, is defined as a person who was born in one country and immigrated into another. *Latina/o* is used to designate both genders and generally refers to a diverse population that includes people from various national origins, including Mexico,

Central America, South America, and the Spanish-speaking Caribbean (Romero, 1997); the term originated within the Spanish-speaking community and is intended to emphasize particular indigenous ancestry. The term *Mexican* refers to a person who is born in Mexico, while *Mexican American* refers to a person with Mexican ancestry born in the United States. For a more comprehensive view of these cultural referents, refer to Comas-Diaz (2001).

Demographics

Latinos constitute about 14.2%, or 40.5 million, of the U.S. population, and Mexicans constitute the largest Latino subgroup at nearly 26 million (U.S. Census Bureau, 2007). Passel and Suro (2005) indicate that approximately 2.5 million immigrants have entered into the United States for foreign humanitarian reasons and another 9 million crossed into the country without documentation. These data would suggest that the number of undocumented immigrants is much greater than the number of legal immigrants. Martin (2003) reports that approximately 1 million legal immigrants each year become legal permanent residents (LPR), which is the initial step toward U.S. citizenship. As such, the number of individuals who attempt to obtain legal status is quite low in comparison to those who have minimal to no intention of pursuing legal status in the country.

Who immigrates and from where

It is estimated that about 42% of Mexican immigrants arrived in the United States before 1990, 37% arrived between 1990 and 1999, and 21% arrived after 2000 (U.S. Census Bureau, 2007). Fussell (2004) states that the motivation for migrating primarily comes from the lack of employment opportunities in Mexico, mainly in rural communities. However, Fussell notes that recently increasing numbers of legal and undocumented immigrants are from interior urban cities, such as Mexico City and Guadalajara.

Cultural values in Mexican families and communities

Latino, including Mexican, cultural values have been described as reflecting collectivistic characteristics (Falicov, 1998) which may be in conflict with mainstream individualistic values of U.S. society. Those specific values and belief systems have included *collectivismo* (collectivism), *familismo* (familism), *compadrazco* (godparentage), *personalismo* (personalism), *respeto* (respect for authority), *fatalismo* (fatalism), *simpatia* (affection), and *dignidad* (dignity) (see Chapter 5, this volume). It is imperative for clinicians, educators, and researchers to be aware that these cultural values greatly influence the overall function-ing of Mexicans and Mexican Americans. Several authors connect cultural values to pro-fessional practice with families (Cervantes & Sweatt, 2004; Santiago-Rivera, Arredondo,

& Gallardo-Cooper, 2002). Cultural values may protect immigrants from experiencing the same level of psychiatric disorders as present in the society to which they immigrate (Grant et al., 2004), but that protection may decrease the longer they reside in the United States (Alegría et al., 2007).

Immigrant families have a wide range of migration experiences, varied acculturation level, generational history, and legal status (Falicov, 2005; Jimenez, 2007; Ramakrishnan, 2004; Wainer, 2006). The migration process significantly impacts how the elements of culture, context, and circumstances play out in the acculturation experience. An illustration of these three elements is now demonstrated with the introduction of two case studies that will be developed throughout this chapter.

Case A: Newly arrived immigrant family

Juan and Guadalupe Osorio crossed over the border from Mexico City approximately three years ago with their young children (Chela, age 8, and Manuel, age 6). The migration journey was traumatic, resulting in the separation of the parents during part of the trip from Tijuana to San Diego. The harrowing hike across the mountain range resulted in Chela being dehydrated, causing mother to stay behind with her and younger son aided by two other women in order not to slow down the rest of the group. Within a few days after hiding in an undisclosed home in San Diego, the family was reunited. They were taken under the cover of night to a relative's home in Los Angeles where the *coyote* was paid the balance of the $4,000 charged for this traumatic crossing. After three months of living with relatives, the family rented a room from a co-worker who resided with his own family in a three-bedroom home.

Case B: Immigrant family with psychological and medical difficulties

Carmen and Mario Lopez are a young couple who met in Guadalajara at a family party. Mario was just finishing medical school and Carmen was a secretary. They married and soon had two boys, Ismael and Raul. However, they had difficulty making ends meet, and decided they might have greater financial and educational opportunities for their family in the United States. After a long process, they gained legal documentation and moved to live with friends in Los Angeles until they could find work and housing. Upon their arrival in the United States the young professional couple had a difficult time adjusting, given their limited English-speaking skills and difficulty finding employment and housing. Being a physician in Mexico, Mario found a job as a medical assistant during the day and worked at a restaurant in the evenings. Carmen then stayed at home with the children in their one-bedroom apartment. As time progressed and about the age of 10, Ismael began to display some particularly odd behaviors. He started to silently mumble to himself and talk back to voices and visions. Carmen and Mario were at a loss, very concerned for the wellbeing of their oldest son, and not aware of how to secure medical services for him.

Migration Process

What happens to immigrants once they arrive in the United States? They are likely to face numerous challenges including learning a new language, unemployment, legal issues, change and expectations about respective family members, and grieving a prior existence and extended family left behind. Undocumented Mexican families may experience the following changes after immigration: separations and changes in the family system, especially when the adult male immigrates prior to moving the whole family (known as step or serial migration); long separations; and family reunification complications, including parent work responsibilities, loss of parental authority at home, minimal family leisure time, and rigid role setting with adolescents (Bacallao & Smokowski, 2007). Other changes which significantly affect levels of coping for families include shifts in values and corresponding family behaviors (Gonzales, Deardorff, Formoso, Barr, & Barrera, 2006); risks of poverty, limited job opportunities, and discrimination (Crowley, Lichter, & Qian, 2006); and exploitation, especially for migrant workers (Parra-Cardona, Bulock, Imig, Villarruel, & Gold, 2006). This section will further conceptualize the process that immigrants and their families go through as they manage their home culture and the U.S. culture.

Acculturation

Acculturation is a key process in the immigration process (Smart & Smart, 1995). Berry (2003) conceptualizes acculturation as four styles, patterns, or trajectories: assimilation, separation, integration, and marginalization. He posits that the particular strategy used by a person is largely governed by the environment, not adopted at random, and consequently may be an outcome of contextual factors that impact an immigrant's adjustment to an adverse environment. Berry (1997) further states that individuals who use an integration acculturative style tend to be better adapted while those that use a marginalization strategy tend to be the least well adapted; the assimilation and separation strategies tend to show intermediate outcomes in adapting. These observations suggest particular ways to conceptualize the post-migration process and assist with predictions of effective treatment strategies.

Adaptations for immigrant families

Sluzki (1979) presented five stages in the migration process: (a) preparatory stage, (b) act of migration, (c) period of overcompensation, (d) period of decompensation, and (e) transgenerational impact. The model explains the behavioral (e.g., developing new family rules and roles), cognitive (e.g., experiencing dissonance in the new country and culture), and emotional (e.g., sadness and depression) changes that the family unit experiences in migration.

The last two stages, decompensation and transgenerational conflict, are especially salient in understanding how families adjust to a new country. The period of decompensation is characterized by conflicts, symptoms, and difficulties, and is usually the time when immigrants will seek therapy. Family members may incorporate polarized and complementary roles and struggle to maintain stability while adjusting to the novel environment. The family may maintain some traits from their home culture while navigating the new learning essential for survival. Children typically acculturate more quickly to the new culture and language than the parents, creating parent–child conflict (Szapocznik & Hernandez, 1988).

Also, the female partner may find employment before the male, potentially challenging previous gender roles. Several studies suggest that immigrant women may experience greater gender role conflict than immigrant men (Espin, 1987), particularly when they work outside the home (Coltrane & Valdez, 1997). Some authors report that in addition to employment outside the home, exposure to more liberal gender roles in the United States may create an imbalance in the traditional power structure of the family (Bacallo & Smokowski, 2007). However, other researchers suggest that Mexican immigrant families become less patriarchal not due to modernization or acculturation but rather as a function of the step migration process (i.e., the male leaves for the United States and the female remains with the family and develops the provider role; meanwhile, men must learn to manage domestic chores while living in the United States) (Hondagneu-Sotelo, 1992). Once families are reunited after step migration, immigrant women and men find they need to reconstruct the patriarchal gender roles, resulting in women gaining power and autonomy, and men losing some of their authority and privilege (Hondagneu-Sotelo, 1992). Sluzki (1998) also suggests that male immigrants may exhibit symptoms of depression or problems with alcoholism. Some families will emerge from this process with new strengths while other families will idolize or denigrate their home country or the host country (Falicov, 2005). This issue will be commented on later in the chapter as it relates to counseling interventions.

The last stage in Sluzki's (1979) model, transgenerational impact, suggests a historical pattern of cyclical disempowerment and emotional impairment. At this stage, whatever issues in adaptation the family members have avoided resurface in the future as conflict between generations. If the family lives in a low-income, socioeconomically compromised neighborhood, limited involvement with mainstream society may delay this process due to survival demands. This delay may set an alarming tone for later emotional and behavioral impairment.

Loss and grieving

In addition to adjusting to a new culture, immigrants are likely to mourn the loss of extended family, friends, and familiar surroundings (Falicov, 2002, 2005). Ainslie (1998) refers to the loss of loved ones due to immigration as a cultural mourning. He argues that the proximity of the countries, as well as the relative fluidity of Mexico's border, allow immigrants to keep closer ties to the mother country. As a result, Mexican immigrants have relatively less to mourn than immigrants from other countries, yet the mourning is lengthened, and consequently, potentially more disruptive to family stability. Ambivalent feelings of cultural mourning may be continuously renewed as unresolved loss (Davis, 1990).

Undocumented border crossings and incidents of trauma and violence

Latina/o immigrants who cross the border into the United States without documentation frequently experience trauma and violence (e.g., being robbed or physically and sexually assaulted) during this process (Falicov, 1998; Jimenez, 2007; Moran-Taylor & Menjivar, 2005; Richards, 2004). Specific reports regarding the undocumented migration experience and border crossings are minimal, likely due to difficulties between self-disclosure and undocumented status. In the future, categorizing border crossings without documentation as traumatic events will allow practitioners and researchers to address interventions appropriately.

Other related traumas include the impact of separation for parents from their children (Miranda, Siddique, Der-Martirosian, & Belin, 2005) and coping with acculturative stress following the immigration process (Salgado de Synder, Cervantes, & Padilla, 1990). This journey for undocumented families is a significant benchmark in their lives and needs to be further addressed in research and practice (Suárez-Orozco, 2007).

Case A

Like many immigrant families, Juan and Guadalupe underestimated the emotional and psychological cost of moving to the United States and found themselves without legal documentation and displaced in a large city where they knew no one. They were the first of their family to emigrate to *El Norte* from their home town, which added more anxiety to the journey. After five to seven years of settling in, this couple was beginning to show signs of distress in their relationship as a result of Juan's working two full-time jobs to support the family and Guadalupe's unemployment. Guadalupe had not worked due to a work-related injury suffered two years prior when she sustained a fall on the slippery concrete floor she was mopping as a maintenance worker; she had been learning to manage chronic pain since then.

Overwhelming emotional and economic stress led this family to couples counseling in order to provide some relief for their life situation, although they also hesitated to seek assistance due to the stigma of telling strangers their problems and their undocumented status. The children, Chela and Manuel, have been model students in the classroom, as reflected by their advanced academic performance in high-achieving classrooms and in their participation on the soccer field.

Case B

Although initially Carmen and Mario had a difficult time getting settled in to the United States, after a few months they felt content to have greater educational and financial opportunities for the family. However, their stressors increased significantly when Ismael began to have auditory and visual hallucinations. Since they did have low-cost insurance, they took Ismael to the pediatrician, who after several routine tests referred them to a psychiatrist. Ismael was prescribed psychotropic medicine to help alleviate his symptoms. However, his symptoms continued to worsen. Since Carmen was at home, she tried to help her son, yet Ismael was becoming violent, and Carmen also felt concern for her younger son. Carmen and Mario were finally referred to counseling.

Carmen and Mario brought Ismael for therapy. It was obvious that he was experiencing psychological instability, but also that the family as a whole was under significant stress. Carmen reported depression and anxiety, missing her friends and family from home, and having difficulty learning English since she was at home. She expressed feeling lost at not knowing the system in the United States and how to assist her children. Mario focused on working and finding resources for his son. Raul was a good student, yet had begun to be rebellious toward Carmen and have behavioral problems at school. The first several sessions focused on coordinating services with the psychiatrist and helping Carmen and Mario navigate the various educational and medical services available to Ismael. Treatment also focused on alleviating some of the stress on the family.

Adjustment and Adaptation in Mexican and Mexican American Children and Adolescents

The majority of research on the adaptation of immigrants, particularly from Mexico and Central America, has focused on adults and not children and adolescents. There are multiple trends that are not well examined due to the diversity of family situations that are encountered: role of family separation and loss due to serial migration patterns (Falicov, 2002; Suárez-Orosco, Todorova, & Louie, 2002); children born in one country and socialized in a foreign country (Portes & Rumbaut, 2001; Ramakrishnan, 2004); acculturation and its impact on children's health (De Garmo & Martinez, 2006; Gonzales et al., 2006); family migration instability (Bacallao & Smokowski, 2007; Phinney, Ong, & Madden, 2000; Zayas, Lester, Cabassa, & Fortuna, 2005); and migration trauma (Perez Foster, 2001). Each of these areas has a distinct impact on the emotional and psychological wellbeing of children (Garcia Coll & Magnuson, 1997).

The professional literature (Portes & Rumbaut, 1996) and experience in clinical practice indicate that there are at least three broad acculturation patterns for children/adolescents with each impacted by distinct, multiple developmental pathways (Ford & Lerner, 1992). These include: children/adolescents born in the United States, those born in Mexico/Latin America and then migrated with family to the United States, and those separated from parents and later reunited.

U.S.-born children with immigrant parents

U.S.-born children who are the offspring of immigrant parents face the following issues: the over-acculturation of the child and the under-acculturation of the parent (Gonzales et al., 2006; Lau et al., 2005; Szapocznik & Hernandez, 1988); the propensity for increased oppositional and defiant behavior on the part of children and adolescents (Asbridge, Tanner, & Wortley, 2005; De Garmo & Martinez, 2006); inequities in school readiness (Crosnoe, 2007); and the overuse of children as translators for parents who do not speak English (Buriel, Perez, DeMent, Chavez, & Moran, 1998).

Despite the challenges that are evident for immigrant parents raising U.S.-born children, there is an expectation of hope, motivation, and resilience that first-generation immigrant families display with respect to their dreams about themselves and for their offspring (Hayes-Bautista, 2004). The resilience of newly arrived immigrant families from Mexico is a significant characteristic and can be underscored in assisting children and adolescents to advance themselves while acknowledging the challenges that may co-exist in their lives (Alegría et al., 2007; Hayes-Bautista, 2004).

Children born in Mexico or other parts of Latin America and migrated to the United States

Little attention has been given in the literature to the generation of children who were born and socialized in a foreign country and then immigrated to the United States at a young age (Ford & Lerner, 1992). Brandon (2002) suggests that the social capital (e.g., social support) of some immigrant families erodes with the rate of changed residence and second-generation status. Crosnoe (2007) found that children from Mexican immigrant families tend to enter lower-status segments of U.S. society, where powerful socio-economic disadvantages are combined with equally potent forces such as segregation and discrimination. As such, opportunities to have children educated effectively are not easily come by, given the disadvantages in U.S. society and the immigrant families' lack of preparedness (Bean & Stevens, 2003). Melia (2004) reports that immigrant adolescents from Mexico and Central America frequently enter the United States thinking that there will be numerous employment opportunities awaiting them. What is not readily recognized is the level of challenge due to the lack of formal education and the pressure from families to take low-level employment in order to survive economically. There is limited information on family relationships and political alliances that build within these family units when children co-exist with siblings from different countries of origin (Suárez-Orozco et al., 2002).

Children separated from parents due to serial migration and subsequent reunification

A last and frequently common family migration strategy is found with those family units where a parent(s) elects to set up the home community in the United States and leave children behind in a foreign country (e.g., Mexico). The specific issue related to this practice typically involves the desire to establish permanency in the United States so that there will be some stability in the reunification of family. As already noted by several authors (Bacallao & Smokowski, 2007; Falicov, 1998, 2002; Sciarra, 1999; Suárez-Orozco et al., 2002), the issues related to leaving family members behind often have a negative and debilitating impact on the family unit. Each of these three strategies of family migration patterns implies a distinct acculturation trajectory in the adjustment of families following the immigration process (Ford & Lerner, 1992).

Relevant Models for Practice with Immigrant Latina/o Families

There are few practice models that have been identified in the literature for effective counseling with immigrant families. Early writing on acculturation and psychological intervention with Latina/o families was reported by Szapocznik et al. (1986) as reflected in their bicultural effectiveness training (BET) model. These authors reported on the role of having open dialogue among and between Cuban American parents and children and the impact that acculturation has within families. The authors designed a parenting course that systematically highlighted themes relevant to the acculturation process in order to facilitate this dialogue and minimize conflict between adolescents and parents.

The Structural Ecosystems Therapy (SET) model (Robbins, Schwartz, & Szapocznik, 2004; see Chapter 24, this volume) acknowledges that an adolescent's behavioral problems may be related to factors within the family but further integrates the role that the greater ecological context plays in the family's functioning. Mejía (in press) describes an application of the SET model to a case example with a Mexican American adolescent and his family.

Other relevant comments about intervention with immigrant families have been reported by Falicov (1998, 2002), Suárez-Orozco (2000), Suárez-Orozco & Suárez-Orozco (2001), and Suárez-Orozco et al. (2002). In brief, their writings reflect a significant shift toward family dialogue that moves from managing generational problems and conflict adjustment to recognizing the forces that are shaping lives and respect individual differences within the family structure (Falicov, 2005; Stone, Gomez, Hotzoglou, & Lipnitsky, 2005).

Bacallao and Smokowski (2005) suggest that the assimilation strategy is a risk factor while the biculturalism strategy is a protective factor for families. These authors provide a prevention program that helps parents and adolescents decrease conflict, cope with discrimination, and increase bicultural coping skills. Their interventions are experiential, developmental, and ecologically focused, addressing parents' reports of anxiety (for the future wellbeing of their children), mourning of losing significant relationships in Mexico, and decreased social support that contribute to the disintegration of family. They and others (Mitrani, Santisteban, & Muir, 2004) advocate for practitioners to pay attention to the accumulation of losses and the grieving process of separated family members and address the relationship issues that develop as a result of serial immigration in order to decrease family ruptures and stressors.

Santiago-Rivera et al. (2002) address the psychological, developmental, and social/cultural tasks for counseling families. Regarding immigrant families, they report that the following considerations should be observed: build continuity and new cultural memories among family members; incorporate the values of the home country with those of the host culture in order to facilitate adaptation; explore coping mechanisms in the acculturative process among the various family members; and utilize experiences of the migration journey to facilitate dialogue. In addition, these authors advocate that an assessment of the immigrant family unit should include a consideration of the family life cycle, age, gender, and language acquisition.

A final descriptive outcome of each of the illustrative cases studies appears below.

Case A

Juan and Guadalupe participated in counseling with a significant level of dread, yet with a motivation to try and improve their relationship. They each recognized the problems that had become increasingly evident due to the lost income from Guadalupe's work-related injuries and the difficulty she was having managing her pain. Further, Juan was able to recognize the more rigid rule setting he had been using over the past year with his children and the fact that they were model students and participated well in their sports activities. Juan's anxiety was fueled both by economic difficulties and by the continued threat of being found by immigration authorities at his job site. Although there had been no raids in the factory where he was employed, there was the threat of this occurring as a result of an actual raid in a similar work environment.

Initiating the dialogue with this couple helped them to manage significant worry that had been accumulating as a result of multiple stressors in their lives. A salient aspect of this stress was the memories of a different life in Mexico and the loss of extended family, which had been absent from their lives since their migration journey. The couple's resolution as they established themselves in the United States was to insure that they all had some regular contact with extended family members in Mexico so that there was a continuity of generational support for the children, Chela and Manuel, as well as not forgetting their cultural and linguistics roots.

Case B

Although Ismael was taking a high regimen of prescribed medications for several months, he continued to experience hallucinations, depression, and angry outbursts. Treatment focused on finding appropriate pediatric bilingual psychiatric services. In coordination with case management services, the appropriate care was secured for the family and his symptoms were finally stabilized. However, Carmen and Mario needed to constantly monitor the various side effects that Ismael was experiencing. Ismael also attended a school to meet his educational needs, as well as behavioral assistance at home on a daily basis.

Therapeutic intervention was a combination of couples, individual, and family therapy. With the in-home assistance, Carmen was able to dedicate more time to her son Raul. Raul began to do better at school and to enjoy more time with his father. The family began to attend a bilingual support group for families with loved ones with a mental illness, and they reported this as being validating and helpful.

Summary and Conclusions

This chapter provides a comprehensive perspective to understanding the immigration process for families of Mexican descent. Coping with the challenge of negative stereotypes, difficult environmental circumstances (Kuther & Wallace, 2003) and the legalization process toward permanent residency status are all fundamental stumbling blocks that make stability a formidable obstacle for most migrants and their families (Hernandez, 1999; Suárez-Orozco, 2000).

Education and training

There are multiple aspects to attend to in training family psychologists to work in this area. These aspects include specific skill sets, language competencies, and professional attitudes that need to be identified as part of effective work with immigrant youth and families (Altarriba & Santiago-Rivera, 1994). In addition, recognizing the post-migration adaptation patterns is an important aspect of this training.

To address these issues, graduate programs can provide didactic and practicum training in psychology of immigration and working with these families. The incorporation of an educational module to develop competency and professional practice with immigrant families and communities would be an important aspect of a family psychologist's professional training.

Practice

This review points to the strong need to develop specific competencies in working with immigrant families. Additional work is needed to develop evidence-based models and interventions for these families. Many of the current interventions need to consider the following in their application with immigrant families.

The three Cs.   The first is *context,* namely the backdrop of salient social, educational, and political forces that have contributed to the seemingly insurmountable challenge for immigrant families that has been stressed in this chapter. Second, *circumstances* have also been illustrated in clinical vignettes that highlighted specific familial patterns and acculturative trajectories for family members. Third, *culture,* namely, the specific beliefs and values of Latina/o families, also plays a salient role. These areas (context, circumstance, and culture) are referred to as the three Cs in assessing immigration issues with Mexican and Mexican American families. They may be instrumental in providing a more comprehensive understanding of these families and their unique life histories. As a baseline level of care, both a family systems framework and a family psychology perspective are recommended approaches with immigrant families.

The importance of self-awareness.   The political climate of immigration is highly charged and filled with conflicted feelings, even among U.S.-born Latina/os (Jimenez, 2007; Lee, Ottati, & Hussain, 2001; National Council of La Raza, 2007). Attitudes of fear, distrust, and protecting one's own home territory and community can also likely be experienced among mental health professionals, inclusive of those who are Latina/o. Awareness of one's attitudes toward immigrant families and the impact of those reactions on psychological care will play a salient role in the effectiveness of the psychological assistance that is rendered to this cultural population. An openness to and awareness of one's reactions with immigrant families are an important consideration in any effective and ethical practice.

Resources

Authors who are addressing issues relevant to Latino families include Jose Szapocnik (Director of Center for Family Studies, University of Miami), Marcelo Suárez-Orozco (Professor and Co-Director of Immigration Studies, New York University), Carola Suárez-Orozco (Professor and Co-Director of Immigration Studies, New York University), and Celia Falicov (Clinical Professor of Psychiatry, University of California San Diego and private practice).

The implementation of the Mental Health Services Act (Proposition 63, which provides funds for prevention, early intervention, and other mental health services for those with severe mental illness) in California has begun to provide much needed resources to underserved populations, including Latinos and immigrants. Visit http://www.dmh.ca.gov/Prop_63/MHSA/default.asp and http://www.lchc.org for further information.

National Council of La Raza. (2007). *Paying the price: The impact of immigration raids on America's children.* Washington, DC: National Council of La Raza.

References

Ainslie, R. C. (1998). Cultural mourning, immigration, and engagement: Vignettes from the Mexican experience. In M. M. Suárez-Orozco (Ed.), *Crossings: Mexican immigration in interdisciplinary perspectives* (pp. 284–300). Cambridge, MA: Harvard University Press.

Alegría, M., Mulvaney-Day, N., Torres, M., Polo, A., Cao, Z., & Canino, G. (2007). Prevalence of psychiatric disorders across Latino subgroups in the United States. *American Journal of Public Health, 97,* 68–75.

Altarriba, J., & Santiago-Rivera, A. L. (1994). Current perspectives on using linguistic and cultural factors in counseling the Hispanic client. *Professional Psychology: Research and Practice, 25,* 388–397.

Asbridge, M., Tanner, J., & Wortley, S. (2005). Ethno-specific patterns of adolescent tobacco use and the mediating role of acculturation, peer smoking, and sibling smoking. *Addiction, 100,* 1340–1351.

Bacallao, M. L., & Smokowski, P. R. (2005). "Entre dos mundos" (between two worlds): Bicultural skills training with Latino immigrant families. *Journal of Primary Prevention, 26,* 485–509.

Bacallao, M. L., & Smokowski, P. R. (2007). The costs of getting ahead: Mexican family system changes after immigration. *Family Relations, 56,* 52–66.

Bean, F., & Stevens, G. (2003). *America's new comers and the dynamics of diversity.* New York: Russell Sage.

Berry, J. (2003). Conceptual approaches to acculturation. In K. M. Chun, P. B. Organista, & G. Marin (Eds.), *Acculturation: Advances in theory, measurement and applied research* (pp. 17–37). Washington, DC: American Psychological Association.

Berry, J. W. (1997). Immigration, acculturation, and adaptation. *Applied Psychology, 46,* 5–68.

Brandon, P. D. (2002). The living arrangements of children in immigrant families in the United States. *International Migration Review, 36,* 416–436.

Buriel, R., Perez, W., DeMent, T. L., Chavez, D. V., & Moran, V. R. (1998). The relationship of language brokering to academic performance, biculturalism, and self-efficacy among Latino adolescents. *Hispanic Journal of Behavioral Sciences, 20,* 283–296.

Cervantes, J. M., & Sweatt, L. I. (2004). Family therapy with Chicana/os. In R. J. Velasquez, L. M. Arrellano, & B. W. McNeill (Eds.), *The handbook of Chicana/o psychology and mental health* (pp. 285–322). Mahwah, NJ: Erlbaum.

Coltrane, S., & Valdez, E. O. (1997). Reluctant compliance: Work–family role allocation in dual-earner Chicano families. In M. Romero, P. Hondagneou-Sotelo, & V. Ortiz (Eds.), *Challenging fronteras: Structuring Latina and Latino lives in the U.S.* (pp. 229–246). New York: Routledge.

Comas-Diaz, L. (2001). Hispanic, Latinos, or Americanos: The evolution of identity. *Cultural Diversity and Ethnic Minority Psychology, 7,* 115–120.

Crosnoe, R. (2007). Early child care and the school readiness of children from Mexican immigrant families. *International Migration Review, 41,* 152–181.

Crowley, M., Lichter, D. T., & Qian, Z. (2006). Beyond gateway cities: Economic restructuring and poverty among Mexican immigrant families and children. *Family Relations, 55,* 345–360.

Davis, M. P. (1990). *Mexican voices/American dreams: An oral history of Mexican immigration to the United States.* New York: Henry Holt.

De Garmo, D. S., & Martinez, C. R. (2006). A culturally informed model of academic well-being for Latino youth: The importance of discriminatory experiences and social support. *Family Relations, 55,* 267–278.

Espin, O. M. (1987). Psychological impact of migration on Latinas. *Psychology of Women Quarterly, 11,* 489–503.

Falicov, C. (2002). Ambiguous loss: Risk and resilience in Latino immigrant families. In M. M. Suárez-Orozco & M. Paez (Eds.), *Latinos: Remaking America* (pp. 274–288). Berkley: University of California Press.

Falicov, C. J. (1998). *Latino families in therapy: A guide to multicultural practice.* New York: Guilford Press.

Falicov, C. J. (2005). Emotional transnationalism and family identities. *Family Process, 44(4),* 399–406.

Ford, D. H., & Lerner, R. M. (1992). *Developmental systems theory.* Newbury Park, CA: Sage.

Fussell, E. (2004). Sources of Mexico's migration stream: Rural, urban, and border migrants to the United States. *Social Forces, 82,* 937–967.

Garcia Coll, C. T., & Magnuson, K. (1997). The psychological experience of immigration: A developmental perspective. In A. Booth, A. C. Crouter, & N. Landale (Eds.), *Immigration and the family: Research and policy on U.S. immigrants* (pp. 91–131). Mahwah, NJ: Erlbaum.

Gonzales, N. A., Deardorff, J., Formoso, D., Barr, A., & Barrera Jr., M. (2006). Family mediators of the relation between acculturation and adolescent mental health. *Family Relations, 55,* 318–330.

Gonzalez, M. G. (2000). *Mexicanos: A history of Mexicans in the United Status.* Bloomington: Indiana University Press.

Grant, B. F., Stinson, F. S., Hasin, D. S., Dawson, D. A., Chou, S. P., & Anderson, K. (2004). Immigration and lifetime prevalence of DSM-IV psychiatric disorders among Mexican Americans and non-Hispanic Whites in the United States. *Archives of General Psychiatry, 61,* 1226–1233.

Hayes-Bautista, D. E. (2004). *La Nueva California: Latinos in the Golden State.* Berkeley and Los Angeles: University of California Press.

Hernandez, D. (Ed.). (1999). *Children of immigrants: Health adjustment and public assistance.* Washington, DC: National Academy Press.

Hernandez, D. J., Denton, N. A., & McCartney, S. E. (2007). Family circumstance of children in immigrant families: Looking to the future of America. In J. E. Lansford, K. Deater-Deckard, & M. H. Bornstein (Eds.), *Immigrant families in contemporary society* (pp. 9–29). New York: Guilford Press.

Hondagneu-Sotelo, P. (1992). Overcoming patriarchal constraints: The reconstruction of gender-relations among Mexican immigrant women and men. *Gender and Society, 6,* 393–415.

Jimenez, T. R. (2007). Weighing the costs and benefits of Mexican immigration: The Mexican-American perspective. *Social Science Quarterly, 88,* 599–618.

Kuther, L. T., & Wallace, S. A. (2003). Community violence and sociomoral development: An African American cultural perspective. *American Journal of Orthopsychiatry, 73,* 177–189.

Lau, A. S., McCabe, K. M., Yeh, M., Garland, A. F., Wood, P. A., & Hough, R. L. (2005). The acculturation gap-distress hypothesis among high-risk Mexican American families. *Journal of Family Psychology, 19,* 367–375.

Lee, Y. T., Ottati, V., & Hussain, I. (2001). Attitudes toward "illegal" immigration into the United States: California Proposition 187. *Hispanic Journal of Behavioral Sciences, 23,* 430–443.

Martin, S. (2003). The politics of U.S. immigration reform. *The Political Quarterly, 74,* 132–149.

Mejía, O. L. (in press). Struggling with research and practice with a Mexican American family: The case of Robert. In M. E. Gallardo & B. McNeil (Eds.), *The clinical casebook of multicultural psychology: Implementation of culturally proficient treatment strategies.* Mahwah, NJ: Erlbaum.

Melia, M. J. (2004). Transatlantic dialogue on integration of immigrant children and adolescents. *International Migration Review, 42,* 123–139.

Miranda, J., Siddique, J., Der-Martirosian, C., & Belin, T. R. (2005). Depression among Latina immigrant mothers separated from their children. *Psychiatric Services, 56,* 717–720.

Mitrani, V. B., Santisteban, D. A., & Muir, G. A. (2004). Addressing immigration-related separations in Hispanic families with a behavior-problem adolescent. *American Journal of Orthopsychiatry, 74,* 219–229.

Moran-Taylor, M., & Menjivar, C. (2005). Unpacking longings to return: Guatemalans and Salvadorans in Phoenix, Arizona. *International Migration Review, 43,* 91–121.

National Council of La Raza. (2007). *Paying the price: The impact of immigration raids on America's children.* Washington, DC: National Council of La Raza.

Ngai, M. M (2004). *Impossible subjects: Illegal aliens and the making of modern America.* Princeton: Princeton University Press.

Parra-Cardona, J. R., Bulock, L. A., Imig, D. R., Villarruel, F. A., & Gold, S. J. (2006). "Trabajando duro todos los dias": Learning from the life experience of Mexican-origin migrant families. *Family Relations, 55,* 361–375.

Passel, J. S., & Suro, R. (2005). *Rise, peak, and decline: Trends in U.S. immigration 1992–94.* Washington, DC: Pew Hispanic Center.

Perez Foster, R. (2001). When immigration is trauma: Guidelines for the individual and family clinician. *American Journal of Orthopsychiatry, 71,* 153–170.

Phinney, J. S., Ong, A., & Madden, T. (2000). Cultural values and intergenerational value discrepancies in immigrant and non-immigrant families. *Child Development, 71,* 528–539.

Portes, A., & Rumbaut, R. (1996). *Immigrant America: A portrait.* Berkeley: University of California Press.

Portes, A., & Rumbaut, R. (2001). *Legacies: The story of the immigrant second generation.* Berkeley: University of California Press.

Ramakrishnan, S. K. (2004). Second-generation immigrants? The "2.5 generation" in the United States. *Social Science Quarterly, 85,* 380–399.

Richards, K. (2004). The trafficking of migrant workers: What are the links between labor trafficking and corruption? *International Migration Review, 42,* 147–168.

Robbins, M. S., Schwartz, S., & Szapocznik, J. (2004). Structural ecosystems therapy with Hispanic adolescents exhibiting disruptive behavior disorders. In J. R. Ancis (Ed.), *Culturally responsive interventions: Innovative approaches to working with diverse populations* (pp. 71–99). New York: Brunner-Routledge.

Romero, M. (1997). Introduction. In M. Romero, P. Hondagneu-Sotelo, & V. Ortiz (Eds.), *Challenging fronteras: Structuring Latina and Latino lives in the U.S.* (pp. xiii–xvi). New York: Routledge.

Salgado de Snyder, V. N., Cervantes, R. C., & Padilla, A. M. (1990). Gender and ethnic differences in psychosocial stress and generalized distress among Hispanics. *Sex Roles, 22,* 441–453.

Santiago-Rivera, A. L., Arredondo, P., & Gallardo-Cooper, M. (2002). *Counseling Latinos and la familia: A practical guide.* Thousand Oaks, CA: Sage.

Sciarra, D. T. (1999). Intrafamilial separations in the immigrant family: Implications for cross-cultural counseling. *Journal of Multicultural Counseling & Development, 27,* 31–42.

Sluzki, C. (1998). Migration and the disruption of the social network. In M. McGoldrick (Ed.), *Re-visioning family therapy: Race, culture, and gender in clinical practice* (pp. 360–369). New York: Guilford Press.

Sluzki, C. E. (1979). Migration and family conflict. *Family Process, 18,* 379–390.

Smart, J. F., & Smart, D. W. (1995). Acculturative stress of Hispanics: Loss and challenge. *Journal of Counseling & Development, 73,* 390–396.

Stone, E., Gomez, E., Hotzoglou, D., & Lipnitsky, J. Y. (2005). Transnationalism as a motif in family stories. *Family Process, 44,* 381–398.

Suárez-Orozco, C. (2000). Identities under siege: Immigration stress and social mirroring among the children of immigrants. In A. Robben & M. M. Suárez-Orozco (Eds.), *Cultures under siege: Collective violence and trauma* (pp. 194–226). New York: Cambridge University Press.

Suárez-Orozco, C. (2007). Reflections on research with immigrant families. In J. E. Lansford, K. Deater-Deckard, & M. H. Bornstein (Eds.), *Immigrant families in contemporary society* (pp. 311–326). New York: Guilford Press.

Suárez-Orozco, C., & Suárez-Orozco, M. (2001). *Children of immigration.* Cambridge, MA: Harvard University Press.

Suárez-Orozco, C., Todorova, I., & Louie, J. (2002). Making up for lost time: The experience of separation and reunification among immigrant families. *Family Process, 41,* 625–643.

Szapocznik, J., & Hernandez, R. (1988). The Cuban family. In C. H. Mindel, R. W. Habenstein, & R. Wright, Jr. (Eds.), *Ethnic families in America* (pp. 160–172). New York: Elsevier.

Szapocznik, J., Rio, A., Perez-Vidal, A., Kurtines, W. M., Herris, O., & Santisteban, D. (1986). Bicultural effectiveness training (BET): An experiment test of an intervention modality for families experiencing intergenerational/intercultural conflict. *Hispanic Journal of Behavioral Studies, 8,* 303–330.

Takaki, R. (1993). *A different mirror: A history of multicultural America.* Boston: Little, Brown.

U.S. Census Bureau. (2007). *The American community – Hispanics: 2004.* Washington, DC: U.S. Census Bureau.

Vigil, I. D. (1998). *From Indians to Chicanos: The dynamics of Mexican American culture.* Prospect Heights, IL: Waveland Press.

Wainer, A. (2006). The new Latino South and the challenge to American public education. *International Migration Review, 44,* 129–165.

Zayas, L. H., Lester, R. J., Cabassa, L. J., & Fortuna, L. R. (2005). Why do so many Latina teens attempt suicide? A conceptual model for research. *American Journal of Orthopsychiatry, 75,* 275–287.

49

International Family Psychology

Florence W. Kaslow

Family psychology differs markedly across countries. It is most developed in the United States as a separate specialty within psychology, with its own body of knowledge and literature, which emphasizes a systemic orientation, graduate school curricula, practica, internships and residencies, and is carried out by researchers, practitioners, professors, supervisors, professional organizations, and board certification.

The field has evolved differently in each country, reflecting its cultural ethos, religious beliefs, academic and professional climate, and traditions. To show this, a kaleidoscopic overview of the evolution in selected regions around the world will be provided. Ten countries are highlighted and others are alluded to as examples of the diversity found in the global scene. Information has been obtained from: (1) the literature; (2) interchanges with colleagues from various countries and experiences the author had when guest lecturing and conducting workshops at universities and international conferences or for organizations in over 50 countries; and (3) conversations and correspondence with "leaders" in the field in multiple countries.

A major dilemma is encountered when trying to differentiate family psychology and family therapy. In many countries portions of the two fields co-evolved; they are intertwined and overlap. Nonetheless, there are distinct variations. (See appendix, which was sent to leaders in various countries who had difficulty making this distinction; some of the data in this chapter were derived from their responses to this form.)

Trends that are seen across a myriad of countries which impact on families and therefore are of concern to family psychologists are highlighted as part of the effort to unify what often is treated segmentally.

Evolution Around the World:
International Academy of Family Psychology

In 1989 a small group of male family psychology professors and researchers from Germany, Italy, Japan, and the United States decided it was time to form an International Academy of Family Psychologists (IAFP). In 1990 in Japan, under the leadership of Luciano L'Abate (1986, 1994) from the United States; Nobuaki Kuniya (1998), Tetsuo Okado, Kenji Kameguchi (2001), Etsuto Sato-Vosburg (2004), and their colleagues from Japan; Klaus Schneewind (1999) from Germany; and Mario Cusinato from Italy, the IAFP was founded. Other charter members who participated at the inception of the IAFP included David Olson (1990, 1996) and Florence Kaslow from the United States. The IAFP has held conferences every 4 years since its founding.

The IAFP is devoted to establishing academic/clinical departments of family psychology that will foster research and theory development. In 1997 the IAFP became the family-focused affiliate organization of the International Association of Applied Psychology (Kaslow, 2000). Each international conference has reflected the culture and traditions of the host country, as well as the increasing globalization of the field. At the first three conferences there were participants from at least 30 countries. The board has been comprised of members from as many countries as possible. Representation from African, Arabic, and some Asian countries has been sparse.

At international gatherings one becomes cognizant of many different constructions of reality. And yet, it becomes apparent that there are some universals – at least in the realm of feelings. Wherever one lives and works, one will meet people who feel sad, happy, joyous, lonely, loving, rejected, resentful, fortunate, anxious, scared, pessimistic, optimistic, angry, desperate, courageous, and confident. What varies is the manner in which these emotions and experiences are expressed; the ways individuals are culturally taught are acceptable for expression or defined as too extreme, and therefore as pathological or "crazy."

Attendance at the last two conferences has decreased and there seems to be less enthusiasm as the founders have become less involved. The original vision of "for family psychologists only" may not be shared by second-generation leaders, some of whom have wanted to merge with family sociologists.

This is why the definition of "who is a family psychologist" and how one acquires this title and identity are such pivotal issues. Throughout the past four decades, family psychologists have struggled to differentiate what they are and do from family therapists, family psychiatrists, and family sociologists. All share an interest in and commitment to the field of family studies – but just as there are many commonalities and areas of collaboration, so there are also some sharp divergences in levels and type of training and education, emphases, research and clinical methodology, and identification with one's own larger professional discipline.

Let us now look to specific countries in different regions of the world to illuminate this discussion and highlight issues, trends, and accomplishments.

Asia: Japan, China, and Singapore

When the first IAFP Conference was held in Tokyo, the Japanese Association of Family Psychologists (JAFP) was already a large, thriving organization (Kuniya, 1998). The scholarly, peer-reviewed *Japanese Journal of Family Psychology* had began publication in 1987, the same year as the (American) *Journal of Family Psychology*. Many of their areas of research and clinical interest parallel our own. By 1990 they were already willing to publish articles by non-Japanese authors in both Japanese and the author's language. At that time none of the American family journals were that cross-cultural in orientation and advanced in policy.

An issue of great concern to Japanese family psychologists has been the school refusal problem encountered with many boys starting school (Kameguchi, 2001) and their mothers, who have trouble letting them go. The long hours many men spend in their work environments, their continuing strong emotional attachments to their own mothers, and the tendency to go out after work with colleagues contribute to the mother's extreme emotional involvement in her children, especially her son – as he is the one expected to repay the devotion when she is elderly. Interventions have included trying to have businesses understand these dynamics and allow men to leave work earlier.

Other major concerns have been the extreme pressure placed on children to study assiduously or practice their sports and musical instruments continually so they can excel and qualify for the best universities. This is a valued way of bringing "honor" and distinction to the family.

When I first went to Japan to present in 1974, I lectured to judges and marital counselors in the Family and Reconciliation Court in Tokyo. All were male. The several marital cases they presented for consultation were all variations on the same theme – the young couple had met in the workplace, fallen in love, and married. Usually they lived with the husband's parents. Once the young woman "had to stay home" to raise the children and take care of her parents-in-law, she became increasingly withdrawn and despondent. Their way of diagnosing and intervening was to interpret her behavior as schizophrenia and hospitalize her. I tactfully suggested that although I knew it might not be applicable in Japan, in my country we might suggest to the husband that they consider moving into their own apartment, thus reducing his wife's responsibilities and her isolation from the larger external world again. By the third case presentation, the men were already incorporating this type of strategy into the approaches they might consider. Assessment and testing in their family court, which was geared to fostering reconciliation, were already well developed. They were utilizing American psychological tests, translated into Japanese, as well as tests they had developed. Treatment was predicated on assessment results.

The changing role of women has proven disruptive to many men who expected their college-educated, career-oriented wives to revert to being like their stay-at-home, devoted mothers after their first pregnancy. Many of these bright, ambitious women spent some of their college or graduate school years in non-Asian countries and became less docile and more "liberated." They have no intention of conforming to this expectation, which they consider to be outdated.

Today family psychologists in Japan are conducting research and addressing the clinical implications of discussing these issues. Because the divorce rate and concerns over child custody issues are rising, family psychologists in Japan are also focusing on this arena.

It was apparent when I keynoted the 1999 sixteenth annual JAFP Conference in Kobe on "Marital Conflict and the Family Life Cycle" that family psychology is at a sophisticated level of training, education, research, and practice in Japan, where it has flourished for over 30 years. Japan is in the forefront in this field in the Asian countries and is trying to organize regional conferences.

There have been a significant number of family therapy workshops and some courses taught in Hong Kong during this same time frame. At some workshops expatriate American therapists residing and working there attend along with the Chinese therapists. There still seems to be a great divide and they treat quite different patient populations. However, they share an eagerness to learn and do mingle, if the workshop is interactive. In the last decade more training opportunities have been offered in mainland China.

The same holds true in Singapore, where the history of family therapy is longer and tied to the social work/social welfare system. There I have had Muslim women therapists, fully veiled, attend, sit silently, and eat totally separately. I am aware of an American colleague who has taught marital and family therapy (MFT) courses several summers in Indonesia. Most of these family therapy trainings have stressed interventions and some theory, not research.

In the past few years some professional schools and graduate departments of psychology on the west coast of the United States have established programs in and around Beijing, China. More Asian psychologists are now getting some of their graduate education outside of their own countries; thus family psychology is more visible.

Western Europe: Italy and Germany

Psychology is one of the most popular undergraduate majors in the huge Catholic universities of Milan and Padua. The latter can have over 1,000 majors at one time. Major professors of family psychology, like Dr Mario Cusinato at Padua and Dr Eugenia Scabini in Milan, have scores of eager, devoted students. However, as recently as 2004 there were no clinically focused graduate family psychology programs in Italy. When students want clinical training in treatment strategies and therapy processes, they either go to graduate or medical school in the United States or United Kingdom, or seek to enroll in a family institute in Italy or abroad. One institute in Italy that has long been a mecca for Italians, Americans, Israelis, Brazilians, etc. is Andolfi's Academia di Psicoterapia Della Familia (Andolfi, Angelo, & deNichelo, 1989; Andolfi & Zwerling, 1980) in Rome. Andolfi, a psychiatrist who did much of his residency training in New York, started the Italian journal of family therapy, *Terapia Familiare*, in the 1970s; he has been editor since its inception. He was also a co-founder of the European Family Therapy Association (EFTA) along with Dr Mony Elkaim, a psychiatrist from Belgium. The other such institute was established in Milan by Drs Gianfranco Cecchin and Luigi Boscolo; the Centro Milanese has been directed by Boscolo alone since Cecchin's death. Here Milan

Systemic Family Therapy as distilled by these two psychiatrists is taught and practiced. Also in Milano, Matteo Selvini, psychiatrist son of deceased psychiatrist Mara Selvini-Palazzoli (Selvini-Palazzoli, Boscolo, Cecchin, & Prata, 1978; Selvini-Palazzoli, Cirillo, Selvini, & Sorentino, 1989), directs the Altevita Formativa del Nuovo Centro per lo Studio Della Famiglia, a program with a more multigenerational and psychodynamic orientation.

With the formation of the European Union and the establishment of the EFTA and the European Psychotherapy Association, the previously independent and autonomous family institutes now must meet certain standards, fulfill proscribed curricula, and offer approved courses for credit. When I was in Milan in 2002, I conducted a full day workshop, the first ever jointly co-sponsored by the two institutes in Milan, on "Children's Role in Parents' Marriage and Sexuality Throughout the Family's Life Cycle." This is course content both institutes must offer for students to graduate and become certified family therapists. These institutes probably represent two of the best clinical family training facilities in the world. However, such institutes are frequently run by family psychiatrists and social workers, with perhaps modest input from and training by psychologists, so that certain aspects of training are not included.

A similar picture emerges from Germany. Places such as the University of Munich have had fine, large undergraduate family psychology programs and small, scholarly graduate programs which emphasize family research, theory development, and preparation for assuming academic responsibilities (Schneewind, 1999). Those wishing to become clinicians, including family therapists, have had the opportunity of attending one of many institutes run by individuals or professional organizations; like elsewhere, these have ranged from fair to excellent in quality. Those initially run by Dr Martin Kirshenbaum, an American family psychologist of German-Jewish ancestry (Luthman & Kirshenbaum, 1974), have tended to be outstanding. Over several decades Kirshenbaum has organized programs throughout Germany, including the former East German sector. Although these emphasize dynamics and treatment, they do not spend much time on comparative theoretical underpinnings and evidenced-based practice, or on the links between research and practice. They produce some very competent practitioners, but few are family psychologists.

Eastern Europe: Czech Republic[1] and Slovak Republic[2]

Czech Republic: Training and education, licensure, and/or certification.   In the Czech Republic (CR), undergraduate education gives only marginal attention to family therapy. Postgraduate programs do not offer systematic long-term studies in this area. Family therapy teaching began in the 1990s. It was based on programs taught by foreign professionals plus further development of the domestic tradition begun in the former Czechoslovakia after the 1970s. The most important early family psychiatrists in both countries were Drs Peter Bos and Jan Spitz. Several organizations in the CR now offer complex education in the area of family therapy/psychology. At the end of the 1990s, a professional psychotherapy society was formed – the Czech Psychotherapeutic Society (CPS). Its aim is to increase the quality of education programs. Health system certification criteria have been created. Currently, there are five certified family education programs in the CR that are recognized by professional associations of psychiatrists and psychologists. The theoretical basis and practical focus of these programs differ.

The historically first and most important is the Family Therapy Institute of Prague, led by Sarka Gjuricova, PhD. This institute's program focuses on the study of families, including gender roles and work on one's own family map. During supervision, participants are trained to understand and conceptualize a problem from the point of view of relationships, to perceive and work with problems from the vantage point of a family, and take into consideration other aspects, such as the social situation and ethnicity.

Second is the Institute of Family Therapy of Psychosomatic Disorders, led by Vladislav Chvala, MD, and Ludmila Trapkova, PhD. Their education program, a 4-year training in family therapy of psychosomatic disorders in Liberec, includes family therapy theoretical basics, skills, and one's own experience in a group and during supervision. Training is geared to students planning to work in clinics and private practices.

Third is the Institute of Virginia Satir. The professional guarantors of this program are Ilona Kot'atkova, PhD, and Milada Radosova, MD. Known as the MOVISA training (an acronym for Model of Virginia Satir), the program's aim is to increase the professional competency of its participants, to facilitate their personal growth, and to provide them with therapeutic skills for working with families, individuals, and groups (Satir, Banmen, Gerber, & Gomori, 1991).

Fourth is the Institute of Systemic Experience, led by Vratislav Strnad in Prague, and established in cooperation with the Hamburg School of Systemic Therapy (under Kurt Ludewig). The fifth institute certified by the CPS is the Institute of Systemic Therapy Brno, led by Josef Zeman, which follows an Austrian school. Common criteria for all training include the theoretical basis of the relevant area, personal (practice) experience, and/or training supervision. Training is designed for university graduates working in the health system or caring professions and usually takes four years.

Apart from the CPS, which carries out the certification of family training in the health system, the Society of Family Therapists (SOFT) also organizes family therapy education programs and provides family therapy (FT) certifications. This organization has its own criteria for complex ft education (programs certified within the health system comply with them automatically) and also criteria for short programs.

Another organization providing family therapy education is the Association of Marriage and Family Counselors (AMFC). Marriage and family counseling is considered a branch of psychology that applies psychological methods to problems in familial relationships; it is taught at all Czech universities as part of psychology studies at faculties of philosophy. Students learn the basics about development, as well as the meaning of family therapy. One of the objectives of the Czech AMFC, founded in 1992, is to further develop professional education in marriage and family counseling, which is based primarily on the systemic approach to interpersonal relationships.

Czech Republic: Roles of family psychologists. Family therapy is taught at universities as part of studies in psychology and social sciences in postgraduate educational programs and also outside these programs. Family psychology *practitioners* work with clients in the medical, education, and social-legal areas (pedagogical-psychological counseling centers, social care, and probation services). *Research* on the family and family psychology is not supported much here. It is conducted mostly as a part of research assignments at universities, primarily at the Faculty of Philosophy in Olomouc. Organizations that provide education in FT specify clear criteria someone must meet to become a *supervisor*, who supervises family therapists either as a part of a complex education program or outside these programs. An official list of supervisors is maintained. *Programs* are continuously updated; they have to apply for a recertification with CPS, which ensures quality is maintained. The number of professionals working in *private medical or counseling practices using family therapy* is growing, as is the number of families using their services. Families with difficult children and couples with partnership problems are encouraged to come for treatment.

Czech Republic: Relationship to other professions.   Family therapy is used in *medical care* much more since the 1989 revolution. However, only certain hospital wards have part-time family therapists. This does not reflect real needs. In non-governmental, private institutions like hospices and institutions providing care to disabled children, the situation is better. Most *psychiatrists'* focus is primarily biological and pharmacological. The situation has been slowly improving, partially due to the FT training certification process. There are many family therapists, particularly among child psychiatrists. *Marriage and family counselors* work on resolving troubled personal, partner, family, and social situations. The number of *social workers* working with families is mounting.

Czech Republic: Changes in the foreseeable future.   Families have to cope with increasing interpersonal and external demands; therefore it can be anticipated that state support of research about families by family psychologists will have to increase. Also, families themselves will begin to see good family relationships as an important value that is closely connected to good health, and thus the demand for family therapy will climb. The need for undergraduate education in family psychology is growing. The influence of FT in the healthcare system will continue to expand with the deepening crisis of medical care perceived by patients. Increasing demands for services that public insurance will not be able to cover are apt to lead to using treatments that are geared toward alleviating the psychological aspects of diseases and mobilizing natural self-healing energy.

The situation in the Slovak Republic (SR) is quite similar; only the differences will be covered. Family psychology as an autonomous subject for academic study does not exist here. It is either a latent part or the byproduct of other scientific subjects in psychology at universities, such as developmental, child, social, educational, or forensic psychology, psychopathology, or psychotherapy and psychological counseling. It is evolving non-systemically; family topics appear only in connection with the social environment of a person, as the condition for normal development, or in cases of individual or family pathology or failure. Theory, research, and practice are fragmented. Until 1993 Josef Langmeier, Zdenek Matejcek, and Karel Balcar developed the foundations for family psychology in Prague in their academic and clinical research and practice. Before the Velvet Revolution in 1989, there were some limits, but under the influence of foreign publications, teachers, trainers, and supervisors from abroad, there was growing interest in family issues. Initially in Europe it was the influence of psychodynamic, cognitive-behavioral, and Gestalt approaches that undergirded family therapy. Later, structural, strategic, and systemic family approaches, Rogerian humanistic psychology, and the Satir model also acquired followers. The Satir movement in the Czech and Slovak Republics developed thanks to Olga Holubova.

Academic education occurred under the "philosophic boards" of the universities until 1993, but there was no separate subject of family therapy. Family topics were taught under psychology boards. Graduates received the title "psychologist" and later "magister of psychology." This issue is now the subject of postgraduate doctoral and internship papers and research.

Training and research in family psychology were initiated in research, clinical, and/or theoretical institutes and centers in Slovakia, such as the International Center for Family Studies in Bratislava, the Center for Experimental Psychology of the Slovak Academy of Sciences, and the Research Center for Child Psychology and Psychopathology. There is a governmental base for family studies and state family policy in the Ministry of Labor, Social Affairs and Family of the Slovak Republic.

Family psychology based on a clearly articulated theoretical framework, including a systemic, humanistic process orientation and a validated model of growth of the person as part of his or her family and the family as a unit, has been studied and practiced in the Institute of Virginia Satir in the SR since 1996. The education of lay people and professionals about optimal family functioning and its deviations is on a voluntary base. From 2007 until 2011 the institute is conducting a 4-year training and education program in psychotherapy based on the teachings of Satir, the founder of conjoint family therapy (Satir, 1964; Satir & Baldwin, 1983), which is accredited in accordance with European Association of Psychotherapy (EAP) criteria by the Ministry of Health under the guarantee of the Slovak Psychotherapy Association.

Slovak Republic: *Roles of family psychologists.*   Theory generation, teaching, and research are conducted by psychologists and psychotherapists. Clinical practice here was connected with the network of over 50 marital and premarital counseling centers from 1972 on, with their focus on healthy pair functioning as the presumption for the healthy family base. In 1991 these centers were transformed into centers for psychology services and counseling for individuals, couples, and families. Therapy was conducted in-agency by psychologists and social workers and externally by lawyers, special educators, sexologists, and sociologists. There was a unified form of education, skills practice training, and supervision for all in this network provided by its central office under the Ministry of Work, Social Affairs and the Family. Since 1990 there have been more U.S. and Canadian trainers (such as John Banmen) coming to do the teaching in family systems theory and therapy. With the political and social transformation of Slovak society, the number of these centers and their clients have decreased and the network is struggling to maintain its existence. Now it is mainly the socially and economically most difficult families and their members and those in foster-family care whom they serve.

Traditionally psychologists have practiced within school counseling centers operated by school psychologists and special educators, and worked with students in the context of their family. Clinical practice has developed within the governmental and private health-care service in hospitals, treatment facilities, and outpatient care, where it is provided by clinical psychologists, psychotherapists, or psychiatrists. All practitioners, after graduate specialization, take postgraduate education and programmed specialization training to obtain licensure for practice, and now the criteria are set to be consistent with the expectations of the European Union.

Slovak Republic: *Status in the community.*   The realities of daily life have led to a more serious focus on family psychology and on making education, research, and practice in family psychology and psychotherapy more valid and effective. There is much public interest, as the family is seen as the institution imprinting the psychic regulation of everyone's life. There is public space created in the media for psychologists to speak and write; there is a project supporting research and trainings. Nonetheless, there is still insufficient status in the academic community for family psychology; all efforts are focused on making more external activities, like conference attendance and publications, possible. There is still no family psychology specialization nor any department of family psychology in Slovakia inside the university educational system.

Slovak Republic: *Changes in the foreseeable future.*   There is now hope for more the-oretical, research, and practical application in the development of family psychology in the SR, and for professional and financial support leading to empowerment of the family psychology network, also under government-supported policy. This means creat-ing a family psychology profession and utilizing resources that exist outside of the SR. There is a need to promulgate a realistic picture of normal family functioning as a model with prevention potential. Family psychology currently is trying to establish itself as a separate discipline that will still be allied to the others in significant ways.

Other Eastern European countries.   For the earliest generation of Hungarian, Polish, Russian, and Yugoslavian (Gacic, Trbic, Markovic & Nikolic, 2004) family professionals, much of the training took place in England or Australia, at workshops at world congresses of psychiatry and later at workshops and institutes throughout the western world. Leaders in these countries also imported well-known trainers from the west and set up their own courses and institutes in some departments of psychiatry. Therapists joined the IFTA from 1989 on and the EFTA from its inception. They have had to treat problems emanating from the numerous upheavals and overwhelming phenomena that have impinged upon their countries. Only in Russia are we aware that there has been a thrust toward establishing and differentiating family psychology (Shapiro, 2004).

Scandinavia: Iceland[3] and Norway[4]

Caring for the young is the most important task of the family, which is considered the cornerstone of Icelandic society. To protect the rights and wellbeing of individuals and to help families fulfill their responsibilities, the government and each municipality has set policies to protect and strengthen the family. An underlying premise is that the family is the milieu for emotional bonding and family life affords children the most security and best opportunity to develop to their fullest potential (Sigrun-Herman, 2004).

To fulfill such a policy touching all sectors of society and covering nearly all aspects of public administration, a wide variety of professionals in Iceland work with families. Professions concerned with family health and wellbeing that fall under the Ministry of Health include family physicians, psychiatrists, psychiatric nurses, psychologists, and addiction counselors.

Higher education and graduate training were limited in Iceland until the 2000s, although undergraduate training was rigorous. Postgraduate training was sought outside the country or at the University of Iceland Continuing Education Center, which offered courses in cooperation with professional associations. Independent associations have also sponsored training for Icelandic professionals. In January 2007 Kristin Ingolfsdottir, rector of the University of Iceland, and Porgerour Katrin Gunnarsdottir, the Minister of Education, signed a 5-year agreement that involves insuring the quality of education and research and the ability to achieve the upward striving of the university.

Students now choose from a variety of professions at different universities. The Universities of Iceland and of Akureyri, for example, offer a 60-credit (2-year) candidate degree in psychology (cand. psych. degree) which fulfills the qualification requirements of the Ministry of Health and Social Security for psychologists. The degree offers a theoretical, pragmatic, and methodological foundation which prepares candidates for general work in psychology. This agreement between the Ministry of Education and the University of Iceland should lead to an even greater variety and depth of education and a possible increase in funding for research at the PhD level.

Specialization in psychology is possible in four areas: clinical, disability, pedagogy, and social and organizational psychology. Family psychology might fall under any of these domains. To specialize, for example, in clinical psychology, at least 4 years of training in addition to a cand. psych. degree are required. The training must include internships in the area of specialization and be within an institution recognized by the Ministry of Education. Psychologists work in all elementary schools in Iceland; their function is to diagnose and assess on the basis of standardized tests and behavior and prepare an intervention plan. They work with teachers and other professionals in the schools who work with the child and family and can supervise their interventions, but they usually do not provide direct therapy. The Association of Psychologists has around 280 members, perhaps 70 of whom can offer psychotherapy.

Icelandic society has changed markedly in the last few decades from a homogeneous society into a multicultural, multireligious, heterogeneous one. Challenges and responsibilities that families face have changed due to the increasing complexities of the society, the influx of immigrants, and both parents working long days. The interplay between work and home has altered family life tremendously and has forced the schools to take a more active role in the socialization of children. The extended family is still important, but the young and elderly increasingly are spending time in institutions. This has called for a larger cadre of professionals whose task is to strengthen individual and family resiliency, health, and adaptation.

Family advocates and those with legalized titles who practice within the realm of the family, such as social workers, psychologists, and family physicians, can work doing family therapy, research, teaching, training, and supervising if they have the necessary prerequisites. Family therapist per se is not a legalized title and family psychology is not defined as a separate discipline. Family therapy is practiced by a wide range of professionals; yet it is recognized as a unique form of therapy which has wide applicability, not only to families but to institutions, and to relations between and within nations. Family therapy in a tradition specific to Iceland has not developed in the academic arena. When and if the lobbying of the EAP and the EFTA is successful and the EU legalizes the profession of psychotherapy, recognizing it as a separate profession, then Iceland will follow suit.

Family psychiatry, therapy, and pastoral counseling have a long and proud tradition in Norway. *The Norwegian Journal of Family Therapy* was begun in 1978. By that time progressive facilities such as Modum Bads Nervesanatorium, a short distance outside of Oslo, were already bringing patients' spouses or families into residential treatment for a month in cottages on hospital grounds. The identified patient and his or her significant others lived and played together, sometimes under observation and direction, and were treated conjointly. This was possible because family members who needed it were provided time released from work with pay by a government that valued treatment. Holm, who conducted a project with agoraphobic patients and their spouses at Modum Bads from 1978 to 1979, described this farsighted treatment and research approach (Holm, 1982).

Since that strong start in the 1970s, family work has burgeoned in Norway; where both the family and welfare system have undergone enormous changes in the post-World War II era. There has been a divide between family therapists and family psychologists. Many of the former became enamored of the postmodern, narrative, constructionist therapy of psychiatrist Tom Andersen (1996). They found listening to, reflecting upon, and reinterpreting stories a mesmerizing approach and easier to teach and learn than many of the other schools of therapy. Andersen's work also has been influential in South Africa, Argentina, and elsewhere.

Conversely, some family psychologists who studied at Norwegian universities and abroad were trained to gravitate toward theories and techniques tested by sound research methodology and refined by being clinically evaluated over time. Wencke Seltzer, PhD, has been one of the psychologists exemplifying the scientific psychology tradition in her work in hospital settings with patients exhibiting *conversion phenomenon*, in her attention to body–mind correlates and neuro-science (Seltzer, 2007), and in her creative co-constructing of culturally relevant rituals with patients in unresolved bereavement situations (Seltzer, 2004). Family psychologists in Norway work in private practices, in hospitals, and in clinics, and teach at universities.

Family therapy has also been taught and practiced in Denmark, Sweden, and Finland for the last 35 to 40 years, with government-approved graduate training programs primarily housed in schools of social work or courses taught in departments of psychiatry, such as at the University of Lund in southern Sweden, formerly under well-respected family psychologist researcher Kjell Hansson, PhD (Hansson, 1999; Kaslow, Hansson, & Lundblad, 1994). But to our knowledge family psychology has not yet emerged as a separate discipline.

Latin America: Argentina

Family therapy has had a proud and illustrious history in Argentina, which is probably the country in South America with the longest record and most sophisticated level of development in the field. Many people who have become world renowned were Argentinean born and bred, including Salvador Minuchin, Braulio Montalvo, Carlos Sluzki, Celia Falicov, and Cloe Madanes. All have long resided in the United States and are identified as family therapists.

Today Argentineans reveal the influence of a variety of schools – initially psycho-dynamic, structural, and strategic, and in the past two decades, also cognitive-behavioral, systemic, integrative, and narrative. The journal of the Systemic Association of Buenos Aires, *Sistemas Familiares*, was begun in 1985; at the time of its launching it had an international editorial board. The first editor, Cecile Rausch Herscovici PhD (2004), is a psychologist who has been involved internationally in the IFTA and in the treatment of eating disorders (Herscovici, 2002), an area of major therapeutic concern she shares with other Argentine psychologists. A professor of psychology at the University del Salvador in Buenos Aires as well as co-director of Tesis Center for Systems Therapies with her family psychiatrist husband, Pedro Herscovici (Herscovici & Herscovici, 1999); she has been an influential teacher, mentor, and therapist throughout her country and other Latin American countries in the last two and a half decades.

The Herscovicis and Ruth Casabianca[5] (2007), a family psychologist/therapist who teaches in the psychology department at the Catholic University in Santa Fe and also is invited to do training in countries throughout Latin America, all indicate that since the political crisis of 2002, and the financial devastation and social upheaval that accompanied it, this country of 35 million inhabitants now has over 50% of its popu-lation living below the poverty line. Current concerns being seen in clinical practice, in addition to those related to family economic reversals, include violence in the streets, in sports, and within families; decrease in respect for parents and breakdown in the traditional extended family system; the increasing number of unmarried couples living together, plus divorce rates rising to around the 33% mark; and many more complex stepfamilies being formed. Considerably more women have had to enter the workforce, which has altered the customary nature of family dynamics and functioning. After the peso was devalued, private practice fees plummeted; they have slowly begun to climb back upward. The mood is optimistic now that the government has been restabilized.

As in many countries of the world, increasingly education and training of therapists are being taken over by universities and the role of private family therapy training institutes, not affiliated with universities or medical schools, is diminishing. This reflects the growing emphasis, here and elsewhere, on promulgation of national and regional standards. But as yet no license to practice family psychology is required (Casabianca, 2007).

Megatrends Affecting Families Around the World

During the past 30 or so years, many megatrends have escalated throughout the globe that have a powerful impact on families and family psychologists, wherever they live, work, relocate, or travel. It is posited here that these trends need to be seriously considered by those shaping curricula; teaching, training, and providing supervision; by experienced clinicians as they select what continuing education workshops to attend; and by researchers contemplating critical issues to study. Because of space limitations, they can only be listed here (see Kaslow, 2008, for more detail).

1   *Strife between different ethnic, religious, racial and/or cultural groups* leading to warfare or ethnic cleansing.
2   *Dislocation, forced migration and relocation.*
3   Massive *immigration* to many new and unprepared recipient countries that may not be very welcoming to hordes of strangers who are "different."
4   *Terrorism and communal violence.*
5   *Violence and abuse in the family* – including child physical, emotional, and sexual abuse, intimate partner violence (Walker, 1994), and elder abuse that may be condoned in certain segments of some societies (Mai, 2006; UN, 2006).
6   The *technological revolution*, which has made worldwide communication easy and instantaneous, providing rapid information, and also potential problems, for families.
7   The *globalization of many businesses and of wealth*, including employee transfers to other countries that entail separation of families.
8   Resultant intercultural intermingling and socialization leading to a great increase in the number of *bicultural, biracial and bireligious marriages.*
9   The *rising separation and divorce rates*, estimated at between 25% and 65% in countries where divorce is not totally forbidden. This has changed drastically how we must conceptualize, view, and define the family in theory, therapy, and research.
10   The *diversity of sexual orientations* and the greater visibility of those who are gay, lesbian, bisexual, and transgender.

These 10 megatrends

> have combined into changing the portrait of what is normative for the family. More forms of families are now perceived: these include not only nuclear and extended families, but also bi nuclear, multicultural, biracial, interreligious, adoptive and foster families, gay and lesbian families, step families, single parent families, and couples or groups of people who live together as if they are a family because of the attachment they feel toward one another, without going through any legal process to formalize the bonds. (Kaslow, 2008, p. 122)

Closing Thoughts: Implications for Family Psychologists Around the World

What emerges clearly is that the fields of family psychology and family therapy remain closely intertwined in many countries. As education and training move from private institutes to universities, and from the undergraduate to the graduate level, the two fields will become more demarcated, as universities and sometimes governmental divisions of the country determine in what department of a university faculty the major will be lodged, and who will be responsible for developing curricula, for teaching, and for supervising students. This shift into academe has coincided with governments and regional communities, such as the European Union, promulgating standards for licensure and/or certification.

As psychologists increasingly treat patients who have lived through various horrendous, disruptive experiences; political and religious persecution; kidnappings; starvation; forced migration; having been a prisoner of war; or natural disasters such as tsunamis (Kalayjian, 2007) or hurricanes, they will need a much richer theoretical foundation and grasp of the larger world; enduring compassion and empathy; and multicultural, multiethnic, multiracial, and multireligious sensitivity and competence (Sue & Sue, 1999). For many of these patients have had experiences that are unfamiliar to their therapists and present with almost unbearable pain.

We must be able to *listen* to each person's story as *they want to tell it*, in bits and pieces, tears, sobs, screams – or *hear the silence* as covering what cannot be said. We must *not push to uncover what is repressed* that they need to keep secret or hidden. This is their *choice*. And *do no harm*.

We need to *go where the clients/patients are* and not wait for them to come to our offices. This may mean the battlefields, behind the scenes in the war zones, or places where earthquakes hit.

We will need to *develop an astute, acute awareness of different systems of meaning and value, of beliefs, of family organization and structure*, and be willing to discard beliefs that our way is "the only right way" of viewing and doing things.

We will need to *become engaged in helping clients solve the most immediate problems at hand* – be that finding the whereabouts of lost family members, shelter, food, income, or school for their children. Talking about restructuring the family hierarchy or improving relationship dynamics before a family's basic needs are addressed will not make sense.

When people tell their stories, and their narratives differ, we must *bear witness* respectfully to each version – for each is expressing their own subjective truth. By bearing witness (Kaslow, 2003), we accept and validate their experience, a necessary step before they can let the past heal.

Psychologists need to *know when to use brief therapies* (Budman, Gurman, & Wachtel, 2002; de Shazer, 1985), including *cognitive and behavioral approaches* (Kaslow & Patterson, 2002). Many clients who have lived through bombings, political oppression, or relocation cannot make a commitment to a long-term process. The only reality is the here and now. Eye movement desensitization and reprocessing (EMDR), combined with family systems therapy, can be very valuable to families where trauma has been experienced (Shapiro, Kaslow, & Maxfield, 2007).

We will need a broad, *integrative foundation and perspective* on life, rooted in our own core ethical beliefs and system of meaning and values, yet remain open to hearing, seeing, and sensing what our clients have experienced, witnessed, intuited, and absorbed, and the meaning they have ascribed to their experiences, and to codetermining what they want from therapy as we co-construct a new reality with them.

We must be attuned to our own capabilities and recognize when we are experiencing duress and nearing burnout. We cannot function well when suffering *compassion fatigue* (Figley, 1997). Good therapist self-care is essential.

We must *focus on our patients' fortitude and courage*, for they have survived tragedies, injustices, and grave losses. We must reframe and expand their construction of reality so they see themselves as *survivors*, and no longer as victims, and build on the resilience they have demonstrated (Walsh, 2006). *Empowering patients to set goals* and strive to attain them, and conveying that you think that they can, can be quite beneficial.

Given the number of complex changes affecting families around the world, in many aspects of their existence, the need for broadly trained, dynamic, multiculturally competent and sensitive family psychologists to function as researchers, theoreticians, academicians, supervisors, and clinicians can only continue to escalate. Hopefully the field, internationally, will be prepared to meet these challenges.

Appendix: Questionnaire sent to family psychologists abroad, July–September 2007

International Family Psychology

I.   *Training and Education:*
     • Where does it occur: Universities, Institutes
     • How many years? What degree granted:
     • Components: Theoretical, clinical, research?
II. *Licensure and/or Certification:*
     • By whom:
     • Is it required?
     • Criteria
III. *Roles of Family Psychologists:*
     • Teaching
     • Clinical Practice – In what realms?
     • Research
     • Supervision and Consultation
     • Program Development
     • Agency Administration
     • Policy and Planning

- Advocacy
- Independent or Private Practice

IV. *Relationship to Other Professions:*
- Medicine
- Psychiatry
- Marriage and Family Therapy – and differentiation from
- Social Work

V. *Status in Community.*

VI. *Trends or Changes in Foreseeable Future.*

Notes

Sincere appreciation and full acknowledgement is expressed to each of the following authors for their contributions on:

1 Czech Republic: S. Gjuricova, O. Hinkova, V. Chvala, I. Kofatkova, M. Radosova, and L. Trapkova, September 2007.
2 Slovak Republic, including Bratislava: Hana Scibranyova and Olga Nemcova.
3 Reykjavik, Iceland: Toby Sigrun-Herman, past president of the IFTA.
4 Norway: Wencke J. Seltzer, past president of the IFTA and former editor of the Norwegian *Journal of Psychology.*
5 Argentina: Ruth Casabianca, former secretary of the IFTA and member of the editorial board of the Argentinian journal.

References

Andersen, T. (1996). Language is not innocent. In F. W. Kaslow (Ed.), *Handbook of relational diagnosis and dysfunctional family patterns.* (pp. 119–125). New York: Wiley.

Andolfi, M., Angelo, C., & deNichelo, M. (1989). *The myth of Atlas: Families and the therapeutic story.* New York: Brunner/Mazel.

Andolfi, M., & Zwerling, I. (Eds.). (1980). *Dimensions of family therapy.* New York: Guilford Press.

Budman, S. H., Gurman, A., & Wachtel, P. L. (2002). *Theory and practice of brief therapy.* New York: Guilford Press.

Casabianca, R. (2007). *How family therapy developed in Argentina.* Part of panel presentation on *Family Psychology Around the World* at the annual conference of the American Psychological Association, San Francisco.

de Shazer, S. (1985). *Keys to solutions in brief therapy.* New York: Norton.

Figley, C. R. (1997). Crisis intervention and compassion fatigue. *Family Therapy News, 15–16,* 21.

Gacic, B., Trbic, F., Markovic, M., & Nikolic, L. (2004). Family life in the context of chronic stress and dramatic social transformation in Yugoslavia. In W. C. Nichols (Ed.), *Family therapy around the world: A festschrift for Florence W. Kaslow* (pp. 3–18). New York: Haworth Press.

Hansson, K. (1999). Family psychology in Sweden. In U. P. Gielen & A. L. Comunian (Eds.), *International approaches to the family and family therapy* (pp. 226–234). Padua: Unipress.

Herscovici, C. R. (2002). Eating disorders in adolescence. In F. W. Kaslow & J. Magnavita (Eds.), *Comprehensive handbook of psychotherapy: Vol. 1. Psychodynamic/object relations* (pp. 133–160). New York: Wiley.

Herscovici, C. R. (2004). Understanding and treating the family in Argentina. In C. W. Nichols (Ed.), *Family therapy around the world: A festschrift for Florence W. Kaslow* (pp. 161–272). New York: Haworth Press.

Herscovici, P., & Herscovici, C. R. (1999). Family therapy in Argentina. In U. P. Gielen & A. L. Comunian (Eds.), *International approaches to the family and family therapy* (pp. 117–138). Padua: Unipress.

Holm, H. J. (1982). The agoraphobic married woman and her marriage pattern: A clinical study. In F. W. Kaslow (Ed.), *The international book of family therapy* (pp. 338–415). New York: Brunner/Mazel.

Kalayjian, A. (2007). Family challenges for post tsunami survivors in Sri Lanka: The bio-psychosocial, educational and spiritual approach. *The Family Psychologist, 22(2)*, 8–11.

Kameguchi, K. (2001). Family psychology and family therapy in Japan. *American Psychologist, 56(1)*, 65–70.

Kaslow, F. W. (2000). History of family therapy: Evolution outside the USA. *Journal of Family Psychotherapy, 11(4)*, 1–35.

Kaslow, F. W. (2003). Descendants' memories and legacies: Post Holocaust highways and byways to and in Chile. *Journal of Family Psychotherapy, 14(2)*, 69–80.

Kaslow, F. W. (2008). Sameness and diversity in families across five continents. *Journal of Family Psychotherapy, 19*, 107–142.

Kaslow, F. W., Hansson, K., Lundblad, A. M. (1994). Long term marriage in Sweden and some comparisons with similar couples in the United States. *Contemporary Family Therapy, 16(6)*, 521–537.

Kaslow, F. W., & Patterson, T. (Eds.). (2002). *Comprehensive handbook of psychotherapy: Cognitive-behavioral approaches: Vol. 2.* New York: Wiley.

Kuniya, N. (1998). *Report from Japan chapter of IAFP.* Sent to Dr F. Kaslow, IAFP president, December 5.

L'Abate, L. (1986). *Systematic family therapy.* New York: Wiley.

L'Abate, L. (1994). *Handbook of developmental family psychology and psychopathology.* New York: Wiley.

Luthman, S. G., & Kirshenbaum, M. (1974). *The dynamic family.* Palo Alto, CA: Science & Behavior Books.

Mai, M. (2006). *Deshonrada/In the name of honor: A memoir* (L. Coverdale, Trans.). New York: Washington Square Press.

Olson, D. H. (1990). The triple threat of bridging research, theory and practice. In F. W. Kaslow (Ed.), *Voices in family psychology 1* (pp. 361–374). Newbury Park, CA: Sage.

Olson, D. H. (1996). Clinical assessment and treatment interventions using the family circumplex model. In F. W. Kaslow (Ed.), *Handbook of relational diagnosis and dysfunctional family patterns* (pp. 59–80). New York: Wiley.

Satir, V. (1964). *Conjoint family therapy.* Palo Alto, CA: Science & Behavior Books.

Satir, V., & Baldwin, M. (1983). *Satir step by step.* Palo Alto, CA: Science & Behavior Books.

Satir, V., Banmen, J., Gerber, J., & Gomori, M. (1991). *Satir model: Family therapy and beyond.* Palo Alto, CA: Science & Behavior Books.

Sato-Vosburg, E. (2004). Toward triadic communication: A crisis in Japanese family communications. In W. C. Nichols (Ed.), *Family therapy around the world: A festschrift for Florence W. Kaslow* (pp. 105–118). New York: Haworth Press.

Schneewind, K. A. (1999). Family psychology and family therapy in Germany: In U. P. Gielen & A. L. Comunion (Eds.), *International approaches to the family and family therapy* (pp. 161–172). Padua: Unipress.

Seltzer, W. (2007). Traditional, modern and postmodern paradigms in Norwegian family therapy/psychology. Part of panel presentation on *Family Psychology Around the World* at the annual conference of the American Psychological Association, San Francisco.

Seltzer, W. J. (2004). Death does not do us part. In W. C. Nichols (Ed.), *Family therapy around the world: A festschrift for Florence W. Kaslow* (pp. 149–160). New York: Haworth Press.

Selvini-Palazzoli, M., Boscolo, L., Cecchin, G., & Prata, G. (1978). *Paradox and counter paradox.* New York: Aronson.

Selvini-Palazzoli, M., Cirillo, S., Selvini, M. & Sorentino, A. M. (1989). *Family games: General models of psychotic processes in the family.* New York: Norton.

Shapiro, A. (2004). The theme of the family in contemporary society and positive family psychology. In C. W. Nichols (Ed.), *Family therapy around the world: A festschrift for Florence W. Kaslow* (pp. 19–38). New York: Haworth Press‘.

Shapiro, F., Kaslow, F. W., & Maxfield, L. (Eds.). (2007). *Handbook of EMDR and family system processes.* New York: Wiley.

Sigrun-Herman, T. (2004). Development and influences on family therapy in Iceland. In W. C. Nichols (Ed.), *Family therapy around the world: A festschrift for Florence W. Kaslow* (pp. 149–160). New York: Haworth Press.

Sue, D. W., & Sue, D. (1999). *Counseling the culturally different: Theory and practice* (3rd ed.). New York: Wiley.

UN. (2006). In-depth study on all forms of violence against women. Retrieved from http://www.peacewomen.org/resources/Human_Rights/SG_VAW_Report2006.pdf.

Walsh, F. (2006). *Strengthening family resilience* (2nd ed.). New York: Guilford Press.

Walker, L. E. A. (1994). *Abused women and survivor therapy: A practical guide for the psychotherapist.* Washington, DC: American Psychological Association.

50

Family Forensic Psychology

Robert Welsh, Lyn Greenberg, and Marjorie Graham-Howard

Family forensic psychology (FFP) is an area of specialized psychological practice that lies at the intersection of family psychology, forensic psychology, and the legal system. It is a notably challenging area of practice that encompasses specialized intervention, evaluation, and consultation. This chapter provides a general overview of the field of FFP focused into two areas. First, we will introduce the practice of forensic psychology and describe elements that differentiate forensic practice from general clinical practice. We will then extend that discussion to the specialty practice of FFP. The second part broadly covers the forensic roles in the specialty practice areas of child custody cases, dependency cases, and juvenile delinquency case. Because of the introductory nature of this chapter, it should not be understood as a satisfactory knowledge base for participating in the work of FFP. Accordingly, we reference important sources to consult throughout the chapter and conclude with recommendations for future education in FFP.

Forensic Psychology and FFP

Forensic psychology has been defined in a number of ways and is currently a source of some disagreement in the field. For this chapter we use the definition of forensic psychology advanced by the American Board of Forensic Psychology (ABFP), which is generally consistent with the current Specialty Guidelines in Forensic Psychology (SGFP: Committee on Ethical Issues for Forensic Psychologists, 1991) and most other forensic specialty standards in the field. According to the ABFP (n.d.), "Forensic Psychology is the application of the science and profession of psychology to questions and issues relating to law and the legal system." Forensic psychologists may serve the judicial system and those involved in it by providing specialized services including evaluation, expert testimony, research, teaching, consultation, or specialized intervention services.

For the purposes of this chapter we define FFP as a special application of family psychology and forensic psychology that provides expert-level services to families involved with the legal system, their attorneys, and the courts. Expert services may be rendered in the form of intervention, consultation, testimony, research, or evaluation. We advance that FFP is defined by three distinctives: (a) the population served; (b) the overlapping fields of interest; (c) the application of a family psychology perspective to the work of forensic psychology. The field of FFP evaluates and intervenes with children and families. A second defining characteristic of FFP is the domain of interest. Kaslow (2000) and Grossman and Okun (2003) have previously written on the overlapping fields of family law, forensic psychology, and family psychology and cited common areas of interest between FFP and family law, elder law, dependency law, and minor law. The final distinctive of FFP is the application of a family psychology perspective or epistemology (see Chapter 1, this volume) to forensic cases. A family psychology perspective involves understanding the complex interaction between interpersonal factors, intraindividual dynamics, and a macrosystemic context.

The Forensic Perspective: Forensically Informed Services v. Routine Clinical Services

Psychologists who interface with children and families in the legal system need to have a basic familiarity with the differences between forensically informed services and routine clinical services. An important distinction needs to be made between the specialized knowledge that qualifies one as a forensic expert and the normal scope of practice governed by licensure as a psychologist. This issue has been addressed both in the previous editions of the American Psychological Association (APA) child custody guidelines, which are currently being updated, and in most other relevant professional standards. Many professionals with clinical practices provide services to children and families involved with the legal system (e.g., conjoint treatment or child treatment); however, the degree of specialized knowledge required for these roles will vary with the characteristics of the case and the types of services needed. In this chapter, we reference the roles of the "forensically informed family psychologist" and the "family forensic psychologist" (also FFP). Responsible practitioners may disagree as to the dividing line between these categories, neither of which has been codified in any formal ethics code or standards. Generally speaking, greater expertise is required to represent oneself as an FFP and to provide services in those roles that clearly imply expert status, such as forensic evaluation or providing a specialized intervention service (e.g. parent coordinator).

Any practitioner who provides services to a court-involved family is likely to find himself or herself impacted by, and potentially impacting, the relevant court case – even if the practitioner never testifies in court. Psychologists may significantly benefit court-involved families, including helping them to focus on the needs of the children. Poor practice in these cases, however, can also cause significant harm. Because of these issues, it is essential that psychologists working with court-involved families maintain a *forensic perspective* throughout their work (Greenberg, Martindale, Gould, & Gould-Saltman, 2004).

Maintaining the forensic perspective includes a more critical evaluation of hypotheses related to the case; careful data collection, as appropriate to the psychologist's role; and carefully limiting advocacy and opinions expressed to what is appropriate to the psychologist's role and available information. Psychologists providing services to a court-involved family need to be familiar with the legal standards governing that type of case, unique limitations and exceptions to confidentiality and privilege, and limitations on opinions and testimony offered in a case. There are a variety of resources detailing the forensic perspective and the boundaries of ethical forensic practice (Bush, Connell, & Denney, 2007; Greenberg, Martindale, Gould, & Gould-Saltman, 2004). Practitioners who neglect or ignore these issues may cause considerable harm to clients and families, and may also find themselves facing malpractice suits and ethics or board complaints.

Family forensic psychology

FFP is well established as an approach to cases that focus on children and the family, such as child custody and juvenile dependency cases. An emerging literature discusses the applicability of FFP to issues such as elder law and family business planning; these emerging areas are beyond the scope of this chapter. Juvenile delinquency cases often involve elements of family and systemic assessment and family-involved treatment (e.g., Hengeller & Lee, 2003; Lipsitt & Lipsitt, 2000).

The practice of juvenile forensic psychology is frequently aligned with criminal forensic psychology; however, given the importance of family and systemic assessment and treatment in juvenile justice cases, we believe that the practice of juvenile forensic psychology fits comfortably within FFP, and we believe that the family forensic perspective has much to offer to the resolution of these cases. These issues are discussed in greater detail below.

When the Family is the Issue: FFP in Child Custody and Juvenile Dependency Cases

Legal and case context

FFP has been most commonly associated with cases that focus on the safety and wellbeing of children. In *child custody* cases, parents may turn to the court to resolve disputes about issues such as parenting time (formerly referred to as physical custody), the right to make decisions on behalf of the child (legal custody), whether the child should relocate with a parent, and other child-related issues such as school choice, extracurricular activities, engagement with extended families or stepfamilies, medical care, psychotherapy, and other issues. Such cases are particularly complex if they involve allegations of domestic violence or abuse. From a legal perspective, both parents are generally presumed to be fit parents unless/until the court sustains an allegation of abuse or endangerment, or the case is transferred to the *Juvenile Dependency Court*. This does not prevent the family court from intervening, ordering evaluations or treatment, or limiting parenting time or authority due to concerns about a parent's behavior; nevertheless, as a general rule, the family court focuses on resolving parental disputes, while the Juvenile Dependency Court focuses on issues of abuse and endangerment.

Juvenile dependency cases are heard in a separate court system in some states, while in other jurisdictions the same judges hear both types of cases. Child Protective Services (CPS) workers are empowered to file cases in Juvenile Dependency Court if they believe that *state* intervention is needed to protect children from one or both parents. In divorce or family law cases, the legal conflict is, at least initially, between two presumably fit parents. In juvenile dependency cases, the state has filed allegations that one or both parents is unfit to care for the child, such that the child has suffered physical abuse, sexual abuse, emotional abuse, or neglect, or is in danger of suffering these events. If the case becomes a juvenile dependency case, a different body of law applies to its resolution. Nevertheless, particularly when a case involves multiple allegations and a long history of conflict, a single family may be involved with each court, or its representatives, at various points during the family's legal struggle.

Many child custody issues are resolved between the parents, either on their own or using a variety of mental health or court-related services such as therapy, specialized parent education, co-parenting therapy, or mediation. The minority of cases that remain unresolved are generally thought to consume disproportionate resources in the court systems due to the level of family conflict and degree of impairment/distress in one or more parties, and, sometimes, the seriousness of the allegations/issues brought to the court. These cases often involve issues such as severe family stress, poor parenting, family conflict, child disability, emotional or behavior problems in children, and allegations of child abuse, domestic violence, or the deliberate undermining of parent–child relationships. Post-divorce stresses, such as blended families or the desire of a parent to relocate with the child, may escalate conflict even in parents who previously cooperated. All of these dynamics may affect the family's interaction with involved mental health professionals (MHP), leading to inaccurate or distorted information presented to the MHP, and/or unusual pressures on psychologists to conform (or prompt a child to conform) to some adult's position in the pending legal action.

Juvenile dependency cases often rest on the intervention of CPS, the agency that files most cases, monitors progress, and may provide resources or other services. Most of those cases are not superimposed on a pre-existing divorce case. When CPS and family law systems do intersect, however, complications can multiply. Generally, the involvement of CPS and the Dependency Court are aimed at addressing specific issues that are thought to be endangering a child, such as physical abuse, with the goal of maintaining or reuniting the child with one or both parents. Psychologists may be called upon to assist such families or children as therapists or parenting coaches, roles which may or may not require significant levels of forensic expertise. FFPs may be retained as consultants by counsel, appointed by the court to conduct forensic evaluations, retained as experts to discuss psychological phenomena, or appointed to provide expert-level intervention (treatment) services to children and families. Some FFPs help families mediate juvenile dependency cases, but this is less common than in child custody cases.

Expertise for forensically informed and family forensic practice

Psychologists undertaking cases in these systems must remain familiar with relevant legal and practice standards and the boundaries of each professional role. Practitioners should be aware of both existing and emerging guidelines, such as those being developed by the APA. This does not require that FFPs be attorneys, nor should they ever attempt to practice law. Rather, they must be sufficiently familiar with the legal practices, court rules, and professional responsibilities relevant to court-involved families to assist them in recognizing ethical issues/challenges, and to recognize the need for professional consultation. FFPs must also be familiar with current research on divorcing/separated families, child development and adjustment, cultural issues, domestic violence and child abuse, the impact of parental conflict on children, children's suggestibility and interviewing, conflict resolution, and the impact of various post-divorce family changes, such as blended families and relocation. Resources such as Kelly and Emery (2003), as well as attention to current child custody journals, can assist FFPs in staying aware of the most current research on these issues. FFPs who specialize in particular issues, such as developmental challenges or child abuse, must have additional expertise in these areas. Family forensic roles require advanced levels of expertise, expanded informed consent procedures, enhanced record-keeping, and careful attention to the conflicting rights, needs, and ethical demands that may arise in these cases.

Given the high rate of divorced and separated parents, it is likely that most psychologists will, eventually, provide treatment to parents or children who are involved in conflict over child custody issues. Such services are common in the treatment community and do not necessarily require a high level of forensic expertise. It is important to note, however, that any case involving a disrupted family can eventually become a legal matter; many contested cases arise long after the initial divorce decree. Therefore, even in community treatment with non-litigating families, it is essential that therapists remain *forensically informed*, attentive to the rights and concerns of both parents and children, and aware of the powerful family dynamics which may impact on treatment in the context of a conflicted child custody case. See Greenberg, Gould, Gould-Saltman, and Stahl (2003) for a more complete discussion of these issues.

Higher levels of forensic expertise are required to provide services in more complex cases, or those with continuing legal involvement. Careful attention to role boundaries is also essential, as will be discussed below. Specialized training is required to effectively fulfill these roles.

FFP roles in child custody/juvenile dependency cases

The FFP may fulfill a variety of roles across different cases, some of which are briefly described below.

Mediator.   When parents are unable to resolve their disputes without assistance, they may utilize the services of a family law mediator to help them resolve the areas of dispute. Traditionally, a mediator is a neutral, expert professional, trained in relevant legal and psychological issues and able to assist the family in formulating and recording an appropriate agreement. In many jurisdictions, the process is confidential. Some jurisdictions, however, have adopted models that blend the role of mediator and evaluator, such that the mediator recommends a resolution to the court if the parents are unable to reach an agreement. This model has been the subject of some controversy. For more information on the role of mediator, consult the Specialty Guidelines drafted by the Association of Family and Conciliation Courts (AFCC) (2000), and the rules of court for each jurisdiction.

Child custody evaluator.　When parents are unable to resolve disputes about a child's parenting plan and the court sees a need for expert psychological assistance, the judge may appoint an MHP to conduct a child custody evaluation with the family. Some jurisdictions have court staff who conduct such evaluations. In more complex cases, and if the family has sufficient resources, the court will appoint an independent expert to conduct a focused or comprehensive evaluation of the family. Such evaluations require a high level of psychological and professional expertise, and both state and national organizations are increasingly adopting court rules and standards to govern them.

The child custody evaluator does not form an alliance with either parent, but rather adopts an objective and investigative stance. Most evaluations are *not* confidential. Current models (Gould & Martindale, 2007) emphasize the *multi-method* approach to gathering evaluation data. Common evaluation methods include individual and conjoint interviews, psychological testing, interviews and observations of the children with each parent and sibling, interview of collateral informants (e.g., friends, neighbors, therapists, teachers), and review of records. Effective child custody evaluators constantly formulate rival hypotheses as to the status of the family and the best plan for the future, and seek information that will support or tend to refute these various possibilities. In a dependency case, the court may reach a preliminary finding regarding the allegations of abuse, but seek expert opinion as to the best options for the child, ongoing safety risks, and potential for reunifying the child with the allegedly abusive parents.

Evaluators are frequently asked to render opinions on *psycholegal* issues before the court, such as the most appropriate parenting plan for a child, whether a child can relocate with a parent, or whether a child is at risk of being abused by a parent or has suffered such abuse. There has been a movement in the literature (Tippins and Wittmann, 2005) to preclude or limit the evaluator from offering such recommendations, otherwise known as *addressing the ultimate issue,* but recommendations are still requested in most jurisdictions. Certainly, evaluators should carefully avoid offering opinions that exceed the scope of available data or the role assigned to the child custody evaluator, and should be careful to articulate the limits of any opinions they do express.

Forensic evaluators are often asked to weigh in on the "big ticket" items in a family dispute, such as how much time the child will spend with each parent. It is equally important, however, that evaluators be attuned to the detailed issues that form the texture of children's daily lives. How will each proposed parenting plan impact the child's ability to master developmental tasks, engage in peer activities, succeed in school, enjoy supportive sibling relationships, adjust to blended or stepfamilies, and engage successfully in each of the systems that impact children's lives? The special expertise and perspective of FFPs may be invaluable in considering these issues.

After a forensic evaluator completes an examination report, he or she often issues a report describing the psychological data collected, methods used, and recommendations reached. Most families reach a settlement after the evaluation is completed, but parents have a right to challenge the evaluator's recommendations in court. In such cases, the evaluator's records may be subject to subpoena, and the evaluator may have to testify in court to explain his or her conclusions. The process, and the mindset required, focus on objectivity, transparency, conclusions that can be supported with available data, and accountability to all concerned. The role of the child custody evaluator is more extensively described in specialty standards/guidelines and well-known texts (AFCC, 2006; APA, 1994; Gould and Martindale, 2007). The APA is currently revising and updating its guidelines for parental responsibility evaluations.

Expert witness/consultant.   FFPs may be retained as expert witnesses, reviewers, or consultants by parents' or children's attorneys in child custody cases. A parent who is dissatisfied with a child custody evaluation may retain an independent expert to review the records and reports completed by the evaluator, and to render an opinion as to whether the evaluation was appropriately completed. An expert who finds deficiencies in an evaluation may be asked to testify in court about those deficiencies. Alternatively, an expert may be retained to serve as a consultant to the attorney, or as a parenting consultant to the parent, to help the parent and counsel prepare or resolve the case. In that case, the consultant's work is covered under the attorney's work-product privilege. Both roles require detailed retainer agreements considering relevant legal standards on psychological practice.

Parenting coordinators.   The role of the parenting coordinator, or special master, is a rapidly developing area for FFPs. A parenting coordinator (sometimes referred to as parenting plan coordinator, PC, or PPC) is an MHP or attorney appointed by the court to assist parents in resolving detailed and daily issues in a parenting plan. Unlike a therapist, the PC is empowered with decision-making authority; in effect, they are "deputized" by the court to make decisions which are considered relatively minor in the overall scheme of litigation, but may be of enormous importance to the child and must be resolved in a timely fashion. For example, a PC may be empowered to make a decision about a child's extracurricular activities or minor adjustments in vacation schedules with each parent. The role of the PC is usually governed by a detailed court order, which empowers the PC to *implement* the overall order established by the court. Parenting coordination may be a powerful tool to reduce conflict, resolve it quickly and, over time, improve parents' ability to co-parent. In some jurisdictions, parents can be ordered to work with a PC. Other jurisdictions require parents to agree to engage such a professional. PCs attempt to form working relationships with parents and children, but they do not provide treatment. They may coordinate or supervise the efforts of other therapists or service providers, and they may be required to periodically submit reports to the court.

Typically, this service is not confidential. Further information about this role is available (AFCC, 2005; Sullivan, 2004).

Expert-level therapists.   The most complex and high-conflict cases may require treating professionals with a level of expertise comparable to that of the forensic expert. Such therapists are often asked to focus on specific issues in parent or child functioning, or parent–child relationships. They may be asked to assist in reunifying a parent and child who have been separated, or assist a child and family in addressing the impact of parental conflict, child abuse, or other issues. Interventions are often focused, systems-oriented, and highly structured, and confidentiality may be limited. Such specialized treatment requires extensive informed consent, careful record-keeping, and attention to detail and the content of evaluation reports and court orders. If required to report or testify, expert-level therapists provide testimony as a *treating expert.* A treating expert may describe treatment progress, interventions attempted, children's or parents' coping skills and relationship progress, and the responses of parents and children to their interventions. Treating experts generally should not express opinions on psycholegal issues such as parenting plans or the validity of child abuse allegations, and children's therapists must use extreme caution to avoid unduly allying with one side or the other in a custody conflict. Biased therapy can approximate the problems associated with repeated, suggestive interviews, and can cause serious harm to children and families. Further information about the treating expert role, and related issues, can be found in Greenberg and Gould (2001) and Greenberg et al. (2003).

Cautions and role boundaries

The nature of family forensic cases may lead to more complex and challenging ethical dilemmas regarding multiple relationships (APA Ethical Standard 3.05, in APA, 2002) so FFPs should be thoroughly familiar with these issues. It is unwise and potentially unethical to fulfill multiple and potentially conflicting roles in any single case. This does not prevent the children's therapist from working with a child and other family members (e.g., helping the child to resolve issues with a parent), with full informed consent procedures in place, unless the role of conjoint therapist has been precluded by the court or assigned to someone else. Such *child-centered* conjoint therapy would be provided to assist the child by engaging parents in the child's treatment, while the therapist's alliance remains with the child. In such circumstances, it is critical that the therapist consider input from both parents, and provide both parents an opportunity to participate if appropriate. Conversely, a *parent's therapist* engenders a significant role conflict, and potential ethical trouble, if he or she suddenly interviews the child, includes the child in the parent's sessions, or makes statements about the best parenting plan or about a parent–child relationship that the therapist had not observed. Most professional standards preclude having a child custody evaluation conducted by an MHP who has a previous relationship with either parent.

Informed consent is paramount in family forensic cases. Standard informed consent procedures do not always anticipate the degree to which confidentiality may be compromised, or the numerous ways in which parents' and children's legal rights may interact with psychological services. Interested readers are referred to Greenberg et al. (2004) and Greenberg, Gould-Saltman, and Gottlieb (2009). Therapists working with court-involved families would be well advised to consult with a forensic psychologist or a trusted family law or professional practice attorney to ensure that their informed consent processes are adequate.

Case Example

Ahiro (father), age 42, was of Japanese descent and was married to Patricia (mother), age 30, for 7 years. After some initial difficulty conceiving they produced one child, Caroline, 4 years old at the time of the case. When Caroline was 2 years 6 months old, her parents separated and ultimately divorced. Father claimed that mother had exploited him for money, and that she didn't take proper care of Caroline. Caroline began attending a demanding preschool at the age of 3, and mother became increasingly concerned that father was demanding and punitive with Caroline when she didn't understand her lessons. Mother claimed that Caroline resisted having overnight visits with father; father alleged that mother was overprotective and that Caroline was fine whenever mother wasn't around. Each filed a court petition seeking primary physical and sole legal custody of Caroline. The parents were ordered to attend mediation, but were unable to resolve their dispute. After a contested custody hearing, father was awarded one weekly overnight and every other weekend with Caroline.

Mother alleged that Caroline dif not want to visit father. She called CPS and alleged that father was emotionally abusing Caroline with his demands about her school performance, but Caroline did not make any allegations of abuse. Father alleged that mother was "brainwashing" Caroline to be afraid of him. Mother then took Caroline to a therapist, without father's consent or knowledge. The *therapist* later issued a letter suggesting that Caroline should not spend overnight visits with father, whom the therapist had never met. Father went to court to request that the therapist be removed from the case due to bias, and the ethical violation of expressing an opinion without sufficient knowledge. A new, *expert-level therapist* was appointed to treat Caroline, with the parents alternating in taking Caroline to therapy. Caroline still resisted visiting with father, at least on some occasions, and mother at times refused to enforce the visitation schedule. Each parent alleged that the other parent put Caroline in the middle of the parental conflict by arguing during parenting transitions and making derogatory remarks about each other in Caroline's presence.

The court appointed a *forensic evaluator* to evaluate the parents' conflicting claims about each other's parenting and relationship with Caroline. The forensic evaluator did not find that either parent was abusive, but did recommend that father see a therapist or *parenting coach* to assist him with developmentally appropriate parenting, and that each parent engage in *conjoint therapy* with Caroline to assist them in supporting the other parent–child relationship. Following the release of the child custody evaluation, father retained an expert to rebut the contention that he needed assistance with his parenting. He stated that his academic demands on Caroline were consistent with his Japanese culture, of which Caroline was also a part, and that the evaluator had neglected to consider these cultural issues. The court upheld the evaluator's recommendations, with increasing time for father contingent upon his cooperation with a parenting coach or therapist and improvements in his parenting skills. The court also ordered mother to consistently ensure that Caroline attend visits with father, and to participate in whatever treatment services were necessary to make this occur. Nevertheless, the parents continued to argue during all custody transitions, dispute the details of the court order, lodge accusations against one another, and interfere with each other's choices about Caroline's friends and activities. Ultimately, upon the recommendation of all professionals, the parents stipulated the services of a *parenting coordinator*, who was empowered by the court to implement the court order, establish detailed transition procedures, consult with all therapists, and approve the progressions in the parenting plan detailed in the court order.

This rather oversimplified example illustrates some of the roles that FFPs may play to assist distressed families in child custody or juvenile dependency cases. Note that the first therapist may have exacerbated the situation, and courted ethical trouble for herself, by aligning with one parent, failing to obtain both parents' consent, and expressing opinions about a parent–child relationship she had never observed. The forensic evaluator had to consider all history of adults questioning Caroline, as well as Caroline's witnessing of parental conflict, cultural issues, and a variety of complex elements in the case. A case involving this level of conflict and complexity likely required intervention professionals (therapists and/or a PC) with a high level of forensic expertise and the knowledge required to establish highly specific procedures for protecting Caroline from the parental conflict.

FFPs are also being engaged in alternative models of dispute resolution, such as collaborative law. Because these cases occur against the critical time frame of children's development, innovative models are constantly being developed to assist families in resolving conflicts more quickly and adjusting more successfully. These emerging roles and models add to the excitement and satisfaction of this particular specialty. Nevertheless, psychologists should approach them with caution, consultation, and clear attention to the issues of forensic perspective, expertise, and other ethical issues described earlier in this chapter and in the associated references (see Greenberg et al., 2004).

When the Child is the Issue: FFP and Juvenile Justice Cases

History of the juvenile court

Prior to 1900, children who committed criminal offenses were adjudicated, sentenced, and housed with adult offenders (Grisso, 1998). The first juvenile court system was established in Cook County, Illinois, in 1899. Within a few years most states had established similar systems. The court systems were informal and advocated rehabilitation. Because the best interest of the child was paramount, juvenile court judges had considerable latitude. From its inception, the juvenile court focused on the family and social background of youth. The probation officer was required to conduct in-home studies, interview parents and other caregivers, and consider numerous family factors when making recommendations to the court. The court was viewed as an extension of parental attempts to discipline and correct wayward youth.

Changes in the juvenile delinquency court occurred in the mid-1970s, through a number of landmark mental health cases. The quasi-criminal and informal proceedings were amended by several Supreme Court cases (*in re Gault*, 1967; *Kent v. United States*, 1966; *in re Winship*, 1970) arguing that juvenile defendants were entitled to the same rights as adults. This included rights to counsel, rights to an appeal, rights to have a written transcription of the hearing, and privilege against self-incrimination. A second wave of procedural and philosophical changes occurred in the 1990s (Grisso, 1998). A rise in juvenile offending, particularly gang-related and violent offending, and mounting public pressure to "get tough on crime," resulted in further changes to the juvenile justice system. The philosophy of rehabilitation was replaced with a more punitive one. Many jurisdictions adopted tougher laws for juveniles, including reducing the age for juvenile transfers, increasing sentencing requirements, and prosecuting juvenile sex offenders formally.

The MHP in juvenile delinquency cases

Psychologists and allied MHPs have played an important role in the juvenile justice system since its inception. When the focus was on rehabilitation, the psychologist identified factors thought to contribute to criminal behavior of minors. Even when the philosophy shifted to a more punitive model, psychologists were still an integral part of the court system. The focus of assessments did shift to a consideration of issues that had not generally been considered before, such as juvenile trial competency, juvenile risk assessment, and juvenile transfer cases. The MHP was afforded more respect and responsibility than professionals working in the adult criminal system.

Types of evaluations in juvenile delinquency cases

Dispositional.   The most common evaluation requested by a juvenile delinquency court involves questions about disposition and treatment. Jurisdictions have differing models for recruiting and using FFPs to perform evaluations. Some jurisdictions refer to agencies contained within the court or probation system itself, while others refer to a panel of private evaluators in independent practice. Regardless of the model, the referral question is the same: who is this minor, why has she or he engaged in criminal behavior, and what should the juvenile court do with the juvenile now? The evaluator assists the court by identifying the presence of mental retardation or developmental delays, disruptive behavioral disorders and other mental health diagnoses, and emerging substance use or abuse problems. Family stressors and problems are of supreme importance in the assessment procedures. The evaluator conducts a parent interview and considers the home life and family stressors as factors in the overall probation plan. After reviewing records, conducting psychological testing, and interviewing the minor, parents, and probation officer, the evaluator will provide an assessment report detailing factors that contribute to delinquent behavior and making recommendations for disposition. The dispositional (sentencing) alternatives for juveniles may include a grant of probation, house arrest or electronic monitoring, placement at a juvenile probation placement, or removal from the community to a secure, locked facility. The evaluator may additionally make recommendations about the type of placement or treatment most fitting for the minor.

Diagnosis/treatment.   Another common referral question occurs when diagnostic clarification or treatment recommendations for youth with identified mental health concerns are needed. Juveniles in delinquency court may have unidentified learning disabilities or school-related deficits in need of remediation. Sometimes there are intellectual or cognitive deficits that should be taken into consideration by the court. For some youth, there are known mental health symptoms that affect the minor's ability to conform to probationary guidelines or remain in the home. The evaluator in these cases makes use of best practice assessment tools to clarify diagnostic issues and assist the court in intervening appropriately. Often the parents can benefit from psychoeducational efforts regarding major mental health disorders. For juveniles with a dual history of criminality and mental health needs, there needs to be coordination between various agencies to ensure services are delivered appropriately.

Competency to stand trial.   A third common evaluation addresses the minor's competency to stand trial. This requires an examination of the juvenile's ability to meet the basic standard of competency, articulated in *Dusky v. US*, 1960. There are two legal criteria to be considered: does the juvenile understand the nature and purposes of the proceeding against him or her, and can the juvenile rationally assist in his or her own defense? While juveniles can be found incompetent for the same reasons as an adult defendant, due to psychiatric symptoms or mental retardation, an additional area of concern is that of developmental immaturity (Grisso, 2005). Developmental immaturity factors may result in a finding of incompetence because the minor lacks the social, interpersonal, or cognitive skills necessary to cooperate with counsel or meaningfully understand the courtroom processes and procedures. Hence, the evaluator must consider additional developmental and social factors not typically considered with adult defendants.

Juvenile transfers.   Juveniles of a certain minimum age who have committed serious or violent crimes may be subject to waiver or transfer to adult court. The criteria for transfer cases vary by jurisdiction but generally require an examination of the adolescent's criminal sophistication, prior criminal record, elements of the crime, age, and amenability to treatment. Psychologists are often asked to assess juveniles to assist the court or attorneys in making decisions about whether to keep a minor in the juvenile justice system, or transfer the case to adult court. In these cases, a thorough social history and use of appropriate testing may assist the courts in making these decisions, since most jurisdictions allow for the consideration of factors, including psychological factors, that would tend to mitigate the seriousness of the offense.

Risk assessment.   Finally, as the literature in violence and sexual risk assessment has expanded to include the juvenile criminal population, psychologists are often asked to conduct risk assessments to assist with decision-making about placement, sentencing, and dispositional alternatives. For these evaluations, the psychologist will consider risk factors with a known relationship to recidivism, and make use of psychological measures designed to systematically assess risk factors. Many psychologists use measures that assess juvenile psychopathy or antisocial tendencies, although there is still debate in the literature about the usefulness of such constructs with a juvenile population (Petrila & Skeem, 2003).

Specialized treatment

In the juvenile justice system there are treating experts, similar to those in the child and dependency courts, who deliver evidence-based interventions designed to decrease recidivism and improve overall functioning in the delinquent adolescent. We want to highlight one treatment that has been widely implemented in the rehabilitation efforts of juvenile justice and captures the systemic focus of the FFP treating experts. Multisystemic therapy (MST: Henggeler & Lee, 2003) is based on a mixture of social ecological and family systems theories and views delinquent behavior and its rehabilitation as a reciprocal and bidirectional relationship between the adolescent and the multiple social networks in which he or she is embedded. In MST, a therapeutic team enters the family, social, and community network of the delinquent adolescent to effect change through education, intervention, and liaising with community support agencies. MST has been successfully used with juvenile sexual offenders, maltreating families, chronic violent offenders, substance dependent delinquents, and youths in psychiatric crisis (Henggeler & Lee, 2003). For a more detailed description of MST refer to Chapter 25, this volume.

As in family law cases, therapists may be contacted for information by forensic evaluators, who will consider the therapists' input in making recommendations to the court. In some cases, therapists will be asked to provide direct reports to probation or the court, or may be asked to provide testimony to amplify or rebut opinions expressed by a forensic evaluator. As in family law and juvenile dependency cases, therapists must be carefully attentive to role limitations, professional objectivity, and bias, and the impact of therapeutic alliance on their perceptions, reports, and testimony.

Training

This chapter demonstrates how diverse and challenging practice in FFP can be. For graduate students who want further training in FFP, we recommend that they attend a training program that offers some specialty training in forensic psychology as part of a broader clinical curriculum. For practicing professionals who want to obtain further training in FFP, we advocate participating in supervised post-doctoral training either in a formal program or under the supervision of a seasoned FFP. For more information on these topics, we refer the interested reader to the reference articles cited throughout this chapter and recommend trainings offered by established organizations dedicated to the practice of forensic psychology, including the continuing education programs offered by the American Academy of Forensic Psychology and the AFCC.

References

American Board of Forensic Psychology. (n.d.). *Brochure*. Retrieved October 27, 2007, from http://www.abfp.com/brochure.asp

American Psychological Association. (1994). Guidelines for child custody evaluations in divorce proceedings. *American Psychologist, 47,* 1597–1611.

American Psychological Association. (2002). Ethical principles of psychologists and code of conduct. *American Psychologist, 57,* 1060–1073.

Association of Family and Conciliation Courts. (2000). *Model standards of practice for family and divorce mediation.* Madison, WI: Association of Family and Conciliation Courts.

Association of Family and Conciliation Courts. (2005). *Guidelines for parenting coordination.* Madison, WI: Association of Family and Conciliation Courts.

Association of Family and Conciliation Courts. (2006). *Model standards of practice for child custody evaluation.* Madison, WI: Association of Family and Conciliation Courts.

Bush, S. S., Connell, M. A., & Denney, R. L. (2007). *Ethical practice in forensic psychology: A systematic model for decision making.* Washington, DC: American Psychological Association.

Committee on Ethical Issues for Forensic Psychologists. (1991). Specialty guidelines for forensic psychologists. *Law and Human Behavior, 15,* 655–665.

Dusky v. US 362 U.S. 402 (1960).

In re Gault, 387 U.S. 1 (1967).

Gould, J. W., & Martindale, D. A. (2007). *The art and craft of child custody evaluations.* New York: Guilford Press.

Greenberg, L. R., & Gould, J. W. (2001). The treating expert: A hybrid role with firm boundaries. *Professional Psychology: Research & Practice, 32(5),* 469–478.

Greenberg, L. R., Gould, J., Gould-Saltman, D., & Stahl, P. (2003). Is the child's therapist part of the problem? What judges, attorneys and mental health professionals need to know about court-related treatment for children. *Family Law Quarterly,* Summer, 39–69.

Greenberg, L. R., Gould-Saltman, D. J., & Gottlieb, M. C. (2009). Playing in their sandbox: Obligations of mental health professionals in custody cases. *Journal of Child Custody, 5,* 192–216.

Greenberg, L. R., Martindale, D. A., Gould, J. W., & Gould-Saltman, D. J. (2004). Ethical issues in child custody and dependency cases: Enduring principles and emerging challenges. *Journal of Child Custody, 1(1),* 7–30.

Grisso, T. (1998). *Forensic evaluation of juveniles.* Sarasota, FL: Professional Resource Press.

Grisso, T. (2005). *Evaluating juveniles' adjudicative competency: A guide for clinical practice.* Sarasota, FL: Professional Resource Press.

Grossman, N. S., & Okun, B. F. (2003). Family psychology and family law: Introduction to the special issue. *Journal of Family Psychology, 17(2)*, 163–168.

Hengeller, S. W., & Lee, T. (2003). Multisystemic treatment of serious clinical problems. In A. E. Kazdin & J. R. Weisz (Eds.), *Evidence-based psychotherapies for children and adolescents* (pp. 301–322). New York: Guilford Press.

Kaslow, F. (2000). *Handbook of couple and family forensics: A sourcebook for mental health and legal professionals.* New York: Wiley.

Kelly, J. B., & Emery, R. E. (2003). Children's adjustment following divorce: Risk and resilience perspectives. *Family Relations, 52*, 352–362.

Kent v. United States, 383 U.S. 541 (1966).

Lipsitt, P. D., & Lipsitt, L. P. (2000). Delinquency and criminality. In F. W. Kaslow (Ed.), *Handbook of couple and family forensics: A sourcebook for mental health and legal professionals* (pp. 188–205). New York: Wiley.

Petrila, J., & Skeem, J. L. (2003). Juvenile psychopathy: The debate. *Behavioral Sciences and the Law, 21*, 689–694.

Sullivan, M. J. (2004). Ethical, legal, and professional practice issues involved in acting as a psychologist parent coordinator in child custody cases. *Family Court Review, 42(3)*, 576–582.

Tippins, T. M., & Wittmann, J. P. (2005). Empirical and ethical problems with custody recommendations: A call for clinical humility and judicial vigilance. *Family Court Review, 43*, 193–222.

In re Winship, 397 U.S. 358 (1970).

51

Families and HIV/AIDS

Willo Pequegnat and the NIMH Consortium on Families and HIV/AIDS[1]

Researchers and health professionals have increasingly recognized the importance of family in health promotion and disease prevention. The family is on the front line in preventing HIV transmission among its members, providing education, and reinforcing risk-reducing HIV-related behaviors in its members. The family is also the de facto care-taker for HIV-infected members. For individuals with access to effective treatments for HIV and related opportunistic infections, HIV infection has become a chronic illness. Healthcare and mental health service providers are being challenged by the need for comprehensive family-based programs because multiple family members can be at risk and already infected (Crystal & Jackson, 1991; Crystal & Sambamoorthi, 1996). Seropositive persons often have other family members who are HIV infected and a constellation of family members who are affected. AIDS is changing the demographics of families in the United States and, in a more pronounced way, internationally.

HIV, AIDS, and Families

Because AIDS was first diagnosed in 1981 among homosexuals and drug users in the United States, family issues initially received little attention, because it was assumed that these groups were alienated from their families (Macklin, 1988). In the third decade of the AIDS epidemic, however, trends have emerged that have made the family prominent in both preventing the spread of HIV and adapting to its consequences. First, as an epidemic ages, the age at which persons become infected is reduced, so 50% of all new HIV infections occur among young people aged 10–24 (World Health Organization, 2005). Second, women, especially monogamous, minority women, who are the capstones of their families, represent an increasing number of new HIV cases. African American gay men who are still in contact with their families are experiencing HIV prevalence rivaling that of sub-Saharan Africa. Men are more likely to have acquired HIV through homosexual contact (59%), women more likely through their primary heterosexual partner (65%).

The NIMH Consortium on Families and HIV/AIDS adopted the definition of family as "a network of mutual commitment" (Pequegnat & Bray, 1997). Despite the fact that family membership can be fluid, it is essential to specify who is a member of the family when providing clinical services or conducting research. Relevant criteria include: (1) blood relationship or extended kinship (including fictive kin) or both; (2) perceived strength and duration of the relationship; (3) perceived support (including financial, emotional, and instrumental); and (4) perceived conflict.

Role of Family in Preventing the Spread of HIV

Families who are infected and affected by AIDS are often burdened with chronic poverty, homelessness, and drug abuse, as well as the social consequences of belonging to a cultural and ethnic minority or an ostracized group (Mellins & Ehrhart, 1994). Certain family dynamics are related to positive or negative adjustment and health of family members. Reciprocal communication, problem solving, warm affect, social support, and caregiving are predictive of positive outcomes (Bray, 1995), while conflict and negative affect are associated with behavioral problems (Donenberg, Paikoff, & Pequegnat, 2007). Parenting dynamics (supervision, monitoring, parental control) are related to prevention of HIV risk behaviors in children and young adults. Stigma can be experienced by the entire family; especially when HIV has been contracted through sex or drugs, stigma about HIV can be a source of conflict and shame for all family members. Conflict, domestic violence, increased risk-taking behaviors, failure to access social support, and poor custody planning can be consequences of secrets and lies. Disclosure of HIV status is inhibited by fear of rejection by family and friends. Families who are at risk for and adapting to HIV are also at risk for serious mental health problems, and families with members who have mental health problems are at increased risk of HIV/AIDS.

Over the past 20 years, NIMH has made a concerted effort to support a research program to develop family-based HIV prevention programs (Bauman, Draimin, Levine, & Hudis, 2000). This work recognizes that adolescents' sexual behavior is part of their social development and that parents have a crucial role to play in guiding and shaping the social and sexual development of their children. Parents are the primary influence on children until adolescence, when youth begin to struggle for autonomy and peer norms have an increasing influence on their social behaviors. Parents, however, continue to have an enduring and direct impact on their children's risk-taking decisions (McCormick et al., 2000; McKay et al., 2000).

Paikoff and colleagues created CHAMP I (Chicago HIV Prevention and Adolescence Mental Health Project) to address increased rates of adolescent HIV/AIDS exposure in minority neighborhoods (Paikoff, 1995). Parents played a pivotal role in guiding adolescents' sexual behavior prior to their becoming sexually active, during a time when sexual possibilities are likely to increase (Paikoff, 1995). Such sexual possibilities are an opportunity to engage in risky behavior because they are not closely supervised. This family-based program had a dual education and skills-building approach: (1) parents-only groups developed skills that enhanced parent monitoring, discipline effectiveness, conflict resolution, support, and comfort in discussing sensitive topics; and (2) children-only groups developed skills to enhance social problem solving, such as an ability to identify risky situations and an ability to be assertive in handling sexual peer pressure (McBride et al., 2007). The overall objective was to promote comfort and communication about puberty, early sexual behavior, and HIV/AIDS. When compared to the control group, families in CHAMP I showed increased family decision-making, improvements in parental monitoring, family comfort in discussing sensitive topics, more neighborhood supports, and fewer disruptive difficulties with children (Miller, McKay, & Baptiste, 2007). The youth in the intervention families reported experiencing significantly less frequent and fewer sexual possibility situations than those in the comparison condition.

Based on findings from the original study, CHAMP II was developed, consisting of a 12-week family intervention for fourth and fifth graders, in partnership with urban parents (McKay et al., 2007). Sixty percent of the youth in the intervention families reported using condoms every time and 72% reported using condoms at last intercourse (Tolou-Shams, Paikoff, McKirnan, & Holmbeck, 2007). The youth also reported less aggressive and disruptive behaviors (Bannon & McKay, 2007).

To further explore how to transfer this family-based prevention program, CHAMP III (Bronx, New York, and Westside of Chicago) was designed to hand off the CHAMP program to community service agencies in Chicago and New York (Baptiste, Coleman, et al., 2007). This work highlights the dissemination process of an evidence-based, efficacious intervention in the real world (McKay et al., 2007).

CHAMP IV – also known as CHAMPSA or the AmaQhawe Family Project – is a culturally appropriate adaptation for families and communities in Durban, South Africa (Bhana et al., 2004). It is based on the theory of triadic influence (TTI) and seeks to address three sources of behavioral influence: (1) an intrapersonal stream, (2) a social normative stream, and (3) a cultural/attitudinal stream (Bell, Bhana, McKay, & Petersen, 2007). Youth and families who participated in CHAMPSA were likely to be better informed about HIV/AIDS transmission, have less HIV-stigmatizing attitudes, have greater parental monitoring of children's activities and adherence to the family rules, and have increased parental comfort communicating about difficult topics. CHAMPSA has significant potential to enhance protective influences in communities and meet international needs (Baptiste, Bhana, et al., 2006).

CHAMP was also adapted for the Caribbean, which has the second highest rate of HIV per capita in the world (Baptiste, Bhana, et al., 2006). Youth in the CHAMP group reported increased frequency of discussions about HIV/AIDS, decreased frequency of discussions about gangs, and increased parental expectations about monitoring children. As with other CHAMP programs, there was strong community participation in the design and administration of the pilot study.

While most family-based prevention programs have been developed for mothers, Krauss et al. (2000) designed PATH, which is a prevention programs for both mothers and fathers, acknowledging fathers' important role in the sexual health of their 10–13-year-old preadolescents. This intervention is aimed at fostering family involvement in the sexual health of adolescents, including delay of sexual intercourse, acquiring information about HIV/AIDS, interacting comfortably with community members and family who may have HIV, and ensuring HIV risk-reduction skills.

Parents participated in four 3-hour group training sessions, given once a week, covering knowledge and safety skills regarding sex, drugs, and HIV; child development; and parent-child communication. The initial parent training was followed by a parent–child session in which each parent and child met alone with a facilitator. Parents chose activities to perform with their child and children had an opportunity to ask questions. The parent group met again after 3 months to discuss real-life situations that had occurred. This study demonstrated that an intervention delivered by either a mother or father can reduce HIV-risk-associated sexual behaviors of adolescents (Krauss, Godfrey, O'Day, Pride, & Donaire, 2002).

DiIorio and colleagues developed a prevention program for mothers and adolescents and a later one for fathers and sons. The primary objective of the mother–adolescent program, called Keepin' it R.E.A.L.! (Responsible, Empowered, Aware, Living), was to enhance the role of mothers in postponing the sexual debut of their 11–14-year-old adolescents (DiIorio et al., 2000). Embedded within Keepin' it R.E.A.L.! are two programs, one based on social cognitive theory (SCT) and the other on problem behavior theory (PBT). The SCT program was built on the recognition that behavior is dependent on a dynamic interaction of personal, environmental, and behavioral factors. The SCT program included sessions on sexual health, HIV transmission and protection, communication skills, and peer pressure. PBT principles propose that problem behaviors in adolescents arise from common underlying psychological attributes. The PBT principles were incorporated into the second program by addressing a wide variety of adolescent behaviors including smoking, violence, sexual intercourse, and school performance. Both programs were designed to be interactive with games, videos, role-plays, and skits to demonstrate and practice skills learned in the sessions. Each participant set a personal goal to be accomplished by the following session. Although there were no differences in delay of sexual intercourse among the three groups, those who participated in the PBT program reported an increase in condom use, and those in the SCT and the control group demonstrated higher levels of knowledge about HIV. Mothers reported more comfort talking about sexual topics with their adolescents and greater confidence over time. Mothers in the SCT program also demonstrated higher levels of HIV knowledge than mothers in the PBT and control groups (DiIrio, Resnicow et al., 2006).

The program for fathers, called R.E.A.L. *(Responsible, Empowered, Aware, Living)*, was designed to enhance the father's role in postponing the sexual debut of their 11–14-year-old adolescent sons (DiIorio, McCarty, Resnicow, Lehr, & Denzmore, 2006). Fathers attended the program once a week for 7 weeks, bringing their sons for the final session. Like sessions for mothers in Keepin' it R.E.A.L.!, the sessions for fathers were interactive and included goal setting and take-home activities. Adolescents whose fathers participated in the SCT program reported significantly higher rates of sexual abstinence, condom use, and intent to delay initiation of sexual intercourse. Fathers in the program reported significantly more discussions about sexuality and greater intention to discuss sexuality in the future with their sons. They also reported more confidence discussing sexual issues with their sons and more positive outcomes associated with those discussions (DiIorio, McCarty et al., 2006).

Another intervention in which the parents assume the role of AIDS educators is Familias Unidas. An ecodevelopmental, Hispanic-specific, ecologically focused, parent-centered preventive intervention, Familias Unidas promotes protection for adolescents against HIV and substance use. This program promotes four major family processes operating at different systemic levels: (1) increasing family functioning (e.g., positive parenting), (2) promoting parent–adolescent communication), (3) fostering proactive connections between the family and other important systems such as peers and school, and (4) gathering external support for parents (Pantin et al., 2003; Pantin et al., 2004). The group format was designed to provide social support for Hispanic immigrant parents by introducing them to other parents in similar situations. This format was efficacious in increasing parental involvement, parent–adolescent communication, and parental support for the adolescent; and in reducing adolescent behavior problems (Pantin et al., 2003). Not surprisingly, active participation in the group was shown to predict engagement and retention in the intervention (Prado, Pantin, Schwartz, Lupei, & Szapocznik, 2006), and in turn engagement and retention have been shown to decrease in behavior problems. Prado et al. (2007) conducted a more extensive evaluation of this program and found similar positive results.

On the basis of over a decade of longitudinal research with rural African American families and youth, Murry and associates designed a family-based preventive intervention to deter HIV-related risk behavior among these youth (Murry, Berkel, Brody, Gibbons, & Gerrard, 2007). The Strong African American Families (SAAF) program is the only randomized prevention trial designed specifically for rural families and youth with demonstrated efficacy in deterring youths' vulnerability to HIV-related risk behavior (Gerrard et al., 2006). The 7-week intervention includes separate programming for youth and their parents, as well as joint activities. Content for the seven sessions is presented on videotapes, depicting family interactions that illustrate targeted intervention concepts. SAAF was implemented in community settings during youths' transition to middle school. Results revealed that SAAF was efficacious in reducing rural African American youths' vulnerability to HIV-related risk behavior through the intervention's effect on parenting practices and its effect on youth intrapersonal protective factors. SAAF-induced effects on parenting behavior deterred not only precursors to risk behavior, such as risk-related attitudes, future orientation, self-regulatory capacity, and resistance efficacy, but also immediate HIV-related risk behavior, including early onset of substance use and sexual intercourse (Murry et al., 2007) and alcohol use trajectories (Brody et al., 2005).

In summary, these studies demonstrate that parents can be taught to be effective educators to reduce the risk and transmission of HIV within their families; they can effectively impart information as well as teach their children skills to protect themselves in risky situations. The studies also provide evidence that the quality of parent-child relations and communication is an important predictor of sexual risk behaviors. Across the studies, adolescents who reported low levels of parental support or more emotional distance from their families were more likely to engage in sexual behaviors at a younger age. Conversely, adolescents' belief that they had a close relationship with their parents was protective against early sexual intercourse.

Role of Family in Adapting to HIV

Although AIDS has become a chronic disease for many individuals in the United States who have access to highly active antiretroviral therapy (HAART), adherence to treatment is challenging and can be complicated by persistent symptoms and side effects. Co-morbid conditions, such as substance abuse, mental illness, or other severe chronic conditions, can further complicate the medical regimen and activities of daily living. Family-based prevention programs for families living with HIV/AIDS must address complex problems, such as treatment adherence, housing instability, and economic uncertainty. Long-standing problems can damage the social environment of the family at a time when they need to be united. Family members may be reticent about discussing problems with the persons living with AIDS, for fear of worrying them and making them sicker. Both the seropositive family member and other family members may experience stress from fear of repercussions if friends and neighbors find out the reason for the illness. HIV changes family functioning in multiple areas (Krishna, Bhatt, Chandra, & Juvva, 2005). There may be developmental or role-changing issues: a previously independent adult may have to be reintegrated into the family for care; an adolescent with chronically ill parents, who is struggling for emancipation, may need to provide care; and a mother who is recovering from drug addiction may need to redefine her role as mother and daughter. Family stress levels depend on how well they problem solve and cope with these issues together.

Over the past 20 years there has been a concerted effort by NIMH to support a research program to develop family-based HIV prevention interventions (Rapkin, Bennett, Murphy, & Munoz, 2000). Secondary prevention programs have focused on developing interventions to help families cope with multiple problems, including stigma, medication adherence, changing parental roles, and custody planning. There are compelling clinical and public health reasons for designing secondary prevention programs aimed at building supportive social networks, increasing coping skills, and reducing stress, risky sexual behaviors, and STDs. First, these programs can reduce unprotected sex and needle sharing. Second, they can improve quality of life among persons living with HIV by reducing stressors, enhancing coping skills, and requiring less need for expensive healthcare. Third, they can reduce risk of HIV transmission to seronegative sexual partners. Finally, they can reduce the risk of HIV transmission by women to their unborn children.

The original family-based intervention entitled Project TALC (Teens and Adults Learning to Communicate), designed for seropositive mothers and their children, has been successful. The goal was to help parents make decisions regarding disclosure and custody, as well as to increase a family's ability to maintain positive daily routines while the parent is ill. The mothers are taught to problem solve stressful situations, maintain their parental role, and make custody arrangements for their children. The adolescents are taught to cope with emotional distress, maintain a healthy, drug-free lifestyle, and explore roles within the family. By 2 years after recruitment, the intervention adolescents and parents reported significantly fewer problem behaviors and less emotional distress than those in the standard care condition. Coping skills were significantly higher among youth, and parents had significantly more positive social support in the intervention condition, compared to the standard care condition (Rotheram-Borus, Lee, Gwadz, & Draimin, 2001). Over 4 years following the delivery of the intervention, fewer adolescents became teenage parents and fewer parents were drug dependent in the intervention compared to the control condition (Rotheram-Borus et al., 2004). Youth in the intervention condition reported significantly less substance use 3 and 6 years later. In addition, positive parental bonds reported at baseline reduced emotional distress at 3 years and increased positive future expectations at 6 years (Rotheram-Borus, Stein, & Lester, 2006).

On the basis of the success of this initial intervention, Rotheram-Borus and colleagues developed a series of adaptations of this intervention for different contexts and countries (Thailand, China, South Africa). These adaptations rest on the premise that there are predictable challenges faced by all families affected by HIV (e.g., disclosure, social support, medication adherence, stigma, transmission behaviors), which are affected by the local culture and social context (Rotheram-Borus, Weiss, Alber, & Lester, 2005).

In order to address the disruptive social and economic circumstances of children whose mothers died from HIV, Project Care was designed to test the efficacy of a short-term preventive intervention (Bauman et al., 2000). The aims of the study were to reduce risk factors and increase protective factors in children to prevent psychological dysfunction after their mothers' AIDS-related death. The intervention enhanced disclosure and communication among seropositive mothers, the designated guardians, and the children. It enhanced the stability and security of the child's future by developing an appropriate custody plan prior to parental death. It enhanced work with the guardian and the child after the death of the mother to facilitate the transition to the new family. It also enhanced access to resources and social support. Thirty-five per cent of mothers disclosed their HIV status to their children (Bauman, Camacho, Silver, Hudis, & Draimin, 2002). If they disclosed to one child, they usually disclosed to all the children.

The Family Health Project teaches AIDS-affected families problem-solving skills (Rapkin et al., 2000). The intervention breaks down problem solving into its component elements and encourages families to follow these steps: (1) create a comfortable climate for problem solving; (2) identify the problem; (3) brainstorm; (4) weigh the consequences of various alternatives; (5) think through together the implementation of possible solutions; (6) set goals; and (7) evaluate solution outcomes. Both patients and family members in the experimental group reported that they were more likely to reinforce one another's problem-solving efforts (Rapkin, Monoz, & Murphy, 2007). They were also more likely to express uncertainty about problems. Although this result was unexpected, it may reflect the fact that the patients in the intervention group and their family members reported more unresolved problems. Despite this, they reported greater ability to care for themselves. Families receiving the intervention attended support groups more often than controls and were more likely to have a case manager. Consequently, these families were also more able to maintain their sense of wellbeing relative to the control group.

Taking another tack, Szpaocznik and colleagues designed an intervention, structural ecological therapy (SET), to improve the quality of the social relations and supports of African American seropositive women (Mitrani, Szapocznik, & Batista, 2000). The intervention focused on changing the quality of relationships, building family trust, increasing mutual support, and reducing blaming and personal attacks (family negativity). This social ecological perspective helped to rebuild a supportive network around the woman and her family that included the family's relation to kin and other neighborhood supports, faith communities, and HIV support groups. The first test of this approach was successful in reducing psychological distress and family hassles, and the reduction of family hassles was partially mediated by the reduction in distress (Pantin et al., 2004). For a full discussion of this intervention, see Chapter 25, this volume.

While SET reintegrates women and men into their existing social support systems, another program that helps seropositive women build new social support networks to enhance and prolong their lives. The WiLLOW Program: Women Involved in Life Learning from Other Women was designed to reduce HIV/STD risk behaviors and enhance psychosocial factors, such as expanding social networks of women living with HIV (Wingood & DiClemente, 2000). These women who live in semi-rural areas feel isolated because of stigma and low rates of disclosure. The four-session, group-administered intervention emphasized gender pride, maintaining current and identifying new network members, HIV transmission knowledge, communication and condom use skills, and healthy relationships. Over the 12-month follow-up, women in the WiLLOW intervention relative to the comparison reported fewer episodes of unprotected vaginal intercourse and had a lower incidence of bacterial infections (chlamydia and gonorrhea). Additionally, participants in the intervention reported greater HIV knowledge and condom use self-efficacy, more social network members, fewer beliefs that condoms interfere with sex, and fewer partner-related barriers to condom use, and demonstrated greater skills in using condoms. This is one of the first trials to demonstrate reductions in risky sexual behaviors and incident bacterial STDS and to enhance HIV preventive psychosocial and structural factors. The Centers for Disease Control and Prevention (CDC) has evaluated and classified WiLLOW as an "evidence-based intervention" and is disseminating it nationally as part of its Continuum of HIV Prevention Interventions for African-American Women (Centers for Disease Control, 2008).

In summary, there is a need to view the families of patients as partners in the treatment process. Until recently, families of patients were not viewed by the medical community as resources in the treatment of the patient. The family is deeply affected – physically and psychologically – by the trauma of serious illness, especially one as devastating as AIDS. The family – whether of origin or of choice – can provide powerful support, guidance, and solace when its considerable resources are marshaled. Although there are common concerns, coping strategies for different stresses may be required, depending on which members of the family are HIV infected. Interventions can restructure familial interactions and communication patterns, enhance family problem-solving skills, enhance a supportive social network, improve quality of life, and ensure HIV risk reduction.

Conclusions

In tackling problems related to preventing HIV infection and adapting to HIV/AIDS within families, it is important to understand HIV-related behaviors in the social context in which they were learned and reinforced. Non-contextual, fragmented approaches may complicate the problem and create a sense of hopelessness on the part of individuals, families, peers, and healthcare workers, rather than promote more effective use of family resources (Rapkin et al., 2000). Several family characteristics have shown consistent relationships with measures of health or illness regardless of the disorder. For example, high family conflict, too permeable or too rigid intra- and extra-familial boundaries, low levels of family organization, and poor spousal or partner support are associated with poor outcomes. When families are functioning in an adaptive way, parents are typically the family leaders, and when they are incapacitated by drug abuse, mental illness, or ill health, family social support may evaporate, which places its members at risk for a host of problems. Social isolation may result from the stigma associated with HIV infection, desire to remain anonymous, and not knowing how or with whom to disclose and talk about their concerns and the pressures they experience due to their HIV infection. Rejection may occur if neighbors and friends blame the seropositive person for his or her infection due to a high-risk lifestyle, even though that may not be the case.

Family research provides a general framework for investigating the processes through which psychological, social, and cultural factors influence the health and wellbeing of all family members. Many of the conditions that contribute to the spread of HIV infection – poverty, drug abuse, and an inadequate healthcare system for the poor – need to be addressed with renewed initiatives in family research. Historically, research on family systems has been based on the report of one family member (Pequegnat & Bray, 1997). Theories and conceptual frameworks that are culturally appropriate and integrate reports from multiple members of the family system are essential if we are to move family-based prevention work forward.

Since 1992 investigators have increasingly enlisted families in research to better understand family process and decision-making in order to prevent and adapt to AIDS. There is a better understanding of the nature of communication within families, the roles of family members in shaping opinion and behavior in the family, and the kinds of incentives under the control of parents and older siblings. Also, the psychological and social factors that characterize families and their response to illness have been identified. From the findings reported in this chapter, it is imperative that community-based programs offer these evidence-based prevention programs for families. New organizations and healthcare systems must be created to respond to the special needs of AIDS patients and their families.

Note

1   The NIMH Consortium includes Laurie J. Bauman, Carl C. Ball, James H. Bray, Colleen DiIorio, Larry Icard, Loretta Sweet Jemmott, Beatrice Krauss, Bruce Rapkin, Mary Jane Rotheran, José Szapocznik, and Gail Wyatt.

References

Bannon, W. M., & McKay, M. M. (2007). *Addressing urban African American youth externalizing and social problem behavioral difficulties in a family oriented prevention project*. Binghamton, NY: Haworth Press.

Baptiste, D., Bhana, A., Peterson, I., Voisin, D., McKay, M. M., & Bell, C. (2006). A community participatory framework for international youth-focused HIV/AIDS prevention in South Africa and Trinidad. *Journal of Pediatric Psychology, 31*, 905–916.

Baptiste, D., Coleman, I., Blachman, D., Leachman, B., Cappella, E., McKinney, L., et al. (2007). Transferring a university-led HIV/AIDS prevention initiative to a community agency. *Social Work in Mental Health, 5*, 269–293.

Bauman, L. J., Camacho, S., Silver, E. H., Hudis, J., & Draimin, B. (2002). Behavioral problems in school-aged children of mothers with HIV/AIDS. *Clinical Child Psychology and Psychiatry, 7*, 39–54.

Bauman, L. J., Draimin, B., Levine, C., & Hudis, J. (2000). *Who will care for me? Planning the future care and custody of children orphaned by HIV/AIDS*. Thousand Oaks, CA: Sage.

Bell, C. C., Bhana, A., McKay, M. M., & Petersen, I. (2007). *A commentary on the triadic theory of influence as a guide for adapting HIV prevention programs for new contexts and populations: The CHAMP-South Africa story*. Binghamton, NY: Haworth Press.

Bhana, A., Petersen, I., Mason, A., Mahintsho, Z., Bell, C., & McKay, M. (2004). Children and youth at risk: Adaptation and pilot study of the CHAMP (Amaqhawe) programme in South Africa. *African Journal of AIDS Research, 3*, 33–41.

Bray, J. H. (1995). Family assessment: Current issues in evaluating families. *Family Relations, 44*, 469–477.

Brody, G. H., Murry, V. M., McNair, L., Chen, Y. F., Gibbons, F. X., Gerrard, M., et al. (2005). Linking changes in parenting to youth self-control: The Strong African American Families program. *Journal of Research on Adolescence, 15*, 47–69.

Centers for Disease Control. (2008). *Best evidence: Women Involved in Life Learning from Other Women (WiLLOW)*. Retrieved April 1, 2009, from http://www.cdc.gov/hiv/topics/research/prs/resources/factsheets/WILLOW.htm

Crystal, S., & Jackson, M. (1991). *Health care and the social construction of AIDS: The impact of disease definitions*. American Sociological Association Presidential Volume. Newbury Park, CA: Sage, in cooperation with American Psychological Association.

Crystal, S., & Sambamoorthi, U. (1996). Care needs and access to care among women living with HIV. In L. Sherr (Ed.), *AIDS as a gender issue: Psychosocial perspectives*. London: Taylor & Francis.

DiIorio, C., Dudley, W. N., Soet, J., Watkins, J., & Maibach, E. (2000). A social cognitive-based model for condom use among college students. *Nursing Research, 49*, 208–214.

DiIorio, C., Resnicow, K., McCarty, F., De, A. K., Dudley, W. N., Wang, D. T., et al. (2006). Keepin' it R.E.A.L.! Results of a mother–adolescent HIV prevention program. *Nursing Research, 55*, 43–51.

DiIorio, C., McCarty, F., Resnicow, K., Lehr, S., & Denzmore, P. (2006). Real men: A group-randomized trial of an HIV prevention intervention for adolescent boys. *American Journal of Public Health, 97,* 1084–1089.

Donenberg, G. R., Paikoff, R., & Pequegnat, W. (2007). Introduction to the special section on families, youth and HIV/family-based intervention studies. *Journal of Pediatric Psychology, 31,* 869–873.

Gerrard, M., Gibbons, F. X., Brody, G. H., Murry, V. M., Cleveland, M. J., & Wills, T. A. (2006). A theory-based dual focus alcohol intervention for pre-adolescents: The Strong African American Families program. *Psychology of Addictive Behaviors, 20,* 185–195.

Krauss, B., Godfrey, C., O'Day, J., Pride, J., & Donaire, M. (2002). Now I can learn about HIV – Effects of a parent training on children's practical HIV knowledge and HIV worries: A randomized trial in an HIV-affected neighborhood (abstract). In M. E. Lyon & L. J. D'Angelo (Eds.), *XIVth World AIDS Conference, Conference Record, 2,* 170.

Krauss, B. J., Godfrey, C., Yee, D., Goldsamt, L., Tiffany, J., Almeyda, L., et al. (2000). *Saving our children from a silent epidemic: The PATH program for parents and preadolescents.* Thousand Oaks, CA: Sage.

Krishna, V. S., Bhatt, R. S., Chandra, P. S., & Juvva, S. (2005). Unheard voices: Experiences of families living with HIV/AIDS in India. *Contemporary Family Therapy, 27,* 483–505.

Macklin, E. D. (1988). AIDS: Implications for families. *Family Relations, 37,* 141–149.

McBride, C. K., Baptiste, D., Paikoff, R. L., Madison-Boyd, S., Coleman, D., & Bell, C. C. (2007). *Family-based HIV preventive intervention: Child level results from the CHAMP family program.* Binghamton, NY: Haworth Press.

McCormick, A., McKay, M. M., Wilson, M., McKinney, L., Paikoff, R. L., Bell, C. C., et al. (2000). Involving families in an urban HIV prevention intervention: How community collaboration addresses barriers to participation. *AIDS Education and Prevention, 12,* 299–307.

McKay, M. M., Baptiste, D., Coleman, D., Madison, S., Paikoff, R., & Scott, R. (2000). Preventing HIV risk exposure in urban communities: The CHAMP family program. In W. Pequegnat & J. Szapocznik (Eds.), *NIMH annual conference: Working with families in the era of HIV/AIDS* (pp. 67–87). Thousand Oaks, CA: Sage.

McKay, M. M., Hibbert, R., Lawrence, R., Miranda, A., Paikoff, R., Bell, C. C., et al. (2007). *Creating mechanisms for meaningful collaboration between members of urban communities and university-based HIV prevention researchers.* Binghamton, NY: Haworth Press.

Mellins, C. A., & Ehrhart, A. A. (1994). Families affected by pediatric acquired immunodeficiency syndrome: Sources of stress. *Journal of Developmental and Behavioral Pediatrics, 15(3 suppl.),* S54–60.

Miller, S., McKay, M. M., & Baptiste, D. (2007). Social support for African American low-income parents: The influence of preadolescents' risk behavior and support role on parental monitoring and child outcomes. *Social Work in Mental Health, 5,* 121–145.

Mitrani, V. B., Szapocznik, J., & Batista, C. R. (2000). *Structural ecosystems therapy with HIV+ African American women.* Thousand Oaks, CA: Sage.

Murry, V. M., Berkel, C., Brody, G. H., Gibbons, F. X., & Gerrard, M. (2007). The Strong African American Families program: Longitudinal pathways to sexual risk reduction. *Journal of Adolescent Health, 41,* 317–418.

Paikoff, R. L. (1995). Early heterosexual debut: Situations of sexual possibilities during the transition to adolescence. *American Journal of Orthopsychiatry, 65,* 389–401.

Pantin, H., Coatsworth, J. D., Feaster, D. J., Newman, F. L., Briones, E., Prado, G., et al. (2003). Familias Unidas: The efficacy of an intervention to promote parental investment in Hispanic immigrant families. *Prevention Sciences, 4,* 189–201.

Pantin, H., Seth, J., Schwartz, S. J., Summer Sullivan, S., Guillermo Prado, P., & Szapocznik, J. (2004). Ecodevelopmental HIV prevention programs for Hispanic adolescents. *American Journal of Orthopsychiatry, 74*, 545–558.

Pequegnat, W., & Bray, J. (1997). Families and HIV/AIDS: Introduction to the special sections. *Journal of Family Psychology, 11*, 3–10.

Prado, G., Pantin, H., Briones, E. S., Seth, J., Feaster, D., Huang, S., et al. (2007). A randomized controlled trial of a parent-centered intervention in preventing substance use and HIV risk behaviors in Hispanic adolescents. *Journal of Consulting and Clinical Psychology, 75*, 914–926.

Prado, G., Pantin, H., Schwartz, S. J., Lupei, N. S., & Szapocznik, J. (2006). Predictors of engagement and retention into a parent-centered, ecodevelopmental HIV preventive intervention for Hispanic adolescents and their families. *Journal of Pediatric Psychology, 31*, 874–890.

Rapkin, B., Monoz, M., & Murphy, P. (2007). *The family problem solving interventions for HIV/AIDS: A progress report submitted to NIMH.* Washington, DC: National Institute of Mental Health.

Rapkin, B. D., Bennett, J. A., Murphy, P., & Munoz, M. (2000). *The family health project: Strengthening problem solving in families affected by AIDS to mobilize systems of support and care.* Thousand Oaks, CA: Sage.

Rotheram-Borus, M. J., Lee, M. B., Gwadz, M., & Draimin, B. (2001). An intervention for parents with AIDS and their adolescent children. *Clinical Child Psychology and Psychiatry, 2*, 201–219.

Rotheram-Borus, M. J., Lee, M. B., Leonard, N., Lin, Y. Y., Franzke, L., & Lightfoot, M. A. (2004). Four-year behavioral outcomes of an intervention for parents living with HIV and their adolescent children. *AIDS, 17*, 1217–1225.

Rotheram-Borus, M. J., Stein, J. A., & Lester, P. (2006). Adolescent adjustment over six years in HIV-affected families. *Journal of Adolescent Health, 39*, 174–182.

Rotheram-Borus, M. J., Weiss, R., Alber, S., & Lester, P. (2005). Adolescent adjustment before and after HIV-related parental death. *Journal of Consulting and Clinical Psychology, 73*, 221–228.

Tolou-Shams, M., Paikoff, R., McKirnan, D. J., & Holmbeck, G. N. (2007). *Mental health and HIV risk among African American adolescents: The role of parenting.* Binghamton, NY: Haworth Press.

Wingood, G. M., & DiClemente, R. J. (2000). *The WiLLOW program: Mobilizing social networks of women living with HIV to enhance coping and reduce sexual risk behaviors.* Thousand Oaks, CA: Sage.

World Health Organization. (2005). *Make mothers and children count.* Retrieved April 1, 2009, from http://www.who.int/world-health-day/previous/2005/en

52

Families, Violence, and Abuse

Daniela J. Owen, Lauren Knickerbocker, Richard E. Heyman, and Amy M. Smith Slep

Yearly prevalence estimates for physical aggression between intimate partners range from 12% to 20%, depending upon the types of questions asked, the time period referenced, and the population being sampled (e.g., Schafer, Caetano, & Clark, 1998). Across surveys, men and women are equally likely to perpetrate less severe acts of intimate partner violence (IPV) (Field & Caetano, 2005). IPV rates in clinics are extremely high; 71% of couples presenting for treatment reported at least one act of physical aggression in the previous year (Cascardi, Langhinrichsen, & Vivian, 1992) but less than 15% listed anger or aggression as a presenting problem (O'Leary, Vivian, & Malone, 1992).

In 2005, approximately 899,000 children in the United States, or 12.1 per 1,000, were victims of substantiated maltreatment (i.e., neglect and physical, emotional, and sexual abuse) (U.S. Department of Health and Human Services [DHHS], 2005). The rate formally substantiated by state Child Protective Services (CPS) has been relatively stable since 2001 (U.S. DHHS, 2005). Neglect accounts for 62.8% of substantiated cases, physical abuse 16.6%, sexual abuse 9.3%, and emotional abuse 7.1%; one third to one half of maltreated children experience more than one type of maltreatment (U.S. DHHS, 2001). When prevalence is studied by combining substantiated CPS reports and substantiatable reports from community sentinels (that may not have reported the suspicions to CPS), the rate of maltreatment is twice as high (about 23.2 per 1,000 children in 1993; Sedlak & Broadhurst, 1996).

In a review of 31 studies examining co-occurring partner aggression and child abuse, Appel and Holden (1998) found co-occurrence rates ranging between 5.6% and 11% in community samples, 51% in samples drawn from battered women shelters, and approximately 45% drawn from identified child maltreatment samples. In another community sample, 45% of homes reported some level of co-occurring partner and child aggression; when limited to severe violence forms (e.g., hit with an object or fist, choked, beat up), and 5% of homes reported experiencing both forms of violence (Slep & O'Leary, 2005).

The Challenges of Defining Maltreatment

Both research and clinical services for partner abuse and child maltreatment suffer from the lack of standardized definitions. Clinicians' thresholds for abuse are often based on their own opinion and researchers' thresholds are typically lower than those used in legal or CPS contexts. Furthermore, studies using varying operationalizations are difficult to compare and the content validity of typical operationalizations is debated, sometimes quite bitterly (e.g., Straus, 1990; White, Smith, Koss, & Figueredo, 2000). To standardize definitions that meet clinical and research needs, Heyman and Slep (2006) created definitions of various forms of partner and child maltreatment that required both a potentially harmful act and demonstrable impact (or high potential for impact) (see resource box for the website address for these definitions). They evaluated the definitions' content validity and then field tested their reliability in five communities, finding over 90% agreement between local decision-makers and master reviewers (Heyman & Slep, 2006).

Risk Factors

A substantial body of literature details risk factors for physical, emotional, and sexual abuse and for child neglect (e.g., Heyman & Slep, 2001). Much of the literature focuses on physical abuse, with less written on other types of maltreatment.

Demographic risk factors

There is some evidence that lower socioeconomic status is a risk factor for all types of maltreatment (e.g., Chaffin, Kelleher, & Hollenberg, 1996; Straus & Kantor, 1987). Living in an area with higher community violence appears to be a significant risk factor for partner and parent–child violence (Lynch & Cicchetti, 1998). In addition, having a larger family may be a risk factor for child physical abuse (Connelly & Straus, 1992), emotional abuse, and neglect (Chaffin et al., 1996).

Younger couples have a higher risk for partner maltreatment (Connelly & Straus, 1992). Likewise, parents' youth is a risk factor for endorsement of minor acts of physical aggression and neglectful omissions (Chaffin et al., 1996). Although Chaffin and colleagues (1996) found an association between neglect and young age of parents in the general population (using data from the Epidemiological Catchment Area study), Zuravin (1987) found that maltreating mothers substantiated by CPS for neglect were significantly older than non-maltreating mothers.

Child maltreatment is the number one cause of death for children between 1 and 4 years old in the United Staes (U.S. Advisory Board on Child Abuse and Neglect, 1995). Children aged 5–12 years are at a greater risk than older children for physical abuse (Wolfner & Gelles, 1993). Children over 7 years of age are at greater risk for emotional abuse

(Sedlak & Broadhurst, 1996; Vissing, Straus, Gelles, & Harrop, 1991) and teens are at greatest risk for sexual abuse (Sedlak & Broadhurst, 1996).

Violence in the family of origin

Maltreatment in the family of origin modestly increases the risk that parents will abuse their own children (e.g., Margolin, Gordis, Medina, & Oliver, 2003). A recent meta-analysis by Stith and colleagues (2000) found a small but significant effect size for the relationship between violence in the home of origin and becoming a perpetrator and/or a victim of partner violence as an adult.

History of childhood abuse and witnessed violence do not automatically result in the intergenerational transmission of violence; 70% of parents with a history of childhood abuse do not become perpetrators of child abuse as adults (compared to 95% of the general parent population) (Kaufman & Zigler, 1987). Similarly, although the biggest risk factor for becoming a perpetrator of sexual abuse is having experienced sexual abuse or another form of abuse oneself, most sexually abused individuals do not go on to perpetrate acts against others (Wilcox, Richards, & O'Keeffe, 2004).

Individual characteristics and behaviors

Factors differentiating men arrested for partner violence from non-violent men include psychological distress, anger, hostility, personality disorders, attachment/dependency problems, alcohol abuse, poor social and communication skills, head injuries, lack of social support and resources, feelings of powerlessness, inability to cope with stress, and witness/experience of violence in their family of origin (see Holtzworth-Munroe, Smutzler, & Bates, 1997).

Substance abuse has been identified as a risk factor for male-to-female partner physical abuse (see Chapter 27, this volume; Thompson & Kingree, 2006) and child physical abuse and neglect (Kelleher, Chaffin, Hollenberg, & Fischer, 1994).

Physically abusive mothers score higher on measures of emotional distress and rigidity (e.g., Caliso & Milner, 1992) and neuroticism (Lesnik-Oberstein, Koers, & Cohen, 1995). Further, abusive and neglectful mothers tend to be more impulsive (Rohrbeck & Twentyman, 1986), have lower self-esteem (Christensen, Brayden, Dietrich, & McLaughlin, 1994), perceive themselves as having less social support, and report more daily stress (e.g., Williamson, Borduin, & Howe, 1991). Physically abusive parents report beliefs that physical force is a necessary means of discipline (Dibble & Straus, 1980), and tend to blame their children's misbehaviors on stable, internal factors (Larrance & Twentyman, 1983).

Parents' perceptions that behavior problems (e.g., conduct disorder, aggression, attention problems) are children's faults put their children at greater risk for physical abuse and neglect (e.g., Larrance & Twentyman, 1983; Whipple & Webster-Stratton, 1991). In addition, children with physical or mental illnesses or disabilities or learning disabilities are up to three times more likely to experience emotional abuse and neglect than are children without such handicaps (Sullivan & Knutson, 2000).

Consequences

Partner physical abuse increases the likelihood of negative physical and mental health outcomes for the victim, including injury (Centers for Disease Control, 1998), functional gastrointestinal disorders (Leserman & Drossman, 2007), chronic pain (Campbell et al., 2002), and major depressive disorder and post-traumatic stress disorder (PTSD) (O'Campo et al., 2006). Victims also are more likely to experience housing instability (Pavao, Alvarez, Baumrind, Induni, & Kimerling, 2007), low satisfaction with life (Varma, Chandra, Thomas, & Carey, 2007), daily activity disruption (Laroche, 2005), increased alcohol and drug use (Lemon, Verhoek-Oftedahl, & Donnelly, 2002), and parenting distress that results in poor parenting behavior (Levendosky & Graham-Bermann, 2000).

In children and adolescents, maltreatment has been shown to have a negative impact on social and academic performance (Iwaniec, Larkin, & Higgins, 2006). Victims of maltreatment are more likely to be reported as acting out, being defiant, and engaging in deviant behavior (e.g., Kelly, Thornberry, & Smith, 1997). Child victims and witnesses of physical abuse often develop hostile models of interpersonal interactions (Cicchetti & Lynch, 1995) as well as poor self-esteem (Okun, Parker, & Levendosky, 1994).

Resilience and Protective Factors

Risk and consequences cannot be discussed without also attending to factors that buffer the impact of maltreatment. Social support and access to community resources (Bender, Cook, & Kaslow, 2003), higher levels of self-esteem (Bradley, Schwartz, & Kaslow, 2005), and financial independence from abusive partners (Anderson & Saunders, 2003) all appear to protect against the negative effects of partner abuse and re-experiencing abuse. African American women with high self-esteem display lower rates of PTSD after experiencing IPV than do those with lower self-esteem (Bradley et al., 2005).

For children, higher intelligence (Jaffee, Caspi, Moffitt, Polo-Tomas, & Taylor, 2007; Luthar, 1991) and more years of education (Lambie, Seymour, Lee, & Adams, 2002) appear to buffer against the negative effects of maltreatment. Sense of personal control (Luthar, 1991) and ego-resiliency (e.g., Flores, Ciccheti, & Rogosch, 2005) predict better outcomes for maltreated children. Children's self-confidence and feelings of acceptance created by supportive environments and relationships with trusted individuals can mitigate the negative impact of maltreatment (e.g., Iwaniec et al., 2006), especially in the case of sexual abuse when the child discloses about the abuse (Conte & Schuerman, 1988). For sexual abuse, the immediacy of disclosure (Kogan, 2005) as well as the child's relationship to the perpetrator, the nature and extent of the abuse (Salter, 1995), and whether they blame themselves or the perpetrator for the abuse (Lev-Wiesel, 2000) all contribute to successful coping. Congruent with a diathesis stress model, the more problems that accumulate as a result of the abuse, the less effective protective factors are at buffering the effects of abuse (Jaffee et al., 2007).

Finally, considering biological factors that protect against the negative impact of maltreatment, the genotype for high levels of monoamine oxidase A (MAOA) was found to protect against antisocial behavior in White males who were neglected, physically or sexually abused, and were rejected by their mothers (Caspi et al., 2002); this was not true in a replication study with non-White males and females (Widom & Brzustowicz, 2006).

Treatment

Prevention of partner violence

Participation in a premarital relationship skills enhancement program may reduce the risk for physical aggression in the early years of marriage (e.g., Markman, Renick, Floyd, Stanley, & Clements, 1993). Similarly, for dating adolescents, participation in prevention programs has been found to reduce both aggression perpetration and victimization (e.g., Wolfe, Wekerle, Scott, Straatman, & Grasley, 2004).

Intervention for partner violence

A recent meta-analysis of battering interventions for men who abuse their partners found very small effects ($d = .09-.34$) on preventing recidivism (Babcock, Green, & Robie, 2004). Such groups are typically comprised of men who have been court mandated, and focus on sensitizing men to their use of power and control tactics against their wives, modifying beliefs about the acceptability of physical and emotional aggression, and developing better cognitive and behavioral control of anger (e.g., Pence & Paymar, 1993).

Dyadic interventions, typically used with non-court mandated, less severely abusive intact couples, have also been developed and tested (e.g., Stith et al., 2005). The Domestic Violence Couple's Treatment (DVCT; Stith et al., 2005) has demonstrated completion rates of 70% and significant reductions in physical and psychological aggression for both partners up to 2 years post-treatment. Although DVCT and other programs have produced significant reductions in aggression following intervention, they too often do not result in complete cessation of aggression and do not necessarily show better results than gender-specific approaches (Stith, Rosen, & McCollum, 2003). Nevertheless, Stith, Rosen, McCollum, & Thomsen (2004) found lower rates of recidivism for a multicouple group treatment in a 6-month follow-up than for couples in individual couple treatment and comparison groups. Emotionally maltreating couples that paused mid-argument to write about their own anger or role in a conflict reported increased marital satisfaction and decreased fighting (Lange, van der Wall, & Emmelkamp, 2000). Couples treatment aimed at reducing substance abuse has also been found to reduce IPV and improve relationship satisfaction (see Chapter 26, this volume).

Prevention of child maltreatment

Home visitation programs designed to prevent child maltreatment (e.g., Barth, 1991) attempt to educate parents about the transition to parenthood, foster realistic expectations for the development of their children, and strengthen and provide social support during this transition. These programs show lower levels of abuse and neglect immediately upon completion (Olds, 1989), as well as continued positive effects up to 15 years later (Olds et al., 2004). A meta-analysis of 23 parenting programs found similar results to home visitation programs with regard to overall effectiveness. In addition, the moderators that significantly enhanced the effectiveness of these programs were the inclusion of a behavioral component, a combination of home and office visits, and individual rather than group settings (Lundahl, Nimer, & Parsons, 2006).

Intervention following child maltreatment

The goal of many targeted programs is to prevent future perpetration or victimization and reduce the harms caused by the previously committed acts of abuse (Tolan & Gorman-Smith, 2002). Treatments often involve parent perpetrators and child victims (Kolko, 2000) and focus on parent training to improve management of child behavior, change distorted and irrational expectations for child behavior and development, and build strategies for anger management (Azar, Wolfe, Mash, & Barkley, 2006) as well as relieving child symptoms. Behaviorally oriented parenting programs tend to improve childrearing practices more than non-behavioral programs do; however, non-behavioral programs fare better at improving parenting attitudes (Lundahl et al., 2006). In a recent meta-analysis investigating the effectiveness of different types of therapy for child maltreatment, Skowron and Reinemann (2005) found moderate effect sizes for treatment regardless of treatment modality (individual, group, family, milieu) or mandated versus voluntary participation.

Diversity Factors

Differences in perpetration

Physical aggression perpetration is higher among Blacks and Hispanics than Whites for both female-to-male and male-to-female partner violence (Field & Caetano, 2005). Klevens (2007) found no significant difference in IPV among Hispanics and non-Hispanics but posited that ethnic differences may exist between the causes of perpetration, such as male dominance and issues related to acculturation. Korbin and colleagues found a positive relation between poverty and perpetration of child maltreatment, especially for Blacks (Korbin, Coulton, Chard, Platt-Houston, & Su, 1998).

Differences in victimization

Some studies have found that African American women experience elevated partner violence victimization rates (Bent-Goodley, 2004) – as well as repeated incidents (Carlson, Harris, & Holden, 1999) and severe abuse (El-Khoury et al., 2004) – compared to White and Latina women. Low acculturation among Hispanic women also results in less reporting of IPV and less use of social services following IPV victimization compared with Black and White women (Lipsky, Caetano, Field, & Larkin, 2006).

For children, rates of sexual abuse are three times greater for females than males, and White female children are the most common victims of parent-perpetrated sexual abuse (Sedlack & Broadhurst, 1996). Male children are at greater risk for serious injury and emotional abuse than female children. White children are more likely to suffer serious injury, whereas non-White children are more likely to suffer moderate injury. Aside from injury, no differences in maltreatment were found by ethnicity (Sedlack & Broadhurst, 1996).

Differences in attitudes about violence

Locke and Richman (1999) found that European Americans (compared with African Americans) and women (compared with men) had more negative attitudes toward IPV. Markowitz (2001) found that males and non-Whites, compared with females and Whites, were more likely to report that use of violence against spouse was acceptable; however, no difference in attitude toward use of violence against children was reported for non-Whites, men, or people of lower socioeconomic status.

Case Study

John and Susan Davies are 28 years old and have been married for 7 years. Throughout their relationship, conflicts have escalated quickly, with John wanting to engage and Susan preferring to withdraw. Although pushing, shoving, and grabbing were initially the most common types of physical violence, their use of violence increased to include punching, scratching, and kicking. John has received bruises, scratch marks, and a welt on his back; Susan has received bruises to her arms, legs, and back and a small bump on her head.

John and Susan have a 7-year-old son, Diego, and a $3^{1}/_{2}$-year-old daughter, Sonia. Both John and Susan were disciplined forcefully by their own parents. Susan witnessed her parents using physical force against each other during arguments. John's father was emotionally but not physically abusive toward his mother. Both John and Susan frequently used spanking and grabbing – and occasionally slapping and pinching – to discipline the children.

The partners were interviewed together and separately. They completed a set of questionnaires, including the Conflict Tactics Scale Revised (Straus, Hamby, Boney-McCoy, & Sugarman, 1996), the Depression, Anxiety, and Stress Scale (Lovibond & Lovibond, 1995), the Dyadic Adjustment Scale (Spanier, 1976), Communication Patterns Questionnaire (Christensen, Noller, & Fitzpatrick, 1988), and the Child Abuse Potential inventory (Milner, 1989).

In establishing a treatment plan, we all agreed that John and Susan's three primary problems were anger management (when dealing both with each other and with their children), decision-making, and communication. We agreed that the escalation to violent conflict needed to be addressed first.

Treatment first focused on anger management. John and Susan identified triggers that caused conversations to escalate and both agreed to be responsible for recognizing these triggers and enacting a conflict plan they negotiated. In creating their conflict plan, they recognized their approach–avoid–pursue conflict style and decided to separate briefly when a problem arose, calm down individually, and re-approach the issue within 15 minutes.

After several weeks, both partners were able to manage their anger during conflicts and violence had ceased. We proceeded to communication skills and problem-solving training and in-session rehearsal. By this point in treatment, conversations were far less conflictual and John and Susan were develop mutually agreeable plans to organize their time, share responsibilities more, and feel less overwhelmed by their busy schedules. They also scheduled a small amount of time alone together to do activities they had both enjoyed before getting married and having children. Treatment concluded with several sessions of behavioral parent training and, finally, the negotiation of a plan to support each other's parenting.

Resources

Family Translational Research Group:
http://www.psychology.sunysb.edu/ftrlab-/supplement.php
This website contains supplemental material to augment this chapter, including family mal-
    treatment definitions.

References

Anderson, D., & Saunders, D. (2003). Leaving an abusive partner: An empirical review of pre-dictors, the process of leaving, and psychological well-being. *Trauma, Violence, and Abuse, 4,* 163–191.

Appel, A. E., & Holden, G. W. (1998). The co-occurrence of spouse and physical child abuse: A review and appraisal. *Journal of Family Psychology, 12,* 578–599.

Azar, S. T., Wolfe, D. A., Mash, E. J., & Barkley, R. A. (2006). *Child physical abuse and neglect.* New York: Guilford Press.

Babcock, J. C., Green, C. E., & Robie, C. (2004). Does batterers' treatment work? A meta-analytic review of domestic violence treatment. *Clinical Psychology Review, 23,* 1023–1053.

Barth, R. P. (1991). An experimental evaluation of in-home child abuse prevention services. *Child Abuse and Neglect, 15,* 363–375.

Bender, M., Cook, S., & Kaslow, N. (2003). Social support as a mediator of revictimization of low-income African American women. *Violence and Victims, 18,* 419–431.

Bent-Goodley, T. B. (2004). Perception of domestic violence: A dialogue with African American women. *Health and Social Work, 29,* 307–316.

Bradley, R., Schwartz, A. C., & Kaslow, N. J. (2005). Posttraumatic stress disorder symptoms among low-income, African American women with a history of intimate partner violence and suicidal behaviors: Self-esteem, social support, and religious coping. *Journal of Traumatic Stress, 18,* 685–696.

Caliso, J. A., & Milner, J. S. (1992). Childhood history of abuse and child abuse screening. *Child Abuse and Neglect, 16,* 647–659.

Campbell, J., Jones, A. S., Dienemann, J., Kub, J., Schollenberger, J., & O'Campo, P. (2002). Intimate partner violence and physical health consequences. *Archives of Internal Medicine, 162,* 1157–1163.

Carlson, M. J., Harris, S. D., & Holden, G. W. (1999). Protective orders and domestic violence: Risk factors for re-abuse. *Journal of Family Violence, 14,* 205–226.

Cascardi, M., Langhinrichsen, J., & Vivian, D. (1992). Marital aggression: Impact, injury, and health correlates for husbands and wives. *Archives of Internal Medicine, 152,* 1178–1184.

Caspi, A., McClay, J., Moffitt, T., Mill, J., Martin, J., Craig, I. W., et al. (2002). Role of genotype in the cycle of violence in maltreated children. *Science, 297,* 851–854.

Centers for Disease Control. (1998). Lifetime and annual incidence of intimate partner violence and resulting injuries – Georgia, 1995. *Morbidity and Mortality Weekly Report, 47,* 849–853.

Chaffin, M., Kelleher, K., & Hollenberg, J. (1996). Onset of physical abuse and neglect: Psychiatric, substance abuse, and social risk factors from prospective community data. *Child Abuse and Neglect, 20,* 191–203.

Christensen, A., Noller, P., & Fitzpatrick, M. A. (1988). *Dysfunctional interaction patterns in couples.* Clevedon, England: Multilingual Matters.

Christensen, M. J., Brayden, R. M., Dietrich, M. S., & McLaughlin, F. J. (1994). The prospective assessment of self-concept in neglectful and physically abusive low income mothers. *Child Abuse and Neglect, 18,* 225–232.

Cicchetti, D., & Lynch, M. (1995). Failures in the expectable environment and their impact on individual development: The case of child maltreatment. In D. Cicchetti and D. J. Cohen (Eds.), *Developmental psychopathology: Vol. 2. Risk, disorder, and adaptation* (pp. 32–71). Oxford: Wiley.

Connelly, C. D., & Straus, M. A. (1992). Mother's age and risk for physical abuse. *Child Abuse and Neglect, 16,* 709–718.

Conte, J., & Schuerman, J. (1988). *The effects of sexual abuse on children: A multidimensional view.* Thousand Oaks, CA: Sage.

Dibble, U., & Straus, M. A. (1980). Some social structure determinants of inconsistency between attitudes and behavior: The case of family violence. *Journal of Marriage and the Family, 42,* 71–80.

El-Khoury, M. Y., Dutton, M. A., Goodman, L. A., Engel, L., Belamaric, R. J., & Murphy, M. (2004). Ethnic differences in battered women's formal help-seeking strategies: A focus on health, mental health, and spirituality. *Cultural Diversity and Ethnic Minority Psychology, 10,* 383–393.

Field, C. A., & Caetano, R. (2005). Longitudinal model predicting mutual partner violence among White, Black, and Hispanic couples in the United States general population. *Violence and Victims, 20,* 499–511.

Flores, E., Ciccheti, D., & Rogosch, F. A. (2005). Predictors of resilience in maltreated and non-maltreated Latino children. *Developmental Psychology, 41,* 338–351.

Heyman, R. E., & Slep, A. M. S. (2001). Risk factors for family violence [Special issue]. *Aggression and Violent Behavior, 6.*

Heyman, R. E., & Slep, A. M. S. (2006). Creating and field-testing diagnostic criteria for partner and child maltreatment. *Journal of Family Psychology, 20,* 397–408.

Holtzworth-Munroe, A., Smutzler, N., & Bates, L. (1997). A brief review of the research on husband violence. Part III: Sociodemographic factors, relationship factors, and differing consequences of husband and wife violence. *Aggression and Violent Behavior, 2,* 285–307.

Iwaniec, D., Larkin, E., & Higgins, S. N. (2006). Research review: Risk and resilience in cases of emotional abuse. *Child and Family Social Work, 11,* 73–82.

Jaffee, S., Caspi, A., Moffitt, T. E., Polo-Tomas, M., & Taylor, A. (2007). Individual, family, and neighborhood factors distinguish resilient from non-resilient maltreated children: A cumulative stressors model. *Child Abuse and Neglect, 31,* 231–253.

Kaufman, J., & Zigler, E. (1987). Do abused children become abusive parents? *American Journal of Orthopsychiatry, 57,* 186–192.

Kelleher, K., Chaffin, M., Hollenberg, J., & Fischer, E. (1994). Alcohol and drug disorders among physically abusive and neglectful parents in a community-based sample. *American Journal of Public Health, 84,* 1586–1590.

Kelly, B., Thornberry, T., & Smith, C. (1997). *In the wake of childhood maltreatment* Washington DC: National Institute of Justice.

Klevens, J. (2007). An overview of intimate partner violence among Latinos. *Violence Against Women, 13,* 111–122.

Kogan, S. (2005). The role of disclosing child sexual abuse on adolescent adjustment and revictimization. *Journal of Child Sexual Abuse, 14(2),* 25–47.

Kolko, D. (2000). Treatment research in child maltreatment: Clinical and research directions. *Journal of Aggression, Maltreatment and Trauma, 4,* 139–164.

Korbin, J. E., Coulton, C. J., Chard, S., Platt-Houston, C., & Su, M. (1998). Impoverishment and child maltreatment in African American and European American neighborhoods. *Development and Psychopathology, 10,* 215–233.

Lambie, I., Seymour, F., Lee, A., & Adams, P. (2002). Resiliency in the victim–offender cycle in male sexual abuse. *Sexual Abuse: Journal of Research and Treatment, 14,* 31–48.

Lange, A., van der Wall, C., & Emmelkamp, P. (2000). Time-out and writing in distressed couples: An experimental trial into the effects of a short treatment. *Journal of Family Therapy, 22,* 394–407.

Laroche, D. (2005). *Aspects of the context and consequences of domestic violence: Situational couple violence and intimate terrorism in Canada in 1999.* Quebec City: Government of Quebec.

Larrance, D. T., & Twentyman, C. T. (1983). Maternal attributions and child abuse. *Journal of Abnormal Psychology, 92,* 449–457.

Lemon, S. C., Verhoek-Oftedahl, W., & Donnelly, E. F. (2002). Preventive healthcare use, smoking, and alcohol use among Rhode Island women experiencing intimate partner violence. *Journal of Women's Health and Gender-Based Medicine, 11,* 555–562.

Lesnik-Oberstein, M., Koers, A. J., & Cohen, L. (1995). Parental hostility and its sources in psychologically abusive mothers: A test of the three-factor theory. *Child Abuse and Neglect, 19,* 33–49.

Leserman, J., & Drossman, D. (2007). Relationship of abuse history to functional gastrointestinal disorders and symptoms: Some possible mediating mechanisms. *Trauma, Violence, and Abuse, 8(3),* 331–343.

Lev-Wiesel, R. (2000). Quality of life in adult survivors of childhood sexual abuse who have undergone therapy. *Journal of Child Sexual Abuse, 9,* 1–13.

Levendosky, A. A., & Graham-Bermann, S. A. (2000). Behavioral observations of parenting in battered women. *Journal of Family Psychology, 14,* 1–15.

Lipsky, S., Caetano, R., Field, C. A., & Larkin, G. L. (2006). The role of intimate partner violence, race, and ethnicity in help-seeking behaviors. *Ethnicity and Health, 11,* 81–100.

Locke, L. M., & Richman, C. L. (1999). Attitudes toward domestic violence: Race and gender issues. *Sex Roles, 40,* 227–247.

Lovibond, P. F., & Lovibond, S. H. (1995). The structure of negative emotional states: Comparison of the Depression Anxiety Stress Scales (DASS) with the Beck Depression and Anxiety Inventories. *Behaviour Research and Therapy, 33,* 335–343.

Lundahl, B. W., Nimer, J., & Parsons, B. (2006). Preventing child abuse: A meta-analysis of parent training programs. *Research on Social Work Practice, 16,* 251–262.

Luthar, S. S. (1991). Vulnerability and resilience: A study of high-risk adolescents. *Child Development, 62,* 600–616.

Lynch, M., & Cicchetti, D. (1998). An ecological-transactional analysis of children and contexts: The longitudinal interplay among child maltreatment, community violence, and children's symptomatology. *Development and Psychopathology, 10,* 235–257.

Margolin, G., Gordis, E. B., Medina, A. M., & Oliver, P. H. (2003). The co-occurrence of husband-to-wife aggression, family-of-origin aggression, and child abuse potential in a community sample: Implications for parenting. *Journal of Interpersonal Violence, 18,* 413–440.

Markman, H., Renick, M., Floyd, F., Stanley, S., & Clements, M. (1993). Preventing marital distress through communication and conflict management training: A 4- and 5-year follow-up. *Journal of Consulting and Clinical Psychology, 61,* 70–77.

Markowitz, F. E. (2001). Attitudes and family violence: Linking intergenerational and cultural theories. *Journal of Family Violence, 16,* 205–218.

Milner, J. S. (1989). Additional cross-validation of the Child Abuse Potential Inventory. *Psychological Assessment, 1,* 219–223.

O'Campo, P., Kub, J., Woods, A., Garza, M., Jones, S., & Gielen, A. (2006). Depression, PTSD, and comorbidity related to intimate partner violence in civilian and military women. *Brief Treatment and Crisis Intervention, 6,* 99–110.

Okun, A., Parker, J. G., & Levendosky, A. A. (1994). Distinct and interactive contributions of physical abuse, socioeconomic disadvantage, and negative life events of children's social, cognitive, and affective adjustment. *Developmental Psychopathology, 6,* 77–98.

Olds, D. (1989). The Prenatal/Early Infancy Project: A strategy for responding to the needs of high-risk mothers and their children. *Prevention in Human Services, 7,* 59–87.

Olds, D., Henderson, C., Cole, R., Eckenrode, J., Kitzman, H., Luckey, D., et al. (2004). Long-term effects of nurse home visitation on children's criminal and antisocial behavior: Fifteen-year follow-up of a randomized controlled trial. In M. A. Feldman (Ed.), *Early intervention: The essential readings* (pp. 238–255). Malden, MA: Blackwell.

O'Leary, K. D., Vivian, D., & Malone, J. (1992). Assessment of physical aggression against women in marriage: The need for multimodal assessment. *Behavioral Assessment, 14,* 5–14.

Pavao, J., Alvarez, J., Baumrind, N., Induni, M., & Kimerling, R. (2007). Intimate partner violence and housing instability. *American Journal of Preventive Medicine, 32*, 143–146.

Pence, E., & Paymar, M. (1993). *Education groups for men who batter: The Duluth model.* New York: Springer.

Rohrbeck, C. A., & Twentyman, C. T. (1986). Multimodal assessment of impulsiveness in abusing, neglecting, and nonmaltreating mothers and their preschool children. *Journal of Consulting and Clinical Psychology, 54*, 231–236.

Salter, A. C. (1995). *Transforming trauma: A guide to understanding and treating adult survivors of child sexual abuse.* Thousand Oaks, CA: Sage.

Schafer, J., Caetano, R., & Clark, C. L. (1998). Rates of intimate partner violence in the United States. *American Journal of Public Health, 88*, 1702–1704.

Sedlak, A. J., & Broadhurst, D. D. (1996). *Executive summary of the Third National Incidence Study of Child Abuse and Neglect.* Washington, DC: U.S. Department of Health and Human Services, Child Welfare Information Gateway.

Skowron, E., & Reinemann, D. H. S. (2005). Effectiveness of psychological interventions for child maltreatment: A meta-analysis. *Psychotherapy: Theory, Research, Practice, Training, 42*, 52–71.

Slep, A. M. S., & O'Leary, S. G. (2005). Parent and partner violence in families with young children: Rates, patterns, and connections. *Journal of Consulting and Clinical Psychology, 73*, 435–444.

Spanier, G. B. (1976). Measuring dyadic adjustment: New scales for assessing the quality of marriage and similar dyads. *Journal of Marriage and the Family, 38*, 15–28.

Stith, S. M., McCollum, E. E., Rosen, K. H., Locke, L. D., Goldberg, P. D., & Lebow, J. L. (2005). *Domestic violence-focused couples treatment.* Hoboken, NJ: Wiley.

Stith, S. M., Rosen, K. H., & McCollum, E. E. (2003). Effectiveness of couples treatment for spouse abuse. *Journal of Marital and Family Therapy, 29*, 407–426.

Stith, S. M., Rosen, K. H., McCollum, E. E., & Thomsen, C. J. (2004). Treating intimate partner violence within intact couple relationships: Outcomes of multi-couple versus individual couple therapy. *Journal of Marital and Family Therapy, 30*, 305–318.

Stith, S. M., Rosen, K. H., Middleton, K. A., Busch, A. L., Lundeberg, K., & Carlton, R. P. (2000). The intergenerational transmission of spouse abuse: A meta-analysis. *Journal of Marriage and the Family, 62*, 640–654.

Straus, M. A. (1990). Ordinary violence, child abuse, and wife beating: What do they have in common? In M. A. Straus & R. J. Gelles (Eds.), *Physical violence in American families: Risk factors and adaptation to violence in 8,145 families* (pp. 403–424). New Brunswick, NJ: Transaction.

Straus, M. A., Hamby, S. L., Boney-McCoy, S., & Sugarman, D. B. (1996). The revised Conflict Tactics Scales (CTS2): Development and preliminary psychometric data. *Journal of Family Issues, 17*, 283–316.

Straus, M. A., & Kantor, G. K. (1987). *Stress and child abuse.* Chicago: University of Chicago Press.

Sullivan, P. M., & Knutson, J. F. (2000). Maltreatment and disabilities: A population-based epidemiological study. *Child Abuse and Neglect, 24*, 1257–1273.

Thompson, M. P., & Kingree, J. B. (2006). The roles of victim and perpetrator alcohol use in intimate partner violence outcomes. *Journal of Interpersonal Violence, 21*, 163–177.

Tolan, P. H., & Gorman-Smith, D. (2002). What violence prevention research can tell us about developmental psychopathology. *Development and Psychopathology, 14*, 713–729.

U.S. Advisory Board on Child Abuse and Neglect. (1995). *A nation's shame: Fatal child abuse and neglect in the United States.* Washington, DC: U.S. Department of Health and Human Services. Retrieved April 30, 2007, from http://ican-ncfr.org/documents/Nations-Shame.pdf

U.S. Department of Health and Human Services, Administration on Children, Youth and Families. (2001). *Child maltreatment*. Washington, DC: U.S. Government Printing Office.

U.S. Department of Health and Human Services, Administration on Children, Youth and Families. (2005). *Child maltreatment*. Washington, DC: U.S. Government Printing Office.

Varma, D., Chandra, P., Thomas, T., & Carey, M. (2007). Intimate partner violence and sexual coercion among pregnant women in India: Relationship with depression and post-traumatic stress disorder. *Journal of Affective Disorders, 102*, 227–235.

Vissing, Y. M., Straus, M. A., Gelles, R. J., & Harrop, J. W. (1991). Verbal aggression by parents and psychosocial problems of children. *Child Abuse and Neglect, 15*, 223–238.

Whipple, E. E., & Webster-Stratton, C. (1991). The role of parental stress in physically abusive families. *Child Abuse and Neglect, 15*, 279–291.

White, J. W., Smith, P. H., Koss, M. P., & Figueredo, A. J. (2000). Intimate partner aggression– what have we learned? Comment on Archer (2000). *Psychological Bulletin, 126*, 690–696.

Widom, C. S., & Brzustowicz, L. M. (2006). MAOA and the "cycle of violence": Childhood abuse and neglect, MAOA genotype, and risk for violent and antisocial behavior. *Biological Psychiatry, 60*, 684–689.

Wilcox, D. T., Richards, F., & O'Keeffe, Z. C. (2004). Resilience and risk factors associated with experiencing childhood sexual abuse. *Child Abuse Review, 13*, 338–352.

Williamson, J. M., Borduin, C. M., & Howe, B. A. (1991). The ecology of adolescent maltreatment: A multilevel examination of adolescent physical abuse, sexual abuse, and neglect. *Journal of Consulting and Clinical Psychology, 59*, 449–457.

Wolfe, D. A., Wekerle, C., Scott, K., Straatman, A.-L., & Grasley, C. (2004). Predicting abuse in adolescent dating relationships over 1 year: The role of child maltreatment and trauma. *Journal of Abnormal Psychology, 113*, 406–415.

Wolfner, G. D., & Gelles, R. J. (1993). A profile of violence toward children: A national study. *Child Abuse and Neglect, 17*, 197–212.

Zuravin, S. J. (1987). Unplanned pregnancies, family planning problems, and child maltreatment. *Family Relations, 36*, 135–139.

53

Serious Mental Illness: Family Experiences, Needs, and Interventions

Diane T. Marsh and Harriet P. Lefley

Family psychologist Elizabeth Clarkson received a call from Delores Martinez, who was referred by the psychiatrist who is treating her 21-year-old son, John. Mrs Martinez said her son had been diagnosed with schizophrenia during his freshman year in college. Although his symptoms had improved with antipsychotic medication, John had no social life or vocational plans, and he experienced periodic relapses that left the entire family feeling hopeless and helpless. Mrs Martinez said that John's illness had devastated the entire family, including his younger siblings, 18-year-old Anna and 16-year-old Michael. She added that she and her husband, Roberto, cannot discuss John's problems without arguing. Roberto feels John should take responsibility for his life and get a job. Delores worries that any pressure on John will result in another hospitalization. Responding to this stressful family environment, Anna tries to support John and to maintain peace in the family. Concerned about her family, she is reluctant to leave for college in the fall. In contrast, Michael is angry that John's illness has caused so much trouble for the family and complains that no one pays any attention to him. How might Dr Clarkson assist the Martinez family?

Like John Martinez, in any given year, approximately 5% to 7% of adults have a serious mental illness, such as schizophrenia, bipolar disorder, or major depression. Serious mental illness typically results in significant impairment in multiple functional areas, including employment, self-care, and social relationships. All of these individuals have family members who share in the tremendous losses and challenges that accompany the illness.

Indeed, with progressive deinstitutionalization, families have become the major care-givers and lifetime support systems for their relatives with serious mental illness (Warner, 2000). In the United States, about 40% of patients reside with predominantly European American families, although reported percentages are typically much higher among

African American and Latino families (Jenkins & Schumacher, 1999; Lefley, 2004). Even when patients live in assisted living facilities or residential housing, families continue to be a significant source of financial, emotional, and social support (Clark & Drake, 1994).

Yet, in contrast to caregivers who are dealing with other chronic conditions, these families have received little attention and support. For example, a landmark study found that fewer than 10% of such families in the United States receive even minimal educational and supportive services (Lehman et al., 1998). Accordingly, professional practice in this area offers a fertile opportunity for family psychologists.

In this chapter, we will explore the family experience of mental illness, professional practice with these families, and family interventions for serious mental illness. In contrast to the past, current practitioners can offer genuine assistance and hope. Recovery from serious mental illness, once thought impossible, has been documented in numerous long-term outcome studies (Davidson, Harding, & Spaniol, 2005). Broadly defined, recovery is the process in which people are able to live, work, learn, and participate fully in their communities (New Freedom Commission on Mental Health, 2003). Moreover, practitioners now have available a growing arsenal of effective treatments for serious mental illness (e.g., Drake et al., 2001).

The Family Experience of Serious Mental Illness

In describing the family experience of serious mental illness, researchers and clinicians have focused on family stress and life-cycle issues. Sources of family stress in coping with serious mental illness are situational, societal, and in some cases iatrogenic (Marsh & Lefley, 2003). Situational stressors involve both objective and subjective family burden, namely, the investments of time and energy required to deal with the illness and the emotional strains on the caregiver. Service system deficits – difficulties in accessing appropriate treatment – are critical stressors for families. Legal constraints, insurance problems, or unavailability of inpatient beds often make it difficult to hospitalize a person in a psychotic state. Premature discharge from crisis units, problems with third-party reimbursements, incarceration of minor misdemeanants in the criminal justice system, or generally inadequate community support systems are all aspects of objective family burden. Subjective burden includes loss, sorrow, grieving, and empathic pain for loved ones who may mourn their own lost aspirations and impoverished lives. Families may have to cope with disruptive or violent behaviors, a patient's rejection of treatment, hostile misjudgments from neighbors or relatives, negative psychological effects on siblings and young children, social isolation, and economic burdens of the illness (Baronet, 1999; Lefley, 1996).

Societal stressors include the still prevailing stigma of mental illness, generalization of stigma to relatives, negative expectancies of recovery, underfunding of research and services, and general public neglect of a devalued subgroup. Iatrogenic stressors are happily diminishing but may still involve attributions of parental causation and ignorance of family burden. Some clinical educators unfortunately still teach theories of family pathogenesis. Reported stressors from clinicians have included failure to provide information and support to caregivers, misuse of confidentiality to deny needed information, attitudinal rejection, and, as some research has demonstrated, years of expensive, ineffective psychotherapy (McGlashan, 1984).

Several recent studies have focused on caregiving gratifications, such as a patient's companionship and contributions to household tasks. Social support is a critical variable in positive perceptions of caregiving (Chen & Greenberg, 2004). Overall, however, the literature has focused on burden. A review of 28 studies of family burden (Baronet, 1999) found that primary objective burdens involved money management, providing transportation, continuous supervision, financial assistance, and limitations on caregivers' own activities. Primary subjective burdens related to safety and potential violence of the sick relative, excessive demands and dependency, symptomatic and embarrassing behaviors, and family conflicts.

The life cycle of the family and the stage and trajectory of the illness are both relevant to family work at any point in time. Schizophrenia and major mood disorders typically have their onset during late adolescence or early adulthood. This means a disruption of the normal transitions of young adults leaving home and becoming independent. At a developmental stage when parents should be experiencing a sense of freedom, they continue to be involved with adult children who frequently depend on them as their major social and economic resource. Elderly parents may endure not only the burdens of caregiving, but ongoing interactions with the mental health, social welfare, and even criminal justice systems.

Despite evidence that persons with severe mental illness do better than expected in later life (Davidson et al., 2005), most are not able to fulfill normative roles in the family life cycle. The majority receiving services have not been able to fulfill adult role responsibilities, marry, raise families, and reverse generational caregiving roles in later life. They generally cannot fulfill age-appropriate roles in society and are frequently locked into the dependency–independence conflicts of adolescence with parental or even sibling caregivers. Spousal relationships of persons with mental illness may involve role disruptions and disparities, childrearing difficulties, economic problems from profligate spending (a common complaint in bipolar disorder), and, as in the case of dysfunctional adult children, displacement of rage onto a caregiving spouse.

With community living, persons with mental illness are increasingly bearing children and becoming parents themselves, with correlative demands and stressors. In New York state, Nicholson and Blanch (1994) reported that 40% of women clients with severe mental illness under the age of 35 had children under the age of 18. Many of these children are being raised by grandparents whose own life-cycle needs are now disrupted. For clients, both childrearing and forced separation from children are unique stressors. Mental health systems offer grossly inadequate help to young mothers who may have few parental skills and their own caregiving needs.

Researchers applying the Thresholds Family Burden Scale attempted to assess how burden relates to the life cycle of the caregivers and the illness. The sample included 222 parents of adults with severe mental illness (mean age 26 years) (Cook, Lefley, Pickett, & Cohler, 1994). Younger parents were significantly more burdened by behavioral problems and control and management issues, older parents by ongoing responsibility and worries about the future. These concerns were confirmed in later studies of aging parents (65 and older), in several different states. Findings indicated intense anxiety about the future of their ill relatives, worries about imposing burden on siblings, and little planning for continued care (Hatfield & Lefley, 2000). A survey of siblings found that they were willing to provide emotional and social support, but rarely the instrumental support provided by parents (Hatfield & Lefley, 2005). Clearly, family interventions would do well to address these realistic life-cycle concerns.

Family Diversity

Reviews of cross-cultural comparisons of families of persons with psychiatric disabilities in the United States have found significant racial and ethnic differences in causal attributions, prognostic expectations, home caregiving, kinship relationship of primary caregivers, hospitalization and service utilization patterns, perceived family burden, and psychological distress (Lefley, 1996). In reviewing 28 studies of family burden, Baronet (1999) reported that significantly higher family burden was experienced by younger, White American caregivers compared to older caregivers from minority group cultures, as well as those living with the ill relative. Age seems particularly relevant. Among Hispanics, lower perceived burden is offset by high rates of depressive symptoms, with younger, less-educated caregivers at particularly high risk (Magana, Ramirez Garcia, Hernandez, & Cortez, 2007). Nevertheless, the most common aspects of burden, across all cultures, are disruptive or threatening behaviors and dependency of the sick relative (Baronet, 1999).

Rationale for a Family-Focused Approach

There is a compelling rationale for a family-focused approach to the treatment of serious mental illness. First, families often serve in essential roles as primary caregivers, informal case managers, de facto crisis intervention workers, and advocates for their relatives. In many respects, the current system of care is as much family- as community-based.

Second, families can play a constructive role in their relative's treatment, rehabilitation, and recovery. They can assist their relative to obtain appropriate services and encourage adherence to the treatment plan. Equally important, during the darkest times, families can offer a life-sustaining message of hope that counteracts the feelings of helplessness and hopelessness that so often accompany serious mental illness.

Third, as we will discuss, effective family interventions are now available for the treatment of serious mental illness. There is strong evidence for the clinical, social, family, and economic benefits of family psychoeducation (Dixon, McFarlane et al., 2001; Falloon, Roncone, Held, Coverdale, & Laidlaw, 2002). In addition, several other family interventions offer potential benefits for families, including family education, family consultation, family support and advocacy groups, and family therapy.

Finally, faced with the catastrophic stressor of a relative's serious mental illness, these families have compelling needs of their own (see Lefley, 1996). Families share in the terrible toll when their relative joins the ranks of the homeless, enters the criminal justice system, or commits suicide, as 10% of these patients eventually do (American Psychiatric Association, 2000).

Engaging and Assessing Families

Particularly at the time of the initial diagnosis or during crises, these families often feel distressed, confused, and overwhelmed. Clinicians can establish rapport by listening to their stories, responding with compassion, and focusing on their expressed needs. They can assist families to identify and prioritize their needs, to deal with illness-related concerns, and to make an informed choice about their use of other available services. Families often appreciate handouts about serious mental illness and suggestions for family resources (e.g., Mueser & Gingerich, 2006).

An initial family assessment enables practitioners to respond to any urgent family needs and begin formulating a family service plan (see Mueser & Glynn, 1999). Assessment usually covers the following:

- current issues facing the family, such as the risk of harm to their relative or to others;
- their knowledge of mental illness, including any misconceptions they have;
- their skills for coping with the illness and with family stress in general;
- their strengths, resources, and potential contributions to their relative's treatment;
- the impact of mental illness on their family unit and on individual members;
- other past or present problems that may affect the family's ability to cope with the illness;
- the level of support available to the family; and
- their immediate and long-term needs and goals.

Families as Caregivers: Role in Treatment

In their final report, the New Freedom Commission on Mental Health (2003) emphasized that mental health systems must be driven by consumers and families. As support systems or actual caregivers, families should participate in treatment to the extent required and assented to by patients. Caregivers do not need to know the confidences of psychotherapy, but they do need information on medications, symptoms, appropriate behavioral expectations, and other aspects of the treatment plan that involve their participation. A skilled practitioner can often influence a patient to agree to an exchange of information with caregivers. A sample release-of-information form may be found in Marsh and Lefley (2003). In any case, thoughtful clinicians should always be willing to receive input from caregivers, understanding that their observations may be important for therapeutic progress.

Dealing with Confidentiality

Practitioners often view confidentiality as a rigid barrier to working with families, although such a stance is rarely in the best interest of patients, family members, or therapists. Professional ethical codes do protect the right of patients to a confidential therapeutic relationship. Nevertheless, families also have rights, particularly if they are serving as primary caregivers, such as information on medications and expected effects. Petrila and Sadoff (1992) have cautioned that there may be legal liability when providers fail to share critical information with families and this leads to adverse consequences, citing various court cases to prove their point. Family psychologists can employ several strategies for resolving potential conflicts related to confidentiality (see Zipple, Langle, Tyrell, Spaniol, & Fisher, 1997). Much non-confidential information regarding serious mental illness is available to the general public and can be shared with families.

When confidentiality does pertain, clinicians can use a release-of-information form designed specifically for families. Early in treatment, patients should be encouraged to make an informed choice about the information that will be shared with family members and the ways in which information will be shared. Because consent requires competence, a decision should be postponed if the patient is experiencing severe psychotic symptoms.

Family psychologists can also function as mediators who negotiate the boundaries of confidentiality to meet the needs of particular patients and families. Working with patients, they can discuss the importance of keeping their families informed. Therapists can work with both parties to decide what specific information is needed. In some settings, different staff members can work with patients and families, or they can meet together to resolve the categories of shared and private information. Because patients suffer acutely from their powerlessness, resolving confidentiality can be a highly therapeutic intervention if the patient is put in control of deciding the areas of information to be shared. With patient consent, families can be actively involved in treatment decisions, sometimes as members of the treatment team.

Practitioners should also be aware that other ethical principles might conflict with – and take precedence over – confidentiality, including the risk of imminent harm to the patient or to others. Under those circumstances, practitioners may be ethically and legally required to contact family members. However, these issues are usually governed by state laws and may vary across jurisdictions.

Family Intervention Models

Several family interventions, some with strong empirical support, offer potential benefits for families: family psychoeducation, family education, family consultation, family support and advocacy groups, and family therapy.

Family psychoeducation

Family psychoeducation, based on numerous well-designed studies, is considered one of the major evidence-based practices (EBPs) for serious mental illness (Dixon, McFarlane, et al., 2001), particularly schizophrenia (Kuipers, Birchwood, & McCreadie, 2002) and bipolar disorder (Miklowitz et al., 2002). Although initially linked to the research on high expressed emotion (EE), namely, to reduction of hostile criticism or emotional overinvolvement in families, international studies demonstrated that worldwide, most families of persons with schizophrenia were actually low EE (Lefley, 1992), but that all benefited from this intervention. The core content of family psychoeducation is support for families, state-of-the-art education about serious mental illness, illness management strategies, problem-solving techniques, and resource information.

A meta-analysis of 25 international studies concluded that psychoeducational interventions are essential to schizophrenia treatment (Pitschel-Walz, Leucht, Bauml, Kissling, & Engel, 2001). Among EBPs is behavioral family therapy, primarily developed by psychologists (see Mueser & Glynn, 1999). Most research has focused largely on relapse and rehospitalization rates of patients with schizophrenia. The Pitschel-Walz et al. (2001) meta-analysis revealed that when families are included in treatment, the relapse rate can be reduced by 20% and the effect was particularly marked if family interventions continued for longer than 3 months. For many researchers, 9 months is essential for an intervention to qualify as an EBP (Falloon et al., 2002).

Except for structured or manualized models with specific time frames, family interventions may vary widely in format and content. Content has been adapted for specific ethnic or cultural groups (Lefley & Johnson, 2002). Other variations include: patient present or absent; single family versus multifamily; time-limited versus ongoing; diagnosis-specific versus serious mental illness; prodromal/first episode versus long-term; mental illness with concurrent substance abuse or criminal offenses; or merged family therapy/psychoeducation.

Family education

In recent years, the focus has shifted to shorter-term educational models with family wellbeing as an outcome variable. Solomon (1996) has differentiated between family psychoeducation and family education on the basis of these two outcomes: symptom and relapse reduction versus reduction of families' distress and burden. Almost all the controlled studies have focused on patient outcome. However, shorter-term manualized programs have also been developed for family groups, with attendant research on participants' knowledge and wellbeing, without regard to other effects.

Brief family education programs have been developed by the National Alliance on Mental Illness (NAMI). Initially designed by psychologist Joyce Burland, Journey of Hope (JOH) is an 8-week manualized course in which carefully trained family members teach other families about the causes and treatment of major mental illnesses and problem-solving skills. Psychologist Susan Pickett-Schenk and her colleagues (Pickett-Schenk, Steigman, Bennett, & Lippincott, 2005) conducted randomized controlled trials of 231 JOH participants and 231 controls. They found that participation significantly increases family members' knowledge and communication skills, decreases depressive symptoms, improves relationships with their ill relatives, and increases family members' satisfaction with mental health services. JOH is offered in a few states.

NAMI's Family-to-Family Education Program is a 12-week course also developed, manualized, and constantly updated by Burland. The program has been administered nationwide to many thousands of families. Evaluation of the program's effectiveness is currently underway, although preliminary results point to significant benefits for families (Dixon, Stewart, et al., 2001).

The Support and Family Education (S.A.F.E.) program was developed specifically for the Veterans Administration hospital system by psychologist Michelle Sherman (2006). It includes post-traumatic stress disorder (PTSD) and was developed as a 14-session professional curriculum for caregivers. Problem-solving skills, creating a low-stress environment, and coping with stigma are emphasized. A 5-year evaluation showed high levels of participant retention and satisfaction. Attendance was positively correlated with understanding mental illness, awareness of resources, ability to engage in self-care, and reduced caregiver distress.

Family consultation

Family consultation assists families to identify and prioritize their needs, make an informed choice about services, and formulate a family service plan. It may be limited to a specific request of families, such as deciding about living arrangements or overcoming concurrent substance abuse. Ongoing consultation services may also be available as needed, to deal with crises, life transitions, or other special needs.

Family support and advocacy groups

Time-limited family interventions, empirically justified in their own right, nevertheless cannot address unexpected problems that arise with cyclical mental disorders. Families benefit greatly from ongoing support groups, such as those offered by NAMI and Mental Health America. McFarlane (2002), finding multifamily psychoeducational groups significantly superior in outcome to individual family psychoeducation, has described the benefits of shared experiences. Family groups normalize reactions of fear, guilt, and grieving. They offer resource information, exchange of coping strategies, a social network for isolated families, enhanced problem-solving capability, connections to advocacy organizations, and positive success stories with renewed hope for recovery. Advocacy organizations such as NAMI, focusing on favorable legislation, funding for research and services, and stigma reduction, offer an action mechanism for families who wish to go beyond mutual support and improve the systems that impact their lives.

Family therapy

Families have three essential needs: for information, skills, and support. Once these needs have been met, some families may continue to experience significant difficulties. Any pre-existing personal, marital, or family problems are likely to be exacerbated by illness-related stress. An individual might experience an unresolved grieving process, incapacitating feelings of guilt and responsibility, or inappropriate anger directed at the relative. A married couple might face significant illness-related conflicts or other relational problems. A family might be unable to support their relative's treatment, rehabilitation, and recovery. On the other hand, some families may manifest none of these problems but nevertheless prefer to meet their needs within the context of a confidential therapeutic relationship. Thus, some families may benefit from psychotherapy in addition to educational and supportive services. At the same time, practitioners should be sensitive to the risks of negative effects when they dispense general prescriptions of family therapy based on assumptions of family pathogenesis or dysfunction or that ignore the needs and desires of particular families (Marsh, 2001).

The Family Service Plan

Although families may play a role in their relative's treatment plan, a separate service plan is designed to address the needs of families themselves. As Bernheim (1994) has discussed, the service plan should specify the nature of family involvement with the patient and the mental health system, the family services that will be provided, and a schedule for reviewing the plan. Depending on the results of assessment, the family's needs and desires, and the available services, the plan might include a referral to an advocacy organization, an occasional telephone call, or some combination of consultative, supportive, educational, skills-oriented, and psychotherapeutic services. Practitioners should request regular feedback from families to ensure that services are responsive to their changing needs.

Given the diversity among families, as well as the shifting needs of families over time, there is no single service plan for all families or even for all members within a given family. The family service plan is also influenced by the patient's history and circumstances, the patient's desire for autonomy and privacy, and the family's desire for involvement in the treatment plan. The overarching goal is to provide an optimal service match for particular families (see Dixon, Adams, & Lucksted, 2000).

Working with the Martinez Family

During her initial session with the Martinez family, Dr Clarkson met with John's parents, Delores and Roberto, and his siblings, Anna and Michael. She listened with compassion to their stories and learned about the impact of John's illness on the entire family. They spoke of the burden his illness had imposed upon the family and of the challenges they faced in coping with illness-related behaviors and an unresponsive mental health system. Dr Clarkson provided some written materials on serious mental illness and community resources, explained the concept of recovery, answered their questions, and addressed their concerns. In addition, she referred them to their local NAMI affiliate and encouraged them to participate in the Family-to-Family Education Program.

A month later, Delores, Roberto, and Anna had already attended several session of the NAMI education program, along with Roberto's mother, Isabel, who played an important role in the family. Michael did not want to receive any services, although he often shared his concerns with his grandmother and seemed relieved that his family was getting help. During the next session, Dr Clarkson discussed other available services, including a family psychoeducation program that was offered through John's treatment center. Delores and Roberto were impressed with the evidence supporting the program, especially regarding the reduced risk of relapse, and decided to follow up with the agency.

Over time, Dr Clarkson held as-needed family sessions, which were sometimes attended by Roberto's mother. Dr Clarkson also met separately with Anna and with Delores and Roberto. Siblings are often profoundly affected by the mental illness of a beloved brother or sister, as Anna was. She shared her parents' feelings of loss and grief, but also worried about her parents' arguments and felt responsible for "keeping the peace." Given her role in the family, Anna was concerned about leaving for college in the fall and wondered if she should attend a local community college instead.

In addition, Anna worried about her peers, saying they often made demeaning comments about people with mental illness. She said she felt guilty for resenting John when he had suffered so much and wondered if she would develop mental illness herself. Dr Clarkson explained that siblings often had similar feelings of grief, anger, and survivor guilt, and that they frequently worried about their own mental health. The therapist also helped Anna to focus on her own interests, relationships, and long-term goals.

In their marital sessions, his parents acknowledged their conflict over John but said there was less disagreement following the NAMI program, which helped them better understand John's mental illness. They asked Dr Clarkson how they could promote John's recovery. She explained the importance of providing a supportive home environment, helped them to enhance their communication and problem-solving skills, and assisted them in developing realistic expectations for John and for themselves.

With the consent of John and his family, Dr Clarkson consulted periodically with John's psychiatrist. John began to develop educational and vocational plans and started to attend a local consumer-run program. With less stress and conflict at home, Anna looked forward to college. Michael had many activities and friends outside the family, and his anger had diminished. Although they still faced occasional illness-related challenges, the Martinez family felt a renewed sense of personal and family satisfaction and looked forward to the future.

Suggestions for Family Psychologists

Family psychologists can take several steps to enhance their effectiveness in working with families that include a member with serious mental illness. They can increase their understanding of serious mental illness and its impact on families, familiarize themselves with family-focused services, and make regular referrals to their local NAMI affiliate. More specifically, practitioners can help families:

- learn about serious mental illness, the mental health system, and community resources;
- access services that can address their needs;
- understand and normalize their experience of mental illness;
- focus on the strengths of the patient and family;
- resolve their feelings of grief and loss;
- create a supportive family environment;
- enhance their coping skills;
- develop realistic expectations for the patient and family;
- play a meaningful role in their relative's treatment and recovery; and
- maintain a balance that meets the needs of all family members.

Additional competencies for involving families in services are listed in Glynn, Liberman, and Backer (1997). As families are empowered to cope effectively with serious mental illness, substantial benefits will accrue for the patient and family, for professionals, and for society.

References

American Psychiatric Association. (2000). *Diagnostic and statistical manual of mental disorders* (4th ed., text revision) [*DSM-IV-TR*]. Washington, DC: American Psychiatric Association.

Baronet, A. M. (1999). Factors associated with caregiver burden in mental illness: A critical review of the research literature. *Clinical Psychology Review, 19,* 819–841.

Bernheim, K. F. (1994). Skills and strategies for working with families. In D. T. Marsh (Ed.), *New directions in the psychological treatment of serious mental illness* (pp. 186–198). Westport, CT: Praeger.

Chen, F., & Greenberg, J. (2004). A positive aspect of caregiving: The influence of social support on caregiving. *Community Mental Health Journal, 40,* 423–435.

Clark, R. E., & Drake, R. E. (1994). Expenditures of time and money of families of people with severe mental illness and substance abuse disorders. *Community Mental Health Journal, 30,* 145–163.

Cook, J. A., Lefley, H. P., Pickett, S. A., & Cohler, B. J. (1994). Age and family burden among parents of offspring with severe mental illness. *American Journal of Orthopsychiatry, 64,* 435–447.

Davidson, L., Harding, C., & Spaniol, L. (Eds.). (2005). *Recovery from severe mental illnesses: Research evidence and implications for practice: Vol. 1.* Boston: Boston University Center for Psychiatric Rehabilitation.

Dixon, L., Adams, C., & Lucksted, A. (2000). Update on family psychoeducation for schizophrenia. *Schizophrenia Bulletin, 26,* 5–20.

Dixon, L., McFarlane, W. R., Lefley, H., Lucksted, A., Cohen, M., Falloon, I., et al. (2001). Evidence-based practices for services to families of people with psychiatric disabilities. *Psychiatric Services, 52,* 903–910.

Dixon, L., Stewart, B., Burland, J., Delahanty, J., Lucksted, A., & Hoffman, M. (2001). Pilot study of the effectiveness of the Family-to-Family Education Program. *Psychiatric Services, 52,* 965–967.

Drake, R. E., Goldman, H. H., Leff, H. S., Lehman, A. F., Dixon, L., Mueser, K. T., et al. (2001). Implementing evidence-based practices in routine mental health settings. *Psychiatric Services, 52,* 179–182.

Falloon, I. R. H., Roncone, R., Held, T., Coverdale, J. H., & Laidlaw, T. M. (2002). An international overview of family interventions. In H. P. Lefley & D. L. Johnson (Eds.), *Family interventions in mental illness: International perspectives* (pp. 3–23). Westport, CT: Praeger.

Glynn, S. M., Liberman, R. P., & Backer, T. E. (1997). *Involving families in mental health services: Competencies for mental health workers.* Northridge, CA: Human Interaction Research Institute.

Hatfield, A. B., & Lefley, H. P. (2000). Helping elderly caregivers plan for the future care of a relative with mental illness. *Psychiatric Rehabilitation Journal, 24,* 103–107.

Hatfield, A. B., & Lefley, H. P. (2005). Future involvement of siblings in the lives of persons with mental illness. *Community Mental Health Journal, 41,* 327–338.

Jenkins, J. H., & Schumacher, J. G. (1999). Family burden of schizophrenia and depressive illness: Specifying the effects of ethnicity, gender, and social ecology. *British Journal of Psychiatry, 174,* 31–38.

Kuipers, L., Birchwood, M., & McCreadie, R. G. (2002). Psychosocial family intervention in schizophrenia: A review of empirical studies. *British Journal of Psychiatry, 160,* 272–275.

Lefley, H. P. (1992). Expressed emotion: Conceptual, clinical, and social policy issues. *Hospital & Community Psychiatry, 43,* 591–598.

Lefley, H. P. (1996). *Family caregiving in mental illness* [Family Caregiver Applications Series, Vol. 7]. Thousand Oaks, CA: Sage.

Lefley, H. P. (2004). Intercultural similarities and differences in family caregiving and family interventions in schizophrenia. *Psychiatric Times, 21,* 70.

Lefley, H. P., & Johnson, D. L. (Eds.). (2002). *Family interventions in mental illness: International perspectives.* Westport, CT: Praeger.

Lehman, A. F., Steinwachs, D. M., and the co-investigators of the PORT Project. (1998). At issue: Translating research into practice: The Schizophrenia Research Team (PORT) Treatment Recommendations. *Schizophrenia Bulletin, 24,* 1–10.

Magana, S. M., Ramirez Garcia, J. I., Hernandez, M. G., & Cortez, R. (2007). Psychological distress among Latino family caregivers of adults with schizophrenia: The roles of burden and stigma. *Psychiatric Services, 58,* 378–384.

Marsh, D. T. (2001). *A family-focused approach to serious mental illness: Empirically supported interventions.* Sarasota, FL: Professional Resource Press.

Marsh, D. T., & Lefley, H. P. (2003). Family interventions for schizophrenia. *Journal of Family Psychotherapy, 14,* 47–67.

McFarlane, W. R. (2002). *Multifamily groups in the treatment of severe psychiatric disorders.* New York: Guilford Press.

McGlashan, T. H. (1984). The Chestnut Lodge follow-up study. II. Long-term outcome of schizophrenia and the affective disorders. *Archives of General Psychiatry, 41,* 586–601.

Miklowitz, D. J., Simoneau, T. L., George, E. L., Richards, J. A., Kalbag, A., Sachs-Ericsson, N., et al. (2002). Family-focused treatment of bipolar disorder: One-year effects of a psychoeducational program in conjunction with pharmacotherapy. *Biological Psychiatry, 48,* 582–592.

Mueser, K. T., & Gingerich, S. (2006). *The complete family guide to schizophrenia.* New York: Guilford Press.

Mueser, K. T., & Glynn, S. M. (1999). *Behavioral family therapy for psychiatric disorders* (2nd ed.). Oakland, CA: New Harbinger.

New Freedom Commission on Mental Health. (2003). *Achieving the promise: Transforming mental health care in America. Final report.* DHHS Pub. No. SMA-03-3832. Rockville, MD.

Nicholson, J., & Blanch, A. (1994). Rehabilitation for parenting roles for people with serious mental illness. *Psychosocial Rehabilitation Journal, 18,* 109–119.

Petrila, J. P., & Sadoff, R. L. (1992). Confidentiality and the family as caregiver. *Hospital & Community Psychiatry, 43,* 136–139.

Pickett-Schenk, S., Steigman, P., Bennett, C., & Lippincott, R. (2005). *Journey of Hope Family Education Course Outcomes Project: Executive summary.* Chicago: University of Illinois at Chicago Center on Mental Health Services Research and Policy.

Pitschel-Walz, G., Leucht, S., Bauml, J., Kissling, W., & Engel, R. R. (2001). The effect of family interventions on relapse and rehospitalization in schizophrenia – a meta-analysis. *Schizophrenia Bulletin, 27,* 73–92.

Sherman, M. D. (2006). Updates and five-year evaluation of the S.A.F.E. program: A family psychoeducational program for mental illness. *Community Mental Health Journal, 49,* 213–219.

Solomon, P. (1996). Moving from psychoeducation to family education for adults with serious mental illness. *Psychiatric Services, 47,* 1364–1370.

Warner, R. (2000). *The environment of schizophrenia.* London: Brunner-Routledge.

Zipple, A. M., Langle, S., Tyrell, W., Spaniol, L., & Fisher, H. (1997). Client confidentiality and the family's need to know: Strategies for resolving the conflict. In D. T. Marsh & R. D. Magee (Eds.), *Ethical and legal issues in professional practice with families* (pp. 238–253). New York: Wiley.

54

Conclusion: The Future of Family Psychology

James H. Bray and Mark Stanton

The field of psychology and the specialty of family psychology are in the process of evolution and change to meet the needs for education, practice, and science in the twenty-first century. With advances in neuroscience, genetics, and collaborative care, family psychology is more relevant than ever. These advances require that we change our traditional understanding of science and practice to take advantage of the new possibilities in contemporary society. Couples, families, and relationships will continue to be at the core of our work, yet family psychology must continue to expand into larger social contexts (e.g., businesses, healthcare, education, and other systems). Many of the chapters in this volume demonstrate how family psychology interventions can be applied to broad systems such as schools and communities. What is lacking is a clear vision for our field and policies that support these efforts.

Future Opportunities for Practice

The excellent work by couple and family researchers demonstrates that family psychology interventions are useful and effective in preventing and treating relationship problems and changing dysfunctional relationships that are related to individual problems for family members. Future practice opportunities will include these evidence-based practices and the further integration of different models of family psychology interventions into integrated treatment packages (see Chapters 21–28, this volume). However, it will be important for future family psychologists to learn multiple models and interventions, as one type of intervention may not work for all families, just like one type of medicine may be generally effective, but not for every person. Individual and group differences require that we have multiple treatments for the same types of problems. The thorough integration of individually based evidence-based practices into systems interventions is a next step for the practice of family psychology.

Future efforts also need to focus on more ways to prevent child, adolescent, and adult health and mental health problems. For example, research by Gottman (1994; see also Chapter 30, this volume) and others on prediction of divorce clearly points to early warning signs for future relationship problems that lead to divorce. It is time to organize this research so that "well couple and family check-ups" can become a routine part of society. Just as children and adult women have "well child" or "well woman" examinations, it is time for society to support the "well couple" or "well family" check-ups.

Given the continuing change in demographics in this country and across the world, a broader understanding of different cultures and norms is necessary to practice (see Chapters 4, 5, and 49, this volume). It is clear that helping couples and families develop healthy and well-functioning relationships is a key not only to happiness, but also to a better quality of life and mental and physical health (Campbell, 2003; see also Chapters 36 and 37, this volume).

Research indicates that major health problems such as diabetes, heart disease, and obesity are due to psychosocial and lifestyle problems that are often family based, yet these issues are not effectively addressed by the medical profession. Minority, underserved, and elderly patients suffer even more from these systems of care. Family relationships and influences are often at the core of the development and treatment of these problems (Campbell, 2003).

Family psychologists are often not involved in the prevention and treatment of these problems because we are not seen as part of the healthcare team. Through our research and practice, family psychologists can provide solutions to effectively prevent and treat health and mental health problems because we are the profession that knows the most about human behavior and how to change it. But we have to become an integral part of the healthcare team (Bray, 2004; see also Chapters 36 and 37, this volume).

The practice of family psychology is often limited because of lack of reimbursement and payment for couple and family treatments in traditional health insurance plans and the frequent absence of these types of services in the public sector. Family psychologists need to work with organizations like the American Psychological Association (APA) and others to have these valuable services covered in standard healthcare insurance plans and public sector services. Continuing to produce scientific evidence on the effectiveness of these interventions will support our efforts toward reimbursement for these services.

Future Opportunities for Science

While family psychology research has made excellent progress in expanding our understanding of couple and family process and outcomes from interventions, there is much more to investigate about both basic family process and interventions to resolve couple, family, and system problems (Liddle, Santisteban, Levant, & Bray, 2002; Pinsof & Lebow,

2005). Family psychology researchers need to develop standards of measurement and agree upon the central concepts for study – we have no gold standards or even agreed-upon instruments (Bray, 1995). The field of psychophysiology made major gains in its research efforts after it developed standards for measuring basic physiological processes. There are consistent and critical family processes (e.g., cohesion, conflict, and communication) that have been identified by research and need standardized measurements that can be used in family psychology research (see Chapter 10, this volume). National panels of family researchers need to identify these critical processes and develop measurement standards. National funding agencies, such as the National Institute of Mental Health or National Institute of Drug Abuse, can play a critical role in facilitating these types of advances.

More basic research that identifies patterns of couple and family relationships related to problem etiology, progression, and treatment is still needed. In particular, more research is necessary regarding family responses to acute and chronic illness, such as HIV/AIDS, cancer, cardiac problems, and trauma, in addition to more traditional mental health areas, such as adolescent conduct problems, attention deficit disorder, alcohol and other drug abuse, and childhood depression. Given the findings with other disorders (e.g., schizophrenia; see Chapter 53, this volume), it is possible that the role of family members can be significant in medication compliance, adherence to treatment regimens, and perseverance in treatment. Research is needed to specify how family members may facilitate more positive outcomes in the treatment of various illnesses and disorders.

With the increase in diversity and globalization, future research needs to focus on these areas and how rapid changes due to wars and disasters impact families. Diversity includes differences due to family structure variations (e.g., single-parent families, stepfamilies), ethnic minorities and cultural differences, and gay and lesbian families. Much of the research on couple and family process and outcomes is based on White, middle-class families. Yet the largest growing segments of our population are ethnic minorities, such as Hispanics, and these families frequently experience high rates of psychosocial problems. There has been only limited research on whether our family assessment tools and instruments are applicable to these ethnic groups and even less research on whether our interventions work with these families (see Chapter 10, this volume; Bray, 1995).

Although research indicates that family psychology interventions are effective, even when compared to non-family-oriented interventions, clinical outcomes, or the clinical meaning and importance of outcomes, the issue is far from settled (Liddle et al., 2002; Pinsof & Lebow, 2005). This point relates to the evolution of questions like "are these interventions effective?" and "what are the circumstances under which these interventions are effective?" to "are these interventions effective enough?" The transportability of different interventions is one of the major research issues facing family psychology interventions. We need to translate and disseminate interventions developed in highly controlled research settings, with manualized treatments and tight supervision, to everyday practice settings with "messy," real-world demands that include integrated healthcare systems. This matter intersects considerably with policy issues and makers and funding agencies for research in these areas.

Future Opportunities for Graduate Education and Training

The two most important issues for the future of family psychology graduate education and training in the United States are: (a) identification or recognition of doctoral programs and pre-doctoral or post-doctoral internships that emphasize couple and family psychology, and (b) accreditation issues related to identification as a family psychology specialty program. The primary issue for family psychology education and training at the international level is the lack of clarity around nomenclature and guilds (i.e., the distinction between psychology, family therapy, and family psychology) and the availability of advanced training in the specialty.

The Division of Family Psychology Task Force on Graduate Education in Family Psychology made substantial progress in identifying doctoral programs that have a strong track or emphasis in family psychology. These programs are listed on the Division of Family Psychology website and may be accessed to guide students who are interested in locating a doctoral program that truly emphasizes the specialty. The next major step, currently underway, is a Task Force on Training in Family Psychology that identifies pre-doctoral and post-doctoral internship programs that emphasize the couple and family specialty. These two steps provide information to the public (i.e., potential students) and are the precursor to possible formal designation and/or organization of the programs into training councils. This is important for the continued development and growth of the specialty. The two groups are constituents of the Family Psychology Specialty Council.

The accreditation of programs in the specialty of family psychology is a more difficult issue. Because family psychology identifies as a broad and general orientation to psychology, it is unlike some specialties where the education and training are primarily post-doctoral. Consequently, it may be possible for doctoral programs to apply to the Commission on Accreditation of the American Psychological Association under the category of Developed Practice Area or under the category that combines two or three practice areas (e.g., Counseling Psychology and Family Psychology; Clinical Psychology and Family Psychology). The latter is most likely for programs that currently identify an emphasis in family psychology. Due to the strong emphasis in psychology on clinical, counseling, or school psychology programs, it is perceived by many students that pre-doctoral and post-doctoral internship sites, as well as potential employers, favor individuals from one of these established practice areas. Many programs that provide a strong foundation in couple and family psychology are currently accredited under one of these three established practice areas, supplemented "with an emphasis in family psychology." The next logical step in the progression is for family psychology to be formally recognized as a developed practice area (following the process of identification by the APA; initial preparation for such application is already complete, including formal guidelines for doctoral education in family psychology; Stanton & Harway, 2007) and for programs to apply for accreditation under the category that combines two or more practice areas and/or under the sole Developed Practice Area alone.

The current lack of clear family psychology nomenclature at the international level and the fact that there is no international standard for family psychology (see Chapter 49, this volume) mean that the specialty is somewhat disjointed worldwide. Because of the variety of education and training currently available in local environments around the world, this may be unavoidable, for now. However, advances in telecommunication (e.g., internet-based education) and the trend toward globalization by academic institutions (e.g., satellite campuses in other countries and/or joint degree offerings between U.S. universities and academic institutions in other countries, such as China) may mean that graduate programs in family psychology will become international in scope. This will require a shift away from some ideas and treatment models that are too western in focus to more global and transcultural models, but a systemic epistemology is readily capable of such adjustment (see Chapter 1, this volume; Marsella, 1998).

Board Certification in the Specialty of Family Psychology

Board certification has become increasingly important in the contemporary practice of psychology in the United States. The American Board of Couple and Family Psychology (ABCFP) is one of the constituent boards of the American Board of Professional Psychology (ABPP), and it coordinates the recruitment and certification of family psychologists. Historically, some have viewed board certification in psychology as a mid-to-late career achievement, but ABPP has moved progressively to clarify that board certification is appropriate for emerging and seasoned professionals. Graduate students are now encouraged to complete the ABPP application while in graduate school in order to facilitate movement to board certification subsequent to licensure and experience.

Until recently, ABCFP specialty-specific requirements specified one year of supervised professional practice in family psychology and either a post-doctoral residency in family psychology or completion of graduate courses and continuing education in family psychology. The ABCFP board recently acknowledged the number of graduate psychology programs with an emphasis on family psychology, and added a new track for specialty-specific qualification that recognizes individuals who received substantial education and training in family psychology during their doctoral experience. This track allows new professionals to complete the specialty-specific qualification process during the fourth year after licensure and move quickly to develop the professional statement (detailing one's theoretical orientation) and practice samples (session video recording) to allow the exam once the candidate has completed 5 years post-licensure.

Board certification denotes competency in the specialty and may facilitate license mobility across states (depending on specific state laws) and qualification for insurance provider boards. It is also consistent with the ethical practice of the specialty (see Chapter 12, this volume) and competent service to individuals, couples, families, and larger groups from a systemic perspective. Individuals who become board certified in family psychology become members of the Academy of Couple and Family Psychology.

Increasing globalization may mean that a need will soon exist for international certification of specialties. This will challenge the post-doctoral specialty boards, such as ABPP, to reconsider qualification standards, since they are currently based on U.S. standards for education and training, including APA accreditation. The spread of global education (noted above) may facilitate such a transition, but it is likely that a number of complications will slow this process.

Conclusions

These are clearly exciting times with many challenging opportunities for the field of family psychology. As we move forward in the twenty-first century, families will continue to form the basis of our society, and the importance of family relationships for healthy functioning will become more apparent. Advances in science and new treatments for chronic diseases all have implications for families, and psychologists will need to be in the middle of these developments to insure not only that we understand the implications of these new discoveries for couple and family relationships, but also to develop effective and efficient interventions for problems that arise in the course of our advances.

Resources

Board certification in family psychology: American Board of Professional Psychology, www.abpp.org

---

References

Bray, J. H. (1995). Family assessment: Current issues in evaluating families. *Family Relations, 44*, 469–477.

Bray, J. H. (2004). Training primary care psychologists. *Journal of Clinical Psychology in Medical Settings, 11*, 101–107.

Campbell, T. L. (2003). The effectiveness of family interventions for physical disorders. *Journal of Marital and Family Therapy, 29*, 263–281.

Gottman, J. M. (1994). *What predicts divorce? The relationship between marital processes and marital outcomes.* Hillsdale, NJ: Erlbaum.

Liddle, H. A., Santisteban, D. A., Levant, R. F., & Bray, J. H. (Eds.). (2002). *Family psychology: Science-based interventions.* Washington, DC: American Psychological Association.

Marsella, A. J. (1998). Toward a "global-community psychology:" Meeting the needs of a changing world. *American Psychologist, 53(12)*, 1282–1291

Pinsof, W., & Lebow, J. (Eds.). (2005). *Family psychology: State of the art.* New York: Oxford University Press.

Stanton, M., & Harway, M. (2007). Recommendations for doctoral education and training in family psychology. *The Family Psychologist, 23*, 4–10.

Subject Index

Author Index